S0-BVY-878

TO THE STUDENT: A partially programmed Study Guide for this textbook is available through your college bookstore under the title *Study Guide for Cost Accounting* by Maurice L. Hirsch, Jr, Joseph G. Louderback III, and Kay Kulfinski. The Study Guide can help you with course material by acting as a tutorial, review, and study aid. If the Study Guide is not in stock, ask the book store manager to order a copy for you.

Cost Accounting

JOSEPH G. LOUDERBACK III

Rensselaer Polytechnic Institute

MAURICE L. HIRSCH, JR.

*Southern Illinois University
at Edwardsville*

Cost Accounting

Accumulation, Analysis, and Use

KENT PUBLISHING COMPANY
Boston, Massachusetts
A Division of Wadsworth, Inc.

KENT PUBLISHING COMPANY
A Division of Wadsworth, Inc.

Senior Editor: David McEttrick
Production Editor: Nancy Phinney
Text Designers: Armen Kojoyian, Carol Rose
Cover Designer: Nancy Lindgren
Production Coordinator: Linda Card

© 1982 by Wadsworth, Inc., Belmont, California 94002.
All rights reserved. No part of this book may be reproduced, stored in a retrieval system, or
transcribed, in any form or by any means, electronic, mechanical, photocopying, recording, or
otherwise, without the prior written permission of the publisher, Kent Publishing Company,
Boston, Massachusetts, 02116.

Printed in the United States of America

1 2 3 4 5 6 7 8 9 — 85 84 83 82

Library of Congress Cataloging in Publication Data

Louderback, Joseph G.
  Cost accounting.

  Includes bibliographical references and
index.
  1. Cost accounting.   I. Hirsch, Maurice L.
II. Title.
HF5686.C8L595   657'.42   81-19288
ISBN 0-534-01026-1   AACR2

Material from Uniform CPA Examination Questions and Unofficial Answers, copyright
© 1968, 1970, 1971, 1973, 1974, 1975, 1976, 1979 by the American Institute of Certified
Public Accountants, Inc., is reprinted (or adapted) with permission.
  Material from the Certificate in Management Accounting Examinations, copyright
© 1973–1980 by the National Association of Accountants, is reprinted (or adapted) with
permission.

Preface

Cost accounting is a changing, diverse field of study that means different things to different people. This book treats the traditional topics of cost accumulation and product costing for determining inventories and income. It also integrates topics and techniques of more recent emphasis, especially quantitative methods and behavioral considerations.

Cost Accounting: Accumulation, Analysis, and Use is designed for several uses. It contains enough material to fill either two quarters (four hours each) or two semesters (three hours each). It is also appropriate for one-term courses of several types. The course could provide a balance of product costing and managerial uses of cost information, or it could emphasize one or the other.

We assume a basic understanding of financial accounting and of the journal entry/T-account framework in the product costing chapters. Students who have had a course in managerial accounting should be able to go through Chapters 2, 3, and 4 fairly quickly, even though these chapters go beyond the typical coverage in basic managerial accounting courses. In using this book a knowledge of statistics would be helpful, but it is not a prerequisite. Students who have had no statistics should first read Appendix A to Chapter 4.

Our objectives in writing this book were straightforward.

1. We wanted to present as much relevant material as possible in as clear, concise, interesting, and straightforward a fashion as possible. Accordingly, we have explained complicated material in an intuitive way, making liberal use of examples and illustrations, as well as nontechnical explanations.

2. We wanted to integrate quantitative techniques and behavioral

dimensions throughout the book where relevant. We do not think that such basic tools as regression analysis and probability estimates should be tacked on in later chapters.

3. We wanted to provide a sequence of chapters that reflects the logical priority of the material. One manifestation of this objective is the early treatment of cost-volume-profit analysis, the analysis of cost behavior, and decision making. We think these topics should precede product costing because they emphasize the uses of accounting information and give students a good perspective of the multiple uses of accounting data.

4. More than any other objective, we wanted to motivate students to learn and to share our view that cost/managerial accounting is valuable, interesting, and challenging. It is worthy of study for its own sake as a general system of thinking and problem solving. In addition, it has specific value in preparing students for work.

The entire text and many problems have been tested in class. We have made liberal use of appendices to chapters for two purposes. Some appendices cover important, but complex points so that instructors can pick and choose from among these materials depending on the objectives of the course and the backgrounds of the students. (For instance, the appendix to Chapter 12 covers matrix inversion for allocations.) Other appendices, such as the one for Chapter 5, cover source documents in job order costing, details of the chapter material that could be distracting if covered in the chapter.

ORGANIZATION AND PLAN

The organization reflects our current thoughts, sometimes conflicting ones, regarding pedagogical advantages and disadvantages. Our overriding objective is logical integration. This is reflected in the early and continual appearance of quantitative techniques, principally regression, statistics, and linear programming.

Part One begins with an introductory chapter that describes a real situation and permits us to explore some of the principal concerns of the book—the various needs for and uses of accounting information. Chapter 2 covers cost-volume-profit analysis, which we consider basic to all other topics. We treat the analysis of cost behavior patterns and decision making in Chapters 3 and 4 before moving to product costing. We think that Part One is necessary to motivate students to learn why and how cost accounting systems and methods provide relevant information and how to proceed when the systems do not routinely provide relevant information.

Part Two treats product costing along with the use of standards for control and evaluation. Chapter 5 covers job order costing and gives a good deal of attention to the managerial uses of product costing information. Continuing with significant attention to managerial concerns, Chapter 6 covers process costing. Chapter 7 treats variances from standards, both revenue and cost. We placed this chapter here because it is difficult to cover these topics before the student has seen how product costing works. It is equally difficult to cover standard costing systems (Chapter 8) without prior exposure to both product costing and standards. Chapter 8, finishing up the main topics in product costing, covers standard costing. Chapters 9 and 10 treat joint products, by-products, scrap, and spoilage. We place these chapters here because the topics are clearly related to product costing and so logically belong here. Both chapters stress the managerial use of cost information generated by typical ways of accounting for these widespread complications.

Chapter 11 covers variable costing and Chapter 12 winds up Part Two with cost allocation. Chapter 12 looks mainly at the allocation of service department costs to operating departments, but devotes some space to the theoretical considerations of allocating and not allocating. It also emphasizes the ubiquity of cost allocations relating to reimbursements by third parties (like Blue Cross and Medicaid), the setting of rates in regulated industries, and government contracts that fall under the Standards of the Cost Accounting Standards Board.

Part Three considers budgeting, beginning with Chapter 13 which looks at the behavioral considerations of the comprehensive budgeting process. Chapter 14 treats the preparation of budgets with some discussion of modern tools that some managers apply to budgeting. Chapters 15 and 16 treat capital budgeting, with the first chapter going through the basic types of decisions and techniques, including income taxes. Chapter 16 looks at refinements like preference rules and comparisons of discounted cash flow techniques. Part Four treats the measurement and evaluation of divisional performance. Either or both could be taken up after Chapter 11.

Part Five considers key areas that seem to us best taken up after students have been through the basics. Even so, some instructors will take up some of these chapters at earlier points with little difficulty. Chapter 19 deals with assessing the significance of variances and could be studied after Chapter 8. Chapter 20, which discusses inventory control, could be examined right after Chapter 4 or could be taken up after Chapter 14.

Chapters 21, 22, and 23 cover topics that we believe are very important and are becoming even more so, but are not usually considered at chapter length in cost accounting books. We have devoted chapters to each topic because we do not think that they can be covered adequately in appendices or as sections of chapters.

Chapter 21 considers the problem of the behavioral aspects of information in much greater depth than space permits in other chapters, such as Chapter 13. Chapter 22 deals with learning curves, an important consideration in many industries, especially ones employing sophisticated technology. Chapter 23 introduces simulation, which (despite its reputation as a last resort technique) has a number of advantages over analytical methods.

ASSIGNMENTS

Assignment material is critical to a cost accounting book. We have provided a wide range of assignments, from simple, straightforward exercises that concentrate on a single fundamental principle to relatively unstructured cases and questions that require students to think logically through the determination of what principles are relevant to the specific method of application required. In between we have problems that provide comprehensive reviews of a chapter or sequence of chapters, as well as ones designed to reinforce specific points like the irrelevance of historical costs to decisions. Some of the assignment material is from CPA and CMA examinations. The Instructor's Manual provides suggestions for assignments to meet specific objectives.

SUPPLEMENTARY MATERIAL

Besides the Instructor's Manual prepared by the authors, there is a Student Study Guide by Kay Kulfinski and the authors. The publisher will supply check figures for nearly every problem, gratis to adopters. Additionally, the publisher will supply free to adopters a deck of cards containing six computer programs in BASIC. The Instructor's Manual describes each of the programs and provides sample terminal sessions. We cannot guarantee that any program will run on any system without modification, but we have paid considerable attention to achieving compatibility.

ALTERNATIVE USES

Although the Instructor's Manual provides suggestions for alternative uses, it is appropriate here to mention a few possibilities. Instructors who want a one-term course that concentrates on managerial uses of accounting information might wish to skip a few chapters in Part Two. Chapters 8, 9, 10, or 12 can be omitted without sacrificing continuity. Succeeding chapters do not rely on these chapters enough to cause serious problems. Then, depending on preferences, you might choose from among all of the chapters in Part Five, none of which presuppose coverage of the chapters just listed.

Instructors wanting a basic course that balances product costing with managerial concerns might go straight through to Chapter 14 or so, depending on whether they want to cover all of the product costing material. The chart below shows the order in which the chapters can be studied and their relationships.

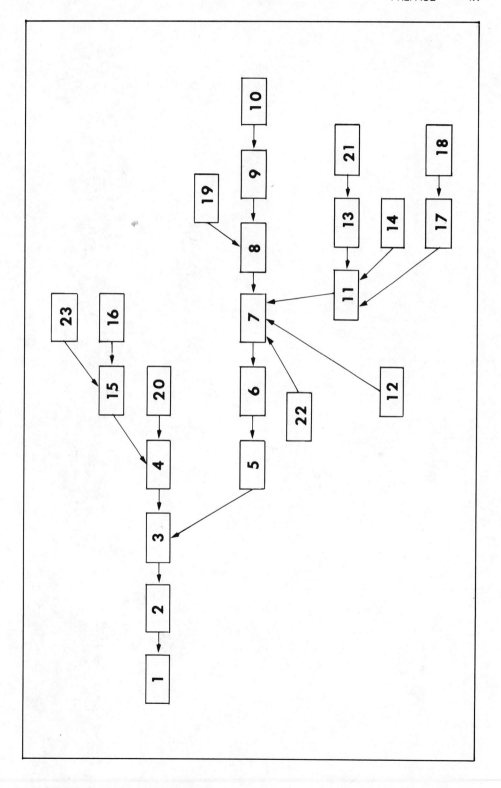

ACKNOWLEDGMENTS

We gratefully acknowledge the kind permission of the Institute of Management Accounting of the National Association of Accountants to use and adapt material from CMA Examinations.

We gratefully acknowledge the kind permission of the American Institute of Certified Public Accountants to use and adapt material from CPA exams.

We wish to thank the following reviewers for their helpful evaluation, criticism, and suggestions during the development of this edition.

Lane K. Anderson	Texas Tech University
David M. Buehlmann	University of Nebraska at Omaha
Curtis Cook	Southern Illinois University at Edwardsville
Werner G. Frank	University of Wisconson
George R. McGrail	The University of Wyoming
C. Stevenson Rowley	Arizona State University
Don P. Schneider	Rensselaer Polytechnic Institute
John P. Seagle	State University of New York—Albany
William O. Stratton	University of Idaho

Contents

Part 1
COST ACCOUNTING FOR PLANNING AND DECISION MAKING

Part 2
PRODUCT COSTING 189

Part 3
BUDGETING AND CONTROL 505

13 *BUDGETING: GENERAL AND BEHAVIORAL ASPECTS 507*

14 *BUDGETING: ANALYTICAL AND TECHNICAL ASPECTS 545*

Part 4
DIVISIONAL PERFORMANCE EVALUATION 669

Part 5
KEY AREAS FOR FURTHER STUDY 759

Cost Accounting for Planning and Decision Making

Part 1

Introduction

Chapter 1

A large firm recently ran a series of commercials asserting that 80 percent of an executive's time was spent in managing information. Among the most significant changes in business in recent decades, certainly, have been the increase in the amount of information available and the rapidity with which it can be communicated. Computers, teleprocessing, and other technological innovations have made it possible to develop more information than any executive can possibly manage. The problem of information management, then, raises questions about what information to provide to managers. How often should particular kinds of information be given to managers? Which managers should receive such information and which should not? Does the form in which information is presented have any effect on its use? How can we tell whether managers are using information effectively? Just what does "using information effectively" mean?

INFORMATION AND ACCOUNTING

Accounting is concerned with providing information to decision makers. For example, investors need financial accounting information. An investor uses this information to evaluate a company. Should she buy stock in this company? What are the expected dividends? How risky is the company? How competitive has management been in products, prices, and costs? Has management dealt with social issues affecting this company? The broad spectrum of information contained in an annual report is the basis for answering many of these questions.

Regulatory agencies also use financial information. Has a company followed all the Securities Exchange Commission rules for disclosure? Have appropriate Financial Accounting Standards Board and Accounting Principles Board pronouncements been followed?

Information also is needed for local, state, and federal taxing authorities. Tax information often varies from financial accounting information. For example, while management may feel that straight-line depreciation most accurately shows how an asset is expiring, it might use accelerated depreciation for tax purposes to get deductions earlier.

A third type of accounting information deals with internal auditing. Here managers are concerned with the safety of the firm's assets and with good controls. For example, a restaurant manager is concerned about cash receipts, and he will want information that tells him whether any employees have been dishonest. We can extend this internal auditing to areas such as inventory, where a manager wants to know how many cases of goods should be in inventory given opening inventory, current purchases, and current sales.

A fourth area of accounting is concerned with information for managerial decision making. Managerial accounting information is used by managers to plan and control company operations. Plans include types of products, pricing decisions, budgets, and equipment purchases. Controls include the comparison of plans with outcomes and the evaluation of divisional or departmental performance.

Although we have looked at them separately, these four functions are interrelated. The financial, tax, audit, and managerial functions all need a common information base and a set of systems to coordinate information flow. Costs and benefits will affect the complexity and sophistication of the accounting information system. The managers of a company are at the center of all these flows. While only they can make decisions relating to company operations, their actions and company performance must be reflected so that external decision makers (investors, SEC, IRS) have adequate information.

Although this book focuses on business firms, many of the techniques and concepts it discusses apply equally to such not-for-profit entities as governments, universities, churches, charities, and social or fraternal groups. In fact, one of the important developments of recent years has been the application of cost accounting concepts and methods to the management of nonbusiness entities.

The objectives of this book parallel the uses of cost accounting information. You should gain an understanding of the methods used to determine costs for financial reporting and income tax purposes. You should become knowledgeable in the uses and limitations of accounting information in the management of economic organizations. Most important, you should learn to think as an accountant. Cost accounting is as much a way of thinking as it is a bundle of techniques and methods. The problems faced by businesses and other economic organizations cannot all be set out with the appropriate solutions: there are simply too many possible problems to allow a cookbook approach to cost accounting. The ability to use what you know in unfamiliar situations is the hallmark of a successful accountant—as it is for any successful person.

MANAGEMENT, ACCOUNTING, AND INFORMATION

In order to highlight the relationships among management, accounting, and information we shall describe a situation that is based on fact. The Mesa Mining case brings up many more questions than this chapter can answer; in fact it raises questions that we shall be considering throughout the book. As you read the case, try to identify the problems the people face and consider the actions you might take to solve some of these problems.

Case Study: Mesa Mining

Bud Norton leaned back in his seat as the jet lifted off for Salt Lake City. In an hour he would be meeting with various members of management of Mesa Uranium Mining Company. Norton began to review the events that led up to this trip.

M. W. Bud Norton was a management consultant specializing in information flows. Norton had an MBA from a large midwestern university, was a CPA, and had extensive training in computer hardware and software. After working in a large public accounting firm for ten years he decided to form his own company to deal specifically with formal and informal flows of information.

A month earlier, Norton had received a call from Jack Block, vice president of finance for Great Midwest Power, Inc. Block had first explained the background of Great Midwest and then told Norton about the problems at Mesa, a subsidiary of Great Midwest.

Great Midwest Power, Inc., was a large electric utility headquartered in Indianapolis that provided power to portions of Indiana, Illinois, and Ohio. Annual sales had recently exceeded $3 billion. From its inception the company had relied on coal-fired plants. In the early 1970s management had begun to consider nuclear generating facilities. Air quality standards had been tightened and the low sulphur coal needed to meet these standards was scarce and expensive. Nuclear facilities seemed to be a cheaper and cleaner way to generate power. Therefore, in 1975 Great Midwest had embarked on a building program that would include three nuclear power plants. Despite environmental issues concerning nuclear facilities, issues heightened by the Three Mile Island incident, management felt that they could solve these problems before the first plant began operations.

In order to ensure a steady supply of fuel, management decided on two concurrent courses of action. For fuel needs in the short run they would contract with firms such as Exxon to provide uranium pellets. To meet long-term needs they would develop a subsidiary, Mesa Uranium Mining Company, to mine and process uranium ore.

Mesa had been in operation for about a year when Block had called Bud Norton. Block was concerned about Mesa for many reasons. He felt that Great Midwest lacked data on Mesa it needed for financial reporting, current tax calculations, and evaluation of the progress, if any, that Mesa was making. He had hired Norton to go to Salt Lake City, investigate the problems, and make recommendations to management regarding Mesa's information system. Norton would work with Great Midwest's auditors, a "Big Eight" accounting firm.

Norton was met at the airport by Sarah Jones, the head of Mesa's accounting and finance department. At company headquarters Jones gave Norton background information on Mesa and on the uranium business.

Norton learned that the major source of nuclear fuel is uranium in a final enriched, pure, pellet state. In the United States, uranium ore is found mainly in Colorado, Wyoming, and Utah. Much of this area is fairly arid or inaccessible and has a very low population density. Great blocks of land in this region are owned by states or by the federal government.

A company wishing to mine uranium must first get the mineral rights to the land. It is unusual to buy the land itself; the usual procedure is either to buy or to lease the rights to mine the land. In order to see whether the rights on a piece of land were worth bidding for and how much to offer, geologists explored the land, tested to see what mining potential existed, and then went through a procedure of staking and filing a claim, defined as an area 600 by 1,500 feet. After a claim had been laid out and filed, the negotiations took place with the owner of the land. Once the mining rights had been acquired, drilling rigs were moved in to obtain samples from beneath the surface. If a seam of ore was found, the firm began mining. Ore contains about 2 pounds of pure uranium (called *yellow cake*) for each ton mined.

Ore is then chemically treated at a mill that separates yellow cake from the balance of the ore. A typical by-product of the process is vanadium, a mineral used to harden steel. Yellow cake (which is formed into brick-shaped cakes) is then sent to a plant that enriches it and puts it into the pellet form needed to fuel nuclear plants.

Jones explained that Mesa was formed to explore for, mine, and process uranium ore. Final enriching of the fuel would be handled by an outside firm specializing in that process. Mesa management obtained funds directly from Great Midwest Power. As funds were needed, Great Midwest purchased additional common stock in Mesa. Thus, Mesa was entirely equity financed and had no long-term debt.

To get a better idea of how Mesa operated, Norton asked for an organization chart and an explanation of who did what and who reported to whom. He found out that no clear table of organization existed. An overall general manager of Mesa operated out of the Salt Lake City headquarters, but at least three people in Indianapolis had areas of authority concerning the Mesa group. Jones herself was an officer of Great Midwest rather than of Mesa.

Norton had read about uranium mining and knew that the issues of prospecting and gaining mineral rights were complex. The field had become quite competitive of late with many power and petroleum companies entering this area. The oil embargo had served to heighten this activity.

If Mesa did sign a contract for a claim or series of claims, the claims on one piece of property had to be accounted for separately for purposes of amortization, allocation, and capital gains. Such a grouping of claims is called a tax property in the trade.

Jones told Norton that the methods of payment for exploration and mining, once Mesa acquired rights on a tax property, were quite numerous. All sorts of fixed fees and royalties were possible. Some royalties had minimum fees that were due even if there was no mining. Most state and federal properties have a provision that a specified minimum amount must be spent on exploration each quarter or the lease will lapse and be up for grabs by other companies.

At the time Norton made his visit, Mesa had about 100 employees divided into five main groups. One group was involved with identifying and purchasing new property rights. A second group operated an ore mine. A third group was buying ore from other small mines for resale in the open market. A fourth group was concerned with overall planning of operations, the operation of the ore processing plant, and the building of a second processing plant. The fifth group handled Mesa's accounting and finance functions.

Mesa was currently buying ore, processing it, and reselling it on the open market. The company had built a buying station where assayers took samples of ore and estimated its percentage of yellow cake. The supplier of the ore was paid 75 percent of the estimated value when the ore was delivered. The other 25 percent payment was made when the ore was processed. If the original 75 percent payment turned out to be greater than the full value of the uranium in the ore, Mesa had no recourse against the supplier. If the original payment was less than full value, then Mesa paid out the balance to the suppliers. If the supplier felt the sum was in error, a third party could be called in to arbitrate. The price per pound changed monthly and was based on quotations in the official trade magazine. Vanadium prices stayed fairly stable at about $0.80 per pound.

As ore was bought, it was stockpiled with other ore of the same estimated uranium concentration. Thus, once it was delivered to Mesa, the individuality of each purchase was lost. Settlement with ore suppliers was based on average yield from a batch of ore.

The ore mine Mesa operated had been bought as a going concern. The previous owner had been on a cash basis for his accounting and had expensed all supplies as purchased, even if most of them stayed on hand in inventory. Mesa had continued this practice. For the first six months it had owned the mine, Mesa had engaged a mining consulting firm to operate it. Mesa had just recently taken over operations itself. Jones told Norton:

> We really have a unique problem to deal with here. Our consultants bought several pieces of new machinery. We do know how much they spent in total, but we don't know exactly what they bought or how much they spent for each individual piece. It's unfortunate in this business that the engineers who run

mines have absolutely no head for business. They expect us to just send them money whenever they have a bill to pay!

Right now we are really swamped and are fighting brushfires all the time. I'm not sure when we will get ahead so we can do some planning. We have our hands full just paying bills. The geology group comes in on a minute's notice and wants large sums to purchase mineral rights. Just yesterday, they rushed in and said that they needed $1,250,000 by this morning to get in a bid before our competition does. Our mining and processing groups and ore-buying people expect their bills and payrolls met. We have to manage all these different kinds of leases to make sure we don't accidentally lose one of them because we didn't live up to our contract. You know, there are times I think this department has been reduced to a bookkeeping function.

Mesa and Accounting Information

Things at Mesa are certainly messy, but what should be done? In particular, what kinds of information should be developed and transmitted among Mesa's managers and from Mesa to Great Midwest? Mesa's managerial problems are generally beyond the scope of this book, but the resolution of some of them will influence the selection of information to be provided by the accounting system. Accounting and management are interdependent and cannot be viewed as two different things.

The discussion that ensues examines the situation at Mesa and indicates areas of improvement. It focuses on the firm's informational requirements and provides a prelude to the remainder of the book, where the individual issues will be discussed and illustrated in detail. The rest of this chapter, then, is essentially an overview of the content of managerial and cost accounting. It raises more questions than it answers.

You may already have some ideas about Mesa's accounting requirements. For example, you saw that Ms. Jones had no idea how much was paid for each piece of mining equipment. Because it is likely that various types of equipment have different useful lives, it is necessary to determine the cost of each piece so that each may be depreciated in a reasonable way. It would be inappropriate to use a single life for pieces of equipment that may have lives ranging from five to fifteen years. Other questions that must be resolved relate to the inventory method to be used for purchased ore, the depletion method to be used for the mine, and the whole cluster of questions associated with the leases of mining rights. These and other questions need to be resolved for financial reporting and income tax accounting as well as for auditing purposes.

From a managerial standpoint, our concerns extend beyond the aforementioned questions. While financial accounting and cost/managerial accounting dovetail in many important respects, they differ in other respects. We will look at the situation from a cost/managerial accounting standpoint.

PLANNING AND CONTROL

Different authors emphasize different aspects of managerial processes and use different terminology to describe managers' functions. Most would agree that planning and control are two extremely important functions of managers. Planning involves setting goals and devising ways to meet them. Great Midwest managers wish to develop the capability of supplying nuclear fuel to their plants, and they decided to establish a separate firm for that purpose. Control involves determining whether things are going according to plan, and if not, what remedies might be applied.

Consider first the role of Great Midwest's management. Great Midwest has been investing heavily in Mesa, and its managers need to know whether the investment is working out satisfactorily or whether corrective action is needed. But what is meant by working out satisfactorily? The answer depends on Great Midwest's objectives in setting up Mesa and on the extent to which Mesa is meeting the objectives. Presumably, Great Midwest set up Mesa in order to obtain uranium fuel more cheaply than it could from other sources. The managers of Great Midwest must have investigated the possibilities of buying fuel from other firms under long-term contracts, perhaps with fixed prices. In any event, management decided that establishing a mining subsidiary was the best action.

When the managers of Great Midwest established Mesa, they must have had some ideas of the progress that should have been made by specific dates. For example, they might have believed that Mesa should be showing a profit by the end of its third year, or that it should be producing 3,000 tons of uranium fuel at a total cost of $26 million by the end of its second year. Because the decision to establish Mesa must have been made by comparing the expected results of owning a mining subsidiary with those of buying from other firms, there must have been some objectives that Great Midwest did use as benchmarks for judging Mesa's progress. Otherwise, the decision was made intuitively, perhaps because Great Midwest managers simply wanted to have a mining subsidiary. However, no rational manager would throw money into a subsidiary without expecting tangible results.

In short, Great Midwest's managers want to know whether Mesa is performing effectively and efficiently. Effectiveness is measured by whether the firm is doing what is expected, whether it is producing the desired quantities of product, whether it is gaining control of enough underground ore to supply Great Midwest's needs. Efficiency is measured by the relationships of input to output. Is the output (fuel) being produced with a reasonable amount of input (cost)? The questions of effectiveness and efficiency are separate. Mesa might turn out to be very efficient but at such low levels of output that it does not fulfill its mission of being Great Midwest's principal long-term supplier of nuclear fuel. It may be very effective in producing fuel, but at a cost that is too high, perhaps higher than Great Midwest would have to pay to other firms to obtain the fuel.

Managers at Mesa have similar considerations. They are concerned with whether the operations under their own control are doing as well as can be expected and where improvements might be made. The manager of the ore-processing plant wants to know whether his costs are under control, as does the manager of the mine. These managers would want much more detailed information about their individual areas of responsibility than would the managers at Great Midwest, who are concerned primarily with overall results. For example, the manager of the ore-processing plant would want information about individual components of cost, such as power, where managers at Great Midwest are concerned less about the details of cost than about the total cost of processing ore.

Responsibility Accounting

Perhaps the most glaring management problem at Mesa is that no one seems to know who is in charge of what and who reports to whom. Norton was told that there was no organization chart and that at least three people at Great Midwest had authority over some aspects of the Mesa operations. Under the circumstances, it is not possible to tell who is doing well and who poorly, except by the crudest means. Unless managers have fairly clear-cut areas of responsibility, their superiors cannot determine anything about their performances. What holds for the management of Great Midwest holds also for Mesa: Great Midwest managers want to know how Mesa is doing, and managers at Mesa want to know how their subordinates are doing.

Responsibility accounting describes the concepts and techniques that underlie reporting on the performance of individual managers. The responsibility accounting system will be based on Mesa's organization and on the scope of each individual manager's responsibility. Regardless of the resolution of Mesa's organizational structure, the responsibility accounting system should provide information about the factors that a manager can control. Managers should not be held responsible for factors beyond their control.

Consider the following example. Suppose that management decides to have separate managers in charge of mining and of the ore-processing plant. The manager of the ore processing plant will be held responsible for earning a *profit* (which is defined as the difference between the market value of the uranium fuel and vanadium produced and the total cost to produce it). Further, part of the total cost is the cost of mining the ore. Since the manager cannot buy ore from independent firms unless the Mesa mine cannot supply his needs, the processing plant is a captive customer of the mine. If the mine is inefficient, its costs may be higher than the processing plant manager would have to pay to buy ore from independent mines. The manager of the processing plant would be evaluated on the basis of a profit figure that included costs over which he had no control and, therefore, would be penalized by the inefficiency of the mine. One solution would be to charge the processing plant with a budgeted cost for ore, a cost that would be incurred if the mine were to operate at a reasonably high level of efficiency.

Another approach would be to charge the plant with the market price of ore, the price that the manager would have to pay to buy ore from independent mines. We shall see in later chapters that both of these alternatives have desirable and undesirable features.

The principle of controllability—that a manager should be held responsible for only that which he can control—is often very difficult to apply in practice. For this reason it may be viewed more as an objective or goal of responsibility accounting than as a rule. We shall find that the principles of cost and managerial accounting are not ironclad and that a great deal of judgment and common sense is required. We shall see some of the reasons for this in a later section of this chapter, where we consider the problems of accounting and human behavior.

Budgeting

Budgets are formal plans for future periods. They detail the firm's objectives and the means by which the firm expects to achieve them. For example, the managers of Mesa should prepare budgets indicating their expectations about production from the mine along with the expected costs of achieving the desired level of production. They should also budget capital expenditures for mining equipment. Additionally, they should budget for acquisition of claims: some goals should be set regarding the total amount of underground ore that Mesa should acquire through claims and the timing and the total cost of acquiring that ore. As things stand, the firm is haphazardly buying up claims with no apparent plans and without considering the total requirements for ore or the long-term availability of funds from Great Midwest.

The lack of budgets makes it impossible to judge whether Mesa is performing according to expectations, since there are no expectations for Mesa save perhaps a vague idea that it should be getting to be one of the big uranium producers. Moreover, the lack of formal budgets means there is little or no control over the activities of Mesa's various groups. There is no consideration of the cost of claims and, therefore, no way of evaluating whether the money being spent to acquire claims has been wisely or unwisely spent. The lack of controls over the mining operation is also apparent. The mining engineers buy equipment without having to justify their expenditures, and apparently there is no indication either of the desired production from the mine or of the efficiency of the mining operation.

Finally, there are no budgets for cash requirements—receipts and disbursements. Mesa's position as a subsidiary of a large firm probably ensures that it will not run out of cash in the near term, but that luxury is not generally available. At some point the management of Great Midwest is going to want to have cash flowing from Mesa to Great Midwest, not the other way around. Firms must carefully budget their cash flows, because running out of cash is a critical event: a firm earning profits, but unable to pay its bills, may be forced into bankruptcy or at least be seriously embarrassed by running out of cash. It would find it difficult to raise cash in the future, because banks and other financial institutions would be wary of lending money to a firm that had been unable to meet its obligations.

At periodic intervals, perhaps monthly or quarterly, managers will compare actual results with budgeted expectations to determine whether the budgeted goals have been met for quantity and quality and at acceptable levels of cost. Thus, budgeting provides feedback to managers and is a tool for exercising control as well as for planning.

One of Norton's first recommendations will be that Mesa begin to budget its operations and that its managers, and those of Great Midwest, make periodic reviews of Mesa's progress toward achieving the budgeted goals. Goals would include such critical matters as the amount of underground ore to be acquired by claims, the amount of ore to be mined from the existing mine, the amount of ore to be put through the processing plant, and the level of profit to be achieved from reselling the ore. The budgets would also relate the goals to the costs of achieving them.

Analysis of Cost Behavior

The development of budgets requires some knowledge of the patterns of behavior of costs—whether costs will change as activity changes or remain the same throughout wide ranges of activity. Consider Mesa's ore processing plant: as the quantity of ore bought and processed increases, the costs of the ore itself as well as of labor, power, and some other items should also increase. However, some costs of operating the plant, such as depreciation and the salaries of the plant manager and clerks, will probably remain about the same no matter what the level of production.

Costs that change in response to changes in the level of activity (processing ore in this case) are called **variable costs.** Costs that remain about the same throughout wide ranges of activity are called **fixed costs.** The graphs opposite show the behavior of both types of costs. The horizontal axis measures the level of activity, which is also frequently called the level of volume. That axis could be measured by sales of products in units, by sales in dollars, or by whatever other activity is important to the firm. Mesa would use the number of tons of ore processed, or perhaps the sales value of ore processed, as the measure of volume for its processing plant. It would probably use the number of tons of ore taken out of the ground as the measure of volume for its mining operation.

As later chapters will show, determining the patterns of cost behavior is often a difficult task. Its importance lies in providing a basis for planning and controlling costs. If the budget for production of ore in the processing plant is set at 4,500 tons with a budgeted cost of $24 million, and if production actually turns out to be 4,100 tons or 4,960 tons, the $24 million budgeted cost figure should not be used to determine whether costs were or were not under control. Suppose that the managers of Mesa determine that the variable cost of processing a ton of ore is $2,000, including the cost of the

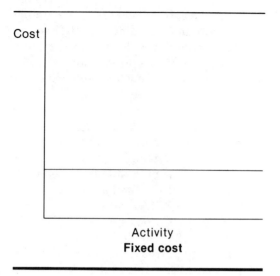

Cost

Activity
Fixed cost

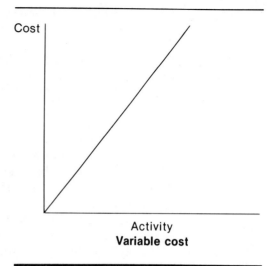

Cost

Activity
Variable cost

ore, the cost of labor, and other costs that vary with the number of tons processed. Further, the fixed costs of operating the plant, depreciation, salaries of personnel required whatever the level of production, and so on, are budgeted at $15 million. Then, at a volume of 4,500 tons, total budgeted costs would be $24 million, consisting of $9 million of variable costs ($2,000 × 4,500) plus $15 million of fixed costs.

At volumes other than 4,500 tons, however, the managers should not expect to incur costs of $24 million. At lower levels of production, costs should be less than $24 million; at higher levels, costs should be higher. The schedule below shows the costs that should be expected at three levels of volume.

	4,100 tons	*4,500 tons*	*4,960 tons*
Variable costs at $2,000/ton	$ 8,200,000	$ 9,000,000	$ 9,920,000
Fixed costs	15,000,000	15,000,000	15,000,000
Total costs budgeted	$23,200,000	$24,000,000	$24,920,000

The three budgeted levels of cost shown above are called the **flexible budget allowances** for the production levels. A flexible budget allowance is simply a budgeted cost based on the actual output achieved. For Mesa, the flexible budget allowance for any level of processing of ore can be expressed as the sum of fixed and variable costs expected at the level of volume achieved. In formula form,

flexible budget allowance = $15,000,000 + ($2,000 × Q)

where Q is the number of tons of ore processed. The advantage of using a flexible budget allowance is that it enables the manager to compare actual costs with costs that should be incurred at the actual level of volume, rather than at the originally budgeted level of volume. The difference between a budgeted amount of cost and the actual amount of cost is called a *variance*. Variances are important when we analyze operations to see, for example, where control may have been poor or where a manager's initiative has pointed the way to more efficient results than planned.

Suppose that the plant actually processed 4,960 tons instead of the 4,500 originally budgeted. Exceeding the production budget may be good or bad, depending on the circumstances. If the increased production had to be sold at greatly reduced prices because of oversupply, producing more than planned was a bad move. If, however, it was profitable to produce the additional 460 tons, then exceeding the original production budget was a good idea. Suppose also that the total costs were $24.91 million. The budget called for a $24 million cost to produce 4,500 tons. Looking at cost behavior, we see that a budget for 4,960 tons would be $24,920,000. Since costs were $10,000 less than budgeted for this level of activity, the plant manager seems to have performed well in keeping costs down. Lacking a knowledge of the cost behavior patterns, someone looking at the difference between the actual costs of $24,910,000 and the original budget of $24 million might have erroneously concluded that something was wrong with the operation.

The classification of costs by behavior is one way in which cost accounting differs from financial accounting. In published income statements, costs that are shown as expenses on the income statement are typically classified by object or by function. An **object classification** simply denotes what the cost is for, such as salaries, heat and light, depreciation, rent, and property taxes. A **functional classification** relates costs to the functional areas of the business, such as cost of goods sold, selling expenses, and general and administrative expenses. The functional classifications will include various object classifications; some salaries will appear as selling expenses, some as general and administrative expenses; depreciation on factory equipment will appear in cost of goods sold, depreciation on office buildings as general and administrative expenses.

In cost accounting, the object and functional classifications are usually secondary to other types of classification. Besides a behavioral classification, there are classifications by responsibility (what manager is responsible for controlling the cost), and by relevance to the intended use of the cost data. An example of the latter is in decision making, where some costs may be relevant for particular decisions but irrelevant for others.

PRODUCT COSTING

Any cost accounting system must provide information on unit costs of products. Inventory on the balance sheet and cost of goods sold on the income statement will be affected by the way in which unit costs are determined. You are already familiar with first-in-first-out, last-in-first-out, and weighted average methods of accounting for inventory. These cost flow assumptions are also used in manufacturing operations. Other questions arise in manufacturing operations; the most fundamental is that of the costs to be included in determining the dollar amount of inventory to be shown on the balance sheet. For financial reporting and tax purposes, virtually all manufacturing costs are included, but for some managerial purposes fixed costs of production will be excluded from inventory. The financial reporting approach is called **absorption costing** (or sometimes **full costing**) while the other method is called **variable costing** or **direct costing.** To give a brief illustration, suppose that the Mesa ore-processing plant has the following results for a year.

Production in tons	5,000
Fixed production costs	$15,500,000
Variable production costs	$ 9,750,000

The per unit amount of inventory calculated under the two methods would be as shown below.

$$\text{Cost per ton, absorption costing} = \$5,050 = \frac{\$15,500,000 + \$9,750,000}{5,000}$$

$$\text{Cost per ton, direct costing} = \$1,950 = \frac{\$9,750,000}{5,000}$$

The $5,050 figure would be used for financial reporting and tax accounting, and the $1,950 would be used for some managerial purposes, especially decision making. The reasoning behind these different approaches will be discussed and illustrated in later chapters.

Other questions still remain. Suppose that Mesa's ore processing plant also contains sales offices. Heat, light, depreciation on the building, and property taxes relate both to production and to selling. Determining how much of these costs to treat as manufacturing costs and, therefore, as part of the cost of inventory, and how much to treat as selling expenses is not easily resolved. Another sticky area is exemplified by Mesa's producing both yellow cake and vanadium from the same ore, in the same process. Products that arise as separate entities only after some processing are called **joint products** (or by-products), and the costs of bringing them to their separate states are called **joint costs.** The problem here, which is discussed fully in later chapters, is how much of the joint cost (cost of ore, labor, and so on) of producing uranium and vanadium should be allocated to each product.

Even though lease management is not a product, the division of common (joint) costs is crucial here, too. Many of the leases of government property call for a minimum amount of money to be spent on each block of claims. Mesa may send a group of geologists and engineers out to do various exploration tasks on hundreds of square miles of land belonging to many private and public owners. These costs must then be assigned to each tax property in an equitable manner in order to meet the terms of the lease.

DECISION MAKING

Making a decision means choosing one course of action from among the available alternatives. The management of Great Midwest decided to establish Mesa rather than take some other action. Presumably, Great Midwest could have decided to ignore nuclear power and continue to use coal, or it could have tried to obtain long-term contracts to obtain nuclear fuel from independent suppliers. The decision to establish Mesa will affect the future of Great Midwest. In fact, all decisions affect the future, not the past. For this reason a manager needs information about the future. However, in the strictest sense, information about the future cannot be obtained, because the future cannot be known with certainty. Therefore, all decisions involve some risk. It may well turn out that Great Midwest would have been better off ignoring nuclear power, but no one can know that for some time.

One of the main jobs of the accountant is to develop information to be used for decision making—that is, information about future revenues and costs. In some cases the information can be developed from the historical data provided by the accounting system. If the ore processing plant manager is concerned with the level of future production costs, the accountant may be able to tell him that costs will be approximately $15 million plus $2,000 per ton processed, as described in a previous section. This formula for predicting costs would be reasonable so long as the manager did not plan any changes in the production process and so long as there were no other changes (such as increases in wage rates) on the horizon. However, the formula does not consider that there are likely to be random fluctuations from the predicted cost. Even such an estimate is subject to uncertainty.

In other cases the accounting system cannot be relied on to provide good predictions. The manager of the processing plant may be considering a change in the production process and, therefore, would wish to know the likely effects on costs. The accountant would work with the plant manager and plant engineers to determine the probable effects on such factors as labor time. It might be that changing the process would reduce labor time by about 10 percent. The accountant would estimate the consequent savings in costs and, together with the other managers, try to determine whether the proposed change would be worthwhile.

Accountants are staff personnel: they do not have the authority to make final decisions on such matters as changing production processes. But they do exercise authority by expertise: their advice is often taken because they are the most knowledgeable managers in their own field. In some situations the accountant may have to expend considerable effort to persuade another manager to take a recommended course of action and may have to educate the other manager in the analysis and interpretation of cost information. We shall see in later chapters that determining what information is relevant for decision making is often a difficult task and that some managers may tend to use information inappropriately. The accountant's choice of information, its presentation, and efforts in persuading managers to use the information wisely may be of great benefit to the firm.

Although the accountant does not have the final say in operating decisions, he or she usually takes part in the analysis and discussion that lead up to the decision. In recent years management scientists have developed a number of sophisticated techniques for dealing with uncertainty. Accountants have been involved in these developments. In later chapters we shall describe and illustrate some of these techniques.

BEHAVIORAL CONSIDERATIONS

A principal area of recent research in cost and managerial accounting is human behavior, especially the effects that various accounting techniques and practices can have on the performance of managers. The study of management from a behavioral standpoint is relatively new. Only in the past fifteen or so years have management courses emphasized behavioral dimensions. Accountants now know that their work can affect managers' behavior, sometimes favorably, sometimes unfavorably. We have glimpsed the problem in the discussion of responsibility accounting, we expand on it briefly here, and we shall consider it in greater detail in later chapters.

This chapter has stressed the development of information for various purposes. It is commonly thought that information can be unbiased, neutral, and objective: that properly presented information will lead a manager to take the best action. This just is not so. *People* make decisions, evaluate subordinates, control their operations. Quantitative information, which is the stock in trade of accounting, does not capture all the relevant factors and may influence managers to take unwise actions.

Consider this example. Managers are often evaluated on the basis of their meeting a budget. Production managers who know they will almost certainly exceed their flexible budget allowance for a certain period may be tempted to take some unwise actions. They could reduce costs, and thereby meet or more closely approach the budget, by postponing expenditures for maintenance, employee training, quality control, and other items. Reducing these costs will increase profits in the short term but could have serious adverse effects in the longer term. Managers would tend to act this way when higher-level managers viewed budgets as strict rules not to be broken.

COST CLASSIFICATIONS

We have seen that different types of costs are used for different purposes. The fixed versus variable cost distinction is important for planning and budgeting, while for responsibility accounting the critical consideration is whether the cost is controllable by a particular manager. Product costing using the absorption costing method requires the calculation of a fixed cost per unit, while variable costing does not.

In the remainder of the book we shall see that a single cost may be treated in several ways for different purposes; that a cost may be relevant for one purpose, irrelevant for another. Our attention will focus on the purposes for which the information is needed and on the development of information with its intended use in mind.

SUMMARY

Cost accounting information is used for many different purposes, and the type of information required for one use may not be the same as that required for others. The principal purpose of cost accounting is to provide information that managers can use to plan and control their operations, make decisions, and evaluate performance. Another important purpose is to provide information used for product costing for financial reporting and income taxation.

The topics of budgeting, analysis of cost behavior, and development of responsibility accounting systems were introduced, along with the very important topic of the behavioral considerations involved in developing and reporting accounting information.

ASSIGNMENTS

1–1 Questions About Accounting. The year has just begun and you have enrolled in a course entitled Cost Accounting. Your roommate, who is not a business school student, asks you the following questions:

1. "Is this cost accounting course like the last accounting course you took? You did all sorts of debits and credits and things like that in the previous course. What makes this course different?"

2. "I was reading over your shoulder while you looked at Chapter 1 and saw something about behavioral considerations in accounting. I thought accounting was just numbers. What is this behavioral stuff and how does it apply to accounting?"

Required: Please answer your roommate's questions.

1–2 Some Basic Questions.

Required: Answer the following questions independently.

1. What are some major differences between a service industry (such as a public accounting firm) and a manufacturing industry (such as a manufacturer of automobile tires)? How would these two differ from or resemble a retailing establishment (such as a department store)?

2. What do you think the differences are between the following companies? The Apex Ship Building Company manufactures luxury yachts to individual customers' specifications. Each boat is unique in design and finish. Broward Chemical Company, on the other hand, puts a single raw material (a petroleum derivative) through a single, continuous, and complex manufacturing process that, with the addition of certain other chemicals at various stages, yields ten different final products.

1-3 Managerial Information. For many years Irving Flycatcher had worked as an engineer in the rate department of Northern-Southern Power Company. Early in 19X1, Flycatcher and Sandy Newburglar, an attorney, decided to open a consulting business specializing in energy and other related matters. Accordingly, the two became partners in a new corporation called Energy Resource Associates.

Both Flycatcher and Newburglar had many talents besides just consulting in the energy field. As an attorney, Newburglar wanted to do some regular corporate work for clients. Flycatcher had much experience in areas of accounting and engineering and could do miscellaneous consulting in those fields.

The usual procedure was that one of the principals in the company would bid a contract to a client for consulting services. Sometimes, when further expertise was needed, the company would hire outside personnel to aid the two partners.

The new corporation had only the two principals as shareholders. The only information that needed to be generated external to the firm would be tax returns. Neither of the two had any experience in setting up an accounting and information system.

Required: Flycatcher and Newburglar have come to you for aid. First give them a description of the kind of business they are in. Then prepare a general discussion and outline of the type of information you think they will need in order to manage their new company. Consider what you would want to know if you were a partner in this business. What information would you need for planning? What for controlling? How would you organize costs?

1-4 Managerial Information. On the advice of a friend, Conrad Archer was employed as a management consultant to Henderson Appliances, a retail store dealing in major appliances such as refrigerators, freezers, washers, dryers, and television sets. Roger Henderson, the sole proprietor, was prompted to call Mr. Archer by various suppliers and by his bank.

Henderson Appliances had been in business for about two years. While

Roger Henderson was basically an honest person, several problems had cropped up. Henderson recommended to Archer that he talk to one of his major suppliers as well as to his banker before visiting. Archer's interview with a major supplier yielded the following:

> I like Roger and I think he is in a position to have a successful business. However, I just don't understand how he has stayed in business this long. When we have called him and asked him about paying a bill, he has always come through. However, on a recent personal visit when this issue came up, I found out that the way he generates cash is to sell some merchandise below cost. Thus, if he is buying a group of washing machines from me, he may dispose of some television sets at below what he paid for them.

An interview with Henderson's banker provided similar information:

> We are willing to stand behind Roger, but we are very concerned about his future. It is not uncommon that we have to hold 20 to 30 checks in the bank because there are not enough funds in Roger's account. Depending on the pressures Roger receives, he comes in and tells us the priority of paying checks as funds become available. In addition, I am concerned that Roger does not know how to differentiate between the direct costs of merchandise that he buys and the entire cost of doing business and earning a profit.

With this information, Mr. Archer met at some length with Roger Henderson. During the interview, Roger Henderson said:

> I know I need help. That is why I called you in. I hope that the information you got from one of my suppliers and my banker has been helpful. I really am confused as to how to run a business. I am not sure what information I need so that I can figure out what prices I should charge, what it costs me to do business, when I should order in new goods, and some way to know if I am making money. I am confused and need your help.

Required: If you were Mr. Archer, what would you identify as the problems that Roger Henderson needs to address? What decisions does Henderson need to make on a daily, monthly, or yearly basis? What kind of information will he need to make these decisions?

1–5 Data and Information. The Fancy Pharmaceuticals Company produces a major line of over-the-counter drugs and a major line of prescription drugs. The company has divided the production and sale of these two lines into separate divisions. Arthur Abraham, general manager of the prescription drug line, has been talking to one of his salespeople, Alice Carney. Carney has been discussing a recent contact she had with a customer:

> Arthur, we have a problem that we need to solve. I went into Ajax Drug Stores the other day and talked with Irving Ajax. We were discussing terms for our new contract. He is interested in adding both our prescription and our nonprescrip-

tion line to his drug store chain. We spent a long time talking about the FDA and how they define the difference between prescription and nonprescription drugs. Irving is concerned over the recent trend in Washington to hold back drugs from the market too long. The FDA seems to require such a very long testing program over so many years that Irving thinks it does not take care of the public at large. Of course, there is the other side that the FDA is really protecting the public by this rigorous program.

Irving's credit seems to be very good. I have talked with the nonprescription division and they are interested in his business. Most of his drug stores are in Peoria, but he does have a few in Matoon. The Matoon market is very interesting with the decrease of the central business district and the addition of those three new shopping malls on the outskirts of town. As I see it, we need to sign a contract with Ajax covering the next three years for a minimum amount of our full line of prescription drugs. I don't know what kind of arrangements the other division is making with Ajax. I just know they are interested in the account as well. If we don't make a deal with them now, Ajax may sign up with Trell Chemical instead. Tell me, boss, what should I do?

Required: What should Abraham's response be to Carney?

Cost-Volume-Profit Analysis

Chapter 2

Accountants and other managers are continually planning operations and making analyses to find the best answers to questions about the probable consequences of following particular courses of action. Such questions would include, among many others: "What will our profits be if we sell 3,000 units? What effects on profits would be likely if we reduced our selling prices and sold more units? Would it be wiser to pay our salespeople a straight commission, straight salary, or some combination of the two?" These and other questions can be approached using cost-volume-profit analysis.

Cost-volume-profit (hereafter CVP) analysis is the most fundamental tool in the accountant's repertoire because it provides straightforward ways to approach the problems implied by the questions posed in the paragraph above.[1] CVP relationships are a basis for virtually all of managerial accounting, and they are essential to the understanding of the value and the limitations of the cost accounting techniques that we discuss in this book.

CVP analysis is a systematic method of examining the relationships among the variables that determine profits: revenues and costs. As a model of these relationships, it simplifies real-world conditions that a firm faces. Like most models that are abstractions from reality, CVP analysis has a number of underlying assumptions and limitations that we discuss later in this chapter. Despite these limitations, it is a powerful tool that can help managers make better decisions.

VOLUME AND COST BEHAVIOR

In CVP analysis, **volume** refers to the level of some activity of the firm. Volume can be measured by sales in units, sales dollars, production in units,

---

[1] Cost-volume-profit analysis is also called breakeven analysis, profit-volume analysis, and volume-cost-profit analysis. All the terms refer to the same basic techniques.

hours worked by employees, or any other activity that might be important. However, either sales in units or in dollars is the measure of volume used most commonly in this context, and we will be concerned with these measures in this chapter. Other measures of volume will become important later on as we analyze the various ways of dealing with costs.

Our original assumption is that all costs can be classified by their behavior, whether or not they can be expected to change in response to changes in volume. Costs that can be expected to change as volume changes are called **variable costs.** Costs that will remain constant over fairly wide ranges of volume are called **fixed costs.** Let us consider an example.

The Quadro Company sells high-quality mechanical pencils for $5 each. It buys them for $2.50 each and pays salespeople a 10 percent commission ($0.50) for each pencil sold. Both of these costs are variable, since each time another pencil is sold, costs increase by $3—a figure that includes the costs of the pencils and the commissions that must be paid.[2] The firm also incurs about $5,000 per month for salaries, utilities, and rent. These costs will not change in total in response to changes in volume and, therefore, are fixed. Please notice that salaries, for example, could easily be changed by managerial decision, since salaried employees could be hired, fired, or given raises. When we call a cost a fixed cost we do not claim that it cannot be changed, but rather that it will not automatically change in response to changes in volume. Finally, notice that variable costs are expressed as per unit amounts while fixed costs are expressed as total amounts per period. In this case the period is a month.

The cost behavior of the Quadro Company can be depicted graphically, as we do in the figures opposite. Fixed costs in total remain constant regardless of sales volume, while total variable costs increase as volume increases, at a rate of $3 per unit. Please remember that we have just started out and will introduce some refinements and discuss assumptions shortly. At this stage we are simply trying to get the basic picture.

Let us look now at the basic relationships of CVP analysis. Profit[3] can be expressed as:

$$\text{profit} = \text{sales} - \text{total costs}$$

Because we have classified costs as either fixed or variable with sales, we also have the following equation.

---

[2] In financial accounting, the term *cost* relates to an expenditure: plant and equipment has a cost, as does inventory. The income statement shows *expenses*, costs that have expired in the earning of revenue. CVP analysis could also be termed expense-volume-profit analysis because it deals with expired costs — expenses. We are not concerned with the purchases of pens made by Quadro Company, but rather with the sales. We use the term cost because it is customary and, as later chapters show, its greater generality makes it a more accurate term than expense.

[3] Terms such as *income* and *income before taxes* are commonly used to denote what we call profit. The term *net income* is normally reserved for income after taxes. We consider income taxes later in the chapter.

$$\text{profit} = \text{sales} - \text{total variable costs} - \text{total fixed costs}$$

In order to relate the terms in the equation above to volume, we have to express sales and total variable costs in per unit amounts. We use the following symbols to denote the key variables.

P = selling price per unit
V = variable costs per unit
F = fixed costs per period
Q = unit sales for period
Z = profit for period

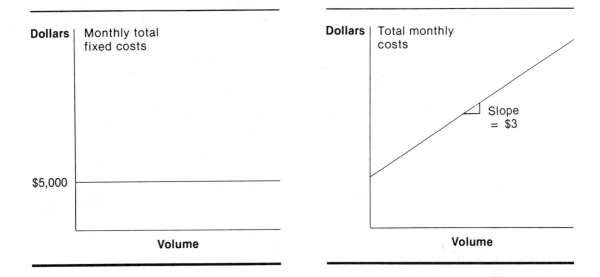

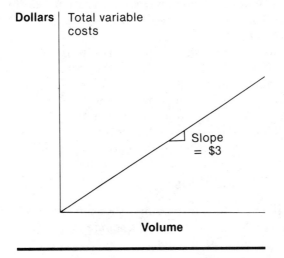

We can now express profit in an equation:

Z	= PQ	− VQ	− F
profit	sales dollars	total variable costs	total fixed costs

Thus, total revenue equals units sold multiplied by price per unit. Profit is determined by subtracting total costs from total revenues. Total costs consist of variable costs per unit multiplied by the number of units sold, plus total fixed costs for the period. Suppose that the managers of the Quadro Company wish to know what profit is likely to be if sales are 4,000 units per month. We substitute the appropriate values into the equation.

$$Z = (\$5 \times 4,000) - (\$3 \times 4,000) - \$5,000$$
$$= \$20,000 - \$12,000 - \$5,000$$
$$= \$3,000$$

We can also express the equation for profit in the following form:

$$Z = (P - V)Q - F$$

Here we express the difference between selling price per unit and variable cost per unit as a single figure $(P - V)$. This amount, called **contribution margin per unit**, is one of the most important concepts in cost and managerial accounting and analysis.

CONTRIBUTION MARGIN

The preceding equation shows contribution margin per unit, but the term **contribution margin** can refer either to the per unit amount or to the total amount. Total contribution margin is equal to contribution margin per unit multiplied by unit sales: that is, the term $(P - V)Q$ is total contribution margin. In a given situation the context will indicate whether the total or per unit amount is meant.

The Quadro Company has a contribution margin of $2 per unit, which is the $5 selling price minus the $3 variable cost. For each unit sold, the firm gains $5 in revenue and sustains $3 in cost, leaving $2 to contribute to the covering of fixed costs and the earning of profits.

Cost-Volume-Profit Relationships

The following income statements for the Quadro Company illustrate some important CVP properties. The income statements reflect results at sales of 6,000 units and 8,000 units.

QUADRO COMPANY
Income Statements

	6,000 Units Sold		8,000 Units Sold	
	$	% of Sales	$	% of Sales
Sales at $5 per unit	$30,000	100.0%	$40,000	100.0%
Variable costs at $3 per unit	18,000	60.0%	24,000	60.0%
Contribution margin at $2 per unit	12,000	40.0%	16,000	40.0%
Monthly fixed costs	5,000	16.7%	5,000	12.5%
Profits	$ 7,000	23.3%	$11,000	27.5%

Sales, total variable costs, and total contribution margin may each be determined by multiplying the appropriate per unit amount by the number of units sold. For example, you could determine that total contribution at 8,000 units sold is $16,000 by multiplying the $2 unit contribution margin by 8,000 units without bothering to compute sales and total variable costs. Additionally, the percentages of variable costs to sales and of contribution margin to sales are constant at 60 percent and 40 percent. Variable cost per unit is 60 percent of the selling price ($3/$5), and total variable costs will be 60 percent of sales. Similarly, contribution margin per unit is 40 percent of selling price ($2/$5), and total contribution margin is 40 percent of sales.

The percentage relationships of fixed costs and of profits to sales do not remain constant. Fixed costs are constant in total and, therefore, decline as a percentage of sales as sales increase. They also decline per unit as sales increase. Once the firm reaches breakeven, profit as a percentage of sales and as a per unit amount increases as sales increase, because profit changes in the same total amount as does contribution margin. It is wrong to use either fixed-cost-per-unit figures or profit-per-unit figures in planning. Such values hold at a single level of volume and cannot be used to predict results at other levels of volume. At 6,000 units, for example, fixed cost per unit is about $0.83 ($5,000/6,000). Using that per unit figure to predict total fixed costs at 8,000 units would yield $6,667, which is greater than the actual fixed costs of $5,000.

Relevant Range

The CVP relationships cannot be expected to hold for all possible volumes. If the Quadro Company managers expected to sell only a few units in a particular month, they would probably cut advertising costs, reduce office hours, and take other steps that would lower fixed costs from the $5,000 level. Similarly, if volume were expected to be 15,000 units, the firm would probably have to increase personnel and take other steps that would increase fixed costs above $5,000. The basic CVP relationships are assumed to hold within a relevant range. The relevant range, then, is self-defining: it is the range of volume where we can expect the CVP relationships to hold reasonably well.

The relevant range might be extremely wide for some firms, quite narrow for others. When we perform the various analyses already illustrated, we are assuming that the volume figures fall within the relevant range. If we have information to the contrary, we make the necessary adjustments.

The concept of a relevant range also has a time dimension. CVP relationships cannot be expected to hold for long periods. We all know that prices change, employees receive salary increases, and so on. The length of time that the relationships remain valid will differ according to the characteristics of the firm. Many authors suggest a year as the likely maximum.

COST-VOLUME-PROFIT GRAPH

Figure 2–1 depicts the revenue and cost functions for the Quadro Company. The horizontal axis is measured in unit sales but could also be measured in dollar sales. Please notice that the lines representing revenues and costs are solid within the relevant range of 2,000 through 9,000 units, dashed outside the range. It is unwise to assume that the behavior of revenues and costs outside the relevant range is the same as it is within the range. Some accountants prefer to draw the lines only within the relevant range; the dashed lines are extended in Figure 2–1 to make it easier to see how the graph is constructed.

Interpreting the Graph

The following points are important in viewing the graph. Profit or loss is measured by the vertical distance between the total-revenue line and the total-cost line at any level of volume. Total variable cost is the vertical difference between the total-cost line and the fixed-cost line at any level of volume. Contribution margin is not so easy to visualize. It is the vertical distance between the total-revenue line and total variable costs at any level of volume. We must determine total variable costs and subtract them from revenues to find contribution margin. Therefore, it cannot be read directly from the graph.

The use of a graph is often helpful in visualizing the effects of changes in volume from currently anticipated levels and in determining how rapidly profits fall if volume falls (or how rapidly they rise if volume rises). Working with the numerical values does not always give this information as clearly as the graph does.

The graphical approach may be especially helpful in assessing the probable effects of changes in the price-cost structure. For example, suppose that the managers of the Quadro Company are considering the possibility of paying salespeople straight salaries of $3,000 per month instead of the

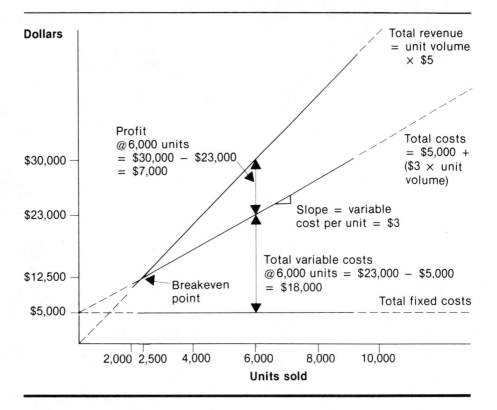

Dollars

Total revenue
= unit volume
× $5

Profit
@ 6,000 units
= $30,000 − $23,000
= $7,000

$30,000 —

Total costs
= $5,000 +
($3 × unit
volume)

Slope = variable
cost per unit = $3

$23,000 —

Total variable costs
@ 6,000 units = $23,000 − $5,000
= $18,000

$12,500 — Breakeven
point

Total fixed costs

$5,000 —

2,000 2,500   4,000   6,000   8,000   10,000

Units sold

FIGURE 2–1
Cost-Volume-Profit Graph, Quadro Company

current $0.50 commission on each unit sold. The proposed change would increase fixed costs from $5,000 to $8,000 per month but would reduce variable cost per unit to $2.50 from $3. The contribution margin percentage would rise from 40 to 50 percent [($5 − $2.50)/$5].

Figure 2–2 on page 30 shows the graph as it would appear under the proposed changes, along with the original results for comparison. Figure 2–2 also uses sales dollars as the measure of volume along the horizontal axis, instead of sales in units. Dollar volume is used at least as often as unit volume and requires only slight changes in constructing the graph. First, the revenue line simply shows the same values on both axes. Second, the total-cost line is developed using the variable-cost percentage of sales instead of the variable cost per unit. Because the variable-cost percentage would be 50 percent under the proposed changes, the total-cost line at any point on the horizontal axis shows the value [(sales dollars × 50%) + $8,000] on the vertical axis.

An examination of Figure 2–2 reveals that the breakeven point would increase to $16,000 in sales from $12,500. We can verify this figure by

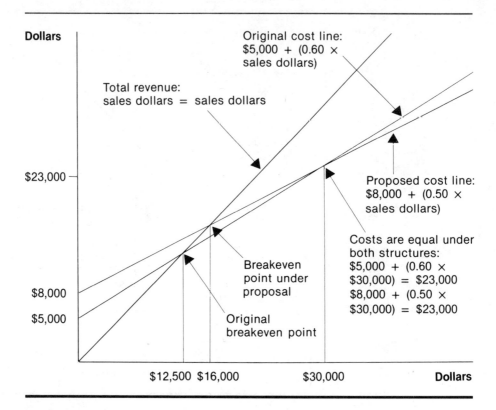

FIGURE 2–2
Alternative Cost Structures, Quadro Company

calculating the new breakeven point. The contribution margin percentage is expected to be 50 percent, fixed costs $8,000. Therefore, $8,000/50% = $16,000. The figure also shows that at volumes below $30,000, total costs would be higher and profits lower under the proposed arrangement than they would under the existing arrangement. However, at volumes above $30,000, total costs would be lower and profits higher under the proposed arrangement.

The decision to make the proposed change would depend on several factors. First, the managers would have to estimate the volumes under each arrangement. If the salespeople were paid straight salary, they might sell fewer units than they would under the commission system, but the reverse could also be true. If sales under both arrangements were expected to be the same, the decision would hinge on whether volume could be expected to exceed $30,000. If it did, the proposed arrangement would be better; if not, the existing arrangement would be better.

Later sections of this chapter outline ways of approaching such decisions. The graphical approach shows the probable effects of changes but does not necessarily indicate that a change should be made.

Alternative Graphical Presentations

Figures 2–3 and 2–4 present two alternative ways of preparing cost-volume-profit graphs for Quadro Company. Figure 2–3 shows a graph with variable costs beginning at the origin and fixed costs added to obtain total costs. This differs from Figures 2–1 and 2–2, where fixed costs were graphed first, with variable costs added to obtain total costs.

This type of presentation allows you to highlight contribution margin, which is difficult to visualize when you use the graph developed in Figures 2–1 and 2–2. In Figure 2–3, contribution margin is the difference between the revenue line and the variable-cost line.

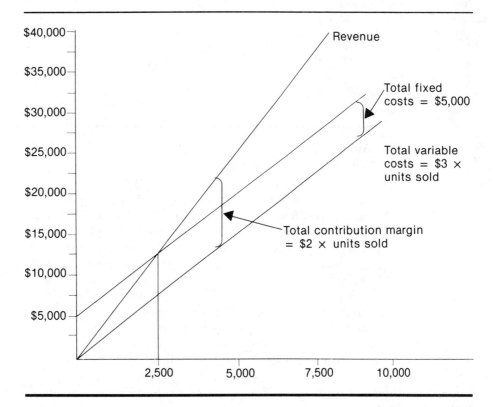

FIGURE 2–3
Alternative CVP Graph, Quadro Company

Figure 2–4 on page 32 shows what is usually called a **profit graph.** The height of the line at any point is profit or loss. The line begins at a negative amount equal to fixed costs. If we assume that fixed costs would be $5,000 at zero volume, the firm would show a loss of $5,000 at zero sales. The line rises at the rate of $2 contribution margin per unit, crossing the zero-profit point (breakeven) at 2,500 units.

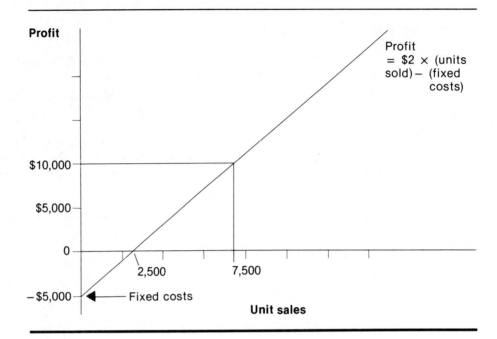

FIGURE 2–4
Profit Graph, Quadro Company

The type of graph shown in Figure 2–4 is helpful in several ways. One is that it has fewer lines and is easier to read. This makes it especially desirable in graphing alternatives, such as the payment of salaries to salespeople instead of commissions. Several alternatives can easily be put on one graph such as Figure 2–4, but not so easily on graphs such as Figures 2–1, 2–2, and 2–3.

These alternatives should give you an idea of the diversity in graphical analysis. Each has advantages and disadvantages, just as the graphs in Figures 2–1 and 2–2. Choosing from among the alternatives depends on your own preferences, on what aspect of your firm's operations you want to highlight, and on the audience that will see your presentation.

TARGET PROFITS

CVP analysis is used to solve for variables other than profit. Sometimes managers will want to know the sales required to earn a particular profit that they have set as an objective. Such a profit is often called a **target profit.** At other times managers may wish to know the sales required to just cover fixed costs without earning any profit or showing any loss. The level of sales required to show a zero profit is called the **breakeven point.** Breaking even is rarely an objective for a business firm but sometimes is a goal of a not-for-profit entity. The executive board of a student union may wish to break even for the year, as might the board of directors of a nursery school. In a business context, the breakeven point is of interest if managers have a reasonably good idea of future sales levels and want to know how much cushion they have between expected sales and sales at breakeven.

Target Profit and Volume

The determination of volume required to earn a target profit starts with the basic equation for profit.

$$(P - V)Q - F = Z$$

For simplicity let $C = (P - V)$.

$$CQ - F = Z$$
$$CQ = Z + F$$
$$Q = \frac{Z + F}{C}$$

In words, the sales volume in units required to earn a particular target profit is the sum of fixed costs and the target profit divided by contribution margin per unit:

$$\text{sales units required} = \frac{\text{target profit} + \text{fixed costs}}{\text{contribution margin per unit}}$$

The breakeven point for the Quadro Company is 2,500 units, calculated as follows:

$$Q = \frac{\$0 + \$5,000}{\$2} = 2,500$$

Similarly, sales required to earn a target profit of $12,000 per month are 8,500 units:

$$Q = \frac{\$12,000 + \$5,000}{\$2} = 8,500 \text{ units}$$

Contribution Margin Percentage

We said earlier that the contribution margin as a percentage of sales remains constant over different volumes. For Quadro Company, the contribution margin percentage is 40 percent, which is $2/$5. We could also find this percentage by looking at an income statement for Quadro

Company that reflected any level of sales. The contribution margin percentage may be used instead of the per unit contribution margin in calculating profits and sales required to earn particular target profits. When the contribution margin percentage is used to solve for required volume, the required volume is expressed in sales dollars, rather than sales units. Starting with the formula for required sales in units,

$$Q = \frac{Z + F}{C}$$

multiply both sides by price (P):

$$PQ = \frac{P(Z + F)}{C}$$

Then divide the numerator and denominator of the right-hand side by P:

$$PQ = \frac{Z + F}{C/P}$$

Since contribution margin per unit divided by price is the contribution margin percentage, the formula may be expressed in words:

$$\text{sales dollars required} = \frac{\text{target profit + fixed costs}}{\text{contribution margin percentage}}$$

Thus, sales dollars required to break even for the Quadro Company are $12,500, calculated as follows:

$$\text{sales dollars required} = \frac{\$0 + \$5,000}{40\%}$$

$$PQ = \$12,500$$

The contribution margin ratio has a distinct advantage over the contribution margin per unit when the firm sells more than one product. A department store may sell articles ranging in contribution margin per unit from a few cents to hundreds of dollars. Similar disparities in unit contribution margin would be found in many other types of firms. A clothing manufacturer might earn $30 contribution margin on one type of sport coat, $18 on a different type. In the face of these different unit contribution margins we cannot work with a single per unit contribution margin for the firm as a whole. Under some conditions, though, we may be able to work with the contribution margin percentage.

First, if all products have the same contribution margin ratio, despite having different per unit amounts, we can perform all standard CVP analyses using the contribution margin ratio. If the ratio were 40 percent across all products, then each $100 in sales would produce $40 in contribution margin no matter which particular products were sold. It could be ten units of one product, fifteen units of another, and 5 units of a third. It could be any combination adding up to $100 in sales.

Second, if contribution margin ratios differ across individual products, but the products are generally sold in about the same relative percentages, the overall contribution margin ratio will be reasonably constant and can be used for CVP analysis. We shall illustrate this principle later in this chapter, but for now we show one example. Suppose that a firm sells two general classes of products, one having a contribution margin ratio of 40 percent, the other a ratio of 50 percent. If the products are usually sold in equal dollar amounts each period, the firm's overall contribution margin ratio will be 45 percent. Half its sales dollars will generate a 40 percent contribution margin, half a 50 percent margin, so that on the average the ratio will be 45 percent.

OTHER PROFIT ANALYSES

Managers are interested in many types of analysis besides the calculation of profits and the volume required to earn a specific target profit. Consider a few such analyses that the managers of the Quadro Company might be interested in making. One possible decision is whether the firm should increase its fixed costs in an effort to secure greater volume. Suppose that the sales manager of Quadro Company believed that an increase in advertising costs of $1,000 per month would result in increased sales of $3,000. Would the advertising costs be a wise investment? Nothing is said about the level of sales expected if the advertising campaign is not undertaken. It is not necessary to know this level, only to know that the expected increase in sales is $3,000.

If sales increase by $3,000 from whatever level they would otherwise attain, total contribution margin will increase by $1,200, which is Quadro Company's contribution margin percentage of 40 percent multiplied by the sales increase of $3,000. Hence the firm would have an additional contribution margin of $1,200 and increased fixed costs of $1,000, leaving an increase in profit of $200. The campaign would appear to be wise if the sales increase did materialize.

Target Return on Sales

Managers sometimes wish to earn a profit that is a given percentage of sales. This ratio, income/sales, is called **return on sales** and is a frequently used measure of profitability, as you may have seen in financial accounting or financial management courses. Sometimes return on sales is viewed as a norm for firms in a particular industry. Some trade associations publish percentage income statements showing what the average firm earns as a percentage of its sales, as well as showing various costs as percentages of sales. A manager might be interested in finding the volume required to earn the industry average return on sales, or perhaps to earn a percentage point or more higher.

Suppose that the managers of the Quadro Company believe that the firm should be able to earn a 15 percent return on sales. The target profit would then be stated as 15 percent of sales. For simplicity, we define S as total sales dollars, $S = PQ$, and M as the contribution margin percentage, $M = (P - V)/P$. Then, using the relationship developed above,

$$MS - F = Z$$
$$.40S - F = Z$$
$$.40S - \$5,000 = .15S$$
$$.25S = \$5,000$$
$$S = \$20,000$$

That is, the firm must have sales of $20,000 to earn a 15 percent return on sales. At that level of sales, profit would be $3,000 [($20,000 × .40 − $5,000)], which is 15 percent of the $20,000 sales. In simplified formula form, the sales required are:

$$\text{sales required} = \frac{\text{fixed costs}}{\text{contribution margin percentage} - \text{target return on sales}}$$

This form of the expression states that the required sales are equal to fixed costs divided by the contribution margin percentage minus the target return on sales. The logic of this formula is that of each dollar of sales, 60 percent (the variable-cost ratio) goes to covering variable costs and 15 percent goes to providing the desired return on sales. Therefore, 25 percent is available for covering fixed costs. In essence, the contribution margin ratio of 40 percent is divided between the 15 percent desired profit and the 25 percent fixed costs.

A Pricing Decision

Suppose now that the managers of the Quadro Company are contemplating a change in the selling price of the product. They believe that sales will be 6,000 units and wish to know what price would yield a $12,000 monthly profit. First, recall that the firm pays $2.50 per unit for its product and that the remainder of the variable cost per unit is a 10 percent commission to salespeople. If the selling price changes, the commission per unit will change, but not the $2.50 purchase price. Starting with the basic CVP equation,

$$(P - V)Q - F = Z$$

we substitute the relevant values:

$$(P - \$2.50 - .10P)(6,000) - \$5,000 = \$12,000$$

The term within the parentheses represents the selling price minus the $2.50 purchase cost minus the commission, which will be 10 percent of the selling price.

$$6,000P - \$15,000 - 600P - \$5,000 = \$12,000$$
$$5,400P = \$32,000$$
$$P \cong \$5.926$$

At a price of $5.93 (rounded) the firm will earn $12,000 monthly, provided that it can sell 6,000 units at that price. Pricing decisions are among the most common made by managers, especially in the consumer goods industries. Most firms have some discretion over prices, but rarely can they set whatever price they please and expect to achieve the same volume that would be achieved at a lower price. We examine the relationship between price and volume later in this chapter; for now we observe that it should be obvious that if competitors of the Quadro Company are selling similar pencils for $4.80 or $5.00, then Quadro will probably have some trouble selling very many at $5.93 per pencil. Prices set using CVP analysis must be reviewed for reasonableness in the light of the competitive conditions in the market in which the firm sells its products. They cannot be too far out of line with the competition.

So far, managers of the Quadro Company have found critical values for unit sales, dollar sales, and selling price. Each analysis has involved a particular arrangement of the basic CVP equation, $Z = CQ - F$. Each problem dealt with so far has had only one unknown. Chapter 4 deals with some decision-making problems with two or more unknowns.

RISK AND RETURN

Anyone would prefer a higher income to a lower income, other things being equal. But other things are not usually equal: if you wish to earn higher incomes (returns), usually you must accept greater risk. If you have saved $10,000 and wish to invest it, you have many choices. You could buy government bonds or notes and earn a virtually certain return of perhaps 7 percent on your $10,000. You could buy a partnership share in an oil drilling expedition that might return 60 percent per year, but you would lose your $10,000 if the operation went broke. In between, you might buy common stocks of well-established firms with the expectation of earning perhaps a 15 percent return. There is the possibility of loss if the stock prices fall, but you would almost certainly not lose your entire investment.

Managers face decisions involving risk and return every day. It is usually riskier to concentrate on new products than on established, existing ones, but it is also potentially more profitable. Increasing the degree of automation in a factory is potentially profitable, but also riskier because it adds fixed costs that will not be avoided if volume does not live up to expectations. Basic CVP analysis is not set up to deal with risk, but it can be adapted to do so in several ways. One method is sensitivity analysis.

Sensitivity Analysis

Sensitivity analysis refers to a number of techniques employed to determine whether a particular factor in a decision is critical. In a CVP context, if a relatively small change in a factor such as unit volume would cause a large change in profit, we would say that profit is sensitive to changes in volume and that volume is a critical factor. Sensitivity analysis finds much of its use in decision-making situations. Consider the two income statements shown below, which portray the expected annual results of two products, A and B. A firm's managers are considering which product to add to the existing line; they will not choose both.

	A		B	
	Dollar Volume	Percent of Sales	Dollar Volume	Percent of Sales
Sales	$800,000	100.0%	$1,000,000	100.0%
Variable costs	600,000	75.0%	300,000	30.0%
Contribution margin	200,000	25.0%	700,000	70.0%
Fixed costs	120,000		600,000	
Income	$ 80,000		$ 100,000	

The expected profits from product B are $20,000 greater than those from product A. If the managers of the firm were certain that the results would be as shown in these income statements, they would prefer product B to product A. However, the figures given are estimates that may not come true, and the managers should go further before deciding. They should determine how profits of each product would be affected by shortfalls.

One common test of sensitivity is the **margin of safety** (MOS). The MOS is the decline in sales that would bring the firm, or product, to breakeven. It may be expressed as a decline in units, dollars, or percentage from the expected level. Product B has a higher contribution margin percentage than product A. This means that the income of product B will be more sensitive to (will increase or decrease more rapidly in response to) changes in sales volume than will that of product A. Equal dollar changes in sales will produce greater income changes for product B. The breakeven points and MOS's are calculated on page 39. We do not have unit data and therefore cannot calculate the MOS in units.

	A	B
Fixed costs	$120,000	$600,000
Divided by: Contribution margin percentage	25%	70%
Equals: Breakeven point in sales dollars	$480,000	$857,143
Margin of safety in dollars:		
$800,000 − $480,000	$320,000	
$1,000,000 − $857,143		$142,857
Margin of safety, percentage:		
$320,000/$800,000	40%	
$142,857/$1,000,000		14.3%

Does it follow that product B is riskier than product A because its margin of safety is lower? Not necessarily. A more complete evaluation would require a great deal more information about the probable ranges within which sales of the two products could be expected to fall. For example, if there are significant probabilities that volumes could be 20 to 25 percent below the expected levels, it would be reasonable to say that selecting product B over product A would entail the firm's taking on more risk. At volumes 20 percent or so below expected levels product B would show losses, while product A would show profits.

The profits of product B are more sensitive to changes in volume than those of product A because the contribution margin percentage of product B is higher than that of product A. Therefore, equal dollar changes in sales volume will produce greater changes in profit for product B on both the upside and the downside.

Sensitivity analysis can be applied to any of the critical variables: price, variable costs, fixed costs, and unit volume. A general procedure is to determine the change in profits that accompanies a specific change in one of the variables. In our example, any percentage change in sales volume would produce greater changes in profits for product B than for product A. However, it might be that volume is relatively certain and that the variable-cost percentages and, therefore, contribution margin percentages are in doubt. The reason could be that the cost of a component of each product is uncertain or that the amount of a sales commission to be given may change from that used in determining the variable-cost percentage.

Suppose that variable costs turn out to be higher than expected and that the managers are concerned about the potential effects on profits. Looking back at the original income statements, we can see that equal percentage changes in variable costs, say 10 percent increases, would affect the profits of product A more than those of product B. A 10 percent increase in unit variable costs would cause a $60,000 decline in product A's profits ($600,000 × 10%) and a $30,000 decline in product B's ($300,000 × 10%).

The use of sensitivity analysis requires consideration of each specific situation. In our example, supposing that sales volume is the only factor that may be different from expected, we might be justified in saying that product B presents better opportunities for higher profits than does product A, but at the risk of having lower profits if expectations do not materialize. Managers who are conservative and inclined to avoid risk at the expense of sacrificing possibly higher profits might choose product A. More venturesome managers might be more likely to choose product B. The whole question of risk and return is extremely complex, and this book can only scratch the surface. An intuitive approach to the trade-off between risk and return is suggested by an anecdote concerning the late Bernard Baruch, a prominent Wall Street financier. A young man approached Baruch seeking advice on investing a newly inherited fortune. Baruch replied, "Young man, do you wish to eat well or sleep well?" That is, if you wish to eat well, you must take some risk in the hope of earning higher returns. If you wish to sleep well, you invest conservatively and accept lower, but more certain, returns.

Indifference Point

One method of testing for sensitivity in a decision-making situation is to determine the **indifference point,** which is the point at which profits will be equal under two different alternatives. The indifference point may be stated in terms of volume, selling price, or any other critical variable. To illustrate, assume that a firm has two possible ways to manufacture an essential component for a major product. One method requires a great deal of labor and little equipment; the other is highly automated and requires much less labor but a great deal of equipment, which would be leased from another firm. Data on the two alternatives are given below. Because the revenue from the product is the same no matter how the part is made, we need only consider costs.

	Labor-Intensive Process	Automated Process
Variable cost per unit	$12	$7
Annual fixed costs	$250,000	$800,000

We first determine the unit volume at which profits will be the same under either alternative. Because selling price is the same either way, we need only solve for the volume where total costs will be the same. Because total cost is $VQ + F$, we have for the labor-intensive process

$$TC = \$12Q + \$250,000$$

and for the automated process

$$TC = \$7Q + \$800,000$$

The indifference point is the value of Q at which total costs are the same for both processes. Calling the indifference point Q_i, we have

$$\$12Q_i + \$250,000 = \$7Q_i + \$800,000$$
$$\$5Q_i = \$550,000$$
$$Q_i = \$110,000$$

At unit volume of 110,000, total costs and profits will be equal under the two alternatives. Notice that the next-to-last step ($\$5Q_i = \$550,000$) simply expresses the difference in variable cost per unit and difference in total annual fixed costs. The calculation answers the question, how many times must we save \$5 per unit in order to make up for an additional \$550,000 in fixed costs?

Suppose now that volume is expected to be 120,000 units per year. The automated process would give \$50,000 lower total costs and higher profits than the labor-intensive process. Each additional unit costs an additional \$12 with the labor-intensive process or \$7 with the automated process. Hence the firm saves \$5 per unit for each unit produced using the automated process. Because total costs are the same at 110,000 units, the additional 10,000 units over the indifference point would cost \$50,000 less under the automated process ($\$5 \times 10,000$ units).

The decision to use the automated process is sensitive to changes in volume. A drop of anything more than 10,000 units, or 8.33 percent, from the expected volume would make the labor-intensive process the better alternative.

The indifference point may also be expressed in terms of other variables. Perhaps the 120,000 volume figure is relatively certain, but the variable cost per unit under the automated process is uncertain. It may turn out to be more than \$7, and we want to find out how high it could go without changing the decision to use the automated process. Volume is known, so we can express the equality of total costs under the two methods as $\$12(120,000) + \$250,000 = V(120,000) + \$800,000$, where V is the variable cost per unit that will equate total costs under the two alternative processes. Solving for V, we find:

$$\$1,440,000 + \$250,000 = 120,000V + \$800,000$$
$$\$1,690,000 - \$800,000 = 120,000V$$
$$120,000V = \$890,000$$
$$V = \$7.417 \text{ (rounded)}$$

That is, if variable costs under the automated process go over the \$7.417 mark, the better decision is to use the labor-intensive process. The \$0.417 increase in variable cost per unit over the estimated \$7 amount is a bit less than 6 percent, which indicates that the decision is also sensitive to the estimate of variable cost per unit for the automated process.

Which process should be adopted? Again, the choice depends on your attitudes about risk and return. There is no one best answer; the choices of individual managers (and students) would indicate whether they preferred lower expected profits accompanied by lower risk, or vice versa.

ASSUMPTIONS OF CVP ANALYSIS

CVP analysis can be used to answer several types of questions and can be helpful in decision making. We have also seen how it can be used when the accountant is uncertain about some of the variables used in the analysis. Even so, can we really expect it to work in practice? What about inflation? Is it really likely that fixed costs will remain fixed and variable cost per unit will remain constant throughout the relevant range? In fact, is it realistic to say that all costs are either fixed or variable with sales?

The following sections discuss the assumptions of CVP analysis and the consequences for the validity of the analysis if the assumptions are not met. We also discuss some ways in which the analysis can be changed to make it more consistent with the critical assumptions.

Conceptual Considerations

Figure 2–5 shows two types of revenue and cost functions. The solid curves are drawn as an economist might portray the operations of a firm, the dashed lines as accountants and other managers typically portray them. The dashed lines do not extend as far as the curves, consistent with the concept of the relevant range. (Most accountants have sufficient knowledge of economic theory to be aware of what is usually called the economist's model of the firm. Accountants and other managers use the linear model primarily for greater simplicity and because it is a good approximation of the behavior of revenues and costs within the relevant range.)

Basic economic theory provides the explanations for the curvilinear behavior of the revenue and cost functions. Taking revenues first, the curve shows that total revenue does not rise at a constant rate, but at a decreasing rate. This behavior results from the law of demand, which states that, other things being equal, the lower the price the higher the quantity buyers will demand and vice versa. As a simple example, GM could not sell an unlimited number of cars at their current prices. If GM reduced its prices, the quantities demanded by customers would be greater than at the higher prices.

Notice our conditional statement above about other things being equal. Changes in tastes, in prices of competing goods, and in other factors may make possible rising volume along with rising prices. The point is that the quantity demanded will be greater at lower prices than at higher prices if price is the only factor being changed.

Now consider the cost curve. Notice that it rises rapidly to point A, then less rapidly to point B, then more rapidly again. The economic interpretation of this form of cost curve is that at both very low and very high levels of volume operations are relatively less efficient than in the middle area. Consider an automobile manufacturer. It has large amounts of fixed costs that will be incurred at zero volume, such as depreciation, property taxes, some

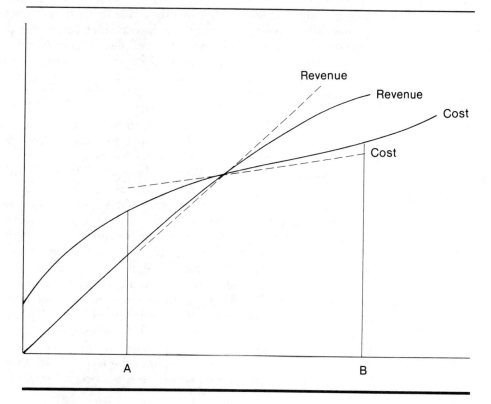

FIGURE 2–5
Linear and Curvilinear CVP Graphs

salaries, and so on. If it operates at very low levels of volume, it must have supervisors, heat, light, and power, inspectors, and enough workers to keep the assembly line going. These workers will be relatively inefficient because they will frequently be idle waiting for additional cars to come along the line. Hence the time they put in might allow for the production of many more cars than they actually produce. The plant will run at normal efficiency at a more reasonable level of volume. However, as production approaches the capacity of the plant, inefficiencies will again arise. Overtime pay will be required at rates higher than straight time, less skilled workers will have to be taken on, more maintenance will be needed because of heavy machine use, and other factors will contribute to more rapidly rising costs.

We meet these theoretical objections to the use of linear CVP analysis by appealing to the relevant range. We assume that linear revenue and cost functions are sufficiently accurate for planning and decision-making purposes within the relevant range. (In fact, we define the relevant range as that area over which linear relationships are reasonably good models.) If the firm is contemplating operations well outside its current relevant range, or if for some other reason it cannot use linear functions, it can still use CVP analysis: it is possible to formulate curvilinear revenue and cost functions and work with them, as we show in the appendix to this chapter.

Practical Considerations

The most pertinent question from a practical point of view is whether *any* curves, linear or nonlinear, can reasonably describe the operations of a modern, complex firm. This question has several aspects.

Managerial Discretion.   We stated early in this chapter that fixed costs are not expected to be absolutely fixed, but that they do not automatically change in response to changes in volume. Managers can raise or lower some fixed costs. Advertising, research and development, and some salaries and bonuses are examples of costs over which managers have discretion. However, costs such as depreciation and property taxes cannot easily be changed in the short term without changing the character of the business.

We assume in CVP analysis that fixed costs will remain constant in that managers will not be changing the levels of costs over which they have discretion. If such changes are being considered, it is still a simple matter to incorporate the probable effects of such changes into the analysis. In fact, one of the basic uses of CVP analysis is determining the probable effects of changes in the key variables. Therefore, the fact that fixed costs may actually be altered by managerial action does not present serious problems for CVP analysis.

Measures of Volume.   We assume that all costs either are fixed or vary with sales. Some costs will probably vary with other measures of volume. Costs of the purchasing department will probably vary with the frequency of purchasing, not with sales volume. Costs of the credit department will probably vary with the number of new customers seeking credit, which in itself may not vary with sales. In short, factors other than sales will cause changes in the level of costs, and therefore our assumption that all costs are fixed or variable with sales is rarely correct.

The fact that some costs will vary with other measures of volume raises two questions. First, are the amounts of such costs likely to be so large that they will harm our analyses? Second, if these costs are large, can we do anything about them so far as CVP analysis is concerned? It is likely that costs that vary with measures of volume other than sales will be relatively low in total and consequently that they will exert very little effect on our analysis. Production costs are an exception because they vary with production, not sales. Production costs provide some problems for CVP analysis, as we discuss later in this chapter and more thoroughly in Chapter 3.

If some costs do vary with other measures of volume, we may still be able to predict them, and prediction is the critical problem. Chapter 3 discusses questions involved in estimating the patterns of cost behavior, and we defer further discussion until then.

Random Fluctuations.   Can we really expect to incur variable costs at a particular amount per unit? Do not the costs of replacing the goods we sell change at fairly frequent intervals? Will not our selling prices change during the next period, perhaps several times? That is, do we honestly expect firms in the real world to be describable by a simple CVP graph or by a simple linear formula for either revenues or costs?

Selling prices, variable costs, and fixed costs are likely to fluctuate over short periods and within the relevant range. We recognize that the selling price might have to be lowered because of competition and that suppliers may raise their prices, thereby increasing unit variable costs. Fixed costs may well fluctuate; heating costs, for example, depend on the weather and cannot be expected to be exactly as predicted. In short, the profits, or the volumes required to earn profits, or any other answers we get from CVP analysis are estimates that cannot be expected to be perfect predictors of actual profits or costs.

Remember that CVP analysis is essentially hypothetical: it answers "what if" questions and requires estimates of the values that key variables will take on. The analysis is not precise. The real question is whether fluctuations in selling prices and costs will be large enough to make significant differences between predicted and actual results. We think that CVP analysis is sufficiently accurate to be of considerable use to managers. It is true that if the firm's selling prices and unit variable costs fluctuate widely over short periods (as is often the case with some agricultural products), then CVP analysis may not be very useful. However, firms facing chaotic situations are relatively rare. The relationships graphed in Figure 2–6 would be appropriate for most firms. The revenue and cost lines in that graph are bands. The single-point estimates that we make are really averages. We usually expect revenues and costs at particular levels of volume to vary somewhat. For example, Figure 2–6 shows the range of expected costs at a volume of 80,000 units. The $250,000 amount is the result of applying CVP analysis, with the $241,000 and $259,000 amounts representing the range of the estimate. That is, we expect that costs will be about $250,000, but we realize that they may be as high as $259,000 or as low as $241,000. Chapter 3 deals in depth with the questions raised by such estimates of the expected range of costs or revenues.

The cost band in Figure 2–6 on page 46 captures much of what we have already said about practical considerations. The effects of managerial discretion over some costs, of the response of some costs to measures of volume other than sales, and of random fluctuations would smear the cost line into a wider band. Chapter 3 treats methods for estimating the ranges of costs. The basic cost-volume-profit model does not provide precise answers but rather gives general ideas about the behavior of revenues and costs.

Sales Mix.   We mentioned earlier that a multiple-product firm would not use a contribution margin per unit but rather an average contribution margin percentage. The reason was that its units might vary greatly in price

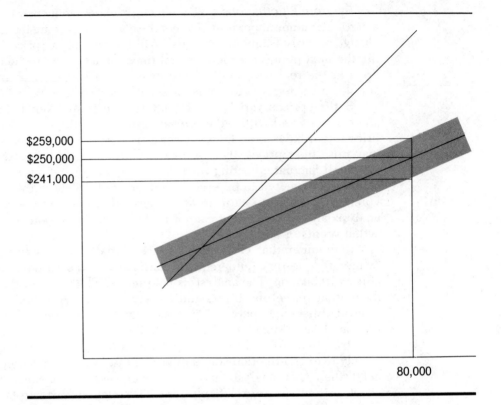

FIGURE 2–6
Cost Band

and contribution margin per unit. We also said that if we were to use the contribution margin percentage, either all products had to have about the same contribution margin percentage, or the mix of sales of individual products had to be relatively constant. The sales mix is the make-up of the relative proportions of products sold. We illustrate below the calculation of a weighted average contribution margin percentage—a percentage that reflects the relative amounts of each product's sales. Data for the illustration are as follows:

	Products			
	A	B	C	Totals
Percentage of dollar sales	40%	25%	35%	100%
Contribution margin percentage	30%	40%	50%	

The weighted average contribution margin percentage is calculated as shown at the top of page 47.

	Products			
	A	B	C	Totals
Sales mix percentage (percentage of dollar sales) × $1 =	40%	25%	35%	100%
Product sales per $1 of total sales ×	$0.40	$0.25	$0.35	$1.00
Contribution margin percentage =	30%	40%	50%	
Contribution margin per dollar of total sales	$0.12	$0.10	$0.175	$0.395
Weighted average contribution margin percentage	39.5%			

The 39.5 percent weighted average contribution margin percentage would be used in making the CVP analyses desired by the managers.

The rationale for these calculations is that of each $1 in total sales, $0.40 comes from product A, and of that $0.40, 30 percent or $0.12 becomes contribution margin. Hence for each $1 in total sales of all three products, product A provides contribution margin of $0.12. Similar reasoning for the other two products leads us to see that the firm gains $0.395 contribution margin for each $1 in total sales, which is 39.5 percent. The calculations can be short-cut so that you simply multiply the sales mix percentage for each product by its contribution margin percentage, then sum the results to get the weighted average contribution margin percentage:

$$39.5\% = (40\% \times 30\%) + (25\% \times 40\%) + (35\% \times 50\%)$$

Please remember: this technique requires that the sales mix remains fairly constant. If the mix changed, say with higher percentages going to product A and lower percentages to product C, the weighted average contribution margin percentage would decline because product A has a lower contribution margin percentage than does product C.

Inventories. Financial reporting practices and income tax law require that fixed production costs be included in the determination of inventory, rather than subtracted from contribution margin as we do in CVP analysis. So long as inventories remain about the same from beginning of period to end of period, the income calculated under the financial reporting and tax method will approximate that calculated by CVP techniques. However, if inventories change significantly, there will be large differences between the income computed under CVP analysis and those under financial-tax requirements. This subject is dealt with in detail in later chapters. We note now that the problem does not invalidate CVP analysis because internal reporting for managerial purposes does not have to conform to that used for financial-tax purposes.

SOME REFINEMENTS

When we take the assumptions of CVP analysis into consideration, we can come up with some modifications in the basic analysis. The distinction between the level of fixed costs expected throughout the relevant range and the level expected at very low operation leads us to classify fixed costs as **avoidable** or **unavoidable.** Avoidable fixed costs are those that can be eliminated by changing the operation, perhaps dropping one product from the firm's line or shutting down a regional sales office. Decisions such as these receive extended treatment in Chapter 4.

Discretionary and Committed Costs

The question whether managers will take action to change costs such as advertising, research and development, employee training, and other costs that may be changed relatively easily leads to another distinction: **discretionary costs** and **committed costs.** Discretionary costs are those that can be changed by management decision within short periods. They are also called managed costs, reflecting the ability of managers to alter them more or less at will. The existence of discretionary costs is the principal reason why some people prefer the term *nonvariable costs* to the term *fixed costs*. These costs do not change automatically and necessarily in response to changes in volume, but they do change, and perhaps frequently, as a result of management decisions.

Analyzing discretionary costs can sometimes present problems. For example, a discretionary cost may appear to be a variable cost because it is incurred at a constant rate of sales. Advertising may always be 5 percent of sales, or research and development 3 percent of sales as a result of a management decision that the firm will base its expenditures for these items on the level of sales. Hence, the costs will hold the same percentage relationships to sales at various levels of volume as the result of management decision, not because of an underlying economic relationship. Cost of goods sold or sales commissions will vary directly with sales because of economic relationships or contractual agreements.

Step-Variable Costs

One reason why we do not expect costs to change in perfectly direct proportion to changes in volume is that some costs are incurred in large chunks, not continuously. For example, a firm may need an additional salaried salesperson for each $10,000 monthly increase in sales. The salary would then behave as shown in Figure 2–7, jumping from one level to the next as each $10,000 increment in sales is reached. These costs[4] are called step-

---

[4] Some writers call these costs *step-fixed* because they remain fixed over some range of volume, then jump to a higher level. We call them step-variable because volume affects their levels.

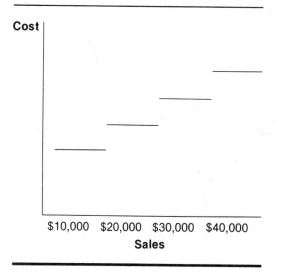

FIGURE 2–7
Step-Variable Cost

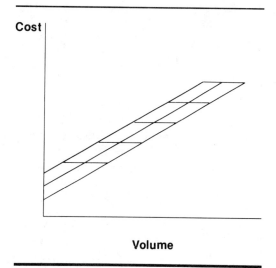

FIGURE 2–8
Planning Step-Variable Costs

variable costs because they vary with volume, but not in direct proportion.

Planning for step-variable costs essentially requires an estimate of the sales level and determination of the number of salaried people required. It is not a matter of multiplying volume by a unit variable cost. If such costs are a large proportion of total costs, planning becomes more tedious, but if they are relatively small in relation to total costs, they may generally be treated as variable costs for firmwide planning.

If step-variable costs are treated as if they were variable, they may be planned for in several ways. Figure 2–8 shows that three different lines could be fitted to the cost behavior pattern. Any one of these lines would yield actual results different from planned costs nearly all the time. The middle line would give the closest estimates on the average and would probably be most useful for that reason.

INCOME TAXES IN CVP ANALYSIS

Our calculations so far have ignored income taxes. Introducing income taxes requires a straightforward modification of our basic profit equation and CVP calculations. We are assuming that income taxes are assessed at a flat rate of pretax income. Tax law, however, is exceedingly complex and requires much careful study; it is not amenable to simple generalizations. For many corporations the flat-rate assumption does little harm to the facts.

The basic equation for profit in the presence of income taxes is given on page 50. The income tax rate is designated T, and income after taxes (or net income) N.

$$N = (PQ - VQ - F)(1 - T)$$

or

$$N = (CQ - F)(1 - T)$$

The term $PQ - VQ - F$ equals income before taxes, what we have previously called Z. Because the government takes a percentage, T, from income before taxes, net income is income before taxes multiplied by $(1 - T)$. The formula to determine the volume required to earn a particular target profit after taxes is found by solving for Q:

$$(CQ - F)(1 - T) = N$$

$$CQ - F = \frac{N}{1 - T}$$

$$CQ = \frac{N}{1 - T} + F$$

$$Q = \frac{\dfrac{N}{1 - T} + F}{C}$$

Please notice that $N/(1 - T) = Z$. That is, net income after taxes divided by 1 minus the tax rate equals pretax income. Expressing this in words, the volume required to earn a particular after-tax profit is the sum of fixed costs and the desired after-tax profit divided by 1 minus the tax rate, all divided by the contribution margin per unit. (The formula also works the same with the contribution margin percentage, giving the answer in dollars of sales.) Dividing the desired after-tax income by $(1 - T)$ gives the pretax profit required to earn the desired after-tax income.

Suppose that the Quadro Company, with its contribution margin of $2 per unit and $5,000 fixed costs, desires an after-tax income of $3,000. The firm is subject to a 40 percent tax rate, including both federal and state income taxes.

$$Q = \frac{\dfrac{\$3,000}{1 - .40} + \$5,000}{\$2}$$

$$= \frac{\$5,000 + \$5,000}{\$2}$$

$$= \$5,000$$

The presence of income taxes does not affect the breakeven point because at that level profits are zero both before and after taxes, there being no income taxes at zero pretax profits.

SUMMARY

CVP analysis is used for planning and decision making. Basic to the analysis is the classification of costs by behavior: whether the cost varies with volume or remains constant through wide ranges of volume. The concept of contribution margin is critical to CVP analysis: it is used to find required volumes and to solve for other important unknowns in various situations.

CVP analysis is underlain by a number of assumptions. It is not expected to be literally true for all firms from zero to high volumes. The analysis will often produce reasonable results that can be used within the relevant range. It can be used to answer questions such as the following: What is the price required to give us a particular target profit? How many units must we sell to justify an increase in fixed costs? Would it be desirable to reduce variable costs and increase fixed costs?

APPENDIX 2–A: CURVILINEAR CVP ANALYSIS

In Figure 2–5 we showed curvilinear revenue and cost functions, which we said are probably more descriptive of the operations of a firm than are linear functions. One implication of linear revenue and cost curves is that the more sold, the greater the profit: that is, the vertical distance between the revenue and cost lines (profit) increases as volume increases without limit. With curvilinear functions of the type we drew in Figure 2–5, profits will increase for a while with increases in volume but will then begin to fall as the revenue curve falls and the cost curve rises more rapidly.

If managers have determined that there is a significant degree of curvature in their revenue and cost functions (or in either one), they may use differential calculus to determine the point at which profits will be maximized.

Revenues

The most commonly used curvilinear revenue function is based on a linear demand curve, where price falls as the quantity demanded rises. Suppose that the firm's demand curve can be expressed as:

$$Q = 10,000 - 400P$$

therefore,

$$P = 25 - \frac{Q}{400}$$

Total revenue could be expressed in terms of either P or Q. If we use Q, total revenue (TR) is:

$$TR = \left(25 - \frac{Q}{400} \right) Q$$

$$= 25Q - \frac{Q^2}{400}$$

Now suppose that total costs (TC) can be described by the function:

$$TC = \$10,000 + \$4Q + 0.0003Q^2$$

The equation for profit (Z) becomes:

$$Z = 25Q - \frac{Q^2}{400} - (\$10,000 + \$4Q + 0.0003Q^2)$$

We solve for the optimal quantity, Q^*, and optimal price, P^*, by finding the first derivative of the profit function and setting it to zero to find Q^*, then solving for P^*. Differentiating with respect to Q,

$$\frac{dZ}{dQ} = 25 - \frac{Q}{200} - 4 - 0.0006Q$$

$$= 21 - 0.0056Q$$

Setting the derivative equal to zero and solving for Q,

$$21 - .0056Q = 0$$
$$Q^* = 3,750$$

With Q^* equal to 3,750, we solve to find the optimal price.

$$P^* = 25 - \frac{3,750}{400}$$

$$= \$15.625$$

Thus the firm will earn maximum profits at a price of $15.625, which would yield volume of 3,750 units.[5] Profits would be $29,375, calculated as follows:

profit = ($15.625 × 3,750) − $10,000 − ($4 × 3,750) − ($0.0003 × 3,750^2)

---

[5] Alert students will note that the second derivative of Z with respect to Q is negative, ensuring that we have a maximum for Z, not a minimum.

Does curvilinear CVP analysis provide any real benefits? It does if the firm's managers find that either revenues or costs can be described by non-linear functions. It is not necessary that the entire firm be so describable, only that one of the products show either nonlinear revenues or costs, in order to make the analysis helpful in the real world.

A final point: some businesspeople might argue that the values we would use are unrealistic and come from nowhere. "How can you say that demand is equal to $10,000 - 400P$ or any other such expression? Where do you get these numbers?" The answer regarding the source of the numbers is that techniques are available to estimate the historical relationship between price and volume and that if the relationship can reasonably be expected to hold in the future, it will provide better guidance than some rule of thumb. Some methods for making such estimates are presented in Chapter 3. More importantly, the same people who might argue that such analyses are un-realistic would be among the first to say that price and volume are inversely related, that in order to increase volume you must often reduce price. They might also say that costs can be expected to rise faster than the rise entailed by a linear cost function. Hence, they do take these factors into considera-tion, but in nonrigorous, intuitive fashion. The method presented here sim-ply makes explicit what is already widely believed and accepted.

ASSIGNMENTS

2–1 Basic CVP Analysis. The following data relate to the Hobart Company, which sells a single product.

Price per unit	$20
Purchase cost per unit	11
Sales commissions, 10 % of selling price	2
Monthly fixed costs	80,000

Required: Answer each question independently of the others.

1. Determine the volume needed to earn $40,000 per month before taxes.

2. Determine the volume needed to earn $40,000 per month after taxes, when the tax rate is 40 percent.

3. Determine the selling price needed to earn $30,000 per month, pre-tax, at a volume of 15,000 units. Remember that commissions are 10 percent of selling price.

4. Suppose that the firm could increase the number of units sold by 2,000 per month (at the $20 price) if it increased fixed promotional expenses by $8,000 per month. By how much, and in what direction, would its pretax income change?

5. The firm's salespeople would like to change their compensation from a 10 percent commission to a 5 percent commission plus $20,000 per month in salary. They now receive only commissions. At what volume (at the $20 price) would the firm earn the same income under the proposed plan as the firm would earn under the existing plan?

2–2 CVP Graph.   The accompanying graph depicts the cost-volume-profit relationships for the Byham Company, a wholesaler of dry goods. Volume is measured by a standard unit, which is a weighted average of selling prices and variable costs for all products that the firm sells.

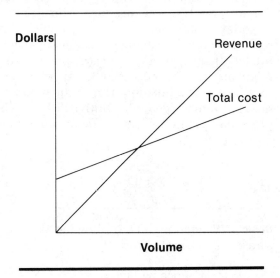

The president of the firm wants your advice about a number of matters. She suggests that you answer the following questions by stating what, if anything, would happen to the revenue line and the total-cost line. (For example, an increase in selling prices would rotate the revenue line up, not affect the total-cost line.)

Required: Treat each case independently of the others.

1. What would happen if the sales mix shifted toward higher percentages of products that have low selling prices and low variable costs?
2. The firm now pays salespeople a 10 percent commission. It will begin paying a 5 percent commission plus a flat monthly salary.
3. The firm will sell more units than previously expected.
4. Both selling prices and purchase costs will rise by 10 percent over all products.
5. Monthly rent will increase by $2,000.

2-3 Product Mix. The Layton Department Store has three major departments, clothing, furniture, and appliances. Annual fixed costs are about $1,600,000. Data on the three departments appear below.

	Clothing	Furniture	Appliances
Sales mix, percentage in dollars	45%	30%	25%
Contribution margin percentage	40%	50%	55%

Required:

1. Determine the dollar volume that will give a pretax profit of $300,000 at the sales mix given above.

2. During the coming year, variable costs of clothing are expected to increase by 10 percent, *not* 10 percentage points. What effect would this change have on the firm's weighted average contribution margin percentage and volume required to earn $300,000 before taxes? You might wish to set up a hypothetical unit to trace through the effects.

3. Using your results from item 2, determine the percentage increase in selling prices in the clothing department that would bring the weighted average contribution margin back to the original value that you used in item 1.

2-4 Basic CVP Analysis. The Rhom Company sells a single product. Data relating to expected operations in 19X6 appear below.

Sales, 100,000 units at $8		$800,000
Variable costs:		
Purchase price of product	$300,000	
Commissions, 10% of sales	80,000	380,000
Contribution margin		420,000
Fixed costs		300,000
Profit before taxes		$120,000

The president of the firm has some questions for you to answer. Each situation is independent of the others.

Required:

1. What is the firm's breakeven point?

2. What unit sales would give a pretax profit of $180,000?

3. If the firm could sell 100,000 units, and wanted a pretax profit of $180,000, what price would it have to charge? (Remember that commissions are a percentage of sales.)

4. If the purchase price of the product increased by 10 percent, what volume would be required to earn a $120,000 pretax profit?

5. What volume would give a 20 percent return on sales?

6. If the selling price of the product increased by 10 percent, what volume would give a pretax profit of $120,000?

2–5 Profit Graph. As the chief staff accountant of Linington Industries, you must on occasion present reports to upper-level management. This afternoon you are to report on three products that the firm could introduce during the coming year. A marketing manager will discuss the prospects for unit sales volume for each product; your job is to show the cost-volume-profit relationships. You would like to make it easy for the assembled managers to see the relationships, so you decide to plot them all on a single profit graph. The following data are supplied to you:

Product	Selling Price	Variable Cost per Unit	Annual Fixed Costs
X-1	$10	$6	$ 60,000
X-2	18	8	200,000
X-3	12	4	120,000

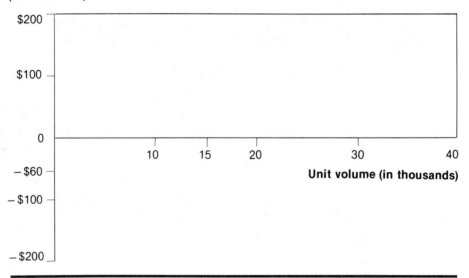

Required: Draw in the lines representing profit or loss for each product and comment on the results.

2–6 Breakeven Pricing. The alumni of Waterford University are having a reunion. The committee in charge of the reunion has decided to hold a dinner dance at the Rockington Hotel. The following estimates of costs are available to the committee.

Rental of ballroom	$ 300
Orchestra	$1,500
Tickets, mailing, etc.	$ 600
Meal, per person	$ 12
Sales tax on meal	7% of price
Favors, programs, door prizes, per person	$ 2.50

The committee expects about 300 persons to attend and wants the affair to break even.

Required:

1. Determine the price per person that will accomplish the committee's objective.
2. One member of the committee wants to price the affair at $20 per person. How many people would have to attend to reach the break-even point?

2–7 CVP Relationships, Taxes. Each of the following situations is independent of the others.

Required: Answer each question on the basis of the available information.

1. A firm in the 40 percent tax bracket with a contribution margin percentage of 30 percent had sales of $1,000,000 and income after taxes of $30,000. What were the firm's fixed costs and its income taxes?
2. A firm with contribution margin of $2 per unit earned $50,000 before taxes and had fixed costs of $200,000. What were its unit sales?
3. A firm with sales of $2,000,000 and fixed costs of $600,000 earned $300,000 after taxes. The tax rate was 40 percent. What were its variable costs?
4. A firm showed a loss of $40,000 (ignoring taxes) on sales of $200,000. In the next period, it earned $10,000 before taxes on sales of $300,000. What was its contribution margin percentage? What were its fixed costs?

2–8 Product Mix. The Raffin Company makes three products. Data follow:

	Product 101	Product 102	Product 103
Selling price	$10	$20	$40
Variable costs	7	12	16

Total annual fixed costs are $840,000. The firm's experience has been that about 20 percent of dollar sales come from product 101, 60 percent from 102, and 20 percent from 103.

Required:

1. Compute the breakeven point in sales dollars. Determine the number of units of each product that would be sold at the breakeven point.

2. Suppose the firm expected to sell $2.5 million at the normal mix. Would it be wise to spend an additional $100,000 on advertising that would increase the mix of product 103 to 30 percent while reducing the mix of product 101 to 10 percent? Total sales would remain at $2.5 million.

3. Assume now that the mix is 20 percent, 60 percent, 20 percent in *unit* sales for products 101, 102, and 103, respectively. What is the breakeven point in total units?

4. Suppose that the firm expects to sell 85,000 total units in the mix given in item 3. Would it pay to spend an additional $100,000 in advertising to shift the mix to 10 percent, 60 percent, and 30 percent for 101, 102, and 103, respectively? Total sales for the firm are still 85,000 units.

2-9 Profit Planning and Inflation.   The following data are from the 19X7 records of the Scagway Household Products Company.

Revenue		$2,560,000
Cost of sales, all variable		1,820,000
Gross profit		740,000
Sales commissions, 10% of sales	$256,000	
Office salaries	198,000	
Rent	36,000	
Heat and light	17,300	
Miscellaneous	13,400	520,700
Profit before taxes		219,300
Income taxes at 40%		87,720
Net income		$ 131,580

For 19X8, the managers of the firm expect purchase prices to rise by an average of 8 percent, selling prices by 6 percent, and physical volume by 10 percent. Operating expenses should rise by 9 percent in all categories, except for commissions, which will remain at 10 percent of sales. The tax rate should be 40 percent in 19X8.

Required:

1. What should the firm's after-tax income be in 19X8?

2. What sales volume would give the firm the same income in 19X8 as it earned in 19X7, with the changes in costs and prices projected for 19X8?

2-10 Service Business. Frank James's automobile repair business employs six full-time mechanics. James himself supervises, takes care of office and administrative work, and occasionally does some repair work.

James charges customers for materials and labor. He charges 20 percent over his cost for materials and multiplies the wage rate of the mechanic by two in determining the labor charge. Late in 19X5 James developed the following estimates for 19X6, based on historical results and expected changes.

Payroll, mechanics	$103,500
Rent	7,500
Utilities	14,300
Insurance	6,500
Other overhead costs	16,600
Materials for repair work, cost	48,500

James estimates that about 85 percent of mechanic time is chargeable to customers, with the remainder being holiday pay, sick leave, vacations, and so on.

Required:

1. What profit should James earn in 19X6?
2. If James wished to earn a $50,000 profit, what multiple of labor cost would he have to charge, all other data remaining as originally given?

2-11 CVP Analysis, Changing Cost Structure. The Tripleweek Book Company publishes paperbacks, principally romantic novels. The firm has acquired the rights to *Echo Valley* by C. M. Jones. Although Jones's books have done well in the past, the president of Tripleweek is not confident about *Echo Valley* because the hardcover edition did not do particularly well.

The critical problem is the first press run. Tripleweek would normally order 200,000 copies from the printer, but the president thinks that it might be better to order 50,000 or 100,000 instead. She has obtained the following prices from the printer.

	Press Run		
	50,000	*100,000*	*200,000*
Set-up	$ 9,000	$ 9,000	$ 9,000
Paper and printing	50,000	92,000	170,000
Totals	$59,000	$101,000	$179,000

The reductions in per copy prices for paper and printing arise because the printer can get quantity discounts on the paper it buys for the book, and some of the savings are passed on to Tripleweek.

The price of the book on the newsstands will be $2.25, of which Tripleweek gets $1.50. Unsold copies are sent to discounters at $0.40 each. As a rule, Tripleweek loses sales that it cannot meet from the first press run. Books such as *Echo Valley* generally sell for about 60 days, then fade away. It takes about 60 days to order and print a new press run, so that Tripleweek either makes it on the first run, or not at all.

Required:

1. For each press run, determine the number of copies that Tripleweek must sell at the regular price in order to break even.
2. Besides the breakeven points you have already calculated, what information can you give the president to assist her in making the decision?

2-12 CVP Analysis, Taxes. The Hobart Company makes a single model garden hose. Expected results for 19X9 appear below.

Sales 200,000 hoses at $4		$800,000
Cost of sales:		
Variable manufacturing costs	$300,000	
Fixed manufacturing costs	200,000	500,000
Gross margin		300,000
Selling and administrative expenses:		
Commissions, 5% of sales	$ 40,000	
Fixed S&A expenses	120,000	160,000
Income before taxes		140,000
Income taxes at 40%		56,000
Net income		$ 84,000

The treasurer of the firm has asked for your assistance in answering some questions about operations. Consider each one independently of the others.

Required:

1. How many units would the firm have to sell to earn an after-tax income of $120,000?
2. What is the firm's breakeven point?
3. What price per unit would the firm have to obtain selling 200,000 units to earn an after-tax profit of $100,000?
4. What volume would the firm have to obtain to earn a 15 percent after-tax return on sales?

2-13 Alternative Cost Structures. Your boss, the president of Nevco, Inc., has informed you that he is considering the lease of a new machine. The lease is $12,000 per month and runs for one year. The machine should reduce labor and other variable costs by about $0.40 per unit. Volume of the product is currently about 50,000 units per month, and you expect it to remain there for the next year.

Required:

1. Determine whether leasing the machine is wise.

2. Suppose that the firm could lease the machine for a five-year period at $10,000 per month. What advantages and disadvantages do you see to the five-year as opposed to the one-year lease?

2–14 Unit Costs.   The controller of the Delpt Company has just handed you the following data relating to the company's budgeted operations for the coming year.

Selling price	$20
Unit cost	19
Unit profit	$1
Volume	40,000
Expected pretax profit	$40,000

The controller told you that she thought the information should be presented this way so that you could concentrate on the critical factors, instead of having to wade through 10 or 15 different types of cost. She added that about $5 of the unit cost represented salaries, rent, depreciation, and utilities, with $14 being the purchase price of the one product that the firm sells.

The president of the firm then entered and asked you the following questions. Answer each independently of the others.

Required:

1. How many units must we sell to earn a $60,000 profit?

2. If we could sell 35,000 units, what price would we have to charge to earn $35,000 profit?

3. Would we be better off reducing our price by $1 to increase our volume 10,000 units (from 40,000 to 50,000 units, and from $20 to $19 price)?

4. How many units must we sell to earn a 10 percent return on sales?

5. How many units must we sell to show a unit profit of $2?

2–15 Product Mix.   The Nelson Sporting Goods Company makes, among other things, golf balls of two types—the Z-flight and the pro-flight. The managers of the firm have been looking for ways to improve profitability and have come up with three suggestions. If none of the suggestions is accepted, they expect the following results. Revenue and cost data are per dozen balls.

	Z-flight	Pro-flight
Suggested retail price	$14.00	$18.00
Net revenue to Nelson, 80% of retail	11.20	14.40
Variable manufacturing costs	4.10	4.80
Sales commissions at 10% of net	1.12	1.44
Total variable costs	5.22	6.24
Contribution margin	$ 5.98	$ 8.16
Expected sales, dozens of balls	80,000	48,000

Nelson sets retail prices, prints them on the packages, and charges retailers 80 percent of the suggested retail. Retailers stick fairly closely to the suggested retail price, although there is some discounting.

The three suggestions and their expected results are as follows.

1. Decrease the suggested retail price of pro-flights by $1 per dozen. The manager who made this suggestion believes that total sales of both balls would go up by 10 percent and that the mix of pro-flights would increase to about 70 percent of the sales of Z-flights.

2. Increase the suggested retail price of Z-flights by $1 per dozen. The manager who made this proposal thinks that total sales of both balls would remain the same, with a shift of 5,000 dozen from Z-flights to pro-flights.

3. Spend $80,000 on advertising pro-flights. The expectation is that sales of pro-flights would increase by 20,000 dozen, with about 30 percent of that increase coming at the expense of sales of Z-flights.

Required: Evaluate each suggestion.

2–16 Committed and Discretionary Costs.   The Moss Company expects to bring out a new product in about three months. The product requires very close tolerances in the manufacturing process, and a computer is needed to ensure quality control. The managers of the firm expect the product to be successful, but they cannot be sure that it will be.

One question the managers must resolve is the lease of a computer to handle the quality control. The particular computer needed can be leased in one of two ways:

1. a month-to-month lease at $3,000 per month;
2. a three-year-lease at $2,400 per month.

The three-year lease cannot be canceled until it runs its course. If the product should prove unsuccessful, the firm will be stuck with the computer because it does not have alternative uses; it is specially designed for products like the one the firm will introduce.

Required: Discuss the factors you would want the managers to consider in reaching a decision.

2–17 Changes in Cost Structure. Levin Calculator Sales, a marketing company, is currently reevaluating how to compensate its retail sales personnel. Salespeople currently earn a 10 percent commission on sales and get a base salary of $10,000 each. A proposed incentive plan would lower base salary to $5,000 but would change the commission to 16 percent. There are six retail salespeople, and average sales are $50,000 per month in the retail outlet. Normal contribution margin is 40 percent (not considering sales costs), and fixed costs other than salaries of salespeople are $40,000 per year.

Required:

1. How would the proposed change affect breakeven for Levin? Why?

2. At what level of sales would management be indifferent between these two plans?

2–18 Cost Classification. The Carmen Company expects to produce 20,000 units of a particular product in the coming year. The product requires 2 pounds of a raw material called Z-gon, which the firm expects to buy at $3 per pound.

Recently the manager of the company that supplies Z-gon suggested that he would be willing to sell 40,000 pounds of Z-gon to Carmen at $2.75 per pound, provided that Carmen agreed to take 40,000 pounds, whether it could use it or not. The 40,000 pounds would be delivered in equal monthly amounts, which would suit Carmen because it generally makes the same quantity of product each month.

Required: Materials are generally considered a variable cost. If Carmen takes the offer, would the cost of materials still be variable? If not, what kind of cost would it be, committed or discretionary? What factors would the managers of Carmen want to consider before accepting the offer? Assume that if Carmen needed more than 40,000 pounds, it could acquire its additional needs at $3 per pound.

2–19 Curvilinear CVP Analysis (Appendix). The Warren Company introduced a new product several months ago and has been gradually raising the price in an effort to find the one that will maximize profit. So far, the managers have tried the following prices and experienced the following volumes.

Month	Price	Volume
1	$18.50	11,500
2	19.00	11,000
3	19.50	10,500
4	20.00	10,000

The managers have concluded that volume seems to be described by the equation, $Q = 30,000 - 1,000P$, where Q = volume and P = price. The product has variable costs of $12 per unit. Fixed costs are negligible because the firm uses existing facilities to make the product.

Required: Determine the optimal price for the product—the one that will maximize profits. Determine the volume that the firm should sell at that price and the profit that it will earn.

2–20 Curvilinear CVP Analysis (CMA adapted) (Appendix). The Hollis Company manufactures and markets a regulator that is used to maintain high levels of accuracy in timing clocks. The market for the regulators is limited and highly dependent on the selling price. Consequently, the managers of Hollis employ a combination of differential calculus and economics to determine the number that they will produce and offer for sale.

The managers have used past relationships between selling price and quantity as well as an informal customer survey to derive the following function, which they believe represents the actual relationship very well:

$$D = 1,000 - 2P$$

where D = annual demand in units and P = unit price. The estimated manufacturing and selling costs for the coming year are:

Variable manufacturing costs	$75 per unit
Variable selling costs	25 per unit

Fixed manufacturing costs relating to the regulator are $24,000 per year and fixed selling costs are $6,000 per year.

Required: Determine the price and volume that will maximize the firm's profit for the coming year.

2–21 Unit Costs. Fred Woodland, plant manager, and Leon Jacobs, a member of the sales department, are discussing the costs associated with a new product. Jacobs is concerned about pricing this new product.

"Look, Leon," says Fred, "you say you want to base your prices on cost plus at least a 10 percent profit. Well, these things should cost us about $27.50 per unit. I guess you could sell them at $30.25 and make your required profit."

As the discussion continued, Woodland gave Jacobs the following breakdown of per unit costs.

Materials	$ 7.50
Labor	10.00
Variable manufacturing overhead	6.00
Fixed manufacturing overhead	4.00
	$27.50

Required:

1. Is $30.25 a price where the company will earn a 10 percent profit? What happens to profits at different sales levels?

2. Would your answer change if you were told that sales and administration costs are $3.50 per unit?

3. Assume that usual volume is 10,000 units and that sales and administration costs of $3.50 per unit are 40 percent variable. What is a price that yields a 10 percent profit?

2–22 CVP Analysis and Sensitivity Analysis. The Mototronics Company makes games and other products that use microprocessors, small computers preprogrammed to perform specific operations. The firm will bring out one of two new products proposed. The president has been trying to decide which one. Both products require the same productive equipment and skilled labor. Lack of equipment prevents the firm from introducing both products.

The following data are the best estimates that the president has received from the firm's market research group, engineers, and accountants.

	Bridge Game	Backgammon Game
Annual volume	40,000	30,000
Selling price	$ 90	$ 160
Variable production costs	$ 40	$ 60
Fixed production costs	$600,000	$ 600,000
Fixed selling and administrative expenses	$450,000	$1,350,000

The higher selling and administrative expenses associated with the backgammon game result from heavier expected advertising and promotional costs, including incentives to dealers who would be reluctant to stock the game. There are far fewer backgammon players than bridge players.

The president realizes full well that the data above are estimates. She is concerned about the likelihood that a product will earn less than $200,000 annual profit (pretax), which is a minimum goal for the firm. Accordingly, she wants to know how sensitive the profit on each product is to changes in the variables (volume, price, variable cost per unit, fixed costs).

Required:

1. Determine the profits expected from each product.

2. Determine the critical value for each variable—that is, the value at which the firm will earn $200,000, assuming that all other variables are as expected. Determine the percentage change to the critical value from the expected value.

3. Make a recommendation and state why you selected the product you did.

2-23 CVP Analysis. Paul Robertson is a tennis buff living in a medium-sized town in New England. The outdoor tennis season there generally runs from early April through mid-October. Robertson has conceived the idea of opening an indoor tennis club that would operate about 180 days each year. He has found a suitable building that he could rent for $20,000 per year on a two-year lease. He would need about $12,000 for equipment, including posts, nets, lockers, and office furnishings. The building could accommodate six courts, locker space, office space, and a lounge.

Robertson has developed the following estimates of operating costs, assuming that he would keep the club open from 10 A.M. to midnight, 180 days per year.

Rent	$20,000
Heat and light	18,000
Salaries of attendants and office staff	42,400
Insurance	10,700
Miscellaneous, including $1,200	
depreciation	7,600
Total	$98,700

In discussion with owners of similar clubs, Robertson has learned that a charge of $13 per court hour for the period from 10 A.M. to 7 P.M. is normal. From 7 P.M. to midnight, the usual charge is $9 per court hour. Thus, if four people played, they would each pay $3.25 or $2.25 per hour, depending on the time period.

Required:

1. Suppose that Robertson could rent 80 percent of the available court time in both time periods. What profit would he earn?

2. Assume now that Robertson could rent 80 percent of the time in the period from 7 P.M. to midnight. What percentage of the time would he have to rent in the period from 10 A.M. to 7 P.M. to earn $50,000?

3. Suppose now that Robertson is confident of renting 80 percent of available time in both periods. He is considering a fixed-fee arrangement where he will offer a group of players an hour every week of the season (26 weeks); the fee will be $195 per group in the period from 7 P.M. to midnight, $285 in the period from 10 A.M. to 7 P.M. He believes that about 50 groups will take advantage of the deal for each time period (100 groups in all). He also believes that if the offer were not available, the takers would probably play about 20 hours during the season during the same period that they would select under the fixed-fee arrangement. Should he institute the fixed-fee arrangement?

4. Robertson knows that the building he is considering has been vacant for over a year, having been occupied by a manufacturing firm that

went bankrupt. He believes that the building's owner would probably accept $17,000 per year rental on a five-year lease. What factors should he consider in deciding whether to pursue the possibility of a five-year lease?

2–24 Profit Improvement. Mr. Jacob Fraher, the owner and president of the Midland Manufacturing Company, was not happy with the results of the first quarter of 19X7 (see below). He had hoped that the firm would be able to show a pretax profit of $50,000 per quarter during the year. After looking at the statement for a while, he called in Art Hamilton, his controller, and told him:

> I want you to determine what we need to do to earn $50,000 per quarter. Look at volume, selling price, variable cost, and fixed costs and come up with some way that we can improve the outlook.

The income statement that distressed Fraher appears below.

Sales, 31,340 units		$385,482
Variable costs:		
Materials	$ 67,370	
Labor	78,590	
Manufacturing overhead	48,510	
Selling and administrative	21,780	216,250
Contribution margin		169,232
Fixed costs:		
Manufacturing	$103,450	
Selling and administrative	36,720	140,170
Income before taxes		$ 29,062

Required: Determine the levels of volume, selling price, variable cost per unit (total only, not by individual component), and total fixed costs that would yield pretax profits of $50,000 per quarter. As you analyze each factor, hold all other factors constant at their existing levels.

2–25 Assumptions of CVP Analysis. Some of your fellow students have found it difficult to understand some of the material and have asked you to help them by answering their questions. You agree to help and hear the following.

1. "The question I have is about inflation," says one student. "I know that prices have been going up and will probably continue that way. I wonder how this is recognized in CVP analysis. After all, you know that you'll be paying higher salaries by year-end, paying more for materials and services, and probably charging more for your product."

2. An economics major took up the discussion. "My courses in economics have shown that companies cannot charge all they want to at all levels of volume. The law of demand states that as the price rises, the quantity demanded falls. Therefore, revenue lines are unrealistic: they should be curves."

3. The economics major continued: "Another point is that companies get what we call economies of scale. As the size of the plant increases, the operation becomes more efficient, with lower variable costs per unit. That is not reflected in the CVP graphs and equations, either."

4. A student who was having some trouble in financial accounting asked why the purchase price of a unit was a variable cost. "Suppose that you buy a unit for $6 and sell it for $10. In March you buy 2,000 and sell 1,000. The graph would show a contribution margin of $4,000. But your sales are $10,000 and your costs are $12,000."

5. A student who had worked in a factory the previous summer chimed in. "My problems are with fixed costs. What about when a firm hires supervisors for the factory, salespeople, or secretaries? Salaries should be fixed costs, but firms hire people, and fire them too. Another point: costs such as advertising, research and development, employee training, and maintenance of buildings don't vary with sales, but management can set them at about any level it wants to and can change them on short notice. So how can they be fixed?"

6. "What bothers me is more fundamental," commented a student who worked in a department store. "I can see that business people really can't predict what their revenues and costs are going to be. Suppliers of merchandise change their prices, and the store might not be able to change its prices because of competition. The store sells a couple of thousand different items, and there is no way to do a chart for each one, even if you knew what costs and revenues would be. I just don't think it is possible to predict in the way the charts and equations imply that you can."

Required: Prepare responses to the questions and comments.

SELECTED REFERENCES

Buzby, Stephen L., "Extending the Applicability of Probabilistic Management Planning and Control Methods," *The Accounting Review*, 49:1 (January 1974), 42–49.

Givens, Horace R., "An Application of Curvilinear Break-even Analysis," *The Accounting Review*, 41:1 (January 1966), 141–43.

Hartl, Robert J., "The Linear Total Revenue Curve in Cost-Volume-Profit Analysis," *Management Accounting*, March 1975.

Hilliard, Jimmy E., and Robert A. Leitch, "Cost-Volume-Profit Analysis Under Uncertainty: A Log Normal Approach," *The Accounting Review*, 50:1 (January 1975), 69–80.

Jaedicke, Robert K., and Alexander Robichek, "Cost-Volume-Profit Analysis Under Conditions of Uncertainty," *The Accounting Review*, 39:4 (October 1964), 917–26.

Cost Estimating and Forecasting

Chapter 3

In Chapter 2 we examined CVP relationships, and we classified costs as either, fixed or variable with sales. We also discussed briefly a number of practical limitations of CVP analysis, including the likelihood that costs would not fall on a single line drawn on a CVP graph. In practice, we would not expect to find that all costs could easily be classified as fixed or variable with sales. Some costs will contain both fixed and variable components. Such **mixed costs** are typified by items such as maintenance of machinery that will have some fixed component related to normal routine maintenance and some variable component related to the number of hours the machinery is used.

This chapter presents some techniques for analyzing cost behavior and for determining the fixed and variable components of individual elements of cost. One question we shall consider is whether variable costs vary with sales or with some other measure of volume. We shall see that some costs vary with measures of activity other than sales. When such costs exist, we must plan for them using the measure of volume with which they vary. We shall consider also the problem of the reliability of estimates of cost behavior—whether we can expect our predictions of costs to be sufficiently accurate for use in planning the firm's operations.

Analysis of costs can be accomplished with both relatively simple and more sophisticated quantitative models. As you will see, the simplest techniques are a good starting point and can serve as checks on more rigorous mathematical models.

The purpose in estimating costs is to plan future activities.[1] While our

---

[1] A distinction can be made between cost estimation, a backward look at what actually happened, and forecasting, a future-oriented measure of expected happenings. We use the terms synonymously, referring to the use of all relevant data to provide estimates related to the future.

discussion focuses on cost forecasting as a tool for pricing and profit planning, the cost accountant can use the techniques we discuss in noncost areas, as in helping the shipping department to minimize delivery times to customers.

COST ESTIMATION

We seek a way to divide costs into fixed and variable components in order to operationalize a basic CVP relationship:

$$total\ cost = fixed\ cost + (variable\ cost)(quantity)$$

Much of our basic information comes from a company's historical cost accounting records. To determine the relevance of these data, we must answer some key questions. Is the range of activity for the next period within the relevant range for the company? Did prices change over the time period? What is the seasonal pattern of activity in the company? Such questions need to be addressed even with the simplest approach.

A critical question in analyzing cost behavior concerns the measure of volume with which the costs seem to be most closely related. Ideally, we would like to be able to relate all cost behavior to sales, but this is not always possible. The primary example is production costs, which should vary with units produced rather than sales. Costs of production will eventually appear on the income statement as cost of goods sold, but not necessarily in the same period in which they are incurred. Managers usually attempt to determine the fixed and variable components of production costs as they vary with the quantity of goods produced, rather than with the quantity sold.

Cost Classification by Account Analysis

In Chapter 2 we described the costs of the Quadro Company as either fixed or variable with sales. We also described the costs by category or object of expenditure: cost of goods sold, commissions, advertising, salaries, and so on. We would like to know about cost behavior, but accounting systems generally classify costs according to the object of expenditure, what the cost is *for*.

Perhaps the fundamental way to determine cost behavior is to analyze a company's various accounts and, based on past experience, classify them as fixed, variable, or mixed. In many smaller firms this method may solve the forecasting problem. In any case, it is a reasonable beginning to cost prediction.

Account analysis should proceed at least at two levels. The first step is to examine account titles and tentatively classify them by behavior. For example, an account entitled Direct Labor, reflecting labor costs as a result of plant activity, would seem to be a variable item. An account called Maintenance of Grounds would seem to be fixed with respect to changes in production volume. The second step is to look beyond the labels and see what kinds of costs appear in these accounts. This step is an analysis of the cost accounting system itself.

Illustration: Analysis of Ronrep Cost Accounts.   The Electric Sweeper Division of Ronrep, Inc., has several departments such as maintenance, computer services, and personnel that provide services to the manufacturing departments. In the maintenance department, costs are entered into three main accounts: Maintenance Wages and Salaries, Maintenance Parts, and Maintenance Overhead. An examination of these accounts shows that, for example, certain wages are hourly and tend to vary with the amount of maintenance performed, while other salaries are fixed (such as the department manager's salary). However, not all of the hourly wages are associated with maintenance service calls in the plant. Inventory of parts must be maintained, clerical work for the department must be performed, and maintenance must be done on the maintenance department's own equipment. Thus, the wages and salaries are a mixed cost, and it is difficult in reviewing the account to identify those costs that are fixed with respect to volume (maintenance activity in operating departments) and those that are variable. It is important for management to go beyond merely knowing that an account contains mixed costs. Thus, later in this chapter we will discuss a mathematical analysis technique to help managers distinguish the fixed and variable portions of such accounts.

Other accounts may have solely fixed costs in them. Perhaps in Ronrep, Inc., the Maintenance Overhead account contains only fixed expenses such as depreciation, heat, light, and other similar costs. However, accounts have different names in different industries and in different companies within an industry. Therefore, it is usually not enough to classify accounts by title. For example, Phil and Scrubby's Car Wash presents you with the following accounts on its income statement: Chemicals, Supplies, Repairs, and Damage to Customer Vehicles. It is not immediately obvious how to classify these accounts. Therefore, it is important to find out what they include. In addition, if Chemicals is classified as variable, what does it vary with? Do different chemicals vary with different things? Soap may vary with the number of vehicles washed, while cold wax (an item added to help dry cars) may vary with humidity and outside temperature as well as with the number of cars washed.

Technological (Engineering) Approach

The technological approach requires direct estimation of cost behavior patterns based on the technological features of particular operations. It is generally most applicable in manufacturing, with more limited applications in administrative functions such as the processing of information. Industrial engineers may be able to determine that a particular product should require, for example, 3 pounds of a given material and 45 minutes of labor time and be able to make reasonable judgments about the behavior of some overhead costs, such as fuel, supplies, maintenance, and indirect labor. The estimates would be based on the engineers' knowledge of the technological relationships among various types of machinery and of workers.

The engineering approach exemplifies the procedure of finding out what inputs (labor, material, overhead) are necessary to produce a unit of output (the final product). When a company uses 300 pounds of material (an input), for example, and each unit is expected to take 3 pounds of material, management should expect 100 finished units of output. To put it another way, to produce 100 units of output *requires* 300 pounds of materials input.

The principal advantage of this approach is that it does not rely on historical data. All other methods discussed in this chapter use historical data, which subjects them to the criticism that they include the inefficiencies of the past. If managers plan for costs based solely on historical results, they are ignoring an important question: *should* the past be used as a guide to the future? The past *may* be used as a guide to the future, but doing so is not always wise. For example, if the workers of a firm have been producing three units of product per hour, the managers may plan on that level of efficiency in the future. But it may be possible to reduce the labor time by improving work methods so that output could rise to 3.5 units or so per hour.

Engineering estimates would also be helpful in situations involving new production methods. If a new machine is to be installed, its operating costs and output are of considerable interest. The firm's managers would have no guides to the probable levels of cost except for estimates prepared by the firm's engineering staff.

We shall have more to say in Chapter 7 about engineering approaches to cost analysis. Such approaches entail difficulties: first, some costs may not be subject to the kind of direct analysis required; second, engineering estimates often give costs that are achievable under ideal conditions, which few firms can expect. Few firms can achieve such high levels of efficiency, and managers who rely heavily on engineering estimates may be overoptimistic.

The Basis for Cost Estimation

Several points emerge from our preliminary discussion. First, classifying costs by account may be more difficult than it sounds. Labels can fool you. Second, accounts must be analyzed to see whether the basic CVP assumptions have been met. Have all the entries been from production during normal operating conditions? If some production levels and costs were well below or above the usual range of company activity, perhaps these costs should be eliminated in any analysis. CVP analysis assumes constant prices and constant mix. If the data available reflect rising prices or a mix that will change in the ensuing period, adjustments should be made.

Relevant range relates to time as well as to volume. Even fixed costs change with time. A radio station commands rates that reflect its share of the market. If its share changes over time, a company's advertising cost to use that station will change. The 1970s and 1980s have been an inflationary period. It is unlikely that a cost for goods or services purchased in 1983 would be the same as in 1979.

Third, the basic account classification analysis must include the identification of the activity (or activities) associated with movement of a variable cost. We will address this problem in more detail in discussing regression and correlation analysis. While CVP analysis implicitly assumes that the activity factor is sales volume, we later show how various activities (called **independent variables**) can affect cost (the **dependent variable**).

Fourth, account analysis should also consider the number of observations in an account. While a single advertising expense for the year might be an appropriate basis for estimation for an upcoming year, a single observation of January labor costs is usually not a sufficient base for an accurate prediction model.

Last, if we can identify specific variable- and/or fixed-cost elements in an account, then we need do no further analysis of these costs. Only when we are faced with mixed costs in a particular area, such as maintenance, factory overhead, or shipping supplies, must we apply the techniques that we discuss next. Even when we use these techniques, we will continue to analyze each account separately.

THE STATISTICAL APPROACH

A systematic statistical approach includes plotting data and using a technique such as simple linear regression to estimate the cost behavior of an account or group of accounts (costs). We have identified cost as a variable that is dependent on the movement of one or more activities (quantities).

High-Low and Scatter Diagram Methods

Just as a CVP graph can be an aid in planning, a scatter diagram can aid in analyzing cost behavior. A **scatter diagram** plots changes that occur in a dependent variable as independent variables change. Note that nothing is implied about cause and effect; we will discuss this problematic area later.

Illustration: Robern Corporation Electricity Costs. Exhibit 3–1 on page 76 shows data from the Robern Corporation, a manufacturer of horse trailers. The company produces two models—economy and deluxe—each able to carry two horses. The company wants to classify the behavior of its costs in order to set prices and make other decisions for the next year. Account classification has produced a pretty solid idea of costs for metal, wood, electrical fixtures, and wiring. However, examination of the electricity costs has not yielded an easy classification. Exhibit 3–1 shows weekly data. The economy model usually needs 100 welds, the deluxe model 125 welds. A scatter diagram for these costs is presented in Figure 3–1 on page 77.

EXHIBIT 3–1
Welding Cost Data, Robern Corp.

Number of Welds	Electricity Cost
3,750	$1,700
7,200	2,250
6,000	1,850
6,000	2,075
4,250	1,850
3,600	1,300
3,750	1,800
5,500	1,975
6,600	1,800
7,300	2,200
5,200	1,700
5,000	1,500
3,750	1,400
7,125	1,900
6,500	2,125
4,600	2,000

The usual format for plotting is to have the independent variable on the horizontal axis and the dependent variable on the vertical axis of the graph. This first example uses an independent variable (number of welds) so that we can progress through the discussion in an orderly fashion and graph the costs in only two dimensions. An inspection of the scatter diagram yields a visual check on the probable form of the cost behavior function. It seems likely that a straight line will be a good predictor of cost behavior. The formula, total cost = fixed cost + (variable cost) × (quantity), now becomes $Y = A + BX$. This means that the total costs (the dependent variable) change as the independent variable changes. We attempt in all our analyses to find the true total-cost line for forecasting. Usually, however, we use only a sample of observations, and we do not know what will happen to cost behavior in the future. Therefore, we classify the line $y' = a + bx$ (y' is called y *prime*) as our estimate of this true cost relationship.

High-Low Cost Estimates

The scatter diagram together with information such as that contained in Exhibit 3–1 can be used to establish a quick estimate of the true cost function. In the **high-low method** you estimate the variable-cost component by solving the following equation:

$$b = \frac{\text{total cost at high volume} - \text{total cost at low volume}}{\text{high volume} - \text{low volume}}$$

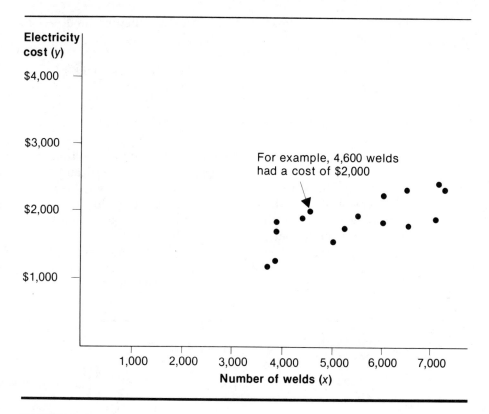

FIGURE 3–1
Scatter Diagram of Welding Electricity Costs

For the Robern data the result would be:

$$b = \frac{\$2,200 - \$1,300}{7,300 - 3,600} = \frac{\$900}{3,700} = \$0.24324$$

Note that the factor determining which values to choose is the total cost *at the highest volume* and the total cost *at the lowest volume.* Since the variable portion has been estimated, the next step is to estimate the fixed portion as follows:

$$\text{high total cost} = a + b \text{ (high volume)}$$

or

$$\$2,200 = a + (\$.24324)(7,300 \text{ welds})$$
$$a = \$425 \qquad \text{(with rounding)}$$

This same estimate of fixed cost could be obtained using low volume and cost:

$$\$1,300 = a + (\$.24324)(3,600)$$
$$a = \$425$$

Figure 3–2 shows the results of this $y' = a + bx$ based on the high-low method. As you can see, the line of $y' = \$425 + (\$0.24324)$(number of welds) is the line that connects the highest-volume and lowest-volume costs. This statement shows both the strength and the weakness of this system of cost estimation. If the high and low values are fairly representative observations, this simple method results in a quite usable cost formula. However, since the line is wedded to these two points, we can also get a cost formula that is quite out of line.

You can see from Figure 3–2 that the majority of the observations occur above the line. For this reason, managers would tend to underpredict costs. Moreover, the high-low method can produce some very poor results if the

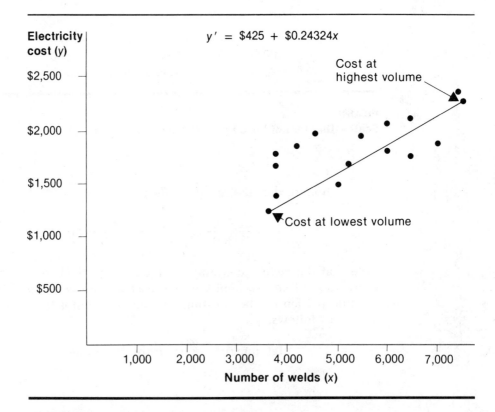

FIGURE 3–2
High-Low Cost Estimate

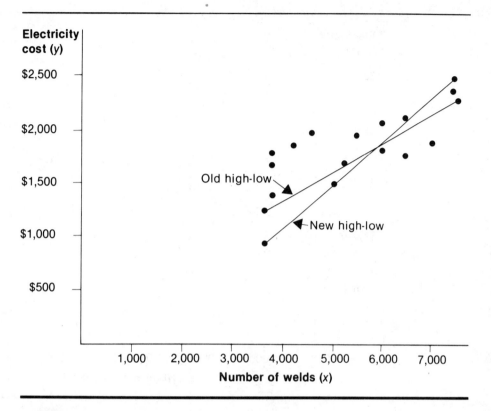

FIGURE 3–3
High-Low Cost Estimate with Two Additional Observations

high and low observations are out of line with the others. Figure 3–3 shows the same observations as does Figure 3–2, but with two additional observations. Notice that the new high-low line is inferior to the old one as a predictor of costs. In short, then, because the high-low method uses only two points to determine the equation (line) for cost prediction, it tends to be less reliable than the methods we now discuss.

A practical modification to the high-low method is to use two points that need not be the high and low volume but are believed to be well within the relevant range. The accountant can select any two points that are considered representative.

Visual Line Fitting

The primary deficiency of the high-low method—its reliance on only two observations—may be partly overcome if we fit a line visually to the plotted data. The objective is to come up with a linear equation for cost that considers all the observations. Figure 3–4 on page 80 shows such a line,

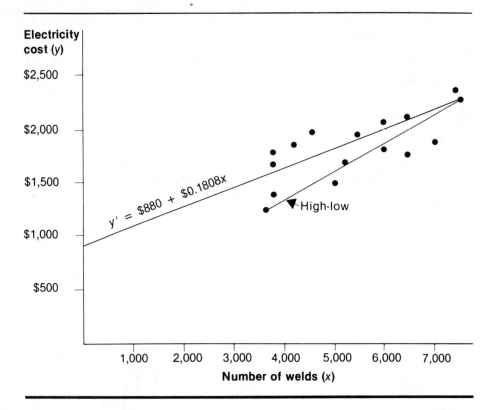

FIGURE 3–4
Visual Line Fitting

along with the line we originally determined using the high-low method. The visually fitted line has about the same number of observations falling on each side of it, and so it would be more likely to provide better estimates of costs.

After fitting the line, we determine the intercept of the equation for total costs by finding the cost where the line hits the vertical axis. We then find the total cost at any other level of volume and subtract from it the calculated fixed component. The remainder is the total variable cost at that level of volume. We then simply divide the remainder by the level of volume to obtain the variable-cost component. We do not mean to imply that the intercept is equivalent to fixed costs at zero volume; this is not true, as we shall develop later in this chapter.

Simple Linear Regression and Correlation

The high-low method is faulty because it uses only two observations. The visual method leaves too much subjectivity in the cost estimate. What we need is a mathematical technique that produces the best description of costs based on the sample observations.[2] In addition, we need a method to see how good a line this best estimate is. These techniques are called **regression** and **correlation** analysis.

Simple linear regression is a tool to describe the movement of a variable based on the known movement of one other variable. The formula is the basic total-cost formula for a straight line. Thus, the simple linear regression formula is $y' = a + bx$.

The data in Exhibit 3–1 on page 76 are only a sample of all possible data to describe electricity cost. The mathematical technique of regression analysis uses data of this kind to estimate the true cost function. Thus, not only is cost (y') an estimate, but the coefficients for the **intercept** (a) and the **slope** (b) are also estimates. A true cost function exists; since we do not know what will happen in the future, however, we cannot find this true relationship, and we must try to estimate it as closely as possible.

Method of Least Squares. A technique called the method of **least squares** is used to estimate the regression line. This method chooses that line that *minimizes the squared vertical distances between observations and the line.* Look back at Figure 3–2. The observations are the points on the scatter diagram. If you were to draw a vertical line between each point and our line estimated by the high-low method, square these deviations from the line, and add them up, the result would be $\Sigma (y - y')^2$ ("Σ" means *sum of*). Regression analysis finds that line that minimizes $\Sigma (y - y')^2$. Note that any observation falling below a line gives a negative value. Thus, we square the deviations, since only one line exists that will minimize $\Sigma (y - y')^2$, while many lines exist that will minimize just $\Sigma (y - y')$.

Normal Equations.[3] We make our estimates for a and b and, therefore, y' by solving the following two normal equations:[4]

$$\Sigma y = na + b \Sigma x$$
$$\Sigma xy = a \Sigma x + b \Sigma x^2$$

Exhibit 3–2 on page 82 shows the required calculations for the Robern example. We now solve the normal equations.

(1) $\qquad 29{,}425 = (16)(a) + (b)(86{,}125)$
(2) $\qquad 162{,}360{,}000 = (a)(86{,}125) + (b)(490{,}365{,}625)$

---

[2] *Best* has several definitions. In this context it indicates the mathematical superiority of this method over competing techniques.

[3] The normal equations and the direct equations for a and b are a result of the calculus in minimizing the sum of the squared deviations. See texts such as Morris Hamburg, *Basic Statistics: A Modern Approach* (New York: Harcourt Brace Jovanovich, Inc., 1974), chap. 10.

[4] Now that we all have access to hand-held calculators and computers that can do this work for us, this material is even more important, so that we keep sight of the relationships that exist in regression and correlation analysis. In addition, since so many programs are available to solve a simple regression problem, one must refer to specific calculator or computer instructions. We cannot begin to cover these instructions in this text.

EXHIBIT 3-2
Calculations for Normal Equations

x	y	xy	x^2
3,750	$1,700	6,375,000	14,062,500
7,200	2,250	16,200,000	51,840,000
6,000	1,850	11,100,000	36,000,000
6,000	2,075	12,450,000	36,000,000
4,250	1,850	7,862,500	18,062,500
3,600	1,300	4,680,000	12,960,000
3,750	1,800	6,750,000	14,062,500
5,500	1,975	10,862,500	30,250,000
6,600	1,800	11,880,000	43,560,000
7,300	2,200	16,060,000	53,290,000
5,200	1,700	8,840,000	27,040,000
5,000	1,500	7,500,000	25,000,000
3,750	1,400	5,250,000	14,062,500
7,125	1,900	13,537,500	50,765,625
6,500	2,125	13,812,500	42,250,000
4,600	2,000	9,200,000	21,160,000

$\Sigma x = 86,125 \qquad \Sigma y = 29,425 \qquad \Sigma xy = 162,360,000 \qquad \Sigma x^2 = 490,365,625$

$$\text{mean of } y = \bar{y} = \frac{29,425}{16} = 1,839.0625$$

$$\text{mean of } x = \bar{x} = \frac{86,125}{16} = 5,382.8125$$

Solve for b by multiplying Equation (1) by 86,125 and Equation (2) by 16. Then subtract (1a) from (2a):

(1a)	$2,534,228,100 = 1,378,000a + 7,417,515,600b$
(2a)	$2,597,760,000 = 1,378,000a + 7,845,850,000b$
(3)	$63,531,900 = \qquad\qquad 428,334,400b$
(4)	$b = 0.14832 \text{ (rounded)}$

Solve for a:

$$29,425 = 16a + (0.14832)(86,125)$$
$$a = 1040.7 \text{ (rounded)}$$

Thus, the line that minimizes $\Sigma (y - y')^2$ is $y' = 1,040.7 + 0.14832x$. This line is shown in Figure 3-5. Compare this to the high-low line in Figure 3-2. There is quite a difference.

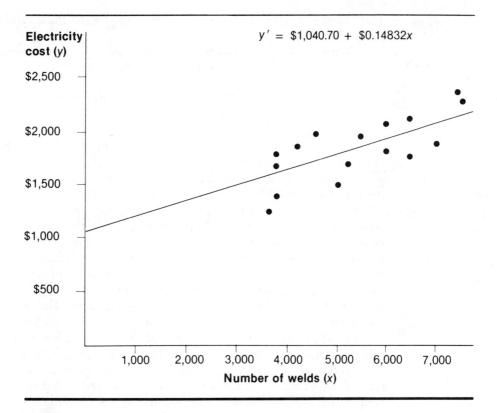

FIGURE 3–5
Least-Squares Regression

A direct method for finding a and b is to solve the following equations:

$$b = \frac{n \sum xy - \sum x \sum y}{n \sum x^2 - (\sum x)^2} = \frac{\sum xy - n\bar{x}\bar{y}}{\sum x^2 - n\bar{x}^2}$$

$$a = \frac{1}{n}(\sum y - b \sum x) = \bar{y} - b\bar{x}$$

For the Robern example these equations would be

$$b = \frac{162,360,000 - (16)(1,839.0625)(5,382.8125)}{490,365,625 - (16)(5,382.8125)^2} = 0.1483 \text{ (rounded)}$$

and

$$a = 1,839.0625 - (0.1483)(5,382.8125) = 1,040.8 \text{ (rounded)}$$

The slight differences in our estimates are due to the rounding in each calculation.

Figure 3–5 was drawn by estimating any y', given a value for x. For example, estimated electricity cost at 6,000 welds is:

$$y' = \$1,040.70 + (\$0.14832)(6,000) = \$1,931$$

Meaning of the Regression Line. Our objective in this example is to be able to forecast electricity costs (the dependent variable) based on the volume of welds (the independent variable). The least-squares equation is $y' = \$1,040.70 + (\$0.14832)(\text{welds})$. The value of \$1,040.70 is an estimate of the intercept. In CVP terms, it would seem that the intercept is an estimate of the fixed portion of total cost. However, the concept of relevant range comes into play. The \$1,040.70 is not necessarily the cost at a zero level of activity. As the data show, the relevant range seems to extend approximately from 3,600 to 7,300 welds. Therefore, we must be careful in defining the meaning of the intercept. It is best thought of as just an intercept to be used in estimating costs when volume is within the relevant range.

The data for Robern show just the relevant range. The object is to find a linear approximation to the cost function in that relevant range. Consider Figure 3–6, where more observations are available at lower volume levels. As can be seen, $y' = 1,040.7 + 0.14832x$ is a good estimate of cost behavior *in the relevant range.* At low levels of output it would not be a good predictor of cost; \$1,040.70 is not a good estimate of true fixed costs, and 14.832 cents is not a good estimate of variable cost (or marginal cost) outside the range.

The b value, \$0.14832, shows the cost to make one more weld within the relevant range. As the number of welds goes up, total cost will increase by about 15 cents per weld. This is a positive relationship, as suggested by the positive sign in the equation. Thus, we know costs will go up as the number of welds goes up. An inverse relationship exists when the sign for b is negative. The resulting line of $y' = a - bx$ is downward sloping to the right.

Bear in mind that regression analysis is based on a normal probability assumption. For example, the prediction for 6,000 welds [$y' = \$1,040.70 + (\$0.14832)(6,000) = \$1,931$] is the *average cost* we would expect at the 6,000-weld level. As we will see in correlation analysis as well as in looking at the variance of regression, we usually expect some deviation from the estimated cost line. If all costs were exactly predicted by the regression line, all observations would fall exactly on the line. As we can see, this is not the case in our example.

Standard Error of the Estimate. The method of estimating an expected value and a variance (or standard deviation) in statistics has an analogy in regression analysis. In fact, y' is the mean line of the sample. The sample variance is calculated in a similar manner to most variances. As we discussed, the least-squares method minimizes $\Sigma\,(y - y')^2$. This minimizes

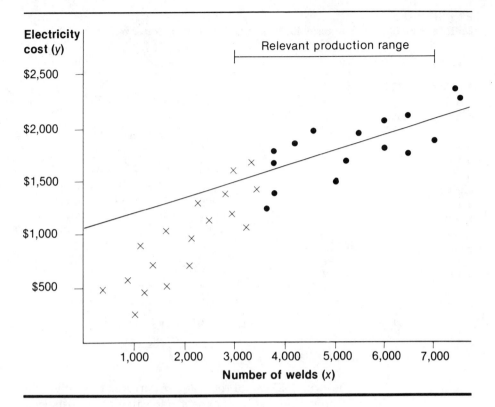

FIGURE 3–6
Possible Costs over Total Range of Production

the squared deviations from the regression line, which, in essence, minimizes the squared deviations from the mean. This concept can now be used to look at the standard error of the estimate. We define this expression by

$$S_e = \sqrt{\frac{\Sigma(y - y')^2}{n - 2}}$$

The squared deviations are divided by the number of observations less the two coefficients that we are estimating. The $(n - 2)$ term is also called **degrees of freedom,** a term to be used later in this discussion. The standard error of the estimate is quite similar to a standard deviation in normal probability analysis. It is a measure of the variability around the regression line. This constant variance is an important assumption of linear regression and is reflected in Figure 3–7 on page 87. The data required to calculate S_e are shown in Exhibit 3–3 on page 86.

$$S_e = \sqrt{\frac{535,967}{16 - 2}} = 196$$

EXHIBIT 3–3

Data for Calculating Standard Error and Coefficient of Determination

x	y	y'	$(y - y')$	$(y - y')^2$	$(y - \bar{y})^2$
3,750	$1,700	$1,597	103	10,609	19,321
7,200	2,250	2,109	141	19,881	168,921
6,000	1,850	1,931	−81	6,561	121
6,000	2,075	1,931	144	20,736	55,696
4,250	1,850	1,671	179	32,041	121
3,600	1,300	1,575	−275	75,625	290,521
3,750	1,800	1,597	203	41,209	1,521
5,500	1,975	1,856	119	14,161	18,496
6,600	1,800	2,020	−220	48,400	1,521
7,300	2,200	2,123	77	5,929	130,321
5,200	1,700	1,812	−112	12,544	19,321
5,000	1,500	1,782	−282	79,524	114,921
3,750	1,400	1,597	−197	38,809	192,721
7,125	1,900	2,097	−197	38,809	3,721
6,500	2,125	2,005	120	14,400	81,796
4,600	2,000	1,723	277	76,729	25,921
			$\Sigma (y - y') = 0^a$	$\Sigma (y - y')^2 = 535,967$	$\Sigma (y - \bar{y})^2 = 1,124,961$

[a] Any small residual is due to rounding, where $\bar{y} = 1,839$.

The principal use of the standard error is to provide us with an indication of how close we can expect our calculated costs (y') to come to the actual costs. For example, we can calculate **confidence intervals,** which are bounds within which we can expect costs to be contained some specified percentage of the time. If we were dealing with a large number of observations (say 30 or more), we could use normal probability tables to calculate confidence intervals. When we have fewer observations, we generally use a Student t table (Table A–2 on page 927). In our example we have 16 observations and, therefore, 14 degrees of freedom. A 95 percent confidence interval using Table A–2 is calculated by

$$y' \pm (t_{0.025})(S_e)$$

For example, we can say we are 95 percent confident that the *true cost* for electricity at 6,000 welds is

$$\$1,931 \pm (2.145)(\$196) \quad \text{or} \quad \$1,511 \text{ to } \$2,351$$

Note that S_e is, in essence, an average variance.[5] We would divide

[5] The standard error of the estimate is most properly used as a measure of variability around the entire regression line, as depicted in Figure 3–7. With a sufficiently large sample, it is possible to establish the kind of confidence intervals shown in this example.

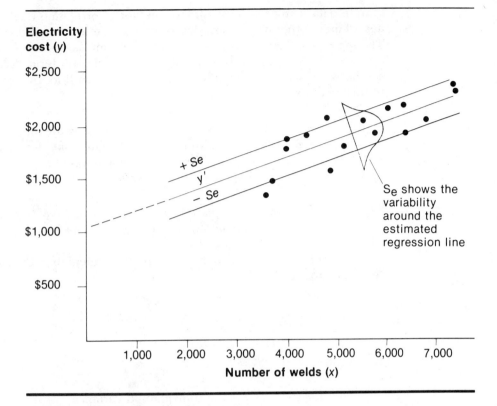

FIGURE 3–7
Variability of Regression Estimate

$\Sigma\,(y - y')^2$ by n for a true average. Dividing by $n - 2$ has a conservative effect, since S_e is a larger figure than a true average. Since we are estimating the true values for A and B by a and b, we need to be conservative to be safe about our estimates.

The value for S_e can also be derived by the formula:

$$S_e = \sqrt{\frac{\Sigma\,y^2 - a\,\Sigma\,y - b\,\Sigma\,xy}{n - 2}}$$

If all observations fell directly on the regression line, S_e would equal zero. This would seem obvious, since there would be no deviations from the line, and $\Sigma\,(y - y')^2 = 0$ in this case. The tighter the observations around the regression line, the lower the value of S_e. When the scatter diagram shows observations all over the chart, we can expect a high S_e, since we need a much bigger band to describe our estimate of true costs.

Correlation Analysis.   Regression analysis describes fitting a line to the sample data using the least-squares method. **Correlation** deals with **goodness of fit.** In other words, how descriptive or usable a line did we calculate? The regression formula of $y' = a + bx$ is the same as $y = a + bx + u$, where $u = (y - y')$. The term u is called the residual or error term. It is the deviation between actual observations and the regression line. In fact, deviations in this analysis can be broken down as follows:

$$(y - \bar{y})^2 = \text{total deviation from an average value for } y$$
$$(y' - \bar{y})^2 = \text{deviation from an average value of } y \text{ described}$$
$$\text{(explained) by the regression line}$$
$$(y - y')^2 = \text{unexplained deviations}$$

$\Sigma (y - y')^2$, the sum of the squared u terms, is a measure of how much of the change in y is not dependent on changes in x. In fact, the u term is considered random and normally distributed.

A measure of goodness of fit is obtained by calculating the **coefficient of determination** for the sample as

$$r^2 = 1 - \frac{\Sigma (y - y')^2}{\Sigma (y - \bar{y})^2}$$

which can be phrased as

$$r^2 = 1 - \frac{\text{unexplained variance}}{\text{total variance}}$$

In our example [see Exhibit 3–3 for $\Sigma (y - \bar{y})^2$],

$$r^2 = 1 - \frac{535,967}{1,124,961} = 1 - 0.4764 = 0.5236$$

An explanation of $r^2 = 0.5236$ is that the regression line $y' = \$1,040.70 + \$0.14832x$ explains about 52 percent of the change in total electricity costs as the number of welds changes. Therefore, about 48 percent of the change in costs is the result of random events or other variables. Note that nothing is said about cause and effect. While it seems fairly obvious in this example that there is a cause-and-effect relationship, this is not always (or usually) the case. Consider the example of overhead costs, where we can only propose why these costs change. Thus, while we may suspect that production volume *causes* overhead costs to rise, we cannot know this to be true. We are just discussing changes of the dependent variable when there is movement of the independent variable. Another explanation of r^2 is that, on average, y' is more than 52 percent better an estimate of total costs than is $\bar{y}$.

The coefficient of determination can be calculated directly by the expression

$$r^2 = \frac{a \Sigma y + b \Sigma xy - n\bar{y}^2}{\Sigma y^2 - n\bar{y}^2}$$

The square root of the coefficient of determination (r) is called the **correlation coefficient.** It takes its sign from the b regression coefficient. If the regression line totally explains y as x changes (thus, x is a perfect predictor of y), r^2 (and r) will equal 1 for a positive relationship (or $r^2 = 1$ but $r = -1$ for an inverse relationship). In this case $\Sigma (y - y')^2 = \Sigma (y - \bar{y})^2 = 0$, since all observations would fall on the regression line.

Graphically this whole relationship is shown in Figure 3–8. At 5,000 welds, electricity cost is observed to be $1,500. Predicted cost is $1,782.30, while, on average, electric cost (regardless of activity level) is $1,839. The term $(y - \bar{y}) = 339$ is the total deviation of the observation from the mean. Of this, $(y' - \bar{y}) = 56.70$ is explained by the regression line. It is explained

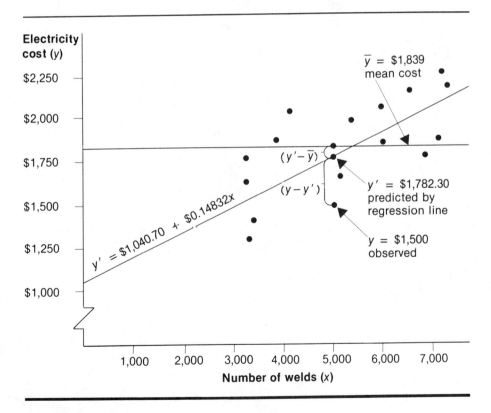

FIGURE 3–8
Explained, Unexplained, and Total Variance

since $\bar{y}$ is constant and y' is a known equation. Finally, the error or residual term $(y - y') = 282.30$ is considered a random, and unexplained, deviation from the regression line. The ratio of the squared explained deviations over the squared total deviation yields r^2.

The terms r^2 and r are measures of goodness of fit or association. They are not measures of causality. It is quite possible to have a high r^2 even if the relationship between y and x is blatantly false.

Standard Error of the Coefficient

We use correlation analysis and the standard error of the regression equation to give us an idea of how accurate our predictions are likely to be. We could fit a regression equation to almost any set of data, but if the spread of observations were nearly random, our predictions would be of little value. In the same vein, we are interested in knowing whether the regression coefficient, b, is a useful predictor of costs. First, if the observations are nearly random, then the coefficient will be close to zero, indicating that changes in volume are not accompanied by significant changes in costs. If the coefficient is not significantly different from zero, in the statistical sense, we cannot rely on it for prediction.

Therefore, we calculate the standard error of the b coefficient and test for significance using classical hypothesis testing where:

$$H_0: B = 0$$
$$H_1: B \neq 0$$

We construct a confidence interval around b to see what the range is for true value, B, where:

$$B = b \pm t_\alpha \frac{S_e}{\sqrt{\Sigma x^2 - n\bar{x}^2}}$$

In this equation, α is half of $(1 - \text{confidence level})$, such as $\alpha = 0.025 = \frac{1}{2}(1 - 0.95)$ for a 95 percent confidence interval. The standard error of the b coefficient is:

$$S_b = \frac{S_e}{\sqrt{\Sigma x^2 - n\bar{x}^2}}$$

Therefore, a 95 percent confidence interval with $n - 2 = 14$ degrees of freedom is:

$$B = 0.14832 \pm (2.145) \frac{196}{\sqrt{490,365,625 - (16)(5,382.8175)^2}}$$

$$= 0.14832 \pm (2.145)(0.03788)$$
$$= 0.06707 \text{ to } 0.22957$$

Thus, we are 95 percent sure that $B \neq 0$ and, in fact is > 0. Another technique to ascertain the same information is to calculate:

$$t = \frac{b}{S_b} = \frac{0.14832}{0.03788} = 3.916$$

The t table shows α is between 0.001 and 0.0005 with $n - 2 = 14$ degrees of freedom when $t = 3.916$. Thus the null hypothesis is rejected at $\alpha < 0.001$. Note above that $t = 2.145$ is the t value for a 95 percent confidence interval. Thus, since the t test yields $t = 3.916$, we know we are more than 95 percent confident that $B \neq 0$.

PROBLEMS IN COST ESTIMATION

We pause to consider some difficulties in using regression analysis and scatter diagrams to estimate the fixed and variable components of costs. We deal first with some problems common to all methods of cost analysis, then proceed to some specific questions of regression analysis.

Measurement Problems

In determining the values for use in regression or for plotting on a scatter diagram, we would generally use the accounting records of the firm. In these records we would find, say, total manufacturing overhead for each of a series of months and the total number of units produced or perhaps total direct labor hours for each month as well. In doing so we would be assuming that the volume (units or labor hours) and the cost (total overhead) relate to the same period. Although this is usually a reasonable assumption, it may not always hold.

For example, suppose that the firm receives its utility bills at the end of each month and that the bills cover 30-day periods ending about the middle of each month. If the firm records each bill as a cost of the month in which it was received, the cost data for each month will contain some costs that applied to the last part of the preceding month and some that applied to the first part of the current month. Therefore, the accountant must use production data from the first half of the current month and the last half of the preceding month to determine the pattern of behavior of utility costs. To use production data and utility costs for April as one observation would be mixing April production with utility costs for the last half of March and first half of April.

Leads and Lags.   It is not uncommon for some costs to lag behind the associated activity. Maintenance costs are one example. We would expect to find maintenance costs increasing as machinery is used more, but the increased costs may not appear in the same period as the heavier use of machinery, because the extra work will be done after the peak period of use is past (or before the peak as a preventative measure). Hence, we might find that maintenance costs have a variable component of, for example, $0.22 per machine hour, but that the variable component shows up in the month after the hours are worked.

In such a case the equation for predicting costs could look about as follows:

$$\left(\begin{array}{c}\text{total maintenance costs} \\ \text{in current month}\end{array}\right) = \$XX + \left[\ \$0.22 \times \left(\begin{array}{c}\text{machine hours} \\ \text{in prior month}\end{array}\right)\right]$$

Lead and lag relationships are more common in sales forecasting than in cost analysis.

Recording Problems.   For the sake of convenience, many firms will record costs in such ways as to make the analysis of behavior difficult. One common example is the practice of recording the cost of some kinds of supplies (for example, wiping rags, or small parts used in maintenance such as nuts and bolts) as they are purchased, not as they are used. Therefore, analysis could not reveal the pattern of behavior. We would expect that such costs would probably be a relatively small proportion of total costs, so that no serious harm would be done.

A much more serious problem can arise because of the widespread practice of allocating some overhead costs to production departments. For example, a firm may allocate fixed maintenance costs to production departments on the basis of the number of maintenance hours used. If accountants included these allocated costs in analyzing the cost structure of the production department, they could reach incorrect conclusions. If the objective is to determine the cost behavior pattern in a single production department, only those costs should be included that are incurred within the department. Allocated costs should be excluded from the analysis.

Economic Sense.   Authors of statistics books relate many instances of what is called **spurious correlation,** a high degree of correlation between two variables that do not seem related at all. Sales of the most expensive liquors might be highly correlated with new housing starts, but the reason is likely to be that both variables are related to the general level of economic activity. When times are good, both expensive liquor and houses sell well.

In analyzing costs, accountants must ask whether the independent variables being considered have some reasonable economic relationship to costs. Factory overhead costs might be closely related to the quantity of scrap produced, but to rely on that observed association for predicting costs might be unwise unless some reason for the association can be found.

Assumptions of Regression Analysis

The use of regression analysis involves several assumptions about the data; if any one of these assumptions is not met, there can be fairly serious problems in using the regression equation and related measures such as the standard error. So long as we are using simple regression analysis we can usually spot some of these potential problems by drawing a scatter diagram. It is always a good idea to draw a scatter diagram, even when we are using regression analysis. The following are some of the assumptions of concern.

Representativeness of Observations.   When applying regression analysis, or any other technique that uses historical data, we are assuming that the observations come from a uniform population. That amounts to saying that we could not use cost data from 1967–1981 to estimate cost behavior in 1982 because the levels of prices have changed greatly and the production process was almost surely not the same during all that time. If the production process has changed, observations should be drawn only from periods after the change. Sometimes we can make adjustments. For example, if the price of electricity has been rising at a known rate, the accountant can adjust the observed cost figures so that they reflected the price currently in effect. Such adjustments, however, are not always possible.

The scatter diagram in Figure 3–9 shows that one unusual observation can have a pronounced effect on the regression line. The reason is that the least-squares criterion for fitting the line gives a great deal of weight to

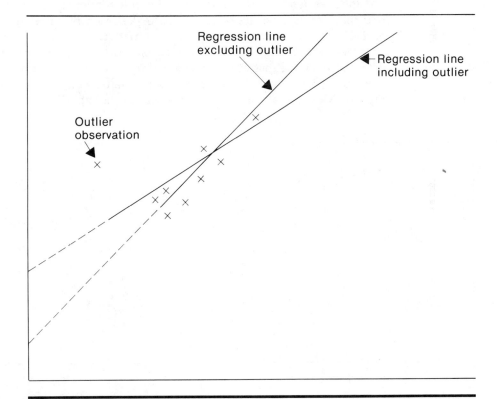

FIGURE 3-9
Effect of Outlier Observation

individual observations. An accountant looking at these observations might decide to throw out the outlier (the unusual observation). It could be caused by some unusual event such as a strike or a plant shutdown for vacation. We should not throw out observations just to get a nice fit of the regression line, but we are justified in omitting observations that are not representative of normal operating conditions. Thus, as well as omitting outliers, we might also eliminate observations well outside the expected range of activity, the relevant range.

Constant Variance. Figure 3–10(a) shows the constant-variance assumption. An example of the violation of this assumption is given in Figure 3–10(b). Notice that the observations spread out as volume increases. We assume that the spread of the observations around the regression line is constant throughout the entire range of observations. When the assumption is met, we say that we have **homoscedasticity;** when it is not met, we have **heteroscedasticity.**

Heteroscedasticity may well be the rule, rather than the exception, in cost data. It is reasonable to expect a higher degree of variability of costs at high levels of volume than at low levels.

Independence.   Stated loosely, the independence assumption requires that the sequence of the observations makes no difference in the levels of cost. For example, costs may follow one pattern as production increases, a different pattern as it decreases. Such patterns are shown in Figure 3–11. The cause of the pattern is the stickiness of costs. As production rises, more workers are hired, but as production falls, workers are not laid off as rapidly. Most firms cannot adjust the size of the labor force immediately in

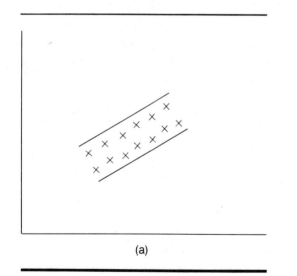

(a)

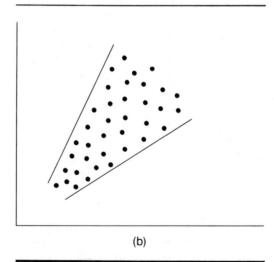

(b)

FIGURE 3–10
(a) Constant Variance (Homoscedasticity), (b) Nonconstant Variance (Heteroscedasticity)

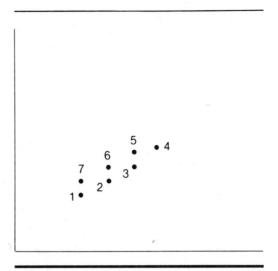

FIGURE 3–11
Autocorrelation

response to changes in production volume; they do not lay workers off in anticipation of relatively small declines in production. Consequently, firms will not see their costs decline as rapidly as they increase. The observations in Figure 3–11 are numbered to show their sequence.

When the assumption of independence of the observations is not met, we say that there is **autocorrelation.** We can detect it not only by plotting and numbering the points, but also by means of statistical tests that are usually performed as part of the output of computer programs. One that is widely employed is the Durbin-Watson test. If autocorrelation is present, the use of dummy variables or first differences may be helpful. We discuss dummy variables in a later section.

Since violation of one or more of the assumptions of regression analysis may cause us serious problems in applying the regression equation, it is always a good idea to prepare a scatter diagram and look at the data. Blind reliance on the results of a regression equation may prove costly: the technique should not be used in cookbook fashion.

Other Scatter Diagrams

The Robern example seems to indicate that $y' = a + bx$ (an upward-sloping straight line) will be a good estimator of cost behavior. The observations all seem to be in one volume range, and costs seem to move upward as volume increases. This is not always the case. As we have seen, the economic model of cost behavior cannot be described by a straight line. Other costs also can behave in a nonlinear fashion. Figure 3–12(a) on page 96 shows a scatter

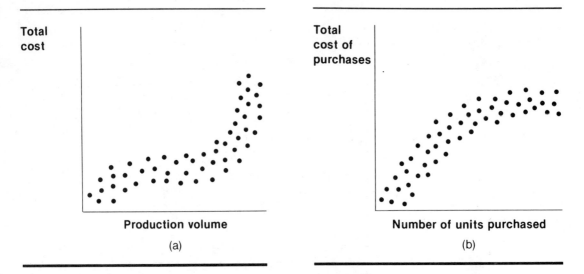

FIGURE 3–12
Alternative Cost Patterns: (a) The Economic Model, (b) Effect of Quantity Discounts

diagram depicting the economic model. Figure 3–12(b) shows total cost where quantity discounts may come into play as purchases increase.

MULTIPLE REGRESSION AND CORRELATION ANALYSIS

Simple linear regression uses a single variable for predicting costs. The basic CVP model assumes that sales volume is the principal determinant of cost levels. In manufacturing firms, production volume is the principal determinant of the level of production costs. However, as the Robern Company example showed, other measures of volume, such as the number of welds made during a period, may also be used to predict cost levels. Recall that the economy model required about 100 welds, the deluxe model about 125. Therefore, the number of trailers produced would not be an accurate predictor of cost levels unless the firm produced about the same proportion of each model in each period. For example, if 30 trailers were produced in one month, the number of welds could range from 3,000 (30 economy models at 100 each) to 3,750 (30 deluxe models at 125 each), or somewhere in between. If Robern also used electricity for air conditioning, it would experience higher electricity costs in the summer, thus introducing a seasonal factor.

Multiple regression and correlation techniques are used when simple linear regression will not produce satisfactory results because more than one factor is critical in determining cost levels. The techniques involve the use of more than one independent variable to predict costs.

Illustration: Predicting Costs for Phil and Scrubby's Car Wash

Phil and Scrubby's Car Wash is trying to determine the total cost of washing a car in order to make decisions for 19X1. Costs include labor, water, electricity, soap, and wax. In addition, brushes must be replaced as they wear down, towels used in touching up cars must be replaced as they wear out, and machinery needs ongoing maintenance. Finally, the car wash business is seasonal, with about 60 percent of yearly volume falling between November and March. As you can see, costs are affected by many factors. In busy months, electricity costs might be lower on a per car basis, since electric motors for brushes and drying would be running constantly rather than repeatedly starting and stopping. However, heavy use in winter months causes more intensive maintenance work. Outside temperature and weather may affect the use of soap and wax. If it has snowed recently, cars are dirtier than normal. Thus, predicting the costs for this car wash calls for consideration of many independent variables.

Multiple Regression Using Three Variables

In using multiple regression, we are still dealing with a linear model. A three-variable regression equation would appear as follows:

$$y' = a + b_1 x_1 + b_2 x_2$$

where b_1 and b_2 are partial regression coefficients associated respectively with the two independent variables x_1 and x_2. Visually this relationship is shown by a plane (see Figure 3–13 on page 98) rather than a line.

As was the case in simple regression, a is the intercept where the plane touches the y axis. However, this analysis involves two slopes. Therefore, b_1 and b_2 are not exactly analogous to the slope of a simple regression. The interpretation of b_1 and b_2 involves looking at one while holding the other constant. If you hold x_2 constant, b_1 is the change in y' as x_1 changes by one unit. Similarly, b_2 is the change in y' when x_2 changes by one unit while x_1 is held constant. This kind of analysis, where everything is held constant except one variable, permeates many accounting models. It is the basis of the "what if" sensitivity analysis in CVP relationships, and it will be the basis of variance analysis as discussed in Chapter 7.

The normal equations for three-variable regression analysis are:

$$\Sigma\, y = na + b_1 \Sigma\, x_1 + b_2 \Sigma\, x_2$$
$$\Sigma\, x_1 y = a \Sigma\, x_1 + b_1 \Sigma\, x_1^2 + b_2 \Sigma\, x_1 x_2$$
$$\Sigma\, x_2 y = a \Sigma\, x_2 + b_1 \Sigma\, x_1 x_2 + b_2 \Sigma\, x_2^2$$

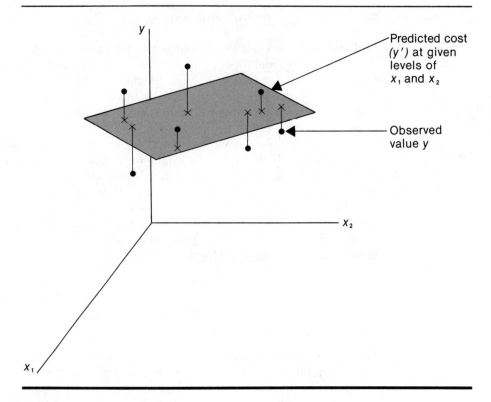

FIGURE 3–13
Three-Variable Multiple Regression

We will not go through a full illustration using these normal equations, since computers can do this task for us. As the number of independent variables expands, so does the number of equations, making hand calculation increasingly more difficult.

As our discussion to this point shows, we have tried to approximate many functions with a line. This is the basis of CVP analysis, for example. However, since we are faced with the problems of possible nonlinear functions and the reality that many costs move with changes in more than one variable, multiple regression may give the decision maker a better predictive tool than simple linear regression.

Standard Error of the Estimate.   The three-variable standard error of the estimate is an extension of the two-variable model. The only difference is that we use $n - 3$ as the denominator (and as the degrees of freedom), since the analysis estimates three parameters (a, b_1, and b_2). We get the same result — the amount of variation in y that is unexplained by the regression plane. Therefore, the same kind of confidence intervals can be constructed as in the simple model.

For ease of explanation the discussion is limited to three variables. Multiple regression techniques can be used with scores of variables if it makes sense to do so. We interpret the results the same as when we are looking at the three-variable model.

Dummy Variables.   Sometimes a factor affecting costs is not entirely quantitative in nature. The winter season in a car wash, for example, is such a variable. Therefore, a **dummy variable** of 1 if it is winter and 0 if it is not winter may be added as an independent variable to help explain cost. In essence, a dummy variable of the 0, 1 type changes the intercept. Assume that a multiple regression produces the following results:

$$y' = 1{,}200 + 14.5x_1 + 100x_2$$

where: y' = total chemical cost
x_1 = number of cars washed
x_2 = 1 in winter, 0 otherwise

If it is winter, $y' = 1{,}300 + 14.5x_1$; in other seasons $y' = 1{,}200 + 14.5x_1$.

Another use of dummy variables is in dealing with autocorrelation. The value 0 may be assigned to periods of rising production, 1 to periods of falling production.

Multiple Correlation Analysis.   With multiple regression there is more than one measure of correlation. Here R^2 is the **sample coefficient of multiple determination** and reflects the ratio of the explained variance over the total variance. Also, there are **coefficients of partial determination** for each independent variable. Assume that a three-variable regression produces the following results:

$$y' = 12{,}500 + 167.9x_1 + 324x_2$$

and

$$R^2 = 0.895$$
$$r^2_{Y2.1} = 0.505$$

$R^2 = 0.895$ means that the plane describes 89.5 percent of the variation of costs. The partial coefficient $r^2_{Y2.1} = 0.505$ means that 50.5 percent of the variation of y is explained by x_1 when holding x_2 constant.

Computer Techniques

With more and more sophisticated computer hardware and programming and with ease of access to such programming through time-sharing networks, even the small firm can benefit from these techniques. Since regression and correlation take so much calculation, computers are the only reasonable solution mode. In fact, with a technique called **stepwise multiple**

regression we can have the computer search for the best two-variable, three-variable, four-variable . . . , n-variable model. Many models exist that look explicitly at seasonality and inflation. As these techniques are more widely used, the problem of estimation takes on a new dimension—interpretation and communication of output.

COST ACCOUNTING REQUIREMENTS FOR STATISTICAL ANALYSIS

We discussed several aspects of cost records in the section on account analysis. When we use regression techniques, we must investigate several important factors. Obviously the cost observations we use come directly from cost accounting records. Unless these records reflect costs recorded in a meaningful form, analysis is useless.

Specification of Observations and Variables

First, at the outset, all factors that might affect the dependent variable should be identified. If you are investigating a sales forecast for the next year, you might identify factors such as prices, mix, inflation, introduction of new products, and limitation of some resources. If you are investigating manufacturing costs, you need to identify all the factors of production. Perhaps even measures of morale or motivation are called for. Since we are generally going to rely on the computer and can use stepwise regression, our search for these factors can be thorough, but not so wild as to throw in factors on mere impulse.

Second, costs are accumulated over specified time periods (days, weeks, months). It is important that the time period be long enough so that current costs are matched with current production. For example, if data are entered only monthly in the cost system, daily observations are not possible. If a lag between costs and activity exists, it needs to be adjusted before data can be used. Thus, the cost time period must be long enough to permit this matching. However, cost periods cannot be too long. Yearly observations, owing to an averaging effect, can mask variability of costs.

Third, while the Robern example shows a fairly large range of observations, imagine that all the observations were over a range of 3,000 to 3,100 welds. With this narrow a range the regression would not be too meaningful. Thus, observations must be over a reasonably broad range.

Fourth, there must be enough observations to have this statistical tool make sense. We are estimating a true cost function based on a sample group of observations. The more observations we have, the better our estimate. As noted earlier, with more than 30 observations we can gain greater confidence in our estimate.

Last, it may be difficult to get needed data for cost estimation. Many costs are common to various products in a department, plant, or company.

Some cost records, too, may include errors. Are costs accurate? Is the independent variable accurate? If not, the regression, its coefficients, and standard errors might be misleading. The shorter the reporting time period, the more devastating the effect of errors. This is especially true if production levels are random and do not have a steadily increasing (or decreasing) pattern.

Multicollinearity

All the assumptions that underlie simple regression analysis apply to multiple regression analysis as well. Multiple regression analysis also may be harmed by **multicollinearity,** which occurs when two or more independent variables are correlated. For example, if production plans call for about twenty minutes of labor time that includes about fifteen minutes of machine time, the two variables will be closely correlated. A multiple regression equation that used both labor time and machine time as independent variables would have multicollinearity.

The chief problem with multicollinearity is that the individual b values have no meaning: they cannot be considered the likely changes in cost arising from a one-unit change in just that variable. The equation itself may be used for predicting total costs, but the coefficients cannot be used as estimates of variable cost of the particular factor. Multicollinearity can exist when the independent variables are either positively or negatively related. The example in the paragraph above showed positive correlation: the more labor time, the more machine time. Sometimes products can be made using either labor or machine time, where using more of the one means that we need less of the other.

Multicollinearity can be found in a variety of ways. One method is to correlate the independent variables. A rule of thumb is that if two independent variables have a coefficient of determination greater than 0.80, multicollinearity exists. As a rule, the standard errors of the coefficients will be relatively large when multicollinearity exists, so that the t values will be relatively low. If t values for two or more independent variables are less than 2, and the coefficient of multiple determination is high, multicollinearity may be inferred.

Cost Estimation and Human Behavior

Communication of relevant information is a key to managerial and cost accounting. As we add sophisticated models to our communication process, we can both help and hinder the information user's understanding. Unless the creators and users of information have the same general technical background and know the strengths and weaknesses of models such as regression and correlation analysis, the results from these newer quantitative techniques can be misinterpreted, unfairly rejected, or overly relied on.

In using a quantitative tool, an information preparer, such as an accountant, must know what a model will do, what it will not do, and how it works. Otherwise, the results and their interpretation can be dangerous. Few managers actually input data for a regression analysis into a computer. Unless managers know the meaning of regression analysis, however, how are they going to use the output?

Even if the accountant understands a quantitative model, the results need to be explained in such a way that a well-informed user can understand them. Every profession uses jargon to explain things. Jargon can stand in the way of common understanding. Imagine the difference between the two conversations from which the following remarks were extracted:

> BILL: I just regressed units and batches against chemical costs and came up with $y' = 2,000 + 0.94x_1 + 3.8x_2$ with $r^2 = 0.9578$ and b significant at 0.0001.

> HARRY: I was investigating chemical costs and related how they change with the number of gallons we produce and the number of batches. What I found was a good relationship between these items and the fact that chemical costs equal about $2,000 per month plus 94 cents for each gallon we produce and plus $3.80 for each batch we start into production.

Bill relies on jargon to produce his message for the listener. If the listener is on Bill's level of expertise, this form of communication might be adequate. However, Bill may be hiding behind the jargon; he may not be able to explain in everyday language what it all means. Harry seems to understand and communicate better.

Computer printouts lead to another kind of information problem. We are all limited in the amount of things we can deal with. If a computer printout includes all sorts of coefficients, t values, probabilities, standard errors, and so on, the user might have too much information to cope with. Therefore, it is the preparer's responsibility to produce an analysis that presents usable results in an understandable and reasonable format. This calls for editing, for deciding what results to show and why, and for selecting the form and format for presentation. Much research is being done in this area, as explained in Chapter 21.

SUMMARY

This chapter deals with both the data and methodology of forecasting. Our answers are only as good as the data we use. We can use past data so long as they are accurate and so long as we expect past conditions and relationships to continue into the future. In Chapter 2 we treated CVP relationships as given facts; in the present chapter we develop techniques to estimate them. Our tools include simple ones such as the high-low method and more complex ones such as simple and multiple regression and correlation analysis. We need to gain a good understanding of these statistical methods in order to use them most effectively.

ASSIGNMENTS

3–1 **Analyzing Cost Behavior.** As the controller of Van Dine Enterprises, you are responsible for the training and development of members of your staff. You recently hired an accounting major from the state university and told her to spend a few days analyzing the cost structure in one of the firm's nearby plants. She has come back with the following questions.

1. "We use the units-of-production method of depreciation for some of our machinery and equipment. Does that make depreciation a variable cost?"

2. "We have a take-or-pay contract with one of our suppliers. We have to pay $600,000 per year for the material for any quantity up to 200,000 gallons. We pay $2.90 per gallon for anything over 200,000 gallons. We use two gallons for each unit of product and generally produce about 110,000 to 115,000 units per year. Is the $600,000 a fixed cost? Are variable costs zero until we get over 100,000 units of product, then $5.80?"

3. "Our union contract requires that we pay each worker who has five or more years of service for thirty-five hours per week even if they work less than that. About 20 percent of our workers have five years or more of service. Are their wages fixed or variable?"

4. "We have a policy that allows each product manager, who is responsible for sales and production of a product or product line, to spend an amount up to 5 percent of sales for advertising and promotion. Are these costs variable?"

Required: Answer the questions above.

3–2 **Cost Analysis.** Managers of the Oxnard Manufacturing Company had not paid much attention to cost behavior in the past because the firm had grown rapidly and had been consistently profitable. It had become obvious to them recently, however, that the days of rapid growth were over and that more attention needed to be paid to planning and controlling costs. The firm's new controller made the following suggestion.

I propose that we determine what costs should be at two levels of volume and interpolate between them. I would suggest that we work with shutdown costs and costs at full capacity because it is relatively easy to determine what costs should be at those levels. In some preliminary analysis, I have determined that our costs at shutdown would be about $94,500 per month, consisting of capacity-related costs such as depreciation and property taxes, minimum maintenance, and salaries of upper-level management. We would save supervisory costs and costs of some departments such as engineering, personnel, accounting, and data processing because we would lay off most of their employees. We would also save on utilities, advertising, and most other similar costs. We have never shut down, but I am still confident about the $94,500. At the top end, we would have a plant running full-tilt twenty-four hours a day. I am not sure what costs we could expect at that level and would like to get together with some of you to see what we might plan on. Once we had the costs at those two levels, we could simply divide the difference in costs by 100 percent, which would give us the variable component of cost, expressed as dollars per percentage point of capacity used. We could use that figure to determine what our costs should be at levels of volume between shutdown and full capacity.

Required: Comment on the suggestion. How would the cost line developed using the proposed method be likely to differ from one developed using a scatter diagram of actual observation of costs?

3–3   Data Requirements and Regression Analysis.   You have asked your assistant to see what relationship, if any, seems to hold between total factory overhead cost and direct labor cost. After initial talks with various people and some independent checking, he has returned with the following.

1. All workers, direct and indirect, received a 12 percent pay increase six months ago.
2. Fuel is a large item of overhead. Its quantity is nearly the same each month, but the price has risen about 2 to 3 percent each month from the beginning of the year.
3. Supplies, which range between 5 and 10 percent of total overhead cost, are recorded when purchased, rather than when used. The firm takes an inventory of supplies only at year end.

Required: You wish to use at least fifteen months' data in the regression analysis. Write out a set of instructions for your assistant, stating what he should do, if anything, about each fact he has brought to your attention.

3–4   Preliminary Cost Classification.   The following is a partial list of accounts for the Rhea Products Corporation.

Sales Expenses	*Occupancy Expenses*
601 Sales Supervisory Salaries	801 Supervisory Salaries
602 Commissions	802 Janitors and Watchmen
612 F.I.C.A. Tax Expense	810 Overtime Premium
616 Unemployment Insurance Expense	832 Janitor Supplies
617 Newspaper Advertising	835 Repairs to Building
619 Convention Expense	842 Heat, Light, Air Conditioning
625 Association Dues	850 Depreciation—Building
634 Automobile Expense	860 Insurance—Building
641 Warranty Expense	

Required:

    1. You are to begin to classify these accounts by analyzing account titles. Discuss each account as to whether it is a fixed, variable, or mixed cost. If it is variable or partially so, what should it vary with?

    2. What are the problems associated with this kind of analysis?

3–5 Analyzing Cost Accounts. The Cunningham Corporation shows the following entries in its Maintenance account during June, 19X0:

    1. Maintenance labor: $3,000

    2. Parts: $5,500

    3. Tools and Supplies: $7,650

    4. Rent: $500

    5. Bookkeeping: $600

Further analysis of these entries shows that labor includes $300 of overtime pay, parts includes a $1,000 motor considered an unusual maintenance cost, tools and supplies includes a $5,650 drill press, and rent and bookkeeping are allocated expenses. Five hundred hours of labor were used. The overtime seemed linked to the major motor replacement.

Required:

    1. What are the relevant costs for CVP analysis that are useful for forecasting future costs? Why?

    2. For July, labor was $2,100, parts $4,500, tools and supplies $1,500, rent $500, bookkeeping $600. Four hundred hours were worked, and there were no overtime costs or extraordinary costs. Use these additional data to develop estimates of fixed and variable components of costs.

3–6 High-Low Forecasting. Tabatha Phelps, president of Alpro Cat Food, shows you the following selected data for the cost of producing one of its products, Tuna Meowt cat snack food.

Date	Production	Cost
March 2	400 cans	$155
April 23	1,100	500
May 7	725	225
June 12	800	375
July 9	475	200
August 27	1,025	425
September 8	1,200	450
October 8	1,150	475
November 6	650	250

You have been asked to use these data and develop a cost-estimating formula based on the high-low method. Assume the data were selected at random from production reports.

Required:

1. Plot the above data.

2. Compute a forecasting equation in the form of $y' = a + bx$, using the high-low method.

3. What would be the effect on your high-low estimate if data for March 2 show 400 cans produced for $125?

4. Using the estimate derived in item 2, what would you forecast for costs at a production of 900 cans?

5. Would you recommend using the high-low method in this case? Why or why not?

3–7 High-Low Forecasting. Assume the following cost and production information for the Apex Service Co.

Number of Service Calls	Cost	Number of Service Calls	Cost
100	$ 800	200	$1,800
125	900	225	1,900
150	1,000	250	2,000

Required:

1. Using all of the data, compute a $y' = a + bx$ forecasting equation by the high-low method.

2. Is your answer to item 1 useful for forecasting? Why or why not? What improvements would you suggest?

3–8 Simple Regression. Ballot Box Company is developing a new costing system. In reviewing data from the past several weeks, its accountant developed the following data.

Week	Maintenance Supply Costs	Maintenance Hours
1	$ 320	22.0
2	352	30.2
3	468	31.0
4	635	29.0
5	500	40.0
6	821	36.9
7	1,020	41.8
8	990	50.0
9	728	36.8
10	905	38.9

Required:

1. Using regression analysis, calculate the intercept and slope.
2. Calculate the coefficient of determination, standard error of the estimate, and standard error of the slope.
3. Evaluate the results of the review for goodness of fit and usefulness.
4. Write a short memo that interprets the results of the review to management.

3-9 Basic Estimating Techniques. A recent review of supply costs and production has been conducted at the Hormutz Manufacturing Company and shows the following:

Supply Costs	Production
$125	3,500 units
175	5,000
200	7,000
100	3,000
125	4,500
200	6,000
150	4,000

These data have been collected over the last two months of production from weekly inputs.

Required:

1. Plot these data points.
2. Using the high-low method, find the intercept and slope based on these data.
3. Can you fit a line visually that is better than the one you calculated in question 2? Why is it better?
4. Using the normal equations, calculate a regression line for these data. Also calculate r^2, S_e, and S_b. Explain the results of all of your calculations.
5. Recalculate the information asked for in item 4, disregarding the observations at 4,500 units and 7,000 units. Again, explain the results. Why would an accountant choose to disregard certain data points?

3-10 Simple Regression Analysis. Febrile Company's consultants have just run a preliminary computer regression and correlation analysis on costs in the packaging department. The independent variable is number of packages, and the dependent variable is cost of packaging supplies. The computer output is shown on page 108.

SIMPLE LINEAR REGRESSION

HOW MANY OBSERVATIONS DO YOU HAVE ? 12

WHAT PERCENTAGE CONFIDENCE LEVEL DO YOU WANT--
70, 80, 90, OR 95? 95

REGRESSION COEFFICIENT A	1090.05
REGRESSION COEFFICIENT B	8.85247
COEFFICIENT OF CORRELATION--R	.796266
COEFFICIENT OF DETERMINATION--R2	.63404

T-TEST OF CORRELATION%

R TIMES THE SQUARE ROOT OF N-2 DIVIDED BY THE SQUARE ROOT OF 1-R2
EQUALS 4.16237

CUMULATIVE T-DISTRIBUTION AT 97.5 PERCENT LEVEL FOR 10 DEGREES OF
FREEDOM EQUALS 2.225

SINCE 4.16237 EXCEEDS 2.225 THE OBSERVATIONS PROVIDE MORE THAN 95
PERCENT ASSURANCE THAT THE X AND Y VALUES ARE RELATED.

OBSERVED X VALUE	OBSERVED Y VALUE	Y VALUE ON REGRESSION LINE AT X	95 PC PREDICTION INTERVAL FOR PREDICTING Y AT X	
			LOWER LIMIT	UPPER LIMIT
132.25	2340	2260.79	1912.68	2608.9
96.75	1940	1946.52	1620.71	2272.34
100.5	1910	1979.72	1655.57	2303.88
120	2300	2152.34	1821.26	2483.43
110.1	2270	2064.7	1740.38	2389.03
110.5	1870	2068.25	1743.78	2392.71
108	1980	2046.11	1722.38	2369.85
105.5	1920	2023.98	1700.54	2347.43
100	1850	1975.3	1650.97	2299.62
127	2310	2214.31	1874.6	2554.02
96	1820	1939.89	1613.62	2266.15
54	1730	1568.08	1164.39	1971.78

Required:

1. Write a memo to management, explaining what simple linear regression is and what these results mean. Do not use jargon. Management has not dealt with many quantitative techniques before.

2. Plot the data. Would your answer to item 1 change? If so, explain.

3–11 Choice of Independent Variables. You are currently involved in estimating overhead costs in the production department. After some research, you have identified three variables as potential predictors of cost. You have collected the following data for the past fifteen weeks.

Week	Overhead Costs	Production Volume #107	#110	#120
1	$12,899	22	25	63
2	9,266	64	96	37
3	7,153	30	62	30
4	11,000	50	0	47
5	11,900	31	77	58
6	8,415	52	7	34
7	10,672	52	85	43
8	12,128	34	43	57
9	8,003	57	53	31
10	10,888	28	51	51
11	10,414	30	59	47
12	10,500	55	54	45
13	11,732	55	16	52
14	7,751	25	68	34
15	12,870	54	45	60

Required: Choose the best variable or variables to predict overhead costs. Justify your choice. Where possible, check the assumptions of regression analysis.

3–12 Simple Regression—Communication and Analysis. The data processing manager enters your office and says: "Well, I've been working on helping you guys in accounting forecast costs. I looked at one production department's costs and came up with a beauty of an analysis." With that, he hands you this:

```
LIST ALL DATA
? Y
VARIABLE    1          2
OBS.
  1 73603.    9914.0
  2 27775.    9774.0
  3 14302.    4110.0
  4 69020.    8450.0
  5 45448.    8586.0
  6 8335.0    4383.0
  7 2850.0    209.00
  8 9208.0    6152.0
  9 75218.    9874.0
 10 74962.    369.00

WHICH VARS
? 1,2
SYMBOL
? *
```

(output continued on pages 110–111)

SCATTER DIAGRAM

VARIABLE 1

```
              782.34     13533.     26283.     39034.     51785.     64535.     77286.
     10399.      + . . . . + . . . . + . . . . + . . . . + . . . . + . . . . + 10399.
                 .                        *                                  **
                 .
                 .
                 .
      8620.0     +                                    *                    +   8620.0
                 .                                                *
                 .                                                    *
                 .
.V                .
.A    6840.8     +                                                          +   6840.8
.R                .
.I                .              *
.A                .
.B    5061.5     +                                                          +   5061.5
.L                .
.E                .
                 .          *
. 2              .              *
                 .
      3282.3     +                                                          +   3282.3
                 .
                 .
                 .
                 .
      1503.0     +                                                          +   1503.0
                 .
                 .                                                          *
                 .          *
     -276.25     + . . . . + . . . . + . . . . + . . . . + . . . . + . . . . + -276.25
              782.34     13533.     26283.     39034.     51785.     64535.     77286.
```

VARIABLE 1

	INTERVAL SPACING	MINIMUM	MAXIMUM
SCALING FOR VARIABLE 1 ---	2125.09	2850.00	75218.0
SCALING FOR VARIABLE 2 ---	254.179	209.000	9914.00

MORE
? N

* * * * * * * * * *

WANT TO EXIT FROM THE PACKAGE (YES OR NO)
? N
WANT ADVANCED USER STATUS (YES OR NO)
? Y

```
SAME DATA
? Y
OUTPUT TO TERMINAL
? Y
TYPE CODE
? RE
```

* * * SIMPLE ONE-VARIABLE REGRESSION * * *

```
DEP. VAR.
? 2
IND. VAR.
? 1
```

INTERCEPT	4225.01
REGRESSION COEFFICIENT	.488393E-01
STD. ERROR OF REG. COEF	.395843E-01
COMPUTED T-VALUE	1.23380
CORRELATION COEFFICIENT	.399831
STANDARD ERROR OF ESTIMATE ...	3671.83

ANALYSIS OF VARIANCE FOR THE REGRESSION

SOURCE OF VARIATION	D.F.	SUM OF SQ.	MEAN SQ.	F VALUE
ATTRIBUTABLE TO REGRESSION	1	.205238E+08	.205238E+08	1.5223
DEVIATION FROM REGRESSION	8	.107859E+09	.134823E+08	
TOTAL	9	.129382E+09		

```
RESIDUAL TABLE
? Y
RESID. TO TEMP. FILE
? N
```

TABLE OF RESIDUALS

OBSERVATION	Y OBSERVED	Y ESTIMATED	RESIDUAL	RES. PCNT OF EST.
1	9914.00	7819.72	2094.28	26.7820
2	9774.00	5581.52	4192.48	75.1136
3	4110.00	4923.51	−813.507	−16.5229
4	8450.00	7595.89	854.106	11.2443
5	8586.00	6444.65	2141.35	33.2267
0	4383.00	4632.08	−249.084	−5.37735
7	209.000	4364.20	−4155.20	−95.2110
8	6152.00	4674.72	1477.28	31.6015
9	9874.00	7898.60	1975.40	25.0095
10	369.000	7886.10	−7517.10	−95.3209

```
TEST OF EXTREME RESIDUALS
   RATIO OF RANGES FOR THE SMALLEST RESIDUAL..................... .348079
   RATIO OF RANGES FOR THE LARGEST RESIDUAL ..................... .245713
   CRITICAL VALUE OF THE RATIO AT ALPHA =.10 ..................... .409000
MORE
? N
```

* * * * * * * * * *

```
WANT TO EXIT FROM THE PACKAGE (YES OR NO)
? Y
```

Required:

1. Carefully explain in simple terms what information has been generated. Do not use jargon in your explanation.

2. The data processing manager said this output was a beauty. What questions do you have about the analysis or its underlying assumptions?

3-13 Explaining Results of Regression Analysis. On your third day on the job as assistant to the controller of ML Industries, the controller approaches you and says: "I have to go overseas tomorrow and I was supposed to give a talk to a group of our managers on regression analysis. Forbes over in the statistical analysis group gave me the output here (see below) to use for illustrative purposes. I want you to give the talk. We would like the people to start using statistics more than they do and so it is important that you give them a good explanation of what the statistics tell them and how they can use them. I'll see you in three weeks."

Required: The output that the controller mentioned appears below. Develop clear and concise explanations of each piece of information in conformance with the controller's request. Both regression equations use samples of 35 monthly observations.

$$TOH = \$346{,}902 + \$6.142X, \quad r^2 = 0.769, \quad S_e = \$19{,}926, \quad S_b = \$2.381$$

where *TOH* is total factory overhead and *X* is direct labor hours.

$$SGA = \$89{,}413 + \$1.27X_1 + \$0.827X_2, \quad r^2 = 0.897, \quad S_e = \$9{,}785,$$
$$S_b \text{ for } X_1 = \$0.814, \quad S_b \text{ for } X_2 = \$0.675$$

where *SGA* is total selling and administrative expenses, X_1 is dollar sales of product 1, and X_2 is dollar sales of product 2.

3-14 Regression Analysis and Inflation. Sam Bozella, the controller of Arway Industries, was discussing a problem with Richard Feister, the president of the firm. Bozzella began:

> We have been using regression analysis to identify cost behavior patterns, but it has not given us the results we want. Part of the problem is that our costs have been rising rapidly over the last year. That is, the prices we pay for utilities, indirect labor, supervision, and other elements of cost are rising.
>
> I can see that there are two ways to handle the problem. One is to use *constant dollars*. That way we multiply each month's costs by the ratio of the price level in the base period, say, at the end of last year, to the price level in the other months.
>
> The other way is to use *current dollars*. We would then multiply the costs in prior months by the ratio of the price level prevailing today to the price level that prevailed during the other month.

Either way, we are simply restating costs in terms of a constant measuring rod. However, I am not sure which way we should go and what use we can make of the new results in planning for levels of cost in future months.

As an example of what he meant, Bozzella provided the following data.

Month	Actual Costs	Price Level	Constant-Dollar Restatement	Current-Dollar Restatement
December	$363,000	110	$363,000	$412,500
May	392,000	120	359,333	408,333
July	377,000	125	331,760	377,000

The constant-dollar restatement uses December as the base level. The costs of the other months are multiplied by the ratio of the price level in December (110) to the price level in the other month. The current-dollar restatement uses the ratio of the price level in the most recent month (July) to the price level in the other month.

Required:

1. Suppose that the quantities of input factors such as utilities, indirect labor, supervision, and so on remained constant in relation to a measure of activity such as direct labor hours. Thus, if prices had not changed, a regression equation based on direct labor hours would have captured quite closely the behavior of costs. What effects would the monthly increase in price of input factors have on the regression results? Would the intercept change? the slope? the measures of goodness of fit?

2. Suppose that the firm adopts one of the methods illustrated above. Given that prices are expected to increase in the future, of what value would a regression equation using either constant dollars or current dollars be in planning for costs?

3-15 Assumptions of Multiple Regression Analysis.   The controller of the Pergman Company has been trying to determine the labor cost of each of the company's four products. She has received information from the firm's industrial engineering staff and has also gotten the following regression equation from the operations research department.

$$TC = \$456,000 + \$0.87X_1 + \$1.18X_2 - \$0.65X_3 + \$2.34X_4$$
$$(\$0.67)\quad (\$0.91)\quad (\$0.88)\quad (\$2.21)$$

$$r^2 = 0.943, \qquad S_e = \$14,823$$

Standard errors of the regression coefficients are in parentheses. TC is total labor cost, and X_1 through X_4 represent the quantities of each product made during the period.

Required: Comment on the usefulness of the equation.

3-16 Regression Analysis and Allocated Costs. One of your jobs as the chief cost accountant of the Dale River plant of MCC, Inc., is to analyze the behavior of costs in the various departments to provide information for planning and control. Your assistant, pursuant to your instructions, has just completed a regression analysis of the milling department. The data he used and the regression results appear below.

Month	Direct Labor Hours	Total Departmental Overhead Costs
January	12,300	$150,685
February	15,600	166,370
March	11,850	153,208
April	13,320	163,694
May	15,240	187,090
June	11,800	145,850

Results of the regression are:

$$\text{overhead cost} = \$61{,}586 + \$7.457DLH$$
$$r^2 = 0.719, \quad S_e = \$8{,}848, \quad S_b = \$2.332$$

He recently discovered, your assistant adds, that the total overhead cost figures above include some general factory costs allocated to individual departments. During the period covered by these cost figures the monthly charge was $2.80 per direct labor hour.

Required:

1. Without performing a new regression analysis, state what differences you expect to find between the results above and the results of a new regression analysis that exclude the allocated general factory costs. For example, would you expect the standard error of the estimate to rise, fall, or stay the same? What about the slope and intercept of the regression equation?

2. Eliminate the allocated costs and perform a new regression analysis, calculating all the measures given above.

3-17 Regression Results and Product Selection. The managers of the Barclay Products Company have been considering two new products. The firm has made a number of units of each in order to get some idea of the costs before putting one or both into full-scale production.

The results of regression analysis on each product prepared by a staff manager are:

	Wall Shelving	File Box
Monthly fixed production cost	$234,210	$186,452
Unit variable production cost	$ 8.52	$ 3.26
Standard error of estimate	$ 42,100	$ 29,543
Standard error of coefficient	$ 3.86	$ 1.18
r^2	.52	.59

The managers estimate that volume for either product would be about 30,000 units per month. The shelving would sell for $19 per unit, the file box for $12.

Required: Suppose that the firm can bring out only one of the two products. Which one would you advise and why?

3–18 **Interpreting Results (CMA Adapted).**   The controller of the Connecticut Electronics Company believes that identifying the variable and fixed components of the firm's costs will enable its managers to make better planning and control decisions. Among the costs the controller is concerned about is the behavior of indirect supplies expense. She believes there is some correlation between the machine hours worked and the amount of indirect supplies used.

A member of the controller's staff has suggested that a simple linear regression model be used to determine the cost behavior of the indirect supplies. The regression equation shown below was developed from forty pairs of observations using the least-squares method of regression. The regression equation and related measures are as follows:

$$S = \$200 + \$4H$$

where S is total monthly costs of indirect supplies and H is machine hours per month. Standard error of estimate $S_e = 100$. Coefficient of correlation $r = 0.87$.

Required:

1. When a simple linear regression model is used to make inferences about a population relationship from sample data, what assumptions must be made before the inferences can be accepted as valid?

2. Assume that the assumptions identified in item 1 are satisfied for the indirect supplies expense of Connecticut Electronics Company.
   a. Explain the meaning of 200 and 4 in the regression equation $S = \$200 + \$4H$.
   b. Calculate the estimated cost of indirect supplies if 900 machine hours are to be used during a month.
   c. In addition to the estimate for the cost of indirect supplies, the controller would like the range of values for the estimate if a 95

percent confidence interval is specified. He would use this range to judge if the estimate of costs indicated by the regression analysis was good enough for planning purposes. Calculate, for 900 machine hours, the range of the estimate for the cost of indirect supplies with a 95 percent confidence interval.

3. Explain briefly:
   a. What does the coefficient of correlation measure?
   b. What does the value of the coefficient of correlation ($r = 0.87$) indicate in this case if Connecticut Electronics Company wishes to predict the total cost of indirect supplies on the basis of estimated machine hours?

3–19 Use of Computers for Regression. The managers of Dallas Division of White Manufacturing have decided to use regression and correlation analysis to help them in establishing cost patterns. One set of data for material costs on product U-101 appears below. All data are from the current year.

Units of Product	Material Cost
267	$10,625
324	14,886
137	5,146
235	9,960
183	7,941
372	15,762
416	18,200
361	15,133
209	8,019
158	6,214

Required: Using an interactive or batch computer program, generate regression and correlation analyses and a plot of the data; interpret results.

3–20 Calculating and Interpreting Results. The sales manager of Paul's Potato Chips is trying to estimate how many salespeople she needs to hire to generate sales of $300,000 per month. Sales in recent months have varied between about $20,000 and $200,000. Paul's is a relatively new company and is trying to establish itself with large supermarket and commercial users. Data for past sales show the following:

Month	Salespeople	Sales Volume
1	3	$ 20,000
2	5	30,000
3	7	100,000
4	8	110,000
5	10	130,000
6	11	200,000

Required:

1. Using hand, calculator, or computer methods, calculate the intercept and slope of these data.

2. Explain your answers derived from item 1.

3. Can these data be used to predict the number of salespeople needed at a volume of $300,000? Why or why not?

3–21 Dealing with Nonlinear Data. Jeff Appleton, controller of the Sleep Products Division, was presented this data for one of the division's products.

Units	Costs
250	$123,177
100	28,648
200	77,857
400	600,307
300	208,274
350	338,606
150	47,305
325	273,945
375	456,720

Required:

1. Plot these data.

2. Since the plot shows a curvilinear (exponential) pattern, Appleton decided to transform the data using logs to see whether a more nearly linear pattern would result.
   a. Using natural logs, transform the cost data.
   b. Plot the transformed data.
   c. Calculate appropriate regression and correlation statistics and interpret the results.

3–22 Multiple Regression Results. Susan Zeller, the marketing manager of Colday Manufacturing, has been looking at the way changes in advertising expenditures and changes in sales price affect sales levels. Over the past few months Zeller has been experimenting with one of the company's products and has the following data to work with.

Price	Advertising	Sales Volume
$ 6	$ 5,000	13,000
6	100	7,000
8	7,000	10,000
8	10,000	15,000
10	5,500	6,500
10	13,000	12,000
12	10,000	11,000
12	14,000	8,000

The results shown below were obtained from a computer multiple regression package using SPSS. The first set of results shows a multiple regression using all variables. The second and third sets of results show simple regression.

ODEPENDENT VARIABLE... SALES

MEAN RESPONSE	10312.50000	STD. DEV.	3011.14003

VARIABLE(S) ENTERED ON STEP NUMBER 1... PRICE, ADVER

MULTIPLE R	.76849
R SQUARE	.59058
ADJUSTED R SQUARE	.42682
STD DEVIATION	2279.70011

ANALYSIS OF VARIANCE	DF	SUM OF SQUARES	MEAN SQUARE	F	SIGNIFICANCE
REGRESSION	2.	37483586.97207	18741793.48603	3.60625	.10
RESIDUAL	5.	25985163.02793	5197032.60559		
COEFF OF VARIABILITY	22.1 PCT				

------ VARIABLES IN THE EQUATION ------

VARIABLE	B	STD ERROR B	F	SIGNIFICANCE	BETA	ELASTICITY
PRICE	-1326.0797	552.03969	5.7703034	.061	-1.0527364	
ADVER	.74816474	.28736578	6.7783560	.048	1.1409918	-1.15731
(CONSTANT)	16205.787	3640.6931	19.813998	.007		.58584

------ VARIABLES NOT IN THE EQUATION ------

VARIABLE	PARTIAL	TOLERANCE	F	SIGNIFICANCE

SUMMARY TABLE

STEP	VARIABLE ENTERED	VARIABLE REMOVED	F TO ENTER OR REMOVE	SIGNIFICANCE	MULTIPLE R	R SQUARE	R SQUARE CHANGE	SIMPLE R	OVERALL F	SIGNIFICANCE
1	PRICE		5.77030	.061	.18854	.03555	.03555	-.18854	3.60625	.107
	ADVER		6.77836	.048	.76849	.59058	.55503	.34364		

ODEPENDENT VARIABLE... SALES

MEAN RESPONSE	10312.50000	STD. DEV.	3011.14003

VARIABLE(S) ENTERED ON STEP NUMBER 1... PRICE

MULTIPLE R	.18854
R SQUARE	.03555
ADJUSTED R SQUARE	0
STD DEVIATION	3194.07003

ANALYSIS OF VARIANCE	DF	SUM OF SQUARES	MEAN SQUARE	F	SIGNIFICANCE
REGRESSION	1.	2256250.00000	2256250.00000	.22116	.65
RESIDUAL	6.	61212500.00000	10202083.33333		
COEFF OF VARIABILITY	31.0 PCT				

------- VARIABLES IN THE EQUATION -------

VARIABLE	B	STD ERROR B	F SIGNIFICANCE	BETA ELASTICITY
PRICE	-237.50000	505.02681	.22115581 .655	-.1895444
(CONSTANT)	12450.000	4683.4260	7.0666141 .038	-.20727

DEPENDENT VARIABLE...   SALES

MEAN RESPONSE   10312.50000   STD. DEV.   3011.14003

VARIABLE(S) ENTERED ON STEP NUMBER   1...   ADVER

		ANALYSIS OF VARIANCE	DF	SUM OF SQUARES	MEAN SQUARE	F	SIGNIFICANCE
MULTIPLE R	.34364	REGRESSION	1.	7495131.97338	7495131.97338	.80343	.40
R SQUARE	.11809	RESIDUAL	6.	55973618.02662	9328936.33777		
ADJUSTED R SQUARE	0						
STD DEVIATION	3054.33075	COEFF OF VARIABILITY	29.6 PCT				

------- VARIABLES IN THE EQUATION -------

VARIABLE	B	STD ERROR B	F SIGNIFICANCE	BETA ELASTICITY
ADVER	.22533279	.25139163	.80342835 .405	.3436447
(CONSTANT)	8492.9377	2299.3403	13.642984 .010	.17644

------- VARIABLES NOT IN THE EQUATION -------

VARIABLE	PARTIAL	TOLERANCE	F	SIGNIFICANCE

------- VARIABLES NOT IN THE EQUATION -------

VARIABLE	PARTIAL	TOLERANCE	F	SIGNIFICANCE

Required:

1. Interpret the results.

2. Is either price or advertising (or both) a good predictor of sales? Why or why not?

3–23 **Assumptions of Linear Regression.** The accompanying scatter diagram and regression information were presented to John Angelis, a supervisor in the management accounting department, by the data processing manager. Variable 1 is maintenance cost and variable 2 is machine hours. One hundred observations are included in this analysis.

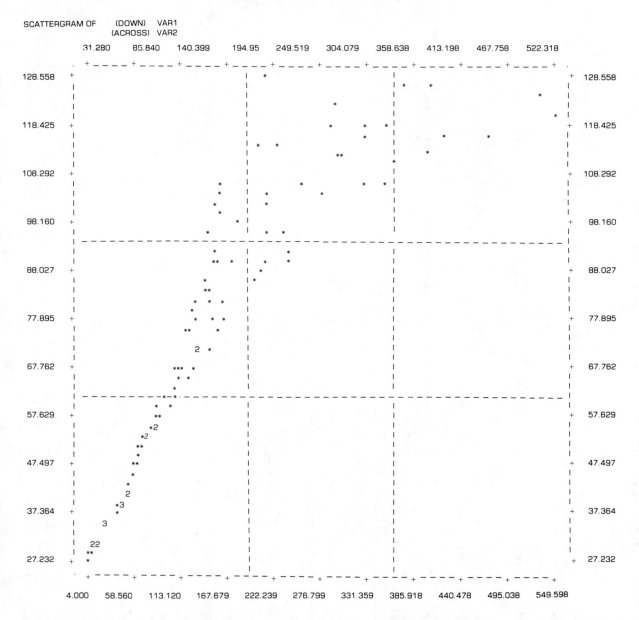

Required: Discuss and analyze these results in light of the assumptions of linear regression.

3-24 Time Series Data. The Grant Company has been in business more than four years. The sales manager requested a regression and correlation analysis of sales over time. The accompanying scatter diagram and set of statistics shows four years of sales. Years are charted with different lines as follows: Year 1 ———, Year 2 ----------, Year 3 · · · · · ·, Year 4 ═══

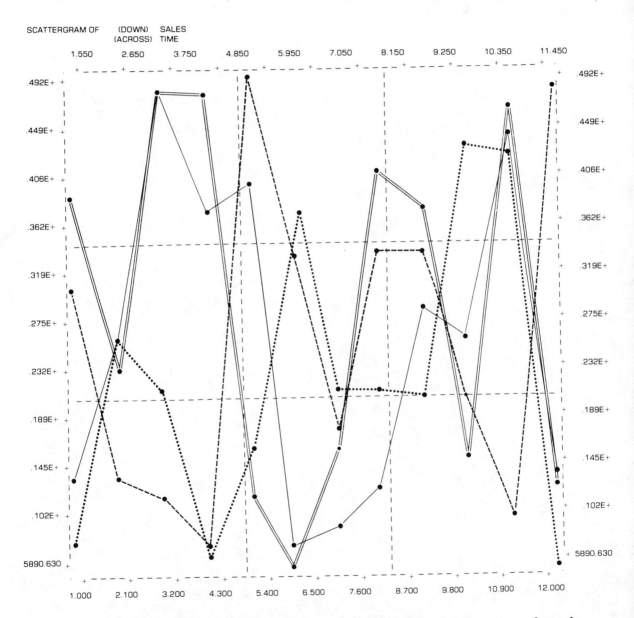

Required: Assuming it is now December of the fourth year, predict sales for January of the following year.

SELECTED REFERENCES

Benston, George, "Multiple Regression Analysis of Cost Behavior," *The Accounting Review*, 41:4, 657–72.

Hamburg, Morris, *Basic Statistics: A Modern Approach*. New York: Harcourt Brace Jovanovich, Inc., 1974.

Jensen, Robert, "Multiple Regression Models for Cost Control—Assumptions and Limitations," *The Accounting Review*, 42:2, 265–72.

Johnston, J., *Econometric Methods*, 2d ed. New York: McGraw-Hill Book Company, 1972.

Lapin, Lawrence, *Statistics for Modern Business Decisions*, 2d ed. New York: Harcourt Brace Jovanovich, Inc., 1978.

Neter, John, and William Wasserman, *Applied Linear Statistical Models*. Homewood, Ill.: Richard D. Irwin, Inc., 1974.

Tactical Decision Making

Chapter 4

This chapter deals with what are known as **short-term, operational,** or **tactical decisions.** Building on the basics of cost behavior and cost estimation, the chapter introduces some new terms, deals with typical tactical decisions, and introduces some applications of probability theory and linear programming.

DECISIONS

What Is a Decision?

A decision is a choice among various alternative courses of action for accomplishing some objective or goal. Before a decision can be made, therefore, a decision maker needs to know what he is trying to accomplish. For example, he might be trying to produce a product of a certain quality as inexpensively as possible, or he might be trying to use existing production facilities in order to generate the largest possible contribution margin. Many goals may be derived from the basic one of increasing the firm's income while taking on an acceptable level of risk.

The decision maker must have at least two alternatives to evaluate (even if one of them is the status quo), or there would be no need to make a decision. In addition, the decision maker is concerned about the future. The past is relevant only if it helps him in forecasting the future.

The Decision Continuum

William T. Morris says in the opening chapter of *Decision Analysis*:

It is sometimes helpful to think of decision-making behavior as characterized along a continuum from random decision making at one extreme, through inspirational decision making, to systematic behavior at the other extreme. By random behavior we might mean decisions with no detectable pattern, order, logic, or consistency. Random decisions are those which we, as observers, find impossible to model, to explain, or to predict. Inspirational decisions are those which feel "good" or "right" to the decision maker himself, but to the observer the explanation of the choice seems highly oversimplified, leaving out most of the obvious considerations present in the situation and placing excessive weight on one or two factors. Systematic deciding implies that the decision maker and the observer can fully see the logic, the pattern, the process that explains choices. Systematic behavior has a sort of consistency, predictability, and clarity that indicate the decision maker knows what he is doing when he decides.

There is a strong belief, and considerable evidence to support the belief, that systematic decision making increases the probability of achieving a good outcome. There is evidence that almost any systematic method of deciding, even though highly simplified, is better than none.[1]

The tactical decisions that we consider in this chapter are solved via systematic means but are usually nonrecurring. (The *type* of decision can recur, but specific decisions are unique.) Routine problems need be solved only once; then procedures can be set up to handle them when they recur.

What Is a Good Decision?

A good decision can be defined as one that is consistent with the information available to the decision maker. Making a good decision does not necessarily lead to a good result: the future may bring events, both favorable and unfavorable, that could not have been predicted by the decision maker. This does not mean that a poor decision was made. If a manager used available information well, then the decision *at the time* was a good one.

RELEVANT INFORMATION

Tactical (or short-term) decisions are those having an immediate rather than long-term economic impact on a firm. Usually such decisions can be quickly reversed. For example, if a price is set too high, it can be lowered. Capital budgeting (or long-term) decisions, on the other hand, deal with projects that will stretch over a span of at least one year and will require a large commitment of resources. Because it can be difficult to determine where short-term effects end, we shall use the term *tactical* rather than *short-term*.

Many of the common decisions we will investigate in this chapter do have longer-term implications. For example, a company's decision to discontinue a particular part of its business will have both short-term and long-term effects on income and cash flow. In many cases, however, we can

---

[1] William T. Morris, *Decision Analysis* (Columbus: Grid, Inc., 1977), p. 1.

model a problem as a single year issue and find that the results of such an analysis hold over a multiyear time frame.[2]

The Criterion of Relevance

Information is **relevant** if it relates to revenues and costs that will differ among the alternative courses of action being considered. For example, the material on cost behavior in Chapters 2 and 3 explains that while variable costs change in total as volume changes, fixed costs remain constant. Therefore, if a manager is deciding how many units to produce next month, fixed costs are irrelevant, since they will not change unless volume moves outside a relevant range. In making tactical decisions, it is important to define what costs are relevant. The decision maker need consider only relevant costs when evaluating information.

Other words for relevant are *incremental* and *differential*. Revenues and costs are **incremental** (or **differential**) if they are expected to differ under different courses of action. For example, some of the incremental costs of buying and driving a new automobile would be the purchase prices and operating costs of various models. Once you have bought the car, though, the incremental costs of continuing to operate it are just the operating costs. The purchase price is no longer relevant to decisions involving how much you will drive the car. In the parlance of decision making, the purchase price has become a **sunk cost.**

Sunk costs are not the only **irrelevant** or **nonincremental costs.** A manufacturing firm's fixed costs are nonincremental with respect to the manager's decision on how many units to produce within the relevant range. At any level within that range fixed costs will be the same. If you are deciding between two competing pieces of machinery and the crews required for each are identical, then the decision process can ignore labor costs (as long as you have decided you will purchase one of the two machines). Once the machine is purchased, then its cost is sunk for future decisions. Sunk costs are always irrelevant.

Models As Abstractions of Reality

If you were intending to buy a new car, you could consider all automobiles sold in the United States as possible alternatives. However, you might limit (**constrain**) your choices to a particular price range, body style, or economy of operation. You could not consider all the information that was available; you might not, for example, seek out information on weight distribution, capacity of the cooling system, or firing sequence of cylinders. You might decide that a few key factors were overwhelmingly important and then investigate these factors.

---

[2] Where we cannot use a single-period model, then we will use discounted cash flow techniques, as explained in Chapters 15 and 16.

Sometimes too much information is available to us; as humans with a limited capacity we can reach a stage of **information overload,** where we are swamped by data.[3] At other times we need more information than we have, but we find that acquiring information is costly. In both these situations we need decision-making models that include only certain variables — we hope the most important ones. While something seems lost in this simplifying process, the decision maker is left with something that is manageable.

Opportunity Costs

Illustration: Phil and Scrubby's Car Wash.   Phil and Scrubby's Car Wash is contemplating repairing a brush that washes car grilles. The current equipment was purchased three years ago for $1,000 and, if sold as is, has a current market value of $100. Even with repairs, this equipment has only a year of life left. Management is contemplating repairs, since the brush was directly responsible for $500 of damages over the last year and they feel it will cause at least this much damage in the coming year. In this example the relevant costs are the amount of damages ($500) and the cost of repairs. The original cost of the equipment is irrelevant and sunk.

The $100 resale value is nondifferential if the decision is solely whether to repair or not repair the equipment. However, if management also is contemplating replacing the existing equipment with new or used equipment, then the $100 is the *opportunity cost* of retaining the old equipment. If the old equipment is retained, the car wash has given up the opportunity to receive $100 (ignoring taxes). Opportunity costs are relevant to decisions.

Defining Opportunity Cost.   An **opportunity cost** is defined as the benefit that is foregone by the choice of one course of action instead of another. By choosing to retain the old car wash equipment, the firm foregoes the alternative of selling it.

Often management has several alternatives open. For example, the grille brush could be sold for some net amount (**net realizable value**). An equivalent brush could be purchased on the used equipment market (**replacement cost**). The current equipment may have alternate uses; perhaps this grille brush can be modified and used as a window brush. This conversion will yield the **next best operating value.** In many cases one or more of these three alternatives does not exist.

Opportunity cost is the lesser of (1) replacement cost and (2) the higher of net realizable value and next best operating value. For example, assume a radio manufacturer is asked to produce a special order of CB radios for a discount chain. The current book value of parts needed to make a CB set is $40. However, the current cost to replace these parts is $45. Most of these parts—some with modifications—could alternatively be used to produce an AM/FM receiver instead of regular AM/FM parts costing $47. The value of this substitution is the *next best operating value.* In other words, if the radio

---

[3] We discuss this topic further in Chapter 21.

manufacturer cannot (or does not) use a part for the purpose originally intended, can it be substituted for another part? Finally, if the CB parts were sold on the open market, they would bring a net of $42. We determine the opportunity cost as follows:

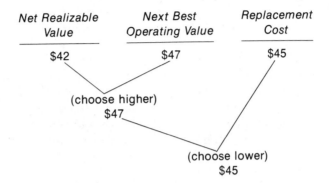

Net Realizable Value	Next Best Operating Value	Replacement Cost
$42	$47	$45

(choose higher)
$47

(choose lower)
$45

By using the parts in making a CB set, the manufacturer gives up the opportunity to keep an asset worth $45.

Whatever opportunity is given up by a particular course of action is the opportunity cost. Regarding relevance, sunk costs and opportunity costs are opposite extremes. No sunk cost is ever relevant, while any opportunity cost is always relevant.

Joint (Common) Costs

Many decisions involve segments of a firm: product lines, individual products, geographical areas in which the firm operates, individual factories, and many others. Costs that are incurred to benefit more than one segment of the firm are called **joint** or **common** to the benefited segments. Joint costs will not change as a result of decisions affecting one of the segments to which they are joint. For example, the fixed costs of producing a particular product are joint to each of the units produced. Producing more or fewer units will not affect total fixed costs, so they are not differential with respect to decisions involving the quantity of production. However, if dropping the product could eliminate the fixed costs, they are differential and relevant.

Joint costs can be variable as well as fixed. An oil refinery produces many different products. The variable costs of labor associated with putting crude oil into the refining process are common to all the oil and petrochemical products that ultimately result.

The principal problem with joint costs is that they are frequently allocated to units of product, product lines, departments of retail stores, and other segments of a firm. These allocations are sometimes made to conform with external reporting requirements: generally accepted accounting principles require that fixed costs of production be allocated to individual units of product, and some regulatory agencies require other sorts of allocations.

If the firm's accounting system is geared primarily to satisfying these external requirements, it will include allocated joint costs that must be removed from consideration in making decisions. In other words, allocated costs are irrelevant. Any cost that is joint with respect to the decision at hand is, by nature, not differential.

It is not always easy to determine what costs are joint; it depends on the particular situation. The salary of a plant manager is joint with respect to the units of product made in the factory. Therefore, it is irrelevant in determining whether to increase or decrease production. But if the decision is whether or not to shut the entire plant down, the salary is relevant because it would be avoided if the plant were closed. The person making a decision must carefully analyze the alternatives and the scope of the decision in order to ascertain which costs are relevant and which are not. It is impossible to develop general rules regarding the relevance of particular types of costs.

COMMON TACTICAL DECISIONS

Perhaps the three most common tactical decisions where we can apply the notions of relevant costs are **make or buy, special orders,** and **drop a segment.** We can deal with these decisions systematically by examining differential revenues and costs.

Make or Buy

When a manager must decide whether to make a part or a product internally or buy it from an outside vendor, she faces a make or buy choice. Many considerations are involved, besides the relevant costs. What are the expected quality or specification differences? Can an outside supplier meet an acceptable timetable for delivery? Will outside buying mean that workers in the firm's plant will be laid off, and, if so, what is the firm's responsibility to them and to the community? Will the supplier offer a long-term pricing structure that will reduce the impact of unknown future inflation? If these qualitative considerations do not eliminate one choice or the other, the manager can use the general approach of examining the differential elements.

Too often in decision making, qualitative factors are ignored. We get so tied into looking at expected cash costs and benefits that we forget the effect of nonquantitative factors on our ultimate decision. Thus, besides looking at differential costs, management needs to consider social issues relating to pollution, community responsibility, safety, and the perceptions that employees, the community and/or customers might have about various decisions. While some of these concerns will have measurable monetary effects on a company, many cannot be accurately quantified. With this in mind, let us look at a typical make or buy situation.

Illustration: Charbroil's Burger Buns.   Charbroil Burgers is a chain of fast food restaurants in Indianapolis. Currently it bakes its own buns at a central plant where it also makes hamburger patties. Costs for a typical month are as follows:

Hamburger meat	$10,000
Hamburger spices	500
Wheat, yeast, etc.	3,000
Electricity–bakery	500
Labor	5,000
Fixed costs (depreciation, rent, manager's salary)	5,000
	$24,000

Assume that labor is evenly divided between the bakery and hamburger production and that output is 40,000 hamburgers and 40,000 buns. A bakery offers a contract to Charbroil to bake and deliver 40,000 buns for 18 cents each. When asked to compute costs per bun at Charbroil, the manager says that costs are 21¼ cents. He made this calculation using the costs of wheat and yeast, electricity for the bakery, half of the labor costs, and half of the fixed costs. He felt that the fixed costs should be allocated on the basis of the relative amounts of labor cost for the hamburger and the buns. Thus, $3,000 + $500 + $2,500 + $2,500 = $8,500, which, when divided by 40,000, gives 21.25 cents per bun. What are the relevant costs in this case? Consider the following cost schedules:

	Make	Buy
Contract (40,000 at 18¢)	—	$7,200
Wheat, yeast	$3,000	—
Electricity	500	—
Labor	2,500	—
Fixed costs	2,500	2,500
	$8,500	$9,700

Even though the fixed costs are included in the analysis, they are not incremental, since they do not change under either alternative. Because they are the same under either alternative, they can be included under *both* alternatives or excluded from both. Incremental costs are:

$$\frac{\$3,000 + \$500 + \$2,500}{40,000} = \$0.15 \text{ per bun}$$

Therefore, a proper comparison is between either *make* at 15 cents versus *buy* at 18 cents or, if fixed costs are included, *make* at 21¼ cents versus *buy* at 24¼ cents (18 cents plus $2,500 fixed costs divided by 40,000). While this illustration shows a quantitative answer to the problem, qualitative factors such as quality or delivery schedules may well be enough to overrule the 3 cents per bun operating savings.

Thus, as a first illustration of tactical decisions, we have the choice to make or buy a basic part of a hamburger sandwich. We see that there is a 3 cents per bun difference between these two options, whether we use solely incremental costs or include some nondifferential costs in both options. This same pattern will be followed in the other examples of tactical decisions.

Special Orders

At times it is advantageous for a company to sell its products at less than normal prices. Some firms make products that are sold under the label of a chain store, as is the case with many products sold by Sears, for example. So long as the special orders do not adversely affect sales at normal prices and the special price exceeds incremental costs, the company can earn additional profits. In its purest form, a company is faced with a one-time special order situation. Practically, firms may face a series of unique decisions.

In January, 19X9, the state of Arkansas approaches the manager of Hawk Table Company with an offer to buy 1,000 tables for a new state government building at $65 each. Sales of 50,000 tables are currently planned for 19X9. The Hawk plant has a capacity of 70,000 tables, and management feels this order would not affect normal demand nor weaken general prices. The Arkansas proposal is a singular problem. The following is the 19X8 income statement for Hawk. Management expects prices and costs to remain relatively stable throughout 19X9. Should Hawk accept the order?

HAWK TABLE COMPANY
Income Statement
Year Ending 12/31/X8

Sales (50,000 tables)	$5,000,000
Less: Cost of goods sold (Schedule 1)	3,000,000
Gross profit	$2,000,000
Other expenses	1,500,000
Income before taxes	$ 500,000

Schedule 1

Cost of goods sold:	
Materials	$1,000,000
Direct labor	1,250,000
Factory overhead — variable	250,000
— fixed	500,000
	$3,000,000

An analysis of the preceding yields the following unit breakdown of relevant data:

Average selling price	$100	
Average materials		$20
Average labor		25
Average variable overhead		5
Unit contribution margin		$50

This analysis assumes either that Hawk only produces one model of table or that the Arkansas order has the same mix of products as Hawk's overall sales mix. Obviously, this is an important assumption.

Hawk is not faced by any capacity constraints, since production was planned at a 50,000-unit level in a facility designed to produce 70,000 units. Therefore, any price exceeding $50 (the average variable cost of a table) will increase profits for Hawk.

If accepting this order would affect normal sales, or if Hawk were currently producing at capacity, management should use a price of $100 for these tables. In both cases normal customers would be displaced and Hawk would have a lower overall profit if it accepted business at less than usual prices. Thus, $100 would be the opportunity cost and, therefore, the relevant price. For example, if Hawk currently were selling 70,000 tables and the offer to buy 1,000 more came in at $65 each, acceptance would reduce Hawk's income.

	Current	Proposed
Sales 70,000 at $100	$7,000,000	
69,000 at $100		$6,900,000
1,000 at $ 65		65,000
	$7,000,000	$6,965,000

Since costs would be unaffected, Hawk would lose $35,000 in profits if it accepted an order at $65 per table when already operating at capacity.

Dropping a Segment

As noted above, **segment** is a general term that can be used to describe a product, product line, type of customer (e.g., wholesale or retail), geographical region, or any other part of the firm that is considered for expansion or reduction. A simple case is that of a retail store operating several departments, one or more of which is being evaluated, possibly to be dropped.[4]

---

[4] As you can see from the examples, it is difficult to sharply distinguish tactical from long-term decisions. Purely tactical decisions are few. However, the point of this chapter is to get us used to thinking in terms of relevant costs no matter what the time frame. Thus, this merging of tactical and longer perspectives is unimportant at this point.

Illustration: Reeding Pharmacy.   Barbara Reed owns Reeding Pharmacy, Inc., a store that carries full lines of drugs, cosmetics, greeting cards, and photographic equipment. Ms. Reed has examined the income statement shown below and is considering the possibility of dropping the photographic equipment and increasing the size of the card department. She feels that because the card department generates a higher profit than the photography department, while using less space, the move could be profitable.

REEDING PHARMACY, INC.
Income by Department
Year Ending 9/30/X2

	Cosmetics and Drugs	Cards	Photographic	Total
Sales	$500,000	$30,000	$150,000	$680,000
Less:				
Cost of merchandise sold	250,000	10,000	100,000	360,000
Sales personnel	100,000	11,000	39,000	150,000
Rent	5,000	900	1,100	7,000
Insurance on inventory	2,500	100	1,000	3,600
General and administrative costs	14,700	900	4,400	20,000
Depreciation on fixtures	3,000	1,500	1,500	6,000
Income by department	$124,800	$ 5,600	$ 3,000	$133,400

The first step that Reed takes is to prepare the schedule below, showing the revenues and incremental costs of the photography department. Reed knows that rent and general and administrative costs are allocated to the departments on the basis of sales and that they will be the same in total whether or not the photography department is dropped. She also eliminates the depreciation on fixtures, because that item represents the allocation of the cost of the fixtures and is sunk. Cost of goods sold is variable. Sales personnel costs are incremental. Insurance on inventory is assessed at 1 percent of cost of sales and, therefore, is also incremental.

Photography Department
Incremental Revenues and Costs

Sales	$150,000
Less:	
Cost of goods sold	100,000
Sales personnel	39,000
Insurance on inventory	1,000
Incremental profit	$ 10,000

If there were no other effects of dropping the department, the income of the firm would drop by $10,000. Therefore, if the department were dropped and the card department expanded, the card department would have to produce an increase in incremental profit of at least $10,000 to make the change profitable.

Ms. Reed's next step is to prepare the income statement shown below. It is called a **pro forma** income statement, which means *for the form*. In this case, *for the form* means the expected results if the photographic department is dropped and the card department expanded. The following assumptions underlie the pro forma statement.

1. Increasing the size of the card department would result in a doubling of card sales; cosmetic and drug sales would be unaffected. This is a key set of assumptions. She is saying that sales in various departments are independent of one another. Any analysis would have to test these statements.

2. The only variable costs are cost of goods sold and insurance on inventory. The latter is 1 percent of cost of sales.

3. Additional salespeople would be needed in the expanded card department at an additional cost of $9,000. Note that this is just the incremental cost over current operations.

4. The fixtures now used in the photography department would be used in the expanded card department, so that no new fixtures would be needed. Otherwise we would consider the resale value of such fixtures and the cost of getting adequate fixtures for the expanded department.

5. Rent and general and administrative expenses are allocated costs that would remain the same in total under either alternative.

REEDING PHARMACY, INC.
Pro Forma Income Statement

	Cosmetics and Drugs	Cards	Total
Sales	$500,000	$60,000	$560,000
Less:			
Cost of goods sold	250,000	20,000	270,000
Sales personnel salaries	100,000	20,000	120,000
Insurance on inventory	2,500	200	2,700
Departmental incremental profit	$147,500	$19,800	$167,300
Joint and unavoidable costs:			
Rent			7,000
General and administrative costs			20,000
Depreciation			6,000
Income			$134,300

Ms. Reeding has a projected income statement that nicely segregates incremental revenue and cost from joint costs. This is an effective way to deal with this information, since it makes it easier for management to analyze what decisions need to be made.

It appears that the move would be wise, resulting in an increase in profit of $900 (from $133,400 to $134,300). However, the monetary difference is close, and the sensitivity of the decision to at least two key factors should be assessed. The key factors are the level of card sales and the assumption that drug and cosmetic sales would not be affected by dropping the photography department. Testing first the sensitivity of the estimate of card sales, we see that cost of sales is 33⅓ percent of sales and that insurance on inventory is 1 percent of cost of sales. Therefore, insurance on inventory is one third of 1 percent of sales, and total variable costs are 33⅔ percent of sales. Contribution margin is then 66⅓ percent of sales. The income statement for the photography department showed incremental profit of $10,000. The incremental fixed costs of additional sales personnel in the card department are $9,000, so that a total of $19,000 in contribution margin is required just to equal current profits. The required *increase* in card sales is about $28,644 ($19,000/0.6633). As proof:

	Current Photographic Department	Required Increase in Card Sales
Sales	$150,000	$28,644
Less:		
Cost of sales	100,000	9,548
Sales personnel salaries	39,000	9,000
Insurance on inventory	1,000	96
Incremental profit	$ 10,000	$10,000

We are comparing the *total* flows of the photography department to the increased portion of card sales. Management has projected an increase of $30,000 in card sales. However, if the estimate of the increase in card sales were off by just $1,356 ($30,000 − $28,644), the change would leave the firm where it would have expected to be without the change. The decision *is* sensitive to the estimate of increased card sales. Now let us look at one of the important assumptions included in the analysis.

Sales in one department of a store often are affected by the presence of other departments. People come to shop for one type of item and wind up buying others, or they tend to patronize stores that carry all, or nearly all, the items they wish to buy on a particular shopping trip. This was the original idea behind the department store and is the current reasoning behind shopping malls. It is possible, then, that sales of drugs and cosmetics could be harmed by the dropping of the photographic department. How much of a drop in these sales, we now ask, would wipe out the anticipated increase in profits of $900 (assuming now that additional card sales will be $30,000)?

Determining the critical drop in drug and cosmetic sales requires determining the contribution margin percentage. Cost of sales is 50 percent of sales ($250,000/$500,000) in this department, and insurance on inventory is 1 percent of cost of sales and, therefore, half of 1 percent of sales. The variable cost percentage of sales is 50.5 percent and the contribution margin percentage 49.5 percent. A drop in sales of $1,818 ($900/0.495) would leave the firm in the same position whether it kept or dropped the photography department. The decision is, therefore, quite sensitive to the assumption that drug and cosmetic sales would not be affected by dropping the photography department. Because of the risk involved in the proposed change, Ms. Reed might elect to continue operating all three departments.

Remember that all our analyses so far are inherently uncertain because they are based on estimates of future results. If it seems that all this estimating injects too much guesswork and subjectivity into the decision-making process, please note that *some decision has to be made* and that *every decision involves some estimate of future results.* If Ms. Reed does elect to continue all three departments, she has made a decision based on prediction just as surely as if she elected to drop the photographic department.

TACTICAL VERSUS LONG-TERM DECISIONS

We distinguished earlier between short-term or tactical decisions and long-term (or capital budgeting) decisions. The main difference is that tactical decisions have an immediate impact, with only lingering long-term effects. For example, if a firm spends an extra $10,000 this quarter on advertising, there is an immediate impact on quarterly earnings and probably some residual impact on future earnings in the near term. At the other extreme is the long-term project. If Reeding is considering buying land and building a new drug store as an additional outlet, this might entail an investment of $1 million or more and would have major effects on the company for many years. The examples offered above illustrating *make or buy, dropping a segment,* and *special orders* decisions fall in a middle ground on this continuum; they are tactical decisions that probably have some long-term implications. In fact, most decisions have some long-term consequences.

DECISIONS UNDER UNCERTAINTY

Barbara Reed had estimated sales lost and sales gained by dropping one department and expanding another. She had estimated that drug sales would remain at current levels and that greeting card sales would double. Sensitivity analysis revealed that if her estimates were off by fairly small amounts, the decision to drop photographic equipment would be unwise. If she overestimated the increase in card sales by more than $1,356 or underestimated the decline in drug sales by more than $1,818, Reeding Pharmacy would make a lower profit than if it kept its current departmental setup. Reed's estimates were of specific values. If just these values are used in the decision-making process, Reed inherently assumes that these sales and cost figures are certain. Even though sensitivity analysis pointed out how important estimates of sales and costs are in this situation, the basic data are based on single, certain estimates.[5] However, it is rare that one can be certain about much in business. Uncertainty exists about sales levels, sales prices, costs, and virtually all other critical factors. If we can somehow quantify this uncertainty (or risk—we will use these terms synonymously), we can better assess the likelihood that events will occur. Some things are more easy to quantify than others. For example, the likelihood that a coin will come up heads when flipped is a lot easier to estimate than the likelihood that it will rain three months hence.

Ms. Reed originally estimated card sales would expand from $30,000 to $60,000. If this estimate was *certain*, there is no problem. However, the $60,000 may have been a *point estimate*, a measure depicting an underlying probability distribution of various sales levels. In order to come up with this estimate, Reed had to unconsciously or consciously (intuitively or systematically) estimate the likelihood of different sales levels. If specific sales levels have specific probabilities assigned to them, the problem is being addressed using a *discrete* distribution. Since sales can take on any level, we could use a *continuous* distribution.

Expected Value

Assume for the sake of this example that total sales in the expanded card department could be $35,000, $50,000, or $75,000 (called **conditional values**). Reed could hire a marketing firm that would give her not only these estimates of sales but also its ideas on the likelihood that these different sales levels would occur. Suppose that Reed did just that and that a market survey revealed the following:

Greeting Card Annual Sales, x_i	Probability of Sales Level, $p(x_i)$
$35,000	.10
50,000	.44
75,000	.46
	1.00

[5] Certainty means that there is no chance a value will be other than expected. Thus, if we are certain that it costs $12.50 to buy a ticket to a baseball game, there is a zero probability of the cost's being other than $12.50. Uncertainty and risk reflect the probabilities of various events when we lack certainty. Classically there is a difference between these two terms: risk describes a situation where there is a reasonable basis for estimating the probabilities of outcomes, and uncertainty exists when there is no way to assign probabilities to outcomes. We deal with risk as thus defined. See Chapters 16 and 21 for a more complete treatment.

Since this example uses a discrete probability distribution, there is the assumption that the probability of *any* other sales level is zero. Obviously this is not a realistic assumption since sales could take on any value from pennies to many thousands of dollars and cents. A continuous distribution can take this into account. However, discrete distributions may be easier to work with and may be quite adequate in dealing with simple risk problems. (The terms used in this chapter, such as continuous and discrete distributions, expected value, and variance are reviewed in Appendix 4–A at the end of this chapter.)

The **expected value** of sales is the various sales values weighted by their probabilities and then summed. Thus, the expected value of sales (noted as $\bar{x}$) is:

$$\bar{x} = (\$35,000)(.10) + (\$50,000)(.44) + (\$75,000)(.46) = \$60,000$$

While $60,000 is the calculated expected value of sales, we must remember that sales will be either $35,000, $50,000, or $75,000. Therefore, if Reed chose to drop one department and expand the card department, there is a 54 percent chance that she would be making a wrong decision—that sales would be either $50,000 or $35,000. At either level she would earn less than she could expect if she kept the photographic department.

This example shows a **discrete probability distribution,** since the **random variable** (sales) can take on only one of three values. Reed can conclude that while the expected value of sales (or **mean** of the distribution) is $60,000, there is a greater than 50 percent probability that sales will be substantially less than this figure.

If Reed and her marketing consultants had estimated probabilities associated with seven, fifteen, or even twenty levels of sales, she would still be modeling the problem using a discrete distribution and would weigh each of the fifteen sales levels (x_i) by its probability of occurrence $[p(x_i)]$ to get the expected value.

Suppose that Reed was not satisfied with the data showing only three sales levels; she ordered a more intensive survey, the results of which appear in Exhibit 4–1 and are graphed in Figure 4–1 on page 138.

Figure 4–2 depicts a continuous probability distribution of sales. In comparing Figures 4–1 and 4–2, we can see how a discrete distribution can be used instead of a continuous distribution (or the reverse where we can use a **normal approximation** of a discrete distribution).

However, as the number of sales levels investigated grows larger, Reed's problem moves closer to those of the real world. As we observed earlier, you can intuitively recognize that actual sales for a year *could* take on *any* value between $0 and some very large figure. Practically we could restrict this range to between $15,000 and $100,000, based on experience or industry averages. By establishing a range of possible sales volumes and by limiting the range, we can make the following points:

1. Because the relevant sales range is limited to between $15,000 and $100,000, there is virtually **zero probability** that sales will be below $15,000 or above $100,000.

2. Because any level of sales between $15,000 and $100,000 will have some chance of occurring, the probability distribution is now considered *continuous*.

EXHIBIT 4–1
Survey of Various Sales Levels for Greeting Cards

Greeting Card Annual Sales x_i	$p(x_i)$
$ 20,000	.02
30,000	.03
40,000	.10
50,000	.20
60,000	.30
70,000	.20
80,000	.10
90,000	.03
100,000	.02

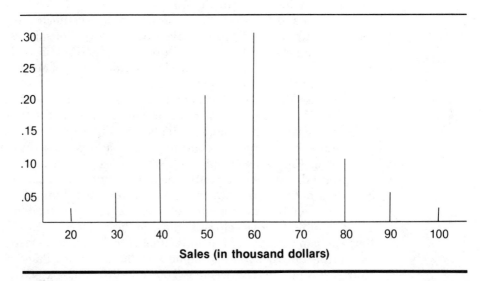

Sales (in thousand dollars)

FIGURE 4–1
Graph of New Probability Assessment

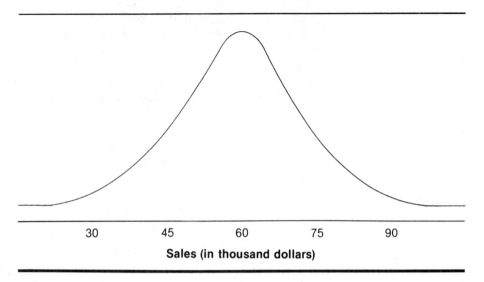

Sales (in thousand dollars)

FIGURE 4–2
Continuous Distribution

Variance and Standard Deviation

An expected value is only one measure of a probability distribution. In the discrete distribution it represents the weighted average value of the variable under study. In a symmetrical continuous distribution it represents the most likely value, the central tendency. Also useful is some knowledge of the dispersion of values around the mean. With the information in Exhibit 4–1 the pharmacy management can get a measure of the divergence of various sales ranges from the mean (expected) value of sales. The **variance** of a distribution is such a measure. The variance is the sum of the squared differences (deviations) of the values of the random variable from the expected value (mean). The square root of the variance, the **standard deviation,** is useful in our analysis. We used this process in Chapter 3 when dealing with variation around the regression line (the standard error of the estimate). The variance for the distribution shown in Exhibit 4–1, $238,000,000 is calculated at the top of page 140.

With a variance of $238,000,000, the standard deviation, is about $15,427. Using the normal probability table, Table A–1 in the Appendix at the back of the book, management can say that actual sales have about a 68 percent chance of being within one standard deviation of the expected value ($60,000 ± $15,427 = $44,573 to $75,427). Management will want to know the probability that card sales will be below the indifference point of keeping the existing departments (alternative 1) and dropping one department while expanding the other (alternative 2). We stated earlier that additional sales in the card department of $28,644 would yield equal profits

Calculation of Variance
(in thousands of dollars)

(1) Sales, x_i	(2) Probability, $p(x_i)$	(3) Squared Deviation from Expected Value, $(x_i - \bar{x})^2$	(4) Col. (2) × Col. (3), $(x_i - \bar{x})^2[p(x_i)]$
$ 20	.02	$1,600,000[a]	$ 32,000
30	.03	900,000	27,000
40	.10	400,000	40,000
50	.20	100,000	20,000
60	.30	0	0
70	.20	100,000	20,000
80	.10	400,000	40,000
90	.03	900,000	27,000
100	.02	1,600,000	32,000
			$238,000

[a] For example: $($20,000 - $60,000)^2 = 1.6 billion.

when compared to the status quo. Thus, if total card sales were expected to be $58,644, management would be indifferent between expanding the card department and retaining the photographic department, all other things being equal and held constant. This figure is 0.09 ($1,356 ÷ $15,427 = 0.09) standard deviations below the expected value of $60,000 in sales. Again, using a normal probability table, there is a 46 percent probability that sales will be below this level, which means that the choice is fairly risky; management therefore may choose alternative 1 instead of alternative 2.

Marginal, Conditional, and Joint Probabilities

In the previous example we explicitly assumed that the probabilities associated with the different levels of card sales were not affected by probabilities associated with drug sales. Thus, the example shows **independent probabilities.** In other words, if card sales are not affected by drug sales, and vice versa, then it can be said that these two are based on independent probability distributions. With independent probabilities, and with the data shown in Exhibit 4–2 about various levels of drug sales, joint probabilities about total sales can be calculated very simply. Exhibit 4–2 shows the marginal probabilities associated with levels of drug sales, while earlier data (Exhibit 4–1, for example) showed the marginal probabilities of different levels of card sales. (Appendix 4–A briefly reviews the concepts of marginal, conditional, and joint probabilities.)

We are now concerned with the joint probability of various levels of *total* sales. For example, we might be interested in the probability of total

EXHIBIT 4-2
Marginal Distribution of
Drug Sales

Drug Sales	Probability
$300,000	.075
400,000	.260
500,000	.350
600,000	.220
700,000	.095
	1.000

sales being $560,000 (drug sales of $500,000 and card sales of $60,000). As developed in Appendix 4-A,

$$p(D, C) = p(D) \cdot p(C)$$
$$p(D = \$500,000 \text{ and } C = \$60,000) = p(D = \$500,000) \cdot p(C = \$60,000)$$
$$= (.35)(.30)$$
$$= .105$$

where D is drug sales and C is card sales. We assume independent probabilities in this example. If, for example, card sales were affected by the level of drug sales, then card sales would be **dependent** on drug sales. In this case the general probability relationship above would be expressed as:

$$p(D = \$500,000 \text{ and } C = \$60,000)$$
$$= p(D = \$500,000) \cdot p(C = \$60,000 \text{ given } D = \$500,000)$$

or

$$p(D, C) = p(D) \cdot p(C \mid D)$$

Objective and Subjective Probabilities

The Reeding example assumes that management could make adequate assessments regarding risk. Actually, probability assessments fall along a continuum from objective to subjective. Basically the likelihood of occurrence of some event would be considered an **objective probability** if a group of impartial observers could agree on it. Classic examples are the probability of a head when flipping a fair coin or the probability of drawing an ace from a full deck of cards. Neutral bystanders would agree the former has an objective probability of .5 and the latter has an objective probability of 4/52 (or .076923). At the other end of the continuum is **subjective probability**. A subjective probability is one person's assessment of a situation. If a person is driving 65 mph in a 55-mph zone, he may feel that there is about a 50 percent chance of getting a speeding ticket, while someone else may feel that there is only about a 40 percent chance.

Most of the everyday business and personal probability assessments that we all make, either explicitly or implicitly, lie between these two extremes. Naturally, if a decision maker is going to compute expected values and variances and use them in a model, the resultant information is only as good as the original estimates of probabilities. This point cannot be taken lightly. Too often models proposed to aid decision makers are unaccompanied by the GIGO warning: if you put garbage in, you will get nothing but garbage out.

ACCOUNTANTS AND QUANTITATIVE METHODS

As accountants we want to provide information in its most useful form. To accomplish this purpose, we need to be able to decide what quantitative models are cost effective to use, and we need to be able to interpret data so we can explain our analyses to management. If we fail to use current mathematical tools or if we ignore behavioral implications, we are doing only part of our job.

DECISION TREES

Multiple Decisions and Events

We look now at a decision-making aid that relies on probabilities. This approach is helpful when the decision maker confronts a multiple decision or multiple-event task.

Illustration: Reeding's Photo and Card Departments. Reeding Pharmacy, for example, may be in the following situation. While they are deciding whether to drop their photography department and expand their card line, another pharmacy signs a lease for a building two blocks away. Reeding's managers are not certain whether the new pharmacy, Glass Drugs, will have a small, medium, or large card department. They do know, however, that the size of Glass Drugs's card department will affect the level of card sales at Reeding.

Exhibit 4–3 presents the Reeding management's assessment of the likelihood (marginal probabilities) that Glass Drugs will have a small, medium, or large competing department as well as the conditional probabilities of Reeding's card sales *given* the size of Glass Drugs's card department. Exhibit 4–3 can be pictured as a **decision tree**, as shown in Figure 4–3. Figure 4–3 depicts a one-decision problem (whether to keep things as they are or to make the photo/card departmental changes) with two **sets of events** (what will be the size of Glass Drugs's card department and what will be the resultant sales level of Reeding's expanded card department). Each set of events in this example can have only one **outcome.** For

EXHIBIT 4–3
Reeding and Glass Card Departments

Marginal Probabilities

p(Glass has small department) = .2
p(Glass has medium department) = .5
p(Glass has large department) = .3

Conditional Probabilities

p(Reeding sales = $60,000 | small Glass department) = .35
p(Reeding sales = $40,000 | small Glass department) = .65

p(Reeding sales = $60,000 | medium Glass department) = .45
p(Reeding sales = $40,000 | medium Glass department) = .55

p(Reeding sales = $60,000 | large Glass department) = .60
p(Reeding sales = $40,000 | large Glass department) = .40

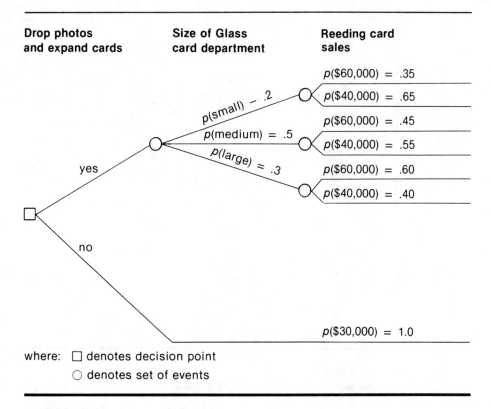

Drop photos and expand cards

Size of Glass card department

Reeding card sales

p($60,000) = .35
p($40,000) = .65

p($60,000) = .45
p($40,000) = .55

p($60,000) = .60
p($40,000) = .40

p(small) = .2
p(medium) = .5
p(large) = .3

yes

no

p($30,000) = 1.0

where: ☐ denotes decision point
        ○ denotes set of events

FIGURE 4–3
Decision Tree

example, Reeding's card sales will be either $60,000 or $40,000. With the decision-tree framework, the expected values (or **expected monetary values** as they are sometimes called) can be calculated from **conditional values**. These values are indeed conditional on the second event (level of sales at Reeding) given the first event (size of Glass Drugs's department). Figure 4–4 shows these conditional values. In order to make the yes or no decision, one must first calculate expected values for each alternative. The expected value of profits for dropping the photo department and expanding the card line is:

$$[(.2)(.35) + (.5)(.45) + (.3)(.60)] \cdot \$134,300 = \$ \ 63,792.50$$
$$+ \ [(.2)(.65) + (.5)(.55) + (.3)(.40)] \cdot \$121,000 = \$ \ 63,525.00$$
$$\text{expected monetary value:} \quad \$127,317.50$$

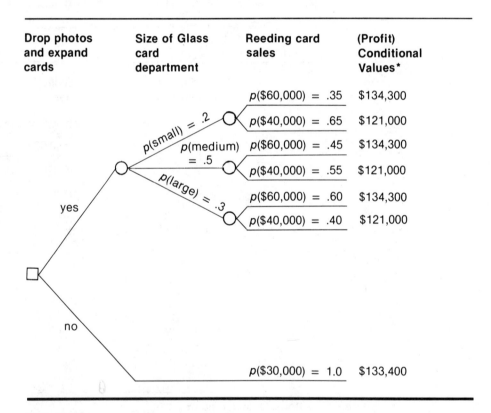

FIGURE 4–4
Decision Tree with Monetary Values

* The figure of $134,300 comes from Reeding's pro forma income statement on page 133, and $121,000 is based on the reduction in contribution margin with $20,000 lower sales.

Since the expected monetary value of changing operations is less than the expected monetary value of the status quo ($133,400), the decision tree points to leaving things as they are.

This first example shows a single decision and two sets of events. Conditional values are predicated on the two events. The choice criterion is to **maximize expected monetary value.** The variance of each event is not considered. This can be a fault of the methodology, and risk should be accounted for in some way. Also, we are looking only at a single decision.

This analysis can easily be expanded to multiple decisions. Here is where the decision tree really shines! Suppose Reeding could offer its merchandise either at regular or at cut-rate prices. Assume also that its potential competitor, Glass Drugs, will have either a very small card department or a very large one. Now there are two decisions to be dealt with: (1) should Reeding expand its card department, and (2) if it does, should it use cut-rate or normal pricing? In addition, there is only one set of uncertain events (the

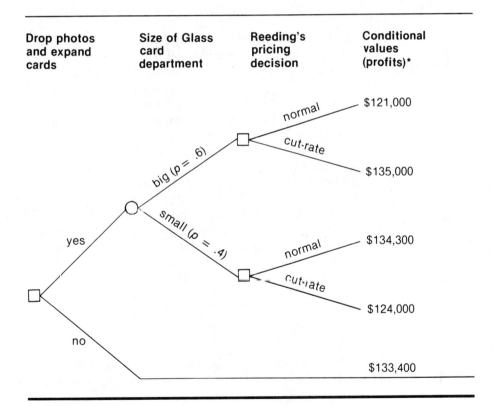

Drop photos and expand cards	Size of Glass card department	Reeding's pricing decision	Conditional values (profits)*

normal — $121,000

cut-rate — $135,000

big (p = .6)

small (p = .4)

normal — $134,300

cut-rate — $124,000

yes

no

$133,400

FIGURE 4–5
Decision Tree—Multiple Decisions

* Conditional values are assumed; they are based on CVP relationships developed in the discussion of dropping a segment at Reeding.

size of Glass's card department). Figure 4–5 depicts the situation with the revised probabilities associated with the assumptions above. You should be able to calculate the expected monetary values of each alternative as $134,720 and $133,400, respectively. This decision tree process works backward to get from the last decision to the first.[6] First you decide the proper action if Glass's department is big (use cut-rate pricing) and if it is small (use normal pricing). From these choices, it is easy to calculate expected values and to decide to expand the card department. The expected value of expanding is $134,720 compared to $133,400 without expanding.

Continuous Distributions and Decision Trees

Our analyses in the brief examples presented in Figures 4–4 and 4–5 are hampered by the need to choose specific sales levels, specific conditional values, and specific probabilities. As the number of decisions and events grows, the decision maker confronts an increasingly more complex decision tree with branches everywhere. Because multiple sets of events add complexity, and because in real life many levels of sales are possible, we will find it useful to consider continuous distributions and decision trees.

With a continuous distribution, the decision tree takes on a different visual aspect. Figure 4–6 is a continuous variable version of Figure 4–4. Almost everything on the tree becomes a continuous random variable depicted by a normal curve. Even if the status quo is maintained, the level of card sales and the level of profits are now both random variables. Each distribution will have a mean, variance, and other measures that can be used to solve the decision tree. If we know the parameters of these distributions, we can use a **stochastic decision tree process**. Usually, however, we do not know all there is to know about the random variables. We can observe card sales in Reeding's current department before competition moves in close by. These observations may give us an indication of what will happen given Glass Drugs's decision, but we cannot *know* expected values or variances associated with future events. Hespos and Strassmann[7] describe a method using computer simulation to estimate the parameters of the distributions associated with various random variables.

LINEAR PROGRAMMING

In discussing tactical decisions thus far we have looked at relevant revenues and costs and derived and used measures of uncertainty regarding them. In

---

[6] A good discussion of discrete decision trees is found in H. Bierman, Jr., C. Bonini, and W. Hausman, *Quantitative Analysis for Business Decisions*, 5th ed. (Homewood, Ill.: Richard D. Irwin, Inc., 1977).

[7] R. F. Hespos and P. A. Strassmann, "Stochastic Decision Trees for the Analysis of Investment Decisions," *Management Science*, 11 (August 1965), 244–59.

Drop photos and expand cards	Size of Glass card department	Reeding's card sales	Conditional values

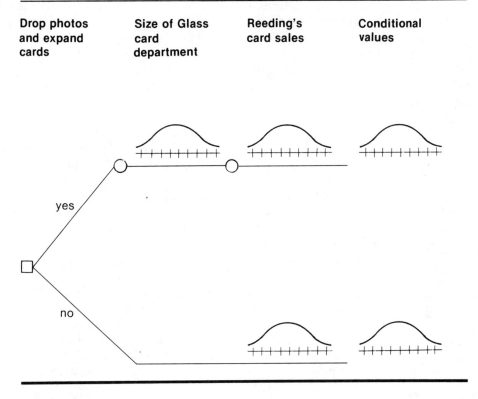

FIGURE 4-6
Stochastic Decision Tree

considering a special order when the firm was already at capacity, we dealt briefly with a constrained resource. In the Reeding Pharmacy example, space is a constraint. Reeding has only a finite amount of retail space and wants to use it to achieve as great a profit as possible. Sometimes there are many constrained (or scarce) resources to deal with. Firms face shortages of such things as material, skills, capacity, and funds. One way in which accountants and other managers can deal with the problem of maximizing contribution margin, for example, given the scarcity of resources, is to use linear programming.

Our discussion here requires some prior knowledge of linear programming and the use of the simplex method. Appendix 4–B discusses the simplex method for those who have not previously formulated or solved linear programming problems.

Linear programming is one of a class of mathematical techniques designed to optimize results. Scarcity of resources is a prerequisite to the use of linear programming. A firm must be limited in such resources as time, money, materials, and delivery commitments in order to profit by using this tool. We are interested in the technique not just for itself but for its use in sensitivity analysis for tactical decisions. Linear programming formulas are based on single values for expected contribution margin of a product or maximum plant capacity. Sensitivity analysis allows us to deal with the issues of uncertainty we dealt with in earlier examples.

Illustration: Broden's Paint and Stain

Broden Paint Company produces two products, paint and stain. The contribution margin per gallon for paint is expected to be $4 and for stain $5.10. Because of a current material shortage, only 50,000 gallons of base mix are available at normal prices. A half-gallon of base mix is required for each gallon of finished paint or stain. The plant capacity is 120,000 gallons per year of paint, or 90,000 gallons of stain, or any linear combination of the two. The formulation of this simple **maximization problem** is presented in Exhibit 4–4. Exhibit 4–5 shows the final tableau from a simplex solution. The formulation and solution to the problem are based on certain figures. Unfortunately, mathematical equations require precise figures. The objective function is based on exact contribution margins. No measure of risk (or dispersion) is included. In our discussion of sensitivity analysis, we will allow one item at a time to vary. This will suggest where we need to get additional data and to quantify various uncertainties.

First we will relax the assumption that only 50,000 gallons of base mix can be purchased. The normal price of the base mix is $2 per gallon. Assume

EXHIBIT 4–4
Objective Function and Constraints

Maximize: $Z = \$4X_1 + \$5.10X_2$
Subject to: $\frac{1}{2}X_1 + \frac{1}{2}X_2 \leq 50,000$ (base mix)
                   $\frac{3}{4}X_1 + X_2 \leq 90,000$ (capacity)
                   $X_1, X_2 \geq 0$

EXHIBIT 4–5
Final Tableau

	C_j	Product Mix	Quantity	$4.00 X_1	$5.10 X_2	$0 S_1	$0 S_2
Paint	$4.00	X_1	40,000	1	0	8	−4
Stain	$5.10	X_2	60,000	0	1	−6	4
		Z_j	$466,000	$4.00	$5.10	$1.40	$4.40
		$C_j - Z_j$		0	0	−$1.40	−$4.40

that another supplier will sell Broden 10,000 gallons of product of the same quality for $3 per gallon. Is it in Broden's interest to buy more base mix? Yes. In fact, any price per gallon up to $3.40 is acceptable. The contribution margin in the optimal solution is $466,000. If Broden purchased an additional 10,000 gallons of base mix at $3.40 per gallon, there would be an additional expense of $14,000. The new optimal solution (shown in Exhibit 4–6) would yield an additional $14,000 before expenses. Therefore, the higher contribution margin and additional expenses cancel each other, proving that any price up to $3.40 is acceptable.

The new solution is derived by taking the matrix of values associated with the slack variables in the final tableau (Exhibit 4–5) and multiplying these values by any new constraints. In this case, only one constraint has changed. The result is a new solution of 120,000 gallons of paint and zero gallons of stain. Check this solution against the constraints in Exhibit 4–4 (with the 10,000-gallon adjustment in base mix availability) and everything is in line. In fact, any additional purchases of base mix over 10,000 gallons could not be used unless the capacity constraint were relaxed.

The final tableau shown in Exhibit 4–5 has a row labeled $C_j - Z_j$. The figures shown in this row are called **shadow prices**. The original formulation of the linear program assumed an absolute value of the amount of available base mix. Usually, however, constraints are not as strictly fixed as the pure mathematical equations imply. Sometimes it is possible to expand capacity or get more raw materials. Here is where sensitivity analysis and shadow prices come into play.

A shadow price is the amount of money one would gain if one more unit of a constrained resource were available, everything else remaining constant. For example, if one additional gallon of base mix were available, the optimal solution would now call for eight more gallons of paint (at $4 per gallon) and six fewer gallons of stain (at $5.10 per gallon). This is a net increase of $1.40.

We can use the shadow price directly to get changes in total contribution margin. We do so by multiplying the shadow price associated with the constraint under study by the addition to the constraint. In the present case we multiply

$$(\$1.40)(10,000) = \$14,000$$

EXHIBIT 4–6
Sensitivity Analysis–Mix

$$\begin{pmatrix} X_1 \\ X_2 \end{pmatrix} = \begin{pmatrix} 8 & -4 \\ -6 & 4 \end{pmatrix} \begin{pmatrix} 60,000 \\ 90,000 \end{pmatrix} = \left\{ \begin{matrix} (8)(60,000) + (-4)(90,000) \\ (-6)(60,000) + (4)(90,000) \end{matrix} \right\} = \begin{matrix} 120,000X_1 \\ 0X_2 \end{matrix}$$

and

$$(120,000)(\$4.00) = \$480,000$$
$$(0)(\$5.10) = \$0$$

Thus, any price less than an additional $1.40 per gallon for these 10,000 gallons would yield a net contribution margin greater than $466,000.[8] This short-cut method gives the new contribution margin, but it does not yield new optimal values for the primary variables.

Now let us examine the other constraint: capacity. Assume that an equipment manufacturer approaches Broden management. The manufacturer has just taken in some good used equipment capable of producing 9,000 gallons per year. The equipment is offered to Broden on a one-year nonrenewable lease. If Broden can get an additional 15,000 gallons of base mix at $3.40 per gallon, how much would they be willing to pay the manufacturer for a one-year lease on this used equipment? Exhibit 4–7 shows that Broden could offer up to $39,600 in rental and be better off than in the current situation.

EXHIBIT 4–7
Sensitivity Analysis—Capacity

$$\begin{pmatrix} X_1 \\ X_2 \end{pmatrix} = \begin{pmatrix} 8 & -4 \\ -6 & 4 \end{pmatrix} \begin{pmatrix} 65,000 \\ 99,000 \end{pmatrix} = \begin{pmatrix} 124,000X_1 \\ 6,000X_2 \end{pmatrix}$$

(124,000)($4.00 cm/gal paint)	$496,000
(6,000)($5.10 cm/gal stain)	30,600
	$526,600
Less: ($1.40)(15,000 gal.)	21,000
New margin	$505,600
Current margin	466,000
	$39,600

Finally, sensitivity analysis can be applied to selling price (or overall variable cost), since any change in selling price or variable cost will affect contribution margin. The $4 and $5.10 per gallon contribution margins have been presented as givens. How certain is management that contribution margins will be as stated? The solution to the original problem (Exhibit 4–5) calls for a fairly even production of paint and stain. Subsequent changes in raw-material availability or capacity severely limited stain production. What change in stain contribution margin will result in this same shift? Obviously, if the stain contribution margin is less than that for paint, the solution will call for no stain production, owing to the capacity constraint. In fact with the original constraints, as long as the stain contribution margin is at any value higher than the paint margin, the current optimal solution will hold. However, if paint's margin drops to below $3.83 (and stain's margin remains at $5.10), the optimal solution will call for zero paint production. An independent analysis shows that stain production is based

[8] There is an upper limit to the number of gallons Broden can purchase without violating other constraints.

on a contribution margin of at least $4.01 (giving a leeway of $1.09 from current levels) while paint production is based on a contribution margin of at least $3.83 (or a leeway of $0.17). Obviously, paint is much more sensitive to changes in price or variable cost than is stain. This new information is an aid to management. They can assess how likely it is that the paint contribution margin will drop more than $0.17 per gallon.

The solutions in Exhibits 4–6 and 4–7 have severely limited or eliminated stain production. We have not included explicit marketing goals or constraints. If Broden customers required a certain percentage of these two products, then other constraints could be added, such as

$$X_1 \geq 25,000 \text{ and } X_2 \geq 25,000$$

Linear programming is a quantitative technique allowing the accountant to look at possible optimal solutions when resources are scarce. We can maximize contribution margin per unit of various scarce resources. Linear programming is limited by requiring single-point estimates for contribution margin, use of constrained resources, and availability of constrained resources. We saw earlier that certainty rarely exists in an organizational environment. Thus, sensitivity analysis becomes an important tool to direct management's attention to prices, costs, usages, or constraints that have the greatest potential impact on profitability. This analysis also allows management to identify areas where specific probability assessments could be cost effective. Management continually asks: "What if . . . ?" Sensitivity analysis pervades the concept of quantitative and qualitative analysis.

SUMMARY

This chapter has covered the general area of tactical decisions. It has explored the larger ideas of decision making along with the more limited realms of deterministic and stochastic tactical decisions. Decision trees and linear programming were presented as tools to help decision makers in processing information and dealing with uncertainty. We saw that tactical (short-term) decisions often are not sharply distinguishable from capital budgeting (long-term) decisions.

APPENDIX 4–A: BASIC CONCEPTS OF PROBABILITY AND STATISTICS

This appendix is a review. If you are unfamiliar with probability and statistics, you may want to consult one of the various references at the end of the chapter as well as reading this material.

Decision making seeks a single, well-defined outcome. Probability theory has the same goal. But, many **events** may be possible. In a simple case, as when you flip a coin, the only events that can occur are heads or tails. In the Reeding example, various possible sales levels are events.

When a coin is flipped, the chance (probability) of heads is 1/2, or 50 percent, and the probability of tails is also 50 percent. Generalizing from this example, the probability of occurrence of any event is greater than or equal to zero. In addition, the sum of the probabilities associated with all possible events equals 1. Symbolically:

$$p(\text{event}) \geq 0 \qquad [\text{or } p(x_i) \geq 0]$$

$$p[\text{sum of all the } p(x_i)] = 1 \qquad \left[\text{or } \sum_{i=1}^{n} p(x_i) = 1 \right]$$

Expected Value

A series (mutually exclusive set) of events and the probabilities of their occurrence are called a **probability distribution**. If events are defined as particular finite values, as was the case in Reeding, then the distribution is **discrete**. If events are an indefinite number of values (perhaps an infinite number), the distribution is **continuous**.

Two general measures we use to assess a probability distribution are the expected value (or mean) and the dispersion (or variance). The **expected value** is the average outcome that will be *likely to occur*. The **variance** is a measure of how much we can expect other values to differ from the expected outcome.

To calculate the average or expected value for a discrete distribution:

$$\bar{x} = \sum_{i=1}^{n} x_i p(x_i)$$

where
$$\bar{x} = \text{the expected value}$$
$$x_i = \text{an event (and there are a total of } n \text{ events)}$$
$$p(x_i) = \text{probability of occurrence of an event}$$

The Reeding expected value on page 137 was calculated as follows:[9]

x_i	$p(x_i)$	$x_i\, p(x_i)$
$35,000	.10	$ 3,500
50,000	.44	22,000
75,000	.46	34,500
$\sum_{i=1}^{n} p(x_i) = 1.00$		$60,000 $= \sum_{i=1}^{n} x_i p(x_i)$

[9] With a discrete probability distribution the expected value can be an unattainable figure. Even though $x = \$60,000$, note that there is a zero probability that sales will be $60,000.

Variance

If we are certain an event will occur, the probability of that event equals 1.0. If we are uncertain about outcomes, we can look not only at a measure of central tendency (the expected value) but also at the dispersion or spread of other events around the mean. The variance is a measure of this dispersion. Dispersion refers to the amount by which other values *deviate* from the mean. Each deviation is noted as

$$(x_i - \bar{x})$$

since it is just the mathematical difference between any value and the expected value. For the example above, the deviations are:

Values, x_i	Deviations from the Mean, $x_i - \bar{x}$
$35,000	$-$25,000
50,000	$-$ 10,000
75,000	15,000

If we use the same method we used for calculating the mean when looking at the deviations, we will always get the sum of zero:

Deviations, $x_i - \bar{x}$	Probabilities, $p(x_i)$	Weighted Deviations $(x_i - \bar{x}) \cdot p(x_i)$
$-$25,000	.10	$-$2,500
$-$ 10,000	.44	$-$4,400
15,000	.46	6,900
		$\Sigma = 0$

The reason is that $(x_i - \bar{x})$ can be negative or positive, and the nature of the calculation of the mean and these deviations insures that their sum equals zero. Therefore, we *square* the deviations and define the variance (σ^2) as:

$$\sigma^2 = \sum_{i=1}^{n} (x_i - \bar{x})^2 \, p(x_i)$$

Our example shows this process:

Deviations, $x_i - \bar{x}$	Deviations Squared, $(x_i - \bar{x})^2$	Probabilities, $p(x_i)$	Weighted Squared Deviation, $(x_i - \bar{x})^2 p(x_i)$
$-$25,000	$625,000,000	.10	$ 62,500,000
$-$10,000	100,000,000	.44	44,000,000
15,000	225,000,000	.46	103,500,000
		Variance $= \Sigma \, (x_i - \bar{x})^2 p(x_i) =$	$210,000,000

The square root of the variance, called the **standard deviation**, is used as the common measure of variation.

$$\sqrt{\sigma^2} = \sigma = \sqrt{\$210{,}000{,}000} \approx \$14{,}491$$

Joint Probability Distributions

Often a manager wants to deal with more than one random variable. Perhaps there are probability distributions associated with sales of various products and the manager wants to know the mean and variance of total sales. Assume, for example, a company sells lawnmowers and chain saws. The probabilities associated with various levels of sales of these products are presented below.

Lawnmower Sales, x_i	$p(x_i)$	Chain saw Sales, y_i	$p(y_i)$
$3,000	.30	$1,000	.20
4,000	.30	1,500	.40
5,000	.40	2,000	.15
		2,500	.25

The probabilities associated with one set of events (such as lawnmower sales) are called **marginal probabilities**; the distribution, then, is a marginal distribution. If the marginal distribution for lawnmower sales is not affected by the level of chain saw sales (and vice versa), then we can look at these two distributions together. The **joint probability** of $3,000 in lawnmower sales *and* $1,000 in chain saw sales is calculated by multiplying the two independent marginal probabilities as follows:

$$p(L = \$3{,}000) = .30$$
$$\times \quad\quad p(C = \$1{,}000) = .20$$
$$\overline{p(L = \$3{,}000 \text{ and } C = \$1{,}000) = .06}$$

where L is lawnmower sales and C is chain saw sales. We have already defined $p(x_i)$ as the probability that an event will occur. We can now say $p(x_i)$ is a marginal probability. A joint probability can then be noted as:

$$p(x_i, y_i) \text{ and } p(x_i, y_i) = p(x_i) \cdot p(y_i)$$

or, more simply,

$$p(A, B) = p(A) \cdot p(B)$$

when events are independent. If the company added a line of lawnmower accessories (leaf sweepers, mulchers, and so on), it is possible this line would have sales dependent on lawnmower sales. For **dependent prob-**

abilities we want to know the probability an event will occur *given* that another event *has occurred.* For example, we would want to know the probability that accessory sales (A) would be $500 *given that* lawnmower sales are $4,000. This is expressed as:

$$p(A = \$500 \text{ if } L = \$4,000) \quad \text{or} \quad p(A = \$500 | L = \$4,000)$$

More generally this is

$$p(z_i | x_i) \quad \text{or} \quad p(B | A)$$

We have seen that $p(A, B) = p(A) \cdot p(B)$ when there is independence. When two distributions are dependent, the basic probability relationship is:

$$\text{joint probability} = (\text{marginal probability}) \cdot (\text{conditional probability})$$
$$p(A, B) = p(A) \cdot p(B | A)$$

We can see that if A and B are independent, then $p(B) = p(B | A)$, since the level of A does not affect the probability of occurrence of any event B.

APPENDIX 4–B: LINEAR PROGRAMMING

This appendix provides a brief introduction to (or review of) linear programming. As the name implies, the basic relationships among the variables that we consider are linear. The material in this appendix is a modification of the excellent material on linear programming contained in the publication *Quantitative Approaches to Management,* 4th edition (1978), by Levin and Kirkpatrick.[10]

Linear programming is a technique for dealing with limited resources. If a machine has only 7,000 hours a year available, and it could be used to produce any combination of a firm's products, the objective is to use this limited resource in a way that maximizes the overall company profits. Linear programming (or LP) results in an optimal combination of products for that machine.

Therefore, in general, if a company wants to achieve an objective (such as *maximizing* profits or *minimizing* costs), if alternative courses of action are open to management, if resources are limited, and if we can express the relationship between variables in mathematical linear terms, linear programming can be a useful quantitative tool.

---

[10] Richard I. Levin and Charles A. Kirkpatrick, *Quantitative Approaches to Management,* 4th edition, 1978, McGraw-Hill Book Company, New York. Used with the permission of McGraw-Hill Book Company.

Graphic Analysis

A good first step in understanding LP is to look at a problem graphically. We will use an example involving a manufacturer of commercial tables. Hawk Table Company produces a standard round table and a standard square table. The contribution margin on the round table is $20, while that on the square table is $15. If there were no limitations on productive capacity, Hawk could produce as many of each product as it could profitably sell. However, the basic process calls for a cutting machine and a laminating machine, each of which has limited capacity. Exhibit 4B–1 shows the relationship that exists in these two production processes.

EXHIBIT 4B–1
Basic Manufacturing Information (hours required for one unit of product)

Department	Round Tables	Square Tables	Total Hours Available per Week
Cutting	2	1	60
Laminating	1	2	48
CM/unit	$20	$15	

The first step is to formally define the objective of maximizing contribution margin. The **objective function** is:

$$\text{maximize:} \quad Z = \$20x_1 + \$15x_2$$

where

Z = total contribution margin
x_1 = number of round tables produced
x_2 = number of square tables produced

The next step is to set up the constraints. Hawk has 60 hours available in the cutting department and 48 hours available in the laminating department. Our solution cannot exceed these hours. Any combination of the two products must use a total of 60 hours or less in cutting, for example. We note this by the following inequalities:

$$2x_1 + x_2 \leq 60$$
$$x_1 + 2x_2 \leq 48$$

The first constraint states that cutting hours cannot exceed 60 per week. Because it takes two hours to cut a round table and one hour to cut a square table, these figures are multiplied by the production of each type of table to formulate the constraint. Finally, we must formally define that the minimum amount we can produce is zero. We cannot produce minus 10 square tables. Therefore, we state:

$$x_1 \geq 0$$
$$x_2 \geq 0$$

In summary, the whole problem is formulated as:

$$\text{Max } Z = \$20x_1 + \$15x_2$$

subject to the following constraints:

$$2x_1 + x_2 \leq 60$$
$$x_1 + 2x_2 \leq 48$$
$$x_1 \geq 0$$
$$x_2 \geq 0$$

The graphical method below is a way to portray these relationships. The

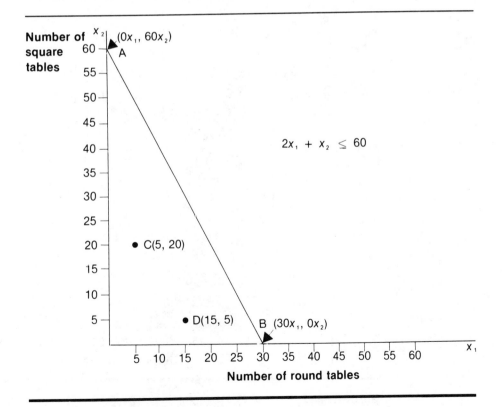

FIGURE 4B–1
Graph Showing First Constraint

equation for the cutting department allows for up to 30 round tables if no square tables are produced $[(30)(2) + (0)(1) \leq (60)]$ or up to 60 square tables if no round tables are produced. Figure 4B–1 shows this relationship. If this were the only constraint, any combination of tables falling to the left of this constraint line would meet the inequality expressed by $2x_1 + x_2 \leq 60$. Other possible combinations are shown in Figure 4B–1 by points C and D. However, only points A and B (or any points falling on the constraint line) use up *all* the available hours.

The same relationship can be drawn for the laminating department. Figure 4B–2 shows both production constraints. Any combination of round and square tables falling within the shaded region on Figure 4B–2 fulfills the inequalities. This area is called the **feasible region,** since it contains all the feasible solutions to the LP problem.

Points A, B, C, and O represent starting points for our analysis, since they lie at the boundary of the feasible region. We can see that points A, B, and C use all the production capacity of at least one department. The contribution margin for each point is shown at the top of page 159.

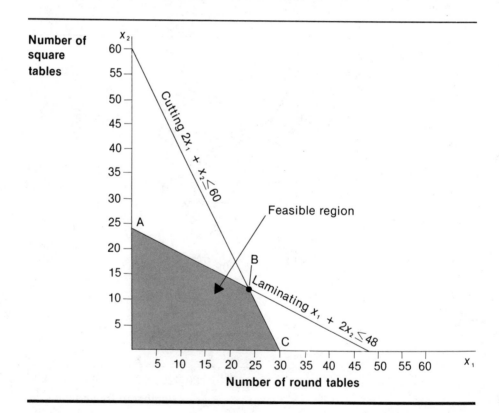

FIGURE 4B–2
Graph Showing Both Constraints

Point O: $(0, 0)$ = ($20)(0)   + ($15)(0)   = 0
Point A: $(0, 24)$ = ($20)(0)   + ($15)(24) = $360
Point B: $(24, 12)$ = ($20)(24) + ($15)(12) = $660
Point C: $(30, 0)$ = ($20)(30) + ($15)(0)   = $600

Point B, where the two constraint lines meet, has the highest contribution margin ($660). This is the only point in the feasible space where all the hours in both departments are used. If we plot the objective function, we can see how this is the logical maximum point. $20x_1 + $15x_2$ can be drawn at any point as long as we define a total contribution margin. If we choose $240, then $240 = $20x_1 + $15x_2$. Using the same technique for plotting as we used for the constraints, we show the objective function in Figure 4B–3. The equation $240 = $20x_1 + $15x_2$ is called an **isoprofit**. If we choose any other total contribution margin, the new isoprofit line will be *parallel* to the one shown in Figure 4B–3. In fact, our optimum solution of $660 = $20x_1 + $15x_2$ is a line parallel to the original isoprofit line that touches the feasible region solely at point B, as shown in Figure 4B–4. Any

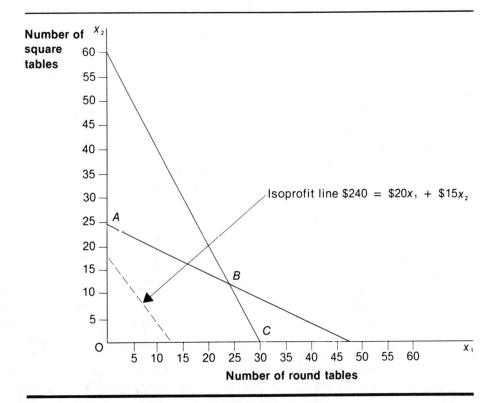

FIGURE 4B–3
Graph Showing Isoprofit Line

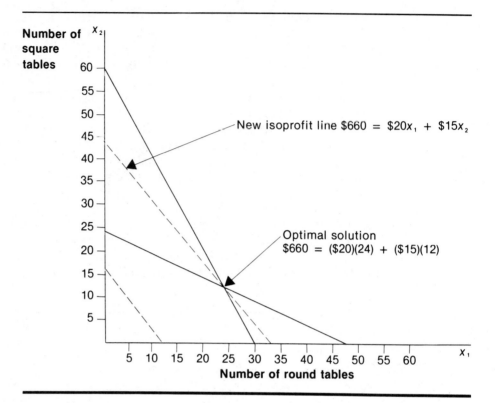

Number of square tables X_2

Number of round tables X_1

New isoprofit line $660 = 20x_1 + 15x_2$

Optimal solution
$660 = (20)(24) + (15)(12)$

FIGURE 4B–4
Graphical Solution

isoprofit line greater than $660 in total contribution margin would violate one or more constraints, since it would be outside the feasible region.

The Simplex Method

While a graphical solution is manageable for two products and two constraints, it becomes impossible when there are many products and many constraints. The **simplex method** of solving linear programming problems is used to solve more complex problems. The simplex method uses a series of algebraic steps to mathematically solve a linear programming problem. Since this method is available on most computer facilities, a knowledge of how it works allows you to better interpret results.

Our basic problem remains:

$$\text{Max } Z = 20x_1 + 15x_2$$

s.t. (subject to)

$$2x_1 + x_2 \leq 60$$
$$x_1 + 2x_2 \leq 48$$
$$x_1 \geq 0$$
$$x_2 \geq 0$$

Since we will use algebra, we need to change the inequalities to equalities by inserting **slack variables** to represent possible unused time on each machine. Calling these variables S_1 for cutting department slack time and S_2 for slack in the laminating department, we have a restated LP formulation:

Max $Z = \$20x_1 + \$15x_2 + \$0S_1 + \$0S_2$ objective function

s.t. $2x_1 + x_2 + S_1 + 0S_2 = 60$ cutting department

$x_1 + 2x_2 + 0S_1 + S_2 = 48$ laminating department

Using the cutting department example, production is limited to 60 hours. Therefore, we account for the 60 hours by the number of tables to be produced multiplied by the hours needed to make them ($2x_1 + x_2$) plus the idle time left over (S_1) if total production time uses less than 60 hours. The cutting department constraint shows $0S_2$, since S_2 represents slack in another department. We set up our original format (called a **tableau**) as shown in Exhibit 4B–2. The simplex solution involves changing values in the rows of the tableau until an optimal solution is found. We follow a set series of steps to get from an initial format (tableau) to a final (optimal) tableau.

Exhibit 4B–3 on page 162 shows the addition of two rows to reflect

EXHIBIT 4B–2
Original Simplex Tableau (in part)

C_j	Product Mix	Quantity	$20 x_1	$15 x_2	$0 S_1	$0 S_2	
$0	S_1	60	?	1	1	0	Coefficients of
$0	S_2	48	1	2	0	1	the constraints
			Real products		Slack time		

where:
C_j = the profits per unit in the current product mix.
Product Mix = the current products in the mix which are zero x_1 and zero x_2 to begin with.
Quantity = quantity of products in current mix. Quantities shown are the full times available in cutting and laminating.
x_1, x_2, S_1, S_2 = the coefficients of the constraints for both real products and slack times.

contribution margin (Z_j) of the solution and ($C_j - Z_j$), a row reflecting the additional contribution of one additional product. The original tableau shows a solution corresponding to point O on Figure 4B–2, where nothing is produced and all time is idle (slack). The solution is shown by the ($\frac{1}{0}$) S_1 column and the ($\frac{0}{1}$) S_2 column. Since the original solution is at point O, where no tables (round or square) are made, there is a zero contribution margin. Therefore, all the figures in the Z_j row are $0.

EXHIBIT 4B–3
Complete Initial Tableau

C_j	Product Mix	Quantity	$20 x_1	$15 x_2	$0 S_1	$0 S_2
$0	S_1	60	2	1	1	0
$0	S_2	48	1	2	0	1
	Z_j	$0	$0	$0	$0	$0
	$C_j - Z_j$		$20	$15	$0	$0

Let us analyze the initial tableau. If Hawk makes one round table, it will use two hours in the cutting department (thereby reducing slack time from 60 to 58 hours) and one hour laminating (so $S_2 = 47$ hours). In addition, contribution margin will equal $20. This is reflected in the ($C_j - Z_j$) row. This trade-off of hours, slack, and profits becomes useful as we reach our constraints and analyze the sensitivity of the optimal solution to the variables.

The next step involves an inspection of the initial tableau to see if we can improve on a $0 contribution margin.

Step 1. Determine the variable that will add the most per unit to profit by looking at positive values in the ($C_j - Z_j$) row. The variable x_1 (round tables) contributes $20, which is higher than x_2's contribution ($15). As long as this highest contribution is greater than $0, we can proceed. Using these criteria, we choose x_1 as the variable to deal with. The x_1 column is defined as the **optimal column**.

Step 2. Now we use algebra to change one row at a time to get to a new solution. First we establish the first row to change, calling it the **replaced row**. Determine the replaced row by looking at the ratio of the elements in the optimal column ($\frac{2}{1}$) and the quantity column and choosing the smaller (or smallest) nonnegative ratio as follows:

S_1 row: $\dfrac{60 \text{ hours available in cutting}}{2 \text{ hours/unit}} = 30$

S_2 row: $\dfrac{48 \text{ hours available in laminating}}{1 \text{ hour/unit}} = 48$

The row that will be replaced first for the next tableau is the S_1 row. All the reasoning so far is shown in Exhibit 4B–4. We now have an *optimal column* and a *replaced row*, and we define the circled figures in Exhibit 4B–4 as **intersectional elements,** since they are at the intersection of the optimal column and the rows.

EXHIBIT 4B–4
Simplex—Step 2

C_j	Product Mix	Quan-tity	$20 x_1	$15 x_2	$0 S_1	$0 S_2
$0	S_1	60	②	1	1	0
$0	S_2	48	①	2	0	1
	Z_j	$0	$0	$0	$0	$0
	$C_j - Z_j$		$20	$15	$0	$0

row to be replaced first   optimal column
                                  intersectional elements

Step 3. Take the row to be replaced and divide the row through by the intersectional element in that row. For example, the **replacing row** is:

$$\$20 \quad x_1 \quad 30 \quad 1 \quad \tfrac{1}{2} \quad \tfrac{1}{2} \quad 0$$

where the old S_1 row has been divided by the intersectional element (2). We show that x_1 is in our new solution by substituting it and its $20-per-unit contribution margin in the first two columns.

Step 4. To complete the second tableau, we calculated new values for all the remaining rows using the following formula:

$$\left(\begin{array}{c}\text{elements in}\\ \text{old row}\end{array}\right) - \left[\left(\begin{array}{c}\text{intersectional}\\ \text{element of old row}\end{array}\right)\right.$$
$$\left.\times \left(\begin{array}{c}\text{corresponding elements}\\ \text{in replacing row}\end{array}\right)\right] = \left(\begin{array}{c}\text{new}\\ \text{row}\end{array}\right)$$

For the S_2 row we have:

$\begin{array}{c}\text{element in}\\ \text{old } S_2 \text{ row}\end{array}$	$-$	$\left[\left(\begin{array}{c}\text{intersectional}\\ \text{element of } S_2 \text{ row}\end{array}\right)\right.$	$\times$	$\left(\begin{array}{c}\text{corresponding element}\\ \text{in replacing row}\end{array}\right)\right]$	$=$	$\begin{array}{c}\text{new } S_2\\ \text{row}\end{array}$
48	–	(1	×	30)	=	18
1	–	(1	×	1)	=	0
2	–	(1	×	½)	=	1½
0	–	(1	×	½)	=	· –½
1	–	(1	×	0)	=	1

Exhibit 4B–5 shows the completed second tableau where the solution now calls for $30x_1$ and $0x_2$. Again, the solution is identified by columns where there is just one 1 and all other values are 0. This solution corresponds to point C in Figure 4B–2. Note that no additional units of x_1 are possible, since $x_1 = 30$ hits the cutting constraint. However, as both Exhibit 4B–5 and Figure 4B–2 show, there are eighteen unused hours in the laminating department.

EXHIBIT 4B–5
Second Tableau

C_j			$20	$15	$0	$0
	Product Mix	Quan-tity	x_1	x_2	S_1	S_2
$20	x_1	30	1	½	½	0
$ 0	S_2	18	0	1½	−½	1
	Z_j	$600	$20	$10	$10	$0
	$C_j - Z_j$		$ 0	$ 5	−$10	$0

where $Z_j = \$20(1) + \$0(0)$ for x_1 column
$ = \$20(½) + \$0(1½)$ for x_2 column
$ = \$20(½) + \$0(-½)$ for S_1 column
$ = \$20(0) + \$0(1)$ for S_2 column

Since there is a positive $(C_j - Z_j)$ figure of $5, the solution is *not* optimal and we can go through the same procedures again (Step 1). The optimum column (Step 2) is now x_2 ($5) and the replaced row is S_2 (18 ÷ 1½ = 12, which is lower than 30 ÷ ½ = 60). Exhibit 4B–6 below shows the next tableau.

EXHIBIT 4B–6
Final Tableau

C_j			$20	$15	$0	$0
	Product Mix	Quan-tity	x_1	x_2	S_1	S_2
$20	x_1	24	1	0	⅔	−⅓
$15	x_2	12	0	1	−⅓	⅔
	Z_j	$660	$20	$15	$8⅓	$3⅓
	$C_j - Z_j$		$ 0	$ 0	−$8⅓	−$3⅓

The steps taken to get from Exhibit 4B–5 to 4B–6 are as follows:

Step 3

$$\frac{18}{1\frac{1}{2}} = 12, \quad \frac{0}{12} = 0, \quad \frac{1\frac{1}{2}}{1\frac{1}{2}} = 1, \quad \frac{-\frac{1}{2}}{1\frac{1}{2}} = -\frac{1}{3}, \quad \frac{1}{1\frac{1}{2}} = \frac{2}{3}$$

These are the new values for the replaced row. We now calculate new values for the x_1 and Z_j rows.

Step 4

old x_1 row	$-$	$\left[\left(\begin{array}{c}\text{intersectional} \\ \text{element } x_1 \text{ row}\end{array}\right)\right.$	$\times$	$\left.\left(\begin{array}{c}\text{corresponding element} \\ \text{in replacing row}\end{array}\right)\right]$	$=$	new x_1 row
30	$-$	($\frac{1}{2}$	$\times$	12)	$=$	24
1	$-$	($\frac{1}{2}$	$\times$	0)	$=$	1
$\frac{1}{2}$	$-$	($\frac{1}{2}$	$\times$	1)	$=$	0
$\frac{1}{2}$	$-$	($\frac{1}{2}$	$\times$	$-\frac{1}{3}$)	$=$	$\frac{2}{3}$
0	$-$	($\frac{1}{2}$	$\times$	$\frac{2}{3}$)	$=$	$-\frac{1}{3}$

New Z_j row

$$
\begin{aligned}
Z_{\text{total}} &= \$20(24) &+ \$15(12) &= \$660 \\
Z_{x_1} &= \$20(1) &+ \$15(0) &= \$\ 20 \\
Z_{x_2} &= \$20(0) &+ \$15(1) &= \$\ 15 \\
Z_{S_1} &= \$20(\tfrac{2}{3}) &+ \$15(-\tfrac{1}{3}) &= \$\ \ 8\tfrac{1}{3} \\
Z_{S_2} &= \$20(-\tfrac{1}{3}) &+ \$15(\tfrac{2}{3}) &= \$\ \ 3\tfrac{1}{3}
\end{aligned}
$$

This is the optimal solution, since no $(C_j - Z_j)$ value is greater than zero. This solution of $x_1 = 24$ and $x_2 = 12$ corresponds to point B in Figure 4B–2. As you can see, the simplex solution moved from a starting place of point O in Figure 4B–2 to point C and then to point B. It is common in simplex solutions for the solution to develop in this manner, moving from corner to corner until it reaches the optimal corner.

ASSIGNMENTS

4–1 Relevant Costs. The Martin Company makes a number of products used by industry. Some time ago the firm bought a large supply of xylon, a chemical it needed for one of its major products. Subsequently the firm stopped using xylon because it found a cheaper substitute. For the past six months the price of xylon has hovered around $2.45 per pound and the firm could buy or sell it at that price. The 3,400 pounds now in inventory cost $3.32 per pound eight months ago and are carried at that value.

The firm now has an opportunity to fill a special order that would require the use of 2,700 pounds of xylon. The substitute could not be used for this order. Total incremental costs associated with the order are $12,540, without considering xylon, and the price is $20,500. The controller is puzzled about the cost to be used for xylon in determining whether or not to accept the order.

Required:

1. Calculate the gain or loss that the firm would show on its books if it accepted the order.
2. Determine whether the firm should accept the order.

4–2 Special Order. The Donna Corporation makes replacement automobile mufflers that it markets under the Touch of Gold label. Sales have been growing at 8 to 10 percent annually and were 1,690,000 in 19X3. At the beginning of 19X4, Colombia Motors approached Donna about an order for 100,000 mufflers for a new car it was planning to produce. Donna's management was asked if it would produce the mufflers, and at what price.

A review of recent cost accounting data shows that an average muffler sold through a franchised dealer has the following costs and revenues:

Average retail price of muffler	$52.00
Cost of installation at dealer	10.00
Cost of muffler to dealer	25.00

Donna makes an average of 15 percent on sales to dealers, and variable costs make up about 60 percent of total costs. Current plant capacity is constrained to 1,900,000 units, owing to a shortage of available skilled workers. New workers could be hired and trained at $15,000 per person. Each new person would add about 75,000 units of capacity.

Required: Should Donna sell to Colombia? If not, why not? If so, why and at what price?

4–3 Relevant Costs. The Moran Furniture Company has received an offer from a European firm that wants to buy 10,000 tables at $70 each. This offered price is well below Moran's customary price of $95. Moran currently has 25,000 tables of the type wanted by the European firm at the following unit costs:

Materials	$33.50
Direct labor	18.40
Variable overhead, 60% of direct labor	11.04
Total variable cost	$62.94

If the firm accepts the order, it will ship tables from inventory, and the customer will pay delivery charges. The tables in question are good sellers, and Moran anticipates selling 90,000 or so during the coming year. Moran has sufficient capacity to fill the order and meet all demand at regular selling prices.

The chief cost accountant for Moran expects some rapid cost increases. Specifically, she believes that materials costs will increase by 10 percent and direct labor by 15 percent within a short time. Variable overhead should continue to be 60 percent of direct labor cost.

Required: Determine whether Moran should accept the order.

4-4   Basic Make or Buy Decision (AICPA adapted).   Standard cost and other data for two parts-components used by the Griffon Electronics Company appear below.

	Part A4	Part B5
Direct material	$0.40	$ 8.00
Direct labor	1.00	4.70
Factory overhead	4.00	2.00
Total unit standard cost	$5.40	$14.70
Units required per year	6,000	8,000
Machine hours per unit	4	2
Unit cost if purchased	$5.00	$15.00

In past years Griffon has manufactured all its requirements of A4 and B5. However, during the coming year the firm will have only 30,000 hours of machine time available for producing components. Accordingly, some of them must be purchased from outside suppliers. In producing parts, the firm applies factory overhead at $1 per machine hour. Fixed manufacturing costs, which are unaffected by the volume of machine hours, are 60 percent of the $1.

Required:

1. Determine the unit costs of A4 and B5 that are relevant to the make or buy decision.

2. Determine the number of units of each component that Griffon should make during the coming year.

4-5   Temporary Shutdown.   The management of the Kalman Company is considering shutting down for the months of October, November, and December. The firm makes food products, largely from corn, and has been experiencing very hard times. Its products sell in highly competitive markets, and selling prices have been forced down by a large supply in the market.

The controller of the firm has prepared the following income statement for the three-month period, assuming that the firm remains open.

Revenue	$4,300,000
Cost of goods sold	3,700,000
Gross margin	600,000
Operating expenses	1,450,000
Expected loss	($ 850,000)

Cost of goods sold includes about $800,000 in fixed costs, and operating expenses includes about $1,100,000 fixed costs. The firm could avoid about 70 percent of the total fixed costs if it shut down. However, shutting down and then reopening the firm would result in additional costs of about $90,000 for mothballing and restarting equipment, severance pay, retraining, and so on.

Required:

1. Determine whether or not the firm should shut down.

2. Determine the level of sales that would make staying open equally attractive (or equally unattractive) to the firm as shutting down. Assume that variable costs would bear the same percentages to revenue that are reflected in the income statement above.

4–6   Trade Agreement.   The Booker Automobile Agency sells a wide variety of cars. Recently its manager was approached by the manager of television station KRZ-TV who proposed the following arrangement. If Booker would provide the station with an automobile, the station would run advertisements for the agency. In particular, the station wanted the car as part of a deal it had swung to hire John Goodlooking, a proven news anchorman, who had demanded a car as part of his compensation. The car that the station wanted retails for $10,000; the cost to the dealer is $7,800.

The costs of a television station are about 90 percent fixed. Its output, the programming it does, is set at eighteen hours per day, seven days per week. Some of the costs are discretionary, but few are variable. Pricing for advertising depends on ratings: the higher the ratings, the higher the price per minute. Prices also depend on the time, with commercials shown in prime time (generally 7:30 P.M. to 11:00 P.M.) selling for about 150 percent of the price charged in nonprime time.

If the two firms were to reach an agreement, KRZ-TV would show advertisements for Booker on a space-available basis; that is, they would appear during periods of commercial time for which there were no paying advertisers. Consequently, Booker could not control the timing of the showings. Since the amount of time devoted to commercials is limited by law, KRZ-TV could not easily slip in commercials for Booker unless it had some unsold time.

Required: Discuss the issues and questions that both Booker and KRZ-TV would consider in trying to reach a price for the car. Decide how much you would try to get, in terms of dollars' worth of time, if you were making the decision for Booker and how much you would be willing to offer if you were on the side of KRZ-TV.

4–7   Relevant Costs.   Rich Miller, treasurer of Fairview Insurance Agency, has a problem. The president of Fairview has asked him to determine whether the firm should ask Henry Daniel, one of its agents, to leave. Fairview is a general insurance agency consisting of twenty agents, an accounting department, data processing department, and an underwriting department. When an agent sells a policy to a client, the commission from the policy is divided 60/40 between the agent and Fairview. In addition, insurance policy writers (carriers) give Fairview an additional commission yearly based on total premium volume. Mr. Daniel, the agent in question, has been generating premiums of about $650,000 per year with average commissions of 6¼ percent. The following costs have been associated with Mr. Daniel:

Secretary	$15,000
Rent	1,000
Telephone	300
Accounting services	2,000
Data processing	250
Miscellaneous	2,150
	$20,700

In analyzing this information, Miller has ascertained the following facts.

1. The secretary works 100 percent for Daniel.
2. Rent is determined on the basis of a square-foot allocation of total rent. Fairview's lease runs out at the end of this year. The offices are in a high-rise downtown building.
3. Telephone includes direct local and long-distance costs.
4. Accounting services and data processing have been allocated on the basis of the number of billing transactions.
5. Miscellaneous expenses include $300 of direct supplies plus an $1,850 share of general expenses, including such items as the office receptionist, the underwriting department, general telephone, and supply costs.

Fairview expects to write policies with premiums of $21,670,000 in the current year.

Required: As Miller, write a memo to Fairview's president recommending whether or not Mr. Daniel be fired. The memo should include an analysis of the relevant data and appropriate calculations.

4–8 Basic Decision Making. The Arnold Company makes a bottle-capping machine used in the soft drink industry. The data below reflect management's expectations of a typical month for the coming year.

Sales $31,000 price for 20 units		$620,000
Manufacturing costs:		
Materials	$ 80,000	
Direct labor	100,000	
Overhead	200,000	380,000
Gross profit		240,000
Selling and administrative expenses		200,000
Income		$ 40,000

All manufacturing costs are variable, except for $120,000 in fixed overhead. Variable overhead is related to direct labor hours. The direct labor rate is $10 per hour, and each machine requires 500 hours. Capacity is 25 machines per month.

Selling and administrative expenses include a $2,000-per-unit variable component, with the remainder fixed.

Unless otherwise instructed, treat each situation below independently of the others.

Required:

1. What is the maximum amount that the firm could earn in a month?

2. Would the firm be wise to accept a contract to deliver ten machines per month to a large soft drink company at $25,000 each? The prospective customer has never bought machines from Arnold before, and the expected volume given above does not reflect any sales to it. Arnold would not incur the $2,000 variable selling and administrative expense on these units.

3. This question assumes the facts from item 2. The limit on Arnold's capacity relates to direct labor hours. Arnold cannot work its own direct laborers more than 12,500 hours per month. An outside contractor could supply suitable workers. These new workers would be as efficient as Arnold's own. Variable overhead would be incurred at the same rate per labor hour on the new workers as on the existing ones. The contractor could supply enough workers to bring Arnold's total capacity to 30 units per month. What is the maximum amount, per month, that Arnold would pay to acquire the workers?

4. The marketing manager believes that Arnold could increase prices by $2,000 per unit and lose sales of only two units per month to competitors. Variable selling and administrative expenses would increase to $2,200 per unit. Would the increase in price be wise?

5. The machine requires a part that Arnold currently makes. Data for the part, one of which is used in each machine, are as follows:

Materials	$180
Direct labor, 20 hours at $10	200
Overhead	400
Total	$780

Variable overhead for making this part is the same per direct labor hour as in any other operation. An outside firm has offered to supply the part for $650. Should Arnold accept the offer?

6. Repeat item 5, except that Arnold is now working at capacity of 25 units per month. Arnold could sell any additional output it could make, and purchasing the part outside would free up enough labor time to make one additional unit. Would it now be wise to purchase the part?

4–9 **Special Order-Pricing (CMA adapted).** Framar, Inc. manufactures automation machinery according to customer specifications. The company is relatively new and has grown each year. Framar operated at about 75 percent of practical capacity during the 19X7–19X8 fiscal year. The operating results for the most recent fiscal year appear below.

FRAMAR, INC.
Income Statement
For the Year Ended September 30, 19X8
(in thousands)

Sales		$25,000
Less: Sales commissions		2,500
Net sales		$22,500
Expenses:		
Direct material		6,000
Direct labor		7,500
Manufacturing overhead—variable		
Supplies	$ 625	
Indirect labor	1,500	
Power	125	2,250
Manufacturing overhead—fixed:		
Supervision	$ 500	
Depreciation	1,000	1,500
Corporate administration		750
Total expenses		$18,000
Net income before taxes		$ 4,500
Less: Income taxes (40%)		1,800
Net income		$ 2,700

The top management of Framar wants to have a more organized and formal pricing system to prepare quotes for potential customers. Therefore, it has developed the pricing formula presented below. The formula is based upon the company's operating results achieved during the 19X7–19X8 fiscal year. The relationships used in the formula are expected to continue during the 19X8–19X9 year. The company expects to operate at 75 percent of practical capacity during the upcoming fiscal year.

APA Inc. has asked Framar to submit a bid on some custom designed machinery. Framar used the new formula to develop a price and submitted a bid of $165,000. The calculations to arrive at the bid price are given next to the pricing formula shown below.

Details of Pricing Formula		APA Bid Calculations
Estimated direct material cost	$XX	$ 29,200
Estimated direct labor cost	XX	56,000
Estimated manufacturing overhead calculated at 50% of direct labor	XX	28,000
Estimated corporate overhead calculated at 10% of direct labor	XX	5,600
Estimated total costs excluding sales commissions	$XX	$118,800
Add 25% for profits and taxes	XX	29,700
Suggested price (with profits) before sales commissions	$XX	$148,500
Suggested total price equals suggested price divided by 0.9 to adjust for 10% sales commission	$XX	$165,000

Required:

1. Calculate the impact the order from APA Inc. would have on Framar Inc.'s net income after taxes if Framar's bid of $165,000 were accepted.

2. Assume APA Inc. has rejected Framar's price but has stated it is willing to pay $127,000 for the machinery. Should Framar Inc. manufacture the machinery for the counteroffer of $127,000? Explain your answer.

3. Calculate the lowest price at which Framar Inc. can supply this machinery without reducing its net income after taxes.

4. Explain how the profit performance in 19X8–19X9 would be affected if Framar Inc. accepted all its work at prices similar to the $127,000 counteroffer described in item 2.

4–10 Opportunity Costs. The managers of Armstrong Machinery are evaluating whether to replace an electric motor on one of their milling machines. The old motor cost $175 two years ago. Because the bushings and windings are becoming worn, electricity costs are about $100 per month; for a new motor they would be about $50 per month. A new motor can be purchased for $250. For $50 Armstrong can convert the old motor to be used efficiently on a grinding machine. The grinding motor has just malfunctioned and a new one would cost $225. If the old milling motor were sold as is, Armstrong would get only $75 for it.

Required:

1. What decisions do Armstrong's managers need to make?
2. List all costs that are relevant to the decision.
3. What is the opportunity cost in this situation? Why? Explain carefully.

4–11 Expected Values (AICPA). During your examination of the financial statements of Benjamin Industries, the president asked your help in evaluating several financial management problems in his home appliances division; he summarized the problems for you as follows:

1. Management wants to determine the best sales price for a new appliance, which has a variable cost of $4 per unit. The sales manager has estimated probabilities of achieving annual sales levels for various selling prices as shown in the following chart:

Sales Level	Selling Price			
(Units)	$4	$5	$6	$7
20,000	—	—	20%	80%
30,000	—	10%	40%	20%
40,000	50%	50%	20%	—
50,000	50%	40%	20%	—

2. The division's current profit rate is 5 percent on annual sales of $1.2 million; an investment of $400,000 is needed to finance these sales. The company's basis for measuring divisional success is return on investment.

3. Management is also considering the following two alternative plans submitted by employees for improving operations in the home appliances division:
   a. Green believes that sales volume can be doubled by greater promotional effort, but his method would lower the profit rate to 4 percent of sales and require an additional investment of $100,000.
   b. Gold favors eliminating some unprofitable appliances and improving efficiency by adding $200,000 in capital equipment. His

methods would decrease sales volume by 10 percent but improve the profit rate to 7 percent.

Required: Prepare a schedule computing the expected incremental income for each of the sales prices proposed for the new product. The schedule should include the expected sales levels in units (weighted according to the sales manager's estimated probabilities), the expected total monetary sales, the expected variable costs, and the expected incremental income.

4–12   Uncertainty.   The Palit Company has forecasted sales of 100,000 pounds of its major product for the upcoming year. In addition, the sales manager has estimated that the probability that sales will be between 90,000 and 110,000 lb is 75 percent.

Required:

1. What is the standard deviation in units?
2. What is the probability that sales will exceed 95,000 lb?
3. If fixed costs are $850,000, if variable costs are $10 per unit, and if selling price is $20 per unit, what is the probability of breaking even?

4–13   Product Selection, Statistics.   As president of the Wehman Company, you make the final decisions on all products. At present you are trying to decide which of two products to bring out next year. Capacity is not sufficient for both, so you must choose either one, or neither. Information about the two products appears below.

	Product 101	Product 102
Expected monthly volume, units	100,000	200,000
Expected selling price	$40	$50
Expected unit variable cost	30	37
Expected monthly fixed costs, all incremental to the product	600,000	2,000,000

Required:

1. Determine which product you would select, based on the information available.
2. You recognize that the expected values may not materialize and that you should perform some sensitivity analysis. Determine how high or low each variable would have to go to bring each product to breakeven. Do each variable independently of the others. (Hold all but one constant at the expected value.) Determine the percentage changes from the expected value to the new one. Does this new information support the decision you made in item 1?

3. Suppose now that you are reasonably certain about all the variables except the variable cost per unit. Pilot studies, statistical analyses, and industrial engineering techniques indicate that variable cost per unit is normally distributed with means as given above and standard deviations of $1.50 and $3 for products 101 and 102, respectively. Would this new information change your decision? Support your analysis with appropriate calculations.

4–14 **Pricing and Expected Values.** The marketing department of your firm has developed the following estimates of volumes at four prices that you are considering for a new product. The estimated ranges of volume at each price reflect uncertainty. The marketing people do not believe that the probabilities are uniform over each range, and they do not consider it reasonable to make more explicit statements about probabilities.

Price	Expected Volume	Range of Volume
$40	10,000	7,000–13,000
35	13,000	11,000–15,000
30	16,000	15,000–17,000
25	18,000	17,000–19,000

Unit variable cost is $10, and incremental fixed costs are $250,000.

Required: Recommend a price, justifying your answer with whatever calculations you believe appropriate.

4–15 **Uncertainty, Including Bayesian Revision.** You are engaged in corporate planning for next year for the Kitchen Company. In order to start the budgeting process, you have talked to various sales, production, and other management people and have some information on the ensuing year.

The company produces and sells two products for gasoline station pumps: nozzles and a metering device. The market consists of both pump manufacturers and wholesalers who supply the replacement market. Sales of the meters are affected by factors including building of new stations, replacement of existing pumps, and replacement of meters. Gas prices began to exceed $1 per gallon in 1979, and many existing meters cannot handle any price over 99.9 cents. In addition, there is the possibility that the United States government will require all gas to be sold in liters instead of gallons. This requirement will mean that most of the 2.5 million meters nationwide will have to be replaced.

Before this new planning period, government sources predicted about a 30 percent chance that there would be government conversion to liters during any of several upcoming years. You have just been to a trade meeting where a reliable speaker said she thought the probability was more like 80 to 90 percent for the coming year.

Recent sales figures show that sales at Kitchen have a 95 percent confidence interval of 97,000 to 103,000 meters and 242,000 to 245,000 nozzles. Kitchen usually has about a 20 percent share in the market in both products.

Required:

1. Using Bayesian revision, what is the updated probability of liter conversion this year?

2. Kitchen has been operating at a mean level of 75 percent of capacity for meters. What is the capacity for meters? What is the probability of its needing full capacity?

3. Given your answers to items 1 and 2, how would you use this information in planning for next year? (Assume additional capacity is possible through a rental agreement calling for a one-year contract payable now. Each 100,000 units in capacity would cost $300,000 in rental fees.)

4-16 Sensitivity Analysis and Statistics. The Gruenwald Thread Company makes a variety of threads, including one used in residential carpeting. The firm recently employed a consultant who developed the following regression equation for this thread:

$$Y = 218,365 + 163.6X, \qquad r^2 = 0.602, \qquad Se = 316,280$$

where Y = monthly sales of thread, in yards
X = the number of housing starts in the geographical region that Gruenwald serves
r^2 = the coefficient of determination
Se = is the standard error of the estimate.

The state commerce department has estimated that regional monthly housing starts will average about 12,400 during the coming year. The thread sells for $1.20 per yard, variable costs are $0.48 per yard, and monthly incremental fixed costs are $1,214,000.

Required:

1. Determine the expected average monthly profit.

2. Determine the probability that sales will be below the breakeven point. Use the normal distribution.

3. The president of the firm wants to know the confidence interval for profits with 95 percent probability. What are the limits of the interval? Use the normal distribution.

4-17 Process Further. Sea Bed Petroleum is considering whether to sell the output of its new petroleum derivative, Oilsoak, or to process this chemical further to produce a more risky end product. Oilsoak is sold to other chemical processors for use as a raw material. The going market price is $20 per gallon. Incremental costs for producing Oilsoak have a mean of $15 and a standard deviation of $0.51.

Company scientists have identified a new product that can be manufactured using Oilsoak as its base. Production costs including those of the current process are estimated to have a mean of $28 with a standard deviation of $3.06. The marketing department feels that the resulting product could be sold for $33.50 on average and that a reasonable range of sales prices would be from $30 to $37. In order to penetrate the market with a new product, at least half the capacity used for Oilsoak would have to be employed.

Required: Should Sea Bed continue producing and selling Oilsoak or should it produce the new product? Include all relevant cost and probabilistic information in your response. [*Hint:* Variance $(X - Y)$ = variance (X) + variance (Y) if variables are independent.]

4–18   Decision Tree. Your firm is the largest manufacturer of word processing equipment, and your competitors usually price their units about $100 below yours. Your equipment is generally thought to be better than your competitors', so that they must charge less to make any inroads into the market.

You have good reason to believe that your competitors might price as much as $175 below you in the coming year in all-out efforts to break your dominance on the market. You have been thinking about two prices, $1,800 and $1,600. At $1,600 you believe there is only a 10 percent probability of your competitors' pricing at $175 below you, but at $1,800 a 60 percent probability.

You believe that your sales will be about 50,000 units if your price is $100 over your competitors', about 30,000 units if you are $175 higher than they. These unit estimates apply at either the $1,600 or $1,800 price. Variable cost is $1,000 per unit.

Required: Analyze the alternative prices, using a decision tree.

4–19   Decision Tree. The managers of Elmar Products are evaluating a series of strategies associated with the possible marketing of a new product. Existing capacity is available on machinery being used for a product that may be phased out. The existing product, Pow-Add, an additive for diesel fuel, has an annual contribution margin of $30,000. Management feels that the new product, Sun-Set, a chemical medium for heat storage for solar heating systems, will prove more profitable.

If Sun-Set is introduced, market research has shown there is a 50/50 chance of demand's being either 8,000 gallons per month or 12,500 gallons per month at a price of $35 per gallon. If Elmar produces this chemical, variable costs of production are uncertain. Sun-Set must be produced in large batches. The firm's engineers think that the batch size should be

10,000, 15,000, or 20,000 gallons at a time. Estimated costs and probabilities of these costs are below. Once the choice of batch size has been made, it cannot be reversed.

Batch Size and Cost per Gallon

10,000 Gallons		15,000 Gallons		20,000 Gallons	
Cost	Probability	Cost	Probability	Cost	Probability
$25	.1	$20	.2	$20	.2
30	.2	25	.2	25	.1
35	.7	30	.6	30	.7

In addition, Elmar has been approached by Wolff, Inc., which has offered a one-year contract to make 100,000 gallons at $2,700,000 or 150,000 gallons at $3,750,000.

Required: Assume that products unsold at year end are worthless.

1. Model this problem using a decision tree. [*Hint:* Identify what decisions are called for and identify what occurrences are probabilistic in nature.]

2. Using the tree in item 1, put in all conditional values and probabilities.

3. Solve the decision tree.

4–20   Linear Programming (AICPA adapted). The Golden Hawk Manufacturing Company seeks to maximize the profits on its three products, for which the following data are available:

	Product A	Product B	Product C
Contribution margin per unit	$2	$5	$4
Production requirements, hours in each department:			
Assembling	2	3	2
Painting	1	2	2
Finishing	2	3	1

Total capacities, in hours, for each department are: assembling, 30,000; painting, 38,000; finishing, 28,000.

Required: Set up the objective function and constraints for the linear programming problem that will maximize Golden Hawk's profits.

4–21 **Linear Programming.** The Little Rock and Sand Company buys gravel from both the Arch Quarry Company and Land Mine Company. Little runs the gravel through a series of screens to get three grades to sell to its customers. Monthly sales have been running at 300 tons of pea gravel, 400 tons of medium gravel, and 250 tons of large gravel. Each ton of gravel from Land Mine has about 500 lb pea gravel, 500 lb medium gravel, and 1,000 lb large gravel. Gravel from Arch is about half pea gravel, with the balance divided evenly between the other two grades. Gravel costs $150 per ton from Arch and $200 per ton from Land Mine.

Required:

1. Formulate this problem so it can be solved using linear programming. [*Hint:* This is a minimization problem.]
2. Graph the constraints and solve graphically.

4–22 **Linear Programming (AICPA).** Select the best answer for each of the following items.

1. In a linear programming maximization problem for business problem solving, the coefficients of the objective function usually are:
   a. marginal contributions per unit.
   b. variable costs.
   c. profit based upon allocations of overhead and all indirect costs.
   d. usage rates for scarce resources.
   e. none of the above.
2. The constraints in a linear programming problem usually model:
   a. profits.
   b. restrictions.
   c. dependent variables.
   d. goals.
   e. none of the above.
3. If there are four activity variables and two constraints in a linear programming problem, the most products that would be included in the optimal solution would be:
   a. 6.
   b. 4.
   c. 2.
   d. 0.
   e. none of the above.
4. Linear programming is used most commonly to determine:
   a. that mix of variables which will result in the largest quantity.
   b. the best use of scarce resources.
   c. the most advantageous prices.
   d. the fastest timing.
   e. none of the above.

5. Assume the following data for the two products produced by Wagner Company:

	Product A	Product B
Raw-material requirements (units):		
X	3	4
Y	7	2
Contribution margin per unit	$10	$4

If 300 units of raw material X and 400 units of raw material Y were available, the set of relationships appropriate for maximization of profit using linear programming would be:

a. $3A + 4B \geq 300$
    $7A + 2B \geq 400$
    $10A + 4B$ max

b. $3A + 7B \geq 300$
    $4A + 2B \geq 400$
    $10A + 4B$ max

c. $3A + 7B \leq 300$
    $4A + 2B \leq 400$
    $10A + 4B$ max

d. $3A + 4B \leq 300$
    $7A + 2B \leq 400$
    $10A + 4B$ max

e.   none of the above.

6. A final tableau for a linear programming profit-maximization problem is shown below:

	X_1	X_2	X_3	S_1	S_2	
X_1	1	0	4	3	-7	50
X_2	0	1	-2	-6	2	60
	0	0	5	1	9	1,200

If X_1, X_2, X_3 represent products, S_1 refers to square feet (in thousands) of warehouse capacity, and S_2 refers to labor hours (in hundreds), the number of X_1 that should be produced to maximize profit would be:

a.   60.
b.   50.
c.   1.
d.   0.
e.   none of the above.

7. Assuming the same facts as in item 6, the contribution to profit of an additional 100 hours of labor would be:

   a. 9.
   b. 2.
   c. 1.
   d. -7.
   e. none of the above.

8. Assuming the same facts as in item 6, an additional 1,000 square feet of warehouse space would:

   a. increase X_1 by 3 units and decrease X_2 by 6 units.
   b. decrease X_2 by 6 units and increase X_1 by 2 units.
   c. decrease X_1 by 7 units and increase X_2 by 2 units.
   d. increase X_1 by 3 units and decrease X_2 by 7 units.
   e. do none of the above.

9. The following is the final tableau of a linear programming profit-maximization problem:

	X_1	X_2	S_1	S_2	
X_1	1	0	-5	3	125
X_2	0	1	1	-1	70
	0	0	5	7	500

The marginal contribution to profit of 5 for each added resource unit S_1 can be maintained if the added resource units do not exceed:

   a. 125.
   b. 100.
   c. 70.
   d. 25.
   e. none of the above.

10. Assume the following per-unit raw material and labor requirements for the production of product A and the production of product B.

	Product A	Product B
Pounds of lead	5	7
Hours of labor	3	4

Assuming that 13,400 lb of lead and 7,800 hr of labor are available, the production of products A and B required to use all of the available lead and labor hours is shown in the following final Gaussian tableau.

$$\left[\begin{array}{cccc|c} 1 & 0 & -4 & 7 & 1,000 \\ 0 & 1 & 3 & -5 & 1,200 \end{array}\right]$$

If the available amounts were increased to 15,000 lb of lead and 8,800 hr of labor, the matrix operation to determine the production schedule that would fully utilize these resources is:

a. $\begin{pmatrix} 5 & 7 \\ 3 & 4 \end{pmatrix} \begin{pmatrix} 15,000 \\ 8,800 \end{pmatrix}.$

b. $\begin{pmatrix} 15,000 \\ 8,800 \end{pmatrix} \begin{pmatrix} -4 & 7 \\ 3 & -5 \end{pmatrix}.$

c. $\begin{pmatrix} -4 & 7 \\ 3 & -5 \end{pmatrix} \begin{pmatrix} 1,000 \\ 1,200 \end{pmatrix}.$

d. $\begin{pmatrix} -4 & 7 \\ 3 & -5 \end{pmatrix} \begin{pmatrix} 15,000 \\ 8,800 \end{pmatrix}.$

e. none of the above.

11. The following schedule provides data for product A, which is processed through processes 1 and 2, and product B, which is processed through process 1 only:

	Product A	Product B
Raw-material cost per gallon	$ 4	$ 9
Process 1 (500-gallon input capacity per hour):		
Processing cost per hour	$60	$60
Loss in processing	30%	20%
Process 2 (300-gallon input capacity per hour):		
Processing cost per hour	$50	
Loss in processing	10%	
Selling price per gallon	$20	$40

If the objective were to maximize profit per eight-hour day, the objective function of a profit-maximizing linear programming problem would be:

a. $20A + 40B - 4A - 4B.$

b. $20A + 40B - 4A - 4B - 60(A + B) - 50A.$

c. $20(0.63A) + 40(0.80B) - 4(0.63A) - 9(0.8B)$
$- 60\left(\dfrac{A + B}{500}\right) - 50\left(\dfrac{0.7A}{300}\right).$

d. $20(0.63A) + 40(0.80B) - 4A - 9B$

$$- 60 \left(\frac{A}{500} + \frac{B}{500} \right) - 50 \left(\frac{0.7A}{300} \right).$$

e. none of the above.

12. Assuming the same facts as in item 11, a constraint of the problem would be:

   a. $0.63A \leq 2{,}400$.
   b. $0.8A \leq 2{,}400$.
   c. $0.7A + 0.8B \leq 4{,}000$.
   d. $0.9A \leq 4{,}000$.
   e. none of the above.

13. The accompanying graph shows engineering estimates of costs of various volumes. In developing the firm's cost function, the point at $x = 0$ would be:

   a. an estimate of variable cost.
   b. an estimate of fixed cost.
   c. the total cost of the first unit.
   d. the slope of the curve.
   e. none of the above.

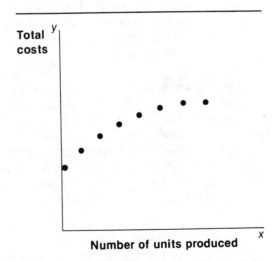

14. Dancy, Inc., is going to begin producing a new chemical cleaner by combining alcohol, peroxide, and enzyme. Each quart of the new cleaner will require ½ quart of alcohol, 1 quart of peroxide, and ⅓

quart of enzyme. The costs per quart are 40 cents for alcohol, 60 cents for peroxide, and 20 cents for enzyme. The matrix operation to determine the cost of producing one quart of new chemical cleaner is:

a. $(\frac{1}{2}, 1, \frac{1}{3}) \begin{pmatrix} 0.40 \\ 0.60 \\ 0.20 \end{pmatrix}.$

d. $\begin{pmatrix} 0.40 \\ 0.60 \\ 0.20 \end{pmatrix} (\frac{1}{2}, 1, \frac{1}{3}).$

b. $\begin{pmatrix} \frac{1}{2} \\ 1 \\ \frac{1}{3} \end{pmatrix} \begin{pmatrix} 0.40 \\ 0.60 \\ 0.20 \end{pmatrix}.$

e. none of the above.

c. $(\frac{1}{2}, 1, \frac{1}{3})(0.40, 0.60, 0.20).$

15. A linear programming model is being used to determine for two products having different profitabilities per unit the quantities of each to produce to maximize profit over a one-year period. One component of cost is raw materials. If both products use the same amount of the same raw material:
   a. This cost may be ignored, because it is the same for each product.
   b. This cost must be ignored, because it is the same for each product.
   c. This cost must be included in the objective function, since it varies with the independent variables in the model.
   d. More information about the products and the other components of the objective function is needed to determine whether to include this cost.
   e. None of the above.

4–23 Linear Programming (AICPA). Beekley, Inc., manufactures widgets, gadgets, and trinkets and has asked for advice in determining the best production mix. Demand for the company's products is excellent, and management finds that it is unable to meet potential sales with existing plant capacity.

Each product goes through three operations: milling, grinding, and painting. The effective weekly departmental capacities in minutes are: milling—10,000, grinding—14,000, and painting—10,000.

The following data are available on the three products:

	Selling Price per Unit	Variable Cost per Unit	Per-Unit Production Time (in minutes)		
			Milling	Grinding	Painting
Widgets	$5.25	$4.45	4	8	4
Gadgets	5.00	3.90	10	4	2
Trinkets	4.50	3.30	4	8	2

Required: Select the single best answer to the following questions.

1. The objective function for this problem using the simplex method might be expressed:
   a. f min $= 4.45X_1 + 3.90X_2 + 3.30X_3 + 0X_4 + 0X_5 + 0X_6$.
   b. f max $= 5.25X_1 + 5.00X_2 + 4.50X_3 + X_4 + X_5 + X_6$.
   c. f max $= 0.80X_1 + 1.10X_2 + 1.20X_3 + X_4 + X_5 + X_6$.
   d. f max $= 0.80X_1 + 1.10X_2 + 1.20X_3 + 0X_4 + 0X_5 + 0X_6$.

2. The requirement that total production time in the painting department may not exceed 10,000 minutes per week might be expressed:
   a. $4X_1 + 2X_2 + 2X_3 \geq 10,000$.
   b. $4X_1 + 2X_2 + 2X_3 > 10,000$.
   c. $4X_1 + 2X_2 + 2X_3 \leq 10,000$.
   d. $4X_1 + 2X_2 + 2X_3 < 10,000$.

3. The variables X_4, X_5, X_6 included in the answers to item 1 are referred to as:
   a. artificial variables.
   b. primary variables.
   c. stochastic variables.
   d. slack variables.

4. The variables X_1, X_2, X_3 included in the answers to item 1 are referred to as:
   a. artificial variables.
   b. primary variables.
   c. stochastic variables.
   d. slack variables.

5. The coefficients for X_1, X_2, and X_3 included in the answers to item 1 are:
   a. the coefficients of the objective function in the problem.
   b. the coefficients of the artificial variables in the problem.
   c. the coefficients of the constraints in the problem and represent the contribution margin for each project.
   d. the shadow prices of the stochastic variables in the problem.

4-24 **Expected Values (AICPA).** Your firm of CPAs audits Food Products, Inc. The president of Food Products recently asked you for help in solving the following problem.

A Food Products plant on the coast produces a food product and ships its production of 10,000 units per day by air in an airplane owned by Food Products. The area is sometimes fogbound, and shipment can then be made only by rail. The plant does not operate unless shipments are made. Extra costs of preparation for rail shipment reduce the marginal contribution of this product from $0.40 per unit to $0.18 per unit, and there is an additional fixed cost of $3,100 for modification of packaging facilities to convert to rail shipment (incurred only once per conversion).

The fog may last for several days, and Food Products normally starts shipping by rail only after rail shipments become necessary to meet commitments to customers.

A meteorological report reveals that during the past ten years the area has been fogbound 250 times for one day and that fog continued 100 times for a second consecutive day, 40 times for a third consecutive day, 20 times for a fourth consecutive day, and 10 times for a fifth consecutive day. Occasions and length of fog were both random. Fog never continued more than five days, and there were never two separate occurrences of fog in any six-day period.

Required:

1. Prepare a schedule presenting the computation of the daily marginal contribution (ignore fixed conversion cost):
   a. when there is no fog and shipment is made by air.
   b. when there is fog and shipment is made by rail.

2. Prepare a schedule presenting the computation of the probabilities of the possible combinations of foggy and clear weather on the days following a fogbound day. Your schedule should show the probability that, if fog first occurs on a particular day:
   a. the next four days will be foggy.
   b. the next three days will be foggy and day 5 will be clear.
   c. the next two days will be foggy and days 4 and 5 will be clear.
   d. the next day will be foggy and days 3, 4, and 5 will be clear.
   e. the next four days will be clear.

3. Assume you determine it would probably be unprofitable to start shipping by rail on either the fourth or fifth consecutive foggy day. Prepare a schedule presenting the computation of the probable marginal income or loss that should be expected from rail shipments if they were started on the third consecutive foggy day and the probability that the next two days will be foggy is .25, the probability that the next day will be foggy and day 5 will be clear is .25, and the probability that the next two days will be clear is .50.

4. In this engagement the CPA should consider the reliability of the data on which any conclusions are based. What questions should be considered regarding:
   a. financial data reliability?
   b. meteorological data reliability?

4-25 **Risk and Return.** "It's tempting to take the sure thing, but if I do I could miss out on some healthy business," mused Joe Bardon. Bardon was the owner and operator of Bardon Construction Company, which specialized in road-building and earth-removing work. Bardon was tempted because Morton Industries, Inc., a large diversified company, had offered to lease some of his equipment for the coming year for $384,000. Morton was building a plant in a remote area and needed road-building and earth-moving equipment. Employees of Morton's construction subsidiary would be doing the work.

Bardon explained some aspects of his business:

Nearly all of my work requires about the same mix of equipment: grader, scraper, a truck or two, and so on. Consequently, I can pretty well measure my volume by using what I call an equipment-day, which is a day's work for the five or six machines that I need. I have five sets of equipment, so that I can do about 1,100 equipment-days working the usual 220-day year. Naturally, I seldom do that much work because of bad weather, breakdowns, and lack of business. I average between 900 and 1,120 days per year.

Morton wants what amounts to two sets, so that I'd have three sets left. They want the newest pieces, of course, so I'll be lucky to get 590 to 610 days out of the three sets even if I can get the business. I had planned to bid on two state jobs, but if I lease to Morton I could only bid on one. I think that I can get either one, and maybe both, but it's no sure thing by any means. I am committed to doing about 350 equipment-days work, and I can probably get close to 700 days if I have the equipment available. I usually charge $2,200 per equipment-day, but on state jobs you have to set a total price, so I would try to get a bit more to give myself a cushion in case I can't finish in the number of days I expect.

Why don't you look at the figures I've pulled together and see what you think? These are my best estimates, and I'm usually fairly close, but you realize that things could change over the year.

The figures that Bardon referred to appear below.

Operating Costs

Variable per equipment-day:		
Fuel, oil	$	95
Wages, fringe benefits, other		870
Total	$	965
Fixed per year:		
Depreciation on equipment		$280,000
General and administrative		595,000

State Contracts

	Job A	Job B
Bardon's estimated bid	$510,000	$880,000
Expected equipment-days required	210	380

Required: Analyze the alternatives, developing information that will be useful to Mr. Bardon. Be prepared to make a recommendation and to support it, based on the information available.

SELECTED REFERENCES

Charnes, A., W. Cooper, and Y. Ijiri, "Breakeven Budgeting and Programming to Goals," *Journal of Accounting Research,* 1:1 (Spring 1963), 16–41.

Feller, William, *An Introduction to Probability Theory and Its Applications,* 3d ed., vol. 1. New York: John Wiley & Sons, 1968.

Hamburg, Morris, *Statistical Analysis for Decision Making,* 2d ed. New York: Harcourt Brace Jovanovich, Inc., 1977.

Hartley, R., "Some Extensions of Sensitivity Analysis," *The Accounting Review,* 45:2 (April 1970), 223–34.

Jaedicke, Robert, "Improving Breakeven Analysis by Linear Programming Techniques," *N.A.A. Bulletin,* 42:7 (March 1961), 5–12.

Lapin, Lawrence, *Statistics for Modern Business Decisions,* 2d ed. New York: Harcourt Brace Jovanovich, Inc., 1978.

Levin, Richard I., and Charles A. Kirkpatrick, *Quantitative Approaches to Management,* 4th ed. New York: McGraw-Hill Book Company, 1978.

Morris, William T., *Decision Analysis.* Columbus: Grid, Inc., 1977.

Product Costing

Part 2

Product Costing:
Job Order Costing

Chapter 5

This chapter begins a sequence on product costing. The main concern of product costing is determining unit manufacturing costs. These unit costs are necessary for financial and income tax reporting as well as for internal use. Accountants need to determine costs of products, and of individual units of product, in order to determine inventories and cost of goods sold. Managers frequently use these unit costs for planning and decision making.

For the most part, we shall be dealing with absorption costing. **Absorption costing** uses fixed manufacturing costs as well as variable manufacturing costs in determining unit costs. We have argued in earlier chapters that calculating unit fixed costs is unwise because fixed costs are not incurred per unit, but in total. However, absorption costing is required for financial reporting and income tax reporting. There are also uses for unit fixed costs in some types of managerial planning and analysis.

Perhaps the most common use of unit fixed costs is in setting long-term prices (as opposed to short-term prices, such as those in the special order problems discussed in Chapter 4). Managers often use unit fixed costs to develop normal, long-term prices to guide their actions. General Motors Corporation reportedly has used a pricing model that incorporates absorption costing data.[1] *Average cost pricing,* which employs absorption costing data, is widespread among firms that have some control over their prices and seek satisfactory profits, rather than the maximum possible profits.

Many sales agreements provide for the price to be based on cost, including some allocated fixed costs. The agreement might specify the price

[1] "General Motors Corporation" case in Robert N. Anthony and John Dearden, *Management Control Systems* (Homewood, Ill.: Richard D. Irwin, Inc., 1980).

as cost plus $20,000 or as 120 percent of cost. Federal government contracts often contain such provisions, as do many contracts in the private sector. The reason may be that the product is not a standard one that the firm regularly makes. The manufacturer might not be willing to set a firm price beforehand because of the risk of setting it too low. It is very difficult to esimate the cost of a one-shot contract. For this reason, as well as others, housing contractors, automobile repair shops, and many other firms work on cost-plus.

When prices are based on costs, it is important that the parties agree on what is included in cost and what is excluded. The Cost Accounting Standards Board, which has had extensive jurisdiction over the cost accounting methods used by government contractors, has issued a number of pronouncements on the acceptability of various methods; we shall deal with some of them later in this book.

Determining the appropriate measure of cost is also of concern in situations where a firm or other organization receives reimbursements for services it performs. Hospitals are often reimbursed for the direct costs of providing services plus a share of the indirect costs. Direct costs would be those traceable to the particular operating segment of the hospital, such as the maternity ward or operating room; indirect costs would include those associated with patient records, admissions, and general administration of the hospital.

While absorption costing combines both the variable and fixed costs of manufacturing, the accounting system can still provide information about cost behavior within the constraints of absorption costing. Accounts for each type of manufacturing cost can be coded to indicate whether the cost is fixed, variable, semivariable, or of some other pattern. The use of computers makes such classifications relatively simple to employ, so that the system can simultaneously provide information for both product costing and managerial use. (The use of computers does not in itself make the determination of the cost behavior pattern a simple matter, but rather makes it easy to use the classifications once they have been analyzed along the lines discussed in Chapter 3.)

FLOWS OF MANUFACTURING COSTS

Up until this chapter we have looked at cost behavior for planning and decision making. However, it is also important to look at the accumulation of costs by product. This means we must trace costs through the manufacturing process. Manufacturing costs are accumulated in various inventory accounts.

A merchandising firm, wholesaler or retailer, generally uses a single inventory account because it has only one type of inventory: goods being held for resale. In contrast, a manufacturing firm may require three types of inventory: one for the materials it uses, another for its finished goods, and a third for goods that are in process—goods on which some, but not all, work has been done. This third account is needed because manufacturing is not instantaneous. It takes time to turn lumber into tables, cloth into pants and coats, wire into nails. Accordingly, the manufacturer has a more complicated record-keeping process than does a merchandiser.

The pattern of cost flows that we describe in the pages that follow applies to any cost accounting system, not just to job order systems. The basic problem for all manufacturing firms is to determine costs for individual products and units of product to assign to inventories and to cost of goods sold.

Two final matters before we proceed. First, throughout this book we shall capitalize account titles when we are referring to the account itself, rather than to the physical products or costs involved. For example, the account Cost of Goods Sold contains the cost of goods sold during a period. The account Materials Inventory contains the cost of materials on hand. This use should help to make clear the important difference between events and the recording of these events.

Second, your previous study of accounting has shown you that terminology differs. Different companies label the same account in different ways. We shall use different, but synonymous, terms to refer to accounts in order to reflect the diversity in practice. For instance, Materials, Inventory of Materials, and Stores are all terms used to designate the account that contains the cost of materials on hand, while Accrued Wages and Accrued Payroll represent the account that shows amounts owed to workers.

Materials

Materials inventory consists of the materials that the firm uses to make its products. Because materials are used in different ways, they are sub-classified as direct and indirect. Roughly speaking, we can say that **direct materials** are those that enter into the product, while **indirect materials** do not become part of the product although they are necessary for its manufacture. For example, the steel that an automobile maker uses is a direct material, while the rubbing compound used to polish the painted parts is an indirect material. The distinction is not hard-and-fast, and various firms in the same industry may classify the same material differently. Thus, one furniture manufacturer might classify wax as a direct material, another as an indirect material. The importance of the distinction is that indirect materials are accounted for as overhead costs and enter the flow of product costs at a different point.

The term **raw materials** is often used synonymously with *materials* or *direct materials*. There is no objection to this usage except that it tends to suggest that the material is fresh from the earth—iron ore, coal, lumber, cotton, and so on. In fact, a material is considered raw if it is bought by the firm. Iron ore is a raw material to a steelmaker, while finished steel is a raw material to an automobile maker. Manufactured products such as cloth, paper, and door hinges are raw materials to the firm that uses them in making its own products.

Since materials are an asset, the Materials Inventory account (or accounts) will be debited when materials are purchased. This is the beginning of the inventory cost cycle that eventually ends in cost of goods sold on the income statement and various inventories on the balance sheet. As materials are used in the production process, Materials Inventory is credited. Any balance (a debit amount) reflects the cost of materials on hand that have not yet been put into production.

Work in Process

Costs flow from the Materials account and other accounts into Work in Process. The ending balance of Work in Process contains the costs of products that are unfinished at the end of a period. At the end of any accounting period most manufacturers will have semifinished units at various stages of completion. A chemical company may have products in mixers, boiling vats, and pipelines. A manufacturer of calculators will have some ready for testing, others partly assembled, others not yet ready for assembly. All manufacturing costs flow through the Work-in-Process Inventory account. The costs of inputs to the production process (materials, labor, and overhead) are debited to the account, the cost of goods manufactured (completed) is credited to it, and its balance represents the cost of goods still in process. The entire inventory cost flow is diagrammed in Figure 5–1. This is a basic flow pattern, no matter what kind of product costing is used.

The determination of what costs are transferred to Finished Goods Inventory and of what the ending balance is in Work-in-Process Inventory can be the most difficult phase of the cost accounting cycle. Some intricate problems may be encountered, as we shall see in later chapters.

Finished Goods

As goods are completed, they are transferred to a finished goods inventory. These goods are ready for sale. The manufacturer's finished goods inventory is analogous to the inventory of a merchandising firm. The principal difference is that the merchandiser debits the account for the cost of goods purchased, while the manufacturer debits the account for the cost of goods manufactured. Both types of firms credit the account for the cost of goods sold.

Finished goods inventory presents few special problems for the manufacturer. The major question concerns the cost of goods manufactured: what costs are to be transferred from Work-in-Process Inventory to Finished Goods Inventory?

The flows of costs through the various types of inventory accounts are summarized in the **statement of cost of goods manufactured and sold.** Usu-

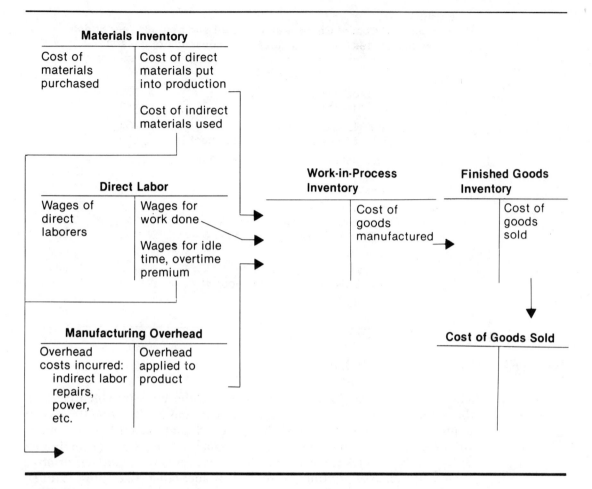

FIGURE 5–1
General Flows of Costs

ally this statement is prepared for internal use only. It provides the back-up detail for the single figure, cost of goods sold, that appears in the income statement in a published annual report. Exhibit 5–1 on page 196 shows an example of the statement. Despite its detail, it is relatively straightforward. Notice that it contains three basic parts: (1) the determination of the cost of materials put into the production process, (2) an analysis of the work-in-process inventory, with its three general inputs of materials, labor, and overhead, and (3) an analysis of the finished goods inventory, culminating in the determination of cost of goods sold.

This statement can be prepared for any type of manufacturing firm, including firms that use job order costing, the subject of the remainder of this chapter.

EXHIBIT 5-1
Statement of Cost of Goods Manufactured and Sold for Year Ended
December 31, 19X7—SLM Company (in thousands of dollars)

Direct materials:		
Inventory of direct materials, January 1	$ 879	
Purchases and freight in	3,456	
Cost of materials available for use	4,335	
Less: Inventory of direct materials, December 31	951	
Cost of direct materials used in production		$ 3,384
Direct labor		12,321
Factory overhead		16,344
Total manufacturing costs		32,049
Add: Work-in-process inventory, January 1		3,897
Less: Work-in-process inventory, December 31		4,065
Cost of goods manufactured		31,881
Add: Finished-goods inventory, January 1		10,306
Less: Finished-goods inventory, December 31		11,015
Cost of goods sold		$31,172

MANUFACTURING OPERATIONS

The types of products that a firm makes and the ways in which it makes them influence its methods of collecting costs and of allocating these costs to products. Consider two firms with quite different circumstances. Bentley Brick Company manufactures a single type of brick in a series of continuous processes. Each brick is virtually identical to every other. Portland Printing Presses, Inc., makes printing presses to customer order. Each press is different, and the range of prices is from a few thousand dollars to over a million dollars.

The informational requirements for the managers of the two firms are considerably different, and so are their product costing problems. Look first at Bentley Brick. Because every brick is nearly the same as every other, the firm can calculate an average cost per brick using a formula such as the following:

$$\text{cost per brick} = \frac{\text{total manufacturing costs for period}}{\text{total number of bricks made during period}}$$

This formula typifies **process costing,** which we treat in detail in Chapter 6. The essential elements of process costing are that it requires the determination of total manufacturing costs *for a period of time* and total unit production *for that same period of time.* The managers of Bentley Brick do not need to know the cost of *this* brick or *that* brick: because of the homogeneity of the units, the average cost is sufficient. The unit cost serves as the basis for determining inventories and cost of goods sold.

In general, firms that make a single homogeneous product in a more or less continuous process use process costing. Flour, sugar, some metals, some chemicals, and cement are examples. Whether or not a firm can use process costing depends on whether the unit cost calculation shown above gives a reasonable result.

Portland Printing Presses cannot make such an average cost calculation: the units it produces differ considerably from one another, and a simple average is not adequate information. Portland's managers need to know whether the cost of a specific printing press was about as planned, whether the profit on a particular press was satisfactory. Moreover, Portland could not value its ending inventory of presses at an average cost that included presses of different sizes. The average cost would probably exceed the selling prices of some presses and be far below the actual cost of others.

JOB ORDER COSTING

Portland would use a **job order cost system.** Such a system accumulates costs by job, by specific unit, or by specific batch of units. Thus, Portland would keep track of the costs of each press, not just of the costs over a period of time.

What constitutes a job varies from firm to firm. In many cases a job is a single unit such as a printing press, office building, or airplane. In other cases a job is a batch of similar units, such as ten desks. In still other cases a job could be a batch of dissimilar items all ordered by the same customer. For example, a furniture maker might treat an order for seventeen sofas and twenty chairs as a single job and not distinguish between the sofas and chairs.

We find job order costing wherever it is necessary to know the cost of a particular unit or batch. Firms that do custom work, such as printers (anything from a few wedding invitations to 100,000 circulars), makers of tools and dies to customer specifications, and construction companies would use job order costing.

Many firms fall somewhere between pure job order and pure process situations. For instance, a furniture manufacturer that produces only a few different items might be able to use a form of process costing. Chapter 8 deals with some cases that fall between the extremes.

Our main concern in this chapter is manufacturing operations, but we should note that service operations use the same basic techniques. A firm of CPAs, consulting engineers, or lawyers would use a form of job order costing because it would need information about the cost of work done for a particular client. Firms could use a form of process costing for repetitive activities such as sorting incoming mail, preparing payroll checks, and filing documents.

General Pattern of Job Order Costing

A job order firm determines the cost of each unit, or batch of units, that it produces. Therefore, the costs of the individual jobs must be kept separate. This is accomplished by the use of a **job order cost sheet** (or job order sheet), an example of which appears in Exhibit 5–2. The job order cost sheet is very much like a subsidiary ledger account, such as one that would show the amount owed to the firm by a particular customer, as opposed to a control account such as Accounts Receivable. As a job is being worked on, the costs of direct materials and direct labor are recorded on the sheet at periodic intervals. The reference column on the sample sheet refers to the original source document from which the posting to the sheet was made.

EXHIBIT 5–2
Sample Job Order Cost Sheet—Imtract Company

Sample Job Order Cost Sheet — Imtract Company

Customer _Wilkins Company_   Job order number   327

Description _10 Casings, #1275_

Date started   2/12

Date finished   3/14

Material Costs			Labor Costs			Factory Overhead		
Date	Reference	Amount	Date	Reference	Amount	Date	Reference	Amount
2-12	M-361	$742.00	2-12	W-1486	$78.00	2-29	J-1011	$1,276
2-15	M-401	1,865.00	2-20	W-1520	560.00			
3-12	M-615	412.50	3-14	W-1606	2,150.00	3-14	J-1115	4,300
Totals		$3,019.50			$2,788			$5,576

Summary

Selling price $ 13,400

Costs:

Materials $ 3,019.50

Direct labor $ 2,788.00

Factory overhead $ 5,576.00

TOTAL COSTS $ 11,383.50

Gross profit $ 2,016.50

The process of going from source documents to the job order sheet is explained in Appendix 5-A.

Overhead costs, which include both variable and fixed items such as indirect labor, indirect materials and supplies, and depreciation on factory equipment are first recorded by the object of the expenditure in descriptive accounts: Indirect Labor, Depreciation on Equipment, and others. These costs are then transferred to a single account called Factory Overhead, Manufacturing Overhead, Factory Burden, or perhaps just Overhead. This account has a clearing function in the sense that the costs simply pass through it on their way to Work-in-Process Inventory. Overhead is periodically applied to individual jobs on the basis of some factor such as direct labor hours, machine hours, or direct labor dollar cost. When this application is made, the overhead account is credited and Work-in-Process Inventory is debited.[2]

The Work-in-Process Inventory account will show the total of all costs recorded on the job order sheets. Therefore, it functions as a control account (in the same sense as Accounts Receivable does) backed up by individual subsidiary records. When a job is completed, its cost as reflected on the job order sheet is credited to Work-in-Process Inventory and debited to Finished Goods Inventory.

For example, the entries associated with Exhibit 5-2 are as follows:

Date			
2-12	Work-in-Process Inventory	$ 820	
	Materials Inventory		$ 742
	Direct Labor		78
2-15	Work-in-Process Inventory	1,865	
	Materials Inventory		1,865
2-20	Work-in-Process Inventory	560	
	Direct Labor		560
2-28	Work-in-Process Inventory	1,276	
	Factory Overhead		1,276
3-12	Work-in-Process Inventory	412.50	
	Materials Inventory		412.50
3-14	Work-in-Process Inventory	6,450	
	Direct Labor		2,150
	Factory Overhead		4,300
3-14	Finished Goods Inventory	11,383.50	
	Work-in-Process Inventory		11,383.50

Job order costing requires several source documents besides the job order cost sheet. Before discussing and illustrating these documents, we will look at an example.

---

[2] We show an alternative method in a later section. We present this treatment first because it is simpler to follow.

Illustration: The Manners Company

The Manners Company manufactures industrial instruments. Although these instruments usually include some standard parts, for example casings, dials, and sensing devices, they require a good deal of fabrication and use of nonstandard parts. The Manners Company, therefore, uses job order costing. Each job is started when an order from a customer is received and approved. Workers analyze the specifications, requisition materials, and do the fabricating and assembly work. After the instruments have been assembled, they are sent to the finished goods storage area to be prepared for shipment.

At the beginning of January, 19X6, the Manners Company had one job in process, EC-25. During January it finished that job and started two others, LP-12 and WW-16. It finished LP-12 during January. Exhibit 5–3 shows the amounts of direct material and direct labor assigned to each job during January.

EXHIBIT 5–3
Data for January, 19X6—Manners Company

| | Jobs | | | |
	EC-25	LP-12	WW-16	Totals
Direct materials used in January	$11,800	$ 9,600	$13,200	$34,600
Direct labor costs for January	9,500	14,500	5,800	29,800
Subtotals	21,300	24,100	19,000	64,400
Beginning inventory	6,500	0	0	6,500
Totals, excluding January overhead	$27,800	$24,100	$19,000	$70,900
Other data:				
Direct labor hours for January	1,950	3,040	1,010	6,000

Total overhead costs incurred in January were $45,400.

At this point we have all the costs that have been accumulated for each job except the overhead to be allocated for January. The $6,500 beginning inventory value for job EC-25 includes both direct costs and allocations of overhead from the previous year. None of the jobs includes an allocation of January's overhead.

Accounting for Overhead

For product costing purposes we must allocate fixed manufacturing overhead to jobs. This information is necessary for the determination of inventory on the balance sheet and, in turn, for income. We must include both fixed and variable overhead in determining the costs of jobs. For planning and control, there is no problem with including variable overhead as a cost of product because it is an incremental cost, like materials and direct labor. The accountant would therefore feel confident in saying that if variable overhead were $6 per direct labor hour, he should include as part of the cost of a job an amount equal to $6 multiplied by the number of direct labor hours worked on the job. However, we cannot be confident about allocating fixed overhead to jobs, because most fixed overhead items are not incremental to specific jobs and are not avoidable. The accountant cannot say that a particular job used $230 worth of heat, light, salaries, and depreciation.

Bases for Allocating Overhead.   Overhead is often allocated on the basis of units produced. That is, total overhead costs are divided by total units to obtain a cost-per-unit figure. Such a calculation is inappropriate in a job order situation because the units are not uniform. It would be absurd to include tables, chairs, and sofas as units produced because these products require different quantities of materials and labor.

The accountant generally uses an input factor such as direct labor hours, machine hours, or direct labor cost as the basis for applying overhead. Total overhead generally depends on the level of some input factor: the more direct labor hours, for example, the more power, supplies, fringe benefits, and other components of overhead. Once the overhead rate per unit of the input factor is calculated, it is used to apply overhead to jobs. Each job will receive a charge for overhead based on the amount of the input factor used to produce it. The amount of overhead for a particular job is the rate per unit of the input factor (such as $3 per direct labor hour) multiplied by the number of units of the input factor worked on the job.

Selection of the Basis.   The selection of the basis (input factor) is important. In general, firms use the same basis for applying overhead that they use for budgeting it. Thus, they will try to find the input factor that correlates most closely with total overhead. Scatter diagrams and regression analysis are tools for selecting the input factor. One way to pick the basis would be to take the one with the highest correlation to total overhead, or the lowest standard error.

Actual Costing

Perhaps the most obvious way to allocate overhead costs to jobs is to determine the actual overhead costs for each period (month, quarter, year), divide the costs by the number of units of the input factor (e.g., direct labor hours, direct labor dollars, or machine hours), then charge each job with its proportionate share of the overhead costs. Firms that use this method are said to use **actual costing** or an **actual costing system.**

For example, using the data for the Manners Company shown in Exhibit 5–3, and allocating the actual overhead cost of $45,400 on the basis of direct labor hours, we would obtain the following results:

$$\text{Overhead rate per direct labor hour} = \frac{\$45,400}{6,000} = \$7.567$$

Charges to jobs:

	Job			
	EC-25	LP-12	WW-16	Total
Direct labor hours	1,950	3,040	1,010	6,000
Overhead rate	$7.567	$7.567	$7.567	
Overhead charged to job (rounded to even dollars)	$14,755	$23,003	$7,642	$45,400

These amounts would be added to the material and direct labor costs to obtain the total cost of each job.

Actual costing systems have some serious drawbacks and are not widely used in practice. We shall look at the reasons why after we consider the more prevalent method of allocating overhead costs, called **actual-normal costing** or simply **normal costing.** It will be easier to see why actual costing is an inferior method after we see how normal costing works.

Normal Costing and Predetermined Overhead Rates

The essence of normal costing is that it uses a predetermined overhead rate to allocate overhead costs to jobs. A predetermined overhead rate is simply a rate calculated at the beginning of a period, usually a year, that is used to determine the overhead cost included in each job worked on during the period. The rate is usually based on the budgeted volume of some input factor such as direct labor hours, direct labor cost, or machine hours. The factor selected is ordinarily the one with which overhead is most closely associated—that is, the input factor that seems to be the causal factor. There is no problem in charging jobs with variable overhead on such a basis, but there is with charging jobs with fixed costs. However, it may be more reasonable to allocate fixed overhead on the basis on which variable overhead seems to be incurred than on some other basis.

Calculation of Predetermined Overhead Rate.   A predetermined overhead rate is calculated as follows:

$$\text{predetermined overhead rate} = \frac{\text{total budgeted overhead costs}}{\text{total budgeted activity}}$$

where total budgeted activity would be expressed as direct labor hours, machine hours, direct labor cost, or some other factor with which variable overhead is closely associated.

Although a rate may be set for a period of any length, by far the most common period is the year. Because total budgeted overhead would consist of a fixed portion and a variable component based on the expected volume of activity, the numerator of the formula may be expressed as

$$\text{budgeted fixed overhead} + \left[\left(\begin{array}{c} \text{variable overhead} \\ \text{per unit of activity} \end{array} \right) \times \left(\begin{array}{c} \text{budgeted} \\ \text{activity} \end{array} \right) \right]$$

Assume that the Manners Company management has analyzed overhead using regression analysis and determined the cost behavior pattern to be $240,000 + ($4 \times$ direct labor hours). The firm expects to work about 80,000 direct labor hours during the year and, therefore, sets the predetermined overhead rate at $7 per direct labor hour, calculated as follows:

$$\text{predetermined overhead rate} = \frac{\$240,000 + (\$4 \times 80,000)}{80,000}$$

$$= \frac{\$560,000}{80,000}$$

$$= \$7 \text{ per direct labor hour}$$

or

$$\frac{\$240,000}{80,000} + \$4 \text{ VOH} = \$7/\text{DLH}$$

where: VOH = variable overhead
           DLH = direct labor hours

The overhead application and total costs are in Exhibit 5–4 on page 204.

Overapplied and Underapplied Overhead. In January, the Manners Company incurred overhead costs of $45,400 (see Exhibit 5–3, page 200), which was $3,400 more than the overhead applied of $42,000. When overhead incurred exceeds overhead applied, overhead has been **underapplied.** Conversely, when overhead applied exceeds overhead incurred, overhead is **overapplied.** It is rare that the overhead applied will equal the actual overhead in any given month or even for an entire year.

A look at the formula for determining total applied overhead will give us some insight. Total applied overhead is the predetermined overhead rate multiplied by actual activity:

$$\text{overhead applied} = \text{actual activity} \times \frac{\text{total budgeted overhead}}{\text{total budgeted activity}}$$

EXHIBIT 5–4
Costs of Jobs—Manners Company

	EC-25	LP-12	WW-16	Totals
January costs:				
Direct materials, from Exhibit 5–3	$11,800	$ 9,600	$13,200	$ 34,600
Direct labor, from Exhibit 5–3	9,500	14,500	5,800	29,800
Overhead applied in January[a]	13,650	21,280	7,070	42,000
Total costs for January	34,950	45,380	26,070	106,400
Plus costs in beginning inventory	6,500	0	0	6,500
Total accumulated costs	$41,450	$45,380	$26,070	$112,900

[a] Overhead applied at $7 per direct labor hour (hours from Exhibit 5–3):

EC-25:	$7 × 1,950 =	$13,650
LP-12:	$7 × 3,040 =	21,280
WW-16:	$7 × 1,010 =	7,070
Total:		$42,000

Thus, if total budgeted activity equals total actual activity *and* total budgeted overhead equals total actual overhead, there will be no over-applied or underapplied overhead (it is also possible that differences could cancel out so that there would be no misapplication, but that is unlikely). However, it is not likely that accountants and the other managers making the predictions will hit them right on the nose.

Consider the formula used by the Manners Company: total overhead costs = $240,000 + ($4 × 80,000 direct labor hours). We see that for the year the firm expects variable overhead costs to be $4 per direct labor. If this budgeted rate is also the actual rate, there will be no overapplied or under-applied *variable* overhead. This is so because total incurred variable over-head would be $4 multiplied by direct labor hours worked, and so would the amount applied. However, the same reasoning cannot be used for fixed overhead, because the firm does not expect to incur fixed overhead at the rate of $3 per direct labor, but rather expects it to total $240,000, regardless of the volume of activity. It is true that if its expectations of cost and volume are realized, the average fixed overhead rate will be $3 per hour, but at any level of volume other than 80,000 direct labor hours the average rate will be different from $3 per hour.

For example, consider the data shown on page 205, which indicate the amounts of variable and fixed overhead *expected* to be incurred and to be applied at 75,000 and 85,000 direct labor hours.

We see that overhead for an entire year can be either underapplied or overapplied. We would expect the same during each month, only more so because of conditions peculiar to individual months. First, even if budgeted volume for the year is achieved, it is unlikely that it will be spread evenly

	75,000 hours	80,000 hours	85,000 hours
Variable overhead incurred at $4	$300,000	$320,000	$340,000
Variable overhead applied at $4	300,000	320,000	340,000
Over- or underapplied	0	0	0
Fixed overhead incurred	$240,000	$240,000	$240,000
Applied at $3 per hour	225,000	240,000	255,000
Over- or underapplied	($15,000)	0	$ 15,000

over all months. Most firms have some seasonal patterns, with some busy months and some slow ones. The Manners Company budgeted 80,000 direct labor hours for the year, which averages 6,167 per month (80,000/12). However, the firm may expect to work at levels above this average during part of the year and below it during other parts of the year. Thus, during relatively slow months we would expect to find underapplied overhead, and during relatively busy months overapplied overhead.

Second, the fixed costs included in the budgeted annual amount will probably not be spread evenly over the year. Heating bills will be higher than normal during the winter months. Property taxes usually will be paid during a single month. Heavy preventive maintenance programs might be carried out during a particular month. Various other factors will affect the pattern of monthly fixed costs, so these costs probably will not be level throughout the year. The Manners Company has budgeted $240,000 fixed overhead for the year, an average of $20,000 per month ($240,000/12). Even if actual costs are about as budgeted, they will probably not be close to $20,000 during several months when seasonal patterns prevail.

Some firms minimize the effects of uneven cost patterns by using accruals and deferrals. For example, you know from financial accounting that if an insurance premium is paid in January, it will be allocated on monthly income statements in equal amounts. The expense will appear evenly over the life of the policy. Similar action can be taken with such costs as property taxes. If property taxes are paid in November, they may still be accrued monthly throughout the year. Each month there will be a debit to the Overhead account and a credit to a current liability for accrued property taxes. Thus the estimated property taxes will be spread evenly over the months of the year. If accruals and deferrals are used, the result will be that monthly or quarterly over- and underapplied fixed overhead will relate primarily to activity, the denominator of the formula.

The two factors just discussed make it likely that actual and applied overhead will differ in most months. Fixed overhead often is the principal reason; actual variable overhead should be about the same as applied variable overhead. There are exceptions: a few variable overhead items will follow uneven patterns. Payroll taxes such as unemployment taxes and the employer's share of social security taxes will tend to fall more heavily in the early part of the year, because these taxes are levied on the earnings of employees only up to certain levels. For example, if the employer's share of social security taxes is 6 percent of earnings up to $18,000, and if the average worker earns $22,000, the taxes will be $1,080 ($18,000 × 6%) per worker. All these taxes will fall in the first nine months of the year. There will be no further taxes in the last three months for employees whose earnings have exceeded the $18,000 limit.

Managerial Analysis of Overhead

Complete analyses of variances between planned and actual results appear in Chapter 7. We make a few important points here regarding overapplied and underapplied overhead.

In looking at over- or underapplied overhead, the manager should consider whether actual overhead was about the same as budgeted overhead for *the particular month*. We have noted earlier that some fixed costs will be incurred unevenly throughout the year. The firm's budgets will usually be prepared by month and will reflect these uneven patterns. For example, the monthly budgets for overhead in the winter will reflect higher heating costs. If the budgeted overhead cost for a month is about the same as the actual amount, the manager has some assurance that things are going more or less according to plan—even if a significant amount of over- or underapplied overhead is being experienced.

The second consideration is whether volume was about as expected for the month. The predetermined overhead rate will be set on the basis of expected volume for the entire year, but the managers will probably have good ideas of expected monthly volumes as well. Therefore, if volume for a particular month is about as expected, even though different from the monthly average, there is generally no cause for concern, even though there is over- or underapplied overhead.

The Manners Company incurred overhead of $45,400 in January, when 6,000 hours were worked. Suppose that budgeted fixed overhead for January was higher than the $20,000 budgeted monthly average because of seasonal factors and was expected to be $21,800. The firm would then expect overhead costs of $45,800 on the basis of the formula:

$$\text{total overhead costs} = \$21,800 + (\$4 \times 6,000 \text{ hours})$$

Overhead, then, was somewhat less than expected, given the activity in January and the budgeted fixed overhead for January.

The same kind of analysis can be done with direct labor hours. The firm worked 6,000 direct labor hours, which was 167 fewer than the budgeted monthly average. If the firm had expected production employees to work 6,500 hours in January, there would be cause for concern, because the shortfall might indicate that total demand for the firm's products for the year, and, therefore, direct labor hours for the year, would be less than originally budgeted. However, if the expected direct labor hours were about 6,000, then no concern would be called for.

Actual Overhead Allocations

Given that under- and overapplied overhead are all-but-inevitable consequences of the use of predetermined overhead rates, why not go ahead and use actual rates? We have to consider this question in two parts, the first having to do with monthly or other interim-period results, the second having to do with an entire year.

If actual overhead costs were allocated monthly, the rates would vary enormously for reasons that we have discussed, including fixed cost patterns and uneven activity in direct labor hours or other measures of activity used to set the rate. Because job order firms will often use costs as the basis for setting, or negotiating, prices, fluctuations in the overhead rate could cause confusion. If the actual overhead rate were $12 per direct labor hour in January, $8 in February, and $11 in March, a manager trying to decide a price for a job to be done in April would be severely handicapped. Moreover, in months of relatively low activity the firm could well show losses on jobs because the overhead rate might be so high as to wipe out any anticipated gross profit.

Advocates of actual overhead costing might argue that it does cost more to operate a factory during the cold months and that it does cost more per direct labor hour to operate in months when there is low volume. Therefore, costs of jobs should reflect the changing conditions under which jobs are produced. The fact that overhead rates may vary considerably from month to month is just a fact of life. The problem with this argument is that it focuses on short periods, rather than on a more reasonable period such as a year. Because the principal source of changes in actual overhead rates from month to month is fixed overhead costs, we can appeal to the following examples to refute the actual-costing argument. Suppose that a manager decides to postpone working on a particular job from March to April because March has been fairly slow and the overhead rate will be fairly high, whereas April is expected to be busy and so the overhead rate will be low. Is work done the first week in April cheaper, so far as fixed overhead is concerned, than it would have been during the last week in March? Obviously not. The total work done in March and April combined would be the same whether the job was scheduled for March or April. Hence to charge actual costs at fluctuating overhead rates per unit creates confusion and may even encourage managers to behave unwisely.

Turning to the annual situation, most firms do end up allocating actual overhead incurred to jobs worked on during the year as a whole. We shall illustrate this procedure shortly. However, even if firms convert from normal costing to actual costing for overhead, they still use a predetermined overhead during the year, rather than waiting until year end to make the allocations of actual overhead to each job. The reason for doing so is that the predetermined rate should provide a reasonable estimate of the actual rate. The total amount of over- or underapplied overhead should not be too great at year end unless the firm's plans are upset by unforeseen conditions.

During the year the firm's managers will be estimating costs and using them to set prices. They will be evaluating individual jobs to see whether they were profitable and, therefore, whether similar jobs should be accepted at similar prices in the future. These kinds of analyses cannot be put off until year end; they must be done continually throughout the year. The best estimate of the actual overhead rate for the year is the predetermined rate. Therefore, it is used to allocate overhead costs to jobs during the year. If circumstances change, so that the budgeted overhead costs or budgeted activity, or both, are no longer expected, the predetermined rate may be changed to incorporate the new information. For example, if the firm receives a large order in May, it may revise its original estimates (budgets) of direct labor hours and overhead costs and change the predetermined overhead rate to reflect the revised budgets.

Journal Entries and Accounts

This section provides journal entries and T-accounts that reflect the operations of the Manners Company for January. Most of the data are from Exhibits 5–2 and 5–3. Other necessary data are added in the descriptions of each entry. The T-accounts summarizing the activities appear in Exhibit 5–5 on page 211. The journal entries are numbered to provide easy reference to the T-accounts. Explanations of individual entries are omitted—both for simplicity and because the purpose of each entry is discussed.

Purchases of Materials. Assume that the firm bought materials costing $41,200 during January, all on account.

(1)	Inventory of Materials	$41,200	
	Accounts Payable		$41,200

When cash is paid, Accounts Payable will be debited and Cash credited.

Issues of Materials. We know from Exhibits 5–2 and 5–3 that direct materials used during January cost $34,600. Assume that indirect materials (supplies, lubricants, abrasives, and so on) costing $2,300 were also issued. These indirect materials are considered part of overhead because they cannot usually be identified specifically with any single job.

(2)	Work-in-Process Inventory	$34,600	
	Indirect Materials	2,300	
	Inventory of Materials		$36,900

Labor Costs. Exhibits 5–2 and 5–3 show that direct labor costs were $29,800 during January. Assume that indirect labor, an overhead cost, was

$3,100. We record the payroll in two steps, its accrual and its payment. At this stage direct labor costs are put into Work in Process.

(3)	Direct Labor	$29,800	
	Indirect Labor	3,100	
	Accrued Payroll		$32,900
(4)	Accrued Payroll	$32,900	
	Cash		$32,900
(5)	Work-in-Process Inventory	$29,800	
	Direct Labor		$29,800

Incurrence of Other Overhead Costs. Actual overhead costs were $45,400 (Exhibit 5–2). So far we have accounted for $5,400 of that total: $2,300 for indirect materials and $3,100 for indirect labor. The following figures are assumed. Except for depreciation, we assume that all the costs were paid in cash.

(6)	Depreciation, Factory and Equipment	$18,500	
	Heat, Light, and Power	12,200	
	Payroll Taxes	3,200	
	Repairs	3,900	
	Miscellaneous	2,200	
	Accumulated Depreciation		$18,500
	Cash		21,500

Collecting Overhead Costs and Applying Overhead. Overhead costs are collected in a single account and then applied to Work in Process.

(7)	Manufacturing Overhead	$45,400	
	Indirect Labor		3,100
	Indirect Materials		2,300
	Depreciation, Factory and Equipment		18,500
	Heat, Light, and Power		12,200
	Payroll Taxes		3,200
	Repairs		3,900
	Miscellaneous		2,200

The balance in Manufacturing Overhead is now $45,400. The entry to apply overhead is:

(8)	Work-in-Process Inventory	$42,000	
	Manufacturing Overhead		$42,000

Completion of Jobs. Jobs EC-25 and LP-12 were completed in January. The costs of these jobs (see Exhibit 5–3) must be transferred to Finished Goods in a total of $86,830 ($41,450 + $45,380).

(9)	Finished Goods Inventory	$86,830	
	Work-in-Process Inventory		$86,830

Sales.   Assume that job EC-25 was sold for $83,500 and that job LP-12 remains on hand at January 31. Assume that the sale was for cash. Entry 11 records the cost of the job sold.

(10)	Cash	$83,500	
	Sales		$83,500
(11)	Cost of Goods Sold	$41,450	
	Finished Goods Inventory		$41,450

Selling and Administrative Expenses.   Finally, assume that selling and administrative expenses for January, all paid in cash, were $22,300. For simplicity, the detailed listing of individual expenses is omitted.

| (12) | Selling and Administrative Expenses | $22,300 | |
| | Cash | | $22,300 |

Let us look more closely at some of these entries. Entries 1, 3, 4, 6 and 12 would be made more or less continuously throughout the period. They relate to purchasing materials, accruing and paying the payroll, recording overhead costs, and incurring and paying selling and administrative expenses. These activities are carried on constantly during a period, in contrast to events such as the sale of a job, as captured in entries 10 and 11. For a job order firm, sales are sporadic, being made at intervals of several days or even weeks. This condition is caused by the firm's making goods to order and making relatively few batches of goods. Of course, some job order firms will finish and sell several batches a week or even a day if they do many small jobs. Printing shops, for example, might operate that way.

Entries 2, 5, 7 and 8 would be made at the end of a period, such as a week or month, depending on how often the firm wants to update its records. These entries reclassify costs from their object categories to product costs—costs that are considered in the determination of inventory. Job order cost sheets may well be more up-to-date than the Work-in-Process general ledger account during a period, but at the end of a period both records should agree.

Trace the flows of costs through the accounts in Exhibit 5–5 to be sure that you understand them.

Disposition of Over- and Underapplied Overhead

At the end of a year over- or underapplied overhead is disposed of in one of two ways. First, if the amount is relatively small, perhaps less than 5 percent of total overhead, it may be included in cost of goods sold. Thus if costs of goods sold including applied overhead were $2,355,500 and underapplied overhead were $2,500, the $2,500 would simply be added to cost of goods sold. In the same way, a small amount of overapplied overhead would be subtracted from cost of goods sold. With this method, underapplied over-

EXHIBIT 5-5
Accounts for the Manners Company

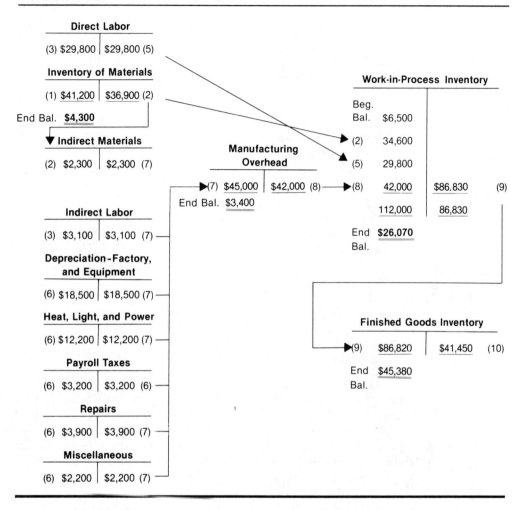

head is treated as a period cost, not as a product cost. Overapplied overhead is treated as a negative period cost.

However, if the amount of over- or underapplied overhead is relatively large, the usual procedure is to allocate it to Finished Goods Inventory, Work-in-Process Inventory, and Cost of Sales in proportion to the amounts of applied overhead included in those categories. This procedure essentially results in the firm's using actual overhead costing for the year. Exhibit 5-6 on page 212 shows how the procedure is employed.

The principal reason for allocating the over- or underapplied overhead and essentially going to an actual costing basis is that financial reporting requires substantially all costs of manufacturing to be included in the de-

EXHIBIT 5–6
Illustration of Proration of Overhead

Data

Total actual overhead	$345,000	
Total applied overhead	305,000	
Underapplied overhead	$ 40,000	

Amounts of Applied Overhead		*Percent of Total*
Work-in-process inventory	$ 45,750	15%
Finished goods inventory	76,250	25%
Cost of goods sold	183,000	60%
Totals	$305,000	100%

Allocations: $40,000 × Percent of Total

Work-in-process inventory:	$40,000 × 15% =	$ 6,000
Finished goods inventory:	$40,000 × 25% =	10,000
Cost of goods sold:	$40,000 × 60% =	24,000
Total underapplied overhead allocated		$40,000

Journal Entry

Work-in-Process Inventory	$ 6,000	
Finished Goods Inventory	10,000	
Cost of Goods Sold	24,000	
Factory Overhead		$40,000

termination of inventory and cost of goods sold. Notice that if a firm has no inventories at the end of the year, all its manufacturing costs including total actual overhead will show up as expenses on the income statement, because they obviously cannot be included in inventory. Hence the procedure shown in Exhibit 5–6 will differ from a direct charge or credit to cost of goods sold only if there are relatively large inventories at year's end.

When allocating overapplied or underapplied overhead, it is important to remember that the basis for allocation is the applied overhead for the current period. Job order costing is essentially a specific identification method of costing, so you must determine where the overhead applied during the current period has gone, ignoring overhead in the beginning inventories of finished goods and work in process.

An example should clarify the procedure. Assume the following facts and that all jobs in the beginning inventories were sold during the period.

Overhead applied during current period	$300,000
Underapplied overhead to be allocated	20,000
Applied overhead in ending inventories	30,000
Overhead in beginning inventories	32,000
Total overhead in cost of goods sold ($32,000 + $300,000 − $30,000)	302,000

We see that $270,000 in overhead applied during the current period is included in cost of goods sold. We could determine this in one of two ways. First, removing the $32,000 overhead in the beginning inventories from cost of goods sold leaves $270,000 ($302,000 − $32,000) that arose during the current period. Second, of the $300,000 applied during the period, $30,000 is in ending inventories so that $270,000 ($300,000 − $30,000) must be in cost of goods sold. The disposition of the $20,000 underapplied overhead is then $18,000 to cost of goods sold [$20,000 × ($270,000/$300,000)] and $2,000 to ending inventories [$20,000 × ($30,000/$300,000)].

A third treatment can be used at interim dates, such as the ends of months, quarters, or halves of the year. This treatment is to show the amount of over- or underapplied overhead, respectively, as a current liability or current asset. Opinion 28 of the Accounting Principles Board recommends this treatment for interim financial reporting.[3] It is appropriate when the firm *expects* to have over- or underapplied overhead at the end of an interim period such as the first quarter or first half of the year. An expected difference between applied and incurred overhead would relate to either or both of the factors we have already discussed—uneven incurrence of some fixed overhead items and uneven amounts of activity in direct labor hours—or to any other measure used to set the predetermined overhead rate.

Conceptually, and procedurally, treatment can best be explained and rationalized using the Anderson Company data below. The firm follows a policy of pricing its products at 150 percent of total manufacturing cost, including applied overhead. For simplicity ignore selling and administrative expenses. There were no inventories on hand at June 30 or December 31.

ANDERSON COMPANY

Predetermined overhead rate for year	$4 per labor hour based on $400,000 budgeted overhead and 100,000 budgeted labor hours

Results of Operations

	January–June	July–December
Direct labor hours worked	40,000	60,000
Applied overhead at $4 per hour	$160,000	$240,000
Actual overhead incurred	190,000	210,000
Over- (under-)applied overhead	($ 30,000)	$ 30,000

[3] Accounting Principles Board, *Opinion No. 28: Interim Financial Reporting* (New York: American Institute of Certified Public Accountants, 1973).

Income statements using actual overhead costs appear below. The figures *cost of sales excluding overhead* are assumed.

Sales	$750,000	$1,125,000
Cost of sales excluding overhead	340,000	510,000
Incurred overhead	190,000	210,000
Total actual cost of sales	530,000	720,000
Gross profit	$220,000	$ 405,000
Gross profit percentage of sales	29.3%	36%

Notice that using actual incurred overhead in cost of sales results in the gross profit ratios' differing greatly in the two periods. These results might mislead investors and managers. The different rates make it appear that the firm was much more profitable in the second six months than in the first six. Using the method recommended under Opinion 28 would provide the following results.

	January–June	July–December
Sales	$750,000	$1,125,000
Cost of sales including applied overhead	500,000	750,000
Gross profit	$250,000	$ 375,000
Gross profit percentage of sales	33.33%	33.33%

The $30,000 in underapplied overhead would appear on the June 30 balance sheet as a current asset. It represents a deferral of costs to the following period, the second half of the year. At the end of the year there would be no balance-sheet effect because there would be no overapplied or underapplied overhead for the year as a whole. The overapplied amount of $30,000 in the second half of the year would cancel out the $30,000 underapplied amount in the first half of the year.

Departmental Overhead Rates

Our illustration involving the Manners Company used a single overhead rate. All labor hours were assumed to contribute equally to overhead whether they were from fabrication, assembly, or any other department in the Manners Company plant. Sometimes the assumption that a single rate can serve is unwarranted; in this case, firms will use departmental overhead rates instead of a single, plantwide rate. A **departmental overhead rate** is used to apply the overhead of a single department. Each department has its own rate, and individual departments might use different measures of volume to allocate overhead costs.

The basic procedures of applying overhead remain the same as in the single-rate case, except that the relevant activity (labor hours, machine hours, labor cost) in each department governs the amount of overhead applied. Additionally, separate overhead accounts are kept for each department so that overapplied and underapplied overhead can be calculated for each.

Two conditions encourage the use of departmental overhead rates. First, different departments' overhead costs may be associated with different measures of activity. Some departments may be very capital intensive, using a great deal of machinery. Such departments may find that overhead costs are closely related to machine hours rather than to labor hours. The use of a machine-hour basis for application would be more accurate than a labor-hour basis. Other departments in the same firm may be labor intensive, using little machinery, and may be best served by rates based on labor hours or dollars. Clearly, if some departments should be using machine hours, others labor hours, a single rate will not suffice.

Second, overhead may vary so much from department to department that a single rate obscures important differences. Consider the data given below. They illustrate the principle that a single rate averages the individual rates and that significant differences in costs would result for products that differed in times spent in different departments.

Department	Budgeted Overhead	Budgeted Labor Hours	Overhead Rate
Department I	$200,000	50,000	$4
Department II	100,000	50,000	2
Total plant	$300,000	100,000	$3

Job	Department I Hours	Department II Hours	Total Hours	Applied Overhead Single Rate—$3	Applied Overhead Departmental Rate[a]
M-3	100	20	120	$360	$440
M-4	20	100	120	360	280

[a] $4 × hours in Department I plus $2 × hours in Department II

The point of this example is that misleading results might follow the use of an overall rate. This problem is especially critical if there is a large variable component in overhead. If, in the example given, all overhead were variable, the firm would seriously miscalculate its costs using the average rate of $3 unless each job required the same labor time in both departments. The firm might accept work prices at less than variable cost if it used the $3 rate for jobs that required much more time in department I than in department II.

SOME REFINEMENTS AND ALTERNATIVES

Having looked at some alternative ways of dealing with overapplied and underapplied overhead, we now examine some alternatives relating to other aspects of product costing.

Multiple Work-in-Process Accounts

Some firms will keep separate Work-in-Process accounts for direct materials, direct labor, and manufacturing overhead, having three accounts instead of one. In such cases the procedures are essentially the same, except that each element of cost is recorded in a separate account. An illustrative journal entry would be:

Work in Process—Direct Labor	$XXXX	
Direct Labor		$XXXX

This entry would have two counterparts: one for direct materials, the other for overhead. So far as end results are concerned, this method does not differ significantly from the single account. The entry to record the completion of a job would have three credits to the work-in-process inventory accounts, rather than one.

Finished Goods Inventory	$XXXX	
Work in Process—Direct Labor		$XXXX
Work in Process—Direct Materials		XXXX
Work in Process—Overhead		XXXX

Manufacturing Overhead Applied

Many firms use an account called Manufacturing Overhead Applied, which is credited for the amounts of overhead applied during the period. Manufacturing Overload is debited for overhead costs incurred but not credited for amounts applied. The difference between the balances in these two accounts is the amount of overapplied or underapplied overhead. If the Manners Company had used these two accounts, they would have appeared as follows at the end of January:

Manufacturing Overhead	Manufacturing Overhead Applied
$45,400	$42,000

The difference between the two amounts is the underapplied overhead for January. At year end, or whenever else the accounts are to be closed, the balances in each account are offset by entries crediting Manufacturing Overhead and debiting Manufacturing Overhead Applied. If the Manners Company had decided to close the underapplied overhead for January to cost of goods sold, it would have made the following entry.

Cost of Goods Sold	$ 3,400	
Manufacturing Overhead Applied	42,000	
Manufacturing Overhead		$45,400

Again, this refinement does not change the final results. Its principal purpose is to keep the major cost account for overhead directly related to actual costs. The balancing entry clearly shows that the $3,400 is under-applied overhead.

Labor and Overhead

We have seen that some labor costs, such as indirect labor, are considered overhead rather than direct labor. Direct labor costs charged to the Work-in-Process account are only those direct labor hours productively worked on specific jobs. Workers classified as direct laborers will frequently work more hours than they charge to individual jobs. If machines are being reset, or if materials have run out, or if some other temporary stoppage of work is experienced, direct laborers will be idle. The cost of idle time is often treated as an overhead cost. It is sometimes treated as an expense of the period, like selling and administrative expenses, and does not enter into the determination of inventory costs.

If idle time is a necessary consequence of the production process and of management decisions, it will be budgeted as overhead and included as an element of total overhead costs. For example, the firm may have a policy of providing some specified minimum number of hours of work for its labor force. The policy might be based partly on the concern that frequent layoffs would result in skilled workers' leaving the firm. It would be reasonable to call such idle time a cost of the products produced and to include the costs as overhead.

When a firm does plan for and budget idle time, it will calculate its predetermined overhead rate based on the budgeted productive hours, rather than total budgeted hours. For example, if the firm expects total direct labor hours to be 100,000, with 5 percent idle time, it will use 95,000 hours in the denominator of the calculation. It will also include 5 percent of expected direct labor cost as an overhead element.

However, if idle time is experienced beyond the normal budgeted amount, it may be considered an expense of the period on the grounds that it does not contribute to the making of products and, therefore, should not be part of the cost of products. Thus, if idle time occurs because of continual machine breakdowns, it may be considered an expense of the period and not part of overhead cost.

Overtime Premium

Overtime premium is the difference between the total wage rate paid for overtime work and the normal wage rate. If a worker who normally receives $5 per hour works an hour of overtime at time and a half, he receives $7.50 for that hour. Of that amount, $2.50 is the overtime premium. Overtime premium is usually considered an overhead cost, not part of direct labor cost. The reasoning is as follows. Overtime work is required because there is more work than can be done during normal working hours. This cost should be borne by all jobs, rather than just by the jobs being worked on during the overtime period. For example, if jobs A and B are worked on during a particular day, it really does not matter which was worked on during normal hours, which during overtime hours. If job B is done during the overtime period, it should not be charged with the overtime premium, because the scheduling was in all likelihood arbitrary. To penalize job B makes no economic sense.

The one exception to the general rule would occur if a rush order were received and accepted, and this order required that the factory work overtime. Then, even if the rush job were worked on during normal hours, it might be charged with overtime premium on the ground that its acceptance was the cause of the overtime.

Departmental Accounts

Job order firms that are departmentalized may use separate accounts for direct labor and overhead costs for each department. Thus there would be accounts such as Direct Labor—Assembly, Direct Labor—Fabrication, Depreciation—Assembly Department Equipment, and so on. Such accounts would be helpful in analyzing overapplied and underapplied overhead by department when departmental rates were used. They would also be helpful in controlling costs because they would be identified by responsibility—the departmental cost accounts reflect the performance of the departmental manager.

The control aspect of departmentalized accounts can be achieved without using such accounts if labor and overhead costs are analyzed by department even though recorded only in total. Many firms use what is called a *departmental cost sheet,* or *departmental expense analysis.* Whatever the title, the sheet is essentially a supplementary record detailing costs by department. The sheet would be used by a manager wishing to determine whether individual departments were staying within their established budgets.

Variable and Fixed Overhead Accounts

Planning, control, and decision making are enhanced by the separation of costs into fixed and variable components. Some firms use separate accounts for fixed and variable overhead. The basic procedures would remain the same, except that the individual overhead costs would be gathered into one or the other account depending on their behavioral patterns. Two different rates would be used to put overhead costs into Work in Process—a variable overhead rate and a fixed overhead rate. Each job would have two entries associated with overhead.

The advantage of using two overhead rates and accounts is that the managers may look at individual jobs from the standpoint of the contribution margin that they generate, rather than the so-called profit, which includes allocated fixed costs. Decisions regarding pricing, accepting special orders, and subcontracting work are better made if information regarding cost behavior is available.

SUMMARY

Absorption costing, in which fixed manufacturing costs are allocated to units of product or to specific jobs, is required for financial reporting and income tax accounting. Absorption costing is not compatible with cost-volume-profit analysis and with planning and control. It is useful and necessary in situations where pricing depends on cost.

Firms that make unique products use job order costing, in which costs are accumulated by individual job. Direct materials and direct labor are charged to jobs as used. Manufacturing overhead is applied to jobs using predetermined rates that are based on budgeted overhead for a period and on budgeted activity for the same period. Activity is usually defined by reference to an input factor such as direct labor cost, direct labor hours, or machine hours.

APPENDIX 5–A: SOURCE DOCUMENTS IN JOB ORDER COSTING

This appendix describes and illustrates the procedures that underlie job order cost accounting systems. The chapter stated that the basic document is the job order sheet, which details the costs of each job and serves as a subsidiary ledger to the Work-in-Process Inventory account. The principal documents that we describe are the materials requisition and the work ticket. These documents are the references for the charges of materials and direct labor to individual jobs.

Because individual pieces of material and individual blocks of labor time must be charged to specific jobs, job order costing requires voluminous records. Therefore, job order systems are expensive to operate and are subject to errors and deliberate deception. From a behavioral standpoint, any recording system that requires workers to specify the time spent on various tasks is open to deception. Consider a foreman in charge of three jobs, one of which is taking much more time than estimated, while the others are running well. He might be tempted to have workers charge some of their time spent on the problem job to the other jobs, so that the records would not draw attention to the slow-moving job.

Direct Materials

All materials, both direct and indirect, are generally stored in a central location. Workers needing materials for individual jobs go to the storeroom and pick up the required items. The issuance of materials is recorded on a requisition, such as the one shown in Exhibit 5A–1. Periodically the requisitions will be sorted by job and the job order sheets brought up to date. The sorted requisitions might be summarized on a worksheet called a Summary of Material Requisitions, or Material Use Summary. This schedule would also serve to make the journal entry to record the issuance of materials.

EXHIBIT 5A–1
Materials Requisition Form and Material Use Summary

BINGHAM MANUFACTURING COMPANY

Material Requisition   Requisition Number_____

Date_____   Department_____   Job Number_____

Quantity	Description	Cost	Total

Received by:_____   Approved:_____

Material Use Summary

Date	Requisition Number	Job Number	Description	Quantity	Cost

Direct Labor

Workers will fill out work tickets (also called job tickets, job time tickets, and time tickets) indicating the time spent on each job. Like material requisitions, these tickets will be summarized periodically and posted to the job order sheets, perhaps through the medium of a labor cost summary or labor cost recapitulation. Examples of these documents appear in Exhibit 5A–2.

EXHIBIT 5A–2
Time Ticket and Direct Labor Summary

BINGHAM MANUFACTURING COMPANY

Time Ticket

Employee_____   Hourly Rate _____

Clock No._____   Date _____

Department _____   Job No. _____

Operation_____   Approved _____

Time Started_____

Time Finished_____

Total Time _____

Direct Labor Summary							
Date	Ticket No.	Job No.	Department	Operation	Hours	Rate	Cost

In many job order firms workers will indicate the time that they do not spend working on particular jobs. As it sometimes happens, there might not be enough work, or workers must wait for materials or wait for machinists to set up or to repair machinery. The total time worked on jobs, plus the idle time, should equal the total time for which workers are paid during a period. Making the reconciliation of the time tickets with the total hours that are paid for should enable managers to determine whether all entries to the job order sheets have been made, although it will not prevent incorrect entries. For example, a worker may charge the wrong job on his time ticket, or a posting could be made to the wrong job order sheet. Again, the complexity and volume of job order records is one of the problems of that type of system. Therefore, management should ensure that there is a good internal auditing system so that records are accurate. Exhibit 5A–3 summarizes the cost flows and source documents for direct materials and direct labor.

EXHIBIT 5A–3
Summary of Cost Flows for Direct Materials and Direct Labor

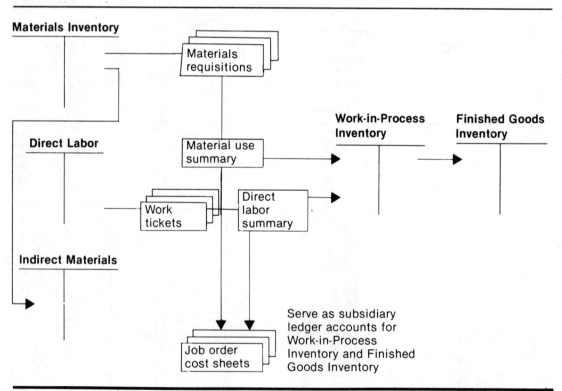

ASSIGNMENTS

5–1 Actual Overhead Cost.   One of your classmates is puzzled at the use of predetermined overhead rates.'Specifically, he asks you: "How is it possible to 'apply' overhead and still have correct figures? If there was one thing I learned in financial accounting, it was that accounting is based on what has actually happened, which seems to me to mean that you should always use actual overhead costs."

Required: Answer your classmate's question.

5–2 Statement of Cost of Goods Manufactured and Sold.   Use the information given below to prepare a statement of cost of goods manufactured and sold for the Cronin Company for the year ended June 30, 19X7. All data are in thousands of dollars.

Direct labor	$2,456
Purchases of materials	1,987
Inventory of materials, June 30, 19X7	171
Inventory of materials, July 1, 19X6	203
Inventory of finished goods, June 30, 19X7	451
Inventory of finished goods, July 1, 19X6	397
Factory overhead	3,124
Inventory of work in process, June 30, 19X7	96
Inventory of work in process, July 1, 19X6	102

5–3 Basic Job Order Cost Flows.   The Nezperse Company makes a variety of industrial fittings to customer order and uses a job order costing system. The following information comes from the records of the firm.

	Materials	Direct Labor
Inventories at July 31, 19X6:		
Finished goods	$12,345	$21,541
Work in process	7,539	12,312
Costs put into process in August, 19X6	$70,634	$90,870
Inventories at August 31, 19X6:		
Finished goods	$11,235	$19,790
Work in process	4,560	11,290

The firm applies overhead at 150 percent of direct labor cost. Actual overhead for August was $128,978.

Required:

1. Determine the total amounts of July 31 inventories of finished goods and work in process.

2. Determine ending inventories of finished goods and work in process.

3. Determine cost of goods sold for August, assuming that any over-applied or underapplied overhead is: (a) deferred until year end and so ignored in monthly income statements; (b) treated as an adjustment to cost of goods sold for the month; and (c) allocated to cost of sales and ending inventories based on the relative shares of overhead applied during the month. For part (c) assume that all beginning inventories of finished goods and work in process were sold during August.

5–4 Overhead Rates. The following data are expected results for the Johnson Company, which manufactures plumbing supplies.

	Department I	Department II	Total
Budgeted overhead for 19X5	$220,000	$245,000	$465,000
Budgeted direct labor cost for 19X5	$ 55,000	$100,000	$155,000

During the year, the firm worked on a number of jobs. Data for two such jobs appear below.

	Job	
	K-65	M-42
Materials	$2,500	$3,800
Direct labor:		
Department I	6,000	2,000
Department II	1,000	8,000

Required:

1. Compute the total cost of each job, assuming that the firm used a plantwide overhead rate, predetermined using the budgeted data given above.

2. Compute the total cost of each job assuming that the firm used departmental overhead rates, predetermined using the budgeted data given above.

3. Comment on the differences in your answers to items 1 and 2. Is there any reason to favor one method or the other?

5–5 Basic Job Order Costing. The Richman Company makes special machinery used for bottling various types of liquids. Each machine differs in some respects from all others, and the firm therefore uses job order costing. The firm had the following jobs in process at March 31, 19X6. It applies overhead using a single, plantwide rate of $2 per direct labor dollar. There was no finished goods inventory in March.

	Job		
	3-12	3-16	3-17
Direct materials	$ 4,120	$ 3,875	$2,685
Direct labor	6,387	8,642	2,375
Overhead	12,774	17,284	4,750
Total costs	$23,281	$29,801	$9,810

During April, 19X6, the firm completed these three jobs and began several others. The materials and labor required to complete the jobs in process at March 31 were as follows.

	3-12	3-16	3-17
Direct materials	$1,820	$2,750	$6,140
Direct labor	1,530	1,956	5,110

The cost of all jobs *started and completed* in April was $147,800, including applied overhead of $74,600. At the end of April the following jobs were in process.

	4-13	4-19
Materials	$1,986	$6,945
Direct labor	2,890	8,985

Actual overhead incurred in April was $124,380. At April 30, jobs in the inventory of finished goods had total costs of $32,680, including $12,456 in applied overhead.

Required: Determine the ending inventory of work in process and cost of goods sold for April. Assume that overapplied or underapplied overhead is written off as an adjustment to cost of goods sold.

5–6 Actual Costing and Normal Costing. The Rosen Company worked on three jobs in April of 19X6. Data on the jobs appear below.

	Job		
	97	98	99
Materials used	$12,500	$9,300	$25,300
Direct labor	11,900	8,500	13,600

The firm incurred factory overhead costs of $74,800.

Required:

1. Determine the total cost of each job, assuming that the firm uses actual costing, allocating total incurred overhead to individual jobs based on the relative amounts of direct labor cost in each job.

2. Determine the total cost of each job, assuming that the firm uses normal costing, applying overhead cost to individual jobs at a predetermined rate of $2 per direct labor dollar.

3. Give two reasons why the overhead costs allocated to the jobs might have differed under items 1 and 2 above.

4. Discuss the advantages and disadvantages of each of the two allocation methods used above.

5-7 Basic Entries. Macon Enterprises has a job costing system based on actual costs. During January the following occurred.

1. Purchases of materials included 70,000 lb of berium and 37,500 lb of tedium for a total cost of $72,650. There was no beginning inventory of materials.

2. At the beginning of the month, work in process included two jobs totaling $14,000 in material and $23,000 in labor and overhead costs. During January $70,000 of new material was used along with $50,000 in direct labor, $26,000 in indirect labor and supplies, and $25,000 in fixed overhead. Ending inventory of work in process included $20,000 in material and $31,000 in labor and overhead.

3. There was no inventory of finished goods at either 1/1 or 1/31.

Required: Make the appropriate journal entries and T-accounts.

5-8 Disposition of Overhead. The Ballston Manufacturing Company uses job order costing. During 19X6 the firm had the following results.

	Jobs Completed and Sold	Jobs in Ending Finished Goods Inventory	Jobs in Ending Work-in-Process Inventory
Materials	$300,000	$ 50,000	$20,000
Direct labor	850,000	100,000	50,000

The firm had actual overhead of $1,450,000. During the year, it used a predetermined overhead rate of $1.50 per direct labor dollar to apply overhead.

Required:

1. Determine cost of sales, ending finished goods inventory, and ending work-in-process inventory using normal costing.

2. Determine the same items that you did above, assuming that the firm prorates overhead that is overapplied or underapplied based on the relative amounts of applied overhead in each category.

5-9 Cost of Goods Manufactured (AICPA adapted). The Halprin Corporation uses a job order costing system, charging actual material and direct labor costs and applied overhead costs to its jobs. The information available is:

1. During 19X7 the firm incurred material costs of $340,000 used on jobs and $300,000 in direct labor costs.
2. The firm incurred overhead of $475,000. It applied overhead at 150 percent of direct labor cost.
3. Cost of goods manufactured, using actual materials and labor and applied overhead, was $1,050,000.
4. Beginning work-in-process inventory was 60 percent of ending work-in-process inventory.

Required: Prepare a statement of cost of goods manufactured.

5-10 Journal Entries. The Arcadia Company, a job order firm, began the month of October with the following balances.

Materials inventory	$22,435
Work-in-process inventory	67,492
Finished goods inventory	37,896

The following events occurred during October.

1. Materials purchases were $96,400.
2. Materials costing $91,200 were charged out to jobs.
3. Direct labor incurred and charged to jobs was $241,360.
4. The firm applied overhead to jobs at a rate of 150 percent of direct labor cost.
5. Actual overhead incurred was $347,500.
6. Jobs costing $657,320 were completed and sent to finished goods storage.
7. Jobs costing $622,480 were sold for $987,600, all sales on credit.

Required:

1. Prepare journal entries to record the events given above. The firm allows overapplied or underapplied overhead to accumulate in Factory Overhead until year end (December 31). Do not write explanations for the entries.
2. Prepare T-accounts for the three inventory accounts and post the appropriate entries to them. Determine the ending balances in the inventory accounts.

5-11 Overhead Rates, Application, and Proration. The Hart Company manufactures pumping equipment. All pumps go through the fabrication and assembly departments, although different types spend different proportions of time in each department. The firm's cost accountant has developed the following equations for budgeting overhead for the coming year, 19X6:

fabrication department overhead = $487,300 + $9.62X_1$
assembly department overhead = $164,200 + $4.21X_2$

where: X_1 = direct labor hours in the fabrication department
          X_2 = direct labor hours in the assembly department

Budgeted direct labor hours for 19X6 are 31,600 for fabrication and 17,650 for assembly.

At the end of 19X5 the firm had inventories of finished goods and work in process with $45,225 in overhead from the fabrication department, $22,105 from the assembly department.

During 19X6 the firm experienced the following.

	Fabrication	Assembly
Total direct labor hours	32,175	16,120
Labor hours on jobs:		
In ending inventory of finished goods	2,165	1,310
In ending inventory of work in process	1,720	880
Actual overhead costs	$821,090	$229,748

Required:

1. Determine the overhead rates for the two departments, using the budgeted overhead costs and budgeted direct labor hours. Round to the nearest tenth of a cent.

2. Determine the amounts of applied overhead in each ending inventory and in cost of goods sold and prorate each department's overapplied or underapplied overhead to the appropriate places. Determine the actual overhead costs in each ending inventory and in cost of goods sold.

5–12 Actual Job Order Costing. The Delvan Company makes small electric machines and uses a job order costing system. The firm uses actual costing: at month end its chief accountant calculates an overhead rate based on actual results and applies overhead to jobs using that rate. The rate is expressed as overhead cost per direct labor dollar.

During March, 19X8, the firm had the following results:

Total overhead cost	$124,200
Total direct labor cost	$ 77,625

The firm worked on the following jobs in March. There were no beginning inventories.

	M-01	M-02	M-03
Materials	$21,365	$15,420	$ 8,760
Direct labor	18,300	39,825	19,500

Jobs M-01 and M-02 were finished. Job M-01 was sold for $97,200. Job M-02 remained in inventory of finished goods, and job M-03 remained in work-in-process inventory. Selling and administrative expenses were $37,230.

Required:

1. Determine the cost of ending inventory of work in process and of finished goods.

2. Prepare an income statement for March.

5–13 Relationships.   The following fragmentary information is available from the records of the QL Company. All data relate to the year ended December 31, 19X8. The firm writes off any overapplied or underapplied overhead to cost of goods sold. The predetermined overhead rate is $2 per direct labor dollar.

Overhead incurred	$_____
Overhead applied	$310,000
Beginning inventories:	
Materials	$ 88,000
Work in process	$110,000
Finished goods	$_____
Ending inventories:	
Materials	$ 95,000
Work in process	$120,000
Finished goods	$104,000
Cost of goods sold, including $3,000 underapplied overhead	$644,000
Cost of goods manufactured, excluding any underapplied overhead	$_____
Cost of materials put into process	$_____
Purchases of materials	$207,000
Direct labor cost	$_____

Required: Fill in the blanks, then check your work by preparing a statement of cost of goods manufactured and sold.

5–14 Dual Overhead Rates.   The controller of Pittston Industries, a job order manufacturing company, developed the following estimated overhead rates for the coming year.

Variable overhead rate	$7.20 per direct labor hour
Fixed overhead rate	5.60 per direct labor hour

The controller told the president that he wanted to apply variable and fixed overhead separately in order to give the firm's managers better information. The president said that he saw no benefits from the procedure and asked the controller why the current policy of using a single overhead rate should not be continued.

Required: Comment on the controller's proposal.

5-15 Overhead Application and Cost Control. The Princeton Electronics Company makes a variety of equipment for industrial customers. The firm uses normal costing, applying overhead to individual jobs at a rate of $6 per direct labor hour. The variable component of the rate is $3.60. The fixed component of $2.40 is based on $288,000 annual budgeted fixed overhead and 120,000 annual budgeted direct labor hours. Fixed overhead is expected to fall evenly in each month of the year.

During the first three months of the year the firm's results were

	January	February	March
Actual variable overhead	$28,800	$34,000	$45,200
Actual fixed overhead	$22,000	$22,000	$26,000
Actual direct labor hours	8,000	10,000	12,000

Required:

1. Determine the amounts of overapplied or underapplied overhead for each month.

2. Using the available information, comment on the causes of the overapplied or underapplied overhead. For example, were actual costs greater than budgeted costs in any month? Was activity, expressed in direct labor hours, above or below normal in any month?

5-16 Actual Costing. The Barnes Company makes small measuring devices for industrial companies. Several of its products are relatively standard, including a pressure gauge, model YZ-361. The firm uses actual job order costing. At the end of each month a clerk divides total factory overhead incurred by total direct labor hours. He then multiplies the overhead rate per labor hour by the number of hours on each job to determine overhead cost for the job.

The firm produced a lot of 50 units of YZ-361 in April, and another in July. The materials and labor for each 50-unit batch appear below.

	April Order	July Order
Materials	$680	$705
Direct labor at $8 per hour	760	736

Total factory overhead and direct labor hours were as follows:

	April	July
Total factory overhead	$162,360	$152,440
Total direct labor hours	12,300	9,200

Required:

1. Determine the total cost of each of the two batches of YZ-361.

2. Do the results of item 1 indicate that the firm was more or less efficient in April than in July? Why or why not? What other information would you need to give an opinion about efficiency?

5-17 Normal Costing.   Some results of the Barnes Company appeared in Assignment 5-16. Suppose now that the firm uses normal costing, with a predetermined overhead rate based on the following budgeted figures:

total annual budgeted overhead = $1,560,000 + $2.50 per direct labor hour

total budgeted direct labor hours = 120,000

The firm's chief cost accountant expects fixed overhead to be incurred about equally in each month, at $130,000. Direct labor hours fluctuate from month to month.

Required:

1. Calculate the predetermined overhead rate from the data given above.

2. Determine the total costs of each of the two jobs described in Assignment 5-16.

3. Determine the amounts of overapplied or underapplied overhead for April and for July.

5-18 Application of Overhead and Pricing Policy.   The Winters Company makes industrial instruments and uses a job order costing system. Customers ask the firm to bid on machines of particular specifications, and Winters must be the lowest bidder to get the job. When the firm receives the specifications, an estimator develops an analysis of the material and labor requirements. He then applies overhead, based on direct labor hours, using the firm's predetermined rate. This analysis goes to the marketing manager, who sets a price, usually 125 percent of total expected production cost.

The firm has typically set its predetermined overhead rate based on direct labor hours at 80 percent of capacity. Capacity is about 400,000 hours per year. The president of the firm has told the controller that he should use 70 percent of capacity to set the rate for 19X6, arguing that "we should absorb our overhead faster so that we can be more certain that we don't have a lot of underapplied overhead."

Budgeted overhead is $1.8 million fixed and about $1.80 variable with direct labor hours. The average wage rate is $10 per hour for direct laborers. The controller believes from prior experience that the cost of materials used is generally about 60 percent of direct labor cost. Selling and administrative expenses, virtually all fixed, are budgeted at $650,000. The firm has negligible inventories.

Required:

1. Compute the predetermined overhead rate that the firm would use if it budgeted direct labor hours (a) at 80 percent of capacity, and (b) at 70 percent of capacity.

2. Suppose that a particular job should take about 50 direct labor hours and that materials will be about 60 percent of labor cost. What would the price of the job be, using each of the two predetermined overhead rates that you calculated above and setting price at 125 percent of production cost?

3. Prepare income statements assuming (a) the firm uses 80 percent of capacity to set the overhead rate and also works at 80 percent of capacity, and (b) the firm sets the overhead rate using 70 percent of capacity and works at 70 percent of capacity. (Notice that there will be no overapplied or underapplied overhead, because actual hours will equal budgeted hours.) Assume the same relationships as in item 2.

4. Suppose that the firm will use 70 percent of capacity to set the predetermined overhead rate. How many hours must it actually work to earn the amount you calculated for 80 percent of capacity in item 3? Because there are no inventories, you can use volume-cost-profit analysis here.

5. What do you recommend?

5–19   Selecting Bases for Overhead Rates.   The managers of the Magill Furniture Company have been thinking about changing the bases that the firm uses to charge overhead to jobs. The firm currently uses a plantwide rate of $4 per direct labor hour but finds that it misapplies overhead by wide margins. One of the managers collected data from the past 24 months of operations and developed the following regression equations. Standard errors of the b coefficients are in parentheses. Y_t is total factory overhead; Y_1 and Y_2 are overhead in the fabrication and assembly departments, respectively; D_t, D_1, and D_2 are direct labor hours—total, fabrication, and assembly, respectively; and M_t, M_1, and M_2 are machine hours—total, fabrication, and assembly.

$$Y_t = \$789,542 + \$1.27D_t, \quad r^2 = 0.237, \quad Se = \$203,245$$
$$(\$0.97)$$
$$Y_t = \$691,452 + \$1.68M_t, \quad r^2 = 0.452, \quad Se = \$143,220$$
$$(\$0.76)$$
$$Y_1 = \$302,350 + \$2.23D_1, \quad r^2 = 0.593, \quad Se = \$63,245$$
$$(\$0.68)$$
$$Y_1 = \$237,980 + \$3.86M_1, \quad r^2 = 0.708, \quad Se = \$39,697$$
$$(\$1.07)$$
$$Y_2 = \$157,320 + \$2.96D_2, \quad r^2 = 0.672, \quad Se = \$28,729$$
$$(\$1.02)$$

$$Y_2 = \$276,230 + \$0.72M_2, \quad r^2 = 0.302, \quad Se = \$78,972$$
$$(\$0.43)$$

Required: Make recommendations to the managers regarding the overhead application rates.

5-20 Overhead Rates and Pricing. The Glenway Company manufactures pumping equipment. Some of its jobs require a great many components and parts that the firm must buy from outside suppliers, while others need a great deal of fabrication, milling, and other operations because the firm must make them to order.

The controller of the firm develops a plantwide overhead rate in advance of each year. Late in 19X4 she used the following data to develop the $3.275 rate that was to be used in 19X5:

	Estimates for 19X5	
Department	Overhead	Direct Labor Hours
Fabrication	$ 486,300	109,900
Grinding and milling	396,500	73,200
Assembly	285,200	173,500
Totals	$1,168,000	356,600

Rate per direct labor hour = $3.275 ($1,168,000/356,600)

The controller has instructed her staff to set prices at 120 percent of factory cost. The wage rates expected to prevail in 19X5 were $8.60 in the fabrication department, $6.40 in the grinding/milling department, and $5.20 in the assembly department.

During 19X5 the firm bid on many jobs, getting some and losing others. Data on two jobs appear below, reflecting expected costs.

	Jobs	
	A	B
Labor:		
Fabrication	$ 37,840 (4,400 hours)	$ 15,480 (1,800 hours)
Grinding/milling	17,664 (2,760 hours)	4,736 (740 hours)
Assembly	5,096 (980 hours)	11,024 (2,120 hours)
Materials	63,400	137,500
Total labor and materials	$124,000	$168,740

Required:

1. Determine the prices that Glenway would have bid for each job.
2. Suppose that a competitor of Glenway has exactly the same departmental setup, cost structure, expectations about labor hours, and

profit objective. The only difference is that the competitor uses departmental overhead rates to determine total factory costs. What would the competitor have bid for each job?

5-21 CVP Analysis in a Job Order Firm.   Armand Forman operates a machine shop that does job order work for larger industrial firms. Forman has been trying to determine what profit he is likely to earn in 19X7 and has amassed the following data:

Expected material cost	$200,000
Expected direct labor hours	40,000
Direct labor wage rate, per hour	$ 9
Expected factory overhead at 40,000 labor hours	$400,000
Expected selling and administrative expenses	$120,000

Forman believes that factory overhead is about 60 percent fixed, 40 percent variable at the budgeted level of direct labor hours and that the variable portion changes closely with direct labor hours. Selling and administrative expenses appear to be virtually fixed. Forman plans to apply overhead to jobs at $10 per direct labor hour and to charge prices at 120 percent of factory cost (materials, direct labor, and *applied* overhead). He keeps minimal inventories.

Required: Answer each question independently of the others.

1. What profit will Forman earn if all his predictions are correct?
2. What profit will he earn if he follows the pricing policy outlined above but is able to generate only 35,000 direct labor hours and $175,000 in material costs?
3. What markup over factory cost would give Forman a $100,000 profit?
4. Does the labor/material mix on Forman's jobs affect profitability? For example, would he earn the same profit on a job that required $2,000 in materials, $8,000 in direct labor, as he would on a job requiring $8,000 in materials, $2,000 in direct labor?

5-22 Overhead Rates and Profitability.   The following data relate to the March operations of Troy Foundry, Inc., which manufactures machinery.

	Department			
	Milling	Machining	Assembly	Total
Direct labor cost	$ 83,900	$225,000	$184,300	$493,200
Departmental overhead	230,400	379,600	147,600	757,600

The controller calculates an actual, plantwide overhead rate each month and uses that rate for costing jobs. He then reviews major jobs to see how profitable they were. The firm sets prices based on a gross profit objective of 20 percent of sales price. Estimators use the most recent available overhead rate in working up prices, which is usually the rate from the prior month.

After determining the March rate to be $1.5361 per labor dollar and costing out the jobs for the month, the controller turned to analyzing profitability, working with the following two jobs.

	Job	
	M-12	M-28
Price	$163,000	$245,000
Materials	$ 17,100	$ 46,700
Direct labor:		
Milling	28,500	8,600
Machining	12,200	39,600
Assembly	4,800	17,300
Overhead at $1.5361 per labor dollar	69,893	100,615
Total costs	132,493	212,815
Gross profit	$ 30,507	$ 32,185

At the levels of operation in March, variable overhead as percentages of total departmental overhead were about 70, 75, and 20 percent in milling, machining, and assembly, respectively.

The controller noted that neither job showed the target gross profit, with job M-28 being especially low.

Required:

1. Calculate the contribution margin earned on each job.
2. Can you offer some reasons why jobs would not show the target gross profit under the system that the firm uses?
3. Would you make any suggestions to the controller? If so, what?

5-23 Job Order Costing, Service Business. Grafton Associates is an engineering consulting firm employing 40 professional engineers and ten office, clerical, and other support personnel. The firm treats each client as a job, preparing a cost sheet that records salaries, overhead, and expenses such as travel and lodging incurred by employees working in the field.

Each employee fills out a weekly time report showing how much time he or she spent on a particular client's business and what expenses were incurred. The sheets also detail time spent on nonchargeable matters such as general administration or idle time between client engagements. The hourly cost of employee time is based on annual salary and a 2,000-hour working year, which is what the employees average. Phillip Grafton, the firm's owner, has instructed the clerks to apply overhead at the rate of 60 percent of salary cost.

Grafton has made the following estimates for the coming year, 19X6:

Salaries of professional staff	$1,188,000
Salaries of support personnel	121,000
Rent, utilities, and other costs not directly billable to clients	565,000

During the first week of January three employees worked on a job involving General Construction Company. Their time and expenses appear below.

Employee	Hours on Client Business	Expenses
Paul White	36	$360
Frederick DePrima	29	185
Ann Connor	22	0

White is a junior engineer earning $23,500 per year, DePrima a senior engineer earning $38,200, and Connor a supervisor earning $47,300. White's and DePrima's expenses related to travel they performed on behalf of the client.

Grafton bills clients for actual expenses (travel, etc.) and for twice the hourly salary cost of employees' work. He expects about 20 percent of the salaries of professional staff and 50 percent of salaries of support personnel to be nonchargeable and considers this nonchargeable time as part of overhead. (The overhead of $565,000 estimated for 19X6 does not include this salary cost. It is included in the salary figures for each category of employee given above.)

Required:

1. Compute the cost of work done for General Construction Company in the first week of January, using the firm's methods.

2. Determine the amount that Grafton will bill General.

3. Determine whether Grafton is likely to overapply or underapply overhead during 19X6.

4. What profit can Grafton expect for 19X6?

5. What overhead rate would Grafton have to use to fully apply overhead costs, including nonchargeable time?

5-24 Disposition of Overhead.   The text mentions three ways of dealing with over- or underapplied overhead. Assume a company has given you the following data.

1. Overhead is applied at $10 per unit based on normal volume of 10,000 units per month. Sixty percent of overhead is variable.

2. During the current month 8,500 units were produced while 10,500 were sold. Beginning inventory of finished goods included 3,000 units, which were all sold. There was no work in process either at the beginning or end of the month.

3. Actual overhead was $91,000.

Required: Using the above information, deal with under- or overapplied overhead in each of the three ways suggested in the text.

5–25 Overhead Rates. The Warner Company makes three products in three departments. It bases its prices on costs, as shown in the schedule below.

	Product		
	A	B	C
Direct materials	$ 10.00	$ 30.00	$ 50.00
Direct labor at $8/hour	40.00	48.00	88.00
Overhead at $7.80/DLH	39.00	46.80	85.80
Total cost	89.00	124.80	223.80
Allowance for profit at 15% of cost	13.35	18.72	33.57
Selling price	$102.35	$143.52	$257.37
Labor time required (hours/unit):			
Department I	0	4	2
Department II	1	0	6
Department III	4	2	3

The overhead rate of $7.80 was based on total estimated overhead and total estimated direct labor hours. Data by department are:

	Department		
	I	II	III
Variable overhead per DLH	$ 7.10	$ 4.10	$ 2.80
Fixed overhead per year	$300,000	$280,000	$171,000

The firm planned to produce 10,000 units of each product during the current year.

Required:

1. Verify the $7.80 overhead rate by determining total estimated direct labor hours and total estimated overhead costs.

2. Develop overhead rates for each department and redo the pricing analysis, using the departmental overhead rates to apply overhead. Are the differences between the prices you determine and the ones given above significant? Why?

5–26   Overhead Rates.   Tom Kowalski was a Certified Public Accountant in practice in a suburb of Los Angeles. One day he received a telephone call from Arnold McEwen, the controller of Newhart Manufacturing Company. McEwen wanted to engage Kowalski to look at the firm's cost accounting system with a view to suggesting improvements. He said that a friend who was a controller at another company had recommended Kowalski because of work he had done for that company. After further discussion, Kowalski accepted the job.

Kowalski first spent several days familiarizing himself with the company's operations and accounting system. The firm had begun as a small machine shop doing specialty work for aircraft companies in Southern California. It had grown steadily through branching out into various types of work but had kept its technological basis by concentrating on the basic metalworking operations of cutting, grinding, stamping, and machining. For example, the firm now made such products as fireplace screens, lamp parts, grates, and many metal components of other products.

Most products were made to customer specifications, although on occasion the firm's salespeople were able to persuade customers to accept one of the more standard products that the firm made more or less continually. These standard items accounted for about 30 percent of revenue, which currently totalled about $9 million annually.

The firm used a job order costing system. Each job was charged with actual material and direct labor costs. Overhead was applied to jobs on the basis of direct labor cost. A predetermined rate was developed quarterly. Toward the end of each quarter McEwen and Richard Winchell, the production manager, developed estimates of direct labor cost and factory overhead for the following quarter. The rate used in the next quarter was estimated overhead for the quarter divided by estimated direct labor cost. McEwen and Winchell usually developed the rate two or three weeks before the quarter began.

McEwen explained to Kowalski that the quarterly rate was used because there was some seasonality in operations and the managers liked to have cost data that were as current as possible.

The costs developed for each job were used for inventory valuation and for analyzing the profitability of individual jobs. Additionally, costs were the principal basis for pricing on nonstandard jobs. Salespeople were free to quote prices on standard work, but on nonstandard items a cost estimator worked up the costs. Winchell and Frank Stein, the sales manager, usually looked at the estimates for large jobs but not small ones (under $500). The general pricing rule was to charge 125 percent of total estimated cost, but this rule was sometimes broken. For example, customers often told salespeople what they thought a fair price was, based on bids from other firms or on work done by Newhart in the past. When the price determined by the formula was significantly different from the fair price suggested by the customer, Winchell and Stein usually made adjustments toward the fair price. These adjustments generally brought the quoted price to within 6 to 10 percent of the fair price.

Other times, Winchell and Stein concluded that a lower price than provided by the formula would be appropriate in order to get a foot in the door of a new customer. In a few cases they raised the price to discourage business that promised to be difficult or that was offered by a slow-paying customer.

Kowalski came to two major conclusions. He believed that departmental overhead rates should be used instead of the plantwide rate currently in effect. He also thought that the rates should be developed on an annual basis, not quarterly.

Kowalski used the firm's existing cost records to see whether his first proposal would be feasible. He found that he could trace over 70 percent of total overhead costs to individual departments. Such items as supervision were easily traced to specific departments, because supervisors worked only in one department. Similarly, depreciation on factory equipment, most supplies and indirect labor, and most maintenance were also clearly associated with individual departments.

Kowalski could not trace such costs as heat and light, depreciation and property taxes on the factory building, and support services such as accounting, engineering, personnel, and general factory administration to individual departments. He decided to allocate these costs to departments on bases that seemed reasonable. He allocated costs related to the factory building on the basis of square feet in each department, costs related to personnel and general administration on the basis of direct labor cost in each department, and so on. He then prepared the analysis shown in Exhibit A.

EXHIBIT A
Kowalski's Memorandum

I have two major recommendations. First, that the firm develop predetermined overhead rates by department, rather than plantwide; second, that these rates be developed annually, instead of quarterly. I have prepared the following material in support of my recommendations.

Effects of Departmental Rates

The following analysis is based on an average quarter's activities.

Department	Direct Overhead Costs	Allocated Costs	Total Costs	Labor Costs	Overhead Rate
Cutting	$ 73,400	$ 22,300	$ 95,700	$ 46,500	$2.058
Grinding	104,200	37,400	141,600	31,500	4.495
Stamping	98,400	34,200	132,600	21,700	6.111
Machining	67,900	28,600	96,500	40,700	2.371
Totals	$343,900	$122,500	$466,400	$140,400	

The plantwide rate would be $3.322 ($466,400/$140,400) per direct labor dollar.

As you can see, the plantwide rate does not reflect the true picture because it ignores differences among the departments. Adopting departmental rates would make for better pricing and analyses of profitability.

Annual Rates Versus Quarterly Rates

Quarterly rates (plantwide) in the past few quarters have ranged from $4.156 down to $2.978 because of differences in total labor costs and seasonal fluctuations in some elements of overhead. Accordingly, prices are set too high in some quarters, too low in others. Confusion results and both management and customers are misled. The year is the basic accounting period, and setting overhead rates annually in advance would further the objectives of making the data more relevant for decision making and control.

I welcome your comments. This memo is only a first step based on preliminary analysis. I shall prepare a more complete report after conferring with interested parties.

The response to Kowalski's proposals was generally unfavorable. No one favored the abandonment of the quarterly rate in favor of annual rates. No one except two departmental supervisors favored the use of departmental rates over a single plantwide rate. The comments that appear below are typical of these that Kowalski received.

RICHARD WINCHELL, PRODUCTION MANAGER: I don't like either proposal. First, the idea of annual rates is bad. We can't budget that far in advance and even if we could I wouldn't favor annual rates. We need up-to-date cost information for control and pricing. As we operate now, we know fairly soon whether the rate is correct or not. We generally have fairly substantial differences between the actual rate and predetermined rate, but if we did it annually we wouldn't know for a full year whether the rate or rates were correct.

Our costs change from quarter to quarter, and so does our labor. We have to reflect different conditions in our pricing policies. For example, our overhead in the winter is heavy because of heating, property taxes (paid in January), and preventive maintenance. You are telling us that we should lose money in the winter and try to make it up in the summer, which is crazy.

Second, the idea of departmental rates leaves me cold. It would involve much more work and would not give us better information. We run a plant, not a group of departments. We have to cover all costs, not just the costs you say are related to individual departments. What are we supposed to do if one department's business falls off? Shut it down? The plantwide rate recognizes the fact that every department has to contribute to the total picture, not just to its own benefit.

FRANK STEIN, SALES MANAGER: I am opposed to the departmental rates for a couple of reasons. First, I've always thought allocating costs wasn't a good idea, and that is exactly what you propose when you throw in building depreciation, general administration, and so on. These costs aren't really associated with any department. If business falls off in, say, the grinding department, you won't lay off any payroll clerks, nor will you save the depreciation on building space that grinding occupies. Your allocations are arbitrary and do not reflect the true costs of the departments. We could play around with your methods of allocation and get quite different rates from the ones you developed. So why go through all of this business when all it will do is add to the costs of accounting and upset the departmental managers? I assume that you would start using the data for evaluating the performance of departmental supervisors, and the allocated costs in there would have nothing to do with whether they were operating efficiently or not.

Required:

1. Determine the total overhead cost and total cost that would be assigned to each of the jobs described below using the $3.322 plantwide overhead rate developed in Kowalski's memo. Each job requires $1,000 in materials.

Department	Required Direct Labor Hours	Hourly Labor Rate	Total Labor Cost
Job L-4757:			
Cutting	132	$5.50⁻	$ 726.00
Grinding	43	5.20	223.60
Machining	38	6.80	258.40
Totals	213		$1,208.00
Job Q-1906:			
Cutting	35	5.50	$ 192.50
Grinding	29	5.20	150.80
Stamping	51	7.20	367.20
Machining	18	6.80	122.40
Totals	133		$ 832.90

2. Redo item 1 using the departmental overhead rates from Kowalski's memo.

3. Why do the differences in overhead costs between the two methods come about? Are they significant for the two jobs described?

4. Comment on Kowalski's two proposals and on the objections raised to them by Winchell and Stein. Can you suggest any improvements?

5. How might your comments in item 4 change if you learned that (a) factory overhead was nearly all fixed, and (b) factory overhead was nearly all variable?

Process Costing

Chapter 6

Job order costing is used by firms that make more than one kind of product. Such firms cannot determine a cost per unit for a period of time because the units would be a combination of different types of products and would, therefore, give a meaningless unit cost figure. Firms that do make the same product more or less continuously will use a variation of **process costing.** Process costing concentrates on the costs and production of individual departments of a firm in determining the unit costs of the product. In other words, it homes in on the production process. Among the kinds of firms that could use process costing are producers of cement, bricks, sugar, flour, some bulk chemicals, and other products for which the units are homogeneous.

The illustrations in this chapter apply equally to actual costing and normal costing. The difference between these methods was described in Chapter 5: actual costing uses actual costs for all productive inputs, while normal costing uses actual material and direct labor costs but applies overhead based on predetermined rates.

DETERMINING PRODUCTION

The principal difficulties encountered in process costing center on the determination of the denominator of the basic formula used to calculate cost per unit. The problems arise because units in process at the beginning and at the end of a period are by definition less than fully complete. Were they complete, they would be included in the finished goods inventory. Thus the firm will have, for example, 2,000 units that are 40 percent complete, or 11,000 units, 75 percent complete, or some other combination of units and percentage of completion. To have a meaningful figure in the denominator of the cost-per-unit formula, we must express these partly completed units in some common form. Clearly, having done 25 percent of the work on 1,000 units is not the same as having done 75 percent of the work on the 1,000 units.

We express partly finished units on a common basis by using the concept of **equivalent unit production** or, more simply, **equivalent production.** The meaning of equivalent production can be readily seen in the following example. If a firm has 3,000 units on hand that are 40 percent complete, we can say that it has the equivalent of 1,200 complete units (3,000 × 40%). We can say this because presumably the firm could have completed 1,200 units in the time required to do 40 percent of the work on 3,000 units. That is the essence of the equivalent production concept, but it is not always so easy to apply.

One common problem in determining equivalent production arises when the inputs of production are not at the same stage of completion. Thus, the various elements of cost are not complete in the same percentages. Consider, for example, the manufacture of bricks. Bricks are made of clay and straw, which are mixed together and formed into desired shapes and sizes. The bricks are then baked in kilns. Thus, when the bricks are ready for the kilns, they are complete so far as materials are concerned: no more materials, and no more materials costs, are required. The bricks are incomplete only insofar as the labor and kiln time required to finish them. Suppose that a firm has 2 million bricks ready for the kilns and that the labor and overhead cost associated with baking the bricks is 25 percent of the total labor and overhead cost. These bricks would be 100 percent complete with respect to materials and 75 percent complete with respect to labor and overhead. As we shall see, this situation requires that we calculate unit costs separately for each cost factor. That is, we must calculate a cost per unit for materials and a separate cost per unit for direct labor and overhead costs.

It is generally assumed that overhead costs follow direct labor hours or costs. Therefore, it is common practice to consider the percentage of completion with respect to overhead to be the same as the percentage with respect to labor. In some cases this assumption may not be warranted, but overall the use of the assumption seems valid. Taken together, labor and overhead costs are usually called **conversion costs.** They are the costs of converting materials into finished, or semifinished, products. For simplicity in calculating cost-per-unit figures, we shall usually lump labor and overhead costs together.

Another matter that arises in the determination of equivalent production is the cost flow assumption, which is usually either weighted average or first-in-first-out (FIFO). The cost flow assumption primarily affects what costs are attached to opening Work-in-Process Inventory. Because FIFO involves some complexities that would take us aside, we shall delay discussing it until later and work with the weighted average method. In order to approach the problem of process costing on a logical, step-by-step basis, we begin with the simple case of a factory that operates a single process, then move to multiple-process production.

THE SINGLE-PROCESS CASE

Our first example is the Winston plant of the Pitman Textile Company. The Winston plant buys wool, spins it into yarn, then sells it to other firms and to other divisions of the Pitman Company. The plant began operations in January, 19X5. Operating results for the first two months of 19X5 appear in Exhibit 6-1. A unit is 100 yards of yarn, and all calculations are made on this basis.

EXHIBIT 6-1
Summary of Operations—Winston Plant

	January	February
Work in Process		
Unit data:		
Beginning inventory	0	8,000
Units put into production	133,000	146,000
Subtotal	133,000	154,000
Units completed	125,000	143,000
Ending inventory	8,000	11,000
Percentages of completion of ending inventories:		
Materials	100%	100%
Conversion costs	60%	30%
Cost data:		
Materials put into production	$332,500	$358,840
Conversion costs incurred	674,960	728,485

Equivalent Production—Weighted Average

Looking at Exhibit 6-1, we see that all units were complete with respect to materials. Although this may seem to be the obvious situation, it does not always prevail. In some production processes materials are added at or near the end of production, and units may be less than fully complete with respect to materials. The percentages of completion for conversion costs (labor and overhead) were 60 percent and 30 percent at the ends of the two months. Weighted average equivalent production is computed by the following formula:

$$\begin{pmatrix} \text{weighted average} \\ \text{equivalent production} \end{pmatrix} = \begin{pmatrix} \text{units} \\ \text{completed} \end{pmatrix} + \left[\begin{pmatrix} \text{units in ending} \\ \text{inventory} \end{pmatrix} \times \begin{pmatrix} \text{percentage} \\ \text{complete} \end{pmatrix} \right]$$

This formula must be applied separately to each cost factor. In our example there are two cost factors: materials and conversion costs. Hence we must apply the formula twice for each month. Exhibit 6–2 employs the formula above to calculate the equivalent production amounts for each cost factor for each month. All data are from Exhibit 6–1.

EXHIBIT 6–2
Equivalent Production—Winston Plant

	Materials	Conversion Costs
January		
Units completed	125,000	125,000
Units in ending inventory:		
Materials 8,000 × 100%	8,000	
Conversion costs 8,000 × 60%		4,800
Equivalent production for January	133,000	129,800
February		
Units completed	143,000	143,000
Units in ending inventory:		
Materials 11,000 × 100%	11,000	
Conversion costs 11,000 × 30%		3,300
Equivalent production for February	154,000	146,300

Before making the unit cost calculations, let us stop for a moment and consider a few important matters. First, the units that are completed during the period are obviously completed with respect to both materials and conversion costs. Therefore, the first figure used in the calculation (units completed) is the same for both cost factors. Second, the ending inventory *in units* is the same for both cost factors (8,000 and 11,000); it is the *equivalent units that differ*. These points may seem simple, but they are frequently overlooked. Further, the weighted average method does not require consideration of the beginning inventory of *units,* or of its percentage of completion, because the cost flow objective of the method is to weight the beginning inventory and production for the period in determining the value of goods completed and ending in-process inventory. Thus, the units in beginning inventory are included in the units completed during the period. That is, the February completed production of 143,000 units included the 8,000 units that were in the January ending inventory and, therefore, in the February beginning inventory.

Unit Cost Calculations

The basic formula for the calculation of unit costs on a weighted average basis is:

$$\left(\begin{array}{c}\text{cost per unit,}\\\text{weighted average}\end{array}\right) = \frac{\left(\begin{array}{c}\text{cost of beginning}\\\text{inventory}\end{array}\right) + \left(\begin{array}{c}\text{costs incurred in}\\\text{current period}\end{array}\right)}{\text{equivalent production}}$$

This is consistent with the calculation of equivalent production, since costs associated with beginning inventory are pooled with current costs to yield an average cost per unit. This formula, like that for equivalent production, must be applied to each cost factor separately.

We are now ready to calculate the unit costs for January. There was no beginning inventory, so the numerator of the formula is simply the cost of each factor incurred during January. Exhibit 6–3 shows the calculations.

EXHIBIT 6–3
Unit Cost Calculations, January—Winston Plant

	Materials	Conversion Costs
Costs incurred during January, from Exhibit 6–1	$332,500	$674,960
Divided by:		
Equivalent production for January, from Exhibit 6–2	133,000	129,800
Equals:		
Cost per unit	$2.50	$5.20

Under the weighted average method, the total unit cost of $7.70 ($2.50 + $5.20) is used to transfer costs of finished units from Work-in-Process to Finished Goods Inventory. However, the cost of the ending inventory of work in process must be determined separately for each cost factor because of the differing equivalent units in the ending inventory. The ending inventory of work in process of 8,000 units is valued at $44,960, calculated as follows.

	Units	Percentage Complete	Unit Cost	
Cost of materials in ending inventory =	8,000 ×	100%	× $2.50 =	$20,000
Conversion costs in ending inventory =	8,000 ×	60%	× $5.20 =	24,960
Total cost of ending work-in-process inventory				$44,960

It would be incorrect to use the $7.70 total unit cost to determine the ending work-in-process inventory, because although the 8,000 units are 100 percent complete with respect to materials, they are only 60 percent complete with respect to conversion costs. Hence the two cost factors must be considered separately. However, for determining the cost of units transferred to the finished goods inventory the $7.70 is perfectly appropriate, because all transferred units are 100 percent complete with respect to both materials and conversion costs. Accordingly, the total debit to Finished Goods Inventory would be $962,500 (125,000 × $7.70). At this point the inventory accounts would be as shown below. Notice two Work-in-Process accounts are kept to keep separate track of materials and conversion costs.

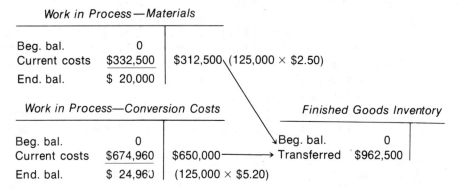

Work in Process—Materials

Beg. bal.	0	
Current costs	$332,500	$312,500 (125,000 × $2.50)
End. bal.	$ 20,000	

Work in Process—Conversion Costs

Beg. bal.	0
Current costs	$674,960
End. bal.	$ 24,960

$650,000 ——→
(125,000 × $5.20)

Finished Goods Inventory

Beg. bal.	0
Transferred	$962,500

Journal Entries. The journal entries in a process costing system parallel those of a job order system. In the system we are considering here, there is one Work-in-Process Inventory account where both direct labor and overhead costs, either actual or applied, are debited, and another account for materials. Transfers to finished goods, or, as we shall see shortly, to another department, require a single debit and multiple credits as suggested by the T-accounts above. The entry to transfer the cost of January completed production to finished goods would be:

Finished Goods Inventory	$962,500	
Work in Process—Materials		$312,500
Work in Process—Conversion Costs		650,000

Winston Illustration: Beginning and Ending Inventories. We have now brought the Winston plant through January and are ready to calculate unit costs for February (Exhibit 6–4). These calculations require consideration of the beginning dollar amounts of work-in-process inventory. The only difference between the calculations here and those in Exhibit 6–3 (unit cost calculations for January), besides the numbers, is the presence of beginning work-in-process inventories.

Again, the unit cost figures would be used in determining the ending inventories of work in process and the amounts transferred to finished goods. Let us now calculate the amounts that should be in the ending inventory for work in process before looking at the T-accounts.

First, we know that 11,000 units remain in the ending inventory and that these units are 100 percent complete with respect to materials, 30 percent complete with respect to conversion costs. The units will therefore be costed in the following way:

$$\text{materials cost in ending inventory} = 11,000 \times 100\% \times \$2.46$$
$$= \$27,060$$
$$\text{conversion costs in ending inventory} = 11,000 \times 30\% \times \$5.15$$
$$= \$16,995$$

EXHIBIT 6–4
Unit Cost Calculations, February—Winston Plant

	Materials	Conversion Costs
Beginning inventory	$ 20,000	$ 24,960
Incurred during February (Exhibit 6–1)	358,840	728,485
Totals	378,840	753,445
Divided by:		
Equivalent production, February (Exhibit 6–2)	154,000	146,300
Equals:		
Cost per unit	$2.46	$5.15

We also know that the costs transferred to Finished Goods Inventory are the total unit costs of $7.61 ($2.46 + $5.15) multiplied by the number of units transferred.

$$\text{Costs transferred to Finished Goods} = \$7.61 \times 143,000$$
$$= \$1,088,230$$

The T-accounts below verify these figures.

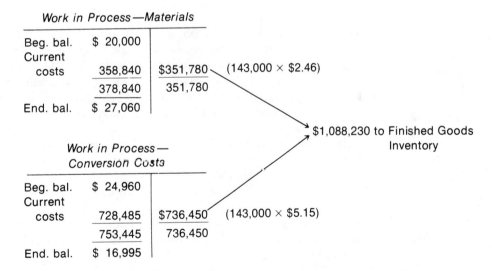

Work in Process—Materials

Beg. bal.	$ 20,000		
Current costs	358,840	$351,780	(143,000 × $2.46)
	378,840	351,780	
End. bal.	$ 27,060		

$1,088,230 to Finished Goods Inventory

Work in Process— Conversion Costs

Beg. bal.	$ 24,960		
Current costs	728,485	$736,450	(143,000 × $5.15)
	753,445	736,450	
End. bal.	$ 16,995		

COST OF PRODUCTION REPORT

At this point we introduce a commonly used statement called the **cost of production report**. This report is prepared for each department. Besides presenting a summary of pertinent data, it enables you to check your work. Exhibit 6–5 on page 250 shows the cost report for February. Note that it

EXHIBIT 6–5
Cost of Production Report, February, 19X5—Winston Plant

Unit Data	
Beginning inventory	8,000
Put into production	146,000
Total to be accounted for	154,000
Transferred out	143,000
Ending inventory	11,000
Total accounted for	154,000

Cost Data	Totals	Materials	Conversion Costs
Beginning inventory	$ 44,960	$ 20,000	$ 24,960
Current period costs	1,087,325	358,840	728,485
Total to be accounted for	$1,132,285	$378,840	$753,445
Transferred out	$1,088,230	$351,780	$736,450
Ending inventory	44,055	27,060	16,995
Total accounted for	$1,132,285	$378,840	$753,445

provides reconciliations of the physical flow of units (from Exhibit 6–1) and of the total of costs for the period and the beginning inventory. In our examples we reconciled the amounts of cost transferred out with the ending inventory in a T-account framework. The cost of production report does this in tabular form. Because it is possible to calculate ending inventory and costs transferred out independently, it is possible to check your work by reconciling the total costs.

The following relationship for unit data must always hold.[1]

$$\left(\begin{array}{c}\text{beginning}\\\text{inventory}\end{array}\right) + \left(\begin{array}{c}\text{units started}\\\text{during period}\end{array}\right) = \left(\begin{array}{c}\text{units}\\\text{completed}\end{array}\right) + \left(\begin{array}{c}\text{units in ending}\\\text{inventory}\end{array}\right)$$

This relationship is for units, not for equivalent unit production. It should be familiar from financial accounting. The following relationship must always hold for cost data:

$$\left(\begin{array}{c}\text{cost of}\\\text{beginning}\\\text{inventory}\end{array}\right) + \left(\begin{array}{c}\text{costs}\\\text{incurred}\\\text{during period}\end{array}\right) = \left(\begin{array}{c}\text{costs}\\\text{transferred}\\\text{out}\end{array}\right) + \left(\begin{array}{c}\text{cost of}\\\text{ending}\\\text{inventory}\end{array}\right)$$

[1] If units are lost or spoiled during production, the equation must be modified. These points are treated in detail in Chapter 10.

This relationship, too, comes from financial accounting. Remember that it must be applied separately to each cost factor. Please notice also that you can independently calculate both cost elements on the right-hand side of the equals sign. For weighted average costing, costs transferred out equals unit cost multiplied by units transferred, and cost of ending inventory equals unit cost multiplied by equivalent units in the ending inventory. Trace these relationships in Exhibit 6–5.

MANAGERIAL USES OF PROCESS COSTING INFORMATION

Our discussion so far has been concerned with the rationale and mechanics of weighted average method process costing. The question that naturally arises is whether the data generated are useful for managerial purposes as well as for product costing.

The simplest answer is no, the information we have been developing so far is not of much importance for managerial purposes, and using it can lead to incorrect conclusions. There are two principal reasons for this answer. First, conversion costs include fixed manufacturing overhead, and so the unit cost for conversion is subject to all the difficulties of any cost figure that includes unit fixed costs. Second, the weighted average method combines unit costs from prior periods with those of the current period. Thus, even if the cost-per-unit figure contains only variable costs, it does not reflect only performance in the current period. To see why this is so, we consider the example for which data are given below.

	Units	Cost
Beginning inventory of work in process—		
materials (percentage of completion = 100%)	1,000	$ 1,000
Units finished during year	9,000	$12,000
Ending inventory of work in process—		
materials	0	0

If we calculate equivalent production, we need simply use the 9,000 units finished, because there is no ending inventory. The total costs from the beginning inventory and those incurred during the period are $13,000 ($1,000 + $12,000), so the weighted average unit cost is $1.444. The $1.444, however, does not represent the unit cost incurred this period but rather a combination of this period and prior periods. We can see that the firm actually put materials into process for 8,000 units during the period (the 9,000 completed less the 1,000 in the beginning inventory). These materials cost $12,000, so that the unit cost incurred during the current period was $1.50 ($12,000/8,000). The units in the beginning inventory had a weighted average cost of $1 ($1,000/1,000), which pulled down the weighted average to

$1.44.[2] Thus, a manager would not be correct in saying that it *currently* costs the firm $1.44 per unit for materials.

Referring for the moment to the Winston plant results, we summarize the cost-per-unit data for the two months in the schedule below.

	January	February
Unit cost of materials	$2.50	$2.46
Unit cost for conversion	5.20	5.15

Both costs declined on a per-unit basis. The costs incurred during February were actually somewhat less per unit than the figures shown, because the January costs, being higher, held up the weighted averages. We could say that the material cost declined and that as a rule this would be considered good, but we cannot say that about conversion costs. The decline in the per-unit amount may simply be due to the spreading of fixed overhead costs over a greater number of units. Hence we cannot draw any conclusions about the relative efficiency of the plant with regard to conversion costs in January as opposed to February.

The FIFO method, as we shall see shortly, avoids the problem of mixing the costs of different periods but does nothing to help the manager in regard to the fixed cost question. Any process costing system that includes fixed costs in unit costs, as must be done for financial reporting and tax accounting, is subject to the criticism about fixed costs.

Of course, it is sometimes possible to keep separate accounts for fixed and variable costs, and doing so would enable the manager to find the information required for planning and special decisions. A well-kept cost accounting system should be able to provide cost data classified behaviorally as well as by the object of the cost.

MULTIPLE PROCESSES

Many firms that use process costing operate more than one process. If the Winston plant of Pitman Company dyed the yarn, it would operate two processes. If it also wove the yarn into fabric, it would have an additional process. In this context, a process may be equated with a department. We could speak of the spinning process or of the spinning department. We shall use the two terms interchangeably throughout the remainder of this chapter.

When products go through more than one department, their costs are transferred from department to department until the last department trans-

---

[2] We can use these data to show that a weighted average calculation is exactly the weighted average of beginning inventory and current-period cost. The 1,000 units in the beginning inventory are one-ninth of the total, and the 8,000 started and completed during the period are eight-ninths. Thus, $(1/9) \times \$1.00 + (8/9) \times \$1.50 = \$1.444$.

fers the costs to finished goods. The procedures are more or less like those for the single department case, but with more Work-in-Process accounts. The additional accounts are required for two reasons. First, each department will have its own Work-in-Process accounts, rather than only one department having them. Second, because the costs must be accumulated from department to department as a product moves through stages of completion, we need a special account to take care of these costs. This account is called **Work in Process—Prior Department Costs,** or **Work in Process—Transferred-in Costs.**

The need for this new account and its basic purpose may be explained best by an example. Suppose that the Winston plant operates a dyeing department as well as a spinning department. The dyeing department receives yarn from the spinning department and dyes it, then transfers it to finished goods. From the standpoint of the dyeing department, the costs incurred in the spinning department are similar to materials cost. That is, it would be possible for the dyeing department to go outside the firm to buy yarn for dyeing, in which case the cost of the yarn would be materials cost. Roughly speaking, the accounts for prior department costs are quite similar to accounts for materials: the finished output of one department is the raw material for the next department.

However, from the standpoint of the firm, or of the plant, the only material cost is that of materials bought from outside. The costs of the spinning department include both materials and conversion costs, not just materials costs. It is therefore more accurate to say that the costs transferred from the spinning department to the dyeing department are costs incurred by the prior department, not materials costs. In addition, transferred-in costs are associated with 100 percent completed units from the prior department. The subsequent department may add more direct materials in such a way as to increase the number of units. For example, the first process in manufacturing a chemical may result in 10,000 gallons of semifinished product. The second process may add materials so that the original 10,000 gallons become 12,000 gallons. Therefore, the equivalent production of units transferred in would have to be adjusted, and separate Work-in-Process accounts would be needed.

For any given department in the flow of production, prior department costs are the cumulative costs of *all* prior departments. Thus, on a per-unit basis, prior department costs will increase as products go through the production departments. The cost of goods transferred to Finished Goods Inventory will then be the sum of the unit costs for all departments multiplied by the number of transferred units.

We illustrate the procedures by changing our example. Instead of simply spinning yarn, the Winston plant also dyes it. Thus, instead of transferring goods and costs from the spinning department to finished goods, it transfers them to the dyeing department and then to finished goods. Exhibit 6–6 on page 254 provides information about the dyeing department for January and February. The units transferred into the dyeing department are

EXHIBIT 6–6
Summary of Operations, Dyeing Department—Winston Plant

	January	February
Production data:		
Units transferred in	125,000	143,000
Units transferred to finished goods	118,000	138,000
Units in process at month end	7,000	12,000
Percentages complete:		
Prior department costs	100%	100%
Materials	80%	90%
Conversion costs	70%	75%
Cost data:		
Materials put into production	$ 27,190	$ 31,997
Conversion costs	$ 52,850	$ 62,276
Costs transferred from spinning department[a]	$962,500	$1,088,230

[a] For January, $7.70 × 125,000 = $962.500.
 For February, $7.61 × 143,000 = $1,088,230.

the units completed by the spinning department, as given in Exhibit 6–1. Please notice that the dyeing department adds materials to the yarn. The cost of materials added is the cost of dye used during each period. The percentages of completion with respect to materials are less than 100 percent because the dye is added at various stages in the process, and some of it is added relatively later in the process. Notice also that the transferred-in (prior department cost) percentages of completion are both 100 percent. This will always be true. Any units in the dyeing department must be complete with respect to costs of the spinning department. The spinning department has done all its work; it has no more left to do. In this respect, the prior department cost is analogous to materials cost when all materials are put into process at the beginning of the process. In that situation any units on hand have all of their material cost.

Finally, the figures shown as costs transferred from spinning department are the amounts that were transferred to finished goods in the original example. They are the total unit-cost figures from Exhibits 6–3 and 6–4 multiplied by the number of units transferred from spinning to dyeing.

Calculations of equivalent production and unit costs for January are given in Exhibit 6–7. Notice that we have three cost categories, rather than the two we had in the original example. Notice also that the cost per unit for prior department costs is $7.70, which was the cost per unit for the spinning department in Exhibit 6–3 ($2.50 + $5.20). This will be true under the weighted average method except for complications such as lost or spoiled units that we consider in Chapter 10.

To clarify the nature of this transfer, we provide the journal entry that would be made when the spinning department transfers the costs for units sent to the dyeing department in January. Credits to the spinning department accounts are the amounts that appear in the T-accounts on page 248.

Work in Process—Dyeing Department, Prior Department Costs	$962,500
Work in Process—Spinning Department, Materials	$312,500
Work in Process—Spinning Department, Conversion Costs	650,000

Notice that we now need to identify each Work-in-Process account not only by type of cost, but also by department.

EXHIBIT 6–7
Dyeing Department—Winston Plant

Unit Cost Calculations for January

	Prior Department Costs	Materials	Conversion Costs
Costs transferred in, 125,000 × $7.70	$962,500		
Costs incurred (Exhibit 6–6)		$27,190	$52,850
Totals	$962,500	$27,190	$52,850
Divided by: Equivalent production (below)	125,000	123,600	122,900
Equals: Cost per unit	$7.70	$0.22	$0.43
Total unit cost equals $8.35			

Equivalent Production for January

	Prior Department Costs	Materials	Conversion Costs
Units completed	118,000	118,000	118,000
Ending inventory:			
7,000 × 100%	7,000		
7,000 × 80%		5,600	
7,000 × 70%			4,900
Total equivalent production	125,000	123,600	122,900

The total unit-cost figure of $8.35 represents not only the costs of the dyeing department, but also those of the spinning department. Hence it is an accumulated cost figure. We show the T-accounts for the dyeing department below. The only difference between these accounts and those of the spinning department are the numbers and the presence of the account for prior department costs. The calculations of unit costs transferred out to finished goods are made in the same fashion as are those of the ending inventory amounts.

Work in Process, Dyeing Department—Prior Department Costs

Beg. bal.	0		
Transferred in	$962,500	$908,600	(118,000 × $7.70)
End. bal.	$ 53,900		

Work in Process, Dyeing Department—Materials

Beg. bal.	0		
Current costs	$27,190	$25,960	(118,000 × $0.22)
End. bal.	$ 1,230		

Work in Process, Dyeing Department—Conversion Costs

Beg. bal.	0		
Current costs	$52,850	$50,740	(118,000 × $0.43)
End. bal.	$ 2,110		

The proofs of the ending inventory amounts are given below. They are slightly rounded because the unit costs for materials and conversion are not exactly $0.2200 and $0.4300.

Ending work
in process—prior department costs   7,000 × 100% × $7.70 = $53,900
                    materials   7,000 × 80% × $0.22 = 1,230
                    conversion costs   7,000 × 70% × $0.43 = 2,110

We now complete the example by looking at February. Exhibit 6–8 shows the unit-cost calculations for February for the dyeing department. Note that the weighted average unit cost for prior department costs is not the $7.61 cost that was transferred in during the period. The reason is that the weighted average method result will depend on how much cost is in the beginning inventory at the prior-period weighted average cost. Although the unit cost of the spinning department is transferred in at $7.61, it is not necessarily transferred out at that amount. The difference between $7.61 and $7.6142 is not great, but it is a difference.

Exhibit 6–9 on page 258 is a cost of production report for the dyeing department for February. Before looking at it, try to make it up yourself, following the format of the report given in Exhibit 6–5. Remember that your objectives are to account for the total costs, beginning inventory plus costs added during the period, for each cost factor. All costs are either transferred out or left in ending inventory.

All data for Exhibit 6–9 down to the section on costs transferred out and costs in ending inventory are from Exhibit 6–8. The calculations of costs transferred out are:

$$\begin{aligned}
\text{transferred-in costs} &= \$1,050,760 = (138,000 \times \$7.6142) \text{ rounded} \\
\text{materials} &= \$30,815 = (138,000 \times 0.2233) \text{ rounded} \\
\text{conversion costs} &= \$60,444 = (138,000 \times 0.438) \text{ rounded}
\end{aligned}$$

Thus, transferred-out costs are the unit costs multiplied by the number of units completed and transferred. The total column is simply the sum of the columns for the individual element of cost. The ending inventories are the costs per unit multiplied by the equivalent units in the ending inventory, which also appear in Exhibit 6–8.

$$\begin{aligned}
\text{transferred-in costs} &= \$91,370 = (12,000 \times \$7.6142) \text{ rounded} \\
\text{materials} &= \$2,412 = (10,800 \times \$0.2233) \text{ rounded} \\
\text{conversion costs} &= \$3,942 = (9,000 \times \$0.438) \text{ rounded}
\end{aligned}$$

EXHIBIT 6–8
Dyeing Department—Winston Plant

Unit-Cost Calculations, February

	Prior Department Costs	Materials	Conversion Costs
Beginning inventory	$53,900	$1,230	$2,110
Transferred-in costs (Exhibit 6–6)	1,088,230		
Incurred during February (Exhibit 6–6)		31,997	62,276
Totals	1,142,130	33,227	64,386
Divided by:			
Equivalent production (below)	150,000	148,800	147,000
Equals:			
Cost per unit	$7.6142	$0.2233	$0.4380

Equivalent Production (Data from Exhibit 6–6)

Units completed	138,000	138,000	138,000
Ending inventory:			
12,000 units × 100%	12,000		
12,000 units × 90%		10,800	
12,000 units × 75%			9,000
Total equivalent production	150,000	148,800	147,000

EXHIBIT 6–9
Cost of Production Report, February, 19X5, Dyeing Department—Winston Plant

Unit Data

Beginning inventory	7,000
Units transferred into department	143,000
Total to be accounted for	150,000
Units transferred out	138,000
Ending inventory	12,000
Total accounted for	150,000

Cost Data

	Total	Transferred-In Costs	Materials	Conversion Costs
Beginning inventory	$ 57,240	$ 53,900	$ 1,230	$ 2,110
Current-period costs	1,182,503	1,088,230	31,997	62,276
Total to be accounted for	$1,239,743	$1,142,130	$33,227	$64,386
Transferred out	$1,142,019	$1,050,760	$30,815	$60,444
Ending inventory	97,724	91,370	2,412	3,942
Total accounted for	$1,239,743	$1,142,130	$33,227	$64,386

FIRST-IN-FIRST-OUT COSTING

We mentioned earlier that the weighted average method of costing units mixes the costs of the current period with those of prior periods. Therefore, even for variable costs, we cannot determine the per-unit amounts incurred during the current period. We can tell whether they were higher or lower than in prior periods by looking at the relationship between the average costs of the latest two periods, but we cannot focus clearly on the variable cost per unit for the current period.

The use of first-in-first-out costing (FIFO)[3] allows us to make unit-cost

---

[3] What we call FIFO costing should probably be called modified FIFO costing. Under a strict interpretation of FIFO, the departments that receive semifinished units from other departments should account separately for the units transferred from the prior department beginning inventory and those transferred from the current-period production. Making this refinement would entail much additional recordkeeping with no apparent benefits.

calculations that relate to current-period activity rather than to a combination of current- and prior-period activity. Of course, the problem of including fixed-overhead costs in conversion costs still renders total-cost-per-unit calculations unsuitable for managerial purposes, but if costs are classified by behavior as well as by object of expenditure, it is possible to analyze variable production costs.

From a procedural viewpoint, FIFO differs from weighted average costing in several important respects. We shall illustrate FIFO costing using our modified example of the Winston plant.

Equivalent Production, FIFO

The first major change from weighted average costing is the calculation of equivalent production. Under FIFO we are trying to calculate the cost of work done *this* period, and we want the equivalent production done *this* period rather than a weighted average of this period and prior periods. The formula for FIFO equivalent production is as follows:

$$
\begin{pmatrix} \text{equivalent} \\ \text{production, FIFO} \end{pmatrix} = \begin{pmatrix} \text{units} \\ \text{completed} \end{pmatrix}
$$

$$
+ \left[\begin{pmatrix} \text{units in ending} \\ \text{inventory} \end{pmatrix} \times \begin{pmatrix} \text{percentage} \\ \text{complete} \end{pmatrix} \right]
$$

$$
- \left[\begin{pmatrix} \text{units in beginning} \\ \text{inventory} \end{pmatrix} \times \begin{pmatrix} \text{percentage} \\ \text{complete} \end{pmatrix} \right]
$$

Notice that the first two terms to the right of the equals sign make up the calculation for the weighted average equivalent production. FIFO equivalent production is equal to weighted average equivalent production minus the equivalent production in the beginning inventory. Think about this for a minute. Because we are trying to determine the amount of work done in the current period, we must subtract the work in the prior period that is included in the units completed during the period. That is, of the units finished this period, some were in the beginning inventory. Work had already been done on those units. That work is expressed by multiplying the number of units by their percentage of completion, and that is what we subtract in the third term.

The percentage of completion used with the beginning inventory is the percentage that applies to that inventory, while the percentage used with the ending inventory is the percentage related to that inventory. Hence only by happenstance will the two percentages be the same (except for transferred-in costs, which will always be 100 percent complete). Like the formula for weighted average equivalent production, this formula must be applied separately to each cost factor.

Let us look at the alternative calculations for the spinning department for the month of February, in tabular form, to highlight the differences that exist.

	Materials	Conversion Costs
Units completed (Exhibit 6–2)	143,000	143,000
Equivalent units in ending inventory (Exhibit 6–2)	11,000	3,300
Equivalent production, weighted average	154,000	146,300
Less: Equivalent units in beginning inventory, which are the equivalent units in the January ending inventory from Exhibit 6–2:		
8,000 × 100%	8,000	
8,000 × 60%		4,800
Equivalent production, FIFO	146,000	141,500

Thus, the two methods differ only in their treatments of the beginning inventory. The weighted average method includes the beginning inventory in equivalent production because it gives a weighted average of the cost of beginning inventory and the cost of work done in the current period. The FIFO method calculates the work done in the current period and therefore excludes the beginning inventory.

An alternative formula concentrates attention on the work actually done in the current period, which is the work done on the beginning inventory to finish those units, plus the work done on units started and completed during the period, plus the work done on the ending inventory:

$$\begin{pmatrix} \text{equivalent} \\ \text{production, FIFO} \end{pmatrix} = \begin{pmatrix} \text{units started} \\ \text{and completed} \end{pmatrix}$$
$$+ \left[\begin{pmatrix} \text{units in ending} \\ \text{inventory} \end{pmatrix} \times \begin{pmatrix} \text{percentage} \\ \text{complete} \end{pmatrix} \right]$$
$$+ \left[\begin{pmatrix} \text{units in} \\ \text{beginning} \\ \text{inventory} \end{pmatrix} \times \begin{pmatrix} 100\% - \\ \text{percentage} \\ \text{complete} \end{pmatrix} \right]$$

Both of the FIFO formulas give the same result. The second looks directly at the work done in the current period, which consists of three elements: the units on which all work was done in the current period, the work done on the units in the ending inventory, and the work done to finish the units in beginning inventory. These three elements correspond to the three terms in the second formula. The first formula looks at total units completed and then subtracts work done in prior periods. The result of either formula is the same: equivalent units of production achieved in the *current* period.

Cost per Unit, FIFO

FIFO evaluates the current-period activity. Therefore, the cost figure that we divide by equivalent production is just the cost of the current period, instead of the sum of the cost in the beginning inventory and the cost of the current period. The formula for computing FIFO cost per unit, then, is:

$$\text{cost per unit, FIFO} = \frac{\text{current-period costs}}{\text{equivalent production}}$$

As usual, this calculation must be done for each cost factor. The numerator of the right-hand term excludes the cost of the beginning inventory, which is included under the weighted average method. Hence we see that both the numerator and denominator are different under the two methods if there are beginning inventories.

Inventories and Transfers

Under weighted average costing, both transferred units and units in ending inventory of work in process were costed using the same unit cost, the weighted average unit cost. Under FIFO, the ending inventory is costed the same way, but transfers are not. With respect to the ending inventory of work in process, each cost factor is determined as follows:

$$\left(\begin{array}{c} \text{ending} \\ \text{inventory} \end{array} \right) = \left(\begin{array}{c} \text{unit} \\ \text{cost} \end{array} \right) \times \left(\begin{array}{c} \text{number of units in} \\ \text{ending inventory} \end{array} \right) \times \left(\begin{array}{c} \text{percentage} \\ \text{complete} \end{array} \right)$$

We would expect this to be the case, because any cost flow assumption assigns a calculated unit-cost figure to the units still on hand.

Transfers are handled differently. We cannot transfer all units using the FIFO unit costs, because under FIFO we assume that the beginning inventory is transferred first, then units that were begun and completed in the current period. The FIFO cost per unit is used to transfer the cost of units started and completed during the current period. It is also applied to the work done this period to finish work in the beginning inventory. The work done last period on the beginning inventory is costed at the prior period FIFO unit cost.

In tabular form, the cost transferred out under FIFO is:

Cost of beginning inventory
Plus:
Current period unit cost × units started and completed
Plus:
Current period unit cost × work done on beginning inventory
Equals:
Cost transferred out

In equation form:

$$\begin{pmatrix} \text{costs transferred} \\ \text{out} \end{pmatrix} = \begin{pmatrix} \text{cost of beginning} \\ \text{inventory} \end{pmatrix}$$

$$+ \left[\begin{pmatrix} \text{current period} \\ \text{cost per unit} \end{pmatrix} \times \begin{pmatrix} \text{units started} \\ \text{and completed} \end{pmatrix} \right]$$

$$+ \left[\begin{pmatrix} \text{current period} \\ \text{cost per unit} \end{pmatrix} \times \begin{pmatrix} \text{units in beginning} \\ \text{inventory} \end{pmatrix} \right.$$

$$\left. \times \begin{pmatrix} 100\% - \text{percentage} \\ \text{complete} \end{pmatrix} \right]$$

An alternative formula that uses the number of units completed, rather than started and completed, is:

$$\begin{pmatrix} \text{costs transferred} \\ \text{out} \end{pmatrix} = \begin{pmatrix} \text{cost of beginning} \\ \text{inventory} \end{pmatrix}$$

$$+ \begin{pmatrix} \text{current period} \\ \text{cost per unit} \end{pmatrix} \times \left\{ \begin{pmatrix} \text{units} \\ \text{completed} \end{pmatrix} \right.$$

$$\left. - \left[\begin{pmatrix} \text{units in beginning} \\ \text{inventory} \end{pmatrix} \times \begin{pmatrix} \text{percentage} \\ \text{complete} \end{pmatrix} \right] \right\}$$

Again the choice between formulas is for convenience alone. Both equations accomplish the objective of allocating the current period cost to the units started and completed during the period and to the work done this period on the beginning inventory, with the beginning inventory itself being transferred at the prior period cost.

Illustration: Winston Unit Cost Calculations

We shall apply FIFO to the month of February for the Winston plant. The results for January under both FIFO and weighted average would be the same, because there are no beginning inventories for January. Exhibit 6–10 shows the unit cost calculations for the spinning department. All data are from Exhibit 6–1.

The costs in the beginning inventories were $20,000 for materials, $24,960 for conversion costs (see Exhibit 6–4). The calculation of costs transferred to the dyeing department is given below:

$$\begin{aligned} \text{material cost transferred} &= \$20,000 + \$2.4578[143,000 \\ &\quad - (100\% \times 8,000)] \\ &= \$20,000 + \$2.4578 \times 135,000 \\ &= \$351,803 \\ \text{conversion costs transferred} &= \$24,960 + \$5.1483[143,000 \\ &\quad - (60\% \times 8,000)] \end{aligned}$$

$$= \$24{,}960 + \$5.1483 \times 138{,}200$$
$$= \$736{,}455$$
$$\text{total transferred} = \$1{,}088{,}258 = (\$351{,}803 + \$736{,}455)$$

These costs transferred should be reconciled with the ending inventories to make sure that we have accounted for all costs. This reconciliation appears below, in T-account form.

Work in Process, Spinning Department—Materials

Beg. bal.	$20,000		
Current costs	358,840	$351,803	transferred to dyeing department
End. bal.	$27,037		

Ending balance = 11,000 × 100% × $2.4578 (rounded)

Work in Process, Spinning Department—Conversion Costs

Beg. bal.	$24,960		
Current costs	728,485	$736,455	transferred to dyeing department
End. bal.	$16,990		

Ending balance = 11,000 × 30% × $5.1483 (rounded)

EXHIBIT 6–10
Spinning Department—Winston Plant

Unit-Cost Calculations for February

	Materials	Conversion Costs
Current costs for February	$358,840	$728,485
Divided by:		
Equivalent production, February (below)	146,000	141,500
Equals:		
Cost per unit	$2.4578	$5.1483
Total unit cost = $7.6061		

Equivalent Production

	Materials	Conversion Costs
Units completed	143,000	143,000
Plus: Ending inventory		
11,000 × 100%	11,000	
11,000 × 30%		3,300
Minus: Beginning inventory		
8,000 × 100%	8,000	
8,000 × 60%		4,800
Equals: Equivalent production	146,000	141,500

Review Problem

To test your understanding of the FIFO method, prepare a schedule of unit costs for the dyeing department for February, determine the costs of ending inventory for each cost factor, and determine the costs transferred to Finished Goods Inventory for each cost factor. Round unit-cost calculations to four decimal places (hundredths of cents). Because of rounding in the unit cost calculations, the total costs of units transferred plus the costs of ending inventories will not add up to total costs to be accounted for. In practice, the costs transferred to Finished Goods Inventory would probably be adjusted.

For your convenience the relevant data are reproduced in Exhibit 6–11. The answers appear in Exhibit 6–12.

EXHIBIT 6–11
Data for Dyeing Department for February—Winston Plant

Unit Data			
Beginning inventory	7,000		
Units transferred in	143,000		
Units transferred out	138,000		
Ending inventory	12,000		

	Transferred-In Costs	Materials	Conversion Costs
Equivalent units, beginning inventory	7,000	5,600	4,900
Costs in beginning inventory	$ 53,900	$ 1,230	$ 2,110
Current-period costs	$1,088,258	$31,997	$62,276
Costs to be accounted for	$1,142,158	$33,227	$64,386
Ending inventory, percentages complete	100%	90%	75%

COMPARISON OF METHODS

Unit cost calculations will not differ significantly under the two process costing methods when costing is done monthly, unless there are violent fluctuations in costs and relatively large inventories in relation to units completed. From a product costing standpoint either method is acceptable, but from a control standpoint FIFO is preferable because it focuses attention on the current-period costs. In addition, when current-period unit costs are being compared with those budgeted or with those of prior periods, only variable costs should be included.

FIFO equivalent production and current-period costs should be used in analyzing cost behavior patterns with production as the independent variable. In using regression analysis or a scatter diagram in which units of production is the independent variable, the weighted average method based production figures would give misleading results.

The weighted average method seems to be prevalent in practice, perhaps because it is simpler to work with than FIFO. Even where FIFO is used, it tends to be a modified FIFO, such as we have illustrated, rather than a strict FIFO that requires the receiving department to keep separate track of units received from the sending department's beginning inventory and its current-period production. Essentially, then, the choice is a matter of preference and should probably be dictated by the cost of maintaining the

EXHIBIT 6–12
Unit-Cost Calculations for Dyeing Department for February—Winston Plant

	Transferred-In Costs	Materials	Conversion Costs
Current-period costs	$1,088,258	$31,997	$62,276
Divided by:			
Equivalent production (below)	143,000	143,200	142,100
Equals:			
Cost per unit	$7.6102	$0.2234	$0.4383
Equivalent production:			
Units completed	138,000	138,000	138,000
Equivalent units, ending inventory	12,000	10,800	9,000
Total	150,000	148,800	147,000
Equivalent units, beginning inventory	7,000	5,600	4,900
Equivalent production	143,000	143,200	142,100
Ending inventory costs:			
12,000 × 100% × $7.6102	$91,322		
12,000 × 90% × $0.2234		$2,413	
12,000 × 75% × $0.4383			$3,945
Costs transferred out:			
$53,900 + $7.6102[138,000 − (7,000 × 100%)]	1,050,836		
$1,230 + $0.2234[138,000 − (7,000 × 80%)]		30,808	
$2,110 + $0.4383[138,000 − (7,000 × 70%)]			60,448
Totals accounted for[a]	$1,142,158	$33,221	$64,393

[a] Differences in total costs accounted for and total costs to be accounted for (bottom of Exhibit 6–11) are rounding errors.

system. By that criterion the weighted average method would more than likely be the choice, but individual circumstances might encourage the use of FIFO.

SUMMARY

Process costing is used by firms that make the same product in more or less continuous processes. For such firms, the unit cost figure given by dividing costs by production is a reasonable figure because all units are more or less the same.

Process costing requires a cost flow assumption. Weighted average and FIFO are the principal assumptions used; each has advantages and disadvantages, and each requires different cost data and different data for equivalent production.

ASSIGNMENTS

6–1 **FIFO and Weighted Average.**

Required: What conditions are necessary for FIFO and weighted average unit costs to be significantly different?

6–2 **Basic Process Costing.**   The data below summarize the operations of Department 202 of the Milton Manufacturing Company.

	Units	Costs
Beginning inventory	800	
Transferred-in costs, 100% complete		$ 1,000
Conversion costs, 70% complete		5,600
Transferred in during period	10,000	11,000
Transferred out	9,000	
Ending inventory, 60% complete for		
conversion costs	1,800	

Department 202 does not add materials to the product. Total conversion costs incurred during the period were $90,800.

Required:

1. Using the weighted average method, determine the amounts of cost transferred to the next department and remaining in Department 202 Work-in-Process Inventory.

2. Repeat item 1, using FIFO.

6–3 **Basic Process Costing—Single Department.** The Wynn Company operates a number of plants. One, the Kelton plant, makes a single product that goes through a mixing process and a drying process. The data below relate to the operations of the mixing department in January and February.

	January	February
Beginning inventory of work in process	0	600
Units put into process	12,400	13,100
Units completed and sent to drying	11,800	13,300
Ending inventory	600	400
Percentage completion of ending inventory:		
Materials	90%	50%
Conversion costs	60%	30%
Costs:		
Materials put into process	$258,640	$271,760
Conversion costs	526,860	569,770

Required:

1. For both January and February, use the FIFO method to determine unit costs of production, transfers out to the drying department, and ending inventories. Round to the nearest dollar.

2. Repeat item 1 using the weighted average method.

6–4 **Basic Process Costing—Second Department.** This assignment is an extension of assignment 6–3. The product that the Kelton plant makes goes from the mixing department to the drying department. The drying department does not add materials. Data for the drying department for January and February appear below.

	January	February
Beginning inventory	0	1,000
Units transferred in	11,800	13,300
Units completed and sent to finished goods	10,800	13,800
Ending inventory	1,000	500
Percentage of completion of ending inventory:		
Transferred-in costs	100%	100%
Conversion costs	80%	70%
Conversion costs incurred	$212,750	$237,620

Required:

1. Assume that the costs transferred in are the FIFO costs of the mixing department, from your solution to assignment 6–3. Determine the unit costs, transfers to finished goods, and ending inventories for the drying department for both months using FIFO. Round unit-cost calculations to four decimal places (1/100 of a cent).

2. Still assuming that the costs transferred in to the drying department are the FIFO costs of the mixing department, repeat item 1 using the weighted average method for the drying department.

6–5 **Journal Entries and T-Accounts.** This problem uses the data and solution to assignment 6–4.

Required: Using the FIFO method for both the mixing and drying departments, prepare the journal entries that affect the Work-in-Process accounts of both departments for January and February. Additionally, prepare T-accounts for the Work in Process of both departments.

6–6 **Cost Flow Relationships.** Each of the following cases is an independent situation. The data relate to conversion costs.

Required: Fill in the blanks, assuming the use of the weighted average method.

Case	Beginning Inventory	Current-Period Costs Incurred	Costs Transferred Out	Ending Inventory	Equivalent Production	Unit Cost
a	$10,000	$210,000	$ _____	$24,000	_____ units	$ 2
b	$ _____	$ 64,000	$ _____	$ 8,000	20,000 units	$ 4
c	$20,000	$ _____	$ 90,000	$ 6,000	_____ units	$10
d	$40,000	$200,000	$180,000	$ _____	15,000 units	$ _

6–7 **Cost Flow Relationships.** Each of the following cases is an independent situation. The data relate to conversion costs.

Required: Fill in the blanks, assuming the use of FIFO.

Case	Beginning Inventory	Current-Period Costs Incurred	Costs Transferred Out	Ending Inventory	Equivalent Production	Unit Cost
a	$ _____	$ 93,000	$ 86,000	$12,000	_____ units	$3
b	$21,000	$ _____	$ _____	$16,000	12,000 units	$8
c	$30,000	$120,000	$ _____	$20,000	10,000 units	$_
d	$10,000	$ _____	$100,000	$ 8,000	_____ units	$4

6–8 **Equivalent Production.** The Brooks Chemical Company makes a product called tricide. Tricide goes through a mixing process in liquid form, then is dried under heat until it becomes powder. The yield rarely changes: each gallon put into the drying process yields six ounces of powdered tricide. The following information is available from the firm's records for the month of August.

	Mixing Department	Drying Department
Beginning inventory	18,000	114,300
Put into process	180,000	?
Ending inventory	26,000	81,200
Transferred out	?	?

Data for the mixing department are in gallons, for the drying department in ounces. All inventories are 100 percent complete for materials, 60 percent for conversion costs, at both July 31 and August 31.

Required:

1. Determine weighted average equivalent production for both departments.
2. Repeat item 1, using FIFO.

6–9 Cost-of-Production Report (Weighted Average). This problem uses the weighted average equivalent production figures from assignment 6–8. The Brooks Chemical Company showed the following figures for August, with the beginning inventory reflecting the use of the weighted average method.

	Mixing Department	
	Materials	Conversion Costs
Beginning inventory	$ 14,800	$ 22,400
Current period costs	146,300	379,800

Required: Prepare a cost of production report for the mixing department for August, using the weighted average method.

6–10 Second Department (AICPA adapted). The wiring department is the second stage of the Flem Company's production cycle. On May 1 the beginning work in process contained 25,000 units that were 60 percent complete as to conversion costs. During May the wiring department received 100,000 units from the first stage of the production cycle. On May 31 the ending work in process contained 20,000 units that were 80 percent complete as to conversion costs. The wiring department adds materials at the end of the process.

Required:

1. Determine equivalent production for transferred-in costs, materials, and conversion costs, using the weighted average method.
2. Repeat item 1, using FIFO.

6–11 Process Costing and Decisions. The Mountainview Brick Company received an order for 300,000 bricks from a large construction company. The price was to be $1,000 per 1,000 bricks and the customer would pay shipping costs. The usual selling price is $1,200 per 1,000, but Mountainview had some excess capacity and accepted the order, even though it necessitated some overtime and expediting costs.

One of the members of the controller's staff made the following analysis before the firm accepted the order.

	Expected Results	
	Reject Order	Accept Order
Beginning inventory	$ 397,400	$ 397,400
Current-period costs:		
Materials	$2,186,900	2,301,500
Conversion costs	3,765,000	3,984,700
Totals	$6,349,300	$6,683,600
Units completed	10,672,000	10,972,000
Equivalent units in ending inventory	886,400	886,400
Total equivalent production	11,558,400	11,858,400
Unit cost	$ 0.549	$ 0.564

Materials and conversion costs are generally about the same percentage complete. The staff member noted that the unit cost would rise somewhat but would still be less than the $1 selling price, and so the firm should accept the order. The actual results for the month turned out about as the staff member had predicted.

Required: Determine whether the firm should have accepted the order.

6-12 **Unit Costs.** The Jordan Company makes a single product, a cloth backpack. The firm does not consider the cutting and sewing processes as different departments, but it does keep track of labor time for each process separately. The data below reflect operations for July. There were no inventories at the beginning of July.

Packs completed	20,000
Packs in process:	
Packs cut, but not sewed	2,000
Packs half sewed	1,000
Conversion costs:	
Cutting operation	$22,540
Sewing operation	$33,210
Material cost of packs put into process	$46,000

Required: Determine the cost of packs completed and the cost of partly finished packs.

6-13 **Process Costing (FIFO), Two Materials.** The Reiner Company makes a single product. The firm heats a chemical called algon for about three hours, then adds another chemical called bygon and heats the mixture for an additional hour. Conversion costs are assumed to be incurred evenly over the process. The firm uses process costing, even though it makes individual batches of the product. The firm has several vats for the heating and mixing and usually has a batch in each vat.

At January 1, 19X5, the firm had twenty batches in process. For fifteen of the batches the percentage of conversion was 40 percent, for the other five it was 90 percent. Material cost for the beginning inventory was $17,000 for algon and $6,000 for bygon, and conversion costs were $54,500. During January the firm completed 350 batches and at the end of the month had ten batches in process. All these batches were 80 percent complete for conversion.

Cost data for January were: algon put into process, $287,000; bygon put into process, $400,200; conversion costs, $1,820,000.

Required:

1. Determine the unit costs for algon, bygon, and conversion for January, using FIFO.

2. Determine the cost of ending inventory of work in process and the cost transferred to finished goods.

6–14 Equivalent Production. The mixing department of one plant of the Chemcol Company experienced the following results in February.

	Pounds
Beginning inventory, three-fourths complete for conversion costs	60,000
Pounds started in process in February	840,000
Pounds transferred out	860,000
Ending inventory, one-fourth complete for conversion costs	40,000

The department does not add materials, only works on product transferred in from the prior department.

Required:

1. Determine equivalent production for prior department costs and conversion costs, using the weighted average method.

2. Repeat item 1, using FIFO.

6–15 Basic Process Costing. The Jardin Corporation uses process costing. Products are started in department 100. For December, beginning work-in-process inventory included 3,500 units that were 90 percent complete in materials and 70 percent complete for labor and other conversion costs. December 31 work-in-process inventory was 4,000 units 100 percent complete in materials and 50 percent complete in conversion costs. January 31 work-in-process inventory was 2,000 units 80 percent complete for materials and 60 percent complete in conversion costs. The firm put 32,000 units into production in December, 25,000 in January.

Required:

1. Using both weighted average and FIFO, calculate equivalent units of production for department 100 for December and for January.

2. Assume that the following costs were recorded.

	Materials	Conversion
Work in process, 12/1	$ 111,037.50	$ 118,825
Current costs—December	$1,164,600	$1,459,350
—January	$ 873,300	$1,244,500

Determine the costs per equivalent unit in December and in January. (Use both weighted average and FIFO assumptions.)

3. Using FIFO, determine the inventories of work in process at December 31 and January 31, and the costs transferred out of department 100 in each of the two months.

6–16 Inventory and Transfers (AICPA adapted).   The Wit Corporation's Department A is the first stage of production. The following data relate to May.

		Materials	Conversion Costs
Beginning work in process		$ 4,000	$ 3,000
Current-period costs		$20,000	$16,000
Units completed	90,000		
Units in ending work-in-process inventory	10,000		

Materials go into process at the beginning of the production cycle. The ending inventory was 50 percent complete as to conversion costs. The firm uses the weighted average method.

Required:

1. Determine the cost of the ending inventory of work in process.

2. Determine the cost of goods transferred to the next department.

6–17 Comprehensive Process Costing (AICPA adapted).   The Ballinger Paper Company makes high-quality paper boxes. The box department performs two separate operations. One group of machines cuts and trims paper to the required dimensions. Another group of machines then folds and creases the paper, forming the boxes. All work in process consists of paper forms cut and trimmed, but not folded and creased. These forms are considered 50% complete as to conversion costs. The firm uses the weighted average method for all of its inventories. One square yard of paper yields four boxes.

Data relating to August, 19X4 appear at the top of page 273.

	Cost	Quantity
Materials (paper)		
Inventory at August 1	$ 82,000	400,000 square yards
Purchases in August	326,000	1,300,000
Inventory at August 31	?	325,000
Box department		
Beginning inventory of boxes in process:		
Material cost	$ 41,700	800,000 boxes cut and trimmed
Conversion cost	22,150	
Boxes completed and transferred to finished goods	?	6,000,000 boxes
Work in process at August 31	?	300,000 boxes
Finished goods		
Beginning inventory	$ 46,400	400,000 boxes
Ending inventory	?	500,000 boxes

Conversion costs for August were $230,000.

Required:

1. Determine the cost of materials put into production.
2. Determine the unit costs of boxes for August.
3. Determine the cost of boxes transferred to finished goods and the ending inventory of work in process.
4. Determine cost of goods sold and the ending inventory of finished goods.

6–18 Comprehensive Process Costing (AICPA adapted). Data related to the August operations of the Ballinger Paper Company appear in assignment 6–17 on page 272. Let us assume that the firm uses FIFO for work-in-process inventory and continues to use weighted average for materials and finished goods.

Required: Redo items 2, 3, and 4 using FIFO. Your answer to item 1 remains valid for the new situation.

6–19 Change in Measure of Units. The Virgule Company makes shaving lotion in two departments, mixing and heating. The mixing department blends dry chemicals and transfers the resulting powder to the heating department, which adds water and heats the mixture. The finished lotion emerges from the heating department. The measure of output in the mixing department is pounds, in the heating department is gallons. Each pound put into process in the heating department results in 0.40 gallon of lotion. Data related to March, 19X0, appear on page 274.

	Mixing Department	Heating Department
Beginning inventory	8,000 lb	4,000 gal
Put into production	74,000 lb	28,000 gal
Completed and transferred	70,000 lb	29,000 gal
Ending inventory	12,000 lb	3,000 gal
Costs		
Beginning inventory:		
Prior department costs	—	$20,200
Materials	$ 3,600	600
Conversion costs	12,000	1,800
Current-period costs:		
Materials	33,300	4,200
Conversion costs	149,950	33,850

The ending inventory of the mixing department is complete for materials, 75 percent complete for conversion costs. The heating department ending inventory is complete for materials, two-thirds complete for conversion costs. The firm uses the weighted average inventory method.

Required:

1. Determine the amount of cost transferred from the mixing department to the heating department.
2. Determine the amount of cost transferred from the heating department to finished goods and the ending inventory of work in process in the heating department.

6–20 Unit Costs. The Bronson Table Company produces a single model table consisting of a top and four legs. The chief accountant, in conjunction with the production manager, has developed the following information about the manufacturing process.

Operation	Labor Time (hours)
Cut sheet of wood to make top	0.10 per top
Sand top	0.05 per top
Cut dowels to make legs	0.05 per leg
Sand legs	0.01 per leg
Glue legs to top	0.10 per table
Paint table	0.20 per table

During March the firm had the following results. There were no beginning inventories.

Tables completed, sent to finished goods   6,000

Work-in-process inventory at March 31:

Tables glued, not painted	800
Sanded tops	300
Sanded legs	1,000
Legs cut, not sanded	500

Total conversion costs for March were $96,000.

Required: Determine the amount of conversion cost transferred to Finished Goods and the amounts remaining in Work in Process. For work in process, determine the cost of *each* component (glued tables, sanded tops, and so on).

6–21 Process Costing and Decisions. The Williams Company operates a plant that weaves cotton. The plant also dyes and waterproofs some of the fabric. The plant currently sells about 40 percent of its output of 2 million square yards after weaving. It dyes the rest and waterproofs half of what it dyes. For technical reasons, it cannot waterproof undyed fabric.

The plant accumulates material and direct labor cost by department (weaving, dyeing, waterproofing) and applies overhead based on a single plantwide rate of $3.55 per direct labor dollar. The statement of gross margin below reflects a typical month's operations, in thousands of dollars.

	Total	Woven Fabric	Dyed Fabric	Waterproofed Fabric
Sales	$1,925.1	$ 640.2	$582.3	$702.6
Cost of sales	1,581.0	496.8	479.5	604.7
Gross margin	$ 344.1	$ 143.4	$102.8	$ 97.9
Gross margin percentages	17.9%	22.4%	17.7%	13.9%
Cost of sales calculations				
Materials		$ 806.0	$ 58.3	$ 42.4
Prior department costs		0.0	745.1	479.5
Direct labor		95.8	34.2	18.2
Overhead at $3.55 per labor dollar		340.1	121.4	64.6
Totals		1,241.9	$959.0	604.7
Transferred to next department		745.1	479.5	0.0
Cost of sales		$ 496.8	$479.5	$604.7

Thus, the cost of sales for woven fabric is 40 percent of the total costs of the weaving department because the firm sells 40 percent of woven fabric, transfers 60 percent to the dyeing department. (Inventories are negligible.)

Some of the managers have expressed concern about the waterproofing operation because of its low gross margin percentage. They have also questioned whether the dyeing operation is sufficiently profitable. The demand for the firm's products exceeds productive capacity. The firm accepts orders for the three different products and schedules production accordingly, within the constraint that it cannot weave more than 2 million square yards per month. Although demand is high, competition is strong, and the firm could not raise prices on any product without suffering a considerable drop in demand.

In analyzing the operations, the controller developed the following information about manufacturing overhead in each department. He had been critical of the practice of applying overhead on a plantwide basis, but he had not pushed for departmental rates because the other managers were not amenable to the change.

	Weaving	Dyeing	Waterproofing
Monthly fixed overhead (thousands)	$343.5	$52.4	$44.1
Variable per labor dollar	$ 0.60	$ 0.65	$ 0.35

Required: Analyze the situation and make whatever recommendations you think wise, supporting them with appropriate calculations and stating your assumptions.

Standards:
Company Plans and Results

Chapter 7

Most financial accounting statements you have seen up to this point reflect current actual performance. Even if a modification is made to use *normal* costing to develop a predetermined overhead rate, results from a period are presented basically as they actually occurred. Actual and normal costing are the basis of job order and process costing as discussed in Chapters 5 and 6. It is important to know actual results. However, as managers we are also interested in a comparison of these results against the plans we made at the beginning of a period.

Our analysis of CVP relationships in Chapter 2 focused on plans. What target profit is projected for the period? This is a basic question because profit is the result of:

1. the number of units sold.
2. the product mix.
3. the prices received for each product.
4. the cost of the products sold:
    a. amount, mix, and cost of various materials.
    b. amount and cost of labor.
    c. amount and cost of fixed and variable overhead.
5. the other costs of the period:
    a. fixed and variable sales cost.
    b. fixed and variable distribution costs.
    c. fixed and variable administration costs.

This chapter develops methods for evaluating performance in relation to plans. These methods address the question of how the critical factors listed above contribute to deviations between planned and actual results.

STANDARDS: COSTS AND PRICES

Plans can range from the very general to the very specific. Increasing sales by 10 percent is a general plan; selling 10,000 more Model fx-12 minicomputers at an average price of $20,500 is a specific plan. When we talk about total revenues and total costs, we can formalize plans into budgets. However, when we talk about looking at planned unit costs and planned unit selling prices, the term we can use is **standards.**

Illustration: Standards for Midwest Brewery

Midwest Brewery produces a single grade of beer. The marketing department has estimated that sales will be 10,000 barrels for the next quarter. Planned results include estimated revenues and sales promotion costs (advertising, store displays, entertainment, and so on). The purchasing agent and production manager will use these plans to order materials and to schedule machinery and workers. Each barrel of beer is more or less like every other barrel, and so it is possible to develop standard costs per barrel. Standard costs would be developed for materials, direct labor, variable overhead, and fixed overhead. The managers of the brewery might have determined that each barrel requires just about 0.40 hour of labor time and that laborers are paid, per union contract, $9 per hour. The standard labor cost per barrel would be $3.60 (0.40 × $9). Similar analyses would be made for each raw material. Variable overhead would be related to labor hours or perhaps machine hours, using techniques described in Chapter 3.

Company chemists, tasters, and engineers use linear programming techniques to establish the least costly combination of raw materials that yield the required quality. Thus, the purchasing agent for Midwest knows how much grain, barley, hops, and other material to buy, given estimated sales of 10,000 barrels. The production manager has standards for machine hours and labor hours for each barrel. Therefore, when the quarter begins, Midwest's managers have operationalized the sales department plans based on operating standards.

MARKETING STANDARDS

Profits are affected by both revenues and costs, and these factors should be discussed separately. Managers predict revenue based on specific sales projections for each product. They project the number of units to be sold, the pricing strategy for each product, and total sales revenue. For a multiproduct firm, total sales revenue is determined by *volume, product mix,* and *sales price per unit.* Deviations of actual results from plans are called *gross margin variances* or *gross profit variances.*

Gross Margin Variances

Since profits are an important measure of success, all the variances we discuss will relate directly to profits. We look first at **gross margin variances.** These variances are the deviation of actual gross margin from planned gross margin caused solely by changes in sales volume, product mix, or sales price.

Variances between plans and actual results occur for a multitude of reasons. If a manager is going to make some sense out of comparing results with plans, he needs to isolate causes as much as possible. The key to analyzing variances is to *look at only one factor at a time.* This key has two levels:

1. What is the total variance caused by divergence of sales volume, mix, and prices from plans *holding everything else constant?*
2. Within that total sales (gross margin) variance, what is the variance caused by sales price when mix and volume are held constant; the variance in sales volume when mix and price are held constant; and the variance in mix of products sold when price and volume are held constant?

Thus, we look at one variance at a time and hold everything else constant. This process moves from actual results back to planned results as we identify variances along the way.

Cause and Effect. It is important to understand what we mean by a variance. At this point, we will simply compare standards with actual performance. A variance will be a dollar reflection of the differences. This comparison does not reveal *why* a variance or series of variances has occurred; it identifies amounts but does *not* establish a *cause-and-effect* relationship. Chapter 19 deals with the investigation of causality. Later discussion in this chapter shows the importance of causality as it relates to the responsibilities of various managers.

Management must have well-developed plans in order to calculate margin variances. Deviations from plans that are ill formed or too broad are impossible to analyze. Plans, budgets, and standards must all be reasonable estimates of anticipated performance if variances are to be used for evaluation and comparison.

The Variance Continuum. While we define a total gross margin variance as the difference between actual gross margin and planned gross margin, how do we look at individual gross margin variances? Exhibit 7–1 on page 280 shows the total gross margin variance, as well as individual

EXHIBIT 7–1
Single-Product Company Gross Margin Variances

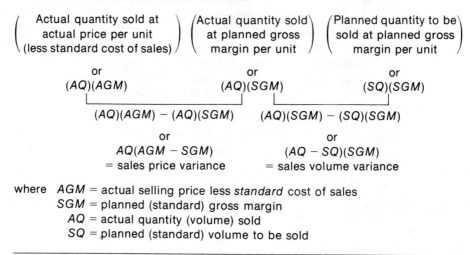

1. Total Gross Margin (Sales) Variance

$$\left(\begin{array}{c} \text{Actual quantity sold at} \\ \text{actual price per unit} \\ \text{(less standard cost of sales)} \end{array} \right) - \left(\begin{array}{c} \text{Planned quantity to be sold at} \\ \text{planned gross margin per unit} \end{array} \right)$$

= total gross margin variance

2. Sales Price and Sales Volume Variances

$$\left(\begin{array}{c} \text{Actual quantity sold at} \\ \text{actual price per unit} \\ \text{(less standard cost of sales)} \end{array} \right) \left(\begin{array}{c} \text{Actual quantity sold} \\ \text{at planned gross} \\ \text{margin per unit} \end{array} \right) \left(\begin{array}{c} \text{Planned quantity to be} \\ \text{sold at planned gross} \\ \text{margin per unit} \end{array} \right)$$

or
$(AQ)(AGM)$

or
$(AQ)(SGM)$

or
$(SQ)(SGM)$

$(AQ)(AGM) - (AQ)(SGM)$ $(AQ)(SGM) - (SQ)(SGM)$

or
$AQ(AGM - SGM)$
= sales price variance

or
$(AQ - SQ)(SGM)$
= sales volume variance

where AGM = actual selling price less *standard* cost of sales
SGM = planned (standard) gross margin
AQ = actual quantity (volume) sold
SQ = planned (standard) volume to be sold

variances: the variance related to selling price and the one related to the quantity of units sold. Exhibit 7–1 shows the continuum from actual results back to planned margin. In keeping with the key to variance analysis, *costs are held constant* by using standard cost of sales. Thus, even though the left-hand column is identified as actual gross margin (AGM), it combines actual price and standard cost. If we included actual costs at this point, we would confuse the issue, since the difference between *true* actual margin and standard margin reflects both sale price *and* cost variances. Some firms make the analysis using contribution margin instead of gross margin.

The Algebra of Gross Margin Variances

Summarizing the variance information from Exhibit 7–1 gives the following formulas for gross margin variances:

Total gross margin variance:

$$GMV_{\text{tot}} = (AGM)(AQ) - (SGM)(SQ)$$

Sales price variance:

$$V_p = AQ(AGM - SGM)$$

Sales volume variance:

$$V_v = (AQ - SQ)SGM$$

Illustration: Analysis for Mencento Chemical.   Mencento Chemical produces a single product. Exhibit 7–2 shows planned and actual sales data. Only two things are involved in this analysis: what were the sales price and the sales volume as compared to plans? To isolate the variance caused by sales price, we look at the difference between the planned price of $5.10 and the actual price of $5.25. Prices were higher than planned by 15 cents per unit. Since Mencento sold 113,000 units at $0.15 per unit *over* planned price, the **sales price variance** is $16,950 Favorable (F) ($0.15 × 113,000 units). Since the actual price is greater than the planned price, resulting in a favorable variance, it follows that the terms **favorable** and **unfavorable** are used to denote the effect of a variance on planned income.

EXHIBIT 7–2
Data for Illustration

	Planned	Actual
Sales during 19X7	115,000 units	113,000 units
Selling price	$ 5.10/unit	$ 5.25/unit
Cost of goods sold	$ 3.75/unit	
Fixed selling expenses	$50,000	$50,000

Not only did the actual price differ from the planned price, but volume was 2,000 units lower than planned (115,000 − 113,000). Planned margin was $1.35 per unit ($5.10 − $3.75). The **sales volume variance** is $2,700 Unfavorable (U) ($1.35 × 2,000 units). Algebraically, these variances are:

$$V_p = 113,000(\$1.50 - \$1.35) = \$16,950F$$
$$V_v = (113,000 - 115,000)\$1.35 = \$(2,700)U$$
$$GMV_{tot} = (\$1.50)(113,000) - (\$1.35)(115,000) = \$14,250F$$

Graphical Analysis.   Figure 7–1 on page 282 is a graph of the data for Mencento Chemical. The shaded rectangle *ABHG* represents plans: planned margin ($1.35) and planned volume (115,000 units). The rectangle *BCFE* shows the favorable sales price variance of 15 cents times actual sales of 113,000 units, while the rectangle *EDGH* shows the unfavorable volume variance arising because actual sales were 2,000 units below planned sales.

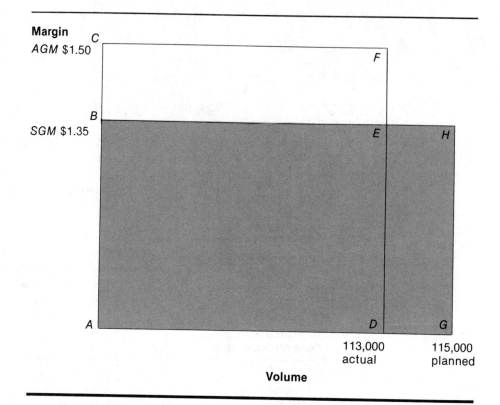

FIGURE 7–1
Marketing Variances

We have been describing variances in terms that go beyond mathematics, so that we can keep track of the inherent logic in the situation. When our descriptions of variances include what is happening, such as a higher-than-expected selling price and a lower-than-expected sales volume, we then have better ways to conclude that a variance is favorable or unfavorable than by relying on the formulas and the sign (+, −) of the answer.

The Multiproduct Company

Most companies market more than one product or service. A sporting goods firm may make football, baseball, tennis, and other equipment. A public accounting firm offers services in tax, auditing, management information systems, and so on. We saw in CVP analysis that company management may be able to forecast a planned, stable mix of products and, using a weighted average contribution margin, employ the basic linear CVP relationship to plan the ensuing period. Identifying a *sales mix variance* involves this same logic. Exhibit 7–3 extends Exhibit 7–1 by looking at the multiproduct company and by identifying three gross margin variances.

Illustration: Mencento Sales Mix Variance.   Assume that the data presented in Exhibit 7–2 represent the weighted average of two products instead of just one. Analysis of the data yields the results presented in Exhibit 7–4.

EXHIBIT 7–3
Multiproduct Company Gross Margin Variances

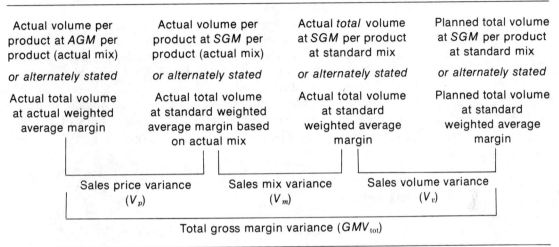

Actual volume per product at *AGM* per product (actual mix)	Actual volume per product at *SGM* per product (actual mix)	Actual *total* volume at *SGM* per product at standard mix	Planned total volume at *SGM* per product at standard mix
or alternately stated	*or alternately stated*	*or alternately stated*	*or alternately stated*
Actual total volume at actual weighted average margin	Actual total volume at standard weighted average margin based on actual mix	Actual total volume at standard weighted average margin	Planned total volume at standard weighted average margin

Sales price variance (V_p) Sales mix variance (V_m) Sales volume variance (V_v)

Total gross margin variance (GMV_{tot})

EXHIBIT 7–4
Data for Illustration

	Planned		Actual	
	Flamex	Retardex	Flamex	Retardex
Sales during 19X7	57,500 units	57,500 units	45,200 units	67,800 units
Selling price per unit	$5.20	$5.00	$5.20	$5.21667
Unit cost of goods sold	$3.95	$3.55		

Since variances are a logical analysis of the facts, we can look at the data in Exhibit 7–4 and identify three things that have differed from plans:

1. Mencento received 21+ cents more per unit for Retardex than they planned ($5.21667 versus $5.00).
2. The mix of the two products was 40%/60% instead of 50%/50% (and Retardex has a higher margin than Flamex).
3. The total sales volume is 2,000 units less than planned (113,000 versus 115,000 total).

Therefore, we should see an unfavorable variance for volume and favorable variances for sales mix and sales price.

The *price variance* isolates changes in price, given actual quantity sold and the actual mix of products.

Flamex: $45,200(\$1.25\,AGM - \$1.25\,SGM) = 0$
Retardex: $67,800(\$1.66667\,AGM - \$1.45\,SGM) = \$14,690F$

The *mix variance* holds total quantity constant and margins constant and looks just at mix differences.

Planned Results for Mencento. Flamex and Retardex were planned to be sold in a 50/50 ratio. Therefore, if 113,000 units in total were sold, 56,500 units of each product should have been sold at a standard margin of $1.25 for Flamex and $1.45 for Retardex. Planned weighted average margin is $1.35 [(0.5)(1.25) + (0.5)(1.45)].

Actual Results for Mencento. Results were that 45,200 units of Flamex and 67,800 units of Retardex made up the total sales of 113,000 units. This is a 40/60 ratio. The actual weighted margin is

$$(0.4)(\$1.25) + (0.6)(\$1.45) = \$1.37$$

and the mix variance is

$$113,000(\$1.37 - \$1.35) = \$2,260\overset{\frown}{F}$$

Finally, the *volume variance* is just 2,000 units below plans times the weighted average standard margin of $1.35, or $2,700U. In the format of Exhibit 7–3, these variances are shown below.

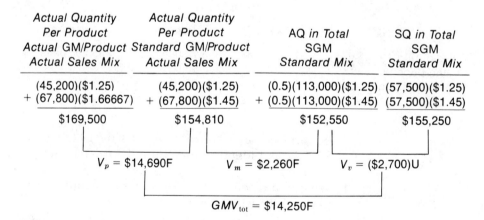

Actual Quantity Per Product Actual GM/Product Actual Sales Mix	Actual Quantity Per Product Standard GM/Product Actual Sales Mix	AQ in Total SGM Standard Mix	SQ in Total SGM Standard Mix
(45,200)($1.25) + (67,800)($1.66667)	(45,200)($1.25) + (67,800)($1.45)	(0.5)(113,000)($1.25) + (0.5)(113,000)($1.45)	(57,500)($1.25) (57,500)($1.45)
$169,500	$154,810	$152,550	$155,250

$$V_p = \$14,690F \qquad V_m = \$2,260F \qquad V_v = (\$2,700)U$$

$$GMV_{tot} = \$14,250F$$

Establishing Marketing Plans

As we will discuss in detail in Chapter 13, the sales forecast is the first step in a company's overall budgeting. Traditionally sales forecasts have not been called standards, although planned costs are termed standard costs.

An important question for the management of any company is "What business are we in?" The answer is needed for both product and pricing decisions. For example, before investors decide to build a chain of car wash/filling stations, they must decide, among other things, what kind of car wash to offer (wash just the car's exterior or also clean the interior), what kind of gas to have (major brand or independent), and what kind of gas/oil products to market (besides regular and no-lead should there be no-lead premium or diesel?).

In order to market and price their products, managements must know who their competitors are. For example, a chain of car wash/filling stations competes against other car washes as well as nearby gas stations.

Many businesses are quite seasonal. Sales are heavier in one month than other months. Even industries such as public utilities are affected, where electric companies need peak power production on hot summer afternoons while natural gas companies deliver the most therms of gas on cold winter nights. A car wash is affected by weather. Winter snow (together with salt on the streets) produces the highest activity while late summer drought or autumn steady rains produce the lowest.

Many firms offer a full line of models and accessories even if small segments of the line are not very profitable. A supermarket offers a special on Pompeii Pizza at a few cents over (or even under) its variable cost as a loss leader to draw in customers who will buy other products at full markup.

Managers can use sophisticated forecasting models based on the multiple regression model to predict sales based on general economic conditions, season of the year, location and activity of competitors, past sales trends, and the like. Many time-sharing networks include forecasting packages, making these models available to even the smallest firm at reasonable cost.

PRODUCTION STANDARDS

In analyzing gross margin variances, we referred to plans as standards for comparison. In many cases, especially in process costing settings, standards can be established for production costs.

In an automobile stamping plant, for example, it is possible to set standards for various costs. Each front fender will use a specified amount of metal of a certain grade and thickness. Standards can be set for how many fenders will be produced each hour. Union contracts provide for required crew size for a machine and for uniform wage rates.

Why Standard Costs?

Basic CVP analysis develops a basic formula for costs:

$$\text{total cost} = \text{fixed cost} + (\text{variable cost})(\text{quantity})$$

Chapter 1 referred to this basic cost formula as a **flexible budget.** If a budget is a plan for the next period, we can specify the assumptions that make up the budget. Production standards, then, are a list of usual (expected) production costs broken down by materials, labor costs, and overhead costs. They are what a product *should* cost to manufacture. Managers do not expect actual results in the future to exactly match these standards, but standard costs can be used as a reference for comparison and control.

Product Costing.   A distinct advantage to setting standards is that these standards can be applied in the product costing cycle. If inventories are all carried at standard, a good amount of bookkeeping is eliminated. Identical products are all carried in inventory at the same cost per unit. Variances from standard are placed into separate accounts, and they are either treated as a period expense or prorated between inventories and cost of goods sold. This subject is covered in detail in the next chapter.

Control.   Standards represent what costs should be. When actual results differ from these standards, management can analyze the variances and evaluate managerial performance as well as decide what actions should be taken. This is the *control* aspect of standards and variances.

Pricing.   Another use of standard costs is in pricing decisions. Since standards are defined as usual or expected costs, they are a logical basis for prices.

For example, Universe Press prints magazines. Assume a new customer approaches management and asks for a quotation on a 96-page magazine, specifying the grade and weight of paper, the size (such as $8\frac{1}{8} \times 10\frac{7}{8}$ inches), and the way in which colors are to be printed (such as a four-color front and back cover and only black and white for the balance of the magazine). The estimating department can go to a set of standards for that type of magazine and use them to establish what it will cost in paper, ink, labor, overhead, and so on to produce the magazine. These costs can be marked up to yield Universe a reasonable profit and then submitted to the prospective client.

Developing Cost Standards

Not all industries can successfully use standard costing or standard costs. For example, a firm making individual unique products may not be able to develop standards for production. However, in companies where there is a fairly homogeneous product, or where nonhomogeneous products require homogeneous operations, standards can be used for planning and control and for product costing.

Standards From Past Records.   A good first step in establishing standard costs is to analyze past records. Past data can be used to predict future costs if operating conditions are fairly constant between past and future time periods. If a new plant has been operating for only a year, these data may not be representative, since the bugs may not all be worked out of the equipment and personnel may still be learning how to efficiently and effectively operate the equipment. (The concept of learning curves is covered in detail in Chapter 22.)

Universe Press, for example, has been in business for many years and has used its current type of printing equipment for the past five years. A review of past records can reveal a clear pattern of costs. Assume this review points to two distinct types of costs: start-up (or makeready) costs and running costs. Start-up costs are the costs of cleaning up a press from the last job, removing the printing plates from that job, mounting new printing plates, threading a new roll of paper through the press, and getting ready to run. Past records show that the more color the job requires and the more expensive the grade of paper, the longer (and more costly) the makeready. Standards can be developed as shown in Exhibit 7–5.

EXHIBIT 7–5
Standard Cost Card

Standard Makeready Costs

Clean up from old job and mount new plate	0.5 hour each 8 pages
Add for each additional color	0.25 hour each 8 pages
Add for coated paper[a]	0.5 hour per job
Standard crew costs	$47.50 per hour
Standard overhead	$40.00 per labor hour
Plus standard paper costs for the equivalent of 200 copies as expected start-up waste	

[a] Coated paper is the glossy kind found in many magazines. In contrast, most newspapers use newsprint.

Running costs include standards for wage rates, running speed, paper and ink costs, and expected paper use. Past records reveal that a 96-page magazine is most economically produced as two 48-page pieces (called sections). The wage rates and crew size and makeup are set by union contract. Shorter-running jobs usually entail a greater cost per unit than longer jobs. The presses will not be able to get up to high-speed operation with short jobs, and expected waste (itself an $a + bx$ relationship) will be higher.

Past records are used here to establish standards in labor hours to be used and paper to be consumed. Current prices can then be applied to these standards to get a standard cost of production.

The principal difficulty with using historical data to establish standards is that inefficiencies may be built into the standards. Past operations may have been inefficient because of inadequate supervision or poor methods or materials. Standards based on past performance do not allow for improvement and, therefore, may not always be reliable.

Engineered Standards. An alternative to using historical data to set standards is the engineering approach. This general approach was discussed in Chapter 3 in connection with cost estimation. Basically, engineers develop standards for materials, direct labor, and variable overhead by studying the product and the production process. Time and motion studies are made to reveal the labor time required for each operation in the production process. Material requirements are estimated on the basis of such factors as the expected normal waste from, for example, cutting circular pieces out of rectangular metal sheets. Variable overhead is estimated on the basis of factors such as fringe benefits for laborers and power requirements for machinery.

Engineered standards are especially useful when managers are evaluating new products. Because the firm has no experience with these products, its historical records are of no value except insofar as they can be related to the operations needed to make the new products. For example, if a new product is expected to require a grinding operation similar to one now used for an existing product, managers may be confident that the grinding time for the new product will be about the same as that for the existing product.

One problem with engineered standards is that they may be too tight, failing to allow for the behavior of workers. The mechanistic approach to management pioneered by Taylor and others in the early 1900s has fallen into some disfavor because it fails to accommodate the attitudes and desires of workers, considering them to be adjuncts to machinery. The range of behavioral problems associated with the setting of standards is discussed later in this chapter.

Standard Costs: Materials

Material standards can be broken down into **material prices** and **material use.** We will use this same analysis when investigating material variances; it is quite like the analysis of gross margin price and volume variances.

Material Prices.   Usually a purchasing department buys necessary materials for a company. Major contracts are often signed for important goods. Contracts are intended to ensure a steady source of supply and provide an orderly process for pricing. For example, a contract can specify current prices and can tie future increases (or decreases) to an index (such as the Consumer Price Index). If a usual source of materials exists or if a contract for materials is in force, management can establish material price standards. Since the purchasing function precedes the production function and actual costs can be compared to standard costs, a material price variance can be isolated at the time of purchase. Not only does this identify a variance as soon as possible, but it also begins the process of a preliminary assignment of responsibility. Raw material inventories can be carried at standard cost, and a production manager is then charged for the actual quantity of material used at the standard cost. If responsibility for a material price variance belongs with a purchasing department, the production manager's costs do not reflect either favorable or unfavorable purchases.

Material Price Variance. Variable cost production variances are almost identical in form to gross margin variances. For a **material price variance** we are interested in comparing prices actually paid with those expected to be paid for the actual goods purchased. The algebra is:

$$\text{material price variance } (V_p) = \text{actual quantity purchased}$$
$$\times \text{ (actual cost per unit}$$
$$- \text{ standard cost per unit)}$$

or

$$V_p = AQ(AP - SP)$$

where AQ = actual quantity purchased
AP = actual price per unit
SP = standard price per unit

To continue the Mencento Chemical example, assume Mencento is a single-product firm with a standard cost per unit as shown in Exhibit 7–6.

EXHIBIT 7–6
Standard Cost Card

MENCENTO CHEMICAL

Standard Cost Per Unit

Direct materials: 2 pounds at $0.50/lb	$1.00
Direct labor: 0.25 hour at $6/hr	1.50
Variable overhead: 0.25 direct labor hour at $2/hr	0.50
Fixed overhead	0.75
Standard cost per unit	$3.75

This cost of $3.75 per unit ties in with Exhibit 7–2 for the calculation of standard gross margin. Assume that fixed overhead is planned to be $112,500 per year and that management has decided to apply overhead based on 150,000 units. Thus, the standard fixed overhead on a per-unit basis is $0.75 ($112,500 divided by 150,000 units). Actual results for Mencento are presented in Exhibit 7–7.

EXHIBIT 7–7
Actual Results—Mencento Company

Materials purchased:	300,000 lb at $0.48/lb
Materials used:	220,000 lb (no beginning inventory)
Current production:	100,000 units of product

The material price variance is:

$$V_p = AQ(AP - SP)$$
$$= 300,000(\$0.48 - \$0.50) = (\$6,000)F$$

In our example of gross margin variances a negative variance was unfavorable, since the actual gross margin was less than the standard gross margin. Therefore, income was reduced. In production variances, however, a negative number is favorable, since actual costs are less than expected costs, thereby increasing income.

Material Quantity Variance.   As goods are entered into Raw Materials at standard prices, the price variance is isolated, and we can now view the production function. We are interested in how much material was used to produce actual finished products (or actual equivalent units of production) as compared to a standard bill of materials. Exhibit 7–6 shows a standard budget of 2 pounds of material per unit of output. Exhibit 7–7 shows that actual production of 100,000 units used 220,000 pounds of raw material. The standard allowance for 100,000 units at 2 pounds per unit is 200,000 pounds. Thus, 20,000 pounds were used in excess of standard. The **material quantity variance**[1] is:

$$V_e = (AQ - SQ)SP$$

where V_e = quantity (or efficiency) variance
   AQ = actual quantity used
   SQ = standard quantity
   SP = standard price per unit

For Mencento, the material quantity variance is:

$$V_e = (220,000 - 200,000)\$0.50 = \$10,000U$$

When we formulate the price variance as $(AQ - SQ)SP$ and when we refer to standard costs, we must remember an important fact. The costs we have developed in Exhibit 7–6 are for *one unit*. When we deal with variances, we use standard costs per unit *given* the actual number of units produced. In the Mencento example, the material use variance is based on comparing actual use to the standard amount called for to produce 100,000 units. The 100,000 units come from Exhibit 7–7. This is the actual production for the period. Given the output of 100,000 units, Mencento should have used 200,000 pounds of material. Since they used more, they were inefficient.

---

[1] The material quantity variance refers to the amount of materials used. Thus, alternative names for this variance are *material use variance*, *material usage variance*, and *material efficiency variance*.

Summary—Material Variances.   Material variances have two parts:

1. Material price variance compares actual prices paid against standard prices for the actual goods purchased $[V_p = AQ(AP - SP)]$.
2. Material quantity variance compares actual material use to standard use at standard prices $[V_e = (AQ - SQ)SP]$.

The total material variance simply adds these two together. In column form, material variances are depicted as follows.

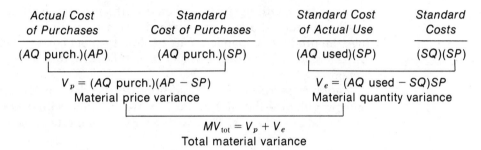

Actual Cost of Purchases	Standard Cost of Purchases	Standard Cost of Actual Use	Standard Costs
$(AQ \text{ purch.})(AP)$	$(AQ \text{ purch.})(SP)$	$(AQ \text{ used})(SP)$	$(SQ)(SP)$

$V_p = (AQ \text{ purch.})(AP - SP)$
Material price variance

$V_e = (AQ \text{ used} - SQ)SP$
Material quantity variance

$$MV_{tot} = V_p + V_e$$
Total material variance

Variances and Responsibility Accounting

The columnar format for material variances shows a division between materials purchased and materials used. The major reason for this division is also a major reason for calculating and reporting variances. Variances, a reflection of how actual results differed from plans, are a natural tool useful in performance evaluation. Thus, it is important to identify variances by nominal areas of responsibility. For example, a purchasing department will usually buy all materials. Thus, identifying the material price variance based on purchases isolates an area of purchasing department responsibility. Likewise, material use is the responsibility of the production manager. We shall see later that such sharp distinctions between responsibilities may not give a true picture. However, isolating variances by apparent responsibility is a valuable first step in analyzing performance.

In addition, there may be an interaction between these variances. For example, the purchasing department may have bought some goods of slightly less than normal quality at bargain prices. However, if this material causes production problems, the favorable material price variance may be more than offset by an unfavorable material use variance and unfavorable conversion-cost variances. These inadequate production results, then, would be the responsibility of the purchasing department.

Standard Costs: Direct Labor

Labor standards can be divided between labor rates and labor use to get a labor rate variance and a labor efficiency variance.

Labor Rates.   It is quite normal for labor rates to be set by union contract or by some other means (such as federal minimum wages). Even so, most companies employ different classes of workers who receive different pay rates.

In the case of Mencento, the contract may call for a crew made up of a lead worker (a foreman for a piece of equipment), a couple of journeymen (regular workers), and one or two assistants. If plant management is short of certain classes of workers, it may substitute a higher- (or lower-) paid employee. This would affect crew costs per hour. In addition, standards reflect normal production. If a heavy workload causes overtime with premium pay, costs per hour will again be affected (although the overtime premium is usually considered a part of overhead rather than direct labor.) Therefore, since the production manager may be able to affect costs per labor hour, we will calculate a labor rate variance that reflects actual hours used for production.

Labor Rate Variance.   In addition to the data in Exhibit 7–7, Mencento provides the data in Exhibit 7–8. We will deal with the overhead items after the labor variances. The algebra for the **labor rate variance** should now be familiar:

$$\text{labor rate variance } (V_p) = AQ(AP - SP)$$
$$V_p = (26,000 \text{ hours})(\$6.25 - \$6.00)$$
$$= \$6,500U$$

The production manager is responsible for the efficient use of labor during a period. As with all variances, we isolate one thing at a time. For a labor efficiency variance we are interested in how much labor was used. We use the standard pay rate, since no matter how much labor was employed, standard wages should have been paid.

EXHIBIT 7–8
19X7 Actual Production Data—Mencento Company

Direct labor:	26,000 hours at $6.25 per hour
Indirect variable overhead:	$2 per direct labor hour
Fixed overhead:	$113,000

Labor Efficiency Variance.   A **labor efficiency variance** (V_e) can be defined as:

$$V_e = (AQ - SQ)SP$$

For Mencento, 26,000 hours were actually used as compared to a standard use of 25,000 hours (0.25 hour times 100,000 units produced). Thus, the labor efficiency variance is:

$$V_e = (26{,}000 \text{ hours} - 25{,}000 \text{ hours})\$6.00 = \$6{,}000U$$

The columnar format below shows the total variance to be the difference between actual labor costs for the period and standard labor costs based on actual output.

Actual Labor Costs	Actual Hours at Standard Rate	Standard Cost for Output
(AQ)(AP)	(AQ)(SP)	(SQ)(SP)
26,000 hours at $6.25	26,000 hours at $6.00	25,000 hours at $6.00

$$V_p = AQ(AP - SP) \qquad V_e = (AQ - SQ)SP$$

$$LV_{\text{tot}} = (AQ)(AP) - (SQ)(SP)$$

Graphical Analysis. Figure 7–2 graphs these relationships. Expected costs are represented by the shaded rectangle *ABED*. This is expected labor use of 25,000 hours times the standard wage rate of $6 or $150,000 total standard costs. Actual costs are represented by the rectangle *ACIG* and are

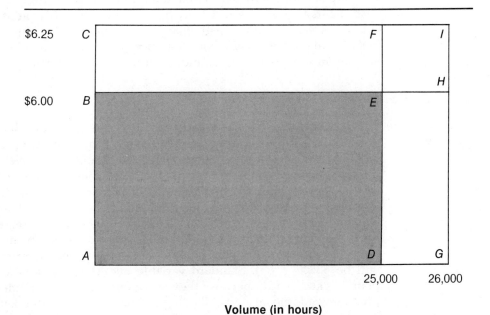

FIGURE 7–2
Labor Variances—Mencento Company

26,000 actual hours at $6.25 actual rate per hour or a total of $162,500. Thus, the total labor variance is $12,500 unfavorable, since actual costs exceed standards by that amount. The labor rate variance is depicted by the rectangle *BCIH*: it is the additional $0.25 per hour ($6.25 − $6.00) above standard wages times the actual 26,000 hours used.

We have identified two variances: labor rate and labor efficiency. The rectangle *EFIH* is the interaction of 1,000 too many labor hours at $0.25 too high a rate. This $250 is an unfavorable *interaction variance*. Thus, a pure labor-rate variance is $0.25 times *standard* hours or $6,250U ($0.25 × 25,000). The labor efficiency variance (*DEHG*) is 1,000 hours over standard use at standard wages of $6 per hour.

In this illustration, where both rate and efficiency variances are unfavorable, the interaction is easy to see and is clearly unfavorable. In situations where one variance is favorable while the other is not, the interaction may be more difficult to visualize and analyze. What would happen, for example, if actual labor use were 24,500 hours instead of 26,000 hours while the rates remained as stated above? The usual variance analysis would now show

$$V_p = (\$6.25 - \$6.00)24,500 = \$6,125U$$
$$V_e = (24,500 - 25,000)\$6.00 = (\$3,000)F$$

The pure rate variance is still $6,250U ($0.25 × 25,000 *standard* hours). The interaction is now $125F, having a rate $0.25 too high but using 500 *fewer* hours than standard. It may be harder to view this variance as favorable, even though we see mathematically it must be. The important point is that even though the interaction variance seems to be an adjustment to the rate variance, it is the outcome of both rate and use results combined.

Overhead Standards

Standard Variable Overhead Rates.   Earlier chapters showed the use of normal costing, allocating overhead to production using a predetermined rate. The use of a predetermined overhead rate allocates overhead to production based on actual direct labor hours (or machine hours, or labor cost). In developing standard costs for units of product, we translate the predetermined overhead rate per (for example) direct labor hour to a per-unit amount. Thus, if four direct labor hours are standard performance for making one unit of product and the variable overhead rate has been estimated to be $8 per direct labor hour, standard variable overhead per unit of product will be $32 (4 × $8). Standard variable overhead amounts are useful for planning and control because they represent expected incremental costs of producing additional units. The higher the level of production, the higher variable overhead is expected to be.

Setting standard variable overhead rates requires that an appropriate activity be associated with overhead costs. Do variable overhead costs change with the number of labor hours? Perhaps they change with the number of units produced. While these are the most common activities associated in a cause-and-effect relationship with variable overhead, other activities may also be used.

Fixed Overhead Rates.   Fixed overhead is not expected to change as production changes. In total amount, it is expected to be constant throughout a relatively wide range of output. Therefore, a standard fixed cost per unit figure is not useful for planning and control purposes. Standard fixed costs are useful for product costing purposes. As we stated in Chapter 5, allocating fixed costs to product is also useful under cost-plus contracts.

Standard fixed costs are determined in much the same way as a predetermined overhead rate. Budgeted fixed production costs for the coming period are divided by some volume figure, such as budgeted unit production. In some cases, other volume figures are used, chiefly normal activity and practical capacity.

Normal activity is generally the expected average annual production over the next three to five years. A longer-range basis than budgeted production for the coming period, the view is that fixed cost per unit figures should reflect average costs over a period longer than a single year.

Practical capacity is generally defined as the maximum output that the firm could achieve, given the usual bottlenecks and interruptions. The usual interruptions would exclude major problems such as strikes, floods, or fires but would include normal breakdowns of equipment and other normal disruptions. Those who advocate the use of practical capacity as the basis for setting standard fixed costs argue that the resulting standards reflect the lowest cost per unit obtainable. That cost, they argue, should be used to value inventory. Any difference between the standard and actual fixed cost per-unit figures reflects the cost of having idle capacity. That is, the firm that fails to produce up to practical capacity has too much capacity.

The selection of an activity level as the basis for setting standard fixed costs is a matter of the managers' preference. Accountants have argued the issue for years. However, recall from Chapter 5 on job order costing that inventory costs must approximate actual costs.

Variable Overhead Variances

Once an appropriate activity has been determined, variable overhead price and efficiency variances are almost identical to labor variance calculation. Exhibit 7–6 shows that Mencento has established direct labor hours (DLH) as the appropriate activity for variable factory overhead and that this overhead is applied at $2 per DLH. Exhibit 7–8 shows that actual costs were $2 per DLH. Thus, there will be no price variance.[2]

$$V_p = (26{,}000 \text{ hours})(\$2 - \$2) = 0$$

[2] Variable overhead price variance is usually called a *rate variance, budget variance,* or *spending variance.*

However, as in the labor variances, since actual hours (26,000) exceed standard hours for this level of output (25,000), we have an unfavorable efficiency variance:

$$V_e = (26,000 - 25,000)\$2 = \$2,000U$$

If variable overhead is applied based on direct labor hours, it makes sense that the efficiency variance is in the same direction as (unfavorable in this example), and proportionate to, the labor efficiency variance. In both cases 1,000 too many labor hours were used. The only difference is in the rate used to establish the variance ($6 per hour for labor or $2 per DLH for variable overhead).

A company will have to establish the activities that seem to affect total variable overhead costs. Examples of these activities are direct labor hours, machine hours, direct labor dollars, or units of production. While Mencento applies variable overhead based on DLH, another company might use DLH as the proper activity for some variable overhead costs but use another activity to reflect others.

Fixed Overhead Variances

Fixed overhead variances fall into two general categories: budget variance and application variance. These variances differ from the variable cost variances, since we are dealing with a new dimension—where costs are fixed. On one hand there is the lump sum of total fixed costs, while on the other hand we are applying overhead on a per-unit basis.

Budget Variances.   A fixed overhead **budget variance** compares total fixed costs as budgeted against total fixed costs actually incurred. For example, we explained earlier that Mencento expected fixed costs to be $112,500 for the period. However, if actual fixed costs were $113,000 for the period, we can say we have a $500 unfavorable fixed overhead budget variance.

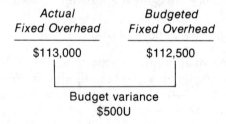

Actual Fixed Overhead	*Budgeted Fixed Overhead*
$113,000	$112,500

Budget variance
$500U

While this budget variance is similar to the price variances we calculate for materials, labor, and variable overhead, it is also different, since activity does not affect fixed costs and we deal only with total fixed costs rather than any per-unit figure.

Application Variances.   Since we apply overhead based on a predetermined rate, if a company does not produce the exact amount of units used in establishing this rate, overhead has been *overapplied* or *underapplied.* For example, Mencento established an application rate of $0.75 per unit based on budgeted fixed overhead of $112,500 and practical capacity of 150,000 units. Therefore, since only 100,000 units were produced, only $75,000 of fixed overhead was applied to these units. However, Mencento management believes fixed overhead will be $112,500. Therefore, we need to deal with the $37,500 difference. This difference is identified as an **application variance** (sometimes called a *volume variance, capacity variance,* or *denominator variance*), since it is caused solely by the rate that management chooses to apply fixed overhead on a per-unit basis. The $37,500 application variance is *unfavorable* and reflects the fact that we have applied less fixed overhead (*underapplied* overhead) than budgeted.

Summary: Fixed Overhead Variances.   We identify two fixed overhead variances: budget and application. In summary form, the Mencento data reveal the following:

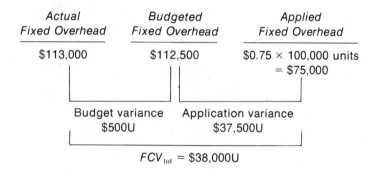

Actual Fixed Overhead	Budgeted Fixed Overhead	Applied Fixed Overhead
$113,000	$112,500	$0.75 × 100,000 units = $75,000

Budget variance $500U   Application variance $37,500U

$$FCV_{tot} = \$38,000U$$

It is important to note that, of all the variances calculated so far, only the application variance has no economic impact on the firm. Actual fixed costs differed from plans by $500. That means Mencento spent an additional $500. The $37,500 unfavorable application variance is a function of bookkeeping on a unit basis. It does not reflect additional funds the company has expended. This ties in directly with the discussion of overapplied and underapplied overhead in Chapter 5.

Combined Overhead Variances

Sometimes management may apply overhead on a combined basis so that the rate includes both fixed and variable components. In order to do this, both elements must be applied based on the same activity. Since the Mencento example shows variable overhead based on labor hours while fixed overhead is based on units of output, all the activities need to be translated into one or the other basis to use this combined technique.

Our efforts in Chapters 2 and 3 were to identify a flexible budget of:

$$\text{total cost} = \text{fixed cost} + (\text{variable cost} \times \text{quantity})$$

When we combine the fixed and variable components of the Mencento overhead, we have

$$\text{total overhead costs} = \$112,500 + \$2 \times \text{DLH}$$

Fixed overhead standard costs are $0.75 per unit (Exhibit 7–6). Since 0.25 hour is required per unit, standard fixed costs *per labor hour* are $3 ($0.75 divided by 0.25). Therefore, we can apply both fixed and variable overhead based on $5 per direct labor hour.

Variable overhead	$2 per DLH
Fixed overhead, $\dfrac{\$112,500}{37,500\ \text{DLH}}$	$3 per DLH
Total	$5 per DLH

We can now identify three variances—spending, efficiency, and application—as follows:

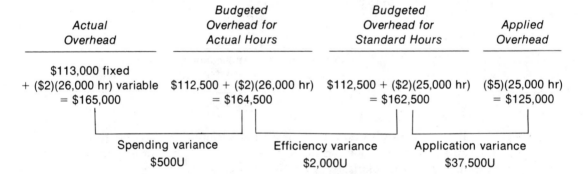

Actual Overhead	Budgeted Overhead for Actual Hours	Budgeted Overhead for Standard Hours	Applied Overhead
$113,000 fixed + ($2)(26,000 hr) variable = $165,000	$112,500 + ($2)(26,000 hr) = $164,500	$112,500 + ($2)(25,000 hr) = $162,500	($5)(25,000 hr) = $125,000
	Spending variance $500U	Efficiency variance $2,000U	Application variance $37,500U

The spending variance could be broken down into fixed and variable components if necessary. It reflects the difference between actual total overhead ($165,000) and a flexible budget for overhead, given the actual amount of hours used. This flexible budget is:

$$\text{overhead costs} = \$112,500 + (\$2)(\text{direct labor hours})$$

The efficiency variance applies only to the variable portion of overhead. Therefore, it reflects the excess 1,000 labor hours used times the variable portion of standard overhead per unit. Finally, the application variance reflects the comparison of the flexible budget based on producing 100,000 units (25,000 labor hours) and overhead applied at $5 per unit. It is no coincidence that the variances are identical to those worked out previously. Only the format has been changed by our looking at total overhead rather than its individual components.

OTHER VARIANCES

The discussion so far has covered gross margin variances, variable production cost variances, and fixed production cost variances. It is possible to set standards in other areas. For example, the sales department may have standards for advertising. These standards may encompass not only a budgeted dollar amount for the period, but also a plan of mix between radio, TV, and the newspapers. At the end of the period, sales management can evaluate performance using the same kind of variance analysis we have used to look at production results.

Behavioral Considerations in Standard Setting

Our discussion of standard costs has centered on the mechanics of establishing such information. Since calculations and analyses of variances are conducted at least in part to help in evaluating managerial performance, we must also investigate the human behavior aspects involved when standards are set. Much of the discussion that follows applies also to the area of budgeting and will be extended in Chapters 13 and 14.

The Conflict

Standards can be used as an aid to planning in such areas as purchasing materials, scheduling workers, estimating cash flow needs, and pricing. For many reasons it is important to know expected sales levels and the flexible budget for expected output. A firm also needs to be competitive. Thus, the expectations included in budgets and standards are based on the most efficient way to produce a given quality of product. Variances can be a key to adaptive and corrective action, thereby saving future costs. A conflict can arise between the objectives of planning, controlling, and profit maximization and the other budgeting objectives of motivating personnel to achieve these ends.

Motivation. Budgets and standards are useless exercises in pencil pushing and computer number crunching unless they are viewed as a set of reasonable goals that managers are willing to try to attain. Each of us has personal, job-oriented goals for such things as monetary rewards, promotion, peer approval, and job responsibility. We have mentioned a few company goals in planning, controlling, and profitability. Ideally a manager should be motivated to act in harmony with and agreement to company goals. Since many authors use the term *goal congruence* to denote this sharing of common goals, the important aspect of how managers *act* in goal-directed ways can be overlooked. We are indeed interested not just in agreeing with company goals but in acting to achieve them.

A Model for Motivation. Some writers have proposed a model to coordinate research and analysis in the area of budgets and motivation.[3] In essence, this model says that motivation is caused by:

1. intrinsic (internal or personally satisfying) rewards from goal-directed behavior—that is, engaging in the activity itself.
2. intrinsic rewards associated with successful performance of a task.
3. various extrinsic (external or managerially administered) rewards associated with the accomplishment of company goals.

The second and third factors are weighted by the probability of achieving a work goal with goal-directed behavior. The third factor also is weighted by the probabilities that goal accomplishment will lead to certain external rewards.

Cook has taken these dimensions and proposes three questions that individuals can raise about their work situation:[4]

"What's in it for me? How important are the available rewards of personal consequences of working at this job for this organization?"

"If I try harder, will it make a difference in my performance? Can I influence my level of performance through my level of effort?"

"Am I rewarded for what I produce? If I increase my level of performance, will I receive an increase in rewards or personal consequences, and vice versa?"

Intrinsic rewards include personal pleasure derived from doing a job. A salesman may enjoy extensive traveling, and this enjoyment motivates him to make efforts to achieve company goals. An actor enjoys the experience of being on stage regardless of other compensation from box-office receipts or favorable reviews. Intrinsic rewards are positive emotions that we feel as we behave in an organizational-goal-directed manner congruent with personal goals.

In contrast, **extrinsic rewards** come from others. They include salary, promotion, level of authority and responsibility, approval of peers and of supervisors, and public recognition of achievement.

Probability of Success.   This model weights these various rewards by the probability that goal-directed behavior will result in goal accomplishment. Here is where standard setting can come into play. A striving by management for greater and greater efficiency can lead to lower and lower standard costs. This would reduce the probability that a budget would be met, and, under the model, would reduce motivation. Conversely, more

---

[3] The model, called expectancy theory, is based on the work of V. H. Vroom, *Work and Motivation* (New York: John Wiley & Sons, 1964) and is extended by L. W. Porter and E. E. Lawler III, *Managerial Attitudes and Performance* (Homewood, Ill.: Richard D. Irwin, Inc., 1968).

[4] Curtis W. Cook, "Guidelines for Managing Motivation," *Business Horizons*, April 1980, p. 63.

lenient standards may be more motivating, but they could run counter to the goal of maximizing efficiency.

Tight and Loose Standards

The terms commonly used to describe the continuum of standard-setting levels is **tight** to **loose**. The basic conflict we mentioned at the outset is manifested when standards are either too tight or too loose.

When standards are tight, it is highly probable that they will be missed more often than met. Variances are deviations from standard. They do not reflect how loose or tight the standard was. They imply inefficient operations rather than ineffective standards. Therefore, it is possible that variance reports can be used as pressure devices, unfairly associating an unfavorable variance with poor managerial performance. However, it may be that tight standards are motivating *because* they are more difficult to achieve. They may be a useful challenge (intrinsic reward) to a manager motivated by a need for achievement, where accomplishment produces a strong feeling of pride and self-reward. Loose standards may be so easy to attain that a manager is not motivated to beat or even meet them.

As is easily seen, there is a trade-off between tightness and looseness. Each situation must be evaluated in light of the production process, the product, and the behaviors of people in determining an answer to the level of tightness chosen.

Participation

The subject of participation will be dealt with more fully in the upcoming chapters on budgeting. It is useful to discuss the basic issues here, however, since they apply to standard setting as well. Put simply, participation involves the question of *who* sets standards. If top management alone sets standards with advice from engineering and accounting, there is said to be no participation. Full participation would mean that all operating personnel from foremen on up are an active part of the negotiating process leading to whatever standard is adopted.

Actual participation usually falls between these two extremes. In addition, real input of lower-level personnel into a final decision may be less in reality than on paper. A firm may purport to involve all its managers in standard setting, while in fact top management rarely takes much advice in reaching a decision.

Like tightness, the degree of participation established depends on both production and human considerations. The act of participation, in the terms of the motivation model, can be intrinsically rewarding and can enhance the probabilities of success and reward. If operating employees believe that their participation really influences standards, the process reduces their feeling of helplessness to influence their work environment. As employees learn to attribute success (in negotiating standards) to their own personal efforts, the probability increases that they will become more achievement striving.

Dual Standards

A possible way to deal with our basic conflict is to establish **dual standards.** For example, engineering studies coupled with production experience would establish standards to be used for planning and pricing. An *additional* (looser) set of standards would be established to be used for variance reporting and performance evaluation. Obviously, to create and maintain dual standards entails a cost. It is also possible that the known existence of two sets of standards can have negative behavioral effects—especially if a *tighter* set of standards is used for performance evaluation.

PROBLEMS WITH VARIANCES AND STANDARDS

With any calculation, be it net income, a CVP relationship, or a linear programming solution, the results are only as good as the information used. The same holds true of variances. If standards are ill formed or out of date, variances have low information content.

Inflation and Standard Costs

Standard costs include both price and quantity components. In an inflationary economy, the price portion of standard costs is open to question. Labor rates are usually fairly predictable, owing to long-term union contracts. Even if a company does not have union employees, wages reflect some combination of federal minimum wages and union wages paid by competitive firms.

Predictability of Material Prices

There is a predictability problem with material costs. Most contracts for materials are entered into in order to assure the purchaser a supply of materials and the supplier a more predictable production level. Prices are set at the beginning of the contract but can be changed as time passes. Thus, as a paper manufacturer experiences rising costs of labor, materials, and overhead, it may increase prices under the terms of its contracts with printers. It is important that the price standards be adjusted for this increase, or else a spurious material price variance will occur. In addition, quantity variances will be understated, since the standard price will be too low.

In businesses where costs change daily, this complication can sharply reduce the usefulness of isolating variances. Assume a manufacturer of feed for cattle and horses has developed various feeds based on a linear programming solution that yields a mix of specific grains, proteins, and vitamins as the least costly way to produce a palatable product of a certain quality. However, prices vary almost daily. Thus, the mix of ingredients will vary with the prices of corn, wheat, bran, soybeans, and hay. The only standards become the level of protein or the amount of vitamin A, for example. Standard costs, as such, and variances have no real value.

Standards need to be based on an ongoing stable process; otherwise variances are hard to interpret. Stability has at least two dimensions. First, we assume that machinery is beyond any break-in period and that production personnel are accustomed to it. Second, we assume that each crew has the same average level of expertise and familiarity with the production process. This means that if a crew on a piece of equipment consists of a specific number of journeymen, assistants, and apprentices, any substitution of labor will result in an equally qualified crew.

After the Fact Variances

Some authors have suggested the need for after the fact, or *ex post* variances,[5] calculated after adjustments are made to standards to reflect different operating conditions. Consider the following example. Corbett Printing Company is a job order shop with two different printing presses, a webfed press used for long jobs and a sheetfed press used for short jobs. Assume that the sheetfed is fully scheduled for the coming month and another short job is received. If there is available time on the webfed press, the job can be run on it, but at a cost of higher material use and makeready time. Conventional variance analysis would show unfavorable variances on the job. However, standards should be adjusted to reflect the scheduling problem to see whether the job was run efficiently on the wrong press. This is the idea of after the fact variances.

SUMMARY

Where a company is producing homogeneous products and/or has homogeneous production processes, expected CVP patterns usually can be formalized into a type of budgeted cost called *standard cost*. Standards can be used as a basis of comparison between plans and actual results. The resulting variances are used as a basis both for adaptive and corrective action and for assessing managerial performance. Obviously, since responsibility comes into play, standard setting is a sensitive issue involving the motivation of employees.

[5] For example, Joel S. Demski, "Analyzing the Effectiveness of the Traditional Standard Cost Variance Model," *Management Accounting*, XLVIII (October, 1967), pp. 9–19.

APPENDIX 7–A: PRODUCTION MIX AND YIELD VARIANCES

In analyzing gross margin variances, we pointed out that most companies sell a variety of products. Therefore, we developed a mix variance. It is also likely that a company may have multiple inputs of materials or labor into a product. If these materials (or labor) are to some extent interchangeable, there can be a **production mix variance.** In addition, a difference between material inputs and expected output may result in a **yield variance.**

Illustration: Mencento Chemical

The original standards for Mencento Chemical reflected a single product with a single input. Exhibit 7A–1, a breakdown of material standards for two products, Flamex and Retardex, shows that Flamex has three materials used in its production. Assume these materials are fairly interchangeable. Actual results for materials are as follows:

Materials Used

25,000 lb Doubleyew
30,000 lb Ex
40,000 lb Wye
125,000 lb Zee
220,000 lb

Current Production

50,000 units Flamex
50,000 units Retardex

We will leave out materials purchased and concentrate on materials used. As in our previous analysis, a logical reading of the data will help us grasp the significance of variances.

EXHIBIT 7A–1
Standard Costs—Mencento Company

			Flamex	Retardex
Direct materials:	½ lb Doubleyew	at $0.80/lb	$0.40	
	½ lb Ex	at $0.80/lb	0.40	
	½ lb Wye	at $0.40/lb	0.20	
	2½ lb Zee	at $0.40/lb		$1.00

When we compare the standard cost data in Exhibit 7A–1 to actual results, two things seem evident. (1) The mix of materials for Flamex was supposed to be 33⅓ percent Doubleyew, 33⅓ percent Ex, and 33⅓ percent Wye, while actual results show 26.3, 31.6, and 42.1 percent, respectively. Wye (with a standard cost of $0.40 per pound) has been substituted for more expensive Doubleyew and Ex ($0.80 per pound). Therefore, we should have a favorable mix variance. (2) While 100,000 total units were produced, instead of using 200,000 lb of the various material inputs at their planned mix, the production process used 220,000 lb. Thus, there should be an unfavorable quantity variance (or yield variance).

Material Mix and Yield Variances

We can use the same logic in analyzing input mix and yield we used in viewing gross margin mix and volume variances.

Material	AQ/Input SP/Input Actual Input Mix		AQ in Total SP/Input Standard Input Mix		SQ in Total SP/Input Standard Input Mix
Doubleyew	(25,000 lb)($0.80)		(⅓)(95,000 lb)($0.80)		(½ lb)(50,000)($0.80)
Ex	+ (30,000 lb)($0.80)	+	(⅓)(95,000 lb)($0.80)	+	(½ lb)(50,000)($0.80)
Wye	+ (40,000 lb)($0.40)	+	(⅓)(95,000 lb)($0.40)	+	(½ lb)(50,000)($0.40)
Zee	+ (125,000 lb)($0.40)	+	(125,000 lb)($0.40)		+(2½ lb)(50,000)($0.40)
	$110,000		$113,333.33		$100,000

Mix variance
($3,333.33)F

Yield variance
$13,333.33U

Comparing the Variances

The single-product, single-input example yielded:

$$V_e = \$10,000U$$

This new multiproduct, multi-input example reveals a subdividing of this total variance into material mix and material yield components.

Why It Is a Yield Variance

The term **yield variance** comes from the fact that if 220,000 lb of materials are put into the process, we expect 220,000 lb of output (110,000 units). However, the process *yielded* only 100,000 units. The amount of Zee (125,000 lb) yielded 50,000 units of Retardex as expected (2½ lb × 50,000). A total of 95,000 lb of the other three materials should have yielded 63,333⅓ units of Flamex (95,000 ÷ 1½ lb) but only 50,000 units were produced. Thus, we have an unfavorable yield.

ASSIGNMENTS

7-1   Gross Margin Variances.   Apple Products uses a standard costing system. Current results show a sales price variance of $4,000F and a sales volume variance of $5,500U. Apple has only a single product. Actual gross margin (actual sales less actual costs) was $137,000, which includes $2,000 of favorable production variances.

Required: Compute total standard gross margin.

7-2   Inputs and Outputs.   Model HS2D of Watertown Industries has the following standard cost card for a batch of ten units.

> Materials: 3 lb at $4.75/lb
> Labor: 5 hr at $12/hr
> Variable overhead at $8/DLH

Required: Consider each of the questions independently.

1. What is the labor required to produce 27,000 units?
2. If standard materials call for $51,300, how many units would management expect to produce?
3. If standard labor was $138,000, what is standard variable overhead?
4. What is the total material cost required to produce 17,000 units?

7-3   Relationships.   Each of the following situations is independent. The only element of cost being considered is direct labor.

Required: Fill in the blanks.

	Actual Labor Costs	Units Produced	Actual Hours Worked	Standard Hours for Production Achieved	Standard Hours per Unit	Standard Rate per Hour	V_p	V_e
a.	_____	2,000	5,600	6,000	___	$ 3	$ 300U	_____
b.	$82,600	_____	8,300	_____	0.5	$10	_____	$1,000U
c.	_____	8,000	_____	_____	2	$ 8	$1,600U	$ 400U
d.	$24,500	_____	_____	6,000	3	___	$ 300F	$ 800U

7-4   Basic Variance Computations.   The Carney Company makes a single product, and 19X6 results showed the following:

Units produced	21,000
Direct labor hours worked	70,000
Rate paid to direct laborers	$ 3.20
Materials purchased	50,000 lb ($102,500)
Materials used in production	46,000 lb
Variable overhead incurred	$150,000

Standards for this product were as follows:

Material, 2 lb at $2.05	$ 4.10
Direct labor, 3 hr at $3.25	9.75
Variable overhead, $2/DLH	6.00
Total standard variable cost per unit	$19.85

Required: Calculate all the variable cost variances.

7-5 Variances—Multiple Choice (CMA). Eastern Company manufactures special electrical equipment and parts. Eastern employs a standard cost accounting system with separate standards established for each product.

A special transformer is manufactured in the transformer department. Production volume is measured by direct labor hours in this department, and a flexible budget system is used to plan and control department overhead.

Standard costs for the special transformer are determined annually in September for the coming year. The standard cost of a transformer for 19X7 was computed at $67, as shown below.

Direct materials:			
Iron	5 sheets	at $2	$10
Copper	3 spools	at $3	9
Direct labor	4 hours	at $7	28
Variable overhead	4 hours	at $3	12
Fixed overhead	4 hours	at $2	8
Total			$67

Overhead rates were based upon normal and expected monthly capacity for 19X7, both of which were 4,000 direct labor hours. Practical capacity for this department is 5,000 direct labor hours per month. The variable overhead costs are expected to vary with the number of direct labor hours actually used.

During October, 19X7, 800 transformers were produced. This was below expectations because a work stoppage occurred during contract negotiations with the labor force. Once the contract was settled, the department scheduled overtime in an attempt to catch up to expected production levels.

The following costs were incurred in October, 19X7:

Direct Material	Direct Materials Purchased	Materials Used
Iron	5,000 sheets at $2.00 per sheet	3,900 sheets
Copper	2,200 spools at $3.10 per spool	2,600 spools

Direct Labor	Amount Used
Regular time	2,000 hours at $7.00
	1,400 hours at $7.20
Overtime	600 of the 1,400 hours were subject to overtime premium. The total overtime premium of $2,160 is included in variable overhead in accordance with company accounting practices.

Overhead	Amount
Variable overhead	$10,000
Fixed overhead	$ 8,800

Required: Select the *best* answer for each question.

1. The most appropriate time to record any variation of actual material prices from standard is:
    a. at year end, when all variations will be known.
    b. at the time of purchase.
    c. at the time of material usage.
    d. as needed to evaluate the performance of the purchasing manager.
    e. at some time other than those listed above.

2. The total material quantity variation is:
    a. $200 favorable.
    b. $400 favorable.
    c. $600 favorable.
    d. $400 unfavorable.
    e. some amount other than those listed above.

3. The labor rate (price) variation is:
    a. $280 unfavorable.
    b. $340 unfavorable.
    c. $1,680 unfavorable.
    d. $2,440 unfavorable.
    e. none of the above.

4. The variable overhead spending variation is:
    a. $200 favorable.
    b. $400 unfavorable.
    c. $600 unfavorable.
    d. $1,600 unfavorable.
    e. some amount other than those listed above.

5. The efficiency variation in variable overhead is the standard variable overhead rate times the difference between standard labor hours of output and:
    a. 2,000 hours.

    b. 2,600 hours.
    c. 2,800 hours.
    d. 3,400 hours.
    e. some amount other than those listed above.

6. The budget (spending) variation for fixed overhead is:
    a. $2,400 unfavorable.
    b. $0.
    c. $800 unfavorable.
    d. not calculable from the problem.
    e. some amount other than those listed above.

7. The fixed overhead volume variation is:
    a. $400 unfavorable.
    b. $2,200 unfavorable.
    c. $2,400 unfavorable.
    d. $1,600 unfavorable.
    e. some amount other than those listed above.

8. An unfavorable fixed overhead volume variation is most often caused by:
    a. actual fixed overhead incurred exceeding budgeted fixed overhead.
    b. an overapplication of fixed overhead to production.
    c. a decrease in the level of the finished inventory of transformers.
    d. production levels exceeding sales levels.
    e. normal capacity exceeding actual production levels.

7–6 **Variances—Multiple Choice (AICPA).** The data below relate to the month of April, 19X6, for Marilyn, Inc., which uses a standard cost system:

Actual total direct labor	$43,400
Actual hours used	14,000
Standard hours allowed for good output	15,000
Direct labor rate variance—debit	$ 1,400
Actual total overhead	$32,000
Budgeted fixed costs	$ 9,000
Normal activity in hours	12,000
Total overhead application rate per standard direct labor hour	$2.25

Marilyn uses a two-way analysis of overhead variances: budget (controllable) and volume.

Required: Select the *best* answer for each question.

1. What was Marilyn's direct labor usage (efficiency) variance for April 19X6?
    a. $3,000 favorable.
    b. $3,000 unfavorable.

    c. $3,200 favorable.

    d. $3,200 unfavorable.

2. What was Marilyn's budget (controllable) variance for April 19X6?

    a. $500 favorable.

    b. $500 unfavorable.

    c. $2,250 favorable.

    d. $2,250 unfavorable.

3. What was Marilyn's volume variance for April 19X6?

    a. $500 favorable.

    b. $500 unfavorable.

    c. $2,250 favorable.

    d. $2,250 unfavorable.

7–7 Marketing Variances. The marketing manager of the Triloff Company believes that he could increase unit volume of the firm's major product, a dishwashing liquid, if he decreased the price. The budget for the coming year shows the following:

Sales	100,000 cases
Contribution margin per case	$ 7
Budgeted contribution margin	$700,000

He is considering a $0.20 reduction per case, which he expects to increase unit volume by 20,000 cases.

Required: Suppose that the manager does reduce the price and gain the additional volume as he expects. What would be the sales price variance and sales volume variance?

7–8 Actual Versus Standard. A report prepared for management of Kueker Products shows the following results for one of their products for October, 19X9:

Planned sales (10,000 units)	$420,000
Standard cost of sales	320,000
Standard gross margin	$100,000
Less:	
Gross margin variances:	
Sales volume	$ 8,000U
Sales price	3,000F
Variable-cost production variances:	
Material price	10,000F
Material use	5,000U
Labor rate	945U
Labor efficiency	3,600U
Adjusted margin	$ 94,455

Production was 12,000 units. All variances are shown as adjustments to cost of sales at the end of each period. Standards for this product are:

> Materials   2 lb at $8.50/lb
> Labor   0.5 hr at $12
> Overhead is applied at $18/DLH

During October, 43,000 lb of material were purchased.

Required:

1. Calculate the following:
   a. actual sales price per unit.
   b. actual sales volume.
   c. actual material price in total (on purchases).
   d. actual material used.
   e. actual labor rate per hour.
   f. actual labor hours used.

2. In this case, management has placed all the variances on the report as period costs. Would the adjusted margin be higher, lower, or the same if the production variances had been treated as product costs?

7–9 Relationships. You are presented with the following data.

Required: Fill in the blanks.

Materials purchased	$68,000 (42,000 lb)
Materials used	32,000 pounds
Actual labor cost	$69,000 (31,500 hr)
Actual variable overhead	$36,000
Standard labor cost per unit	_____
Standard material cost per unit	$ 45
Standard variable overhead cost per unit	_____
Material price variance	$ 5,000 U
Material use variance	_____F or U
Labor rate variance	$ 6,000 U
Labor efficiency variance	$ 3,000 U
Variable overhead spending variance	_____F or U
Variable overhead efficiency variance	_____F or U
Standard labor rate	_____
Standard direct labor hours per unit	30
Variable overhead rate per DLH	$ 1.15

7–10 Production Variances. Pilcher Products has the following production standards for a model PF-14 plastic tub used for farming applications:

Materials—plastic: 2.25 lb at $3/lb
Materials—metal reinforcement rings: 3 at $0.25 each
Labor: 0.04 hr per tub
Labor rates: $14/hr

Overhead is applied at $30 per labor hour, consisting of $13 in variable costs and $17 in fixed costs. Budgeted annual volume of 100,000 tubs was used in determining fixed costs per unit.

Actual results for April, 19X0, showed that 18,000 tubs were made using 700 labor hours at a cost of $10,000. During the month 39,300 lb of plastic were used, while 63,000 lb were purchased for $195,300. There were no beginning inventories of plastic. A total of 54,000 rings were used, and 20,000 rings were purchased at $0.23 each. Variable overhead amounted to $9,600, while fixed overhead was $6,000.

Required:

1. How many standard hours of labor are required to produce 18,000 tubs?

2. How many standard pounds of plastic are required to produce 18,000 tubs?

3. What is the expected cost *per tub* for overhead?

4. Calculate the following variances:
   a. material price, material use.
   b. labor rate, labor efficiency.
   c. overhead spending, efficiency, and application.

5. Explain the overhead variances.

6. Explain possible causes of the material and labor variances.

7–11 Overhead Variances.   The following data apply to June, 19X8, production of Sabre Company.

Overhead incurred	$20,000
Direct labor hours	400

The firm uses an overhead rate of $48, based on 5,500 direct labor hours per year. At 5,500 hours, 37½% of total budgeted overhead is variable. Of the overhead incurred during June, 60% was fixed.

The controller reported the following to the president. "Our fixed overhead variances totaled zero, and variable cost variances were $250 favorable even with an $800 unfavorable spending variance. The performance is partly due to our working only 400 hours, instead of the normal 458⅓."

Required:

1. Determine the fixed overhead budget and application variances and the variable overhead spending and efficiency variances.

2. Does the method of calculation used by the controller give good information? Why or why not?

7-12 Standards—Job Order (CMA adapted). The Justin Company has recently installed a standard cost system to simplify its factory bookkeeping and to aid in cost control. The company makes standard items for inventory, but because its line includes many products, each is manufactured periodically under a production order. Before the installation of the system, job order cost sheets were maintained for each production order. Since the introduction of the standard cost system, however, the job order cost sheets have not been kept.

The fabricating department is managed by a general supervisor who has overall responsibility for scheduling, performance, and cost control. The department consists of four machine/work centers. Each work center is manned by a four-person work group or team, and the centers are aided by a twelve-person support group. Departmental practice is to assign a job to one team and expect the team to perform most of the work necessary to complete the job, including acquisition of materials and supplies from the stores department, machining, and assembling. This departmental practice has been practical and satisfactory in the past and is readily accepted by the employees.

Information regarding production cost standards, products produced, and actual costs for the fabricating department in the month of March is presented below.

Unit Standard Cost

		Part	
	A7A	C6D	C7A
Material	$2.00	$ 3.00	$1.50
Direct labor	1.50	2.00	1.00
Overhead (por direct labor dollar):			
Variable	3.00	4.00	2.00
Fixed	0.75	1.00	0.50
	$7.25	$10.00	$5.00

The departmental standard overhead rates are applied to the products as a percentage of direct labor dollars. The labor base was chosen because nearly all the variable overhead costs are caused by labor activity. The departmental overhead rates were calculated at the beginning of the year as follows:

Departmental Overhead Rates

	Variable (including indirect labor)	Fixed
Estimated annual cost	$360,000	$ 90,000
Estimated annual department direct labor dollars	$180,000	$180,000
Overhead rate	200%	50%

Analysis of the Fabricating Department Account for March

Charges

Materials:

Job No. 307-11	$ 5,200	
Job No. 307-12	2,900	
Job No. 307-14	9,400	$17,500

Labor charges:

Job No. 307-11	$ 4,000	
Job No. 307-12	2,100	
Job No. 307-14	6,200	
Indirect labor	12,200	24,500

Variable overhead costs (e.g., supplies, electricity, etc.)		18,800
Fixed overhead costs (e.g., supervisor's salary, depreciation, property tax and insurance, etc.)		7,000
Total charges to department for March		$67,800

Credits

Completed jobs:

Job No. 307-11, 2000 units part A7A at $7.50	$14,500	
Job No. 307-12, 1000 units part C6D at $10	10,000	
Job No. 307-14, 6000 units part C7A at $5	30,000	$54,500

Variances transferred to the factory variance account

Materials[a]	$ 1,500	
Direct labor[b]	1,300	
Variable overhead	9,000	
Fixed overhead	1,500	13,300
Total credits		$67,800

---

[a] Material price variances are isolated at acquisition and charged to the Stores Department.
[b] All direct labor was paid at the standard wage rate during March.

Required:

1. Justin Company assumes that its efforts to control costs in the fabricating department would be aided if variances were calculated by jobs. Management intends to add this analysis next month. Calculate all the variances by job that might contribute to cost control under this assumption.

2. Do you agree with the company's plan to initiate the calculation of job variances in addition to the currently calculated departmental variances? Explain your answer.

7-13 **Standards and Variances (from a problem prepared by Professor Jack R. Blann).** At the end of 1923 Al Kapon, vice-president of the Chicago Syndicate, Inc., stared out of the window of his posh west side office in dismay. His expectations for a highly profitable year were dashed. The disappointing results appear below.

	Plan	Actual	Variance
Sales	$500,000	$456,000	$44,000
Direct materials	50,000	48,000	(2,000)
Direct labor	200,000	201,000	1,000
Variable overhead	100,000	92,000	(8,000)
Total variable costs	350,000	341,000	(9,000)
Contribution margin	150,000	115,000	35,000
Fixed costs	100,000	98,000	(2,000)
Syndicate profit	$ 50,000	$ 17,000	$33,000

Mr. Kapon realized that because sales were down, expenses too should fall, such that profit should be somewhat more than $17,000. His organization, which made only one product (the identity of which cannot be disclosed), incorporated the following data in its plans.

Standard Cost and Contribution Margin

Selling price		$10 per unit
Direct materials (2 quarts at $0.50)	$1	
Direct labor (0.80 hour at $5)	4	
Variable overhead ($2.50 per labor hour)	2	7
Standard contribution margin		$ 3

The firm planned sales of 50,000 units, but sold only 48,000 at an average price of $9.50 per unit. Materials averaged $0.48 per quart for the 100,000 gallons bought and used. Direct labor hours were 40,000. Production was 48,000 units.

Mr. Kapon made you an offer that you could not refuse, and so you accepted the assignment laid out below.

Required:

1. Prepare an income statement at standard. That is, given that sales were 48,000 units at $9.50, and assuming that variable costs were incurred at standard (prices and quantities), and that fixed costs were incurred as budgeted, determine the income that the organization would have earned.

2. Calculate the gross margin variances, using contribution margin as gross margin. Their sum should equal the difference between the income you determined in item 1 and the $50,000 that the firm planned.

3. Calculate the price and quantity variances for the variable costs. Does the sum of those variances equal the difference between the actual income ($17,000) and the income you computed in item 1? If not, what is missing? What would you call this variance?

4. Prepare a memo to Mr. Kapon explaining what possible causes gave him his difficulties. Be sure that he will understand your explanation, as he becomes violent (occasionally) when business is bad.

7–14 Comprehensive Variance Analysis. The Gorton Company makes a device that returns soccer balls kicked into it. The device has been very successful over the past few years, and therefore the managers of the firm were not especially happy when they saw the following results for 19X6, in thousands.

	Budget	Actual
Sales	$854.0	$830.0
Standard cost of sales	550.0	495.0
Standard gross margin	304.0	335.0
Production variances (favorable):		
Materials		12.4
Direct labor		8.1
Overhead		(3.4)
Actual gross margin		317.9
Selling and administrative costs	140.0	162.0
Income before taxes	$164.0	$155.9

Other information given with the report was that unit volume was 10 percent below budget, but that increased prices had softened the potential blow. Higher advertising expense also helped, in the view of the sales manager. The average labor time to make a unit was 0.60 hour, which was above the 0.55 hour used in budgeting. The direct labor rate is $7 per hour and variable overhead $6 per direct labor hour. During the year the firm produced 20,000 units and sold 18,000. Budgeted sales and production were both 20,000 units. The firm uses budgeted production to set its standard fixed overhead costs.

Materials prices from suppliers rose about 4 percent over standard for the year. Materials cost per unit of product is $12.

Required: Identify as many variances as you can, so that you can tell the managers why profits were below budget. You will not be able to find all the variances, but you can determine a good many.

7-15 **Variances and Standard Setting.** The Saric Corporation used a regression and correlation program to help calculate overhead standards in the assembly department. Based on this analysis, overhead standards were set at $3,500 per month plus $3.50 per direct labor hour. During November 34,000 actual units were assembled. Overhead costs were $125,000, and 36,000 actual labor hours were used. Standards call for 1 hour per unit. Overhead is applied at $4 per DLH.

Required:

1. Calculate the overhead budget, efficiency, and application variances.

2. The regression and correlation analysis used for establishing the standards showed the following.

Intercept	$3,367.50
Regression coefficient	$ 3.43875
Correlation coefficient	0.947
Standard error of the estimate	$5,047.43
Standard error of the regression coefficient	$ 0.6926
Number of observations	25

Using this additional information, evaluate the variances calculated in item 1.

7-16 **Marketing Variances.** Professors Shank and Churchill have suggested a method of calculating marketing variances in which they analyze the sales quantity variance into two portions: market size and market share.[a] These variances are calculated as follows:

market size variance = (expected total market − actual total market)
    × (expected market share)
    × (budgeted contribution margin per unit)

market share variance = (expected market share − actual market share)
    × (actual total market)
    × (budgeted contribution margin per unit)

[a] John K. Shank and Neil C. Churchill, "Variance Analysis: A Management-Oriented Approach," *The Accounting Review*, (October 1977), pp. 950–57.

Positive values are unfavorable, negative values are favorable. As an example, suppose that a firm had the following expectations and actual results:

	Expected (budgeted)	Actual
Total market for product	100,000 units	90,000 units
Company sales	30,000	28,800

Budgeted contribution margin per unit is $4. The total sales quantity variance is $4,800 unfavorable [(30,000 − 28,800) × $4]. Analyzing the variance using the Shank/Churchill method gives:

market size variance = $12,000 unfavorable
market share variance = $7,200 favorable

Required:

1. Verify the calculations of the market size and market share variances.

2. Discuss the benefits of the division of the quantity variance into the two components. For example, using the normal quantity variance, would you be inclined to say that the sales manager had done a good job or a poor job? Would your impression be different after making the calculations of size and share variances?

7–17 Interpretation of Variances.   The Scorum Company uses standard costs for all input factors. Two components of variable overhead appear below.

Cost Factor	Standard Quantity per Direct Labor Hour	Standard Rate per Direct Labor Hour
Indirect labor	0.10 hr	$1.20
Fuel	0.40 gal	0.36

These costs are expressed in terms of standard labor hours following the general practice of relating variable overhead to an input factor like direct labor hours or machine hours. Expressed per unit of finished product for one of the firm's many products, the costs are:

Cost Factor	Price per Unit of Cost Factor	Quantity per Unit of Product	Standard Cost per Unit of Product
Indirect labor	$12/hour	0.20	$2.40
Fuel	$ 0.90/gal	0.80	0.72

A unit of product requires two standard labor hours, so that the standards per direct labor hour are half of the standards for a unit of finished product. In March the firm made 1,000 units of the product using 2,050 direct labor hours. Actual indirect labor cost was $2,376 for 198 hours, and actual fuel cost was $765 for 850 gallons bought and used. The usual approach to computing variances gives the following:

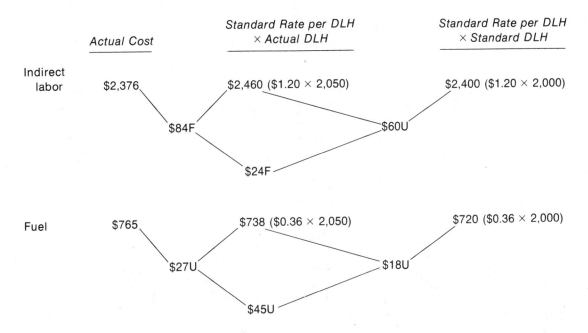

Required: Comment on the variances calculated above. Do they accurately reflect what they should? What changes would you recommend?

7–18 Dividing Variances.   Sunrise Corporation uses standard costing for its operations. Nancy Linek, a recent accounting graduate, has just come up to you with a question:

> I was looking at January's results for the Beloit plant on job M-73. Let's look at labor costs. The standards for that job called for 27 hours at $18.50 per hour. The job sheet shows labor costs are $414 and 23 hours were used. I remember something from my cost accounting course about pure variances and interactions. Could you explain these variances to me?

Required: Answer Nancy's question by explaining in numbers and words the sources of the variances.

7–19 Variances: Good Output; Causes (CMA).   The Felton Company manufactures a complete line of radios. Because a large number of models have plastic cases, the company has its own molding department for producing the cases. The month of April was devoted to the production of the plastic case for one of the portable radios—Model SX76.

The molding department has two operations—molding and trimming. There is no interaction of labor in these two operations. The standard labor cost for producing ten (10) plastic cases for Model SX76 is as follows:

Molders	0.50 hr at $6 =	$3
Trimmers	0.25 hr at $4 =	1
		$4

During April, 70,000 plastic cases were produced in the molding department. However, 10 percent of these cases (7,000) had to be discarded because they were found to be defective at final inspection. The purchasing department had changed to a new plastic supplier to take advantage of a lower price for comparable plastic. The new plastic turned out to be of a lower quality and resulted in the rejection of completed cases.

Direct labor hours worked and direct labor costs charged to the molding department are shown below.

Direct Labor Charged to the Molding Department

Molders	3,800 hr at $6.25 =	$23,750
Trimmers	1,600 hr at $4.15 =	6,640
Total labor charges		$30,390

As a result of poor scheduling by the production scheduling department, the foreman of the molding department had to shift molders to the trimming operation for 200 hours during April. The company paid the molding workers their regular hourly rate even though they were performing a lower-rated task. There was no significant loss of efficiency caused by the shift. In addition, the foreman of the department indicated that 75 hours and 35 hours of idle time occurred in the molding and trimming operations, respectively, as a result of unexpected machinery repairs required during the month.

Required:

1. The monthly report that compares actual costs with standard cost of output for the month of April shows the following labor variance for the molding department:

Actual labor costs for April	$30,390
Standard labor cost of output (63,000 × $4/10)	25,200
Unfavorable labor variance	$ 5,190

This variance is significantly higher than normal, and management would like an explanation. Prepare a detailed analysis of the unfavorable labor variance for the molding department, showing the variance resulting from
   a. labor rates.
   b. labor substitution.

      c. material substitution.

      d. operating efficiency.

      e. idle time.

2. The foreman of the molding department is concerned with the large variances charged to his department. He feels that the variances due to labor substitution and change in raw materials should not be charged to his department. Does the foreman have a valid argument? Briefly justify your position.

7–20 **Sales Mix Variance.** The president of the Corham Company was discussing the performance of the marketing manager, using the data given below. The president was pleased at the favorable quantity variances but was critical of the unfavorable mix variance.

| | Products | | | |
	Regular	Deluxe	Super	Totals
Budgeted volume	10,000	6,000	4,000	20,000
Actual volume	12,000	7,000	4,500	23,500
Budgeted contribution margin (equals actual contribution margin)	$3	$5	$8	

The marketing manager felt it was unreasonable to say that there was an unfavorable mix variance. "After all, my job is to get as much volume as we can at favorable prices, and I did just that. To criticize me for not increasing sales of all products at the same rates is unfair and does not present a true picture of my performance."

Required:

1. Calculate the sales quantity and sales mix variances.

2. Comment on the position taken by the marketing manager.

7–21 **Gross Margin Variances.** The income statement for Franklin, Inc., is presented below. Franklin makes men's shirts.

FRANKLIN, INC.
Income Statement
19X3

Sales	$646,800
Cost of sales	380,000
Gross profit	$266,800
Sales expenses	50,000
Administrative expenses	45,000
Income before taxes	$171,800

Sales consist of 12,000 units divided as follows: 40 percent deluxe designer shirts, 30 percent western style shirts and 30 percent dress shirts. The average prices were $30 for the dress shirts, $35 for the western shirts, and $86 for the designer shirts. Plans for the period called for sales of 5,250 designer shirts, 4,500 western shirts, and 5,250 dress shirts.

The 19X3 cost of sales includes $5,000 unfavorable variable cost variances. Standard costs of sales for designer shirts are $44.6425 and for dress and western shirts $22.3213 each. Standard prices for the line call for $80 designer, $40 western, and $30 dress shirts.

Required:

1. Calculate the gross margin price, volume, mix, and total variances.

2. Explain these variances.

7–22 Labor Mix and Yield Variances (CMA) (appendix). Landeau Manufacturing Company has a process cost accounting system. An analysis that compares the actual results with both a monthly plan and a flexible budget is prepared monthly. The standard direct labor rates used in the flexible budget are established each year when the annual plan is formulated and held constant all year.

The standard direct labor rates in effect for the fiscal year ending June 30, 19X8 and the standard hours allowed for the output for the month of April are shown in the schedule below:

	Standard Direct Labor Rate per Hour	Standard Direct Labor Hours Allowed for Output
Labor class III	$8	500
Labor class II	$7	500
Labor class I	$5	500

The wage rates for each labor class increased on January 1, 19X8, under the terms of a new union contract negotiated in December, 19X7. The standard wage rates were not revised to reflect the new contract.

The actual direct labor hours worked and the actual direct labor rates per hour experienced for the month of April were as follows:

	Actual Direct Labor Rate per Hour	Actual Direct Labor Hours
Labor class III	$8.50	550
Labor class II	$7.50	650
Labor class I	$5.40	375

Required:

1. Calculate the dollar amount of the total direct labor variance for the

month of April for the Landeau Manufacturing Company and analyze the total variance into the following components:

   a. direct labor rate variance.

   b. direct labor mix variance.

   c. direct labor performance (efficiency) variance.

2. Discuss the advantages and disadvantages of a standard cost system
   in which the standard direct labor rates per hour are not changed
   during the year to reflect such events as a new labor contract.

7–23 **Marketing Variances in a Service Firm.** Jan McMinn, the managing partner of
McMinn & Co., consulting engineers, gave you the following data regarding budgeted and actual revenue for 19X8.

	Budgeted	Actual
Chargeable hours	65,000	65,470
Total revenue	$1,885,200	$1,870,600

Virtually all costs are fixed, so that revenue is the critical determinant of
profit. McMinn wants you to analyze the figures to give him an idea why
there was a shortfall in revenue.

Required: Give McMinn an appropriate analysis.

7–24 **Marketing Variances in a Service Firm (continued).** McMinn later gave you
the following additional data that show actual and budgeted results by
category of engineer that the firm employs:

	Budgeted		Actual	
	Chargeable Hours	Average Rate	Chargeable Hours	Average Rate
Junior engineer	45,700	$21.75	47,100	$21.60
Senior engineer	13,300	35.20	12,650	35.30
Partner	6,000	70.50	5,720	71.10

Required: Determine the sales mix, sales price, and sales volume variances. Round your calculations of values for revenues to the nearest $100.

7–25 **Interpretation of Variances.** McMinn looked at the analysis that you prepared for assignment 7–24 and made the following comments:

I see what you mean about the mix of engineers changing from the budgeted
one, but wasn't my real problem the shortfalls in chargeable hours for seniors
and partners? Granted, the ratio of juniors increased over the budget, but that
was because I was able to use juniors more than I had originally planned. Look,
why don't you do a price and volume analysis for each category, treating them
as individual firms, and drop the mix variance. That might help me more.

Required: Do as McMinn suggests. Compare the results with those you obtained in the preceding assignment and comment on the differences, especially with regard to the information that they give McMinn.

SELECTED REFERENCES

Beyer, Robert, and D. Trawicki, *Profitability Accounting for Planning and Control*, 2d ed. New York: The Ronald Press Company, 1972.

Dickey, Robert I., ed., *Accountants' Cost Handbook*, 2d ed. New York: The Ronald Press Company, 1960.

Ferrara, William L. "Production Costs," in Sidney Davidson, ed., *Handbook of Modern Accounting*, New York: McGraw-Hill Book Company, 1970.

Landekich, Stephen. "Setting Standards and Reporting Standard Costs," in Homer A. Black and James Don Edwards, eds., *The Managerial and Cost Accountant's Handbook*, Homewood, Ill.: Dow Jones-Richard D. Irwin, Inc., 1979.

Standard Costing

Chapter 8

In Chapter 7 we developed a full range of variances relating to sales, purchasing, and production. The algebra of variances shows how to compute the differences between planned performance and actual results. This chapter relies on that algebra but considers how firms use standard costs and variances in product costing.

Standard costing is the use of standard costs in product costing, especially in the cost accounting cycle from Materials Inventory through Work-in-Process Inventory to Finished Goods Inventory and, finally, to Cost of Goods Sold. Under standard costing systems, inventories of materials, work in process, and finished goods are kept at standard cost, not actual or normal cost. Standard costing may be used by processing firms such as those in Chapter 6 and also by job order firms that produce the same basic products over and over. A furniture manufacturer that produces only a few basic models could use standard costing. Most large firms, and many small ones, use standard costing because of several advantages it offers.

ADVANTAGES OF STANDARD COSTING

First, the calculations required under standard costing are somewhat less cumbersome than those under actual or normal costing, especially for processing firms. Second, the use of standard costs in the accounts ties the planning and control aspects of standard costs into the accounting system. Firms that use actual or normal costing for product costing purposes and that calculate variances from standard only to judge sales and production effectiveness and efficiency divorce the managerial aspects of standards from the accounting system.

Third, standard costing is much the best choice for multiproduct firms. Consider a firm that makes 1,000 or so different products in the same factory. The products may differ in size, like panes of glass, or in qualitative ways, like different models of automobiles. Consider an automobile assembly plant. Keeping track of costs for each individual car would be prohibitively costly, as well as nonsensical. Yet the plant could not use straightforward process costing, because the cars differ in so many important respects that no single denominator could be used to determine a cost-per-car figure. The use of standard costing would be cheaper and more informative than would some version of actual or normal costing.

RECORDING STANDARD COSTS

Standard costing parallels actual and normal costing so far as the basic flows of costs are concerned. The flows from Materials Inventory, Direct Labor, and Factory Overhead accounts through Work-in-Process Inventory to Finished Goods Inventory to Cost of Goods Sold are essentially the same under all costing methods. Standard costing usually involves transfers at standard cost, or at least at standard prices of input factors. The nature of the transfers depends on the way in which the system is operated.

In one type of standard costing system, all costs put into Work-in-Process Inventory, taken out to Finished Goods, and finally to Cost of Goods Sold are at standard. Thus, the amount debited to Work-in-Process Inventory when materials are put into process is the standard cost of materials for the number of units produced, the direct labor cost put into Work-in-Process Inventory is the standard direct labor cost for the number of units produced, and so also with factory overhead. Such a system can be used if the entries in the accounting system are made after production for a period is known. That is, in order to know the standard labor cost (material cost, overhead cost) of units produced, you must know actual production.

Entries under the standard costing system described are made periodically: once a week, once a month, whenever the production for a period is known. If entries are made before production is known, they cannot reflect standard costs, but they can reflect standard prices. Thus, entries to Work-in-Process Inventory can reflect the actual quantity of materials, labor, and overhead put into process, but at standard prices per pound and rates per hour, not the actual costs. This type of standard costing system essentially does for materials and labor what normal costing does for overhead, since it applies them at standard, or predetermined, rates.

In Figure 8–1 production is known and management has isolated variances immediately. Under this system the inventories are all carried at standard, and variances are, therefore, treated as a period expense. Later in the chapter we will discuss how to dispose of variances.

Basic Information: Labrea Carpet Illustration

We begin by showing a standard costing system where entries are made after production is known. Later we shall illustrate standard costing where actual quantities of input factors are put into Work-in-Process Inventory at standard prices. The basic illustration uses data from Labrea Carpet Com-

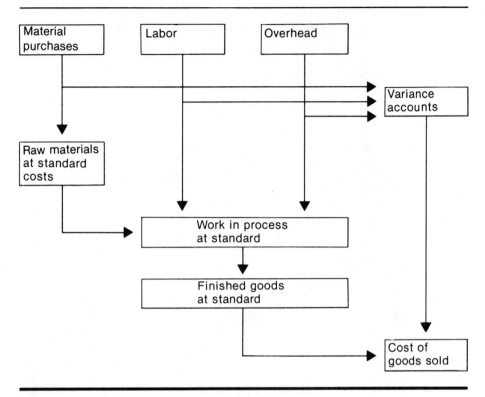

FIGURE 8–1
Inventory Flow—Standard Costs

pany. Labrea's Doltown mill makes two grades of industrial carpeting. Ultimate use of products from Doltown include offices, hospitals, retail stores, and other heavy-traffic locations. Both grades of carpet use the same basic raw material, a synthetic yarn made of newlon. The other principal raw materials include a fabric backing and rubber cushion (or padding). The production process involves weaving the newlon in a specific pattern, using the fabric backing. Rolls of semifinished carpets are made at the end of the automatic weaving machine. All rolls are 12 feet wide and 1,000 feet long. Semifinished rolls are transported by a crane to another machine, where the rubber padding is affixed with an adhesive, using heat and pressure. Final rolls in shorter lengths are then cut and wrapped for shipment. Special designs are available for the deluxe grade; their complexity slows down the production process on the weaving machine. This is the sole difference between the two grades. There is little time lost changing between regular and deluxe on any of the manufacturing equipment. The standard cost card for the regular grade is shown in Exhibit 8–1 on page 328. Exhibit 8–2 on page 328 summarizes the standard costs for the deluxe grade. The Doltown plant buys newlon either directly through major yarn manufacturers or through brokers handling smaller producers. Rubber padding is purchased from one supplier under a long-term contract.

EXHIBIT 8–1
Standard Cost Card—Labrea Carpet Company

Mill: *Doltown*
Model: *Indestructo Regular*
Material specification—0.003 in. multistrand commercial grade newlon
   —$^1/_{16}$ in. standard carpet backing
   —⅜ in. foam rubber padding

Standard Costs per 100 Square Yards

Materials: 150 lb newlon fiber at $1.10	$165.00
25 lb carpet backing at $0.50	12.50
200 lb foam rubber padding at $0.25	50.00
Labor: weaving—0.4 hr × 6 people × $9/hr	21.60
padding—0.6 hr × 5 people × $6/hr	18.00
Factory overhead—5.4 DLH at $12/hr	64.80
	$331.90

EXHIBIT 8–2
Summary of Standard Costs—Execusuite
Deluxe Carpet

	Cost per 100 Yd
Material: newlon	$165.00
carpet backing	12.50
foam rubber	50.00
Labor: weaving—0.6 hr × 6 people × $9/hr	32.40
padding—0.6 hr × 5 people × $6/hr	18.00
Factory overhead: 6.6 DLH at $12/hr	79.20
	$357.10

Carpets are available in regular or deluxe weave in various colors. There is no difference in the cost of buying any of these colors of newlon yarn.

Both fixed and variable overhead are included in the $12 per DLH overhead standard. Fixed factory overhead is expected to be $300,000 for the year, $25,000 per month. Variable overhead is $9 per DLH and includes indirect labor and materials. Practical capacity for this plant has been chosen as the denominator for applying fixed overhead. Labrea operates two processes, weaving and padding, but could not readily use process costing because it makes two different products. To use actual or normal process costing would require considerable allocation of material, labor, and overhead costs. It will be necessary, however, to convert standard costing results to actual costing for determining inventory and cost of sales for financial reporting and tax purposes. This is illustrated later in the chapter.

Materials Inventory

Since it is company policy in this case to isolate variances as soon as possible and to carry inventory at standard costs, the first variances can occur when materials are purchased. During March, 19X1, the purchasing department bought newlon and backing. The invoices from various suppliers showed the following.

Newlon fiber, 340,000 lb	$370,600
Standard backing, 37,000 lb	18,500
	$389,100

There was enough foam rubber padding in inventory so that none was purchased in March. An analysis of Exhibit 8–1 shows that the standard cost for newlon is $1.10 per pound and for backing $0.50 per pound. Material price variances can be identified as follows:

$$V_p \text{ (newlon)} = \$370,600 - (340,000 \times \$1.10) = (\$3,400)\text{F}$$
$$V_p \text{ (backing)} = \$18,500 - (37,000 \times \$0.50) = 0$$

The materials purchased will be used for both the Indestructo Regular and the Execusuite Deluxe Carpet. When a material price variance is identified at purchase, the costs of carpeting in process and in finished goods do not reflect the level of efficiency or inefficiency of the purchasing department. The entry for these purchases would be as follows:

1. Materials Inventory—newlon	$374,000	
Materials Inventory—backing	18,500	
Material Price Variance—newlon		$ 3,400
Accounts Payable		389,100

The amounts in this entry can be verified by referring to the calculations for V_p above. The favorable variance is shown as a credit entry, since it has a positive effect on income.

Work in Process

As work is processed through a plant, materials are converted into various products, and labor and overhead costs are incurred. Exhibit 8–3 on page 330 shows facts regarding March production. Assume fixed costs are incurred evenly throughout the year. Also assume that work in process consists solely of carpeting that has been woven but not run through the padding machine. We will relax this assumption later on in a discussion of standard process costing. The entries for the information contained in Exhibit 8–3 can be broken down into those for materials, labor, and overhead as costs are first recorded and then entered into Work-in-Process Inventory. In addition, as goods are finished, they move into Finished Goods Inventory.

EXHIBIT 8-3
Data for March, 19X6—Labrea Carpet Company

Production

	Deluxe	Regular
Put into process, hundreds of yards	29,550	118,200
Beginning inventory of work in process	1,000	4,000
Total	30,550	122,200
Completed	30,000	115,000
Ending inventory of work in process	550	7,200

Materials used

Newlon	221,000 lb
Backing	37,000 lb
Foam rubber	290,000 lb

Labor

| Weaving | 3,800 hr | $34,580 |
| Padding | 4,400 hr | $26,400 |

Overhead

| Fixed | $25,000 |
| Variable | $72,000 |

Efficiency Variances

Chapter 6 made the point that calculations of equivalent production on a FIFO basis were superior for control purposes to those made using a weighted average basis. The reason is that the weighted average basis mixes the results of the current period with those of prior periods, while FIFO concentrates on the work done in the current period. Under standard costing, efficiency variances are calculated using FIFO equivalent units of production as the relevant output of the period.

The managers of Labrea would like to evaluate the weaving and padding operations separately and, therefore, would calculate equivalent production for each operation. We could calculate the equivalent production in work in process by using the basic techniques shown in Chapter 6, or we could simplify the calculations by looking at the operations separately.

The calculations of equivalent production for Labrea are relatively straightforward. The only work in process consists of carpet woven but not padded. Therefore, we can easily determine the quantities woven and padded during the period and use those quantities to determine the efficiency variances. From Exhibit 8–3 we see that 30,000 yards of deluxe and 115,000 yards of regular grade carpet were padded during the period. The efficiency variance for direct labor in the padding operation is:

Direct Labor Efficiency Variance–Padding

Standard hours, $\dfrac{(30,000 \times 0.6 \times 5) + (115,000 \times 0.6 \times 5)}{100}$	4,350
Actual hours	4,400
Excess actual over standard	50
Standard rate per hour	$6
Labor efficiency variance—padding	$300 unfavorable

The material use variance for foam rubber, the only material added in the padding operation, is zero. Actual use of 290,000 lb equals standard use. At 200 lb of foam rubber per 100 sq yd of both grades, standard use is (30,000 × 200) + (115,000 × 200), which is 290,000 lb.

The equivalent production of the weaving operation requires the following calculations, because the quantity sent to the padding operation is not equivalent production for the period. The calculations are simplified, however, because all the work required in the weaving operation, as well as materials put into the weaving operation, is 100 percent complete.

	Deluxe	Regular
Transferred to padding	30,000	115,000
Ending work in process	550	7,200
Subtotal	30,550	122,200
Beginning work in process	1,000	4,000
Equivalent production	29,550	118,200

These figures are used to determine the standard quantities of weaving labor, newlon, and backing, from which the efficiency and use variances will be calculated.

Direct Labor Efficiency Variance—Weaving

Standard hours, $\dfrac{(29,550 \times 0.6 \times 6) + (118,200 \times 0.4 \times 6)}{100}$	3,900.6
Actual hours	3,800.0
Excess of standard hours over actual hours	100.6
Standard rate per hour	$9
Direct labor efficiency variance—weaving	$905.40 favorable

Material Use Variance—Newlon

Standard quantity, $\dfrac{(29{,}550 \times 150) + (118{,}200 \times 150)}{100}$	221,625 lb
Actual quantity	221,000
Excess of standard quantity over actual quantity	625
Standard price per pound	$1.10
Material use variance—newlon	$687.50 favorable

Material Use Variance—Backing

Standard quantity, $\dfrac{(29{,}550 \times 25) + (118{,}200 \times 25)}{100}$	36,937.5 lb
Actual quantity	37,000.0
Excess of actual over standard	62.5
Standard price per pound	$0.50
Material use variance—backing	$31.25 unfavorable

Overhead Variances

The firm does not have separate records for overhead by operation. We must use the total direct labor hours to determine the variable overhead efficiency and rate variances. There was no fixed overhead budget variance. Total standard hours will also be used to determine the application variance.

Variable Overhead Efficiency Variance

Total standard hours, 3,900.6 + 4,350	8,250.6
Total actual hours, 3,800 + 4,400	8,200.0
Excess of standard hours over actual hours	50.6
Variable overhead rate per labor hour	$9
Variable overhead efficiency variance	$455.40 favorable

The 50.6 hr favorable is a combination of the 100.6 hr favorable in the V_e for weaving labor and the 50 hr unfavorable in the V_e for padding labor.

Fixed Overhead Application Variance

Total standard hours	8,250.6
Application base 100,000 hours/12 months	8,333.3
Excess of expected application over standard	82.7
Standard rate per hour	$3
Application variance	$248.20 unfavorable

Variable Overhead Rate Variance

Total actual cost	$72,000
Total actual hours at standard rate	
[(3,800 hr + 4,400 hr) × $9]	73,800
Variable overhead rate variance	$ 1,800 favorable

Recording Costs Incurred

Now that several actual costs, standard costs, and variances have been determined, it is time to record these facts. The first entries record costs incurred during March. Material purchases were dealt with under entry 1 on page 329.

2.	Direct Labor—weaving	$34,580	
	Direct Labor—padding	26,400	
	Wages Payable		$60,980
3.	Variable Factory Overhead	$72,000	
	Fixed Factory Overhead	25,000	
	Various credits		$97,000

All these costs are recorded at actual quantities and actual prices (costs). The accounts shown as debits in both entries 2 and 3 are used to identify specific costs, since identification of labor and overhead is lost when costs are attached to products in work in process.

Transferring Costs to Work in Process

In this example we are making summary entries for the month. It would be quite usual that weekly entries would be made instead of monthly ones. The basic idea behind transferring costs into Work-in-Process Inventory is to value this inventory at standard. Thus, any variances are identified and placed in separate variance accounts. Materials Inventory is already at standard costs. Entry 4 reflects material use.

4.	Work-in-Process Inventory	$334,756.25	
	Materials Use Variance		$ 656.25
	Materials Inventory—newlon		243,100.00
	Materials Inventory—backing		18,500.00
	Materials Inventory—foam rubber		72,500.00

The total materials use variance is the sum of the separate variances for newlon and backing calculated earlier. If costs versus benefits warrant, separate entries could be made for each of the two material use variances (newlon and backing).

The entry to Direct Labor includes possibly both wage rate and labor efficiency variances. Entries 5 and 6 reflect isolating these wage rate and labor efficiency variances when the labor costs are transferred to work in process.

5.	Work-in-Process Inventory	$35,105.40	
	Labor Rate Variance	380.00	
	Labor Efficiency Variance		$ 905.40
	Direct Labor—weaving		34,580.00
6.	Work-in-Process Inventory	$26,100	
	Labor Efficiency Variance	300	
	Direct Labor—padding		$26,400

The labor rate variance can be calculated from information in Exhibit 8–3. While we can calculate separate rate and efficiency variances for weaving and padding, it is impossible to identify these variances with the regular or deluxe carpeting with just the information given in Exhibit 8–3.

While entry 3 shows overhead costs as incurred, these costs are applied at $12 per direct labor hour. Entry 7 shows this application.

7.	Work-in-Process Inventory	$99,007.20	
	Overhead Application Variance	248.20	
	Variable Overhead Rate Variance		$ 1,800.00
	Variable Overhead Efficiency Variance		455.40
	Variable Factory Overhead		72,000.00
	Fixed Factory Overhead		25,000.00

Transferring Costs to Finished Goods

Since all inventories are at standard cost, there is no need to make an inventory flow assumption such as FIFO or weighted average. As Exhibit 8–3 shows, 30,000 square yards of the deluxe grade and 115,000 square yards of the regular grade carpeting were foam-rubber padded and, therefore, finished. The entry to record such a transfer is:

8.	Finished Goods Inventory—regular	$381,685	
	Finished Goods Inventory—deluxe	107,130	
	Work-in-Process Inventory		$488,815

Exhibit 8–4 on page 336 shows T-accounts and, keyed to the entry numbers, traces the cost flows from incurrence to work in process and to finished goods. We assume that the various raw material inventories identified in entries 1 and 4 will be subsidiary accounts to a general Materials Inventory account. The beginning balance of this account (assumed to be $100,000) contained sufficient foam rubber for this period. Entries to factory overhead and finished goods are also reflected on a master account basis, and we assume a beginning inventory of $161,537 in finished goods.

Transferring Costs to Cost of Goods Sold

Assume that the firm sold 120,000 square yards of regular carpeting at $8 per yd and 30,000 square yards of deluxe at $11 per yd during March. As in the transfers from Work-in-Process Inventory to Finished Goods Inventory, the transfer from Finished Goods to Cost of Goods Sold is at standard cost.

9. Cost of Goods Sold		$505,410	
	Finished Goods Inventory—regular		$398,280
	Finished Goods Inventory—deluxe		107,130

DISPOSITION OF VARIANCES

As we proceeded through the production cycle, we incurred costs, and, using standard costing, recorded these costs at standard in Raw Materials, Work-in-Process, and Finished Goods accounts. Variances were identified as soon as possible and placed in several variance accounts. The following production cost variances have been recorded:

Material Price Variance—newlon	($3,400)F
Material Use Variance	(656.25)F
Labor Rate Variance	380 U
Labor Efficiency Variance—weaving	(905.40)F
Labor Efficiency Variance—padding	300 U
Variable Overhead Efficiency Variance	(455.40)F
Variable Overhead Rate Variance	(1,800)F
Application Variance	248.20 U

What do we do with these variances? When the period is concluded, all costs that a firm incurs are classified as either assets or expenses. Assets are reflected in appropriate balance sheet accounts, while expenses appear on the income statement. How shall we classify production variances for control purposes? There are two general approaches.

Income at Standard

The first approach is to classify all production variances as expenses. If we can assume with some degree of confidence that the standards that management has developed are reflections of what products should cost to make, then under normal circumstances we would expect actual production costs to be nearly equal to standard costs for the quantity produced. Any savings from standard (favorable variances) or costs in excess of standard (unfavorable variances) would then be considered abnormal.

Also helpful in this discussion is a definition of an asset. An **asset** is

EXHIBIT 8-4
T-Accounts

Materials Inventory

Beg. bal.	$100,000	$243,100	(4)
(1) newlon	374,000	18,500	(4)
(1) backing	18,500	72,500 foam rubber	(4)
End. bal.	$158,400		

Materials Price Variance

$3,400 newlon	(1)

Work-in-Process Inventory

Beg. bal.^{a}	$ 11,647	$488,815	(8)
(4)	334,756.25		
(5)	35,105.40		
(6)	26,100.00		
(7)	99,007.20		
End. bal.^{b}	$17,800.85		

Material Use Variance

$656.25	(4)

Labor Rate Variance

(5) $380	

Direct Labor—Weaving

(2) $34,580	34,580	(5)

Labor Efficiency Variance

(6) $300	$905.40	(5)

Direct Labor—Padding

(2) $26,400	26,400	(6)

Variable Overhead Efficiency Variance

$455.40	(7)

Factory Overhead

(3) $72,000	$72,000	(7)
(3) 25,000	25,000	(7)

Overhead Application Variance

(7) $248.20	

Finished Goods Inventory

Beg. bal.	$161,537	398,280	(9)
(8)	381,685	107,130	(9)
(8)	107,130		
End. bal.	$144,942		

Variable Overhead Rate Variance

$1,800	(7)

^{a} Consists of 1,000 yd deluxe at $2.531 and 4,000 yd regular at $2.279, which includes newlon, backing, weaving labor, and overhead on weaving labor hours. ^{b} Consists of 550 yd deluxe at $2.531 and 7,200 yd regular at $2.279.

something of future value to a company. Since costs can be treated in two ways (as assets or as expenses), management can ask whether variances have future value to the firm in a planning or control sense. If management concludes that inventories costed at standard reflect assets better than if part of the variances were included, then the way is open to classify variances as **period expenses.** Thus, the balance sheet would show the raw materials, work-in-process, and finished goods inventories at standard while the income statement would show all variances in their entirety as period expenses (as separate items or as an adjustment to cost of goods sold.) If Labrea followed this procedure, the income statement would appear as in Exhibit 8–5 below. This exhibit treats all variances as adjustments to gross profit.

EXHIBIT 8–5
Partial Income Statement, Month Ending 3/31/X6—
Labrea Carpet Company

Sales, (120,000 × $8) + (30,000 × $11)		$1,290,000
Standard Cost of Goods Sold		505,410
Standard Gross Margin		784,590
Plus: Material Price Variance—newlon	$(3,400)	
Material Use Variance	(656)	
Labor Rate Variance	380	
Labor Efficiency Variance—weaving	(905)	
Labor Efficiency Variance—padding	300	
Variable Overhead Efficiency Variance	(455)	
Variable Overhead Rate Variance	(1,800)	
Application Variance	248	6,288F
Gross Margin		$ 790,878

PRORATING VARIANCES

From a control and managerial accountability standpoint, assigning all variances as expenses seems the most appropriate method. However, financial reporting and tax accounting generally require the use of actual costing. In developing financial statements for those purposes, therefore, variances must be prorated to inventories and cost of sales.

The variances of Labrea Carpet Company were not material and, therefore, could reasonably be written off as adjustments to cost of sales. However, if variances for a full year are material, they must be allocated to inventories and cost of sales. *Accounting Research Bulletin 43* requires that standard costs, to be acceptable for financial reporting purposes, be "adjusted at reasonable intervals to reflect current conditions so that at the balance-sheet date standard costs reasonably approximate costs computed under one of the recognized bases."[1] The recognized bases are FIFO, LIFO, and weighted average cost flow patterns.

As a general rule, each type of variance (materials, direct labor, overhead) is allocated (prorated) to each ending inventory and to cost of sales on the basis of the relative amounts of standard cost for that factor in each account. Data appear in Exhibit 8–6. To save time and concentrate on the problem at hand, we have presented the data assuming that all variances, equivalent production, and so on have been calculated. Familiarize yourself with the data first, making sure that you see how the figures for standard costs in the ending inventories and cost of sales were developed. For simplicity we ignore beginning inventories here; they are covered in Appendix 8–A.

EXHIBIT 8–6
Data for Illustration

	Standard Cost of Product	
Materials, 3 pounds at $2	$ 6	
Conversion costs	12	
Total	$18	

	Units	Standard Cost of Materials at $6	Standard Conversion Costs at $12	Total Standard Costs
Sales	40,000	$240,000	$480,000	$720,000
Ending inventory of finished goods	20,000	120,000	240,000	360,000
Work in process:				
Materials, 8,000 units 100% complete		48,000		
Conversion costs, 8,000 units 60% complete			57,600	
Total work in process				105,600

Additionally, there were no beginning inventories and the inventory of materials was 10,000 pounds, with a standard cost of $20,000.

	Variances	
Material price variance	$15,000	unfavorable
Material use variance	10,000	favorable
Conversion cost variances	80,000	unfavorable

---

[1] Committee on Accounting Procedure, *Accounting Research Bulletin No. 43, Restatement and Revision of Accounting Research Bulletins* (New York: American Institute of Certified Public Accountants, 1953), p. 17.

Because all conversion cost variances will be prorated the same way, there is no need to break them down into individual items. However, the material price and use variances must be treated separately from the conversion cost variances because of the different equivalent productions and ending inventories of work in process. Additionally, the material price variance is allocated separately because it relates to all ending inventories and to cost of sales. The other variances relate only to ending inventories of work in process and finished goods and to cost of sales.

Material Price Variance

There are several ways to allocate the material price variance. Some accountants allocate it to each of the ending inventories, cost of sales, and material use variance on the grounds that this gives the most accurate representation of actual costs. Other accountants ignore the material use variance in allocating the material price variance because they believe that the increase in accuracy is not worth the additional effort. The schedule below shows the allocation of the material price variance.

Account	Standard Cost	Percentage of Total	Allocation of Material Price Variance (Rounded)
Materials Inventory	$ 20,000	4.79%	$ 719
Work-in-Process Inventory	48,000	11.48	1,722
Finished Goods Inventory	120,000	28.71	4,306
Cost of Sales	240,000	57.42	8,613
Material Use Variance	(10,000)	(2.40)	(360)
Totals	$418,000	100.0%	$15,000

Notice that the allocation to the material use variance is negative because the material use variance was favorable. Essentially, this allocation recognizes the fact that less material than the standard quantity was required to produce the units. The resulting allocation of the material use variance, augmented by the share of the material price variance, will give the same results as the use of actual costing. The reason is that the standard costs of materials in the ending inventories of work in process and finished goods and in cost of sales reflect standard quantities of material, not the actual quantity used.

Material Use Variance and Conversion Cost Variances

The schedules below show the allocations of the material use variance and of the conversion cost variances based on the relative amounts of standard cost in each account. This part of the allocation should present no problems: the procedures are similar to other allocations that we have dealt with in this book.

Material Use Variance

Account	Standard Cost	Percentage of Total	Allocation of Material Use Variance
Work-in-Process Inventory	$ 48,000	11.77%	$ 1,219
Finished Goods Inventory	120,000	29.41	3,047
Cost of Sales	240,000	58.82	6,094
Totals	$408,000	100.00%	$10,360

Notice that the total amount of material use variance allocated is $10,360, which is the original variance of $10,000 favorable, plus the favorable allocation from the material price variance. In journal entry terms, the unfavorable material price variance is a credit to Material Use Variance, debits to the other accounts.

Conversion Cost Variances

Account	Standard Cost	Percentage of Total	Allocation of Conversion Cost Variances
Work-in-Process Inventory	$ 57,600	7.41%	$ 5,925
Finished Goods Inventory	240,000	30.86	24,692
Cost of Sales	480,000	61.73	49,383
Totals	$777,600	100.00%	$80,000

Finally, the schedule below summarizes the prorations and shows the inventory valuations that would be used for financial reporting purposes.

Account	Standard Cost	Unfavorable Material Price Variance	Favorable Material Use Variance	Unfavorable Conversion Cost Variances	Actual Cost
Materials Inventory	$ 20,000	$ 719			$ 20,719
Work-in-Process Inventory	105,600	1,722	($1,219)	$ 5,925	112,028
Finished Goods Inventory	360,000	4,306	(3,047)	24,692	385,951
Cost of Sales	720,000	8,613	(6,094)	49,383	771,902

Variances and Control

The purpose in identifying variances is to open the way to an orderly investigation of why results differed from plans by looking at various areas of responsibility. Accordingly, it is logical from a control and from a responsibility accounting perspective to show any variance as an adjustment to income. This is exactly what happens when each full variance appears as an expense in Exhibit 8–5.

STANDARD JOB ORDER COSTING

Chapter 5 described job order costing as a method that requires accumulating actual direct material and direct labor costs for each job, with overhead generally being applied on the basis of labor hours, labor cost, or machine hours. Job order firms can use standard costing if there is sufficient repetition in their products or in operations common to most products. For example, if a firm makes 40 to 50 different optical instruments that contain several standard components, such as lenses and frames, and that require similar operations, such as drilling, grinding, and chamfering, it might be able to make good use of standard costing.

The procedure for a job order standard costing system would be about the same as those for Labrea Carpet. Individual jobs would be charged with the standard cost of direct materials and direct labor, standard quantities times standard prices, and Work-in-Process Inventory would then consist of the standard cost of work done on each job to date. This assumes that production is known at the completion of particular operations; otherwise, we could not use standard quantities until the jobs were completed.

For example, suppose that the standard cost card for a particular optical instrument calls for a grinding of one edge to take a half-hour. If the standard labor rate is $8 per hour, each grinding has a standard cost of $4. The worker would mark his job ticket with the number of edges ground during the time he worked on the job. The clerk would then be able to determine the total standard hours allowed for grinding all the pieces.

ALTERNATIVE COST FLOW PATTERNS

In some cases accounting entries are made before production is known. It is then impossible to make debits to Work-in-Process Inventory at standard prices times standard quantities because standard quantities depend on production. Firms that do make entries to Work-in-Process Inventory as the period progresses, and without knowing total production, will use standard prices and actual quantities for direct labor and materials. They will probably apply overhead at the end of the period, based on actual production.

Transfers from Work-in-Process Inventory to Finished Goods Inventory and, ultimately, to Cost of Goods Sold will be made at standard cost per unit times the number of units involved.

The basic difference between the flows under the two possibilities is that the material use variance and direct labor efficiency variance go into Work-in-Process Inventory because actual quantities, not standard quantities, are used to make the debits to the account. At the end of the period these amounts will be transferred out of Work-in-Process Inventory and it, as well as the other inventory accounts, will appear at standard cost per unit times the number of equivalent units in process.

Because overhead usually is applied at the end of the period when production is known, the entries for overhead would appear like those used by Labrea Carpet Company in the illustration. In actual practice many variations are possible, but the essence of standard costing is that inventories and cost of sales be shown at standard, with variances isolated in separate accounts. Because variances are shown in accounts, instead of simply being computed, they become part of the basic accounting records. The value is that the accounting records then support and tie into the information needed for planning and control.

SUMMARY

Standard costing involves reflecting standard costs and variances in a company's product costing system. We have shown the entries needed for such a system. Some companies use a standard costing system and assign all variances to an income statement made up for planning and evaluation purposes. However, in order to create both financial and tax reports, management must prorate significant variances between various inventories and cost of goods sold. The examples in this chapter merely illustrate basic standard costing systems. Each company, based on its history, current needs, size, and cost-benefit trade-offs, will establish its own specific standard costing system.

APPENDIX 8–A: VARIANCE PRORATION WITH BEGINNING INVENTORIES

When a firm has beginning inventories, the proration of variances cannot be done in the straightforward fashion illustrated in the chapter. When there are no beginning inventories, there is no need to adopt a cost flow assumption such as FIFO or weighted average. A cost flow assumption must be adopted when beginning inventories are present. FIFO is the best cost flow assumption for control purposes, because it isolates variances of current-

EXHIBIT 8A–1
Data for Illustration—Cooper Products Company

Standard Cost per Unit

Material, 3 gallons at $2	$ 6	
Conversion costs	9	
Total standard costs	$15	

Equivalent Production for Period

	Materials	Conversion Costs
Completed during period	40,000	40,000
Equivalent units in ending inventory of work in process	8,000	6,000
Equivalent units in beginning inventory of work in process	(6,000)	(5,000)
Equivalent production, FIFO	42,000	41,000

Variances

Material price, $0.10 per gallon for 130,000 gallons purchased	$13,000 unfavorable
Material use	6,000 favorable
Labor and overhead variances, total	54,000 unfavorable

Inventories

	Gallons of Materials	Units of Finished Goods
Beginning inventory	30,000	12,000
Added during period	130,000	40,000
Used in production or sold	(123,000)	(38,000)
Ending inventory	37,000	14,000

period work. Therefore it seems reasonable to adopt it for prorating variances as well. The data presented above in Exhibit 8A–1 serve for our illustration.

Using FIFO, we assume that all beginning inventories of finished goods were sold first, that all beginning inventories of work in process were completed first and sold after the beginning inventory of finished goods, and that all beginning inventories of materials were put into production before any materials purchased in the current period. Again, we begin with the material price variance, which is allocated first to the ending inventory of materials in the schedule at the top of page 344.

Ending inventory of materials	37,000 gallons
Material price variance per gallon ($13,000/130,000)	$ 0.10
Material price variance allocated to materials inventory	$3,700
Material price variance remaining	$9,300

The remaining material price variance relates to current-period purchases used in current-period production and can be allocated along with the material use variance. To make the allocation, we must determine where the current-period equivalent production for materials wound up. Similarly, to allocate the conversion-cost variances, we must determine where equivalent production with respect to conversion costs wound up. These calculations are needed because under FIFO we assume all beginning inventories wound up in cost of sales before any current-period production was sold.

	Disposition of Current-Period Production	
	Materials	Conversion Costs
Total equivalent production for period	42,000	41,000
Equivalent units in:		
Ending inventory of work in process	8,000	6,000
Ending inventory of finished goods	14,000	14,000
Total current period equivalent production in ending inventories	22,000	20,000
Equivalent production in cost of sales	20,000	21,000

The purpose of these calculations is to keep separate the flow of production for the current period and the beginning inventories of the period. The method gives the same results that actual costing would under the FIFO assumption, as you may wish to verify. The allocations appear in the schedule opposite.

Prorating the variances would result in the following values for inventories and cost of sales (see schedule opposite).

One point remains: the treatment of variances in the beginning inventories prorated from the prior period. Using FIFO, we assume that all beginning inventories are completed and sold before any current-period production. Therefore, any variances in the beginning inventories would be carried to cost of sales so long as the beginning inventories were less than the amount sold during the period, which is usually reasonable to expect.

You might wish to verify that the method shown here duplicates the results that would be obtained using actual costing under the FIFO assumption. You might also wish to verify that the method illustrated in the chapter will not give the same results in situations where beginning inventories are present.

Allocation of Variances

Materials Variances, $3,300 Unfavorable ($9,300 − $6,000)

Standard Costs of Materials

	Amount	Percentage	Variance Allocation
Work-in-process inventory, 8,000 × $6	$ 48,000	19.1%	$ 630
Finished goods inventory, 14,000 × $6	84,000	33.3	1,100
Cost of sales, 20,000 × $6	120,000	47.6	1,570
Totals	$252,000	100.0%	$3,300

Conversion Cost Variances, $54,000 Unfavorable

Standard Conversion Costs

	Amount	Percentage	Variance Allocation
Work-in-process inventory, 6,000 × $9	$ 54,000	14.6%	$ 7,884
Finished goods inventory, 14,000 × $9	126,000	34.2	18,468
Cost of sales, 21,000 × $9	189,000	51.2	27,648
Totals	$369,000	100.0%	$54,000

Prorating of Variances

	Materials Inventory	Work-in-Process Inventory	Finished Goods Inventory	Cost of Sales
Standard costs	$74,000	$102,000	$210,000	$570,000[a]
Material price variance	3,700			
Material price variance and use variance		630	1,100	1,570
Conversion cost variances		7,884	18,468	27,648
	$77,700	$110,514	$219,568	$599,218

[a] This figure is total cost of sales at standard cost, not just the standard cost of sales relating to current period production, which was used to determine the relative share of the variances going to cost of sales.

ASSIGNMENTS

8–1 Analysis of Records (AICPA adapted). The Bovar Company began to manufacture a new mechanical device called the Dandy on May 1, 19X6. The firm also introduced a standard cost system at that date. Standard costs per unit of Dandy are:

Raw materials	6 lb at $1/lb	$ 6.00
Direct labor	1 hr at $4/hr	4.00
Overhead	75% of direct labor cost	3.00
		$13.00

The following data come from Bovar's records for May, 19X6.

Unit production of Dandy	4,000
Unit sales of Dandy	2,500

	Debit	Credit
Sales		$50,000
Purchases of raw materials, 26,000 pounds	$27,300	
Material price variance	1,300	
Material quantity variance	1,000	
Direct labor rate variance	760	
Direct labor efficiency variance		800
Manufacturing overhead total variance	500	

The amount shown for the material price variance applies to material purchased in May.

Required: Compute each of the following items for Bovar, showing computations in good form.

1. Standard quantity of raw materials allowed, in pounds.
2. Actual quantity of raw materials used, in pounds.
3. Standard direct labor hours allowed.
4. Actual direct labor hours.
5. Actual direct labor rate.
6. Actual total overhead.

8–2 Standard Job Order Costing (AICPA). Milner Manufacturing Company uses a job order costing system and standard costs. It manufactures one product whose standard cost is as follows:

Materials	20 yd at $0.90/yd	$18
Direct labor	4 hr at $6/hr	24
Total factory overhead	Applied at five-sixths of direct labor (the ratio of variable costs to fixed costs is 3 to 1)	20
Variable selling, general, and administrative expenses		12
Fixed selling, general, and administrative expenses		7
Total unit cost		$81

The standards are set based on normal activity of 2,400 direct labor hours.

Actual activity for the month of October, 19X5, was as follows (see data at the top of page 347).

Materials purchased	18,000 yd at $0.92/yd	$16,560
Materials used	9,500 yd	
Direct labor	2,100 hr at $6.10/hr	12,810
Total factory overhead	500 units actually produced	11,100

Required:

1. Compute the variable factory overhead rate per direct labor hour and the total fixed factory overhead based on normal activity.
2. Prepare a schedule computing the following variances for the month of October 1975:
   a. materials price variance.
   b. materials usage variance.
   c. labor rate variance.
   d. labor usage (efficiency) variance.
   e. controllable (budget or spending) overhead variance.
   f. volume (capacity) overhead variance.
   Indicate whether each variance is favorable or unfavorable.

8-3 Overhead Activity. Enterprise, Ltd., has projected fixed overhead per month in various operating ranges as follows:

Shutdown of facilities	$ 35,000
Normal activity	160,000
Practical capacity	180,000

Management thinks that direct labor hours are a good way to apply overhead. Practical capacity of the plant is 120,000 direct labor hours, while normal activity is 80,000 hours.

During March, 85,000 labor hours were used for current production. Jeff Market, a staff accountant, has calculated the following variances for March. Actual overhead was $165,000.

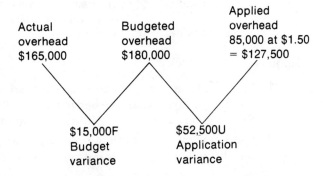

Actual overhead $165,000	Budgeted overhead $180,000	Applied overhead 85,000 at $1.50 = $127,500
	$15,000F Budget variance	$52,500U Application variance

Market had some comments on his report, including the following: "It looks like we controlled costs well in March with that favorable budget variance. Obviously, however, we will have to increase production during the year to wipe out the activity variance like we experienced in March."

Required: Comment on Market's analysis and comments. Suggest any improvements you believe would help management.

8–4   Basic Journal Entries.   The Glow Lantern Corporation uses standard costing and identifies and isolates variances as soon as possible. The following data apply to activity in February, 19X2, for its single product.

1. 2,087 pounds of a chemical named Askarben were purchased for $118,959.

2. 3,200 hours of direct labor were worked at a cost of $22,000, which includes $1,200 in overtime premiums.

3. There were 2,000 units in beginning inventory work in process 100 percent complete in materials and 80 percent complete in conversion costs.

4. 10,000 units were completed and sent to the warehouse. The firm sold 12,000 units, which equaled budget. Revenue was $856,800. There was no ending inventory of work in process.

5. 13,800 feet of steel were used in production and 2,250 pounds of Askarben.

6. Other factory overhead was $59,280 during February. Budgeted overhead, virtually all fixed, was $60,480. The firm does not use separate rates for fixed and variable overhead.

Standards for Glow include:

Askarben	$52 per pound; ¼ pound per unit
Steel	$15 per foot; 1½ feet per unit
Labor	$6.50 per hour; 0.4 hour per unit
Overhead	$18 per direct labor hour, based on 3,360 standard labor hours
Sales price	$68 per unit

Required:

1. Record all the above events, isolating variances as soon as identified. All ending inventories are carried at standard. Variances are put into cost of goods sold at the end of each quarter.

2. Use a T-account for work in process to verify that ending inventory is zero by reflecting proper entries from item 1.

8–5   Journal Entries—Job Order.   You have been given information relating to production at the Dancen Company for January, 19X0. Company policy is to accumulate all the information for the month and enter it into the books at month end. Dancen is a job order company that usually deals with only a few large jobs at a time. The following data relate to January:

Direct labor hours worked,	6,000 hours
including 4,000 hours journeyman	
2,000 hours apprentice	
Standard pay scale: journeyman	$13/hour
apprentice	$ 7/hour
Overhead (mostly fixed) applied at $12 per journeyman hour and $10 per apprentice hour based on 5,000 total hours per month, two-thirds for journeymen, one-third for apprentices.	
Materials issued: Job 1-A5	$24,500
Job 1-A3	$16,750

There were no inventories of work in process or finished goods at the beginning of the month. At month end, Job 1-A5 was 100 percent complete in materials, 50 percent complete in conversion costs. Job 1-A3 was delivered to the customer in January. The estimating department developed the following standards for 1-A3 and 1-A5:

	Job	
	1-A3	1-A5
Materials:		
Steel	$10,300	$14,900
Plastic	5,625	6,500
Joints and hardware	1,260	2,890
Labor hours (⅔ journeymen, ⅓ apprentices):		
Machining	650 hr	790 hr
Drill press	1,780	980
Lathe	25	600
Miscellaneous/assembly	1,200	1,700

A single Work-in-Process account is used, and costs are segregated by jobs when they are moved to finished goods. All variances (except material price variances) are removed from the Work-in-Process account at month end. The chief cost accountant computes variances for each job.

Required:

1. Record all the appropriate standard costing entries from the information given so far. Do not record any variances yet.

2. Month-end information includes the following breakdown of labor hours: Job 1-A3, 3,950 hr; Job 1-A5, 2,050 hr. Record all the variances you can identify for Job 1-A3. Verify that ending Work-in-Process Inventory includes only costs associated with Job 1-A5. How would you handle the application variance?

3. What variances have not been identified?

8-6 **Process Costing—Actual and Standard.** The Barry-Davis Company uses FIFO process costing. Current practice is to use actual costs incurred. However, Jane Barry, president, has proposed that standard process costing be used. November data for one of their products, weeding formula 1121, are as follows:

November—Actual Costs

Beginning inventory— work in process	3,000 gal $ 6,500 material (80% complete) $17,350 labor and overhead (50% complete)
Current costs	$21,890 material (2,067 lb used) $98,875 labor and overhead (2,860 hr)
Transferred to finished goods	9,600 gal
Ending inventory— work in process	1,000 gal (75% complete materials; 40% complete labor and overhead)

Current costs include $24,000 in fixed overhead, $40,040 in labor costs, and $34,835 in variable overhead.

Required:

1. Using FIFO actual costing, calculate equivalent units of production, equivalent unit costs, and the value of ending inventory—work in process.

2. Ms. Barry has asked the accounting department and manufacturing department to develop standards for various products. Standards for weeding formula 1121 are shown below:

100 gallons—weeding formula 1121

Material, 25 lb at $11.20/lb	$ 280
Labor, 32 hr at $14.375/hr	460
Variable overhead at 90% of labor dollars	414
Fixed overhead at $8.625/DLH	276
	$1,430

    a. What are equivalent units of production under FIFO standard costing?

    b. What are the equivalent unit costs?

    c. What is the value of ending inventory?

    d. Calculate all relevant variances.

Assume that fixed overhead is budgeted at $25,000 per month and normal activity is 8,000 gallons.

8–7 Standards and Variances. The Throwbridge Company buys copper wire in 0.05-in. diameter and draws it through dies to stretch it and make it smaller. The smaller wire is needed in many electronic components. As a rule, two or more drawings are necessary to bring the wire to the desired diameter. Data on three of the firm's best-selling diameters appear below, representing operations at normal levels of efficiency.

	Diameter		
	0.025 in.	0.010 in.	0.008 in.
Feet of 0.05-in. stock per foot of product	0.51	0.215	0.182
Number of drawings	2	3	3
Time for drawings, total hours per 1,000 ft of product	0.80	1.30	1.50

There is considerable waste in the process so that, for example, it is not possible to get 4 ft of 0.025 diameter wire from 1 ft of 0.05 diameter. Similarly, the stretching and drawing time depends partly on the diameter to which the firm is aiming, so that the total drawing time is not linear with respect to the number of drawings.

Standard prices and rates are as follows:

Copper stock, 0.05 in.	$ 0.18/ft
Direct labor	12.50/hr
Variable overhead	6.25/DLH
Fixed overhead, based on 12,000 normal hours per month	15.00/DLH

During March the firm experienced the following results:

Purchases of copper stock, 3,680,000 ft	$647,300
Stock used	3,527,400 ft
Direct labor, 12,700 hr	$157,280
Overhead	$268,660
Production:	
0.025 in.	4,155,000 ft
0.010 in.	3,817,000 ft
0.008 in.	2,710,000 ft

Required:

1. Develop standard costs for each of the three diameters of wire. Make the standards for 1,000-ft batches.

2. Calculate variances for March. For overhead, calculate a total budget variance and an application variance. The firm cannot determine the fixed and variable portions of actual overhead costs.

8–8 **Journal Entries—Two Alternatives.** The following data apply to December production for Ree United, Inc.

1. Purchases were 4,300 lb of plastic for $9,725. A total of 2,560 lb were used in production.
2. Conversion costs included: labor—1,200 hr, $7,896; overhead—$1,836 variable, $2,550 fixed.
3. Beginning inventory consisted of 100 units 50 percent complete on all costs. Ending inventory was 325 units 80 percent complete on all costs. Four hundred units were transferred to finished goods and sold for $29,000.
4. Standards for the sole product are:

Material, 4 lb at $2.25/lb	$ 9.00
Labor, 2 hr at $6.50/hr	13.00
Overhead at $3.50/DLH[a]	7.00
	$29.00

[a] Based on $2,400 fixed cost, 1,200 expected labor hours, and $1.50 per DLH variable overhead.

5. All variances are treated as an adjustment to cost of goods sold.

Required:

1. Record these transactions using a FIFO standard costing system where variances are identified as a part of work-in-process entries.
2. Record these transactions, assuming a FIFO standard costing system whose variances are identified at the end of the period after actual costs have been entered into Work in Process.

8–9 **Standard Costing—Journal Entries.** The Wapello Corporation makes a single product. Its standard costs are as follows:

Materials (2 lb at $4.50)	$ 9
Direct labor (3 hr at $5)	15
Variable overhead ($7 per DLH)	21
Fixed overhead (based on normal capacity of 50,000 units)	10
	$55

At the beginning of 19X2 there were no inventories. During 19X2 the following events occurred:

1. Material purchases were 120,000 lb for $511,000.

2. Direct labor was $790,750 for 151,000 hr worked.

3. Variable overhead incurred was $1,046,000.

4. Fixed overhead was $490,000.

5. 95,000 lb of materials were used.

6. 48,000 units were produced. There were no unfinished goods at the end of 19X2.

7. Sales were 45,000 units at $120 each.

Required:

1. Prepare journal entries to record these events. Isolate variances as early as possible. Assume that production managers are responsible for all variances except material price and labor rate.

2. Calculate ending inventory and cost of goods sold, assuming:
   a. standard process costing.
   b. actual process costing.

8–10 Proration of Variances.

Required: Given the results you obtained in assignment 8–9 on the Wapello Corporation, prorate the variances to appropriate inventories and cost of goods sold. Show all work. Allocate part of the material price variance to the material quantity variance in the proration procedure.

8–11 Standard Costs, Prices, and Profitability. The managers of the Davis Plastics Company have argued for some time the merits of standard costs. The firm uses a standard costing system, with overhead allocated to products based on their relative machine times. At a recent meeting, one of the managers said that the standard costs got in the way of good pricing decisions because of the fixed costs included in the standard. Another manager pointed out that the factory required equipment, supervision, and other inputs that led to the incurrence of fixed costs and that incorporating the fixed costs into the standards was a rational way to allow for them.

One of the managers put the following data on a blackboard.

	#762	#456	#206
Selling price	$20	$15	$30
Variable costs	8	4	14
Fixed costs[a]	4	2	8
Total costs	12	6	22
Profit	$ 8	$ 9	$ 8
Machine hours required	1	½	2

[a] Fixed costs are allocated at $4 per machine hour. The firm has 10,000 machine hours per month available.

The manager commented that the pricing was pretty good, but not perfect. He said that the firm should raise the prices of #762 and #206 by $1 to make them equally profitable with #456. The manager who had said that standard costs got in the way of good pricing responded that the firm was operating at capacity and could sell all of any product that it wanted to, and he did not think that just raising those prices by $1 would do the trick. He asserted that the firm should receive an adequate profit from the machine hours it used but that the standard åmount per hour was not a good reflection of that adequate profit.

Required: Determine the prices that the firm should charge for #762 and #206 to make them equally as profitable as #456. Assume that the firm can sell all its output of any product at the prices you determine and that it is limited in machine-hour capacity.

8-12 Practical Capacity and Normal Activity. The controller of the Charleston Manufacturing Company developed the following estimates of total factory overhead costs.

	Volume	
	80,000 Direct Labor Hours	100,000 Direct Labor Hours
Variable overhead at $6.50	$ 520,000	$ 650,000
Fixed overhead	855,000	904,000
Totals	$1,375,000	$1,554,000

Fixed overhead is higher at practical capacity of 100,000 direct labor hours because of increased requirements for supervisory personnel, higher utility costs, and the like. The controller had given some thought to using practical capacity as the basis for applying overhead, but she realized that it could create a problem. Specifically, she wondered how to compute the overhead budget variance and overhead volume variance. She fully expected actual volume to be about 80,000 direct labor hours.

Required:

1. Calculate the fixed overhead application rate, using the cost and volume at practical capacity.
2. Assuming that actual direct labor hours are 81,000 and that actual fixed overhead is $886,400, calculate the fixed overhead budget variance and volume variance.
3. Comment on the results of item 2 and make a recommendation.

8-13 Prorating Variances. The Jambalaya Corporation uses standard process costing. For February, 19X3, actual results were as follows:

Beginning inventory—work in process	2,000 units
(100% complete in material, 50% complete	
in conversion costs)	
Ending inventory—work in process	1,500 units
(100% complete in material, 66⅔% complete	
in conversion costs)	
Goods completed during February	8,000 units
Ending inventory—finished goods	1,000 units
Sales	7,000 units
Materials—ending inventory	5,000 lb

There were no beginning inventories in Materials or Finished Goods. The following costs were incurred in February.

Materials purchased (36,000 lb)	$342,000
Labor (23,000 hr)	$276,000
Overhead	$580,000

Standard costs are:

Materials	4 lb at $10/lb	$ 40
Labor	3 hr at $12/hr	36
Overhead	$25/labor hour	75
		$151

There had been no variances in January.

Required:

1. Calculate material, labor, and overhead variances. (Remember: this is process costing.)

2. Prorate all variances to Materials Inventory, Work in Process, Finished Goods, and Cost of Goods Sold. (Ignore prorating first to Materials Use Variance.)

3. Calculate the actual values for inventories and the actual values for cost of sales by adjusting standard costs by the amounts prorated in item 2.

4. Verify the actual costs calculated in item 3 by calculating FIFO process costing actual values for ending inventories and Cost of Sales. (Use T-accounts.)

8–14 Comparison of Methods.   The president of Bolton Industries wants to know what the differences are among actual costing, normal costing, and standard costing. He gives you the following data for Bolton Industries, which makes a single product. There were no inventories at the beginning of 19X2.

	19X2	19X3
Sales in units at $10 each	10,000	8,000
Production in units	12,000	10,000
Materials and labor	$25,000	$19,000
Manufacturing overhead	$30,600	$31,000
Selling and administrative costs	$15,000	$15,000

Required:

1. Prepare income statements for the two years using actual costing and FIFO.

2. Prepare income statements for the two years using normal costing and assuming that the firm uses 11,000 units to set the normal overhead rate, and sets budgeted manufacturing overhead using the formula, total manufacturing overhead = $22,000 + $0.80 × units produced. The firm uses this formula, and 11,000 units, in both years. Any overapplied or underapplied overhead is treated as an adjustment to cost of sales.

3. Prepare income statements for both years, using standard costing. The overhead standard is the same as given in item 2. The standard materials and labor cost, combined, is $2 per unit. Show variances as adjustments to standard cost of sales, separately identified to the extent that you determine particular variances.

8-15 **Proration of Variances—Financial Statements (CMA adapted).** Nanron Company uses a standard process cost system. All inventories are carried at standard during the year. The inventories and cost of goods sold are adjusted for all variances considered material in amount at the end of the fiscal year for financial statement purposes. All products are considered to flow through the manufacturing process to finished goods and ultimate sale in a first-in, first-out pattern.

The standard cost of one of Nanron's products manufactured in the Dixion Plant, unchanged from the prior year, appears below.

Raw materials	$2
Direct labor (0.5 DLH at $8)	4
Manufacturing overhead	3
Total standard cost	$9

Owing to the nature of the product and the manufacturing process, there is no work-in-process inventory of this product.

The schedule appearing at the top of page 357 reports the manufacturing and sales activity measured at standard cost for the current fiscal year.

	Units	Dollars
Product manufactured	95,000	$855,000
Beginning finished goods inventory	15,000	135,000
Goods available for sale	110,000	$990,000
Ending finished goods inventory	19,000	171,000
Cost of goods sold	91,000	$819,000

The balance of the Finished Goods Inventory, $140,800, reported on the balance sheet at the beginning of the year included a $5,800 adjustment for variances from standard cost. There were unfavorable variances for labor for the current fiscal year consisting of a wage rate variance of $32,000 and a labor efficiency variance of $20,000 (2,500 hr at $8). There were no other variances from standard cost for this year.

Required:

1. Management has decided that the $52,000 labor variances are material. Prorate these variances as appropriate to cost of goods sold and finished goods inventory. Determine the full amount to be shown at year end for these two accounts.

2. What would be the effect on the proration process of a beginning or ending inventory of work in process?

8–16 **Proration—Adjusting Cost of Goods Sold (AICPA).** The Longhorn Manufacturing Corporation produces only one product, Bevo, and accounts for the production of Bevo using a standard cost system.

At the end of each year, Longhorn prorates all variances among the various inventories and cost of sales. Because Longhorn prices its inventories on the first-in, first-out basis and all the beginning inventories are used during the year, the variances allocated to the ending inventories are immediately charged to cost of sales at the beginning of the following year. This allows only the current year's variances to be recorded in the variance accounts in any given year.

Following are the standards for the production of one unit of Bevo: 3 units of item A at $1 per unit; 1 unit of item B at $0.50 per unit; 4 units of item C at $0.30 per unit; and 20 minutes of direct labor at $4.50 per hour. Separate variance accounts are maintained for each type of raw material and for direct labor. Raw material purchases are recorded initially at standard. Manufacturing overhead is applied at $9 per actual direct labor hour and is not related to the standard cost system. There was no overapplied or underapplied manufacturing overhead at December 31, 19X2.

After proration of the variances, the various inventories at December 31, 19X2, were priced as indicated in the material appearing at the top of page 358.

Raw Material:

Item	Number of Units	Unit Cost	Amount
A	15,000	$1.10	$16,500
B	4,000	0.52	2,080
C	20,000	0.32	6,400
			$24,980

Work in Process: 9,000 units of Bevo were 100 percent complete as to material items A and B, 50 percent complete in item C, and 30 percent complete as to labor. The breakdown of this inventory is as follows:

Item	Amount
A	$28,600
B	4,940
C	6,240
Direct labor	6,175
	45,955
Overhead	11,700
	$57,655

Finished Goods: 4,800 units of Bevo composed and valued as follows:

Item	Amount
A	$15,180
B	2,704
C	6,368
Direct labor	8,540
	32,792
Overhead	16,200
	$48,992

Following is a schedule of raw materials purchased and direct labor incurred for the year ended December 31, 19X3. Unit cost of each item of raw material and direct labor cost per hour remained constant throughout the year.

Purchases:

Item	Number of Units or Hours	Unit Cost	Amount
A	290,000	$1.15	$333,500
B	101,000	0.55	55,550
C	367,000	0.35	128,450
Direct labor	34,100	4.60	156,860

During the year ended December 31, 19X3, Longhorn sold 90,000 units of Bevo and had ending physical inventories as follows:

Raw Materials:

Item	Number of Units
A	28,300
B	2,100
C	28,900

Work in Process: 7,500 units of Bevo which were 100 percent complete as to items A and B, 50 percent complete as to item C, and 20 percent complete as to labor, as follows:

Item	Number of Units or Hours
A	22,900
B	8,300
C	15,800
Direct labor	800

Finished Goods: 5,100 units of Bevo, as follows:

Item	Number of Units or Hours
A	15,600
B	6,300
C	21,700
Direct labor	2,050

There was no overapplied or underapplied manufacturing overhead at December 31, 19X3.

Required: Answer each of the following questions. Supporting computations should be prepared in good form.

1. What was the charge or credit to cost of sales at the beginning of 19X3 for the variances in the December 31, 19X2, inventories?

2. What was the total charge or credit to the three material price variance accounts for items A, B, and C for the year ended December 31, 19X3?

3. What was the total charge or credit to the three material quantity variance accounts for items A, B, and C for the year ended December 31, 19X3?

4. What was the total charge or credit to the direct labor rate variance account for the year ended December 31, 19X3?

5. What was the total charge or credit to the direct labor efficiency variance account for the year ended December 31, 19X3?

8–17 Comprehensive Review of Chapters 6, 7, and 8. During March, 19X3, the Northland division of Blann, Inc., had the following events regarding their sole product at the Jennings plant.

March 3	Purchased 40,000 lb of metal for $138,300
March 14	Paid wages for 4,000 hr worked in first part of March: $26,144
March 17	Paid various indirect labor costs and indirect expenses of $12,250 (all variable), all applying to March production
March 22	Purchased 10,000 lb of metal for $32,000
March 24	Paid various fixed costs of March equaling $6,500
March 30	Paid for materials purchased on March 3
March 31	Paid the balance of wages for March: 5,200 hr, $33,987
March 31	Paid various indirect labor costs and indirect expenses of $16,000 (all variable), all applying to March production

Inventories as of March 1, 19X3, were:

Material—metal	5,000 lb; $17,500
Work in Process	1,000 units; $8,145 (100% complete in materials; 50% in conversion costs)
Finished Goods	2,500 units; $24,625

Standard costs called for the following:

Materials: 2 lb of metal at $3.20	$6.40
Labor: ⅓ hr at $6.45	2.15
Overhead: $3.75 per DLH	1.25
	$9.80

Overhead includes $8,000 in budgeted fixed costs per month at a denominator activity of 10,000 hr.

Inventories as of March 31, 19X3, were:

Materials	3,500 lb
Work in Process	1,500 units (100% complete in materials and 50% in conversion costs)
Finished Goods	1,000 units

During March 26,250 units were sold. Northland division used FIFO standard process costing. Entries are made as events occur. At month end entries are made to the Work-in-Process account at standard costs. Material price variances and labor rate variances are identified when costs are incurred. At month end all variances under $1,000 are charged to Cost of Goods Sold, while all other variances are prorated as appropriate to Materials, Work-in-Process, Finished Goods, and Cost of Goods Sold.

Required:

1. Prepare proper journal entries to record the events of March. Post your entries to appropriate T-accounts. Assume a single account is used for overhead incurred and applied.

2. Prorate variances as appropriate. Remember that there are beginning inventories.

3. Record journal entries to adjust accounts based on the proration of variances in item 2. Post these to your T-accounts.

4. Assume the Northland division prepares its statements using normal costing with fixed overhead applied on the basis of the information given in the problem. What would be the amount of underapplied or overapplied overhead? If this amount differs from the total fixed overhead variance calculated in item 1, explain the difference.

8–18 Standard Costing System. John Moroney, the controller of Garden Products Corporation, had just returned to his office after attending a three-day seminar on standard costing. He was enthusiastic about the possibility of putting some of the ideas he had gained into practice. He called on Anthony Hobson, the firm's president, to discuss his ideas and received the go-ahead to develop a proposal for adopting a standard costing system. Hobson cautioned Moroney that the upper-level managers would have to be convinced of the value of the system before he would order it put in place.

Moroney spent several days going through his notes and other materials he had gathered, refining his ideas about how the system should work at Garden Products. Eventually he wrote the material that appears below to clarify his thoughts and give the other managers the opportunity to see what he had in mind.

We currently use an actual-normal job order cost system. We charge actual materials and labor to each job and apply overhead based on a predetermined rate developed annually. Most of our production is standard (about 95 percent by dollar volume) and we have good data on the material and labor quantities needed for each model of lawnmower, tiller, snowblower, and so on.

We presently initiate production based on our estimates of demand in the coming months. Stan Phillips, production manager, writes up production orders and assigns a number to each batch. Copies of the order go to the departmental supervisors and to my office. One of my clerks blanks up a job order cost sheet putting in the product number, quantity, and a few other items. The supervisors schedule the job and assign workers. The workers obtain the necessary materials from the storeroom, filling out materials requisitions. A copy of the requisition comes to my office, where a clerk uses it to update our inventory records. Another clerk determines the FIFO cost of the materials issued and posts it to the job order cost sheet. The form is then filed.

Once a month, clerks go through the files of material requisitions and compare them to the Material Inventory accounts and a list of jobs in process. If there are discrepancies, someone goes down to investigate. We don't have many problems here, just a few lost requisitions each month. The physical inventory that we take once a year usually comes pretty close to our perpetual records.

Workers use time slips to indicate how much time they spend on each job and how much nonproductive time they have, such as waiting for materials and setting up machinery. My clerks receive these slips, sort them by job every day, and post them to the cost sheet after getting the worker's pay rate from the book we keep. The slips then go to another section where clerks use them to prepare the payroll records. They also check to see that the times on the slips for each worker correspond to the times on their clock cards. When a worker has overtime, the cost entered on the cost sheets is at regular time, with the overtime premium being debited to an account that is included in factory overhead.

When production notifies us that a job is complete, we apply overhead to the job order cost sheet, then move the sheet to the file for finished goods. When we are notified that part of the job has been sold, we note that on the cost sheet and also make an entry to debit Cost of Sales and credit Finished Goods Inventory. When the entire job has been sold, we put the cost sheet into the file of sold jobs, noting the price on the sheet. Tony (Hobson) uses the sheets to analyze the profitability of various models.

Once a month, we apply overhead to all jobs still in process, based on direct labor cost. Each department has a different rate, so that we also keep track of the department that each worker is in on the cost sheets. Monthly, we reconcile the cost sheets with the general ledger totals for Work in Process and Finished Goods. We have to make sure that all direct labor costs have been accounted for either on jobs or in accounts such as Idle Time and Vacation Pay.

My proposal is that we develop standard costs for each of our models, or at least for the high-volume items. We would then keep track of the number of units of each model made each month, but not of the costs of individual batches. When my office is notified that a batch is completed, one of my clerks will debit Finished Goods Inventory and credit Work-in-Process Inventory for the standard cost of the completed units. Similarly, we will debit Cost of Sales and credit Finished Goods Inventory when we are notified of a sale.

We would still use the materials requisition slips to control inventory and update the perpetual records. But we would debit Work-in-Process Inventory for the standard prices times the actual quantities of materials issued, which would save a good deal of work over finding the actual FIFO prices. Incoming materials would be debited to Materials Inventory at standard prices, so that we would identify and isolate material price variances at the time of purchase.

We would no longer need the detailed time slips from each worker every day. Instead, we would simply debit Work-in-Process Inventory for actual labor costs each week, using the clock cards for determining payroll.

Once a month we would determine the total standard cost of all work done by looking at the Work-in-Process Inventory and transfers to Finished Goods. There would be more work involved here, because we have to determine how far along each job was in order to get the standard cost of the work done to that point. Once we did that, we would remove the variances from Work-in-Process Inventory, putting them into individual variance accounts, so that month-end Work-in-Process Inventory would show standard costs.

Our procedures on overhead would be about the same as now. The principal difference would be that we would apply overhead once a month based on the standard labor cost for the month, not the actual labor cost. We would not apply overhead to individual jobs, however, which would give a substantial saving in clerical time.

In general, I would not anticipate significant labor rate variances. Our work force is pretty stable and we usually make sure that each hourly employee gets at least 40 hours per week. If we used a standard rate for each department based on the current average hourly wage in the department, the variance would be minimal even though the rates do vary considerably among workers.

In addition to the savings in clerical work, we would have better information for planning and control. We would be able to see which departmental supervisors are keeping costs in line and which are going over. We can tell that now only in very crude terms.

Moroney showed his proposal to various managers. Virtually all had some comments. On the plus side, a number of managers stated that any reduction in bookkeeping was desirable so long as it did not lessen the quality of the information they would receive. Moroney summarized the comments under the following headings in order to be able to discuss each point that the managers brought up.

Need for Actual Costs. A few people argued that it would be a mistake to abandon the actual costing system because they would not be able to spot changes in costs of specific models. The costs of individual jobs, and therefore of specific models, would be smeared and no one would be able to see unfavorable trends so long as total costs for all models were in line with standards.

Responsibility for Variances. Several managers, notably the supervisor of the assembly department, argued that variances in one department were not necessarily its fault. The supervisor of the assembly department told of a recent incident where a batch of mowers came to him with improperly lined-up bolt holes. One of his workers had to do some redrilling to make the holes line up. This extra time in his department would show up on his performance report but would be the fault of another department. He also felt that work would get sloppy because of pressure to meet the standards.

Fineness of Standards. Several managers said that they could understand developing standard times for all of the operations in a given department as a whole, but not for each of the multitude of operations. Yet, if output were to be measured accurately, it would be necessary to break down each operation and develop a standard for it. Without such breakdowns it would be impossible to evaluate partially completed work. Developing such breakdowns would be costly and subject to a great deal of inaccuracy. It would also cause problems, because workers would be held responsible for each operation, not for the overall task.

Required:

1. Discuss the pros and cons of Moroney's proposed system. Would you favor it? Be sure to comment on the reservations expressed by the managers.

2. How would your answer to item 1 change, if at all, if you were to learn that month-end work-in-process inventory is quite large?

8–19 **Job Order Costing—Journal Entries.** Use the facts developed in assignment 8–2 for Milner Manufacturing Company.

Required:

1. Record the events of October, 19X5, in a standard costing system.

2. How would you calculate an application variance if there was an ending inventory in work in process? Assume that the 500 units consist of 400 that were started and completed this period and 200 that were 50 percent complete in all cost elements.

8–20 **Actual, Normal, and Standard Process Costing.** The managers of Alltrue Manufacturing are discussing whether to use actual, normal, or standard process costing. During October, 19X0, the following occurred regarding their single product:

	Units
Beginning inventory—work in process	
(100% complete—materials; 60% complete—conversion)	1,000
Transferred to finished goods	90,000
Ending inventory—work in process	
(90% complete—materials; 40% complete—conversion)	1,500

Beginning inventory included $15,750 in materials and $48,000 in conversion costs.

Proposed standard costs:

Materials	10 lb at $1.50	$15.00
Labor	2 hr at $17.50	35.00
Overhead	$20/labor hour	40.00
		$90.00

Actual costs:

Materials used, 993,850 lb	$1,540,467
Labor, 166,500 hr	2,913,750
Overhead:	
Variable	1,665,000
Fixed	6,000,000

Overhead for normal or standard costing is based on annual fixed overhead of $20 million and a normal activity of 2 million hours plus variable overhead of $10/DLH. All proposed systems would use FIFO. During October 80,000 units were sold. There was no inventory of finished goods at the beginning of October.

Required:

1. Record journal entries for actual costing for October.

2. Record journal entries for normal costing for October (show only those entries that would change). All underapplied or overapplied overhead is treated as an adjustment to cost of goods sold.

3. Record journal entries for standard costing. Identify as many variances as you can. All variances are treated as adjustments to cost of goods sold.

4. List the following for each system:
    a.   ending inventory of work in process.
    b.   ending inventory of finished goods.
    c.   cost of goods sold.
    Explain the differences among the three different systems.

8–21 Actual, Normal, and Standard Costing—Relationships. The following questions apply to the data presented in assignment 8–20.

Required: Consider each question independently.

1. If all other things were held constant except that actual hours worked were 200,000 instead of 166,500, what would be the effect on actual costing income? normal costing income? standard costing income?

2. If all things were held constant except that variances were prorated instead of being treated as an adjustment to cost of goods sold, what would be the effect on actual costing income? normal costing income? standard costing income?

Joint Products and By-Products

Chapter 9

Many manufacturing processes inevitably produce more than one output. Sometimes the firm's managers can control the relative quantities of each output, sometimes they cannot. An oil refiner may increase the amount of gasoline and decrease the amount of other outputs (for example, kerosene) obtained from a batch of crude petroleum, but some of the other products are inevitable. It is impossible to produce a gallon of gasoline from a gallon of crude petroleum.

When two or more products of relatively high value emerge from a single process, they are called **joint products.** The process that gives rise to them is called a **joint process,** and the costs of operating the joint process are called **joint costs.** Usually one or more raw materials enter the joint process and at a later time the joint products appear as separate entities. The point at which the joint products appear is called the **split-off point;** it is only at split-off that the joint products become individually identifiable.

Some joint products are sold just as they come out from split-off, others require further processing to make them saleable, and some may be sold either at split-off or after additional processing. We are usually concerned with this last type in decision making involving joint products. An example is a meat packer who may sell hides or process them into tanned leather.

Some outputs of a joint process have little or no value. Metal shavings may be collected and sold, but the revenue from selling them is usually inconsequential. In a technical sense, metal shavings, sawdust, and other such materials that are a normal part of any production process are joint products. However, the term *joint product* is usually limited to products with relatively high value. The terms *by-product, scrap,* and *waste* are used to refer to outputs of little or no value. The differences among these outputs are to a great extent terminological. Different people will use different terms to refer to the same thing. Let us look briefly at the distinctions in the use of the terms.

Waste is a term usually reserved for material that has no value, or even negative value because it must be disposed of at some cost. Waste presents no accounting problems. It is neither inventoried nor sold.

By-product may denote almost anything that is a necessary consequence of a production process. We speak of smoke as an undesirable by-product of burning coal to generate electricity. In accounting, the term is usually reserved for a joint product that has some value, but relatively little in relation to the one or more other joint products. The joint products of relatively high value are often called **main products** to distinguish them from the relatively low-value by-products.

Scrap is also a joint output because it emerges as a normal consequence of the production process. The difference between scrap and by-products is not always clear, and one firm might call something scrap that another calls a by-product. As a rule, scrap is the leftover part of raw materials, whereas by-products are different from the material that went into the process. Metal shavings and sawdust would usually be considered scrap. Distillates from chemical processes would usually be considered by-products. The term scrap is usually limited to material that has some use. It may be sold or reprocessed. Scrap is one of the topics of Chapter 10.

When a product is processed beyond its split-off point, it is considered a by-product, not scrap. However, the mere fact that a product is not processed further does not mean that it will be considered scrap. The criterion noted before, that by-products are different from the material that went into the production process, would generally control the classification. Both scrap and by-products require accounting treatment because they are sold or reprocessed. In some cases the same accounting treatment could be used for either one. As we shall see later, by-products that are processed beyond split-off require special treatment.

PREVALENCE OF JOINT PRODUCTS

We cited earlier a few examples of joint products, but it might be helpful to list some more to show how common they are and therefore how widespread the problem is for accountants.

Virtually all meat and leather products are joint. Steaks, roasts, hamburger, and hides come from cattle; pork chops, ham, and pigskin from hogs. Most basic wood products are joint. Planks and boards of various sizes, studs, sheets of veneer, and chips used for composition board all come from logs. In most cases a specific log will yield several products (pieces of different sizes), so that all are joint.

Many plastics result from joint processes, as do chemicals and gases. The list could go on, but the point should be clear: joint products are everywhere. In fact, the more difficult economic times of recent years have stimulated the search for new uses of joint products, especially by-products or scrap that once were discarded. Recycling heat generated by computers to reduce fuel requirements is one prominent case.

DECISION MAKING WITH JOINT PRODUCTS

Firms that make joint products face two basic decisions: (1) whether to sell joint products at the split-off point or process them further; and (2) whether to operate the joint processes at all.[1] In the first type of decision the joint costs are irrelevant because they are sunk. The joint products have been produced (or the firm plans to produce them), and the only decision left is whether to sell them at split-off or process them further. In the second type of decision the *avoidable costs* of operating the joint process (for example, the cost of materials and direct labor) are relevant.

We introduced the concepts of differential analysis and incremental costs in Chapter 4. The decision to sell a joint product at split-off or to process it further is the same kind of tactical decision as make or buy, or dropping a segment. Thus, different costs are relevant in different decision settings. The following illustration should clarify these basic points.

Illustration: Walton Chemical's Joint Products

The Walton Chemical Company produces three joint products, 101, 102 and 103. The data in Exhibit 9–1 reflect average monthly results. Notice that we use the term *sales value* in the exhibit rather than *sales*. Sales value is the total quantity of current output at selling prices, not just the quantity sold. For example, the firm may have had sales of less than $40,000 for product 101, or greater than $40,000 if there was a beginning inventory. Figure 9–1 on page 370 diagrams the operations.

EXHIBIT 9–1
Data for Walton Chemical Company

	Joint Products		
	101	*102*	*103*
Monthly output (lb)	40,000	20,000	20,000
Sales value at split-off	0	$ 30,000	$105,000
Sales value after further processing	$40,000	$100,000	$150,000
Avoidable costs of further processing	$18,000	$ 40,000	$ 57,000
Joint process—monthly costs:			
Avoidable	$80,000		
Unavoidable[a]	$20,000		

[a] Consists of fixed costs such as allocated costs and depreciation on equipment.

[1] The following discussion applies also to by-products (which are joint products), but for brevity we shall use the term joint products.

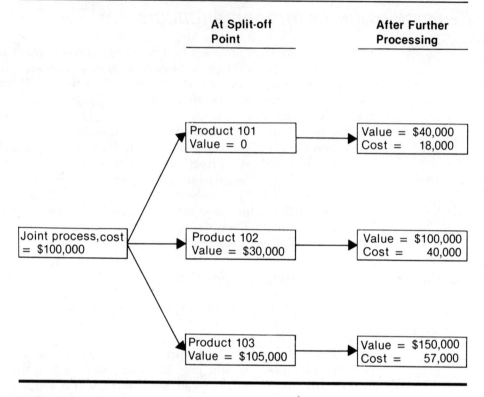

	At Split-off Point	After Further Processing

Joint process, cost = $100,000

Product 101
Value = 0

Value = $40,000
Cost = 18,000

Product 102
Value = $30,000

Value = $100,000
Cost = 40,000

Product 103
Value = $105,000

Value = $150,000
Cost = 57,000

FIGURE 9–1
Walton Chemical Company

We first examine the decision whether to process joint products beyond the split-off point. The schedule opposite shows that 101 and 102 should be processed beyond the split-off point, while 103 should be sold at split-off. It is important to point out that only avoidable costs of further processing, those costs that are incremental if further processing is done, should be used in the analyses. Notice that even though product 101 cannot be sold at split-off, we still evaluate the decision to process it further. If the avoidable costs of further processing exceeded the sales value of product 101 after further processing, and if the firm could simply junk it at the split-off point (dispose of it with no cost), the firm would be better off dumping it at split-off. The following schedule shows the gain or loss of processing beyond split-off.

In the schedule opposite the emphasis is on the respective margins—one from processing further, the other from selling at split-off. An alternative method that would give equivalent results would be to subtract the sales value at the split-off point from the sales value after further processing to get the incremental revenue from further processing.

	101	102	103
Sales value after further processing	$40,000	$100,000	$150,000
Avoidable costs of further processing	18,000	40,000	57,000
Margin from further processing	$22,000	$ 60,000	$ 93,000
Less: Sales value at split-off point	0	30,000	105,000
Net gain (loss) from further processing	$22,000	$ 30,000	($ 12,000)

If these values exceed the incremental, avoidable costs of further processing, the products should be processed further; if not, they should be sold at split-off. This alternative method is illustrated below.

	101	102	103
Sales value after further processing	$40,000	$100,000	$150,000
Sales value at split-off	0	30,000	105,000
Incremental revenue from further processing	40,000	70,000	45,000
Incremental costs of further processing	18,000	40,000	57,000
Net gain (loss) from further processing	$22,000	$ 30,000	($ 12,000)

The sales value at split-off is the opportunity cost of processing the joint products further. In some cases it may be negative, as with products that must be disposed of at some cost if they are not processed further. Some kinds of acids or other noxious products fit this category.

Any unavoidable costs associated with further processing are not relevant to decisions about the timing of the sale of a joint product. They are sunk and therefore irrelevant. Similarly, in deciding whether to process joint products beyond the split-off point, all the costs of the joint process are irrelevant. However, the firm does not have to operate the joint process, and its managers should be aware that shutdown is a possible course of action. In determining whether or not to operate the joint process, the relevant data are the margins achievable from making the best decisions about the further processing of the joint products, and the avoidable costs of operating the joint process.

The schedule on page 372 shows the total margin obtainable from selling each joint product at its most advantageous point. The total margin is greater than the avoidable costs of operating the joint process, and so the firm should continue to operate it.

	Total	101	102	103
Revenue	$245,000	$40,000	$100,000	$105,000
Avoidable costs of further processing	58,000	18,000	40,000	0
Product margin	$187,000	22,000	60,000	105,000
Avoidable costs of joint process	80,000			
Advantage to operating joint process	$107,000			

ALLOCATING JOINT COSTS TO JOINT PRODUCTS

For financial reporting and income tax purposes the inventory valuation for joint products must include a portion of the joint costs of production as well as the separable, additional costs of further processing (if any). The major constraint on the selection of an allocation method for the joint costs is that the inventory valuation should not exceed the net realizable value of the product—its expected selling price less costs to complete and sell. From a standpoint of financial reporting and income tax accounting, this requirement is virtually the only one that need be satisfied. You may recall from financial accounting that net realizable value is the ceiling on the market value of inventory in the application of the lower-of-cost-or-market rule.

As we discussed in earlier chapters, the allocations made for financial reporting and income tax purposes are of no value for managerial purposes. Misleading information can result from such allocations, and they should be ignored by managers. For one thing, the joint costs that will be allocated to the joint products are the total joint costs of operating the joint process ($100,000 for the Walton Company), not just the avoidable costs ($80,000 in our example). About all that we can ask of an allocation method for internal, managerial purposes is that it does not get in the way of making good decisions. In general, the two methods that we discuss shortly will not prove harmful in the sense that managers would make the wrong decisions using the allocated costs.

Bases used to allocate joint costs to joint products fall into two general categories: physical measures such as pounds, gallons, and square feet; and value measures such as selling price and net realizable value. The use of physical measures is unwise, because it may easily result in showing book losses for products that are in fact profitable in the sense that they contribute to the covering of joint costs and earning of profits, and it may also result in inventory valuations that violate the lower-of-cost-or-market rule by showing products at amounts greater than their net realizable values.

To illustrate, assume that the Walton Company (Exhibit 9–1) had no beginning inventories and sold 30,000 lb of product 101 of the 40,000 lb produced. The total selling price was $30,000, three-fourths of the total sales value of $40,000 for the 40,000 lb. If joint costs were allocated on the basis of relative weight, 50 percent would go to product 101 [40,000/(40,000 + 20,000 + 20,000)]. An income statement for product 101 would show the following results.

Sales		$30,000
Production costs:		
Additional, beyond split-off	$18,000	
Joint $100,000 × 50%	50,000	
Total	68,000	
Ending inventory, 25%	17,000	
Cost of goods sold		51,000
Loss		($21,000)

Using this base for allocation results in showing a loss on product 101, whereas the product contributes to the covering of joint costs and earning of income. Additionally, the $17,000 inventory figure is greater than the sales value of $10,000 ($40,000 total sales value less $30,000 sales) and is therefore unsuitable for financial reporting purposes. Unless physical measures closely parallel values of joint products, their use may give misleading results, and therefore they should be avoided.

Net Realizable Value Method

One of the most commonly advocated methods for allocating joint costs is the net realizable value method, under which the allocations are made in accordance with the net realizable values of the products. The **net realizable value** of a joint product that can be sold at the split-off point is simply its selling price at split-off less any expected selling costs. If the product has no market at split-off, its net realizable value is its selling price after further processing minus the costs of further processing and any selling costs expected. In either case, the basis for the allocation is the total net realizable value of the quantity produced during the period, not the actual sales for the period.

The net realizable values of the Walton Company's products are shown below, with all data from Exhibit 9–1.

	Total	101	102	103
Sales value at split-off	$135,000	—	$30,000	$105,000
Sales value after further processing minus costs of further processing	22,000	$22,000		—
Net realizable value	$157,000	$22,000	$30,000	$105,000
Percentage of total	100%	14%	19%	67%

Using these data, we obtain the allocations of the joint costs of $100,000 as well as the total inventoriable costs of each product. Only production costs, separable and joint, are included in the inventory valuation. If we had expected selling costs for one or more of the products, we would not include them in inventory although they would be used to determine the net realizable values.

	Total	101	102	103
Allocated joint costs	$100,000	$14,000	$19,000	$67,000
Additional processing costs	58,000	18,000	40,000	—
Total costs	$158,000	$32,000	$59,000	$67,000
Pounds of output (Exhibit 9–1)		40,000	20,000	20,000
Cost per pound		$0.80	$2.95	$3.35

The net realizable value method has two important results so long as the total net realizable value for all the joint products exceeds the total production costs.[2] First, all products will appear profitable on the income statement; second, the inventory valuations on the balance sheet will be less than net realizable values, thereby conforming to the lower-of-cost-or-market rule.

Constant Gross Margin Rate Method

An alternative to the net realizable value method is the constant gross margin rate method. This method results in all joint products' showing the same percentage rate of gross margin; in other words, it assumes that each product contributes an equal percentage amount per dollar of sales. This method works backward from gross margin to joint cost allocations. (1) You first find the overall rate of gross margin (gross margin/sales value) assuming that the optimal decisions have been made for the individual joint products. (2) You then multiply this rate by the sales value of each product and subtract the result from the sales value, giving the total cost of each product. The further processing costs and selling costs (if any) are then subtracted from the total-cost figures to give the joint cost allocations. Using our example:

Step 1

	Total	101	102	103
Sales value—best decisions	$245,000	$40,000	$100,000	$105,000
Further processing costs	(58,000)	18,000	40,000	0
Joint costs	(100,000)			
Gross margin	$ 87,000			
Gross margin rate, 35.51%	$87,000/$245,000			

---

[2] Technically, we must also assume that all joint products have either positive split-off values or sales values after further processing in excess of further processing costs. Products that violate these conditions would not usually be considered main products, but rather by-products. Additionally, we can sometimes get inventory values exceeding net realizable value if the joint costs exceed the total split-off values.

The gross margin rate is applied to the individual products and joint cost allocations are calculated as follows:

Step 2

Sales value	$40,000	$100,000	$105,000
Gross margin at 35.51%	$14,204	35,510	37,286
Total costs	25,796	64,490	67,714
Less: Additional processing costs	18,000	40,000	0
Allocated joint costs	$ 7,796	$ 24,490	$ 67,714

Total allocation equals $100,000

The constant gross margin method has the same properties as the net realizable value method: all products will show profits and will be valued for inventory determination at less than net realizable value. The net realizable value method is used more in practice, but the constant gross margin rate method has an advantage if managers do pay attention to the full costs of the joint products. The advantage is that the constant gross margin rate method will give income statements by product, and for the entire group of joint products, that show the same gross margin rate no matter how much of the output is sold and how much remains in inventory. The net realizable value method will not necessarily do this. Exhibit 9–2 on page 376 shows that the two methods can produce different income statement results. The assumptions of Exhibit 9–2 are that all the output of products 101 and 103 is sold, but none of the 102. Beginning inventories are assumed to be zero.

The overall gross margin rate was lower under the net realizable value method because product 102, which has a rate of 41 percent ($41,000/$100,000) under the net realizable value method, was not sold but remained in inventory. If in the following month the sales of product 102 are double the usual amount, thereby using the ending inventory for the current period plus next month's production, the gross margin rate will increase under the net realizable value method. However, the rate will be the same under the constant gross margin rate method so long as selling prices and costs remain constant. The constant gross margin rate method is not widely used in practice.

ACCOUNTING FOR BY-PRODUCTS AND SCRAP

Several methods may be used to account for by-products, but scrap is usually accounted for in only one way in actual and normal costing systems. We consider standard costing systems in a later section. Recall from earlier discussion that the difference between what is called scrap and what is called by-product may be very hazy. The names given to different outputs are not of great importance. In fact, the first method we describe in this section can be used for both by-products and scrap.

EXHIBIT 9–2
Comparison of Net Realizable Value and Constant Gross Margin Rate Methods

	Net Realizable Value Method			
	Total	*101*	*102*	*103*
Sales	$145,000	$40,000	$ 0	$105,000
Further processing costs	58,000	18,000	40,000	0
Allocated joint costs	100,000	14,000	19,000	67,000
Totals	158,000	32,000	59,000	67,000
Ending inventory	59,000	0	59,000	0
Cost of sales	99,000	32,000	0	67,000
Gross margin	$ 46,000	$ 8,000	0	$ 38,000
Gross margin rates	31.7% ($46,000/$145,000)			

	Constant Gross Margin Method			
	Total	*101*	*102*	*103*
Sales	$145,000	$40,000	$ 0	$105,000
Further processing costs	58,000	18,000	40,000	0
Allocated joint costs	100,000	7,796	24,490	67,714
Totals	158,000	25,796	64,490	67,714
Ending inventory	64,490	0	64,490	0
Cost of sales	93,510	25,796	0	67,714
Gross margin	$ 51,490	$14,204	0	$ 37,286
Gross margin rates	35.51% ($51,490/$145,000)			

Other Income Method

The simplest method of accounting for by-products and scrap is to ignore them for inventory determination, simply crediting Other Income, Miscellaneous Income, or Income from Sales of By-Products (or Scrap) when they are sold. This method predominates in accounting for scrap. It is also used for by-products that are not processed beyond the split-off point and are of so little value that leaving them out of inventory would have an imperceptible effect on the firm's financial statements.

The firm may keep records of the physical quantities of an item for control purposes, but the only effect on the financial statements would occur in the period of sale (an increase in income). The main product, or products, would be allocated all of the costs of production. Thus, the only journal entry required would be at the time of sale, and would appear about as follows:

Cash (or Accounts Receivable)	xxxx	
Income from Sale of Scrap (or By-Product)		xxxx

Net Realizable Value Method

By-products are frequently inventoried at net realizable value, especially if they require processing beyond split-off. If a by-product requires processing past split-off, the costs beyond split-off should be inventoried, and so the other income method is inappropriate. Suppose that a by-product is expected to sell for $400. Before it can be sold, it must be separately processed at a cost of $120. At the time of sale the firm expects to incur selling costs of $20 for sales commissions. The net realizable value is $260 ($400 − $120 − $20). At the time of split-off the following journal entry would be made:

Inventory of By-Product	$260	
Work-in-Process Inventory		$260

When the additional processing has been done, the entry would be:

Inventory of By-Product	$120	
Cash, etc.		$120

And at the time of sale, assuming the sale is for cash and commissions are accrued:

Cash	$400	
Inventory of By-Product		$380
Accrued Commissions		20

Under the net realizable value method no profit or loss is recognized on the by-product so long as expectations are correct. If the selling price or selling costs turn out to be different from expectations, a gain or loss would be recognized at the time of sale. For example, if the selling price had been $415, a $15 gain would be recognized.

Essentially, the net realizable value method reduces the cost of the main product or products. The credit to Work-in-Process Inventory in the first entry above results in $260 less cost to be charged to the main product and therefore $260 more profit when the main product is sold. Thus, if the costs of the process that generated the by-product totaled $24,000, the main product(s) would be charged $23,740 ($24,000 − $260), reducing inventory valuations and reducing the subsequent cost of goods sold.

The net realizable value method is sometimes criticized because it may result in premature recognition of profit. The inventory of a by-product is shown at market value (less additional expected costs), which results in all of its profit being recognized on sales of the main product. The premature recognition of profit would occur if at the end of a period all of the main product had been sold and the by-product remained in inventory. In that case, showing the inventory of by-product at net realizable value leaves no profit to be recognized on the sale of the by-product in the next period.

So long as the amounts involved are not material, we may safely ignore the problem of premature profit recognition. If the amounts are material, some accountants would modify the method by reducing the amount allocated to the by-product by a normal profit. Thus, if a normal profit on sales of $400 were assumed to be $30, the first entry given above would show a debit to Inventory of By-Product of $230 ($260 − $30). A profit of $30 would then be shown at the time of sale. The entry could appear as follows:

Cash	$400	
Inventory of By-Product ($230 + $120)		$350
Accrued Commissions		20
Income from Sales of By-Product		30

In this modification of the net realizable value method, the weak point is the *normal* profit. Because a by-product is a joint output, along with the main product or products, there is really no such thing as its *cost*, just as there is no such thing as *the* cost of a joint product. Consequently, any allocation that gives inventory costs conforming to the lower-of-cost-or-market rule is at least defensible in the context of financial reporting. In fact, if a normal profit is defined as the overall gross margin expected multiplied by the sales value, this method produces the same results as the constant gross margin rate method would, treating the by-product as a joint product.

VARIABLE PROPORTIONS

It is often possible to control, within limits, the quantities of joint products that emerge from a single batch of raw materials. The amounts of gasoline, oil, and kerosene that a refiner can obtain from a barrel of crude petroleum are subject to some control, as are the number of boards of various sizes (2 by 4 inches, 4 by 8 inches, and so on) that a sawmill can get from a log. If the control is complete, so that the firm can get any amount of any one product that it wants, then the process is no longer a joint process.

When the quantities are controllable within some limits, the decision making and allocation become slightly more involved, but they still follow the basic patterns we have already outlined. The firm will seek to increase the quantity of one product at the expense of others as long as it is profitable to do so. The allocations under the net realizable value or constant gross margin rate methods then depend on the final quantities produced.

Illustration: *Molton's Joint Products*

The Molton Company produces products A and B from a joint process. Each 10,000 lb of raw material yields 9,000 lb of the two products, with 1,000 lb lost in processing. The maximum and minimum amounts of A and B, in pounds, are:

	A	B
Maximum	7,000	6,000
Minimum	3,000	2,000

The total output of products A and B is limited to 9,000 lb. Suppose now that product A sells for $10/lb at split-off and that product B sells for $8/lb after additional processing that costs an incremental $1/lb. Also, the joint costs of production are $50,000. The firm would prefer to produce as much of product A as it could, because its value is greater than B's. The schedule below shows the amounts, revenues, and allocations of joint costs under the net realizable value method.

	A	B	Total
Production in pounds	7,000	2,000	9,000
Revenue at $10 and $8	$70,000	$16,000	$86,000
Additional processing costs	0	2,000	2,000
Net realizable values	70,000	14,000	84,000
Joint costs, 5/6, 1/6	41,667	8,333	50,000
Gross margin	$28,333	$ 5,667	$34,000

Some types of joint processing decisions are amenable to linear programming, as the article by Hartley shows (see Selected References). In fact, one of the early uses of linear programming was in the petroleum industry, which still employs it widely. Additionally, the statistical techniques of Chapter 3 can also be valuable in analyzing joint processes when the output of the individual products is stochastic.

SUMMARY

Joint products and by-products abound in manufacturing and refining processes. Costs incurred up to the split-off point are joint to all of the products and must be allocated to the joint outputs for product costing purposes. Making these allocations may create problems in analyzing the profitability of individual products. The allocated joint costs are irrelevant to decisions involving whether or not to process the products beyond the split-off point. For planning and control purposes, the major objective is to make the allocations in such a way that they do not interfere with decision making.

The net realizable value method of allocating joint costs, as well as the constant gross margin method, will ordinarily satisfy the objective of allocating in a way that will not interfere with decision making.

Accounting for by-products, which are joint products of relatively low value, varies greatly in practice. Because of the relatively low value of by-products, the choice of a method is largely governed by the cost of operating the accounting system.

ASSIGNMENTS

9–1 Basic Joint Cost Allocation. The following data relate to the operations of the MLL Company for April. The firm produces three joint products, all of which require additional processing beyond the split-off point. There were no beginning inventories.

	Product		
	100	101	102
Production in gallons	18,000	12,000	10,000
Sales	14,000	12,000	8,000
Ending inventory	4,000	0	2,000
Selling price per gallon	$ 2	$ 4	$ 10
April sales	$28,000	$48,000	$80,000
Costs of additional processing	$ 9,000	$ 9,600	$15,000

Total joint processing costs were $60,000. The ending inventories have been through all processing and are ready for sale.

Required:

1. Allocate the joint costs using the net realizable value method and prepare a statement of gross margin for April, by product.

2. Repeat item 1, using the constant gross margin rate method to allocate the joint costs.

9–2 Processing Decisions. The LMC Company produces two chemicals in a joint process. Both X-on and Y-on emerge in quantities of 5,000 lb from each 10,000-lb batch of raw materials. X-on sells for $10/lb, Y-on for $2/lb. Neither product receives processing beyond split-off. One of your staff has prepared the following analysis, which, he says, shows that the firm would do better to dump the Y-on.

	X-on	Y-on
Revenue per batch	$50,000	$10,000
Material costs	(10,000)	(10,000)
Labor and overhead	(8,000)	(8,000)
Profit (loss) per batch	$32,000	($ 8,000)

The labor and overhead are variable with the number of batches processed. The raw material costs $2/lb.

Required:

1. Determine the profit that the firm would earn per batch if it dumped Y-on at split-off.

2. Suppose the firm could process Y-on into another product it could sell for $5/lb. Additional processing would have variable costs of $1/lb and monthly incremental fixed costs of $20,000. The firm processes three batches per month. Should it process Y-on beyond split-off?

9-3 By-Product Costing. Marquette Company makes three chemicals in a joint process. March data appear below. There were no beginning inventories. The firm sells product Y-16 at split-off, the others after further processing.

| | Product | | |
	X-202	Y-16	Y-18
Pounds produced	48,000	4,000	6,000
Selling price at split-off, per pound	$1.65	$0.70	—
Additional processing costs, beyond split-off, per pound	0.20	—	0.08
Selling price after further processing, per pound	2.25	—	0.97
Selling costs per pound	0.08	0.02	0.04

Monthly joint costs are $78,000. The firm regards product X-202 as its main product, the others by-products. At the end of March 1,200 lb of Y-18 were on hand that had not been processed beyond split-off. There were 500 lb of Y-16 on hand. All X-202 was sold. The firm inventories Y-18 at its net realizable value and uses the other income method of accounting for Y-16.

Required:

1. Determine inventory at March 31.

2. Prepare an income statement for March.

3. Suppose that the 1,200 lb of Y-18 on hand at March 31 had gone through the additional processing and were ready for sale. What differences would there have been in your answers to items 1 and 2? Do not make new calculations; just describe the differences.

9-4 Allocations and Decisions. Your assistant enters your office and proclaims that you made a costly mistake in recommending that product 106 be processed beyond its split-off point. He shows you the following analysis.

| | Product 106 | |
	Sold at Split-off	Sold After Further Processing
Revenue	$34,400	$61,800
Costs:		
Further processing		21,100
Joint	17,315	28,502
Gross profit	$17,085	$12,198

Total joint costs were $151,000, and the total sales value of joint products at split-off was $300,000, including the $34,400 for product 106. All products except 106 were sold at split-off. Total sales value was then $327,400, with product 106 sold after further processing, and that figure was used to make the allocation of $28,502.

Required:

1. Verify the calculations of allocated joint costs, as you were told the assistant performed them.

2. Determine whether you made an error in recommending that product 106 be processed beyond split-off. If you did not err, prepare a suitable explanation for your assistant.

9–5 Main Products and By-Products, Comparison of Methods.   The following data relate to the operations of the Foster Company in July, 19X6. There were no beginning inventories.

	Product	
	X-con	Z-con
Pounds produced	10,000	2,000
Selling price per pound	$12.00	$3.00
Selling costs per pound sold, all variable	$ 2.50	$0.50
Pounds sold	8,000	1,500

Both products arise from a joint process. The joint costs for July were $50,000.

Required:

1. Prepare an income statement for July, with separate columns for each product, assuming that the two products are both treated as main products and that joint costs are allocated using the net realizable value method.

2. Prepare an income statement for July, assuming that Z-con is treated as a by-product and is inventoried at net realizable value, with its inventory valuation used to offset the costs of X-con.

9–6 Processing Decision.   The Zeeco Company manufactures a number of chemical products, mostly industrial solvents. The processes used to make the major products generate joint products of lesser value. The firm maintains a large research and development staff to examine ways to make better use of the joint products.

The firm presently makes 400,000 gal of X-diampyl per month, which is all that it can sell. The process also generates about 0.5 gal of a chemical called chlorogen for each gallon of X-diampyl. Chlorogen sells for $0.40/gal.

Recently, a chemist in R&D developed a way to make chlorogen into two new products, X-chloro and Y-chloro. Preliminary investigations indicate that these products would bring $0.44 and $0.90 per gallon, respectively. Each 1,000-gal batch of chlorogen would require about $30 in other ingredients and would yield about 390 gal of X-chloro and 440 gal of Y-chloro, with the rest lost to evaporation. Labor costs would be about $40 per batch. The firm's standard overhead rate is $2.40 per direct labor dollar, including a fixed component of about $1.50. The process would not add to the firm's fixed costs.

Required:

1. Determine whether the firm should process chlorogen beyond split-off.
2. Suppose that further processing would add $15,200 to monthly fixed costs, required for additional supervision and other costs not considered in item 1. Would your recommendation be the same as it was in item 1?

9–7 Multiple Split-off Points. The Corcoran Chemical Company operates a plant that has three departments. In department I, a raw material costing $60 per ton is processed into Algon and Betagon. Department II processes Algon into Trigon and Zygon, while department III processes Betagon into Betaplus. The plant can handle 800 tons of raw material per month. Yields of products, along with other data, appear below.

Department I: 1,200 lb Algon and 600 lb Betagon per ton of raw material.
Department II: 0.60 lb Trigon and 0.25 lb Zygon per pound of Algon.
Department III: 0.90 lb Betaplus per pound of Betagon.

All losses are from evaporation and cannot be reduced with the existing techniques for processing. Cost data by department are:

Department	Unavoidable Monthly Fixed Costs	Avoidable Monthly Fixed Costs	Variable Cost per Hour of Processing
I	$20,000	$55,000	$12
II	11,000	37,000	14
III	9,000	17,000	9

The unavoidable fixed costs consist of depreciation and allocated costs like rent.

Processing times are as follows: department I, 2 hr per ton of raw material; department II, 2 hr per 1,000 lb Algon; department III, ½ hr per 1,000 lb Betagon.

Prices and variable selling costs are:

	Algon	Betagon	Trigon	Zygon	Betaplus
Price per pound	$0.12	$0.10	$0.34	$0.20	$0.14
Selling expense per pound	0.02	0.01	0.04	0.04	0.01

Required:

1. Determine the firm's optimal processing decisions and the profit it will earn by making those decisions.

2. Determine the price of Betaplus where the firm would be indifferent between selling Betagon and processing it into Betaplus. Assume that unit selling expenses would remain as given.

3. Suppose that some new machinery could be leased for $12,000 per month. The machinery would enable the firm to increase the yield of Algon to 1,300 lb per ton of raw material. The yield of Betagon would remain at 600 lb. Would it be financially advantageous to acquire the new machinery if all other cost and revenue data remained the same?

9–8 Processing Decision. The Walker Pork Company makes a number of pork products and also processes the hides into tanned leather for sale to other firms. The assistant controller has developed the following income statement for a typical month, which he believes shows that the firm should stop tanning the hides and sell them after they come off the animals. The price per hide would be $6 without tanning.

	Meat	Hides	Total
Sales (10,000 hogs processed)	$840,000	$120,000	$960,000
Cost of hogs	437,500	62,500	500,000
Processing costs:			
Separation of hide and meat	131,250	18,750	150,000
Separate processing	220,000	23,000	243,000
Total costs	$788,750	$104,250	$893,000
Profit	$ 51,250	$ 15,750	$ 67,000

The separate processing costs are all incremental. About 70 percent of the costs of separating the hides and meat are incremental.

Required: Analyze the assistant controller's proposal.

9–9 Joint Cost Allocation. The Quanto Company makes three joint products. It allocates joint costs to each product using the net realizable value method. It also uses FIFO. Data for April, 19X7, appear at the top of page 385.

	Product		
	896	451	341
Units in beginning inventory	2,000	0	6,000
Units produced during April	25,000	46,000	20,000
Units in ending inventory	4,000	8,000	0
Units sold	23,000	38,000	26,000
Cost of beginning inventory	$7,800	0	$60,600
Selling price at split-off	$3	$0	$7
Selling price after further processing	$9	$12	$15
Selling expenses per unit, at split-off			
and after additional processing	$0.40	$0.20	$0.80
Additional processing costs for April	$30,000	$120,000	$80,000

Total joint costs, $600,000

All products were processed beyond the split-off point. Selling expenses are incurred when the products are sold.

Required: Prepare an income statement for April together with necessary supporting schedules.

9–10 Joint Costs—Selling at Split-off. Byron Gumbo, controller of Rice Manufacturing, Inc., has been looking over the costs of making the company's two main products, Filé and Flambe. In order to make these two products, a common raw material is used in a joint process to produce Filé powder and Flambe cake. Further work is required to bring both products to a finished stage of Filé liquid concentrate and Flambe pellets. The standard costs for the joint process are as follows.

Standard Costs to Produce
1 lb Semiprocessed Filé Powder
and ½ lb Semiprocessed Flambe Cake

Raw materials: 2 gal at $25	$ 50
Direct labor: 15 hr at $12	180
Variable overhead at $15/DLH	225
Fixed overhead[a]	40
Standard joint cost	$495

[a] Based on $1,600,000 per year and 40,000 gal (standard use) of raw material.

During 19X4, Rice plans to produce 20,000 lb of Filé powder and 10,000 lb of Flambe cake. Flambe cake cannot be sold as an intermediate product and must be processed into pellet form at a cost of $500,000 for the planned production. Flambe pellets sell for $300/lb. There is a market for both Filé powder and liquid concentrate. The semifinished product can be sold for $350/lb, while the liquid concentrate sells for $800/gal. It takes 2 lb of powder to produce 1 gal of concentrate. Further processing costs are $120,000 for each 1,000 gal.

Required: Should Gumbo sell Filé at split-off?

9-11 **Joint Products and CVP Analysis.** The Marcot Company processes a raw material into three joint products. Data relating to a single batch appear below.

	Joint Products		
	X-10	Y-15	Z-20
Gallons per batch of material	40	120	30
Selling price at split-off, per gallon	$1	$3	$ 7
Additional processing costs, variable per gallon	$3	$2	$ 5
Selling price after further processing, per gallon	$5	$7	$11

Monthly fixed costs, all unavoidable, are $110,000. The raw material cost per batch is $180, and direct labor and variable overhead associated with each batch are $60.

Required:

1. How many batches must the firm process to earn $40,000 each month?

2. Suppose that the firm could increase the output of Z-30 by 10 lb per batch if it used a new raw material that costs $210. Direct labor and variable overhead would remain constant, as would the yields of the other joint products. Would it be to the firm's advantage to use the new material?

3. Assume that the firm is using the old material. If the price of Z-30 after further processing increased to $14, how many batches would the firm have to produce to earn a $40,000 monthly profit?

9-12 **Make or Buy Decision.** The Thorson Company manufactures a number of products. Among them are three chemicals that arise from a single raw material put through a single process. Data on these products for a typical month appear at the top of page 387.

The firm processes product 101 beyond split-off at a cost of $100,000, sells 102 and 103 at split-off. The joint costs of $600,000 are allocated using the net realizable value method. Of the $600,000, about $100,000 is unavoidable cost such as depreciation.

The firm currently buys a chemical outside for $8/gal, using it in a product made in another department. The manager in charge of that product

		Product		
	Total	101	102	103
Output in gallons	100,000	60,000	30,000	10,000
Revenue	$1,100,000	$720,000	$180,000	$200,000
Cost of sales	700,000	472,000	108,000	120,000
Gross margin	$ 400,000	$248,000	$ 72,000	$ 80,000

has discovered that he could use product 102 in place of the chemical he now buys, provided that he put 102 through some additional processing. The additional processing would cost $1.50/gal variable, and incremental fixed costs would be about $15,000 per month. He would need 20,000 gal of 102 per month.

Looking at the data above, the manager made the following calculation to show that it would be better for the firm to process 102 and stop buying the chemical outside.

Processing cost of product 102, $108,000/30,000	$3.60
Variable processing cost	1.50
Fixed processing cost per unit, $15,000/20,000	0.75
Total unit cost	$5.85

"That's less than the $8 we now pay, so it should be a good deal to use 20,000 gallons inside," was the conclusion.

Required: Determine whether the manager is correct.

9–13   Relationships (AICPA adapted).   The Bensom Company makes three joint products. The following data are available from operations from August, in thousands of dollars.

	Product			
	N	O	P	Total
Sales value at split-off	$ __	$__	$50	$200
Allocated joint costs	$ 48	$__	$__	$120
Sales value if processed further	$110	$90	$60	$260
Additional costs, if product processed beyond split-off	$ 18	$14	$12	$ 44

The firm allocates joint costs using the relative sales values at split-off. It also made the best decisions about selling at split-off or processing further.

Required:

1. Fill in the blanks above.

2. Determine the gross profit that the firm earned. There were no inventories at either the beginning or end of August.

9-14 Joint Products—Variable Proportions. The Tyndall Company produces three bulk chemicals in a joint process. The process and raw materials allow the firm to vary, within limits, the proportions of each product that emerge from a single batch. Information about the percentages of each product that can be produced, and about other characteristics of each product, appears below. The firm can process 100,000 lb of raw materials per month, yielding 100,000 lb of the three joint products.

Product	Output— Range of Percentages		Price at Split-off	Price After Further Processing	Cost per Pound of Further Processing
	High	Low			
Nalgon	30%	20%	$3.20	$3.80	$.40
Norphyll	40	30	2.50	3.10	.80
Kryton	50	20	1.80	3.70	.70

Required: Develop a production plan for the firm, including the quantities of each product that it should make and the disposition of each product (sell at split-off or process further).

9-15 Negative NRV. Blackman Company runs a joint process that produces two saleable products and a toxic waste. Data for a typical month follow.

	Saleable Products		
	CZ-60	MR-42	Waste
Quantity produced, in pounds	60,000	35,000	5,000
Selling price at split-off	$10/lb	$8/lb	0

Monthly joint costs are $550,000. The firm currently pays an outside contractor $20,000 a month to haul the waste to a safe dump.

Required:

1. For product costing purposes, how would you treat the $20,000 paid to haul away the waste? As an expense? As part of the cost of producing the saleable products? Why?

2. Suppose that the firm could process the waste into a saleable product at a cost of $24,000 per month. The new product would sell for $2/lb. Would it be advantageous for the firm to do the processing?

3. Assume that your answer to item 2 was that it would benefit the firm

to process the waste. For product costing purposes, how would you allocate costs to each product?

9-16 **Variable Proportions, Calculus.** The Braton Chemical Company makes two chemicals, beon and zeon, in a joint process. The process takes 10,000 gal of raw material and heats it under pressure to yield the joint products. The output of the process depends on the running time: the longer it runs, the more zeon and the less beon. However, there is evaporation, which increases rapidly as the time increases. The equations below give the quantities of beon and zeon, expressed as functions of the number of hours each batch stays in the process.

$$Q_b = 10,000 - Q_z - 100H^2$$
$$Q_z = 1,000H$$

where $Q_b =$ number of gallons of beon
$Q_z =$ number of gallons of zeon
$H =$ number of hours the process runs for each batch

The last term in the first equation, $-100H^2$, represents evaporation. Thus, the total yield is always less than 10,000 gal.

Beon sells for $10/gal, zeon for $20. The cost of the raw material is $65,000 per 10,000 gal. The variable cost to operate the process is $500/hr.

Required: Determine the optimal time for operating the process, the quantities of each product that the firm will make, and the gross profit at the optimal mix.

9-17 **Comprehensive Joint Products Problem.** The Steger Chemical Company buys a single raw material for $0.10/lb. The material is put through a process from which three products emerge. The processing is done in batches of 1,000 lb of material and requires 10 labor hours per batch. The joint process has associated fixed costs of $2,200 per month, of which $1,200 is avoidable. The output of a 1,000-lb batch is as follows:

Product	Quantity in Pounds	Selling Price per Pound
Algex	300	$0.90
Gamex	200	1.80
Deltex	400	0.75
Waste	100	0

Each of the three usable products can be put through further processing. Algex can be made into two new products, Nonex and Querex. The variable cost to process a 100-lb batch of Algex is $40 for labor and overhead. Fixed costs associated with the process are $12,000 per month, of which $4,800 is avoidable. The output per 100 lb of Algex is:

Product	Quantity in Pounds	Selling Price per Pound
Nonex	45	$3
Querex	40	2
Waste	15	0

Gamex can be processed further and sold for $1.90/lb. The additional processing requires one labor hour per 100 lb.

Deltex can be refined and sold for $1.20/lb. The additional refining requires three-fourths of a labor hour per 100 lb put into the refining process. Evaporation during the process takes 10 percent of the quantity put into the process. The refining process also has incremental, avoidable fixed costs of $2,200 per month.

For all processes, the cost per hour of labor time is $20, which includes labor and variable overhead. The firm can process 10 tons of raw material per month and can sell all of any product it makes. Selling and administrative expenses are $1,600 per month.

Required: Answer each question independently of the others, unless otherwise stated.

1. Determine the firm's best production plan. Which products should be sold at split-off, and which processed further?

2. Prepare an income statement for a month, based on your answer to item 1.

3. The selling prices of some of the products might change in the next few months. The president of the firm is concerned about the possibilities and is concerned about the potential effects on the firm's operations. Specifically, the president asks you the following questions.

   a. At what price per pound for Querex would the firm earn the same profit processing Algex into Nonex and Querex as it would selling Algex at split-off?

   b. At what price per pound for Gamex, after further processing, would the firm earn the same profit processing it further as it would selling it at split-off?

4. The firm has the opportunity to rent equipment for $2,000 per month. Using the equipment would enable the firm to increase its capacity to 12 tons of raw material per month. No other costs would be affected. All additional output of any product could be sold at the prices given. Determine the effect on the firm's monthly profit if the equipment is rented.

5. The president of the firm has learned of a new process. The process could be used to make a new product called Postex. Each 100-lb batch of Postex requires 50 lb of Nonex and 50 lb of Gamex (as it emerges from the joint process). Postex could be sold for $4/lb. The combining process would require two labor hours per 100-lb batch.

Additional fixed costs of $800 per month would also have to be incurred. Determine the effect on monthly profit of making Postex.

6. Another new process is also available. In this process the firm would combine Algex and Gamex (after Gamex has been further processed) into Zentex. A 100-lb batch of Zentex requires 50 lb of each of the other products and 3 labor hours. Additional fixed costs would be $1,500 per month. Zentex can be sold for $2.50/lb. Determine the effect on the firm's monthly profit of making Zentex.

9–18 Adding a Department (CMA adapted). The management of Bay Company is considering a proposal to install a third production department within its existing factory building. With the company's present production setup, raw material is passed through department I to produce materials A and B in equal proportions. Material A is then passed through department II to yield product C. Material B is presently being sold "as is" at a price of $20.25/lb. Product C has a selling price of $100/lb.

The per-pound standard costs currently being used by the Bay Company are as follows:

	Department I (Materials A and B)	Department II (Product C)	(Material B)
Prior department costs	—	$53.03	$13.47
Direct material	$20.00	—	—
Direct labor	7.00	12.00	—
Variable overhead	3.00	5.00	—
Fixed overhead:			
Attributable	2.25	2.25	—
Allocated ($\frac{2}{3}$, $\frac{1}{3}$)	1.00	1.00	—
	$33.25	$73.28	$13.47

These standard costs were developed by using an estimated production volume of 200,000 lb of raw material as the standard volume. The company assigns department I costs to materials A and B in proportion to their net sales values at the point of separation, computed by deducting subsequent standard production costs from sales prices. The $300,000 of common fixed overhead costs are allocated to the two producing departments on the basis of the space used by the departments.

The proposed department III would be used to process material B into product D. It is expected that any quantity of product D can be sold for $30/lb. Standard costs per pound as proposed, developed by using 200,000 lb of raw material as the standard volume, are at the top of page 392.

Department D would occupy space that is not currently used, and there are no foreseeable alternative uses for the space. The firm's managers expect sales and production levels to continue at their present levels. They also expect selling prices to hold at their present levels.

	Department I (Materials A and B)	Department II (Product C)	Department III (Product D)
Prior department costs	—	$52.80	$13.20
Direct material	$20.00	—	—
Direct labor	7.00	12.00	5.50
Variable overhead	3.00	5.00	2.00
Fixed overhead:			
Attributable	2.25	2.25	1.75
Allocated ($\frac{1}{2}$, $\frac{1}{4}$, $\frac{1}{4}$)	0.75	0.75	0.75
	$33.00	$72.80	$23.20

Required:

1. Determine whether the firm should make product D.

2. Suppose now that the managers expect the price of product D to be $30/lb about 75 percent of the time, $25 about 25 percent of the time. Other prices are expected to remain constant. The attributable overhead of department III is unavoidable once the department is set up, but the firm can avoid the variable costs of producing product D if it sells material B at split-off. Should the firm install department III under these conditions?

9–19 Determine Joint Costs, Constant Gross Margin (AICPA adapted). O'Conner Company manufactures products J and K in a joint process. During a recent month the firm produced 4,000 units of product J, which had a value at the split-off point of $15,000. Processing product J would have given revenue of $20,000. The additional processing costs would have been $3,000. For product K, 2,000 units were produced having a sales value at split-off of $10,000. Processing product K further would have yielded revenues of $12,000 and additional processing costs of $1,000.

The firm used the relative sales values of the products at the split-off point to allocate the joint costs. Product J received $9,000 of allocated joint costs.

Required:

1. Determine the total joint costs for the month.

2. What would have been the allocations of joint costs if the firm had used the constant gross margin method and had made the best decisions regarding each product (sell at split-off or process further)?

9–20 Processing Decisions. The Wilkinson Company manufactures a variety of furniture, all from wood. The firm operates several integrated factories, each with its own sawmill for cutting timber into pieces of desired sizes, and with other departments that make the finished products. The factories sometimes sell cut lumber, rather than convert it into finished goods, especially when they cannot operate the finishing departments at full capacity. Because the output from the sawmill is rough-cut, the lumber department must do additional work before it sells the lumber. Sales of lumber are usually about 7 to 8 percent of total physical output of the sawmill.

In March of 19X6 the general manager of the Marathon Plant, which specialized in pine furniture, received the following income statement, with dollars in thousands. The Marathon Plant operated three departments: lumber, office furniture, and home furniture.

			Furniture	
	Total	Lumber	Office	Home
Sales	$743.2	$96.5	$369.3	$277.4
Materials and sawmill costs	334.4	43.4	166.2	124.8
Added materials	11.9	0.0	7.6	4.3
Direct labor	126.7	6.2	77.3	43.2
Overhead	163.3	21.2	91.1	51.0
Cost of sales	636.3	70.8	342.2	223.3
Gross margin	106.9	25.7	27.1	54.1
Selling/administrative expenses	87.8	11.4	43.6	32.8
Profit (loss)	$ 19.1	$14.3	($ 16.5)	$ 21.3
Percentage of sawmill output	100.0%	18.8%	47.2%	34.0%

From consultations with the controller, the manager knew the following:

1. The materials and sawmill costs were allocated to operations on the basis of relative sales dollars. These costs were about 80 percent variable at the present level of operations, which was nearly full capacity for the sawmill.

2. Added materials and direct labor were variable. (Added materials consisted of hardware and other nonwood items.)

3. Variable manufacturing overhead was about 60 percent of direct labor across all departments. Fixed overhead was about 80 percent avoidable, again across all departments.

4. The controller allocated selling and administrative expenses on the basis of sales. He did so because the only variable component was a 5 percent commission on all products (including lumber), so that total expenses depended only on sales volume.

5. The home furniture department was operating at capacity, but the office furniture department was at 70 percent capacity. The manager expected this situation to continue. Severe competition in the office furniture business had resulted in drops in prices and an oversupply on the market. Demand for lumber was strong.

The general manager was disturbed by the results for the office furniture department but was unsure what to do.

Required: Analyze the situation and make a recommendation based on the available information. State clearly any assumptions that you must make. List items of information that you would want in order to better ground your recommendation.

SELECTED REFERENCES

Bierman, Harold, Jr., "Inventory Valuation: The Use of Market Prices," *The Accounting Review*, 42:4 (October 1967), 731–37.

Edwards, J. O., "Accounting for Joint and By-product Costs," in Homer A. Black and James Don Edwards, eds., *The Managerial and Cost Accountant's Handbook*, Homewood, Ill.: Dow Jones-Irwin, Inc., 1979.

Hartley, Ronald V., "Decision Making When Joint Products Are Involved," *The Accounting Review*, 46:4 (October 1971), 746–55.

Jensen, Daniel L., "The Role of Costs in Pricing Joint Products: A Case of Production in Fixed Proportions," *The Accounting Review*, 49:3 (July 1974), 465–76.

National Association of Accountants, *N.A.A. Research Report 31: Costing Joint Products*, New York: National Association of Accountants, 1957.

Spoilage, Lost Units, and Scrap

Chapter 10

Chapter 9 introduced the basic ideas of joint products. We stated that by-products, waste, and scrap fell under the general category of joint products because they are often inevitable. We noted that distinctions among these outputs were largely terminological, and that different firms would give different names and use different accounting methods for the same basic product, such as sawdust or metal shavings. This chapter treats scrap in more detail, but its primary subject is another type of joint product—lost and spoiled units.

LOST AND SPOILED UNITS

Lost and spoiled units abound in manufacturing processes. Input of 1,000 gallons of raw material may yield 800 gallons of finished product, and other types of shrinkage reduce output in other processes. Cracked bricks, warped pieces of lumber, and broken chairs are produced along with good units of these products. Some of these losses are normal and expected. Attempts to reduce them below a certain level may be more costly than allowing them to continue.

Another type of loss occurs when the firm puts more finished product into containers than the label states. For example, a maker of instant coffee may put out four-ounce jars. It may set its machinery so that it is 98 percent sure that each jar contains at least four ounces. Given the tolerances available, the average weight of the coffee in a jar may be 4.08 ounces. However, failure to have four ounces or more in a large percentage of its jars may bring fines and unfavorable publicity if the shortages are detected by government agencies, hence the firm plays safe and often overfills jars. The extra cost of coffee is more than offset, the managers believe, by the potential costs of underfilling.

The managerial problems of lost and spoiled units center on the question of the costs and benefits of reducing losses. Questions asked include: Are losses within acceptable ranges, given the techniques used? What does it cost us to lose units, and what would it cost to reduce the losses by specified amounts? The accounting questions center on the question of inventoriable costs. Are the costs of lost and spoiled units to be treated as expenses of the period or as part of the cost of the good output? In the following discussion we use the term **spoilage** to refer to all the types of losses described above. This usage will provide brevity and does no harm, because the accounting for each type of loss is generally the same.

Normal and Abnormal Spoilage

Spoilage is classified into two types, normal and abnormal. **Normal spoilage** is the amount expected, given the manufacturing techniques used by the firm and assuming that the manufacturing process is under control. Thus, normal spoilage for one firm may be about 10 percent of good output, while for another firm in the same industry using more advanced equipment the rate may be about 6 percent. **Abnormal spoilage** is unexpected and, therefore, is total spoilage minus normal spoilage.

Throughout the remainder of the discussion we shall speak of normal spoilage as a single number of units or single rate. However, from both conceptual and practical standpoints, normal spoilage should be viewed as a range, not as a point estimate. Even highly automated processes operating under near-laboratory conditions will show differing amounts of spoilage in different periods, especially if the periods are short (say, days or weeks as opposed to months or quarters). The principles developed in Chapter 3 (regression analysis) and explored in Chapter 19 (analyzing the significance of variances) are relevant to the determination of a range of normal spoilage.

When we speak of normal spoilage being, say, 200 units, we should interpret that figure as the midpoint of a range, say from 170 to 230 units. One important reason for keeping in mind the notion of a range of normal spoilage is that managers will be more likely to investigate spoilage that is called abnormal than spoilage called normal. Failure to recognize that normal spoilage is a range may result in excessive investigation and therefore excessive costs.

Accounting for Spoilage

Accountants agree that normal spoilage costs should be allocated to the good output, because normal spoilage is an inevitable consequence of the production process. There is also wide agreement that the costs of abnormal spoilage should be expensed in the period incurred, not inventoried. The reasoning is that abnormal spoilage is not a necessary consequence of producing good output and is therefore not part of the cost of good product.

Accounting for Abnormal Spoilage. In a process costing situation, either actual costing or normal costing, the determination of spoilage costs requires the calculation of equivalent production including the abnormally spoiled units. This figure is then used to determine a cost per unit amount in the same fashion as was done in Chapter 6. The number of units spoiled abnormally is multiplied by the cost per unit, the result being shown as an expense on the income statement.

Often a careful analysis of the physical flow of units is required to determine how many were lost or spoiled. In some cases—for example, where losses are due to evaporation—you do not know the amount lost; you have to determine it from information about the beginning inventory, quantity put into process, quantity completed, and ending inventory.

To illustrate, we assume the following facts about a manufacturing process.

Units in beginning inventory	1,000
Units put into process during the period	12,000
Units completed during the period	10,000
Units in ending inventory	2,000

We have to reconcile the physical flow to determine how many units were lost or spoiled.

Units in beginning inventory	1,000
Units put into process	12,000
Units to be accounted for	13,000
Units completed	10,000
Units in ending inventory	2,000
Total	12,000
Units lost or spoiled (13,000 − 12,000)	1,000

A reconciliation like this one is the first step in dealing with lost or spoiled units, unless you know the amount lost or spoiled. It is important to recognize that the data used are not equivalent units: they are physical units, no matter what the percentage of completion. That is, you are trying to determine the number of units lost or spoiled; the determination of equivalent production follows this reconciliation. Exhibit 10–1 on page 398 provides the data for an illustration. The firm detects spoiled units at the end of the production process.

The calculations of equivalent production and unit costs under both the weighted average and FIFO methods are shown in Exhibit 10–2 on page 399. Again, the only difference between these calculations and the ones you already know from Chapter 6 is the inclusion of the abnormal spoilage in the unit-cost calculations through its inclusion in equivalent production.

The unit costs in Exhibit 10–2 are now used to determine the amounts of cost transferred from Work-in-Process Inventory to Finished Goods Inventory (or to the next department) and the amounts of cost to be shown in

EXHIBIT 10–1
Data for Illustration

Physical Flow

Beginning inventory	1,000
Units put into production	12,000
Total to be accounted for	13,000
Completed and transferred	10,000
Ending inventory	2,000
Spoiled	1,000
Total accounted for	13,000

Percentages of Completion

	Materials	Conversion Costs
Beginning inventory	100%	70%
Ending inventory	100%	60%

Costs

			Total
Beginning inventory	$ 1,760	$ 2,675	$ 4,435
Current-period costs	24,240	33,925	58,165
Totals	$26,000	$36,600	$62,600

the ending inventory of work in process, as well as the amount to be expensed as Abnormal Spoilage Expense. The determinations follow the usual techniques of Chapter 6. Exhibit 10–3 on page 400 shows T-accounts for Work-in-Process Inventory under the two cost flow assumptions, along with the appropriate calculations. You may wish to review the formulas in Chapter 6 before checking the calculations. Notice that the cost of spoiled units under both cost flow assumptions is simply the number of spoiled units multiplied by the cost per unit that is calculated in Exhibit 10–2 on page 399.

Let us now pause a minute and review the procedure. *Essentially, you are calculating the unit costs based on the equivalent production of all units, whether good or spoiled.* You are calculating a cost-per-unit, not a cost-per-good-unit figure. You then use the unit costs in determining the amounts to be transferred to Finished Goods Inventory, left in Work-in-Process Inventory, and sent to the income statement as Spoiled Goods Expense, or other descriptive title.

Accounting for Normal Spoilage.   Two general methods are used to account for normal spoilage. One is to ignore the normally spoiled units in

EXHIBIT 10–2
Unit Cost Calculations[a]

Equivalent Production

	Materials	Conversion Costs
Units completed	10,000	10,000
Ending inventory (2,000 × 100%), (2,000 × 60%)	2,000	1,200
Spoiled units	1,000	1,000
Equivalent production—weighted average	13,000	12,200
Beginning inventory (1,000 × 100%), (1,000 × 70%)	1,000	700
Equivalent production—FIFO	12,000	11,500

Unit Costs—Weighted Average

	Materials	Conversion Costs
Beginning inventory costs plus current-period costs	$26,000	$36,600
	÷	÷
Equivalent production—weighted average	13,000	12,200
Cost per unit	$2	$3

Unit Costs—FIFO

	Materials	Conversion Costs
Current-period costs	$24,240	$33,925
	÷	÷
Equivalent production—FIFO	12,000	11,500
Cost per unit	$2.02	$2.95

[a] All data from Exhibit 10–1

the calculations of unit cost by leaving them out of the computations of equivalent units. The other is to include normally spoiled units in these calculations, just as we did previously with abnormally spoiled units. The cost of normally spoiled units is then computed the same way as the cost of abnormally spoiled units, and this cost is transferred to the next department or to Finished Goods. The first method, ignoring the spoilage, is simpler but does not allow the manager to see the cost of spoilage because it is not computed.

Let us use the data from Exhibit 10–1 again, only assume that all the spoilage is considered normal. Exhibit 10–4 on page 401 shows the calculations and results of using the first method—ignoring spoilage in the determination of equivalent production. Because we omit spoilage from equivalent production, the unit costs are higher than they were in Exhibit 10–2.

Again, this method is deficient because it obscures the quantity and cost of spoilage. The other method recognizes the cost of normal spoilage, treating it as part of the transfer to Finished Goods.

To illustrate the second method, we change the assumption of spoilage to read that 800 units were normally spoiled, 200 abnormally spoiled. Mak-

EXHIBIT 10–3
Disposition of Costs

	Work-in-Process Inventory— Weighted Average			Work-in-Process Inventory—FIFO		
Beginning. balance	$ 4,435			$ 4,435		
Current-period costs (from Exhibit 10–1)	58,165			58,165		
		$50,000	To Finished Goods		$50,050	To Finished Goods
	———	5,000	Abnormal Spoilage Expense	———	4,970	Abnormal Spoilage Expense
	62,600	55,000		62,600	55,020	
Ending inventory	$ 7,600			$ 7,580		

Calculations: Weighted Average

Transferred to Finished Goods, $5 × 10,000	$50,000
Abnormal Spoilage Expense, $5 × 1,000	5,000
Ending inventory, ($2 × 2,000) + ($3 × 1,200)	7,600
Total accounted for	$62,600

Calculations: FIFO

Transferred to Finished Goods:[a]		
Materials, $1,760 + $2.02(10,000 − 1,000)	$19,940	
Conversion costs, $2,675 + $2.95(10,000 − 700)	30,110	$50,050
Abnormal Spoilage Expense, ($2.02 + $2.95) × 1,000		4,970
Ending inventory, ($2.02 × 2,000) + ($2.95 × 1,200)		7,580
Total accounted for		$62,600

[a] Recall the formula from Chapter 6: cost of beginning inventory + unit cost × (units transferred − equivalent units in beginning inventory).

ing this change allows us to illustrate how we can treat both types of spoilage in the same situation.

Exhibit 10–5 on page 402 presents the results. For comparison, we show summary results from Exhibit 10–3. The equivalent unit calculations are exactly the same as those in Exhibit 10–2. Both normally and abnormally spoiled units are included. The resulting unit costs are employed in determining the transfers to Finished Goods and to Abnormal Spoilage Expense. The only differences between Exhibits 10–5 and 10–3 are that part of the spoilage cost goes to Finished Goods in Exhibit 10–5, part to Abnormal Spoilage Expense, whereas in Exhibit 10–3 it all goes to Abnormal Spoilage Expense. The ending inventories of work in process are the same in both exhibits.

EXHIBIT 10–4
Disposition of Costs—Normal Spoilage Ignored

Equivalent Production
(see Exhibit 10–2)

	Materials	Conversion Costs
Units completed	10,000	10,000
Ending inventory, equivalent production	2,000	1,200
Equivalent production—weighted average	12,000	11,200
Beginning inventory, equivalent production	1,000	700
Equivalent production—FIFO	11,000	10,500

Unit Costs—Weighted Average
(see Exhibit 10–2)

	Materials	Conversion Costs
Beginning inventory costs plus current-period costs	$26,000	$36,600
	÷	÷
Equivalent production	12,000	11,200
Unit costs	$2.1667	$3.268

Unit Costs—FIFO

	Materials	Conversion Costs
Current-period costs	$24,240	$33,925
	÷	÷
Equivalent production	11,000	10,500
Unit costs	$2.204	$3.231

Disposition of Costs

Weighted Average

Transferred to Finished Goods ($2.1667 + $3.268) × 10,000	$54,347
Ending inventory ($2.1667 × 2,000) + ($3.268 × 1,200)	8,255
Total accounted for ($2 rounding error)	$62,602

FIFO

Transferred to Finished Goods
  Materials $1,760 + $2.204 × (10,000 − 1,000) $21,596
  Conversion costs $2,675 + $3.231
    × (10,000 − 700)   32,723 $54,319
Ending inventory ($2.204 × 2,000) + ($3.231 × 1,200)   8,285
  Total accounted for ($4 rounding error) $62,604

EXHIBIT 10–5
Disposition of Costs: 800 Normally Spoiled Units, 200 Abnormally Spoiled Units

			Results From Exhibit 10–3
FIFO			
Transferred to Finished Goods:			
Good units, from Exhibit 10–3	$50,050		$50,050
Normal spoilage ($2.02 + $2.95) × 800	3,976		0
Total transferred to Finished Goods		$54,026	50,050
Ending Inventory, from Exhibit 10–3		7,580	7,580
Abnormal Spoilage Expense ($2.02 + $2.95) × 200		994	4,970
Total accounted for		$62,600	$62,600
Weighted Average			
Transferred to Finished Goods:			
Good units, $5 × 10,000	$50,000		$50,000
Normal spoilage, $5 × 800	4,000		0
Total transferred to Finished Goods		$54,000	50,000
Ending Inventory, from Exhibit 10–3		7,600	7,600
Abnormal Spoilage Expense, $5 × 200		1,000	5,000
Total accounted for		$62,600	$62,600

Because the cost of normal spoilage goes to Finished Goods, we have to recalculate the unit costs of the transferred units. The 10,000 units completed would have a per-unit cost of $5.4026 in Finished Goods under FIFO, which is the total transfer of $54,026 divided by 10,000. The cost would be $5.40 under weighted average ($54,000/10,000). Basically, the cost of normal spoilage is allocated to the good units transferred to Finished Goods. The units remaining in ending Work-in-Process Inventory receive no allocation because they are not yet inspected and we do not yet know how many will turn out to be spoiled.

Spoilage Detected During Production

The previous examples have assumed that spoilage was detected at the end of the production process. All spoiled units were 100 percent complete for both materials and conversion costs. At times, inspections during the production process will detect spoiled units before they are 100 percent complete for conversion costs. They would be 100 percent complete for materials if materials were put into process before the detection point, or they would be less than 100 percent complete if materials were added throughout the process.

For example, suppose that spoiled units are detected when units are 40 percent through the process. Put another way, the spoiled units are 40 percent complete with respect to conversion costs when they are detected and removed. Suppose further that all materials are put into process at the beginning, so that the spoiled units are 100 percent complete with respect to materials. The following data are the basis for the example.

Units in beginning inventory, 60% complete for conversion costs	3,000
Units put into process	30,000
Units completed and transferred out	26,000
Units in ending inventory, 80% complete for conversion costs	5,000
Spoiled units, detected when 40% through the process (3,000 + 30,000 − 26,000 − 5,000)	2,000

The calculations of equivalent production, weighted average and FIFO, appear below.

	Materials	Conversion Costs
Units completed	26,000	26,000
Ending inventory (100%, 80%)	5,000	4,000
Spoiled units	2,000	800 (2,000 × 40%)
Equivalent production—weighted average	33,000	30,800
Beginning inventory (100%, 60%)	3,000	1,800
Equivalent production—FIFO	30,000	29,000

Notice that the only difference between these calculations and those in Exhibit 10–2 arises because the spoiled units did not receive all the conversion work. Because the 2,000 units were removed after they had gone 40 percent of the way through the process, they received 40 percent of the conversion work. Accordingly, the unit-cost calculations will reflect only 800 equivalent units of conversion cost, not 2,000 units.

This refinement does not change the basic calculations of unit costs. The appropriate cost figures (current-period costs for FIFO, current-period costs plus beginning inventory costs for weighted average) are divided by the equivalent unit figures.

ANALYZING SPOILAGE COSTS

We have explored the accounting treatment of spoilage, which also applies to units lost through evaporation or other shrinkage. However, the costs of spoilage calculated in the preceding pages are not suitable for managerial purposes such as decisions to change the production process in order to reduce spoilage. In earlier sections we implicitly assumed that spoilage was detected at the end of the process and, therefore, that the spoiled units contained all the materials and conversion costs, just like the good units.

There are two general ways to reduce spoilage costs. One is to reduce the number of spoiled units, the other is to catch spoilage earlier in the process so that no more work is done on the spoiled units. For example, if an inspection made after 75 percent of the conversion work has been done will catch all spoiled units, the firm can save 25 percent of the variable conversion costs on spoiled units by inspecting then rather than at the end of the process. A numerical example will make this point clear.

Suppose that a firm makes the same product in two different processes. Units made in process A cannot be inspected until the end of the process, while units made in process B can be inspected after all materials are added and 75 percent of conversion costs incurred. This inspection catches all spoiled units: that is, no spoilage occurs after 75 percent of conversion costs have been incurred. The variable conversion costs are $10 per equivalent unit on both spoiled and good units in both processes. During one month the firm produces 1,000 good units and 200 spoiled units in each process. What is the saving resulting from being able to inspect units earlier in process B?

The total variable costs of conversion are given below.

	Process	
	A	B
Good units produced	1,000	1,000
Work done on spoiled units	200	150 (200 × 75%)
Total equivalent production	1,200	1,150
Variable conversion costs at $10	$12,000	$11,500

The firm saves $500 for each 200 spoiled units in process B as opposed to process A. This saving does not occur because fewer units are spoiled in process B, but rather because the units spoiled in process B receive only 75 percent of the total work required to complete a unit, whereas those spoiled in process A receive all of the work. It is important to include only variable costs in this type of analysis. The firm would not save fixed costs by detecting spoiled units early. Additionally, it is important to compare the savings with the cost of early inspection, as opposed to later inspection. Thus, if it costs $200 per period to inspect at the end of the process or $800 to inspect at the 75 percent mark, earlier inspection would be unwarranted since it would cost more than the $500 benefit.

Our example was intended to make a point and was therefore simplified. In some cases there could be savings in material costs if inspection revealed units spoiled before some materials were added to the product. A more likely complication is that only some of the spoiled units would be discovered at the earlier inspection point or that some units would be spoiled after reaching the early inspection. For example, suppose now that the early inspection in process B catches only 70 percent of the defective units. Thus, of each 200 spoiled units, 140 (200 × 70%) would be caught at the early inspection and discarded. The remaining 60 would go through the rest of the process. The savings in variable conversion costs would then be $350, determined as follows:

Total variable conversion costs, process A		$12,000
Total variable conversion costs, process B		
Cost of 1,000 good units at $10	$10,000	
Cost of 60 spoiled units at $10	600	
Cost of 140 spoiled units, on which 75% of		
work is done: (140 × 75% = 105) × $10	1,050	11,650
Saving from process B		$ 350

The previous analyses assume that capacity is not a problem, that the firm cannot profitably make more than 1,000 good units in each process. Refer back to the original situation where all spoiled units were caught at the inspection point and assume that the firm can sell all the output it can produce. However, each unit requires a half-hour of labor time and there are only 600 labor hours available in each process. The half-hour requirement is per equivalent unit, so that at output of 1,000 good units and 200 spoiled units, process A is operating at full capacity. Process B is operating at 575 labor hours and is therefore below capacity [575 hours are needed to make 1,000 good units (500 hours) and do 75 percent of the work on the 200 spoiled units (200 × 0.75 × 0.50 = 75 hours)]. In a situation where resources are limited, an opportunity cost approach is desirable. Assume that the selling price of each unit is $30 and that conversion costs are the only variable costs. We shall consider material costs later, but for now we want to focus on the question of capacity. We also assume that spoiled units are 20 percent of good units produced.

The question now is the value of finding spoiled units at the 75 percent mark and therefore being able to use the saved hours to produce additional units. First, let Q equal the number of good units produced. With $0.20Q$ being the number of spoiled units, and 75 percent of the work being done on those units, we have:

$$0.50Q + (0.50 \times 0.20Q \times 0.75) = 600 \text{ hours}$$
$$0.575Q = 600$$
$$Q = 1,043 \text{ (rounded)}$$

That is, the firm can produce 1,043 good units in process B using 600 labor hours. Spoiled units will total about 209 (1,043 × 0.20).

Labor hours for good units, 1,043 × 0.50	521.5
Labor hours for spoiled units, 209 × 0.50 × 0.75	78.4
Total labor hours required	599.9 (rounding error)

What is the value of the additional 43 good units? The selling price of $30 each gives a total of $1,290. However, the total variable conversion costs are the same in both processes, because they both use 600 labor hours. Process B shows an advantage of $1,290 over Process A if the firm can work at capacity.

Consider one final complication. Suppose that materials cost $5 per unit and are all added at the beginning of the processes. This additional information would reduce the gain in process B, because more units are started in process B and therefore more materials used.

	Process	
	A	B
Total units started	1,200	1,252 (1,043 + 209)
Material cost per unit	$ 5	$ 5
Total cost of materials	$6,000	$6,260

The $260 difference would reduce the advantage to process B to $1,030 ($1,290 − $260).

SCRAP AND SPOILAGE IN STANDARD COSTING SYSTEMS

Standard costs generally allow for some measure of normal scrap and spoilage. For example, if a piece of copper plate weighing 300 ounces is used to produce three units of product, with 60 ounces of scrap normally resulting from the cutting process, the standard cost of materials could be reduced by the expected value of the scrap. Suppose that the copper plate costs $9 ($0.03 per ounce) and that scrap is sold for $0.009 per ounce. The normal scrap from each plate would sell for $0.54, or $0.18 per unit of output ($0.54/3 units per plate). The standard material cost per unit could be calculated as follows.

Copper plate, 100 oz bought at $0.03	$3.00
Less normal scrap, 20 oz at $0.009	0.18
Net material cost	$2.82

The mechanics of accounting for the recovery value of scrap can be exceedingly complex. Two alternatives appear in Appendix 10–A, but for now we can say that the simplest procedure is to credit Work-in-Process Inventory with the expected recovery value of scrap, debiting an account called Inventory of Scrap or possibly a subsidiary account under Manufacturing Overhead. If the recovery value is insignificant, it might even be ignored. Sales of scrap would appear as Miscellaneous Income.

Normal spoilage can similarly be worked into the standard cost. Careful attention must be given to the point at which spoilage is detected or is assumed to take place. The principal difference between a standard cost allowance for scrap and one for spoiled units is that the former is usually related only to materials, while the latter is related to all cost factors. This is because the firm works on the spoiled units, just as it does the good units, while it does not do any work on scrap.

Suppose that the Baltural Manufacturing Company has the following standard costs per unit of product:

Materials, 2 lb at $2	$ 4.00
Direct labor, ½ hr at $8	4.00
Variable overhead at $6 per labor hour	3.00
Fixed overhead at $7 per labor hour[a]	3.50
Total standard cost	$14.50

[a] Based on budgeted monthly costs of $4,200 and normal activity of 600 labor hours.

Additionally, assume that the firm normally produces 20 spoiled units for every 100 good units. Spoilage is detected at the end of the process, so that all work done on good units is also done on spoiled units. The standard cost would be revised as follows:

Unadjusted standard cost	$14.50
Allowance for normal spoilage, 20%	2.90
Standard cost per good unit	$17.40

Please notice that we do not adjust the individual cost factors. For example, we would expect to use 2.4 lb of material (2 lb × 120%) for each good unit produced, but we do not incorporate that into the standard cost. The reason is that we want to be able to calculate variances based on both effectiveness and efficiency. The variances that will reflect effectiveness are variances related to abnormal spoilage. The variances that will reflect efficiency are the usual cost variances familiar from Chapter 7. Assume the following results for March:

Production:	
Good units	1,000
Spoiled units	300
Materials used at standard price, 2,700 lb	$5,400
Direct labor at standard rate, 620 hr	$4,960
Variable overhead	$3,720
Fixed overhead	$4,200

First, we see that the firm had abnormal spoilage of 100 units (300 spoiled − 200 normal spoilage). We calculate an abnormal spoilage variance for each cost factor, using the standard cost per unit for each factor.

Abnormal spoilage variances:

Materials, $4 × 100 units	$400
Direct labor, $4 × 100 units	400
Variable overhead, $3 × 100 units	300
Fixed overhead, $3.50 × 100 units	350
Total variance	$1,450

Next we calculate the usual variances based on output of 1,300 units. There were no price variances and no fixed overhead budget variance.

Material use variance, [2,700 − (1,300 × 2)] × ($2)	$200 U
Direct labor efficiency variance, [620 − (1,300 × 1/2)] × ($8)	$240 F
Variable overhead efficiency variance, [620 − (1,300 × 1/2)] × ($6)	$180 F
Fixed overhead application variance, (650 standard hours − 600 normal activity hours) × ($7)	$350 F
Total variances	$570 F

The reconciliation of actual and standard costs is as follows:

Total actual costs ($5,400 + $4,960 + $3,720 + $4,200)		$18,280
Standard cost of 1,000 good units finished at $17.40		17,400
Difference		$ 880
Consisting of:		
Abnormal spoilage variance	$1,450 U	
Other variances (above)	570 F	$880

The principal advantage of this treatment is that it highlights the excessive costs incurred because of abnormal spoilage. These costs are not like the usual efficiency variances because they do not reflect wastefulness of materials and labor, but rather ineffective production—work done, and perhaps done efficiently, but done on abnormally spoiled units. The major defect in the method is that it shows a fixed cost variance for abnormal spoilage. This variance is not an economic cost of abnormal spoilage, but simply an allocation of fixed costs to abnormal spoilage. It should be ignored for managerial purposes, along the lines of the analysis of early detection of spoilage described in a previous section.

SUMMARY

Some losses and spoilage are inevitable in many manufacturing processes. Sometimes it would be possible to reduce losses and spoilage, but the cost to achieve the reductions would be greater than the savings. To the extent that losses and spoilage are below the limit stated to be normal, the costs are appropriately considered to be part of the costs of producing good units.

Accountants treat the costs of normal spoilage and loss as part of the cost of producing good units.

When losses or spoilage are greater than normal, they are considered abnormal, and the accountant treats the cost as an expense of the period. The rationale is that inventoriable costs include the necessary costs of production and that abnormal spoilage is by definition unnecessary.

From a managerial point of view, the critical question is whether or not it would be wise to take measures to reduce spoilage and losses. For this purpose, the incremental costs of producing spoiled units are relevant, not the absorption costs of the spoiled units.

APPENDIX 10-A: SCRAP AND SPOILAGE RECOVERY IN STANDARD COSTING SYSTEMS

This appendix illustrates a technique for dealing with the estimated recovery values of scrap and spoiled units. We employ the following example. The standard cost of a unit of product 509 appears below.

Materials: 4 lb at $2	$ 8.00
Less, allowance for scrap, ½ lb at $0.80	(0.40)
Net material cost	7.60
Direct labor and overhead	12.00
Total standard cost	19.60
Allowance for normal spoilage at 10% of good output	1.96
Adjusted cost	21.56
Less, estimated recovery of spoiled units at $1.50 × 10%	(0.15)
Standard cost	$21.41

In this example we ignore the differences among labor cost, variable overhead, and fixed overhead to concentrate on the subject at issue. The allowance for scrap indicates that a finished unit requires 3½ lb of material and ½ lb is normal scrap that can be resold for $0.80 per pound. The allowance for normal spoilage indicates that an amount equal to 10 percent of good output is spoiled under usual working conditions. These adjustments were covered in the chapter. The $0.15 recovery value of spoiled units requires a bit more consideration. Each spoiled unit can be sold for $1.50, and each good unit is normally accompanied by one-tenth of a spoiled unit (each ten good units by one spoiled unit), so that the average recovery per individual good unit is $0.15, 10 percent of $1.50. Accordingly, if all goes according to plan, each unit should cost $21.41 after allowing for the recovery of scrap material and spoiled units.

Suppose that the firm experienced the following results in March. There were no beginning or ending inventories.

Production of good units	2,000
Production of spoiled units	300
Materials used	9,100 lb
Direct labor and overhead costs	$29,500

First, we see that abnormal spoilage was 100 units [300 − 2,000(0.10)]. Using the technique illustrated in the chapter, we would compute the cost of abnormally spoiled units separately from efficiency variances. Accordingly, we could compute the following variances based on total production of 2,300 units.

$$\text{material use variance} = \$200 \text{ F} \quad [9,100 − 4(2,300)] \times \$2$$
$$\text{labor and overhead variances} = \$1,900 \text{ U} \quad [\$29,500 − \$12(2,300)]$$

We would then compute the abnormal spoilage variance as follows, using the total standard cost figure from the analysis above.

$$\text{abnormal spoilage variance} = \$1,960 \text{ U} \quad (\$19.60 \times 100)$$

The T-account for Work-in-Process Inventory would appear as follows, assuming no beginning or ending inventories.

Work-in-Process Inventory

Materials (9,100 × $2)	$18,200	$42,820	2,000 good units at $21.41
Other costs	29,500	1,960	Abnormal spoilage variance
Material use variance	200	1,900	Other cost variances
		920	Scrap recovery (2,300 × $0.40)
		300	Recovery of normal spoilage (2,000 × $0.15)
	$47,900	$47,900	

All the entries should be self-explanatory except the last two credits. The standard allowance for expected scrap recovery is based on the total number of good and spoiled units produced, consistent with the calculation of the material use variance based on the same amount of production. The entry representing the expected recovery on normally spoiled units is a bit different; its rationale is as follows. Good units leave Work-in-Process Inventory at standard cost, fully adjusted for recovery on normally spoiled units and scrap. However, the costs incurred should, at standard performance, amount to the gross cost, without allowance for recovery. Accordingly, the expected recovery must also come out of Work-in-Process Inventory in order that ending inventory reflect the standard cost of units still in process. In this example, no units remain and the balance should be zero.

The debits offsetting the two credits that we have just discussed could be to overhead accounts or to inventory accounts. Either way, the account would be credited when the scrap or spoiled units were sold. Using inventory accounts might be conceptually superior, but it might also be tedious and no more informative than using an overhead account.

The technique illustrated here is not the only one that could be used. Any technique must result in Work-in-Process Inventory being shown at standard cost, but otherwise there are no restrictions.

ASSIGNMENTS

10-1 **Basic Spoilage, Three Alternatives.** The Farnsworth Company makes machine parts. One department specializes in a small gear used in precision instruments. The gears are ground to small tolerances and are inspected at the end of the process. Spoiled gears must be thrown out. During March the department showed the following results:

Good gears completed	10,000
Spoiled gears	2,000
Ending inventory of work in process	3,000

Conversion costs in the beginning inventory and incurred during March totaled $81,420. The ending work-in-process inventory was 60 percent complete for conversion costs. We ignore materials to reduce calculations. The firm uses the weighted average method.

Required: Determine unit conversion costs, ending work-in-process inventory, and transfers to finished goods, under each of the following assumptions:

1. Spoilage is ignored.
2. Spoilage is considered normal and its cost is computed.
3. Spoilage is considered abnormal.

10-2 **Normal Spoilage, Comparison of Methods.** "I don't see why you go through all those calculations of spoiled units when it all comes out the same." Your boss made that comment to you as you were calculating the unit cost for the current period, as shown below. He went on: "Why don't you just ignore the spoiled units and calculate unit costs based on good output? It would work out the same, wouldn't it?"

Your firm uses the weighted average method and detects spoilage at the end of the process. Your calculations are:

	Materials	Conversion Costs
Units completed (good)	100,000	100,000
Ending inventories, 100% and 60% complete	20,000	12,000
Spoiled units (all normal)	10,000	10,000
Equivalent production	130,000	122,000
Total costs from beginning inventory and incurred during the period	$1,300,000	$1,830,000
Unit costs	$ 10	$ 15
Costs transferred to Finished Goods:		
Good units	$1,000,000	$1,500,000
Normal spoilage	100,000	150,000
Total	$1,100,000	$1,650,000
Ending Work-in-Process Inventory	$ 200,000	$ 180,000

Required:

1. Calculate unit costs, amounts transferred to Finished Goods, and ending Work-in-Process Inventory as your boss has suggested you do.

2. Comment on the differences between your calculations in item 1 and those in the problem.

10-3 Reducing Scrap Losses. The Gorgan Company makes a number of products out of sheet metal. The firm generally experiences scrap losses of about 20 percent of the total metal that it uses. The scrap sells for $0.60/lb and the firm now generates about 10,000 lb of scrap per month.

The production manager has been working on ways to cut the losses and has learned of a new process that he estimates could cut the company's losses to about 6 percent. The machinery required for the process costs $15,000 per month to rent. On average, the company pays $2.50/lb for sheet metal.

Required: Determine whether the firm should rent the machinery.

10-4 Abnormal Spoilage (FIFO). The Crittendon Company makes a single product. Data for August appear below.

Unit data:

Beginning inventory, work in process	1,200
Started in production	8,000
Completed, sent to finished goods	8,500
Ending inventory, work in process	500

Percentages complete:

	Materials	Conversion Costs
Beginning inventory	100%	70%
Ending inventory	100%	40%

Cost data:

	Materials	Conversion Costs
Beginning inventory	$ 4,120	$ 9,980
Current period costs	33,600	112,840

All spoilage is considered abnormal and its cost is expensed on the income statement for the month. Spoilage is detected at the end of the process. The firm uses FIFO.

Required:

1. Determine the number of units spoiled in August.
2. Determine the cost of spoiled goods, costs transferred from Work in Process to Finished Goods, and cost of ending inventory of work in process.

10–5   Abnormal Spoilage (Weighted Average)

Required: Repeat assignment 10–4 using the weighted average method instead of FIFO.

10–6   Spoilage, Normal and Abnormal (FIFO). The Barnett Company makes a single product. Data for March appear below.

Unit data:

Beginning inventory, work in process	2,000
Started in production	13,000
Completed, sent to finished goods	13,000
Ending inventory, work in process	1,200
Units spoiled	800

Cost data:

	Materials	Conversion Costs
Beginning inventory	$ 79,000	$ 91,080
Current-period costs	611,000	1,172,160

Normal spoilage is 500 units. All inventories were 100 percent complete for materials, 60 percent for conversion costs. All spoilage is detected at the end of the process. The firm uses FIFO.

Required: Determine the costs of normal spoilage, abnormal spoilage, ending Work-in-Process Inventory, and transfers to Finished Goods. Be sure that you account for all costs, beginning inventory, and current-period costs.

10–7 **Spoilage, Normal and Abnormal (Weighted Average)**

Required: Repeat assignment 10–6 using the weighted average method instead of FIFO.

10–8 **Evaporation.** The Kermit Company makes a number of products, one of which is an industrial cleaning liquid used to remove grease from machinery and floors. The firm heats the ingredients for 2½ hours, resulting in considerable evaporation. The plant's industrial engineers have been working on ways to reduce evaporation and have found that using some more expensive ingredients and heating the mixture for a longer period, but at lower temperatures, reduces the loss considerably.

The plant manager and controller have assembled the following data.

	Existing Process	Proposed Process
Cost of ingredients per 10,000-gal batch	$480	$515
Heating time in hours	2.5	2.8
Cost of heating at $300/hr	$750	$840
Yield in gallons[a]	8,100–8,300	8,950–9,050

[a] The yields generally fall evenly throughout the ranges given.

Required:

1. On the basis of the information given, determine whether the firm should adopt the proposed process.

2. Suppose that the $300 cost per hour contains a fixed component of $200 per hour. Determine whether the firm should adopt the process.

3. Suppose that the cost structure is the same as in item 2, and that you have the following additional information.

Selling price per gallon	$0.22
Additional variable costs per gallon	0.03
Capacity in batches per week	20 batches

The firm can sell all the cleaner it can produce. Determine whether the firm should adopt the process.

4. Assume the data from item 3 except that the capacity of the heating operation is 60 hr per week. The firm cannot process a fractional batch. Determine whether the firm should adopt the new process.

10–9   Tracing Normal Spoilage. The Argon Company produces a single type of fountain pen in a single process. The firm experiences normal spoilage of 5 percent of good output, detected at the end of the process. During the process, materials and conversion costs are continuous, so that we need consider only total costs. Additionally, all of the production costs are variable. The firm began April with no work-in-process inventory, completed 200,000 good units during the month, spoiled 10,000, and had 21,000 units 40 percent complete at the end of the month. Total production costs were $2,184,000.

Required:

1. Determine the firm's equivalent production, considering normal spoilage.

2. Determine the cost of the ending work-in-process inventory and the cost transferred to Finished Goods.

3. Given that normal spoilage is 5 percent of good output, and assuming that April costs are under control, what is the unit cost per *good* unit? Does this unit cost correspond to the costs transferred to finished goods from your answer to item 2?

4. How many of the units in ending work-in-process inventory should turn out to be spoiled? Does the cost-per-good unit that you computed in item 3 correspond to the unit cost of the ending Work-in-Process Inventory, considering that work in process is only 40 percent complete?

10–10   Scrap and Decisions. The Wilson Millwork Company makes a variety of wooden products including doors, windows, framing studs, and plywood. It also collects a great deal of scrap wood and sawdust from its cutting and finishing operations. In the past, the firm has burned the scrap and sawdust, but its managers are now considering alternatives. Other firms are willing to buy the scrap and sawdust at a price of about $4.80 per ton. These firms would grind up the scraps and form the resulting sawdust into pellets to burn in their furnaces. Wood pellets provide substantial quantities of heat and are often more economical than coal or oil.

Wilson Millwork's chief engineer has suggested that the firm consider burning its waste wood, rather than selling it. Wilson Millwork could have another firm grind and pelletize its scrap for about $2.10 per ton, including freight both ways. Wilson now uses coal, which costs about $23 per ton and provides about three times as many BTUs as wood pellets. In other words, Wilson Millwork would need to use three tons of pellets to replace one ton of coal.

The plant produces about 220 tons of scrap and sawdust per month and uses about 150 tons of coal, so it could not satisfy all of its needs from its own scrap and would continue to use some coal.

The controller has developed the following information regarding the choices.

	Wood Products	Scrap and Sawdust	Total
Sales value	$319,500	$1,056	$320,556
Total costs	275,390	910	276,300
Profit	$ 44,110	$ 146	$ 44,256

The controller allocated all costs to the products using the relative sales value method. He felt that because scrap and sawdust arose from nearly all the firm's operations, it was proper to consider all costs to be joint. Thus, the $910 is given by $276,300 × ($1,056/$320,556). His next step was to develop the analysis shown below, that indicates that the firm would save $1,079 per month by having scrap and sawdust pelletized and burned in its own furnaces.

Sales value of scrap and sawdust	$1,056
Cost	910
Profit from sales	146
Cost of pelletizing 220 tons × $2.10	462
Total cost	608
Savings on coal, 220/3 × $23	1,687
Net benefit of pelletizing	$1,079

Required: Analyze the controller's work to determine whether it is appropriate. Calculate the monthly advantage or disadvantage of pelletizing in the manner you believe correct, if you disagree with the controller's work.

10–11 **Tracing Spoilage in a Standard Costing System (appendix).**   The Trotter Company makes a single model of table. The firm usually experiences one spoiled table for each ten good ones made. Without considering any allowance for spoilage, the table has a standard variable cost of $50. (We limit the analysis to variable costs for simplicity and to focus on the main point.) Spoiled tables sell for $10.

During April the firm made 1,100 tables, of which 1,000 were good, the other 100 spoiled. Total variable costs incurred were $55,000.

Required:

1. Determine the standard cost of a table, using the 10 percent spoilage rate to set an allowance for spoiled units.

2. Reconcile the difference between the standard cost of good tables and the total actual variable cost incurred.

10–12 **Tracing Spoilage in a Standard Costing System (appendix).**   Refer to the data from the previous problem. Suppose that in May the firm made 1,000 good tables, 125 spoiled ones. Total variable costs were $56,250.

Required:

1. Compute the abnormal spoilage variance.
2. Reconcile the total actual variable costs with the standard cost of the good tables produced.

10–13 **Tracing Scrap in a Standard Costing System (appendix).** The Marlowe Company makes a lamp that consists mainly of sheet metal, cut and formed. The firm buys sheets that are 8 ft by 4 ft and cuts enough pieces for two lamps from each piece. The remainder, which is 2 sq ft, sells as scrap for $0.50 ($0.25/sq ft). Each lamp, then, requires 15 sq ft. A sheet of 32 sq ft costs $64.

During the month of July the firm made 1,000 lamps. It used 500 sheets and sold the scrap for $250. It used exactly 15,000 sq ft to make the lamps and had 1,000 sq ft of scrap.

Required:

1. Compute the standard materials cost per lamp.
2. Verify that the firm did not have a material use variance in July. That is, determine the total standard material cost for 1,000 lamps, the total cost of metal used at the standard price, and reconcile the difference, if any.

10–14 **Tracing Scrap in a Standard Costing System (appendix).** Refer to the data for assignment 10–13. Suppose that in August the firm made 1,000 lamps using 510 sheets of material.

Required: Compute the actual cost of materials, the standard cost of materials, and the material use variance. Reconcile the difference between the actual cost and the standard cost of materials.

10–15 **Spoilage and Standards.** The Layton Millwork Company uses standard costs with no allowances for spoilage, even though its managers expect that spoilage will normally amount to 15 percent of the number of good units produced. The firm detects spoilage at the end of the production process. The standard costs for materials and labor of one product made in a single department are given below.

Materials, 12 lb at $4/lb	$48
Direct labor, ½ hr at $10/hr	5

During a recent month the department produced 500 good units and 90 spoiled ones. It used 7,000 lb of material and 300 direct labor hours. These variances appeared on the performance report of the department manager.

Material use variance	$4,000 unfavorable
Direct labor efficiency variance	$500 unfavorable

Required:

1. Determine how the variances given above were calculated.

2. Assuming that the 15 percent spoilage rate represents currently attainable performance, evaluate the performance of the department. Support your contentions with appropriate calculations.

10–16 Lost Units, Comparison of Methods. The Norwalk Chemical Company manufactures a number of products in different plants. The Eastbourne Plant makes polycoat, which is used in the making of furniture waxes. The controller of the plant has been ignoring spoilage, which takes place in the form of evaporation. The plant engineers usually determine whether or not the amount of evaporation is within normal limits and take corrective action if it is not. In any case, the controller considers all evaporation to be normal and simply does not count it in determining unit costs.

The controller recently attended a seminar where a speaker argued that it was wise to calculate the cost of spoilage because it gave managers more information than they would otherwise have. The controller decided to try it using the prior month's data, but was unsure how to proceed. The data appear below.

Inventory at beginning of month, gallons	14,000
Gallons put into production	120,000
Gallons completed and sent to finished goods	102,000
Gallons in ending inventory	20,000
Gallons lost in processing	12,000
Cost of beginning inventory:	
Materials	$ 29,900
Conversion costs	51,300
Current-period costs:	
Materials	239,500
Conversion costs	732,600

Inventories were complete with respect to materials at the beginning and ending of the month. The beginning inventory was 60 percent complete for conversion costs and the ending inventory 40 percent complete. The firm uses FIFO. The plant engineers believe that the losses take place very near the end of the production process, largely because of overheating.

Required:

1. Calculate the unit costs of production, both materials and conversion costs, ignoring the lost units, as the controller has been doing.

2. Calculate the unit costs of production, both materials and conversion costs, including the lost units.

3. Looking at the results in items 1 and 2, do you see any advantage to using one method or the other?

10–17 Scrap, Spoilage, and Standards. "I'm really confused," said Bob Gibbons, the production manager of the Rivers Manufacturing Company. He went on to explain:

> The reports I get always show unfavorable variances from standard costs, but the controller tells me not to worry unless they are 10 percent or more. He says that we expect some scrap and spoilage and that he considers them when he looks at variances. The thing is, I have no idea whether 10 percent is reasonable or not. I do know that we have perfectly normal scrap losses of about 8 percent of the total material that we use in production and that we spoil units equal to about 10 percent of our good output when we are operating at normal efficiency. It would be costly to reduce scrap or spoilage any more, so we don't try. But I have a devil of a time trying to figure out whether or not we are operating at normal efficiency.

The standard cost of a unit of product appears below, with no adjustments for scrap or spoilage, as used by the firm.

Materials, 10 lb at $2	$20
Direct labor, 2 hr at $12	24
Overhead at $15 per direct labor hour	30
Total standard cost	$74

During the most recent month, Gibbons received a report that contained the following information:

Units produced, good	1,000
Spoiled units	120

Costs were reported as follows:

	Standard for 1,000 Units	Actual Costs at Standard Prices	Unfavorable Variances
Materials	$20,000	$25,000	$5,000
Direct labor	24,000	26,500	2,500
Overhead	30,000	31,400	1,400
Total unfavorable variances			$8,900

The firm includes only variable costs in the standard cost. There is no recovery of scrap or spoilage. The production manager is not responsible for prices, so that the actual costs at standard prices figures represent actual quantities of inputs at standard prices for the input factors.

Required:

1. Compute revised standard costs reflecting the normal scrap and normal spoilage.

2. Compute a new set of variances that will be more informative to Gibbons and the controller.

10-18 **Spoilage and Process Costing.** Eatright Manufacturing presents the following information for February, 19X7.

Beginning inventory—work in process:
Materials	$27,850
Conversion costs	40,800

(1600 units 75% complete for materials and 60% complete in conversion costs)

Ending inventory—work in process:
(2000 units 50% complete in materials and 40% complete in conversion costs)

Units put into production during February	13,600
Units completed during February	12,000

Current production costs:
Materials	$290,000
Conversion costs	$525,000

Assume that spoilage occurs and is identified on average when units are 50 percent complete both for materials and conversion costs.

Required:

1. How many units were spoiled? What does this translate to in equivalent units?
2. If Eatright uses weighted average and accounts for this spoilage as abnormal, what is the value of ending inventory—work in process for February?
3. If Eatright uses FIFO and accounts for this spoilage as normal and ignores it, what costs are transferred to finished goods?
4. If the company followed the procedure in item 2, what would be the journal entry to record the month end events?

10-19 **Spoilage and Decisions.** The superintendent of the Walpole Plant of BGH, Inc., has been unhappy with the spoilage rate, which currently runs about 15 percent of good output. He believes that inspecting units midway through the process would reduce the rate to about 5 percent. (Spoilage is now detected at the end of the process.) He believes that most spoilage results from small flaws that show up soon after the units start into process. Correcting these flaws at the midway point would be relatively easy.

It would cost about $8,500 per month to maintain a testing station. This cost includes the additional labor that would be needed to correct the flaws detected at the station. Data for a typical month appear at the top of page 421.

Good output, units	60,000
Spoiled output	9,000
Monthly costs:	
Materials	$147,000
Conversion	$303,000

At the current level of output, about 30 percent of conversion costs are fixed.

Required: Determine whether the firm should set up the testing station.

10–20 Abnormal Spoilage, Two Departments (AICPA adapted). The Dexter Production Company makes a single product, using a machining process and a finishing process. Company records for June, 19X4, showed the following.

	Machining Department	Finishing Department
Units in process, June 1	0	0
Units transferred from prior department	0	60,000
Units started in production	80,000	0
Units completed and transferred out	60,000	50,000
Units in process, June 30	20,000	8,000
Percentages of completion of June 30 work-in-process inventories:		
Materials	100%	100%
Conversion costs	60%	70%

Spoiled units have no salvage value and are 50 percent complete with respect to materials and conversion costs. The firm's policy is to charge all spoilage to expense because all spoilage is considered abnormal.

Cost records showed the following for June.

	Machining Department	Finishing Department
Materials	$240,000	$ 88,500
Conversion costs	216,000	164,140

Required:

1. For the machining department, determine the cost of ending inventory and of units transferred to the finishing department.

2. For the finishing department, determine the cost of ending inventory, the cost of units transferred to finished goods inventory, and the cost of abnormal spoilage.

10–21 Scrap, Spoilage, and Standards. "The reports I get just don't help me to control my operations," lamented Bill Halston, the manager of the Conway plant of Temco Products Company. Temco was a diversified company; the Conway plant concentrated on metal products. The plant had begun to use a standard costing system in the prior year, and the reports based on the system were given to Halston, several other managers at the plant, and to corporate headquarters.

Halston went on:

> I really can't see that the standard costing system is doing us any good. You look at these figures and see that we seem to be using too much material every period, but that's because the standards don't include any allowance for scrap and spoilage. In an operation like ours, you cannot get finished parts out of every foot of rod. You have to take the rod in the lengths that the suppliers provide, so there is some loss in trimming. You always spoil a few parts at the start of each run, and there is also some unavoidable spoilage because of the nature of the process. My controller knows this, but he says that we should strive for less scrap and spoilage and that using standards that don't consider them will be better for motivation. I couldn't agree less, but he is appointed by headquarters and what he says goes as far as accounting is concerned.

Standard costs developed by the controller for two high-volume parts appear below, per 100 units of each part.

	Part Number	
	65-388	65-041
Materials, steel rod at $0.90/ft	$10.80	$12.60
Direct labor at $8/hr	4.80	5.60
Factory overhead at $16/DLH	9.60	11.20
Totals	$25.20	$29.40

Before these standards were developed, an industrial engineer had studied the production process at the Conway plant. Among other things, he concluded that scrap of about 1 ft of rod per 100 units of part 65-388 and 1.4 ft per 100 units of part 65-041 was unavoidable because of the trimming needed. He also believed that spoilage of about 10 percent of good output should be considered normal and no cause for alarm. Spoilage was detected at the end of the process and consisted primarily of units that were improperly shaped or had sustained cracks at joints.

Scrap rod and spoiled units could be sold for the value of the metal, which usually ran about $0.10 per pound. The rod weighed 1 lb per foot.

The data at the top of page 423 are illustrative of the information that Halston received each month.

Scrap sales, both trimmed rod and spoiled units, are generally made about twice a month and consist of the scrap accumulated during the time since the latest sale. Accordingly, they do not usually reflect the scrap and spoilage that occurred during the production for the month.

	Production, in Hundreds of Units		
	Good Output	Spoiled Output	Total
Part 65-388	22,500	3,000	25,000
Part 65-041	19,600	2,050	21,650

Material use	651,000 ft
Material price	$0.92/ft
Direct labor hours	30,040
Direct labor cost	$242,300
Factory overhead	$468,350

Variances

Materials	$108,960 U
Direct labor	24,540 U
Factory overhead	32,830 U
Total	166,330
Less, scrap and spoilage sales	8,650
Net variances	$157,680

Required:

1. Explain the variances shown above by analyzing them into price and quantity variances, so far as is possible with the data. Ignore allowances for spoilage.

2. Prepare standard costs for each part based on the information available regarding normal scrap and spoilage.

3. Prepare a new set of variances that will indicate better how well the plant performed during the month.

4. What suggestions would you make beyond those implicit in your answers to the above requirements?

Variable Costing

Chapter 11

Chapters 5, 6, and 8 presented the basics of absorption costing for actual, normal, and standard costing in both job order and process situations. Chapters 2 and 4 stressed a contribution margin approach to the determination of net income, with all fixed costs shown as expenses on the income statement. This chapter focuses on a product costing technique that is consistent with a contribution margin approach. The method is called **variable costing** or **direct costing.** The essence of the method is that it excludes fixed production costs from the inventory flow and valuation, treating them as expenses in the period incurred. The income statements for manufacturers that we prepared in Chapters 2 and 4 were variable-costing income statements. The technique, therefore, is not new.

Because variable costing stresses contribution margin and shows total fixed costs as expenses, it is more compatible with managerial analyses than is absorption costing. For example, cost-volume-profit analyses cannot readily be made using absorption costing. It is possible to develop contribution margin information from an absorption costing system by isolating fixed and variable costs. However, income determined under absorption costing will be affected not only by the level of sales, but also by the level of production. Under variable costing, income is strictly a function of sales and is unaffected by production levels. This is a significant advantage for variable costing, as we shall see shortly.

While variable costing is not acceptable for financial reporting and tax purposes, it may be used for internal reporting, since generally accepted accounting principles and tax law have no effect on internal reporting. Therefore, some firms will use variable costing for internal purposes and switch to absorption costing for financial reporting and income tax accounting. Variable costing is a complete alternative to absorption costing. It can be used by job order firms and by processing firms. It can be used with actual, normal, or standard costing.

Until now we have considered costing systems in two basic ways. A system is job order or process depending on whether costs are accumulated by individual unit or batch of units, or by department for each period. A system is actual, normal, or standard depending on whether unit costs contained actual costs for all inputs, actual labor and materials with a predetermined overhead rate, or standard costs for all inputs. We now have a third type of classification: whether the system includes fixed costs in the determination of inventory cost per unit for internal reporting purposes.

All product costing systems must include a selection from each of these three dimensions.

Production Method	Type of Costs	Treatment of Fixed Costs
Job order	Actual	Absorption
Process	Normal	Variable
	Standard	

Thus, a system can be actual variable process costing, normal absorption job order costing, and so forth.

ABSORPTION COSTING, INCOME, AND PRODUCTION

The data in Exhibit 11–1 relate to the operations of the Coulson Company for a two-month period. The firm uses standard absorption costing and writes off application variances as a separate expense on the income statement each month. The income statements given in Exhibit 11–1 conform to the firm's policies. In this illustration we assume that there are no variances from standard variable costs and no fixed cost budget variances.

The statements in Exhibit 11–1 show an interesting result. Income decreased in April even though sales increased. This result is counterintuitive, because we would expect income to increase if sales increased and the cost structure remained constant. The reason for this result is that production was higher in March than in April, so that a good portion of the fixed production costs incurred in March were deferred in ending inventory. Because sales were higher than production in April, the total fixed costs expensed on the income statement exceeded the amount incurred, a point we shall return to shortly. If we prepared income statements using standard variable costing and the data from Exhibit 11–1, they would appear as shown in Exhibit 11–2 on page 428.

Comparing Exhibits 11–1 and 11–2 reveals the following points. First, both methods exclude selling and administrative expenses from inventory. These costs are expensed on the income statement in the period incurred. Using language from financial accounting, selling and administrative costs are period costs, not product costs. Second, under absorption costing, some or all of both fixed and variable manufacturing costs are considered to be product costs. In this example, all standard manufacturing costs are treated as product costs, with variances treated as expenses of the period. Variances could also be prorated to inventories and cost of sales as illustrated in Chapter 8. Then all manufacturing costs would be treated as product costs,

EXHIBIT 11-1
Operating Data and Income Statements—Coulson Company

Unit Data

	March	April
Beginning inventory	0	3,000
Production	12,000	9,000
Total available	12,000	12,000
Sales	9,000	10,000
Ending inventory	3,000	2,000

Cost and Price Data

	March	April
Sales at $15 per unit	$135,000	$150,000
Variable production costs at $6	72,000	54,000
Variable selling costs at $1	9,000	10,000
Fixed production costs	40,000	40,000
Fixed selling and administrative expenses	20,000	20,000

Standard cost of goods sold is $10; $6 variable plus $4 fixed based on $40,000 monthly budgeted fixed production costs and 10,000 units normal activity.

Income Statements

	March	April
Sales	$135,000	$150,000
Beginning inventory	0	30,000
Current-period production costs:		
Variable at $6 per unit	72,000	54,000
Fixed, applied at $4 per unit	48,000	36,000
Totals	120,000	120,000
Ending inventory at $10 per unit	30,000	20,000
Standard cost of sales at $10 per unit	90,000	100,000
Application variance[a]	8,000 F	4,000 U
Actual cost of sales	82,000	104,000
Gross margin	53,000	46,000
Selling and administrative expenses	29,000	30,000
Income	$ 24,000	$ 16,000

[a] $(10,000 - 12,000) \times \$4 = \$8,000F; (10,000 - 9,000) \times \$4 = \$4,000U.$

EXHIBIT 11–2
Income Statements, Variable Costing—Coulson Company

		March		April
Sales		$135,000		$150,000
Beginning inventory	0		$18,000	
Variable production costs	$72,000		54,000	
Total available for sale	72,000		72,000	
Ending inventory at $6/unit	18,000		12,000	
Variable cost of sales		54,000		60,000
Variable gross margin		81,000		90,000
Variable selling expenses		9,000		10,000
Contribution margin		72,000		80,000
Fixed costs:				
Production	$40,000		$40,000	
Selling and administrative	20,000	60,000	20,000	60,000
Income		$ 12,000		$ 20,000

because prorating variances essentially converts standard costing to actual costing. Under variable costing, the only costs considered to be product costs are the variable manufacturing costs, with fixed manufacturing costs treated as period costs. The treatment of fixed manufacturing costs gives rise to the differences in incomes under the two methods.

We pointed out earlier that under absorption costing, income is affected by the level of production as well as by the level of sales. That is not true under variable costing. Income under variable costing can be determined using the basic cost-volume-profit equation from Chapter 2. Thus, in March, variable costing income is given by:

$$\text{sales} \quad - \text{ variable costs} - \text{ fixed costs} = \text{ income}$$
$$(9{,}000 \times \$15) - (9{,}000 \times \$7) - \quad \$60{,}000 \quad = \$12{,}000$$

Notice that production data are not required, only sales and cost data. Notice also that what we subtract from sales is not total variable costs incurred, but rather variable cost per unit multiplied by unit sales. Variable costing does recognize inventories: some of the variable manufacturing costs incurred during a period are deferred in inventory. However, all fixed manufacturing costs are expensed.

Exhibit 11–3 shows how the level of production influences income under absorption costing. The level of production determines how much fixed manufacturing cost is deferred in inventory at the end of a period. When production exceeds sales (inventory increases), then the amount of fixed cost expensed through cost of sales and application variances is less than the amount incurred during the period. When sales exceed production (inventory decreases), the reverse is true. When sales equal production, the amount of fixed costs expensed equals the amount incurred, and absorption costing income will then equal variable costing income. (A review problem coming up shortly illustrates this point.)

EXHIBIT 11–3
Reconciliation of Absorption Costing and Variable Costing Incomes—Coulson Company

Flows of Fixed Production Costs—
Absorption Costing

	March	April
Fixed production costs in beginning inventory	0	$12,000
Fixed production costs incurred during period	$40,000	40,000
Totals	40,000	52,000
Fixed production costs in ending inventory[a]	12,000	8,000
Fixed production costs expensed during period[b]	$28,000	$44,000

Flows of Fixed Production Costs—
Variable Costing

	March	April
Fixed production costs expensed during period	$40,000	$40,000
Differences, equal differences in incomes for periods	($12,000)	$ 4,000

[a] Inventories: end of March, 3,000 units at $4 standard fixed cost = $12,000; end of April, 2,000 units at $4 = $8,000.
[b] These figures may also be found by taking the amount of standard fixed costs included in cost of goods sold for each month plus the unfavorable application variance or minus the favorable application variance for the month. In March, fixed production costs, at standard, in cost of sales were $36,000 (9,000 × $4) and the application variance was $8,000 favorable, giving the $28,000 total fixed production costs expensed in March.

Under standard costing, the difference in income between variable and absorption costing can be calculated simply by using the following formula:

$$ ACI - VCI = \left(\begin{array}{c} \text{increase in inventory} \\ \text{in units} \end{array} \right) \times \left(\begin{array}{c} \text{standard fixed} \\ \text{cost per unit} \end{array} \right) $$

where ACI = income under absorption costing
        VCI = income under variable costing

Naturally, if inventory in units decreases, then variable costing income is greater than absorption costing income. This formula also presupposes that the standard fixed cost-per-unit figure used for the beginning inventory is the same as the one used for the ending inventory. Applying the formula for March and April gives:

$$\text{March} = (3{,}000 \times \$4) = \$12{,}000$$
$$\text{April} = (-1{,}000 \times \$4) = -\$4{,}000$$

This type of reconciliation suggests an alternative way to handle the problem of possible misinterpretations of absorption costing results. The accountant could prepare an absorption costing income statement that had an adjustment for the change in fixed costs in inventory at the bottom, giving as a final figure the income that would have been shown had the firm used variable costing. The income statements given in Exhibit 11–1 would then have the following format.

	March	April
Absorption Costing Income (last line from Exhibit 11–1)	$24,000	$16,000
Inventory adjustment for fixed costs	(12,000)	4,000
Variable Costing Income	$12,000	$20,000

The advantage of such a presentation is that it highlights the effect on income of the change in fixed costs in the inventories. Therefore, it allows the manager to see how the firm's production affected its income as reported using absorption costing.

Review Problem: Coulson Company

Suppose that in May the Coulson Company produced and sold 10,000 units. The cost structure remained the same as in the previous months (variable cost per unit and total fixed costs). Prepare income statements for May using absorption costing and variable costing. The solution appears in Exhibit 11–4.

Exhibit 11–4 shows that when production and sales are equal, incomes under the two methods will be the same. This is true so long as standard costing (or normal costing) is used and the fixed cost per unit does not change from the prior period to the current period. Both methods will give the same total incomes over the life of a firm, since at both the beginning and end of its life a firm will have no inventory. However, at any time during the firm's life when it does have inventory, cumulative income under absorption costing will be higher than cumulative income under variable costing. Over a period of time during the firm's life (such as a year or five years), if its inventories and cost structure remain relatively stable, incomes under the two methods for that period will be about the same. If fixed costs rise over time, the difference between absorption costing and variable costing inventories and incomes will widen, even if the physical amount of inventory remains reasonably constant.

EXHIBIT 11–4
Income Statements—Coulson Company

Absorption Costing				Variable Costing			
Sales			$150,000	Sales			$150,000
Beginning inventory	$20,000			Beginning inventory	$12,000		
Production costs:				Variable production costs	60,000		
Variable	60,000			Total	72,000		
Fixed	40,000			Ending inventory	12,000	60,000	
Total	120,000			Variable gross margin		90,000	
Ending inventory	20,000	100,000		Variable selling expenses		10,000	
Standard gross profit		50,000		Contribution margin		80,000	
Selling and administrative							
expenses		30,000		Fixed costs		60,000	
Income		$20,000		Income		$20,000	

ACTUAL COSTING RESULTS

If the Coulson Company used actual costing, it would not show application variances as expenses but would prorate them to inventory and cost of sales. Similarly, if it experienced other production cost variances, it would prorate them as well. If the application variance were quite large, there might be a significant difference between actual and standard absorption costing. Actual and standard variable costing results would differ significantly only if there were large variable cost variances. A large fixed overhead budget variance would not result in actual and standard variable costing incomes being different because it would always be shown as an expense.

Suppose that the Coulson Company establishes a standard variable production cost of $6 per unit and budgeted fixed monthly production costs of $40,000, which are the actual costs used in the earlier examples. During October the firm had the following results. There was no beginning inventory.

Production	12,000 units
Sales at $15 per unit	9,000 units
Variable production costs	$73,500
Fixed production costs	$39,500
Total selling and administrative expenses	$29,000

Income statements using actual and standard absorption costing appear in Exhibit 11–5, along with statements using actual and standard variable costing. The results above show the same production and sales as in March of the original example (refer to Exhibit 11–1). The difference is that in October there are production cost variances netting $1,000 unfavorable (variable cost variances and fixed overhead budget variance). Income under standard variable costing is exactly $1,000 less in October than it was in March, reflecting these variances. Income under standard absorption costing is also $1,000 less than it was in March, reflecting those same variances.

Notice that the fixed overhead budget variance is shown separately in both variable costing income statements. Even though the firm might prepare variable costing income statements based on actual costs, rather than standard costs, it might still show variances as separate items or as supplementary information. Variable costing income statements are intended for managerial use and should therefore be as informative as possible. It is informative to know whether or not fixed overhead costs were incurred as budgeted.

TERMINOLOGY–DIRECT COSTING AND VARIABLE COSTING

Many accountants and businesspeople use the term direct costing to refer to what we have been calling variable costing. Dictionaries of accounting terms usually define the two as synonyms. We have chosen variable costing because it seems to be more descriptive of the cost system. Some variable production costs are direct, such as direct materials and direct labor. Others, however, such as the variable portions of indirect labor, supplies, maintenance, and power, are not direct to individual units of product. These costs will vary with the amount of production but cannot be traced to specific units. Thus, the term direct costing, which implies that only direct costs are included in inventory, is potentially confusing because some variable costs are indirect.

Another source of potential confusion in using the term direct costing goes back to earlier discussions of separable and joint costs. Separable costs can be fixed or variable depending on the segment being examined (product, department, plant, etc.) and can be thought of as direct to that segment. Fixed production costs may be direct to the period, or to the product, but not to individual units of product. Thus, supervisory salaries are direct to the department in which the supervisor works and to the entire period's production taken as a whole, but not to any specific unit of product. Although both terms are widely used, variable costing seems to be more descriptive and less confusing than direct costing.

EXHIBIT 11–5
Income Statements for October—Coulson Company

Variable Costing

	Standard Costing	Actual Costing
Sales, 9,000 × $15	$135,000	$135,000
Variable cost of sales:		
Production costs	72,000	73,500
Ending inventory[a]	18,000	18,375
Variable cost of sales	54,000	55,125
Variable gross margin	81,000	79,875
Variable production cost variances	1,500 U	—
Actual variable gross margin	79,500	79,875
Variable selling and administrative costs	9,000	9,000
Contribution margin	70,500	70,875
Fixed production costs, budgeted	40,000	40,000
Budget variance	500 F	500 F
Selling and administrative costs, fixed	20,000	20,000
Total fixed costs	59,500	59,500
Income	$11,000	$11,375

Absorption Costing

	Standard Costing	Actual Costing
Sales 9,000 × $15	$135,000	$135,000
Production costs:		
Fixed	48,000	39,500
Variable	72,000	73,500
Total available for sale	120,000	113,000
Ending inventory[b]	30,000	28,250
Cost of sales	90,000	84,750
Gross margin	45,000	50,250
Production cost variances:		
Variable cost variance	1,500 U	
Application variance	8,000 F	
Fixed cost budget variance	500 F	
Actual gross margin	52,000	50,250
Selling and administrative costs	29,000	29,000
Income	$23,000	$21,250

[a] $73,500/12,000 = $6.125 × 3,000 = $18,375.
[b] $113,000/12,000 = $9.4167 × 3,000 = $28,250.

EVALUATION OF METHODS

Two considerations are involved in evaluating variable costing and absorption costing: their relative suitabilities for internal and for financial reporting purposes. These two purposes must be separated, because different factors influence the arguments supporting each of the two methods. Some accountants may favor variable costing for internal purposes, absorption costing for financial reporting.

Internal Reporting—Absorption Costing

Proponents of absorption costing for internal reporting purposes do not deny the importance of contribution margin and the related concepts of cost behavior for planning and some decision making. Virtually all accountants would agree that an isolated short-term tactical decision should be based on contribution margin and any incremental fixed costs involved. That is, if the decision will have no effects beyond its immediate, direct ones, it should be based on incremental profit.

Those who prefer absorption costing point out that concentrating on contribution margin, and therefore on variable costs, may be habit forming. They foresee managers applying the contribution margin criterion to normal, recurring decisions—with potentially disastrous effects. Pricing policy is one area where such effects are likely to be felt. Managers who concentrate on contribution margin may tend to price products so low that the firm cannot recover its fixed costs and earn a satisfactory profit in the long term.

A proponent of absorption costing would go on to point out that all costs are variable in the long run. Commitments in fixed assets and manpower levels may be adjusted over time so that capacity may be set at any desired level, given time to adjust. Fixed costs are largely a function of long-term commitments, and for the most part these are the ones that can get firms into trouble. Variable costs represent short-term commitments—hours of labor time, kilograms of materials, and so on. These commitments do not have the same potential for plunging the firm into bankruptcy as do the long-term commitments represented by fixed costs. Accordingly, managers should always bear in mind the possible consequences of fixed costs, and the best way for them to do so is to use absorption costing. This argument is heavily behavioral, focusing on the possible unfavorable effects of managers' failing to consider fixed costs.

Another argument advanced by proponents of absorption costing is that variable costing does not necessarily provide information about incremental costs. Fixed costs may change if the level of production moves from one relevant range to another. Step-variable (or step-fixed) costs such as supervision may change with fairly small changes in the level of output. Therefore, to limit product costs to those that are strictly variable is to misstate the actual cost behavior of the firm.

Finally, it may be argued that absorption costing data should be used to set fair and equitable prices. We saw in earlier chapters that firms may set prices based on the variable costs of production plus allowances for fixed production costs, selling and administrative expenses, and a profit margin.[1] Pricing formulas such as variable cost plus 15 percent for overhead and 10 percent for profit are not uncommon. Using variable costing data to set prices may be unfair if different products use different amounts of fixed assets and, therefore, different amounts of fixed cost. For example, if a firm sets prices at 250 percent of variable cost, it may, the argument goes, be charging some customers too little and some too much. Products that require substantial investment in fixed assets should be priced higher than those that do not, so that they bear a fair share of the costs associated with the higher investment.

Internal Reporting – Variable Costing

Proponents of variable costing argue that it does not downplay the importance of fixed costs: it shows them clearly on the income statement as a single figure (or as several figures) in one place, highlighting their impact on profits. They argue that the *total* fixed costs are important, not per-unit amounts that can change with changes in volume under actual costing. Even under normal and standard costing, the total of the fixed costs applied to product on a per-unit basis may not equal the total incurred costs. With absorption costing, fixed costs show up in cost of sales and in application variances, which makes it difficult to determine their overall impact.

Advocates of variable costing also point out that absorption costing is inconsistent with determining a full cost, since it does not unitize selling, general, and administrative expenses, which may be quite large in relation to manufacturing costs. Thus, managers who consider per-unit fixed production costs in pricing decisions are not including all the costs that must be covered to earn a profit.

Advocates of variable costing do argue that prices should be set to recover fixed costs and provide a profit. They do not see that unitizing fixed costs is useful in such decisions. Consider a multiproduct firm. Fixed costs will be allocated to product lines and then to units of product. Suppose that a particular product shows a loss on an absorption costing basis but does have a positive incremental profit (contribution margin less avoidable fixed costs). A manager might be tempted to raise the price of the product to make it pay its way. The economic law of demand states that as prices rise, the quantity demanded falls, and vice versa. We might then expect to see a decline in volume of the product. The decline might more than offset the increased price, so that incremental profit drops. The decline would also trigger reallocation of fixed costs, which would affect the apparent profitability of other products. If the absorption cost results after the price increase

---

[1] Chapters 2, 5, and 6 made this point.

were worse than before, the manager might raise the price again or even consider dropping the product, both of which could be very unwise decisions.

Prices can be set using variable costing data and considering total fixed costs. Again, no one argues that fixed costs are unimportant, only that they should not be expressed as per-unit amounts, because doing so fulfills no useful purpose.

A final argument is that variable costing is better for evaluating the effects of decisions. Most firms will perform post-audits of decisions, especially major decisions. Managers will determine whether the decision worked out as expected and, if not, what adaptive and corrective actions need to be undertaken and what lessons can be learned for use in making future decisions. A manager who has determined a product mix using linear programming would be able to evaluate the results of this decision and determine whether things went according to plan using variable costing. It would be more difficult to do so using absorption costing.

Consider the simple situation depicted in the partial income statements below. The firm uses standard absorption costing, and one of its managers is considering a request for a special order of 10,000 units at $12 each. The order would not affect sales at regular prices and, because variable costs are $5 per unit, the manager believes that the sale would be wise. Because inventory is high, the order would be filled from inventory.

	Without Special Order	With Special Order
Sales: 80,000 at $20	$1,600,000	
80,000 at $20, 10,000 at $12		$1,720,000
Standard cost of sales at $13[a]	1,040,000	1,170,000
Standard gross margin	$ 560,000	$ 550,000

[a] Standard variable cost is $5, standard fixed cost $8 based on $800,000 budgeted fixed manufacturing costs and 100,000 units normal activity. Production for the period is 100,000 units, so there is no application variance.

These results suggest that the firm would lose money on the special order. The problem arises because the fixed costs of $80,000 on 10,000 units are shown as additional cost of sales under standard absorption costing. If the sale is not made, these costs will remain in inventory. Thus, the effects of the sale are a $70,000 increase in contribution margin [($12 − $5) × 10,000] and an $80,000 charge for fixed costs, giving the $10,000 reduction shown above. Variable costing income statements would show a $70,000 increase in contribution margin and profit. Accepting the order would be a wise decision despite the effects on the absorption costing income statements. This type of analysis is covered in Chapter 4, and we illustrate it again to integrate our basic discussion of relevant costs in that chapter with our discussion of variable costing.

External Reporting

Generally accepted accounting principles for financial reporting require the use of absorption costing. The major theoretical underpinning of the position seems to be the matching concept. Essentially, the **matching concept** states that costs should become expenses when they no longer provide benefits. Thus, the wages paid to direct and indirect laborers should be treated as assets, because those wages created service potentials in the form of units of product. Similarly, annual depreciation on equipment represents a decline in service potential of the equipment, but that decline is at least partly offset by the service potential of the units of product made on the equipment. Therefore, these costs (wages and depreciation) and other costs of manufacturing should be expensed in the period in which the units are sold, because it is when the units are sold that the service potential expires.

According to this line of reasoning, to treat the costs of production as expenses in the period when they were incurred would violate the matching concept. The matching concept is broad enough to encompass the use of standard costing and the charging of variances to the income statement. Variances can be thought of as costs of the period, rather than of the product, on the ground that they represent inefficient uses of resources that do not contribute to the making of product and, therefore, have no future value to the firm.

Proponents of the use of direct or variable costing for external reporting purposes employ a number of arguments. Some are related to the confusing effects on income of the changes in inventories under absorption costing. Others point to the usefulness of variable costing as a managerial tool and ask why it should not therefore be used for external reporting.

Perhaps the most compelling argument for the use of variable costing for financial reporting centers on the definition of an asset.[2] Most accountants agree that an asset is an economic resource, something that provides future benefits to the firm. Inventory is an asset because it can be sold and, therefore, represents a source of future cash inflows. However, a firm usually can produce more inventory, so that we might think of the future benefits of existing inventory as the costs that we avoid in not having to produce so much in the future. Fixed manufacturing costs do not reduce, or obviate, to use Professor Green's term, the need to incur costs in the future. Variable manufacturing costs incurred now do obviate the need to incur such costs in the future. Thus, fixed manufacturing costs do not comply with the meaning of an asset in the sense described and should not be included in inventory cost.[3]

---

[2] The argument described here leans heavily on an exposition by Professor David Green, Jr., in "A Moral to the Direct Costing Controversy?" *The Journal of Business*, 33:3 (July 1960), 218–26.

[3] Professors George H. Sorter and Charles T. Horngren developed a method called relevant costing. Under their criteria, fixed costs could be included in inventory if they obviated the need to incur costs in the future, or reduced the future requirements. Thus, if variable costs

Tax Considerations

We noted earlier that variable costing is not acceptable for income tax accounting. However, firms may use normal costing with practical capacity as the basis for allocating fixed production costs to units of product for tax purposes.[4] The application variance may be expensed, but other variances (variable cost variances, fixed cost budget variances) must generally be prorated among inventories and cost of sales. Because the use of practical capacity gives the lowest possible fixed cost per unit figure, results will be closest to those of variable costing. Hence, using practical capacity and expensing application variances will reduce taxable income in periods of rising inventories or increase taxable income when inventories fall, in comparison to actual costing or normal costing using a lower basis for determining fixed cost per unit.

It should not be difficult to see why the Internal Revenue Service would not allow variable costing. In most years, inventories will rise because most firms grow. Even if physical inventories do not rise, the dollar value of inventories is likely to rise because prices rise. In such periods, tax payments would be lower if firms used variable costing than if they used absorption costing.

BEHAVIORAL CONSIDERATIONS

Throughout this book we have seen that behavioral considerations are an important part of cost and managerial accounting. Chapters 7 and 8 emphasized the importance of behaviorally sound reporting, identifying variances by responsibility and considering the effects of poor performance in one area on the performance in other areas. Because the departments in a firm are dependent on one another, it is usually not possible to identify responsibility perfectly.

Income reporting is subject to the same considerations as expense reporting. Most firms prepare income statements by product, product line, geographical area, or some other segmented basis. These income statements will frequently serve as bases for evaluating the performance of individual managers. Therefore, we must consider the potential problems in evaluation posed by absorption costing and variable costing income statements.

---

were to increase or if expected sales were greater than current productive capacity, the fixed costs of the current period would obviate the need to incur the higher future variable costs or would provide benefits in the form of units of product that the firm would not be able to produce in the future. Under such circumstances, they would allow fixed costs to be included in inventory. See "Asset Recognition and Economic Attributes: The Relevant Costing Approach," *The Accounting Review*, 37:3 (July 1962), 391–99.

[4] Regulation 1.471-11 (1975).

The most obvious possible problem under absorption costing is that managers can manipulate income by altering production levels. Because income can be increased (decreased) by increasing (decreasing) production, a manager has the opportunity to meet budgeted profit goals at least partly by changing production. This possible abuse is the basis for several instructive examples, one of which appears as a problem at the end of this chapter.[5] Such manipulation can easily be discovered if it takes place over several years. If inventory levels increase beyond their usual amounts expected to meet future sales, we would be inclined to investigate, and we might expect to see that production has been at levels much too high to be economically justifiable.

Another behavioral problem of interpretation arises with seasonal businesses. Such firms usually produce more in slack seasons than they do in the busy season, because they need high inventories entering the busy season. For example, toy manufacturers will find their sales concentrated in the fall of the year, production in the spring and summer. Absorption costing income statements may indicate that income is higher when production is high and sales low than vice versa. The example used in the first part of this chapter is a case in point. The question is whether managers can interpret the absorption costing results better than variable costing results. Poor decisions might be made by managers who used information incorrectly.

Whether or not poor decisions are made by managers using one type of information as opposed to another is important. It is also important to note that if managers see counter intuitive results such as falling income with rising sales, they may become distrustful of the system. If that occurs, they may ignore the information produced by the accounting system. They will almost certainly not improve performance because they distrust the accounting system.

The effects of production on income may be particularly severe in segmented reporting, such as reporting by product, product line, or geographical area. A method and format for such reporting that seems to meet the basic requirements of managers is to use variable costing, showing fixed costs as avoidable or unavoidable. An example of this type of reporting is given in Exhibit 11–6 on page 440. This income statement shows both variable costs and incremental fixed costs associated with each product. Because it uses the variable costing approach, it avoids all the problems of the effects of production on income, while it highlights the fixed costs that could be expected to change if the product were dropped.

This type of income statement is compatible with the principle of controllability in management reporting. It highlights the costs that are controllable in the short term, both variable costs and avoidable fixed costs. It shows unavoidable costs, including costs joint or common to the various segments, in one place, distinguishing them from the controllable costs. We assume that a manager is responsible for each product line. Other managers

---

[5] Also see Sorter and Horngren, *op. cit.*, for an example of the problem.

would be responsible for individual departments or other subunits within the three broad categories of product line.

EXHIBIT 11–6
Product-Line Income Statement, 19X5—Crawford Company
(in thousands of dollars)

	Total	Valves	Fittings	Pipe
Sales	$2,345	$978	$648	$719
Variable production costs	1,035	453	313	269
Variable selling expenses	97	38	16	43
Total variable costs	1,132	491	329	312
Contribution margin	1,213	487	319	407
Avoidable fixed costs	456	204	109	143
Incremental profit	757	$283	$210	$264
Common and unavoidable fixed costs	684			
Income before taxes	$ 73			

FLOWS OF COSTS UNDER VARIABLE COSTING SYSTEMS

Firms that use variable costing for periodic internal reporting may keep their cost accounting systems on either a variable costing or an absorption costing basis. Either way, they will have to make adjustments. If they keep the system using variable costing, they will have to make an adjustment to absorption costing for financial reporting and tax purposes. If they keep the system on an absorption costing basis, they must make adjustments to develop variable costing information.

The basic flows of costs under a variable costing system are the same as under an absorption costing system, save that fixed production costs are not carried through Work-in-Process Inventory, Finished Goods Inventory, and Cost of Goods Sold. At year end, or whenever external financial statements are to be issued, the firm will allocate fixed manufacturing overhead to inventories and cost of sales. The procedure is much the same as that used to prorate variances in going from standard costing to actual costing. The following illustration shows the process.

Illustration: Cornwall Company

The Cornwall Manufacturing Company allocates fixed manufacturing overhead according to the relative amounts of variable manufacturing overhead in the various categories. An analysis of 19X7 data reveals the following:

Total fixed manufacturing overhead		$9,874,000
Variable manufacturing overhead included in:		% of total
Cost of Sales	$3,720,000	74.7%
Ending Work-in-Process Inventory	272,000	5.5
Ending Finished Goods Inventory	986,000	19.8
Total	$4,978,000	100.0%
Allocation of fixed overhead:		
To Cost of Sales	$7,375,880	($9,874,000 × 74.7%)
To Work-in-Process Inventory	543,070	($9,874,000 × 5.5%)
To Finished Goods Inventory	1,955,050	($9,874,000 × 19.8%)
Total	$9,874,000	

These allocations would not have to be reflected in the accounts. They could simply be made as worksheet adjustments so that the accounts would continue to show variable costs.

Determining Variable Costs

Many costs need to be estimated. While we may be sure of the fixed nature of property taxes, we may not know the fixed and variable portions of many other costs. This is one of the reasons proposed for the use of regression models in planning. However, even with sophisticated mathematical models to aid in CVP analyses and standard cost setting, the manager is still left with an estimate. It would be unusual to find perfect correlation between costs and volume. It would be extremely rare for actual costs to equal standard costs for a period. Finally, not only are standard costs per se estimates of expected total costs per unit, but the division of fixed and variable costs (especially in overhead) is an estimate. Even under actual costing or normal costing the estimate of the fixed and variable portions of mixed costs exists. Under absorption costing the effect of this estimate is minimized, since fixed as well as variable costs are included in the inventory flow. Since variable costing treats fixed production costs as a period expense, firms using variable costing can experience more pronounced errors if estimates prove to be unreliable. Thus, even in product cost accumulation our books are just as good as the estimates used.

SUMMARY

Variable costing is a product costing alternative that is consistent with cost-volume-profit analysis. Variable costing treats fixed production costs as period costs, in contrast to absorption costing, where fixed production costs are inventoried. The two methods give differing income statement results when sales and production differ. Variable costing income is lower than absorption costing income when production is greater than sales, and vice versa. Variable costing is an alternative for internal reporting only. It is not acceptable for financial reporting or income tax accounting.

ASSIGNMENTS

11-1 Directness of Fixed Costs. An argument advanced by some advocates of variable costing is that fixed costs are not directly associable with units of product and should, therefore, not be inventoried. However, one can also argue that some fixed costs can be associated with changes in the level of production and consequently are direct to small batches of production.

For example, suppose that a firm needs one foreman for each ten direct laborers and that each laborer makes 1,000 units of product per month. It is possible to argue that the salaries of foremen are direct to each 10,000 units of product, perhaps even variable because they will change in fairly close proportion to changes in output.

Required: Discuss whether costs such as the foremen's salaries discussed above can be considered inventoriable under variable costing.

11-2 Basic Variable Costing and Absorption Costing. The data below are operating results for the Blanchard Company for 19X6, 19X7, and 19X8.

	19X6	19X7	19X8
Beginning inventory	0	2,000	2,000
Production	12,000	12,000	8,000
Sales in units, price $20/unit	10,000	12,000	10,000
Ending inventory	2,000	2,000	0

Variable production costs were $8 per unit each year and fixed production costs were $60,000 each year. Selling and administrative expenses, all fixed, were $40,000 each year.

Required:

1. Prepare income statements for each year using variable costing.

2. Prepare income statements for each year using absorption costing, with 10,000 units used to set a standard fixed cost of $6 per unit. Application variances are to be charged to the income statement as a gain or loss.

3. Prepare income statements for each year, using actual absorption costing and FIFO.

11-3 Relationships

Required: Treat each of the following cases independently.

1. A firm had income of $100,000 using absorption costing with a fixed overhead rate of $10 per unit. Inventory at the end of the period was 2,000 units lower than at the beginning of the period. What was income under variable costing?

2. A firm had income of $100,000 under variable costing, $80,000 under absorption costing with a fixed overhead rate of $5 per unit. What was the difference between sales and production?

3. A firm had $60,000 income using variable costing, $100,000 using absorption costing with a fixed overhead rate of $2 per unit. What was the difference between the beginning and ending inventories, in units?

11-4 Costing Methods and Profitability Analysis. The sales manager of the Jamestown Furniture Company was attempting to analyze the profitability of three models of chairs. The three models accounted for about 35 percent of the firm's total revenues. All three models were manufactured in the Vahalia plant, one of four plants that Jamestown Furniture operated. At the request of the sales manager, a staff member had developed the following income statement from the previous year's operations. Dollar figures are in thousands.

			Model	
	Total	Aragon	Balway	Dorham
Unit sales and production	22,780	6,540	11,800	4,440
Revenue	$2,808.3	$1,013.7	$1,062.0	$732.6
Materials and components	526.4	164.8	139.2	222.4
Direct labor	469.8	206.7	180.5	82.6
Factory overhead, 200% of direct labor	939.6	413.4	361.0	165.2
Selling and administrative expenses at 25% of revenue	702.1	253.4	265.5	183.2
Total costs	2,637.9	1,038.3	946.2	653.4
Profit (loss)	$ 170.4	($24.6)	$ 115.8	$ 79.2

The sales manager was distressed by the figures. She had thought that the Aragon line was profitable and had planned to increase advertising expenditures aimed specifically at increasing its sales. In consultation with the firm's chief cost accountant, she learned that variable factory overhead was about 60 percent of direct labor cost and that variable selling and administrative expenses were about 8 percent of sales revenue, principally for commissions.

She also received the following estimates of fixed costs that were directly associated with each model and could be avoided if the line were dropped. Costs are in thousands of dollars.

	Total	Aragon	Balway	Dorham
Direct fixed factory overhead	$121.4	$46.5	$39.8	$35.1
Direct fixed selling and administrative costs	85.0	36.2	27.5	21.3
Total direct fixed costs	$206.4	$82.7	$67.3	$56.4

Required: Prepare an income statement for the year using the format shown in Exhibit 11–6. Compare and contrast this income statement with the one above from the standpoint of the uses that managers might make of the two statements.

11–5 Basic Variable Costing and Absorption Costing. The data below relate to the one product of the Eastern Company.

Selling price	$12
Production costs, per unit:	
Variable	$5.50
Fixed	3.50
Selling and administrative costs, per unit:	
Variable	0.50
Fixed	1.50

The unit costs are based on normal volume of 8,000 units per month. During June the firm produced 7,500 units and sold 7,000. During July it produced 8,500 and sold 9,000.

Required: Prepare income statements for June and July using (a) absorption costing and (b) variable costing. Treat any application variances as adjustments to gross margin.

11–6 Standard Costing. The Arno Company makes two models of its sold product, a sophisticated trap for rodents. Data relating to each model appear below.

	Regular Model	Deluxe Model
Standard material cost	$10	$20
Standard labor cost	5	8

All overhead is fixed and the firm uses budgeted direct labor cost for the coming year, 19X6, as the basis for determining standard cost. During 19X6 the managers expect to make 4,000 units of each model, for total direct labor cost of $52,000. Budgeted overhead is $104,000. There were no beginning inventories.

Operations for the year showed the following results:

	Regular	Deluxe
Production	4,200	3,600
Sales	4,000	3,200
Selling prices	$40	$70
Costs:		
Materials	$108,000	
Direct labor	54,000	
Overhead	98,000	
Selling and general, all fixed	35,000	

Required:

1. Prepare an income statement, using standard absorption costing. Identify all variances separately, to the extent that you have the necessary information to do so.

2. Prepare an income statement, using standard variable costing.

11-7 Standard Process Costing. The Exco Company makes a single product. Standard cost data follow.

Materials, 3 gal at $2	$ 6
Direct labor, ½ hr at $8/hr	4
Variable overhead at $6 per labor hour	3
Fixed overhead at $10 per labor hour	5
Total standard cost	$18

Annual budgeted fixed overhead is $500,000. There were no inventories at the beginning of 19X6. The firm's transactions during the year were:

1. Material purchases were 330,000 gal at $1.90.

2. Material use was 304,000 gal.

3. Direct laborers worked 47,500 hr at $8/hr.

4. Variable overhead was $285,000.

5. Fixed overhead was $512,000.

6. The firm completed 97,000 units and sold 90,000 at $25 each. Work in process at year end was 3,000 units complete as to materials, 60 percent complete as to labor and overhead.

7. Selling and administrative expenses were $450,000.

Required:

1. Determine ending inventories at standard cost, Materials, Work in Process, and Finished Goods.

2. Prepare an income statement using standard absorption costing, identifying all variances separately.

3. Without preparing a new income statement, determine what income would have been if the firm had used standard variable costing.

11–8 Income Statements (AICPA adapted). The Bicent Company makes a single product. Cost data are, per unit:

Direct material (all variable)	$30.00
Direct labor (all variable)	19.00
Manufacturing overhead:	
Variable	6.00
Fixed, based on 10,000 units per month	5.00
Selling, general, and administrative:	
Variable	4.00
Fixed, based on 10,000 units per month	2.80

The product sells for $80 per unit. The following data reflect estimates for June, 19X7, in units.

Beginning inventory	2,000
Production	9,000
Available for sale	11,000
Sales	7,500
Ending inventory	3,500

Required:

1. Prepare an income statement for June, assuming the use of absorption costing with any application variance charged or credited to cost of goods sold.

2. Prepare an income statement for June, using variable costing.

11–9 Replacement Costs. The controller and the sales manager of B&M Enterprises were arguing about the desirability of selling some inventory to a large chain store. The price was to be $60 per unit, which was well below the usual $85 price. In support of his position, the sales manager offered the following data regarding the product. The cost figures are from operations of the previous month.

	Unit Costs
Materials	$12
Direct labor	25
Variable overhead, $0.80 per direct labor dollar	20
Total variable cost	$57

The sales manager said that accepting the offer would increase the firm's income by $3 for each unit sold. The controller, he declared, had advocated the use of variable costing precisely because it provided information that would be useful in making decisions like the present one.

The controller opposed the sale. She stated that, although variable costing had advantages over absorption costing, it was not a cure-all. She pointed out that labor cost had risen by 10 percent since the units on hand were made, and that the variable overhead rate per direct labor dollar had stayed at $0.80 because much of variable overhead was fringe benefits and other costs that were related to labor cost, not to labor time. She went on to say that the firm should always consider the cost to replace units, not the historical cost, because replacement cost was a measure of opportunity cost.

Required: Determine whether the firm should make the sale to the chain store, supporting your position with appropriate calculations and making your assumptions explicit.

11–10   Variable Costing and Income Taxes

Required: What would happen if variable costing were made acceptable for income tax purposes? Comment from the standpoint of the federal government.

11–11   Variable and Absorption Costing Standards.   The following data relate to the operations of the Cramer Company for 19X5 and 19X6. There were no inventories at the beginning of 19X5.

	19X5	*19X6*
Production, in units	10,000	8,000
Sales, in units, at $10 per unit	$70,000	$90,000
Variable production costs incurred	30,000	24,000
Fixed production costs incurred	20,000	20,000
Selling and administrative expenses	15,000	15,000

Standard variable production cost is $3 per unit; budgeted fixed production costs are $20,000 per year.

Required:

1. Prepare income statements for the two years, using variable costing.
2. Suppose that the firm uses 8,000 units to set its standard fixed cost for determining absorption costing inventories and income for tax purposes and financial reporting. Prepare income statements for the two years, using standard absorption costing. Treat any application variance as an adjustment to standard gross profit, so that actual gross profit is standard gross profit plus or minus any application variance.

11–12 **"How's That Again?"** The president of your firm is considering the use of standard absorption costing. She has asked you to develop a few examples to illustrate the effects on income of various events. You develop the following basic data.

Selling price, per unit	$ 50
Standard variable production cost, per unit	10
Annual budgeted fixed production costs	300,000
Standard fixed cost per unit, based on 10,000 units at normal activity	30

You assume, for simplicity, that selling and administrative expenses are zero. You then prepare the following income statement, assuming a beginning inventory of 1,000 units and production and sales of 10,000 units.

Sales	$500,000
Beginning inventory	40,000
Variable production costs	100,000
Applied fixed production costs	300,000
Ending inventory	(40,000)
Standard cost of sales	400,000
Standard gross margin	100,000
Application variance	0
Actual gross margin	$100,000

Required: The president asks you to redo the income statement to show the effects of each of the following events. Consider each event independently, so that you will prepare five new income statements. In each case where production changes from the original 10,000 units, assume that actual production costs equal budgeted production costs for the new level of production.

1. Production increases to 10,001 units, sales remain at 10,000 units.
2. Production increases to 10,001 units, sales increase to 10,001 units.
3. Sales increase to 10,001 units, production remains at 10,000 units.
4. Sales decrease to 9,999 units, production increases to 10,001 units.
5. Sales increase to 10,001 units, production decreases to 9,999 units.

11–13 **Analysis of Income Statements.** The president of the Myoko Company, a small manufacturer of automotive parts, has asked for your assistance in analyzing the firm's recent income statements.

"Profits don't seem to be responding to increases in sales. I just don't understand what's going on," says the president. "My production supervisor tells me that his costs are under control, with fixed costs running at about $86,000 per month and variable costs averaging about 40 percent of selling

	July	August	September
Sales	$232,417	$296,385	$247,811
Cost of sales	156,220	240,499	176,049
Gross margin	76,197	55,886	71,762
Selling and administrative costs	53,120	56,215	54,267
Profit before taxes (loss)	$ 23,077	($329)	$ 17,495

price for all our products. Selling and administrative expenses seem to be running about as budgeted, too, so I don't see where the problem lies. I have some other data that you might like to see." He then gives you the following information.

Inventories:	June 30	$ 97,320
	July 31	188,415
	August 31	106,434
	September 30	88,712

The firm uses actual absorption costing for inventories.

Required: Prepare an explanation for the president.

11-14 Pricing Dispute.   You have been serving as the chairman of a local charitable drive. You asked the manager of the Wheaton Bakery to donate loaves of its rye bread for door prizes. The manager agreed to give you the bread at cost, which he stated was 43¢ per loaf. Knowing that the retail price of a loaf is 74¢, you decided to investigate further. The manager of the bakery provided the following information.

Retail price per loaf		$0.74
Wholesale price to Wheaton		$0.53
Cost to manufacture and sell:		
Ingredients	$0.18	
Direct labor	0.08	
Overhead, manufacturing	0.14	
Overhead, selling and administrative	0.03	
Total cost		$0.43
Profit		$0.10

Both manufacturing and selling/administrative overhead are largely fixed and based on expected operations, at about 85 percent of capacity.

Required: Prepare a letter to the manager of the Wheaton Bakery explaining what you believe is a fair price and why.

11-15 Product Costing and Profitability.   The manager of the Greg Division of the General Products Company presented the following report to the president of the firm.

Income Statements—Greg Division

	March	April	May
Sales at $50 per unit	$1,000,000	$1,200,000	$1,380,000
Standard cost of sales	750,000	900,000	1,035,000
Standard gross profit	250,000	300,000	345,000
Production cost variances	30,000 F	40,000 F	55,000 F
Actual gross profit	280,000	340,000	400,000
Selling and administrative costs	350,000	380,000	380,000
Income (loss)	($70,000)	($40,000)	$ 20,000

"We really have it going now," the manager said. "We had to spend a good bit on promotion, as evidenced by the increases in S&A expenses, but we are now out of the woods and should be able to keep sales at the May level from here on out." Upon questioning, the manager told the president that the production cost variances related to fixed costs. He explained: "We use a $10-per-unit standard fixed production cost, and the variances arise because our production exceeds our normal activity of 30,000 units, which is the basis for determining the standard cost."

Required:

1. Determine the standard variable cost per unit.
2. Determine production in each of the three months.
3. Is the division manager's optimism justified? Why or why not?

11-16 Analysis of Performance. The president of the Dorwaldt Company was not happy with the results for July and August, the first two months of the firm's fiscal year. She knew that income in those months should be less than the average budgeted monthly income of $40,000, because sales in the summer were slower than in the winter. Average budgeted monthly sales were $300,000.

Income Statements—Dorwaldt Company

	August	July
Sales	$200,000	$210,000
Standard cost of sales	120,000	126,000
Standard gross margin	80,000	84,000
Manufacturing variances, unfavorable	20,000	22,000
Actual gross margin	60,000	62,000
Selling and administrative expenses	80,000	80,000
Loss before taxes	($20,000)	($18,000)

The president asked the controller what was going wrong and heard that nothing was: sales were on target based on the monthly budgeted amounts for each month, and all costs were incurred as expected. The controller explained that output was relatively low, which accounted for the losses. Variable production costs were about 30 percent of sales dollars. Unit standard fixed costs were based on expected volume for the year.

Required:

1. Determine the firm's breakeven point (monthly), assuming that production equals sales.

2. Is the controller correct in saying that the unfavorable application variances are the reason for the losses? Show why or why not.

11-17 Explaining Differences in Incomes. Operating results for 19X5 and 19X6 for the Ulseth Company appear below. There were no inventories at the beginning of 19X5. All costs represent both actual and budgeted amounts.

	19X5	19X6
Sales at $10 per unit	$200,000	$190,000
Unit production	25,000	18,000
Production costs:		
Variable at $3 per unit	$ 75,000	$ 54,000
Fixed	$ 50,000	$ 50,000
Selling and administrative costs	$ 40,000	$ 40,000

Required:

1. Prepare an income statement under variable costing for each year.

2. Prepare an income statement for each year under absorption costing, assuming that the firm uses 20,000 units as the basis for absorbing fixed overhead. Treat any application (volume) variances as adjustments to standard cost of sales.

3. Prepare a formal reconciliation of incomes under the two methods for each year.

11-18 Variable Costing. Vernon Allbright, the president of Vincent Products, has just been to a seminar on variable costing. He tells you:

I am excited about the possibilities of using variable costing for planning. I think we can make better tactical decisions and can see better how everybody is doing under such a system. I am worried, though, that it will be costly keeping two separate sets of books, since we'll continue to need full costing information for our shareholders and the IRS. Is there anything we can do short of having duplicate systems to allow us to use variable costing while retaining the necessary parts of absorption costing?

With that, Allbright hands you the following income statement for 19X9. Vincent uses FIFO.

Income Statement, 19X9—Vincent Products

Sales (115,000 units)		$6,545,000
Cost of Sales:		
Beginning inventory	$ 418,500	
Current production	4,567,500	
Goods available for sale	4,986,000	
Less: Ending inventory	207,600	
Cost of Goods Sold		4,778,400
Gross Profit		1,766,600
Less: Sales Expenses		625,000
General Expenses		450,000
Interest		190,000
Income Before Taxes		$ 501,600

Beginning inventory of finished goods consisted of 10,000 units ($12 in materials, $19.85 in conversion costs, and $10 in fixed costs per unit). Current production included 110,000 units transferred to finished goods. In addition, there was no beginning inventory of work in process, but an ending inventory of 4,000 units 100 percent complete for materials and 75 percent complete in conversion costs. Current production costs consist of $12 per unit in materials, $10.26 in labor, $9.26 in variable overhead, and $10 in fixed costs. Fixed overhead incurred in 19X9 was $1,130,000.

Required: Assume Vincent's books were kept using variable costing but management wants an absorption costing income statement and balance sheet. Considering Work in Process, Finished Goods, Cost of Goods Sold, and any other relevant accounts, show the entries to adjust the accounts from variable to absorption costing to have proper financial statements. Allocate fixed overhead on the basis of total variable conversion costs.

11–19 **Actual Versus Standard: Variable and Absorption Costing.**   The Mayme Company presents the following data for 19X3:

	Actual
Beginning Inventory (units)	0
Production (units)	100,000
Sales (units), at $30	90,000
Costs for production of 100,000 units:	
Direct Materials	$350,000
Direct Labor	$610,000
Variable Overhead	$400,000
Fixed Overhead	$110,000
Selling, general and administrative expenses	$250,000

Required:

1. Prepare income statements for 19X3, using:
   a. actual absorption costing.
   b. actual variable costing.
2. Standard costs for the product appear below.

Standard Cost per Unit

Direct Materials: 2 lb at $1.50/lb	$ 3.00
Direct Labor: 1 hr at $6.25/hr	6.25
Variable Overhead: $4.10/DLH	4.10
Fixed Overhead[a]	1.25
Total	$14.60

[a] Fixed Overhead is based on $112,500 per year and 90,000 units of production.

Prepare income statements for 19X3, using:
a. standard absorption costing.
b. standard variable costing.
You may show one variance for each cost element. Show all variances as adjustments to cost of goods sold.

3. By doing items 1a, 1b, 2a, and 2b, you have come up with four income figures. Explain the differences.
4. If production had been 90,000 units instead of 100,000 units, how would that have affected the four income numbers? (Do not do new statements to answer this question.)

11–20 Product Costing and Decisions. The controller of Harding Products, Inc., was considering whether or not to accept an offer from Lacy Stores, a large chain of retailers. Lacy had offered to buy goods for $650,000, which was about $250,000 below the normal selling prices. Harding was overstocked and would fill the order from inventory. The controller prepared two pro forma income statements for the current year, one assuming that the firm accepted the order, the other assuming that it did not.

	Do Not Accept	Accept
Sales	$9,320,000	$9,970,000
Standard cost of sales	6,617,000	7,256,000
Standard gross margin	2,703,000	2,714,000
Manufacturing variances, unfavorable	67,000	67,000
Actual gross margin	2,636,000	2,647,000
Selling and administrative expenses	2,104,000	2,120,000
Income before taxes	$ 532,000	$ 527,000

The controller was surprised at the results. He knew that the sale would cause some increase in selling and administrative expenses, and his estimate of a $16,000 rise seemed reasonable. Standard cost of sales was about 71 percent of normal selling prices on all products, so the increase there also seemed right.

In discussing the decision with you, his new assistant, the controller stated that standard variable cost of sales was about 45 percent of normal selling prices for all products and that the manufacturing variances consisted largely of an application variance (about $55,000), the remainder being variable cost variances. Finally, he said that the beginning inventory at standard cost was about $456,000. The ending inventory would be about $1,330,000 if the firm did not accept the offer.

Required: Determine whether or not the firm should accept the offer.

11-21 Multiple Products. The Morton Manufacturing Company makes a wide variety of products. The firm uses standard costing—absorption costing for tax purposes, variable costing for internal reporting. The following information pertains to 19X9.

Beginning inventory at standard cost (6,500 standard hours):	
Absorption costing	$ 312,000
Variable costing	$ 195,000
Standard labor hours for 19X9 production	45,000 hr
Standard variable production cost for output achieved	$1,350,000
Budgeted fixed production cost	$ 900,000
Normal activity in standard labor hours, used to set	
per-unit standard fixed costs	50,000 hr
Variable cost variances and fixed cost budget variance	$ 30,000 U
Selling and administrative expenses	$ 850,000
Sales	$3,200,000

The number of units sold corresponds to about 41,000 standard labor hours. The material content of each product is about the same as the labor content. You may assume that all variable production costs may be expressed in terms of labor hours. Standard costs in 19X8 were the same as in 19X9.

Required: Prepare income statements for 19X9, using:

a. absorption costing.

b. variable costing.

11-22 Costing Methods, Decisions, and Analysis of Results. Jay Dixon, the president of QBM Company, had expected the month of May to show a turnaround. The firm had been barely breaking even in recent months, and toward the end of April Dixon had ordered an across-the-board cut in prices of about 10 percent and an increase in advertising and promotional expenses of about $30,000 per month. Early sales reports in May showed that unit volume was up by about 25 percent, and Dixon was therefore shocked at the May income statement.

Income Statements—QBM Company (in thousands)

	May	April
Sales	$2,251	$1,994
Cost of sales	2,076	1,496
Gross margin	175	498
Selling and administrative expenses	528	497
Income (loss) before taxes	($353)	$ 1

Ray Stout, QBM's controller, was also at a loss to explain the results. He told Dixon that costs were incurred as budgeted in both April and May. There were small shifts in the product mix from April to May, but because standard cost of sales was about 75 percent of selling price for all products (before the price reduction), that factor could not be important. Stout did say that production was well below normal in May. The firm had built up excess inventories in the early part of the year but had worked them down to normal in May.

In April, sales had approximately equaled production, and the level of activity in April was about the level used to set the standard fixed cost for each product. Monthly fixed production costs were about $800,000, and selling and administrative expenses were virtually all fixed. The firm writes off any variances to cost of sales during the month.

Dixon was convinced that he had made good decisions on prices and promotion, but the May results did not bear him out. He did not want to see any more months like May. He did expect that volume would hold at the May level if he kept prices and promotional expenses at their current levels.

Required: Prepare an analysis for Dixon, indicating whether he should keep prices and promotion at their current levels or go back to the former levels.

11–23 Absorption Costing in Production Planning. The Corts Company produces two products, basic widgets and deluxe widgets. Several of its managers had been arguing for some time about the wisdom of the firm's policy with respect to fixed overhead costs. The firm used the practical capacity in each of its two departments—stamping and assembly—to determine figures for fixed cost per hour. These figures were used to set the standard costs of the two products. The schedule below shows the most recent results.

	Basic Widgets	Deluxe Widgets
Selling price	$25	$35
Variable costs	15	22
Contribution margin	10	13
Fixed costs	7	6
Profit per unit	$ 3	$ 7

The fixed costs were based on the hourly rates for fixed overhead in the two departments and the hours required to make each unit. Monthly fixed overhead was $5,000 in stamping, $18,000 in assembly, with available hours of 10,000 and 9,000, respectively, giving rates of $0.50 and $2. Basic widgets require 2 hr of stamping time, 3 hr of assembly. Deluxe widgets need 4 hr of stamping and 2 hr of assembly.

Demand for both products exceeds capacity. During the most recent month the firm produced and sold 2,500 deluxe widgets, no basic widgets. This resulted in an unfavorable application variance of $8,000, which caused the managers a good deal of concern.

Required: Determine the optimal production plan for the firm.

11–24 Unit Costs and Pricing Policies. The Calgary Machine Works makes tools and dies for industrial companies. The firm has recently adopted a new pricing policy that calls for pricing all products by the following formula:

$$\text{price} = \frac{\left(\begin{array}{c}\text{variable}\\\text{manufacturing cost}\end{array}\right) + \left(\begin{array}{c}\text{applied fixed}\\\text{manufacturing cost}\end{array}\right)}{0.70}$$

Applied fixed manufacturing cost is calculated at $8 per machine hour used for the product. This figure is based on budgeted fixed manufacturing costs of $1,200,000 and budgeted machine hours of 150,000. Dividing the total manufacturing cost by 70 percent provides an allowance for selling and administrative expenses and for profit. Selling and administrative expenses are budgeted at $745,000 fixed plus $0.08 per sales dollar.

In general, variable manufacturing costs average $10 per machine hour, but that average does not apply to every product. Inventories are negligible.

Required:

1. Determine the profits that the firm would earn at the following levels of machine hours:
   a.   140,000.
   b.   150,000.
   c.   160,000.

2. Suppose that the firm has 160,000 machine hours available and more demand than it can satisfy. Its managers also believe that the profit

calculated in item 1c above is a satisfactory target. However, they wonder whether the pricing formula will yield that profit if the mix of products changes so that variable manufacturing costs per machine hour change. Determine whether the policy would work if variable manufacturing costs dropped to an average of $8 per machine hour.

3. Can you develop a formula that would yield the target profit no matter what variable manufacturing costs become? Assume that the firm can get all the business it can handle at 160,000 machine hours. Remember that the firm makes many different products, and you are developing a formula that should apply to any given product.

SELECTED REFERENCES

Fremgen, James M., "The Direct Costing Controversy—An Identification of Issues," *The Accounting Review*, 39:1 (January 1964), 43–51.

Green, David O., Jr., "A Moral to the Direct Costing Controversy?" *Journal of Business*, 33:3 (July 1960), 218–26.

Grinnell, D. Jacque, "Using Linear Programming to Compare Direct and Absorption Costing," *The Accounting Review*, 52:2 (April 1977), 485–91.

National Association of Accountants, *N.A.A. Research Report 37: Current Applications of Direct Costing*, New York: National Association of Accountants, 1961.

Sorter, George H., and Charles T. Horngren, "Asset Recognition and Economic Attributes—The Relevant Costing Approach," *The Accounting Review*, 37:3 (July 1962), 391–99.

Cost Allocation

Chapter 12

Earlier chapters covered some of the principal aspects of cost allocation, especially as they relate to product costing. Chapters 5, 6, 8, and 9 showed how the costs of operating departments are allocated to units (or jobs) that pass through them. The costs of operating departments that are allocated to units of product include their own separable, or direct, costs plus costs allocated *to* the operating departments from service departments that perform plantwide functions. That is, the costs of operating departments include some of the costs of building security, personnel, general factory administration, cost accounting, and other service functions that support the manufacturing activities.

It might be better to speak of service *centers* than of service *departments*. Depreciation on building is not a department in the usual sense, but it does represent a cost that provides service—shelter for the manufacturing and other operations carried out in the building. For brevity, we shall use the term department to refer to the activities that generate costs.

This chapter considers the problems of allocating service department costs to operating departments, as well as some other important allocation problems. In prior chapters we have been concerned with allocating costs to units of product (broadly defined to include the providing of services as well as physical products), which we may call **final allocations.** Our principal concern in this chapter is with **intermediate allocations**—allocations made before the final allocation to individual units of product. The process is shown graphically in Figure 12–1 on page 460.

The process outlined in Figure 12–1 relates to product costing by business firms and to a great many other situations. Many of the prices that we pay are based on allocated costs, as we shall see shortly. First, we consider some of the theoretical bases for allocation and one of the principal counterarguments.

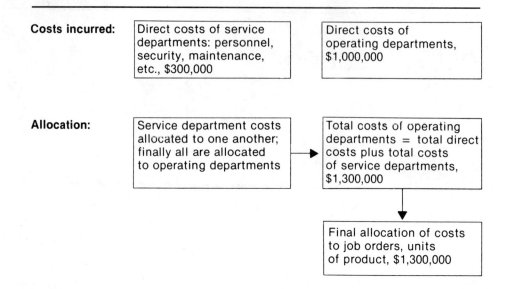

Costs incurred:

| Direct costs of service departments: personnel, security, maintenance, etc., $300,000 | Direct costs of operating departments, $1,000,000 |

Allocation:

| Service department costs allocated to one another; finally all are allocated to operating departments | → | Total costs of operating departments = total direct costs plus total costs of service departments, $1,300,000 |

Final allocation of costs to job orders, units of product, $1,300,000

Example: Depreciation on building would be allocated to service departments as well as to operating departments. The amounts allocated to service departments would in turn be allocated to operating departments as part of the cost of a service center.

FIGURE 12–1
Cost Allocation Process

ALLOCATIONS—THEORETICAL JUSTIFICATION
The Matching Principle

The theoretical justification for cost allocation comes from the principles of financial accounting, especially the matching principle. The essence of the **matching principle** is that costs should be reported as expenses in the period when they cease to have future benefits. Thus, the cost of merchandise is reported as an expense when the merchandise is sold, because the revenue received from the sale constitutes the benefit. When the benefits of a particular cost are not so directly traceable to particular revenues, the cost is often allocated over the periods assumed to be benefited in a rational and systematic manner. Thus, depreciation is the allocation of a cost over an estimated useful economic life—the period over which the firm will benefit from owning the asset.

In a manufacturing situation, the notion that all costs of production should be treated as assets (costs that will provide benefits in the future) has long been recognized, and it forms the basis of the most prominent allocation that accountants make—the allocation of production costs to units of output. The idea is that all production costs are incurred to produce the firm's output, and so each unit of product receives some benefits from these costs. It follows that each unit of output should be charged with some of the costs. The line of reasoning is sometimes called *costs attach* to denote the position that individual units of product pick up costs as they proceed through manufacturing processes.

Additionally, in the long run the fixed production costs become variable; that is, the firm can build a plant of any size it wants, and it must renew the commitments that cause fixed costs. There is no doubt that fixed production costs and the costs of service departments such as maintenance, engineering, general factory administration, and factory accounting are necessary for the production of the firm's products.

In general, most accountants would accept the position that the costs mentioned above are joint to individual units of product. The costs are required in order that the firm might produce all of its products during a period, but they are not specifically traceable to specific units. This is where those who do not accept the allocation of joint costs part company with those who do.

Arbitrariness of Allocations

Whenever we have costs that are joint, we cannot allocate them in a single, perfectly defensible way. There are always alternative ways of making the allocations that someone else could favor, and we cannot say that they are wrong.

Chapter 9 considered the problems of joint products, such as the various cuts of meat that come from cattle and the different products that come from crude petroleum. We saw there that we could make allocations of the costs of the joint process, including the cost of the raw material, in several ways. But we cannot say that each joint product has a true cost. Neither the net realizable value method nor the constant gross margin rate method yields allocations that we can say tell us exactly what the cost of a steak, roast, or pound of hamburger actually is. The joint costs are associated with the output as a whole, not with any given unit of any given product. The same is true with fixed production costs: they cannot be identified with specific units of product or hours of direct labor. They relate to the entire output of a period.[1]

Accordingly, allocations of joint costs are arbitrary, because we can make them in different ways and no one can win an argument about which method is correct. Nevertheless, accountants must allocate for product cost-

[1] Arthur L. Thomas has written extensively on the problems of allocations. See the selected references at the end of the chapter.

ing purposes. Moreover, allocations pervade modern life and affect our taxes and the prices that we pay, as the next section discusses.

ECONOMIC AND SOCIAL EFFECTS OF ALLOCATIONS

Cost-plus pricing, as used by many business firms, is one economic consequence of allocations: the prices charged for various products will be affected by the allocations. The prices that the federal government pays for goods produced by private firms, especially defense contractors, often include cost allocations as provided under various standards of the Cost Accounting Standards Board. Other examples exist throughout a wide range of entities.

Hospitals are reimbursed under Medicaid and various insurance plans such as Blue Cross according to formulas that include the allocation of indirect costs. Hospitals will allocate the costs of service departments such as admissions, medical records, laundry, and others to the departments that provide patient services (surgery, pediatrics, maternity, and so on). In turn, these costs will be allocated to patient-days. State and local governments, universities, community service agencies, and others receive grants-in-aid from the federal government. Sometimes these grants allow for the inclusion of indirect costs in the reimbursement.[2] For example, part of the costs of operating the mayor's office, the central administrative services department, and the personnel department of a city will be charged to a grant that provides assistance to the aged, or to juvenile authorities. Selecting one allocation method over another may result in significantly different reimbursements. The allocations have important economic consequences to the entities.

The rates that we all pay for electricity, natural gas, and telephone service are generally determined by state utility commissions. Again, allocations are critical. For example, electric utilities (and other utilities) have largely fixed operating costs, with fuel being the only significant variable cost. Utilities serve several classes of customers: residences, small businesses, light industry, heavy industry, streetlighting, and so on. The huge fixed investment in generating equipment is used to serve all customers. The investment is often allocated to various customer classes, then the fixed costs are similarly allocated and variable costs added to the fixed costs for each class. Total costs are subtracted from revenues from each class to obtain an income figure. The income figure for each class is divided by the allocated investment to get a rate of return by customer class. These rates of return are used by the utility management, public service commissions, and

---

[2] See, for example, *A Guide for Non-Profit Institutions: Cost Principles and Procedures for Establishing Indirect Cost and Other Rates for Grants and Contracts with the Department of Health, Education, and Welfare* (Washington: U.S. Department of Health, Education, and Welfare, August 1974). This department is now called Human Services.

interested lobbying groups (household users, industrial users, and so on) to see whether each class is paying its fair share. Requests for increases in rates are advocated, and disputed, against this background.

The allocation question in rate setting and elsewhere has often been viewed as a cost accounting question, with the emphasis on determining the accuracy of an allocation scheme. However, because all allocations are arbitrary, because there is no such thing as the true cost of (say) providing electricity to homes, the issues would be better addressed from the standpoint of welfare economics and social policy. No one argues that customers should pay only the direct costs of service: someone must pay for the generating capacity, administrative overhead, interest on debt, and so on. What one can say is that we might all be better off if the arbitrariness of allocations were openly admitted and if the fact that true costs usually do not exist were acknowledged, so that we could avoid wasting time and effort in arguing about justifying one allocation method versus another.

One final example: Corporations pay income taxes to states and cities as well as to the federal government. A firm that operates in several states must allocate some of its costs to the business it does in each state in order to avoid multiple taxation. Multiple taxation would arise if the firm earned, say, a total of $100,000 and paid income taxes on $60,000 of income in each of two states because it did not allocate all its costs between the business done in the two states. Obviously, firms would prefer to allocate more cost to business done in states with high tax rates, less to that done in states with low rates. State taxing authorities will sometimes attempt to disallow such allocations, so that multiple taxation may be unavoidable.

TERMINOLOGY

In order to establish a common frame of reference, we first discuss terms used in this area: cost objective (or cost object), cost pool, and allocation base. A **cost objective** is the recipient of the allocation, as when a unit of product receives a share of overhead costs. More generally, a cost objective is any segment of the firm or any activity to which an allocation is made. Some examples of cost objectives are divisions that are allocated general corporate costs, operating departments that are allocated service department costs, and programs or projects such as research and development that are allocated general overhead costs.

A **cost pool** is an amount to be allocated during a period. The costs of a service department (such as data processing) that are to be allocated to operating departments constitute such a cost pool. In a different context, the general and administrative expenses of a city may form a cost pool that will be allocated to programs such as public safety, recreation, education, and economic development. Cost pools are developed in a number of ways and may contain all, or only a part of, the costs of a service department. For example, as we will discuss, the only costs of a maintenance department that wind up being allocated to operating departments may be budgeted costs, rather than actual costs. In addition, some costs that are not allowable under reimbursement contracts, such as fund-raising costs of a hospital, may be excluded.

An **allocation base** is the measure of activity used to make the allocations. In earlier chapters we have seen measures of activity, such as direct labor hours, machine hours, or units of production, that were used to assign indirect overhead. The selection of an allocation base is given a great deal of attention, sometimes much more than it deserves. As we saw earlier, the allocation of costs may well confuse rather than enlighten and rarely produces valuable information for planning, control, and decision making. In many cases it makes little difference what allocation base is used, but in others, such as those mentioned at the beginning of the chapter, it can make a significant economic difference to companies, public agencies, and consumers.

Indirect Costs

An allocation is essentially the distribution of indirect costs to cost objects. The contrast is that direct cost can be specifically traced to a cost object, while an **indirect cost** cannot be directly traced to the cost object of current attention. Any cost is direct to *some* cost object, but that cost object might not be the one of interest. For example, the salary of the vice-president for production is direct (separable) to the manufacturing function considered as a whole, but is indirect (joint) with regard to individual factories, departments within factories, and units of product. Costs that are directly associated with a relevant cost object need not be allocated. What we are concerned with are costs that are not directly attributable to the cost objects of our current attention.

Indirect costs may be fixed or variable with respect to a given cost object. Much variable manufacturing overhead is indirect in a strict sense, even though we treat it as incremental. For example, we might estimate that maintenance costs change at the rate of $0.05 per machine hour, and so we would include this amount in determining the variable cost of making products. However, the $0.05 cannot be specifically traced to each machine hour. Rather it is an average cost relationship that holds over a relevant range. Such variable costs of service departments usually are allocated to production departments, just as fixed costs are. There is no theoretical or practical problem in allocating indirect variable costs, as long as the measure of activity (allocation base) is a fair indicator in a cause-and-effect relationship with the cost.

Similar costs for different firms may be direct to a production department in one firm, indirect in another. A firm in which maintenance workers are employed by production departments would show their wages as direct to the departments. A firm that has a separate maintenance department would consider the wages as direct to the maintenance department, but indirect to the production departments. Hard-and-fast rules tend to be of little use in accounting in general and in cost accounting in particular. In both firms mentioned above, however, maintenance costs would be indirect to units of product and would have to be allocated to those units.

Cost Objectives

The selection of cost objectives is usually a straightforward process no matter what entity we deal with. For a manufacturing firm, the ultimate cost objectives are units of product. For a hospital they are the basic patient services rendered by maternity, medical, surgical, and pediatrics departments. For a defense contractor they are individual projects or jobs, such as a particular batch of airplanes. Cost objectives may be intermediate or final (ultimate). An **intermediate cost objective** is one to which allocations will be made and from which other allocations will be made.

An example of an intermediate cost objective is a service department such as a computer center. Costs for depreciation on the building and a share of the costs of the personnel department may be allocated to the computer center. These costs, as well as the direct costs of operating the center, will then be allocated to other departments. Thus, allocated costs can pass through intermediate cost objectives en route to their final destinations. This means that the full cost developed for a unit of product can include many levels of cost allocation. The complexities in some cases such as utility cost allocations to various customer classes become enormous.

Cost Pools

Developing Cost Pools.   A cost pool may consist of the costs in a single account, or in a group of accounts that would be allocated using the same basis. Thus, depreciation on a building might be a separate cost pool, or the pool might consist of depreciation as well as other costs. Property taxes, heat and light, building maintenance, and janitorial service might be included along with depreciation in a single cost pool, because they could all reasonably be allocated using the same base such as relative amounts of space occupied.

Cost pools frequently consist of costs incurred by a particular department, especially a service department. A service department is generally defined as one that does not work directly on the product. Payroll, personnel, maintenance, accounting, data processing, and engineering are examples of service departments. Many illustrations of the cost allocation process are drawn from service departments. Additionally, service departments sometimes bring up some interesting problems in cost determination and estimation, as well as allocation, as we shall see later in this chapter.

The amounts in cost pools can be affected if there are intermediate allocations. Two techniques that we describe later require that costs be allocated from one service department to another. For example, some of the costs of the personnel department may be allocated to the maintenance department and then in turn allocated to various production departments.

Costs Included in Pools.   Often the costs included in pools are actual, incurred costs, but there are exceptions. Some costs may not be allowable under reimbursement contracts and must therefore be excluded from the pool. Certain costs of defense contractors are not allowable under regulations of federal government procurement agencies. The effect of excluding costs from pools is that the ultimate allocations to cost objects will be lower than if the costs were allowable. The determination of allowability is a matter between the parties to a contract.

Another instance of excluding costs from allocation occurs when only budgeted or standard costs are allocated, while variances are not. The practice of allocating only budgeted or standard costs is wise, because it insulates the operating manager from the inefficiencies of service departments. For example, suppose that the maintenance department of a large firm incurs costs of $245,000 during a particular month. The flexible budget allowance for the amount of work done is $228,000. Allocating the $228,000 to the operating departments that used maintenance services makes more sense than allocating the $245,000. The operating managers are not responsible for the efficiency of the maintenance department. The head of the maintenance department is responsible for the $17,000 variance, and the operating managers should not be penalized (or rewarded) for inefficiencies (or efficiencies) of the maintenance department.

Allocation Bases

Chapter 5 on job order costing made the point that the base for allocating costs should be the one that has the closest cause-and-effect relationship with the cost objective. Thus, factory overhead costs may be allocated using direct labor hours, machine hours, direct labor cost, or some other base thought to be the causal factor in the incurrence of overhead. Pronouncements of the Cost Accounting Standards Board also stress the use of a base that reflects cause-and-effect relationships or benefits received.[3] The benefits-received criterion as outlined in CASB Standards is similar to the cause-and-effect criterion. Both require the accountant to look at the activities of the service departments (or, more generally, the cost pools) and of the cost objectives (specific government contracts, for example) to determine how the service department benefits are distributed.

Bases Commonly Used.   Some commonly used allocation bases appear opposite. Some seem perfectly reasonable, others may seem tenuous. To argue that, for example, it makes more sense to allocate building depreciation on the basis of cubic footage occupied rather than square footage is wasting time and effort. (The argument would run that because some de-

[3] Cost Accounting Standards Board, Standard No. 403, *Allocation of Home Office Expenses to Segments*, and Standard No. 418, *Allocation of Direct and Indirect Costs.*

partments, especially production departments, occupy space with very high ceilings to accommodate equipment, they should be charged more than departments that occupy space with ceilings of normal height.) One important point is that allocations must be made and, therefore, that some base must be used.

Common Bases for Allocation

Cost	Possible Bases
Personnel	Number of employees, hours worked, dollar payroll
Data processing	Computer time used
Central purchasing	Number of purchase orders, dollar volume of orders
Telephone	Number of calls, number of telephones
Employee fringe benefits	Dollar payroll, hours worked

Dual Allocation Bases.   Firms might use two allocation bases—one for variable costs, one for fixed costs. The reasoning is that variable costs can be associated with the use of a service, whereas fixed costs are incurred to provide the capacity to render the service. For example, having $220,000 in maintenance equipment does not provide services, but it provides the capacity to provide services that could not be provided without the equipment. When a firm develops the capacity to provide services to its operating departments, it does so with some consideration of the expected long-run use of these services. Because the managers of the operating departments may participate in the decision to develop a particular amount of capacity, it may be reasonable to allocate the fixed costs in proportion to their expected long-run use. An example showing how the dual allocation bases would work appears below.

Costs of Maintenance Department

Variable $24,000
Fixed $80,000

	Operating Departments	
	Fabrication	Assembly
Hours of maintenance service used	1,000	2,000
Expected long-run average use	40%	60%
Allocations:		
Variable costs 1/3, 2/3	$ 8,000	$16,000
Fixed costs 40%, 60%	32,000	48,000
Totals	$40,000	$64,000

ALLOCATION METHODS FOR
SERVICE DEPARTMENT COSTS

Three general methods are used to allocate service department costs to operating departments. The *direct method* allocates all the costs of a service department at once to the operating departments. These allocations use the relative shares that each operating department bears to the allocation base. If a service department supports other service departments, no consideration is given to this fact under the direct method. The *step-down* (or *step*) *method* allocates service department costs both to operating departments and to other service departments by proceeding in steps until all service department costs have been allocated to operating departments. This method gives some recognition to the support that service departments give to other service departments (called *reciprocal services*) but does not give them full recognition. Finally, the *reciprocal method* uses simultaneous equations or matrix operations to give full recognition to reciprocal services. This method is often cited as the ideal, and in some situations it can be the only correct method to use.

The first step in applying any method is to determine the amounts in the cost pools and the percentages of service that each service department gives to other departments. The latter determination requires the selection of allocation bases for each service department and the determination of the relative shares of the service that other departments use. Each of the three methods requires somewhat different calculations of these relative shares. We shall illustrate each method using the data in Exhibit 12–1 opposite.

Notice that no percentages are shown in the cells representing the work done by a service department for itself. For example, no value is entered in the space showing personnel services for the personnel department. If we simply added up the total number of people working in all departments, we would, obviously, find that some people work in personnel. Similarly, the building services department probably occupies and maintains space, which is the basis used to allocate its costs. We ignore the percentages of work done by departments for themselves—that is, self-service costs. Doing so has both theoretical and practical merit.[4] Thus, there could be 110 employees, of whom ten are in the personnel department, so that the total used to determine the percentages would be 100.

Direct Method

The **direct method** requires that we determine solely the percentages of service that the operating departments consume, and it ignores those con-

---

[4] See the article by Robert S. Kaplan cited in the selected references at the end of the chapter.

EXHIBIT 12–1
Data for Illustration

Percentages of Service

| | Service Performed For | | | | | |
| | Service Departments | | | Operating Departments | | |
Service Performed By	*Personnel*	*Plant Administration*	*Building Services*	*Molding*	*Extruding*	*Totals*
Personnel	—	20%	10%	20%	50%	100%
Plant administration	20%	—	—	50%	30%	100%
Building services	15%	10%	—	50%	25%	100%
Direct costs of departments— before allocation	$30,000	$210,000	$80,000	$680,000	$800,000	$1,800,000

Statistical Bases

Personnel: number of employees[a]	—	20	10	20	50	100
Plant administration: managerial estimates of relative efforts spent on each department, no statistical estimates						
Building services: square footage occupied	3,000	2,000	—	10,000	5,000	20,000

[a] Self-service omitted; see text.

sumed by other service departments. Exhibit 12–1 presents all the percentages of use, so that we must restate the percentages related to the operating departments in order to allocate all of the service departments' costs. The calculations for the allocations are given, along with the results, in Exhibit 12–2 on page 472.

The final results—$873,154 total overhead for the molding department, $926,846 for the extruding department—would be used to determine the actual overhead rates for the two departments if the firm used actual costing. If the firm used normal costing, these figures would be the amounts of actual overhead that would be used to determine the amount of overapplied or underapplied overhead. Additionally, the calculations made in Exhibit 12–2 could be done before the period, using budgeted data. The total overhead figures would then be used in setting the predetermined overhead rates for the two operating departments.

Step-down Method

The **step-down method,** or simply **step method,** gives partial recognition to the services that one service department performs for other service departments. The method has a number of variations, but usually it requires as many steps as there are service departments. In our example there will be three steps. In some cases, especially with local governments, step-downs may be done in just two or three steps even though there are many service departments.

In applying the step-down method you begin by allocating the costs of one service department to the other departments that it supports, both service and operating. Then you select another service department and allocate its costs, continuing this process until all service department costs have been allocated to the operating departments. Two important points of procedure must be kept in mind. First, the costs that end up being allocated include not only those incurred by the particular service department, but also any costs allocated to it from other service departments. For example, if service department A has incurred costs of $40,000 and has been allocated an additional $5,000 from one or more other service departments, you must allocate the $45,000 total when department A costs are allocated to other departments. Second, once you have allocated the costs of a particular service department, you do not reallocate any other costs back to it. These points should be clear after we go through the example.

A question that arises when the step-down method is used is the order in which the departments will be selected. Should we begin with personnel, with plant administration, or with building services? There are three general rules. One is to select the sequence based on the number of other departments, both service and operating, that the service departments support. Thus, if service department A provides support to two operating departments and one other service department, its costs will be allocated before those of service department B that supports only one operating department and one service department.

Another criterion is to select departments according to the percentages of their service that go to other service departments. The service departments are ranked in descending order according to these percentages. Thus if 30 percent of department A's services were consumed by other service departments, and 20 percent of department B's services were consumed by other service departments, the costs of department A would be allocated before those of department B.

A third criterion for selecting departments is to take them in descending order of the dollar amounts of service that they perform for other service departments. This criterion requires that you transform the percentage data on service to dollar data. These two latter criteria are often used as tiebreakers when the first criterion is used and two or more service departments support the same number of operating and service departments.

The reason for having some criterion for determining the order of allocation is that the step-down method aims to recognize the services performed by service departments for other service departments, so it is desirable to try to give the best possible recognition of these reciprocal services. None of these criteria can be judged better than the others if the results of the reciprocal method are taken as the ideal method of allocation. However, there are many practical reasons why the step-down method is used. Therefore, some criterion must be selected.

Illustration: Data From Exhibit 12–1.   We now use the data from Exhibit 12–1 to allocate the service department costs using the step-down method. We shall use the criterion that departments be selected in descending order of the percentage of their services used by other service departments. Thus, the order is personnel, building services, and plant administration. The results are given in Exhibit 12–3 on page 472.

As you look at the exhibit, keep the following points in mind. First, once you have allocated the costs of a department, you do not allocate any more costs *to* it. For example, the services provided *to* personnel by the other service departments are ignored, because personnel costs are the first to be allocated. Second, the costs cumulate. The costs allocated from building services include not only its directly incurred costs, but also include the costs allocated to it from personnel. Similarly, the costs allocated from plant administration include its incurred costs plus the allocations from the other two service departments. Finally, be sure you understand the determination of the percentages used to make the allocations. In each case, they are the percentages from Exhibit 12–1 divided by the total of the percentages of each department to which allocations will be made. This step is easy to check. You should make sure that the costs allocated *to* the other departments equal the costs allocated from the department you are currently handling.

The step-down method improves on the direct method because it at least partially considers reciprocal services, although not fully. For example,

EXHIBIT 12-2
Cost Allocations—Direct Method

	Personnel	Plant Administration	Building Services	Molding	Extruding	Total
Overhead costs before allocation	$30,000	$210,000	$80,000	$680,000	$800,000	$1,800,000
Personnel, 20/70, 50/70[a]	(30,000)			8,571	21,429	
Plant administration, 50%/80%, 30%/80%[a]		(210,000)		131,250	78,750	
Building services, 10,000/15,000, 5,000/15,000[a]			(80,000)	53,333	26,667	
Totals				$873,154	$926,846	$1,800,000

[a] The ratios used to determine the allocations are based on the operating departments' relative shares of the use of the service. Thus for the personnel department, of the 70 employees in the two operating departments, 20 are in molding, 50 in extruding. Plant administration devotes 50 percent of its efforts to the molding department, 30 percent to extruding, for a total of 80 percent.

EXHIBIT 12-3
Cost Allocations—Step-down Method

	Personnel	Plant Administration	Building Services	Molding	Extruding	Total
Overhead costs before allocation	$30,000	$210,000	$80,000	$680,000	$800,000	$1,800,000
Personnel, 20%, 10%, 20, 50%[a]	(30,000)	6,000	3,000	6,000	15,000	
Building services, 10%/85%, 50%/85%, 25%/85%[a]		9,765	(83,000)	48,824	24,411	
Plant administration, 50%/80%, 30%/80%[a]		(225,765)		141,103	84,662	
Totals				$875,927	$924,073	$1,800,000

[a] Percentages: Personnel, from Exhibit 12-1. Building services, from Exhibit 12-1, 10 percent to plant administration, 50 percent to molding, 25 percent to extruding, total 85 percent. Plant administration, from Exhibit 12-1, 50 percent to molding, 30 percent to extruding.

the services that the personnel department provides to the other service departments are considered in the first allocation, but the fact that the other departments provide services to the personnel department is never considered.

Reciprocal Method

The **reciprocal method** fully considers all reciprocal services, thereby overcoming one problem associated with the use of the direct and step-down methods. Two techniques may be used: simultaneous equations and matrix inversion. Matrix inversion is a linear algebra technique that has certain advantages over the use of simultaneous equations. It is illustrated in Appendix 12–A.

In setting up an equation to determine how to allocate the costs of each department we are essentially determining the total costs of the department including the costs of the services provided to them by other service departments. We will use the following notation:

P = total costs of the personnel department
A = total costs of the plant administration department
B = total costs of the building services department

These total-cost figures will include not only the direct costs of operating the departments (for example, the $30,000 incurred by the personnel department), but also the costs allocable to them from the other service departments. In order to solve for these total costs, we solve the following equations:

(12–1) $P = \$30,000 \qquad\qquad\quad + 0.20A + 0.15B$ (personnel)
(12–2) $A = \$210,000 + 0.20P \qquad\qquad + 0.10B$ (plant administration)
(12–3) $B = \$80,000\ \ + 0.10P$ (building services)

The terms in each of these equations correspond to the *columns* in Exhibit 12–1. The logic of setting up the equations this way may require some discussion. Take the personnel department as an example. Personnel *receives* 20 percent of the services performed by plant administration and 15 percent of those performed by building services. Thus, the total cost to run the personnel department is not only the $30,000 direct cost, but also 20 percent of plant administration cost and 15 percent of building services costs.

However, both plant administration and building services use the services of the personnel department, and so on. Accordingly, we must solve for the total costs of all departments simultaneously. We have three equations and three unknowns. Solving the three equations simultaneously can be done in various ways. In this case one relatively straightforward method is to substitute the equations for A and B into the equation for P. This substitution gives:

$$\text{(12-1a)} \quad P = \$30,000 + 0.20\overbrace{[\$210,000 + 0.20P + 0.10(\$80,000 + 0.10P)]}^{\text{equation for } A}$$
$$+ 0.15\overbrace{(\$80,000 + 0.10P)}^{\text{equation for } B}$$

Multiplying the terms in parentheses by the coefficients gives:

$$\text{(12-1b)} \quad P = \$30,000 + \$42,000 + 0.04P + \$1,600 + 0.002P$$
$$+ \$12,000 + 0.015P$$

Collecting terms gives:

$$\text{(12-1c)} \quad 0.943P = \$85,600$$
$$P = \$90,774.13$$

We now solve for A and B, using the value for P. Beginning with B, we have:

$$\text{(12-3a)} \quad \begin{aligned} B &= \$80,000 + 0.10P \\ &= \$80,000 + 9,077.41 \\ &= \$89,077.41 \end{aligned}$$

Solving for A:

$$\text{(12-2a)} \quad \begin{aligned} A &= \$210,000 + 0.20P + 0.10B \\ &= \$210,000 + \$18,154.83 + \$8,907.74 \\ &= \$237,062.57 \end{aligned}$$

As we noted before, each of these costs exceeds the direct costs of each department. The personnel department total cost of $90,774 is more than three times its direct costs of $30,000.

When we allocate these costs to the operating departments, we must use the percentages originally given in Exhibit 12–1 without adjusting them. Since 30 percent of the personnel department costs have already been allocated to service departments, we shall allocate 20 percent of the personnel department's costs of $90,774 to the molding department and the remaining 50 percent to the extruding department. The allocations are given in Exhibit 12–4. Note that this procedure results in the correct total of $1,800,000 in overhead costs (both direct and allocated) shown in the operating departments.

Although Exhibit 12–4 provides complete data for the allocation of costs to the operating departments, it does not show the details of the intermediate allocations of service department costs to other service departments, nor does it show how the direct costs of the service departments are accounted for. As a check on the accuracy of the solution, Exhibit 12–5 on page 476 shows the entire allocation process including the simultaneous allocations of the service department costs to the other service departments. You may wish to trace these allocations to satisfy yourself that all the costs are accounted for correctly. Each entry is the final service department cost figure multiplied by the percentages in Exhibit 12–1, which are reproduced in Exhibit 12–5 for your convenience.

EXHIBIT 12–4
Final Cost Allocations—Reciprocal Method

	Combined Service Departments	Molding	Extruding	Total
Costs before allocation	$320,000	$680,000	$800,000	$1,800,000
Allocations (to nearest dollar):				
Personnel				
($90,774 × 0.20)		18,155		
($90,774 × 0.50)			45,387	
Plant administration				
($237,063 × 0.50)		118,531		
($237,063 × 0.30)			71,119	
Building services				
($89,077 × 0.50)		44,539		
($89,077 × 0.25)			22,269	
Totals		$861,225	$938,775	$1,800,000

Evaluation of Methods

There is one case in which only the reciprocal method should be used: when the service department costs are variable. In that case, the information given by applying the reciprocal method is valuable for planning, control, and decision making. This point is covered in the following section. If, as we discussed before, variable costs are allocated separately from fixed costs, the question how the fixed costs should be allocated is usually inconsequential so long as the allocations are not used for reimbursement, pricing, and other decision-making purposes.

As earlier chapters have constantly pointed out, allocating fixed costs is undesirable for planning, control, and decision making. If fixed costs are allocated by any of the methods described and if managers use those allocated costs for managerial purposes, they will be committing a serious error. If the allocated fixed costs are used only for product costing purposes, any of the methods can be used without providing misleading information. The same comment applies to selecting bases for allocation and to grouping departmental costs into cost pools. So long as we are considering only fixed

EXHIBIT 12–5
Intermediate and Final Cost Allocations—Reciprocal Method

	Personnel	Plant Administration	Building Services	Molding	Extruding	Total
Costs before allocation	$30,000	$210,000	$80,000	$680,000	$800,000	$1,800,000
Allocations:						
Personnel	(90,774)	18,155	9,077	18,155	45,387	
Plant administration	47,413	(237,063)		118,531	71,119	
Building services	13,361	8,908	(89,077)	44,539	22,269	
Totals	0	0	0	$861,225	$938,775	$1,800,000

		Work Done For				
Work Done By	Cost	Personnel	Plant Administration	Building Services	Molding	Extruding	Total
---	---	---	---	---	---	---	---
Personnel	$ 90,774	—	0.20	0.10	0.20	0.50	1.00
Plant administration	237,063	0.20	—	—	0.50	0.30	1.00
Building services	89,077	0.15	0.10	—	0.50	0.25	1.00

costs, there is no correct method of allocating these costs for managerial purposes. Throughout this book we have discussed the theoretical issues leading to this conclusion.

In general, then, the criteria to be used for selecting an allocation method depend on whether variable costs are included in the cost pools. If not, then the basic criterion is the cost to the firm of using one method rather than another. The direct method is the easiest to apply and, therefore, the cheapest, but the use of computers makes it relatively easy and cheap to employ the reciprocal method. The step-down method may not be costly to use, but the decisions required on the sequence in which departments are selected make its use sometimes seem arbitrary. Of course, any allocation of fixed costs is arbitrary, but if the method is consistently applied, there may be less irritation to managers than if it is changed at frequent intervals.

VARIABLE COSTS OF SERVICE DEPARTMENTS

A special problem exists when service department direct costs are mainly variable and these departments provide support to other service departments. The true variable cost to operate such departments includes not only the direct variable costs, but also a portion of the variable costs from the supporting departments. These same problems may apply in determining the true variable costs of operating departments. This whole matter is best addressed by an example.

Illustration: The Thornton Company

The data in Exhibit 12–6 on page 478 describe the operations of the Thornton Company during a typical month. Maintenance and power are service departments, while fabrication and assembly are operating departments. All cost data are for variable costs only.

Presumably the $9 and $2 variable cost-per-unit figures could be used for planning, control, and decision making were it not for the reciprocal relationships. That is, if maintenance and power were not dependent on one another, increasing maintenance by one hour would increase maintenance cost by $9. But if we do increase maintenance, we must also increase power, which in turn increases maintenance, and so on. Therefore, the variable cost figures required for planning must be determined by solving the simultaneous equations to determine the total costs of the two departments.

Proceeding as before, we set up equations for each department's cost:

(12–4) $$M = \$9,000 + 0.20P$$
(12–5) $$P = \$4,000 + 0.10M$$

where M = total costs of the maintenance department
P = total costs of the power department

EXHIBIT 12–6
Thornton Company

Units of Work and Percentages

| | *Work Done For* | | | | |
| | Maintenance | Power | Fabrication | Assembly | Total |
Work Done By					
Maintenance, in hours	0	100 (10%)	700 (70%)	200 (20%)	1,000 (100%)
Power, in kilowatt hours	400 (20%)	0	1,200 (60%)	400 (20%)	2,000 (100%)

Technological Requirements

Each hour of maintenance requires the use of 0.40 kwh of power (400/1,000), since the 1,000 hr of maintenance work required the consumption of 400 kwh. By the same reasoning, each kilowatt hour of power requires 0.05 hr of maintenance (100/2,000).

Cost Data

	Direct Variable Cost per Unit	Total for Period
Maintenance	$9/hr	$9,000
Power	$2/kwh	$4,000

Substituting the equation for P into the equation for M:

$$M = \$9,000 + 0.20(\$4,000 + 0.10M)$$
(12–4a) $\quad 0.98M = \$9,800$
$$M = \$10,000$$

Solving for P,

(12–5a) $\quad \begin{aligned} P &= \$4,000 + 0.10(\$10,000) \\ P &= \$5,000 \end{aligned}$

Dividing these adjusted total costs by the outputs of each department gives new variable-cost-per-unit figures, which we shall call **adjusted variable costs:**

$$\text{maintenance} = \$10\ (\$10,000/1,000)$$
$$\text{power} = \$2.50\ (\$5,000/2,000)$$

These adjusted variable costs are the relevant ones for planning and decision making, as we now illustrate.[5]

Illustration: External Versus Internal Purchase

Suppose the firm could buy its power from an outside company for $2.50/kwh. If our calculations of the adjusted variable costs are correct, the firm should incur the same total direct costs of $13,000 ($9,000 + $4,000) for the two activities. If power is bought outside, the firm no longer needs the services that the maintenance department provides to the power department. Therefore, total maintenance time will be 900 hr (700 for fabrication, 200 for assembly) at the current level of activity of the operating departments. The total power requirements will be 1,600 kwh for the operating departments, plus 0.40 kwh per hour of maintenance. (See the technological requirements section of Exhibit 12–6.) In equation form, letting K = required number of kilowatt hours of power,

$$K = 1,600 + 0.40(900)$$
$$K = 1,960$$

The total direct variable cost will then be $13,000, as shown below:

Maintenance, 900 × $9	$ 8,100
Power (bought from outside source), 1,960 × $2.50	4,900
Total	$13,000

However, if power is bought internally, the adjusted variable costs of $10 and $2.50 for maintenance hours and kilowatt hours of power are relevant to any situation in which the activity of one department is to be increased, so long as the technological relationships (0.40 kwh per hour of maintenance and 0.05 hr of maintenance per kilowatt hour of power) are expected to hold.

The allocations of the service department costs to the operating departments are also relevant for planning and decision making. These alloca-

---

[5] Alternatively, we could solve directly for the variable costs using the following equations:

$$V_M = \$9 + 0.40V_P, \qquad V_P = \$2 + 0.05V_M$$

where V_M is the variable cost per hour of maintenance and V_P is the variable cost per kilowatt hour of power. (Each hour of maintenance requires 0.40 kwh. Each kilowatt hour requires 0.05 hr of maintenance.) Replacing the equation for power with the equation for maintenance, we get:

$$V_M = \$9 + 0.40(\$2 + 0.05V_M)$$
$$0.98V_M = \$9.80$$
$$V_M = \$10$$
$$V_P = \$2.50$$

tions are given below. Figures come from Exhibit 12–6 and from the new, total variable costs calculated above.

		Fabrication	Assembly
Maintenance,	700 × $10	$ 7,000	
	200 × $10		$2,000
Power,	1200 × $2.50	3,000	
	400 × $2.50		1,000
Totals		$10,000	$3,000

Suppose that the managers of the firm use the $9 and $2 figures for planning. Suppose further that the manager of one operating department is considering a change in operations that will increase maintenance requirements by 100 hr per month but will save $950 in other costs. If he uses the $9 variable cost, he will make the change, because there will be a $50 monthly saving [$950 − (100 × $9)]. But if maintenance requirements in an operating department increase by 100 hr, power requirements of the maintenance department increase. In turn, because maintenance serves power, maintenance requirements will increase further. We can show that the actual cost increase will be $1,000 (100 × $10), using the following equations:

(12–6) $M' = 100 + 0.05P'$
(12–7) $P' = 0.40M'$

where M' = the total increase in maintenance hours
          P' = the total increase in kilowatt hours of power

The relationships of 0.40 kwh per hour of maintenance and 0.05 hr of maintenance per kilowatt hour were given above. Solving by substituting (12–6) into (12–7) gives:

$$M' = 100 + 0.05(0.40M')$$
$$0.98M' = 100$$
$$M' = 102.04 \text{ (rounded)}$$
$$P' = 40.82 \text{ (rounded)}$$

Using the direct variable costs of $9 and $2 gives a total cost increase of $1,000 ((102.04 × $9) + (40.82 × $2)), which is the same result we would get using the $10 adjusted variable cost for maintenance.

BEHAVIORAL CONSIDERATIONS OF ALLOCATIONS

Earlier chapters stressed the principle of controllability—that managers should be held responsible only for what they can control. Managers cannot control allocated joint costs, and so these costs should not be shown on a manager's performance reports. There is no reason why costs allocated for product costing purposes have to appear on performance reports. It is quite possible, then, to allocate for product costing but not for control and performance evaluation.

Some accountants, and other managers, take the position that managers who receive services (benefit from the activities of service departments) should have to bear some of the cost of those services. They argue that cost allocations are therefore appropriate for performance reporting. The question is whether the costs that are allocated to operating departments are a reasonable reflection of the benefits that managers receive from the service departments.

Dual Allocation Rates

Earlier in this chapter we discussed the notion of dual allocation rates: one for variable costs, the other for fixed costs. The major advantage of that scheme is that the costs charged to a particular manager depend only on his or her use of a service, not on the use that other managers make of the service. In contrast, when all service department costs, both variable and fixed, are allocated on the basis of relative use of the service, each department's share is dependent on the use of other departments. An example should make this point clear.

Monthly service department costs are $100,000 + $5/hr.

	Operating Departments	
	Molding	Finishing
Use of service, January	1,000 hr	2,000 hr
February	1,000	1,000

If allocations were made on the basis of relative use, January would show the following:

	Molding	Finishing
Variable Costs	$ 5,000	$10,000
Fixed Costs	33,333	66,667
Totals	$38,333	$76,667

And February would show:

	Molding	Finishing
Variable Costs	$ 5,000	$ 5,000
Fixed Costs	50,000	50,000
Totals	$55,000	$55,000

The molding department received a higher allocation in February than it did in January, solely because of the increased allocation of fixed costs under the relative share allocation base. The idea behind a true dual rate system is that the allocation of fixed service department costs to both departments would be based on their relative long-run expected use of the service. If, for example, the relative long-run expected use was 40 percent for molding, 60 percent for finishing, the allocations of fixed costs each month would be $40,000 and $60,000, respectively, and would be unaffected by relative use. Thus, the only change in the allocation from month to month would be the result of using greater or fewer hours, and it would be shown solely in the variable-cost allocation.

Whenever an allocation scheme involves the allocation of fixed costs on the basis of actual relative use of the service, managers will find that their allocations differ because of the actions of other managers. This situation is considered undesirable. Managers may postpone using the service for fear that the allocation will be high in a particular month, even though it may be desirable to use it. For example, postponing of maintenance services may be to the long-run detriment of the department, and of the firm, but may be commonplace because managers wish to keep down their allocated costs.

An additional way to avoid behavioral problems in allocating costs is to allocate standard or budgeted costs, rather than actual costs, as discussed earlier in this chapter (pages 466–467). The use of standard variable costs and budgeted fixed costs for allocations does not penalize (reward) the operating manager for inefficiencies (efficiencies) of the service departments. Variances between actual and standard or budgeted costs are left with the service department so far as performance evaluation is concerned, even though they may be allocated to products through operating departments for product costing purposes.

Transfer Prices

Some firms do not use cost allocations for performance evaluation. Instead they use **transfer prices,** which are preset charges for goods or services provided by one segment of the firm to another. That is, instead of allocating some dollar amounts based on the costs of the service departments, the firm charges the consuming department a price for the services. The price might be based on the market price that the segment would have to pay to obtain the service, and such prices might add up to a great deal more than the cost of running the service department.

Transfer prices are discussed in detail in Chapter 18. They are especially prevalent in decentralized companies where operating divisions deal with one another as well as with outside firms. We are interested here in how transfer prices can help us with the problems of allocating actual costs, budgeted costs, or standard costs.

Transfer prices may be valuable from a behavioral standpoint, especially if they approximate market prices. A manager who buys a service from another department in the firm may feel better about it if he knows that it would cost him about the same amount to buy the service outside. In some firms, managers who believe they can get the service cheaper outside are permitted to do so. So if the computer center charges $80 per hour for computing time, and time on a similar machine costs $70 from an outside firm, managers may decide to buy the service outside.

So long as transfer prices approximate market prices, they satisfy the criterion that managers should be charged for the services from which they receive benefits. Moreover, the use of transfer prices, rather than allocated costs, entails that managers who do not use the service do not pay for it. Transfer prices are charged only for services used, whereas allocations are frequently based on other criteria, so that even if managers make little or no actual use of a service, they receive allocations of its costs.

Another important advantage of transfer prices over cost allocations is that they can be used to encourage or discourage the use of various services. By setting the transfer price of, say, maintenance time, very low, upper-level managers encourage department managers to use the service more than they otherwise would. If regular maintenance is highly desirable, the low transfer price will have a favorable behavioral impact. If managers begin to overuse a service because of a low transfer price, upper-level management may raise the price to discourage increases in use. This kind of flexibility is not available with cost allocations.

Finally, it is important to note that product costing requires cost allocation and that transfer prices are generally not appropriate in that context. Transfer pricing is used for motivation and performance measurement, but usually not explicitly for product costing or income tax accounting. The reason is that financial reporting is based on the cost principle, and transfer prices do not necessarily approximate costs.

SUMMARY

Cost allocations are prominent in product costing and in the pricing of various types of goods and services. They are therefore of interest to accountants despite their irrelevance to decisions, planning, and control. Several methods are commonly used to allocate service department costs to operating departments. The direct method fails to consider the services that departments provide to each other, while the step-down method gives them partial recognition. The reciprocal method gives full recognition to the services performed by one department for another. It is especially valuable when the service department costs are variable.

Cost allocations can affect the behavior of managers. Upper-level management may decide to use transfer prices for services, rather than allocating costs. Transfer prices can be used to encourage or discourage the use of services as upper-level managers desire.

APPENDIX 12–A: MATRIX SOLUTIONS TO COST ALLOCATION AND COST DETERMINATION PROBLEMS

Matrix algebra techniques provide some significant advantages over the use of simultaneous equations in solving problems of cost allocation and, in the case of variable service department costs, of determining adjusted variable costs. Using the problem on pages 477–480, we employ the following notation, which is more general than that used in the chapter:

$$S_1 = \text{costs of the maintenance department}$$
$$S_2 = \text{costs of the power department}$$

The first step in setting up the problem for matrix solution is to rearrange the original equations:

$$S_1 = \$9,000 + 0.20S_2$$
$$S_2 = \$4,000 + 0.10S_1$$

to read:

$$S_1 - 0.20S_2 = \$9,000$$
$$-0.10S_1 + S_2 = \$4,000$$

That is, S_1 and S_2 appear in the same columns. In matrix algebra, the equations above are solved using the following format. The coefficients of S_1 and S_2 form a matrix, A, the values for S_1 and S_2 (the solution) form a column vector, x, and the direct costs of the departments form another column vector, b. In matrix notation:

$$\overset{A}{\begin{bmatrix} 1 & -0.20 \\ -0.10 & 1 \end{bmatrix}} \overset{x}{\begin{bmatrix} S_1 \\ S_2 \end{bmatrix}} = \overset{b}{\begin{bmatrix} \$9,000 \\ \$4,000 \end{bmatrix}}$$

That is, the vector x multiplied by the matrix A gives the vector b. To solve, we multiply both sides of the equation by A^{-1}, the inverse of the matrix A:

$$A^{-1}Ax = A^{-1}b$$

The inverse of a matrix multiplied by the original matrix gives an identity matrix, I, which has ones along the main diagonal (upper left through lower right) and zeros elsewhere. Therefore $A^{-1}A$ is $\begin{bmatrix} 1 & 0 \\ 0 & 1 \end{bmatrix}$ in this case. Multiplying a vector by the identity matrix leaves the vector unchanged, so that $Ix = x$. Therefore $A^{-1}b = x$.

Determining the inverse of a matrix can be time consuming. However, when the matrix to be inverted is 2×2 (two rows, two columns) with ones along the main diagonal, as is our matrix A, the procedure is simple and quick.

Step 1. Subtract from 1 the product of the off-diagonal elements (upper right element multiplied by lower left element). In our example, the result is 0.98 $[1 - (-0.20 \times -0.10)]$.

Step 2. Change the signs of the off-diagonal elements and divide all elements by the result from step 1. The result is the inverse:

$$A^{-1}$$
$$\begin{bmatrix} 1/0.98 & 0.20/0.98 \\ 0.10/0.98 & 1/0.98 \end{bmatrix}$$

which equals:

$$A^{-1}$$
$$\begin{bmatrix} 1.0204 & 0.2041 \\ 0.1020 & 1.0204 \end{bmatrix}$$

We can now solve for the vector x using matrix multiplication.[6]

$$\begin{array}{ccc} A^{-1} & b & x \end{array}$$
$$\begin{bmatrix} 1.0204 & 0.2041 \\ 0.1020 & 1.0204 \end{bmatrix} \begin{bmatrix} \$9{,}000 \\ \$4{,}000 \end{bmatrix} = \begin{bmatrix} \$10{,}000 \\ \$\ 5{,}000 \end{bmatrix}$$

The allocations to the operating departments are simply the adjusted costs multiplied by the percentages of each service consumed by each operating department:

$$\text{fabrication} = \$10{,}000 = (\$10{,}000 \times 70\%) + (\$5{,}000 \times 60\%)$$
$$\text{assembly} = \$3{,}000 = (\$10{,}000 \times 20\%) + (\$5{,}000 \times 20\%)$$

The elements on the main diagonal of A^{-1} have special significance. Divided into the corresponding elements of x, they give the savings in cost that would come from eliminating the department. Thus, they give the maximum amount that the firm could pay to obtain the service outside without reducing profits. This assumes that the level of operations would remain the same. For S_2, which we showed in the chapter had incremental costs of \$4,900 (page 479), we obtain:

$$\$5{,}000/1.0204 = \$4{,}900$$

and for S_1:

$$\$10{,}000/1.0204 = \$9{,}800$$

[6] $S_1 = \$10{,}000$ from $(1.204 \times \$9{,}000) + (0.2041 \times \$4{,}000)$.
$S_2 = \$5{,}000$ from $(0.1020 \times \$9{,}000) + (1.204 \times \$4{,}000)$.

In applying this technique, remember that the corresponding elements must be used. In the 2 × 2 case, both elements on the main diagonal are the same. The 1.0204 we used above for S_2 is the lower right element. Thus, the element to use is the one in the same row as the cost you are considering. When the matrix is 3 × 3 or greater, the same values will probably not show all along the main diagonal.

Cost Determination—An Alternative Setting

Let us consider our example from a different standpoint. So far we have worked with percentages of service provided to other departments and with total units of service provided. These data, from Exhibit 12–6, may come from observation of the results for a period, or from planning prior to a period. In the latter case, the percentages and totals would have to be derived from unit data regarding the operating departments' requirements for services, as well as the service departments' requirements for services. The data in Exhibit 12A–1 below relate to the technological requirements of a single unit of product. We use P_1 to refer to the fabrication department, P_2 for the assembly department.

Our first objective is to determine the amounts of service required from S_1 and S_2 to make a single unit of product. The direct requirements of service to the operating departments are simply the requirements in Exhibit

EXHIBIT 12A–1
Technological Requirements

Units of Product

Two hours in each operating department.

Operating Department Requirements

Requirements per hour of time in operating department:

	P_1	P_2
S_1	0.35	0.10
S_2	0.60	0.20

Service Department Requirements

From Exhibit 12–6:

		Consuming Department	
		S_1	S_2
Providing	S_1	0	0.05
Department	S_2	0.40	0

12A–1 multiplied by the hours of operating time required to make a unit of product. The reciprocal service department requirements also come from Exhibit 12A–1. Letting S_1' = units of service department 1, S_2' = units of service department 2, P_1 and P_2 = the times in operating departments 1 and 2 per unit of product, we have:

$$S_1' = 0.35P_1 + 0.10P_2 + 0.05S_2'$$
$$S_2' = 0.60P_1 + 0.20P_2 + 0.40S_1'$$

Because both P_1 and P_2 are 2 hours per unit of product, we have:

$$S_1' = 0.90 + 0.05S_2' \qquad [0.90 = (0.35)(2) + (0.10)(2)]$$
$$S_2' = 1.60 + 0.40S_1' \qquad [1.60 = (0.60)(2) + (0.20)(2)]$$

Restating in matrix form:

$$
\underset{B}{\begin{bmatrix} 1 & -0.05 \\ -0.40 & 1 \end{bmatrix}}
\underset{x}{\begin{bmatrix} S_1' \\ S_2' \end{bmatrix}}
=
\underset{b}{\begin{bmatrix} 0.90 \\ 1.60 \end{bmatrix}}
$$

Solving by finding B^{-1} and multiplying by b:

$$
\underset{B^{-1}}{\begin{bmatrix} 1.0204 & 0.051 \\ 0.4082 & 1.0204 \end{bmatrix}}
\underset{b}{\begin{bmatrix} 0.90 \\ 1.60 \end{bmatrix}}
=
\underset{x}{\begin{bmatrix} 1 \\ 2 \end{bmatrix}}
$$

This result means that one unit of S_1 and two units of S_2 are needed to make one unit of product. These values include the reciprocal requirements of $0.05S_1$ per unit of S_2 and $0.40S_2$ per unit of S_1. The total service department variable cost per unit of product is $13. That amount can be obtained by multiplying the final values of x given above by the direct variable costs of $9 and $2 [(1 × $9) + (2 × $2)] or by multiplying the final variable costs of $10 and $2.50 by the b vector [(0.90 × $10) + (1.60 × $2.50)]. The difference between this solution technique and the one shown earlier lies in the statement of the problem. Here we dealt directly with the technological coefficients required; earlier we dealt with percentages of service. The earlier method can be used only when the results for a period are known, so that one can determine the percentages of reciprocal service.

The matrix inverse may also be used to determine the total requirements of the service departments at any level of activity. The values for the b vector are simply the requirements for service department work at the expected level of output ($0.90S_1$ and $1.60S_2$ per unit of product) multiplied by the inverse.

It may seem a waste of time to invert a 2 × 2 matrix rather than simply to solve two simultaneous equations. However, as noted before, the matrix inverse gives some information that the other method of solution does not.

Additionally, in realistic situations (say, eight to twenty service departments), solving by matrix inversion is more efficient and is also the method used by many computer programs. A large system of simultaneous equations may take hours to solve by hand, but milliseconds by computer.

ASSIGNMENTS

12–1 **Importance of Cost Allocations.** Late in 1978, a syndicated columnist wrote about a case that the federal government was developing against one of the largest firms in the United States. The columnist made the following points, attributed to inside sources from the federal government.

1. The company used "a bit of bookkeeping sleight-of-hand" that resulted in placing the "entire burden of its research and development costs, both foreign and domestic, on its United States operations." The U.S. operations included sales to the federal government.

2. The company also allocated "an overly generous amount for selling and marketing expenses which, by rights, should have been allocated to its nongovernmental domestic operations."

3. The result was that the company was able to "boost the price of products sold to the government." The firm's "allegedly inflated costs" made it appear that it was earning less than it actually was.

The column contained the terms *price gouging, profit hype,* and *excess profits.*

Required: Comment on the issues involved in cost-plus pricing and on the implications of the statements given above.

12–2 **Basic Cost Allocation.** The Barner Company makes several products in a single factory that has three operating departments and two service departments. The controller is currently developing overhead rates for the operating departments and has asked for your assistance. Budgeted data for the coming year appear below. S means service department.

	Square Feet	Employees	Total Direct Overhead Costs Before Allocation
Fabrication	900	40	$265,000
Assembly	2,000	80	420,000
Building Services (S)	100	20	165,000
Personnel (S)	200	20	90,000
Administration (S)	900	30	320,000

The controller believes that the correct bases for allocation are: Building Services, square footage; Personnel and Administration, employees.

Required:

1. Allocate the service department costs using the direct method. Determine the total costs that the controller will use to set the overhead rates for each operating department.

2. Allocate the service department costs using the step-down method. The sequence you should follow is the percentage of service given to other service departments. (Begin with the service department that provides the greatest percentage of its services to other service departments.)

12–3 Step-Down Allocation. The controller of the Plainview Manufacturing Company has prepared the following information related to operations for 19X6.

	Operating Departments		
	Milling	Refining	Finishing
Direct labor hours	141,000	235,000	162,000
Direct labor cost	$1,385,000	$2,416,000	$1,586,000
Direct overhead	$2,740,000	$1,934,200	$1,017,000

Using various allocation bases, the controller developed the following estimates of percentages of service department effort devoted to other departments.

Percentages of Effort to Other Departments	Service Departments		
	Personnel	Administration	Engineering
Personnel	0%	5%	0%
Administration	10	0	8
Engineering	8	11	0
Milling	17	21	38
Refining	41	35	34
Finishing	24	28	20
Service department costs	$165,000	$486,000	$292,000

Required: Allocate the service department costs, using the step-down method. Begin with the department that performs the largest percentage of service for other service departments. Determine the total overhead rates per labor hour for each operating department after all allocations.

12–4 Joint Costs and Pricing. The Town of Nacandaga is in a resort area. About 3,000 of the 10,000 houses in the town are owned by people who occupy them only during the summer season, which runs for about four months in that area.

The town operates a water company that supplies virtually every house in the town. The charge for water has always been a flat rate per 1,000 gallons: it is currently $3.50/1,000. Recently some of the year-round residents have begun to complain that the summer residents do not carry a fair share of the costs of the water company. The town does not have a minimum monthly charge, so that the summer residents pay only during the time that they occupy their houses and use water.

The town controller has developed the following information.

Variable cost of water	$0.20 per 1,000 gal
Annual fixed costs	$2,500,000
Annual consumption	780,000,000 gal

The water company is expected to break even each year, not to show a profit.

Required: Devise a pricing method that you consider fair and equitable. State the reasoning that you used in developing the method.

12-5 Reciprocal Allocations. During February the Cronin Company experienced the following results.

Percentage of Work Performed For	Service Department		
	Maintenance	Engineering	Administration
Maintenance	0%	10%	15%
Engineering	5%	0%	10%
Administration	5%	0%	0%
Milling	60%	40%	45%
Machining	30%	50%	30%
Totals	100%	100%	100%

The service department direct costs were: maintenance, $60,000; engineering, $90,000; administration, $200,000.

Required: Allocate the service department costs to the operating departments, using the reciprocal method.

12-6 Allocating Fixed Costs. Managers of the operating departments of the Morton Company have been unhappy with the allocation of power costs. Several years ago the firm built its own generating unit, which now supplies all the power needed in the plant. The costs of generating power are allocated to the operating departments based on their relative use, which has created some problems, because the allocation to each department depends on the use it makes of power and also on the use that other departments make.

Variable costs of generating power are about $0.03 per kilowatt hour; and monthly fixed costs are about $320,000. The generating plant has monthly capacity of 500,000 kwh, and the operating departments have the following use:

	Department		
	Foundry	Machining	Coating
Average monthly use	200,000 kwh	180,000 kwh	80,000 kwh
Maximum monthly use	230,000	190,000	120,000

The controller has been thinking of using the average or maximum monthly needs as the basis for allocating the fixed portion of power costs, with variable costs assigned on the basis of actual use. The peak loads in each department do not occur in the same months, so that the 500,000-kwh capacity is sufficient.

Required:

1. Determine the amount of monthly fixed cost that would be allocated to each operating department, using their average requirements as the basis.

2. Determine the amount of monthly fixed cost that would be allocated to each department, using the maximum requirements as the basis.

3. Which basis, average or maximum, would you recommend? What are the arguments for and against your choice?

12–7 Variable Service Department Costs. The Rock Ridge Plant of the York Steel Company is located in a remote area near a major source of iron ore. There are also several coal mines nearby, which are also owned by York. The plant has its own electrical generating equipment, which uses some of the coal.

The plant requires 250,000 tons of coal and 10,000,000 kilowatt hours of electricity for the steelmaking process. Additionally, each 100 kwh of electricity require 1 ton of coal, and mining 1 ton of coal uses about 10 kwh. The variable cost to produce a kilowatt hour, apart from the cost of coal, is $0.10, and the variable cost to mine a ton of coal, apart from the cost of electricity, is about $8.

Required:

1. Determine the total annual requirements of coal and electricity for the steelmaking process.

2. Determine the total variable cost per ton of coal and per kilowatt hour of electricity.

12–8 Reciprocal Allocations (AICPA adapted). The 4N Company has two service departments (designated below as S_1 and S_2) and three production departments (designated as P_1, P_2, and P_3). The schedule at the top of page 492 shows overhead directly attributable to each department, along with the percentages of service that each service department performs for other departments.

Service Department	Percentages to Be Allocated to Departments				
	S_1	S_2	P_1	P_2	P_3
S_1	0	10%	20%	40%	30%
S_2	20%	0	50	10	20
Overhead before allocation	$98,000	$117,600	$1,400,000	$2,100,000	$640,000

The firm uses the reciprocal method of allocation.

Required: Determine the amounts of cost allocated to each production department.

12-9 **Cost Accounting Standards Board Allocation Method.** Cost Accounting Standard No. 403, *Allocation of Home Office Expenses to Segments*, sets up an allocation scheme for home office expenses that cannot be allocated to segments (departments, plants, divisions) on some basis of benefits or causality. The method works in the following way. You determine the percentages that each segment has to the total of each of (a) total payroll, (b) operating revenues, and (c) tangible capital assets plus inventories. These percentages are then added together and divided by 3 to get an unweighted average. The segment then receives an allocation equal to the total cost to be allocated multiplied by the unweighted average percentage.

For example, if a plant has 20 percent of total firm payroll, 15 percent of revenues, and 30 percent of tangible capital assets plus inventories, its share of the "residual," or leftover home office expenses, will be 21.667 percent, calculated as 65% (20% + 15% + 30%) divided by 3.

It is important to note that the expenses allocated in the manner described are residual expenses, those that cannot be reasonably allocated in some other fashion. The Board stated that such expenses should be relatively low and should consist primarily of such items as the expenses associated with "the chief executive, the chief financial officer, and any staff which are not identifiable with specific activities of segments."

The General Militronics Corp. home office had these 19X6 expenses:

Data processing	$2,500,000
Central purchasing	800,000
General corporate staff and officers	940,000

Data related to the firm's three divisions are (in millions):

Division	Operating Revenue	Payroll	Material Purchases	Tangible Capital Assets Plus Inventories	Data Processing Transactions
Instruments	$26.4	$14.2	$ 8.6	$19.0	2,700
Vehicles	55.0	22.1	19.6	28.0	4,500
Armament	17.3	6.3	7.8	9.5	800

Required: Allocate the three home office expenses in conformity with the CASB Standard.

12-10 Matrix Solution (appendix). You instructed your assistant to develop a matrix solution to your cost allocation problem. Because he had not worked with reciprocal allocations, you wrote out the following equations and told him to use MRIX, which is a time-sharing computer program that solves matrix problems.

$$S_1 = \$120,000 + 0.20S_2 + 0.15S_3$$
$$S_2 = \$176,000 + 0.05S_1 + 0.25S_3$$
$$S_3 = \$103,000 + 0.20S_1 + 0.15S_2$$

where S_1, S_2, and S_3 represent the costs of the three service departments.

Required:

1. Set up the equations in matrix form.

2. Assume that the inverse of the matrix is:

1.0561	0.24414	0.21945
0.10972	1.06433	0.28254
0.22768	0.20848	1.08627

Determine the final amounts of costs of each service department.

3. Suppose that all the service department costs are variable. Determine the amount that the firm could save if it were able to eliminate each of the departments.

12-11 Fairness of Cost Allocations. Mr. Able employed a landscaper who came to his house each Monday to mow the lawn, trim the hedges, and do other work. Able paid $20 per week for the service. One day Mr. Baker, who lived next door to Able, asked the landscaper how much he would charge to do his lawn work. The landscaper said that he would do it for $17 per week if he had to come on a day other than Monday. However, he told both Able and Baker that he would do both of their yards for $30 in total if he could do them on the same day. That would save him a trip.

Able and Baker agreed to accept the offer to do both yards for $30 per week. They were unsure how much each should pay and came to you for advice.

Required: List a few fair ways that Able and Baker could split the $30 cost.

12-12 Cost Allocations—Revenue Base. The Sweeten Company has three managers, each in charge of a separate product line. The firm's practice is to allocate joint costs to the product lines using revenue as the base. The firm had the following results in two recent months, in thousands.

		Product Line		
		Suits	Sweaters	Accessories
June Results				
Revenues		$400	$200	$300
Direct costs (variable and separable fixed costs)		180	90	120
Product margin		$220	$110	$180
Total joint costs	$450			
July Results				
Revenues		$400	$300	$300
Direct costs		180	160	120
Product margin		$220	$140	$180
Total joint costs	$450			

The manager of the sweater line conducted a promotional campaign in July and also lowered selling prices to increase the product margin.

Required:

1. Allocate the joint costs to product lines for June and July and determine the income figure for each line in each month.
2. Comment on the practice of using revenue as the allocation basis.

12–13 Cost Allocations and Decisions. The Schoenfeldt Company allocates joint costs to product lines based on their total revenues. The most recent month for the firm showed the following results for the industrial equipment line and all others combined, in millions:

	Total	Industrial Equipment	All Others
Sales	$32.0	$8.0	$24.0
Direct costs	20.0	5.4	14.6
Product-line margins	12.0	2.6	9.4
Joint costs	10.0	2.5	7.5
Income	$ 2.0	$0.1	$ 1.9

Of the direct costs of the industrial equipment line, about $4 million are variable with the quantity sold, $1.4 million fixed. In a later month the manager of the industrial equipment line raised selling prices by 25 percent, which resulted in lower unit volume amounting to 60 percent of that sold in the month shown above. All other lines performed the same as shown above.

Required: Prepare a segmented income statement as shown above for the later month, reallocating the joint costs (still $10 million) in accordance with the new relative revenue figures. Was the decision to raise prices wise for the manager of the industrial equipment line? For the firm as a whole? The managers of product lines are evaluated based on the income figures, not product-line margins.

12-14 Cost Allocations and Decisions. Refer to the data for assignment 12–13. Suppose that the Schoenfeldt Company allocated joint costs based on relative direct costs, rather than revenues.

Required:

1. Redo the segmented income statement given in assignment 12–13, using direct costs as the base for allocating joint costs.

2. Prepare a segmented income statement for the month when the manager of the industrial equipment line raised prices and had reduced volume. Would his decision be wise from his own point of view?

12-15 Dual Allocation Rates. The Brinson Company operates its own electric power plant. In the past, the controller has allocated the costs of generating power to the users (other departments of the firm) based on their relative actual use each month. One result has been widely fluctuating allocations, in part caused by the high fixed costs of the plant and the wide variations in monthly use. The controller has decided to try a different scheme, allocating variable costs based on actual use and fixed costs based on expected long-term use. Data that the controller has developed appear below.

Variable cost per kilowatt hour		$0.40
Monthly fixed costs	$1,500,000	
Expected long-term use:		
Department I		20%
Department II		40%
Department III		40%
Use during a recent month:		
Department I		60,000 kwh
Department II		90,000 kwh
Department III		100,000 kwh

Required:

1. Determine the total costs of the electric power department for the month described and allocate the costs to the departments, using the relative-actual-use basis.

2. Allocate the costs to the departments, using the controller's proposed method.

3. Which basis seems better to you? Why?

12-16 Variable Service Department Costs. During March the following results occurred in the operations of the Kimball Company.

Service	Percentage of Service Performed For				
Performed By	Power	Engineering	Foundry	Grinding	Total
Power	0	20%	30%	50%	100%
Engineering	25%	0	60%	15%	100%

The variable costs of the service departments are: power, $30,000; engineering, $50,000. The total quantities for the service departments are: power, 200,000 kwh; engineering, 4,000 hr.

Required:

1. Determine the total variable costs of each service department, and the "adjusted variable cost" per unit of service for each service department.

2. Determine the amounts of variable service department costs allocated to each production department.

3. Show that if the firm buys power from an outside supplier at the variable cost per kilowatt hour that you calculated in item 1, it will show the same total variable costs for power and engineering that it now does ($80,000). Remember that the firm will not need to provide engineering services to obtain power and that its power requirements will be lowered because the engineering department will need less power.

12-17 Homogeneity of Cost Pools.   The Cost Accounting Standards Board requires that government contractors accumulate indirect costs in homogeneous pools and allocate the costs in the pools to the final cost objectives "in reasonable proportion to the beneficial or causal relationship of the pooled costs to cost objectives. . . ." (See *Cost Accounting Standard No. 418*). The following data relate to a firm that has a single contract with a governmental agency, contract A.

	Fabrication Department	Assembly Department	Totals
Labor cost at $8/hr	$2,400,000	$4,000,000	$6,400,000
Indirect costs	$4,800,000	$2,000,000	$6,800,000
Indirect cost rate per labor dollar	$2	$0.50	$1.0625
Labor cost on contract A	$100,000	$800,000	$900,000

Required:

1. Allocate the indirect costs to contract A, using the plantwide rate.

2. Allocate the indirect costs to contract A, using the departmental rates.

12-18 Multiple Bases for Allocation (CMA adapted).   The Herbert Manufacturing Co. uses a job order accounting system. Overhead consists primarily of supervision, employee benefits, maintenance costs, property taxes, and depreciation and is applied on the basis of actual direct labor hours required for each product.

During October, Herbert added a new product line, furniture for fast-food restaurants, to its line of custom restaurant furniture. Management has been analyzing the results for January through September and comparing them to the results for October. These results are indicated below (in thousands):

Herbert Manufacturing Company

	Fast-Food Furniture	Custom Furniture	Consolidated
Nine months, year-to-date, 19X8			
Gross Sales	—	$8,100	$8,100
Direct Material	—	$2,025	$2,025
Direct Labor:			
Forming	—	758	758
Finishing	—	1,314	1,314
Assembly	—	558	558
Overhead	—	1,779	1,779
Cost of Sales	—	$6,434	$6,434
Gross Profit	—	$1,666	$1,666
Gross Profit Percentage	—	20.6%	20.6%
October, 19X8			
Gross Sales	$400	$ 900	$1,300
Direct Material	$200	$ 225	$ 425
Direct Labor:			
Forming	17	82	99
Finishing	40	142	182
Assembly	33	60	93
Overhead	60	180	240
Cost of Sales	$350	$ 689	$1,039
Gross Profit	$ 50	$ 211	$ 261
Gross Profit Percentage	12.5%	23.4%	20.1%

Management has been discussing whether allocation of overhead based on direct labor hours continues to be appropriate. The accounting manager has suggested that supervision and employee benefits should be allocated on direct labor hours but that the balance of the costs seem more machine related and should be allocated on machine hours.

The actual direct labor hours and machine hours for October are:

	Fast-Food Furniture	Custom Furniture
Machine Hours:		
Forming	660	10,700
Finishing	660	7,780
	1,320	18,480
Direct Labor Hours:		
Forming	1,900	9,300
Finishing	3,350	12,000
Assembly	4,750	8,700
	10,000	30,000

Supervision and employee benefits totaled $108,000 in October, and the balance of the overhead items were a total of $132,000.

Required:

1. Reallocate October overhead according to the accounting manager's recommendation.

2. Based on your results in item 1, recalculate gross profits and gross profit percentages for October. What conclusions can you draw from this analysis?

12-19 Allocation Formulas in Budget Appropriations. The vice-president for administration of the NMC Company recently issued the following directives regarding the staffing of the firm's personnel department and general administration department.

> The authorized size of the personnel department is to be determined as follows: The department shall have 50 employees for every 1,000 production workers, and 20 employees for every 1,000 nonproduction employees. Employees of the personnel department shall count as nonproduction employees for the purpose of this calculation.
> The authorized size of the general administration department shall be 100 employees for every 1,000 production workers and 60 employees for every 1,000 nonproduction employees. However, the employees of the general administration department shall *not* be counted for the purpose of this calculation.

This states that the size of the personnel department depends in part on itself, because its employees are counted in determining its authorized size. However, the size of the general administration department is not affected by its own size, but only by the sizes of the other departments.

Required:

1. Assume that the firm has 100,000 production workers. Determine the

authorized size of the personnel department and of the general administration department.

2. Assume that the costs of operating the personnel department are $100,000, those of the general administration department $200,000. Further, assume that the firm has 50,000 workers in each of two production departments, I and II. Use the reciprocal method to allocate the costs of the two service departments. The basis for the allocations is the number of employees in each service department serving the other departments. Remember that the personnel department has employees who serve itself, and you should ignore them in determining the percentages.

12-20 Revenue Centers and Reimbursements. The administrator of Burrows Hospital has been grappling with some problems associated with reimbursements under a medical insurance plan. Although the hospital can charge patients whatever rates it chooses, its reimbursements under the plan, for patients covered by it, are limited by the following formula:

total annual reimbursement = total annual cost

$$\times \frac{\text{charges to covered patients}}{\text{total charges to patients}}$$

The total annual cost figure is the annual cost of each revenue center. The hospital currently treats the following departments as revenue centers: medical/surgical, outpatient, emergency room. The total annual cost figure includes costs allocated from nonrevenue centers such as admissions, dietary, administration, and building depreciation.

The administrator has developed the following information about the medical/surgical department, in thousands of dollars:

	Total	Medical	Surgical
Total annual costs	$300,000	$100,000	$200,000
Total patient charges	400,000	120,000	280,000
Charges to covered patients	80,000	60,000	20,000

The hospital now considers medical/surgical to be a single department. The figures above for each of the types of service are the ones that would be used if the department were separated into two revenue centers.

Required:

1. Calculate the reimbursement that the hospital would receive if it treated the medical and surgical services as a single revenue center (the present practice).

2. Calculate the reimbursement when each service is treated as a separate revenue center.

12–21 When to Allocate (CMA). Bonn Company recently reorganized its computer and data processing activities. The small installations located within the accounting departments at its plants and subsidiaries have been replaced with a single data processing department at corporate headquarters responsible for the operations of a newly acquired large-scale computer system. The new department has been in operation for two years and has been regularly producing reliable and timely data for the past twelve months.

Because the department has focused its activities on converting applications to the new system and producing reports for the plant and subsidiary managements, little attention has been devoted to the costs of the department. Now that the department's activities are operating relatively smoothly, company management has requested that the departmental manager recommend a cost accumulation system to facilitate cost control and the development of suitable rates to charge users for service.

For the past two years, the departmental costs have been recorded in one account. The costs have then been allocated to user departments on the basis of computer time used. The schedule below reports the costs and charging rate for 19X5.

Data Processing Department
Costs for the Year Ended December 31, 19X5

(1)	Salaries and benefits	$ 622,600
(2)	Supplies	40,000
(3)	Equipment maintenance contract	15,000
(4)	Insurance	25,000
(5)	Heat and air-conditioning	36,000
(6)	Electricity	50,000
(7)	Equipment and furniture depreciation	285,400
(8)	Building improvements depreciation	10,000
(9)	Building occupancy and security	39,300
(10)	Corporate administrative charges	52,700
	Total costs	$1,176,000
	Computer hours for user processing[a]	2,750
	Hourly rate ($1,176,000 ÷ 2,750)	$ 428

[a] Use of available computer hours:

Testing and debugging programs	250
Setup of jobs	500
Processing jobs	2,750
Down-time for maintenance	750
Idle time	742
	4,992

The department manager recommends that the department costs be accumulated by five activity centers within the department: Systems Analysis, Programming, Data Preparation, Computer Operations (processing), and

Administration. He then suggests that the costs of the Administration activity should be allocated to the other four activity centers before a separate rate for charging users is developed for each of the first four activities.

After reviewing the details of the accounts, the manager made the following observations regarding the charges to the several subsidiary accounts within the department:

1. Salaries and benefits—records the salary and benefit costs of all employees in the department.
2. Supplies—records punch card costs, paper costs for printers, and a small amount for miscellaneous other costs.
3. Equipment maintenance contracts—records charges for maintenance contracts; all equipment is covered by maintenance contracts.
4. Insurance—records cost of insurance covering the equipment and the furniture.
5. Heat and air-conditioning—records a charge from the corporate heating and air-conditioning department estimated to be the incremental costs to meet the special needs of the computer department.
6. Electricity—records the charge for electricity based upon a separate meter within the department.
7. Equipment and furniture depreciation—records the depreciation charges for all owned equipment and furniture within the department.
8. Building improvements—records the amortization charges for the building changes required to provide proper environmental control and electrical service for the computer equipment.
9. Building occupancy and security—records the computer department's share of the depreciation, maintenance, heat and security costs of the building; these costs are allocated to the department on the basis of square feet occupied.
10. Corporate administrative charges—records the computer department's share of the corporate administrative costs. They are allocated to the department on the basis of number of employees in the department.

Required:

1. For each of the ten cost items, state whether or not it should be distributed to the five activity centers, and for each cost item that should be distributed, recommend the basis upon which it should be distributed. Justify your conclusion in each case.
2. Assume the costs of the Computer Operations (processing) activity will be charged to the user departments on the basis of computer

hours. Using the analysis of computer utilization shown as a footnote to the department cost schedule presented in the problem, determine the total number of hours that should be employed to determine the charging rate for Computer Operations (processing). Justify your answer.

12–22   **Alternative Allocations (AICPA).**   Thrift-Shops, Inc., operates three food stores in a state that recently enacted legislation permitting municipalities within the state to levy an income tax on corporations operating within their respective municipalities. The legislation establishes a uniform tax rate that the municipalities may levy, and regulations that provide that the tax is to be computed on income derived within the taxing municipality after a reasonable and consistent allocation of general overhead expenses. General overhead expenses have not been allocated to individual stores previously and include warehouse, general office, advertising, and delivery expenses.

Each of the municipalities in which Thrift-Shops, Inc., operates a store has levied the corporate income tax as provided by state legislation and management is considering two plans for allocating general overhead expenses to the stores. The 19X9 operating results before general overhead and taxes for each store were as follows:

	Store			
	Ashville	Burns	Clinton	Total
Sales, net	$416,000	$353,600	$270,400	$1,040,000
Less cost of sales	215,700	183,300	140,200	539,200
Gross margin	200,300	170,300	130,200	500,800
Less local operating expenses:				
Fixed	60,800	48,750	50,200	159,750
Variable	54,700	64,220	27,448	146,368
Total	115,500	112,970	77,648	306,118
Income before general overhead and taxes	$ 84,800	$ 57,330	$ 52,552	$ 194,682

General overhead expenses in 19X9 were as follows:

Warehousing and delivery expenses:		
Warehouse depreciation	$20,000	
Warehouse operations	30,000	
Delivery expenses	40,000	$ 90,000
Central office expenses:		
Advertising	18,000	
Central office salaries	37,000	
Other central office expenses	28,000	83,000
Total general overhead		$173,000

One-fifth of the warehouse space is used to house the central office and depreciation on this space is included in other central office expenses. Warehouse operating expenses vary with quantity of merchandise sold.

Delivery expenses vary with distance and number of deliveries. The distances from the warehouse to each store and the number of deliveries made in 19X9 were as follows:

Store	Miles	Number of Deliveries
Ashville	120	140
Burns	200	64
Clinton	100	104

All advertising is prepared by the central office and is distributed in the areas in which stores are located.

As each store was opened, the fixed portion of central office salaries increased $7,000 and other central office expenses increased $2,500. Basic fixed central office salaries amount to $10,000 and basic fixed other central office expenses amount to $12,000. The remainder of central office salaries and the remainder of other central office expenses vary with sales.

Required:

1. For each of the following plans for allocating general overhead expenses, compute the income of each store that would be subject to the municipal levy on corporation income:

    Plan 1.   Allocate all general overhead expenses on the basis of sales volume.

    Plan 2.   First, allocate central office salaries and other central office expenses evenly to warehouse operations and each store. Second, allocate the resulting warehouse operations expenses, warehouse depreciation and advertising to each store on the basis of sales volume. Third, allocate delivery expenses to each store on the basis of delivery miles times number of deliveries.

2. The managers of the firm believe that they can expand sales by $50,000 in any one of the three stores, but not more than one. Expanding would increase fixed operating expenses of the store by $7,500 and require ten additional deliveries from the warehouse. Determine which store the company should expand.

SELECTED REFERENCES

Churchill, N., "Linear Algebra and Cost Allocations: Some Examples," *The Accounting Review*, 39:4 (October 1964), 894–904.

Cost Accounting Standards Board, Washington, D.C., *Cost Accounting Standards* (various titles and dates).

Eckel, Leonard G., "Arbitrary and Incorrigible Allocations," *The Accounting Review*, 51:3 (October 1976), 764–77.

Kaplan, Robert S., "Variable and Self-Service Costs in Reciprocal Allocation Methods," *The Accounting Review*, 48:4 (October 1973), 738–48.

Moriarity, Shane, "Another Approach to Allocating Joint Costs," *The Accounting Review*, 50:4 (October 1975), 791–95.

Thomas, Arthur L., "The Allocation Problem in Financial Accounting Theory," *Studies in Accounting Research*, No. 3. Sarasota: American Accounting Association, 1969.

_____, "The Allocation Problem: Part Two," *Studies in Accounting Research*, No. 9. Sarasota: American Accounting Association, 1974.

Budgeting and Control

Part 3

Budgeting: General and Behavioral Aspects

Chapter **13**

The **master budget,** or **comprehensive budget,** is a set of plans for achieving various goals. It is also used in the control process to determine whether operations are going according to plan. The budgeting process involves setting goals and objectives and developing forecasts of revenues, costs, production quantities, cash flows, and other important factors. Budgeting also involves communication within the organization. In fact, budgeting involves nearly all the functions of management.

RELATIONSHIPS OF BUDGETING TO EARLIER CHAPTERS

Virtually all the material covered earlier in this book is tied up in the budgeting process. Budgets for revenues and expenses reflect cost-volume-profit (CVP) analysis, the analysis of cost behavior, and the evaluation of available resources as exemplified in linear programming. Budgets for costs are built on the techniques used to set standard costs. The budgeting process includes reporting on performance, of which variance reporting is one aspect and costing methods (absorption and variable) are another.

Budgeting does much more. It ties together the concepts of responsibility accounting, the design of information systems, and the entire managerial process of setting goals and objectives and assembling the resources required to achieve them. In short, the budget is the firm's master plan for a period of time and the basis for evaluating performance. It is the most formal statement of the goals of upper-level management, and it serves to communicate these goals to lower-level managers. It may be one of the most powerful tools for motivation that managers possess. Yet, poorly handled, the budgeting process may work to the firm's disadvantage.

At this point in the book, you have most of the knowledge required to understand the mechanics of preparing budgets. The illustration in the next chapter ties things together; it is involved largely with the relationships among various components of financial statements (for example, sales, accounts receivable, and cash inflows). The sections that follow consider the more important problems of effectively developing and using a master budget to improve the firm's performance.

THE BUDGETING CYCLE

Figure 13–1 diagrams the overall budgeting cycle. The arrows going back and forth from one activity to another indicate a process that moves, not one-way, but to-and-fro. There is a considerable amount of reappraising, redeveloping, and reevaluating at every stage. It is a continuing and dynamic process that looks to the future by evaluating the present.

The goals set by managers may originally be expressed in very general terms, such as *increase market share* or *improve cost control*. However, budgeting plans must be quite specific. The budget must specify how mar-

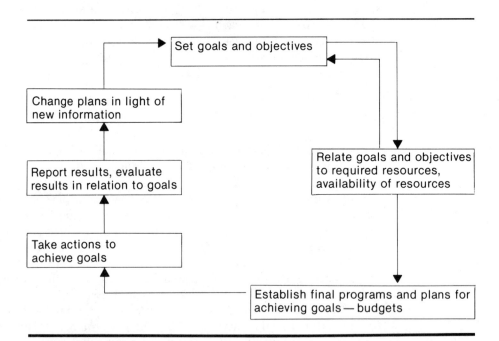

FIGURE 13–1
The Budgeting Process

ket share is to be increased. What combination of pricing, advertising, distribution, and other factors can be expected to provide the desired market share? In the formulation of strategies designed to meet overall goals and objectives, there are usually a few key factors (sometimes called **key result areas** or **critical success factors**).[1] These factors vary from industry to industry, and only a few examples can be given here. In some consumer products industries, especially personal care products (soap, toothpaste, and the like), market share is vitally important, because the products bear heavy selling and promotional expenses and require very high volumes to be profitable. For some manufacturing companies, quality of product and tight cost control are of overriding importance.

The importance of identifying critical success factors is that they enable managers to focus on a few areas, not to try to watch everything. In the budgeting cycle, managers of each segment of a company would pay a great deal of attention to these factors. Budgets for, say, engineering would be scrutinized carefully by managers in a firm where cost control was critical. Resources such as personnel, and the money required for payrolls, would be directed at improving performance in the critical areas. Put another way, managers must analyze the means required to achieve their goals and must have reasonable ideas of the probable effectiveness and efficiency of different means of achieving them. This is how a budget is operationalized.

The reporting of actual results compared with budgeted results is the first step in the control phase of budgeting. Chapters 7 and 8 dealt with standards and the analysis and reporting of variances. Variances should be signals designed to alert managers to potential problems. They do not tell the manager what is wrong, only that something may be going awry and that giving some attention might prove wise. We saw as early as Chapter 1 that evaluation of progress is impossible without goals expressed in budgets. The managers of the parent company of Mesa Uranium Mining Company had no formal expectations and, therefore, could not receive feedback information that would have allowed them to determine whether operations were going according to plan. Even control is future oriented. The comparison of results to expectations is a step in planning for the next cycle of business activity. The major structure of goal setting and planning through evaluation and new planning is contained in the master budget.

BUDGETS AND PLANNING

Forecasts in the Budget

A master budget consists of an interrelated, coordinated group of forecasts—plans for the future. Some of the forecasts are in financial state-

---

[1] See J. R. Daniel, "Management Information Crisis," *Harvard Business Review*, 43:5 (September–October 1961), for an analysis of informational requirements related to success factors. Robert N. Anthony and John Dearden, *Management Control Systems*, 4th ed. (Homewood, Ill.: Richard D. Irwin, Inc., 1980), also discuss the points in their Chapter 4.

ment form. Examples are a budgeted income statement, budgeted balance sheet, and budgeted statement of changes in financial position. These statements are often called **pro forma** financial statements as well as budgeted statements. A pro forma statement is a statement made *for the form,* including the hypothetical transactions planned for the coming period rather than historical transactions that have already been experienced.

Other forecasts in the budget include production quantities and costs, capital asset requirements, personnel requirements, levels of activity in various departments, and new financing through short-term debt, long-term debt, and common stock. Most of these forecasts are developed using techniques already covered in this book. For example, production costs are budgeted using standard costs, often with techniques such as regression analysis. As we proceed, you will see other instances of familiar techniques being used to develop budgets.

Developing Budgets

Budgets may be developed in one of two general ways. Upper-level managers might state what they expect from their subordinate managers in regard to production, sales, costs, personnel, and other factors. Lower-level managers may then try to negotiate with the upper-level managers the items that they do not think reasonable. For example, if upper-level management sends down a budgeted sales figure of $400,000 to a district manager, he may try to have it modified on grounds that it is not realistically achievable. As another example, the data processing manager might be given a budget that requires cutting two employees. She might argue that such a cut would severely impair the service that the department can provide. Whether these negotiations work out as the lower-level managers hope is another matter.

The other basic way of developing budgets is to start at the bottom, with managers of responsibility centers proposing what they expect to accomplish and what resources (principally personnel and cash) they believe are necessary to achieve their goals. Upper-level managers then make revisions and suggestions, offer questions regarding the importance of various activities, and perhaps require a resubmission. For example, a district sales manager might ask for six additional salespeople and an increase in his travel and entertainment budget over the prior year's figure. His requests would probably be accompanied by an explanation of how he planned to use the salespeople and travel money, why the firm would benefit, and what unfavorable results might come from a failure to meet his requests. A good deal of thrashing back and forth would take place between the district manager and upper-level managers before they reached agreement. As you can see, both general methods usually involve negotiation and revisions until a final budget is accepted.

BUDGETING AND RESPONSIBILITY ACCOUNTING

A good budgeting system is an indispensable component of a responsibility accounting system. Each responsibility center, which is a subunit of the firm under the control of a manager, will usually have budgeted objectives and budgeted resources for accomplishing them. As mentioned earlier, budgeted resources include personnel, machinery, space, and the money needed to acquire them. The budget then indicates what is required of each manager, and comparisons of budgeted and actual results will enable managers to see whether particular centers were effective in meeting their objectives, and efficient in the use of resources.

The assignment of responsibility to centers is often facilitated by a careful examination of budgets. This is especially true when the budgets submitted by individual managers show clearly what the money is needed for—what the department (center) expects to accomplish. Duplication and gaps may become apparent when budget requests detail the objectives of the centers. In contrast, when budgets are simply requests for money based on prior-year amounts or on some expansion of activities, the manager evaluating the budget request has no real idea what the firm is getting for its money.

Many organizations, especially governments, follow the practice of **line budgeting.** Individual managers submit budget requests detailing the items of expenditure—salaries, supplies, travel, and so on—with no indication of the contribution that the unit should make to the goals of the organization. Indeed, it is sometimes difficult to see what the goals and objectives of the unit are by examining its budget request. In contrast, **program budgeting** focuses on objectives; it requires managers to justify their budget requests by showing what they will accomplish with the resources given them. Program budgeting also forces managers to show how the accomplishment of the departmental goals contributes to the accomplishment of the organization goals.

ADVANTAGES OF BUDGETING

Systematic Planning

Businesspeople sometimes say that budgeting is not worthwhile because the uncertainties facing the firm are so great that no managers can expect to carry out plans as originally formulated. One version of this position is that after a while, no one pays any attention to the budgets anyway. This attitude reflects the position that managers must be flexible in adapting to changing conditions, and that they not be tied to meeting specific goals and objectives.

There are several counterarguments to this general position. First, no advocate of budgeting argues that a budget must be followed down to the last letter. Budgets are usually viewed as plans for guidance, subject to adaptive and corrective action if conditions change. Second, whether managers use formal budgets or not, they do plan, at least implicitly. Every action a manager takes implies some expectations, whether stated or not. Budgets make these plans and expectations explicit, which makes it possible to evaluate them. For example, if the treasurer of a firm that does no cash budgeting lines up a source of short-term credit, he is making some assumptions about the firm's future cash flows. Explicitly or not, they are there. Requiring a cash budget would force the treasurer to think about why and under what conditions he should be seeking short-term credit.

The idea that managers should be concerned only with running the firm's day-to-day operations, not worrying about the future because it is likely to be different from what they expect, can be disastrous. The future is to a great extent a product of the past and present; and the actions that managers now take or do not take can affect the future greatly. The most common example is the financial difficulties that growing firms run into because they do not consider the future financing requirements that growth will bring.[2] Paradoxically, it is successful, growing firms that experience cash shortages, together with the threat of bankruptcy.

The fact that budgets force managers to plan is important. Managers must state their premises and expectations and consider the possible consequences of their actions. A formal budgeting process provides a systematic framework for planning and control, which is more likely to be successful than a wait-and-react approach to management.

Chapter 4 emphasized systematic decision making, as opposed to the random or inspirational type.[3] Budgeting is a form of systematic decision making, because the plans that a firm makes require decisions about numbers of workers to hire, quantities of various products to make and raw materials to buy, and many other matters. If conditions change and the original budget no longer seems feasible, it will still have served a purpose, because it will make it easier for managers to adapt to the changed conditions. That is, managers who have a budget can adapt better to changing circumstances than managers without one. The discipline of developing the formal relationships involved in the budgeting process will help them understand how changed conditions should affect their planning and decision making in the future.

Coordination

Coordination of activities has always been an important aspect of management in any firm; it is especially so in modern firms because of the inter-

---

[2] Peter Drucker made several points regarding the management of small and medium businesses in the *Wall Street Journal,* April 21, 1977. One was that firms should plan their cash requirements at least two or three years ahead.

[3] See especially the quotation from Morris, *Decision Making,* on page 123 in Chapter 4.

dependence among the various functions. Marketing, production, finance, and general administration activities must work together. Success requires that managers work together and perform their assigned tasks satisfactorily and on time. Budgeting is extremely useful in coordination, and it may help managers to spot potential problems and conflicts. Different managers have different points of view about many aspects of the firm, and these divergent views must be harmonized.

Consider the question of credit policy. Most firms have credit departments that must approve sales on credit. The department may have to approve the credit for all new customers and for orders over specified amounts for existing customers. Checking on a customer's credit takes time and may result in lost sales. This would be unwise from the standpoint of the sales manager and salespeople, but wise from the standpoint of the treasurer, who is concerned with the firm's cash flow.

Salespeople and sales managers would probably like to see credit terms loosened, because sales would be higher if the firm could offer generous terms (say, 60 days instead of 30 days). However, loosening credit policy would probably lead to higher bad debts and higher accounts receivable, which must be financed. The treasurer would probably favor tighter credit policies than would the sales manager. How should this conflict be resolved?

One solution that is consistent with the principles of responsibility accounting would be to allow the sales manager to control credit policies, but to charge his operating budget with the costs of credit. These costs would include the cost of the credit department, which would be under his control, the cost of bad debts, and the opportunity cost on the cash tied up in accounts receivable. Doing all this would have motivational effects. The sales manager would now be responsible for credit and would be charged with the costs associated with that responsibility. However, many firms do not allow the sales manager to be responsible for granting credit, because their managers believe that the credit department should be independent of sales.

BUDGETING AND HUMAN BEHAVIOR

Earlier in this book we have discussed behavioral considerations in various contexts. The overall budgeting process, which includes the development of standards and analysis of variances, provides an opportunity to delve into some behavioral material in a more systematic way. This section describes some of the traditional, or classical, theories of human behavior as they relate to management and accounting. It also discusses some more modern theories of behavior derived from research in the behavioral sciences and management, as well as implications for accounting, especially budgeting.

First, any management control system, of which budgeting is one type, is effective only if it influences behavior in directions that will advance the best interests of the firm. In addition, *any* system will have some influence on behavior. The problem is that many such influences may be dysfunctional—against the best interests of the firm. Because control systems influence behavior, the design and operation of a system will reflect some theory, or parts of several theories, of human behavior. In most cases the underlying theory is not made explicit, but it is there. Therefore, in order to understand why certain features of budgeting systems work well and others poorly, the accountant must be aware of behavioral assumptions. The accountant must also be able to recognize why some types of dysfunctional behavior may plague the budgeting process and what might be done to overcome the problems.

Exhibit 13–1 lists two sets of behavioral assumptions, one labeled *traditional* the other *modern*. These assumptions are not exhaustive. Various writers have proposed different formulations of some of those listed here, and other writers have proposed additional assumptions. Those listed should provide an understanding of the basic attitudes that underlie the two viewpoints.

EXHIBIT 13–1
Some Behavioral Assumptions

Traditional

1. People work principally for money and do not derive any intrinsic satisfaction from work.

2. People are generally lazy, inefficient, and apt to avoid working unless closely supervised.

3. Two important jobs of the manager are to control workers through close supervision and to find more efficient ways for workers to accomplish their tasks (especially through making their jobs simpler).

4. The role of the accounting and budgeting system is to provide information that helps managers to control their subordinates by highlighting inadequate performance.

Modern

1. People work for many reasons, including satisfaction. They are motivated by many needs, which differ in relative importance over time.

2. Managers usually cannot be effective unless their subordinates accept their authority and believe that they will advance their own goals if they work toward their superiors' goals.

3. Accounting and budgeting systems should serve to communicate and to provide feedback that allows people to perform better. Accountants should recognize that the information they present, and the ways that they present it, can affect the behavior of people receiving the reports.

These are only a few of many assumptions that we could list. The selected references at the end of the chapter, especially the work of Caplan, provide fuller discussions.

Authoritarian Management

The traditional behavioral assumptions depict the human as a being of very limited dimensions, very nearly as a beast of burden. The implications for management were articulated by the "scientific management" school that flourished in the early part of the twentieth century.[4] The proponents of scientific management were concerned with finding the best way to perform a task. Time and motion study was an important part of the analysis. Because a worker could not be expected to show any initiative, it was up to the manager to tell him exactly how to perform his task. It was also important to limit the number of operations each worker performed. In that way, workers would become more efficient, because they would do the same few operations over and over. The assembly line was the logical outgrowth.

The early theorists did not foresee difficulties with their approach. If people work only for pay, and are indifferent to the tasks they perform, it follows that they will do as they are told so long as they are paid and watched. The tendency of workers to be lazy, wasteful, and inefficient requires close, direct supervision. Foremen and second-level managers were expected to ensure that workers were performing as upper-level management intended. That is, they were to exercise tight control over operations in order to achieve peak efficiency.

Managers who accept the traditional assumptions believe that the flow of authority is downward. A manager's position in the hierarchy gives him authority over others, and he in turn is subject to the authority of his superiors. Each manager's authority is unquestioned and accepted automatically by his or her subordinates. The manager's job is to use this authority to accomplish the objectives set out by upper-level managers.

The problem with this approach is that it does not always work. Managers who exercise extremely tight supervision may find relatively low productivity among their subordinates. In fact, it seems to be the case that groups of workers or managers develop their own ideas or **norms** of how they should behave at work, and these norms tend to be more powerful controls than those controls used by the supervisor.[5] Norms relate to many aspects of group behavior, including productivity, treatment of superiors and other group members, attitudes toward the firm, and other aspects of behavior.

Workers who exceed the group norms for production may find themselves ostracized or even physically punished. The rate buster is rarely a popular person. Because most people value friendship and acceptance by

---

[4] The classic is Frederick W. Taylor, *The Principles of Scientific Management* (New York: Harper & Bros., 1911).

[5] Many studies have explored the various aspects of group norms and their effects on behavior. Synopses of some of the more prominent studies, such as the Bank Wiring Room, appear in books on organizational behavior. One good source is Paul W. Lawrence, Louis B. Barnes, and Jay W. Lorsch, *Organizational Behavior and Administration*, 3d ed. (Homewood, Ill.: Richard D. Irwin, Inc., 1976).

others, it is not common to find people willing to violate the norms of a group.

In contrast, workers who support the group norms are often viewed as leaders. These leaders derive their leadership not from the organizational structure but from their co-workers, who are very concerned with the preservation of group norms.

Budgeting and Authoritarian Management

An upper-level manager who accepts the traditional assumptions will be very wary of relinquishing any authority. The manager will not trust subordinates and will want to keep a close watch on them. This is because the appropriate response to the traditional assumptions is close, direct supervision. However, it is usually not possible for upper-level managers to exercise such supervision. They simply do not have the time to control everything themselves.

McGregor has argued that authoritarian managers work out of this problem by using staff personnel such as accountants and engineers.[6] The job of the staff is to collect information that the manager can use to control the operation. Budget and standard cost variances are prominent examples of such types of information. The accountant serves as one part of the eyes and ears of upper-level management, and the information that accountants develop substitutes for direct supervision.[7] In such a setting, accountants are viewed with suspicion by line managers.

Under the authoritarian school, budgets are developed from the top down. Upper-level managers set the goals and objectives with only limited participation or consultation of their subordinates. The budget is then used as a club to pressure employees, both subordinate managers and workers, into meeting the goals of the upper-level managers. Subordinates simply provide information to their superiors.

Given the assumptions of the traditional school, the view of the budget as a managerial device for ensuring that employees conform to the expectations of upper-level managers is perfectly reasonable. The problem is that employees charged with meeting budgets frequently behave dysfunctionally. There is a great deal of evidence to show that employees often succeed in circumventing the budgeting system.[8]

Hopwood found some very disquieting effects of what he termed a **budget-constrained** style of leadership, where the supervisor evaluates sub-

---

[6] Douglas McGregor, *The Human Side of Enterprise* (New York: McGraw-Hill Book Company, 1960).

[7] Caplan found that managerial accountants tended to accept traditional behavioral assumptions in about the same proportion as line managers. Edwin H. Caplan, "Behavioral Assumptions of Management Accounting—A Report of a Field Study," *The Accounting Review*, 43:2 (April 1968), 342–62.

[8] The classic is Chris Argyris, *The Impact of People on Budgets* (New York: Financial Executives Research Foundation, 1952).

ordinates primarily on whether they meet short-term budgets.[9] He contrasted this with what he called a **profit-conscious** style, where the important criterion is increasing the long-term effectiveness of the firm. Costs play an important role for this style of manager, but cost and other budgetary data are used more flexibly than by budget-constrained managers. Budget-constrained managers, Hopwood found, tended to preside over departments that had poor-quality service to customers, a low level of innovation, and higher processing costs. Additionally, tension and mistrust were higher among the subordinates of budget-constrained managers.

What many researchers have found is that concentration on achieving a single objective, such as meeting a short-term cost budget, frequently leads to behavior that appears good from the standpoint of the single objective but that does not further the long-term goals of the organization.[10] Because budgets often specify a single goal, such as achieving a particular level of cost, workers and managers may have ample opportunity for dysfunctional behavior. For example, workers could meet production or cost goals by working rapidly and cutting corners, which could adversely affect the quality of the product. Foremen could postpone preventive maintenance to stay within budget. Plant managers could reduce spending on employee training, engineering, and other discretionary cost items. All these actions could improve short-term performance but be detrimental in the long term.

Goal Congruence

The examples given in the paragraph above illustrate a lack of **goal congruence.** Goal and behavior congruence exist when the goals of the manager or worker are in line with those of the organization. Achieving goal congruence is often very difficult—precisely because individuals usually are evaluated on the basis of achieving subgoals rather than organizational goals.

For example, earning a satisfactory profit is a common goal for a business firm, but it is usually not possible to evaluate units within the firm based on profitability: many units within the firm do not earn revenues, only incur costs. Accordingly, it is necessary to establish subgoals. However, ensuring that achieving the subgoals will also ensure achieving the overall organizational goals is rarely a simple, straightforward process. Meeting cost budgets in various departments does not necessarily result in meeting long-term profit goals, as examples above showed.

Unnecessary Spending.   A lack of goal congruence may arise in other

---

[9] Anthony G. Hopwood, "An Empirical Study of the Role of Accounting Data in Performance Evaluation," *Empirical Research in Accounting: Selected Studies, 1972,* Supplement to *Journal of Accounting Research;* and "Leadership Climate and the Use of Accounting Data in Performance Evaluation," *The Accounting Review,* 49:3 (July 1974), 485–95.

[10] The whole problem of dysfunctional consequences of attempts to measure performance using a single criterion is articulately discussed by V. F. Ridgway, "Dysfunctional Consequences of Performance Measurement," *Administrative Science Quarterly,* 1:2 (September 1956), 240–47.

ways. Suppose that a manager has a $12,500 travel budget. Obtaining this budget allowance took a good deal of negotiation with his superior and required considerable justification. Having kept travel costs low during the year, the manager finds toward the end of the year that he will underspend the budget by about $3,000 (expenditures of $9,500). Assuming that there are no good uses for additional expenditures, it would be in the firm's best interest for the manager to stop spending. However, from the manager's standpoint, underspending might be unwise. If he underspends this year, he may find that next year's budget is reduced. His superior may be all the more skeptical: "You got along fine on $9,500, so your budget for next year will be $9,500."

The manager might decide to spend the entire $12,500 in order to avoid the anticipated reduction in the coming year: "Spend it or lose it." This action would not be in the firm's best interest but might be in the manager's. This configuration is all too prevalent, leading to many unwise expenditures near the ends of budget years.

Falsification of Information.   A serious form of dysfunctional behavior attributed to control systems is the deliberate falsification of data. For example, workers may wish to show relatively steady production figures day by day. Sometimes they will produce over the desired level for a few days, but report less than the actual amount. The excess serves as a cushion for later days when they fail to meet the desired level. The objective in this example is to prevent management from finding out how rapidly they can work. Presumably, workers feel that higher levels achieved would soon become the standard level.

McGregor reported that subordinate managers will develop their information systems in order to stay ahead of the staff (such as the accounting department). He described a case where one division of a large firm had reported erroneous data on costs, production, and quality control for several years without anyone discovering it. A change in top management of the division led to the uncovering of the practices.[11]

Slack and Budgetary Pressure

The authoritarian use of budgets encourages managers and workers to respond in order to protect themselves. One method they use is the creation of **budgetary slack,** a cushion to avoid the likely penalties for failure to meet the budget.[12] Managers may underestimate revenues and overestimate costs in their budget requests to create slack. Workers may attempt to fool time-and-motion-study people or use other means to prevent management from learning how rapidly they can work.[13]

---

[11] McGregor, *The Human Side of Enterprise.*

[12] Mohamed Onsi, "Factor Analysis of Behavioral Variables Affecting Budgetary Slack," *The Accounting Review,* 48:3 (July 1973), 535–48.

[13] A wealth of cases based on field research show ways in which workers deceive time-and-motion people. Many appear in books on organizational behavior, such as Lawrence, Barnes, and Lorsch, *Organizational Behavior and Administration.*

Managers submitting inflated cost budgets, or underestimated revenue budgets, usually count on having better access to information than their superiors do. Clearly, if the superior to whom the request is submitted knows as much as the subordinate, there will be no opportunity for introducing slack.

Is slack per se undesirable? There is no unanimous agreement on this point. One argument in favor of some slack is that it will reduce the potential impact of uncertainty by providing a hedge. Additionally, a manager who knows that he has some slack to work with may feel less pressured because he is reasonably sure that he can meet the budget. His actual performance may even be somewhat better under a slack budget than under a tight one. Consider an example from everyday life. If your instructor were to set a goal (budget) of covering three chapters of this book each week, most students would become so frustrated that they would lose heart; they might not even cover one chapter per week. If the goal were set at one chapter per week, most students would probably be able to maintain that pace.

MODERN ORGANIZATIONAL THEORIES
Diversity of Human Behavior

Modern organizational theories are diverse, and no single set of assumptions can describe the entire field. The assumptions listed in Exhibit 13–1 are those that are most relevant to our purposes.

Modern theories of organizational behavior recognize diversity in human beings. People do care about the kind of work they do. People can be motivated by factors other than money. People have various personal goals and will try to further their achievement of those goals as they work in an organization. The acknowledgment of diversity in human behavior presents some problems. We can no longer offer simple rules, such as "Pay them well and watch them closely," as we could under the traditional theory.

Consider a fairly straightforward question: What are the effects on productivity of different styles of supervision? The traditional school emphasizes close, direct supervision. A contrasting style is that of general supervision, where the supervisor provides basic information about the tasks, leaves the details of accomplishing them to the employees, and stands ready to assist when problems arise. The supervisor does not watch everyone closely. This style is an implication of the modern assumptions in Exhibit 13–1. Research into the relationship between supervisory style and productivity *generally* supports the hypothesis that traditional close supervision is associated with lower productivity. The evidence is mixed, and other factors seem to be important in given situations.[14] We should expect to

[14] Chapter 4 of Paul Hersey and Kenneth H. Blanchard, *Management of Organizational Behavior*, 3d ed. (Englewood Cliffs, N.J.: Prentice-Hall, Inc., 1977), provides a good summary of the available evidence.

see many competing theories, and differing empirical results, in organizational behavior. Many, many factors influence human behavior. Some of them may be important in one situation, negligible in another. Many of them are not subject to measurement in the same way that physical properties are. For example, no unit measures self-esteem the way pounds measure weight. It may be possible to state that one person has more self-esteem than another, but not that one has twice as much, or three times as much as another.

Accordingly, the application of findings in management and worker behavior to budgeting and other areas of interest to accountants is not usually straightforward. One or more theories may sometimes help to explain behavior of people who operate in a budgeting environment, but not always. Moreover, the implications of various behavioral science findings for improving budgeting and other control systems do not always hold in practice.

Because the most critical behavioral question in budgeting is motivation, we shall concentrate on motivation in the discussion that follows. We shall draw on a limited portion of behavioral research and present conclusions very tentatively, indicating some areas where research provides conflicting results.

Theories of Human Motivation

Two theories of motivation that speak to the budgeting question are need hierarchy theory and expectancy theory.[15] Many researchers have refined and modified the basic theories, as well as applied them to explain various forms of observable behavior. The relevance of these theories for budgeting is found in several areas. Both have implications for the ways in which budgets should be set and the levels of performance that should be expected.

Need Hierarchy.   The **need hierarchy** theory states that people have needs of quite different types, and that these needs may be arranged in categories such as the following:

1. physiological needs for food, shelter, and other basic requirements of life.
2. safety needs for protection against danger and threat.
3. social needs for belonging, friendship, acceptance.
4. ego needs for self-esteem, self-confidence, status, respect of peers.

---

[15] See Abraham Maslow, *Motivation and Personality* (New York: Harper & Row, Publishers, 1954); McGregor, *The Human Side of Enterprise,* and R. J. House, "A Path-Goal Theory of Leader Effectiveness," *Administrative Science Quarterly,* 16:3 (September 1971), 321–38.

5. self-realization or self-fulfillment needs, which relate to creativity, realization of one's potential, and continued self-development.

Proponents of the need hierarchy theory argue that satisfied needs cannot serve as motivation. Poorly paid workers may be inclined to work harder for more money than well-paid ones. Labor unions become more concerned with job security, a safety need, once their members are receiving reasonable wages.

McGregor has argued that the traditional theories of management focus almost exclusively on the lower-level needs. People are expected to satisfy their higher-level needs away from work. It is little wonder, he comments, that managers complain that they pay their workers well and provide good job security, but suffer from low productivity.

Once people have acquired a high degree of job safety and a reasonable salary, they look to other things. They become more concerned about social and personal needs—the respect of their peers, their self-esteem, the needs that cannot be satisfied on the job with money. Accordingly, management must help employees (both workers and subordinate managers) to achieve their personal goals in order to motivate them to act in the firm's best interests. McGregor summed up part of his argument by saying that management must treat people as adults, rather than as children, which is how he viewed their treatment under the classical school.

Two important elements in McGregor's recommendations are job enlargement and participative-consultative management. **Job enlargement** refers to the process of allowing workers to control the way they work. Rather than use assembly-line techniques, workers could switch jobs among themselves to reduce boredom. They could decide how to organize each operation, rather than having their supervisor order them to perform in specified ways. In short, they would be urged to take on more responsibility. They would not be viewed as indolent, indifferent robots, as they were under the classical assumptions.

Participation and consultation among various levels of the organization, workers and managers, would bring the participants into the stream of the decision-making process. Workers and subordinate managers would have a voice in the control process, and their ideas and advice would be sought out by their superiors. Again, they would have greater responsibility. McGregor argued that these steps, combined with others, would create an atmosphere where employees could satisfy their needs and, therefore, would be more likely to identify with the goals of the firm, rather than just with their own goals.[16]

---

[16] McGregor, *The Human Side of Enterprise,* cited the Scanlon Plan as a manifestation of participative and consultative management. The Scanlon Plan is a way of compensating workers that treats the entire work force as a single unit. The firm pays bonuses to all workers if productivity rises. Part of the rationale for the plan is that workers will be better able to organize the operations of the firm than foremen and managers because they are closer to the actual operations.

Expectancy Theory.   According to **expectancy theory**, individuals behave in accordance with (1) their expectations about the outcomes from various kinds of behavior and (2) the utility they expect to gain from each outcome in the form of satisfying their personal goals.[17]

Expectancy theory uses the term **valences** to refer to the utilities of outcomes. There are two types of valences, called intrinsic and extrinsic. **Extrinsic valences** are rewards bestowed by others: praise, bonuses, promotions, and other forms of pay are the most obvious examples. **Intrinsic valences** come in two varieties. One is the satisfaction associated with the work itself; the more the person likes the work, the higher the valence. The other type consists of internal satisfactions that follow successful completion of the work. Enhanced self-esteem, self-confidence, the feeling of a job well done, and satisfaction gained by meeting the goal are examples of intrinsic valences.

According to the theory, people assign probabilities of two types. One is the probability of success, the other is a set of probabilities associated with each extrinsic valence. That is, the person will evaluate the likelihood that each extrinsic valence will actually be forthcoming upon successful completion. If a manager has been told that accomplishing a particular task will yield a bonus, the probability will be very close to one. If the manager believes that a promotion will follow successful completion, but is not assured of it, the probability will be less than one, perhaps even close to zero.

The higher the probabilities of both types, the higher the motivation. The greater the valences, the greater the motivation. Maximum motivation is achieved when the work itself is very satisfying, the intrinsic and extrinsic valences are high, the probability of successful completion is high, and the probabilities that the extrinsic valences will follow successful completion are also high.

The theory can be formulated in mathematical terms but cannot be verified mathematically. Usually not every valence can be identified, nor can the individual probabilities be precisely measured. Testing of the theory has yielded the usual conflicting results. However, it does provide suggestions about the likely effects on motivation of different factors. For example, a superior who promises assistance to a subordinate may be increasing the subordinate's estimate of the probability of accomplishing a task. Obviously, few people will state that they believe the probability of success is 0.785 or some other precise figure. However, people will make some gross estimates of the chances for success in many endeavors, both at and away from their jobs, and will act accordingly. The amount of time that you devote to studying for a final examination depends partly on your belief about the likelihood of raising or lowering your grade. If there is very little likelihood of either, your motivation to study is low.

---

[17] J. Ronen and J. L. Livingstone provide an excellent discussion of expectancy theory in a budgetary setting in their article, "An Expectancy Theory Approach to the Motivational Impacts of Budgets," *The Accounting Review*, 50:4 (October 1975), 671–85.

Consider an example. Suppose that a manager is offered a difficult task. If he succeeds, he expects to gain a promotion earlier than he otherwise would and also to gain a great deal of respect from his peers. Moreover, the work he will have to do on the task is intrinsically satisfying. Presumably, if he succeeds, he will also enhance intrinsic valences not specifically associated with the work, but rather with his self-confidence and self-esteem.

Obviously, the manager would not formulate the problem in mathematical terms, assigning probabilities to each of the intrinsic and extrinsic valences associated with a successful outcome. However, he would surely make some estimates of the probability of success and of the probabilities of enhancing some valences. If he believed that a larger bonus for the year would be fairly likely, given a successful outcome, he would be somewhat more motivated. If the work were not intrinsically satisfying, he would be less likely to accept the task, and less motivated if he did accept it.

Again, expectancy theory cannot be relied on to give precise numerical values to motivation. What it can do is suggest directions in which motivation is likely to go, given some specific factors. The theory may help us understand why some types of incentives may be motivational and others not in specific situations.

BUDGETING AND MOTIVATION

Many writers have made specific suggestions for improvements in the budgeting process and in other aspects of control systems. These suggestions generally have some behavioral theory behind them, although not necessarily any theory that we have discussed so far.[18] In this section we discuss several of these suggestions, relate them to the previous discussion of motivation, and survey the evidence that either supports or tends to disconfirm them.

Participation

McGregor and others have recommended participation in all phases of the management process. The concept also finds a great deal of support in the literature on budgeting and control systems. Among the asserted benefits of having employees participate in the budgeting process are the following:

1. Employees who participate will be more likely to internalize the goals in the budget, to accept them because they had a hand in developing them. Participation should increase the commitment of employees to the budget.
2. Employees who participate in developing budgets are experiencing

[18] Recall the warning that many kinds of behavior can be equally well explained by different theories.

job enlargement. Their responsibilities are greater than those of employees who do not participate. Enlarging an employee's job should bring greater satisfaction and self-esteem.

3. Employees who participate are likely to have more positive attitudes toward the firm, which should lead to higher levels of performance and morale.

These arguments may be supported by both the need hierarchy and expectancy theories. From the standpoint of the need hierarchy theory, participating employees receive the opportunity to satisfy needs higher than the physiological, safety, and social. The job enlargement that they experience provides greater self-esteem, status, and respect of peers.

The expectancy theory also speaks to the question of participation. First, the process of participating involves the superior and subordinate in discussions about the feasibility of achieving various goals, the development of alternatives such as substituting overtime for the hiring of new workers, and the setting of goals that all parties find reasonable.[19] The employee may experience some enhancement of intrinsic valences because of his or her contribution to the process. Achieving the goal might be more important to the employee who has contributed to setting it.

Participation may also result in the subordinates' having higher estimates of the probability of achieving the goals, which would increase the motivation to perform. These higher estimates could come from the very process of participating, as well as from specific statements and attitudes of the superior. If the superior recognizes the problems, provides assistance where needed, and is genuinely supportive of the subordinates, they are likely to be more confident of reaching the goals.

Does it work? Do employees, both workers and managers, perform better when they participate in the budgeting process? The evidence, as you would expect, is mixed. Empirical studies have found that participation improves performance, and that it does not.[20] Again, it depends on the circumstances.

What appears to be participation may not be. Simply consulting with subordinates before setting budgetary goals is not participation. Subordinates called in and asked for their views may not see such conferences favorably if they believe they are just another of management's tricks. That is, if subordinates (perhaps foremen) do not trust management, they will be suspicious of attempts to inject participation into the budgetary process.

Becker and Green have hypothesized that participation may lead to

---

[19] Of course, the process might not result in the setting of goals that everyone considers reasonable. At this point, the superior might impose goals or there might be additional negotiations with higher-level managers.

[20] Summaries of empirical findings and references appear in Ken Milano, "The Relationship of Participation in Budget-Setting to Industrial Supervisor Performance and Attitudes: A Field Study," *The Accounting Review*, 50:2 (April 1975), 274–84. Articles cited in the selected references at the end of the chapter contain numerous references as well.

either higher or lower performance.[21] Participation will involve greater interaction among the employees, which interaction may increase group cohesiveness. High cohesiveness exists when the group's members value their membership highly and, therefore, tend to accept the norms of the group in order to continue as members. If the cohesiveness of the group increases as a result of greater interaction, and if this cohesiveness is positively correlated with incentives for either better or poorer performance, then participation may result in higher or lower levels of performance.

In other words, if high performance is a group norm, participation will probably improve performance. If low performance is a group norm, participation will probably lower performance.

Becker and Green also point out that participation at higher levels of management may foster more positive attitudes in supervisors, which may be carried through to their subordinates, so that higher levels of performance may result.

In short, participation has often been found to correlate well with increased morale, better attitudes toward the firm and the job, and other factors. However, these factors themselves do not always correlate well with better performance. Participation by itself cannot be expected to increase performance, but it is a factor important in improving performance.

Currently Attainable Budgetary Goals

Accountants, we noted in Chapter 8, generally support the position that standard costs should be set at currently attainable levels, rather than at levels very hard or very easy to attain. The same thinking applies to budgetary goals. The term **aspiration level** describes the level of performance (goal) that someone decides to achieve and intends to devote maximum effort to reach.

Where subordinates participate in the budgeting process, they are unlikely to allow goals to be set at unattainable levels. Superiors, however, can often affect goal levels. In one study, subordinates performed better when the supervisor set a specific standard than when he set a very low standard or no standard at all.[22] In another study, one group was told a standard and its members were then asked to set their own goals. Another group was asked to set goals, then was given the standard. The second group set higher goals and also performed better than the first group.[23] A rule of some current popularity is that performance is best when there is roughly a 50-50 chance of achieving the goal.

[21] See Selwyn W. Becker and David O. Green, Jr., "Budgeting and Employee Behavior," *Journal of Business*, 35:4 (October 1962), 392–402.

[22] D. J. Cherrington and J. O. Cherrington, "Appropriate Reinforcement Contingencies in the Budgeting Process," presented at the *Accounting Empirical Research Conference*, University of Chicago, May 1973.

[23] Andrew C. Stedry, *Budget Control and Cost Behavior* (Englewood Cliffs, N.J.: Prentice-Hall, Inc., 1960).

One advantage of using reasonably attainable goals is that achieving a goal seems to help, while failure to achieve a goal may harm, performance in the future.

Budgetary Feedback

Ideally, managers compare actual results with budgeted results so that they can make any changes necessary to achieve budgeted goals in future periods. Thus, the January report would be used to spot problems and perhaps revise some plans so that results in subsequent months would improve.

In practice, superiors also compare actual and budgeted results in order to evaluate the performance of their subordinates. The behavioral problems thereby created have been discussed earlier—dysfunctional consequences including the falsification of information. Here we have a potential behavioral dilemma. People would like frequent feedback on their own performance so that they can adapt to changing conditions. However, if such reports are also used to evaluate their performance and to affect their rewards or penalties, they are encouraged to beat the system by engaging in various types of dysfunctional behavior.

Hopwood's conclusions about the dysfunctional effects of budget-constrained styles of leadership are relevant here. Superiors who concentrate on the budget invite dysfunctional behavior. Superiors should not be overly concerned with whether short-term goals are met, because this might be achieved at the expense of long-term results.

Some Final Comments

Human behavior is critical in any management control system, including the use of budgeting and standard costs. The diversity of human responses makes it difficult to generalize and to offer recommendations that will meet every situation.

It is not, however, impossible to generalize. Participation, the use of currently attainable goals, and feedback do seem to help make budgeting systems more effective. It also seems clear that top management must support the budgeting system and convey its importance to managers and workers throughout the firm. Unless employees believe that the system is important, they will pay it scant heed. The problem is to avoid the potential dysfunctional consequences of the crude use of using a budgeting system. This area of study is receiving a great deal of attention from accountants and behavioral scientists, and some progress is already apparent. More progress should be forthcoming.

SUMMARY

Budgeting is a complex process that involves the entire firm. It provides a comprehensive plan for the firm, specifying goals and objectives, the strategies and policies required to achieve them, and the particular tactics selected to implement the strategies and policies. Budgeting is also an important aspect of the control process, encompassing standard costs and variance analysis. It provides a framework for evaluating the performance of managers and their subordinates.

Much of budgeting is behavioral. Budgets may encourage or discourage good performance; they may motivate managers for better or for worse. An understanding of the important role that human behavior plays in budgeting is essential to its successful use.

ASSIGNMENTS

13-1   Budgeting—Spending and Requests. Many organizations, especially governmental units, follow the practice called incremental budgeting. What this practice boils down to is that the upper levels of management approve next year's budget on the basis of the current year's *spending*. For example, if a state agency spent $300,000 out of its $320,000 budget this year, and the total state budget was to be 10 percent higher next year, the agency's budget would be $330,000 next year ($300,000 × 1.10), not $352,000 ($320,000 × 1.10).

Required: Discuss the practice. What potential dysfunctional consequences do you see?

13-2   Budgetary Slack. Lee Widner, the president of Safco, Inc., recently read an article that described ways that managers introduced slack into their budget requests. He decided to begin a new policy: he would reduce each manager's budget request by 10 percent across the board. Although he had no reason to believe that his managers were padding their requests, he thought it wise not to take any chances.

Required: Comment on Widner's proposed action. Is it wise? Is it likely to have the desired effect of reducing budgetary slack?

13-3   Line Budgeting. Many organizations, especially governmental units, follow the practice called *line budgeting*. Under line budgeting, the budget for a responsibility unit, such as a department, factory, school, or entire firm, is broken down by individual categories (lines)—telephone, travel, postage, salaries, equipment purchases, overtime, part-time help, and so on. The manager of the unit is held accountable for meeting each and every line, not just the total budget. Managers are not permitted to shift expenditures from one line to another without express permission. For example, the chairman of an accounting department who had a budget of $800 for telephone and $1,100 for travel could not spend $900 for telephone and $1,000 for travel, even though the total spent would equal the total budgeted.

Required: Comment on the practice. Do you think it promotes the welfare of the organization? Why or why not?

13–4 Budgeting, Compensation, and Motivation. The upper-level managers of Gorb-Warren Company have not been happy with cost control in their manufacturing operations. In an effort to achieve better control, they have decided to experiment with three systems of compensation for department managers.

System A—The manager receives a $2,000 bonus during any month in which he shows a favorable budget variance.

System B—The manager receives a bonus equal to 20 percent of any favorable budget variance in a given month. There are no penalties for failing to meet the budget in a month.

System C—The manager receives a bonus of $6,000 if he meets the budget over a three-month period. No attention is paid to individual months within the period.

The schedule below shows the variances of managers X, Y, and Z over a six-month period. Each was compensated according to one of the systems described above, and no two managers were compensated under the same system. Each manager is in charge of a large production department. Budgeted costs include materials, labor, and various overhead items such as repairs and maintenance, supplies, employee training, and utilities. The budgets are flexible, based on output, and average about $100,000 per month. Output fluctuates, and so do the budgets. For the manager under system C, months 1, 2, and 3 are one period, months 4, 5, and 6 are another. Parentheses denote favorable variances.

	Month 1	Month 2	Month 3	Month 4	Month 5	Month 6
Manager X	$10,000	$6,000	$14,000	($2,000)	($1,000)	$2,000
Manager Y	28,000	(13,000)	(12,000)	24,000	(19,000)	(11,000)
Manager Z	(500)	17,000	(1,000)	(1,200)	22,000	(900)

Required:

1. Determine which manager was compensated under which system. Support your answer. Assume that each manager wished to maximize his or her compensation.

2. Describe some of the ways that a manager operating under each of the compensation systems could beat the system, earning bonuses even though not acting in the firm's best interests.

13–5 Budgetary Pressure. Grading systems used in colleges are similar to budgets in the sense that they establish standards for performance and result in rewards or punishments. Presumably, a student's principal goal in taking a course is to learn. Suppose that you enrolled for a course and read the following on the assignment sheet.

A passing grade in this course is 90, with 93 being a C and 95 being a B. An A requires a 99. You will have a quiz every day on the material assigned for that day, and these quizzes will be 80 percent of your grade, with a final examination being 20 percent.

Required: Comment on the policies described above and relate them to the material in the chapter.

13-6 Organizational Goals and Group Norms. Some workers are on piecework, which means that they are paid for their output, not for their time. A person who is reasonably talented and works hard can earn more than co-workers who are less talented or less ambitious.

Required: Do you think that those who work very hard to improve their incomes are popular with their fellow workers? Respected by them?

13-7 Budgets and Responsibility. Bill Stasiuk, the purchasing manager of Northcote Products, was upset about his performance report for July. The report showed that he had overspent his July budget for telephone by $250 and that he had paid $2.30/lb for 22,000 lb of plyton, a raw material used in one of the firm's products. The standard price of plyton is $2.12/lb.

Stasiuk had been buying plyton at the standard price from two suppliers in accordance with the purchases budget approved at the beginning of the year. Early in July the sales department accepted a rush order for the product that required plyton, and the production manager agreed to make it. However, there was not nearly enough plyton on hand, so that Stasiuk had to find the additional 22,000 lb required. Neither of the firm's regular suppliers could fill the need, so Stasiuk spent several days on the telephone trying to track down the required amount. Eventually he did locate the plyton and managed to have it delivered in time to meet the production schedule.

Required: Discuss the issue and recommend a solution.

13-8 Responsibility for Costs. The MBI Corporation, a large multinational company, runs an extensive training program for newly recruited college graduates. Each graduate spends from one to three months in each of six different departments in order to gain some understanding of various phases of the firm's operations.

In the past, the salaries of the trainees were charged to a general administration account and would subsequently be reallocated to other departments as part of the overall allocation process. The basis for the allocation was the total costs of each department.

The controller now intends to charge the salaries directly to the departments where the trainees work. He believes that this will give a fairer picture of the costs. Some departmental managers are not happy with the proposal. A typical complaint follows:

I don't really mind paying for the costs of trainees through the allocation. Someone has to pay it. The allocations of all costs are lumped together, anyway, as an uncontrollable cost, so that they don't affect my performance report. The problem that I see arising is that the direct charge will make us less eager to take trainees. If the cost is to be considered controllable, the departmental managers will be hurt. The trainees are really no good to us: by the time they learn something they're about to go to the next stop.

Required: Comment on the proposal and on the current system. You might wish to use the department manager's comments as a basis for yours.

13–9   Responsibility.   The budget director of a medium-sized manufacturing company recently told you his troubles:

My purchasing manager is responsible for buying materials and components at standard prices, and that is how we evaluate his performance. The production manager is responsible for meeting budgeted production goals at budgeted costs. The system does not seem to be working out.

The production manager keeps telling me that the purchasing manager is so intent on getting goods at prices below standard that he buys inferior goods and uses unreliable suppliers. He claims that his costs are higher because of these actions and that he sometimes fails to meet his production budget because he doesn't have an adequate supply of a material or component.

He also tells me that the purchasing manager often buys in huge lots to get a good price. He is then responsible for storing and safeguarding the goods, which also adds to his costs. He says that it's always feast or famine: either he has a huge oversupply or an inadequate supply.

When I talk to the purchasing manager, he says that he is doing just what he is expected to do and won't change so long as he is evaluated by whether or not he gets materials and components at standard prices. I'm telling you, it's a real mess.

Required: What suggestions can you make?

13–10   Budgeting and Goal Congruence (CMA adapted).   In late 19X1 Mr. Sootsman, the official in charge of the State Department of Automobile Regulation, established a system of performance measurement for the department's branch offices. He was convinced that management by objectives could help the department reach its objective of better citizen service at a lower cost. The first step was to define the activities of the branch offices, to assign point values to the services performed, and to establish performance targets. Point values, rather than revenue targets, were employed because the department was a regulatory agency, not a revenue-producing agency. Further, the specific revenue for a service did not adequately reflect the differences in effort required. The analysis was compiled at the state office, and the results were distributed to the branch offices.

The system has been in operation since 19X2. The performance targets for the branches have been revised each year by the state office. The revisions were designed to encourage better performance by increasing the

Barry County Branch Performance Report

	19X2		19X3		19X4	
	Budget	Actual	Budget	Actual	Budget	Actual
Population served	38,000		38,500		38,700	
Number of employees:						
Administrative	1	1	1	1	1	1
Professional	1	1	1	1	1	1
Clerical	3	3	2	3	1½	3
Budgeted Performance Points[a]						
1. Services	19,500		16,000		15,500	
2. Citizen comments	500		600		700	
	20,000		16,600		16,200	
Actual Performance Points[a]						
1. Services	14,500		14,600		15,600	
2. Citizen comments	200		900		200	
	14,700		15,500		15,800	
Detail of Actual Performance[a]						
1. New drivers licenses						
a. Examination and road						
tests (3 pts)	3,000		3,150		3,030	
b. Road tests repeat—failed						
prior test (2 pts)	600		750		1,650	
2. Renew drivers licenses (1 pt)	3,000		3,120		3,060	
3. Issue license plates (0.5 pt)	4,200		4,150		4,100	
4. Issue titles						
a. Dealer transactions						
(0.5 pt)	2,000		1,900		2,100	
b. Individual transaction						
(1 pt)	1,700		1,530		1,660	
	14,500		14,600		15,600	
5. Citizen comments						
a. Favorable (+0.5 pt)	300		1,100		800	
b. Unfavorable (−0.5 pt)	100		200		600	
	200		900		200	

[a] The budget performance points for services are calculated using 3 points per available hour. The administrative employee devotes half time to administration and half time to regular services. The calculations for the services point budget are as follows:

> 19X2: 4½ people × 8 hours × 240 days × 3 pts × 75% productive time = 19,440 rounded to 19,500
> 19X3: 3½ people × 8 hours × 240 days × 3 pts × 80% productive time = 16,128 rounded to 16,000
> 19X4: 3 people × 8 hours × 240 days × 3 pts × 90% productive time = 15,552 rounded to 15,500

The comments targets are based upon rough estimates by department officials. The actual point totals for the branch are calculated by multiplying the weights shown in the report in parentheses by the number of such services performed or comments received.

target or reducing resources to achieve targets. The revisions incorporated noncontrollable events, such as population shifts, new branches, and changes in procedures.

The Barry County branch is typical of many branch offices. A summary displaying the budgeted and actual performance for three years appears on page 531.

Mr. Sootsman has been disappointed in the performance of branch offices because they have not met performance targets or budgets. He is especially concerned because the points earned from citizens' comments are declining.

Required:

1. Does the method of performance measurement encourage goal congruence? Why or why not?

2. The Barry County branch came closer to its budgeted points in 19X4 than in either previous year. Does this mean that it improved its performance in 19X4? Why or why not?

13–11 Budgeting and Responsibility Accounting (CMA adapted). The Argon County Hospital is located in a well-known resort area. The county population doubles in the May–August period and hospital activity more than doubles during these months, owing to vacation-related accidents and ills. The hospital is organized into several departments and, despite its small size, has attracted a very competent staff.

The hospital hired an administrator a year ago to improve the business aspects of its operation. Among the new ideas he introduced was responsibility accounting. He announced the program in a quarterly cost report supplied to each department head. In the past, department heads had received cost reports infrequently and at irregular intervals. Excerpts from the announcement and the report to the head of the laundry department appear below.

> The hospital has adopted a *responsibility accounting system.* From now on you will receive quarterly reports comparing the costs of operating your department with budgeted costs. The reports will highlight the differences (variations) so you can zero in on the departure from budgeted costs (This is called management by exception). Responsibility accounting means you are accountable for keeping the costs in your department within the budget. The variations from the budget will help you identify what costs are out of line, and the size of the variation will indicate which ones are the most important. Your first such report accompanies this announcement.

The annual budget for 19X3 was constructed by the new administrator. Quarterly budgets were computed as one-fourth of the annual budget. The administrator compiled the budget from analysis of the prior three years' costs. The analysis showed that all costs increased each year, with more rapid increases between the second and third year. He considered establish-

ARGON COUNTY HOSPITAL
Performance Report—Laundry Department
July–September 19X3

	Budget	Actual	(Over) Under Budget	Percent (Over) Under Budget
Patient days	9,500	11,900	(2,400)	(25)
Pounds processed				
—laundry	125,000	156,000	(31,000)	(25)
Costs:				
Laundry labor	$ 9,000	$ 12,500	$ (3,500)	(39)
Supplies	1,100	1,875	(775)	(70)
Water, water heating and softening	1,700	2,500	(800)	(47)
Maintenance	1,400	2,200	(800)	(57)
Supervisor's salary	3,150	3,750	(600)	(19)
Allocated administration costs	4,000	5,000	(1,000)	(25)
Equipment depreciation	1,200	1,250	(50)	(4)
	$ 21,550	$ 29,075	$ (7,525)	(35)

Administrator's Comments: Costs are significantly above budget for the quarter. Particular attention needs to be paid to labor, supplies, and maintenance.

ing the budget at an average of the prior three years' costs, hoping that the installation of the system would reduce costs to this level. However, in view of the rapidly increasing prices he finally chose 19X2 costs less 3 percent for the 19X3 budget. The activity level measured by patient days, and pounds of laundry processed was set at 19X2 volume, which was approximately equal to the volume of each of the past three years.

Required:

1. Comment on the method used to prepare the budget.

2. Does the report effectively communicate the level of efficiency of the laundry department? Why or why not?

13–12 Compensation Plans and Goal Congruence (CMA). The Parsons Co. compensates its field sales force on a commission and year-end bonus basis. The commission is 20 percent of standard gross margin (planned selling price less standard cost of goods sold on a full absorption basis), contingent upon collection of the account. Customer's credit is approved by the company's credit department. Price concessions are granted on occasion by the top sales management, but sales commissions are not reduced by the discount. A year-end bonus of 15 percent of commissions earned is paid to salesmen who equal or exceed their annual sales target. The annual sales target is usually established by applying approximately a 5 percent increase to the prior year's sales.

Required:

1. What features of this compensation plan would seem to be effective in motivating the salesmen to accomplish company goals of higher profits and return on investment? Explain why.

2. What features of this compensation plan would seem to be countereffective in motivating the salesmen to accomplish the company goals of higher profits and return on investment? Explain why.

13–13 Budgetary Slack (CMA adapted).   The Noton Company has operated a comprehensive budgeting system for many years. This system is a major component of the company's program to control operations and costs at its widely scattered plants. Periodically the plants' general managers gather to discuss with the top management the overall company control system.

At this year's meeting the budgetary system was severely criticized by one of the most senior plant managers. He said that the system discriminated unfairly against the older, well-run and established plants in favor of the newer plants. The impact was lower year-end bonuses and poor performance ratings. In addition, there were psychological consequences in the form of lower employee morale. In his judgment, revisions in the system were needed to make it more effective. The basic factors of Noton's budget include:

1. announcement of an annual improvement percentage target established by top management.
2. plant submission of budgets implementing the annual improvement target.
3. management review and revision of the proposed budget.
4. establishment and distribution of the final budget.

The target percentage for improvement is the same for all plants, which was one of the matters that most concerned the plant manager. In support of his arguments, he also compared the budget revisions and performance results. The older plants were expected to achieve the improvement target but often were unable to meet it. On the other hand, the newer plants were often excused from meeting a portion of this target in their budgets. However, their performance was usually better than the final budget.

He further argued that the company did not recognize the operating differences that made attainment of the annual improvement factor difficult, if not impossible. His plant had been producing essentially the same product for its twenty years of existence. The machinery and equipment, which had undergone many modifications in the first five years, had had no major changes in recent years. Because they were old, repair and maintenance costs had increased each year, and the machines were less reliable. The plant management team had been together for the last ten years and worked well together. The labor force was mature, with many of the employees having the highest seniority in the company. In his judgment, the significant improvements had been wrung out of the plant over the years so that merely keeping even was difficult.

For comparison he noted that one plant opened within the past four years would have an easier time meeting the company's expectations. The plant was new, containing modern equipment that was in some cases still experimental. Major modifications in equipment and operating systems had been made each year as the plant management obtained a better understanding of the operations. The plant's management, although experienced, had been together only since its opening. The plant was located in an area that had previously had very little industry, and the work force was relatively inexperienced.

Required:

1. Evaluate the views of the manufacturing manager.
2. Discuss how managers of both old and new plants could incorporate slack into their budgets.

13–14 Conflicting Goals. William Jacobs founded the WMJ Company fifteen years ago, after leaving his job as chief engineer of Ramsey Industries. He believed he could make some industrial measuring devices that were vastly superior to those available at that time, and subsequent events proved him right. WMJ Company flourished and now employs 2,500 people.

The company maintains an extensive engineering department that is constantly working to improve the product line, and Jacobs spends nearly half his time either supervising or working with that department. The firm's products are well known for quality and are priced somewhat above those of its competitors.

In recent years the firm has lost some business to competitors who make less accurate devices. Some customers do not need devices of the quality of WMJ's for some applications and accordingly seek out cheaper ones. Jacobs has refused to make less accurate devices and considers his firm to be the standard of quality of the industry. The manufacturing superintendents have complained that the engineers require such low tolerances that nearly 10 percent of the units fail to pass final inspection.

The firm's financial vice-president, Allen Rose, has become distressed during the two years that he has been with the firm. Rose has often commented to Jacobs that the firm keeps unreasonably high inventories and accounts receivable. One reason for the high inventories is that Jacobs insists on being able to supply a customer's needs quickly. The high receivables are due in part to Jacobs's unwillingness to pressure old and valued customers for prompt payment. The current level of interest rates encourages customers to withhold payments as long as they can.

Rose believes that the company is headed for trouble. The high investment in current assets has been financed largely with bank loans at very high interest rates.

The firm uses only the most up-to-date manufacturing equipment, and Rose has never known Jacobs to deny a request from the engineering department for personnel, instruments, or other equipment. Rose has prepared budgets, but Jacobs has dismissed them with the comment that he didn't build the firm with budgets. In fact, Jacobs recently told Rose to keep to his own area of interest and not to meddle in the operations of the business.

Required: What are the probable reasons for the situation, and what would you suggest be done?

13-15   **Effect of Tight Budget (CMA adapted).**   Tom Emory and Jim Morris strolled back to their plant from the administrative offices of Ferguson & Son Mfg. Company. Tom was manager of the machine shop in the company's factory; Jim was manager of the equipment maintenance department. The men had just attended the monthly performance evaluation meeting for plant department heads.

"Boy, I hate those meetings!" Tom exclaimed. "I never know whether my department's accounting reports will show good or bad performance. I'm beginning to expect the worst."

Tom had just received his worst evaluation ever in his long career with Ferguson & Son. He had been promoted from machinist to machine shop supervisor when the company expanded and moved to its present location. The president (Robert Ferguson, Sr.) had often stated that the company's success was due to the high quality of the work of machinists like Emory. As supervisor, Tom stressed the importance of craftsmanship.

When Robert Ferguson, Jr., became plant manager, he directed that monthly performance comparisons be made between actual and budgeted costs for each department. The departmental budgets were intended to encourage the supervisors to reduce inefficiencies and to seek cost-reduction opportunities. The company controller was instructed to have his staff tighten the budget slightly whenever a department attained its budget in a given month; this was done to reinforce the plant supervisor's desire to reduce costs.

Tom Emory remarked further to Jim Morris:

I really don't understand. We've worked so hard to get up to budget, and the minute we make it they tighten the budget on us. We can't work any faster and still maintain quality. I think my men are ready to quit trying. Besides, those reports don't tell the whole story. We always seem to be interrupting the big jobs for all those small rush orders. All that set-up and machine adjustment time is killing us.

The accountants seem to know everything that's happening in my department, sometimes even before I do. I thought all that budget and accounting stuff was supposed to help, but it just gets me into trouble.

Tom Emory's performance report for the month in question is reproduced below. Actual production volume for the month was at the budgeted level.

Machine Shop—October 19X8
T. Emory, Supervisor

	Budget	Actual	Variances
Direct labor	$ 39,600	$ 39,850	$ 250 U
Direct materials	231,000	231,075	75 U
Depreciation—equipment	3,000	3,000	0
Depreciation—buildings	6,000	6,000	0
Power	900	860	40 F
Maintenance	400	410	10 U
Supervision	1,500	1,500	0
Idle time	0	1,800	1,800 U
Set-up labor	680	2,432	1,752 U
Miscellaneous	2,900	3,300	400 U
	$285,980	$290,227	$4,247 U

Required:

1. Identify the problems in Ferguson & Son Mfg. Company's budgetary control system and explain how they may reduce the system's effectiveness.

2. Explain how the budgetary control system could be revised to improve its effectiveness.

13–16 Participation, Standards, Overhead Allocation (CMA). The Kelly Company, founded twenty years ago, has achieved a moderate degree of success. The company manufactures and sells pottery items. All manufacturing takes place in one plant, which has four departments. Each manufacturing department produces only one product. The four products of Kelly Company are plaques, cups, vases, and plates. Sam Kelly, the president and founder, attributes the company's success to the well-designed quality products and to an effective cost control system. The system was installed early in the firm's existence to improve cost control and to serve as a basis for planning.

The company establishes standard costs for material and labor with the participation of plant management. Each year the plant manager, the department heads, and the time-study engineers are invited by top management to recommend changes in the standards for the next year. Top management reviews these recommendations and the records of actual performance for the current year before setting the new standards. As a general rule, top management sets tight standards representing very efficient performance, so that no inefficiency or slack will be included in cost goals. The plant manager and department heads are charged with cost control responsibility, and the variances from standard costs are used to measure their performance in carrying out this charge.

No standards are set for factory overhead because the management believes it is too difficult to predict overhead and relate it to output. The actual factory overhead for the departments and the plant is accumulated in a single pool. The actual overhead is then allocated to the departments on the basis of departmental output. The schedule below is a three-year summary of overhead allocation among the departments.

	19X5	
Department	Units Produced	Allocated[a] Overhead
Plaques	300,000	$120,000
Cups	250,000	100,000
Vases	200,000	80,000
Plates	250,000	100,000
Totals	1,000,000	$400,000

	19X6	
Department	Units Produced	Allocated[a] Overhead
Plaques	330,000	$126,000
Cups	270,000	103,091
Vases	220,000	84,000
Plates	280,000	106,909
Totals	1,100,000	$420,000

	19X7	
Department	Units Produced	Allocated[a] Overhead
Plaques	180,000	$ 60,000
Cups	360,000	120,000
Vases	300,000	100,000
Plates	360,000	120,000
Totals	1,200,000	$400,000

[a] Dollar amounts are rounded to the nearest dollar.

The company's executives are convinced that more effective cost control can be obtained. A review of cost performance for recent years disclosed several factors that led them to this conclusion:

1. Unfavorable variances were the norm rather than the exception, although the size of the variances was quite uniform.
2. Department managers took steps that, while benefiting their own departments, were detrimental to overall company performance.
3. Employee motivation, especially among first-line supervisors, appeared to be low.

Required:

1. What are the probable effects, if any, on the motivation of the plant managers and departmental heads from:
   a. The participative standard cost system?
   b. The use of tight standards?
   Explain the reasons for your conclusions.
2. What effect, if any, will the practice of applying actual overhead costs on the basis of actual units produced have on the motivation of the department heads to control the overhead costs? Explain your answer.

13-17 Allocations and Transfer Prices. The National Electronics Company is a large, decentralized firm. One of the activities that is centralized is research and development (R&D). Managers of operating divisions suggest projects for R&D, and the individual section heads in R&D (for example, fiber optics, lasers, solid state physics) also authorize and carry out projects that they believe desirable. The head of R&D makes the final decisions on project selection, as there are always more requests (both from operating divisions and from section heads) than time and money. The ability of a section head to gain approval for his projects often determines what projects will survive.

The president of the firm is not satisfied with the current arrangements. R&D is a cost center, so that the operating managers are not billed for any work that they request. The president also believes that R&D people spend too much time on projects that interest them but are of little economic promise. He believes that the scientists who run R&D are more interested in their fields of expertise than in the firm. A number of the scientists are internationally known for their research, but a good deal of their research has not yet borne fruit for the firm.

The president is now considering two plans. One is to allocate both the costs and investment of R&D (about $26 million and $65 million, respectively) to the operating divisions on the basis of sales or total divisional investment. The other is to make R&D into a profit center. R&D would have to sell its services to the operating divisions, convincing the operating managers that they should pay to support particular research projects.

Required: Discuss the merits and disadvantages of each proposed plan, as well as the current situation.

13–18   Advertising and Promotional Budgets.   The Hampton Corporation makes and markets a wide variety of household products including dishwashing liquids, detergents, floor care products, and furniture polishes and waxes. The firm is organized into several divisions, each concentrating on a single line of products. A regional manager is in charge of operations of each division in each of the geographical areas that the division serves. Each division has from four to eight regional managers. Both divisional and regional managers are responsible for profits.

Advertising and promotion (newspaper coupons are the major promotional cost) are extremely important in the markets that Hampton serves. A great deal of effort is involved in the budgeting of these expenses.

Each regional manager submits a budget for the coming year. The divisional manager reviews them, frequently asking for more justification and revision. After approval at the divisional level, the budgets go to the corporate budget committee, which also makes frequent requests for additional justification and often demands revisions.

During the year, regional managers make many requests for supplemental amounts to meet changing circumstances, such as heavier promotion by competitors. These requests go through the divisional manager, and if he or she concurs in the request, it goes to the budget committee. The committee meets once a month and grants about half the requests by number, about one-third by dollar amount.

The system satisfies very few managers. The regional and divisional managers complain that they cannot get quick enough action from the budget committee. Too often, by the time the request for additional funds has been granted, if it is granted, it is too late. Sales have been lost to competitors who have been more aggressive. One of the regional managers related a typical case:

> I was faced by an increase in advertising of a competitor's liquid detergent. Its sales were increasing rapidly and we were doing nothing about it. I asked for a 20 percent increase in my budget to go for advertising and newspaper coupons giving 10 cents off the regular price. The request was eventually granted, but it took five weeks from the time I decided to take the action and initiate the request. By then we had lost two percentage points of market share in my geographical area, and smaller, but significant, amounts in others.

Members of the budget committee were equally unhappy. Their feelings were expressed by the treasurer of the firm:

> These guys just won't try to understand that we cannot approve changes instantly. First, all of us have jobs to do besides looking at these requests. We

could spend half our time in meetings going over these requests, and that seems to be what the regional managers want. I have recommended that we give the divisional managers the authority to shift funds around among their regions. Right now, a divisional manager can't reduce spending in one area to increase it on another. Some of the members of the committee are against it because they feel that the regional managers will all be clamoring for money and the one with the loudest voice will get it. Still, it's obvious that we have to do something soon.

The president of the firm was well aware of the situation and had asked a management consultant to make confidential recommendations. She had not yet discussed these recommendations with anyone because she wanted to give them very careful consideration.

In essence, the consultant recommended two major changes. One was to give the divisional managers the authority to reallocate funds from region to region, as the treasurer had recommended. The second was to set formulas for governing the total advertising and promotional budget for each division. These formulas would permit the divisional manager to spend an amount equal to some specified percentage of sales. The budget would then be flexible, not static. The percentages used would be negotiated by the divisional managers and the budget committee, but the consultant expected that historical ratios of advertising and promotion to sales dollars would be the bases.

The sales figures to be used would be quarterly. Each quarter, the budget would be the specified percentage of the sales of the previous quarter. Quarterly sales figures were usually available by the second week of the subsequent quarter. The consultant had stated that it was important to keep the budget current, so that basing the current year's budget on the prior year's sales was unwise. However, he also said that using monthly sales figures to determine the following month's budget would cause confusion and be difficult to implement.

The consultant argued that the proposed changes would have a number of benefits. The budget committee would no longer be involved in the continual evaluation of supplemental requests. Only in rare cases would divisional managers request changes during the year. The firm's regional managers could respond more quickly to competitive pressures, because they could go straight to the divisional manager with supplemental requests. The time involved in the budget committee review would be eliminated, so that actions could be taken when they would still be effective.

The continual updating of the budgets would keep them more current, more in line with current requirements. The divisional managers would also understand that they had to earn their budgets. Higher sales would lead to higher budgets and lower sales to lower budgets. Total budgets would then be in line with the firm's ability to pay.

Required: Evaluate the consultant's recommendations. Make your own recommendations to supplement those of the consultant, or to replace those that you do not agree with.

13-19 Responsibility Accounting (AICPA adapted).   For some years the Avey Company has used a standard cost system for production costs, and its managers have been happy with the results. However, distribution expenses have risen rapidly, and the managers are not able to determine whether or not they are under control. They have decided to give each local manager an income statement for his or her territory showing monthly and year-to-date results for the current and prior year. Each territory is assigned to a single manager, who is responsible for sales and distribution expenses. The local managers forward sales orders to the main office. A central warehouse ships the goods. The main office also handles all billing and collection.

   The managers at the main office have decided to classify costs by function, then allocate them to each territory in the following ways:

Function	Allocation Basis
Sales salaries	Actual
Other selling expenses	Relative sales dollars
Warehousing	Relative sales dollars
Packing and shipping	Weight of package
Billing and collection	Number of billings
General administration	Equally

Required:

1. What objectives are the managers of Avey trying to achieve by the territorial income statements? Will the comparative income statements serve their needs?

2. Discuss the allocation bases that the managers have proposed.

SELECTED REFERENCES

Argyris, Chris, *The Impact of Budgets on People*, New York: Financial Executives Research Foundation, 1952.

Becker, Selwyn W., and David O. Green, Jr., "Budgeting and Employee Behavior," *Journal of Business*, 35:4 (October 1962), 392–402.

Benston, George J., "The Role of The Firm's Accounting System for Motivation," *The Accounting Review*, 38:2 (April 1963), 347–54.

Caplan, Edwin H., "Behavioral Aspects of Management Accounting," *The Accounting Review*, 41:3 (July 1966), 496–509.

_____, *Management Accounting and Behavioral Science*. 2d ed. Reading, Mass.: Addison-Wesley Publishing Co., Inc., 1982.

DeCoster, D. T., and J. P. Fertakis, "Budget Induced Pressure and Its Relationship to Supervisory Behavior," *Journal of Accounting Research*, 6:2 (Autumn 1968), 237–46.

Ferrara, William L., "Responsibility Accounting—A Basic Control Concept," *N.A.A. Bulletin*, 46:1 (September 1964), 11–19.

Hersey, Paul, and Kenneth H. Blanchard, *Management of Organizational Behavior*, 3d ed. Englewood Cliffs, N.J.: Prentice-Hall, Inc., 1977.

Hopwood, A. G., "An Empirical Study of the Role of Accounting Data in Performance Evaluation," *Empirical Research in Accounting: Selected Studies, 1972*. Supplement to *Journal of Accounting Research*, 10, 156–82.

Maslow, Abraham, *Motivation and Personality*. New York: Harper & Row, Publishers, 1954.

McGregor, Douglas, *The Human Side of Enterprise*. New York: McGraw-Hill Book Company, 1960.

Onsi, Mohamed, "Factor Analysis of Behavioral Variables Affecting Budgetary Slack," *The Accounting Review*, 48:3 (July 1973), 535–48.

Rockness, Howard O., "Expectancy Theory in a Budgetary Setting," *The Accounting Review*, 52:3 (October 1977), 893–903.

Ronen, J., and J. L. Livingstone, "An Expectancy Theory Approach to the Motivational Impacts of Budgets," *The Accounting Review*, 50:4 (October 1975), 671–85.

Schiff, Michael, and Arie Y. Lewin, "The Impact of People on Budgets," *The Accounting Review*, 45:2 (April 1970), 259–68.

Budgeting: Analytical and Technical Aspects

Chapter 14

Chapter 13 dealt with general aspects of budgeting and concentrated on behavioral considerations; this chapter deals with the analytical and technical aspects. We shall consider the difficult problem of forecasting and budgeting sales, from which all other budgets flow. A principal goal is to see how the budgeting process explicitly relates means and ends, resources and goals. The development of cash budgets is of special importance: firms, especially fast-growing ones, get into more difficulty from running short of cash than from any other situation.

Managers of firms and of other economic organizations spend a great deal of time preparing budgets. One reason is that modern, complex organizations have many interrelated activities, most of which must be taken into consideration in developing budgets. Thus there may be a good many intermediate steps between a sales forecast and a cash budget.

COMPONENTS OF THE MASTER BUDGET

The set of budgets prepared by the managers of a firm are collectively called the **master budget** or **comprehensive budget.** Different firms will prepare different individual budgets, but the following list is representative.

budgeted income statement, or pro forma income statement, showing the income expected for the budget period

sales budget, perhaps by product, territory, class of customer (such as government, commercial), or other segment of interest

production budget, by product, by plant

purchases budget, by type of raw material

labor budget, by type of worker required, in hours or in number of workers

production cost budget, by product, by plant

budgets for other expenses, by category depending on the relative importance of various types of expenses (selling, general, administrative, research and development, and so on)

cash receipts budget

cash disbursements budget

cash budget, summarizing receipts and disbursements, indicating financing requirements

budgeted balance sheet, or pro forma balance sheet, showing the balance sheet expected at the end of the budget period

Time Frames of Budgets

Budgets are almost always prepared for a year. Some firms will also budget two to five years in advance. Most firms, especially those with seasonal operations, will budget for shorter periods as well as for a year. Depending on the sharpness of the seasonal patterns of business, a firm might budget quarterly, monthly, or even weekly for some important factors. Cash would be one item that a firm might budget for very short periods.

Some firms follow the practice of **continuous budgeting.** Each month the managers add an additional month to the budget, thus keeping a twelve-month budget always available. At the end of January, for example, the firm would have budgets through the end of the following January, and so on. Continuous budgeting keeps the firm's plans ahead. If the firm prepares only annual budgets, its plans will be formalized only through the end of the current year. Toward the end of each year it will have to prepare a new budget for the coming year. The budgeting process involves a great deal of work, and the use of continuous budgeting spreads it throughout the year instead of concentrating it near the end of each year.

Some budgets are oriented not to time but to events. This is typical of project budgets and capital budgets. A **project budget** is one related to a large job, like the construction of a new plant. A **capital budget,** as discussed in Chapters 15 and 16, is related to the firm's overall spending plans for new assets.

Relationships Among Budgets

Chapter 13 discussed and diagrammed the overall process of budgeting. This chapter works with the budgets themselves. Figure 14–1 diagrams the relationships among various budgets. The figure is simplified: the relationships and interrelationships are very complex. For instance, managers developing production budgets from the sales budgets might find that they could not produce the required amounts because of shortages of labor, materials, or machinery. The process would then have to start over, and the firm might change its strategies regarding particular products. Because it could not make all the units originally called for, it might raise prices or lower promotional expenses.

There could be similar to-and-fro movement between sales budgets and credit policy, and virtually all other budgets and policies. A completed first run at a master budget is like a smooth pond: a stone tossed into it will send ripples in all directions and for considerable distances. Changing credit terms from 60 to 30 days payment in an effort to collect cash more rapidly could adversely affect sales and profits, as could reducing the quantity of inventory of finished goods to save interest expense.

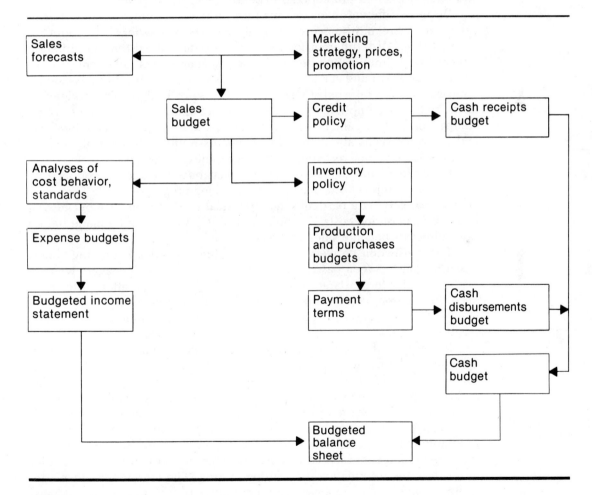

FIGURE 14–1
Relationships Among Budgets

SALES BUDGETING

The sales budget is the starting point in the development of the master budget. From it flow the production budget and flexible expense budgets for all costs that vary with sales and production. Sales budgeting usually begins with forecasts of sales of individual products. These forecasts may be by region, by class of customer, or by some other breakdown that is important to the firm. Sales forecasts are based on many assumptions, some explicitly stated, some left implicit. Examples of such assumptions are the prices to be charged by the firm and by its competitors, economic activity in the geographical areas the firm serves, number of salespeople in the field, and advertising and promotional expenditures.

Because different managers may use different assumptions about critical factors, there may be many different forecasts of sales for each product or product line. Also, different forecasts may be developed through different forecasting techniques. As described below, managerial judgment, historical trend analysis, and statistical techniques may all be used in developing forecasts. Therefore, a sales forecast is not a sales budget. The budget reflects, sometimes implicitly, one particular set of assumptions about prices, competitors' actions, and other critical factors. Managers must take forecasts and make decisions about the critical factors under their control, such as prices, sales force, advertising, and geographical coverage.

Upper-level managers may decide that one product or product line should be deemphasized because of poor long-range potential. They may decide that serving a particular geographical market is unwise because of heavy transportation costs. A whole host of decisions must be made before sales forecasts become sales budgets.

The distinction between sales forecasting and sales budgeting comes down to that between passive and active management. Managers who accept particular forecasts are acting passively. Those who attempt to influence the environment by altering policies and strategies are being active, making decisions and taking actions that they expect will improve the firm's position.[1]

In the interplay of forecasting and budgeting, the accountant plays an important role. Some sales managers are conscious of only a few factors, such as total volume and market share. They may not analyze the benefits and costs of changing strategies. The accountant may be involved in determining whether, for example, an increase in sales volume obtained by reducing prices and increasing advertising expenditures would be more profitable than the original strategy. The accountant may also be involved in the development of forecasts, because he or she is the principal provider of much of the information used in forecasting. The following sections describe some of the commonly used techniques of forecasting.

[1] The references to internal and external locus of control in Chapter 21 discuss this point.

Statistical Approaches

Statistical approaches to the forecasting of sales come in two general types, time series analysis and indicator analysis. **Time series analysis** uses the techniques of regression analysis (and scatter diagrams) to predict future sales based on patterns of historical sales. In general, the dependent variable in the regression equation is sales and the independent variable is time. We have already seen that the past is not necessarily an accurate guide to the future, and time series analysis is therefore unreliable when the environment is changing.

When no major changes in the basic environmental conditions are expected, time series analysis may be a valuable tool in forecasting sales. However, it is useful only for forecasting, not necessarily for budgeting, because it fails to consider whether management action in the past was good, bad, or indifferent. This criticism parallels the one made in Chapter 7 regarding the use of historical performance for setting standard costs. The observed fact that unit sales have risen at a 4 percent annual rate says nothing about the effectiveness of managerial action: the market for the product may have been rising at a 6 percent rate and the firm in question may have been lax in not achieving a higher rate of growth. Time series analysis may be extremely valuable in forecasting industry sales, and if the firm has been able, or expects to be able, to capture a specific percentage of the market, a good forecast of company sales may be obtainable. Such a forecast could be at least a starting point for development of a sales budget.

The major tools of **indicator analysis** also are regression analysis and scatter diagrams. The independent variable is the **indicator,** the variable that is closely correlated with the sales of the firm or the industry. Indicators that firms may find valuable range from the Gross National Product to the number of marriages, the number of building permits, and the sales of another product. Like time series analysis, indicator analysis may be most helpful in forecasting industry sales, from which the managers of a particular firm will have to develop budgets for their own firm based on an expected market share.

Indicators vary in value. The best indicator is one that *leads* the firm's sales. That is, the indicator rises before sales of the firm rise, falls before sales of the firm fall. If the indicator rises and falls right along with sales, it is of little value for forecasting, because it provides its signals too late for management to take any action. For example, a manufacturer of cement used largely for building foundations could not use building starts as an indicator. By the time the number of building starts was published, the demand for the cement would already have manifested itself, because foundations are poured very early in the building process. However, the cement manufacturer might be able to use building permits as an indicator because they are issued several months before actual building begins. As building permits rose or fell, the manufacturer could adjust production to meet the changing demand.

Indicators are also valuable if they are predictable, even if their rises and falls accompany rises and falls of the firm's sales. The Gross National Product is usually predictable within fairly narrow limits, and firms whose sales closely follow GNP are usually able to predict sales quite well. Some firms use extremely complex econometric models that include a great number of variables. Other firms buy the services of universities or companies that develop models of the economy and use them in their own sales forecasting and overall business planning.

Judgmental Approaches

Sales budgets are often set through consultations of salespeople, sales managers, and top management. Individual salespeople may submit budgets that would probably be revised by (say) district sales managers. The revised budgets would be sent to upper levels of sales management (such as the vice-president for sales) and finally to the firm's chief executive officer. He or she, in turn, might make some revisions, consult with the sales vice-president, and send the budgets back down the line. Another round or two of this process might ensue before the budget was finally adopted.

The major disadvantage of this type of process is that it lacks analytical content. People setting budgets may be motivated by many factors, and the lack of some objective standard by which to judge the reasonableness of the budget makes the process somewhat iffy. On the plus side, the consultation and adjustment that take place will involve the people responsible for carrying out the plans and meeting the goals. To the extent that participation is desirable, such consultation is desirable. Additionally, the method relies on the experienced judgment of people who should have a reasonably good idea of market conditions. At times, the judgment of experienced salespeople and sales managers may validly modify or override a budget based on a statistical forecast.

DEVELOPING THE MASTER BUDGET

Once the sales budget and the relationships among sales and the other critical variables are known or assumed, the actual development of the budgets is primarily a matter of technical analysis. In fact, this part of the budgeting process may often be done by computer, or in simple cases even by a programmable calculator. Determination of the relationships among the different variables is most important, because if some of them are incorrectly estimated, any resultant budget will be misleading and will not serve planning and control functions. The importance of this matter is heightened because we will base a whole set of interrelated budgets on given relationships and assumptions.

There are several alternative sequences for developing the budgets, but the sales budget must be done first. With this basic budget in hand, the production and purchases budgets as well as the cash receipts budget may be prepared. The cash disbursements budget must await the completion of the production and purchases budgets. The budgeted, or pro forma, balance sheet is usually prepared last. We shall use the data in Exhibit 14–1 to prepare the comprehensive budget for the Enco Company for March and April. The month of May will be presented later as a review problem.

The balance sheet in Exhibit 14–1 reveals that Enco's finished goods inventory of 11,800 units is less than the 13,500 units that we would expect, given the March sales budget of 9,000 units and the policy of keeping 150 percent of the coming month's budgeted sales in finished goods inventory. The inventory of raw materials is also lower than would be expected, but this is not obvious from the balance sheet because we do not yet know budgeted production for March, which would determine how much raw material Enco would budget to have on hand.

The reason for the shortfall in finished goods inventory could be that February sales were higher than budgeted, with February production being based on the lower budgeted figure. It could also result from a problem in the production process and/or from deliberate management action. The policies stated for Enco are simplified. Firms may adopt different policies for different conditions. For example, a firm might wish to keep its inventory of finished goods at 80 percent of the coming month's budgeted sales during its slow selling season, and at 200 percent during the busy season. We shall see why shortly. The point here is that budgets are based on expectations. We do not expect that actual results will precisely reflect budgeted results. Hence the budgets to be prepared should be regarded as plans, not as commitments to be met regardless of future conditions.

EXHIBIT 14–1
Data for Comprehensive Budget—Enco Company

Product Data

Selling price		$25
Costs (at standard):		
Raw materials (4 lb at $0.50)	$ 2	
Direct labor (½ hr at $6)	3	
Variable overhead (at $8 per DLH)	4	
Fixed overhead	5[a]	
Total manufacturing cost	$14	
Selling and administrative costs		
Variable (commissions)	$2 per unit	
Fixed	$35,000 per month	

Sales Budget

March, 9,000 units; April, 12,000 units; May, 11,000 units; June, 10,000 units; July, 12,000 units.

[a] Based on budgeted fixed costs of $60,000 per month and normal activity of 12,000 units per month. Depreciation is $15,000 per month.

EXHIBIT 14–1 (*Continued*)

Other Data

1. *Cash collections.* About 20 percent of sales are collected in the month of sale, another 78 percent in the month after sale, with about 2 percent becoming bad debts.

2. *Inventories.* Finished goods inventory is generally kept at about 150 percent of the coming month's budgeted sales requirements. Raw material inventory is held about equal to 80 percent of the coming month's budgeted production requirements.

3. *Cash disbursements*
   a. Purchases of raw materials are paid, on average, 60 percent in the month of purchase, 40 percent in the month after purchase.
   b. All other production costs requiring cash disbursements are paid 80 percent in the month of production, 20 percent in the following month. All production costs require cash disbursement except the $15,000 monthly depreciation.
   c. Fixed selling and administrative expenses all require cash and are paid in the month incurred. Variable selling expenses (commissions) are paid in the month after they are earned.
   d. The firm expects to declare and pay a $5,000 cash dividend in April.

4. *Income taxes.* The income tax rate is 40 percent. The taxes payable on the February 20 balance sheet will be paid in April. Taxes accrued on income for March and April will be paid in July.

Balance Sheet as of February 28, 19X0

Assets		Equities	
Cash	$ 52,000	Accounts payable (raw materials)	$ 6,600
Accounts receivable, net	154,000	Taxes payable	15,000
Inventories:		Commissions payable	16,000
Finished goods,		Accrued expenses	
11,800 units at $14	165,200	(production costs)	22,000
Raw materials, 35,200			
lb at $0.50	17,600		
Plant and equipment:		Common stock	1,700,000
Cost	2,460,000		
Accumulated depreciation	(940,000)	Retained earnings	149,200
Totals	$1,908,800		$1,908,800

As we go through individual components of the master budget, first attempt to determine how each budget would appear, then check your answers in the appropriate schedule in Exhibit 14–2. Be sure that you understand each schedule thoroughly before proceeding to the next, because the results are cumulative. Most of the schedules depend on prior schedules.

EXHIBIT 14–2
Comprehensive Budget for March and April—Enco Company

Schedule A—Cash Receipts Budget

	March	April
Collections of current month's sales, 20%	$ 45,000	$ 60,000
Collections from prior month, 78%	154,000[a]	175,500
Total budgeted receipts	$199,000	$235,500
Net accounts receivable at month end, 78% of month's budgeted sales	$175,500	$234,000

[a] Accounts receivable balance from February 28 balance sheet. All net receivables at end of a month are collected in the following month.

Schedule B—Production Budget

	March	April	May[b]
Desired ending inventory[a]	18,000	16,500	15,000
Budgeted sales	9,000	12,000	11,000
Total requirements	27,000	28,500	26,000
Beginning inventory	11,800[c]	18,000	16,500
Production	15,200	10,500	9,500

[a] 150% of following month's budgeted sales—for example, March ending inventory = 12,000 × 150%.
[b] May production figures are needed in order to find April purchases.
[c] From balance sheet for February 28.

Schedule C—Purchases Budget—Pounds

	March	April
Desired ending inventory[a]	33,600	30,400
Used in production[b]	60,800	42,000
Total requirements	94,400	72,400
Beginning inventory	35,200[c]	33,600
Purchases budgeted	59,200	38,800
Dollar purchases at $0.50/lb	$29,600	$19,400

[a] 80% × coming month's budgeted production × 4 lb.
[b] Current month's budgeted production × 4 lb.
[c] From balance sheet for February 28.

Schedule D—Production Cost Budget

	March	April
Direct labor at $3 per unit	$ 45,600	$ 31,500
Variable overhead at $4 per unit	60,800	42,000
Fixed overhead	60,000	60,000
Total production costs	$166,400	$133,500
Less depreciation	15,000	15,000
Production costs requiring cash payments	$151,400	$118,500

EXHIBIT 14–2 (Continued)

Schedule E—Cash Disbursements Budget

	March	April
Materials purchases—		
prior month (40%)	$ 6,600[a]	$ 11,840
current month (60%)	17,760	11,640
Production costs—prior month (20%)	22,000[a]	30,280
current month (80%)	121,120	94,800
Commissions, $2 × prior month's sales	16,000[a]	18,000
Fixed selling and administrative expenses	35,000	35,000
Taxes	—	15,000[a]
Dividends	—	5,000
Totals	$218,480	$221,560

[a] From February 28 balance sheet.

Schedule F—Cash Budget

	March	April
Beginning balance	$ 52,000[a]	$ 32,520
Receipts (from receipts budget)	199,000	235,500
Total available cash	251,000	268,020
Disbursements		
(from disbursements budget)	218,480	221,560
Ending balance	$ 32,520	$ 46,460

[a] From February 28 balance sheet.

Schedule G—Budgeted Income Statement
March and April, 19X0

Sales $25 × (9,000 + 12,000)		$525,000
Standard cost of sales $14 × 21,000		294,000
Standard gross margin		231,000
Volume (application) variance[a]		8,500 F
Actual gross margin		239,500
Selling and administrative expenses:		
Variable, 21,000 × $2	$42,000	
Fixed	70,000	
Bad debts, 2% × $525,000	10,500	122,500
Income before taxes		117,000
Income taxes at 40%		46,800
Net income		$ 70,200

[a] Production of 25,700 units for the two months minus 24,000 units normal activity, multiplied by $5 standard fixed cost per unit.

EXHIBIT 14–2 (Continued)

Schedule H—Pro Forma Balance Sheet as of April 30, 19X0

Assets		Equities	
Cash (from cash budget)	$ 46,460	Accounts payable[e]	
Accounts receivable, net[a]	234,000	(materials)	$ 7,760
Inventories:		Taxes payable[f]	46,800
Finished goods,		Commissions payable[g]	24,000
16,500[b] × $14	231,000	Accrued production	
Raw materials,		costs[h]	23,700
30,400[c] × $0.50	15,200	Common stock	1,700,000
Plant and equipment	2,460,000		
Accumulated depreciation[d]	(970,000)	Retained earnings	214,400
Totals	$2,016,660		$2,016,660

[a] 78% × April budgeted sales of $300,000.
[b] From production budget, Schedule B = 1.5 × budgeted May sales of 11,000 units.
[c] From purchases budget, Schedule C = 0.80 × budgeted May production of 9,500 units × 4 lb per unit.
[d] $940,000 beginning balance plus $30,000 depreciation for March and April.
[e] 40% of April purchases of $19,400, from purchases budget, Schedule C.
[f] From income statement.
[g] $2 × April budgeted sales of 12,000 units.
[h] 20% × April budgeted production costs requiring cash, from production cost budget, Schedule D.
[i] Beginning balance of $149,200 plus net income of $70,200 minus dividend of $5,000.

Each of the balance sheet figures can also be determined using standard financial accounting analysis. For example, accounts receivable at the end of April are equal to the beginning balance of $154,000 plus sales of $525,000 minus collections of $434,500 ($199,000 + $235,500) and bad debts of $10,500. Similar analyses may be used for inventories and liabilities.

Cash Receipts Budget

The pattern of collection of sales depends on the firm's credit policies and its customers' behavior. Some firms will offer discounts for payment within some specified period, such as 10 days. Firms may offer 30 days, 60 days, or some other period for payment without a discount, depending on trade practice and the creditworthiness of customers.

All other things being equal, a firm would prefer that its customers pay immediately on receipt of the goods, or even in advance of delivery. Collection would be certain, and the firm would not have to finance the investment in accounts receivable. When a firm has receivables, it must obtain cash to pay current bills while awaiting the receipt of cash from credit customers. Securing these funds has at least an opportunity cost to the firm, since they are tied up and cannot be used for any other purpose. This idea will be developed further in Chapter 15 on capital budgeting. However, a requirement for immediate cash payment would severely reduce sales for many firms, because their customers would patronize more accommodating firms. Some firms do prefer that their customers take plenty of time to pay, because they charge high interest rates. For example, the interest rate on some retail stores' charge accounts may run to 18 percent or more, which is a good return on the investment in receivables.

The Enco Company cash receipts budget appears in Schedule A of Exhibit 14–2. March receipts are budgeted at 20 percent of March sales plus receivables at the end of February. April receipts are equal to 20 percent of April budgeted sales plus 78 percent of March budgeted sales. Net accounts receivable at month end (accounts receivable less allowance for doubtful accounts) are equal to 78 percent of the sales of the month. We do not distinguish between gross accounts receivable and the allowance for doubtful accounts. The balance in the allowance account depends on how soon the firm writes off the individual bad debts as they become known.

Production and Purchases Budgets

Production levels and levels of purchases are governed by the firm's inventory policy. Inventory of finished goods is typically held equal to some budgeted sales requirements, such as twice the coming month's budgeted unit sales. This is done in order to meet extraordinary demands and as a hedge against short-term breakdowns or work stoppage. Inventory of raw materials is generally kept at some desired amount based on budgeted production for coming periods. For example, the Enco Company keeps its raw materials at 80 percent of the budgeted requirements for the coming month's production.

Inventory policy is governed by a number of factors. It is costly to hold inventory: insurance, taxes, cost of the capital invested (opportunity cost), obsolescence, and pilferage can amount to 20 to 25 percent of the cost of inventory over a year. However, carrying very little inventory of finished goods may result in lower sales, and carrying small quantities of raw materials may result in stoppages in production. Inventory is also bought as a hedge against price increases.

Wide swings in production may be very costly. A firm that produces at 50 percent of capacity one month and 85 percent the next month may find it is losing good workers, who get tired of being laid off in slack months. Overtime pay during high production periods may also be costly. Such companies may decide to downplay inventory levels and keep production at a more or less level rate throughout the year. Inventory would then rise rapidly in months of low sales and decline as sales pick up. Models for determining the optimal amount of inventory to carry and to buy or produce are presented in Chapter 20.

From a technical standpoint, the determination of required production or purchases in units is based on the familiar equation:

beginning inventory + production − ending inventory = units sold

Rearranging the equation gives:

production = ending inventory + units sold − beginning inventory

Purchases of raw materials for a manufacturer will be expressed as follows:

units purchased = ending inventory + units used in production − beginning inventory

The two equations have the same general form, the difference being that material purchases are based on production, not on sales, and are expressed in units of material (pounds, gallons, and so on), not units of finished product.

A merchandising firm may express its required purchases of merchandise using the first formula expressed in dollars of cost:

purchases in dollars = cost of ending inventory + cost of goods sold − cost of beginning inventory

In general, a manufacturing firm must solve for production in units, rather than cost, because of the presence of fixed manufacturing costs. Raw material purchases may be solved for in terms of either units or cost. Enco's production and purchases budgets appear in Schedules B and C of Exhibit 14–2. Its budget for production costs is shown in Schedule D.

Cash Disbursements Budget

The cash disbursements budget relies on the patterns of payments for materials and other production costs and for selling and administrative expenses. In general, firms will not pay for raw material purchases in cash at delivery, but in 10 days, 30 days, or some other time depending on the supplier of the particular material. Workers are not paid as soon as they work, but perhaps a week later. Thus we would not expect cash disbursements to match costs incurred in the same period. Costs incurred but not paid will show up as accounts payable and accruals in the current liability section of the balance sheet. The cash disbursements budget also contains sporadic items such as dividends, insurance premiums, property taxes, quarterly payments of estimated income taxes, and purchases of plant and equipment. Schedule E of Exhibit 14–2 presents Enco's cash disbursements budget.

Cash Budget

This budget is an extremely important part of the planning process. Firms are severely embarrassed and may go into bankruptcy if they run out of cash, or allow cash to get so low that emergency financing is required. A banker considering whether to lend to a firm would be more favorably disposed if the firm could show why it needed cash and how soon it could expect to repay the loan. If the treasurer of the firm rushed into the bank at the last minute, just as cash was about to run out, the banker would be reluctant to grant a loan because the firm's performance would indicate poor planning. Anticipating cash requirements and seeking financing well in advance of the need would give the firm a much better chance of obtaining the loan and would probably help to ensure a lower rate of interest than would a distress loan.

The other side of the coin is excess cash. Cash on deposit in a checking account does not (generally) earn interest. A firm that expects a surplus of cash above its normal desired balance would try to invest it in income-producing securities. A surplus that is expected to last for three months might be invested in 90-day government notes or other securities due within the three-month period. Schedule F gives Enco's cash budget.

Budgeted (Pro Forma) Income Statement

Schedule G shows the budgeted income statement for the two-month period. We could prepare this statement earlier in the process, but it sometimes happens that the cash budget will show that the firm needs to borrow money and it will then have interest expense that has to be reflected in the budgeted income statement. We show the effects of financing shortly.

The budgeted income statement is important to the managers: they want to know whether budgeted operations will produce a satisfactory profit, and if not, what they might do to increase profits. Here again, the interplay of budgets is important. The managers might decide to raise prices, offer more generous credit terms in the expectation of increasing unit volume, or increase advertising and promotional expenses. They would then redo the set of budgets to see what would result if their expectations were borne out.

Additionally, the budgeted income statement shows the budgeted income taxes for the period, which the firm will have to pay in July (see item 4 of Other Data in Exhibit 14–1). This piece of information is needed for the budgeted balance sheet, as is the budgeted net income, which we shall add to retained earnings at February 28 in determining the April 30 balance of retained earnings.

Budgeted (Pro Forma) Balance Sheet

The treasurer of a firm is extremely interested in the cash budget, because obtaining financing and investing surplus cash are among his duties. The budgeted balance sheet is also helpful to the treasurer, because it shows some sources and uses of cash in the period after its date. In our example, the treasurer would see from the pro forma balance sheet (Schedule H) that the firm should expect to collect about $234,000 from outstanding receivables. He would also see that cash requirements for accounts payable and other current liabilities are already in place. The pro forma balance sheet does not indicate all sources and uses of cash for the coming period. Cash will be collected from sales made in the coming period and cash will be paid for purchases and production to take place in the coming period.

Another reason for being interested in the pro forma balance sheet is that it might be part of a package of budgeted statements prepared for an application for a bank loan, or it might be published for stockholders and other interested external parties (especially if dated at the end of a fiscal year). Some firms will have loans requiring that a certain working capital (current assets minus current liabilities) or a certain current ratio (current assets divided by current liabilities) be maintained. If these requirements are not met, the loan may fall due immediately. In such cases the treasurer would want to see whether the firm might be in default on any of these provisions and, if so, take some corrective action. He might arrange for the sale of some additional common stock, postpone purchases of plant and equipment, or seek to reduce production in order to conserve cash.

In practice, many more schedules would make up the comprehensive budget. Labor hours by department, overhead costs in itemized form, several products, and several raw materials would probably be involved in the budgets for a real firm. The increased complexity would not require any changes in the basic procedures already illustrated: there would simply be more budgets of each type.

Cash Shortages and Financing

One serious problem arises if the firm's cash budget shows that it will have a negative balance, or even a positive balance that is below the minimum required. No large firm would attempt to operate with $50 budgeted cash at the end of a coming month. Errors in estimating the flows of cash could easily turn that low an amount into a sizable deficit. Remember that we are dealing with expectations, so we cannot be sure that the budgeted results and the actual results will be the same.

Dealing with an expected shortage of cash requires a few additional steps in the cash budget. Let us illustrate, using the Enco Company and assuming that it has a minimum required cash balance of $40,000, that it can borrow at 1 percent interest per month, and that it borrows and repays in multiples of $10,000 (the last assumption is for simplicity). The cash budget from Exhibit 14–2 is reproduced below, along with the financing plan to cover the temporary shortage for March.

Revised Cash Budget—Enco Company

	March	April
Beginning balance	$ 52,000	$ 42,520
Receipts	199,000	235,500
Total available	251,000	278,020
Disbursements	218,480	221,560
Indicated balance	32,520	56,460
Minimum desired balance	40,000	40,000
Excess (deficiency)	(7,480)	16,460
Borrow (repay)	10,000	(10,000)
Interest	—	(200)[a]
Balance (equals indicated balance plus borrowing/minus repayment and interest)	$ 42,520	$ 46,260

[a] $10,000 × 1% × 2 months.

If the firm followed the policy of keeping cash above $40,000, it would borrow at the beginning of March and repay at the end of April. The cost would be $200 interest expense, but it might be well worth while to take the loan rather than risk running out of cash.

OTHER BUDGETING TECHNIQUES

Pro Forma Balance Sheets

Cash budgeting is sometimes done using pro forma balance sheets, especially when a manager wants to know how much cash is likely to be available at some future date to meet a specific obligation. For example, a firm may have a bond issue falling due in six months, a payment on a large plant expansion due in one year, or a target dividend due to be paid in eight months. The treasurer of the firm wants to know whether sufficient cash will be available, and if not, what steps might be taken.

The analytical methods used in such problems may vary according to the circumstances and preferences of the managers involved. One method is to determine the total asset requirements other than cash, and the total available equities. Cash is then a plug figure, which may be positive or negative, and it is compared with the minimum balance that the firm wishes to keep on hand. To illustrate, we use the data in Exhibit 14–3. They related to the Beach Company, a retailing firm. Its treasurer is determining whether the firm will be able to pay off its 9.5 percent debt due on December 31, 19X5.

EXHIBIT 14–3
Data for Beach Company

Balance Sheet as of December 31, 19X4

Cash	$ 168,000	Accounts payable	$ 81,000
Accounts receivable	374,000	Other current liabilities	145,000
Inventory	244,000	9½% Bonds payable, due	
		December 31, 19X5	450,000
Net fixed assets	1,210,000	Common stock	1,260,000
		Retained earnings	60,000
Totals	$1,996,000		$1,996,000

Budgeted Income Statement for 19X5

Sales	$2,400,000
Cost of sales	960,000
Gross margin	1,440,000
Selling, general, and administrative expenses[a]	1,100,000
Income before taxes	340,000
Income taxes	167,000
Net income	$ 173,000

Other Data

1. Sales are expected to be evenly spread throughout the year.
2. Accounts receivable are collected in 60 days, on the average. Thus, receivables generally approximate sales for the prior two months.
3. The firm generally carries about a three-month supply of inventory. Sales in the first quarter of 19X6 are expected to be about $660,000 with the same cost-of-sales percentage as 19X5.
4. Purchases of fixed assets will be about $440,000 in 19X5.
5. Accounts payable generally run at about one-third of inventory. Purchases are paid for about 30 days after purchase.
6. At the end of 19X5 *other current liabilities* are expected to be about $153,000.
7. The firm's treasurer hopes to pay a $75,000 dividend in 19X5.

[a] Includes $240,000 depreciation and $42,750 interest on 9½% bonds.

A pro forma statement of required assets and available equities appears in Exhibit 14–4 on page 562. It shows that if the firm does pay off the 9½ percent bonds, it will have a negative cash balance of $415,000. Its assets needed to operate will be $2,074,000 exclusive of cash, while its available equities will be only $1,659,000. A negative cash balance is generally not possible; the firm will have to raise additional cash to bring the budgeted balance above zero, with a corresponding increase in equities.

EXHIBIT 14-4
Budgeted Required Assets and Available Equities—Beach Company
December 31, 19X5

Assets Required		Available Equities	
Accounts receivable[a]	$ 400,000	Accounts payable[d]	$ 88,000
Inventory[b]	264,000	Other current liabilities[e]	153,000
Net fixed assets[c]	1,410,000	Common stock	1,260,000
		Retained earnings[f]	158,000
Totals	$2,074,000		$1,659,000

Indicated cash balance = ($415,000) = $1,659,000 − $2,074,000

[a] From other data items 1 and 2. Sales of $2,400,000 evenly spread gives average monthly sales of $200,000 ($2,400,000/12). Two months sales will be uncollected at year end.
[b] From other data item 3, sales in the first quarter of 19X6 are expected to be $660,000. Cost of goods sold is 40% of sales ($960,000/$2,400,000 from 19X5 budgeted income statement). The inventory of a three-month supply is then $660,000 × 40%.
[c] Beginning balance of $1,210,000 plus purchases of $440,000, from other data item 4, minus depreciation for the year of $240,000 from the note to the 19X5 budgeted income statement.
[d] From other data item 5, accounts payable are about one-third of inventory.
[e] Given in other data item 6.
[f] Beginning balance of $60,000 plus net income budgeted at $173,000 minus dividends budgeted at $75,000.

This method has some advantages over preparing a cash budget for the year. It is much shorter, because to prepare a cash budget you would have to determine the year-end balances of some of the balance sheet items anyway, and there would be many more calculations. Variations of the method are used for making rough estimates of long-term financing requirements.

Budget Simulations

We discuss the techniques of simulation in Chapter 23. At this point we say merely that many companies use computer programs to develop budgets under various assumed conditions. Once the firm has a program that does the calculations, it is relatively easy to test a large number of alternatives to see what happens. For instance, the managers of a firm might be uncertain about the total market for its products during the coming year, but they might have in mind a range that seemed reasonable and achievable. They could run the simulation several times, using different levels of sales, to get some idea of the ranges of such important variables as income and cash flow.

In some cases a budget simulation could use regression analysis. The managers might put historical data into the computer, from which the program would develop estimates of relationships such as accounts receivable to sales, inventory levels to cost of sales, and so on. The program would then use these regression results along with the managers' forecasts of sales to develop budgeted income statements, balance sheets, and cash flow statements. There are commercial programs that have these capabilities.

Firms might also develop simulation models of parts of their operations, perhaps using linear programming or other forms of mathematical programming to locate optimal actions. Some models allow the manager to simulate the behavior of competitors. For instance, the manager could see what would happen if the firm raised prices and competitors raised their prices by a lesser amount. Such a model requires estimates of the effects on volume of changes in prices and in the relative prices that all the firms charge.

Simulation models are costly to develop but relatively cheap to run. The programming effort can be utterly huge, requiring the services of many people over a fairly long period. Commercially available models are likely to be cheaper but are also likely to require some modification to fit the firm's particular circumstances. Nevertheless, firms will probably continue to develop models of varying size and complexity to help them to simplify the enormous complexity of modern business operations.

BUDGETING FOR DISCRETIONARY EXPENDITURES

The budgeting that we have so far described relates primarily to production and sales. We have considered selling and administrative expenses but have not clearly distinguished them from production and sales. Costs of production activities are relatively easy to determine and to relate to output (units of product). In contrast, costs such as research and development, advertising, employee training (including executive development), and the myriad of administrative support activities (accounting, data processing, and so on) present in any large firm do not lend themselves easily to analyses of output/input relationships.

The activities described above are to some extent discretionary; the firm may, within limits, increase or decrease the amounts spent on them more or less at will. Cutting back on some of these activities may be extremely unwise, but it is rarely easy to determine that in the short run. Short-term reductions in cost may be accompanied by long-term deterioration in sales (if research and development is reduced), efficiency (if employee training is reduced), and so on. Thus, the principal problem in budgeting for these activities is that they do not have short-term outputs that can be examined and analyzed. Their effects are going to be felt in the long term, and even then it will be difficult to trace particular effects back to particular expenditures made in earlier periods.

Research and development (R&D) is the classic case. Managers hope that work of the R&D group will show up in increased sales in periods far removed from the one in which the expenditures are made. It now takes about ten years to bring a new drug on the market, from research through development and testing. In fact, a new product may be the joint output of a number of expenditures for various types of testing and experimentation. In such cases it is impossible to trace the benefits back to specific costs.

To make matters worse, many expenditures for discretionary activities may never bear fruit. Highly trained employees may leave the firm. R&D efforts might come to naught. The problem is that you cannot tell in advance that efforts will be wasted. If you could, you would not authorize them to begin with. For some activities also there is a serious question regarding the definition and the measure of output. The computer center of one organization displays the sign "Satisfaction Guaranteed or Double Your Data Back." This is a facetious statement of a real problem. The output of a computer center may be measured by the number of jobs processed, hours of time used, or pages of printed output. However, these measures have no necessary relationship to benefits. Valuable output and frivolous output are counted the same.

What, then, is the solution to budgeting for discretionary activities? Some general guidelines are possible, but exceptions will always exist. First, upper-level managers must determine the general objectives of the discretionary activity and translate them into required resources and costs. Participants in this process should include the head of the department and the users of the service (for example, the head of data processing and the heads of the other departments that make the most use of the computer center). A good deal of give-and-take may be needed to resolve the concerns of each party about what is important.

In the Mesa case (Chapter 1) we noted that professionals such as engineers, lawyers, and accountants have goals that may not coincide with those of upper-level managers. Professionals often want to have the best department around, and this is not always desirable. In the Mesa case we saw that the mining engineers wanted the latest equipment, giving little attention to its cost. Similarly, the head of a legal department may want to be absolutely sure that no contract goes through without the most careful, minute examination, even if the sum involved is only a few hundred dollars per year. For a manufacturing process the cost of trying to achieve a zero defect record may be way out of proportion to the benefits. Upper-level managers must recognize the benefit-cost relationships of staff activities and determine reasonable levels.

Second, management should establish some performance goals, even though outputs may not be subject to easy measurement. For example, a data processing center might be expected to keep turnaround time (the time from the submission of a job to its completion) under four hours 90 percent of the time. The legal department might be required to process routine transactions within two days, instead of studying them to death to ensure that no conceivable problem could develop. Of course, all transactions with legal implications might contain potential problems, but the mortgage on a $200,000 piece of land may not need the same study as a complex application for a patent.

The developing of objectives and the setting of goals for performance interact. Setting objectives without some idea of how to determine whether the responsible manager is achieving them is fruitless. So is establishing performance goals without relating them to objectives. Does the firm really need to provide a four-hour turnaround time on *all* data processing jobs?

If this interactive process works well, one important result should be that upper-level managers come away with a good understanding of what the firm is getting for what it is spending. It is not possible to quantify the benefits of, say, spending $X to reduce the time that it takes to prepare sales reports, but it is possible to make the judgment that the expenditure seems worthwhile or is probably not worth it. In many cases, such qualitative judgments are all that managers can make.

Third, it may be possible to develop some general ideas about the efficiency of some centers by looking at industry averages. A bank manager may be able to determine that the data processing costs of his bank are greatly higher than those of similar banks. Statistics of R&D spending are generally available, and comparisons with other firms can easily be made. It may be possible to determine whether performance is improving or deteriorating by looking at historical trends. The rate of increase in administrative personnel could be compared with the rate of increase in production workers; advertising expenses per dollar of sales could be plotted for several years.

The principal problem in analyzing discretionary expenses by using either industry averages or historical trends is that they are relative measures, but not relative to a standard. It is not necessary to believe that the industry average of R&D spending represents good performance, or that a ratio of 0.45 administrative employees to each production worker is a good or a bad figure. The problem is essentially the same as that of developing standard costs from historical data. Actual results, whether in your firm or in others, do not necessarily represent currently attainable performance.

One commonly used method of budgeting for some discretionary activities, especially R&D and advertising, is to provide a flexible budget allowance based on sales. Thus, R&D could be 1.5 percent of sales; advertising could be 2 percent. This is essentially an ability-to-pay method, and it is not conducive to good results. It fails to relate benefits to costs and ignores the long-run aspects of costs such as R&D, employee training, and management development. Its use could result in reducing expenditures during periods when they are most needed. This result is obvious with advertising, which may not need to rise during periods of high sales but perhaps should rise during periods of low sales. The flexible budgeting method would give the opposite effects.

Often, upper-level management will simply make policy statements: "Each manager at the third level will have the opportunity to attend at least two seminars per year." "We shall increase our spending on R&D at a rate at least 2 percent above the rate of inflation." Sometimes such policy statements are about the only ones that management can make, but before resorting to them, management should try to make more analytical judgments.

SUMMARY

This second chapter on budgeting focused on the development of budgets. We saw that a large array of budgets may be necessary to get a fairly accurate portrayal of the firm's operations and its requirements for resources, especially cash.

The sales forecast is the beginning step in the development of budgets. Sales forecasts, along with assumptions derived from experience or specified by company policy, are the foundation on which the remaining budgets are built.

Budgets for manufacturing operations are developed with the aid of techniques described in earlier chapters. Budgets for selling and administrative activities are more difficult to prepare, because there are no well-developed standards for performance. In fact, the unit of output of a discretionary expense center might be undefinable. In these areas the accountant is on soft ground.

ASSIGNMENTS

14–1 Cash Flow. It is not uncommon to hear businesspeople use the term *cash flow* to mean net income plus depreciation. This definition refers only to operating cash flows, not to borrowings, issues of stock, purchases of plant assets, and other short- and long-term sources and uses of cash.

Required: What is wrong with the definition? Does it leave anything out? Does it include too much?

14–2 Cash Receipts Analysis. The data below reflect the sales, receivables, and cash receipts for the Allen Company for the past five months.

	March	April	May	June	July
Sales	$64,000	$ 81,000	$ 75,000	$ 92,000	$114,000
Receivables, end of month	89,000	113,000	115,500	129,500	160,000
Cash collections	90,000	57,000	72,500	78,000	83,500

Required: Determine the pattern of collection of sales. (For example, sales are collected in 30 days.)

14–3 Cash Disbursements Budget. The Farnsworth Manufacturing Company makes a number of products. The firm uses normal costing, charging direct labor and materials at actual cost and applying overhead at a rate of $4.80 per direct labor hour. Variable overhead is about $3 per direct labor hour and fixed overhead is budgeted at $54,000 per month, including $6,500 depreciation.

Both direct labor and variable overhead are paid for 75 percent in the month incurred, 25 percent in the following month. Fixed overhead requiring cash is paid in the month incurred. All direct laborers earn $8 per hour. An assistant to the controller has prepared the following budgets of production cost. Material purchases are budgeted separately.

	April	May	June	July
Direct labor	$226,500	$284,200	$310,100	$295,600
Overhead at $4.80/DLH	135,900	170,520	186,060	177,300

The assistant has used these figures in budgeting cost of goods manufactured but is unsure how to use them in budgeting cash disbursements.

Required: Prepare cash disbursements budgets for May, June, and July for direct labor and overhead.

14–4 **Basic Comprehensive Budget.** The following data pertain to the Newhall Company, which operates a wholesale business.

Sales Forecasts—19X6

January	$ 80,000
February	100,000
March	120,000
April	110,000
May	100,000

Balance Sheet, December 31, 19X5

Cash	$ 20,000	Accounts payable	$ 27,000
Accounts receivable, net	70,000	Accrued commissions	9,000
Inventory	115,000	Common stock	220,000
Net fixed assets	190,000	Retained earnings	139,000
Totals	$395,000		$395,000

Other data:

1. All sales are on credit. About 40 percent of sales are collected in the month of sale, 58 percent in the month after sale, with 2 percent bad debts.

2. Cost of sales runs about 60 percent of sales.

3. A 7 percent commission on sales is the only variable cost, besides cost of sales. The commissions are paid in the month after they are earned.

4. The firm keeps inventory about equal to a two-month supply.

5. The firm pays for its merchandise in the month after purchase.

6. Fixed operating costs are $12,000 per month, including $4,000 depreciation.

Required:

1. Prepare a budgeted income statement for the quarter ending March 31. Do not break it down by month.

2. Prepare a cash budget and all necessary supporting schedules for each of the first three months of 19X6.

3. Prepare a pro forma balance sheet as of March 31, 19X6.

14–5   Cash Budget.   The Lyman Company is a wholesaler of school supplies. The firm's busy season is July through September, with sales then tailing off. In June of 19X7 the controller was preparing a cash budget to determine whether he would have to use the firm's line of credit at a local bank. He had amassed the following information.

Sales forecasts: June, $217,500; July, $325,600; August, $337,200; September, $296,400; October, $243,100; November, $211,300.

Cost of sales averages 60 percent of sales. Operating expenses are $37,400 per month plus 10 percent of sales, all paid during the month incurred except for $2,800 in depreciation. The firm tries to keep a two-month supply of inventory on hand and pays for its purchases in 30 days. Its customers pay, on average, in 60 days.

The controller would like to keep a cash balance of at least $30,000 and was therefore not happy at the projected balance of $28,750 at the end of June (see below). Balance sheet data expected at June 30 appear below.

Cash	$ 28,750
Accounts receivable	416,300 ($198,800 from May, $217,500 from June)
Inventory	367,200
Accounts payable	198,240 (anticipated from expected purchases in June)

Required: Prepare a cash budget by month from July through September and supporting schedules showing whether the firm will need to use its line of credit and when it can pay off any loans. Assume that borrowings against the line of credit, if needed, are made in multiples of $10,000. Ignore interest.

14–6   Basic Budgets for Production and Purchases.   The Morlin Company makes a single product. Data appear at the top of page 569.

Raw materials, 2 lb at $3/lb

Inventory requirements, two-month supply of finished goods, one-month supply of raw materials (based on production needs).

Sales forecasts (in units): January, 1,000; February, 1,200; March, 1,300; April, 1,500; May, 1,400; June, 1,600.

The firm began January with 1,800 units of finished goods; 2,300 lb of raw materials.

Required:

1. Prepare production budgets for months January through April.

2. Prepare budgets of purchases of raw materials, both in pounds and in dollars, for as many months as you can. Explain why you had to stop where you did.

14-7 **Cash Budget—Manufacturer.** The treasurer of Malta Manufacturing Company has been developing information to prepare a cash budget for the period August–October. He has amassed the following:

Sales forecast. August, 68,000 units; September, 82,000 units; October, 70,000 units; November, 64,000 units; December, 61,000 units.

Price and cost data. The selling price is $10 per unit. Material cost is $2 per unit, direct labor and variable manufacturing overhead are $4 per unit. Fixed factory overhead is $120,000 per month, including $15,000 depreciation. Selling and administrative expenses are $42,500 per month (all cash costs), plus $0.80 per unit sold (commission).

Inventory policy. The firm tries to keep finished goods inventory at 1½ times the coming month's budgeted sales. It keeps raw material inventory at twice the coming month's budgeted production. It makes purchases evenly over a month.

Collection of sales. Sales are collected about 40 percent in the month of sale, 58 percent in the following month, with 2 percent bad debts. Bad debts are not included in the cost data given above.

Cash disbursements. The firm pays for two-thirds of its materials in the month after purchase, one-third in the second month after purchase. Selling and administrative expenses are paid in the month incurred, except that the $0.80 commission is paid in the month after sale. Manufacturing costs, other than for materials, are paid in the month incurred.

Balance sheet data. At the end of July the firm should have about $78,000 in cash, $348,000 in net accounts receivable, 95,000 units of finished product, and $288,000 in raw material inventory. Accounts payable due in August from July purchases are $126,000, from June purchases are $67,000. Another $63,000 is due in September from July purchases. Sales commissions payable in August are $48,000 from July sales.

Required: Prepare a cash budget by month for the August–October period. Keep cash at least at $50,000 by borrowing and repaying in $10,000 multiples. Ignore interest.

14–8 Balance Sheet Data

Required: Use your solution to assignment 14–7 to develop as many items as you can that would appear on Malta Manufacturing's balance sheet as of the end of September. Assume that the firm uses variable costing for its finished goods inventory.

14–9 Cash Budget—One Month.   The Burlington Dry Goods Company makes all its purchases on credit, paying in 10 days in order to obtain the 2 percent discount offered by all its suppliers. The firm records its inventory net of the discount and tries to keep inventory at gross cost about equal to the sales requirements budgeted for the next two months. The firm sells on credit, with 40 percent of its customers paying within 20 days to take advantage of the 1 percent discount that Burlington offers for prompt payment. The remainder pay in 60 days. Cost of sales (gross) averages 47 percent of sales.

The following additional information is available.

Sales:	
August (actual)	$340,000
September (actual)	404,000
October (budgeted)	385,000
November (budgeted)	410,000
December (budgeted)	390,000
Inventory at September 30	365,500
Purchases in September (net of discount)	176,000
Operating expenses budgeted for October	144,000 + 6% of sales
Cash at September 30	53,500

The 6 percent variable operating expenses is for sales commissions. Depreciation included in the $144,000 is $12,500. All operating expenses requiring cash are paid in the month incurred. Sales and purchases are made evenly throughout each month. Assume that each month has 30 days.

Required: Prepare a cash budget for October.

14–10 Sales Forecasting, Regression Analysis.   The sales manager of the Bramon Cement Company has collected the following data in an effort to get an idea of the relationship, if any, between the firm's sales and total dollars spent on construction in the geographical area that Bramon serves. All dollar amounts are in millions.

Year	Total Construction	Sales of Bramon
19X1	$3,200	$27
19X2	3,600	30
19X3	2,400	22
19X4	3,100	24
19X5	3,900	35
19X6	3,800	32

Required:

1. Develop a regression equation that relates Bramon's sales to total construction spending. Find the standard error of the estimate and of the b coefficient, and the value of r^2.

2. The sales manager has read a series of forecasts of construction spending in 19X7. They range from $3,500 to $3,700 (in millions). What would you forecast for Bramon's sales for 19X7, and how much confidence would you have in your forecast?

14-11 **Pro Forma Balance Sheet.** The Whittaker Company is a wholesaler of dry goods. The firm has a $200,000 line of credit with a local bank that its treasurer expects to use during the coming period. In fact, she is not sure whether the firm will be able to get by with only $200,000 and has decided to prepare a pro forma balance sheet as of the end of April, 19X7. She has assembled the following information in preparation for the task.

Month	Sales Forecast	Purchases Forecast
January	$280,000	$210,000
February	315,000	382,000
March	476,000	302,000
April	490,000	156,000
May	375,000	138,000

Other data are:

1. Cost of sales averages 60 percent of sales.

2. All sales are on credit, with payments made in 60 days.

3. The firm generally maintains an inventory of about twice the coming month's budgeted sales requirements. The purchases forecasted above reflect this policy.

4. The firm pays for its purchases in 30 days.

5. Operating expenses, all fixed, are $130,000 per month. They are paid as incurred, except for depreciation, which is $10,000 per month.

6. The dividend payable shown below will be paid in April.

The expected balance sheet at December 31, 19X6, is given below.

Balance Sheet (Expected), December 31, 19X6—Whittaker Company

Cash	$ 80,000	Accounts payable (merchandise)	$ 165,000
Accounts receivable	650,000	Dividend payable	40,000
Inventory	328,000	Long-term debt	400,000
Plant and equipment (net)	920,000	Stockholder equity	1,373,000
Totals	$1,978,000		$1,978,000

The treasurer believes that $70,000 is the minimum balance of cash that the firm needs to operate.

Required: Determine whether the firm will need more than $200,000 at the end of April by preparing a pro forma balance sheet as of April 30, 19X7. You need not prepare cash budgets for each month to make the determination.

14–12 Sales Forecasting. Multitronics, Inc., is a large manufacturer of various high-technology products. The budget director of the firm has been working on sales budgets for each major line and has run intô a problem with the semiconductor segment of the business.

The firm generally captures about 15 percent of the total semiconductor market, with 13 percent the lowest share in recent years and 16.5 percent the highest. A recent article in a trade journal forecast a 20 percent increase in semiconductor sales for the coming year, assuming that economic conditions did not deteriorate. A mild recession, the article stated, would drop the increase to about 12 percent, while a severe recession would reduce it to 4 percent. Total industry sales for the current year should be about $68 million.

The sales manager has told the budget director that he expects Multitronics to sell about $14 million worth of semiconductors in the coming year.

Reports from government agencies and private economic consulting firms indicate that the probability of a mild recession is about 25 percent, of a severe recession, 15 percent.

Required: Develop an optimistic forecast for Multitronics, a pessimistic one, and one that you would use for budgeting production, manpower, and other items for the coming year. Be prepared to defend the figure you elect to use for budgeting.

14–13 Cash Collection Patterns. The following independent situations describe the cash collection experiences of various firms.

1. A firm makes 20 percent of its sales for cash. Its credit sales, except for bad debts equaling 2 percent of credit sales, come in 30 days after sale.
2. A firm's records show that its accounts receivable equal sales for the current month plus 40 percent of sales for the prior month.
3. A firm's accounts receivable turnover (sales/accounts receivable) is four times per year.
4. A firm offers a 2 percent discount for customers paying within 10 days after sale. Customers accounting for 80 percent of total sales pay within the discount period, with the remainder paying in 60 days.

5. A firm makes 10 percent of its sales for cash. It makes available a 1 percent discount to the customers who pay within 20 days, and the cash customers get that discount. Of the credit sales, about 1 percent become bad debts, 40 percent of the total credit sales are paid within the discount period, and the remainder are collected in 60 days.

Required: Assuming that sales are made evenly throughout each month, and that each month has 30 days, write an equation to determine cash collections for each firm. Use the notation C_t = cash collections in month t, S_t = sales in month t, S_{t-1} = sales in the prior month, and so on.

14–14 Cash Budget—Two Months. The Craven Company is a wholesaler in the dry goods business. The firm is growing rapidly, and its owner is wondering whether she will need short-term financing over the next two months. She has amassed the following information for you to use to develop a cash budget for the next two months (July and August).

Sales forecasts: July, $100,000; August, $140,000; September, $160,000.
Cost of sales is 40 percent of sales.
The firm keeps inventory at 150 percent of the following month's forecasted sales requirements.
Collections of sales are as follows: month of sale, 30 percent; month after sale, 68 percent; bad debts, 2 percent.
Monthly expenses, other than cost of sales and bad debts, are 10 percent of sales for commissions and other variable costs, and $40,000 fixed, including $5,000 depreciation.
The firm pays for its purchases of merchandise (goods) in 30 days and for operating expenses as incurred.

The balance sheet at June 30 is expected to be as follows. Inventory is lower than the firm's policy would indicate, because June sales were higher than expected.

Cash	$ 18,000	Accounts payable (merchandise)	$ 43,000
Accounts receivable, net	85,000	Taxes payable, due July 15	28,000
Inventory	35,000	Common stock	100,000
Furniture and fixtures, net	110,000	Retained earnings	77,000
Totals	$248,000		$248,000

Required: Prepare cash budgets for July and August. If you determine that cash will go below $15,000, which is the minimum balance that the owner considers acceptable, assume that the firm borrows enough to bring the balance up to $15,000.

14–15 Budgeting (AICPA adapted). The Helpat Corporation, a retail store, had the following balance sheet at January 31, 19X7.

Cash	$ 8,000	Accounts payable, merchandise	$ 61,875
Accounts receivable, net of	38,000		
$2,000 allowance for			
doubtful accounts			
Inventory	16,000	Common stock	50,000
Fixed assets, net	40,000	Retained earnings (deficit)	(9,875)
Totals	$102,000		$102,000

Sales budgets are: February, $110,000; March, $120,000. The firm collects 60 percent of its sales in the month of sale, 38 percent in the following month, and 2 percent are uncollectible. Gross margin is 25 percent of sales. Purchases are 75 percent of the following month's budgeted sales requirements (at cost). Accounts payable are paid in 30 days. Other expenses are $21,500 per month, including $5,000 depreciation.

Required:

1. Prepare a budgeted income statement for February.
2. Determine budgeted cash collections for February.
3. Determine budgeted accounts payable at the end of February.
4. Determine sales for January.
5. Determine cash disbursements for February.

14–16 Inventory Policies and Purchasing Requirements. Each of the following situations is independent of the others, except that the following budgeted sales figures apply to all cases.

Sales Budgets (in units)

March	8,000	May	13,000
April	10,000	June	11,000

Cases:

1. The firm maintains an inventory equal to the next two months' budgeted sales.
2. The firm maintains an inventory equal to budgeted sales for the next 45 days.
3. The firm has an annual inventory turnover of four times, based on average monthly data.
4. The firm buys inventory three months before it sells it.

Required: For each case determine budgeted purchases for March, assuming that the March 1 (or February 28) inventory equals the amount implied by the policy.

14–17 **Receipts and Disbursements (AICPA adapted).** The controller of Patsy Corporation has estimated the following activity for December, 19X1.

Sales	$350,000
Gross profit percentage of sales	30%
Increase in gross accounts receivable during month	$ 10,000
Increase in inventory during month	$ 5,000
Variable selling and administrative expenses, as a percentage of sales, including 1% estimated bad debts	15%
Fixed selling and administrative expenses	$ 35,500
Depreciation, included in fixed S&A expenses	$ 20,000
Change in accounts payable during month	$ 0

Required:

1. Determine the estimated cash receipts for December.

2. Determine the estimated cash disbursements in December.

14–18 **Sales Budgeting, Regression Analysis.** The sales manager of Cleanhair Products, Inc., has asked you to help him understand the results of regression analyses that one of his assistants has developed. The notation used is: Y = monthly sales of Glowbright, one of the firm's products, X_1 = dollars spent on advertising Glowbright in magazines, and X_2 = dollars spent on advertising Glowbright on television. Standard errors of the coefficients are in parentheses.

$$Y = \$467,000 + \$3.98X_1, \qquad r^2 = 0.47, \quad Se = \$64,320$$
$$(\$1.73)$$

$$Y = \$381,000 + \$4.23X_2, \qquad r^2 = 0.53, \quad Se = \$54,060$$
$$(\$1.86)$$

$$Y = \$752,300 + \$0.87X_1 + \$0.91X_2, \quad r^2 = 0.876, \quad Se = \$34,210$$
$$(\$0.79) \qquad (\$0.99)$$

"What does all of this mean, should I advertise or not, and where? I don't get it."

Required: Comment on the results.

14–19 **Pro Forma Balance Sheet.** One of your first duties on taking over as controller of Clete Products Company, a small manufacturer of camping equipment, was to determine whether or not the firm could meet two goals set by Howard Clete, the company president. Mr. Clete wanted to buy $140,000 in new equipment and to pay a $40,000 dividend without having to borrow or sell additional common stock. He wanted to buy the equipment and pay the dividend before March 31, 19X6, the end of the firm's current fiscal and tax year.

You began your task in late September of 19X5 and collected the following information.

1. Sales forecasts, October 19X5 through January 19X6, $130,000 per month; February 19X6, $180,000; March 19X6, $200,000; April through July $150,000 per month. The firm collects receivables in 45 days.

2. Variable manufacturing cost is 45 percent of sales, and there is a 5 percent sales commission paid on all sales. The commission is paid in the month after earned. Raw materials are about 70 percent of variable manufacturing costs.

3. The firm generally keeps a three-month supply of finished goods and a one-month supply of raw materials. It uses variable costing for finished goods inventory.

4. Fixed manufacturing costs, including depreciation of $13,000, are about $35,000 per month. Fixed selling and administrative expenses are about $20,000 per month, including $2,000 in depreciation.

5. The firm pays for its purchases of raw materials in 30 days. Except for commissions and taxes (below), all expenses requiring cash are paid as incurred.

6. Clete has told you that the firm will make a payment on estimated income taxes in December. The payment will cover taxes due for income for the first half of the 19X6 tax year (April 1, 19X5, to September 30, 19X5). The firm will not pay any estimated amount on income for the last half of the tax year. In other words, the liability at March 31, 19X6, will be equal to taxes on income from October 1, 19X5, to March 31, 19X6. The tax rate is 40 percent.

7. At September 30, 19X5, the firm will have about $750,000 in net plant and equipment and about $1,050,000 in stockholder equity.

Required: Prepare a pro forma balance sheet as of March 31, 19X6, to see whether or not Clete will be able to buy the equipment and pay the dividend without borrowing money.

14-20 Pro Forma Balance Sheet, Ratio Analyses.   The controller of the Towson Company has been planning the firm's cash requirements for the coming year, 19X6. Before going into a detailed month-by-month cash budget, he wants to get a first cut at the end-of-year results to get some idea of the firm's financing needs. He has gathered the following information.

1. Sales in 19X6 should be about $2 million, cost of sales about $1.4 million, and operating expenses $250,000. The income tax rate is 40 percent.

2. Sales in 19X7 should be about 10 percent higher than in the coming year, and cost of sales should remain constant as a percentage of sales. Sales are fairly even throughout each year.

3. The firm generally has about 60 days' sales in accounts receivable, 90 days in inventory.

4. The minimum required cash balance is $80,000.

5. By the terms of agreements related to long-term debt, current liabilities must be no more than 50 percent of current assets. The long-term debt is $450,000, and no payments are planned for the coming year (except interest, which is included in operating expenses above).

6. At year end, according to budgeted purchases and depreciation, net fixed assets will be about $950,000.

7. Stockholder equity at the beginning of the year is $640,000, and the firm plans a dividend of 60 percent of its income after taxes.

Required: Prepare a pro forma balance sheet as of December 31, 19X6, to determine whether or not Towson Company will need additional financing, and if so how much. Make whatever assumptions you think are reasonable.

14–21 Budgeting and Regression Analysis. The president of Holton Industries has asked for your assistance. The firm has recently begun to use statistical analyses in developing its budgets, and the president believes that some managers will not be receptive to the idea. He wants you to give a seminar on the use of regression analysis in budgeting, concentrating on sales forecasting and cost estimation. He gives you the following regression equations that one of his staff developed for use as examples (standard errors are in parentheses):

$$\text{sales} = \$2,367,000 + \$4.723 \text{ (advertising expenditures)}$$
$$(\$2.560)$$
$$r^2 = 0.57, \quad Se = \$489,345$$

$$\text{factory overhead cost} = \$1,096,356 + \$3.77 \text{ (direct labor hours)}$$
$$(\$1.58)$$
$$r^2 = 0.71, \quad Se = \$104,234$$

Required: Prepare a set of comments as the basis for the presentation requested by the president.

14–22 Budgeting and Linear Programming. The Hooper Chair Company makes many different chairs in two basic models, the modern and the traditional. The materials and labor requirements for all the modern chairs are about the same, and the materials and labor requirements are about the same for all the traditional chairs. Accordingly, the managers of the firm consider that they have two products.

The sales manager has estimated the maximum amounts of each model that the firm could sell as 60,000 modern, 50,000 traditional. The production manager knows that he cannot produce all the chairs that the firm could sell and decides to use a linear program to determine the optimal mix. The schedule below gives the times that each chair requires in the two departments and the total available times in them.

| | Required Times, Hours | | Total |
	Modern	Traditional	Available Time
Cutting	0.80	1.50	70,000
Assembly	1.60	0.50	100,000

The direct labor rate is $10 per hour in both departments. The variable overhead rates are $4 per hour in cutting, $6 in assembly. Contribution margins on each chair are as follows:

	Modern	Traditional
Selling price	$64.00	$73.00
Material cost	15.20	24.00
Direct labor	24.00	20.00
Variable overhead	12.80	9.00
Total variable costs	52.00	53.00
Contribution margin	$12.00	$20.00

Total fixed manufacturing costs are $410,000, and selling, general, and administrative expenses are $145,000.

Required:

1. Find the optimal production mix, solving graphically the linear programming problem.

2. Determine the total profit that the firm will be earning at the optimal mix.

14–23 Budgeting, Linear Programming, and Sensitivity Analysis. The president of the Hooper Chair Company (see the preceding assignment) looked at the production schedule that the managers developed. She wondered about the overhead rates, especially in the assembly department. The rates came from regression equations, and the standard errors of the coefficients (the variable overhead rates) were $0.65 in the cutting department and $2 in the assembly department.

"Let us suppose," the president said, "the true rate in the assembly department is $8, which is one standard error above what the mean is. Will this really hurt us badly if we stick to the mix of 57,500 modern chairs and 16,000 traditional chairs? What will the optimal schedule be if the rate is $8?"

Required:

1. Determine the effects on the contribution margins of modern and traditional chairs if the variable overhead rate in the assembly department were $8 per labor hour.

2. Determine the optimal product mix under the new circumstances. You need only find the contributions at each of the mixes you analyzed in the preceding assignment. The corner points remain the same as they were in that assignment.

3. Would you recommend that the firm stick to the original mix or change to the one you determined in item 2?

14-24 Cash Budget: Not-for-Profit (CMA adapted).   United Business Education, Inc., (UBE) is a nonprofit organization that sponsors a wide variety of management seminars throughout the United States. In addition, it is heavily involved in research into improved methods of educating and motivating business executives. The seminar activity is supported largely by fees and the research program from member dues.

UBE operates on a calendar-year basis and is in the process of finalizing the budget for 19X9. The following information has been taken from approved plans, which are still tentative at this time.

In the seminar program, UBE expects $12 million in revenue for the year. Programs totaling $1,440,000 will be offered in each of the first five months of the year; the remaining revenue will be split evenly through the months of September, October, and November. No programs are offered in the other four months of the year. Revenue is collected in the month a program is given. All programs are budgeted to produce the same amount of revenue.

Seminar expenses consist of instructors' fees, facility fees, and annual promotional costs. Instructors' fees are paid at the rate of 70 percent of the seminar revenue in the month following the seminar. Facilities are $5.6 million annually and are paid in the month a program is given. Promotional costs are $1.2 million annually, spent equally in each month.

The research program has a large number of projects nearing completion. The other main research activity this year includes the feasibility studies for new projects to be started in 19Y0. As a result, the total grant expense of $3 million for 19X9 is expected to be paid out at the rate of $500,000 per month during the first six months of the year.

UBE expenses include the following:

Office lease—annual amount of $240,000 paid monthly at the beginning of the month.

General administrative expenses (telephone, supplies, postage, and so on)—$1,500,000 annually or $125,000 a month.

Depreciation expense—$240,000 a year.

General UBE promotion—annual cost of $600,000 paid monthly.

Salaries and Benefits

Number of Employees	Annual Salary Paid Monthly	Total Annual Salaries
1	$50,000	$ 50,000
3	40,000	120,000
4	30,000	120,000
15	25,000	375,000
5	15,000	75,000
22	10,000	220,000
50		$960,000

Other information:

Membership income—UBE has 100,000 members, each of whom pays an annual membership fee of $100. The fee for the calendar year is invoiced in late June. The collection schedule for the organization is as follows:

July	60%
August	30%
September	5%
October	5%
	100%

Capital expenditures—The capital expenditures program calls for a total of $510,000 in cash payments to be spread evenly over the first five months of 19X9.

Cash and temporary investments at January 1, 19X9, are estimated at $750,000.

Required:

1. Prepare a budget of the annual cash receipts and disbursements for UBE, Inc., for 19X9.
2. Prepare a cash budget for UBE, Inc., for the first six months of 19X9.
3. Using the information you developed in items 1 and 2, identify two important operating problems of UBE, Inc.

14–25 Budgeting and Receivables (CMA). Weldon's Bike Shop has been in business for five years. The shop buys medium- to high-quality bicycles and related bike accessories for resale to customers.

The bike shop has shown profits for the past four years. The projected results for the current year are presented on page 581.

WELDON'S BIKE SHOP
Projected Statement of Income
for the Year Ended December 31, 19X8

	Dollars (in thousands)	Percent
Sales revenue	$300	100%
Cost of goods sold	180	60
Gross margin	$120	40%
Operating expenses:		
Sales commissions	$ 15	5%
Fixed expenses:		
Advertising	9	3
Salaries	21	7
Rent	18	6
General administration	12	4
Total operating expenses	$ 75	25%
Net income before taxes	$ 45	15%
Income taxes (40%)	18	6
Net income	$ 27	9%

The sales figure results from strict cash sales only. No personal checks are accepted, nor are credit or credit card sales made. Ann Weldon, the owner, is deciding whether to accept these payment methods:

personal checks only

bank credit cards only

both personal checks and bank credit cards

Ann believes that sales will increase if she accepts other payment methods in addition to strict cash. She also realizes that some cash customers will change to a different method of payment if alternative payment methods are available. The schedule below presents Ann Weldon's estimates of how sales will increase under each of the proposed three payment methods and how total sales will be collected under each:

Alternatives	Percentage Increase in Sales	Percentage of Total Sales Paid By		
		Cash	Check	Credit Card
Payment by check	10%	60%	40%	—
Payment by bank credit card	20%	50%	—	50%
Payment by check and bank credit card	25%	20%	40%	40%

If checks are accepted as a method of payment, approximately 10 percent of all check sales can be expected to be returned for nonsufficient funds (NSF). Half of the NSF checks (5 percent of total sales) will be collectible through a collection agency at a cost of 25 percent of the amount collected. The remaining half of the NSF checks will never be collected. In addition, the merchandise paid for by NSF checks will not be recovered.

Bank credit card sales can be deposited daily as if they were cash. However, the bank charges a 4 percent discount fee when credit card sales are deposited.

The cost behavior patterns of the existing costs and expenses are expected to be unchanged regardless of the payment method.

Required: Prepare an analysis that shows the effect each of the proposed payment methods being considered by Weldon's Bike Shop would have on the shop's net income. Based upon your analysis, explain whether Weldon's should accept any of the proposed payment methods in addition to strict cash, and if so identify the method which should be selected.

14-26 **Master Budget—Manufacturer.** "It looks as if we are in good shape," said Roland Eustis, president of the E&W Manufacturing Company. Eustis was looking at the budgeted income statement for the first two months of 19X6.

E&W Manufacturing Company
Budgeted Income Statement—
January–February, 19X6

Sales		$9,300,000
Cost of sales:		
Materials	$ 600,000	
Labor and variable overhead	2,736,000	
Fixed overhead	1,700,000	5,036,000
Gross margin		4,264,000
Selling and administrative expenses		2,830,000
Income before taxes		$1,434,000

E&W makes two models of the same basic product: regular and deluxe. Additional data appear below and on page 583.

	Regular Model	Deluxe Model
Unit selling price	$200	$250
Materials, in pounds	2	4
Direct labor hours	3	4
Sales collection period, in days	30	60

Material cost per pound	$ 5	
Direct labor cost per hour	$10	
Variable overhead per direct labor hour	$ 9	
Sales commissions, percentage of sales	10%	
Monthly fixed manufacturing overhead	$850,000	(including $100,000 depreciation)
Monthly fixed selling and administrative expenses	$950,000	(no depreciation)

The firm tries to keep finished inventories at 200 percent of budgeted sales for the coming month and raw material inventories at production requirements budgeted for the coming month. Sales budgets by month and product are, in units:

	Regular Model	Deluxe Model
January	10,000	7,000
February	14,000	11,000
March	18,000	9,000
April	17,000	11,000

Selected balance sheet information, as of December 31, 19X5, is:

Cash	$ 648,000
Accounts receivable:	
Regular model	2,800,000
Deluxe model	3,750,000
Accounts payable, materials	143,000
Accrued payroll, direct labor	240,000
Accrued commissions	330,000

Of the receivables for the Deluxe model, 40 percent are from sales in December, 60 percent from November. The firm expects to have 17,000 units of the regular model on hand at December 31, 19X5, 12,000 units of the Deluxe model, and 90,000 lb of materials.

The firm pays for materials in 15 days. It pays sales commissions in the month after they are earned. It pays 80 percent of direct labor cost in the month incurred, 20 percent in the following month. It pays all other expenses requiring cash in the month incurred. The firm makes sales and purchases evenly over each month.

Mr. Eustis was happy with the budgeted income statement, but he also wanted to see how much his cash position would improve as a result of the profitable operations.

Required: Prepare the following budgets for January, February, and for the two-month period as a whole:

1. cash receipts budget.
2. production budget, by product.
3. material purchases budget.
4. budgets of direct labor and variable overhead cost.
5. cash disbursements budget.
6. cash budget.

14-27 Cash Flow and Income.   You have prepared and submitted the budgets to E&W (see assignment 14–26). Mr. Eustis's response follows:

> You can't be serious! We expect to earn over $1,400,000 in January and February and you tell me that we'll run out of cash? Show me why, and you'd better make it good.

Required: Show Mr. Eustis why the firm will run out of cash, even if all goes according to budget. Make it good.

14-28 Cash Budgeting Model (CMA adapted).   Over the past several years, the Programme Corporation has encountered difficulties estimating its cash flows. The result has been a rather strained relationship with its banker.

Programme's controller would like to develop a means by which he can forecast the firm's monthly operating cash flows. The following data were gathered to facilitate the development of such a forecast.

1. Sales have been and are expected to increase at 0.5 percent each month.
2. Thirty percent of each month's sales are for cash; the other 70 percent are on open account.
3. Of the credit sales, 80 percent are collected in the first month following the sale and the remaining 20 percent are collected in the second month. There are no bad debts.
4. Gross margin on sales averages 25 percent.
5. Programme purchases enough inventory each month to cover the following month's sales.
6. All inventory purchases are paid for in the month of purchase.
7. Monthly expenses are: payroll, $1,500; rent, $400; depreciation, $120; other cash expenses, 1 percent of that month's sales. There are no accruals.
8. Ignore the effects of corporate income taxes, dividends, and equipment acquisitions.

Required: The controller asks you to develop mathematical expressions of the following elements of cash flow using the following notation: S = sales in current month, t = number of months in the future the forecast is desired.

1. Sales t months from now.
2. Cash collections t months from now.
3. Purchases t months from now.
4. Cash disbursements t months from now.

SELECTED REFERENCES

Ferrara, William L., and Jack C. Hayya, "Toward Probabilistic Profit Budgets," *Management Accounting*, 52:4 (October 1970), 23–28.

Gershefski, George W., "Building a Corporate Financial Model," *Harvard Business Review*, 47:4 (July–August 1969), 61–72.

Godfrey, James T., "Short-Run Planning in a Decentralized Firm," *The Accounting Review*, 46:2 (April 1971), 286–97.

Naylor, Thomas H., "The Future of Corporate Planning Models," *Managerial Planning*, March–April 1976, pp. 1–9.

Seed, Allen H., III, "Strategic Planning: The Cutting Edge of Managerial Accounting," *Management Accounting*, May 1980.

Capital Budgeting Decisions

Chapter 15

These next two chapters concern decisions about the replacement and acquisition of major capital assets. Starting with profit plans and sales budgets, management must analyze current facilities and equipment to see if they are adequate for ensuing periods. As new projects and manufacturing processes become available, managers need techniques to evaluate them. The basic models we will use for such evaluations are called *discounted cash flow* (DCF) models and rely on the basic notion of the *time value of money*. The appendix to this chapter explains the time value of money, while Tables A–3 and A–4 in the appendix at the end of the book contain discount factors used in these models. If you need to learn or to review the basics of the time value of money, read the appendix to this chapter at this point. The full discussion of capital budgeting will include expected cash flows, their timing, and the uncertainty surrounding them.

CAPITAL RESOURCE ALLOCATION

In Chapter 4 we explained tactical decisions as those that have their major economic impact in the short term. In contrast, capital budgeting decisions usually involve long-term considerations as well as the committing of substantial resources. For example, building a new 100,000-square-foot factory and putting in new production equipment is a decision (or series of decisions) that could commit $25 million of resources and could have a fifteen- to twenty-year impact on the company. Success or failure could affect the firm's very existence. Thus, managers need to have models to aid in the decision-making process that consider the size, timing, and variability of alternatives open to the firm.

In general, managers can use available investment funds in many ways. Certain older equipment may be wearing out and must be replaced. In other areas newer equipment has entered the field, and current production processes can be evaluated against the new developments. New projects can be proposed by the research and development or marketing departments. Finally, these funds could be invested or used to reduce outstanding indebtedness, pay dividends, or buy treasury stock. Investment decisions to buy new equipment and facilities are, therefore, competing with other productive uses of the same funds.

While some firms will generate enough cash to meet all their needs, most companies will need to secure funds through such means as selling stock or bonds or entering into other long-term financing arrangements with banks, insurance companies, or leasing companies. Obviously, any form of funds obtained from an outside party has a cost in the form of dividends or interest. Unless overall corporate returns can at least cover these payments, investors and creditors will no longer make funds available to the firm. Therefore, the question remains what are the best alternatives for a company to follow, given an available supply of cash resources generated by profits or acquired from external sources. In order to begin this analysis, we will first explore the size and timing of cash flows.

CASH FLOWS

We explore here some models that consider the time value of money (DCF models) and some that do not. Most models are based on the cash inflows and outflows resulting from particular alternatives.

Cash Flow Versus Net Income

In evaluating a decision, we ask what the economic impact of each alternative will be, and we look at an incremental analysis of this impact. For capital budgeting decisions we focus on expected incremental cash flows. Since this is a departure from the traditional accounting stress on net income, it is desirable to discuss why cash flows are the relevant data for consideration.

First, over the life of a firm, net income and net cash inflow will usually be the same.[1] However, the timing of the incomes and cash inflows may differ substantially. Given the time value of money, it is better to receive cash now rather than later, because cash can be invested to earn more cash. For example, we would prefer to own firm A rather than firm B in the schedule below. Both firms have lives of two years, and the cash flow from each is returned to us as it occurs.

---

[1] Differences between net income and net cash inflow may arise when assets are acquired through the issuance of stock, but for our purposes these differences can be ignored.

		Firm A	Firm B
First year:	net income	$20,000	$40,000
	cash inflow	20,000	0
Second year:	net income	20,000	0
	cash inflow	20,000	40,000

Firm A returns cash yearly, while firm B returns cash only at the end of the second year. If you received $20,000 at the end of the first year from firm A, you could invest it at 10 percent, for example. Thus, while you would receive only $40,000 in total from firm B after two years, you would receive $42,000 in total [($20,000 × 1.1) + $20,000] if you had invested in firm A.

Net income is an accounting measure based, in part, on the matching concept. Costs become expenses as they are matched against revenue. The actual timing of cash inflows and outflows is ignored. Certain expenses do not even require a cash outflow. Depreciation is the best example of this type of expense. Even though depreciation is deducted from revenue on a yearly basis, no cash is paid to anyone. Rather, the cash payment is made when the asset is bought. Regardless of where investment funds are acquired, a supplier of machinery or a building contractor will be paid upon delivery of a finished capital asset. In the next chapter we will discuss the difference between deciding to invest in a project and how to finance it. In whatever way an asset is financed, it is, in essence, paid for at the beginning of the project. The chapters on budgeting clearly point out the differences between an income statement and a cash budget. With these differences in mind, we can proceed and define what the relevant cash flows are for capital budgeting decisions.

Cash Flows and Taxes

Since we are interested in cash flows, it is only natural to use *after-tax* cash flows. Various actions will have various consequences under current IRS regulations. Since this is not a tax course, we will simplify tax aspects for analysis at this point. Our discussion of various types of cash flows will include tax considerations. In Chapter 16 we will explore more thoroughly the tax code and its effect on both investing and financing decisions.

Types of Cash Flows

Cash flows associated with a new production process, for example, could include investment-related flows, cash flows from operations, changes in working capital, and other miscellaneous flows.

Investment, Life, Ultimate Sale. In general, three types of flows are associated with buying a piece of machinery: the original investment, the tax effects of depreciation over its life, and the net after-tax inflows (or outflows) upon selling or disposing of the asset when its economic life is finished.

EXHIBIT 15–1
Data for New Product—Dahl Corporation

Cost of machinery	$320,000
Useful life	5 years
Expected salvage value	$ 70,000
Annual straight-line depreciation	50,000
Expected incremental revenues	500,000
Expected incremental cash costs	350,000

For example, the Dahl Corporation is considering buying a machine to make a new product. To keep the illustration simple we will use a five-year life. Assume a marginal tax rate of 40 percent and data about the machine appearing in Exhibit 15–1. Thus, the firm will pay $320,000 to the equipment dealer. We will depreciate the equipment to the expected salvage value, which gives a total depreciation of $250,000 over its five-year life ($320,000 − $70,000 salvage value), or $50,000 per year. An income statement for the incremental business generated would show

Revenue	$500,000
Expenses:	
Operating	350,000
Depreciation	50,000
Income before taxes	$100,000
Taxes	40,000
Net income	$ 60,000

If cash receipts are $500,000 during the period and if cash disbursements are made on a current basis, what is the net cash inflow for this period? The $350,000 in operating expenses and taxes of $40,000 (40 percent of income) will be outflows. Depreciation is not a cash expense and will *not* be an outflow. A comparison of income and cash items would be as follows:

	Income	Cash Flow
Revenue	$500,000	$500,000
Expenses:		
Operating	350,000	(350,000)
Depreciation	50,000	
Income before taxes	$100,000	
Income taxes (40%)	40,000	(40,000)
Net income	$ 60,000	
Net cash flow		$110,000

If cash receipts and revenue are coincident and if operating expenses and disbursements also coincide, we can view yearly cash flows as:

1. Net income *plus* depreciation. If the $50,000 in depreciation is added

back to $60,000 in income, the result is the $110,000 cash flow.

2. Segregate cash flows from operations and depreciation. For this example, you would do the following:

a. Cash flows from operations:

$$\$500,000 - \$350,000 = \$150,000 \text{ before taxes}$$
$$\$150,000(1 - \text{tax rate}) = \$90,000 \text{ after taxes}$$

b. Savings in taxes due to depreciation:

$$\$50,000 \text{ depreciation} \times 40\% \text{ tax rate} = \$20,000$$

c. Total net cash flows:

$$\$90,000 + \$20,000 = \$110,000$$

In this second method, revenues and cash expenses are multiplied by *1 − tax rate* in order to deduct taxes and achieve a net cash flow. However, since depreciation itself has no cash flow associated with it, its value in a cash-related analysis stems from the *taxes saved* because depreciation can be deducted as an expense. Thus, depreciation is multiplied by the *tax rate* in order to get the net cash effect of depreciation. This is also called the **tax effect of depreciation** or the **tax shield of depreciation.**

Although this company expects to receive $70,000 for the machinery, it will probably get some other amount. Predicting a salvage value five years away is obviously subject to substantial error. To illustrate gains and losses, first assume that the machinery can actually be sold for $80,000, then that it can only be sold for $55,000. The analysis appears below. To simplify this procedure assume that gains and losses are taxed at ordinary rates.[2]

Cash Flow—Gains and Losses

	Gain	Loss
Net book value of asset	$70,000	$70,000
Net selling price[a]	80,000	55,000
Gain (loss)	$10,000	($15,000)
Tax of 40% on gain (loss)	(4,000)	6,000
Net cash received:		
Selling price	$80,000	$55,000
Tax consequences	(4,000)	6,000
	$76,000	$61,000

[a] Net selling price is cash received less any costs of removal.

[2] Chapter 16 includes a section dealing specifically with tax consequences of capital gains and losses.

As you can see, the existence of the $10,000 gain reduced the net cash received by the 40 percent tax ($4,000) on that gain. However, with a $15,000 loss, a company will *save* $6,000 in taxes, and net cash inflow is cash received from the sale *plus* the taxes saved because of a book loss. As with depreciation, the gains and losses are important not in themselves but because of tax consequences. Notice that the sale at a gain still brings in more cash. Selling at a loss simply to get a tax deduction is usually unwise.

Salvage Value and Depreciation.   If the expected salvage value of a piece of machinery exceeds 10 percent of the original purchase price, the IRS allows a company to depreciate the asset down only to that expected salvage value. This would be the case in the current example, where a machine costing $320,000 has an expected salvage value in five years of $70,000. However, if this machine had a $20,000 expected salvage value, the company would have the option of (1) depreciating a total of $300,000 over five years so that net book value would equal salvage value at the end of that period, or (2) depreciating a total of $320,000, the entire purchase price, leaving a zero net book value at the end of the asset's life. Given this option, it is to the company's advantage to depreciate all the cost of the asset and pay taxes on the gain. The following calculations demonstrate this point:

	Option 1	Option 2	Difference
Total depreciation:	$300,000	$320,000	+ $20,000
Net book value, year 5:	$ 20,000	$ 0	− 20,000
Tax saving from depreciation:			
Year 1	$ 24,000	$ 25,600	+ $ 1,600
Year 2	24,000	25,600	+ 1,600
Year 3	24,000	25,600	+ 1,600
Year 4	24,000	25,600	+ 1,600
Year 5	24,000	25,600	+ 1,600
Net salvage value, year 5	20,000	12,000	− 8,000
	$140,000	$140,000	0

For option 1, tax savings from depreciation are ($300,000 ÷ 5) × 0.40 = $24,000; for option 2, they are ($320,000 ÷ 5) × 0.40 = $25,600. Net salvage value is $20,000 for option 1, since salvage value equals book value; for option 2, where there is a $20,000 gain, $20,000 − ($20,000)(0.40) = $12,000. While the amounts of net cash received from both tax savings from depreciation and net salvage value are the same, option 2 allows receipt of the cash *earlier*. The time value of money makes this more advantageous.

Investment Tax Credit.   Another tax consequence is the **investment tax credit.** The federal government has, from time to time, offered companies what amounts to a discount on specific capital assets (mainly machinery) if they meet certain rules. This credit is a direct reduction of taxes. Therefore, if the investment tax credit is 10 percent, the firm can deduct $32,000 ($320,000 × 10%) from its tax bill in year zero. The required investment in year zero is $288,000. This is a one-time tax credit and is subject to being recaptured (returned to the government) if an asset is sold before the end of a specified period (such as five years). In summary, Exhibit 15–2 shows net investment at the beginning of a project and net salvage value at the end of a project, considering both investment tax credit and taxes on gains. We have assumed that actual salvage value will be $80,000 and net book value $70,000.

EXHIBIT 15–2
Cash Flow Format

	Year					
	0	1	2	3	4	5
Cash flows:						
1. Buy machine	$(320,000)					
Investment tax credit	32,000					
2. Salvage value						$80,000
Taxes on gain						(4,000)
3. Tax savings from SL depreciation		$20,000	$20,000	$20,000	$20,000	$20,000
Total	$(288,000)	$20,000	$20,000	$20,000	$20,000	$96,000

This treatment of taxes has been superficial. We have ignored state and local taxes and used marginal tax rates. We have assumed that a company can always use any tax benefits realized, such as taxes saved due to a book loss. This is a complex issue with many ramifications. Our simplification will make it easier to deal with the other complexities of capital budgeting.

Depreciation Tax Shield Timing. No matter what method we use to depreciate the machinery, total accumulated depreciation will equal $250,000 after five years if we estimate a $70,000 salvage value. Under straight-line depreciation this would be a $50,000 per year. We now show the effects of using **sum-of-the-years'-digits** (SYD) depreciation.

The denominator for SYD is

$$\frac{(n) \cdot (n + 1)}{2} = \frac{(5) \cdot (6)}{2} = 15$$

Year	SYD		
1	5/15 × $250,000 =	$	83,333.33
2	4/15 × $250,000 =		66,666.67
3	3/15 × $250,000 =		50,000.00
4	2/15 × $250,000 =		33,333.33
5	1/15 × $250,000 =		16,666.67
			$250,000

This yields tax savings from SYD depreciation of

Depreciation	Tax Rate	Tax Effect of Depreciation (rounded)
$83,333.33	40%	$33,333
66,666.67	40%	26,667
50,000.00	40%	20,000
33,333.33	40%	13,333
16,666.67	40%	6,667

Another accelerated depreciation method is **double-declining-balance** (DDB), which would yield the following (including a switch over to straight-line in years 4 and 5):

Year	DDB			Tax Effect
1	40% × $250,000 =	$100,000		$40,000
2	40% × 150,000 =	60,000		24,000
3	40% × 90,000 =	36,000		14,400
4	50% × 54,000 =	27,000		10,800
5	27,000 =	27,000		10,800

In year 4, the DDB amount is $21,600 compared to $27,000 for SL. Since the IRS code allows a switch from DDB to SL, this switch has been shown. Exhibit 15–3 shows all three methods compared.[3]

EXHIBIT 15–3
Timing of Tax Shield From Depreciation

Method	Year					Total
	1	2	3	4	5	
Straight-line	$20,000	$20,000	$20,000	$20,000	$20,000	$100,000
SYD	33,333	26,667	20,000	13,333	6,667	100,000
DDB/SL	40,000	24,000	14,400	10,800	10,800	100,000

As we noted, all methods depreciate the original investment of $320,000 a total of $250,000 down to estimated salvage value of $70,000 in year 5. Thus, all three methods will yield a total of $100,000 in tax savings. However, the *timing* of these flows differs. One reason many firms choose an accelerated depreciation method such as SYD or DDB for taxes while using straight-line for financial reporting is to receive the tax benefits from

---

[3] Certain assets qualify for a method called ADR (Class Life Asset Depreciation Range). This is a complexity we need not address in detail. Under certain circumstances it allows things such as DDB with a switchover to SYD. Refer to a current Commerce Clearing House *Federal Tax Course* manual for a full definition.

depreciation *sooner*, since money has a time value. This timing difference is clearly shown in Exhibit 15–3.

Cash Flows From Operations.   In general, cash flows from operations include both current sales dollars receipts and operating expense disbursements. Since we will usually look only at yearly flows, our problem is less acute than, say, a weekly or monthly cash budget. In planning, it is logical to make some assumptions about yearly cash flows much as we did in the chapters on budgeting. Since the tax effect of depreciation was handled separately above, operating cash flows per se would not include the tax effect from depreciation. In our original example there were cash inflows of $500,000 and operating outflows of $350,000. Thus, net after-tax cash flows from operations would be $90,000 ($150,000 less 40 percent taxes), as we developed before. To generalize, after-tax cash flows from operations are found by multiplying before-tax flows by "1 – tax rate." Note that this relationship holds whether you are talking about net inflows or net outflows.

Working Capital and Cash Flows

Cash budgeting illustrated the timing differences between, for example, sales and cash receipts or purchases and cash disbursements. In many cases, changing a production process by replacing old equipment or adding a new product line will have an impact on cash balances, accounts receivable, inventory, and accounts payable.

For example, if a company is going to enter a new product area, management may decide to keep higher cash balances on hand to meet emergencies, may need to expand inventory with raw materials for the new products, and can expect some delay in receiving payments on goods sold. Perhaps the easiest way to illustrate the problem is to assume a new company is being formed.

Illustration: Forming a Subsidiary.   Skywalker, Inc., has decided to make and market a fad product that is expected to have no more than a three-year life. Management has formed a wholly owned subsidiary, Floorborne, Inc., to make and market this new product. Management has decided that it needs $5,000 average cash balance in order to get credit from suppliers and avoid paying C.O.D. In addition, a policy of having two months' inventory of raw materials on hand means buying $50,000 of plastic parts as business begins. The supplier requires payment within 30 days. Finally, it is expected that customers will pay on a net 30 day basis. Thus, even with sales of $100,000 per month, there would be no cash receipts until the beginning of the second month of operation. Exhibit 15–4 on page 596 summarizes this information.

Let us analyze each element of Exhibit 15–4. If management has decided that the cash balance should be no less than $5,000, then there will be $5,000 of idle funds in a checking account for the three-year expected life of the project. Any funds in excess of this amount could be used to pay off accounts payable, reduce outstanding loans, or be invested. Only the $5,000 remains idle during the life of the company.

EXHIBIT 15–4
Working-Capital Requirements—Floorborne, Inc.

	By Month				
	1	2	3	. . .	12
Cash balance	$ 5,000	$ 5,000	$ 5,000		$ 5,000
Inventory	50,000	50,000	50,000		50,000
Receivables:					
Beginning balance	0	100,000	100,000		100,000
+ Sales	100,000	100,000	100,000		100,000
− Collected	0	(100,000)	(100,000)		(100,000)
Ending balance	100,000	100,000	100,000		100,000
Payables:					
Beginning balance	0	(50,000)	(50,000)		(50,000)
+ Purchases	(50,000)	(50,000)	(50,000)		(50,000)
− Paid	0	50,000	50,000		50,000
Ending balance	(50,000)	(50,000)	(50,000)		(50,000)

Similarly, $50,000 must be paid for inventory during the first 30 days of business. Therefore, $50,000 will be tied up in inventory and not available for other uses. As funds come in during month 2, purchases can be paid for to maintain this inventory level. For the life of the project, however, $50,000 in funds will be in inventory and cannot be used in any other way. With 30-day payment terms, the supplier allows Floorborne's management to delay the impact of this inventory purchase. The increase in accounts payable offsets the increase in inventory in this case.

During the first month, funds will be needed for expenses other than purchases. Salaries, wages, rent, insurance, and other current payables will come due before the first cash from sales is received. It is possible that up to $100,000 will be needed to pay these current obligations. In any case, cash receipts lag sales by an average of $100,000.

In summary, then, a net total of $105,000 is either tied up in a state where it can earn no interest or return (cash and inventory balances) or is a lag in receipts (receivables). In essence this $105,000 can be thought of as a cash outflow that occurs during the first month of operation. However, this project will exist only for three years. At the end of that time Floorborne, Inc. will be liquidated and cash returned to Skywalker. Thus, $5,000 in cash will be available for other uses, $50,000 from current receipts will no longer be needed to replenish inventory, $50,000 will be needed to pay for the final round of material purchases, and receivables of $100,000 will come in during the month following the final month of sales. Therefore, the net of $105,000 will come back to the firm at or near the end of year 3. It is important to include this timing of an outflow at the beginning of the project and an inflow three years later, since the money was tied up and unavailable for other productive uses for that three-year period.

While this example has involved the launching of a new project using a subsidiary corporation, the same kind of analysis is valid for ongoing firms. It is also possible for working-capital needs to go *down* because of a project or process change. If inventory levels were to *decrease* at the start of a project, this would be reflected as an inflow, since the cash freed up from inventory could be put to use in other places.

Other Cash Flows.   So far we have looked at cash flows associated with original investment, operations, and working capital. There may also be other regular or irregular flows to consider. Perhaps a machine needs a major overhaul every four years, or management decides to spend extraordinary amounts on advertising during the first year of a new product. These kinds of cash flows need to be reflected in their applicable after-tax form. Let us tie all these notions of cash flows together into an example.

Illustration: *Cash Flows for Waterway Barge*

Waterway Barge Co. has heretofore transported only grain in its river barges. Its managers are considering undertaking the handling of liquids such as petroleum products. They intend to buy three barges costing a total of $1,500,000. Barges last about twenty years and then are worth about $10,000 each as scrap. Waterway has decided to use straight-line depreciation down to estimated net salvage value. Yearly operating costs and expected revenues are as follows:

Revenue	$ 443,500
Labor	(100,000)
Maintenance	(25,000)
Other costs	(30,000)
Pretax net inflow	$ 278,500

A new parts inventory of $20,000 will have to be maintained, and receivables are expected to increase by about $40,000. Finally, besides regular maintenance, a full overhaul will be needed in the tenth year, costing a total of $45,000. This amount must be amortized for tax purposes; that is, it cannot be deducted in the year incurred. Exhibit 15–5 on page 598 reflects all these cash flows. It is assumed that there is a 40 percent marginal tax rate and that all cash flows take place at the end of a period. We shall use this example as we discuss capital budgeting models as well.

CAPITAL BUDGETING MODELS

Having analyzed the types and timing of cash flows associated with a long-term project, we next consider several models that use this information in order to judge the desirability of various courses of action. Capital budgeting models fall into two general classes. The first class includes models that consider the time value of money: *net present value, internal rate of*

EXHIBIT 15–5
Cash Flows—Waterway Barge Co. (in thousands of dollars)

			Year		
Description	0	1 through 9	10	11 through 19	20
Original investment	(1,500)				
Overhaul			(45)		
Salvage					30
Operations					
$278,500 \times (1 - 0.40)$		167.1	167.1	167.1	167.1
Tax effect, depreciation[a]		29.4	29.4	31.2	31.2
Inventory	(20)				20
Receivables	(40)				40
Totals	(1,560)	196.5	151.5	198.3	288.3

[a] Depreciation is computed as:

$$\frac{\$1,500,000 - \$30,000}{20 \text{ years}} = \$73,500 \text{ per year}$$

and

$$(73,500)(0.40) = \$29,400 \text{ for years 1 through 10}$$

However, the additional $45,000 investment at the end of year 10 yields $4,500 of depreciation (45,000 ÷ 10 years) or $1,800 additional tax shield for the last ten years of the project.

return, and *present value index*. The second class does not consider money's time value: *payback* and *book rate of return*.

Present-Value Models

The three models listed above that all consider the time value of money are based on the present-value model. As our example of Waterway Barge illustrates, cash flows can occur over a number of years. Using the principle of the time value of money, we can discount these various flows to their present values. After exploring the basic algebra of all present-value models, we will discuss the three basic types of present-value models themselves.

The Algebra of Present-Value Models.   As the appendix to this chapter demonstrates, yearly discount factors are calculated by:

$$\text{discount factor} = \frac{1}{(1 + r)^t}$$

where

r = the interest rate
t = the year when the cash flow occurs from year 0 to a final year n. (Thus $t = 0$ to n.)

The **total present value** can be defined as the present value of all future cash flows, be they received as a single sum, a series of equal sums (annuity), or a series of sums that vary from year to year. If we define C_t as a cash flow in year t, present value can be represented as follows:

$$(15\text{--}1) \qquad \text{present value} = \sum_{t=0}^{n} \frac{C_t}{(1 + r)^t}$$

Net Present Value.   Equation 15–1 shows the present value of a series of cash flows, be they positive (inflow) or negative (outflow). Since the present value of any sum received (or spent) *now* equals that sum $[1/(1 + r)^0 = 1]$, we can rewrite the basic present-value formula 15–1 to yield:

$$(15\text{--}2) \qquad \text{net present value} = \sum_{t=1}^{n} \frac{C_t}{(1 + r)^t} - I_0$$

where I_0 = original investment (outflow) in year 0.

Net Present Value and Waterway Barge.   Let us apply this model to the Waterway Barge example. Exhibit 15–5 shows the various cash flows as:

$$\text{net } I_0 = \$1{,}560{,}000$$

$$C_t = \begin{cases} 196{,}500 & \text{for } t = 1\text{--}9 \\ 151{,}500 & \text{for } t = 10 \\ 198{,}300 & \text{for } t = 11\text{--}19 \\ 288{,}300 & \text{for } t = 20 \end{cases}$$

What discount rate shall we use to bring all these sums back to their present value? The next section addresses this topic. For now, assume for ease of computation that all cash flows occur at the end of each year and that 10 percent is the relevant discount rate to use. Exhibit 15–6 shows various ways to bring the cash flows back to present values by using different combinations of Tables A–3 and A–4. The results are all the same: a positive net present value of $113,217. As explained above, this positive net present value means that the proposal yields a return greater than 10 percent.

Internal Rate of Return

The **internal rate of return** (IRR), sometimes called the **true rate of return** and **time-adjusted rate of return,** is the interest rate that yields a zero net present value.[4] In NPV analysis, the interest rate (r = 10 percent) was given

---

[4] As Chapter 16 will show, there are several methods that are called "true" rate of return. This term should probably not be used.

EXHIBIT 15-6
Net-Present-Value Analysis—Waterway Barge Co.

Net Cash Flows (in thousands of dollars)

		Year		
0	1–9	10	11–19	20
(1,560)	196.5	151.5	198.3	288.3

Net Present Value

Method 1

a. ($196,500)(9-year annuity PV factor from Table A–4)
= ($196,500)(5.759) = $1,131,648
b. ($151,500)(received in 10 years PV factor from Table A–3)
= ($151,500)(0.3855) = $58,410
c. ($198,300)(9-year annuity for years 11 thru 19 PV factors
from Table A–4) = ($198,300)(8.3649 − 6.1445) = $440,305
d. ($288,300)(received in 20 years PV factor from Table A–3)
= ($288,300)(0.1486) = $42,854
e. NPV summary:

NPV = $1,131,648 + $58,410 + $440,305 + $42,854 − $1,560,000 = $113,217

Method 2

Parts a, b, and d are the same.

c. Instead of using the PV factor for an annuity of 19 years less the PV factor
for an annuity of 10 years used in method 1, take the PV of an annuity of 9
years and multiply this by the PV factor for a single sum received in 10
years. Thus the PV factor to be multiplied by $198,300 is:

method 1: (8.3649 − 6.1445) = 2.2204
method 2: (5.759)(0.3855)   = 2.2203

(Difference is due to rounding.)

Method 3

It is possible to go to Table A–3 and add up the PV factors for 10 percent for
years 11 through 19. As you would expect, this adds up to 2.2204.

---

and we solved for the net present value. IRR, on the other hand, starts with a
known NPV (NPV = 0) and solves for r. Algebraically:

(15–3) $$\text{IRR:}\quad \sum_{t=1}^{n} \frac{C_t}{(1 + r)^t} - I_0 = 0$$

or

$$(15\text{--}4) \qquad \text{IRR:} \qquad \sum_{t=1}^{n} \frac{C_t}{(1 + r)^t} = I_0$$

Thus, IRR is the rate of return that equates the present value of the inflows with the investment. Equivalently, it is the rate that makes the NPV = 0.

For even flows, computing IRR is easy—just use Table A–4. If an investment of $100 yields $58.39 per year for two years, then:

$$(C_t)(\text{PV annuity factor}) = I_0$$
$$(\$58.39)(\text{PV annuity factor}) = \$100$$
$$\text{PV annuity factor} = 1.7126$$

Looking at Table A–4 for two years, we find that this factor corresponds to an 11 percent rate. Thus, $r = 11$ percent and the IRR is 11 percent.

With uneven flows, as in our Waterway Barge example, the IRR is more difficult to ascertain. Certain calculators or a computer program can be used to solve for r. In addition, Tables A–3 and A–4 can be used in a hunt for the IRR. We know from our net-present-value analysis that $r > 10$ percent, since there was a positive NPV. Various rates can be tried out to find NPV = 0. The following shows the results of discounting the cash flows from Exhibit 15–5 at 10, 11, and 12 percent. In this case the IRR is 11 percent.

$$\text{NPV at } 10\% = \$113{,}217$$
$$\text{NPV at } 11\% = 0$$
$$\text{NPV at } 12\% = (\$94{,}139)$$

Among other things, IRR eliminates the scale of an investment by focusing on its percentage return. We know that IRR > 10 percent because the NPV at 10 percent is positive. If NPV = 0 at 10 percent, then the IRR would be 10 percent.

Present-Value Index

A method that also eliminates scale is the **present-value index** (PVI), also called **benefit-cost ratio** (BCR) or **profitability index** (PI). The PVI is a ratio of the present value of cash inflows over the present value of outflows. In our same notation, this would be:

$$(15\text{--}5) \qquad \text{PVI} = \frac{\displaystyle\sum_{t=1}^{n} \frac{C_t}{(1 + r)^t}}{I_0}$$

If the NPV is positive, the PVI will be greater than 1.0; if the NPV is negative, then PVI < 1.0; and if NPV = 0, then PVI = 1.0.

In addition, as we shall see, payback is related to internal rate of return. It is a valuable aid in the search for an IRR. Book rate of return is closely tied to return on investment (ROI), a common measure of profitability and a ratio used in evaluating segment performance, as will be discussed in Chapter 17. The use of these models is widespread and that alone makes them a valid subject to discuss.

Payback

Payback is a method that asks, simply, "How long does it take to recover the original investment?" For example, a $100 investment that produces cash flows of $30 per year for ten years would have a four-year payback.[5] This can be shown as follows:

```
Year  0 = ($100)  investment
      1 = $ 30    inflow ⎫
      2 =   30           ⎪   Payback = 4 years
      3 =   30           ⎬   4 × $30 > $100
      4 =   30           ⎪
      .                  ⎭
      .
      .
     10 =   30
```

Thus, payback merely looks at the cumulative *amount of inflow* and ignores timing within the payback period. For example, assume that another investment of $100 would produce the following inflows:

```
Year 0 = ($100)  investment
     1 =  $60    inflow ⎫
     2 =   15           ⎪
     3 =   15           ⎬   Payback = 4 years
     4 =   30           ⎪
     5 =  180           ⎭
```

Again, payback is four years.[6] However, two things have changed. First, instead of even payments of $30 per year, this new investment has uneven cash flows. Second, instead of being received over ten years, the total of $300 is received over only five years. The earlier receipt of funds is seen not only in the shorter life but also in the way the first $100 (the payback) is received. While payback would rate both of these projects the same (four years), either the NPV or IRR criterion would produce a result showing the second opportunity to be more favorable than the first.

---

[5] Again, assume all cash flows occur at year end.

[6] We say that payback is four years in both of these examples, since we are assuming all cash flows are received at year end. If they were received evenly throughout the year, we *could* say payback is 3⅓ years.

In addition, payback ignores profitability. If a project costing $90 returns $30 per year for three years, its payback is three years, but it is obviously an unwise project, since the discounted cash flows yield a negative NPV at any rate of interest.

When using the payback method, you set a maximum acceptable period. The length of the period will differ among firms: some may use four years, others three years, and so on. You then accept projects with payback periods equal to or less than the cutoff period. Additionally, in ranking investment opportunities, you use the different payback periods to compare the opportunities.

Payback in Practice.   Although the payback method ignores profitability and is conceptually inferior to DCF techniques, it does have some uses and is widely employed in industry. First, it provides a rough screen. A project with a long payback period is likely to rank low in internal rate of return and present value. In fact, payback is automatically calculated when you have equal cash flows and use the internal rate-of-return method: the present-value factor for an annuity is the payback period, I_0/C_t. For this purpose, we compute payback with fractional years. For instance, we would use $3\frac{1}{3}$ years for the project above where we expected $30 annually from a $100 investment.

Second, when risk is an important consideration, payback gives some guidance, because the longer the payback, the less certain you can be that the investment will turn out well. The further away the cash inflows, the less you can be sure of their amounts. Most businesspeople rightly feel that they are safer if they believe they can get their money out of an investment in a short period.

Payback Reciprocal.   Payback is the number of years needed to recapture the original investment. For even cash flows, this would be:

$$\frac{I_0}{C_t} = \text{payback}$$

If you refer back to the section on internal rate of return, you will see IRR defined as:

$$\text{PV inflows} = \text{PV outflows}$$
$$(C_t)(\text{PV annuity factor}) = I_0$$

when there are even cash flows. This can be easily arranged to yield the payback. In fact, the payback is the same as the present-value factor for an annuity found in Table A–4.

As we show in Appendix 15–A, the factors found in Table A–4 are all calculated from the formula:

(15–6)
$$PV = C_t \frac{1 - \dfrac{1}{(1 + r)^t}}{r}$$

As the life of the project, t, becomes very large, the term $1/(1 + r)^t$ becomes very small, so that the numerator approaches one. In this case:

(15–7) $$PV = C_t\frac{1}{r} \quad \text{or} \quad PV = \frac{C_t}{r}$$

Multiplying both sides by r and dividing both sides by PV gives:

(15–8) $$r = \frac{C_t}{PV}$$

C_t/PV is the payback reciprocal, since for IRR the present value (PV) of the inflow equals the investment (I_0). Thus, $r = C_t/I_0$. The payback reciprocal usually is a good estimator of the IRR if the economic life of a project is at least twice as long as the payback period. Graphically the relation between IRR and the payback reciprocal is shown as follows:

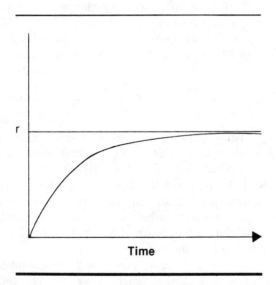

Waterway Barge. Waterway Barge cash flows are summarized in Exhibit 15–6. Payback is eight years.

$$I_0 = \qquad\qquad\qquad (\$1,560,000)$$
$$C_t = \$196,500 \times 8 \text{ years} = \quad 1,572,000$$

This measure ignores when flows are received, and payback totally disregards cash flows occurring after the payback period. The payback reciprocal is:

$$\frac{1}{8} = 0.125$$

We saw that the IRR of this project is 11 percent. While 12.5 percent is a bit higher, it does yield a reasonable upper bound for finding the internal rate of return.

Book Rate of Return

The **book rate of return**[7] is the only model that deals with income figures and not solely with cash flows. This model yields an accounting measure of an average income return on investment. Its most common definition is **average book rate of return** (ABRR), shown as follows:

$$\text{average book rate of return} = \frac{\text{average yearly income}}{\text{average investment}}$$

Thus, if a project costs $100 and yields cash flows from operations of $58.39 per year for two years, we can calculate the book rate of return by· (1) taking into account depreciation of $50 per year straight-line, thereby yielding an $8.39 income figure ($58.39 − $50) and (2) translating the $100 investment into an *average* investment of $50 over the two-year life ($100 at the beginning, $0 at the end—thus, $50 average):

$$\text{average book rate of return} = \frac{\$8.39}{\$50} = 0.168$$

On average, then, this project has an average book rate of return of 16.8 percent. If this measure were based on original investment, as it sometimes is, the return would be 8.4 percent ($8.39 ÷ $100).

This measure has the deficiencies of payback in that it also ignores the timing of flows and combines everything in an average. Second, as we pointed out earlier, cash flows are the important measure of project desirability, since cash flows can have alternative uses and can be reinvested, while income per se cannot.

The yearly cash flows and depreciation need to be averaged. In addition, nonincome cash flows are ignored. Thus, a translation of the information in Exhibit 15–6 to income terms would be:

$$I_0 = \$1,500,000 \quad \text{(machinery only)}$$
$$I_{10} = 45,000$$

(years 1–10)   Income = $196,500 − $73,500 depreciation = $123,000
(years 11–20)   Income = $198,300 − $78,000 depreciation = $120,300

Average income is $121,650 [($123,000 + 120,300) ÷ 2], and average investment is about $761,250 if you consider the overhaul.

---

[7] Book rate of return is also called *accounting rate of return*. The idea is that it is calculated on the basis of historical accounting numbers rather than cash flows.

$$1,500,000 \div 2 = \$750,000 \text{ for 20 years}$$
$$45,000 \div 4 = \underline{\quad 11,250} \text{ for last 10 years}$$
$$\$761,250$$

Thus ABRR is calculated as follows:

$$\text{ABRR} = \frac{\$121,650}{\$761,250} = 0.16$$

The ABRR really has more implications for ongoing project and manager performance evaluation than for making a capital budgeting decision. This topic will be discussed in Chapter 17.

Summary

We have been exploring various models that are useful in capital budgeting decisions. We have identified three discounted cash flow models (NPV, IRR, and PVI), one nondiscounted cash flow model (payback), and a model that relies on income rather than any form of cash flows (ABRR). In general, the DCF models yield a more useful result.

The argument is sometimes advanced that too many assumptions must be made in order to use such sophisticated models as NPV. What is the life? the cash flows? the discount rate? changes in working capital? As you can see, even the simple models require basically the same assumptions. While any model is only as good as the data and a set of underlying assumptions, mere sophistication of a model is not a cause for doubting its ultimate practical usefulness.

This discussion has, in the main, focused on cash flows and has assumed a relevant discount rate. The next section discusses this aspect of DCF models.

RELEVANT DISCOUNT RATE

This chapter opened with a discussion of the relevancy of cash flows, since funds have alternative uses. The manager weighs alternative uses of funds generated by current operations, and the individual investor weighs alternative uses for personal funds. Since corporations receive the bulk of their financing from stockholders and bondholders, these two perspectives become intertwined.

Weighted Average Cost of Capital

Many texts refer to a relevant discount rate as the **cost of capital** or more properly as the **weighted average cost of capital** (WACC). The WACC is the cost of obtaining equity and debt funds. It is a measure of the average dividend return required by investors in stock and the average interest rate and life required by investors in bonds. The weighting is the proportion of equity and debt funds needed. As many a finance book will point out, this concept is easy to explain theoretically but extremely tough to implement on a practical level.

If only common stock and bonds were offered, we could say that a prospective bond investor looks at (1) the present value of interest payments and (2) the present value of the face amount of a bond. These present values when compared to alternative uses of the same funds would produce an investing decision. The common stockholder looks, in the main, solely at the present value of an infinite stream of dividends. That present value should be the price the investor will pay. Thus, each investor has his own alternative use of funds and own risk/reward structure. Theoretically the result is an average return required by different investor classes.

For example, if we have a company whose dividend is $2 per share and investors are buying that stock at $20 per share, it can be inferred that investors are anticipating a 10 percent return over a long time horizon. (This assumes that investors do not anticipate growth in dividends. If they do, the analysis becomes more complex.) Bondholders may have bonds maturing in ten years ($1,000 face value per bond) and receive an 8 percent cash return yearly. Their full expected return is $1,000 (the present value of $1,000 received in ten years plus the present value of $8 received annually) if they purchase the bond at its face value. Thus, with a debt/equity mix of 50/50, the weighted average cost of capital is 9 percent.

The Problem.   Many equity and debt instruments are available today. Eliciting these data on an average-investor-needs basis is infeasible. Thus, the WACC is more a theoretical than practical way to establish a relevant discount rate for capital budgeting decisions. We do not mean that a firm *cannot* calculate WACC, only that the difficulty of doing so is substantial.[8]

While the classical approach is to measure the cost of all of the debt and equity of a firm, at least two other views of WACC (or a reasonable estimate of it) can be advanced. The first is a *risk premium for the firm* and the second is *average riskiness of the firm's projects.*

Risk Premium.   In most economies there is some sort of riskless investment. In the United States this would be U.S. Treasury bills and notes.[9] Thus, any interest rate greater than a riskless rate is a reflection of investors' views of the riskiness of the firm. Most investors want a higher return, the more risk is associated with an investment. Any WACC, then, is a combination of a riskless rate and the risk premium for the firm.

Average Firm Risk.   A firm has from a few to many projects. Taking a mean-return and a variance-of-returns viewpoint, we can gain some idea of

[8] For a discussion of this subject, see J. Osteryoung, *Capital Budgeting*, 2d ed. (Columbus, Ohio: Grid, Inc., 1979), H. Bierman, Jr., and S. Smidt, *The Capital Budgeting Decision*, 5th ed. (New York: The Macmillan Company, 1980), and W. F. Sharpe, *Investments* (Englewood Cliffs, N.J.: Prentice-Hall, Inc., 1978).

[9] See Sharpe, *Investments;* and J. F. Weston and E. F. Brigham, *Essentials of Managerial Finance*, 5th ed. (New York: Dryden Press, 1979).

the average riskiness of the firm. This average riskiness should be reflected in what returns are demanded by investors.

We have advanced three complementary theories of weighted average cost of capital. The same problems exist in calculating any of the three methods. For this reason, many managers set a *hurdle rate* or *cutoff rate* as a surrogate for WACC.

Goal-Oriented Cutoff Rate

Managers strive to have a series of products and projects that, when combined, will yield a return at least as great as the actual WACC of a firm. Our discussion of decision making has stressed the necessity of looking at separable costs and benefits. Thus, individual projects must have returns *in excess* of an overall WACC in order to cover joint costs of the company. This is necessary because costs of the sales department or accounting department, for example, would not be assigned to any specific product or project.

In addition, managers may want to raise the attractiveness of their company by earning at a higher rate of return than currently attained. Thus, management can set goals for a required return on investment. With these goals in mind, a hurdle rate or cutoff rate can be established as a criterion for acceptance of any new projects.

SUMMARY

This chapter deals with cash flows, capital-budgeting models, and basic decision-analysis frameworks. We concentrated on DCF models, which are theoretically superior to nondiscounting models like payback and ABRR. In the next chapter we shall discuss different types of capital-budgeting decisions, problems with IRR and PVI, investing versus financing, uncertainty of cash flows, inflation, qualitative factors, and other advanced topics.

APPENDIX 15–A: TIME VALUE OF MONEY

Suppose you received a call from a radio station announcing that you had won its grand prize of $100 in a contest, and you had the choice of getting $100 now or $100 in a year. You would choose receiving the $100 now, since you could (1) spend it a year earlier or (2) put it in a bank and earn interest for a year, thereby having more than $100 at year end.

Now let us change the situation slightly. Assume that your choice was between $100 now and $109 in one year. In order to see which choice was economically better, you would have to see what you could do with $100 received now. All of this relates to the fact that money has a time value. If the only possible use of $100 received now was to put it in a savings account earning (here is the *value* part) at 10 percent per year (*time*), you would have $110 in a year ($100 × 1.10).

Present and Future Values

The example above illustrates the time value of money. Money received now can earn some positive cash return (interest) over time. Thus $100 in the present (called a **present value**) is worth $110 a year in the future (a **future value**). Since ($100)(1.10) = $110, we can say that, for one year:

$$\text{(present value)}(1 + \text{interest rate}) = \text{(future value)}$$

or
$$(PV)(1 + r) = FV$$

If you could invest $100 for *two* years at 10 percent, you would have a future value of $121 in two years:

$$(\$100)(1.10) = \$110 \text{ at end of year 1}$$
$$(\$110)(1.10) = \$121 \text{ at end of year 2}$$

We could write this as one step:

$$[(\$100)(1.10)](1.10) = \$121$$

or
$$(\$100)(1.10)^2 = \$121$$

This **compound-interest formula** translates present values into future values. If t denotes the number of years in the future, this formula becomes:

(15A–1)
$$(PV)(1 + r)^t = FV$$

Thus, if we know a future value (a cash flow occurring in the future), we can rearrange equation 15A–1 and get:

(15A–2)
$$PV = \frac{FV}{(1 + r)^t} \quad \text{or} \quad PV = FV\left[\frac{1}{(1 + r)^t}\right]$$

In words, the present value of a sum received t years in the future at r rate of interest is the PV shown in equation 15A–2. In the $100 example:

$$\$100 = \$121\left[\frac{1}{(1 + 0.10)^2}\right]$$

$$\$100 = (\$121)(0.8264)$$

The portion of the formula shown by:

(15A–3)
$$\frac{1}{(1 + r)^t}$$

is called a **present-value factor** of receiving $1 in t years at r rate of interest. Discount factors for present values for various periods and various rates of interest are shown in Table A–3 in the appendix at the back of the book. While an interest factor is used to move a present sum to a future sum, a present-value factor or **discount factor** is used in going from the future to the present. Equation 15A–3 can be used to find the present-value factor for any number of periods or rates of interest, even if they are not shown on a table.

Present Value of an Annuity

So far we have looked at a present value ($100) and a future value received as a lump sum in two years ($121). Let us assume that you could receive even payments of $57.62 each year for two years. The receipt of even cash flows each year is called an **annuity.** What is the present value of these even cash inflows?

$$PV = (\$57.62)\left[\frac{1}{(1.10)}\right] + (\$57.62)\left[\frac{1}{(1.10)^2}\right]$$

$$= (\$57.62)(0.9091) + (\$57.62)(0.8264)$$
$$= (\$57.62)(0.9091 + 0.8264)$$
$$= (\$57.62)(1.7355)$$
$$= \$100$$

Thus the present value of an annuity is found by adding together all the PV factors for each year. Since this is tedious, Table A–4 shows these discount factors for receiving $1 *per year* for t years at various discount rates. These factors are found by using the following formula:

$$(15A-4) \qquad \frac{(1 + r)^t - 1}{r(1 + r)^t} \quad \text{or, alternatively,} \quad \frac{1 - \dfrac{1}{(1 + r)^t}}{r}$$

Formula 15A–4 is found by a geometric progression summing up various years.

An annuity of $57.62 per year (received at the end of each year) has a future value at 10 percent interest of:

$$(\$57.62)(1.10) + (\$57.62) = \$121$$

The concepts of present value and future value as well as the receipt of a single sum or an annuity are all parts of a time continuum tied to a relevant rate of interest.

	Cash Received		
Present Value	Year 1	Year 2	Future Value
$100		$121	$121
$100	$57.62	$ 57.62	$121

The choice offered at the beginning of this discussion was between receiving $100 now or $109 in one year. While the answer, assuming a 10 percent rate of interest, is obvious, the following illustrates the choice of receiving $100 now.

	Present Value	Future Value
Alternative 1 ($100 now)	$100	$110
Alternative 2 ($109 in 1 year)	$ 99.09	$109

Thus, from either a present- or a future-value perspective, alternative 1 is superior.

As a final illustration, assume that you have $100 now and place it in a bank at 10 percent interest. You can withdraw $57.62 per year for two years, since you are earning 10 percent interest. This is illustrated as follows:

	(a) Beginning Balance	(b) 10% Earnings	(c) [(a) + (b)]	(d) Withdraw	(e) Ending Balance [(c) − (d)]
Year 1	$100	$10.00	$110.00	$57.62	$52.38
Year 2	$ 52.38	$ 5.24	$ 57.62	$57.62	0

Summary

Money can be invested over time. Therefore, it has a time value. Present-value factors can be calculated for a single sum received in the future or for a steady stream of sums (annuity). By using compound interest we can translate present sums to future sums. By using present-value (discount) factors we can translate future sums to present sums. Since we are dealing with cash flows, the decision models based on this concept are called *discounted cash flow models* (DCF).

ASSIGNMENTS

15-1 Present and Future Values

Required: Answer each question independently.

1. If an investor wants an after-tax return on her money of 8 percent and is offered a cash return of $1,000 annually for three years, how much would she be willing to invest if the tax rate was 50 percent?

2. Assume an investor wants to have $5,000 in five years. Ignoring taxes, how much would he have to invest now at 10 percent to achieve that goal? How much at 8 percent? At 12 percent?

3. A student borrows $1,500 per year for four years from the government and will have to repay the loan five years after graduation at 5 percent interest compounded annually. How much will she have to repay? Borrowing takes place at the beginning of each year.

15–2 **Sunk Costs.** The Solidon Company has a number of old typewriters. Its office manager plans to sell some of them and replace them with newer models. The president of the firm has told the office manager to be sure to sell the ones that are fully depreciated, so that the firm will make a profit on the sale. The firm uses straight-line depreciation for tax and financial reporting purposes.

Required: Comment on the president's suggestion.

15–3 **Relevant Cost.** Your firm has a machine that cost $10,000 earlier this year. It is capable of producing 1,000 units of a product, after which it will collapse. It has produced 400 units so far, and accumulated depreciation using the units-of-production method is $4,000.

Required: Is the $10-per-unit depreciation a variable cost? An incremental cost? An opportunity cost? A relevant cost in making decisions?

15–4 **Basic Cash Flows.** The SaraSoda Company is considering expanding its product line by producing a nonalcoholic soft drink that tastes like beer.

Required: Using a format like that of Exhibit 15–2, show the timing of the effects of the following. The marginal tax rate is 40 percent. Assume all cash flows occur at the end of a period.

1. Equipment that will last five years will be purchased at a cost of $300,000. Expected salvage value is $20,000. The firm has decided to use sum-of-the-years'-digits for depreciation for tax purposes and straight-line depreciation for financial reporting purposes.

2. Annual sales for the life of the project are expected to be $480,000. It is expected that the firm will have an average of 1½ months' sales in receivables.

3. Cash balances of $10,000 additional to current balances will be maintained, and $100,000 in additional inventory will have to be carried over the life of the project.

4. Operating expenses (exclusive of depreciation) are expected to be $250,000 per year, and various payables will increase by $40,000.

15–5 **Questions About Cash Flows.** You and your fellow students are discussing capital budgeting, and the following questions are asked.

Required: Respond to each statement or question.

1. "This whole thing about depreciation not being a cash flow really baffles me. I've looked at lots of cash flow statements and they take net income and add depreciation. If that's not a cash flow, what is it?"

2. "I was looking at a problem where inventory went up by $100,000 and the project had a life of three years. In my analysis I showed an outflow of $100,000 for each year. That's right, isn't it?"

3. "We keep hearing about after-tax cash flows. I'm confused about what to do when you buy a piece of equipment. Say you spend $250,000 and the tax rate is 50 percent, wouldn't you show a net cost of $125,000 after taxes?"

4. "If receipts from sales on our new project are $100,000 per year and cash outflows from operations are $40,000, what is the net annual cash flow with a 40 percent marginal tax rate and a 10 percent investment tax credit?"

5. "If working capital increased by $100,000 at the beginning of a project, what can I expect to recover at the end of the project with a 40 percent marginal tax rate?"

15–6 Basic DCF Models. Sonata Company has embarked on a new project that will cost $250,000 and will last eight years. Annual cash flows from operations will be $90,000, not including depreciation and taxes. The company expects no salvage value. The tax rate is 40 percent.

Required:

1. If straight-line depreciation is used, what is the net present value if the relevant discount rate is 18 percent?

2. Is the internal rate of return 18 percent? Higher? Lower? Why?

3. Solve for the internal rate of return.

4. Solve for the payback.

5. Recompute item 1 if DDB depreciation is used, with a switch to straight-line in year 5. Explain the difference between this result and your answer to item 1.

6. Using your results from item 5, find the benefit-cost ratio of this investment.

15–7 Effect of Taxes. Both the Columbia Corporation and the Manatee County Hospital are evaluating the same computer system. The Columbia Corporation has an after-tax discount rate of 12 percent, considering its 40 percent marginal tax rate. The hospital is exempt from taxes, owing to its not-for-profit status. Thus, its relevant discount rate is 20 percent.

The computer costs $300,000 and has an expected salvage value in five years of $30,000. Columbia's managers will use SYD depreciation for the entire $300,000. Expected pretax savings of the new system are $95,000 per year for both organizations.

Required: Evaluate this investment opportunity for both the corporation and the hospital, using net present value.

15-8   Basic DCF Relationships

Required: Answer each of the following cases independently.

Investment	Present-Value Straight-Line Tax Effect of Depreciation	Annual After-Tax Cash Flows (excluding depreciation)	Present Value of Inflows	Life	Tax Rate	Discount Rate
1. ?	$33,158	?	$100,000	3 years	0.40	0.10
2. $250,000	$99,818	$33,000	$231,577	5 years	?	?
3. $ 20,000	?	$ 7,010	$ 30,000	?	0.45	0.08
4. $ 40,000	?	$10,000	?	4 years	0.40	0.10

15-9   IRR and Payback Reciprocal.   The Vino Company is contemplating a project that is expected to last ten years. Annual cash flows are planned at $3,000, and an original investment of $9,000 is required. Vino is subject to a marginal tax rate of 40 percent and has an after-tax hurdle rate of 9 percent.

Required:

1. What is the net present value of the project?
2. What is the payback?
3. Using the payback reciprocal as a guide, find the internal rate of return.

15-10   Alternative Use of Funds.   Geemat Company is considering two alternative investment opportunities. First, management can invest in municipal bonds that will cost $50,000 and that pay a tax-free yield of $4,000 annually. The alternative investment, a new project within the company, will cost $50,000. Pretax cash flows (excluding depreciation) are expected to be $15,500 annually. Straight-line depreciation will be used, and the applicable tax rate is 40 percent. Both projects will last five years. Management has only approximately $50,000 available to invest this year. The new project will require $5,000 additional in net current assets, which will be recovered at the end of the project. All cash flows take place at the end of the year.

Required:

1. Which project yields the highest return?
2. If the after-tax cost of capital for this firm is 11 percent, should management invest in the bonds or in the new project?

15-11   Basic Cash Flows and DCF Models.   The following facts apply to a project being considered by the Adele division of Marie Corporation.

1. New equipment will be purchased for $150,000.
2. Revenues are expected to be $20 per unit on sales of 9,000 units annually.

3. Costs were determined using a regression analysis of similar operations. The results of that analysis are:

Intercept	$10,527
Regression coefficient	$7.635
Standard error of slope	$0.935
Coefficient of determination	0.863

4. Cash costs other than those for production above are $50,000 annually.

5. A special investment tax credit of 10 percent will apply to this project.

6. The project is expected to last five years.

7. The marginal tax rate is 40 percent, and the corporation has set a hurdle rate of 10 percent.

8. Working capital is expected to increase by $30,000 at the outset of the project.

9. There is expected to be a $1,000 salvage value on the machinery in five years.

10. Sum-of-the-years'-digits depreciation will be used, depreciating the asset to zero after five years.

11. All cash flows occur at the end of a period.

Required:

1. Outline the cash flows, using the Exhibit 15–2 format in the chapter.
2. What is the net present value of these cash flows?
3. What is the internal rate of return?
4. What is the present-value index?
5. Using the data from the regression analysis, what is the approximate probability that this project will have less than a zero net present value?

15–12 New Product. The ICL Company is considering a new product that it expects to have a useful life of five years. Other estimates relating to the product appear below.

Annual volume	40,000 units
Selling price	$20
Unit variable manufacturing costs	$8
Unit variable selling expenses	$1
Annual fixed cash manufacturing costs	$150,000
Annual fixed selling expenses	$100,000

The product requires machinery that costs $400,000 and should have about $30,000 salvage value at the end of five years. The firm uses straight-line depreciation and is permitted to ignore salvage value in calculating depreciation. Therefore, it will depreciate the entire $400,000 over five years and have a taxable gain of $30,000 at the end of the investment.

The tax rate is 40 percent and cost of capital is 15 percent.

Required:

1. Determine the net present value of the investment.
2. Determine the payback period.
3. Determine the approximate internal rate of return.
4. Determine the volume that the product needs to make the investment yield just 15 percent.

15-13 Purchasing Alternatives. The Klero Corporation uses about 35,000 tons of coal per year. The president of the firm expects that rate to continue for the next four to five years. He is also interested in obtaining coal on long-term contract to ensure a steady supply at a reasonable cost. He has investigated widely and has come down to the following three alternatives.

Acme Coal Company will deliver 140,000 tons within the next few months at a price of $22 per ton. The payment must be made at the time of delivery and will not be tax deductible in the current year. The tax deductions will arise as the firm uses the coal.

Berman Coal Mines will agree to deliver exactly 35,000 tons per year for the next four years, with payments at year ends. The price for the first year will be $23 per ton and will be subject to renegotiation in each subsequent year. Berman will have to justify any price increase on the basis of increases in its production costs. The increase cannot be more than $2 per ton in any year.

Carlson Coal Company will agree to deliver anywhere between 30,000 and 40,000 tons per year for four years at a set price of $26 per ton.

Klero uses a 15 percent discount rate and has a tax rate of 45 percent.

Required: Determine the best course of action.

15-14 Disposal Decision. The Hardison Manufacturing Company owns two drill presses. Because of a decline in business, the firm can get by with only one, and the managers are trying to decide which one to sell. Data on the two presses appear below.

	Press A	Press B
Original cost	$80,000	$100,000
Accumulated depreciation, tax and book	$80,000	$75,000
Estimated remaining useful life	5 years	5 years
Current market resale value	$12,000	$21,000
Estimated resale value at end of life	0	0

Both presses have the same operating costs, exclusive of depreciation. Press B has two years of life remaining for purposes of tax depreciation at

$12,500 per year. Press A is fully depreciated because it was acquired when a special fast-writeoff provision was in the tax code.

One of the managers has suggested that press A be sold because it is fully depreciated and the firm would therefore show a $12,000 profit. The firm has a tax rate of 40 percent and cost of capital of 15 percent.

Required: Determine which press the firm should sell, supporting your answer with appropriate calculations.

15–15 Working-Capital Investment.   The Cramer Company has an opportunity to invest in a new product. Data appear below.

Required Investment	
Plant and equipment, 10-year life	$1,000,000
Accounts receivable, 25% of annual sales	
Inventory of work in process and finished goods,	
40% of annual production	
Annual Returns	
Expected revenue, 50,000 units at $60	$3,000,000
Variable production costs	$30/unit
Fixed production costs, annual, including $100,000	
depreciation	$ 800,000
Fixed selling and administrative expenses, annual	$ 140,000

Cost of capital is 15 percent. The firm uses straight-line depreciation. Ignore taxes.

Required:

1. Determine the number of units the firm will produce in the first year, assuming it will reach the stated level of inventories by the end of the year.

2. Determine the cash outflows associated with manufacturing the product in the first year.

3. Determine the cash inflows expected from sales in the first year.

4. Determine the investment in working capital that the firm will carry over the life of the product.

5. Determine whether the investment is desirable.

15–16 Basic DCF Relationships.   The Ronnie Company is looking at a project costing $200,000 with an expected life of five years and no salvage value. The marginal tax rate is 40 percent, and the after-tax cost of capital is 10 percent.

Required:

1. If straight-line depreciation is used, what must the minimum before-tax cash flows be to yield a net present value of $10,000?

2. What must before-tax cash flows be if sum-of-the-years'-digits depreciation is used?

The present value of the cash inflows over the original investment for Waterway Barge Co. is as follows:

$$\text{PVI at } 10\% = \frac{\$1,673,217}{\$1,560,000} = 1.073$$

We would expect a PVI > 1.0, since the net present value is $113,217 at a 10 percent discount rate.

Decision Making and Present-Value Models

These three models (NPV, IRR, and PVI) all give a quantitative solution to the question, "Is this a worthwhile project?" The NPV decision criterion is to accept projects yielding a zero or positive net present value. The IRR decision criterion is to accept projects where the IRR is at least equal to the relevant discount rate (and we shall define relevancy next). A manager using PVI would accept projects where PVI ≥·1.0. These three models, then, comprise the main discounted cash flow (DCF) models. We shall discuss a few modifications as we proceed.

It is difficult to recommend which model is best in a particular situation. All the models can be appropriate. We tend to stress NPV as the least flawed model using discounted cash flows, but many people who want to relate returns to a percentage figure find IRR very useful. Rather than prescribing, we can look at the strengths and weaknesses of each measure and decide which is the most useful for each of us.

Quantitative analysis is but one part of any decision-making process. Our approach has been to analyze cash flows and then, using one of the present-value models, discount the flows and make a decision. However, many factors that are not quantifiable directly may have a great affect on a decision. Qualitative factors may be important enough that, for example, a project with NPV > 0 would be rejected while another project with NPV < 0 would be accepted. We shall discuss the qualitative factors in some depth in Chapter 16.

Non-DCF Models

Two general models ignore the time value of money: *payback* and *book rate of return*. Since this chapter and its appendix point out the importance of considering the time value of money, the reader may ask why we would discuss models that ignore this important aspect.

There is a time and place for the simplest of models. Even though they ignore the time value of money, in a small decision context or over a very short period these methods yield a reasonable input to the decision-making process. These models can be used as a rough screen for the present-value models, and they can be valuable in cases where liquidity is a pressing concern for management.

3. If expected after-tax cash flows from operations are $30,000 annually, what must the purchase price of the equipment be to yield a $10,000 net present value using straight-line depreciation?

4. If expected after-tax cash flows from operations are the following, what must the purchase price of the equipment be to yield a $10,000 net present value using straight-line depreciation?

Year	After-Tax Cash Flows
1	$30,000
2	30,000
3	60,064
4	40,000
5	40,000

5. Ronnie's management is concerned about its after-tax cost of capital. It is fairly certain that annual after-tax cash flows will be $36,596. If the machinery costs $200,000 and straight-line depreciation is used, what must the discount rate be to yield a $10,000 net present value?

15-17 Payback and IRR. The managers of Sea Oats Company have been considering a project that has an estimated life of ten years. Revenues and expenses (not including depreciation) should be as follows:

Year	Revenues	Cash Expenses
1	$300,800	$166,200
2	300,800	166,200
3	300,800	166,200
4	323,850	170,000
5	323,850	170,000
6	335,400	171,950
7	335,400	171,950
8	325,500	171,650
9	303,400	168,800
10	295,500	180,100

The equipment necessary for the project will cost $300,000 and will be subject to 10 percent investment tax credit. The expected salvage value is $45,000. Sea Oats has a marginal tax rate of 48 percent and uses straight-line depreciation. The managers think that working capital will increase by $100,000 because of this project.

Required: Using the payback reciprocal as a guide, find the internal rate of return of this project. [*Hint:* There is a trick to this, since there are uneven net cash flows. Also, since no estimates can be exact, it might be useful to do a little rounding to ease the computations. You might first try the payback reciprocal and then 1 percent higher or lower as indicated by your answer.]

15-18   Timing of Tax Effects of Depreciation. Assume that the current corporate tax rate is 48 percent on ordinary income and capital gains. The Razorback Company is investigating the best way to depreciate a new asset they have purchased for $100,000. It is expected that the asset will last ten years and have a salvage value of $10,000. Options open include straight-line, sum-of-the-years'-digits, and double-declining-balance (with a switchover to straight-line). The cost of capital is 10 percent.

Required:

1. If management depreciates the asset down to expected salvage value, what is the present value of the tax effect of each method of depreciation and the salvage value?

2. If management depreciates the asset down to zero, what is the present value of the tax effect of SYD depreciation and the net salvage value?

3. Assume that the asset will last three years and there will be no salvage value. Compute the present value of the tax shield from SYD and DDB.

15-19   Net Income and Cash Flows. Joplin Corporation has approached the Pine County Bank for a loan. Mr. Scott, the president of Joplin, has presented the following income statement to the loan officer at the bank.

Income Statement, 19X0	
Sales	$300,000
Cost of sales	150,000
Gross margin	$150,000
Sales and	
administrative expense	50,000
Income before taxes	$100,000
Taxes	40,000
Net income	$ 60,000

Mr. Scott feels that net income will grow at about 5 percent per year. In the declining economy of the time, receivables are expected to go up by 10 percent of sales yearly. For example, at the beginning of 19X0, receivables increased by $30,000. Depreciation makes up $20,000 of sales and administrative expenses. Marginal taxes are at 40 percent. The bank is offering a loan floating with prime rate for five years that is expected to average 15 percent over the life of the loan. Mr. Scott hopes to pay 50 percent of net income to investors as a dividend. Cost of sales are all variable.

Required: If you were the bank officer, how much would be the maximum amount you would lend Mr. Scott? The loan would be repaid at the end of 19X4.

15–20 **Cash Flows and Discount Rate.** The managers of Ferris division are contemplating a new product for their line of automobile accessories, special design wheels. Equipment is available to manufacture this product at $700,000. In order to accommodate the new product, some of the warehousing space in the plant will be turned into manufacturing space. This will mean that additional warehouse space will have to be leased at $10,000 per year with rent due at the beginning of each year. The management expects that the net of accounts receivable, cash, and inventory in excess of accounts payable to increase by $125,000 immediately. They feel that after two years they will be able to reduce the working-capital level by $25,000. Sales are expected to be 10,000 units the first year and 15,000 the second year. Sales are then expected to grow at 10 percent per year. The equipment, according to the manufacturer, has a life expectancy of eight years; it will then have little, if any, salvage value. Ferris's marginal tax rate is 48 percent, and the new equipment purchased will qualify for a 10 percent investment tax credit. Straight-line depreciation will be used for book and tax purposes.

There has been a discussion regarding the appropriate discount rate to use. Mr. Courtenay, the vice-president of finance, has proposed three alternatives. He estimates that current after-tax cost of capital is about 11 percent. However, owing to current inflation, the prime rate has been rising, with current short-term borrowing rates of 12 percent and higher expected in the next few years before rates again level off at near 10 percent. Thus, a rate tied to short-term rates could be used. Mr. Carver, the president and a major shareholder, has suggested to Courtenay that a goal-oriented rate be established, based on corporate goals for the next five years. This rate was set at 15 percent.

The sales department has estimated that the sales price will be $50 per wheel to begin with, but should be raised at $5 per wheel per year until it reaches $70. Other manufacturing fixed costs requiring cash that are associated with this project are $130,000 in the first year. Fixed costs are expected to go up $10,000 per year. Variable cost of goods sold (materials, labor, variable overhead) is estimated to be $30 per unit and, owing to inflation, will rise at about 8 percent per year. All cash flows (except rent) are assumed to occur at year end.

Required:

1. What is the appropriate discount rate? Justify your answer.

2. What is the net present value of this project, using the discount rate you have chosen in item 1? Round units sold to the nearest hundred, and round costs to two places.

3. Evaluate your NPV analysis from item 2.

15–21 **Contrasting Methods of Capital Budgeting.** Jeffrey Lawrence, manufacturing director of Millbrook Enterprises, is considering some new product lines. Corporate management of Millbrook has developed several measures for evaluating projects. Projects expected to last under five years are judged under the payback method, with a required payback of two years or less for moderately risky projects and of three years for moderately safe projects. In addition, the risky projects must show a 15 percent after-tax average book rate of return.

On longer projects, management uses multiple measures of net present value and internal rate of return. The estimated cost of capital for Millbrook is 12 percent. However, management has established goal-oriented rates including expected inflation of 18 percent for moderately risky projects and 14 percent for moderately safe projects. Millbrook uses straight-line depreciation. Taxes are 50 percent.

Required:

1. One project will cost $30,000 in equipment, will last an expected four to five years, and is considered relatively risky. Net income is expected to be $3,300 per year. Evaluate this project under Millbrook's criteria.

2. The other project will cost $50,000 in equipment, will last about six years, and is considered moderately risky. After-tax cash flows are expected to be $14,000 per year, including the tax savings from depreciation. Evaluate this project under Millbrook's criteria.

3. Discuss the criteria that management has developed for capital budgeting decisions. What are their strengths and weaknesses? Use the examples from items 1 and 2 to illustrate your discussion.

15–22 **By-Product and Capital Budgeting.** The Shull Company operates a combined factory/office building that it currently heats with natural gas at a cost of about $250,000 annually. The production process requires a great deal of heat, which is also supplied by natural gas at an annual cost of about $1,240,000. One of the plant engineers believes that it would be economical to recycle the heat from the production process and use it to heat the building. He estimates that the move would reduce consumption of natural gas by about $200,000 in the first year alone. The saving would relate to the $250,000 now spent to heat the building.

Recycling the heat would require large fans, considerable ductwork, and other equipment, with an aggregate cost of about $600,000 and a useful life of five years. The tax rate is 40 percent and cost of capital is 15 percent. The best estimates available indicate that the price of natural gas will rise at about 10 percent per year for the next five years. The firm uses straight-line depreciation for tax purposes.

Required: Determine whether the firm should install the system.

15–23 **Cost of Capital, Pretax and After-Tax.** Your firm has been using the net-present-value method of evaluating capital investments for several years. One manager has suggested that it would simplify the calculations if the firm used pretax, rather than after-tax, data. The hurdle rate, after-tax, is 15 percent. Because the tax rate is 40 percent, the manager argues, the firm could get the same results (accept or reject an investment) if it used a 25 percent rate to discount pretax cash flows. The 25 percent is 15 percent divided by 60 percent, which is one minus the tax rate.

Required: Evaluate the manager's suggestion. For comparability with the work of other students, show the results that you would get using the present method and the proposed method with the following hypothetical investment:

Investment required, all depreciable assets	$10.0 million
Annual pretax operating cash flows	$2.75 million
Life of investment	10 years

Use straight-line depreciation (no salvage value) in doing the after-tax analysis.

SELECTED REFERENCES

Clark, John J., Thomas J. Hindeland, and Robert E. Pritchard, *Capital Budgeting: Planning and Control of Capital Expenditures*. Englewood Cliffs, N.J.: Prentice-Hall, Inc., 1979.

Copeland, Thomas E., and J. Fred Weston, *Financial Theory and Corporate Policy*. Reading, Mass.: Addison-Wesley Publishing Company, Inc., 1979.

Osteryoung, Jerome S., *Capital Budgeting: Long-Term Asset Selection*. Columbus, Ohio: Grid, Inc., 1979.

Capital Budgeting: Complexities

Chapter 16

Chapter 15 covered the basics of capital budgeting: the determination of net cash flows and use of both discounted cash flow and other capital budgeting techniques. The decisions in Chapter 15 may be called **new-asset decisions:** management considered either expanding or introducing new equipment to reduce operating costs. In this chapter we consider several other types of decisions. We also consider preference rules for use in situations where only one, or a limited number of investments, can be made and the problem is to decide which to accept. We consider leasing as a special type of financing decision and take up several other complexities in capital budgeting.

REPLACEMENT DECISIONS

A **replacement decision** involves an investigation of new methods of production compared to existing machinery and technology. Managers of a firm can choose to retain current equipment (the status quo) or they can opt for new equipment. Of course, if the status quo is to be a viable option, existing equipment must be serviceable.

In many cases management has equipment that is becoming technologically obsolescent. While it is effective, it is not as efficient as newer equipment. Or a situation may involve a labor- versus machine-intensive trade-off, where, for example, new automated machinery may eliminate the need for some labor. This latter phenomenon has been occurring in the newspaper industry for the last ten years.

Cash Flows and Replacement

The analysis of a replacement decision parallels that of any other decision. The question is whether the incremental net cash flows from replacement justify the investment. The determination of net cash flows and investment for a replacement decision is more complicated than for the decisions considered in Chapter 15—for several reasons. First, the investment is usually not the cost of the proposed new equipment, because the old equipment may have some resale value or there may be tax effects of selling or scrapping it. Second, the depreciation tax shield from replacement is associated not with the depreciation on the new equipment but with the difference between depreciation on the new and on the existing equipment.

Illustration: Alpedo, Inc.

Assume Alpedo, Inc., is currently making its sole product on a piece of machinery bought five years ago, and a new piece of machinery has just been put on the market. Data for the firm and for these two pieces of equipment are as follows:

	Current Machine	Proposed Machine
Cost	$800,000 (5 years ago)	$750,000
Life	20 years	15 years
Depreciation, straight-line	$ 40,000/year	$ 50,000/year
Current book value	$600,000	—
Estimated salvage value now	$600,000	—
Estimated salvage value at end of life	0	0
Direct operating costs	$ 50,000/year	$ 30,000/year
Material savings		$ 5,000/year
Marginal tax rate: 40%		
Hurdle rate: 9%		

Thus, the net cash flows would be:

1. net investment of $750,000 − $600,000 salvage value on the old equipment.
2. annual operating savings of:
   a. $50,000 − $30,000 = $20,000 in direct operating costs
   b. $5,000 in savings on materials
   c. $50,000 − $40,000 = $10,000 additional tax shield from depreciation, which, after tax, would be

$$(\$20,000 + \$5,000)(1 - 0.40) + (\$10,000)(0.40) = \$19,000/\text{year}$$

With the 9 percent hurdle rate (goal-oriented discount rate), the following DCF measures can be made regarding this replacement decision:

$$\text{net present value} = \text{PV of savings} - \text{net investment}$$
$$= (\$19,000)(8.0607) - \$150,000 = \$3,153$$

$$\text{internal rate of return} = \frac{\text{net investment}}{\text{annual savings}}$$
$$= \frac{\$150,000}{\$19,000} = 7.895 \quad \begin{array}{l}\text{present-value factor for 15}\\\text{years or about 9.35\%}\end{array}$$

$$\text{present-value index} = \frac{(\$19,000)(8.0607)}{\$150,000} = 1.02$$

As you can see, all three DCF models indicate that this is a worthwhile project. Note that the payback is calculated as a result of the internal-rate-of-return process (eight years).

In this illustration the net book value ($600,000) is the tax basis for the old asset. However, some firms use one type of depreciation for financial reporting (straight-line, for example) with accelerated depreciation such as sum-of-the-years'-digits for tax purposes. In those cases, the book value and tax basis of an asset will nearly always be different. The book value of the asset is irrelevant, but the tax basis is important. It will determine the taxable gain (or loss) on disposal of old equipment and, therefore, the cash flow consequences from the saving of taxes or payment of additional taxes.

For example, the old machine cost $800,000 five years ago and has a current book value of $600,000. Assume the worst: the machine is worthless today. Thus, the firm would receive nothing if it were to sell the asset. The books would be adjusted to show a loss of $600,000. However, did the firm have a cash inflow or outflow of $600,000? The only cash flow would be the taxes *saved* owing to the loss. The $600,000 loss per se has *no cash consequences*.

The approach outlined above dealt with incremental cash flows. It would have been just as logical to look at separate cash flows associated with the current and the proposed equipment. The results would have been the same. Here we determine the present value of future flows associated with each choice. The one with the lower present value is better.

Keep old equipment:

$$\text{operating costs} = (-\$50,000)(1 - 0.40) = -\$30,000$$
$$\text{tax shield from depreciation} = (\$40,000)(0.40) = \$16,000$$
$$\text{present value} = (\$16,000 - \$30,000)(8.0607) = -\$112,850$$

Buy new equipment:

$$\text{purchase new equipment} = -\$750,000$$
$$\text{sell old equipment} = \$600,000$$
$$\text{operating costs} = (-\$30,000)(1 - 0.40) = -\$18,000$$
$$\text{savings in material} = (\$5,000)(1 - 0.40) = \$3,000$$
$$\text{tax shield from depreciation} = (\$50,000)(0.40) = \$20,000$$
$$\text{present value} = (\$20,000 + \$3,000 - \$18,000)(8.0607)$$
$$- \$150,000 = -\$109,700$$

The difference between the two alternatives is $3,150 (off due to rounding). Both alternatives yield *negative* present values. The idea is to choose the alternative with the lowest cost. As you can see, the new equipment fits this criterion.

CAPITAL BUDGETING SENSITIVITY ANALYSIS

Capital budgeting sensitivity analysis asks "what if" questions about the various inputs. The basic components of a discounted cash flow analysis are the original investment, depreciation schedule, an estimated salvage value of new equipment, ongoing operating costs, current salvage value of existing equipment, working-capital requirements, and estimated economic life. In addition to length of economic life, managers need to know an expected pattern of sales of a new product or service.

Economic Life

Managers are not concerned solely with physical life. Many pieces of manufacturing equipment can produce efficiently for thirty years or longer. However, if a machine becomes technologically obsolete or if the product made by a special-purpose machine becomes unwanted or obsolete, the asset's economic life is over. Economic life most concerns managers, not physical life. With this in mind, let us look at another use of breakeven analysis and the present-value model.

Discounted Payback

The payback concept is concerned with the number of years it takes to recover an initial investment. This concept can be modified to include the time value of money. With **discounted payback** or **breakeven net present value** we can ascertain the number of years it will take for the present value of future cash flows to equal the net investment. This is an important piece of sensitivity analysis because, like margin of safety in CVP breakeven analysis, it alerts managers to how sensitive a project is to its projected economic life.

Illustration: Discounted Payback for Waterway Barge.   The managers of Waterway Barge Company are considering the purchase of a barge that will accommodate loaded railroad cars. The tax rate is 40 percent and Waterway's hurdle rate is 10 percent. Expected results appear below.

Total annual tonnage	215,000
Revenue at $4.67/ton	$1,004,050
Variable costs at $0.66/ton	$141,900
Fixed costs, annual	$660,000
Pretax cash flow from operations	$202,150
After-tax flow at (1 − 0.40)	$121,290
Cost of barge	$1,000,000
Useful life	20 years (no salvage value)
Working-capital requirements	$60,000

Exhibit 16–1 shows the present values of the future flows, assuming sum-of-the-years'-digits depreciation and rounding the after-tax operating cash flows to $121,000. Remember that we are dealing with estimates of results many years in the future, so we should not try to be overly precise with the numbers.

EXHIBIT 16–1
Net-Present-Value Analysis, Flat Railroad Barge—Waterway Barge Co.

Present Values

SYD Tax Shield	Depreciation	Tax Shield × PV Factor
20/210	$1,000,000 = $95,238	$(38,095)(0.909) = $ 34,628
19/210	1,000,000 = 90,476	(36,190)(0.826) = 29,983
18/210	1,000,000 = 85,714	(34,285)(0.751) = 25,748
17/210	1,000,000 = 80,952	(32,380)(0.683) = 22,116
16/210	1,000,000 = 76,190	(30,475)(0.621) = 18,925
15/210	1,000,000 = 71,428	(28,570)(0.564) = 16,113
14/210	1,000,000 = 66,666	(26,665)(0.513) = 13,679
13/210	1,000,000 = 61,904	(24,760)(0.467) = 11,563
12/210	1,000,000 = 57,142	(22,885)(0.424) = 9,703
11/210	1,000,000 = 52,380	(20,950)(0.386) = 8,087
10/210	1,000,000 = 47,618	(19,045)(0.350) = 6,666
9/210	1,000,000 = 42,856	(17,140)(0.319) = 5,468
8/210	1,000,000 = 38,094	(15,235)(0.290) = 4,418
7/210	1,000,000 = 33,332	(13,330)(0.263) = 3,506
6/210	1,000,000 = 28,570	(11,428)(0.239) = 2,731
5/210	1,000,000 = 23,808	(9,520)(0.218) = 2,075
4/210	1,000,000 = 19,046	(7,615)(0.198) = 1,508
3/210	1,000,000 = 14,284	(5,710)(0.180) = 1,028
2/210	1,000,000 = 9,522	(3,805)(0.164) = 624
1/210	1,000,000 = [a]4,760	([a]1,900)(0.149) = . 283
		$218,852[b]

Annual cash operating flows for 20 years, ($121,000)(8.5136)	$ 1,030,146
Tax shield—depreciation (above)	218,852
Recovery of working capital in 20 years, ($60,000)(0.1486)	8,916
Working capital	(60,000)
Investment in barges	(1,000,000)
Net present value	$ 197,914

[a] Off due to rounding
[b] Tables exist that eliminate this longhand way of getting the PV of SYD or DDB depreciation tax shields. See Table A–5 in the appendix at the end of this book. To use this table, take the factor times the tax rate times the investment. Thus, ($1,000,000)(0.40)(.547) = $218,800.

If the project lasts for twenty years, current estimates show a positive NPV of almost $198,000. How many years must the project last at these levels for a discounted payback or NPV breakeven? We need to make a couple of assumptions to answer this question. Assume that if the barge were sold before twenty years, the net salvage value would approximate the net book value.[1] Thus, at the end of ten years, for example, the barge would have a salvage and book value of $261,905 (55/210 times $1,000,000). In addition, the $60,000 in working capital would be recovered in full whenever the project terminated. Exhibit 16-2 shows the adjustments that can be made to the original NPV calculation of $197,914.

For example, if the project lasted eighteen years, Waterway would lose annual cash flows of $121,000 per year for years 19 and 20, would lose the last two years of tax savings from depreciation, would recover the $60,000 in working capital two years earlier, and would gain a salvage value equal to net book value. This adds up to a $34,232 reduction in present values, thereby changing the NPV to $163,682. The breakeven point is between ten and eleven years. Therefore, the discounted payback (or net-present-value breakeven) is about eleven years. As you can see, this project is not too sensitive to economic life. In practice, the schedule in Exhibit 16-2 would probably arise from computer output. The manager would try a few values by hand, say twelve years, then eight years, to get a ballpark estimate of the needed life. As an exercise at the end of this chapter you will be asked to verify Exhibit 16-2 by calculating net present values for ten and eleven years from scratch.

Sensitivity Analysis—Other Variables

The example above for discounted payback looked at a breakeven net present value when the variable in question was economic life. This same breakeven technique can be used for any other factor in a DCF analysis. In most schedules of cash flows associated with net-present-value analysis, managers are more confident about some estimates. For example, a manager may be more confident about the cost of a piece of machinery, the yearly depreciation, and the tax rate than he is about needed working capital, expected annual sales, expected costs, estimated salvage value, and economic life. Thus, a manager might want to look at the most pessimistic estimate and do some sensitivity analysis.[2]

---

[1] We could make other assumptions. The most pessimistic would be that the barge has no salvage value. Scrapping it would then result in a tax saving equal to the tax basis multiplied by 40 percent.

[2] See G. V. Henderson and A. H. Barnett, "Breakeven Present Value: A Pragmatic Approach to Capital Budgeting Under Risk and Uncertainty," *Management Accounting*, January 1978, pp. 49–52.

EXHIBIT 16-2
Discounted Payback (all figures present values)

Economic Life in Years	(1) Cumulative Lost Annual Cash Flows	(2) Cumulative Lost Tax Shield Depreciation	(3) Recovery of Working Capital	(4) Lost Recovery of Working Capital, Year 20	(5) Salvage Value	(6) Net Present Value
20	$ 0	$ 0	$ 8,916	$8,916	$ 0	$197,914
18	37,770	907	10,792	8,916	2,569	163,682
15	109,805	5,518	14,363	8,916	17,097	105,135
11	244,238	21,641	21,030	8,916	75,101	19,250
10	286,648	28,307	23,133	8,916	100,970	(1,854)

Illustration: Waterway Barge Operating Cash Flows. If we assume that a twenty-year life is reasonable for Waterway Barge's flat barge and that we are fairly certain about everything except annual cash flows, we can ask what the level of annual cash flows has to be to have a net-present-value breakeven. Exhibit 16–3 on page 632 shows the necessary calculations. The top portion of the exhibit shows the total investment to be recovered. The present values of the depreciation tax shield and recovery of working capital are subtracted to determine the present value of after-tax operating flows needed to achieve the NPV breakeven. This value is divided by the present-value factor for twenty years at 10 percent to find the annual flows needed. Basic CVP analysis is then used to determine the required tonnage.

Exhibit 16–3 shows that the reduction in after-tax operating flows to bring the project to NPV breakeven is 19 percent, which suggests that the decision is not too sensitive to cash flow estimates. However, when we look at the drop in volume of tonnage needed to bring the project to NPV breakeven, we see a different picture. A decline in volume of only 4.6 percent will give the 19 percent decline in cash flows. The high fixed costs are the reason. Contribution margin per ton is high, so cash flows are very sensitive to changes in volume. The managers would also analyze the sensitivity of selling price per ton and variable cost per ton to complete this phase of the analysis.

This type of sensitivity testing relies on the basic relationships of cost-volume-profit analysis. Consequently you should verify for yourself that if the estimate of annual tonnage of 215,000 is taken as given, a decline in selling price or an increase in variable cost per ton (that is, a decline in contribution margin per ton) of about $0.18 would also bring the project to NPV breakeven.

Sensitivity analysis is a method of seeing how sensitive our DCF analyses are to changes in any of the parameters. Thus, we can even question future rates of reinvestment opportunities to see how sensitive a project is to

EXHIBIT 16–3
Breakeven Net Present Value

Investment in barge	$1,000,000
Investment in working capital	60,000
A. To be recovered	$1,060,000
Present value of depreciation tax shield (Exhibit 16–1)	$ 218,852
Present value of recovery of working capital	8,916
B. Total	$ 227,768
Amount to be recovered through operating net cash flows (A − B)	$ 832,232

Annual net cash flows required for 20 years:[3]

$$\frac{\$832,232}{8.514} = \$97,753$$

Percentage drop from original estimate:

$$\frac{\$121,000 - \$97,753}{\$121,000} \cong 19\%$$

Required Volume in Tonnage per Year

After-tax flow	$ 97,753
Divided by: (1 − tax rate)	0.60
Pre-tax flow required	$162,922
Add fixed costs requiring cash payment	660,000
Required contribution margin	$822,922
Divided by: Contribution margin per ton ($4.67 − $0.66)	4.01
Required annual tonnage	205,218

Percentage drop from original estimate:

$$\frac{215,000 - 205,218}{215,000} \cong 4.6\%$$

---

this factor. Note that we are not assessing the risk associated with each variable. We do not know how likely it is that an economic life of a project will be drastically shortened. Once we have determined the factors that can severely affect present values of cash flows, then we can decide to do a more thorough analysis of key variables.

[3] We deal here with equal annual flows. Actually, flows can be uneven as long as the present value of such flows (at 10 percent) equals $832,232.

PREFERENCE RULES

So far we have considered investments from the standpoint of acceptability: they either do or do not have positive net present values or internal rates of return in excess of the cutoff rate (of course, a positive net present value entails a profitability index greater than 1). We have considered these decisions independently of other capital budgeting decisions facing the firm. These decisions, then, require that the manager either accept or reject the investment proposal.

In many cases managers face **preference** or **ranking decisions.** This type of decision requires that the manager select one or more investments and reject others that may meet the net-present-value and IRR criteria of acceptance. There are two general situations where managers must make preference decisions. First, some decisions involve *mutually exclusive alternatives.* Two or more investments are available, but only one can be chosen. For example, a firm needing one delivery truck can pick from among several makes and models. A manufacturer needing materials handling equipment can choose either fork lift trucks or a conveyor system. Selecting one investment precludes selecting others, because one is enough.

The second type of situation where preference is important arises *under capital rationing:* the firm has a limited amount of cash available for investment, and the cost of investment opportunities that pass the NPV or IRR tests exceeds the available funds. The decisions already considered assume the availability of funds for investment. In theory, a firm should be able to raise a sufficient amount of capital at some cost, even though the cost could well be above the current cost of capital. However, in practice the managers will find that funds are limited, owing to the capital structure of the firm, size, risk, current market availability of funds, and many other factors. When management is faced with several competing alternatives or limited funds, the problem is one of ranking or preference, not simply of acceptability.

The major difficulty involved with preference decisions is that the three basic criteria (NPV, IRR, PVI) may give different rankings of projects. For example, if there are three mutually exclusive projects up for consideration, it could well be that one has the highest NPV, another the highest IRR, and the third the highest PVI. When the criteria give conflicting answers, the problem is to determine which criterion should be used to set the rankings.

Preference rules are the source of much of the current argumentation in capital budgeting. Some of the considerations can become extremely complex, and the range of assumptions used to justify different rules is wide. We consider only a few of the problems, because a deeper analysis should be the subject for a course in managerial finance. However, because accountants are intimately involved in capital budgeting decisions, they must have some understanding of the problems and of the assumptions that underlie each of the discounted cash flow models.

COMPARING DCF MODELS

The internal rate of return is a percentage, the net present value is a dollar figure, and the profitability index is a ratio. One reason for the popularity of the IRR in practice is that businesspeople are used to thinking in percentage terms. For example, financial ratio analysis such as you probably studied in financial accounting or finance courses emphasizes percentages and ratios in order to make different firms more comparable. The problem with percentages and ratios is that they eliminate size—and size can be very important. For example, if you had $10,000 to invest and had only two choices, invest the entire amount at 15 percent, or invest $1,000 at 80 percent and leave the other $9,000 idle, you would be better off taking the 15 percent return on the $10,000. Your total return would be $1,500 ($10,000 × 0.15), which exceeds $800 ($1,000 × 0.80). This is an extreme case, but relevant, as we shall see shortly.

The DCF models differ in one extremely important respect: the rate of return on reinvested cash flows. All DCF models assume reinvestment of the periodic cash flows, but the NPV and PI models assume reinvestment at the discount rate used to determine the NPV, while the IRR model assumes reinvestment at the IRR. The reinvestment-rate assumption creates virtually all the problems in making preference decisions. The following sections show how the three models can give conflicting results and how to overcome the problem.

IRR Versus NPV

Assume that a firm has the following investment opportunities. They are mutually exclusive, so only one can be chosen. Their rankings on the NPV and IRR criteria differ, with investment B showing a higher NPV than A, and investment A a higher IRR than B.

	Investments	
	A	B
Cash flow—year 0 (investment)	($1,000)	($1,000)
year 1	775	0
year 2	775	1,695
NPV at 10%	$345	$400
IRR	35%	30%

The reason for the conflicting rankings is that project A returns its cash flows faster than does project B. In general, the IRR method emphasizes the speed with which cash flows come in, because it assumes that they are reinvested at the IRR. Thus, when the IRR is greater than the cutoff rate (10 percent in this example), the cash is assumed to be reinvested at the IRR for a longer period.

The selection of the project depends on the assumed reinvestment rate. If the rate is 10 percent, then project B is superior to project A. This can be shown by analyzing the terminal values of the investments, as advocated by Solomon.[4] He proposed that the manager should determine the rate at which the flows from either project would be invested and determine which investment had the higher terminal value (the amount of cash available at the end of the life of the investment). At a rate of 10 percent, the two projects would have the following amounts of cash available at the end of year 2.

	Investment	
	A	B
Cash flow from year 1 × 1.10	$ 852.50	0
Cash flow from year 2	775.00	$1,695
Total available cash	$1,627.50	$1,695

In this example the superiority of investment B is clear, because both projects required the same initial cash outlay of $1,000. If the amounts of investment are unequal, Solomon advocates calculating a true rate of return using the terminal values and investments.[5] The rate is calculated using the present value of a single payment, which is the amount of cash available to the firm at the end of the life of the investment. These calculations are given below.

	Investment	
	A	B
Investment at time zero	$1,000.00	$1,000.00
Divided by		
Cash available at end of life	$1,627.50	$1,695.00
Equals		
Present-value factor[6] for $n = 2$	0.614	0.590
Approximate rate of return	28%	30%

The terminal-value method overcomes some of the problems in preference decisions and elsewhere. It is not widely used, probably because it does not have the intuitive appeal of the IRR or NPV. It requires accumulating cash flows reinvested, thus works with future values rather than present

---

[4] Ezra Solomon, "The Arithmetic of Capital Budgeting," *Journal of Finance*, April 1956.

[5] Several versions of the rate of return are called the true rate. Each is true given its assumptions.

[6] This is derived from, for example,

$$\frac{1}{(1 + r)^2} \, \$1,627.50 = \$1,000 \quad \text{and} \quad \frac{1}{(1 + r)^2} = 0.614$$

This is the same as $(1 + r)^2 = 1/0.614$ or 1.6287. Thus $1 + r = \sqrt{1.6287}$ or 1.276 (approximately 28 percent). The rate of return can also be determined from Table A–3 in the appendix at the end of this book.

values. (Our example required only one calculation: the reinvestment of the cash flow for project A received at the end of year 1. In other cases the future-value factor of a single payment or of an annuity would be used to calculate the terminal value.)

Figure 16–1 shows the net present values of projects A and B graphed against various discount rates. Assuming that the discount rate used is equal to the reinvestment rate, the figure shows that project B is preferable to project A so long as the rate does not exceed 18.7 percent. Above that rate, project A is superior to project B. Solomon recommends that the reinvestment rate be used as the discount rate, whether or not it approximates cost of capital.

We conclude that the NPV criterion is better than the IRR criterion in cases where the reinvestment rate is the same as the discount rate used to determine the NPVs of the mutually exclusive projects. If the reinvestment rate is greater than the discount rate, the terminal-value method will indicate the appropriate choice. One final point: we have assumed that the reinvestment rate is the same for the two projects. It may not be. Investing

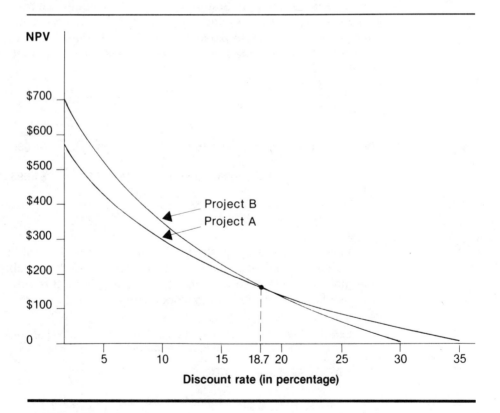

FIGURE 16–1
Net Present Values at Various Discount Rates

in one project may provide opportunities to invest in others at different rates from those that would be available if one invested in the other project. This situation requires the use of the terminal-value method.

NPV Versus PV Index

We now consider the net-present-value criterion and present-value-index criterion. These criteria give the same ranking if the investments are equal, so we must use illustrative projects with different investments.

	Investments	
	C	D
Cash flows—time 0 (investment)	($1,000)	($500)
year 1	800	450
year 2	800	450
NPV at 10%	$388	$281
Present-value index, $1,388/$1,000	1.388	
$781/$500		1.562

As a point of interest, the IRR of project D is greater than that of project C. In considering the present-value index as a criterion, we are eliminating the scale of the investments, reducing them to a common denominator of present value of future cash flows to dollar of investment. Again, the critical assumption is the reinvestment rate, but in this analysis the question is what amount is to be invested at the current time. Suppose that the firm has a total of $1,000 to invest and that if it chooses project D, it will invest the remaining $500 ($1,000 − $500 for D) at 10 percent. Applying the terminal-value approach, we see that more cash is available at the end of year 2 if project C is selected.

	Investment	
	C	D
Cash flow for two years	$800	$450
Multiplied by:		
Future-value factor for annuity for two years at 10 percent	2.10	2.10
Cash available from reinvestment	$1,680	$945
Investment of $500 at 10 percent, future value of single amount, $500 × (1.10)^2		605
Total available	$1,680	$1,550

In this situation we consider the alternative use of the $500 difference between the investments in projects C and D. Project C should be selected if the reinvestment rate is 10 percent. This technique is used in capital-rationing situations, where the amount of cash available to finance projects is limited.

Unequal Lives

All the examples so far have assumed that alternative projects have equal economic lives. The reason for this constraint is the reinvestment question. How do you compare the following two projects?

	Cash Flows	
Year	Project A	Project B
(original investment)	($10,000)	($10,000)
1	2,000	3,242
2	2,000	3,242
3	2,000	3,242
4	2,000	3,242
5	2,000	3,242
6	2,000	
7	2,000	
8	2,000	
9	2,000	
10	2,000	

Both projects have a net present value of $2,289 at a 10 percent discount rate. Project B has an IRR of about 18 percent, while that of project A is about 15 percent. If project B is accepted, specific assumptions must be made about the reinvesting of funds in years 6 through 10. This is the same problem that we analyzed using Solomon's future values. However, investment opportunities five years hence are not known. Therefore, owing to uncertainty and comparability, we recommend comparing alternatives *as if* they had equal lives. To do this, one may have to make some assumptions about some of the cash flows. For example, when comparing the alternatives above, you might estimate the salvage value of the first project at the end of five years and, in essence, compare the two on a common time horizon.

Obviously, there is some uncertainty about future cash flows stretching over ten years, as illustrated in project A. It may be possible to be as certain about reinvesting in another project B in five years as it is about receiving $2,000 per year those last five years with project A. Therefore, a limited way to deal with unequal lives may be to make some specific assumptions about a replacement chain of like projects. While this may be reasonable for looking at a two-year project as compared to a four-year one, it is less likely to be useful if you need to compare a two-year project against one that could last twenty years.

CAPITAL RATIONING

Capital rationing is the term used to express the idea that firms have limited funds in any particular period. While a firm may identify several projects that are acceptable under the net-present-value criterion, funds may not be available to go forward on all these projects. Capital becomes a scarce resource and must be used optimally.

Internal and External Rationing

Capital rationing can be internal or external. **Internal rationing** means that management decides to limit the amount of projects to funds currently being generated from within the firm. Perhaps the company has an acceptable debt and equity structure and the managers and owners do not want to change it. Shareholders may want no dilution of their holdings.

External rationing comes about because of limited availability of funds. Finance theory states that there is a strong capital market and that funds should be available at some rate.[7] However, at certain times funds may not be available. For example, in 1980 when interest rates hit new highs, lending institutions did not have money available since their own cost of borrowing was so high. As another illustration, the size or relative riskiness of a firm may lead to limited equity markets and virtually nonexistent debt markets.

Solutions for Capital Rationing

Managers can deal with this problem using a variety of approaches. The major idea is to find that group of projects that will best use available capital resources.

Solution by Inspection. With a limited number of projects, managers can group those found acceptable when discounted at the cost of capital and pick the set of projects that maximizes present value. Assume Rubber Tire Company is considering several projects but has only $100,000 in funds available this year. A list of projects and needed investment appears below. None of these projects are mutually exclusive.

	Cost	Net Present Value
1. New aligning machine	$50,000	$65,000
2. Expanded retail facilities	75,000	37,000
3. Computer for inventory, billing	25,000	24,000

[7] Thomas E. Copeland and J. Fred Weston, *Financial Theory and Corporate Policy.* Reading, Mass.: Addison-Wesley Publishing Company, 1979.

As you can see, several combinations of these three projects are available. With unlimited funds, there are 2^n (or eight in this example) possible combinations. However, with the capital constraint of $100,000, the only feasible combinations are as follows:[8]

	Cost	Net Present Value
Project 1	$ 50,000	$65,000
Project 2	75,000	37,000
Project 3	25,000	24,000
Projects 1 and 3	75,000	89,000
Projects 2 and 3	100,000	61,000

Thus, assuming no more funds are available, the combination of projects 1 and 3 will yield the maximum present value. Excess funds can be invested at the cost of capital.

Solution by the Discount Rate.   A common technique used by many companies is to raise the hurdle rate to reflect limited funds. Thus, only the projects yielding the highest return will have positive net present values. Owing to the problems we discussed earlier, this seems a better alternative than ranking by internal rates of return.

Mathematical Solution Techniques.   Our original discussion of this problem identified capital rationing as a limited resource. Therefore, it can be dealt with like other limited resources in a mathematical programming context. Both linear and integer programming techniques are useful. We will not undertake a complete discussion of these models but will outline a single example, so you can see how they fit into the general mathematical programming framework.[9]

Let us expand the Rubber Tire Company problem to include limited fund availability now plus limited funds in a year. Assume that the company has the following four projects to consider:

Project	Funds Needed Now	Funds Needed in One Year	NPV
A	$20,000	−$10,000	$ 4,000
B	30,000	− 10,000	6,000
C	20,000	30,000	10,000
D	20,000	50,000	12,000

If this firm has $40,000 it can invest now and $60,000 in a year, this problem can be formulated as an integer program:

Maximize: $Z = 4{,}000X_1 + 6{,}000X_2 + 10{,}000X_3 + 12{,}000X_4$

[8] To be complete, we could include *no projects* as a feasible alternative.
[9] For a complete discussion, see J. Osteryoung, *Capital Budgeting* (Columbus, Ohio: Grid, Inc., 1979), chap. 7.

Subject to: $20,000X_1 + 30,000X_2 + 20,000X_3 + 20,000X_4 \le 40,000$
$-10,000X_1 - 10,000X_2 + 30,000X_3 + 50,000X_4 \le 60,000$
$X_1, X_2, X_3, X_4 = 0 \text{ or } 1$

Other constraints can be added for such things as limited machine capacity, supplier availability, supervision time, and environmental concerns.

Mathematical programming rests on several assumptions. In this case, we assume (to name a few) that funds cannot be transferred between periods, that we know the cash flows with relative certainty, that the constraints and objective function are linear, and that the projects are fully independent. Some authors point out that relaxing these assumptions tends to weaken the model.[10] However, in defense of an integer programming solution, other authors propose an extensive use of sensitivity analysis to deal with this problem.[11]

Summary

In the majority of cases, managers will be faced with the need to select projects in light of constrained capital resources. In simpler situations, techniques such as raising the discount rate or selecting by inspecting all combinations of projects are appropriate. As the number of projects increases and the number of constraints goes up, more sophisticated techniques involving various forms of mathematical programming can be used. Finally, as we relax more and more assumptions of, say, known life and cash flows, techniques such as simulation can be used to find an optimal solution.[12]

ADLER'S RATE OF RETURN

All the techniques so far discussed assume that all cash flows are reinvested at some rate. In practice, however, firms do not reinvest all cash flows. They must make some periodic payments to suppliers of capital (dividends, interest, and principal on debt). Professor Michael Adler proposed a method of analyzing investment projects that avoids the assumption that all cash flows are reinvested.[13] Adler's method works with uneven cash flows as well, but for simplicity we present it under the assumption of even cash flows. He argued that it was reasonable to assume that the firm would reinvest only

---

[10] Copeland and Weston, *Financial Theory and Corporate Policy*, pp. 53–56.

[11] J. Clark, T. Hindelang, and R. Pritchard, *Capital Budgeting: Planning and Control of Capital Expenditures.* (Englewood Cliffs, N.J.: Prentice-Hall, Inc., 1979), Chapters 12, 13, and 14.

[12] See Chapter 4 and see R. Hespos and P. Strassmann, "Stochastic Decision Trees for the Analysis of Investment Decisions," *Management Science*, 11 (August 1965), 244–59.

[13] M. Adler, "The True Rate of Return and the Reinvestment Rate," *Engineering Economist*, 15:3 (1970), 185–87.

enough of each cash inflow to maintain the value of the investment. The remaining cash flows, in equal annual amounts, would be consumed (for example, paid as dividends). If cash flows are received in equal annual amounts, the following equation describes the process:

$$I = (C_t - kI)f_r$$

where I = the original investment
C_t = the equal annual cash flows
k = the rate of return
f_r = the **future-value factor** for an annuity at the reinvestment rate, $r, [(1 + r)^t - 1]/r$

The equation above states that some amount of each equal annual cash flow must be reinvested at the rate, r, in order that the original amount invested can be returned. The amount $C_t - kI$ is reinvested at rate r to yield an amount equal to the original investment at the termination of the project. The amount kI is consumed each year and represents income on the investment. In effect, the method results in viewing an investment project as if it were a bond bought at face value, with the annual interest being consumed and the face value being returned at maturity. You know from financial accounting that a bond bought at face value has an effective yield equal to the nominal yield.

Rearranging to solve for k gives the following:

$$I = C_t f_r - kI f_r$$

$$kI f_r = C_t f_r - I$$

$$k = \frac{C_t}{I} - \frac{1}{f_r}$$

To give an example, assume that a project is available with the following characteristics:

Investment required	$1,000,000
Annual cash flows, 10 years	$250,000
Reinvestment rate	15%

The future value of an annuity of $1 at 15 percent for ten years is $20.30—$[(1 + 0.15)^{10} - 1]/0.15$—and, therefore,

$$k = \frac{\$250,000}{\$1,000,000} - \frac{1}{20.30}$$

$$= 0.25 - 0.049$$

$$= 0.201$$

Thus, the firm could take approximately $201,000 (0.201 × $1,000,000) out of the annual cash flows and distribute it to shareholders or other suppliers of capital, while reinvesting $49,000 at 15 percent to give $1 million at the end of the ten-year life of the project. As you can see, the formula for Adler's k involves the payback reciprocal (C_t/I), and the results (25 percent) can be compared to the IRR of 21.4 percent for this example. The payback reciprocal is an upper bound for both IRR and Adler's k.

The reinvestment rate in this model could be the cost of capital, or it could be a different rate, depending on the opportunities available. The most appealing aspect of the model from a practical standpoint is its recognizing that "you have to eat." You do not normally reinvest all the cash flows produced by a project. The method will give the same results as the others in evaluating single projects so long as the reinvestment rate is set equal to cost of capital. That is, projects that would be acceptable under the NPV and IRR methods would also be acceptable using Adler's k, where the cutoff rate for $k = r =$ cost of capital or discount rate used for NPV.

INVESTING AND FINANCING DECISIONS

Our discussion in Chapter 15 focused on the alternative uses management has for funds. The previous discussion on rates of reinvestment also highlighted alternative uses and opportunity costs. With this in mind, we will look at the difference between investing and financing decisions.

The Investing Decision

If management uses NPV, IRR, or PVI, it will have set a goal-oriented cutoff rate or hurdle rate of return. In net-present-value terms, a project is acceptable only if it has a positive net present value when discounted at this goal-oriented rate. The rate chosen usually reflects many aspects regarding cost of capital and risk of the project. It is possible the goal-oriented hurdle rate should be higher than the weighted average cost of debt and equity financing. DCF analysis looks at separable costs associated with a project. In some cases joint costs may increase over time but not be associated directly with specific projects. If so, the hurdle rate should take this into account, or some measure of those joint costs should be included in the cash flow analysis. So, it is important to judge any proposal by a relevant discount rate. This is the **investing decision.** Is a proposal worthwhile when judged, quantitatively at least, against the hurdle rate? That is the information a manager wants. Once that question is decided positively by weighing all the quantitative and qualitative data, the use of DCF models per se is over.

The Financing Decision

If a project is accepted, management must have knowledge not only of the pool of funds available for capital projects, but also of the rates and terms of payment of these funds. The **financing decision** is the choice of the cheapest way to fund a project, taking into account all relevant terms and tax considerations.

It is important to separate the investing decision from the financing decision. Consider the following examples shown in Exhibit 16–4. Assume that this firm has a tax rate of 40 percent and a hurdle rate of 10 percent after taxes. In project 1, the returns are $16,500 per year for ten years, and the equipment is offered by the manufacturer on a delayed-payment basis. The firm must pay $120,000 at the end of one year. It is obvious that there is interest included in a payment to be made a year later. If we assume that the equipment could be purchased now for $100,000 (reflected in alternative 2), the NPV calculation shows the problem when investing and financing decisions are mixed together. The project would be unwisely rejected if judged at a 10 percent hurdle rate, since the after-tax rate of interest offered by the equipment seller is 20 percent. However, if the project (alternative 2) is viewed as an investing decision only, then it would be properly accepted using the 10 percent rate. The same kind of example can be drawn to show that specific financing at a rate less than 10 percent can, if included in an NPV analysis, make a project that actually returns less than 10 percent look as if it were acceptable.

EXHIBIT 16–4
Investing Versus Financing

	Alternative 1	Alternative 2
Yearly net cash flows (10 years)	$ 16,500	$ 16,500
Payment to manufacturer:		
Year 0		100,000
Year 1	120,000	
Net present value at 10%	($433)	$1,385

where ($120,000)(PV factor 1 year) = $100,000; thus $120,000 in 1 year = $100,000 discounted at 20 percent. The $20,000 is deductible as interest and, therefore, the net payment is $112,000 in a year.

LEASING

In recent times, leasing has become a major source of financing. Note that leasing a piece of equipment cannot be compared to buying the equipment for cash on delivery. The cash paid had to be obtained at some cost. If a firm purchases an asset, funds can come from equity investment, debt, or other sources. When leasing, funds are being provided by the lessor at some cost.

Thus, the cost of leasing can be compared to the cost of owning to find out which is the cheapest way to finance a project that has already been found acceptable.

The Effective Interest Rate: Mann's Method

Since leasing is a financing alternative, the cost of the lease can be expressed as an interest rate just like the cost of a loan. However, the tax consequences of leasing are different from those of owning. Thus, the effective lease rate can be calculated and compared to other sources of funds. Several authors have proposed ways of finding this rate, including Ferrara,[14] Mann,[15] and Osteryoung.[16] Several methods have been proposed to find the implicit interest rate included in a lease. In most of these methods two factors are important. One is the comparison of interest rates in the lease to alternative sources of financing. The second is the comparison of depreciation under owning to implicit depreciation under a lease.[17] We discuss Mann's method to deal with these problems, but other equally justified techniques could be used.

The basic difference between owning and leasing has to do with different tax consequences. If a firm owns an asset, it can deduct depreciation and interest expenses and reduce taxes. In addition, if an investment tax credit is available, this direct credit to taxes is available to reduce the cost. However, a firm can deduct only the lease payments when leasing an asset. There is no depreciation.

Mann's method looks for the interest rate that equates a cash purchase price to the present value of lease payments less the difference between the lease payments and depreciation. For example, a manager considering an investment of $50,000 for a project with a five-year life may be offered a lease at $12,000 per year. The manager wants to find the implicit interest rate in this lease, including the tax differences due to leasing rather than owning. Exhibit 16–5 on page 646 shows such a method. The $12,000 yearly payments are deductible for tax purposes if the firm leases. The exhibit shows the relevant sum-of-the-years'-digits (SYD) depreciation that could be deducted if the asset were owned. The difference between the two is the excess of lease payments over depreciation. The savings are in taxes, and this is shown in the last column. The company will pay the leasing company $12,000 per year, and the net cash flow difference of taxes saved is deducted from that payment to get the net incremental outflow. The present value of this outflow can be compared to the cash purchase price of $50,000.

[14] William L. Ferrara, "Capital Budgeting and Financing or Leasing Decisions," *Management Accounting*, July 1968, pp. 55–63.

[15] Clifton D. Mann, "Evaluating the Cost in a Lease Proposal," *Management Accounting*, July 1971, pp. 56–58.

[16] Osteryoung, *Capital Budgeting*, chap. 8.

[17] Lanny G. Chasteen, "Implicit Factors in the Evaluation of Lease vs. Buy Alternatives," *The Accounting Review*, 48:4 (October 1973), 764–67.

As the exhibit shows, the after-tax rate is about 4¼ percent. Thus, before tax it would be 7 percent. This 7 percent rate can be compared to rates on alternative sources of funds. If the rate is greater than the borrowing rate, the firm should buy the asset.

EXHIBIT 16–5
Mann's Effective-Interest-Rate Method

Year	Cash Lease[a]	SYD Depreciation	Excess (Deficiency) Lease Over Depreciation Tax Shield	Net Excess (Deficiency) Lease Tax Shield at 40%
1	12,000	$16,667	(4,667)	($1,867)
2	12,000	13,333	(1,333)	(533)
3	12,000	10,000	2,000	800
4	12,000	6,667	5,333	2,133
5	12,000	3,333	8,667	.3,467

Computations to find effective interest rate:

	At 4⅛%	At 4¼%
Present value of lease payments	$53,235	$53,048
Less: Present value of net excess lease tax shield	3,071	3,046
Total	50,164	50,002
Purchase price	50,000	50,000
	164	2

Therefore, the effective interest rate is approximately $0.0425/(1 - 0.40) = 7\%$.

[a] Assuming lease payments are made at year end.

Other Reasons for Leasing

In the entire discussion of cash flows and tax effects, a common assumption has been that enough positive income exists in a firm that taxes will be saved by deducting depreciation or receiving an investment tax credit. However, situations do exist where firms have had a series of poor years or where extraordinary events have adversely affected profits. Thus, there may be no taxable income expected in the near term, and the advantages of investment tax credit and accelerated depreciation are virtually lost.

Before illustrating this consideration, we must discuss one of the properties of current federal income tax law. Firms that show losses on their tax returns are permitted to carry the loss *back* for three years, and *forward* for five years, offsetting the loss against taxable income in those years.[18] When the loss is carried back, the firm gets a refund of prior-year taxes; when carried forward, the taxable income and, therefore, income tax is reduced.

The following example shows the effects of the carryback and carryforward. The tax rate is 40 percent in all years.

Year	Taxable Income	Income Tax (refund)
1	$ 40,000	$16,000
2	$ 30,000	$12,000
3	$ 50,000	$20,000
4	($200,000)	($48,000)
5	$ 60,000	0
6	$ 50,000	$12,000

In year 4 the firm gets a refund from carrying the loss back three years. Because the loss exceeded the taxable income in those years ($200,000 − $40,000 − $30,000 − $50,000 = $80,000), the firm has an $80,000 carryforward to apply against taxable income for the next five years. In year 5 it uses $60,000 of the carryforward, and pays no tax. In year 6 it uses the remaining $20,000, thus paying tax on $30,000 ($50,000 taxable income − $20,000 remaining carryforward).

Now, if a firm has sustained a large loss and has carryforwards that exceed its expected taxable income for the next five years, it will pay no tax for those years. If it has been operating at near zero taxable income and expects losses for the next five years, it will also pay no tax. If we consider the example above in the context of such a firm, the analysis changes. All the tax considerations are dropped. Essentially we need to find the discount rate that will equate the $12,000 yearly lease payments over five years to the $50,000 outright purchase price. This would be 6.4 percent and would not have to be adjusted again to make it pretax.

INFLATION

Inflation seems a way of life in most of the economies around the world. The 1970s were a heightened inflationary period, spurred by many factors including the increasing price of energy. For this reason, a schedule of cash flows that extends into the future should consider inflation.

Depreciation and Salvage Value

While the original investment in a project is known, inflation has effects on the tax shield from depreciation and estimated salvage values. Depreciation

---

[18] The provision is known as the net-operating-loss carryback and carryforward. It does not apply to all losses, as you may learn in a tax course.

is set when an asset is acquired. A depreciable life and depreciation method are chosen according to existing tax code regulations. Therefore, assuming tax regulations are unchanged, the nominal cash flows from tax savings due to depreciation are known at the outset. However, with inflation these cash flows when received are worth less than planned.

For example, a $10,000 tax savings from depreciation received in one year given a hurdle rate of 10 percent would have a present value of $9,090. However, if inflation were 12 percent per year, the $10,000 received in one year would buy only as much as $8,928 would today ($10,000/1.12). Thus the present value of this cash flow at 10 percent is $8,116, with $974 in purchasing power lost to inflation. Naturally, compounded inflation over a project's life can sharply reduce the worth of cash flows arising from the tax effect of depreciation.

Salvage also can be affected by inflation. Any estimate of an ultimate salvage value in ten years must include a prediction not only of the value of the used equipment but also of how that value will be affected by technology and inflation.

Project Versus Process

Discounted cash flow techniques are designed to analyze a project. For example, when evaluating a replacement opportunity, managers tend to look at the costs associated with a new machine until its economic life is over. The analysis rarely includes subsequent replacements ten, twenty, and thirty years down the line. To do so would be to look at the entire *process* until it was over. Firms entering new product areas and spending a good deal for investment capital do not usually plan to abandon the area when the first set of equipment wears out. However, managers should at least implicitly look at expected replacement costs as influenced by inflation as part of the original decision to get into a product line in the first place.

Discount Rates and Inflation

A couple of suggestions can be made for handling inflation. One is to adjust the discount rate to include the manager's estimates of inflation. Cash flows for future years should also be adjusted to reflect the effects of inflation. For example, if it is expected inflation will raise a firm's hurdle rate from 10 to 12 percent, then 12 percent will be the relevant discount factor. If we assume that cash flows were expected to be $10,000 per year, these cash flows would have to be revised upward at roughly 2 percent compounded yearly.

A second suggestion is to keep both the cash flows and the discount rate in current dollars. Thus, only noninflation-related changes would be reflected in future years' cash flows.

It would be quite usual for operating cash flows to be affected by inflation while items such as the tax effect of depreciation remained constant. Thus, the total cash flows might increase at a different rate than the inflation-adjusted discount rate. An example is shown in Exhibit 16–6. If revenue and cash costs are expected to rise at 2 percent and the nominal discount rate is 10 percent, the following analysis would yield a proper inflation-adjusted present value:

$$PV = \sum_{t=1}^{3} \frac{\left(\begin{array}{c}\$10,000 \text{ operating} \\ \text{cash flows}\end{array}\right)(1.02)^t + \left(\begin{array}{c}\$3,000 \text{ tax-effect} \\ \text{depreciation}\end{array}\right)}{[(1.10)(1.02)]^t}$$

This would yield

$$PV = \frac{(10,000)(1.02) + 3,000}{1.122} + \frac{(10,000)(1.0404) + 3,000}{1.259}$$
$$+ \frac{(10,000)(1.0612) + 3,000}{1.412}$$

$$= 11,765 + 10,647 + 9,640 = \$32,052$$

This can be compared to $32,329 if the flows were not adjusted for inflation. While this example uses a minimal inflation rate, one can easily see the effect that inflation of 10 or 12 percent annually would have. In practice, the nominal rate and inflation adjustment are often just added together, since little is gained in precision by the multiplication. Thus, if an unadjusted rate is 9 percent and inflation is expected to be 8 percent, a 17 percent discount rate is used instead of 17.72 percent (1.09 times 1.08).

These methods are fairly unsophisticated, yet effective. The point is to make the cash flows and the discount rate compatible so that the resultant net present value or internal rate of return reflects real economic effects.

EXHIBIT 16–6
Inflation Example

Assume: Project with three-year life;
       cash flows for the first year as follows:

Revenue	$40,000
Cash costs	20,000
Straight-line depreciation	6,000
Income before taxes	$14,000
Taxes (50%)	7,000
Net income	7,000
Plus: Depreciation	6,000
Cash flow	$13,000

BEHAVIORAL AND QUALITATIVE FACTORS

Our discussion until now has focused on DCF models as a way to maximize the NPV of the firm's future cash flows. As seen in earlier chapters, profitability is just one aspect of an ultimate decision. Some projects are undertaken for health, safety, or other social reasons even if an economic analysis reveals that they will not produce an adequate return. A firm may decide to install pollution-control devices in excess of legal requirements because of a commitment to the social good and a belief that consumers will reward such actions in the marketplace. Certain health and safety investments must be made due to OSHA or other governmental regulations.

It is possible that behavioral issues will affect the choice of alternatives. The most profitable machinery available might have adverse effects on the morale of customers or workers. For example, the equipment used in tunnel-type car washes can frighten customers who drive through the wash. Thus, managers of such an enterprise must look at efficiency of equipment design and the way in which that design affects customer attitudes.

Some new-equipment alternatives might mean laying off some workers while retraining others. Management must consider not only the cash consequences of retraining and severance pay, but also its responsibility in finding other positions for displaced workers.

Problems With Book Losses

One of the most serious behavioral problems in capital budgeting results from the use of book income for evaluating the performance of managers. Lower-level managers are evaluated by upper-level managers, and upper-level managers are evaluated by stockholders and other outside parties. Book income is not the only criterion for evaluation, but it is usually an important one. Although we cover this problem in Chapter 17, it is appropriate to give a single example here.

The president of Argo Products is considering a substantial increase in the capacity of one of the firm's plants. The increased capacity would be used to absorb the production of another plant that would be closed and sold. The data below show that the move would be wise on the basis of discounted cash flows.

Existing Plant

Original cost	$2,400,000
Current book value and tax basis	1,000,000
Current market value	300,000
Annual straight-line depreciation over 5-year remaining useful life	200,000

The proposed addition to another plant would cost $3 million, have a five-year life, no salvage value, and would save $250,000 in cash operating costs the first year, $1,300,000 for each of the next four years. The tax rate is 40 percent and cost of capital is 14 percent. The proposed investment is desirable, as shown below.

Required Investment

Cost of addition	$3,000,000
Less: Selling price of existing plant	(300,000)
Tax saving from sale,	(280,000)
($1,000,000 − $300,000) × 0.40	
Net required investment	$2,420,000

Annual Savings

	Year	
	1	*2–5*
Savings in cash costs	$250,000	$1,300,000
Change in depreciation ($3,000,000/5) − $200,000	400,000	400,000
Change in taxable income	(150,000)	900,000
Increase (decrease) in tax	(60,000)	360,000
Change in net income	($ 90,000)	$ 540,000
Net cash flow	$310,000	$ 940,000
Present value at 14%	$272,000	$2,402,000
Total present value: $2,674,000		

In the year of the investment (year zero) the firm will show a loss on the sale of the existing plant of $700,000, less the tax saving of $280,000, for a net of $420,000. In year 1 the effect on book income of the investment will be a negative $90,000. Years 2 through 5 will show profits from the investment. The president of the firm may be uncomfortable with the proposal because of the adverse effects on book income for the first two years. He might feel that stockholders and creditors could lower their appraisals of the firm, perhaps making it difficult to raise needed funds at reasonable rates. It is not uncommon for managers to be reluctant to take losses in order to show higher profits later on. If the loss is serious enough, the manager could lose his job and never reap the benefits of the decision.

The loss on disposal of the existing plant is irrelevant to the decision. The tax effect of the loss is relevant, but that loss is determined by the tax basis, not the book value per se, as we discussed earlier.

Qualitative Factors and Uncertainty

Classic definitions of risk and uncertainty are that uncertainty exists when one cannot make some reasonable predictions about probabilities of events occurring, while risk assumes that one can make these assessments. Under this definition, some qualitative aspects of decisions can be thought of as factors involving uncertainty. How does having more pollution-abatement equipment than the law requires ultimately affect sales? While some firms saw the effects of consumer boycotts due to environmental considerations in the late 1970s, how can a manager quantify a positive consumer response?

For example, suppose that a company is putting in new equipment that requires a cooling system. Given the current state of technology, an electric cooling system offers the lowest discounted cost. However, experimental solar-powered equipment is available at a higher cost and with less knowledge about its performance. A strict profit-maximization model would opt for the more predictable, lower-cost electric equipment. How does a firm quantify the trade-off between this analysis and considerations of how consumers will act and what the effect on costs may be in ten, twenty, and thirty years? Sensitivity analysis may be useful. Another option might be for managers to decide to use the solar-powered equipment as a matter of policy, overriding the quantitative analysis.

ONGOING EVALUATION

We present several DCF methods for making an original investing decision. An area often overlooked is that of control—the ongoing evaluation of how projects are coming along when compared to both original plans and updated information.

Evaluation

In variance analysis the actual costs are compared to the budget (standard), and deviations are dealt with. In that context, risk is reduced, since managers are dealing with fairly short periods. However, as we have seen, capital-budgeting projects may last for several years. As each year passes, the ultimate cash flows become more and more certain. After four years of a ten-year project, not only does management have actual cash flows from four years in hand, but it also may have a better estimate of what the risk will be over the final six years. Thus, the original project evaluation can be updated. To be consistent, the idea of terminal values can be used. Managers can compare originally expected terminal values with updated estimates.

Several areas can be updated in such a yearly analysis. Marketing surveys can be made more current. Production costs can be predicted with greater certainty. Osteryoung identifies four areas of concern:[19]

1. Cost experience and other accounting information can be updated.
2. General and specific economic information should be revised.
3. If alternative investment opportunities exist, these should be evaluated.
4. Any policy changes that might significantly alter an organization's goals should be looked at to see the effect on specific projects.

These areas can be combined into a systematic evaluation scheme. Obviously, such techniques are necessary to see if projected funds are forthcoming for new projects and to determine if a project should be continued.

Abandonment

An important part of the evaluation procedure is to see whether a project should be abandoned. Have cash flows varied enough that the firm is better off by ceasing operations in that area? That is the abandonment question.

This question can be rephrased into two parts, either of which should signal abandonment. First, what is a project's updated NPV? If it is negative, then other options should be explored. Second, even if a project has a positive NPV, can the firm get an even higher NPV by ceasing one project and beginning another? In times of capital rationing, this is an important consideration, since funds as well as other more optimally used resources might be available if certain areas were abandoned.

SUMMARY

Chapters 15 and 16 have provided an overview of the main topics of concern in dealing with capital budgeting. As accountants, we must know how various models work and what their strengths and weaknesses are. While it is tempting to deal at even greater depth with this area, we leave that to courses in finance.

ASSIGNMENTS

16-1 **"Is Capital Budgeting Now a Losing Battle?"**   Roger Lopata, writing in the September 8, 1980, issue of *Iron Age,* discusses not only the basics of capital

---

[19] Osteryoung, *Capital Budgeting,* p. 241; and Chapter 10 of that book deals extensively with this subject.

budgeting, but also his concern about capital budgeting and today's environment:

> If capital budgeting is a game, it is one played in deadly earnest. In this game, losing a turn or getting sent back five squares can cost a company its profits and its managers their job.
>
> And the game isn't getting any easier these days. In fact, what financial planners spent so many years turning from seat of the pants judgements into a highly formalized and reputedly scientific process may run into hard times in the future. And some corporations may turn back to the simpler planning techniques of days gone by.
>
> For companies that have worked long hard years trying to develop a planning process that includes capital budgeting in some form of expenditure analysis, a whole new series of ugly problems has raised its head.
>
> It's not time to junk the concept yet, but most firms agree that the current climate of economic volatility calls for a more adaptable and dynamic planning process.
>
> In technical terms of economics, the heart of the problem facing today's capital planner is the exogenous variable, really just another way of saying a surprise. The problem is the surprises, the exogenous variables, seem to be coming a lot faster these days.

Required: The material on capital budgeting in this text presents a series of techniques for dealing with capital budgeting decisions. Are these techniques obsolete, given today's economic and political climate? How would you respond to the above remarks by Mr. Lopata?

16–2   Verifying Exhibit 16–2

Required: Using the data leading up to Exhibit 16–2, calculate the net present values if the project lasts ten years and if it lasts eleven years. Show all your work.

16–3   Leasing

Required: Consider the firm outlined in Exhibit 16–5. If it has sufficient reason to believe that current operating results combined with past losses will yield no income taxes due in the next five years, calculate the effective interest rate of the lease.

16–4   Replacement Decision.   The Worthington Manufacturing Company owns a machine with the following characteristics:

Current market value	$30,000
Net book value (equals tax basis)	20,000
Remaining useful life	5 years
Capacity in units of output	14,000
Fixed cash operating costs	$18,000/year
Annual depreciation	$4,000

The product made on the machine sells for $5 and has variable costs of $2. The sales manager of the firm believes that he could sell 20,000 units per year at $5 if the firm had more capacity.

A new machine with a capacity of 22,000 units per year is available. Data follow.

Cost	$60,000
Fixed cash operating costs	$24,000/year
Useful life	5 years

Neither machine would have any salvage value at the end of five years. The firm uses straight-line depreciation for both tax and book purposes. The tax rate is 40 percent and cost of capital is 20 percent.

Required: Determine whether the firm should replace the existing machine with the new one.

16–5 **Reinvestment of Funds.** The Robin Corporation is considering two new pieces of equipment to replace an existing manufacturing process. The existing process is labor intensive and, since the equipment is getting old, maintenance costs are rising and both quality and efficiency are suffering. The production manager working with the cost accounting staff has narrowed possible new equipment purchases to machines from Gray, Inc., and from Leah Company. Fred Lyon, the production manager, has written the following memo to Walter Reid, manufacturing vice-president:

TO: Walter Reid, Manufacturing Vice-President
FROM: Fred Lyon, Production
SUBJECT: Replacement Equipment

As we have discussed, I am sending you this memo to summarize the costs and benefits from purchasing equipment from Gray or Leah. Either piece of equipment will last about five years and will produce equally high-quality products. The net cash flows (after all tax considerations) comparing each of these pieces to our existing equipment is as follows:

	Gray	Leah
Net investment	$130,000	$130,000
Annual net savings (5 years)	36,510	35,000
Expected net salvage value	0	9,695

Not only am I indifferent between the two from a production point of view, but also feel we are indifferent financially since both yield an identical 12½% internal rate of return.

Required:

1. Verify that the IRR of both projects is about 12½ percent.

2. If the firm has a hurdle rate of 10 percent, what is the NPV of each project? Which project would you choose and why?

3. If it is possible for Robin's managers to reinvest funds at 15 percent, which alternative would you choose and why?

16-6   Basic Replacement Decision.   The controller of Tantrum Enterprises wants to know whether it would be advantageous to replace a current piece of machinery. The current machine was purchased for $400,000 ten years ago and is expected to last another ten years. Depreciation was set up on a sixteen-year basis at purchase. Current operating costs for labor, material, and variable overhead are $240,000 annually. If the old machine were sold now, the firm would get $100,000. It is expected that if it were sold in another ten years, it would bring $20,000.

A manufacturer has offered Tantrum new pieces of equipment costing a total of $750,000. Of this amount, about $500,000 qualifies for a 10 percent investment tax credit. The expected life of the new equipment is ten years and there is no expected salvage value. Operating costs are expected to be $150,000 in the first year and $100,000 per year thereafter.

The firm uses straight-line depreciation and a hurdle rate of 15 percent. Assume all cash flows occur at the end of each period. The tax rate is 40 percent.

Required:

1. Using an incremental analysis, compare the cash flows of the new machines with those of the old.

2. Calculate the net present value of these differences and make a recommendation to management.

16-7   Internal Rate of Return.   Beryl Products is considering two pieces of machinery. The first machine costs $50,000 more than the second machine does. During the two-year life of these two alternatives, the first machine has a $155,000 additional cash flow in year 1 and a $110,000 lower cash flow in year 2, compared with the second machine. All cash flows occur at year end.

Required:

1. Which machine should be purchased if the relevant discount rate is 8 percent? 15 percent? 125 percent?

2. Which machine should be purchased if evaluated using IRR?

16-8   Investing and Financing.   Doe Manufacturing has an investment opportunity to embark on a project where yearly revenues for five years are expected to be $4,000 and operating costs $1,048. The equipment costs $10,000, and straight-line depreciation will be used for book and tax purposes. No salvage value is expected at the end of the project's life. The corporation has a 40 percent marginal tax rate and a 10 percent cost of capital. The equipment manufacturer has offered a delayed payment plan of $5,605 per year at the end of the first and second years. Assume all cash flows take place at the end of each year. There will be no changes in working capital.

Required: Should Doe Manufacturing invest in this project? If not, why not? If so, why—and how should this project be financed?

16-9 Capital-Budgeting Criteria. The president of the Crowlton Company is considering three investment opportunities, which are summarized below (in thousands of dollars):

	A	B	C
Investment	$2,500	$9,745	$6,645
Cash inflows, net:			
Year 1	0	1,000	3,000
Year 2	0	2,000	4,000
Year 3	0	3,000	1,000
Year 4	0	7,000	1,000
Year 5	8,650	6,000	0

The firm's cost of capital is 15 percent. The IRRs of the projects are: project A, 28 percent; project B, 20 percent; project C, 17 percent.

Required: Assuming that the projects are mutually exclusive, which one would you pick? Which one would be your second choice?

16-10 Alternate Uses of Facilities (AICPA). Marshall Manufacturing, Inc., has produced two products, Z and P, at its Richmond plant for several years. Management is going to drop P from the product line as of January 1, 19X3. Marshall manufactures and sells 50,000 units of Z annually, and this is not expected to change. Unit material and direct labor costs are $12 and $7, respectively.

The Richmond plant is in a leased building; the lease expires December 31, 19X7. Annual rent is $75,000. The lease provides Marshall the right of sublet; all nonremovable leasehold improvements revert to the lessor. At the end of the lease, Marshall intends to close the plant and scrap all equipment.

P has been produced on two assembly lines, which occupy 25 percent of the plant. The assembly lines will have a book value of $135,000 and a remaining useful life of seven years as of January 1, 19X3. This is the only portion of the plant available for alternative uses.

Marshall uses one unit of D to produce one unit of Z. D is purchased under a contract requiring a minimum annual purchase of 5,000 units. The contract expires December 31, 19X7. A list of D unit costs follows:

Annual Purchases (units)	Unit Cost
5,000– 7,499	$2.00
7,500– 19,999	1.95
20,000– 34,999	1.80
35,000– 99,999	1.65
100,000–250,000	1.35

Alternatives are available for using the space previously used to manufacture P. Some may be used in combination. All can be implemented by January 1, 19X3. Should no action be taken, the plant is expected to operate profitably, and manufacturing overhead is not expected to differ materially from past years when P was manufactured. Following are the alternatives:

1. Sell the two P assembly lines for $70,000. The purchaser will buy only if he can acquire the equipment from both lines. The purchaser will pay all removal and transportation costs.

2. Sublet the floor space for an annual rental of $12,100. The lease will require that the equipment be removed (cost nominal) and leasehold improvements costing $38,000 be installed. Indirect costs are expected to increase $3,500 annually as a result of the sublease.

3. Convert one or both P assembly lines to produce D at a cost of $45,500 for each line. The converted lines will have remaining useful life of ten years. Each modified line can produce any number of units of D up to a maximum of 37,000 units at a unit direct material and direct labor cost of $0.10 and $0.25, respectively. Annual manufacturing overhead is expected to increase from $550,000 to $562,000 if one line is converted and to $566,000 if both lines are converted. The marginal tax rate is 40 percent. The relevant discount rate is 15 percent. Straight-line depreciation is used.

Required: Prepare a schedule to analyze the best utilization of the following alternatives for the four years ended December 31, 19X7.

1. Continue to purchase D; sell equipment; rent space.
2. Continue to purchase D; sell equipment.
3. Produce D on two assembly lines; purchase D as needed.
4. Produce D on one assembly line; purchase D as needed.

16–11 Reinvestment Assumptions.   T. Young Freud was analyzing an investment decision for his company. A new product was being considered. Equipment costing $700,000 would have to be bought. The product was expected to have a ten-year economic life and the equipment could be depreciated over a ten-year life as well, using straight-line depreciation. Intermediate receipts during the life of the project were expected to be reinvested at an average of 12 percent. It was expected that after-tax cash flows (not including the tax effect from depreciation) would be $100,000, assuming a 40 percent tax rate.

Required: Can Freud distribute $85,000 per year to stockholders as dividends and still pay off a loan for $700,000 after ten years? [*Hint:* Freud uses Adler's method to solve this problem.]

16–12 **Sensitivity Analysis.** The management of Stump Iron Works, a company involved in fabricating metal parts, was investigating a new stamping process. Jack Stump, company vice-president of production, estimated that the entire installed cost of this new process would be $100,000. He also knew that the company would have to experiment with this equipment, and he expected to spend $20,000, $10,000 and $5,000, respectively, for research in each of the first three years of the project. Stump also estimated that the net increase in cash balances, inventory, and receivables offset by expected payables would be $30,000 immediately and $20,000 in the first year. Stump uses straight-line depreciation for both financial accounting and tax purposes. The relevant marginal tax rate is 40 percent, and Stump requires that projects earn at least 15 percent after taxes. Assume all cash flows occur at the end of each period.

Required:

1. If annual fixed costs are $60,000 and the project has a five-year life span, what annual total pretax contribution margin is needed to break even on a present-value basis?

2. If the pretax contribution margin is estimated to be $130,000 annually and the fixed costs, working-capital needs, original investment, and life remain as stated above, what is the average annual amount of research funds that Stump could expend in years 1 through 3 and still have a positive net present value of $10,000?

3. If the pretax contribution margin is estimated to be $130,000 annually and the fixed costs, original investment, and research estimates are as in item 1, how long would the project have to last in order to yield at least a $30,000 positive net present value? Assume for this item that the project would require *no* changes in working capital. Also assume the asset would be fully depreciated over its economic life.

4. Discuss the use of sensitivity analysis in capital-budgeting decisions. Use examples from this assignment to illustrate your points.

16–13 **Discounted Payback.** Gene Etics, the manager of Equine Products, has decided to use sensitivity analysis coupled with discounted cash flow techniques in evaluating a new product. He plans to do some market research and to estimate the probabilities of this project's lasting various lengths of time. If he knows how sensitive various factors are to the time dimension, he can use this information in making a decision about the project.

The project involves providing a new way to supply minerals to horses. The entire concept includes manufacturing a disposable mineral feeder and two different mineral blocks—one for calcium and one for phosphorus.

He expects that new manufacturing equipment will have to be bought totaling $500,000. The physical life of the equipment is fifteen years, but IRS regulations will allow a ten-year SYD depreciation. This ten-year life seems a more reasonable maximum period to deal with all cash flows. This is special-purpose machinery and would have minimal salvage value if any. There would be an initial advertising budget in the first year of $100,000, and current plans are for $40,000 per year thereafter. It is expected that inventories and receivables would build which, when offset against increased payables, would result in the following changes in working capital:

Year	Change in Working Capital
0	$200,000
1	150,000

The firm has a 40 percent marginal tax rate. Owing to the riskiness of this project, management wants to use an 18 percent discount rate. Annual fixed costs of production are expected to be $500,000, not including depreciation.

Required: Model this as a project with a potential ten-year life span. Assume all cash flows are at the end of each period.

1. What total yearly pretax contribution margin is needed to break even on a net-present-value basis?

2. If operating cash flows before taxes and the tax effect of depreciation are $400,000 per year, how many full years would it take to break even on a net-present-value basis? For ease, assume straight-line depreciation.

16–14   Leasing, Unequal Lives.   The president of Jasmin Corporation is evaluating two new projects that have been proposed by the director of manufacturing. Owing to financial and space constraints, only one project will be accepted, if any.

One project is to produce a solar-powered water heater. Various equipment would have to be purchased to fabricate the solar panels and heater system. The total installed price being quoted by the manufacturers of this equipment is $3,500,000. It is expected that completed heater systems would sell for $2,500 each for a 50-gallon model and $3,500 for a 100-gallon model. Marketing research has led the sales department to believe that the sales mix will be about three-fourths 50-gallon units and one-fourth 100 gallon units. They think that they will sell a total of 1,000 units the first year, 2,000 the second year, and that sales will grow by 400 units a year thereafter. Manufacturing costs are expected to be as follows:

	50-Gallon System	100-Gallon System
Materials	$ 800	$1,400
Labor	400	400
Variable overhead	300	300
	$1,500	$2,100

Fixed manufacturing overhead and additional sales costs are $500,000 (not including any depreciation) and are expected to increase by 15 percent per year.

It is expected that the technology for solar heaters will remain stable for at least seven years. Working-capital requirements are estimated to be $500,000 and will be fully recoverable at the end of the life of the project.

The other proposal is to make projection television sets. The price for these sets is $3,000 each. Management is proposing that almost all the sophisticated parts of the set be made internally, while the cabinet would be purchased from an outside source. This venture is expected to last ten years. Investment in equipment will be $3 million. Costs of starting up in year 1 will be $300,000 (fully deductible), and $200,000 in additional working capital (fully recoverable) is expected to be needed. Variable costs of manufacturing and buying components are expected to be $1,800 per unit. Fixed manufacturing costs (excluding depreciation) will be $400,000 per year. Advertising and sales costs are planned at $300,000 to begin with and will increase proportionally to sales. Sales volume is expected to start at 1,500 units and increase at 10 percent per year (rounded to the nearest 50 units).

The hurdle rate that management has set is 20 percent after taxes. Prices and variable costs are to be kept stable per unit for this analysis. The marginal tax rate is 40 percent. No equipment is expected to have a salvage value. The investment tax credit would not apply to either project. Straight-line depreciation is used for financial and tax purposes.

Required:

1. Evaluate the water-heater system based on its expected life.

2. Evaluate the television project based on its expected life.

3. Since one project is expected to last three years longer than the other, state how you would choose between them. What information would you need?

4. The management of Jasmin has been offered 18 percent financing from its major bank and has been offered a lease by the manufacturer of the equipment for the television project as follows: ten equal payments of $611,500 to be paid at the beginning of each year. Assuming that these are the only two viable financing alternatives open at this time, which should be chosen if management decides to invest in the television project?

16–15 **The Abandonment Option.** It has been suggested that the decision-tree framework for dealing with probabilities can be used in dealing with the abandonment option. When managers assess a project, it is likely they have an idea about possible cash flows and the probabilities of achieving these flows. In the decision-tree framework of Chapter 4, we dealt with events and cash flows occurring in the *same* time period. Let us extend this analysis to multiple time periods. We have a single decision to make: do we invest in a project? The events are cash flows in each year of a project's life.

One new aspect is the idea of an *abandonment value*. An easy way to think of this concept is to think of a plant nursery built on land in a suburb to a city. If you abandon the nursery business, the land itself has a sales value. When the current net sales value is greater than the net present value of the future flows from operating the business, it may be a good idea to abandon the business and sell the land.

Assume the Hiburgler Company has an opportunity to invest $11,000 in a project expected to last three years. Cash flows and the probabilities that management thinks are associated with them appear opposite. The relevant discount rate is 10 percent.

Required:

1. Draw these cash flows and probabilities in a full decision-tree framework. To do this, you need to calculate joint probabilities and conditional values discounted at 10 percent. For example, the probability that cash flows in year 1 $(C_1) = \$2,000$, $C_2 = \$1,000$, and $C_3 = \$600$ is $.7 \times .2 \times .6 = .084$. The conditional value (present value at 10 percent) associated with that same chain of cash flows is $(\$2,000)(.9091) + (\$1,000)(.8264) + (\$600)(.7513) = \$3,095$. You need to calculate the joint probabilities and conditional values for the other eleven branches. Round all figures to the nearest dollar.

2. Using the joint probabilities and conditional values, calculate an expected net present value.

3. Without considering any abandonment values, you should have come to a few-hundred-dollar *negative* NPV in item 2. Now assume that if you abandon the project at the *end* of year 1, you can receive a net abandonment value of $5,000. In other words, you will receive a cash flow at the end of year 1 of either $2,000 or $4,000 *and* an additional $5,000 if the project is abandoned at that time. Use the decision-tree framework and see if it is wise to abandon the project after one year. What you are doing is seeing whether the expected present value of cash flows at the *end* of year 1 is greater than $5,000. Thus, you will be repeating the same methodology you used in items 1 and 2 *except* you will be dealing only with a two-year time frame (years 2 and 3), with the year 1 cash flow not considered. You should see that you do *not* have to do this for the whole bottom half of the tree where $C_1 = \$4,000$, since all the NPVs in that half are positive. Thus, just do it assuming $C_1 = \$2,000$.

Net Cash Flows

Year 1		Year 2		Year 3	
Cash Flow	Probability	Cash Flow	Probability	Cash Flow	Probability
				$600	.6
		$1,000	.2		
				1,000	.4
				3,000	.5
$2,000	.7	2,000	.5		
				5,000	.5
				5,000	.4
		4,000	.3		
				7,000	.6
				6,000	.6
		5,00ι	.2		
				8,000	.4
				10,000	.5
4,000	.3	8,000	.5		
				13,000	.5
				14,000	.4
		10,000	.3		
				18,000	.6

4. In item 3, the expected PV of the cash flows will be greater than
$5,000. Thus, you would not want to abandon after one year. Now
assume that the abandonment value at the end of two years is $4,000.
Look at a one-year time frame (year 3) given year 2 cash flows of
$1,000, $2,000, or $4,000 and see whether the expected value of year
3 flows is greater or less than $4,000.

5. In item 4, you should find out that if C_2 = $1,000 or $2,000, it would
be better to abandon the project at the end of year 2 rather than
continuing on into year 3. Amend the decision tree in items 1 and 2
by including this information. To redraw the tree, you will be dealing with the following cash flows:

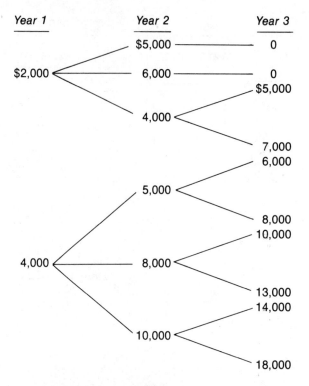

	Year 1	Year 2	Year 3

Put in the proper discounted conditional values and joint probabilities. Calculate a new expected NPV, given the inclusion of the abandonment option.

16–16 **Capital-Budgeting Criteria.** The capital-budgeting manual of the Turnburry Manufacturing Company contains the following statements.

Investments will be defined in one of the following ways: new product or new market; expansion of capacity for existing products; replacement; and required by government regulation. The criteria for acceptance of investments in each category follow.

New product or market. These investments are more speculative than the others and so must show higher returns. Any investment in this category must show an internal rate of return (IRR) of 18 percent after taxes and a payback period of no more than eight years. Cash flows to be included at the end of the eighth year for determining whether the payback criterion is met should include a 90 percent recovery of working-capital investment and recovery of 50 percent of the net book value of fixed assets, adjusted for appropriate tax effects.

When fixed assets have unequal lives, the useful life calculation shall be the weighted average. For example, if an investment of $400,000 has a ten-year life and another investment of $600,000 a fifteen-year life, the weighted average is thirteen years (40% × 10) + (60% × 15).

Expansion. These investments must show an IRR of 15 percent after taxes, along with a payback period not to exceed three fourths of the useful life of the fixed investment.

Replacement. Investments that replace existing facilities must earn a 12 percent after-tax IRR. There is no payback criterion.

Government-required investments. Any investment required by governmental regulation will be made. Managers should determine the least-cost method of complying with the regulation, as measured by the present value of the total required outlay, both investment and operating costs, using an 18 percent discount rate.

Additional criteria. The IRR and payback criteria given above assume that the investment is special-purpose, so that the machinery, equipment, and buildings could not be converted to general use. Where the investment is in general-purpose assets, the IRR for each category should be reduced by two percentage points and the payback period increased by two years (if applicable). These additional criteria reflect the lower risk associated with general-purpose investments.

Required: Assume that the cost of capital for the firm is about 13 percent. Discuss the criteria the firm uses, making sure to comment about the likely purpose of each criterion and whether it should accomplish the purpose. (For example, why include a payback criterion?) What problems do you see in using these criteria?

16–17 **Eliciting Information and Capital Expenditure Analysis.**[20] Junior Executive has been asked to determine whether his company should trade in its old airplane and purchase a new one. The company manufactures and sells highly specialized, complex machinery, which often requires extensive technical selling, installation, and subsequent service. The airplane is used in the business for two purposes: (1) to transport company executives to plants of potential new customers or to bring the executives of potential customers to the company's home office for sales demonstrations, and (2) to provide quick troubleshooting and repair service to customers.

The problem involves whether to replace a single-engine Arrow airplane with a twin-engine Navajo model. The company is considering the larger plane for two reasons. First, its greater seating capacity will allow more people to be transported for sales demonstrations. Second, its ability to fly in adverse weather conditions will result in even faster repair service, thus enhancing the firm's reputation for reliable service. The president of the company finds it impossible to quantify the increased value of the larger airplane. Instead he has asked Junior to estimate by how much the new airplane would have to increase yearly sales to economically justify its purchase. Junior also is supposed to determine whether to lease the new airplane or to buy it outright, if the company decides to acquire it.

The company is using a four-seat Arrow purchased a year ago on January

[20] Earl A. Spiller, Jr., "Capital Expenditure Analysis: An Incident Process Case," *The Accounting Review*, 56:1 (January 1981), 158–165.

5, 19X9, at a cost of $58,000. The airplane was flown more than 1,000 hours during the first year. It is common practice to have an extensive engine overhaul or exchange every 1,600 to 1,700 flying hours with this type of aircraft. Because the Arrow will be scheduled within the year for this overhaul, the president thinks that now is the ideal time to consider buying a larger plane.

The larger aircraft being considered is a six-seat Navajo. The dealer has offered the Navajo at a cash price of $294,500. The Arrow would be sold for $42,000 as a used airplane. Alternatively, the dealer will buy the Arrow for $50,000 and lease the Navajo to the company under a six-year noncancellable lease at a monthly rental of $5,200. The rental fee covers only the basic use of the aircraft and property taxes.

Junior has asked you to help him. He has access to all company data but has trouble deciding which data are relevant or how to formulate the decision framework. He must report to the president by January 10, 19Y0.

Required: You will be a member of a team that will consult with Junior Executive. Your instructor will give you more complete instructions. You will be meeting with Junior Executive and submitting questions to him. The results of your analysis will be a complete written report to management recommending actions and supporting these recommendations with appropriate financial and other data.

16–18   **Uncertainty.**   Anthrax Company is considering two mutually exclusive projects. After estimating the cash flows of each and calculating the present values based on appropriate discount rates, they determined the following approximate probability distributions of net present values:

Project 1		Project 2	
Probability	NPV	Probability	NPV
.3	$30,000	.3	$ 1,000
.4	40,000	.4	35,000
.3	50,000	.3	70,000

Required:

1. What is the expected NPV and the standard deviation for each project?
2. Which is preferable and why?

16–19   **Uncertainty—Conditional Probabilities.**   The SMU Division of Diel Products is evaluating a new project that has an initial cost of $8,000. The relevant discount rate is 8 percent. Cash flows in year 2 of this project are dependent on flows received in year 1. Management has assessed both marginal and conditional probabilities for cash flows for each year. These are presented below with various cash flows.

	Year 1		Year 2	
Marginal Probability	Net Cash Flows		Conditional Probability	Net Cash Flows
			.1	$3,000
.2	$4,000		.7	4,000
			.2	5,000
			.3	4,000
.6	$5,000		.4	5,000
			.3	6,000
			.3	5,000
.2	$6,000		.6	6,000
			.1	7,000

Required:

1. Use this information to calculate an expected net present value for this project. [*Hint:* Find the expected present value for each year separately, using the marginal probabilities for year 1 and joint probabilities for year 2.]

2. Find the standard deviation as follows. Calculate the nine possible NPVs. Use the answer from item 1 as your expected value and use the joint probabilities to weight the squared differences.

3. Comment on this method of quantifying risk, and evaluate this project.

16–20 Capital Rationing—Integer Programming. The Amorsh Company has the following cash constraints: they can invest $50,000 now, $40,000 in a year, and $30,000 in two years. It will not be possible to transfer funds between years. Management is evaluating four projects with the following characteristics:

			Net Cash Flows	
Project	Net Present Value	Original Investment	Year 1	Year 2
1	$4,000	$12,000	$ 6,000	$12,760
2	5,000	10,000	40,000	−25,850
3	3,000	18,000	−18,000	45,210
4	6,000	36,000	24,200	24,200

Required: Using the techniques described in Chapter 4 on linear programming, set up this rationing problem with an objective function and appropriate constraints. (Do not actually solve the problem.)

16–21 Leasing. The managers of Choi Products are evaluating how to finance a project. Using a hurdle rate of 15 percent, the project has a positive net present value. Financing alternatives include a loan with 16⅔ percent interest on the unpaid balance or a lease with annual payments of $14,500 at the beginning of each year. The project has an investment cost of $40,000, none of which is subject to an investment tax credit. The project will last four years and can be depreciated using SYD. Choi's marginal tax rate is 40 percent. There is no anticipated salvage value. Maintenance is expected to be $1,000 per year, a cost that would be avoided under the provisions of the lease.

Required: Which form of financing should management choose?

SELECTED REFERENCES

Clark, John J., Thomas J. Hindelang, and Robert E. Pritchard, *Capital Budgeting: Planning and Control of Capital Expenditures*. Englewood Cliffs, N.J.: Prentice-Hall, Inc., 1979.

Copeland, Thomas E., and J. Fred Weston, *Financial Theory and Corporate Policy*. Reading, Mass.: Addison-Wesley Publishing Company, Inc., 1979.

Dudley, Carlton L., Jr., "A Note on Reinvestment Assumptions in Choosing Between Net Present Value and Internal Rate of Return," *The Journal of Finance*, 27:4 (September 1972), 907–915.

Henderson, Glenn V., Jr., and Andrew H. Barnett, "Breakeven Present Value: A Pragmatic Approach to Capital Budgeting Under Risk and Uncertainty," *Management Accounting*, January 1978, 49–52.

Osteryoung, Jerome S., *Capital Budgeting: Long-Term Asset Selection*. Columbus, Ohio: Grid, Inc., 1979.

Schall, Lawrence D., Gary L. Sundem, and William R. Geijsbeek, Jr., "Survey and Analysis of Capital Budgeting Methods," *The Journal of Finance*, 33:1 (March 1978), 281–87.

Solomon, E., *The Management of Corporate Capital*. New York: The Free Press, 1959.

Divisional Performance Evaluation

Part 4

Decentralization: Measures of Performance

Chapter 17

Earlier chapters developed the idea of a responsibility center and described the role of accounting information in planning and controlling the operations of some types of centers, particularly cost centers. Recall that a cost center is an activity that incurs costs but does not produce revenues. Most departments in a factory are cost centers, as are most administrative departments such as finance, personnel, data processing, and legal services. Chapters 7 and 8 examined some of the ways of evaluating cost centers, particularly through the use of standard costs. Chapters 13 and 14 examined budgeting, which is used to plan and control the activities of various segments of the firm.

This chapter and the next go beyond budgeting and standard costs, looking at the performance-evaluation aspect of control. The material ties into various planning phases, including operational and capital budgets. In addition, the perspective of performance evaluation involves not only the various segments of the firm, but also the managers of those segments. These chapters look at profit centers and investment centers within the framework of a decentralized company.

A **profit center** is a unit that controls both revenues and costs. An **investment center** is one that controls revenues, costs, and investment. There are very few pure profit centers: almost any unit that controls revenues and costs requires assets ranging from receivables through plant and equipment. Units that sell services, such as consulting firms or law firms, could have relatively little investment, but most profit-seeking activities require capital investment. In practice, the term profit center is often used to describe both profit centers and investment centers. No harm arises from this usage so long as people know what type of center they mean.

THE DECENTRALIZED STRUCTURE

A **decentralized firm** is one where individual managers have a great deal of authority and autonomy: they are free, within some limits, to make important decisions such as product mix, selling prices, and sources of supply for materials and components. In contrast, a **centralized firm** is one where individual managers are constrained by upper-level management. Managers in highly centralized firms are not permitted to make many decisions: they must follow directives.

Let us consider an example. Figure 17–1 shows partial, simplified organization charts of two hypothetical steel companies. Notice that both firms are vertically integrated, controlling virtually the entire process from the mining of iron ore and coal through the making of various types of steel through the marketing to customers.

The charts in Figure 17–1 show that both firms are organized into divisions and that each division has subunits, individual mines, plants, and sales offices. The organizations differ in the degree of autonomy of the managers of the divisions and subunits within them, although the charts do not necessarily show it. The division managers of the Carnoustie Company are free to deal as they like. The managers of the mining operations may sell ore to the steelmaking division or to outside firms. The managers of the steelmaking division are free to set prices, determine product mix, select suppliers (that is, buy from the firm's mining divisions or from mines owned by other companies), and, to a degree, operate as if they were separate companies.

The degrees of autonomy may vary within the divisions of Carnoustie. The mining division may give a good bit of autonomy to the manager of each mine, while the steelmaking division might give little autonomy to plant managers. The opposite could also be true. The point is that a firm could make varying uses of decentralization at different levels, or in different divisions at about the same level.

The general level of autonomy at Carnoustie can be compared to that in Devon Company, where the managers are not so autonomous. Central headquarters dictates whether the steelmaking division may buy from outsiders and whether the mines can sell to outsiders. Prices, product mix, and other factors are also determined by central management. Thus, the role of a division manager in the Devon Company is to carry out the orders of central headquarters. The Carnoustie Company is highly decentralized, while the Devon Company is highly centralized.

One way to express the difference between the two firms is to say that the divisional managers of the Carnoustie Company, and some managers of subunits within divisions, have **profit responsibility**. They are responsible for generating revenues, controlling costs, and earning a satisfactory return on the capital invested in their operations. The managers of the Devon Company do not have profit responsibility. The steel fabricating plant man-

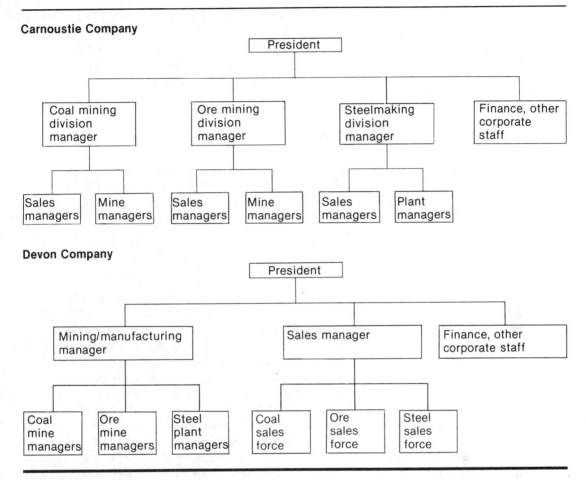

FIGURE 17–1
Alternative Organizational Structures

ager has no control over sources of supply, mix, or selling prices. All these responsibilities have been assumed by corporate top management.

For our purposes, the most important consideration that arises from differing responsibilities is the evaluation of managerial performance. The managers of highly autonomous units may be evaluated by many measures, including profits and return on investment. The managers of units with little autonomy must be evaluated by different measures, including meeting sales quotas or meeting budgeted production goals within budgeted costs. Standard costs and variance analyses are ways to evaluate managers of cost centers.

No firm is likely to give a divisional manager complete autonomy. In all firms, for example, central headquarters will normally control long-term financing and capital expenditures. Even where divisions issue long-term debt or common stock (if they are separate corporations), the decisions to do so come from top management as a part of overall corporate financing strategies. In addition, in even the most decentralized firms, major capital expenditures are usually approved by central headquarters.

BENEFITS OF DECENTRALIZATION

Proponents of decentralization point to a number of advantages, not all of which can be achieved by all firms, since the degree of benefit depends on the operating characteristics of the firm. It would seem that the benefits are substantial, because the trend in recent years has been to greater decentralization.[1]

Diversity of Operations

One advantage arises from the size and complexity of modern firms, especially diversified firms. Diversified firms operate in many lines of business, sometimes related, sometimes not. A steel company that operates coal mines is extending its control over the supply of raw materials; a steel company that owns a chain of retail stores is operating in a quite different line of business—one that has little, if anything, to do with the steel business. Conglomerates—firms that have divisions or subsidiaries in a wide range of businesses—are the most prominent example of diversification.

It would be almost impossible for central headquarters to run 15 to 25 different types of businesses. The managers of each division would be expected to have the expertise to run their particular operations, whereas central headquarters could not be expected to have the necessary specialized knowledge.

Timeliness of Decisions

Spreading the authority to make decisions throughout the firm is likely to lead to better and quicker decisions. The managers of the individual divisions are closer to the situation and are in a much better position to evaluate circumstances and act quickly. If, for example, a division manager had to obtain permission to make a price concession in order to secure a large order, he might not receive it until the customer had gone elsewhere and the sale had been lost. Whether accepting the sale at a reduced price would be wise is important, but the presumption must be that the division manager is in the best position to make that determination.

---

[1] McGregor, cited on page 516 in Chapter 13, and many others have argued for greater decentralization as a better way to manage.

Motivation

Behavioral research has indicated that workers and managers tend to have higher morale and higher productivity when their tasks are broadened. Workers who perform simple repetitive chores such as those done on assembly lines tend to be dissatisfied. The term **job enlargement** is used to describe the broadening of responsibility and authority. In the same way, managers who are nearly autonomous are likely to be better motivated than those whose actions are severely constrained.[2]

The broad responsibility that accompanies decentralization provides good training for future corporate managers, since managers who have been responsible for profit, rather than just revenues or costs, have acquired a more comprehensive outlook. Divisional managers with high degrees of autonomy provide a good pool of talent for the top slots in a firm.

Segment Performance Evaluation

Another positive aspect of decentralization is the aid it offers in the evaluation of various divisions and division managers. In a centralized company, it is often difficult to assess how well each part of the firm is performing. For example, if the wholesale and retail divisions of a marketing firm are combined, it is difficult for top management to evaluate the profitability of each segment and the performance of managers. This makes it difficult to give specific feedback regarding performance and to decide where corrective actions need to be taken.

Decentralization, however, means that a manager who has profit responsibility can be better evaluated. Part of this process is the selling of goods or services among the decentralized divisions. The full issue of transfer pricing with its economic, accounting, and behavioral consequences is discussed in Chapter 18.

Service Centers

In some firms, service centers such as maintenance, data processing, legal services, and others are structured as either profit or investment centers. The service department costs would not be allocated to user divisions and departments. Instead, the service department would charge a price for the service. The user would be charged with the price of services received, and the providing department would be credited with revenue.

The appeal of making service centers into profit centers is that it might help to spot poorly run service centers. If operating managers do not use the

---

[2] The two theories of motivation discussed in Chapter 13, expectancy theory and the need hierarchy theory, support the position that decentralization provides greater motivation to managers.

firm's data processing facilities because they can buy the services elsewhere more cheaply, it might be a sign that the data processing department is not well run. Measures of performance of service departments that do not act as profit centers are limited, as a rule, to measures of work done, not the value of work done. The data processing department manager might argue that he is performing well because his department processed 30 million transactions in the past month. The unanswered questions are whether all of those transactions should have been processed and at what cost. If the department charged users for the service and showed a reasonable profit at prices approximating market prices for the same service, it would indicate that the department was operating reasonably well. This entire area is fraught with problems, and it is rash to make broad generalizations.

PROBLEMS WITH DECENTRALIZATION

Decentralization is not a cure-all. It requires a large number of very competent managers who can be trusted by central management. Complete decentralization is not always feasible or cost effective. Some activities and services can be performed much more efficiently if they are centralized. Most firms centralize research and development, legal services, data processing, and cash management. The financial functions relating to long-term debt and common stock are administered centrally. To the extent that the first activities are decentralized, the autonomy of the division increases, but the cost would probably be higher than if they were centralized. Duplication of effort may be very costly.

The chief problem of decentralization is probably motivational: specifically, the achievement of goal congruence. How does central management ensure that division managers will work in the best interests of the firm? When managers are evaluated on the basis of performance of their own operations, they will naturally take actions that benefit themselves. Under some circumstances the actions that divisional managers take to benefit their divisions will also benefit the firm. Frequently, however, the action of one divisional manager will benefit his own division but harm the firm as a whole. When managers act in ways that benefit themselves, while harming the firm, they are said to be acting in a *suboptimal* or *dysfunctional* way. The literature is replete with references to such behavior, and we shall see some examples soon.

If divisions within a particular firm are highly interdependent, dealing primarily with one another, it is very difficult to decentralize profit responsibility. If for reasons of technological dependence or management strategy the divisions are not free to deal with outsiders, they probably should not be profit centers. The reason is that the essence of profit centers is independence: if the manager is not free to operate reasonably independently, it is not possible to evaluate performance by looking at profit. The manager does not have profit responsibility, because he or she does not have autonomy and freedom to deal with other firms.

BASES FOR DECENTRALIZATION

Even when upper-level management has decided to decentralize, it still faces choices. Firms can decentralize in various ways, and which way is best is not always obvious. Most modern firms are also in a more or less constant process of changing. Old markets dry up, new markets open, technological changes occur, and governmental regulations evolve.

For example, a firm in a high-technology business such as semiconductors might start a new division to take over the manufacture and marketing of new products such as LCD (liquid crystal display) digital watches. The justification for starting a new division might be that the firm now deals only with industrial customers and has little experience in the consumer product area. The firm might wish to hire managers who have such experience, and one of the inducements it might offer is great autonomy in the new division.

Firms consolidate divisions for several reasons. Divisions that make competing products might be allowed to go on for some time, but then might be combined to achieve economies of scale in production and marketing. Two or more divisions serving particular geographical areas might be consolidated for similar reasons.

There are several ways in which firms can logically decentralize. The selection of a basis for decentralizing will depend on the characteristics of the firm, the attitudes of upper-level managers, and a host of other factors. Some of the more common bases are discussed below.

Product Lines

This basis would seem to be best where the firm's products are quite different and require different skills and experience. Managers dealing with consumer products such as toothpaste require skills and knowledge quite different from those who deal with structural steel or bulk chemicals. Both technological and marketing differences are involved in these examples.

Product-line decentralization is not usually possible when a single plant makes several different products and product lines. The large amount of joint costs makes it difficult to evaluate each product or product line separately. Unless it is reasonably easy to make such evaluations, it is not advisable to decentralize, because pinpointing responsibility for profit is crucial to evaluating decentralized operations.

Type of Customer

Some firms use classes of customers as the bases for assigning profit responsibility. One investment center might deal exclusively with governmental work, another with commercial work, a third with colleges and universities. This type of classification will most often be used when different types of customers have special needs, so that salespeople, engineers, product designers, and other personnel need expertise of a particular sort in order to compete with other firms.

Geographical Areas

Most multinational firms decentralize by geographical area as well as, perhaps, by product line. Domestic companies might decentralize by region, with regional managers being in charge of all products made and sold in their areas. In some industries, each individual plant is an investment center serving a limited area. This occurs when shipping costs are extremely high or other factors limit the market to a fairly small geographical area.

Technological Similarity

Some investment centers will produce quite different products but use the same basic production process for all of them. An obvious example is in industries where joint products are prevalent. Many chemical processes provide gases used in other industries. A chemical division would therefore also produce and market gases that have no similarity to its chemicals save that they arise from the same process.

A slightly different type of example develops when a production process can be used to make quite different products. Tires, vinyl wallpaper, credit cards, and several other products are all made using the same basic process. Here, the division would be taking advantage of technical expertise to broaden its markets.

MEASURES OF DIVISIONAL PERFORMANCE

Evaluating the performance of a division is not the same thing as evaluating the performance of its manager. Different measures and different standards should be applied in these two types of evaluation. We shall return to this point later, after discussing some of the techniques most commonly used, and misused, for both types of evaluation. At the outset, let us point out that the major considerations in selecting measures of performance are behavioral. Will the measures encourage managers to act in the best interests of the firm (goal congruence) and will they provide a fair and equitable assessment of how well the managers have performed their jobs? If either question is answered negatively, the evaluation system could work against the firm.

Return on Investment (ROI) and
Residual Income (RI)

Return on investment (ROI) is the most commonly used measure of divisional performance.[3] It is defined as income ÷ investment. The two terms, income and investment, may be measured in a variety of ways that we shall consider in a later section. For now, we point out that ROI is a ratio. The use of ratios in analyzing performance has the advantage, and disadvantage, of eliminating the effects of size. Thus, if a firm has two divisions, A and B, with data as shown below, division B is better than division A using the ROI criterion.

	Division A	Division B
Annual divisional income	$1,200,000	$ 300,000
Divisional investment	6,000,000	1,000,000
ROI	20%	30%

Notice that although division B has a much higher ROI than division A, it contributes far less dollar profit to the firm. In contrast to ROI, residual income (RI) focuses on dollars of profit after a charge is assessed for the cost of the investment in the division. RI is given by the formula:

RI = divisional income − (divisional investment × required ROI)

The required rate of return in this calculation would theoretically be cost of capital. In most cases, it will be a cutoff rate based on the firm's overall strategy and objectives. The excess of the divisional income over this "charge" for the use of capital is the residual that the division returns to the firm. For the two divisions in the example above, we obtain the following RIs, assuming that the minimum required return is 15 percent.

	Division A	Division B
Incomes	$1,200,000	$300,000
Less: Required return:		
$6,000,000 × 0.15	900,000	
$1,000,000 × 0.15		150,000
Residual incomes	$ 300,000	$150,000

We see that the picture has changed: using the RI criterion, division A is better than division B because it returns a higher amount to the firm after allowing for the cost of funds invested in the divisions. It is by no means universally true that it is easier to earn higher rates of return by investing smaller amounts, but it tends to be true. As divisions grow, it frequently becomes more difficult to find investments that have ROIs in excess of the current rate. In addition, older divisions have investments made in many prior periods when the firm may have had different profitability objectives. The use of RI specifically addresses the problem that increasing both size and ROI are usually incompatible objectives.

---

[3] See the studies by Mauriel and Anthony and by Reece and Cool cited in the Selected References at the end of the chapter.

The purpose of using RI is to focus attention on the dollar contribution that a division makes to the firm. Using terms from capital budgeting, RI may be viewed as *analogous* to net present value, while ROI may be viewed as *similar* to the internal rate of return. We say analogous and similar because book values are most frequently used to calculate ROI and RI, and book values are not compatible with discounted cash flow measures. But, just as a policy of maximizing the internal rate of return is generally inferior to one of maximizing net present value, a policy of evaluating divisions and managers based on ROI is usually inferior to one based on RI. The major reasons are behavioral, as the illustration below shows.

Illustration. Two divisional managers within the same firm are considering investment proposals. The firm has cost of capital of 15 percent and uses ROI to evaluate performance.

One manager is considering a project that would add $100,000 to divisional income and increase divisional investment by $500,000. Thus, the project has a book ROI of 20 percent. The division manager expects to earn ROI of 26 percent without the investment and so would probably reject it. Acceptance would reduce ROI below the 26 percent expected level—to the detriment of the manager's perceived performance.

The other manager is considering a $500,000 project that would increase divisional profit by $40,000, giving an 8 percent ROI. He expects the division to show an ROI of 4 percent without considering the investment, and so he would probably accept it. The divisional ROI would increase, even though the project would be unwise if it were evaluated using discounted cash flow techniques. The internal rate of return could not be greater than 8 percent, even if the project had an unlimited life.

In cases where the life of a project is very long, the book ROI and internal rate of return approach one another. Suppose that that is the case with both investments described above. The first investment is desirable and the second is not, but the first would be rejected and the second accepted. If RI were used to evaluate the divisions and managers, the picture would change. At a minimum required rate of 15 percent, the first investment would be acceptable to both managers and the second unacceptable to both.

Thus, RI overcomes some of the objections to ROI. This technique focuses on a hurdle rate in the same way that the net present value does. While it is not a discounted cash flow method, its results tend to encourage wise projects and discourage unwise ones more consistently than ROI.

Other Problems. A related, but slightly different problem arises when we consider more typical investments: ones with shorter lives. The book ROI and internal rate of return rarely coincide in such cases, as we know from Chapter 15. Moreover, if the investment has low cash flows in the early years, high flows in later years, it may result in a reduction of both ROI and RI for some time. Suppose that the manager of the division currently earning a 26 percent ROI can invest $500,000 now and obtain cash flows of $200,000 in the first year, $480,000 in the second year. The project has an internal rate of return of about 20 percent, but the book results for the first year would be disappointing, as the data below show.

	Year 1	Year 2
Cash flow	$200,000	$480,000
Depreciation, straight line	250,000	250,000
Income (loss)	($50,000)	$230,000

Obviously, both ROI and RI in the first year would be lower than they would have been if the investment had not been accepted. They would also both be higher in the second year. The two-year life was used to minimize calculations. However, a more realistic example would be likely to show the same result: lower ROI and RI in the early years of the life of a project. It is easy to say that a manager should be patient, but it is not so easy to be patient when it is your performance that is being evaluated. Later in this chapter we show a way to overcome this problem by using compound-interest depreciation.

The problem of managers' accepting unwise projects can be alleviated by requiring that capital investments be justifiable on a discounted cash flow basis. If ROI or RI would be lowered in the early years of the life of a desirable project, the managers could be evaluated on the basis of whether they achieve budgeted results rather than the values of ROI or RI. So long as actual results were close to budgeted results, the manager and the division would be considered to be performing adequately. Budgeting for declines in ROI and RI may take discipline and patience. Most managers and investors are used to comparing current performance against the prior period. With inflation and the emphasis on growth in profits, managers might find it hard to explain to their superiors that they have started projects expected to lower current earnings but to increase future earnings. Encouraging managers to take the best long-term action, even at the expense of the short term, is a difficult behavioral problem.

The use of RI does not eliminate all problems of undesirable behavior. Both ROI and RI are short-term measures, and managers can improve them by taking actions that could hurt the firm in the long run. Reducing or postponing expenses such as maintenance, research and development, employee training, and engineering will improve short-run results, including both ROI and RI. However, the long-term effects could be harmful. Both measures are also subject to criticism because of their reliance on book figures, and it is to such problems that we now turn.

MEASURING INCOME AND INVESTMENT

Several interrelated questions are involved in selecting methods for determining both income and investment for calculating ROI or RI. Two basic types of questions must be answered: what items are to be included, and how are they to be measured? There is reasonable agreement among accountants and other managers that income should be based on controllable items and that investment should be limited to the assets (and perhaps liabilities) that a divisional manager can use for the generation of income.

Income

Determining the revenues and expenses that a divisional manager can control is not simple. There is certainly reason to exclude allocated costs such as the costs of central headquarters on the ground that the manager cannot control them. Some managers, however, feel that allocating such costs is desirable because it alerts divisional managers to the need to cover all costs, not just the costs direct to the division.

The divisional income or divisional profit figure used in calculating ROI and RI does not usually include any provision for income taxes. Taxes on income are determined by the multitude of rules and regulations of tax law and do not reflect the operating performance of divisions. Income taxes are considered in making capital budgeting decisions, but they are rarely included as expenses in a divisional income statement because they are not controllable by divisional managers.

Similarly, it would be rare to find interest expense on corporate debt allocated directly to divisions, because divisional managers do not control the issuance of debt and common stock. However, it is not uncommon to see an imputed cost of the capital employed in the division charged to it. In fact, that is exactly what is done when residual income is calculated. Other variations of this type of imputation of opportunity cost can be found in the practice of charging interest based on the divisional investment in receivables and inventory. Such interest charges are not controllable in the usual sense of the term, but the amount of investment in receivables and inventory is, within limits, controllable by many divisions. Interest on corporate debt, however, especially long-term debt, is not controllable at the divisional level.

Most firms will put divisions on the same accounting methods to achieve greater comparability. Thus, all divisions will generally use either FIFO or LIFO for inventory, and straight-line, sum-of-the-years'-digits, or double-declining-balance depreciation, and so on. Exceptions will arise. A firm might have ten divisions using LIFO, but one or two using FIFO, average cost, or specific identification, because they cannot use LIFO. An obvious example is a division that does mainly job order work. It could use LIFO for materials but would have to use specific identification for finished goods and work in process.

Cash Flow

One way to avoid some of the problems of accounting measurements of income is to use cash flow as the numerator in ROI and RI calculations.

Cash flow could be roughly defined as income plus depreciation, or it could also include changes in current assets and current liabilities. For example, an increase in accounts receivable means that cash collections from customers were less than sales. An increase in accrued wages means that payments were less than the expense.

The appeal of using the crude form of cash flow, income plus depreciation, is that it eliminates the problems of useful life, salvage value, and depreciation method from the analysis. The more refined version of cash flow, which includes all operating cash flows, has the further advantage of providing a measure that indicates what the division is "releasing" to the firm for reinvestment. Recall from the capital-budgeting chapters that reinvestment of cash flows is an important part of the investment decision. The firm cannot use large buildups of accounts receivable and inventories: it needs cash to invest.

Although some firms do use cash flow, rather than income, most probably do not. Managers are leery of return figures that do not include depreciation. Upper-level corporate managers may not be comfortable with cash flow figures and may prefer to evaluate their divisional managers and divisions using the more common income measures.

Investment

Determining the elements of investment, and measuring those elements, presents some extremely difficult problems. First we consider the question of the elements of investment; then we examine some alternative measurement bases.

Some firms consider investment to be the total assets employed by a division, with no consideration of liabilities. Others subtract current liabilities (such as trade accounts payable and accrued expenses) from total assets employed to determine investment. The concept of leverage and of various definitions of investment in a context of financial statement analysis may be familiar to you from earlier courses in accounting and finance. The example described below shows the effects of leverage of ROI and RI under different definitions of investment.

Data for Illustration: Semtrol, Inc.   The Bergen Division of Semtrol, Inc., has the following data for 19X5.

Divisional income	$ 2,500,000
Assets employed by division	16,000,000
Current liabilities of division	1,800,000
Minimum required ROI	12%

The schedule at the top of page 684 shows ROI and RI when current liabilities are included and excluded in determining investment.

As the example shows, both ROI and RI are increased by including current liabilities in determining net investment. This seems justified, since current liabilities of various divisions relate to ordinary operating matters.

	Include Current Liabilities	Exclude Current Liabilities
Income	$ 2,500,000	$ 2,500,000
Investment	14,200,000	16,000,000
ROI	17.6%	15.6%
RI at 12% required return	$ 796,000	$ 580,000

Accounts payable and accrued expenses for payroll and utilities are liabilities arising out of normal divisional operations.

Long-term liabilities are not usually considered, because divisions typically do not issue long-term debt. Moreover, divisions are usually viewed as operating units, and to deduct interest expense on long-term debt from divisional income, as well as deducting long-term debt from divisional investment, would blend measures of operating effectiveness with measures of financial effectiveness. Leveraging or trading on the equity is not usually considered part of the responsibility of operating (divisional) management.

Another significant issue in divisional performance evaluation is whether to allocate assets to divisions. Should divisions be allocated a portion of the investment in central research and development, and central headquarters? For the most part, accountants and other managers would answer no. Investment in centrally directed activities is not controllable by divisional managers and should not be part of their responsibility. However, in many cases it is reasonable to impute investment, as well as costs, to divisions.

In some firms the central headquarters handles nearly all the cash disbursements required to operate the divisions. Often it is best for the firm as a whole to centralize cash management. Divisions then carry very little cash, only enough to cover minor disbursements made locally, such as freight charges. It is then quite reasonable to impute some cash to each division for purposes of calculating ROI and RI. The amount allocated to each division is based on some idea of how much cash each division would have to carry if central headquarters did not handle its disbursements.

Leases. Before the issuance of Financial Accounting Standard No. 13, long-term noncancellable leases were not usually capitalized.[4] The annual lease payments were shown on the income statement as expenses, but no asset (right to use leased property) or liability for the present value of the future payments was recognized. Presumably, divisions followed the same practices as the consolidated firm, so that managers of divisions could increase their ROIs and RIs by leasing assets rather than buying them. That option is no longer available if the lease meets certain requirements of Standard No. 13. However, the potential subterfuge is still alive and well.

Consider the following situation. A division leases computing machinery on a ten-year noncancellable lease for $300,000 per year. The ma-

[4] Financial Accounting Standards Board, *Statement No. 13, Accounting for Leases* (Stamford, Ct.: FASB, 1976).

chinery is likely to have negligible salvage value at the end of ten years, so the lease would be capitalized under Standard No. 13. Assuming a 9 percent interest rate, the present value of the future payments is $1,925,400 ($300,000 × 6.418). Capitalizing the lease would give the following journal entry at the inception of the lease:

Capital Lease (asset)	$1,925,400	
Liability under Capital Lease		$1,925,400

That is, the lease would be treated somewhat the same as a purchase of the machinery. Presumably, the cash price of the machinery would approximate $1,925,400, so that an asset and liability would result from the signing of the lease. Before Standard No. 13, the lease might have been treated as a simple rental, with a $300,000 debit to Lease Expense and credit to Cash each year.

Suppose further that the machinery provides operating savings of $370,000 per year. Under the old method, the division would show $70,000 higher income each year, with no additional investment, thereby increasing its ROI and RI. However, if the lease is capitalized, the payment is treated as part interest, part repayment of principal, and the asset is amortized. If the division uses straight-line amortization for the asset, as prescribed by Standard No. 13, it would show the following results in the first year:

	Expense
Amortization, $1,925,400/10	$192,540
Interest, $1,925,400 × 0.09	173,286
Total	$365,826

The increase in income from the savings in operating costs would give a net saving of only $4,174 ($370,000 − $365,826). The ROI in the first year, based on the beginning-of-year investment of $1,925,400, is only 0.002, which would help the ROI of very few divisions and would harm the RI of nearly any division. The internal rate of return on the investment is about 14 percent, so that the investment would be wise if the target rate were less than 14 percent. Again, the wise decision might not be made if corporate management emphasized short-term ROI.

Suppose now that the division could lease the same machinery on a year-to-year basis for $320,000. The extra $20,000 rental would compensate the lessor for the risk that the division might cancel at any time. Such a lease would not qualify as a capital lease under Standard No. 13 and would probably be treated as an operating lease for purposes of analyzing divisional performance. An operating lease is accounted for by treating the payment as an expense, and there is no capitalization of the liability and asset. The division would then increase its income by $50,000 per year ($370,000 − $320,000), with no increase in investment, again boosting its ROI and RI, but the decision to lease year-to-year might be inferior to the ten-year lease. If the divisional manager expects to continue leasing the same machinery for ten years at $320,000, the decision to accept the non-cancellable ten years lease is clearly superior, but the book results could point the manager in the wrong direction.

Bases for Determining Investment and Income

Historical Costs. Very few firms use bases other than historical cost for evaluating divisional performance. The principal questions involved are whether to use gross or net book values for fixed assets and whether to subtract liabilities from assets to determine investment. The use of gross book values (original costs with no accumulated depreciation) is sometimes recommended on grounds that net book values reflect estimated useful lives and different depreciation methods, making it difficult to compare divisions.

An additional argument for using gross book values is that ROI and RI will tend to increase with time if they are based on net book values. We saw an example of this problem earlier, but an extended example will make the difficulty clearer. The example uses uniform cash flows. In practice, we would be much more likely to find cash flows increasing for some part of the life of the investment. The increasing ROI and RI would be even more evident with increasing cash flows. If cash flows decrease during the latter part of the investment's life, the phenomenon of increasing ROI and RI could still occur. It would depend on whether the decline in cash flows was more rapid than the decline in the investment.

Illustration. Suppose that a division increases its plant and equipment by $1 million, expecting to obtain annual net cash flows of $350,265 for four years. (We use this figure in order to obtain a 15 percent internal rate of return.) If the division uses straight-line depreciation, it will show the following results, assuming the use of beginning-of-year book values for calculating ROI and RI. The division is evaluated on both ROI and RI, with a minimum required return of 15 percent.

Year	Cash Flow	Depreciation	Income	Net Book Value of Investment	ROI	RI at 15%
1	$350,265	$250,000	$100,265	$1,000,000	10.0%	($49,735)
2	350,265	250,000	100,265	750,000	13.4	(12,235)
3	350,265	250,000	100,265	500,000	20.1	25,265
4	350,265	250,000	100,265	250,000	40.1	62,765

The implication of these results is that the manager will appear to be doing well if he keeps new investment to a minimum. The ROI and RI on the existing investment will rise, and the lack of new investment will not penalize performance. It is also worth noting that if an accelerated depreciation method, such as SYD, were used, the problem would be worse. ROI and RI would start out very low and then increase enormously.

The use of original cost (gross book value) would eliminate the problem of rising ROI and RI for investments that have equal annual cash flows. However, in most cases we would expect some decreases in cash flows toward the end of the life of a project, which would then penalize divisions with older assets. DuPont is one of the most prominent firms to use gross book values. One reason is the rising ROI. Another is its managers' belief that because they maintain assets in top shape throughout their lives, the manager should be responsible for earning a satisfactory return on gross book value.[5] The theoretical solution to the problem of rising ROI and RI is the use of compound-interest depreciation.

Compound-Interest Depreciation. Compound-interest depreciation is calculated using the internal rate of return. That rate is applied to the investment at the beginning of the period to determine income for the period. Depreciation is then the difference between cash flow and income. Depreciation represents the recovery-of-capital portion of cash flow. The process is illustrated in Exhibit 17–1.

EXHIBIT 17–1
Compound-Interest Depreciation

Year	(a) [prior value − (d)] Investment at Beginning of Year	(b) Cash Flow	(c) [(a) × 0.15] Income at 15%	(d) [(b) − (c)] Depreciation Expense
1	$1,000,000	$ 350,265	$150,000	$ 200,265
2	799,735	350,265	119,960	230,305
3	569,430	350,265	85,414	264,851
4	304,579	350,265	45,686	304,579
Totals		$1,401,060	$401,060	$1,000,000

Exhibit 17–1 shows that the compound-interest method provides a constant book ROI and RI (zero at 15 percent in this case). The method thereby overcomes two objections to the use of net book value in calculating ROI: the low ROI in the early life and the rising ROI in the later life of an investment. If the minimum required return were less than 15 percent, RI would be positive, and would be the same amount each year, not an increasing amount as would be shown if straight-line depreciation were used.

Although the method shown in Exhibit 17–1 is the easiest way to determine compound-interest depreciation, it is not the only way. You may also determine each year's depreciation by subtracting the present value

[5] Frank R. Rayburn and Michael M. Brown, "Measuring and Using Return on Investment Information," in Homer A. Black and James Don Edwards, eds., *The Managerial and Cost Accountants Handbook*, Homewood, Ill.: Dow Jones-Irwin, 1979, p. 331.

of the future cash flows at the end of a year (beginning of the next year) from the present value at the beginning of the year. You may wish to verify that the investment figures shown in Exhibit 17–1 all represent the present value of the remaining cash flows. (For example, at the beginning of year 3, or end of year 2, there are two payments of $350,265 left to receive. The factor for a two-year annuity at 15 percent is 1.6257, which gives $569,426, with the difference due to rounding.) Thus, using compound-interest depreciation also results in showing investments at the present values of their future cash flows.

If expected cash flows do not materialize, the schedule of depreciation would have to be modified to reflect the different internal rate of return. It would then be obvious that things were not going according to plan. ROI would drop below the originally calculated internal rate of return, and residual income would be negative.

Compound-interest depreciation is rarely, if ever, found in practice. One reason is that it usually gives a rising amount of depreciation expense, which managers might think is unconservative and inappropriate. If cash flows fall markedly from period to period, compound-interest depreciation will give straight-line or even decreasing depreciation expense, but the fall has to be quite rapid. The apparent complexity of the method as well as the problems involved in estimating cash flows has probably also contributed to its disuse.

Finally, some investments are not made on economic (discounted cash flow) grounds. Firms must invest in pollution-control equipment, safety devices, and other types of equipment because of regulations of state and federal governmental units and as matters of company policy regarding social responsibility and corporate citizenship. Investments that do not increase cash flows cannot be depreciated using the compound-interest method because their rates of return are negative.

Additional Decision-Making Problems.   We have already seen that the use of ROI and RI may discourage managers from making sound acquisition decisions. Capital budgeting also encompasses disposal decisions, and here again ROI and RI based on book data may be dysfunctional. This is especially likely where gross book values are used for determining the investment base. Consider the following data for two divisions, one evaluated using gross book value, the other using net book value.

	Gross Division	Net Division
Divisional profit	$ 250,000	$ 200,000
Divisional investment	$2,500,000	$1,200,000
ROI	10.0%	16.67%

Both divisions have machinery that originally cost $500,000 and now has a net book value of $100,000. The remaining useful life is five years, and annual straight-line depreciation is $20,000. The machinery could now be sold for its net book value, but selling it would result in increased cash operating costs of $34,000 for additional labor and associated variable overhead. First, assume that cost of capital is 18 percent. Then the $34,000 cash savings has a present value of $106,318 ($34,000 × 3.127), so the machinery should be kept. The calculations below show that the divisional managers would be tempted to sell the machinery because of the boost in their ROIs. Notice that the income of Gross Division is reduced by the full cash saving, while the income of the Net Division is reduced by the cash flow lost minus the depreciation on the machinery. If the Gross Division income included depreciation, which is inconsistent with using gross book value, the increase in its ROI would be even greater, because the reduction in income would be lower.

$$\text{gross division ROI} = \frac{\$250,000 - \$34,000}{\$2,500,000 - \$500,000} = \frac{\$216,000}{\$2,000,000} = 10.8\%$$

$$\text{net division ROI} = \frac{\$200,000 - \$34,000 + \$20,000}{\$1,200,000 - \$100,000} = \frac{\$186,000}{\$1,100,000} = 16.9\%$$

The Net Division ROI will be lower in later years if it sells the machinery than if it keeps it, but the one-period increase in ROI might be tempting to the manager. Generally, the use of net book value is much less likely to encourage dysfunctional decisions than is the use of gross book value, especially when fully depreciated assets are involved.

Suppose that the two divisions have fully depreciated machinery with an original cost of $300,000. The machinery is expected to save $10,000 per year in cash operating costs for the next three years. Its salvage value is zero. Starting from the original ROI data for the two divisions, and assuming the scrapping of the machinery, we would obtain the following results:

$$\text{gross division ROI} = \frac{\$250,000 - \$10,000}{\$2,500,000 - \$300,000} = \frac{\$240,000}{\$2,200,000} = 10.9\%$$

$$\text{net division ROI} = \frac{\$200,000 - \$10,000}{\$1,200,000 - 0} = \frac{\$190,000}{\$1,200,000} = 15.8\%$$

In this case the use of net book value does not encourage the manager to scrap the machine, because there is no reduction in the investment base. The Gross Division manager would be inclined to scrap the machinery, but the decision would be unwise.[6]

---

[6] Reece and Cool studied the practices of 620 firms, 96 percent of which used profit or investment centers. They found that 65 percent used only ROI, 2 percent used only RI, and 28 percent used both ROI and RI for evaluation. About 85 percent of firms used net book values for plant assets, 14 percent used gross cost, and 2 percent used replacement costs. About 51 percent included current payables in the investment base, 49 percent did not allocate corporate

Problems in Interpretation.   The use of historical costs, either gross or net, suffers from a defect widely noted in connection with financial reporting—the problem of price changes. An old plant may have been bought at prices much lower than those currently prevailing, which would tend to make its ROI and RI higher than that of a newer plant doing the same work. However, older plant is likely to be considerably less efficient than newer plant and probably requires much higher maintenance costs. These factors tend to offset the lower historical cost. It is not possible to generalize about the net effects of having older plant. The lower cost and consequent lower investment and depreciation may be much more significant than the increased maintenance and lower efficiency, or vice versa; it depends on the particular circumstances.

The following sections describe some alternatives to historical cost that have been recommended in the literature; these may become more popular as inflation makes comparisons of plant acquired at different times an extremely difficult job.

Present Values

The use of present values of future cash flows for asset valuation is often argued to be the theoretically best method. But there are several problems with attempting to value assets in that manner. One is that interest rates, the cost of equity capital, and, therefore, the weighted average cost of capital are subject to change. If we attempted to value assets at present values based on cost of capital, we would have a good deal of disagreement determining just what cost of capital was at any given time.

Additionally, it is usually not possible to value individual assets on the basis of future cash flows, but only collections of assets. This is the interaction problem: a single asset may not produce any cash flows by itself but may be essential to the production of cash flows. A factory building without machinery will not produce cash flows from operations, nor will machinery that is not properly installed inside a building. Hence, we would have to determine present values for batches of assets, not just individual items.

The present value of future cash flows (after tax) is the appropriate valuation to be used if the management of the firm is considering a sale of the division. The present value is compared to the best price offered to determine whether the sale should take place. This, of course, is a capital-budgeting decision at the firm level, rather than at the divisional level. Sales

---

costs, and 84 percent did not allocate corporate assets. See the article in the Selected References.

An earlier study by Mauriel and Anthony found 52 percent using only ROI, 6 percent using only RI, and 41 percent using both. They also found 18 percent using gross book value, 73 percent using net book value, and 3 percent using replacement costs. See the article in the Selected References. The percentages above do not add up to 100 percent because of "other" and "no answer" responses in both studies.

of individual assets would be considered at the divisional level using standard capital-budgeting techniques.

Market Resale Prices

For some purposes, the individual assets of a division should be valued at their current resale prices. The most common case is when the divisional manager is considering the sale of one or more specific assets. Entire divisions are sometimes sold, or the individual assets are sold. If the corporate management is trying to decide whether to sell the entire division as a whole, or to sell the individual assets piecemeal, the question is whether the price offered for the entire division is greater than the expected selling prices of the individual assets.

If ROI based on current selling prices is low, and is expected to remain low, the assets should probably be sold and the funds invested elsewhere. The key point here is whether the low ROI is expected to continue. A low current ROI is obviously not something to be happy about, but if corporate management expects improvements, the division might be kept. We see, then, that market resale prices are valuable primarily in determining whether to dispose of a division, or of some of its assets, or to continue operating. ROI based on market resale values is not particularly useful for evaluating the performance of divisional managers. Many divisional assets, such as specialized machinery, will have very low selling prices, and ROI will appear to be quite high if it is based on selling prices of such assets.

Replacement Costs

Some accountants advocate using replacement costs in evaluating the performance of divisions and their managers. **Replacement costs** are the amounts estimated to be needed to replace the existing inventory and fixed assets, expressed as the capability of generating future cash flows. They are not necessarily the amounts needed to replace the firm's existing assets with similar assets, because the firm might not replace an asset with a physically similar one.

Advocates of using replacement costs for divisional performance evaluation point out that a manager is given the responsibility of using the assets under his or her control in a prudent and profitable manner. The monetary measure of those assets is replacement cost, not historical cost, because replacement cost represents the amount estimated to be needed to provide the existing capacity. It is that cost, not historical cost, on which managers should be required to earn an adequate ROI.

Using replacement costs would also eliminate many of the problems in interpreting historical-cost results that we discussed earlier. Managers would all be put on the same cost basis, so that those with old assets would not have the advantage of a low investment in calculating ROI and residual income. Each division, and manager, would be evaluated as if it had just begun operations. Depreciation expense based on replacement cost would also better reflect the current costs of operating the division than does historical-cost based depreciation.

Despite the arguments put forth by the advocates of replacement costing, it is not widely used in practice. Its use may grow, because the information must now be collected for reporting purposes and so the cost to develop the information is sunk. Little additional cost would be needed to use the data in evaluating divisional performance.

Price-Level Adjustments

There is an unfortunate tendency among some people to lump replacement-cost accounting and price-level accounting together. The two methods are quite different, although they sometimes use similar techniques. **Price-level accounting** emphasizes changes in the general purchasing power of money. Price-level adjusted valuations of assets represent the current purchasing power invested in the asset, not the replacement cost. Changes in the general price level are reflected in changes in broad indexes of prices, such as the Gross National Product Implicit Price Deflator. Such an index averages the prices of a whole host of goods and services; it tells you nothing about the changes in prices of specific items.

An illustration should clarify the difference between the two techniques. Assume that land was bought for $100,000 when the general price-level index was 80. The general price-level index has advanced to 120, a 50 percent increase [(120 − 80)/80]. A specific price index for land of the same type is now at 180 and was 100 when the land was bought. The specific price index will often be used to estimate the replacement cost, as shown below, along with the general price-level adjusted cost.

Replacement cost	$100,000 × 180/100	$180,000
General price-level adjusted cost	$100,000 × 120/80	$150,000

The general price-level adjusted cost represents the current purchasing power invested in the land. The general purchasing power of the dollar has declined, so that $1.50 is needed now to buy the same goods and services that cost $1 when the land was bought. But that $1.50 represents the average prices of many goods and services, not necessarily land or any other specific item. Because general price-level adjustments do not reflect the current costs of the assets that a division operates, they are of doubtful value in evaluating divisional performance.

ANALYZING ROI

The basic equation for ROI can be expanded into two (or more) components, depending on how detailed the accountant wishes to make the analysis. We can look at ROI as composed of investment turnover and return on sales:

$$ROI = \frac{sales}{investment} \times \frac{income}{sales}$$

This expansion enables the accountant to look at the relative performance of a division in regard to two components, rather than one. A division might have a high turnover (sales/investment) but a low return on sales (income/ sales). The result could be a high or low ROI, depending on the relative magnitudes of the components. Comparisons of each component with those of firms in the same industry or with divisions within the same firm may highlight areas of possible improvement. Additionally, firms in different industries, or firms in the same industry using different strategies, frequently depend on either a high turnover (with low return on sales) or high return on sales (with low turnover) to achieve satisfactory ROIs. Discount stores of various types are the classic case of dependence on turnover. The profit margin (return on sales) of a discount record store, drug store, or department store is usually considerably lower than that of a conventional operation. The high turnover of the discount store often makes up for the lower profit margin.

Consider the two divisions for which data are given below. They both provide the firm an ROI of 20 percent, but do so in quite different ways. The jewelry chain has a high profit margin and low turnover, the chain of food stores the reverse.

	Jewelry Chain	Food Chain
Sales	$22,000,000	$560,000,000
Income	2,200,000	11,200,000
Investment	11,000,000	56,000,000
Turnover, sales/investment	2 times	10 times
Return on sales, income/sales	10%	0.2%
Return on investment	20%	20%

Analyzing return on investment using its components has several advantages. It allows managers to focus on the key result area, which for most firms will be one component or the other. That is, many firms will rely on keeping one measure relatively high, and managers will watch that component closely.

Consider some steps that managements might take to increase ROI. One is to reduce investment while holding other values constant. Another is to increase income without increasing investment. Notice that an increase in sales, with both income and investment remaining constant, would have no effect on ROI, because the increase in turnover would cancel the decrease in profit margin. Inventory and receivables are two elements of investment subject to a reasonable degree of managerial discretion. Receivables can be reduced by tightening credit terms, inventory by stocking less. The problem is that changes in one variable may not be easily made in a vacuum: reducing inventory might also lead to reduced sales and reduced income. Tightening credit terms might have the same effect. Accountants and other managers must always be alert to the possible interactions involved in decisions, especially the undesirable side effects described above.

DIVISIONAL PERFORMANCE AND MANAGERIAL PERFORMANCE

Both divisions and their managers are evaluated. A division might be dropped, enlarged, or left at about its present size. Its manager's requests for capital expenditures might be turned down or approved. Evaluation of the division revolves around the best alternative uses of company funds and the importance of the division to the firm. Evaluating the manager of a division is a separate matter. The obvious example is that of a highly competent manager being put in charge of a poorly performing division to straighten it out. The manager might be doing a superb job in raising its ROI from 2 percent to 5 percent and reducing its negative RI. It may turn out that the firm will drop the division, but that is not a reflection on the performance of the manager.

At the other extreme, the most profitable division in the firm might be managed by an incompetent. Such a division might be capable of earning an ROI of 35 percent or so, with corresponding high RI, but might actually earn 25 percent. The practice of management by exception, where top managers focus their attention on problem areas, may be conducive to such results. Putting all your attention on the poorly performing divisions might not be an optimal policy. The firm might benefit more if attention were directed at improving already profitable divisions than by concentrating on less profitable ones.

Performance Report

Exhibit 17–2 gives an income statement format and calculation of investment bases that reflect, however imperfectly, the differences between the performance of the manager and that of the division. In making this distinction, we want to concentrate on the factors that the manager currently in charge of the division can control, as opposed to those to which previous managers have committed the division through their decisions. Any effort to distinguish between what the incumbent manager can and cannot control is bound to be imprecise, but much can be done.

The controllable profit and investment relate to the manager, while the noncontrollable items (costs and investment) relate to the division itself. Noncontrollable items could include allocated corporate expenses and assets as well as items to which previous managers committed the division.

EXHIBIT 17-2
Sample Report of Managerial and Divisional Performance
(millions of dollars)

Sales	$46.5
Variable costs	28.2
Contribution margin	18.3
Controllable fixed costs	6.2
Controllable profit	$12.1
Noncontrollable costs	5.0
Divisional profit	$ 7.1
Current assets less current liabilities	$18.2
Controllable fixed assets	17.9
Controllable investment	36.1
Noncontrollable investment	10.2
Total divisional investment	$46.3
ROI on controllable investment ($12.1/$36.1)	33.5%
RI on controllable investment, 12% minimum	$ 7.8
ROI on total investment ($7.1/$46.3)	15.3%
RI on total investment	$ 1.5

Standards for Comparison

The use of any measure of performance presupposes some idea of good performance. Is 15 percent a satisfactory ROI? Is $23,500,000 a satisfactory RI? The value of a performance measure must be related to some standard or norm. A 15 percent ROI is, all other things being equal, better than one of 8 percent. The problem is that all other things are rarely equal. In general, managers will evaluate divisions in several ways. They will compare ROI and RI figures for each division within the firm. They will probably try to compare ROIs of particular divisions with those of independent firms in the same industry. Thus, if a division is exclusively engaged in packaging, upper-level management might compare its ROI with that of one or more companies in the packaging business. Some industry associations publish data showing averages of various operating characteristics of firms in the industry, including ROI. If such statistics are not available, upper-level management might turn to annual reports of firms comparable to the division.

Corporate management might also compare current-period ROI and RI with those of prior periods, looking for improvement or deterioration. Corporate management would also be interested in whether the division earned its budgeted ROI or RI. Budgeted results are, in fact, probably the most common basis for comparison, and they have some advantages over the other bases mentioned so far. Budgeted results represent management's best judgment of what a division should do. Comparisons of divisions with others within the firm suffer from the defect that divisions operating in different industries should be expected to have different ROIs. For example, ROIs in consumer-goods industries are generally higher than those in producers'-goods industries such as industrial equipment.

Comparisons with independent firms operating in the same industry as a division are not always possible. It might be quite difficult to find a firm with a business approximating that of your division. There could be so few firms that comparisons are not reliable guides. Additionally, a division of a large firm should have higher ROI and RI than an independent firm of about the same size, because it should benefit from centrally provided services. The division would not have to provide a staff for finance, legal services, and other such activities. The charges that might be made for such services would probably be less than the cost that an independent company would have to incur.

Comparing actual current-period results with those of prior periods does not indicate whether performance is good or bad, only the direction it seems to be taking. The problem here is the same as in using historical results to set standard costs.

Even granting the subjectivity in budgeted ROI and RI, comparisons of actual and budgeted results may be the best of the comparisons we have mentioned. The problem of comparing historical and current-period results extends to comparing divisions within the firm and comparing divisions with independent companies outside the firm. There is no guarantee that the standards used for comparison constitute good performance.

RISK, ROI, AND RI

The previous discussion assumed that the risks involved in all divisions were the same, which is certainly not likely to be true in practice. Where divisions engage in lines of business of different risk, their ROIs should be different. A division in a high-risk business should earn a higher ROI than one in a low-risk business. The high-risk division should also earn RI based on a higher minimum required return. In fact, it could be argued that different types of investment should earn different ROIs.

Burlington Industries, Inc., has used a technique that recognizes the relative riskiness of different types of investment.[7] The Burlington system employs a Use of Capital Charge (UOCC) that is based on corporate management's estimates of the cost of capital and the proportions of total investment in three classes. The classes, from least risky to most risky, are: accounts receivable, net of accounts payable; inventories; and plant and

[7] See Donald R. Hughes, "Burlington Industries, Inc.," in Thomas J. Burns, ed., *The Behavioral Aspects of Accounting Data for Performance Evaluation* (Columbus, Ohio: College of Administrative Science, The Ohio State University, 1968), pp. 49–65.

equipment. The corporation charges each division a dollar amount based on the amounts of assets in each class and the applicable rates.

For example, the following schedule shows the calculation of the UOCC using hypothetical data.

Assets	Amount	Required ROI	UOCC
Receivables less payables	$ 2,300	7%	$ 161
Inventories	8,400	12%	1,008
Plant and equipment	18,600	22%	4,092
Totals	$29,300		$5,261

Weighted average UOCC = 18% ($5,261/$29,300)

This technique recognizes the relative riskiness of investing in different types of assets. The risk rises as the investment is committed for longer periods and is accordingly less liquid.

The use of different required returns for different divisions on the basis of relative riskiness is not prevalent in practice. However, managers recognize different degrees of riskiness by informally requiring higher ROIs for riskier divisions. A corporate manager expects a division in a high-technology, rapidly changing, and therefore risky field such as lasers to earn a higher ROI than one in a relatively stable field such as food processing.

SUMMARY

Divisional performance evaluation is a constant problem for accountants and other managers. Much depends on these evaluations, because they are used for determining which managers should receive praise (and rewards), which should be penalized. They are also used to determine if the firm should remain in a particular line of business, expand the line, or drop it.

ROI is a criterion frequently used for evaluating performance of both divisions and their managers, but it is generally inferior to residual income. Problems of determining how income and investment should be defined for the purpose of calculating ROI and RI are quite serious. There are no easy solutions. Accountants and managers advocate many different ways to make the required measurements, and controversy abounds.

ASSIGNMENTS

17-1 Investment Bases. At a recent seminar, several presidents of decentralized companies were discussing the asset bases that they used to calculate ROI and RI. Summaries of their comments appear below. All the firms use historical costs.

PRESIDENT SMITH: We use total assets with no reduction for liabilities or for accumulated depreciation. Our belief is that operating managers are just that—operating managers—and don't have anything to do with financing the business. Further, using gross book value for fixed assets allows us to overcome the problems of different useful lives and different depreciation methods.

PRESIDENT JONES: We use net book value for fixed assets. We also use working capital, instead of total current assets. We think that our managers should get the benefit of short-term liabilities' being included in the base because they are really related to operations, not to financing.

PRESIDENT BROWN: We use net book value for fixed assets. We also allocate corporate debt to the divisions, so that their net investment amounts added together equal the stockholder equity of the firm. This way, the weighted average ROI for the divisions equals the return on stockholder equity for the firm as a whole. We allocate income taxes and interest to the divisions as well.

Required: Comment on each method, citing both strong and weak points.

17-2 Allocated Assets. The Ponta Mona Company is a decentralized firm with eleven operating divisions. Each division keeps a small amount of petty cash (from $10,000 to $60,000 depending on the size of the division) while paying for materials, labor, and other cash costs directly from the company bank account.

In determining the ROI of each division, the controller of the company allocates cash to each division in the amount of 30 days' average cash disbursements. The company bank account generally contains about 30 days' requirements, with any excess invested in short-term securities. Naturally, the division managers are not happy with this allocation.

Required: Present arguments for and against the firm's policy on allocating cash. What would you do if you were the president of the company?

17-3 ROI and RI. The operating data for the three divisions of IML Industries appear below, in millions of dollars.

	Automotive Parts	Consumer Products	Industrial Equipment
Income	4.5	14.6	6.1
Investment	17.8	43.6	40.7

Required:

1. Determine ROI for each division.

2. Determine RI for each division at a minimum required return of (a) 15 percent and (b) 20 percent.

17-4 Compound-Interest Depreciation. The Glen Company is considering the acquisition of machinery that will have a five-year life and produce after-tax cash flows of $33,435 per year. The machinery will cost $100,000 and have no salvage value.

Required: Prepare a schedule of depreciation for the equipment, using the compound-interest method.

17–5 **Behavior of ROI and RI.** The general manager of the Rebach division of Continental Products, Inc., has the opportunity to invest $2 million in plant and equipment that will have a useful life of four years. The investment should add income before depreciation of $700,000 annually. The proposed investment meets the firm's capital-budgeting criterion of a 15 percent internal rate of return.

Because the general manager is evaluated on the basis of a combination of ROI and RI, he wants to know the likely effects of the investment on these two results. The division now earns an ROI of 20 percent, and the minimum required ROI is 15 percent. The firm uses straight-line depreciation on all assets and calculates ROI using end-of-year amounts of net assets (cost less accumulated depreciation).

Required: Prepare a schedule showing the ROI and RI on the proposed investment in each year.

17–6 **ROI and Decisions.** The general manager of the Warren division of MNI, Inc., is trying to decide about several matters. He has projected the divisional income for the coming year at $2 million and divisional investment at $10 million without considering the effects of taking the following possible courses of action.

1. The division has old equipment that is fully depreciated but is still in service. Replacement equipment costing $100,000 and having a ten-year life is available. That equipment would provide savings of $25,000 per year. The division uses straight-line depreciation. At the firm's cost of capital, the investment would be desirable using discounted cash flow methods.

2. The division also has equipment with a book value of $200,000 and annual depreciation of $40,000. It could be sold at book value, with the proceeds returned to corporate headquarters and therefore not included in the division's investment. If the equipment were sold, labor costs would rise by $70,000. The sale would not be desirable using discounted cash flow techniques.

Required: Considering each case independently, determine whether the manager would be likely to make a decision that is bad from the standpoint of the firm. The manager is evaluated on the basis of book ROI.

17–7 **ROI, RI, and Investment Decisions.** The general manager of the Wyner division of General Industries, Inc., expects income of $250,000 on an investment of $1 million without considering the opportunities listed below.

Investment Opportunity	Income	Investment
A	$40,000	$ 80,000
B	60,000	300,000
C	40,000	250,000
D	25,000	98,000

Required:

1. Assuming that the manager is evaluated on the basis of ROI, which investment opportunities would he accept?

2. Assuming that the manager is evaluated on the basis of RI with a minimum required return of 20 percent, which investments would he accept?

17-8 Improving ROI. George Petty, the president of the Wycomb division of QMC Group, Inc., received the following budgeted data from his controller. The information relates to 19X6.

Sales	$8,000,000
Cost of sales, 60% variable	6,000,000
Gross profit	2,000,000
Selling and administrative expenses, all fixed	1,200,000
Divisional profit	$ 800,000
Investment	
Cash, 5% of sales	$ 400,000
Receivables, 25% of sales	2,000,000
Inventories, 40% of cost of sales	2,400,000
Plant, net	5,000,000
Total investment	$9,800,000

Petty was not happy with the expected ROI and wondered about taking some actions to improve it. He expected that cash and receivables would maintain their percentage relationships to sales, inventories would maintain the percentage relationship to cost of sales, and plant and equipment would remain at $5 million, unless otherwise specified.

Required: Treating each of the following actions independently of the others, determine the ROI that the division would earn if the action produced the stated effects.

1. An increase in selling expenses of $80,000 coupled with a 10 percent increase in selling prices would reduce unit volume by 10 percent.

2. Increased selling expenses of $300,000 would increase unit volume by 12 percent.

3. Customers now pay their bills, on average, in 90 days. Allowing them more time to pay would increase unit volume by 5 percent and increase the percentage of accounts receivable to sales to 40 percent.

17–9 Analyzing Divisional Performance.   Horner Industries is a large conglomerate with highly decentralized divisions. The Parker division is in the cosmetics business and had been growing very slowly until Phillip Bates became its manager early in 19X4. Bates had been a marketing vice-president for many years and undertook aggressive campaigns to increase the division's sales.

Selected results for the first three years of his tenure appear below, in millions of dollars.

	19X4	19X5	19X6
Sales	$10.0	$12.0	$15.0
Income	2.0	2.5	3.2
Investment:			
Receivables	1.0	1.9	3.0
Inventory	2.0	2.7	4.4
Net fixed assets	4.0	4.6	5.4
Total investment	$ 7.0	$ 9.2	$12.8

The divisions do not keep cash. Corporate headquarters pays all bills directly. In 19X3, the year before Bates took over the division, it had earned $1.2 million on sales of $8.7 million. ROI was 29.4 percent.

Required:

1. Appraise the performance of the Parker division during Bate's tenure.

2. The assignment states that Bates acted to increase sales. Do any of the results shown above suggest what some of his actions might have been?

17–10 Value of Division to Firm.   The York Company has eight divisions. Data on three appear below (in millions of dollars):

	Division		
	Wellington	Heathcliff	Nelson
Sales	$160	$225	$600
Income	16	20	45
Investment	80	120	300
Depreciation, included in determining income	10	15	40

The three divisions are all relatively mature. Their current assets and liabilities remain fairly constant from year to year. The firm has a minimum required ROI of 10 percent. The other five divisions are all growing rapidly, and their invested capital increases commensurately.

Required: Rank the divisions in order of their contributions to the firm, using three different criteria.

17–11 Interdependence.   The Poladak Company makes cameras and film, each in a separate division. The film division makes one particular type that fits only one camera, the model ZX-22, which the camera division now sells for $180. Data on the camera and film appear below.

	Camera ZX-22	Film, per pack
Selling price	$180	$4.20
Variable cost	90	0.90
Contribution margin	$ 90	$3.30
Annual volume	60,000	780,000

The manager of the film division has argued for several years that the camera division should reduce the price of the ZX-22, because additional sales of the camera would stimulate additional sales of film. Both divisional managers agree that a reduction to $150 would probably result in sales of about 80,000 cameras annually. In general, the firm sells about 13 packs of film for each camera over its life.

The divisional managers are evaluated on ROI. Investment does not vary significantly with volume, because nearly all customers pay cash and the divisions keep very low inventories.

Required:

1. Would the camera division benefit by reducing the price of the ZX-22 to $150?

2. Assuming that sales of film were about 13 rolls per camera sold, would the firm as a whole benefit if the camera division reduced its price?

3. If your answers to items 1 and 2 conflict, try to suggest a solution that would not force either manager to act against his division's best interests.

17–12 ROI and Internal Rate of Return.   The manager of the Knute division of Montauk, Inc., has been considering an investment in new fixed assets. He expects the investment to yield annual net cash flows of $386,250 for its four-year life. The cost is $1 million. The firm has a minimum required rate of return on investment of 15 percent. The calculation of the minimum required dollar return is based on net assets (cost less accumulated depreciation) at the beginning of each year. The firm uses straight-line depreciation. Ignore taxes.

Required:

1. What is the internal rate of return of the investment?

2. Prepare a schedule showing the residual income (or loss) that the investment would give in each of the four years of its life.

3. Can you suggest a way to reconcile the conflict?

17-13 ROI and Investment. The Carpenter Company operates a number of divisions, including the Drake division, which manufactures automotive ignition parts. The division has been having a great deal of difficulty in recent years, owing to its inability to produce electronic parts, which have been taking over the market.

Three years ago, George Maxwell became the division manager at Drake. The division then showed income of $80,000 on an investment (book value) of $3 million. The division is now earning about $350,000 on an investment of $2 million at book value. Maxwell cut down on expenses and on working capital but has gone about as far as he can. There have been almost no replacements of fixed assets in the past five years. Annual depreciation is about $200,000.

The one bright note is that the division is located in an area where real estate values have been increasing. The land that the division occupies is currently worth about $6,000,000, although the building and equipment are nearly valueless.

Required: As president of the firm, what would you do?

17-14 ROI, RI, and Decisions. The M-Tronics Company operates several divisions that specialize in various types of electronic components. Budgeted data for two divisions appear below.

	Z-Tron Division	Excelsior Division
Divisional profit	$ 1,300,000	$1,600,000
Divisional investment	$13,200,000	$6,800,000

There is an investment opportunity that either division could take. Its expected profit is $300,000 on an expected investment of $1,600,000.

Required:

1. Suppose that the division managers are evaluated on ROI. Would either divisional manager accept the project?

2. Suppose now that the managers are evaluated on residual income. The minimum required return is 15 percent. Would either manager accept the project?

3. If a 15 percent return reflects cost of capital, would it be in the firm's interest for one of the divisions to accept the project?

17–15 DuPont ROI Analysis. The diagram below depicts the DuPont method of analyzing the components of ROI. The method expands the basic margin-times-turnover model by building up the individual elements so that the manager can look more closely at them to see where he might make improvements.

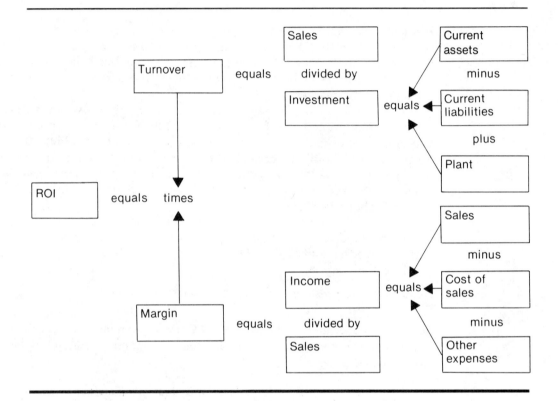

The Abington Company operates a number of divisions. Data for the Kraftone division appear below, along with other data that reflect averages for the construction supplies industry, which is where Kraftone operates (all data in millions):

	Kraftone	Industry Average
Sales	$121.7	$100.0
Cost of sales	(86.3)	(64.2)
Other expenses	(21.4)	(20.0)
Income	$ 14.0	$ 15.8
Current assets	$ 27.7	$ 31.6
Current liabilities	18.6	15.6
Plant and equipment, net	54.4	55.8

Required:

1. Analyze the industry and the Kraftone division, using the DuPont model.

2. Comment on the significant differences between Kraftone and the industry and suggest some possible reasons for the differences. For example, does Kraftone perhaps charge higher prices, require faster payment of receivables, hold lower inventories? You cannot be sure of any suggestion, but you should be able to support your reasoning.

17–16 ROI, CVP Analysis, and Variable Investment. The manager of the Anderson division of General Industries, Inc., expects the following results in 19X7, dollar amounts in millions.

Sales		$49.60
Variable costs, 60% of sales		29.76
Contribution margin		19.84
Fixed costs		12.00
Profit		$ 7.84
Investment:		
Plant and equipment	$19.51	
Working capital	14.88	$34.39
ROI, $7.84/$34.39		22.80%

The division has a target ROI of 30 percent, and the manager has asked you to determine how much sales volume the division would need to reach that. He states that the sales mix is relatively constant so that variable costs should be close to 60 percent of sales, that fixed costs and plant and equipment should remain constant, and that working capital (cash, receivables, and inventories) should vary closely with sales in the percentage reflected above.

Required: Determine the sales volume that the division needs to reach the 30 percent ROI target.

17–17 Corporate Charges and Behavior. Like many other corporations, Borthwick Industries charges its divisions a management fee. Borthwick levies the fee on total invested capital at a rate of 5 percent. It defines total invested capital as assets under divisional control less current liabilities associated with divisional operations (mostly trade payables and accruals). The charge usually approximates the costs of operating corporate headquarters, including interest on corporate debt. About 95 percent of total assets for the firm are controlled by divisions; about 75 percent of the firm's current liabilities are associated with divisional operations.

The manager of the Gregson division is considering a promotional campaign designed to increase sales over the next few years. His staff people have developed the following estimates, in millions of dollars, of the incremental effects of the campaign:

Sales	$4.9
Cost of sales	2.8
Gross margin	2.1
Operating expenses, including promotion	1.3
Income	$0.8

The division's receivables typically run about 30 percent of sales and its inventories about 25 percent of cost of sales. Trade payables average 50 percent of inventory and accruals are negligible. The division would also need about $0.8 million in additional equipment.

The firm evaluates divisions and their managers using ROI. The manager of Gregson expects ROI to be in the 28 to 30 percent range without considering the promotion. The effects of the corporate charge on invested capital are not reflected in the information given above.

Required: Determine whether or not the manager would undertake the campaign, based on his own best interests. Is it likely that his decision is not in the best interests of the firm? Why or why not?

17–18 Corporate Charges and Behavior.   Assume the same facts as in assignment 17–17 except that the corporate charge is 2 percent of revenue instead of 5 percent of investment.

Required:

1. Determine whether or not the division manager would undertake the campaign, based on his own best interests.
2. Will his decision be in the firm's best interests? Why or why not?

17–19 Multiple Required Rates of Return.   One difficulty with using residual income is that a single rate of return fails to consider the relative riskiness of different types of assets under divisional control. Requiring an ROI of, say, 20 percent on plant and equipment might be reasonable, but it is less likely to be reasonable for accounts receivable. A lower rate would better reflect the lower risk in receivables.

One way to circumvent this problem is to use different ROIs for different assets. The following data relate to two divisions of the Walton Company, in millions of dollars.

	SCC Division	Trutone Division
Cash and receivables	$ 18.6	$ 9.4
Inventories	37.2	17.9
Net plant and equipment	63.5	97.0
Totals	$119.3	$124.3
Profit	$ 27.5	$ 33.5

Required:

1. Calculate the RI for each division, assuming that the firm uses a 20 percent minimum required ROI on all assets.

2. Calculate the RI for each division, assuming that the firm uses the following minimum ROIs: cash and receivables, 12 percent; inventories, 15 percent; plant and equipment, 24 percent.

3. Comment on the differences between the results in items 1 and 2. Does the idea of using different minimum required ROIs seem reasonable to you? Why or why not?

17-20 **Bases for ROI.**   The Fulmer Company operates three divisions and has been calculating ROI for each division using controllable profit and controllable investment. Recently, the president of the firm decided that it would be wise to allocate corporate assets, debt, and expenses to each division so that divisional ROIs would more closely reflect the return that the firm earns on its stockholder equity.

Controllable profit for the divisions does not include any allocated corporate expenses and is pretax. Controllable investment includes only the assets under the control of the divisions, with no liabilities, either corporate or related to the divisional operations, included. The following data relate to divisional operations for the current year (in millions):

	Cooper Division	Dalmas Division	Brockton Division
Controllable profit	$160	$150	$ 300
Controllable investment	400	600	1,000

Total corporate expenses, largely for interest on long-term debt, are $150 million. Corporate assets not controlled by divisions total $200 million, mostly investments in long-term securities. Income on securities is netted against expenses. Corporate debt is $880 million. The tax rate is 40 percent, and no income taxes are reflected above.

The president wants you to calculate the return on equity of each division, and for the firm as a whole. He asks that you allocate corporate expenses to divisions on the basis of their relative controllable investments, then determine after-tax income for each division. He also wants corporate assets and liabilities allocated on the basis of relative controllable investments. Thus, the equity figures computed for each division should add up to the firm's total stockholder equity of $1,320 million.

Required:

1. Calculate the ROI for each division, using controllable profit and controllable investment.

2. Calculate the return on equity for each division in accordance with the president's instructions.

3. Does the president's method seem reasonable to you? Why or why not?

17-21 Lease-Buy Decision. The manager of the CCM division expects income of $50,000 on an investment of $200,000 for the next ten years without considering some new machinery that she will acquire. The machinery costs $20,000, has a ten-year life with no salvage value, and would save $9,000 in pretax cash operating costs each year. The firm uses straight-line depreciation for tax and book purposes, and the tax rate is 40 percent. Capital-budgeting techniques show that the investment is desirable.

The machinery is also available on a year-to-year lease, cancellable by both lessor and lessee, for $5,000 per year, paid at year end. The manager wonders whether it might be better to lease instead of buy, especially since her performance is judged by book ROI. The income figure used for ROI is pretax, and investment is net book value of assets at the beginning of the year. The relevant discount rate for deciding whether to lease or buy is 10 percent. The lease is an operating lease, so it would not affect investment.

Required:

1. Evaluate the lease or buy decision by comparing: (1) the present value of the after-tax lease payments, and (2) the purchase price less the present value of the depreciation tax shield. The smaller present value indicates the better choice.

2. Determine the effects on book ROI of buying versus leasing for the first three years.

17-22 ROI, Special Order. The manager of the Granger division of Mildyne Industries is considering an offer from the Meers Company, a large retail chain. Granger makes a line of high-quality appliances that it markets through independent dealers, and Meers wants to buy 250,000 units of various appliances during the coming year, to be sold under its own label. The average price per unit that Meers has offered is $23, and the mix of appliances is about the same as that reflected in the following budgeted data (dollar values in thousands):

Sales, 1,000,000 units at average price of $38	$38,000
Cost of sales	22,000
Gross margin	16,000
Selling and administrative expenses	5,500
Divisional profit	$10,500
Required cash, 5% of sales	$ 1,900
Receivables	6,800
Inventories, at variable production cost	4,400
Net plant and equipment	16,200
Total investment	$29,300

Cost of sales includes $5,000,000 in fixed manufacturing costs. Selling and administrative expenses include a charge of 5 percent of sales levied by the parent company and are otherwise fixed. The charge is for centrally provided services such as data processing, research and development, and finance.

The manager of the Granger division expects sales at regular prices to fall by 5 percent if he accepts the offer from Meers. He anticipates that cash requirements would remain at 5 percent of sales and that inventories would change proportionately with the net change in volume ensuing from accepting the offer. He also expects that Meers will follow its usual practice of paying for its purchases in 120 days.

Corporate management at Mildyne evaluates divisional managers based on ROI.

Required: Determine whether the manager of the Granger should accept the offer, both from his standpoint and from the standpoint of the firm. Make whatever assumptions you feel you need, and be prepared to justify them.

17–23   Corporate Resources and Growth.   "I've done a good job with this division over the past eight years, and the people at corporate headquarters have told me so, but they turn around and cut my requests for capital expenditures by nearly two-thirds." John Bolinski, the general manager of the heavy equipment division of General Industries, was lamenting the fact that the firm seemed to view his division as a cash cow, a generator of funds for use in other, faster-growing divisions.

He went on: "They say that they want to put the money where it will do the most good. My equipment is getting out of date and we ought to be replacing it a lot faster than they are allowing. All of my proposals show internal rates of return of 15 percent or so, which ought to make them satisfactory, but all I get money for is replacements that just have to be made. I generated over $14 million in cash flow last year, including $5.2 million in depreciation, yet my replacements are running at only $3.2 million. My ROI is 22 percent, which is better than some of the divisions where they are pouring in the money. It is awfully discouraging."

Required: Comment on the issues raised. Does the behavior of the corporate headquarters seem reasonable? Why or why not?

17–24   Compensation System.   Porter & Campbell was a large diversified company making industrial parts and some consumer goods. The firm was organized into fourteen divisions that were nearly autonomous. Each division concentrated on a line of products, and there was almost no overlap among them. For some years the divisional managers had been paid salaries that were determined largely by the sizes of their respective divisions. Although there was no explicit formula, a manager of a division twice the size of another (measured by total investment) would receive about 50 percent more pay. There were also bonuses for divisional managers, based on the firm's profits and the managers' salaries. Each manager's bonus was the same percentage of salary, so that a manager earning 30 percent more salary than another would receive a 30 percent larger bonus. Bonuses had averaged about $22,000 in recent years.

Albert Hodges, the president of the firm, was not satisfied with the compensation system and requested a proposal for changing it so that it recognized merits of the individual managers. The proposal, prepared by Bill Morris, an assistant to the president, was as follows.

Each manager would receive a salary at his or her current level. The bonus would be calculated in two parts. The first part of the bonus, which could not exceed $20,000, was 2 percent of the difference between the division's current-year profits and 110 percent of the average profit of the division over the past three years. Morris called this part of the bonus the profit-growth portion and supported it by appealing to the firm's goal of steadily increasing profits.

The second part of the bonus, which could not exceed $15,000 (so that the maximum possible bonus was $35,000), was based on return on investment. Each division had the same target ROI, which was 105 percent of the firmwide average ROI over the past three years. The ROI portion of the bonus was to be calculated as follows:

$$\text{ROI bonus} = 0.02 \times \left\{ \left(\begin{array}{c} \text{divisional} \\ \text{profit} \end{array} \right) - \left[\left(\begin{array}{c} \text{target} \\ \text{ROI} \end{array} \right) \times \left(\begin{array}{c} \text{divisional} \\ \text{investment} \end{array} \right) \right] \right\}$$

In words, the ROI portion of the bonus was to be 2 percent of the excess of divisional profit over a target profit based on a target ROI. The justification for this portion of the bonus was that ROI was also an extremely important factor that divisional managers should be concerned with, and therefore it should be a factor in their compensation. The firm's ROI had averaged 12 percent in the past three years.

Failure to meet either criterion would not carry a penalty. That is, there would not be a negative value for one portion offset against the other. Thus, if profits were lower than 110 percent of the prior three-year average, there would be no bonus for increasing profits, but there could be one for meeting the ROI target.

Required: Evaluate the proposed system.

17-25 **Decentralization—Or Is It? (CMA adapted).** Edwin Hall, chairman of the board and president of Arrow Works Products Company, founded the company in the mid-1970s. He is a talented and creative engineer. Arrow Works was started with one of his inventions, an intricate diecast item that required a minimum of finish work. The item was manufactured for Arrow Works by a Gary, Indiana, foundry. The product sold well in a wide market.

The company issued common stock in 19X2 to finance the purchase of the Gary foundry. Additional shares were issued in 19X5, when Arrow purchased a fabricating plant in Cleveland to meet the capacity requirement of a defense contract.

The company now consists of five divisions. Each division is headed by a manager who reports to Hall. The Chicago division contains the product development and engineering department and the finishing (assembly) operation for the basic products. The Gary plant and Cleveland plant are the other two divisions engaged in manufacturing operations. All products manufactured are sold through two selling divisions. The eastern sales division is located in Pittsburgh and covers the country from Chicago to the east coast. The western sales division, which covers the rest of the country, is located in Denver. The western sales division is the newest operation and was established just eight months ago.

Hall, who still owns 53 percent of the outstanding stock, actively participates in the management of the company. He travels frequently and regularly to all of the company's plants and offices. He says, "Having a business with locations in five different cities spread over half the country requires all my time." Despite his regular and frequent visits he believes the company is decentralized, with the managers having complete autonomy. "They make all the decisions and run their own shops. Of course they don't understand the total business as I do, so I have to straighten them out once in a while. My managers are all good men, but they can't be expected to handle everything alone. I try to help all I can."

The last two months have been a period of considerable stress for Hall. During this period, John Staple, manager of the fabricating plant, was advised by his physician to request a six-month sick leave to relieve the work pressures that had made him nervous and tense. This request had followed by three days a phone call in which Hall had directly and bluntly blamed Staple for the lagging production output and increased rework and scrap of the fabricating plant. Hall made no allowances for the pressures created by the operation of the plant at volumes in excess of normal and close to its maximum rated capacity for the previous nine months.

Hall thought he and Staple had had a long and good relationship prior to this event. Hall attributed his loss of temper in this case to his frustration with several other management problems that had arisen in the past two months. The sales manager of the Denver office had resigned shortly after a visit from Hall. The letter of resignation stated he was seeking a position with greater responsibility. The sales manager in Pittsburgh asked to be reassigned to a sales position in the field; he did not feel he could cope with the pressure of management.

Required: Present a memo to Mr. Hall covering these points:

1. How do centralized and decentralized management differ?

2. Analyze whether Arrow Works Products Company is as decentralized as Edwin Hall believes. Explain your answer.

3. Advise Mr. Hall, on the basis of the facts presented in the problem, whether the events that have occurred over the past two months in Arrow Works Products Company should have been expected. Explain your conclusion in a way that will be useful to Mr. Hall.

17–26 Performance Evaluation (CMA adapted).   George Johnson was hired as assistant general manager of the Botel division of Staple, Inc., on July 1, 19X2. It was understood that he would be promoted to general manager of the division on January 1, 19X4, when the then current general manager retired. This was duly done. In addition to familiarizing himself with the division and with the duties of the general manager, Johnson was specifically charged with developing the budgets for 19X3 and 19X4. As general manager in 19X4 he was, of course, responsible for the 19X5 budget.

The company is a highly decentralized, multiproduct firm where the divisions are quite autonomous. The corporation staff approves operating budgets prepared by the divisions, seldom making changes. The corporate staff is active in decisions involving capital expenditures and makes the final decisions. Divisional management is responsible for carrying out the capital-investment program. Divisional managers are evaluated principally on Contribution Return on Division Net Investment. The following budgets and actual results are available. The budget for 19X5 will not be revised, even though 19X4 results departed from the approved budget.

BOTEL DIVISION
(in thousands of dollars)

| | Actual | | | Budget | |
Accounts	19X2	19X3	19X4	19X4	19X5
Sales	1,000	1,500	1,800	2,000	2,400
Less: Division variable costs:					
Material and labor	250	375	450	500	600
Repairs	50	75	50	100	120
Supplies	20	30	36	40	48
Less: Division managed costs:					
Employee training	30	35	25	40	45
Maintenance	50	55	40	60	70
Less: Division committed costs:					
Depreciation	120	160	160	200	200
Rent	80	100	110	140	140
Total	600	830	871	1,080	1,223
Division net contribution	400	670	929	920	1,177
Division investment:					
Accounts receivable	100	150	180	200	240
Inventory	200	300	270	400	480
Fixed assets	1,590	2,565	2,800	3,380	4,000
Less: Accounts and wages payable	(150)	(225)	(350)	(300)	(360)
Net investment	1,740	2,790	2,900	3,680	4,360
Contribution return on net investment	23%	24%	32%	25%	27%

Required:

1. Identify Mr. Johnson's responsibilities under the management and measurement program described above.

2. Appraise the performance of Mr. Johnson in 19X4.

3. On the basis of your analysis, recommend to the president any changes in the responsibilities assigned to managers or in the measurement methods used to evaluate division management.

17–27 **Evaluating Divisional Managers (CMA adapted).** The divisional managers of the Texon Company are responsible for all components of ROI, revenue, expenses, and acquiring and financing assets. Two such managers are now under consideration for the vice-presidency for general operations, which will become vacant shortly. Both managers took over their divisions in late 19X5. Data related to their performances since then appear below (in thousands):

	Division A			Division F		
	19X6	19X7	19X8	19X6	19X7	19X8
Estimated industry sales —market area	$10,000	$12,000	$13,000	$5,000	$6,000	$6,500
Division sales	$ 1,000	$ 1,100	$ 1,210	$ 450	$ 600	$ 750
Variable costs	$ 300	$ 320	$ 345	$ 135	$ 175	$ 210
Managed costs	400	405	420	170	200	230
Committed costs	275	325	350	140	200	250
Total costs	$ 975	$ 1,050	$ 1,115	$ 445	$ 575	$ 690
Net income	$ 25	$ 50	$ 95	$ 5	$ 25	$ 60
Assets employed	$ 330	$ 340	$ 360	$ 170	$ 240	$ 300
Liabilities incurred	103	105	115	47	100	130
Net investment	227	235	245	123	140	170
Return on investment	11%	21%	39%	4%	18%	35%

The two divisions serve different geographical regions. The manager of division A served as assistant manager for five years before being appointed manager. The manager of division F served as assistant manager of division B before being promoted to manager of division F. Division F is relatively new, having been formed in 19X4, while division A is in its fifteenth year of operation.

Required: On the basis of the financial information available, which manager would you promote to the vice-presidency? What other information would you seek before deciding?

SELECTED REFERENCES

Anthony, Robert N., and John Dearden, *Management Control Systems*, 4th ed. Homewood, Ill.: Richard D. Irwin, Inc., 1980.

Dearden, John, "The Case Against ROI Control," *Harvard Business Review*, 45:3 (May–June 1967).

Mauriel, John S., and Robert N. Anthony, "Misevaluation of Investment Center Performance," *Harvard Business Review*, 48:3 (March–April 1966).

Reece, James S., and William R. Cool, "Measuring Investment Center Performance," *Harvard Business Review*, 56:3 (May–June 1978).

Solomons, David, *Divisional Performance: Measurement and Control.* Homewood, Ill.: Richard D. Irwin, Inc., 1965.

Vancil, Richard F., *Decentralization: Managerial Ambiguity by Design.* New York: Financial Executives Research Foundation, 1979.

Transfer Pricing

Chapter 18

Chapters 12 and 17 mentioned transfer prices: the prices that divisions charge one another for goods and services. In decentralized companies these prices can be extremely important, because they affect the revenues of the selling division and costs of the buying division. Both divisional managements and corporate management may spend a good bit of time and effort in developing policies on transfer pricing.

A transfer price may induce a divisional manager to make a decision that would lower (or raise) the income, ROI, or residual income of the firm. It is for that reason that corporate management pays attention to transfer prices. However, in and of itself, a transfer price does not affect the firm's income. Because the revenue to one division is cost to the other, they wash each other out. If a transfer price increases, the selling division earns more revenue, but the buying division has higher costs. So long as the divisions continue to transfer the same quantities of product as they had in the past, there is no effect on income for the firm, only for the divisions.[1] However, if a change in a transfer price induces a manager to increase or decrease the quantity bought from or sold to another division, there may be an effect on the income of the firm. A common example is when a division begins to buy products from outside suppliers that it had previously bought inside. Another example is when increased orders from another division cause the selling division to turn away outside buyers.

---

[1] A special problem arises when goods transferred internally are in the inventory of the buying division at the end of an accounting period. For financial reporting and tax purposes, the accountant eliminates the profit on the transferred goods so that all inventories are shown at cost to the firm. Courses in advanced accounting devote a good deal of coverage to this problem.

PROBLEMS OF TRANSFER PRICING

The ways in which transfer prices are set, the mechanisms for resolving disputes among divisional managers, and the policies regarding the amounts of autonomy divisional managers may exercise have important behavioral consequences. It is critical that the system work in the best interests of both the divisional managers and the firm, that the divisional managers perceive it as fair, and that it is easily understood. No one system can always guarantee success, but any system should provide an atmosphere that is at least relatively conducive to success.

Because transfer prices are revenues to selling divisions, costs to buying divisions, divisional managers will regard them much as they would external market prices. They use transfer prices to decide whether to make a component or buy it from another division, whether to use existing capacity to supply a sister division or outside customers, whether to increase productive capacity, and so on through the entire range of decisions that managers customarily make.

From the standpoint of the firm as a whole, the critical question is whether or not the transfer should take place, not the price. If one division transfers components to another that uses them in the assembly of a finished product, the question is whether the selling division can make the components for less than the buying division could acquire them from an outside supplier. From the standpoint of the firm, the decision is whether to make or buy.[2]

Accordingly, corporate management wants the transfer price to encourage the divisional managers to take the actions that are best for the firm as a whole. Naturally, the divisional managers want to take the actions that are best for their divisions. If the transfer price serves to signal the divisional managers to take the best action for the firm, as well as for their divisions, it is doing its job: it is promoting goal congruence.

Research into the problems of transfer pricing shows that it is not possible to make flat statements. Whether or not a particular transfer price fosters goal congruence depends on a host of factors such as the type of market and the cost structure faced by the divisions. Like other generalizations, those made about transfer pricing are subject to a number of exceptions because of the range and complexity of the topic. Obviously, goal congruence (and motivation) is affected by many factors. Transfer pricing is an important one, since divisional managers may be judged on the things that transfer prices affect: profit, return on investment, and residual income.

Chapter 12 (on cost allocation) described how transfer prices might be

---

[2] We could also look at the decision as one involving further processing. The question could be put as follows: should the firm sell the components in their current state of completion or process them into other products? Looking at the decision in this way presupposes a market for the components. The existence of a market is a critical point that we return to later.

used to motivate managers to demand more or less of a service provided internally. When corporate management wishes to encourage the use of some service such as data processing or engineering, it may do so by charging a very low transfer price. Conversely, if demand for a service is greater than corporate management believes desirable, the price may be raised. Thus, transfer prices may have the motivational impact of encouraging or discouraging the use of internally provided goods or services.

MARKET PRICES

Chapter 17 noted that an autonomous divisional manager should be just as free to deal with outside firms, both to buy and to sell, as with internal divisions. If this extent of autonomy is present, and if there are outside markets for the goods, then a transfer price will often approximate market price. If the selling division is operating at capacity and can sell its output to outside customers at, say, $10 per unit, it will not accept less than $10 from an inside customer because doing so would reduce divisional profits. It could also reduce corporate profits. (In practice, the actual transfer price could be less than $10, because the selling division might have lower costs on inside sales than on outside sales. Shipping, commissions, and bad debts could be significantly less on inside sales.) If the selling division is operating at capacity, it should charge another division the market price (less any costs avoided by inside dealing). The market price is the opportunity cost of the goods—the amount that the firm, as well as the division, can get by selling them outside.

If the selling division is not operating at capacity, it will probably be inclined to accept a lower price for sales to a sister division. Consider the following example. The Verguenza division of the Sarducci Company makes a variety of pumps, fans, and other equipment used in heating and air-conditioning equipment. Data relating to the expectations of the divisional manager for sales of a model 3405 blower appear below.

Sales, 2,000 units at $100 per unit	$200,000
Variable costs at $40	80,000
Contribution margin	120,000
Separate fixed costs	70,000
Profit	$ 50,000

The Lakehart division of Sarducci Company makes equipment that could use the model 3405 blower. Its manager asks the manager of Verguenza to give him a price.

First, it should be obvious that if Verguenza could produce only 2,000 blowers, it should charge Lakehart the full $100 (less any savings from dealing internally). Any reduction in price to Lakehart would reduce overall profits because sales at $100 would be lost. However, suppose that Verguenza has the capacity to produce 2,500 units without having to reduce production of other products. In that case, any transfer price over the $40 variable cost would increase Verguenza's profits. From the standpoint of the manager of Verguenza, it is a special order problem of the sort discussed in Chapter 4. The reason that the manager of Verguenza will accept a price below the market price is that he does not expect to sell more than 2,000 blowers at $100. With the variable cost as a lower bound, the transfer price for units over 2,000 will be whatever can be negotiated between Lakehart and Verguenza.

Advantages of Market Prices

If market prices exist, there is much to recommend them as transfer prices. If a division is operating at capacity, a market price is the opportunity cost of the goods. It is also the incremental cost to the buying division, because that division would have to buy the goods in the market if it could not get them from another division within the corporation.

The use of market prices as transfer prices also makes it possible to evaluate divisions as if they were independent companies. A division that cannot succeed by selling its products at market prices to other divisions presumably could not succeed as an independent firm. Market prices discipline managers to act as if they were managing independent companies. In fact, any attempt by corporate managers to impose transfer prices that are significantly different from market prices will meet the justified criticism that they are tampering with the autonomy of the divisional managers. Thus, market prices best fit the goals of decentralization, autonomy, and responsibility accounting.

Limitations of Market Prices

Market prices may be obtained in a variety of ways, depending on the type of product. There are very active markets for many raw materials, especially agricultural commodities, with quotations easy to get. It is also a simple matter to get reliable prices for a variety of manufactured products, especially ones that are made by several companies and are relatively standard, such as sheet steel or paper. Prices for such goods may be obtained directly from the companies and are likely to be reliable, provided that the outside firms can meet the required delivery schedules and perform any other services that a related division supplying the same goods would.

A problem exists when divisions make products that they sell exclusively to other internal divisions. There might not be an outside market for the products and, therefore, no opportunity to test the market. If the division transfers a significant portion of its output (measured by cost or labor time) internally, it is not an independent, autonomous unit. It is to a great extent a captive of the divisions it supplies. There is serious doubt that such divisions should be treated as profit centers, because their success or failure is not determined by the market.

The firm might make some effort to determine what a reasonable market value would be by seeking quotations from outside suppliers. Unfortunately, outside firms might not give quotations that reflect what the market would be. If the outside firm does not really expect to get the business, it will not be likely to spend much time working up a quotation. It may quote a price much higher than would be reasonable to charge the buying division. The reverse could also be true: an outside firm might quote a very low price for a limited quantity of the product in order to use excess capacity. The outside firm might have lower variable costs, and higher fixed costs, than the internal supplier, and it might be willing to quote a low price in order to get the business. It might be fine in the short run for the buying division to accept a price that is below the variable cost of the selling division. However, the selling division might reduce its capacity or take other measures that would impair its ability to supply the buying division in the longer run. If the outside supplier later raised the price, the firm as a whole could suffer considerably.

Often there are products or components that the firm will neither buy nor sell outside for strategic reasons. Among the reasons are: ensuring a steady, reliable source of supply; quality control; protection of trade secrets; and encouraging technological progress. Market prices do not help here, even when the amounts of product involved are relatively low in relation to the selling division's total business, nor are quotations from potential suppliers useful, because the firm has no intention of going outside for business.

However, in some cases it might be possible to refer to external markets to develop transfer prices. If the selling division could operate at capacity without the internal business, it should not have to lose profits because it serves the other division. It would be reasonable for the transfer price to be high enough to keep the total profit of the selling division where it would have been if it had kept the external business.

Finally, there are circumstances in which market prices may induce managers to take actions that are unwise from the standpoint of the firm.[3] In order to show how this can happen, we shall present some economic analyses of transfer pricing, dealing with three different situations. The analyses will show that managers may make unwise decisions (from the firm's point of view) in two common types of situations. Then we turn to cost-based transfer prices, which may give satisfactory, if not optimal, results.

---

[3] It would not be an exaggeration to say that 90 percent or more of the extensive literature on transfer pricing deals with the reconciliation of goal congruence and autonomy. The principal objective of most transfer-pricing proposals is to achieve both. See the Selected References at the end of the chapter.

SOME ECONOMIC ASPECTS OF TRANSFER PRICING

Economists and management scientists devote a good deal of attention to the problems of transfer pricing.[4] Their analyses are somewhat more abstract than managers might be accustomed to seeing, but they are nonetheless relevant because they highlight some potential shortcomings of conventional wisdom on transfer pricing. One finding is that under some very prevalent circumstances there may not be a transfer price that ensures goal congruence in the sense of optimizing output for the firm while still preserving divisional autonomy. This conclusion is disturbing. The fact that under some conditions there is no easy way to achieve goal congruence and to preserve divisional autonomy in a simple case argues that the solution would be at least as elusive in more complex, more realistic cases.

For the following examples, we shall use a firm that has two divisions, A and B. Division A makes product A. Division B buys product A and performs additional work to convert it into product B. We shall consider several combinations of different market conditions. Before we begin, we reiterate that market price is the ideal transfer price when the selling division is operating at capacity. All the analyses that follow assume excess capacity.

Perfectly Competitive Market for Intermediate Product

Economists define perfectly competitive markets very strictly. From our standpoint, the most important aspect of **perfect competition** is that the seller of a product can sell all that it wishes to at a given price. The question then is the quantity to be offered for sale. The familiar rule is to offer a product until its marginal revenue equals its marginal cost. Under perfect competition, marginal revenue equals price. There is no need to reduce price to obtain more volume. Marginal cost is closely akin to what we have called incremental cost in this book.

Economists and accountants both recognize that marginal cost will tend to rise. The linear total-cost functions used in cost-volume-profit analysis assume constant marginal cost that is equal to variable cost per unit. We still recognize that as production rises, variable cost per unit will also tend to rise because of overtime premium, the hiring of less skilled workers, and so on.

Figure 18–1 on pages 722–723 depicts three possible situations. The price of the intermediate product, A, is $P(A)$. The marginal-revenue line for product A is straight and horizontal, reflecting the assumption that product A is sold in a perfectly competitive market. Division A will not accept a

---

[4] Professor Jack Hirshleifer did much of the early work in this area and this section draws on that work. See the Selected References at the end of the chapter.

price less than $P(A)$ from its sister division, B, because to do so would be to reduce its profits. Accordingly, division A will produce up to the point where its marginal-cost curve, denoted $MC(A)$, hits its marginal-revenue curve, $P(A)$. To simplify the graphs, we have used only one line to denote division B's activities. The line labeled $NMR(B)$ represents the marginal revenue of division B less the marginal cost that division B incurs in further processing product A. Thus, $NMR(B)$ is net marginal revenue to division B and does not include the transfer price that division B would pay to division A. Accordingly, it represents the change in profit that division B experiences at a given volume, excluding the transfer price. The line slopes down to the right, which could reflect a falling price per unit as volume rises, increasing marginal costs of making product A into product B, or a combination of the two. Division B maximizes its profits where its net marginal revenue equals the transfer price. The transfer price is a marginal cost to division B.

Graph (a) of Figure 18–1 shows that production of A, $Q(A)$, equals that of B, $Q(B)$. In other words, division A sells all its output to division B, which in turn converts it into product B and sells it to outside firms. Graph (b) shows that when the profit-maximizing output for product A is greater than that of product B, division A will sell some of its output in the external market. Finally, graph (c) shows the case where the profit-maximizing output for product B is greater than that for product A. Here, division B will buy additional units of product A from the outside market, while still taking all of division A's output.

We see from Figure 18–1 that the market price of product A is a good transfer price in the sense that it encourages both managers to maximize not only the profits of their divisions, but also the profits of the firm. The manager of division A will sell units of product A to whomever wants them until marginal revenue equals marginal cost. The manager of division B will determine the profit-maximizing output of product B and will buy as many units of product A as he or she needs, either from division A or from outside firms.

Perfect competition is a limiting case: we cannot expect it to prevail in the real world. As we move toward more realistic situations, we find that it becomes extremely difficult to obtain both goal congruence and divisional autonomy. The fact that market prices provide ideal transfer prices only in the limiting case of perfect competition gives us pause to consider whether decentralization may be expected to be effective in an imperfectly competitive environment, a characterization of the markets in which most companies buy and sell.

No Intermediate Market

Let us begin with an extreme case. Assume that product A can be used only by division B, so that there is no external market for this intermediate product. Further, assume that, at least in the short run, no other firm makes

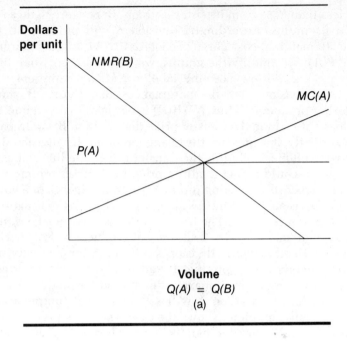

Volume
Q(A) = Q(B)
(a)

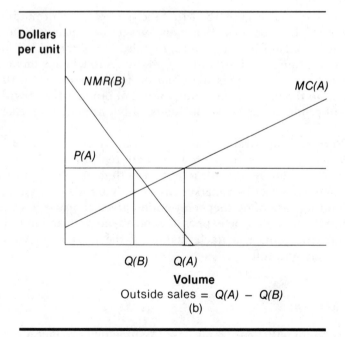

Volume
Outside sales = Q(A) − Q(B)
(b)

FIGURE 18–1
Profit-Maximizing Outputs—Perfect Competition for Intermediate Product

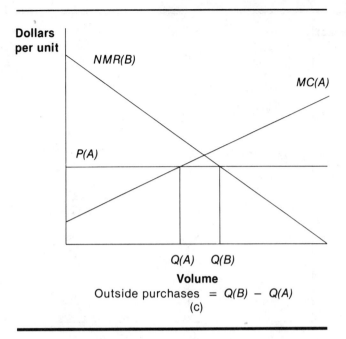

Dollars per unit

NMR(B)

MC(A)

P(A)

Q(A)   Q(B)

Volume

Outside purchases = Q(B) − Q(A)

(c)

product A, so that division A is division B's sole supplier. In this situation, the ideal transfer price is the marginal cost of product A. This is true because, from the standpoint of the firm, the distinction between the two divisions is irrelevant: the question is at what level of output of product B the firm is best off, in the sense of maximizing profits. This situation parallels the one described earlier, where the selling division is essentially a captive supplier.

The profit-maximizing output of the firm is simply the point where the net marginal revenue of division B (which is the NMR of product B) equals the marginal cost of product A. Figure 18–2 on page 724 shows that this output is 96 units. The figure also shows that the manager of division A would earn higher profits by restricting output to 62 units. It is at that point that division A maximizes its profits. The reason is that net marginal revenue of division B is also the average revenue of division A. Division B will pay an amount up to the NMR of product B to obtain product A. This is true because the transfer price of product A is the marginal cost to division B.

The line labeled MR(A) is the marginal-revenue curve for division A and is derived from the demand curve for product A (the NMR curve of division B). The manager of division A would seek to equate marginal revenue and marginal cost, which occurs at 62 units and a price of $68. This level of output is below the 96 units that is optimal output from the standpoint of the firm.

The appendix to this chapter provides a mathematical example that shows how the manager of a division might be better off restricting output.

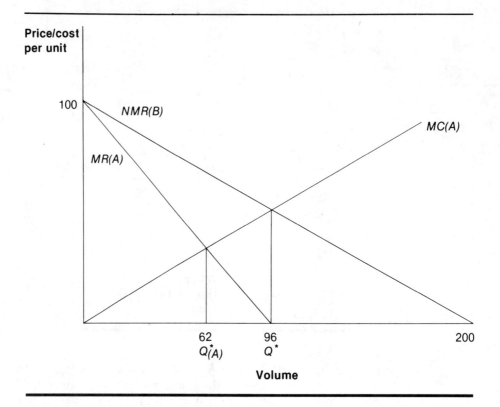

FIGURE 18–2
Profit-Maximizing Outputs—No Intermediate Market

Similarly, the manager of division B would like to obtain additional units of product A until the price equals the net marginal revenue of product B. The extreme case is that the manager of division B would like to acquire 200 units of product A at a price of zero. It is at that point where the net marginal revenue of product B is zero, which is the point of profit maximization for division B.

Let us look at a numerical example to illustrate the point. We shall use different numbers from those implied in Figure 18–2. Suppose that the Lakehart division makes a component for the Verguenza division and is the sole source of supply. Data for the component and the final product appear below, excluding the transfer price.

| | | Incremental Cost | | Revenue | Profit |
Quantity	Lakehart	Verguenza	Firm	to Verguenza	to Firm
10,000	$100,000	$50,000	$150,000	$200,000	$50,000
12,000	122,000	60,000	182,000	235,000	53,000

The firm as a whole makes a higher profit at 12,000 units than it does at 10,000 units. Suppose now that the manager of Lakehart decides to set the transfer price at $13. The manager of Verguenza will then see the following data:

| | | Total Costs | | |
| | | Transfer | Additional | |
Quantity	Revenue	Price	Costs	Profit
10,000	$200,000	$130,000	$50,000	$20,000
12,000	235,000	156,000	60,000	19,000

Thus, the manager of Verguenza will be inclined to take only 10,000 units, because his profit is higher at that volume. If the price were the marginal cost of $11 per unit, he would make the best decision from the standpoint of the firm. The marginal cost of $11 is the difference between total cost that Lakehart incurs at 12,000 units and at 10,000 units ($122,000 − $100,000 = $22,000) divided by 2,000 units (12,000 − 10,000). Of course, the manager of Lakehart would not accept that price because he could earn more selling 10,000 units at $13 than he could selling 12,000 units at $11. In the following section we show that the two managers might be able to work out an arrangement that benefits both of them as well as the firm.

The case of the captive division indicates that when a division exists primarily to serve the needs of another, there is considerable doubt whether the captive should be treated as a profit center. The reason is that from the standpoint of the firm, the ideal transfer price is marginal cost, which might be reasonably close to variable cost for most firms. But the manager of the captive division would certainly balk at selling at marginal cost because his or her profits would be less than they would be at a higher price and lower output. Since goal congruence is incompatible with divisional autonomy in this admittedly unrealistic case of perfectly straight revenue and cost functions, it is difficult to see how the two features would be compatible in a more realistic situation.

Imperfect Competition

We deal with one final case in this section. The producing division faces a declining price curve (demand curve) for its product. Selling price is no longer equal to marginal revenue. The division that buys the intermediate product, processes it further, then sells it, also faces a declining demand curve.[5] Again, we shall see that the selling division would show its highest

---

[5] We could also assume that it faced rising marginal costs and drop the assumption of a declining demand curve. The assumption that we use is simpler to employ in developing the numerical example that follows.

profit if it restricted output below the amount that would be optimal for the firm. Here, we shall again use the Sarducci Company.

Lakehart division of the Sarducci Company makes a particular model that has variable costs of $300, not including the transfer price of a component made by the Verguenza division. The market research staff of Lakehart estimates that it could sell 13,000 units at $900 or 17,000 units at $800. The variable cost of the component that Verguenza supplies is $100. Verguenza's managers expect that they could sell 7,000 units on the open market at $250 or 10,000 units at $200.[6]

The schedules below show that the optimal actions for the firm are to sell 7,000 units of the component to outsiders at $250 and to sell 17,000 units of the finished product at $800. The analysis for the finished product includes the variable cost incurred by both Lakehart and Verguenza, totaling $400. The market prices that Verguenza could obtain are relevant only for determining how many units of the component to sell outside. Because Verguenza does not operate in a perfectly competitive market, it cannot sell all that it wishes to at a given, constant price. Similarly, Lakehart cannot buy all the components it wishes to at a given price from outside suppliers. If the transfer price were set at the $100 variable cost, the schedules below would also reflect the results of each division. The 17,000 units of the component that Verguenza would make and transfer to Lakehart would bring no additional contribution margin to Verguenza, because the price would equal variable cost.

Finished Product (Lakehart)

Price	Unit Contribution Margin (Price − $400)	Volume	Total Contribution Margin
$900	$500	13,000	$6,500,000
800	400	17,000	6,800,000

Outside Sales of Component (Verguenza)

Price	Unit Contribution Margin (Price − $100)	Volume	Total Contribution Margin
$250	$150	7,000	$1,050,000
200	100	10,000	1,000,000

[6] We limit the choices to make the calculations more straightforward. The point of the example would remain valid if we allowed additional levels of volume at different prices.

Now let us look at the situation from the standpoint of the manager of Verguenza. Begin by supposing that he refuses to sell to Lakehart except at the $250 price that he can obtain on the market. At that transfer price, the manager of Lakehart would restrict his output to 13,000 units, as shown below.

Price	Unit Contribution Margin (Price − $300 − $250)	Volume	Total Contribution Margin
$1900	$350	13,000	$4,550,000
800	250	17,000	4,250,000

The $250 transfer price would induce the manager of Lakehart to make fewer units of the finished product. While this is a good decision from his point of view, it is a bad one from the point of view of the firm. The firm would have earned $7,850,000 contribution margin if Lakehart had made 17,000 units (the sum of $6,800,000 from outside sales of the finished product and $1,050,000 from outside sales of the component). At the $250 transfer price, and 13,000 units for Lakehart, the divisions would show the following results.

	Lakehart	Verguenza
Sales:		
Finished product, 13,000 at $900	$11,700,000	
Component, 20,000 at $250		$5,000,000
Variable costs—at $550 ($300 + $250)	7,150,000	
—at $100		2,000,000
Contribution margin	$ 4,550,000	$3,000,000

Total contribution margin for the firm is $7,550,000 ($4,550,000 + $3,000,000), which is $300,000 below the level that would have been achieved if Lakehart had produced 17,000 units. Notice that we could also work simply with the contribution margin on sales to outsiders. The finished product would show total contribution margin of $6,500,000 from the first schedule and the outside sales of the component $1,050,000. The distribution of the $6,500,000 would be $4,550,000 to Lakehart and $1,950,000 to Verguenza. The $1,950,000 is $150 multiplied by 13,000. While the transfer price is irrelevant for determining the total profit of the firm (because it washes out as revenue to one division, expense to the other), a bad transfer price could affect the actions of a manager and thus affect the total profit of the firm.

The manager of Verguenza would show total contribution of $3,000,000 if he insisted on the $250 price, which is $1,950,000 greater than he would show if he altruistically made the transfer at $100. Let us make one final check to see whether the two managers could reach a solution that would be optimal for both of them and for the firm. Suppose that corporate management were aware of the market research study performed by Lakehart and had asked the divisional managers to come up with a transfer price that would encourage optimal decisions.

The transfer price would have to result in both divisions' preferring the transfer of 17,000 units. It is possible to make the managers of both divisions better off by transferring 17,000 units, because the total profit to the firm would be higher and that additional profit could be shared by the divisions.

The problem is that the two managers must agree on both a transfer price and an amount to be transferred. Simple agreement on price will not necessarily work to the advantage of the firm.

Let us begin by determining the minimum transfer price that the manager of Verguenza would accept if he were to transfer 17,000 units to Lakehart. The manager knows that he can transfer 13,000 units at $250, which will provide a contribution margin of $1,950,000. He would therefore be willing to transfer 17,000 units at a price that would give total contribution margin of $1,950,000 or more. Accordingly, the minimum acceptable price is $214.70 using basic CVP relationships. The calculations are as follows:

$$\text{required price} = \frac{\text{total required contribution margin}}{\text{unit volume}} + \text{variable cost per unit}$$

$$= \frac{\$1,950,000}{17,000} + \$100$$

$$= \$114.70 + \$100$$

$$= \$214.70$$

The manager of Lakehart can earn a contribution margin of $4,550,000 if he buys 13,000 units at $250, as calculated above. He must obtain a transfer price for 17,000 units that would give at least $4,550,000 in contribution margin to induce him to make 17,000 units. Here, we need to solve for the maximum variable cost that would give that contribution margin. The selling price for 17,000 units of the final product is $800. Again using CVP relationships:

$$\text{maximum variable cost} = \text{selling price} - \frac{\text{total contribution margin}}{\text{unit volume}}$$

$$= \$800 - \frac{\$4,550,000}{17,000}$$

$$= \$800 - \$267.65$$

$$= \$532.35$$

Lakehart incurs $300 variable costs of its own, so that the maximum allowable transfer price is $232.35 ($532.35 − $300).[7]

Lakehart's maximum is above Verguenza's minimum, so the two managers could well come to an agreement somewhere in the middle. However, they might not for various reasons. The manager of Verguenza might refuse to lower the price, however unwisely. Corporate management might have to intervene to force the managers to make decisions that are optimal from the firm's standpoint. Please notice especially that the *market price* of the component does not *provide the information needed* for optimal decisions. Negotiation and compromise are required.

Other Assumptions

The previous analysis requires that the divisions be independent in the sense that the actions of one do not affect the results of the other. If the assumption does not hold, the divisions are interdependent and the analysis becomes quite complex. Two types of independence are of especial importance: revenue and cost. Taking revenue first, the divisions are independent if the price that one charges does not affect the demand for the product of the other. In this respect, the divisions of a large automobile manufacturer would not be independent. An increase in the price of Oldsmobiles, for example, would probably result in higher demand for Chevrolets.

Cost independence requires that the output of one division not affect the level of costs of the other. If two divisions compete for resources, their costs are likely to be interdependent. For example, if two divisions require highly skilled labor, the more that one division demands, the higher the wages that both divisions will have to pay.

If divisions are significantly interdependent, it is extremely difficult to evaluate them as if they were separate, autonomous units. An example is the extreme case of the division that makes a product without an intermediate market and can set the level of output of the final product by setting the

---

[7] If the managers, or corporate management, consider only the transfer price, not both the transfer price and the quantity to be transferred, the analysis above is derailed. The manager of Lakehart is better off selling (and buying from Verguenza) only 13,000 units so long as the transfer price is greater than $175. If the manager of Verguenza offers to sell any quantity at a price above $175, the manager of Lakehart will take 13,000 units. Let X = the contribution margin per unit at sales of 13,000 units. Then $X − \$100$ is contribution margin per unit at sales of 17,000, because the price at which Lakehart could sell 17,000 units is $800, compared to $900 at 13,000 units. The indifference contribution margin, X, is

$$13,000X = 17,000(X − \$100)$$
$$4,000X = \$1,700,000$$
$$X = \$425$$

For a contribution margin of $425 at 13,000 units, $325 at 17,000 units (both of which would yield $5,525,000 total contribution), total variable costs must be $475 ($900 − $425 or $800 − $325). Subtracting the $300 leaves $175 for the component from Verguenza.

level of the intermediate product. As already seen (no intermediate market), there is no use in treating the divisions as separate profit centers.

Concluding Remarks

The most disturbing conclusion of the economic analyses is that market prices serve as good transfer prices only in the presence of perfectly competitive markets for intermediate products, or if the selling division is at capacity. Even then, revenue and cost interdependencies are possible. If they exist, market prices may not be ideal transfer prices. In the real world, we would not expect to find many perfectly competitive markets. Markets for agricultural products are about as close as we could come. In most other markets, including those for raw materials such as metals, there are some very large buyers or sellers whose actions affect the market price.

Accordingly, it does not seem possible to achieve both goal congruence and autonomy in practice. Of course, if intrafirm transfers are relatively small, the loss of some autonomy or of some profits from suboptimal decisions may not be worth worrying about. However, there is an additional point to consider. The economic analysis assumes that managers have perfect knowledge of demand curves and cost curves. (More precisely, it assumes that they have single-point expectations regarding these curves, rather than ranges of expectations.) The question is whether managers operating in practice will tend to make more goal-congruent decisions than ones pictured in economic analyses.

In the absence of perfect knowledge, managers are likely to be somewhat more cautious than the all-knowing ones described above. Most notably, they would probably set prices based on costs and on competition (which need not mean perfectly competitive markets), then strive to sell a budgeted quantity. In dealing with sister divisions, they might tend to act as if they were dealing with just another customer, using their selling prices to outsiders as the basis for negotiating transfer prices. In short, they might very well make decisions that did not provide the greatest profit to the firm.

The gloom is not unrelieved. Very few managerial situations (or any others, for that matter) present clear-cut choices of all good or all bad consequences. It may be that the possible losses in profits resulting from suboptimal decisions are more than offset by higher profits resulting from dealings with outside firms. Suboptimal decisions involving intrafirm transfers might be a small price to pay for decentralization. Corporate management simply cannot respond as quickly as divisional management when circumstances change and opportunities arise.

There is an interesting and instructive parallel given by centrally controlled economies, such as those of socialist countries.[8] Central planners

---

[8] A good deal of the theory of transfer pricing owes an intellectual debt to researchers who were trying to develop optimal methods of allocating resources in centralized economies. The use of mathematical programming techniques, described briefly later in this chapter, is a direct descendant of such research.

make decisions regarding prices and quantities in many countries. Their records are not unblemished. Newspapers and magazines provide numerous accounts of shortages of some products, gluts of others. Black-market activities are notoriously common when prices are centrally controlled. Economic dislocations are prevalent. To cite one example, it has been argued that the United States Department of Energy, which has acted as a central planner in such matters as allocating gasoline to various states and locales, made the gasoline shortage of the summer of 1979 worse than it would have been had it simply kept hands off. We are not taking a position here on the role of government or of the oil companies. We simply point out that central planners must possess knowledge that is exceedingly difficult to develop. Decentralization in national economies seems to work much better than centralization.

The energy crisis has stimulated the development of wood-burning stoves, greater use of insulation, and other measures. It is doubtful that a central planner would have been able to determine, for example, how many wood stoves should be produced and at what price they should have been sold. Business firms are in a much better position to make these decisions. In fact, even if all industry were governmentally owned, we would be better off if the managers of the firms made decisions, rather than central planners.

COST-BASED TRANSFER PRICES

When the selling division is operating below capacity, marginal cost is the ideal transfer price. When it is at capacity, market price is ideal. The problem with using marginal cost is that corporate management destroys autonomy by imposing transfer prices. However, if the products involved are a relatively small part of the output of a division, some type of cost-based transfer price might satisfy all the managers.

Additionally, in some situations managers cannot be allowed complete freedom. A division that makes a patented component used by another division might be required to sell only to that division and refuse offers from outsiders. Other strategic considerations such as ensuring a reliable long-run supply of a good might make it sensible to require internal purchase and sale. In such situations, the rule that a division should be able to treat a sister division just like any other customer or supplier could not prevail. Cost-based prices might be the only alternative available.

In effect, cost-based transfer prices are allocations, subject to all the objections and problems that we described in Chapter 12. Allocations involving service departments are optional for managerial purposes even though required for financial reporting and tax purposes. However, when one division sells goods to another, some credit must be given to the selling division and some charge made to the buying division if they are profit centers. Accordingly, the problem is how to make the allocations, not whether to make them. As usual, there are several alternatives, each with some points in favor and some against.

Actual Costs

Perhaps the worst basis for setting transfer prices is actual cost, either absorption or variable cost. The reason is that actual cost does not encourage the manager of the selling division to control costs: someone else is going to pay them. On occasion, the use of actual cost may even encourage the manager of the selling division to allow costs to rise deliberately. This may occur when a margin for profit is included in the pricing formula.

Consider an example. Suppose that the manager of Lakehart division orders 1,000 fans from the Verguenza division. The transfer price is to be actual full cost (with fixed overhead applied) plus a 10 percent allowance for profit.[9] The fan usually requires 2 labor hours, and total variable costs should be $20 per fan. Verguenza applies fixed overhead at a rate of $4 per direct labor hour. The transfer price would be $30.80 per fan, calculated as follows:

Total variable cost	$20.00
Applied fixed overhead	8.00
Total cost	28.00
Allowance for profit (0.10 × $28)	2.80
Price	$30.80

Suppose that through inefficiency, total labor time per unit increased to 2.5 hours and total variable costs increased to $25. Fixed overhead would then be $10 ($4 × 2.5), total cost $35, and the transfer price $38.50 ($35 + $3.50). The manager of Lakehart would be charged with the inefficiency of Verguenza, and in fact would pay even more for it because both fixed overhead and the profit margin are affected by actual labor hours.

The situation would be worse if actual fixed costs, rather than applied fixed costs, were used. First, fixed overhead budget variances would be incorporated into the transfer price. Second, the activity of the period would affect the rate per direct labor hour, which in turn would affect the overhead cost allocated to the fans, and the transfer price. The manager of Verguenza could be tempted to schedule the production of the fans in periods of low volume, so that the rate would be higher, with a corresponding increase in the transfer price.

The use of actual variable cost, rather than actual absorption cost, would relieve one problem: the level of activity during the period would not affect the transfer price. However, assuming that the transfer price is set at some multiple of variable cost to allow for some recovery of fixed costs, the objection that the manager has no incentive to control costs still holds.

Standard or Budgeted Costs

In some cases, variable cost will approximate marginal cost, making variable cost an excellent transfer price so long as it represents efficient opera-

[9] The price is based on normal cost because of the application of fixed overhead. We consider the "pure" actual cost case shortly.

tion. Standard variable costs should fulfill that requirement: they should be representative of efficient operation and, therefore, they overcome the problem of failing to motivate the manager to control costs.

If standard variable costs do serve as transfer prices, with no allowance for recovery of fixed costs and contribution to profit, the manager of the selling division is being penalized. He or she is expected to produce goods for another division in an efficient manner and show no increase in total profit. Obviously, managers of selling divisions will not be delighted with this. The only chance of showing any profit on transfers is to make the goods at less than standard variable cost. Accordingly, there may be some motivation to cut corners and otherwise try to reduce costs. This tendency might be beneficial, but it could also be harmful if quality suffered. There are some alternatives that might prove satisfactory, and we next consider a few of these.

Standard Absorption Cost.   One possibility is to use standard absorption cost, with or without a markup. This would overcome the problems associated with using actual costs, but it would not provide a transfer price that reflects the marginal cost of the transferred goods, and so it could lead to poor decisions.

Suppose that there is no real market for the fans that Verguenza is to make for the Lakehart division. Assume further that the $20 variable cost is standard and that the transfer price is $30.80 as calculated above. Now, the manager of Lakehart might solicit bids from outside firms for the fans. Suppose that an outside firm offers to supply them at $26 per unit. If the manager of Verguenza does not meet that price, the manager of Lakehart will buy from the outside firm.

Buying the fans outside would reduce profits for the firm. The incremental (marginal) cost of production internally is $20 per unit, which is less than the $26 outside price. As we noted earlier, this is a make-or-buy decision from the standpoint of the firm. The manager of Verguenza should be willing to meet the price because it would provide $6 per unit in contribution margin and increased profit. However, the standard full cost transfer price does not encourage optimal action. Notice that this case does not conform to a market situation. It might be argued that the $26 outside bid is a market price, but it is not a price that could be used for decisions stretching beyond the single sale. If Lakehart needed 1,000 fans per year for several years, it would not use the $26 price for a single year's supply as the basis for making the long-run decision. The supplier could turn out to be unreliable or could raise the price after the first year.

The main advantage of using standard absorption costing, with a markup, is that it might reflect the price that would prevail if there were a market for the goods. The reasoning is as follows. If other firms were making the same product, they would probably base their prices on absorption cost plus a markup. If their cost structures and markup policies were similar to those of the internal division, their prices would approximate the transfer price. There is some evidence that firms sometimes set transfer prices by building up costs and markups based on what a hypothetical outside firm would do if it were going to market the product.

Standard Variable Cost Plus Lump Sum.   We recommended this method of allocating service department costs in Chapter 12. It is also a possible basis for transfer pricing and has some distinct advantages. As an allocation method, it works as follows: The user is charged a flat amount per period based on expected long-run use of the service and a variable amount that depends on actual use in each period. In a transfer-pricing context, the selling division would charge the buying division some flat amount per month or per year. It would then charge an amount approximating variable cost per unit for the number of units actually transferred during a given period.

For example, the Verguenza division might charge the Lakehart division $30,000 per year for the fans, plus $20 per fan. The $30,000 could be determined in a number of ways. It could represent a share of fixed costs based on the expected share of direct labor hours that the fans would require over a three-year period. It could also include some margin for profit. It could also be a figure negotiated by the two managers, without an attempt to do much analysis of fixed costs.

The major advantage of this method of transfer pricing is that it results in the individual units' being transferred at an amount that approximates marginal cost. The buying division incurs the flat fee no matter how many units it buys—it is a sunk cost and is irrelevant in deciding how many units to buy from the inside supplier. Because the individual units are transferred at variable cost, make-or-buy decisions are simplified. If an outside supplier is willing to provide the units at less than the internal variable cost, it should be welcome to do so. (Of course, this conclusion assumes that the supplier is able to meet delivery schedules, quality standards, and so on.)

Dual Pricing

A method that offers the best of both worlds is to charge the buying division with the marginal cost of the transferred goods and to credit the selling division with a higher amount. The higher amount could be a market price or a figure based on standard absorption costs with an allowance for profit. This method is not widely used, at least partly because revenue to the selling division is greater than cost to the buying division, which strikes many managers and accountants as extremely artificial. The incomes of the divisions will exceed the income of the firm, even if all corporate costs are allocated to divisions. The differences are wiped out on the corporate books.

The major advantage of the system is that both divisions benefit. The managers are likely to make goal-congruent decisions because each is working with a relevant value. The manager of the buying division is confronted with a make-or-buy or a further-processing decision, and the marginal cost of the goods is a critical datum. The manager of the selling division is not penalized for dealing internally and, therefore, does not care where the goods go.

Besides its strangeness, the method has another drawback. The manager of the selling division is not motivated to keep costs down unless the transfer price is a market price. If a cost-plus formula is used, the manager of the selling division may become complacent because he has a near-captive customer. The manager of the buying division is unlikely to find an outside supplier whose prices are less than the marginal costs of producing internally, and so he is almost certain to be bound to the selling division.

Gaming and Misinformation

One of the problems of using cost-based transfer prices is that they may encourage misestimations of costs. Consider the following example. Division A makes a number of products in a single factory. It sells them all to outside customers except for product X, which it sells exclusively to division B, which makes it into another product. Corporate management, as well as the manager of division B, would like the transfer price of product X to approximate its variable cost.[10] Corporate management would like to see variable cost as the transfer price, because the principal decision is whether to process product X beyond the point to which division A brings it.[11]

The manager of division A will have a different view. Even if he or she decides to supply the needs of division B at variable cost, there is still room to maneuver. The manager of division A will likely try to build some cushion into the variable-cost figure used by overstating costs. It is rarely possible to estimate variable costs with certainty, and the estimates of the manager of division A may be significantly higher than the actual costs. The problems here are obvious. The firm would not be using valid data for deciding on the various matters related to product X (whether to process it further, whether to seek an outside supplier, and so on).

The manager of division A is clearly in a better position than corporate management and the manager of division B to determine variable cost. It is, therefore, likely that he or she would be able to get a price somewhat above the optimal, which is variable cost. In fact, if the manager of division A is not in a better position to develop and interpret information regarding the operations of division A, there is no need to decentralize. One of the principal benefits of decentralization is that people who are close to the information needed to make decisions are the ones who do make the decisions.

---

[10] For variable cost, we could well substitute marginal cost. We assume for simplicity that variable cost equals marginal cost.

[11] There might be outside sources of product X, so that division B and the firm as a whole could also be looking at a make-or-buy decision. However, if other firms made product X, it is likely that division A could sell the product to someone else. Other firms would not be likely to make a product that had no market. Of course, other firms might make product X in order to process it further into product Y. Such a firm would be interested in serving division B.

NEGOTIATED TRANSFER PRICES

A possible solution to the transfer-pricing problem is to allow the divisional managers to negotiate the prices among themselves, with corporate management intervening only if an impasse arises. There is much to recommend this proposal. Divisional managers negotiate such matters as delivery schedules, specifications, and quantities on interdivisional transfers, so it may seem reasonable to allow them to negotiate prices as well.[12]

The usual objection to negotiated transfer prices is that the performance of a divisional manager would be affected by his or her skill as a negotiator, as well as by efficiency and effectiveness in operating the division. The counter to this objection is that negotiating ability is part of the package of talents that a manager needs. Divisional managers negotiate with their peers within the firm and they also negotiate with outsiders on many of the same kinds of matters, as well as others.

One aspect of a transfer-pricing system that allows negotiation is some provision for appeal to a higher level. The corporation might have a board or a single arbitrator who steps in when the divisional managers cannot agree and something must be done. Appeal to a higher authority does lessen the degree of autonomy, but it may be necessary if the well-being of the firm is at stake. For example, the manager of the buying division may dispute the cost data that the manager of the selling division is providing to support his claim for a particular price. If the transfer is clearly in the interests of the firm, it would be reasonable for corporate management to intervene and set a price.

PROGRAMMED PRICES

We have seen that when the selling division is operating at capacity it should transfer goods at the outside market price (less any costs avoided by dealing inside instead of outside) because the market price is the opportunity cost of the goods. Linear programming provides opportunity costs of using scarce resources—the shadow prices on the constraints. Moreover, a large firm that does extensive inside transferring could use linear programming to determine the best overall mix of dealing inside and outside.

The idea is that transfer prices should be the variable costs of a division, including any transfer prices it has paid, plus the opportunity costs (shadow prices) of the scarce resources that the division uses in making the product. The central headquarters of the firm would determine the optimal overall mix, and the divisional managers would then implement it. Unfortunately, as several writers have pointed out, there can be some very sticky questions

---

[12] See the article by Watson and Baumler in the Selected References at the end of this chapter.

and potentially dysfunctional behavior on the part of divisional managers.[13]

We consider a simple example. To the extent that problems arise in a simple case, we would expect even worse difficulties in a more realistic one.

Illustration

The ABC Company operates three divisions, A, B, and C. Division A makes a product that it can sell only to division B. In turn, division B can sell outside or to division C, which sells only to outsiders. We assume for simplicity that all costs are fixed, so that selling price equals contribution margin. The work that each division does requires one unit of capacity for each unit of product. No other firm makes the product. The following schedule shows the selling prices that each division can obtain, along with its capacity.

Division	Selling Price	Capacity
A	none	100
B	$15	110
C	20	60

Letting A, B, and C denote the quantities sold outside by the respective divisions, we have the following linear programming problem.

Maximize: $\$0A + \$15B + \$20C$

Subject to:

$$
\begin{aligned}
A + B + C &\le 100 \quad \text{(division A constraint)} \\
B + C &\le 110 \quad \text{(division B constraint)} \\
C &\le 60 \quad \text{(division C constraint)} \\
A, B, C &\ge 0
\end{aligned}
$$

The optimal solution is $40B$ and $60C$, which uses all the capacities of divisions A and C, while leaving 10 units of division B capacity idle. The shadow price on division A capacity is $15. Because any additional units that division A could make should go through division B and then be sold at $15, the shadow price exceeds the market price of units sold outside after division A has processed them. The shadow price on division B capacity is zero, because the division cannot work at capacity. Thus, division B would sell to division C at the transfer price that division B pays division A (which is division B's variable cost).

If we interpret the opportunity costs strictly, division A would charge division B $15 per unit. Division B would then earn zero contribution margin because it would pay $15 and sell for $15, both outside and to division

---

[13] Good discussions of this area appear in Onsi, in Manes, and in Dopuch and Drake, cited in the Selected References at the end of the chapter. Thomas provides an extensive discussion and a comprehensive bibliography.

C. Now, market prices would be fine as transfer prices here, if we had a market price for units made by division A.

Of course, it might be possible to work out acceptable arrangements among the divisions, but the corporation would be imposing its will on the divisional managers if it developed a product mix program and set the transfer prices. Thus, one of the salient objections to the use of linear programming is that it destroys, or at least seriously impairs, divisional autonomy.

Lest we too quickly assume that mathematical programming has no place in transfer pricing, let us point out that it is useful just as the economic model is useful. Any transfer price should be based on a notion of cost and optimality. Even if managers decide to follow different criteria for decisions on product mix, quantity, and transfer prices, accountants will want to provide incremental cost, marginal cost, and programmed solutions as information to be used in various decisions.

SUMMARY

Transfer pricing is an extraordinarily complex and difficult topic. Even in relatively simple situations it is unwise to expect that transfer prices will both promote goal congruence and foster autonomy of divisions. Therefore, in more realistic situations, we would expect gaming and other dysfunctional behavior.

Market prices are good transfer prices so long as markets are competitive and the individual firm does not affect market prices by its own actions. This is unlikely in large firms. Cost-based transfer prices are frequently used, but they should be used with great care because they can lead to very bad results.

APPENDIX 18–A: TRANSFER PRICING— NO INTERMEDIATE MARKET

This appendix gives a mathematical solution to the transfer-pricing problem depicted in Figure 18–2. The figure shows net marginal revenue from sales of product B, marginal cost of product A, and marginal revenue of product A derived from net marginal revenue of product B. We provide here a more complete treatment that should help you understand how such functions are developed. We begin with the net marginal-revenue curve of product B, which is given by:

$$(18A–1) \qquad NMR(B) = 100 - 0.50Q$$

where $NMR(B)$ = net marginal revenue of product B
Q = the number of units of product B sold

Because product B requires product A, and because division A is the only supplier of product A and division B is the only buyer of product A, the quantities of products A and B must be equal. (We ignore inventories.) Therefore, Q equals the number of units of product A and of product B sold during the period.

Net marginal revenue is the marginal revenue less the marginal cost of product B, without considering the transfer price that division B pays to division A. Accordingly, net marginal revenue is the change in profit resulting from a change in quantity of product sold and, therefore, is the first derivative of the profit function of product B (again, excluding the transfer price, which is a cost to division B). We can write the equation that depicts the profit of division B before the transfer price:

$$(18A-2) \qquad NR(B) = 100Q - 0.25Q^2 - F$$

where $NR(B)$ = profit for division B before transfer price
F = fixed costs of division B

Fixed costs would disappear in determining the first derivative of $NR(B)$, and we shall assume that they are zero in order to reduce calculations and notation. Including fixed costs would have no effect on the results of our analysis.

We now turn our attention to division A. The total costs of division A are assumed to be:

$$(18A-3) \qquad TC(A) = F + 4Q + 0.25Q^2$$

where $TC(A)$ = total costs of division A
F = fixed costs of division A

Again, we assume that fixed costs are zero, without diminishing the significance of the results. Division A's marginal cost, $MC(A)$, is the first derivative of total cost:

$$(18A-4) \qquad MC(A) = 4 + 0.50Q$$

The profit-maximizing output for the firm occurs where the net marginal revenue from product B equals the marginal cost to produce product A. Using equations 18A–1 and 18A–4, we get:

$$100 - 0.50Q = 4 + 0.50Q$$
$$Q = 96$$

At an output of 96 units of product B, the marginal cost of product A will be $52, which is the optimal transfer price. ($52 = 4 + 0.50Q$). The net revenue, or profit excluding the transfer price, from product B is $7,296, determined by equation 18A–2:

$$NR(B) = 100Q - 0.25Q^2$$
$$= 100(96) - 0.25(96)^2$$
$$= \$7,296$$

The total costs of division A are $2,688, from equation 18A-3:

$$TC(A) = 4(96) + 0.25(96)^2$$
$$= \$2,688$$

Total profits for the firm are $4,608. Using the $52 transfer price, profits for division A are $2,304 [$52(96) − $2,688] and for division B are also $2,304 [$7,296 − $52(96)]. The equality of profits is coincidental.

A couple of other points should be mentioned here. At a transfer price of $52, division B maximizes its profits by taking 96 units of product A and changing them into product B. This is because the transfer price is a marginal cost to division B, and it maximizes its profits when its net marginal revenue equals its marginal cost. Thus, if its marginal cost is $52, it maximizes profits at 96 units. Using equation 18A-1:

$$100 - 0.50Q = 52$$
$$Q = 96$$

Division A also maximizes its profits, again given the transfer price of $52, at an output of 96 units. The $52 is marginal revenue to division A and so it will produce until its marginal cost equals $52, which is at 96 units. Unfortunately, as we show in the next section, both divisions could do better (although not both at the same time) by acting suboptimally.

Divisional Standpoints

Let us begin with division B. It would naturally like the lowest possible transfer price. In fact, it would like a transfer price of zero. At that price, division B would take 200 units and would earn total profits of $10,000. A transfer price of zero gives the manager of division B a marginal cost of zero. Therefore, he would take units until his net marginal revenue became zero. Using equation 18A-1, we find:

$$100 - 0.50Q = 0$$
$$Q = 200$$

Total profits will be given by equation 18A-2:

$$NR(B) = 100(200) - 0.25(200)^2$$
$$= \$10,000$$

However, the firm as a whole will show a loss of $800 because division A will incur costs of $10,800, as given by equation 18A-3:

$$TC(A) = 4(200) + 0.25(200)^2$$
$$= \$10,800$$

Would it be possible for the manager of division B to somehow get 200 units of A at a transfer price of zero? Probably not, but he or she certainly has some inducement to persuade corporate management that the transfer price should be lower than its current level and that division A should supply all of division B's needs. The manager of division B might argue that the manager of division A is not controlling costs well, or is overstating costs in order to get a higher transfer price. The manager of division B wants the lowest transfer price obtainable and has a good deal of inducement to seek that objective.

The manager of division A can also act unwisely, and perhaps more easily than can the manager of division B. We saw above that the manager of division B must somehow get the transfer price lowered and get as many units of product A as he needs to maximize profits. The manager of division A, if he is able to act autonomously, can increase his divisional profit by reducing the supply of product A and charging a higher price. The net-marginal-revenue curve of division B is the demand curve, or price curve, for division A. This is because division B's manager will pay an amount up to net marginal revenue to get a given number of units of product A. Division B's manager would prefer to pay less, but he will pay up to net marginal revenue if forced. The following analysis shows why.

The price curve facing division A is equation 18A–1. Therefore, the total-revenue curve facing division A is equation 18A–1 multiplied by Q. Thus, total revenue to division A from sales to division B are given by equation 18A–5:

(18A–5) $$TR(A) = 100Q - 0.50Q^2$$

Therefore, marginal revenue to division A is the first derivative of equation 18A–5, given by equation 18A–6:

(18A–6) $$MR(A) = 100 - Q$$

The manager of division A maximizes profits where marginal revenue equals marginal cost:

$$100 - Q = 4 + 0.50Q$$
$$96 = 1.5Q$$
$$Q = 64$$

The manager of division A will charge \$68 per unit, relying on equation 18A–1:

$$NMR(B) = 100 - 0.50(64)$$
$$= \$68$$

And the manager of division B would take 64 units at the $68 price. The manager of division A would increase profits to $3,072, given by equation 18A–5 minus equation 18A–3:

$$\text{profit} = 100(64) - 0.50(64)^2 - [4(64) + 0.25(64)^2]$$
$$= 6,400 - 2,048 - 256 - 1,024$$
$$= \$3,072$$

The income of the firm will fall to $4,096. Division B will show a profit of $1,024, from equation 18A–2 and the transfer price:

$$\text{profit} = 100(64) - 0.25(64)^2 - 68(64)$$
$$= 6,400 - 1,024 - 4,352$$
$$= \$1,024$$

What is to prevent the manager of division A from restricting output to obtain a higher transfer price? Either altruism or a directive from corporate headquarters would do the job. It is unlikely that a manager would be motivated by altruism if he or she were evaluated on the basis of profits (or ROI, or RI, both of which depend on profits). And if corporate headquarters imposes a solution, the autonomy of the divisions is lost. The answer in the limited case considered here was given in the text: make division A a cost center instead of a profit center. The lack of an outside market makes it unwise to evaluate managers on the basis of profits.

ASSIGNMENTS

18–1   Market Price and Variable Cost. The Gorman Company has several operating divisions that are expected to act autonomously. The firm maintains a central data processing department that recently became a profit center and began to charge divisions for the work it did at market prices. Market prices for data processing services are easy to obtain, so the prices are reliable indicators of what the divisions would have to pay to acquire the services outside.

The manager of one operating division has data processing requirements that would cost $12,500 if bought either outside or from the internal department. He could develop the required information using clerical labor at a cost of $9,500. The variable cost to provide the services through the internal data processing department is about $2,800.

Required: Discuss the issues and problems involved in the situation.

18–2   Transfer-Pricing Dispute. The Industrial Products Division (IPD) of Chemco Inc. has been leasing warehouse space from the Consumer Products Division (CPD) for several years. The agreement provides that CPD will reserve 20 percent of its available space in each of five warehouses for IPD at a rent of $90,000 per year.

Until recently, IPD has used all of its allotment, but demand for some of its products has fallen and it will not use more than about 60 percent of its allotted space in the coming year. The manager of IPD informed the manager of CPD, who was able to find customers for the space that IPD would not use. The aggregate rentals from the space are $37,000 for the year. The manager of IPD has asked for a reduction in his rental payment to $53,000. He argues that CPD will not be losing money, as its total rentals will still be $90,000 for the space.

The manager of CPD retorts that he will not accept any reduction because he was willing to provide the space, had IPD needed it. He further points out that he has gotten the additional $37,000 through his own efforts and has no intention of giving it up.

Required: Discuss the issues and make a recommendation.

18-3 **Transfer Pricing—Data Processing Services.** The manager of the billing department of Conway Industries received the following charges for computer use:

	March	April
Central processing unit:		
5,890 minutes at $0.984	$ 5,795.76	
6,102 minutes at $0.783		$ 4,777.87
Storage:		
597 units at $33.47	19,981.59	
537 units at $37.23		19,992.51
Other	1,203.67	1,451.32
Total	$26,981.02	$26,221.70

The manager is held responsible for data processing costs and has consistently been over budget during the past six months. His inquiries to the data processing manager have brought the following information.

Data processing costs are largely fixed. Each department that uses DP services receives charges based on actual use for the period. The controller's office has prescribed allocations of DP costs into central processing unit, storage, and other, based on formulas published in trade journals. Accordingly, each user is charged with a proportionate share of the cost of each of the three basic components of use.

Required: Comment on the system that the firm uses to charge for data processing costs. Would you recommend any changes?

18-4 **Transfer Prices and Decisions.** The Tourny division sells its one product to outsiders and to the Crayton division, which is also part of National Products Company. Crayton uses the product as a component of one of its products. The income statement below gives budgeted results for the Tourny division for the coming year.

	Total	Outside Sales	Sales to Crayton Division
Sales	$350,000	$200,000	$150,000
Variable costs	160,000	80,000	80,000
Contribution margin	190,000	$120,000	$ 70,000
Fixed costs	120,000		
Income	$ 70,000		
Assets employed	$280,000		

The selling price to outside customers is $20, to Crayton division $15. Divisional managers are evaluated on ROI.

Required:

1. The manager of the Crayton division receives an offer from an outside firm to supply the product at $11. If the manager of the Tourny division will not meet the price, he will take the business outside. Tourny cannot increase its sales to outsiders. It will save $20,000 in fixed costs and reduce its assets employed by $40,000 if it loses Crayton's business. From the standpoint of the Tourny division, should its manager reduce the transfer price?

2. Suppose now that if the Crayton division went outside for the product, the Tourny division could increase its outside sales by 4,000 units. Its fixed costs would be $120,000 and its assets employed would be $260,000. From the standpoint of the Tourny division, what action should its manager take? Assume also that Tourny cannot increase its outside sales unless it drops the Crayton business because of capacity limitations. Further, the outside supplier will not supply fewer than 10,000 units at the $11 price, so that Tourny supplies either 10,000 units or none to Crayton.

3. Answer items 1 and 2 from the standpoint of the firm.

18-5 Transfer Pricing (AICPA adapted). The Mar Company operates two decentralized divisions, X and Y. Division X has been buying a component from Division Y at a price of $75 per unit. Because Division Y plans to increase the price to $100, Division X has looked for and found an outside supplier who will furnish the component at $75 per unit. Division Y incurs the following costs.

Variable cost per unit of component	$70
Annual fixed costs	$15,000
Annual production of component	1,000 units

If Division X does buy from an outside supplier, the facilities that Division Y devotes to producing the component would be idled.

Required: Select the *best* answer to the following question: What would be the effect of Mar Company's enforcing a transfer price of $100 and requiring Division X to buy from Division Y?

1. It would be suboptimization for the firm, because X should buy from an outside supplier at $75 per unit.
2. It would provide lower overall company profit than a transfer price of $75.
3. It would provide higher overall company profit than a transfer price of $75.
4. It would be more profitable for the company than allowing X to buy from an outside supplier at $75 per unit.

18–6 Prices and Market Conditions. The Oliver Company has several divisions that deal in different types of electronic products. The Nason division makes integrated circuits, selling about 90 percent of its output to outside firms. The division is operating well below capacity because of oversupply of the type of circuit that it makes.

Recently, the Frith division, which makes consumer products, developed an electronic bridge game that could use the circuit made by the Nason division. The manager of the Nason division quoted a price of $72 per circuit, which would provide a $41 contribution margin. The price is somewhat below the current market price of the circuit.

The controller of the Frith division developed the following estimates of costs for the bridge game.

Materials, including $72 for one circuit from Nason	$157
Direct labor	22
Factory overhead	80
Selling and administrative expenses	14
Total cost	$273

Factory overhead is about 50 percent fixed, and selling and administrative expenses contain $4 variable cost, with the remainder fixed.

Frith division's head of marketing submitted the following estimates of volumes at different selling prices.

Price	Volume
$400	4,000 units
350	6,000
300	9,000
250	13,000

Nason has enough capacity to meet the 13,000 maximum volume that Frith could obtain. Divisional managers are evaluated on ROI, and total investment would be the same for any of the volumes that Frith may sell.

Required:

1. As the manager of the Frith division, what price would you charge for the bridge game?
2. As the president of the firm, what price would you like Frith division to charge for the game?
3. If your answers to items 1 and 2 conflict, suggest a way to achieve goal congruence, while maintaining the autonomy of the divisional managers.

18-7 Prices and Market Conditions. Refer to the preceding assignment. Suppose that the Nason division has no excess capacity even without the business from the Frith division. The market price of the circuit that Nason could supply to Frith is $72.

Required:

1. What is the optimal price of the bridge game from the standpoint of the firm?
2. If Nason charges Frith $72 per circuit, what is the optimal price of the bridge game from the standpoint of the Frith division?
3. What is the optimal transfer price, or the range of optimal transfer prices, in the sense of fostering goal congruence and maintaining autonomy?

18-8 International Transfers. The RSE Company operates divisions in several nations. The Moore division operates in country A, the Bowton division in country B. Bowton division wants to buy a component from Moore division for $100, while Moore wants the price to be $150. Variable cost to Moore is $40. Bowton incurs an additional $50 cost per unit and sells the finished item for $250.

The tax rate in country A is 42 percent, in country B 46 percent. Additionally, country B levies a duty of 12 percent of the price of any goods imported into it. (Bowton would pay the duty.) The duty is tax deductible.

Required: Determine which transfer price would be better from the standpoint of the RSE Company.

18-9 No Intermediate Market (appendix). The SP Company has two divisions. Division P manufactures a single product and transfers it to division S, which sells it with no further processing. The revenue and cost functions appear below.

$$NMR(S) = \$350 - \$3Q \qquad \text{(the net marginal revenue for division } S)$$
$$\text{profit}(S) = \$350Q - \$1.5Q^2$$
$$TC(P) = \$1,000 + \$10Q + \$0.20Q^2$$

Required:

1. Determine the output that will maximize the profits of the firm.

2. Determine the output that division S would select to maximize its profits.

18–10 Interdependence. The Priam division of the Chester Company requires an electric motor for a new lawnmower that it intends to market next summer. The purchasing manager of the division has secured three bids from outside firms and one from the Jay division of Chester. Jay bid $60 for the motor and would incur variable costs of $47. Jay has excess capacity, and making the motors would not bring the division up to capacity operations.

The bids submitted by the outside firms are summarized below. Norton Motors bid $54. Jasper Electric bid $57, but would buy parts for the motor from the Monroe division of Chester for $22. The $22 is market value for the parts, and Monroe earns about 60 percent contribution margin. Monroe would operate at capacity whether or not it sold parts to Jasper Electric, and its manager has assured Jasper that it would meet its needs, after being informed that the motor was for the Priam division. Coulton, Inc., bid $58 for the motor and would buy parts from the Allen division of Chester for $28. Allen division has excess capacity and would incur variable costs of $15.

Required: Determine what the manager of Priam would do in his own best interests and what he should do in the firm's best interests. If your answers conflict, suggest a way to resolve the problem.

18–11 Transfer Prices and Profit Centers. The PS Company has been centralized for some years. The sales manager orders units from the production manager, who is obligated to supply as many as are ordered. The sales manager is evaluated on total revenue, the production manager on unit cost. Recently the president of the firm decided it might be worthwhile to set up the sales and production functions as profit centers, evaluated on the basis of profits. The two managers would negotiate the transfer price.

The following schedule shows the possible selling prices of the product on the outside market, the volume associated with each price, and the total production cost for that level of output. The selling division has no costs. The production manager cannot sell directly to the market: his only customer is the sales manager.

Selling Price	Volume	Total Production Costs
$10	100,000	$ 880,000
9	120,000	930,000
8	150,000	1,026,000
7	180,000	1,131,000
6	200,000	1,203,000

These relationships have held in the past and are expected to continue. Under the proposed setup, the transfer price must be an even dollar amount.

Required:

1. Determine the number of units that the sales manager would have been ordering under the old arrangement, where he was evaluated based on total revenue.

2. What is the optimal outside price/volume combination for the firm?

3. Suppose that the production manager sets a transfer price and the sales manager decides how many units to take at that price. How many units will the sales manager buy at transfer prices of $9, $8, $7, and $6?

4. At what transfer price would the sales manager be indifferent between (a) selling 100,000 units at $10 and 120,000 at $9 and (b) selling 120,000 units at $9 and 150,000 at $8?

5. What suggestions would you make to the president, who has asked your advice in helping him decide whether to decentralize?

18–12 Prices and Actions (CMA adapted). The manager of the Frigidwind division of National Industries, Inc., believes that he can increase sales of his air conditioners if he reduces the selling price by $20. A budgeted income statement for the coming year, without considering the proposed reduction, is given below.

Sales, 4,000 units at $400	$1,600,000
Variable costs at $200 per unit	800,000
Contribution margin	800,000
Fixed costs	420,000
Profit before taxes	$ 380,000

The proposed price reduction would increase volume by 500 units, according to a market research study in which the manager has a great deal of confidence. Part of the variable cost of the product is a compressor that the division now buys for $70 from an outside supplier. The manager approaches the manager of the compressor division of National Industries and offers to pay $50 per unit for a compressor that the division currently makes and sells exclusively to outside firms. The manager of Frigidwind will not accept fewer than 4,500 units.

Data for the compressor division are given below.

Budgeted sales, 17,000 units at $100		$1,700,000
Variable costs:		
Production	$510,000	
Selling	102,000	612,000
Contribution margin		$1,088,000

The compressor division has the capacity to produce 20,000 units per year. The division would not incur the variable selling costs on units sold to Frigidwind.

Required:

1. Determine whether the compressor division should supply the 4,500 units to Frigidwind. The managers of divisions are evaluated on the basis of profit earned.

2. Determine whether it would be in the best interests of the firm for the compressor division to supply the units to Frigidwind division.

3. Determine the lowest price that the compressor division could accept for the units without reducing profits below what they would be if none were sold to Frigidwind.

18-13 Opportunity Costs and Transfer Prices. The Morton division of United Industries, Inc., has in the past sold its products only to outsiders. Recently, Morton was approached by the Crago division, which needed a component for one of its products. Morton does not now make the component for outsiders, but it could produce it by making extensive modifications and combining several of the products it now makes. The component would be unique, and there would be no market price available to guide the setting of a transfer price. Data related to the component appear below.

Material cost	$ 7.50
Direct labor (½ hour)	4.50
Overhead at $11 per labor hour	5.50
Total estimated cost	$17.50

Variable overhead is about $7 per direct labor hour, fixed overhead about $4 at normal activity. Morton's budgeted income statement for the coming year is as follows:

Sales	$21,500,000
Cost of sales	13,400,000
Gross margin	8,100,000
Selling and administrative expenses	6,300,000
Profit	$ 1,800,000

The division's inventories will be about the same at the beginning and end of the year. Materials included in cost of sales are about $5,400,000, and direct labor is about $3,600,000. All direct laborers receive very close to the same hourly wage. Selling and administrative expenses are virtually all fixed. Morton's investment would be unaffected by doing the work for Crago.

Required:

1. Suppose that the Morton division has excess capacity and could easily accommodate Crago division's needs. What is the minimum transfer price that Morton division's manager would accept, acting in his own best interests? (He is held responsible for ROI.)

2. Suppose now that Morton expects to work at full capacity (measured by labor hours) without considering the component for Crago. On the basis of the information that you have available, estimate the transfer price that Morton would demand. Make your assumptions clear.

18-14 Transfer Price, Personnel. Ron Goode, the manager of the ITM division, approached Earl Robinson, the manager of the Fleeton division, with a proposal to buy some labor time. Goode offered to pay the workers' usual hourly wage plus fringe benefits to employ them on a project that he expected to begin soon. The factories of the two divisions are adjacent, so that no travel or lodging costs would be involved.

Robinson was reluctant to accept the proposal because he was running the division at full capacity. He collected the following data:

Wage rate	$12/hr
Total budgeted labor hours	120,000 hr
Total budgeted contribution margin	$2,400,000
Variable overhead rate per direct labor hour	$8/hr

Robinson could not replace the hours that Goode would use, because the workers have special skills and it is impossible to hire and train others on short notice.

Required:

1. What would you, acting in Robinson's place, charge Goode for each hour of labor time that you sell him?

2. Assuming that Robinson has excess capacity, and that fringe benefits are $2 per hour out of total variable overhead of $8 per hour, how much should he charge Goode? Robinson would continue to pay their wages and fringe benefits. All variable overhead except fringe benefits relates to hours worked, not hours paid.

18-15 Transfer Pricing and ROI. The divisional managers of the Argive Company are evaluated on ROI. Recently, the manager of the Selmon division offered to buy 4,000 units per month of a particular component from the Franklin division at a price of $44. The chief cost accountant of the Franklin division estimated the variable cost of the component at $40. He also determined that the division would not need to add to its plant and equipment to service Selmon, but it would require increased investment in working capital, which he estimated as follows:

Raw materials inventory	$45,000
Inventory of finished components	two months' supply
Accounts receivable	one month's sales

The firm values inventories at variable cost. It also provides for one month's credit on intracompany business, so that the selling division will have a receivable and the buying division a payable in the same amounts. In calculating total investment for a division, the firm includes current liabilities.

Franklin is currently earning a 30 percent ROI, and its manager wants to know whether or not the $44 price will maintain it.

Required:

1. Determine whether Franklin would earn a 30 percent ROI on the business with Selmon.

2. Comment on the firm's policy of recognizing intracompany receivables and payables in determining the investment base. Would it lead to goal congruence or hinder it?

18–16 Transfer-Pricing Dispute, Linear Programming. The BCH Company operates several divisions. The manager of the Compto division is planning on bringing out a new product, a desk-top computer that will sell for about $350. He has approached the manager of the electronics division with a proposal that electronics make a component for the computer. Satisfactory components are available from outside firms at $47 each. The manager of the electronics division developed the following data and quoted a price of $53. The electronics division does not now make the component.

Materials cost	$14
Direct labor cost	12
Overhead at 150% of direct labor	18
Total cost	44
Allowance for profit at 20% of cost, rounded	9
Quoted price	$53

The manager of the Compto division was unhappy with the quotation, citing the market price as an upper limit. He said, "I know that your overhead is only about 40 percent variable, so you are really trying to get rich on me." The manager of the electronics division replied that he was operating at capacity and would have to forego other business if he made the component for Compto. He said, "My operations research people tell me that the shadow price for direct labor time is $22 per hour. The component requires one hour, which would reduce my profits if I didn't charge you based on my usual formula."

Required: If you were the manager of the electronics division, what price would you have quoted?

18–17   Promotion Decisions and Transfer Prices.   The Marchmont division of ICC Industries supplies the Cooper division with 100,000 units per month of an LED (light-emitting diode) that Cooper uses in a calculator that it makes and sells. The transfer price of the LED is $8, which is the market price. However, Marchmont does not operate anywhere near capacity.

The variable cost to Marchmont of the LED is $4.80, while Cooper incurs variable costs (excluding the transfer price) of $12 for each calculator. Cooper's selling price is $32.

Cooper's manager has been considering a promotional campaign. The market research department of the division has developed the following estimates of additional monthly volume associated with additional monthly promotional expenses.

Additional Monthly Promotional Expenses	Additional Monthly Volume
$ 80,000	10,000 units
120,000	15,000
160,000	18,000

Required:

1. As the manager of Cooper division, which level of additional promotional expenses would you select?

2. As the president of the firm, which level would you like Cooper division to select?

3. If your answers to items 1 and 2 are different, make a recommendation to resolve the problem.

18–18   Perspective of Selling Division (CMA adapted).   MBR Inc. consists of three divisions that have operated as if they were independent companies. Each division has its own sales force and production facilities. Each division management is responsible for sales, cost of operations, acquisition and financing of divisional assets, and working-capital management. The corporate management of MBR evaluates the performance of the divisions and division managements on the basis of return on investment.

Mitchell division has just been awarded a contract for a product that uses a component manufactured by the Roach division as well as by outside suppliers. In preparing its bid for the new product, Mitchell used a cost figure of $3.80 for the component manufactured by Roach. This cost figure was supplied by Roach in response to Mitchell's request for the average variable cost of the component and represents the standard variable manufacturing cost and variable selling and distribution expense.

Assume that Roach's regular selling price for this component is $6.50. The two divisions are at an impasse. Roach has offered to sell the component to Mitchell for $6.50 less variable selling and distribution expenses. Mitchell's management has countered with an offer of paying the standard variable manufacturing cost plus 20 percent. A corporate vice-president has suggested a compromise of standard full manufacturing cost plus a 15 percent markup. Both divisions have rejected this suggestion.

The unit cost structure for the Roach component and the three suggested prices are shown below.

Regular selling price	$6.50
Standard variable manufacturing cost	$3.20
Standard fixed manufacturing cost	1.20
Variable selling and distribution expenses	0.60
	$5.00
Regular selling price less variable selling and distribution expenses ($6.50 − 0.60)	$5.90
Variable manufacturing plus 20 percent ($3.20 × 1.20)	$3.84
Standard full manufacturing cost plus 15 percent ($4.40 × 1.15)	$5.06

Required:

1. How would Roach's management rank each of these three proposed prices in relationship to how Roach itself is evaluated?

2. What is the role of negotiation and the role of corporate management in this case?

18–19 Transfer Pricing. The Morgan Company operates 22 divisions in various industries. The divisions are relatively decentralized, and the managers are responsible for earning a satisfactory ROI. A large percentage of their compensation comes from bonuses related to ROI. The ROI calculation has been based on the direct profit earned by the division. Corporate overhead is allocated to divisions, but is "below the line" and does not reduce the profit figure used to determine ROI.

The treasurer of the firm wants to develop a transfer-pricing scheme for legal services performed for the divisions. The workload of the legal department, and its costs, have been rising rapidly in the face of increased governmental regulation and costly litigation ranging from suits over product liability to charges of discrimination in hiring and promoting practices.

The treasurer believes that making the department into a profit center and billing its services to divisions would make sense because the divisions are the beneficiaries of the services, even of those performed on general corporate work such as bond issues. He has decided that standard hourly rates be developed for all the lawyers and paraprofessionals in the department, but he is still open on the question whether the rates should be set to cover costs or to provide a profit.

There is no question about the growing demand for legal services from the divisions. Much of the demand is forced by directives from corporate headquarters. For example, any new-product proposal must be submitted to the legal department for review regarding potential liability. Divisions must also submit capital-investment proposals to the department for review for conformity with various governmental regulations.

The treasurer anticipated objections from the divisional managers and was concerned with developing rebuttals. He was convinced that the size of the cost made it imperative to charge the divisions, and he wanted to be well prepared for the objections that were certain to come.

Required:

1. As a divisional manager, prepare arguments against the proposed system.

2. As the treasurer, rebut the arguments you developed.

3. Make any recommendations that you think would help to make the system more palatable to the divisional managers.

18–20   **Role of Arbitration (CMA adapted).**   The Lorax Electric Company is organized into several autonomous divisions. Corporate management is pleased with the results of decentralization and evaluates divisions on profits and return on investment.

The devices division, currently operating at capacity, has been asked by the systems division to supply a large quantity of integrated circuit IC378. Devices currently sells this circuit to its regular customers at $40 per hundred.

The systems division, which is operating at about 60 percent of capacity, wants this particular component for a digital clock system. It has an opportunity to supply large quantities of these digital clock systems to Centonic Electric, a major producer of clock radios and other popular electronic home entertainment equipment. This is the first opportunity any of the Lorax divisions have had to do business with Centonic Electric. Centonic Electric has offered to pay $7.50 per clock system.

The systems division prepared an analysis of the probable costs to produce the clock systems. The amount that could be paid to the devices division for the integrated circuits was determined by working backward from the selling price. The cost estimates employed by the division reflected the highest per-unit cost the systems division could incur for each cost component and still leave a sufficient margin so that the division's income statement could show reasonable improvement. The cost estimates are summarized at the top of page 755.

As a result of this analysis, the systems division offered the devices division a price of $20 per hundred for the integrated circuit. The bid was refused by the manager of the devices division, because he felt the systems division should at least meet the price of $40 per hundred that regular customers paid. When the systems division found that it could not obtain a

Proposed selling price		$7.50
Costs excluding required integrated		
circuits (IC378):		
Components purchased from		
outside suppliers	$2.75	
Circuit board etching—labor		
and variable overhead	0.40	
Assembly, testing, packaging—		
labor and variable overhead	1.35	
Fixed overhead allocations	1.50	
Profit margin	0.50	6.50
Amount that can be paid for		
integrated circuits IC378		
(5 at $20 per hundred)		$1.00

comparable integrated circuit from outside vendors, the situation was brought to an arbitration committee, set up to review such problems.

The arbitration committee prepared an analysis showing that $0.15 would cover variable costs of producing the integrated circuit, $0.28 would cover the full cost including fixed overhead, and $0.35 would provide a gross margin equal to the average gross margin on all the products sold by the devices division. The manager of the systems division responded: "They could sell us that integrated circuit for $0.20 and still earn a positive contribution toward profit. In fact, they should be required to sell at their variable cost of $0.15 and not be allowed to take advantage of us."

Lou Belcher, manager of devices, countered: "It doesn't make sense to sell to the Systems division at $20 per hundred when we get $40 per hundred outside on all we can produce. In fact, systems could pay us up to almost $60 per hundred and still have a positive contribution to profit."

The recommendation of the committee, to set the price at $0.35 per unit ($35 per hundred), so that devices could earn a fair gross margin, was rejected by both division managers. Consequently the problem was brought to the attention of the vice-president of operations and his staff.

Required:

1. What would be the immediate economic effect on the Lorax Company as a whole if the devices division were required to supply IC378 to the systems division at $0.35 per unit—the price recommended by the arbitration committee? Explain your answer.

2. Discuss the advisability of intervention by top management as a solution to transfer-pricing disputes between division managers such as the one experienced by Lorax Electric Company.

3. Suppose Lorax adopted a policy requiring that the price paid in all internal transfers by the buying division equal the variable costs per unit of the selling division for that product and that the supplying division be required to sell if the buying division decided to buy the

item. Discuss the consequences of adopting such a policy as a way of avoiding the need for the arbitration committee or for intervention by the vice-president.

18–21 Market Prices and Transfers. The Allied Company operates a number of decentralized divisions, some of which deal extensively among themselves. The IMC division currently makes a type of cathode ray tube (CRT) that the Balkan division could use in a new product that it has just developed. The new product is a device for measuring the viscosity of liquids, and the CRT would allow the operator to monitor the viscosity continuously, which is important in some manufacturing processes.

IMC expects to produce and sell 20,000 of the CRTs during the coming year. The expected price is $300 and the variable cost $150. The division has sufficient capacity to produce 25,000 units, but it would have to drop its price to about $240 to sell 25,000.

The Balkan division's manager has estimated the following with regard to the new product, excluding the transfer price for the CRT.

	Selling Price	
	$800	$750
Expected variable costs:		
Materials and purchased components	$75	$75
Direct labor and variable overhead	200	200
Expected volume	4,000 units	4,800 units

The manager of the IMC division has quoted the market price of $300 as the transfer price to the Balkan division. One CRT is needed for each measuring device. The manager of the Balkan division believes that the transfer price should be the variable cost of $150 and has approached you, the president of Allied, to intercede.

Required: As the president of the firm, what would you do? Prepare any analyses that you believe are relevant.

18–22 Transfer-Pricing Formulas. The controller of the Inverness Company has been concerned for several years about the firm's transfer pricing policies. There were often prolonged and acrimonious discussions between divisional managers, with subsequent hard feelings. The controller thought it would be possible to develop a formula, or set of formulas, to use for all products that did not have competitive market prices. He decided that the transfer price should consist of the following components:

1. standard variable production cost.
2. a fair share of fixed production costs, measured by standard cost per direct labor hour or machine hour.
3. a satisfactory return on investment on the plant and equipment and inventories associated with the output to be transferred.

The firm did not record accounts receivable or payable on interdivisional business, so there was no need to include a provision for return on receivables. The investment in inventories would be calculated as the standard absorption cost divided by the normal inventory turnover. Investment in plant and equipment was to be based on a measure of capacity such as direct labor hours or machine hours. Thus, the controller would compute a figure called investment per labor hour (or machine hour) and use it to determine the component of the transfer price that would give the ROI on this investment. The firm used ROI to evaluate divisional managers.

The controller decided to test his ideas by working out the transfer price of a gear box that the Sharp division was to make for another division. He gathered the following data regarding Sharp division and the gear box.

	Sharp Division
Normal activity in direct labor hours	200,000
Plant and equipment (net)	$2,000,000
Inventory turnover	5 times
Standard fixed production cost per direct labor hour (based on normal activity)	$8
Target ROI	20%

	Gear Box
Standard variable cost per unit	$22.00
Standard fixed cost (4 standard hours)	32.00
Total standard cost	54.00
ROI component:	
Plant ($2,000,000/200,000 × 4 × 0.20)	8.00
Inventory ($54/5 × 0.20)	2.16
Transfer price	$64.16

Required:

1. Suppose that the Sharp division expects the following results without the internal business (in thousands):

Sales	$7,600
Standard cost of sales	4,100
Standard gross margin	3,500
Underabsorbed overhead	240
Actual gross margin	3,260
Selling and administrative expenses	2,173
Income	$1,087
Accounts receivable	$3,080
Inventory	815
Plant and equipment	2,000
Total investment	$5,895

These results are based on 85 percent utilization of normal capacity. Determine the income and investment that the division would have after the internal business at the transfer price that the controller calculated. The internal business will not affect selling and administrative expenses.

2. Calculate a new transfer price, using practical capacity of 250,000 direct labor hours to determine the standard fixed production cost and the investment per labor hour figure.

3. Comment on the general approach taken by the controller. What problems do you foresee?

SELECTED REFERENCES

Abdel-Khalik, A. Rashad, and Edward J. Lusk, "Transfer Pricing—A Synthesis," *The Accounting Review*, 49:1 (January 1974), 8–23.

Benke, Ralph L., Jr., and James Don Edwards, *Transfer Pricing: Techniques and Uses*. New York: National Association of Accountants, 1980.

Dopuch, N., and D. Drake, "Accounting Implications of a Mathematics Approach to the Transfer Pricing Problem," *Journal of Accounting Research*, 2:1 (Spring 1964), 10–24.

Hirshleifer, Jack, "On the Economics of Transfer Pricing," *Journal of Business*, 29:3 (July 1956), 172–84.

————, "Economics of the Divisionalized Firm," *Journal of Business*, 30:2 (April 1957), 96–108.

Manes, Rene P., "Birch Paper Company Revisited: An Exercise in Transfer Pricing," *The Accounting Review*, 45:3 (July 1970), 565–72.

Onsi, Mohamed, "A Transfer Pricing System Based on Opportunity Cost," *The Accounting Review*, 45:3 (July 1970), 535–43.

Schroeder, Richard G., and Calvin A. Vobroucek, "Transfer Pricing," in Homer A. Black and James Don Edwards, eds., *The Managerial and Cost Accountant's Handbook*. Homewood, Ill.: Dow Jones-Irwin, 1979.

Solomons, David, *Divisional Performance: Measurement and Control*. Homewood, Ill.: Richard D. Irwin, Inc., 1965.

Stone, Williard E., "Legal Implications of Intracompany Pricing," *The Accounting Review*, 36:1 (January 1964), 38–42.

Thomas, Arthur L., *A Behavioural Analysis of Joint-Cost Allocation and Transfer Pricing*. Champaign, Ill.: Stipes Publishing Company, 1980.

Watson, David J. H., and John V. Baumler, "Transfer Pricing: A Behavioral Context," *The Accounting Review*, 50:3 (July 1975), 466–74.

Key Areas for Further Study

Part 5

Variance Investigation

Chapter 19

Our discussion of standard costs and variances in Chapters 7 and 8 included identifying variances, assigning responsibility for variances, and recording variances in a standard costing system. As various illustrations have shown, variances may range from fairly small to quite large. In addition, while it may be easy to classify a variance, it is more difficult to determine cause.

For example, while an unfavorable material use variance may mean that the production department used too much material, there is no evidence in the mere variance number whether the cause was poor-quality material (not the responsibility of production), sloppy workmanship, faulty production equipment, or some other cause. Thus, it is not enough to know the dollar amount of a specific variance. Other questions must be addressed. For example, was a variance a random happening or was it a sign that something of a more permanent nature is happening with the production process? Can anything be done to correct an out-of-control situation? If so, what will it cost to bring the process back under control?

TWO CONCERNS OF INVESTIGATION

There are two distinct concerns that management can have when a variance is calculated. First, since a variance has economic consequences, managers are interested to see what corrective actions are warranted and possible, given a set of variances. Identifying the cause of variances will let a manager see whether unfavorable variances in one area, for example, were caused by favorable variances in another. It is not enough to know that a variance occurred. We also need to know why and how it is interrelated with other variances. If the changes reflected by a variance are more or less permanent, then management needs to make appropriate changes in standard costs and, perhaps, in product mix or production processes to reflect this new reality.

Second, a basic reason for identifying variances is to assign responsibility. Therefore, managers need a system not only to calculate variances but also to assess their degree of importance. Only in this way can a manager's efficiency be determined. With this in mind, we shall develop a rationale and methods for going beyond merely calculating and reporting variances.

WHY VARIANCES OCCUR

There are several reasons why actual results differ from standards. A simple, yet often overlooked, cause is the accuracy of the data. A second cause could be that production conditions, and therefore costs, have changed so that new standards are needed. Third, variances can be caused by random happenings. Finally, variances can result from especially efficient or inefficient operations.

Inaccurate Data

If reported results differ from standard costs, it might be wise to check the source data. Were costs recorded properly in the purchasing department? Were labor costs and use accurately calculated? One might check the journal entries to see if they were properly done. This check-out of data should include separable as well as joint costs. Overhead application can be tricky and needs to be examined.

The data an accountant obtains result from many steps and many people. Products go through several departments. Multiple-shift operations mean that different people handle a product within the same department. In many three-shift operations, there are fewer supervisory personnel on the 11 P.M. to 7 A.M. shift than on the others. For these and many more reasons, recorded data can be inaccurate. A good managerial accounting system includes ways to check incoming data for accuracy and reasonableness. In this way, errors can be detected before any use of the data in the financial or cost system of the firm.

Out-of-Date Standards

Standard costs might be outdated. Ongoing inflation makes it difficult for standard prices to be realistic over periods of six months or even less. Therefore, price variances may mean that standard prices need to be adjusted.

Perhaps new machinery has replaced older equipment, or crews are generally more experienced than was contemplated when the standards were set. If these efficiencies seem ongoing, then standards can be revised. However, as we have discussed, tightening standards too much with each new indication of efficiency can have serious behavioral repercussions, just as can standards that are too lax.

Random Happenings

Standards are set as a result of engineering studies, behavioral considerations, and various other factors. The standard cost of a product includes
many separate standards for price and use of materials and conversion costs.
In essence, each standard is an expected value. Managers expect costs to
fluctuate around the standard cost within reasonable limits, even under
ideal working conditions. The statistical model we will discuss later in this
chapter identifies a reasonable band of costs around the standard cost. Thus,
any result falling within these control limits can be considered random and
not a cause for concern.

Out-of-Control Operations

Finally, it is possible that a bearing is wearing out, making a motor increasingly inefficient, or a pump is adding an improper mix or consistency of
materials. The process is changing from the efficiency level used when
establishing standards. Statistical techniques can be used to identify trends
and then to assess the cost and benefit of investigating and trying to cure the
cause of the inefficiency.

WHEN TO INVESTIGATE

As we have seen, there are various reasons why variances occur. Managers
need to decide whether or not they want to spend resources in investigating
the causes of variances so that appropriate corrective action can be taken. In
many companies managers set arbitrary policies. For example, management
could state that any variance of at least $1,000 or greater than ±10 percent
from standard will be reviewed. Other companies may rely on statistical
methods such as control charts.

Management by Exception

Information is costly. If every variance from standard were investigated or
reviewed, the ongoing investigation costs might exceed the variances. Additionally, managers would be swamped with reports, which would soon lose
any sense or meaning. Therefore, from both cost and human information-
processing perspectives, it is reasonable for guidelines to be set for variance
investigation. Managers will see only the exceptions to normal variability.

Cost Versus Benefit

Investigating a material price variance may mean a couple of hours on the
phone with the purchasing department and various suppliers. However, a
material use or labor use variance may be much more complex and more

costly to investigate. It is possible that the investigation will be in vain: the cause of the variance might not be identifiable, or, if identifiable, not correctable. Finally, a large variance can occur randomly, and even if nothing is done the variance will disappear the next period. Therefore, a manager needs to have estimates of both the expected costs and the potential benefits of investigation.

As with many models, it is reasonable to start off with some simple assumptions and relax them later. If we know that the cost (C) of investigation is fixed and certain and if we also know the benefit (B) of investigation (the variance would virtually disappear the next period, owing to corrective action), a simple decision rule can be developed: we investigate if the expected benefit is greater than the expected cost. This is the same as saying: investigate if the probability that the process is out of control times the benefit is greater than or equal to the cost of investigating. This would be represented algebraically as $PB \geq C$.

Suppose that a manager has determined through prior experience that 95 percent of the time when material use is more than 10 percent over standard, the machinery is incorrectly set (out of control). He has also determined that only 12 percent of the time that the variance is 10 percent or less over standard is the machinery incorrectly set. He has collected extensive data to support these estimates. If we *do not* investigate when there is a small variance, we run a 12 percent chance of making the wrong decision. If we *do* investigate a large variance, we run a 5 percent chance of making the wrong decision.

In our example, we would investigate if $0.95B \geq C$ if a 15 percent variance occurred. Assume that the cost to investigate is $400 while expected savings are $750, which constitutes a variance of 15 percent over standard. Thus, since $(0.95)(\$750) \geq \$400$, the decision would be to investigate. What is the critical "breakeven point" for the percentage, P? It is the point where:

$$PB = C \quad \text{or} \quad P = \frac{C}{B}$$

In our example, $C/B = 400/750 = 0.533$. Thus, if the probability that the process is out of control given a variance exceeding 10 percent of standard is at least 53⅓ percent, we would investigate all such variances. Obviously, 95 percent is well above this breakeven level.

Expected Value and Investigation

Payoff tables and expected value (EV) can also be used to help in investigation decisions. Investigation may prove fruitless, since perhaps the cause of the variance either cannot be identified or cannot be corrected. Thus, we have the following set of circumstances:

	Investigation	
	Success	Failure
Decision Investigate	+$	−$
Do Not Investigate	0	0
	p	1 − p Probability of Success

If we investigate and are successful, the benefit will exceed the cost. If investigation was in vain, we are out the investigation cost and have no benefits. Naturally, if we do not investigate, there is neither a cost nor a benefit.

For example, if an investigation would cost $400 and expected benefits are a maximum of $750 and if the probability of finding a correctable cause is 40 percent, the payoff table would be as follows:

	Investigation	
	Success	Failure
Decision Investigate	750 − 400	−400
Do Not Investigate	0	0
	.40	.60 p (Success)

Then EV(investigate) is ($350)(.40) − ($400)(.60) = −$100. Therefore, the decision would be to *not* investigate, since EV(do not investigate) = $0.

Sensitivity analysis also can be employed. Managers can find out how high costs can be or how low benefits can be where an investigation is still called for.

STATISTICS AND OPERATING VARIANCES

Because a standard is an expected value, the basic framework for investigating variances should use this expected value and its standard deviation.[1] First we shall establish normal bounds for costs. Then we shall deal with investigation costs and probable benefits.

Control Limits

We discussed confidence intervals and sampling in Chapters 3 and 4. In variance analysis, the observations would be daily, weekly, or monthly production data. As each week (day, month) passes, production results can be

---

[1] We have a word problem in this section, since we are dealing with operating *variances* and statistical *variance*. Where at all practicable, we shall deal with a standard deviation for statistical purposes and save the use of the word variance to refer to operating variances.

observed and a mean and standard deviation calculated. This sample mean ($\bar{x}_i$) is an estimate of the true cost of production (μ).

As time goes by, we can accumulate larger samples. If we average the sample means of several periods, the result is the **grand mean** denoted as $\bar{\bar{X}}$ (read as X double-bar). As we have noted before, the larger the sample, the more confident we can be that $\bar{\bar{X}}$ is a good estimator of the true cost, μ.

We shall assume initially that the observations of actual cost are normally distributed. If a manager is fairly confident that observations are normally distributed but wants to use fewer than 30 observations, he can then use a t distribution.[2] The variance of the distribution of sample means is denoted as $\sigma_{\bar{x}}^2$ and is calculated by dividing the true variance of costs by the sample size. Thus:

$$\sigma_{\bar{x}}^2 = \frac{\sigma_x^2}{n}$$

and $\sigma_{\bar{x}}^2$ decreases as n increases. It is quite usual that μ is unknown. Thus we estimate μ by $\bar{\bar{X}}$. In the same way, σ_x^2 is also unknown and we estimate it by s^2. We calculate s, the sample standard deviation, by:

$$s = \sqrt{\frac{\Sigma(x_i - \bar{x})^2}{n - 1}}$$

and s is an unbiased estimator of the standard deviation.

Illustration: Labrea Carpet

The managers of Labrea Carpet (see Chapter 8) developed standards for materials, labor, and overhead. One standard was that each square yard of carpet should take 1.5 lb of newlon fiber, with a standard price of $1.10 per pound. The standard material cost for newlon was $1.65 per yard of carpet. The $1.65 is not the true cost, μ, but rather is the best estimate of the true cost, given that the process is operating at normal efficiency. The estimate was based on engineering studies and actual observations made under close supervision to ensure that they reflected operations under normal efficiency.

Naturally, some of the observations were different from $1.65 despite the close supervision. Suppose that the standard deviation of the sample means was $0.06, using the $1.10 standard price per pound of newlon. Remember that we are interested in the material use variance separate from the material price variance. The managers of Labrea can now make the

---

[2] Actually, the use of a t distribution is warranted when the variance, σ_x^2, is unknown. However, as the number of observations increases, the values of the t distribution shown on a t table approach values on a table for a normal distribution (a Z table). Finally, even if the underlying variable has an unknown distribution, the distribution of sample means will be normal.

same kinds of statements about whether future observed values are within certain limits as we did when looking at the standard error of a regression equation or of the slope of the regression line.

We shall be testing the hypothesis that future actual observations come from a distribution with a mean of \$1.65 and standard deviation of \$0.06. Therefore, we denote $\bar{\bar{X}}$ as \$1.65 and $\sigma_{\bar{x}}$ as \$0.06.

Suppose that in April, actual use of newlon is 247,500 lb and production is 150,000 sq yd of carpet. At the standard price of \$1.10/lb, the cost is \$1.815/yd of finished goods. A mean of \$1.815 is 2.75 standard deviations above the grand mean, where, for a normal distribution:

$$Z = \frac{1.815 - 1.65}{0.06} = 2.75$$

Therefore, as you can see from Table A–1 on page 926, there is only a .003 probability that the \$1.815 observation is from a distribution with a mean of \$1.65 and a standard deviation of \$0.06. It is extremely likely that this observation comes from another distribution and that material use, at least for this period, has shifted upward. In other words, it is very unlikely that the observation comes from a distribution with a mean of \$1.65 and a standard deviation of \$0.06.

CHOOSING CONTROL LIMITS

Whatever statistical technique (or nonstatistical technique as well) the manager uses, he or she must set some limit beyond which there will be an investigation. The limit could be the 99 percent range, 95 percent range, or any other. An observation that lies outside the selected range would be investigated; observations within it would not be.

In deciding whether to investigate a variance, we are taking one of two risks. If we investigate and find that the process is in control (variance caused by some random factors), we have accepted a false hypothesis (that investigation was called for) and have wasted time and effort in the investigation. If we do not investigate, and later find that the process is out of control and that the variance continues, we have rejected a true hypothesis (that investigation was called for) and have borne the extra costs of variances that we might have been able to avoid by taking corrective action.[3] In statistical theory these are called Type I and Type II errors, respectively.

In a later section we develop some explicit rules for investigating. At this point we offer some basic suggestions. First, suppose that we have decided to use a 99 percent confidence interval and, therefore, investigate

---

[3] Notice that we say "might have been able to avoid." A variance may be caused by some factor that we cannot correct, and so it would continue even if we investigated it. We return to this important point shortly.

only when an observed cost has a ½ percent or lower probability.[4] If we lower the interval to, say, 85 percent, we increase the likelihood that we will incorrectly judge a sample mean falling outside this range to be a candidate for corrective action. However, we also increase the likelihood of catching out-of-control operations and reducing future variances. There is a cost/benefit trade-off.

Because investigation is costly, managers would like to investigate only when there is clear reason to do so or when the consequences of failing to investigate may be very costly. Managers would, therefore, set relatively narrow control limits for relatively high-cost factors, and wide limits for low-cost factors. If direct labor is 75 percent of total variable cost, an uncorrected problem can do a great deal more damage than if labor were 15 percent of total variable cost.

CONTROL CHARTS

We can calculate limits for each element of price and quantity that goes into standard costs. Much as we can graph CVP relationships, we can also graph charts for various levels of production. Figure 19–1 shows such a chart for newlon material use. Managers can easily check current costs in order to see if they are within the normal range for that level of production.

Statistical Control Charts

If managers at Labrea have a fairly large sample to draw on, they can establish a 99 percent control range of $\bar{\bar{X}} \pm 2.57\sigma_{\bar{x}}$ or $1.8042 to $1.4958. Graphically these control limits are shown in Figure 19–2 on page 770. The top line is called the **upper control limit** (UCL) and the bottom line the **lower control limit** (LCL). The middle line is the standard cost. As sample data become available, they are plotted on this chart. Note that Figure 19–2 is based on per-unit cost data while Figure 19–1 deals with total cost and volume. Figure 19–2 also allows trends to be identified over time, as the mean of each sample is plotted weekly, for example.

Control Chart for Range

As we have pointed out, a basic mean-standard deviation relationship underlies this statistical analysis. As a way to deal with the variance, we can examine the data to find the *range* of values in each sample. Just as we calculated control limits and drew a control chart for $\bar{x}$, the sample mean, we can do the same thing for the range (which is usually denoted as R). Standard charts are available for different sample sizes for $\bar{x}$ and R control charts. Statistically there is a reason to investigate results when either the UCL or

---

[4] We are dealing with both tails of the distribution.

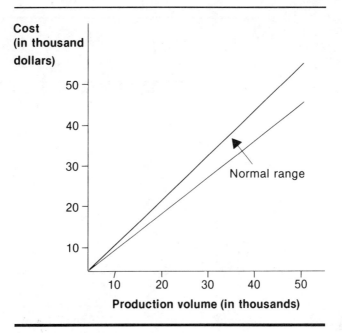

FIGURE 19–1
Newlon Material Use

LCL is "violated" on *either* control chart. We shall address the cost-benefit part of an investigation decision later in this chapter.

Illustration: Weight Range for Carpeting.   Each yard of carpet that has gone through the weaving process should contain 1.5 lb of newlon fiber and 0.25 lb of backing. Thus, carpeting at this stage should weigh 1.75 lb/sq yd. During the month of January samples of carpeting that had gone through just the weaving process were inspected every other working day. For simplicity, we use samples of 5 yd. The results are as follows:

	Day	Sample No.	Weight per Square Yard Measured					$\bar{x}$	R
Jan.	2	1	1.76	1.70	1.72	1.74	1.73	1.73	0.06
	4	2	1.80	1.79	1.81	1.78	1.71	1.78	0.10
	8	3	1.83	1.82	1.83	1.85	1.84	1.83	0.03
	10	4	1.60	1.69	1.67	1.70	1.73	1.68	0.13
	12	5	1.75	1.71	1.80	1.76	1.77	1.76	0.09
	16	6	1.70	1.76	1.68	1.73	1.72	1.72	0.08
	18	7	1.70	1.74	1.74	1.73	1.75	1.73	0.05
	22	8	1.88	1.89	1.86	1.87	1.92	1.88	0.06
	24	9	1.82	1.72	1.78	1.78	1.76	1.77	0.10
	26	10	1.82	1.82	1.89	1.83	1.82	1.84	0.07

Figures 19–3A and 19–3B on page 771 reflect the control limits (estab-

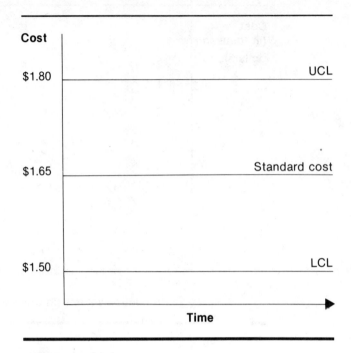

FIGURE 19–2
$\bar{x}$ **Control Chart**

lished when standard costs were set) that management established for $\bar{x}$ and R. The overall mean from these ten new samples is 1.77 (rounded), and $\bar{R}$ is 0.077. These results can be compared to the standard of 1.75 and 0.075, respectively. Thus, not only do none of the new sample data fall outside the pre-established control limits, but also the overall mean and the average range of these new samples are close to standard. Finally, the control charts show visually the fairly random fluctuations with no apparent pattern or trend.

BAYESIAN REVISIONS AND INVESTIGATION

In a previous example, we assumed that if a variance was 10 percent or less over standard, there was an 88 percent chance that the process was in control. This is our **prior probability** about the process. This prior probability includes all the information we have to date. We can use Bayes' theorem to revise this prior probability with the inclusion of current data.

Illustration: Materials Use Variance for Carpeting

The materials use variance in April for newlon fiber is 16.5 cents per yard ($1.815 − $1.65). This is exactly 10 percent above the mean (standard) cost

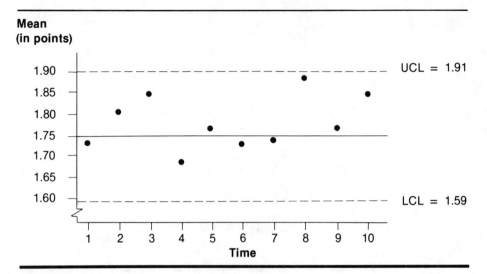

FIGURE 19–3A
$\bar{x}$ **Chart**

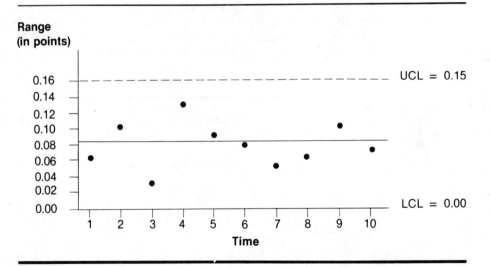

FIGURE 19–3B
R **Chart**

of $1.65. In earlier discussion we developed a standard deviation of $0.06. Figure 19–4 on page 772 shows this relationship plotted as a normal curve. You can see that the likelihood that the $1.815 observation comes from this distribution is quite small—.003, as we established earlier. It is possible, then, that the process is out of control. Assume that management has informa-

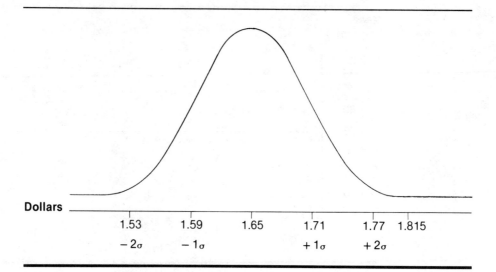

FIGURE 19–4
In-Control Distribution

tion regarding this equipment based on past experience. Past data show that if there is bad bearing wear, the production process can be considered out of usual control limits, and costs are expected to average $1.87 with a standard deviation still of $0.06. Figure 19–5 shows both the in-control and out-of-

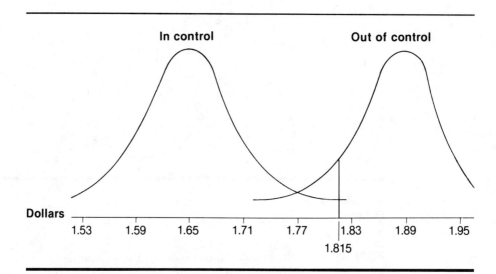

FIGURE 19–5
In-Control and Out-of-Control Distributions

control distributions. Let us see how the $1.815 observation fits into this new distribution. The $1.815 figure is 0.9167 standard deviations below the $1.87 mean of the out-of-control distribution. This translates to a probability of approximately .321.

Bayes' theorem allows us to obtain the **posterior probability** that the process is in control by using these data. Relying on the notation developed in Chapter 4, we write the posterior probability as:

$$\frac{p(B \mid A) \cdot p(A)}{p(B \mid A) \cdot p(A) + p(\bar{B} \mid \bar{A}) \cdot [1 - p(A)]}$$

where $\bar{A}$ is not A and $\bar{B}$ is not B. In our example, the standard deviation of both distributions is $0.06. Therefore, we can refer to standard normal tables for the exact probability of $1.815 for each distribution.[5] The value of $1.815 is 2.75 standard deviations above the mean of the in-control distribution or a probability of .00909. This same value is .9167 standard deviations below the mean of the out-of-control distribution or a probability of .26209. Using these likelihoods [the label for the terms such as $p(B \mid A)$ in the equation], we get

$$\frac{(.00909)(.88)}{(.00909)(.88) + (.26209)(.12)} = \frac{.008}{.03945} = .203$$

Thus, with the $1.815 observation, there is a 20.3 percent chance that the process is in control. Our prior experience would have indicated that there was an 88 percent chance that the process was in control. We have used our prior experience and current results to obtain this revised (posterior) probability.[6]

It is hard to argue that managers know the prior probability that the process was in control was exactly 88 percent. This may be an approximation. However, the Bayesian revision clearly shows a major shift in our assessment of the situation. This is much more important than finding an exact probability such as .203. In addition, it is important to point out that management would have assessed the 88 percent chance before observing current production. With the posterior probability of only 20 percent that

[5] Refer to basic statistics books for the probability density function of a normal distribution. Note that we are seeking an exact probability rather than one greater than or less than some value. Thus we are interested in the probability density function rather than the cumulative distribution function we use for interval estimates.

[6] If the variances of the two distributions had been different, an adjustment would have been made in this procedure. Assume the standard deviation for the out-of-control distribution is $0.11 while it remains $0.06 for the in-control distribution. Referring to the standard normal distribution, the exact probability for 2.75 standard deviations above the mean is now .00909 divided by 0.06 or .1515. The probability of being .50 standard deviations below the mean of the out-of-control distribution is .35207, which must be divided by 0.11 to yield 3.2006. Using these likelihoods results in a posterior probability of 25.7 percent that the process is in control.

the process is in control, management can weigh the costs of investigating, the likelihood that a correctable cause can be found, and expected benefits in light of very clear evidence that the process is seemingly out of control.

INVESTIGATION AND DECISION MAKING

Our emphasis on standard costs has been one of product costing as well as planning and control. Since much attention has been devoted to variances, it is easy to assume that control, responsibility, and evaluation of managers is more important than the planning phase. This is not so. In fact, variances and variance investigation, while occurring at the control stage of the business cycle, are keys to planning for upcoming periods.

Setting New Standards

Variance analysis can point out that current standards are inadequate; therefore, new standards must be established. This opens the door to possible new decisions on product mix, quality, prices, and so on. For example, if standard prices on a material such as a certain grade of plastic have changed, a television and radio manufacturer might analyze other materials available to do the same job at a lower price. If labor costs for a hand-made product are rising rapidly, managers need to examine alternative methods of production.

Decision Models

A company may have used some quantitative models to decide on current courses of action. If the parameters of these models have changed, the models should be solved again for an updated optimal solution. For example, assume that a linear programming model was employed to find an optimal product mix for a firm. Statistical variance investigation could point out that one of the production processes was out of control and that the cause was too costly to correct. Thus, the basic CVP relationships for that process would have changed, and the old optimal linear programming solution should be revised.

If Labrea Carpet had set production levels for its two products by linear programming, the kind of information we developed in the example of posterior probabilities would be helpful to formulate a new solution. Given the evidence in that example, management could decide that material use for newlon be based on a distribution with a $1.87 mean instead of a $1.65 mean, the old standard cost. This new cost could be included either in sensitivity analysis or in formulating a new objective function and constraints in order to calculate a new optimal solution. While this example involves linear programming, the same point holds for other optimizing models that are employed to aid decision making.

Reasons for Investigating Favorable Variances

Unfavorable variances that continue from period to period cost money, and it is obvious that at some point they should receive attention. It is not so obvious that favorable variances may require attention. With management by exception, it seems reasonable to be concerned when things are going poorly, unconcerned when they are going well. There are several reasons why favorable variances should be investigated, provided that they are large enough to warrant attention.

In some cases, favorable variances might be caused by poor work, by cutting corners. Foremen might feel pressured to show favorable variances and might pressure workers to speed up output. The resulting decline in quality could have disastrous effects, such as huge recalls of products and lawsuits brought by people injured by faulty performance of the products.

In other cases, workers might concentrate on one aspect of performance to the exclusion of others. This is the problem of dysfunctional consequences of performance measurements. For example, if the ratio of defective units is emphasized, workers will probably try to perform well on that measure, which could result in excessive costs of material use and labor time. This problem may be resolvable if several measures of performance are used. However, when the measures conflict, managers must decide which one to emphasize, and the problem may remain. Here the question is one of benefit/cost. Is a rise in the percentage of defective units more costly than unfavorable labor and material variances? The accountant would supply a good part of the information needed to make this decision.

Occasionally, a failure to investigate favorable variances might result in a failure to spot improved methods of operation. It is not uncommon for workers to be able to beat standards. A host of material in the organizational behavior literature testifies that workers have the ability to keep standards at low levels. Remember that standards are often set by industrial engineers who observe workers in action. The standards developed in this way may be quite loose, because the workers may be able to produce more than they show when they are observed.

There are extremely tough behavioral problems in attempting to encourage workers to increase output. Courses and textbooks in organization behavior show how subtle and intractable these problems can be, and accountants need to be aware of these difficulties.

PRACTICAL USE OF STATISTICS

The examples regarding probabilities and variance investigation assume that a manager can adequately estimate various probabilities. Ideas such as Bayesian revisions and Chebychev's inequality may sound nice as academic theory but look impractical in the everyday business world. How do managers determine probability-distribution characteristics? Can they estimate the parameters of in-control and out-of-control operations? The simple decision rule for investigation assumes certain costs and benefits. Can we really know these costs with certainty? And what has all this statistical material to do with accounting? Should we leave this field to the engineers, foremen, or quality control people?

Obviously, this material is integral to cost and managerial accounting, or it would not have been presented. The emphasis throughout this book is on useful information for managerial decision making. In this chapter we are faced with decisions to investigate and decisions to *not* investigate. Statistical data can help the manager in making these decisions. While it is possible to make such decisions without statistical data, often a systematic approach to the problem will yield better decisions. Therefore, even if estimates of probability distributions are somewhat inaccurate, they can still provide a framework that assists managers to direct their efforts in a profitable way.

It is true that foremen and forewomen as well as other first-line supervisors, the people who observe daily operations first hand, are in a position to determine whether operations are going relatively well or poorly. However, certain things can remain undetected without proper analysis. In addition, higher-level managers cannot personally observe the ongoing production process. Thus, they must rely more on reports and must have a working knowledge regarding an acceptable range of costs. Accountants can provide all levels of management with information about the production process, thereby calling attention to items in need of investigation.

Consider an example. If you own a car, you may keep track of gas mileage and use that information to decide whether to take the car to a garage for an inspection to see whether something is wrong. For example, you might take the car in for a check-up and possible action (tune-up, repairs) if gas mileage drops below some level that you believe is satisfactory. You realize that mileage will be lower than normal if you do a good deal more city driving than usual, so low mileage after a period of high city driving would not cause you as much concern as it would after a period of average city-highway driving. Accordingly, you make decisions based on available information such as mileage and performance. Your decision rule could be fairly simple, such as take the car in every six months or 8,000 miles unless something is obviously wrong. If you operated a fleet of cars, you would probably adopt a more sophisticated decision rule, such as one derived from the statistical analysis we have illustrated. Although the cost of taking your one car to a garage might be significant, it is not likely to be so great as to require a control chart and Bayesian analysis. If you operated 150 cars, however, you might be well advised to use such analysis.

DEPENDENCE OF CERTAIN VARIANCES

Our discussion to this point has implicitly assumed the independence of the variances that are identified. We have assumed that material price, material use, and labor efficiency variances, for example, are all independent—that the occurrence of one variance will not affect any other variance. As we stated in Chapter 7, in many cases variances are dependent.

To illustrate, assume that a purchasing manager bought parts from an untried source at a low price, generating a sizeable favorable price variance. That variance seemingly is to his credit. However, when these parts were used in assembling the products in the factory, excessive waste occurred and efficiency suffered. Thus, much of the unfavorable labor and overhead variances and material use variances is the responsibility of the purchasing manager, because these variances were dependent on his material purchase. Therefore, while it is usual practice to isolate variances as soon as possible to assign responsibility and to evaluate managers, dependence of variances cannot be overlooked. Investigation may cause a reassignment of responsibility based on dependence. In fact, some models have been developed to deal with this problem.[7]

VARIANCE REPORTS

We have discussed the mathematics of variance identification and the statistics surrounding possible investigation. Chapter 7 dealt with a key use of variances—as a way to assess responsibility and evaluate various managers. This section deals with the timing, format, and use of variance reports. Naturally, it will discuss the behavioral problems that can occur as we lend our own perceptions to reports we prepare and use.

Timing of Reports

A formal variance report must await the collection of data, over a week or month or quarter, and a report form typed or generated by data processing equipment. As timely as reports can be, they are still after the fact. They summarize events that took place last month, while people are already dealing with current problems in the middle of a new month.

There is a trade-off between timeliness and accuracy. Certain interim information of a tentative nature can be feedback to line personnel on an hourly or daily basis. However, a complete and accurate report will have to follow. The interim feedback allows for ongoing monitoring and corrective action, while the formal variance report is a summary of a whole week or month.

It is logical to ask whether variance reports are relevant for current decisions in a production department. In fact they can be. Consider the use of control charts. A manager may look at the trends that are developing or may even use a computer-based forecasting model to predict future trends.

---

[7] See Baruch Lev, "An Information Theory Analysis of Budget Variances," *The Accounting Review*, 44:4 (October 1969), 704–710. See also Henri Theil, "How to Worry About Increased Expenditures," *The Accounting Review*, 44:1 (January 1969), 27–37.

A slowly deteriorating process can be identified and alternatives formulated. It is also possible that variance reports will verify seat of the pants information (also called *heuristic* information) with hard data.

Basic Reports

Exhibit 19–1 shows a basic report covering the Labrea example from Chapter 8. All variances are reported on one form, and it is assumed that analysis has revealed that the variances are independent. This example is offered as a basis for discussion rather than as an illustration of a suggested report format. Since we did not develop gross margin variances in the Labrea example, the figures shown are assumed.

EXHIBIT 19–1
Summary of Variances, March 19X1—LABREA CARPET

Sales department:		
Gross margin price—deluxe	$ 1,000F	
Gross margin price—regular	500U	
Gross margin mix	2,000F	
Gross margin volume	2,500F	
Net		$ 5,000F
Purchasing department:		
Price—newlon		3,400F
Production scheduling:		
Labor rate—weaving		380U
Production operations:		
Material use—newlon	687.50F	
Material use—backing	31.25U	
Labor efficiency—weaving	905.40F	
Labor efficiency—padding	300.00U	
Variable overhead price	1,800.00F	
Variable overhead efficiency	455.50F	
Net		3,371.19F
Capacity:		
Application		248.20U
March total		$10,317.99

This report is a monthly summary. It simply lists variances by responsibility area. There are relatively few breakdowns of gross figures. There are no editorial or descriptive comments. The order is that in which we isolated variances in our previous discussion. We list these characteristics as starting points for discussing the form and format of these reports.

Form and Format of Variance Reports

There is no single, standard type of report that companies use. Rather, managers must address the reasons why these reports are generated and how they are perceived in order to create a useful set of variance reports.[8]

Responsibility.   An important consideration is responsibility. If a variance is listed as part of production operations, the assumption is that the variance is indeed attributable to that department and controllable by its manager. For example, Exhibit 19–1 shows a $1,800 favorable variable overhead price variance under the heading of production operations. If this variance was caused by a change in supply costs not contemplated at the beginning of 19X1, the production operations manager cannot be held responsible (or given credit) for it. For this reason, a variance report should carefully distinguish between controllable and uncontrollable variances in order to yield a fair view of each manager.

Exhibit 19–1 lists variances with no way to compare them. This makes interpretation difficult. Is the material use variance 2 percent over standard or 20 percent over? Is it about the same as January or February use variances? Unless all users have a common frame of reference when looking at these figures, their perception of the value, materiality, and effect of the variances is left open, allowing for possible misinterpretation.

As part of a frame of reference, variances that are material should be highlighted and differentiated from those that are minor. Perhaps variances that violate control limits should be listed separately from those that do not.

Order and Aggregation.   Current research has shown that the order in which variances are presented can affect user perception of how efficient the manager in question is.[9] Will the listing of all unfavorable variances first have a different effect on user perception than the listing of all favorable ones first instead? Level of aggregation is another question to be dealt with. How much should information be summarized (aggregated) and how much should it be presented in detail (disaggregated)?[10] Will the level of aggregation affect the usefulness or perception of the report? These order, format, and aggregation questions are still to be answered. The answers may indeed vary with specific firms and specific individuals holding managerial jobs. Chapter 21 covers these and other behavioral aspects of information.

Exception Reports.   Managers are often deluged with piles of reports and other paperwork. Certainly, to increase the usefulness of variance reports the idea of **exception reporting** should be employed. The number and detail of variances reported would be less for the plant manager than for a

---

[8] Chapter 21 discusses behavioral questions associated with information.

[9] L. D. Bourne, *Order Effects in Accounting Variance Reports: A Laboratory Experiment* (unpublished Ph.D. dissertation, Washington University, 1976).

[10] J. Ronen, "Nonaggregation Versus Disaggregation of Variances," *The Accounting Review*, 49:1 (January 1974), 50–60.

line foreman. The plant manager is not interested in the details of every variance. She is interested in a report that draws her attention to key problem areas that warrant her investigation. Therefore, the question of materiality is not just one of size of a variance, but also of who is going to see that variance.

Verbal Analysis

Accounting reports that consist merely of a set of numbers can be incomplete. If causality is known or if corrective action has taken place, it is good to communicate this to the user in the form of remarks.

It is important in a report such as this to distinguish facts from opinions, inferences, and assumptions. Facts are the result of unbiased procedures, such as statistical analysis of the figures. Other facts might include establishing that a worn part was the cause of a specific variance. The opinions or judgments derived from an investigation of the facts should be listed as such, along with evidence to support these interpretations of the results.

Too often variance reports can be used as a way to fix blame. We have even said that variances should be isolated by managerial responsibility. However, a verbal analysis of variances can show respect and caring for line managers. Favorable variances that were caused by efficient operations can be praised. If a manager has taken steps to correct an unfavorable situation, that can be pointed out. The idea behind variance analysis includes adaptive, corrective action. Management should be more concerned with problem solving for future periods than it is with blame fixing for the past. As a motivational footnote, repeated blaming (for failure) of a person not high in achievement motivation can increase that person's internal acceptance of failure and increase the tendency to *avoid* accepting the challenge of taking corrective action.

Cost-Benefit and Reporting

As can be seen from the preceding discussion, there are many behavioral dimensions to variance reporting. The discussion of standard setting in Chapter 7 pointed out how sensitive managers are about standards, because tight standards will likely produce unfavorable variances—a negative connotation, to be sure. Our analysis of the costs and benefits of collecting data and preparing variance reports is colored by these many behavioral considerations.

Computer Reports.   Variance reports can be generated economically as a by-product of the gathering of data in a financial accounting system that employs standard costs. With data processing equipment, variances can be identified and printed out. While this one report has a relatively low monetary cost, care must be given when assessing the true cost. A carelessly prepared report just listing variances can be costly in human terms for the reasons discussed above.

Beyond the Computer.   It is important to deal specifically with issues of form and format, cost, and the benefits derived. Overt decisions in this area allow management to deal with raw variance data generated by any system—computer or human.

Our discussion in Chapter 4 on linear programming pointed out an iterative process (the simplex method) for arriving at an optimal solution. Reporting can be an iterative process in two ways. First, each new report can be the result of learning from past reports. As managers receive and use reports, they can feed back information designed to increase the effectiveness and efficiency of the reports. This feedback coupled with a cost-benefit analysis can be used to determine the form and content of reports for the next period. Obviously, as a situation becomes relatively static, the reports will become fairly routine and consistent in form.

Second, reports can be designed so that each level of management is able to add numerical, analytical, or descriptive data as a report moves from the production foremen through the general superintendent to the plant manager and beyond. These new data can be additional facts about such things as material tolerances or the cost to replace or adjust faulty parts. They can include any corrective action that has taken place. At higher levels, specific appraisals of performance can be included. The object is to design reports that are optimal at each level of use.

SUMMARY

This chapter along with Chapters 7 and 8 covers the idea of standards and variances, how to record standard costs in the accounting system, and statistical methods for analyzing variances. In Chapter 19 we have looked beyond simple variance calculations. Our approach is to combine on-the-job experience and analysis of the cost recording system with various statistical techniques. These statistical tools are not an answer in and of themselves. However, with computers available to handle the mechanics of such methods, we can effectively use statistics to aid us and, hopefully, to help management save money. This is the goal of all the models from control charts through Bayesian revision. Finally, since variances from standard can be used as part of performance evaluation, we must be continually aware of how we transmit variance information so that managers will use it creatively to enhance motivation.

APPENDIX 19–A: SMALL SAMPLE SIZE OR UNKNOWN DISTRIBUTION

In Chapter 3 we introduced the use of a t distribution for small numbers of observations. The same rules developed there would apply here. If t-values are used, the control range will be wider, since we are less sure of the estimates because of the limited number of sample points (and an unknown population variance). For example, with 10 observations a 99 percent confidence interval would be $\overline{\overline{X}} \pm 3.25\sigma_{\overline{x}}$, where $df = n - 1 = 9$. In the Labrea illustration this would increase the range to \$1.845 to \$1.455. Even with small samples, we cannot strictly use the t distribution if we are not willing to say that the sample is approximated by a normal distribution.

It is possible to make some probabilistic estimates even if a manager is unsure of the underlying distribution of the random variable, x_i. Chebychev's inequality provides a way to make such estimates.[11] Basically this is a conservative fall-back rule. In order to understand this rule, first refer back to the 99 percent control range determined when a normal distribution was assumed. The control range was $\overline{X} \pm 2.57\sigma_{\overline{x}}$. With a t distribution (assuming $df = 9$), a t statistic of 2.57 equals approximately a 97 percent range. As we illustrated, it would take a t value of 3.25 to achieve a 99 percent confidence interval.

Chebychev's inequality says that C percent of any set of numbers will fall within the range of $\overline{x} \pm h\sigma$, where

$$C = 1 - \frac{1}{h^2}$$

Thus, if we define h equal to 2.57, about 85 percent of observations must fall within the limits of $\overline{x} \pm 2.57\sigma$ regardless of the distribution $\{C = 1 - [1/(2.57)^2] = 0.8486\}$. For C to equal 99 percent, h would have to be 10. That is quite a large difference from 2.57 for a normal distribution. The following figures reflect the comparison between a normal distribution, a t distribution, and an unknown distribution:

	$\overline{X} \pm 2.57\sigma_{\overline{x}}$	99 Percent Control Limits
Normal distribution	99% range	\$1.80 to \$1.50
t Distribution	97% range ($df = 9$)	\$1.85 to \$1.46
Unknown distribution	85% range	\$2.25 to \$1.05

ASSIGNMENTS

19–1   Questions About Variances

Required: Respond to each question or comment independently.

1. A friend has just read some material on variances and says to you, "I would think you would want to really look at all variances and find

---

[11] See a basic text on statistics.

out why they happened no matter what their size. Oh, I might overlook a $10 variance, but anything that is bigger should be investigated."

2. "It would seem to me," another student says, "that if the production variances are bad, then the person in charge of that production facility should be held responsible for the poor performance."

3. A friend has done a problem where she had to find a critical value for the probability of success in investigating a variance. She tells you, "So I solved the problem and found the answer to be 58 percent. How am I ever going to know in a practical setting whether the probability of success is 58 percent?"

19-2 High Productivity Through Statistical Analysis. An article in a recent issue of *People* magazine (September 8, 1980) discussed Dr. W. Edwards Deming and his work in Japan and the United States regarding statistical analysis. The article reminds us that "Made in Japan" used to be a joke and a synonym for shoddiness. Today Japanese products are highly regarded for their quality. Dr. Deming was instrumental in working with industry in Japan and is currently working with industry in the United States to increase quality and productivity.

Asked why American industry has not adopted his methods, Dr. Deming criticized it for not being willing to commit to a long training program for all workers. He added: "And, to my horror, I have discovered that most American companies think they already have statistical control of quality. What they have is lots of printouts full of irrelevant and out-of-date information."

Dr. Deming asserted that management has much more responsibility in declining productivity than do the workers. As an example, he discussed the purchase of inferior material that caused unfavorable efficiency variances in the production line. Management had not directed its attention to the correlation between material quality and production efficiency. Asked what could be done about ineffective management, he said:

> For one thing, our business schools have to change. Their graduates get good economics, law, finance—overall a good education. But they don't teach statistical methods in research and production. For instance, they don't teach the connection between what people need, the cost of materials and what can be produced economically.

He went on to recommend using statistical methods to improve quality. He criticized final inspection of products or inspection at major assembly points as being inefficient and ineffective. Instead, he said, we must rely more on the statistical methods available to us for quality control.

Required: Comment on the philosophy espoused by Dr. Deming in light of the material presented in this chapter.

19–3 Control Chart The Portland Carpet Company maintains a standard costing system and keeps a set of control charts like the one below, which relates to direct labor cost per unit of a particular model carpet. The firm investigates a variance when the actual unit cost goes outside the limits drawn on the chart.

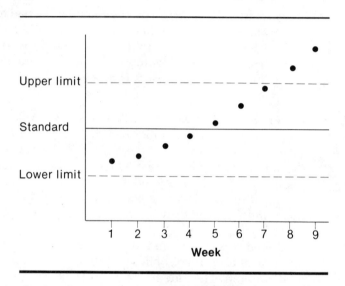

Control Chart—Direct Labor, Model 397

Required:

1. Using the firm's criterion for investigating a variance, when would it first investigate direct labor cost for carpet model 397?
2. Do you have any suggestion for the firm?

19–4 Variance Investigation. The Porter Corporation's controller has determined that it costs $400 to investigate a variance and that in one out of five cases investigated corrective action is possible. A variance of $1,000 unfavorable has just been reported. Owing to a major overhaul of equipment scheduled for a month from now, any savings would last only a month if corrective action could be taken.

Required: Should the variance be investigated?

19–5 Variance Investigation: Expected Values. Blake, Inc., has experienced a $2,500 unfavorable variance. The production manager believes there is a 30 percent chance that the variance is a unique occurrence and will not continue. She believes that if an investigation is made, the chance of correcting the variance is 40 percent (and, therefore, the chance of not correcting it is 60 percent). It costs $700 to investigate a variance. It is expected that the most that will be lost if the variance continues is $3,000.

Required:

1. Calculate the expected costs of investigating and not investigating the variance.
2. Should an investigation be made?

19–6 **Variance Investigation: Expected Values.** Current variance reports from the Schlechter Company show an unfavorable $2,000 variance this month. The production supervisor has analyzed past data and estimates that about 30 percent of the time a variance of this size is experienced there is nothing wrong with the process and the variance stops. When there is a problem with the process, about 60 percent of the time the variance continues for two additional months (at $2,000 per month) and 40 percent of the time it continues at $2,000 per month for three months.

Just investigating the variance would cost Schlechter $800. A correctable problem usually occurs about 40 percent of the time (for either two-month or three-month variances). If a correctable cause is found, it is estimated that another $600 would be spent to solve the problem.

Required: Determine the expected costs of investigating and of not investigating.

19–7 **Decision to Investigate.** Standard costs for the Crawford Frozen Foods Company include the following for one of its largest-selling products.

Standard Material Costs
Chinese Beef and Asparagus Dinner
per 8-oz Package

Choice grade sirloin strips—8 oz uncooked weight at $3/lb	$1.50
California select thin asparagus—3 oz uncooked weight at $1.50/lb	0.28
Secret blend of herbs and spices—½ oz	0.20

The production process starts in the food preparation department, where all raw foodstuffs are cut. From there, the raw foods go to the cooking department, where workers combine the ingredients according to Crawford's recipes. Portion control is very important from the standpoint of cost as well as that of quality and consistency. Foods shrink when cooked; it is expected that the net weight of a package after shrinkage is 8 oz. Management has set up control limits as follows, using a three-sigma range for the finished product:

$\bar{X}$: 7.92 to 8.16 oz
R: 0 to 0.12 oz

Crawford is limited by federal government rules to providing packages that weigh no less than 99 percent of the stated weight. Thus, while the upper control limit is three sigmas, the lower limit is truncated for $\bar{X}$.

During February the following samples were taken at random over a one-week period:

Sample	Work Shift	Sample Packages			
		1	2	3	4
1	1	7.95	8.09	8.06	8.03
2	2	8.16	8.13	8.18	8.11
3	2	8.14	8.19	8.12	8.15
4	1	8.05	7.93	8.07	8.05
5	1	8.05	8.03	8.02	8.15
6	2	8.12	8.20	8.15	8.17

Required:

1. Plot the data on $\bar{X}$ and R charts.

2. On the basis of these data, what recommendations would you make to the managers of Crawford?

19-8 Developing Control Charts. Rather than calculating control limits for $\bar{\bar{X}}$ (and $\bar{R}$) by using $\bar{X}$ and σ_x, tables are available to use just $\bar{\bar{X}}$ and $\bar{R}$ in the calculations. Under this method, control limits for $\bar{X}$ are

$$\bar{\bar{X}} \pm F\bar{R}$$

where F is a factor (Table 19–8A) for three standard deviations (a confidence interval of 99.73 percent using the normal distribution). Limits for $\bar{R}$ are:

upper limit: $U\bar{R}$
lower limit: $L\bar{R}$

where U and L (Table 19–8B) also are three standard deviations from the mean, $\bar{R}$. In both cases, n refers to the number of items in each sample.

Assume the Tercela Company produces a chemical called Plake that is delivered to customers in 5-lb buckets. As part of cost control it is important to check that the net weight of each bucket of Plake is within reasonable limits of 5 lb. On January 28 management sampled production runs over an eight-hour shift. The weights found in Table 19–8C were recorded for samples taken at random during each hour:

Required:

1. Using the techniques described above, establish upper and lower control limits for $\bar{X}$ and $\bar{R}$.

2. Use the techniques in the chapter to confirm a three-standard-deviation UCL and LCL calculated for $\bar{X}$ and $\bar{R}$ in item 1.

TABLE 19–8A
Control-Limit Factor
for $\bar{\bar{X}}$ Charts, F

n	F
2	1.880
3	1.023
4	0.729
5	0.577
6	0.483
7	0.419
8	0.373
9	0.337
10	0.308
12	0.266
14	0.235
16	0.212

TABLE 19–8B
Control-Limit Factors
for R Charts, U and L

n	U	L
2	3.268	0.000
3	2.574	0.000
4	2.282	0.000
5	2.114	0.000
6	2.004	0.000
7	1.924	0.076
8	1.864	0.136
9	1.816	0.184
10	1.777	0.223
12	1.716	0.284
14	1.671	0.329
16	1.636	0.364

TABLE 19–8C   Tercela Company Production Runs

	Samples (in pounds)					
Hour	1	2	3	4	5	6
1	5.22	5.06	4.97	5.11	5.02	5.03
2	4.95	5.18	5.08	5.00	5.06	5.12
3	5.11	5.09	5.06	5.13	5.10	5.01
4	4.98	5.00	5.06	4.96	5.07	5.10
5	5.05	5.18	5.01	5.15	5.01	5.09
6	5.11	5.04	5.06	5.10	5.18	5.20
7	5.07	5.11	5.08	4.99	5.00	5.02
8	5.13	5.02	5.09	5.08	5.15	5.10

19–9 **When to Investigate.** Frank Strout, manager of Midcourse, Inc., has been accumulating data over several years concerning the costs, benefits, and probability of success when seemingly excessive variances have been investigated. These data show that about 90 percent of the time that material use is higher than 2½ standard deviations from standard, the process can be considered out of control. Past records also show that use under 2½ standard deviations from standard means that there is an 85 percent chance the process is in control.

Required:

1. What is the probability that the process is in control given each of the following situations?

a.

	Standard Cost per Unit	σ
Materials	3 lb at $4	$1
Actual use:	1,000 units produced using $15,000 of materials at standard prices	

b.

	Standard Cost per Unit	σ
Materials	4 gal at $5	0.2 gal
Actual use:	1,000 units produced using 4,400 gal	

2. If we assume that the cost to investigate variances is $1,500 and the expected savings are $2,000 in item 1a, what is the breakeven point for investigation? Would you investigate in this case? What about item 1b?

19–10 **Investigation Decisions.** Studies by the industrial engineering staff have indicated that the direct labor time on product 804 should average 12.6 hours. The distribution should be about normal, with a standard deviation of 1.4 hours. You have established 95 percent confidence limits of 9.8 and 15.4 hours for deciding whether or not to investigate labor efficiency variances. Results for the past seven weeks appear below.

Week Number	Average Labor Time
1	12.4
2	12.9
3	12.7
4	13.4
5	13.6
6	14.0
7	14.3

Week 7 is the most recent week for which you have data. You have not investigated any variances during the seven-week period because labor time has remained well within the 95 percent confidence limits.

Required: Discuss whether you would investigate the labor efficiency variance even though labor time is within the 95 percent confidence limits. Would your answer be different if the product were a high-volume item with a contribution margin of $28 per unit when labor time was 12.6 hours, and if total labor and variable overhead was $9.50 per labor hour?

19–11 **Linear Programming and Variance Investigation.** Many companies use linear programming to help them in resource allocation. The constraint on labor time, for example, may include standard times for each different unit produced. If actual times vary either favorably or unfavorably beyond some point, the company would be better off to produce a different mix than the mix of products called for using a linear programming solution.

Assume that cost data for the Egrad Company are as follows:

	Product 1	Product 2
Sales price	$20.00	$21.00
Materials at $1/lb	3.00	5.00
Labor at $2/hr	5.00	4.00
Overhead	6.00	4.80
Margin	$ 6.00	$ 7.20

Constraints are as follows:

Materials	200 lb
Labor	100 hr

Required:

1. Use the simplex method, a computer solution, or a graphical analysis and solve the product mix called for by a linear program.

2. What level of labor would be required to change the solution reached in item 1? [*Hint:* Use sensitivity analysis as developed in Chapter 4.]

3. During the current month, variances on product 1 for 1,000 equivalent units were as follows:

Material use variance	$ 600U
Labor efficiency variance	$1,200U

If these variances are investigated and found to be rather permanent in nature, should the production be changed or kept the same? If it is changed, what is the new solution?

19-12 Variance Reports. The Doonsberry Division of Zonker Enterprises produces footballs, basketballs, and soccer balls for home, school, and professional use. The following is a variance report issued on January 11, 19X1, for production during November 19X0.

Variance Report, Footballs—Model H25

Sales variances	$1,200F
Production variances:	
Material use variance	$ 300U
Labor rate variance	200U
Labor efficiency variance	800U
Variable overhead efficiency variance	600U
Material price variance	400F
Variable overhead rate variance	100F
Fixed overhead spending variance	1,000F
Fixed overhead application variance	400F

Required: Comment on this report and offer suggestions for improvement.

19–13 Bayesian Revision. Harris Stowe, the production manager of Redeye Manufacturers, has been developing data on one of the main pieces of manufacturing equipment. As a cost accountant, you have been using these data in looking beyond simple variance calculations. The main forming machine usually produces parts that are within standard tolerances. For example, the standards for a #80-H shaft include a diameter of 2.5 cm and an acceptable variance of 0.01 cm. However, internal parts of the machine are subject to wear. Past experience indicates that when average diameter is 2.9 cm and the variance is 0.09 cm, the process is out of control and repairs are called for costing $38,000 at current prices. During December, production data combined with standard costs showed $8,000 in unfavorable variances associated with the production of #80-H shafts. You have been asked to give Mr. Stowe information to help him decide whether to order the $38,000 overhaul. December production reports show an average diameter for #80-H shafts of 2.75 cm.

Required: If management is currently 90 percent confident that a variance of 10 percent or less means that the production process is within normal ranges of tolerance, calculate an updated probability estimate for Mr. Stowe, given the current production information. (A table of selected exact probabilities, also called ordinates, is given below.)

$\dfrac{x - \mu}{\sigma}$	Ordinate
0.25	.38667
0.50	.35207
0.75	.30114
1.00	.24197
1.25	.18265
1.50	.12952
1.75	.08628
2.00	.05399
2.25	.03174
2.50	.01753
2.75	.00909
3.00	.00443

19–14 Investigation Decision. In Assignment 19–13 you were asked to calculate the posterior probability that the forming process was in control. Assume Redeye management thinks that if $38,000 is spent on an overhaul, there is only an 80 percent chance they can solve an out-of-control situation. Also assume that if the process is out of control, abnormal variances will be $90,000 per year.

Required: Using a one-year time frame, should management order an overhaul? (Use the information you calculated in the previous assignment.)

19–15 Variances and Make-or-Buy Decision. The Richards Company has been making an electronic subassembly that it uses in several of its products. The manufacturing process for the subassembly is very precise, and machine settings are critical. The following data regarding production times under two sets of conditions attest to the problem.

	Correct Setting	Incorrect Setting
Average labor time, hours per unit	10	14
Standard deviation of labor time	1	3

The times, under both the correct setting and the incorrect setting, are normally distributed about their respective means. Incorrect settings occur about 30 percent of the time. The total variable cost per labor hour, including labor cost and variable overhead, is $22.

There is now new machinery on the market that is less sensitive to settings. However, the Richards Company does not make enough of the subassemblies to warrant buying the machinery. Another firm that has bought the machinery and has some excess capacity has offered to do the work on the subassemblies for $250 each. Richards would supply the material.

Required: Make a recommendation supported by whatever calculations you deem relevant.

19–16 Variances—A Chance to Review Standards. The standards for overhead in the Kermit Glove Company were set using linear regression and correlation analysis. Based on this analysis, variable overhead was set at $1.10 per direct labor hour. After the first six months of operations, the plant manager has pointed to the following variable overhead variances and has asked that they be investigated.

Variable Overhead Spending Variance,
January–June, 19X1

	Production Level	Variance
January	3,000 units	$ 500F
February	3,500	1,000U
March	4,000	100U
April	4,200	500F
May	3,800	500U
June	3,300	100U

The production manager states that the last six months are typical of good production and he does not see why there has been this big swing in variances. Further investigation reveals that the data used for the standards are as follows:

Direct Labor Hours	Overhead Costs
7,200	$11,982
6,600	10,721
5,800	9,552
6,300	10,004
8,030	12,017
6,850	11,325
7,500	12,031
6,700	11,197
6,500	10,578
7,850	12,040
7,000	11,930
8,120	12,006
5,500	9,505

It takes two labor hours to produce one unit based on standard costs. The efficiency variances have been fairly minimal over the last six months.

Required:

1. The production manager says that the stated variances do not seem reasonable to him. Check the standards for variable overhead by calculating a regression equation by hand, calculator, or computer. What reply do you make to the production manager?
2. Plot the original data. Does this change your thinking? Explain.

19–17   Variances and Decisions. The Carlton Company makes two models of high-quality radios, called model X and model Y. Data on each model appear below.

	Model X		Model Y	
Selling price		$150		$230
Standard material cost	$25		$30	
Standard labor cost:				
Department I	10		20	
Department II	15		20	
Standard variable overhead				
at 200% of direct labor	50	100	80	150
Contribution margin		$ 50		$ 80

All direct laborers earn $10 per hour, and the variable overhead rate of 200 percent of direct labor cost applies to both departments. Department I does the basic assembling operations on the chassis, while department II does the final assembling. The firm has 500 direct labor hours available per week in department I, 600 hours in department II. The firm operates at capacity because it can sell all of either model that it can make.

The managers of the firm have used the data to develop the following weekly production plan: model X, 200 units; model Y, 150 units. This plan is the result of solving the linear programming problem:

$$
\begin{aligned}
\text{Maximize:} \quad & \$50X + \$80Y \\
\text{Subject to:} \quad & X + 2Y \leq 500 \\
& 1.5X + 2Y \leq 600 \\
& X, Y \geq 0
\end{aligned}
$$

After a time, the managers have observed that it takes 2½ hours to do a unit of model Y in department I about half the time. The department begins each week working on model Y, then uses the remaining available hours to work on model X. The reason has to do with the technology of the process. In addition, the managers must decide on the production schedule before the week starts: it is very costly to change it during the week.

Accordingly, when it does take 2½ hours to get a unit of model Y through department I, the firm can make 150 units of Y, but only 125 units of model X. (Subtracting 2.5 × 150 from the available hours in department I, 500, gives 125 hours for making model X.) Additionally, the contribution margin on model Y falls by $15 because the combined labor and variable overhead per hour is $30.

Required: Analyze the alternatives and make a recommendation.

19–18   **Bayesian Revisions—Two Periods.**   The Fondar Corporation has established probability distributions for the production process being in control and out of control as follows:

In Control		Out of Control	
Waste Percentage	Probability	Waste Percentage	Probability
0.10	.05	0.13	.05
0.09	.10	0.12	.05
0.08	.20	0.11	.15
0.07	.30	0.10	.35
0.06	.20	0.09	.20
0.05	.10	0.08	.10
0.04	.05	0.07	.10

In March, 19X0, the prior probability of being in control is .80. If the probability of being in control falls below 40 percent, then the company will investigate the situation.

Required:

1. During April, a sample was taken revealing a 10 percent waste. Should the company investigate?

2. During May, a sample revealed 8 percent waste. Should the company investigate? (Use the probability developed in item 1 as your new prior probability.)

19-19 **Variance Investigation (extension of assignment 8-17).** Refer to Assignment 8-17 for the basic data for this problem (relating to Northland division of Blann, Inc.).

Required:

1. When standard costs for labor and materials were developed, standard deviations from standard costs were also developed as follows:

	Standard Cost	Standard Deviation of Standard Cost
Materials	$6.40	$0.23
Labor	2.15	0.06

Overhead standards were developed from a regression and correlation analysis, where:

$$\text{overhead costs} = \$7{,}980 + \$2.963/\text{labor hour}$$

Where $r^2 = 0.9476$
$S_e = 753.07$
$S_b = 0.06$

Management has decided to accept as normal any variances falling within a 95 percent confidence interval of standard costs. Evaluate the results obtained and list for management the variances that might be investigated.

2. Assume that management is deciding whether or not to investigate the labor efficiency variance (and the variable overhead efficiency variance, since it is tied to labor hours worked). If they investigate this variance, it is estimated that costs will be $1,500. If a correctable problem is found, another $4,200 is expected to be spent. Past experience has shown that management can expect to find a correctable cause of a labor efficiency variance about 40 percent of the time. In most cases this variance is a random event that will not reoccur. Even if a correctable cause is found, management estimates that ongoing savings should be based on the limits of the confidence

interval calculated in item 1. Should management investigate these variances? Assume a relevant time period is three years and the relevant interest rate is 10 percent.

19-20 **Variance Reports—A Case.** The World's Fair Printing Company, located in a large Midwest city with plants throughout Ohio and Indiana, is a large printer of books and catalogs. The company was founded in the 1920s with a plant in Dayton. Over the ensuing years several suburban and rural plants have been built. Currently the company does $200 million in sales annually. The corporate headquarters are in Dayton. The general organizational structure is mostly decentralized with respect to all functions except finance and sales. These functions are carried out and coordinated by the corporate headquarters.

The Troy, Ohio, plant primarily prints catalogs for various stores and mail-order companies. The plant itself consists of a preparatory department where the plates for the offset presses are made, a pressroom containing fifteen offset presses, a bindery where the sections of each catalog are collected, bound, and made ready for shipment, and a shipping department where orders are staged and shipped via truck and rail.

Purchasing consists of paper, ink, and preparatory, binding, and shipping supplies. Paper contracts are negotiated companywide by a committee consisting of the various plant managers under the direction of the vice-president of production at corporate headquarters. Paper contracts tend to be long-term insofar as supply commitments are concerned, but prices vary with the market. Several mills supply paper to the Troy plant. Ink contracts for both price and quantity are negotiated by each plant manager. In some plants there are various suppliers; in other plants an ink company has installed an in-house plant for producing ink right next to the particular production facility. This is the case at Troy. The purchasing department at each plant is responsible for the various supplies that are bought. Aluminum of a certain weight and thickness as well as various supplies and chemicals are needed for the preparatory department. Photographic materials also must be purchased, although they usually come from a major supplier such as Kodak. Wire, glue, and other supplies must be purchased for binding and shipping. The contracting for boxes and bags is handled separately from that for paper for printing. In the case of boxes and bags, the local purchasing department makes the necessary contacts.

The operations of the preparatory department are as follows: material is sent in from various customers in what is called camera-ready form. This means that all type has been set, sized, and pasted down onto thin sheets of cardboard, so that only one photo is needed per page of type. Photographs are provided loose, showing any cropping and sizing that is necessary. Thus, each photograph will require one photo. This camera-ready art work is taken to the camera room, where large horizontal cameras take pictures of both the type and the photographs needed for each page. Film is processed through an automatic film-processing machine and is given to a worker at a light table (a large table with a piece of glass on top and fluorescent lights underneath) to put together into eight-page groupings. The presses are set up so that each part of a catalog that is printed is basically a sixteen-page section. There are eight pages on each side of this section. Depending on the size of the press used, sixteen, 32, or 48 pages may be printed at one time. After the worker has assembled eight pages using special paper and tape, a contact print of the finished sheet (sometimes called an eight-page flat) is made on another large piece of film.

In another part of the preparatory department, thin sheets of aluminum are coated with a special chemical substance that is heat and light sensitive. The full eight-page negatives are placed on top of the aluminum plates. This sandwich is exposed to high-intensity light, which hardens all the material on the aluminum exposed through clear areas in the film. The printing plate is put through a chemical process by which the soft areas (those areas that were black on the negative) are washed away. A caustic substance is used to etch into the plate, and a copper solution is introduced into this area. When this process is completed, the remaining treated area of the plate is removed. As a final result, all areas that will print have been filled with a copper substance, and all areas that will not print remain aluminum. The plate is then treated with a preservative and sent to the press room. Given the number of presses at the Troy plant and the average length of production runs, an average of 50 to 60 plates are produced in each eight-hour shift. The plant generally runs three shifts a day.

The general cost accounting system for the Troy plant, like that for most of the other plants in the company, is basically job order costing. The costs are accumulated by each catalog for analysis by both the production department and the sales department.

Required: Plant management has just instituted a standard cost system in the preparatory department. Expected costs have been developed for the various aspects of the production process in this department. You have been asked to prepare a recommendation for variance reports reflecting the performance of the preparatory department. The variance reports will be used as appropriate by various levels of management. Part of your recommendation should include the audience and format of your reports. State all assumptions you have made. If you have questions that need to be answered before final recommendations are made, make sure to list these questions.

SELECTED REFERENCES

Dittman, David, and Prem Prakash, "Cost Variance Investigation: Markovian Control Versus Optimal Control," *The Accounting Review,* 54:2 (April 1979), 358–73.

Duvall, Richard M., "Rules for Investigating Cost Variances," *Management Science,* 13:12 (June 1967), 631–41.

Dyckman, T. R., "The Investigation of Cost Variances," *Journal of Accounting Research,* 7:2 (Autumn 1969), 215–44.

Kaplan, Robert S., "Optimal Investment Strategies with Imperfect Information," *Journal of Accounting Research,* 7:1 (Spring 1969), 37–43.

————, "The Significance and Investigation of Cost Variances: Survey and Extensions," *Journal of Accounting Research,* 13:2 (Autumn 1975), 311–37.

Noble, Carl E., "Calculating Control Limits for Cost Control Data," *N.A.A. Bulletin,* 35:10 (June 1954), 1309–17.

Zannetos, Zenon S., "Standard Costs as a First Step to Probabilistic Control: A Theoretical Justification, an Extension and Implications," *The Accounting Review,* 39:2 (April 1964), 296–304.

Inventory Control

Chapter 20

In Chapter 14 we considered inventory policy by looking at relationships between budgeted inventories and budgeted levels of sales. We noted that the selection of a particular value (such as finished goods inventory budgeted to be 120 percent of the coming month's budgeted sales) depends on a number of factors. We noted also that managers might state policies in terms of production, rather than inventory per se. This would be likely when sales were seasonal and when fairly level production throughout the year would be considerably less costly than wide fluctuation.

Inventory policy is usually much more complex, requiring considerable time and effort for its formulation. Consider a firm that makes several hundred products using forty or so types of material and hundreds of purchased components. The managers responsible for purchasing, production scheduling, and inventory control must ensure that enough finished units are available to meet demand. They must also ensure that sufficient quantities of each material and component are available to meet production schedules.[1]

One answer is to stock enough of everything required for a long period, perhaps a year. Such a policy would be prohibitively costly for nearly any firm. The costs of insurance, pilferage, and obsolescence could be incredibly high because they would probably vary closely with the level of inventory. Moreover, the firm would be tying up a great deal of capital and would have to finance the inventory. Interest charges alone could be enormous, but interest charges do not capture the true opportunity cost of investment. As Chapter 15 points out, the firm's cost of capital measures the opportunity cost of investment, and cost of capital is higher than the interest rate on debt.

---

[1] We shall usually speak of manufacturing firms, but the basic analysis holds also for merchandising companies.

At the other extreme, a firm might keep its inventories at minimal levels, buying and making only as needed to meet sales and production requirements. The problem here is that the firm would make its products in very short production runs and buy its materials and components at frequent intervals. Short production runs are usually costly because of setup time. Changing over from one product to another may require shutting down production for an hour or more, idling workers and losing production. Buying materials and components in small quantities at frequent intervals would give rise to high freight charges and mountains of paperwork with high clerical costs. Additionally, if the firm attempted to get by with minimal inventories of materials and components, it would run the risk of failing to meet production schedules and thereby experiencing shortages of finished goods. In turn, shortages of finished goods might result in lost sales in the current period. Perhaps worse, customers might go to other firms in the future if they had difficulty obtaining the goods in the current period. An obvious example is that people often stop going to retail stores that do not have good selections.

This chapter examines two questions of inventory policy: how much to make or buy at a time, and at what level to replenish inventory. We shall discuss and illustrate several models designed to minimize the costs of inventory. These costs come in three basic types: the cost of having inventory, called *holding costs* or *carrying costs;* the costs of setting up a production run or of placing a purchase order; and the costs of being out of inventory, called *stockout costs.* Examples of these costs appear in Exhibit 20–1.

The costs relevant to determining inventory policies are the incremental costs of setup, carrying, and stockout. Some of these costs are extremely difficult to measure because they are opportunity costs and so are not recorded. The cost of the capital tied up in inventory is one example. That cost is not the interest that has to be paid to borrow funds to carry inventory, but is the opportunity cost—the return that could be earned if the funds were invested elsewhere. This important point was discussed in detail in Chapter 15. The cost of lost sales is also an opportunity cost, and while usually it cannot be measured or estimated accurately, it is for some firms the most important of all the costs listed. (Again, if you shun retail stores that you have found do not offer enough selection, you are living proof of this statement.)

Some of the costs listed in Exhibit 20–1 are likely to be step-variable. The cost of clerks in the purchasing department is probably step-variable with the number of purchase orders. Storage might be step-variable, especially for the wages of stores clerks and materials handlers. Some costs would change only with drastic shifts in policy: rent on storage space would be fixed within very wide ranges of inventory, but would increase if the quantity stored rose so much that additional space was needed. Storage space owned by a firm might have alternative uses and, therefore, opportunity costs. As we have repeatedly emphasized, the cost accountant must analyze individual elements of cost to determine their probable patterns of

EXHIBIT 20–1
Inventory-Related Costs

Setup (Ordering) Costs

1. Contribution margin of production lost during changeover, if operations at capacity
2. Wages paid to workers idle during changeover, if operations below capacity
3. Unloading and inspecting order
4. Clerical and data processing costs of purchase orders

Carrying (Holding) Costs

1. Opportunity cost of investment in inventory
2. Incremental storage
3. Insurance, personal property taxes
4. Obsolescence

Stockout Costs

1. Opportunity cost of lost sales
   a. contribution margin on sales lost during stockout period
   b. contribution margin on lost future sales (customer ill will)
2. Idle time of workers (assuming that sales are not lost because of stockout)
3. Disruptions and changeovers in production schedules
4. Airfreight versus surface transportation and other expediting costs

behavior: costs do not come with labels indicating their relevance to particular decisions.

ECONOMIC ORDER QUANTITY (EOQ)

The **economic order quantity**, also called the **economic lot size**, or **economic production quantity**, is the optimal amount of product to be made in a single production run. Obviously, a processing firm that makes a single product more or less continuously usually does not have to worry about the EOQ, because it operates evenly all the time. However, such a firm does buy materials and components and must be concerned about the EOQ in controlling these items of inventory.

Basically, the EOQ is the quantity that minimizes the sum of holding costs and setup or ordering costs. Stockout costs are not included in determining the EOQ because they relate to how low inventory falls before it is replenished, not how much to make or buy at a time. We consider stockout costs in determining the reorder point. The costs of following a given policy can be expressed by the following equation:

$$\text{total cost} = \text{annual carrying cost} + \text{annual setup cost}$$

$$TC = \left(\frac{Q}{2} \times h\right) + \left(\frac{D}{Q} \times k\right)$$

where TC = total holding cost plus setup cost
   Q = quantity produced on each run (or purchased)
   h = holding cost per unit per period
   D = expected demand for the period
   k = setup cost for each run

The term $Q/2$ reflects average inventory and is the amount on which the firm incurs holding costs. The term D/Q gives the number of runs of each product or component during the period.

   This expression of total costs assumes that demand for the product, material, or component is even throughout the period. Otherwise, $Q/2$ does not reflect the average inventory. We can determine the optimal value for Q, which we call Q^*, the EOQ, by differentiating the equation with respect to Q and setting the derivative equal to zero.[2]

$$Q^* = \sqrt{\frac{2kD}{h}}$$

Illustration: The Ascot Company

Assume the following data:

Setup cost	$250 per run
Carrying cost	$12 per unit per year
Expected annual demand	25,000

The EOQ is about 1,021 units:

$$Q^* = \sqrt{\frac{2 \times \$250 \times 25,000}{\$12}}$$

$$= \sqrt{1,041,667}$$

$$\cong 1,021$$

---

[2] The derivative of the total-cost equation is

$$\frac{dTC}{dQ} = \frac{h}{2} - \frac{kD}{Q^2}$$

Setting the derivative equal to zero gives $h/2 = kD/Q^2$. Solving for Q:

$$Q^* = \sqrt{\frac{2kD}{h}}$$

The optimal policy is to produce 1,021 units at a time, which means that there will be about 24.5 production runs per year (25,000/1,021). This figure is obviously an average, because you cannot have fractional runs. As a practical matter, the firm would probably make 1,000 units each run. The cost of violating the EOQ by 21 units is trivial, as we show below. First, note the total cost of following the EOQ policy is about $12,248, calculated as:

Carrying costs = (1,021/2) × $12		$ 6,126
Setup costs = (25,000/1,021) × $250		6,122
Total costs		$12,248

We can also determine the EOQ by using a trial-and-error method. The schedule below shows calculations of total costs working with various numbers of orders per year. We could also use various order quantities, the choice is a matter of personal preference. So long as total costs fall as we increase the number of orders, we should continue the schedule. When total costs begin to rise, the optimal number of orders has been passed.

(a) Runs per year	20	22	24	25	26
(b) Setup cost = (a) × $250	$ 5,000	$ 5,500	$ 6,000	$ 6,250	$ 6,500
(c) Units per run = 25,000/(a)	1,250	1,136	1,042	1,000	962
(d) Average inventory = (c)/2	625	568	521	500	481
(e) Carrying costs = (d) × $12	$ 7,500	$ 6,816	$ 6,252	$ 6,000	$ 5,772
(f) Total costs = (b) + (e)	$12,500	$12,316	$12,252	$12,250	$12,272

The figures above show that setup costs increase as the number of runs increases, which is expected, and that carrying costs decline as the number of runs increases because the average inventory falls as the number of runs increases. In the basic EOQ model, carrying costs equal holding costs at the EOQ, subject to rounding errors, as shown above. When we introduce factors like quantity discounts, the equality does not necessarily hold.

We see that the total cost does not change dramatically near the vicinity of the EOQ. The difference between the cost of 22 production runs and 25 runs is only $66 ($12,316 − $12,250). The relative insensitivity of total costs to the quantity produced (or, equivalently, to the number of runs per period) is confirmed by Figure 20–1 on page 804, which depicts the behavior of costs for the situation that we have been using. Notice the relatively long range over which the total-cost curve is fairly flat.

Sensitivity Analysis: Cost Estimation

Figure 20–1 showed that total costs do not differ significantly from the lowest obtainable so long as the order quantity is reasonably close to opti-

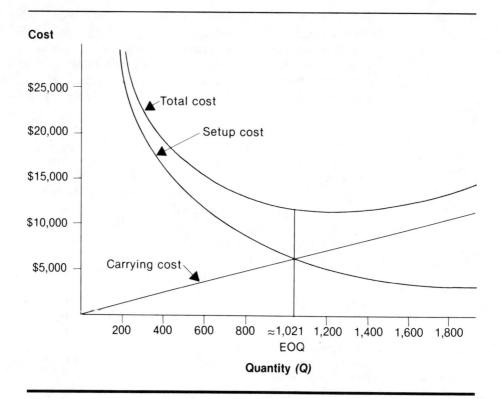

FIGURE 20–1
Cost of Inventory Policy

mal. We now consider the effects on costs if the firm bases its order quantity on the EOQ model, but makes substantial errors in estimating the costs of setting up and the costs of carrying inventory. Let us assume that the firm incorrectly estimates setup costs at $500, which is double the original figure of $250. The cost of making this error is the difference between the cost of following the optimal policy of making 1,021 units per run and the actual costs that would be incurred if the firm were to base its EOQ on $500 setup costs.

Using the incorrect $500 setup cost, the firm would set the EOQ at 1,443 units:

$$Q^* = \sqrt{\frac{2 \times \$500 \times 25{,}000}{\$12}}$$

$$\cong 1{,}443$$

The order quantity of 1,443 units would yield total costs as follows:

Carrying costs, 1,443/2 × $12	$ 8,658
Setup costs, 25,000/1,443 × $250	4,331
Total costs	$12,989
Cost at correct EOQ	12,248
Difference	$ 741

The $741 difference is about 6 percent of the cost of following the optimal EOQ. Thus, a 100 percent error in the estimate of setup costs results in increased costs of about 6 percent. Suppose now that the carrying costs are incorrectly estimated at $24, rather than $12, and that setup costs are correctly estimated at $250. The EOQ that is calculated would be about 722 units:

$$Q^* = \sqrt{\frac{2 \times \$250 \times 25,000}{\$24}}$$

$$\cong 722$$

Using an order quantity of 722, total costs would be:

Carrying costs, 722/2 × $12	$ 4,332
Setup costs, 25,000/722 × $250	8,657
Total	$12,989

The cost is the same as for an order quantity of 1,443 units, so it also is about 6 percent over the lowest obtainable cost. Thus, we see that the total cost in this case is not very sensitive to estimation errors of either cost factor. Incidentally, if the estimation errors were 50 percent low ($125 for setup, $6 for carrying) the results would be the same as shown above. That is, halving setup costs has the same effect on the EOQ as doubling carrying costs and vice versa.

Quantity Discounts

Purchased products, materials, and components often are subject to discounts on individual orders exceeding certain specified quantities. For example, the unit price of a material might be $2 for orders less than 1,000 units, $1.97 for orders from 1,000 units through 1,999 units, and $1.93 for orders of 2,000 or more. The EOQ model that we have used does not provide for consideration of quantity discounts. They must be worked in ad hoc, as we shall see below. Quantity discounts create an additional problem. Part of the carrying costs of an item depend on the cost of the item: they are not a constant amount per unit. The opportunity cost of funds invested in inventory is dependent on the cost per unit, as is insurance based on cost, and personal property taxes levied on inventories.[3] Other costs, such as storage, depend on units, not on cost per unit. Thus, some of the carrying costs will change if the cost of a unit changes, and these changes also must be worked into the analysis.

Let us assume that the product that we have been dealing with so far is purchased, not made. The $250 setup cost is now the incremental cost of placing and handling a single order. Suppose further that the price per unit is $100 for orders up to 5,000 units, $99 for orders of 5,000 through 12,499 units, and $98 for orders of 12,500 or more units. Finally, assume that $2 of annual per-unit carrying costs are constant per unit, and that the remaining $10 consists of interest, insurance, and other costs that are 10 percent of the purchase price. Thus, carrying costs will drop to $11.90 if the firm pays $99 for each unit [$2 + (0.10 × $99)] and to $11.80 if the price is $98 [$2 + (0.10 × $98)].

We already know that the EOQ without considering quantity discounts is 1,021 units. We also know the cost of following this policy. All we need to do to determine the new EOQ is to test the costs, including the quantity discounts, of following policies of buying 5,000 units at a time and 12,500 units at a time to see which is the least expensive overall. The schedule below shows the costs of each policy.

		1,020	5,000	12,500
(a)	Order size			
(b)	Number of orders per year = 25,000/(a)	24.5	5	2
(c)	Order cost = $250 × (b)	$ 6,125	$ 1,250	$ 500
(d)	Average inventory = (a)/2	510	2,500	6,250
(e)	Carrying costs = $12 × (d)	$ 6,120		
	= $11.90 × (d)		$29,750	
	= $11.80 × (d)			$73,750
(f)	Quantity discount = $1 × 25,000		($25,000)	
	= $2 × 25,000			($50,000)
(g)	Total costs = (c) + (e) − (f)	$12,245	$ 6,000	$24,250

The results show that buying 5,000 units five times per year is the least-cost policy. The additional $25,000 quantity discount that could be

---

[3] For manufactured goods, the opportunity cost of funds tied up in inventory depends on incremental production costs. Allocated fixed costs that are not incremental are irrelevant because they are incurred at any level of production within the relevant range. However, if taxes and insurance or other carrying costs are based on absorption costs, the allocated fixed costs must be considered, because they affect the amounts of relevant costs. The situation is analogous to the role of depreciation in capital budgeting: it does not affect cash flows per se but affects income taxes that are cash flows.

obtained by ordering only twice a year would be more than offset by increased carrying costs. In some cases there may be savings in manufacturing large quantities at one time, rather than making smaller quantities more often. The analysis shown here can be applied to those situations. We illustrated the analysis using quantity discounts on purchased items because that is a more prevalent source of savings.

REPLENISHMENT POINT

The **replenishment point,** often called the **reorder point,** is the level of inventory at which an order is placed. For the finished product of a manufacturer it is the level of finished goods that triggers a production order. For materials, components, and merchandise, it is the point at which a purchase requisition is initiated, and an order sent to a supplier. In general, there is some lead time between ordering more units and receiving them. It takes time to process production orders, set up for a production run, and make the units. It takes time to process a purchase order and for the supplier to deliver the goods. **Lead time** is the period, usually measured in days, required from the initiation of the order to the receipt of the goods.

Because units are being withdrawn during the lead time, it is necessary to place the order before inventory goes to zero. In addition, the demand for units during the lead time might be greater than normal, or the lead time might be longer than usual. Both factors argue for the use of safety stock. **Safety stock** is a self-defining term: it is the amount of inventory carried in excess of the expected use during the lead time to provide a cushion and guard against stockouts. Thus, the replenishment point is the sum of the expected use during the lead time and the safety stock. In formula form:

$$RP = (\text{average daily use} \times \text{lead time in days}) + \text{safety stock}$$

where RP = the replenishment point

It is possible to express the lead time and average use in weeks or months, and for some items the lead time might be quite long. In most cases, lead times are short enough to use days, usually working days rather than calendar days. The average daily use is simply the expected demand for the period divided by the number of working days in the period.

The behavior of the level of inventory under certainty is shown in Figure 20–2A on page 808. Notice that there is really no need to have safety stock under certainty because the use during the lead time is always equal to 150 units, the daily use of 15 units multiplied by the lead time of 10 days. Figure 20–2B on page 809 shows the behavior under uncertainty. The declines in inventory are not always the same amount per day, and the lead time is not always the same. Even with safety stock, there is some probability of running out, as occurs on the third cycle in Figure 20–2B.

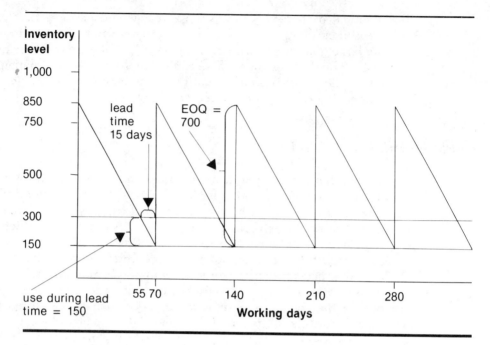

FIGURE 20–2A
Inventory Behavior Under Certainty*

* Assumptions: EOQ = 700; lead time = 15 days; average use = 10 units per day; replenishment point = 300 units; safety stock = 150 units.

Determining the replenishment point under uncertainty could involve some very sophisticated methods. We shall illustrate two fairly straightforward ones. Our objective in determining the replenishment point is to minimize the sum of the carrying costs on safety stock and the costs of stockouts. Recall that the basic EOQ model does not consider the cost of carrying safety stock. The EOQ is independent of the replenishment point, and the costs of holding safety stock are not incremental to the EOQ but only to the quantity of safety stock carried.

Setting the amount of safety stock requires the use of expected values. Assume that the cost accountant of a firm has collected the following data from historical records and has no reason to believe that patterns have changed.

Number of orders placed per year (determined using EOQ) is 20.

Use During Lead Time	Probability
1,000	.30
1,100	.60
1,200	.10

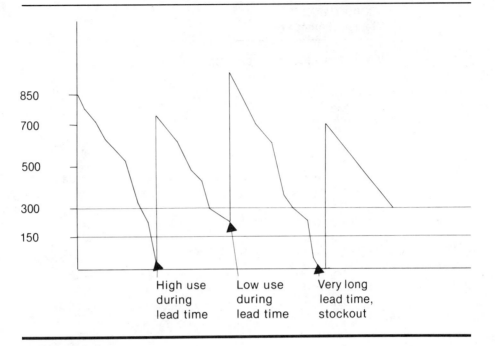

FIGURE 20–2B
Inventory Behavior Under Uncertainty*

* Assumptions: Same as for Figure 20–2A but daily demand and lead time are uncertain.

Estimated stockout cost per unit (excess of air freight over trucking and other expediting costs)	$2
Estimated carrying cost per unit per year	$6

The firm could adopt any number of replenishment points, including ones that would virtually guarantee stockouts, such as any point substantially less than 1,000 units. In some cases it might be most economical to allow stockouts, as when stockout costs are near zero. That is not the case for the firm in our example, as we show in Exhibit 20–2 on page 810. The expected stockouts when the replenishment point is set at each of the possible values of use during the lead time appear there, along with the costs of following each policy. For example, if the replenishment point is 1,100 units, the firm would have 100 units of safety stock above the minimum expected demand, giving carrying costs of $600 (100 × $6), while it would expect stockouts of 100 units twice a year (20 orders × .10 probability of demand's being 1,200 units), giving expected stockout costs of $400.

The policy of ordering when inventory is 1,100 units provides the lowest total cost. This policy gives safety stock of 100 units above the minimum expected use during the lead time.

EXHIBIT 20-2
Replenishment Point

Expected Stockouts per Year

Replenishment Point	Use During Lead Time			Stockouts
	1,000	1,100	1,200	
1,000	0	1,200	400	1,600
1,100	0	0	200	200
1,200	0	0	0	0

Each calculation is the number of orders per year (20) multiplied by the probability of use during the lead time multiplied by the number of units short. For example, for a policy of replenishing at 1,000 units and use during the lead time of 1,100, we have $20 \times .60 \times 100 = 1,200$.

Costs of Replenishment Policies

Replenishment Point	Safety Stock	Stockout Costs	Additional Carrying Costs	Total Costs
1,000	0	$3,200	0	$3,200
1,100	100	400	$ 600	1,000
1,200	200	0	1,200	1,200

In this example the uncertainty was not specifically identified with either the lead time or the average daily use, or both. It could be that the lead time is known to be 10 days and that average daily demand is either 100, 110, or 120 units. Or it could be that the average daily demand is always 100 units, but the lead time could be 10, 11, or 12 days. Either situation would give the same total-use figures. In practice, there are likely to be uncertainties regarding both factors, and then the joint probabilities must be calculated. An example appears in Exhibit 20–3 on page 811. The technique illustrated there was introduced in Chapter 4. Obviously, in a real situation there would be many possible levels of use during the lead time.

Service Levels

When the probability distribution of use during the lead time is continuous, or contains so many possible values that calculation by hand is awkward, managers might use simulation (see Chapter 23) or might simply set the safety stock at a level that provides for stockouts less than some specified percentage of the time, say 5 or 10 percent. For example, suppose that the cost accountant has found that demand during lead time is normally distributed with mean of 1,000 units and standard deviation of 150 units. The

EXHIBIT 20-3
Sample Calculations of Probabilities of Use During
Lead Time

Data

Lead Time in Days	Probability	Average Daily Use	Probability
8	.20	80	.10
9	.50	110	.70
10	.30	130	.20

Uses and
Joint Probabilities

Lead Time	Average Daily Use	Total Use	Joint Probability
8	80	640	.02
9	80	720	.05
10	80	800	.03
8	110	880	.14
9	110	990	.35
10	110	1,100	.21
8	130	1,040	.04
9	130	1,170	.10
10	130	1,300	.06
Total probabilities			1.00

Each joint probability is the product of the probabilities of each of the two events, lead time and daily use. For example, the joint probability of a lead time of eight days combined with daily use of 80 units is $.20 \times .10 = .02$.

firm's managers have set a policy of replenishing inventory soon enough to keep stockouts from occurring more than 10 percent of the time. Thus, we wish to find the number of standard deviations that corresponds to a 10 percent level of probability of being exceeded just in one tail. We use a one-tail test because we are concerned only with cases where demand is high during the lead time, not where it is low.

Using Table A-1 on page 926, we find that the probability of 10 percent in one tail corresponds to about 1.28 standard deviations. We are searching for the standard deviation such that 40 percent of the area above the mean is included within the range z to the mean. Using this information, the managers would set the replenishment point at:

$$1,000 + (150 \times 1.28) = 1,192$$

This approach to determining the replenishment point does not involve explicit consideration of the costs of safety stock and of stockouts. Given the difficulties in estimating stockout costs, such a policy might be about as well as the firm can do.

Other Techniques

The use of EOQ and of various models for setting the replenishment point can be very costly. We have already mentioned that firms may have a manager whose principal job is inventory control, which indicates the importance of the topic. However, inventory control is not equally important for all products, components, and materials. A low-volume product that is not essential to the sales of other products does not require constant attention. A material or component with low value that can be stored outside is not one that managers need to watch as carefully as a high-value item.

ABC Method.   Managers recognize the benefits and costs of various levels of control by using the ABC method. Inventoried items are classified A, B, or C depending on their value. High-value products are classified as A's and are watched carefully; low-value products are classified as C's and given little attention. Those classified as B's fall in the middle. In some firms, the percentages of products are inversely related to their total dollar volume. For instance, 10 percent of the products might account for 65 percent of sales, while 70 percent of them contribute only 20 percent of sales. Formal models could be used for the A's and some "eyeballing" techniques used for the C's. The items classified as B's might receive more regular review and analysis than the C's but less than the A's.

In general, the ABC method works best with finished products. Low-value materials and components might be essential in the production process, and shortages could cause high stockout costs. A way to deal with these items is to keep them in two bins. When one bin is empty, an order is placed and the contents of the other bin are used. The order will usually be received before that bin is empty. Variations on this method include placing tags in stacks of items. When the unit just above the tag is removed, the tag is sent to the purchasing department, which will then order another batch. The height at which the tag is placed indicates the relative value of the item: the higher in the stack, the higher the replenishment point.

Perpetual Inventory Methods.   Firms that keep perpetual inventory records will frequently set a replenishment point that triggers an order. This method relies on the records, not on a physical count as do the two-bin method and its variations. Its accuracy, therefore, depends on the accuracy of the perpetual inventory records. The elaborate cash registers now in use in many stores are called point-of-sale terminals. They not only record the sales, but also update perpetual inventory records through computer linkages.

Managers may receive printouts daily that show the quantities of each product on hand as well as information on sales. The data will help managers to determine which products are moving rapidly and which slowly and can be used as the basis for replenishing. Sales personnel also use these data to make tactical decisions on special prices or special promotion on slow-moving items.

PERISHABLE PRODUCTS

A special problem arises when a firm deals in perishable products. The term *perishable* refers to economic life, not necessarily to physical life. Thus, fresh fruits and vegetables are physically and economically perishable. Newspapers, magazines, and programs for athletic and cultural events are economically perishable even though physically they might last for years. Very few day-old newspapers or month-old magazines are sold. The general problem is determining the quantity to order or make when unsold units must be disposed of at a loss. Again, the problem involves expected values and risk-return trade-offs.

Illustration: The Ascot Company

The Ascot Company makes a variety of products, including fad items. It has developed a toy that its managers think could be a big seller at Christmas but will have almost no sales afterward. The managers must decide now how many units to produce, because the firm will not be able to produce any more and get them into the hands of department stores once the selling season starts. The firm will charge retailers $20 for each toy, but will also agree to take back any unsold units by January 10 of the coming year. The variable cost of production is $7, and returned toys can be sold for $2 each in bulk lots. Based on previous sales of similar items and other analyses, the sales manager has made the following forecasts and estimated probabilities. To make the calculations tractable, we have limited the values that demand can take on to four. We shall consider more realistic continuous distributions in the next section.

Demand	Probability
10,000	.10
12,000	.40
14,000	.30
16,000	.20
Total	1.00

Problems of this sort are often met by using a payoff table, which is similar to a decision tree and easier to work with when several actions are possible. We assume for now the firm can produce, or the manager has decided to produce, one of the quantities given above. That is, the firm will not produce 13,000 units, or 12,400 units, but one of the estimated levels of demand.

The payoff table appears in Exhibit 20–4. Each entry is the profit that the firm would expect to earn, given the demand and the quantity produced. The figures are conditional values because they depend on the action (production) and the event (demand). The table at the bottom of Exhibit 20–4 shows the expected values of profit for each production strategy. Using the expected-value criterion, the firm would produce 14,000 units.[4]

EXHIBIT 20–4
Payoff Table for Production Strategies—Ascot Company

Profit—Conditional Values

| | Strategy (Production) | | | | |
Demand	10,000	12,000	14,000	16,000	Probability
10,000	$130,000	$120,000	$110,000	$100,000	.10
12,000	130,000	156,000	146,000	136,000	.40
14,000	130,000	156,000	182,000	172,000	.30
16,000	130,000	156,000	182,000	208,000	.20

The quantity sold is the lesser of demand or production. If demand is equal to or greater than production, profit is simply demand × $13. If production exceeds demand, the calculations are as follows: (sales × $13) − [(production − sales) × $5] or (sales × $20) − (production × $7) + [(production − sales) × $2]. For example, if 14,000 units are produced and 12,000 sold, (12,000 × $13) − (2,000 × $5) = $146,000.

Expected Values of Profit (Conditional Values × Probabilities)

| | | Production | | | |
Demand	Probability	10,000	12,000	14,000	16,000
10,000	.10	$ 13,000	$ 12,000	$ 11,000	$ 10,000
12,000	.40	52,000	62,400	58,400	54,400
14,000	.30	39,000	46,800	54,600	51,600
16,000	.20	26,000	31,200	36,400	41,600
Totals	1.00	$130,000	$152,400	$160,400	$157,600

Note: When the conditional values for several levels of demand are the same, you can simply add the probabilities of the equal conditional values and multiply the sum by the conditional value. For example, the expected value of the strategy of producing 12,000 units is ($120,000 × .10) + ($156,000 × .90) = $152,400.

[4] Notice that the expected value of profits under each action, except producing 10,000 units, is not equal to any one of the profit figures that could occur. For example, the expected profit of $160,400 from producing 14,000 units cannot be realized under our assumptions: it does not correspond to the conditional profit for any level of demand. This occurs because of the assumption that demand can take on only one of four values.

Selecting the action with the greatest expected value is only one possible decision rule. The expected-value criterion for selection depends on the law of large numbers. It assumes that the decision recurs often enough so that the events will occur in proportion to their assessed probabilities. However, the Ascot Company faces this decision only once. Consider an analogy in a different setting. Suppose that someone offered you the opportunity to toss a fair coin, heads you win $20,000, tails you lose $5,000. The expected value of the game is $7,500 [$20,000(.50) − $5,000(.50)]. You probably would not play the game if you had only one chance, because you could lose $5,000. But if you could play it 1,000 or so times, you probably would, because the number of heads would be fairly close to half of the tosses. Playing the game only once, or even six to eight times, does not give the laws of probability enough time to operate in your favor.

In Chapter 4 we introduced the concept of variance and its role in decision making. It is obvious from Exhibit 20–4 that the variance of profit increases as production increases. The strategy of producing 10,000 units has a zero variance, with all values being equal to the expected value of $130,000. This strategy is the safest. Every other one has some probability of showing profits below $130,000. A very risk-averse manager might select 10,000 units for that reason.

A venturesome manager might decide to produce 16,000 units because of the probability of a $208,000 profit. Managers using the same information may arrive at different decisions because they have different attitudes about risk and return, a point that we have made many times in this book.

Value of Information

Suppose now that the example we have been using is for daily or weekly activity, so that the expected value of profits becomes a stronger decision criterion than it is under the assumption of a unique event. How much would a manager be willing to pay to forecast demand accurately and thereby know in advance how many units to produce? While it is rare that a manager could obtain perfect information, it is also rare that he could not obtain some information that would narrow down the possible events or improve his probability estimates. Let us first look at the value of perfect information, which is the extreme case but nonetheless instructive. First, if our example were for a firm that made production decisions weekly, the firm would probably make 14,000 units per week because that would give the highest expected profit over a good number of weeks. The value of perfect information is the difference between expected profits with perfect information and the expected profits given the optimal strategy without perfect information.

If the managers of the Ascot Company knew demand in advance, they would produce the quantity to be demanded. The expected value of profit would then be the sum of the elements on the main diagonal (upper left to lower right) of the payoff table that shows expected values of profit—that is,

$13,000 + $62,400 + $54,600 + $41,600 = $171,600$. The expected value of perfect information is then $11,200 ($171,600 − $160,400). Look at it in a slightly different way. Out of each ten weeks the firm would sell 10,000 units once (0.10), 12,000 units four times (0.40) and so on. Thus, because they would produce exactly what was demanded, the firm would show profits of $130,000 once, $156,000 four times, $182,000 three times, and $208,000 twice. Total profits for the ten weeks would then be $1,716,000. (The $1,716,000 is also $171,600 multiplied by 10.) If the firm produced 14,000 units each week it would expect to earn $110,000 once, $146,000 four times, and $182,000 five times, for total profits of $1,604,000, which is $112,000 less than $1,716,000. Hence the value of perfect information for each of the ten weeks is $11,200 ($112,000/10).

Obviously, perfect information is hard to come by. However, sample information is usually available. Market research surveys and test marketing are methods of acquiring additional information and perhaps of narrowing the range of the probability distribution.

A General Approach

The perishable-products problem can be approached more generally than the use of payoff tables. The analytical method that we describe here can be used for both discrete and continuous probability distributions and has some characteristics that make it adaptable to practical use.

First, to maximize profits the firm must set production or purchases so that the expected value of selling an additional unit equals the expected value of the loss of making or buying the unit but not selling it. The expected value of selling the unit is the contribution margin multiplied by the probability of selling the unit, and the expected value of the loss is the variable cost minus salvage value multiplied by the probability of not selling the unit. The probability of not selling the unit is $(1 − p)$, where p is the probability of selling the unit. In equation form, the expected value of profit is maximized when:

$$cp = h(1 − p)$$

where c = contribution margin per unit
$\quad\ h$ = the loss sustained if a unit is not sold, which is variable cost per unit less salvage value per unit, if any

$$cp = h − hp$$

$$p = \frac{h}{c + h}$$

In words, the critical value of p is the ratio of the loss on unsold units to the sum of the contribution margin and loss. The firm that seeks to maximize the expected value of profits will produce up to the critical value of p.

In the Ascot Company case, the values are as follows: $c = \$13$, $h = \$5$. Solving for p:

$$p = \frac{\$5}{\$13 + \$5} = .278$$

The Ascot Company should produce to the point where the probability of selling at least one additional unit is .278. This is another way of saying that it should produce up to the point where the cumulative probability of demand's being less than production is .722, which is $1 - .278$. Let us look at the probability distribution for Ascot.

Demand	Probability	Cumulative Probability
10,000	.10	.10
12,000	.40	.50
14,000	.30	.80
16,000	.20	1.00

The cumulative probability column shows the total probability that demand will be equal to or less than each level of demand. Thus, there is an 80 percent probability that demand will be equal to or less than 14,000 units. The critical ratio, .278, is greater than the probability of demand's being 16,000 units. It is also greater than the probability of demand's exceeding 14,000 units, because the only level of demand above 14,000 units is 16,000 units. The ratio indicates that the optimal level of production is somewhat below 14,000 units, but because this example is limited to four discrete levels of demand, 14,000 units is the optimal production quantity. At production of 12,000 units there is a 50 percent probability that demand will exceed production, which is considerably greater than the 27.8 percent value that we seek.

The critical value of p is easier to interpret when demand is more realistically assumed to take on a continuous probability distribution. Obviously, most firms will not find demand limited to four values. The problem with using continuous probability distributions is that calculating expected profits from following a strategy requires a computer and a great many calculations. Suppose that a manager believes that demand is reasonably well described as normally distributed with mean of 10,000 and standard deviation of 1,800. To calculate expected profits with production of 11,000 units requires a separate calculation for each possible level of demand. Each calculation is the profit at that level of demand, given production of 11,000 units, multiplied by the probability of occurrence of that level of demand. Even though it would be reasonable to use, say, intervals of five or ten units instead of one unit, the calculations would be overwhelming if done by hand.

However, determining the optimal production level is straightforward.

Assume that a firm faces the demand distribution just stated, mean of 10,000 and standard deviation of 1,800, and that the critical value for p is .278. The optimal level of production is shown visually in Figure 20–3. The objective is to find the number of standard deviations from the mean that corresponds to .278 of the area under the curve falling to the right. From Table A–1 we find that the z value for the standard deviation is about .59. Optimal production is then 11,062 units, which is 10,000 + .59(1,800).

This method does not require a complete specification of the probability distribution of demand. It only requires an estimate of the demand level corresponding to (or reasonably close to) the critical value of the probability of selling an additional unit.

In some cases, a manager may be willing to make statements about the probability that demand will be greater than some particular amount, even though he or she is unwilling to make estimates about means, standard deviations, or the shape of the probability distribution of demand. For instance, a sales manager may be willing to say that there is about 30 percent probability of demand's being greater than 20,000 units, a 50 percent probability of its exceeding 17,000 units. In a situation such as this, the data developed by the cost accountant could be very helpful. Suppose that the accountant has estimated contribution margin at $12 and the loss on unsold units at $2. The critical value for the probability of selling an additional unit

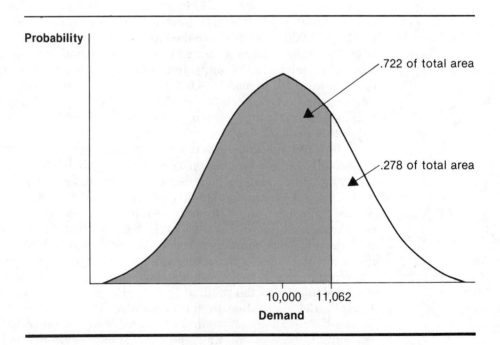

FIGURE 20–3
Probability Distribution of Demand

is .143, which is \$2/\$14. Thus, the optimal policy is to produce the quantity that gives a .143 probability that demand will exceed production. The sales manager may have no idea what that demand is, but if he is confident that the probability of demand's being greater than 20,000 is about .30, then a level of production somewhat above 20,000 units is likely to be a reasonable level. If the critical ratio were .45, then somewhere around 17,000 units would be indicated.

Practical Considerations

We mentioned earlier that illustrating the concept of expected value requires unrealistic data. Few firms would face only four levels of demand. The calculations required for a more realistic probability distribution are easy to handle on a computer. However, the question of the value of probabilistic techniques remains. The essential question is whether managers can in fact make reasonably accurate estimates of the probability distributions of demand.

Some firms can probably do so with reasonable success. Publishers of newspapers and magazines amass a great deal of experience in estimating newsstand sales. Bakeries and other firms making perishable food products also gain a good deal of experience in estimating probable levels of demand. One of the points made in Chapter 13 on budgeting can fruitfully be repeated here. Managers must make decisions. They must, for example, decide on levels of output. A manager's subjective judgment or feel is one basis for deciding, but it is haphazard and likely to be inconsistent.

Market research techniques offer ways to elicit probabilistic statements regarding demand. Firms will frequently test-market a product in a relatively small geographic area to see how well it does before committing themselves to major marketing efforts. Test marketing is one way of obtaining sample information. Perfect information is rarely obtainable no matter what the cost. Over a reasonable period, it is likely that such sample information will help managers to make better decisions.

Chapter 23 shows ways to simulate the behavior of profit to get an idea of the probability distribution and to select strategies that do not maximize expected profits, but are safer.

The Accountant's Role

Accounting data regarding costs and revenue play a large part in decision making. So do data that the accountant develops for special purposes, such as estimates of holding costs and stockout costs. At the very least, the accountant will be involved in providing information, interpreting it, and explaining its significance. At times, the accountant will be able to show that one course of action is so potentially profitable that it is clearly the best choice. At other times accounting data will show an action to be so costly that it should be ruled out.

The accountant's role is especially important because other kinds of managers are sometimes less concerned with costs than with sales volume, production scheduling, or whatever they are experts about. The accountant may be in a position to determine what conditions are necessary to make a proposed action desirable.

SUMMARY

Inventory control is important because the costs of following poor inventory policies can be very high. Some of the costs of poor policies are opportunity costs, which are not routinely recorded in the accounts and are therefore hard to identify, let alone measure. As in virtually all situations where costs are important, the accountant is involved in determining and evaluating inventory policies by providing data relevant to the analysis.

The accountant requires some knowledge of the basic models and methods used to control inventory so that he or she can determine what information is relevant and what is not. These models include the EOQ, replenishment point, and payoff tables.

ASSIGNMENTS

20-1 **Assumption of Level Demand.** The chapter states that the EOQ model is correct only if demand is level throughout the period. Thus, if annual demand were 12,000 units, with alternate months showing demands of 1,000 and 3,000 units, the EOQ based on annual data would not be correct.

Required: Can you reason out why the assumption of level demand is necessary?

20-2 **Basic EOQ and Replenishment Point.** The Braintree Wholesale Company experiences relatively constant demand of 24,000 units per year for one of its products. The product, an electric mixer, costs the firm $30. Placing an order costs about $200, and annual carrying costs are about $2 per unit. The firm works 200 days per year and desires a safety stock of 300 units. The lead time for an order is fifteen working days.

Required:

1. Determine the economic order quantity and the costs (ordering and carrying) associated with it.
2. Determine the replenishment point.

20–3 **Quantity Discounts.** The Ramsey Company requires 10,000 subassemblies per year that it buys from a single supplier. The supplier recently published a new price list keyed to the quantity ordered at a time. The prices and quantities are:

Price	Quantity
$10.00	up to 999 units
9.90	1,000 to 1,999 units
9.80	2,000 and up

Ramsey's chief accountant has estimated incremental ordering costs at $50 per order. He also estimates incremental carrying costs at $1 per unit, plus 20 percent of purchase price for the required return on investment.

Required: Determine the optimal number of units that Ramsey should order at a time.

20–4 **Sensitivity Analysis.** The Burgoyne Furniture Company uses about 200,000 yards of a particular fabric each year. The fabric costs $2.50 per yard. The current policy is to order the fabric four times per year. Incremental ordering costs are about $200 per order and incremental carrying costs are about $0.75 per yard, much of which represents the opportunity cost of the funds tied up in inventory.

Required:

1. Determine the total annual costs of following the current policy.
2. Determine the EOQ and the total annual costs associated with it.

20–5 **Relevant Costs.** The Warren Company uses 30,000 pounds of strip steel per year in making its own products. The firm manufactures evenly over the year and uses steel evenly over the year. The following data relate to the purchase and use of steel.

Cost per pound	$0.80
Carrying costs:	
Annual warehousing costs, salaries, and rent	$64,000
Insurance	$ 0.20 per pound
Taxes, levied on the basis of average inventory	$ 0.08 per pound
Shrinkage	2% of inventory is lost from various causes
Return on investment, at cost of capital	15%
Ordering costs:	
Clerical salaries, annual total	$43,000
Forms, postage, telephone	$1.50 per order
Freight	$1,000 per order
Receiving and handling	$23,000 annually plus $40 variable cost per order for extra help

Required: Determine the EOQ. Be prepared to explain why you included or excluded individual items of cost.

20–6 Basic Safety Stock. The Newman Company orders one of its raw materials ten times per year using the EOQ model. The firm's cost accountants have estimated that annual carrying costs for the material are $2 per pound. Stockout costs seem to be about $3 per pound, as best the accountants can estimate them.

Recent records show the following amounts of use of the material during the lead time and the associated probabilities:

Use During Lead Time (pounds)	Probability
800	.40
900	.40
1,000	.20

Required: Determine the optimal replenishment point.

20–7 Relationships. Each of the following situations is independent of the others.

Case	EOQ	Ordering Cost	Carrying Cost per Unit, per Year	Annual Demand
a	1,000	$50	—	10,000
b	2,000	——	$2	50,000
c	2,000	$100	$5	——

Required: Fill in the blanks.

20–8 Finding Annual Demand (AICPA adapted). Garmar, Inc., has determined the following for a given year:

EOQ	5,000 units
Total cost to place orders for year	$10,000
Cost to place one order	$50
Cost to carry one unit for one year	$4

Required: Determine the annual use.

20–9 Payoff Table. Horton Publishing Company generally has a press run of 100,000 copies of *Daily*, a newsmagazine that comes out once a week. The managers have been wondering whether this is optimal and have amassed the following information about demand, which they believe should hold true in the future.

Demand	Probability
60,000	.20
80,000	.30
100,000	.30
120,000	.20

The magazine sells for $1 and variable cost to print is $0.30. Unsold magazines are burned.

Required: Set up a payoff table to determine the optimal strategy and determine the value of perfect information.

20-10 Service Level (AICPA adapted). Helms, Inc., operates a number of sales offices. The manager of one such office has developed the following probability distribution of daily sales of a perishable product. The office restocks the product each morning.

X (units sold)	P(sales = X)
100	.20
150	.50
200	.20
250	.10

Required: The firm desires a 90 percent service level in satisfying sales demand. What should the initial stock balance be for each day?

20-11 Probabilities. *The Easton News-Leader* is a daily newspaper with wide circulation throughout several small towns in New England. The paper is plagued with returns of unsold copies, for which it gives dealers full credit. That is, the company buys back the papers at the wholesale price of $0.09. The variable cost of printing a copy is about $0.03 and the unsold copies bring about $0.005 as waste paper.

The publisher has been trying to determine how many copies to print per day. Information available from past records indicates that sales are uniformly distributed between 5,000 and 7,000 copies per day. Any value between 5,000 and 7,000 is equally likely, or so close as not to matter. For example, there is a 50 percent probability that sales will be greater than 6,000 copies, a 25 percent probability that they will exceed 6,500 copies, and so on.

Required: Determine the number of copies that the paper should produce each day.

20-12 EOQ and Relevant Costs. The Wininger Company makes a number of products. Data for model M-2203 appear at the top of page 824.

Cost of production:

Variable	$10 per unit
Fixed, based on 12,000 units	$4 per unit
Cost to set up production run	$1,000
Carrying costs:	
Storage	$2 per unit
Insurance	$4 per unit

Storage cost is allocated based on square footage normally occupied by each product. The firm has ample storage space, and the space has no alternative use. The firm also requires a 15 percent return on investment. The 12,000 units normally demanded during a year are spread evenly throughout the year. Insurance costs are variable with the number of units that are in inventory.

Required:

1. Determine the economic lot size.
2. Determine the total annual costs associated with the answer to item 1.
3. Determine the total annual costs associated with producing *double* the economic lot size.

20–13 Sensitivity Analysis. Jordan Jeans orders one of its major products twenty times a year. Carrying costs on the product are about $2 per unit annually, and the sales manager and treasurer have been arguing about the stockout costs for some time. The sales manager believes it desirable that the firm never run out, while the treasurer would like to keep a relatively low amount of safety stock to minimize carrying costs. The treasurer is on record as having said: "He [the sales manager] would keep the place full to bursting just to make sure he doesn't lose $5 in sales." The sales manager holds an equally complimentary view of the treasurer.

As the new controller, you have landed smack in the middle, and both parties have appealed to you to support their positions. You have gathered some information about the use during lead time of the product and associated probabilities, but are not yet sure whether you have a handle on stockout costs.

Use During Lead Time	Probability
1,000	.20
1,200	.30
1,500	.45
1,800	.05

The product has a contribution margin of $4, and the sales manager is sure that anyone coming in to buy the product who cannot get it will go elsewhere. The treasurer is equally sure that a good many customers do wait until Jordan has the product in stock. He believes that no more than 25 percent of stockouts result in lost sales.

Required: Make a recommendation on the replenishment point.

20–14   Replenishment Point.   The United Millwork Corporation uses 12,000 lb of a particular raw material each year. The EOQ is 1,200 lb, so that the firm orders it ten times per year. Carrying costs are $2 per unit, stockout costs $6 per unit. The following schedule shows both lead times and average daily use with their associated probabilities.

Lead Time	Probability	Average Daily Use	Probability
10 days	.30	40 units	.20
12 days	.70	60 units	.60
		80 units	.20

Required: Determine the optimal replenishment point.

20–15   Cost Analysis.   The treasurer of the Delmar Company has insisted on ordering very small quantities of materials and components with the objective of keeping the inventories at a minimum. As a consequence, the workload of the purchasing, receiving, and bookkeeping departments has grown quite rapidly.

The president of the firm has asked you to serve as a consultant on the matter of inventory policy. As you begin your study, you pick out one high-volume component, part M-302. The firm uses about 120,000 units of the part per year and currently orders it from its supplier twice a month. You have satisfied yourself that $0.20 per unit per year is a reasonable estimate of the carrying cost of the part. However, you are unable to make a good determination of the incremental ordering costs because the part is only one of many that the firm uses. Nevertheless, you believe that the twice-a-month ordering policy is unsound.

Required: Prepare whatever analysis you believe appropriate to support the position that ordering twice a month is too often. You need not determine the optimal order quantity, only make a plausible argument that the current policy is unsound.

20–16   Finding Setup Costs (CMA adapted).   Pointer Furniture Company manufactures and sells office furniture. In Pointer's line of desks each model is unique. Thus, a changeover (setup) is required on the manufacturing equipment whenever a batch of each model is put into production.

One model (JE 40) is a junior executive desk. The accounting department has been asked to determine the setup costs for this model.

The equipment maintenance department consists of ten employees who are paid $9 an hour plus employee benefits of 20 percent of wage costs. This department is responsible for changeover adjustments on the production line. Other costs in the maintenance department are $50,000 per year, which includes items such as supervision, depreciation, and insurance.

Two men are required to make the change on the desk line for Model JE 40. They are expected to spend three hours on machinery changes, one hour on testing, and one hour readjusting the machinery. The manufacturing line requires five workers who must be present during changeover. However, they are idle 40 percent of the time during changeover.

Production workers are paid $7.50 per hour. Overhead for these workers is applied as follows:

	Based on Direct Labor Hours	Based on Machine Hours
Variable	$2.75	$ 5.00
Fixed	2.25	15.00
	$5.00	$20.00

These rates are based on an expected activity of 10,000 direct labor hours and 1,500 machine hours. Other setup costs include $200 in direct materials. However, $50 is recovered through salvage of these materials.

Required: Estimate the setup cost for Model JE 40. For each cost item you identify, justify the amount and the reason for including this cost item in your estimate. Also explain the reason for excluding any cost item.

20–17 Safety Stock (AICPA adapted). The Polly Company management wants to determine the amount of safety stock that it should maintain to minimize the costs of product D. The following information is available.

Carrying cost	$2 per unit per year
Number of orders	5 per year

Units of Safety Stock	Probability of Stockout
10	50%
20	40%
30	30%
40	20%
50	10%
55	5%

If the firm runs out of product D, it must fly in units at a cost of $80, no matter how many units it requires. There are no other stockout costs.

Required: Determine the safety stock that the firm should carry.

20–18 Relevant Costs. In response to your request for information bearing on the EOQ and replenishment point for one of your firm's major products, your assistant gave you the following data.

Annual demand	20,000 units
Selling price per unit	$100
Purchase price per unit	$60
Freight in by railroad	$1.50 per unit plus $500 per shipment
Delivery to customer	$0.90 per unit plus $100 per delivery to each customer
Insurance	$0.80 per unit
Storage	$2.50 per unit
Pilferage and shrinkage	2% of inventory
Postage, forms, and other incremental ordering costs	$90 per order
Annual clerical salaries and other costs of purchasing department	$87,000
Opportunity cost of funds	20%
Sales commissions	$10 per unit

The firm can rush-order units at some additional cost. Air freight is $7 per unit plus $1,200 per shipment. The firm also incurs the $90 ordering cost if it places special orders.

Required:

1. Determine the ordering costs and carrying costs needed to determine the EOQ.

2. Determine the stockout costs needed to determine the replenishment point, assuming that:
   a. The firm can fill all sales by using air freight to obtain the units.
   b. The firm cannot fill sales using air freight and so loses sales when it stocks out.

20-19 **Stockpiling and Price Changes.** The purchasing manager of Westcott Industries recently approached the treasurer and asked if he could buy 200,000 lb of glycol, a raw material that the firm uses in great quantities. He wanted to make the purchase now because he expected the price to rise from the current $2.90/lb to $3.15 within a few weeks.

The treasurer promised to look into the matter and get back within a day. He then assembled the following information.

EOQ in current use	13,100 lb
Annual carrying cost per unit, including 20% required return on investment of $2.90	$0.70
Incremental ordering cost	$300 per order

Annual demand is about 200,000 lb, so that the purchasing manager in effect wants to buy an entire year's supply.

Required: Evaluate the purchasing manager's proposal.

20-20 Quantity Discounts, Supplier's Viewpoint. CZM Company supplies the Morgan Company with 45,000 units of part A-506 per year. Morgan uses an EOQ model with estimated order costs of $200 and estimated carrying costs of $2 per unit to determine that it should order 3,000 units fifteen times per year.

CZM sets up and runs the component each time Morgan orders it, incurring setup costs of $2,000 each time. It is not possible for CZM to carry an inventory of part A-506 because of space limitations, and its managers have given some thought to offering Morgan quantity discounts if it would order larger amounts less frequently. CZM ships the finished parts quickly and has no carrying costs.

Required:

1. The managers of CZM have asked you to determine the largest quantity discount that they could offer Morgan to buy only twice a year. That is, they want the upper limit, where CZM would earn the same income that it does now.

2. Determine whether or not the discount you calculated in item 1 would be enough to induce Morgan to buy only twice per year.

3. Repeat items 1 and 2, assuming that CZM wants to induce Morgan to order once per year. Treat this part independently of items 1 and 2. That is, assume that CZM and Morgan have not agreed on a discount that would reduce the number of orders to two per year.

20-21 Payoff Table. The Wycomb Company makes corsages that it sells through salespeople on the streets. Each sells for $2 and has variable production costs of $0.80. The salespeople receive a $0.50 commission on each corsage they sell, and the company must spend $0.05 to get rid of each unsold corsage. The corsages last for only one week and cannot be carried in inventory.

The managers of the firm have estimated demand per week and associated probabilities as follows:

Demand	Probability
100,000	.20
120,000	.20
140,000	.30
160,000	.30

Required: Determine the optimal weekly production of the corsage and the value of perfect information.

20-22 Inventory, Expected Value, and Information (CMA adapted). The Jessica Company has decided to use the expected-value model in a small department in order to see if this model will help in decision making. This department buys and resells a perishable product. A large purchase at the beginning of each month provides a lower cost than more frequent purchases and also assures that Jessica Co. can buy all of the item it wants. Unfortunately, if too much is purchased, the product unsold at the end of the month is worthless and must be discarded.

If an inadequate quantity is purchased, additional quantities probably cannot be purchased. If any should be available, they would probably be of poor quality and be overpriced. Jessica chooses to lose the potential sales rather than furnish poor-quality product. The standard purchase arrangement is $50,000 plus $0.50 for each unit purchased for orders of 100,000 units or more. Jessica is paid $1.25 per unit by its customers.

The needs of Jessica's customers limit the possible sales volumes to only four quantities per month—100,000, 120,000, 140,000, or 180,000 units. However, the total quantity needed for a given month cannot be determined before the date Jessica must make its purchases. The sales managers are willing to place a probability estimate on each of the four possible sales volumes each month. They note that the probabilities for the four sales volumes change from month to month because of the seasonal nature of the customers' business. Their probability estimates for December, 19X8, sales units are 10 percent for 100,000, 30 percent for 120,000, 40 percent for 140,000, and 20 percent for 180,000.

The following schedule shows the quantity purchased each month, based upon the expected-value decision model. The actual units sold and the product discarded or sales lost are shown also.

	Quantity (in units)			Sales Units Lost
	Purchased	Sold	Discarded	
January	100,000	100,000	—	20,000
February	120,000	100,000	20,000	—
March	180,000	140,000	40,000	—
April	100,000	100,000	—	80,000
May	100,000	100,000	—	—
June	140,000	140,000	—	—
July	140,000	100,000	40,000	—
August	140,000	120,000	20,000	—
September	120,000	100,000	20,000	—
October	120,000	120,000	—	20,000
November	180,000	140,000	40,000	—

Required:

1. What quantity should be ordered for December, 19X8, if the expected-value decision model is used?

2. Suppose Jessica could ascertain its customers' needs before placing its purchase order rather than relying on the expected-value decision

model. How much would it pay to obtain this information for December?

3. The model did not result in purchases equal to potential sales except during two months. Is the expected-value model unsuitable in this case, or is this a characteristic of the model? Explain your answer.

20-23 **Payoff Table, Alternative Strategies.** Robert Jablonski, the owner of a large produce market, has been trying to work out a strategy for purchasing merchandise. The average crate of produce costs him $6 and he sells it for $10. He must order in advance for each week and must discard all produce unsold at the end of the week. He has developed the following probability distribution of demand:

Demand in Crates	Probability
10,000	.10
14,000	.20
18,000	.20
22,000	.50

He asks you to determine the strategy with the highest expected value of profit. Also he wants to know, for each possible strategy, the probability that profits will equal or exceed each of the following targets: $40,000; $50,000; and $60,000. That is, for each strategy, what percentage of the time should profit equal or exceed each of the targets?

Required: Do the analyses that Jablonski has asked for and recommend a strategy.

20-24 **Order Strategy.** The Boston Flower Shop sells corsages. It must order them in advance, at the beginning of each week, and cannot obtain any more once the week begins. The purchase price is $1.50, the selling price $4. Any unsold corsages are discarded. An examination of demand in previous weeks indicates that demand is approximately normally distributed, with a mean of 5,000 and standard deviation of 1,200. The owner of the shop wants to maximize the expected value of profits.

Required:

1. Determine the optimal number of corsages to order each week.

2. Without making any additional calculations, answer the following questions:
   a. What would be the effect on the optimal order quantity if the purchase price increased, with the selling price held constant?
   b. What would be the effect on the optimal order quantity if the standard deviation of demand were greater than 1,200 units?

Behavioral Aspects of Information

Chapter **21**

This chapter deals with a frontier in accounting: the behavioral aspects of accounting information. Interest in this area has grown within the last fifteen years. Accounting researchers have drawn more and more on studies conducted by psychologists and sociologists and have developed both theories and practical applications. This chapter is more abstract than others, since it contains no formulas or methods for recording cost data. Its object is to give you a new perspective on the preparation and use of information.

INFORMATION AND BUSINESS DECISIONS

While it may seem obvious, almost every subject we deal with either implicitly or explicitly concerns an interface between the creators and users of information. Let us look at some examples from earlier chapters. In Chapter 7 we discussed the behavioral consequences of setting standards where the amount of participation can affect motivation. In Chapter 13 we discussed budgeting. Obviously, there is a motivational impact when a very tight or a very loose budget is received. Less obvious is the fact that the budget contains information about more than just dollar limits on spending; it can contain information also about corporate priorities and managerial attitudes.

For example, if research and development funds are held at a constant level and requests for expansion into new areas are denied, this indicates corporate management's attitude about the future role of the department. Managers can use this information for decisions that go beyond just the budgeting cycle. In Chapter 18 we discussed transfer pricing: direct behavioral consequences are involved in negotiating transfer prices between divisions or in having transfer prices imposed.

These examples are clear evidence of behavioral dimensions in accounting. They show reactions to participation, to budgets, and to negotiating, and they involve motivation as a key ingredient. However, in many ways they are one step removed from the major subject of this chapter.

As accountants, we must be concerned that the information that decision makers use will result in the best decisions possible at the time. What data did a manager see before participating in standard setting or budgeting? How many of these data became relevant information to that manager? How did the manager *use* the information? The advent of sophisticated word processing machines and newer generations of computers also requires that we make more explicit choices on the form, order, format, content and complexity of information that we produce. This choice will depend partly on the decisions at hand, a benefit-cost analysis of how much information to report, and—most importantly—the audience: the decision makers who need the information. These decision makers are the major focus of what follows.

Information and the Accountant

Accountants recognize that one of their principal functions is to provide information to facilitate decision making for planning and control. For many years it was implicitly assumed that accounting information is "objective, unbiased, neutral."[1] In recent years that view has been challenged. For example, Caplan argued that

> The objectivity of the management accounting process is largely a myth. Accountants have wide areas of discretion in the selection, processing, and reporting of data.[2]

Some people assume that an accountant's role is to provide unbiased information for decision making. They tell the accountant: "Just give me the facts and I'll make the decision." The assumption is that there is a single set of facts waiting to be reported and that the accountant's job is to *find* them. This view has been challenged; accountants now argue that the selection of data for reporting to decision makers is not a neutral, unbiased activity. The facts are too numerous, so the accountant must consciously and unconsciously make choices. In some cases the accountant might even wish to influence the decision, and this wish would be reflected in the information he or she chose to present.

[1] Accounting Principles Board, *Basic Concepts and Accounting Principles Underlying Financial Statements of Business Enterprises* (New York: American Institute of Certified Public Accountants, 1970), 10, 37.

[2] Edwin Caplan, *Management Accounting and Behavioral Science* (Reading, Mass.: Addison-Wesley Publishing Company, Inc., 1971), p. 31. Also see A. Thomas, "Useful Arbitrary Allocations," *The Accounting Review*, 46:3 (July 1971), 472–79.

This is a good point at which to differentiate between *data* and *information*. **Data** are all the facts and impressions that exist. In any context, however, some facts are relevant while others are not. **Information** is intended to be useful in decision making: it is some subset of data purposely selected from an overall set.

For example, during an energy shortage in the late 1970s, the management of Naro Paints wanted to look at the profitability of keeping its stores open on Sundays. Naro's retail outlets were located in a large metropolitan area covering two neighboring states. One state allowed Sunday sales while the other did not. There are a lot of data that management could have chosen. General categories include the weather, time of year, competition, availability and price of gasoline, and customer count and makeup. Let us look at just this last item. Employees could do a car count in the parking lot to determine state of registration, number of adults arriving in each vehicle, city of owner, and so on. The point is that not all of the data are relevant to the analysis of whether to stay open on Sunday. Some facts might be totally irrelevant to Naro, while others might be relevant in *other* decision contexts, but not this one. Thus, there is the need to decide *what* data can be relevant information and *how* to present that information so it is most useful.

Information and the Individual

The accountant is going to make choices on what information to present and how to present it. Our personal psychological makeup is a part of this decision process. Each of us possesses a set of biases, techniques, and structures that affects our perceptual choices both in the presentation and in the use of information. Our choices are made in light of who we are as individuals.[3] Let us look now at some dimensions of information perception, use, and selection.

HUMAN INFORMATION PROCESSING

Human information processing is a field of study taking us beyond the premise that all you need in order to make good decisions are the facts. Many studies in this area have shown that different people use information differently. Some people seem able to understand and *use* much more complex information than others. Some need a greater quantity of information for decisions. Some people are more comfortable with numerical information than others. Equations might be useful for some decision makers, while anything mathematical might turn others off. A person's experience and

---

[3] Norton Bedford discusses the concept of the individual and how accounting research needs to include behavioral dimensions in "Behavioral Science and Accounting Research," in W. Bruns and D. DeCoster, *Accounting and Its Behavioral Implications* (New York: McGraw-Hill Book Company, 1969).

personality can affect his or her use and perception of information. We are also learning more about how form, order, and level of aggregation of information can affect decision-making behavior. Accountants are amassing hard evidence in this field that can be used and expanded.

We referred earlier to new developments in word processing and computer technology. With easy access to sophisticated programs and equipment, an attitude has grown up that more is better. People even thought that the computer would replace human judgment, because with all the data that can be generated, much routine decision making would become trivial. However, we know now that people do not respond well to too much data. They reach a saturation point that is called **channel** or **information overload**. It is a lot like trying to fill a soda bottle from a 55-gallon drum: only so much liquid gets in while the rest is wasted. We see direct applications of this concept in studies by both Revsine and Miller[4] in the area of financial reports. Each concludes that too much information actually reduces a person's ability to use any of the information.

Cognitive Complexity

Cognitive complexity is one of the subjects studied in human information processing. Before we explain this area, let us consider a case example.

Illustration: Corbett Printing Company.   Corbett Printing Company has a computer-based job order costing system. Corbett prints various trade magazines, catalogs, and specialty work such as posters and promotional material. Some jobs are quite regular in format and scheduling, while others come in last-minute and are very diverse in specifications. Chris Bendt, president, and Alice Perez, the company's chief accountant, want to report job cost information for the use of lead workers on various equipment, departmental forepersons, the scheduling and production staff, the company's estimating staff, and for themselves. While issues of cognitive complexity are not really handled independently of other information-processing problems, we can look at how Bendt and Perez need to make choices in this area.

A lot of data are available regarding the costs of a job. There are actual cost and standard cost data. Data are available from the various departments (camera work, printing, binding, shipping) in the production sequence. There are fixed costs and variable costs. Some jobs create overtime because they are received behind schedule, while others are run on overtime at the convenience of Corbett's management.

As Bendt and Perez have remarked, various people need to have some of this information to make relevant decisions. We can assume for the sake of this illustration that Bendt is more able to deal with complex data and can better use complex information than the shipping department foreman.

[4] L. Revsine, "Data Expansion and Conceptual Structure," *The Accounting Review*, 45:4 (October 1970), 704–711; and H. Miller, "Environmental Complexity and Financial Reports," *The Accounting Review*, 47:1 (January 1972), 31–37.

Bendt might be very comfortable with an organized computer output showing various dimensions of actual and standard costing along with variances, a breakdown by department of fixed and variable costs, as well as a dimension of controllability, just to mention a few. As president, he has an ongoing interest in bidding new jobs and seeing how profitable each current job has been. His decisions include not only short-range planning and control but also long-range issues of supplier contracts, union negotiations, new printing or binding equipment, new market segments, and so on. The decisions are complex, and the job cost data with all their complexity are but one part of Bendt's full set of information. He needs to be flexible in his use of information from various sources both within and without the company. He needs to organize all this information in such a way that he can best use it for the decisions at hand.

The shipping department foreman has a different need for information. His decisions regard crews, supply costs, scheduling, and efficiency. Not only is he less comfortable with complex data, but he also needs less information in order to do his job. While he needs to be flexible in his use of information, his approach can be much more ordered and regular than Bendt's or Perez's. While Bendt concerns himself with complex external issues such as the economy or market research, the department foreman may have only specific worker problems to deal with (sickness, a new baby) as external concerns. The internal issues confronting the foreman also are limited to the scope of his department. Thus, this foreman needs a simpler set of information and simpler ways of using it than does top corporate management.

However, even within top management there are differences in how information is used and how much is needed. Perez and Bendt may have different abilities to handle complex information. For example, Perez may be able to handle more complexity and ambiguity than Bendt, but her job entails using fewer dimensions of information than does Bendt.

Several factors are evident in Corbett Printing. They include the need to provide relevant information to people at different levels of management. These people have different needs for information: the information must be relevant to each person's area of decision making. Some people seem better able to deal with abstract information, while others need more details. The study of human information processing (HIP) offers us ways to explore these factors.

One of the main bodies of HIP research is concerned with **cognitive complexity**. Several authors propose two dimensions in the use of information for decision making. Driver and Mock[5] call these dimensions the

[5] See M. Driver and J. Mock, "Human Information Processing, Decision Style Theory, and Accounting Information Systems," *The Accounting Review,* 50:3 (July 1975), 490–508, for a good review of the literature and references on this area. Also see H. M. Schroder, M. J. Driver, and S. Struefert, *Human Information Processing* (New York: Holt, Rinehart and Winston, Inc., 1967), chaps. 1–3; and P. L. Hunsaker, "Incongruity Adaptation Capability and Risk Preference in Turbulent Decision-Making Environments," *Organizational Behavior and Human Performance,* 2 (1975), 173–85.

amount of information used and the degree of focus. A person who uses a minimal amount of information and focuses on one, clear-cut solution to a problem is at one end of the continuum; at the other end is a person who uses all the relevant data that he can get (obviously weighed by benefit versus cost) and develops multiple analyses and solutions. Keep in mind that we are dealing with two dimensions and not just one. A person might be quite able and willing to use a lot of information but not able to move beyond a simple focus on a singular solution.

Assume that Corbett Printing's management is considering new product lines. If Bendt is able to use a lot of information successfully and can focus on multiple solutions, he might review all the operating specifications of current equipment along with production schedules and cost reports to determine the time available and the type of job Corbett would be able to handle. In addition, he would call in various equipment manufacturers, sound out competitors and customers, and seek other information relevant to what compatible types of work were available and who was currently printing these jobs. Just with this set of concerns, Bendt could accumulate quite a bit of information to review.

However, if Bendt wanted to use only a minimal amount of information, he might concentrate on a few simple items. He would not expand this data set, but rather would be satisfied with just enough information to yield some answers.

The other dimension is the focus of Bendt's analysis. A simple focus would be to find one product that would use existing slack time in a reasonably profitable way. The focus at the other extreme would be to find several products or sets of products to use existing capacity as well as options entailing new equipment and perhaps new buildings.

Now put these two dimensions together. If Bendt is both a minimal information user and has a singular focus, he may come up with a short-range plan based on limited data to fill existing capacity. It may very well be nonoptimal in either the short or long term. If he has a multiple focus, he may use a limited amount of information to propose several alternatives. However, he will have very little hard information on each of the alternatives.

If Bendt can use a maximum amount of information but has a single-solution focus, he may choose the alternative with the highest expected value. His analysis will be thorough but directed toward a singular problem. The ultimate style is being able to use a maximum amount of information while also looking at multiple objectives and solutions. This will yield a complete analysis and a full set of options together with an assessment of the strengths and weaknesses of each.

Decision Styles.   Driver and Mock[6] use the term **decision style** to describe the combination of these two dimensions. The four styles that they note are:

[6] Driver and Mock, "Human Information Processing."

Style	Information	Focus
1. Decisive	Minimal	One solution
2. Flexible	Minimal	Multiple solutions
3. Hierarchic	Maximum	One solution
4. Integrative	Maximum	Multiple solutions

While research has shown most people are dominant in just one style, mixed styles are possible. People who have hierarchic and integrative styles use a maximum of information and are **cognitively complex**. Thus, a person who successfully uses a lot of information can, by definition, deal with complexity.

Conceptual Levels

So far we have seen that people can use different amounts of information and they can focus on a unique or on multiple solutions in decision making. As accountants, we are interested not just in this general taxonomy, but with knowing more about how information is used. Miller and Gordon[7] look at a level of cognitive complexity called the **conceptual level.** For example, let us compare the conceptual level of the decisive style and that of the integrative style. The decisive style (using minimal information directed toward a singular solution) implies that the decision maker will satisfice rather than optimize and will have an intolerance for much information. Such a person will look at summary figures such as total variances or earnings per share or just the return on investment of a project and may make reasonable decisions, but based on very little information. A decision maker with an integrative style (using maximum information directed toward multiple solutions) can look into the figures in a report, analyze the assumptions, integrate external factors, and consider various perspectives in the process of arriving at a set of solutions. Thus, the decisive style involves a low conceptual level and the integrative style a high one.

Environmental Complexity. Even if each of us has a dominant decision style, there is some range of complexity (conceptual level) over which we vary. While our ability to use information is in part learned behavior, it is affected by what is happening now in our environment. This factor is called **environmental complexity.** Consider a well-organized report that is full of recognizable relevant information, and compare it with an unorganized, poorly labeled report containing the same information. In the first instance we would be better able to *use* the information (or some of it), no matter what our decision style. In the second instance our ability to use the information would be impaired by an environmental factor: the poor organization of the material.

[7] D. Miller and L. Gordon, "Conceptual Levels and the Design of Accounting Information Systems," *Decision Sciences,* 6 (1975) 259–69. This article contains a good bibliography on the subject.

The dimensions of conceptual level and environmental complexity are illustrated in Figures 21–1 and 21–2. Figure 21–1 shows that each individual has an optimal level of abstractness. If a person is presented with one piece of information and no more, he or she is not motivated to use much more than a simple decision style. At the other end of the spectrum, if an individual is swamped with too much information, he or she will retreat to a simple style to be able to deal with this overload. Thus, the idea that accountants and others (engineers, market researchers, personnel experts) should simply give managers all the facts can lead to the managers' throwing up their hands and using very simple decision rules. Somewhere in the middle lies an optimal range of complexity and conceptual level for decision making.

Figure 21–2 compares people who have different abilities to use complex information. The lowest (curve a) might be someone with a decisive style, the highest (curve c) a person with a hierarchic or integrative style.

Accounting Issues.   This discussion has direct application to accounting information. For example, both Revsine and Miller[8] have looked at recent trends to expand data in corporate annual reports. Each author concludes that too much information can reduce a person's ability to deal with abstract ideas.

Differentiation and Integration

Some of the original work in HIP was done by Schroder, Driver, and Streufert.[9] This work precedes that cited earlier by Driver and Mock. They define dimensions called differentiation and integration. **Differentiation** refers to the parts of information we use or the number of variables we examine as decision makers. **Integration** refers to the ways in which we put these parts together.[10] Consider how two different investors might buy securities. One might look at ten years' worth of annual reports and 10-K forms, while the other might just look at earnings per share and the price/earnings ratio. The first investor uses a highly differentiated set of information, the second a nondifferentiated set.

The integration function involves the way in which these investors combine this information in a useful way to yield a decision. A simple integrative structure involves a static set of rules. One investor might have a very organized way of proceeding through an information set and might never deviate from it. Another might start with different information each time and might seek whole new sets of data, given what he sees in a pre-

---

[8] Revsine, "Data Expansion and Conceptual Structure"; and Miller, "Environmental Complexity and Financial Reports."

[9] See Schroder, Driver, and Struefert, *Human Information Processing.*

[10] This same terminology is used adroitly by D. Watson and J. Baumler in discussing decentralization and negotiated transfer pricing in "Transfer Pricing: A Behavioral Context," *The Accounting Review*, 50:3 (July 1975), 466–74.

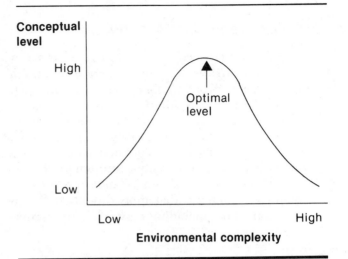

FIGURE 21–1
A Person's Optimal Level of Abstractness

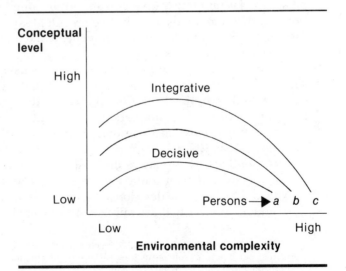

FIGURE 21–2
Persons Differing in Ability to Use Abstract Information.

liminary investigation. This second person would be more integrated (and flexible) than the first. Note how these examples illustrate the decision styles described earlier.

Cognitive Complexity and Cost Accounting

Information that accountants prepare for other managers can be of various levels of diversity and structure. For example, the advent of the computer and of canned programs for certain analyses (such as regression and correlation analysis) has resulted in managers' receiving nearly every piece of information that can be generated. The format may be designed by a statistician with no regard for relevancy to the problem at hand. Given this bewildering array of data, it is no wonder that the manager might look at some summary piece of information and ignore the rest.[11]

The area of human information processing includes topics other than cognitive complexity that apply directly to the creation and use of accounting information, including most of those discussed below.

Cognitive Limits

All the maximization models that we use (such as linear programming and expected value) are based on the assumption that an **economic person** is the decision maker. Economic person is characterized as an expected utility maximizer. He or she is rational—a perfect information processor. However, few people fit this idealized framework.[12] Most of us are administrative persons.[13] The **administrative person** cannot cope with every bit of information and therefore tends to look at key result areas. For example, in considering a product's value to the company, he or she might look only at contribution margin or market share.

Administrative people seem to want to satisfice rather than maximize. Thus, when a reasonable solution is found, they accept it, and there is no drive to find an optimal solution. As part of this process, they tend to limit the search process for information; they want to look at familiar situations and perpetuate existing decisions. This orientation has also been called **bounded rationality**.[14]

Accountants as preparers and users of information are faced with a conflict. They and their audience are limited by levels of cognitive complexity and by the basic decision style they use. In addition, all the quantitative models we use that are supposed to promote optimal behavior are in

[11] Managers tell various horror stories about, for example, some 50 pages of PERT diagrams they receive from subcontractors. If there is information contained in the 50 pages, it is ignored, since the data set is just too complex.

[12] For a full discussion of various sources for this material, see S. Kerr, R. J. Klimoski, J. Tollier, and M. A. Von Glinow, "Human Information Processing," in J. Leslie Livingstone, *Managerial Accounting: The Behavioral Foundations* (Columbus, Ohio: Grid, Inc., 1975), 169–92.

[13] The pioneering ideas were set forth by Herbert A. Simon, *Administrative Behavior: A Study of Decision Making Processes in Administrative Organization*, 2d ed. (New York: The Free Press, 1975).

[14] *Ibid.*

opposition, in some ways, to a person's natural tendency to satisfice. No wonder that the adopting of sophisticated techniques has lagged behind the development of the techniques themselves.

PERSONALITY DIMENSIONS AND INFORMATION USE

The material presented earlier on cognitive complexity shows that different people can fall on different complexity curves, and it introduces us to the topic of how personality traits affect information use. Each of us brings into a job situation the sum total of who we are and what we have learned. Our personal history includes how we deal with our feelings, what our self-image is, and what our need structure is at the time, to name just a few dimensions.[15] We are the product of our own choices as conditioned by what we have learned from parents, teachers, and supervisors over the years. We possess various communication skills that we have learned and developed. All these factors and more are part of our personality and style and have an effect on how we use information. As accountants, we should know what variables affect the use of information so that we understand better what choices we have to make when selecting and presenting information. For example, a group of authors looking at human information processing propose that *locus of control* can affect how an individual uses information.[16]

Locus of Control

Locus of control is a concept originated by Rotter to describe how a person perceives the question of who controls his destiny.[17] If a person thinks that he is in control, he has an internal framework (locus of control). If, on the other hand, a person feels he is at the mercy of his environment, that he has little personal control, then his locus is external. Tests have been developed to measure relative positions on this continuum, and added dimensions of internality and externality rather than just an overall scale have been posited.[18] Some researchers have demonstrated that people with an internal

---

[15] For references regarding feelings and self-image, see such books as M. James and D. Joungeward, *Born to Win* (Reading, Mass.: Addison-Wesley Publishing Company, 1971); T. Harris, *I'm OK, You're OK* (New York: Harper & Row, Publishers, 1967); C. Rogers, *On Becoming a Person* (Boston: Houghton Mifflin Company, 1961). Refer also to A. Maslow's hierarchy of needs as described in his book, *Toward a Psychology of Being*, 2d ed. (New York: Van Nostrand-Reinhold Company, 1968).

[16] Kerr and others, "Human Information Processing," and J. Dermer, "Human Information Processing and Problem Solving: Implications for Accounting Research" in Livingstone, *Managerial Accounting: The Behavioral Foundations*, 169–208.

[17] See J. B. Rotter, "Generalized Expectancies for Internal Versus External Control of Reinforcement," *Psychological Monographs*, 80:609 (1966), 1–28.

[18] For example, B. Collins, "Four Components of the Rotter Internal-External Scale: Belief in A Difficult World, A Just World, A Predictable World, and A Politically Responsive World," *Journal of Personality and Social Psychology*, 29:3 (1974), 381–91.

locus of control make different decisions and seem to use information differently from those more externally oriented.[19]

n-Achievement

Another dimension that has received attention is n-achievement, a measure of the achievement motivation of an individual.[20] High achievers tend to set reasonable goals that may have some moderate degree of risk but seem normally attainable. A person with a high motivation to achieve usually is a problem solver, a person who is willing to assume responsibility. The idea of accepting a moderate degree of risk (not wanting a situation either too easy or too risky) is borne out in many studies in psychology.[21] As with locus of control, n-achievement is measurable.

Recent research suggests that the need for achievement and the elements of locus of control (or attribution) are related.[22] Persons who attribute successes to themselves (internal locus of control) tend also to experience pride in accomplishment. Because positive esteem-enhancing feelings mediate from self-attribution of success, these persons tend eagerly to approach future task challenges. So long as this association pattern is repeated whenever progress or accomplishment is perceived by an individual, he or she sets in motion the conditions to develop a higher-than-average need for achievement.[23] After all, the achievement motive long has been characterized as the capacity for taking pride in accomplishment.[24] However, persons who attribute success to luck, powerful others, or easy tasks do not experience pride in accomplishment (since they do not see themselves as the cause of success) and thus are ambivalent about future task challenges. Persons who are strong external attributers thus do not form the mental-emotional associations necessary for developing achievement motivation.

Personality Dimensions and Accounting Information

The dimensions of the psychological and behavioral makeup of a person include where he is on a needs hierarchy, his self-image, a position on the

---

[19] M. Hirsch, "Disaggregated Probabilistic Accounting Information: The Effect of Sequential Events on Expected Value Maximization Decisions," *Journal of Accounting Research*, 16:2 (Autumn 1978), 254–69.

[20] D. C. McClelland, J. D. Atkinson, R. A. Clark, E. L. Lowell, *The Achievement Motive* (New York: Appleton-Century-Crofts, Inc., 1953).

[21] See, for example, Ward Edwards, "Behavioral Decision Theory," *Annual Review of Psychology*, 12 (1961), 473–98.

[22] Bernard Weiner, *Achievement Motivation and Attribution Theory* (Morristown, N.J.: General Learning Press, 1974).

[23] Curtis W. Cook and Ruth E. Cook, "Achievement Motivation Can Be Managed: A Coaching Strategy of Attribution Change," Southern Illinois University at Edwardsville, School of Business, working paper.

[24] J. W. Atkinson, *An Introduction to Motivation* (New York: Van Nostrand-Reinhold Company, 1964), p. 241.

internal-external locus of control dimension, a measure of achievement motivation, and many more. The few we have explored are just a sample. Our purpose is to raise the issue that information will be used by different people in different ways. If we can develop and test models that allow us to predict decision-making behavior based on personality characteristics, we will have greatly added to our effectiveness as accountants. As you might expect, only preliminary steps have been taken in this area. Human predictability is elusive.

Social scientists have only recently begun to explore the extent to which personality dimensions can affect information use. One difficulty in this research is that there is some dependency between the decision at hand and the personality characteristics of the decision maker. For example, a person who is high in n-achievement might react differently in one capital budgeting decision when compared to another capital budgeting decision.[25] A recent study looked at decision style and tolerance for ambiguity. The authors found that it was difficult to develop a useful predictive model based on these two dimensions. Our problem is that, while we know that an information user's personality affects how information is processed and what decisions are made, we have not yet developed clear, useful models to apply.

FORM, ORDER, FORMAT OF INFORMATION

We have discussed cognitive complexity (a part of the study of human information processing) and have looked at some personality dimensions that can affect how we use information in decision making. Too much or too little data can limit the use of information in the decision-making process. People who have an internal locus of control may make different decisions and may make greater effort to follow through on them than those who are more externally oriented. In addition, the very form, format, and order of information can affect the decision-making process. We now turn to some of the considerations and choices that accountants confront in presenting information.

Order of Information

One choice to make is the **order of information.** For example, assume that a company is using standard costing and that current results show various favorable and unfavorable variances, including material price, material use, labor rate, labor efficiency, overhead spending, overhead efficiency, and overhead volume variances. The discussion in Chapters 7 and 8 points out that one purpose of calculating variances is to evaluate how a manager is

[25] W. McGhee, M. D. Shields, J. G. Birnberg, "The Effects of Personality on a Subject's Information Processing," *The Accounting Review*, 53:3 (July 1978), 681–97.

doing. How should this current variance information be presented? Several alternatives include:

1. listing alphabetically.
2. listing in descending order of dollar value.
3. listing all unfavorable first and then all favorable.
4. listing all favorable first and then all unfavorable.
5. listing the material price variance under *purchasing department,* the labor rate variances under *scheduling,* and the volume variance under *noncontrollable* with all other variances under *current operations.*

The list could go on, and these are not mutually exclusive alternatives; many of them can be combined in a final ordering. A recent study shows that the order of variances can affect an evaluator's perception of a manager's performance.[26]

Order can affect the perceived relevancy of information. If minor points are covered first, the reader may be led to assume that the body of a report is irrelevant. For this reason, many writers tend to summarize major points at the beginning of a report and then develop these issues in the main text.

Order can affect the perceived ranking of various alternatives. Assume that a company is investigating several ideas for new product lines and that, after much analysis, a group of managers is ready to present its recommendations to top management. Often the various alternatives can be broadly classified into excellent, good, and fair opportunities. Within each classification, the ordering is not quite so clear. There are trade-offs among expected profits, risk levels, economic life, social concerns, and so on. How should this management committee order its list of excellent opportunities? Choices include:

1. alphabetical;
2. NPV (or IRR, terminal value, PVI, and so on);
3. degree of risk;
4. amount of investment;
5. market segment;
6. plant affected.

and many more. Will the order affect the perceived ranking of these opportunities?

In fact, the order chosen and the rationale for it may be an ideal way for the committee to come to a final overall preference list of the various alter-

---

[26] See L. Bourne, *Order Effects in Accounting Variance Reports: A Laboratory Experiment* (unpublished Ph.D. dissertation, Washington University, St. Louis, 1976).

natives. Consider the need to rank several investment projects because of limited funds. A management committee could look at the NPV of each project and use that measure as a preliminary ranking. Then, the managers could consider issues such as how each project would affect workers at various plants or how each would affect energy conservation and other environmental concerns. The degree of risk of each project could be considered. The result would be a ranking that considered many dimensions.

Level of Aggregation

Aggregation refers to how detailed or summarized a set of information is. For example, earnings per share is a highly aggregated figure, while a list of all the accounts receivable would be disaggregated information. While issues involving cognitive complexity are concerned with what various types of information to present, choices about aggregation have to do with the *level of summarization* of whatever type is chosen.

Aggregation can have an effect on information on both the input and output sides. A manager must choose what data to use to define the benefits and costs of an alternative course of action. Aggregating too much can distort information or at least reduce the amount of information in a set of data. Consider the example in Chapter 19 on investigating variances. A model was proposed where current performance was to be compared against standard costs in order to see whether an investigation was warranted. The procedure includes calculating a standard deviation of the sample means. This standard deviation is *different* from one calculated from all sample data, since some of the variability of the data has been removed just in the aggregating process of figuring several sample means.

Our discussion of variances showed the difference between looking at an overall material variance (aggregated) or at material price, mix, and use variances (disaggregated). Another example of aggregation is the use of a weighted average contribution margin. The individual contribution margins in dollars and in percent are lost by this aggregation.

Aggregation certainly is an issue at the output end. In fact, certain management principles implicitly assume increasing levels of aggregation. The idea of *management by exception* is built on giving fewer and fewer details in reports as they go to higher and higher levels of management.

Managers need to make explicit choices on the aggregation issue. Various studies show that level of aggregation or disaggregation can have an effect on perception and decision-making behavior. Malcom discusses this choice in the context of sales variances.[27] He shows that if a firm has four similar products, there are eighteen different ways to present sales data. Aggregating one way or another may tend to hide certain trends and may

[27] R. E. Malcom, "The Effect of Product Aggregation in Determining Sales Variances," *The Accounting Review*, 52:1 (January 1978), 162–69.

lead managers to improper conclusions. He concludes that sales variances should be aggregated only if the products are homogeneous in most respects.

Quite a few studies, including work by Barefield, by Ronen, and by Hirsch, have explored the issue of aggregation and accounting information.[28] Barefield looked at whether decision makers made better choices when given condensed (aggregated) information regarding operating variances or when they were given more (disaggregated) information. In this experiment, Barefield found that the subjects did better with *more* information.

However, both Ronen and Hirsch show that simple disaggregated information can lead people to make nonoptimal choices. As defined earlier, economic man is an expected-value maximizer.[29] In a simple decision setting with all other factors being equal, most decision makers will choose that alternative with the highest expected value. However, both Ronen and Hirsch show that people will choose an alternative with a lower expected value when given certain disaggregated information.

Therefore, there is a conflict on level of aggregation just as there is in the cognitive-complexity area. How aggregated should data be? How aggregated should reports be? Highly aggregated information tends to hide or even cut out certain items that might be of great value in a particular analysis. Too much disaggregation may lead to suboptimal decisions from a different perspective.[30] Like the other concepts considered in this chapter, level of aggregation interacts with many other variables.

Stochastic Versus Deterministic Information

Many chapters in this book discuss assessment of risks, measurement of uncertainty, and sensitivity analysis. However, most of the information we see is deterministic. An annual report shows a single figure for net income, and each account balance is reported as a single figure in the balance sheet. Cost-volume-profit models and discounted cash flow models generally use single values. We use specific data for an objective function and constraints in linear programming. In all these cases a full set of information includes some assessment of risk. Accounts receivable or inventory could be expressed using a 95 percent confidence interval. Discounted cash flow models and linear programming can reflect uncertainty through simulation and

---

[28] R. Barefield, "The Effect of Aggregation on Decision Making Success: A Laboratory Study," *Journal of Accounting Research*, 10:2 (Autumn 1972), 229–42; J. Ronen, "Some Effects of Sequential Aggregation in Accounting on Decision-Making," *Journal of Accounting Research*, 9:2 (Autumn 1971), 307–32; Hirsch, "Disaggregated Probabilistic Accounting Information."

[29] Assume that expected value and expected utility are identical. While this may not always be the case, it holds sufficiently so that this is not a restrictive assumption.

[30] Another interesting discussion of aggregation is in J. Ronen, "Nonaggregation Versus Disaggregation of Variances," *The Accounting Review*, 49:1 (January 1974), 50–60.

sensitivity analysis. However, there is a problem regarding the use of such information. As one report states:

> Certainly a more complete decision model may be specified using probabilities, but do users deal with probabilities in a consistent, "rational" way, as every good "economic man" should? The information specialist should know the answers to such questions. . . .[31]

This is a crucial question pertaining to all aspects of behavior and information. It is quite easy to say that mathematical models are better than heuristic ones or that specifically dealing with uncertainty is more complete than just making point estimates. However, we have very little evidence on how people use this information. For example, much of our thinking about how people use stochastic information comes from studies involving gambling odds and decisions from the psychology literature.[32] Any extrapolation of these studies into accounting is tenuous at best.

THE ELICITING OF INFORMATION

Certain information is fairly easy to obtain from the usual data that management collects. Variable and fixed components of costs can be calculated by the use of regression equations. A standard costing system usually yields a full range of variances. However, other information is not as readily available. The most difficult area is that of probabilities.

Risk and Uncertainty

Our discussion of most elements of planning and control has assumed we can produce various probabilities reflecting the risk inherent in any situation. Our original discussion has not distinguished between *risk* and *uncertainty*.

If an event is not certain, the main question is how well we can quantify probabilities. If there is no way to assess probabilities, then the situation is **uncertain**. However, if we can reasonably assign probabilities regarding an event, we are quantifying **risk**.

Objectivity and Subjectivity

We can think of risk and uncertainty as part of a continuum. At one end is pure uncertainty, where it is virtually impossible to do anything but guess.

---

[31] Report of Committee on Managerial Decision Models, American Accounting Association, *The Accounting Review* (Supplement 1969), 42–76.

[32] Ward Edwards did a whole series of such studies in the 1950s and 1960s. For example, see "Probability Preferences in Gambling," *American Journal of Psychology*, no. 66 (1953), 349–64, and "The Prediction of Decisions Among Bets," *Journal of Experimental Psychology*, 50:3 (1955), 201–14.

At the other end are objective probabilities. Objective probabilities are hard to find when it comes to business situations. Managers must usually formulate probabilities with some degree of subjectivity. Even if estimates are based on past data, they still involve the subjective judgment that this assessment of risk will apply to the future.

Illustration: Liza Fashions.   Liza Fashions is a manufacturer of women's robes. Elaine Mars, president, needs to make several estimates that involve subjective probabilities. Any new line will have a chance of succeeding or failing (or falling somewhere in between). While market research can provide some information regarding success potential, Mars must integrate this information with other data and use her own experience to come up with her estimate of sales. This same procedure is applicable for existing product lines, for estimates of material costs, and for other areas of the business. While most of these risk assessments can be quantified, some are closer to the uncertainty end of the spectrum than others. The question we are dealing with here is how to elicit these subjective probabilities in order to yield useful information.

Eliciting Probabilities

Earlier discussion in this chapter has shown that while theoretically we can say that models are more useful if they explicitly recognize risk, we are less sure how people *use* information containing probabilities. The elicitation of probabilities is another area of concern.

There are three dimensions to the problem of eliciting probabilities.[33] First, does the manager elicit information from himself, or do others (such as the accounting department) elicit information either orally or in writing?

Second, how is probability information thought about and presented? One way is to get direct assessments regarding probabilities, odds, means and variances, and so on. Another way is to get some specific dollar figures. For example, a manager could say it is equally likely to have the following three sales ranges: $100,000 to $300,000, $300,001 to $700,000, and $700,001 to $900,000.

Third, should probabilities be elicited directly or indirectly? A direct estimation is illustrated by the manager's statement above. An indirect method is to infer probabilities *given* that decisions have been made. This involves going backward from the decision to the probabilities. For example, the accountant could ask a manager to state his estimate of profits if 100,000 units of product A were produced at a variable cost of $75 with a selling price of $125 per unit. This estimate could be compared to estimates based on other production levels, variable costs, selling price, and so on. The accountant could then derive a probability distribution based on these various values.

---

[33] For a good summary and complete references see G. R. Chesley, "Elicitation of Subjective Probabilities: A Review," *The Accounting Review*, 50:2 (April 1975), 325–37.

Eliciting Other Information

Managers elicit many forms of information. Probabilities are but one area where information is needed. While probabilities may be implicit in most information, accountants are involved in a wide range of data-gathering activities that do not explicitly include risk assessment. All information that accountants present is intended to aid a decision maker, as we have emphasized throughout this book. However, the accountant may be facing a circular problem in that he must first get certain information from a decision maker before he can evaluate it, decide how best to present it, and then have the decision maker use it. The elicitation process has a direct bearing on use. It is as difficult to elicit unbiased information as it is to present it.

THE SELLING OF INFORMATION

Assume, that in the future accounting managers have a good grounding in quantitative techniques, and they are aware of and responsive to various personality dimensions and their effects on information use. How, then, does the accountant sell all this better information to line management?

For example, Norton Dudley has just been hired as the chief accounting officer at Eagle Products. Dudley's background is diverse. He has acquired considerable quantitative knowledge in five years of working in a computer consulting firm. In addition, his last job was with a market research firm, where he gained insights into how consumers make decisions. In his new job at Eagle, Dudley wants to combine his work in computer science and behavioral research to improve the management information system and decision-making process.

Eagle is a successful company that has been run for fifteen years by its founder, John Brand. Brand went to college in the early 1960s when computer facilities were limited, and so, while he has heard of some of the newer techniques, he does not use them himself. Brand has developed his own decision-making style. In many ways he does a lot of implicit modeling in his head as he puzzles through a problem.

A conflict could arise between Dudley and Brand. Not only is Brand the president, but the firm has been successful under his leadership. Dudley, however, thinks that the firm could prosper even more if more scientific methods were used. He believes that if Brand could use more sophisticated information and knew more about his own decision-making style, he would be an even better manager. To avoid conflict, Dudley needs to work with Brand to enhance Brand's style. Studies show that Brand will be most receptive to change if it is self-directed and if he owns new ways of doing things as if he had thought of them.[34]

---

[34] An interesting discussion of this is found in W. T. Morris, *Decision Analysis* (Columbus, Ohio: Grid, Inc., 1977), chap. 13.

Thus, as accountants, we have to be concerned with acquiring knowledge not only about better ways to present and process information but also about how to sell these ideas to management at all levels.

SUMMARY

This chapter raises many questions while proposing few definite answers. Each of us has different capacities to process information. Our personality itself has a bearing on how we perceive information. Since accounting is the heart of any management information system, we must be aware that the creation of useful information is a difficult and complex task. This problem is bounded not only by cost/benefit considerations, but also by issues of human information processing, ranging from our increasing capacity to create reams of data from sophisticated computer models to our limited capacity to deal with information and the distinct possibility of information overload.

Even though few answers can be provided, it is important to raise the concerns. If we are aware that these issues exist, then we can make conscious choices as to how we will address them. Entire courses and books are devoted to each of the subjects we discuss in this chapter. We have crammed a good bit of new material into a few pages. This material is integral to other areas such as budgeting, variances, and the use of quantitative techniques. We can use this chapter's introductory presentation as a springboard for further exploration of these subjects.

ASSIGNMENTS

21–1 General Concepts

Required: Using examples from your own experiences, explain and illustrate major ideas in the chapter including the issues of human information processing; personality and information use; form, order, and format of information; and the eliciting and selling of information.

21–2 Behavior and Information.   Edwin Caplan has observed that:

The efficiency and effectiveness of human behavior and decision making within organizations is constrained by: (1) the inability to concentrate on more than a few things at a time; (2) limited awareness of the environment; (3) limited knowledge of alternative courses of action and the consequences of such alternatives; (4) limited reasoning ability; and (5) incomplete and inconsistent preference systems. As a result of these limits on human rationality, individual and organization behavior is usually directed toward attempts to find satisfactory—rather than optimal—solutions.[35]

Required: Comment on this quotation, referring to the chapter material and bringing in specific examples to illustrate your discussion. Be sure to do the following:

1. Explain the five constraints Caplan proposed.
2. Explain how these constraints are important to managerial and cost accounting.

21-3 Human Resource Accounting (CMA adapted). During the 1970s several authors wrote about human resource accounting (HRA).[36] The idea was not only to recognize the investment in land and equipment that a manager is held responsible for, but also to evaluate that manager on how he or she develops human resources. In a company that uses residual income or return on investment and ignores human assets, it is possible that managers will choose to maximize short-term profits by eliminating training seminars and conferences, company-financed college programs, and the like. This may achieve a better ROI in the current period, but it may have negative effects on future profits. With this as a brief introduction to HRA, consider the following situation.

The consumer products division of the Liberty Manufacturing Company experienced reduced sales in the first quarter of 19X8 and has forecasted that the decline in sales will continue through the remainder of the year. The profit budgeted in the original 19X8 profit plan was about 40 percent less than that of the prior year. Fortunately, Liberty's other divisions budgeted improved profits in 19X8 over 19X7.

The top management of Liberty believes in a decentralized organization, and division managers have considerable latitude in managing the operations of their divisions. Division managers receive bonuses of a specified percentage of division profits in addition to their annual salaries.

At the end of the first quarter of 19X8, John Spassen, the manager of the consumer products division, felt that drastic action was needed to reduce costs and improve the performance of his division. As one step to reduce costs he dismissed twenty highly trained, skilled employees. Only five of them are expected to be available for reemployment when business returns to normal in 19X9.

The top management, upon reviewing the steps taken by Spassen, was concerned about the consequences of releasing the twenty skilled employees. Company officials had recently attended seminars on human resource accounting and wondered whether Spassen would have taken that particu-

[35] E. Caplan, *Management Accounting and Behavioral Science*, pp. 31–33.
[36] See R. Likert, *The Human Organization* (New York: McGraw-Hill Book Company, 1967); and E. Flamholtz, *Human Resource Accounting* (Belmont, Cal.: Dickinson Publishing Co., Inc., 1974).

lar action had a cost-based human resource accounting system been in operation.

Required:

1. Evaluating human assets or resources is a difficult question. Some authors propose a cost-based system founded on measurable costs, while others advocate a more general approach such as a present value of future worth to the company. Using this situation as an example, what is accounted for in a cost-based HRA system?

2. How could the company use information from a cost-based HRA system in deciding whether to dismiss the twenty skilled employees?

3. What other information would be useful in evaluating this decision?

21–4 The Issue of Control.   One of the theories discussed in this chapter, that of cognitive complexity, involves the idea of confusion. Obviously, knowledge should be designed to reduce confusion. Some authors have stated that we humans are very intolerant when faced with confusion. In fact we may even accept someone who is a dictator as long as we will be given order (and confusion will disappear). Recent history has lent some support to this proposition.

Required: Using the resources of this chapter (and additional resources if so requested by your instructor), discuss the issues of control and confusion reduction. What is the management accountant's role in these matters?

21–5 Human Information Processing.   The Shop 'n Save Corporation is run by Robert Lennon. The company operates a chain of retail quick-shop stores that are open 24 hours a day. All the stores are located in a major eastern metropolitan area. The company started ten years ago with one store and over the years has expanded to fifteen stores. Mr. Lennon is the majority shareholder in the company, and the other shares are owned by two other persons. Mr. Lennon is a C.P.A. and a lawyer. He is quite bright in simple mathematics and algebra but has had no formal training in subjects such as calculus. He has a good memory and can recall details of various events affecting the company and financial data about the company. The management team in the central office is fairly small; besides the president, Mr. Lennon, there is an accountant-bookkeeper and an administrative vice-president. John Carlton, the vice-president, has had little formal education. While he completed high school, he did not complete college. However, he is both bright and industrious.

Mr. Lennon likes to be in control of most situations. He tends to centralize decision making. In addition, he tends to keep a lot of information in his head rather than having a management information system. Even the financial accounting data must sometimes be explained to the other shareholders, since various adjustments between stores and differences between cash and accrual accounting have caused some confusion in the interpretation of financial statements. Several of these discrepancies grew with the business. While the accounting system was adequate for a single store, it needs improvement for the multiple-store current status.

The nature of this business is high-volume, low-profit. While the company has grown, it has encountered severe cash flow difficulties from time to time. All the investors have had to put in investment capital or lend money to the corporation over its life. Up until now the minority investors have been fairly inactive in an ongoing review of the business. They have accepted information given to them by Mr. Lennon at face value and have accepted his analysis of current situations. However, with increasing interest rates and increasing investment in the company, the outside investors want to improve the information network at the company so that they might better determine how the company is doing.

Required: Assume that you have been hired as a consultant to the outside investors. Describe and critique the current situation and the problems that you see. Your description and analysis should include the concepts outlined in this chapter as well as appropriate concepts from other chapters. What recommendations would you make to the outside investors and to management, and how would you implement these recommendations?

21–6 **Assessing Risks.** The managers of Rose, Inc., are contemplating several new projects. Rubin Stein, company treasurer, is aiding the various managers in these analyses. Mr. Stein and his staff are responsible for presenting net-present-value data and other pertinent information to Charles Largo, company president, who will make the final decision on which project or projects to accept.

Rose is a decentralized company. The projects under consideration are from five different divisions. Divisional managers have done some preliminary gathering of data to analyze the projects, but they are looking to the accounting staff to help them get together all the information needed. The operating divisions are classified by central management as expense centers. In addition to these operating divisions, there is a sales division. Operating divisional managers and the sales manager have met to discuss the viability of the various projects. These meetings have been preliminary, and more are needed.

The equipment division is contemplating entering the building of car-wash equipment. The sales division would set up regional wholesalers of the equipment. This type of equipment is modular and would have both an original-equipment and replacement-equipment market.

The electronics division is considering a new cordless telephone. The technology for making such a telephone is quite new, and research and development costs would be entailed if the company were to embark on the project. The units could be marketed both to the government and to wholesalers and retailers.

The chemical division is considering a line of car-wash chemicals, which would be manufactured even if the equipment division did not produce car-wash equipment. The technology for these chemicals is fairly straightforward. Marketing would be handled by the sales force of Rose.

The other two projects under consideration are similar in nature to the three described above.

Required:

1. How should members of the accounting staff work with the various managers in this case?

2. What information is necessary in order to make an adequate analysis for the president?

3. How would the staff aid in eliciting this information and in assessing risks for each of the three projects outlined above?

21-7   Time and Information: A Conflict?* In a recent article in *Harvard Business Review*, a trio of authors[37] traced the corporate strategy planning process through four distinct phases. They reported in part:

Most companies trace the origins of a formal planning system (Phase I) to the annual budgeting process where everything is reduced to a financial problem. Procedures develop to forecast revenue, costs, and capital needs and to identify limits for expense budgets on an annual basis. Information systems report on functional performance as compared with budgetary targets. . . .

A principal weakness of Phase II and III strategic planning processes is their inescapable entanglement in the formal corporate calendar. Strategic planning easily degenerates into a mind-numbing bureaucratic exercise, punctuated by ritualistic formal planning meetings that neither inform top management nor help business managers to get their jobs done. . . .

Required:

1. This quotation seems to outline a possible conflict between the information-generating process and an annual timetable. Does such a conflict exist? How does it curtail the flow of useful information?

2. What are the processes by which this conflict is resolved and information becomes more useful for strategic planning purposes?

21-8   How Specific Should Information Be? It often is claimed that if information is to be useful for decision making, the data supplied to managers must become more general and abstract as the manager occupies a higher position in the organizational hierarchy.

---

* The source for Assignments 21-7 through 21-15 is Curtis W. Cook.

[37] Frederick W. Gluck, Stephen P. Kaufman, and A. Steven Walleck, "Strategic Management for Competitive Advantage," *Harvard Business Review*, 58:4 (July–August 1980), 154-61.

Required: Select a specific functional area within an organization (such as R&D, production, sales) and provide an example of information moving from highly specific to general as it applies to four levels of management. Comment on how this relates to environmental/organizational complexity.

21-9   Administrative Person.   Two of the basic tenets of *administrative person* are the concepts of *bounded rationality* and *satisficing*. As psychological processes that limit cognitive complexity and data overload, they involve (1) limited search for information and (2) choice of the first available alternative that resolves a problem.

Required: To what extent do these phenomena suggest that accountants reduce or narrow the scope of data they provide managers? What do they suggest about the nature of face-to-face interaction between accountant and manager?

21-10   Locus of Control.

Required: Would a manager high in internal locus of control (perceiving self as a critical causal element in controlling environmental outcomes) be more likely to review accounting data carefully than a manager who is external in locus of control? Discuss.

21-11   *n*-Achievement.

Required: Should a managerial accountant be high in the need to achieve? How might the level of achievement motivation vary by level of responsibility within the organization? Explain and offer examples. How high are your achievement needs?

21-12   Aggregation.

Required: Why do many reports to management begin with a brief summary and statement of recommendation(s)? In what ways does this relate to the order of presentation of information? How does it relate to the aggregation effects of condensation and possible managerial performance in decision making or action taking on the basis of that report?

21-13   Probabilistic Information.   A successful manager once commented: "The only useful information for managers represents at best only some probability of being true."

Required: What does this mean in terms of how accountants view and present their factual data?

21-14   Oral Versus Written Information.   Recent research into human performance suggests that people differ in the extent to which their information processing is dominated by oral, visual, or physical stimuli. In an unrelated line of investigation, O'Reilly concludes: "In the studies reported here, subjects who report having more information and being more satisfied may be less able to select and use relevant information because of pressures and distractions that reduce the time available for processing as well as because of the difficulty in identifying relevant information from the total set available."[38]

Required: What informational shortfalls are likely to occur if accountants rely exclusively (or almost exclusively) upon presenting data in tabular or written report form? How might verbal discussion help identify relevant data for managerial users while possibly accommodating to the users' dominant/preferred mode of information sensing?

21–15 Stages of the Problem Cycle. An unconventional approach to problem solving was suggested by Cook as involving a three-stage cycle of "(a) problem seeking, (b) problem finding, and (c) problem solving." Cook contended:

> . . . that the problem solving process, especially in the realm of complex policy and strategy issues, begins within a context of seeking out data and splicing together threads of information. Through hypothesis guided data discovery, decision makers weave pieces of information into a patterned fabric wherein challenges and issues take on form and meaning.[39]

Required: Comment on this viewpoint with respect to the accountant's role in helping managers to seek problems. What are the responsibilities and limits of the managerial accountant in supplying problem hypotheses as well as data to managers?

SELECTED REFERENCES

Bruns, W. J., Jr., and D. DeCoster, *Accounting and Its Behavioral Implications.* New York: McGraw-Hill Book Company, 1969.

Caplan, E. H., *Management Accounting and Behavioral Science.* Reading, Mass.: Addison-Wesley Publishing Company, 1971.

Hopwood, A., *Accounting and Human Behavior.* Englewood Cliffs, N.J.: Prentice-Hall, Inc., 1976.

Libby, Robert, *Accounting and Human Information Processing: Theory and Applications.* Englewood Cliffs, N.J.: Prentice-Hall, Inc., 1981.

Livingstone, J. L., *Managerial Accounting: The Behavioral Foundations.* Columbus, Ohio: Grid, Inc., 1975.

Morris, W. T., *Decision Analysis.* Columbus, Ohio: Grid, Inc., 1977.

Schiff, M., and A. Y. Lewin, *Behavioral Aspects of Accounting.* Englewood Cliffs, N.J.: Prentice-Hall, Inc., 1974.

Schroder, H. M., M. J. Driver, and S. Streufert, *Human Information Processing: Individuals & Groups Functioning in Complex Social Situations.* New York: Holt, Rinehart and Winston, Inc., 1967.

[38] Charles A. O'Reilly, III, "Individuals and Information Overload In Organizations: Is More Necessarily Better?" *Academy of Management Journal,* 23:4 (December 1980), 692.

[39] Curtis W. Cook, "Policy Unfolding through Data Discovery Techniques," *Exchange: The Organizational Behavior Teaching Journal,* 5:4 (1980), pp. 30–34.

The Learning Effect

Chapter 22

As accountants we are interested in predicting costs as accurately as possible for all the pricing, planning, and control uses that are outlined in many previous chapters. Our discussion of costs from basic CVP relationships through product costing and standard costing has treated variable costs per unit as a constant. In Chapters 2 and 3 we proposed a linear model as a predictor of costs. However, we also looked at the economist's model. Here such items as labor costs are expected to go down on a per-unit basis as a plant gets into its most efficient production range.

EFFECT OF LEARNING ON PRODUCTIVITY

In fact, research has shown that in many situations workers increase their efficiency as they produce more units. The time required to produce a unit declines as workers learn their jobs. This phenomenon is called the **learning effect** or the **learning curve** (or other similar names).[1] Where it occurs, our knowledge of its effects can supply management with much better information for a variety of planning and control applications including production scheduling, budgeting, setting standard costs and analyzing variances, pricing, and a host of special decisions.

The learning curve may be expressed in several ways. One common statement is that as cumulative production doubles, the cumulative average time required to make a unit, or a batch, declines by a particular percentage. The percentage varies from situation to situation. Early studies of the learning curve in the aircraft industry showed a 20 percent decline.[2] As a rule, the learning curve is expressed by reference to the value *to* which cumulative average declines, not the value *by* which it declines. Thus, a decline of 20 percent would bring the new value to 80 percent of the former one and

---

[1] Other terms used include *progress curve, improvement curve,* and *manufacturing efficiency curve.*

[2] An early example is T. P. Wright, "Factors Affecting the Cost of Airplanes," *Journal of Aeronautical Science,* (February 1936), 122–28.

we would say that the learning curve is 80 percent. Similarly, if cumulative average time declined by 15 percent, the learning curve would be expressed as 85 percent, and so on.

Illustration: *Learning Curve for the Gordon Company*

The Gordon Company produces small industrial products. The purchasing manager of Morehead Industries has approached Gordon Company for a bid on 32 batches of components that Morehead needs for one of its products. Other firms will also bid on the job. The managers of Gordon must make some estimates of the total cost to produce the components, and one part of that cost is direct labor. Industrial engineers have estimated that the first batch would take about 100 labor hours, and that the firm should experience an 80 percent learning curve throughout the remainder of production. The expected times at various doubling points (where cumulative production doubles) appear in Exhibit 22–1.

EXHIBIT 22–1
80 Percent Learning Curve—Gordon Company

Batches	Cumulative Average Time	Total Time[a]
1	100 hours	100 hours
2	80 (100 × 0.80)	160
4	64 (80 × 0.80)	256
8	51.2 (64 × 0.80)	409.6
16	40.96 (51.2 × 0.80)	655.36
32	32.768 (40.96 × 0.80)	1,048.576

[a] Equals the product of the number of batches and cumulative average time through that number of batches. For example, for eight batches, 256 = 4 × 64.

Notice that we do not make separate computations for each batch. Using the tabular method, we are limited to working with doubling points, 2, 4, 8, 16, and 32. We could use a formula to determine values of cumulative average time and total time at levels of production that are not doubling points, and we will do so in the following section.

Notice that the total time estimated to complete the 32 batches is 1,048.576 hours. This is considerably less than we would expect if there were no learning effect and each batch required 100 hours. The total time would then be 3,200 hours (100 × 32). We are not saying it will take 1,048.576 hours to complete the work, only that this is the estimate, given an 80 percent learning curve. The actual time could be somewhat different.

Assume that total incremental costs other than labor and labor-related costs for the entire job are expected to be $85,000. For example, costs of materials will probably not decline as much as labor and labor-related costs. There could be some savings in materials, but they are unlikely to be as great as savings in labor. Also assume that variable cost per direct labor hour is $12, including wages, fringe benefits, and overhead that varies with direct labor hours. The estimated total costs of the job under assumptions of no learning and an 80 percent learning curve appear below.

	No Learning Effect	80% Learning Effect
Total hours	3,200	1,050 (rounded)
Rate per hour	$12	$12
Total labor and labor-related costs	$ 38,400	$12,600
Other costs	85,000	85,000
Totals	$123,400	$97,600

The difference is significant. Should the Gordon Company managers base their bid on the assumption of an 80 percent learning curve, no learning at all, or something in between? Clearly, if competing firms have similar cost structures and profit goals, and incorporate some learning effect in their bids, Gordon will not get the job if it assumes no learning in setting its bid. A bid based on an assumption of no learning would be higher, and therefore safer, than one based on an 80 percent learning curve, but it would likely result in someone else getting the job.

At the other end, if the managers do base the bid on an 80 percent learning curve and do not achieve it (say, labor hours are 1,300 or so), the firm will make less profit than expected. One factor in making the decision is the confidence in the estimate of 100 hours for the first batch and an 80 percent learning curve. The more confident they are in those estimates, the more likely it is that they will both shave the bid and get the business.

The data in Exhibit 22–1 do not answer the question of the bid price, but they are useful in developing a bid and in analyzing the sensitivity of profit to the learning curve assumed.

Later we consider decision making learning curves in more detail. Here we return to the curve itself, expressed in mathematical form.

THE BASIC FORMULA

The learning curve may be expressed by the following formula:

(22–1)
$$Y = aX^b$$

where Y = cumulative average time (or cost)
a = time (or cost) for the first unit or batch
X = cumulative production
b = the learning exponent

We shall spend a good deal of time working with the exponent and with some alternative formulations. For now, let us put equation 22–1 into linear form by using logarithms. Raising a number to a power (X^b) is equivalent to multiplying the logarithm of the number by the exponent. Accordingly, taking logarithms of both sides of the equation gives us the following:

(22–2) $\log Y = \log a + (b \times \log X)$

Figure 22–1 shows the data from Exhibit 22–1 plotted on an ordinary scale and on a logarithmic scale. The logarithmic form is linear; the ordinary form is not. The linearity of the logarithmic form allows us to do a great deal. We can use scatter diagrams and regression analysis to determine the parameters a and b. We can also use logarithms to make calculations of the values of cumulative average time at any point, rather than just at doubling points. (If you have a calculator that performs exponentiation, you may use the ordinary form given in equation 22–1 instead of using logarithms.)

The advantage of a formula not restricted to doubling points is seen if we modify the company's decision to make the contract call for 45 batches instead of 32. The doubling point after 32 is 64, so the contract falls far short of that amount. But, we can solve for the cost using equation 22–2.

For an 80 percent learning curve, the value of b is about -0.3219. Table 22–1 on page 876 gives base 10 logarithms for use in solving for $\log Y$, $\log a$, and $\log X$. We use natural (base e) logarithms because most calculators can determine natural logarithms and antilogarithms. We use ln to denote natural logarithm. Note that any logarithms will give the same final results.[3]

$$\begin{aligned}
\ln Y &= \ln a + b \ln X \\
&= \ln 100 + (-0.3219) \ln 45 \\
&= 4.605 + (-0.3219)(3.8067) \\
&= 3.3796
\end{aligned}$$

The antilogarithm of 3.3796 is about 29.36, which is cumulative average time for the first 45 batches. Total time is about 1,321 hours (29.36 × 45).

Determining the Exponent (b)

Because the slopes of both lines in Figure 22–1 are negative, the exponent b is also negative.[4] The value of b is expressed as:

---

[3] Using logarithms to the base 10 in our example, $\log_{10} Y = 2 + (-.3219)(1.6532) = 1.4678$. Y, the antilogarithm, is about 29.36, as determined above.

[4] Some accountants prefer to state equation 22–1 as $Y = aX^{-b}$, and you will come across this formulation in the literature. In this form the exponent, b, is a positive number, so that $-b$ is negative. The positive sign of b results from a different method of calculation, but the numerical value is always the same as it would be using equation 22–3. The two formulations are equivalent and give the same results. Both require raising X to a negative power. Selecting one version or the other is a matter of convenience.

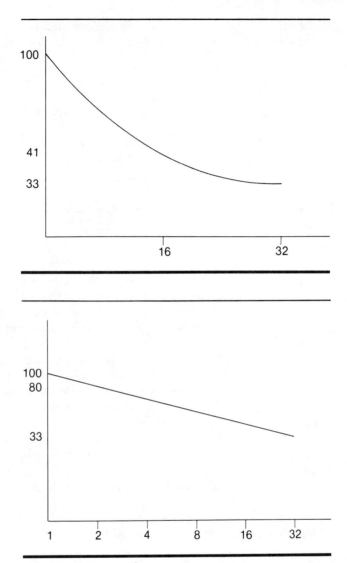

FIGURE 22–1
Ordinary and Log-Log Plots of Cumulative Average Time

(22–3)
$$b = \frac{\ln \text{ learning percentage}}{\ln 2}$$

We can show why b is determined in this way by looking at the logarithmic form of the equation. Suppose that we calculated the value of Y at two points, one of which is double the other. We could use the two equations on page 862:

$$(22\text{-}4) \qquad\qquad \ln Y_2 = a + b \ln 2X$$
$$(22\text{-}5) \qquad\qquad \ln Y_1 = a + b \ln X$$

where Y_2 = cumulative average time at the output level $2X$, which is double output X

Y_1 = cumulative average time at output X

Subtracting equation 22–5 from 22–4 gives the following:

$$\ln Y_2 - \ln Y_1 = b(\ln 2X - \ln X)$$

$$b = \frac{\ln Y_2 - \ln Y_1}{\ln 2X - \ln X}$$

$$b = \frac{\ln (Y_2/Y_1)}{\ln 2}$$

The ratio Y_2/Y_1 is the learning percentage when Y_2 is determined at the value of X that is double the value where Y_1 was determined. In our example, at $X = 2$, $Y = 80$ and at $X = 4$, $Y = 64$, so that we get 64/80 = 0.80. (Also, at $X = 1$, $Y = 100$ and at $X = 2$, $Y = 80$; 80/100 = 0.80. Thus, any values of X and, therefore, $2X$ will yield the 80 percent learning curve. To prove this, try it with $X = 8$ batches from Exhibit 22–1.) In fact, any matched values of Xs and Ys will work. They need not be doubling points.

The general formula for finding the value of b parallels the high-low method of estimating the fixed and variable components of a cost. Additionally, the value of a can also be found. The general formula for b that follows is a necessary part of a solution for a. As an example, suppose that we have determined the values of Y for the Gordon Company's operation at $X = 4$ and $X = 45$. We already know that these values are 64 (from Exhibit 22–1) and 29.36 (from the calculation made earlier). Suppose we have obtained these values from observing the firm's operations and wish to determine the learning curve. We then have the following:[5]

$$b = \frac{\ln 29.36 - \ln 64}{\ln 45 - \ln 4}$$

$$b = \frac{\ln (29.36/64.0)}{\ln (45/4)}$$

$$b = \frac{\ln 0.45875}{\ln 11.25}$$

$$b = -.7793/2.4204$$
$$b = -0.32197 \quad \text{(difference from rounding)}$$

[5] Using base 10 logarithms, $b = (.6616 - 1)/1.0512 = -0.3219$.

Now we can solve for a using either of our starting points. For example:

$$\ln 64 = \ln a + (-.32197) \ln 4$$
$$\ln a = 4.1589 + (.32197)(1.3863)$$
$$\ln a = 4.6052$$
$$a = 100$$

Total Time and Incremental Time

It is relatively simple to calculate the total time expected to complete some number of units by multiplying the cumulative average time at that level of output by the number of units. For several reasons, one of which is computational ease, managers often rely on a modified version of equation 22–1. If we multiply both sides of equation 22–1 by X, the number of units, the left-hand side will show the total required time, rather than the cumulative average time (number of units times cumulative average time per unit equals total time):

(22–7) $$XY = XaX^b$$

The right-hand side simplifies to aX^{b+1}. (The exponent, $b + 1$, is sometimes denoted as c.) Thus, we have the following equation to solve for total time at any level of output:

(22–8) $$XY = aX^{b+1}$$

This equation in logarithmic form is as follows:

(22–9) $$\ln XY = \ln a + (b + 1) \ln X$$

Finally, managers are often interested in incremental time. For example, the managers of the Gordon Company might wish to know how many hours it should take to produce batches 45 through 61. Equation 22–8 or 22–9 solved for $X = 61$ and $X = 44$ would give the total time required for production of 61 batches and 44 batches. The total required for 44 batches would then be subtracted from the total required for 61 batches to determine the time required for the 45th through 61st batches.

Batches and Units

We have said that cumulative production (X) may be individual units or batches of a number of units. Of course, for the calculations to be valid, the number of units in each batch must be the same. At times, the accountant will have to work with fractional batches. For instance, she might have the total labor time or cost for the first 1,000 units of a new product and might wish to estimate the cost of 13,500 units. The value that she would use for cumulative production would then be 13.5 (13,500/1,000). All calculations would be the same as if the number of batches were an integer value.

It would not be unusual for the accountant to have cost data for the first five, first 35, or some other number of units, rather than the cost for the first unit. It might be unwise or impractical to determine the time or cost of the very first unit. One reason is that there would probably be wide variations in observed times depending on which worker made the first unit. In order to smooth out random fluctuations, we would probably want to observe the time for a sizable number of units, not just one unit because our estimates depend heavily on the value of a, the time or cost of the first unit or batch.

DATA REQUIRED FOR ANALYSIS

One of the problems in analyzing data to determine whether a learning effect is present, and if so, what it is, is that data are not routinely collected in the form of the cost to produce the first unit, or cumulative average costs, or even cumulative production to date. It is possible to determine total output of any product as of a given date. It is also likely the firm's records would show the total number of hours, or total cost, expended to produce that quantity. In some cases it might be necessary to go back through records to determine total output of a product, because the cumulative total might not be routinely reported. Once data are available, both scatter-diagram and regression techniques will help to determine parameters of interest, cost to produce the first unit (a), and learning-curve exponent b (or c).

Scatter Diagram

The scatter-diagram method may be used in two ways. One is to plot logarithms of cumulative production (X) and resultant average production time (Y) on ordinary graph paper. The other is to use log-log paper for a plot of the data. Intercept and slope of such plots can be used in determining cost of the first unit (a) and the learning curve $(b$ or $b + 1)$. Assume the following data. We provide the natural logarithms that we shall use in regression.

Total Number of Units		Average Hours per Unit	
X	In X	Y	In Y
2	.6932	8.9	2.1861
3	1.0986	7.2	1.9741
5	1.6094	7.0	1.9459
8	2.0794	5.7	1.7405
15	2.7081	5.4	1.6864

The data do not show doubling points, which does not create a problem because we shall work with the formula, rather than with a schedule. Figure 22–2 found below shows the values of X and Y that are plotted on log-log paper. The line fitted to the points shows the intercept and slope estimated visually.

The individual points fall very close to the line, indicating a good fit. The result should be suitable for planning, so long as there are no major changes in operating techniques. The next step is to determine the intercept and learning rate. Determining the value of a, the time for the first unit, is straightforward. All that is necessary is to read the value, because the horizontal axis begins at one, not at zero. The intercept is 10 hours. Finding the learning rate requires finding the ratio of values for cumulative average time at two points. Any two may be used, so long as one represents twice the level of production as the other (for example, 2 and 1, 4 and 2, 6 and 3). The ratio of cumulative average time at the higher level to the value at the lower level is the learning rate. Here, we could use the values at outputs of one

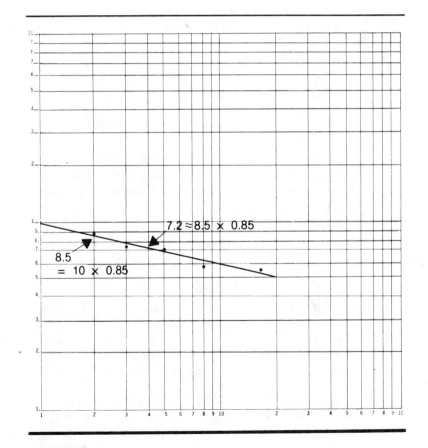

FIGURE 22–2
Log-Log Plot

unit and two units. The time for one unit is 10 hours, for two units is about 8.5 hours. The rate is therefore about 85 percent (8.5/10).

Regression Analysis

The scatter diagram is helpful, but it gives only an eyeball look at the closeness of fit. Regression analysis would enable us to make more precise determinations. The same points that held true in Chapter 3 hold here as well. In using regression analysis, we first convert the X and Y values to logarithms, then use the logarithms to perform the regression. This is done to retain a linear format of $Y = a + bx$. Regressing the natural logarithms of production and cumulative average time gives the following equation and measures:

$$\ln Y = 2.303 + (-0.2418) \ln X, \quad r^2 = 0.921, \quad S_e = 0.065, \quad S_b = 0.041$$

The next step is to convert the logarithm values. The antilogarithm of 2.303 is 10, which corresponds to the value that we determined using the scatter diagram. The value for b, -0.2418, may be used to determine the learning rate as already illustrated.

$$b = \ln \text{ learning rate}/\ln 2$$
$$-0.2418 = \ln \text{ learning rate}/.6931$$
$$\ln \text{ learning rate} = -.1676$$

The antilogarithm of $-.1676$ is 0.8457, which is just about the value of 0.85 that we estimated from the scatter diagram. The regression results allow us to make predictions with more rigor and confidence than those obtained from the scatter diagram.

Sensitivity Analysis

In their roles as providers of cost information for planning and control, accountants will be involved in the estimation of future costs of new products or contracts where the learning curve is assumed. The accuracy of the estimate of the learning curve can be extremely important, especially when large quantities of product are concerned. The accountant would be well advised to analyze the sensitivity of total costs and profits to changes in the assumed learning curve.

The schedule below shows that relatively small changes in the learning curve can have significant impacts on total costs subject to the learning curve. We assume that the first unit requires 50 hours and that labor and labor-related costs are $15 per hour.

Total Labor and Labor-Related Costs

Quantity Produced	Learning Curve			
	90%	85%	82.5%	80%
25	$ 11,495	$ 8,815	$ 7,674	$ 6,652
50	20,691	14,986	12,662	10,643
100	37,244	25,476	20,893	17,030
200	67,039	43,309	34,473	27,247
400	120,670	73,626	56,880	43,596

The impact of a misestimation of even 2½ percentage points (82.5 from 85 percent, or 80 from 82.5 percent) can be significant, especially at high levels of output.

CONDITIONS FOR LEARNING

The learning effect is not an automatic natural phenomenon. Not all production processes will show increased efficiency, and among those that do, the differences in learning rates will be substantial. Various researchers have offered guidelines for predicting learning rates, but they are just guidelines, not rules for automatic application.

In general, the higher the labor content the more opportunity for learning. Highly automated processes offer relatively little opportunity for improvement. This would seem reasonable. The more the automation the more the pace of the job is controlled by machinery, not by the worker. However, where workers exercise a good deal of control over the machinery, they may be able to increase the speed at which they can operate.

A different kind of consideration involves the amount of preplanning done before a new product is manufactured or new contract begun. Suppose that the managers of the firm spend a good deal of time and effort in developing production techniques, such as the flow of materials and product through the plant, the scheduling of different operations, and the assignment of personnel. Then the labor time on the first batches will be lowered and the apparent learning effect reduced. The more preliminary work done, the lower the initial time is likely to be, with a correspondingly lower learning rate. In contrast, if a product is put into mass production with little planning in advance, its early production time will be high, but improvement will be rapid. It is wise, then, before projecting results into the future, to determine whether early data are from a process that had been pretty well ironed out. A high rate of learning (say, a 70 percent or so learning curve) might not be sustainable for very long because it partly reflects rushing into production and getting some of the bugs out, as well as the learning effect.

That is, the improvement occurs partly through learning and partly through other factors.

The learning curve relates only to improvements in performance of workers doing the same job using the same operating equipment. Increases in productivity stemming from improved machinery, better materials, or changes in the sequence in processing are not learning-curve phenomena. These factors are important to the firm—increases in productivity from any source are welcome—but they do not have anything to do with learning curves.

In analyzing data to determine whether a learning curve exists, you should try to remove the effects of nonlearning increases in productivity. It may be a very difficult job to isolate the effects of learning from other effects, and that difficulty may show up in lower correlations between time and production.

COSTS AND LEARNING CURVES

So far we have addressed the learning curve as it relates to labor time. Obviously, labor time translates into labor and labor-related costs such as overhead that vary with direct labor time. So long as labor and labor-related costs will remain fixed per hour, the calculations made using labor time can also be made using costs, simply by multiplying required time by cost per hour.

The learning curve may also relate to materials. As workers become more efficient, they may reduce scrap and waste, thus increasing the efficiency of materials as well as of labor. However, it is unlikely that gains in the efficient use of materials will be as great as those in labor time.

CESSATION OF LEARNING

It is usually not reasonable to expect learning to continue forever. At some point workers will reach maximum efficiency and will not continue to improve performance. The term **steady state** is often used to describe this situation. Naturally, the question when the steady state arrives is of utmost importance to managers. For example, if they expect that learning will continue throughout the duration of a contract and find that it ceases about halfway through, they will show lower profits than they originally anticipated.

Determining where learning stops is an empirical matter. Managers may observe different points on different types of products and in different types of production processes. In some cases, workers may approach some theoretical limit imposed by constraints on machinery or on the human body. For example, a worker using a power saw cannot go any faster than the saw will allow. A new saw with higher cutting speed might allow for some improvement, but that is a technological change. Constraints on the human body vary among individuals. Some people can work faster than others, and even the fastest usually reach some limit beyond which they cannot improve.

In other cases, learning per se might not stop, but improvement might stop because of externally imposed constraints. Union regulations frequently provide for maximum outputs. An example is the speed of an assembly line. In the automobile industry, managers often plan for a period of learning in the early part of a new model year. The assembly line runs slower during that period, gradually increases, and finally reaches a maximum that is negotiated between the management and the union. It is possible that the workers could improve further, but they do not because of the negotiated regulation.

If managers had reasonably good information about the likely point at which learning stops, they would incorporate it into decisions. They would assume that the learning effect on a new product or contract would continue over a given period of time or amount of production, then stop. If the learning effect lasted longer than expected, costs would be lower than expected, and vice versa.

To say that learning stops means that incremental time stabilizes, not that cumulative average time stabilizes. Incremental time is less than cumulative average time. For cumulative average time to stabilize, incremental time would have to increase. That is, unlearning would have to occur. The schedule below shows that cumulative average time continues to fall after learning stops. The assumptions in the schedule are that the first batch requires 100 hours, the learning effect is 90 percent, and learning stops after the fourth batch. The incremental time per batch stabilizes at 70 hours.[6] Accordingly, the cumulative average times and total times after the fourth batch are determined from the incremental time, instead of vice versa.

Number of Batches, X	Cumulative Average Time, Y	Total Time, XY	Incremental Time per Batch
1	100	100	100
2	90	180	80
4	81	324	72
8	75.5 (604/8)	604 [324 + 70(4)]	70
16	72.75 (1,164/16)	1,164 [604 + 70(8)]	70
32	71.375 (2,284/32)	2,284 [1,164 + 70(16)]	70

[6] The incremental time for the fourth batch is just about 70 hours, the difference between total time for four batches and total time for three batches. The theoretical incremental time, assuming perfectly continuous learning throughout each unit as well as each batch, is the first derivative of the function for total time. Thus $XY = aX^{b+1}$ and $dXY/dX = a(b + 1)X^b$. In the example above, the result is 68.69, which is not significantly different from 70, when we consider that we are dealing with estimates.

Contrast these results with the ones we would get if learning continued through the 32nd batch. Cumulative average time for eight batches would be 72.9 hours (81 × 0.90), through sixteen batches, 65.61 hours (72.9 × 0.90), and through 32 batches, 59.049 hours (65.61 × 0.90). Total time for 32 batches would be about 1,889 (59.049 × 32), a good many fewer than the 2,284 shown above. If managers anticipate that learning will stop, they must plan for it in order to develop reasonable estimates of cost.

Managers may develop estimates of learning curves from regression analysis. They should watch out for the problem of a learning curve's applying for a while, then stopping. Regression results can be misleading if some of the data come from periods after learning has stopped. The learning curve will be misestimated, and the correlation and standard error of the estimate and of the b coefficient will also be off. Again, the scatter diagram is helpful in such cases because managers will be able to see the behavior of cumulative average time.

SOME ADDITIONAL APPLICATIONS OF THE LEARNING CURVE

The learning curve is clearly relevant for planning costs and therefore is important in bidding on contracts, as illustrated briefly in the Gordon Company example. The learning curve is also important in pricing decisions involving new products. Managers frequently have a range of choices in setting prices, with each price likely to lead to a different volume. In general, the lower the price, the more volume. Applying the learning curve could well indicate that the managers would be wise in setting a relatively low price in order to gain high volumes. The example below illustrates the point. We ignore the time value of money for simplicity. Incorporating it would only require determining the expected cash flows by year and discounting them.

	$10 Price	$13 Price
Total volume, five-year life	500,000	350,000
Total variable costs, first 10,000 units	$90,000	$90,000

The learning curve is 80 percent, and we assume for simplicity that all variable costs are subject to the learning curve.

Without the learning curve, the $13 price is better. Contribution margin would be $4 per unit ($13 − $9) for a total of $1,400,000 ($4 × 350,000). The $10 price gives contribution margin per unit of $1 ($10 − $9) and total contribution margin of $500,000. However, when we incorporate the learning curve, the picture changes. Given that the first batch is 10,000 units, we have 50 batches (500,000/10,000) to produce at the $10 price and 35 batches at the $13 price. The exponent, $b + 1$, for an 80 percent learning curve is 0.67807 (1 − 0.32193), so that we have the following results:

	$10 Price	$13 Price
Total revenue:		
500,000 × $10	$5,000,000	
350,000 × $13		$4,500,000
Total variable costs:		
$90,000 × $50^{0.67807}$	1,277,212	
$90,000 × $35^{0.67807}$		1,002,833
Total contribution margin	$3,722,788	$3,547,167

The analysis indicates that the firm would be better off at the $10 price. Of course, the values used for volume and for the learning curve are estimates and might prove wrong. Because the difference in total contribution margin is not overwhelmingly in favor of the $10 price, the managers might well decide to set a $13 price on grounds that it would be safer. As we have pointed out several times earlier, decision making relates to the future, which is generally uncertain, and accounting data are estimates, not known quantities.

Production Planning

Decisions involving quantities of output usually have a time horizon. A decision to accept a special order at a price below the normal one usually requires that the firm produce and deliver the goods within a specified time. Contracts usually state delivery dates, and the seller can be penalized for failing to meet the agreed schedule.

In determining whether the firm will be able to produce some specified quantities by given dates, a manager would consider many factors. One factor might well be the learning curve. Consider the following example.

The Cipolla Company makes industrial equipment. A skilled crew is currently working on an order of twenty large machines. The first machine required 1.5 weeks, and the firm usually experiences an 85 percent learning curve. The order must be completed within six months. The firm also has the opportunity to bid on another contract that must be completed within six months and that would require five weeks of the time of the same skilled crew.

In order for the firm to accept the new contract, it must be able to complete the existing order in 21 weeks (the 26 weeks in six months minus 5 weeks for the new contract). The expected total time to complete the existing order is given by the following equation (the exponent, $b + 1$, for an 85 percent learning curve is 0.76553):

$$XY = 1.5 \times 20^{0.76553} = 14.86 \text{ weeks}$$

The firm should have plenty of time available to work on the new contract, if the 85 percent learning curve holds for the existing contract. In fact, the firm will have time to produce both orders unless the learning effect is greater than 92 percent, since $XY = 21$ when the learning curve is at this level. When we wish to find the learning rate that will allow us to achieve an objective, such as being able to fill the new contract in this example, we must solve for the exponent, b. In the Cipolla example, we need to solve:

$$21 = 1.5 \times 20^{(b+1)}$$
$$\ln 21 = \ln 1.5 + (b + 1) \ln 20$$
$$3.044 = .405 + (b + 1)(2.996)$$
$$b + 1 = .881$$
$$b = -.119$$

$$b = \frac{\ln \text{ learning rate}}{\ln 2}$$

$\ln$ learning rate $= -.083$
The anti-log is 0.921, for a 92% rate.

Standard Costs and Budgets

When there is a learning effect, the accountant must make some adjustments to standard cost information and budgets. Because he expects labor time and cost to decline as production increases, he cannot compare actual costs against a predetermined average unit cost based on the life of a product or contract. An example should make the point clear.

The Royal Aircraft Company has begun production of its new model 477 long-range private plane. The firm's engineers and accountants expect an 80 percent learning effect over the first 1,000 planes, at which time learning will cease. The total labor time on the first ten planes should be about 10,000 hours. The standard wage rate is $9.50 per hour.

It is not likely that the $9.50 wage rate will prevail over the period needed to produce 1,000 planes. Accordingly, there is little merit in calculating a total standard labor cost for the 1,000 planes unless we estimate wage rates into the future. Obviously, we would do that for planning purposes, but that is not our concern here.

We can calculate the expected hours to complete the first 1,000 planes and the average hours per plane. Because a batch is ten planes, there will be 100 batches. Total time, XY, is given by the following equation, where 0.67807 is the coefficient, $b + 1$, of an 80 percent learning curve:

$$\ln XY = \ln 10,000 + (0.67807 \times \ln 100)$$
$$= 9.2103 + (0.67807 \times 4.6052)$$
$$= 12.3329$$

The antilog is about 227,040, giving an average standard labor time of 227.04 hours per plane over the first 1,000.

We cannot use the 227.04 hours to determine whether production is going as expected until the first 1,000 planes are completed. At any point along the way, we must compute the expected time based on actual production to date to see whether operations seem to be in line with expectations.

Suppose that in the last quarter of 19X6 the firm began production and finished 54 planes using 33,790 direct labor hours. Any labor rate variance would be calculated in the usual way. The labor efficiency variance must be calculated based on the expected time to complete 54 planes, not by using the 227 hours per plane expected over the entire 1,000 units. Working with total time, XY, we calculate the expected time for 5.4 batches (54/10):

$$\ln XY = \ln 10,000 + (0.67807 \times \ln 5.4)$$
$$= 9.2103 + 1.1435$$
$$= 10.3538$$

The antilog is about 31,376. The labor efficiency variance is $22,933 unfavorable, calculated as follows:

$$\text{labor efficiency variance} = \$9.50 \times (33,790 - 31,376)$$
$$= \$22,933 \text{ unfavorable}$$

Inventory Valuation and Reporting

One important aspect of learning curves is that costs in the early stages of production are considerably higher than those in the later stages. In some cases, unit costs of early batches could exceed the selling prices. That would give rise to a serious problem in valuing inventory and in reporting inventory and cost of goods sold. Earlier chapters showed that actual cost is the usual basis for inventory valuation. However, the lower-of-cost-or-market rule states that inventory should not be shown at an amount greater than net realizable value (selling price minus cost to complete and sell).[7] Accordingly, if cost exceeds net realizable value, the difference must appear on the current-period income statement as a loss or as part of cost of sales. The following example illustrates the problem. Epco Company has a contract to produce and deliver 16,000 components. The data below summarize operations over a two-year period:

	19X6	19X7
Units produced	2,000	14,000
Units delivered	1,000	15,000
Price per unit	$14	$14
Cost of production	$40,000	$123,840

[7] "Market" is defined as replacement cost with a ceiling of net realizable value and a floor of net realizable value less a normal profit margin. In situations where the learning curve exists, replacement cost will be lower than actual cost (barring increases in material prices, labor rates, and prices of other inputs). If actual cost exceeds net realizable value, it is likely that replacement cost also will exceed net realizable value, so that "market" will usually be net realizable value.

The cost-of-production figures reflect an 80 percent learning curve on all production costs (assumed for computational ease). The average cost of production in 19X6 was $20 per unit ($40,000/2,000), which is higher than the $14 selling price. The maximum valuation of the ending inventory for 19X6 is $14,000. The following partial income statements show results for the two years.

	19X6	19X7
Sales at $14	$14,000	$210,000
Beginning inventory	0	$ 14,000
Production costs	40,000	123,840
Ending inventory, at net realizable value	14,000	0
Cost of sales	26,000	137,840
Gross profit (loss)	($12,000)	$ 72,160

The income statements for both years are misleading in the sense that they do not reflect the economics of the situation. The circumstances were not as bad as depicted by the 19X6 statement, nor as good as shown in the 19X7 statement.

Some writers have argued that inventory and cost of sales should be shown at the expected cumulative average cost, not the actual cost.[8] The difference between actual costs and expected cumulative average costs would appear in two places. First, any variances such as we described in the previous section would be expensed in the period incurred (actual cost minus standard cost for the cumulative output). Second, expected variances would be deferred as an asset on the balance sheet. In our example, cumulative average cost for the entire lot of 16,000 units is $10.24, ($40,000 + $123,840)/16,000. Cost of sales and inventory for 19X6 would be shown at $10.24, with deferred production costs of $19,520 calculated as follows:

19X6 cost of sales	$10,240	(1,000 × $10.24)
19X6 ending inventory	10,240	(1,000 × $10.24)
Total	20,480	
Actual costs	40,000	
Deferred production costs	$19,520	

The $19,520 would appear as an expense on the 19X7 income statement. Gross profit in total for the two years would be the same, but now 19X6 would show $3,760 ($14,000 − $10,240) and 19X7 $56,400 ($210,000 − $10,240 beginning inventory − $123,840 production costs − $19,520 deferred production costs).

[8] For example, see Wayne J. Morse, "Reporting Costs that Follow the Learning Curve Phenomenon," *The Accounting Review*, 47:4 (October 1972), 761–73.

SUMMARY

The learning phenomenon is important to accountants because it affects total costs and therefore profits. Accountants must be alert to the possibility of a learning effect in order to develop reliable estimates of costs for pricing, bidding on contracts, production planning, and the development of standards and budgets. Estimates of cost are often very sensitive to the estimated value of the learning curve, so that it is a very critical variable.

The general form of the learning curve is that as cumulative output doubles, cumulative average cost falls to some percentage of its previous level. The learning curve is a function that contains an exponent, and it can be put into a linear form using logarithms.

COMMON LOGARITHMS

Common logarithms consist of a characteristic and a mantissa. The **mantissas** appear in Table 22–1 on pages 876–877. There is an implicit decimal point to the left of each. The **characteristic** appears to the left of the decimal point and may be positive or negative. The characteristic tells you how many digits to put to the left or right of the decimal point of the antilogarithm.

For example, the logarithm of 4.5 is .6532. The characteristic is zero. The logarithm of 45 is 1.6532. The antilogarithm has one more than the characteristic places to the left of the decimal point, when the antilogarithm is equal to or greater than one. Thus, the logarithm of 4,500 is 3.6532 and the antilogarithm of 4.6532 is 45,000.

Negative numbers do not have logarithms, but logarithms can be negative. A negative logarithm indicates that the antilogarithm is less than one. The characteristic is the number of zeros appearing to the right of the decimal point of the antilogarithm.

To find the logarithm of a number less than one, look up the mantissa and subtract from it the number that is one more than the number of leading zeros to the right of the decimal point. Thus, the logarithm of .45 is −.3468, which is .6532 − 1. There are no leading zeros to the right of the decimal point. The logarithm of .00450 is −2.3468, which is .6532 − 3. The first nonzero digit, 4, appears in the third place.

To convert a logarithm with a negative characteristic to its antilogarithm, reverse the process. Add the number that is one greater than the characteristic to the logarithm; this gives you the mantissa. The number of zeros just to the right of the decimal point is equal to the characteristic. For example, the logarithm −1.3468 gives the antilogarithm .045.

$$\text{mantissa} = -1.3468 + 2$$
$$= .6532$$

antilogarithm = .045, with one zero just to the right of the decimal point.

TABLE 22-1
Common (Base 10) Logarithms

N	0	1	2	3	4	5	6	7	8	9
1.0	0000	0043	0086	0128	0170	0212	0253	0294	0334	0374
1.1	0414	0453	0492	0531	0569	0607	0645	0682	0719	0755
1.2	0792	0828	0864	0899	0934	0969	1004	1038	1072	1106
1.3	1139	1173	1206	1239	1271	1303	1335	1367	1399	1430
1.4	1461	1492	1523	1553	1584	1614	1644	1673	1703	1732
1.5	1761	1790	1818	1847	1875	1903	1931	1959	1987	2014
1.6	2041	2068	2095	2122	2148	2175	2201	2227	2253	2279
1.7	2304	2330	2355	2380	2405	2430	2455	2480	2504	2529
1.8	2553	2577	2601	2625	2648	2672	2695	2718	2742	2765
1.9	2788	2810	2833	2856	2878	2900	2923	2945	2967	2989
2.0	3010	3032	3054	3075	3096	3118	3139	3160	3181	3201
2.1	3222	3243	3263	3284	3304	3324	3345	3365	3385	3404
2.2	3424	3444	3464	3483	3502	3522	3541	3560	3579	3598
2.3	3617	3636	3655	3674	3692	3711	3729	3747	3766	3784
2.4	3802	3820	3838	3856	3874	3892	3909	3927	3945	3962
2.5	3979	3997	4014	4031	4048	4065	4082	4099	4116	4133
2.6	4150	4166	4183	4200	4216	4232	4249	4265	4281	4298
2.7	4314	4330	4346	4362	4378	4393	4409	4425	4440	4456
2.8	4472	4487	4502	4518	4533	4548	4564	4579	4594	4609
2.9	4624	4639	4654	4669	4683	4698	4713	4728	4742	4757
3.0	4771	4786	4800	4814	4829	4843	4857	4871	4886	4900
3.1	4914	4928	4942	4955	4969	4983	4997	5011	5024	5038
3.2	5051	5065	5079	5092	5105	5119	5132	5145	5159	5172
3.3	5185	5198	5211	5224	5237	5250	5263	5276	5289	5302
3.4	5315	5328	5340	5353	5366	5378	5391	5403	5416	5428
3.5	5441	5453	5465	5478	5490	5502	5514	5527	5539	5551
3.6	5563	5575	5587	5599	5611	5623	5635	5647	5658	5670
3.7	5682	5694	5705	5717	5729	5740	5752	5763	5775	5786
3.8	5798	5809	5821	5832	5843	5855	5866	5877	5888	5899
3.9	5911	5922	5933	5944	5955	5966	5977	5988	5999	6010
4.0	6021	6031	6042	6053	6064	6075	6085	6096	6107	6117
4.1	6128	6138	6149	6160	6170	6180	6191	6201	6212	6222
4.2	6232	6243	6253	6263	6274	6284	6294	6304	6314	6325
4.3	6335	6345	6355	6365	6375	6385	6395	6405	6415	6425
4.4	6435	6444	6454	6464	6474	6484	6493	6503	6513	6522
4.5	6532	6542	6551	6561	6571	6580	6590	6599	6609	6618
4.6	6628	6637	6646	6656	6665	6675	6684	6693	6702	6712
4.7	6721	6730	6739	6749	6758	6767	6776	6785	6794	6803
4.8	6812	6821	6830	6839	6848	6857	6866	6875	6884	6893
4.9	6902	6911	6920	6928	6937	6946	6955	6964	6972	6981
5.0	6990	6998	7007	7016	7024	7033	7042	7050	7059	7067
5.1	7076	7084	7093	7101	7110	7118	7126	7135	7143	7152
5.2	7160	7168	7177	7185	7193	7202	7210	7218	7226	7235
5.3	7243	7251	7259	7267	7275	7284	7292	7300	7308	7316
5.4	7324	7332	7340	7348	7356	7364	7372	7380	7388	7396
N	0	1	2	3	4	5	6	7	8	9

TABLE 22-1
Common (Base 10) Logarithms (cont.)

N	0	1	2	3	4	5	6	7	8	9
5.5	7404	7412	7419	7427	7435	7443	7451	7459	7466	7474
5.6	7482	7490	7497	7505	7513	7520	7528	7536	7543	7551
5.7	7559	7566	7574	7582	7589	7597	7604	7612	7619	7627
5.8	7634	7642	7649	7657	7664	7672	7679	7686	7694	7701
5.9	7709	7716	7723	7731	7738	7745	7752	7760	7767	7774
6.0	7782	7789	7796	7803	7810	7818	7825	7832	7839	7846
6.1	7853	7860	7868	7875	7882	7889	7896	7903	7910	7917
6.2	7924	7931	7938	7945	7952	7959	7966	7973	7980	7987
6.3	7993	8000	8007	8014	8021	8028	8035	8041	8048	8055
6.4	8062	8069	8075	8082	8089	8096	8102	8109	8116	8122
6.5	8129	8136	8142	8149	8156	8162	8169	8176	8182	8189
6.6	8195	8202	8209	8215	8222	8228	8235	8241	8248	8254
6.7	8261	8267	8274	8280	8287	8293	8299	8306	8312	8319
6.8	8325	8331	8338	8344	8351	8357	8363	8370	8376	8382
6.9	8388	8395	8401	8407	8414	8420	8426	8432	8439	8445
7.0	8451	8457	8463	8470	8476	8482	8488	8494	8500	8506
7.1	8513	8519	8525	8531	8537	8543	8549	8555	8561	8567
7.2	8573	8579	8585	8591	8597	8603	8609	8615	8621	8627
7.3	8633	8639	8645	8651	8657	8663	8669	8675	8681	8686
7.4	8692	8698	8704	8710	8716	8722	8727	8733	8739	8745
7.5	8751	8756	8762	8768	8774	8779	8785	8791	8797	8802
7.6	8808	8814	8820	8825	8831	8837	8842	8848	8854	8859
7.7	8865	8871	8876	8882	8887	8893	8899	8904	8910	8915
7.8	8921	8927	8932	8938	8943	8949	8954	8960	8965	8971
7.9	8976	8982	8987	8993	8998	9004	9009	9015	9020	9025
8.0	9031	9036	9042	9047	9053	9058	9063	9069	9074	9079
8.1	9085	9090	9096	9101	9106	9112	9117	9122	9128	9133
8.2	9138	9143	9149	9154	9159	9165	9170	9175	9180	9186
8.3	9191	9196	9201	9206	9212	9217	9222	9227	9232	9238
8.4	9243	9248	9253	9258	9263	9269	9274	9279	9284	9289
8.5	9294	9299	9304	9309	9315	9320	9325	9330	9335	9340
8.6	9345	9350	9355	9360	9365	9370	9375	9380	9385	9390
8.7	9395	9400	9405	9410	9415	9420	9425	9430	9435	9440
8.8	9445	9450	9455	9460	9465	9469	9474	9479	9484	9489
8.9	9494	9499	9504	9509	9513	9518	9523	9528	9533	9538
9.0	9542	9547	9552	9557	9562	9566	9571	9576	9581	9586
9.1	9590	9595	9600	9605	9609	9614	9619	9624	9628	9633
9.2	9638	9643	9647	9652	9657	9661	9666	9671	9675	9680
9.3	9685	9689	9694	9699	9703	9708	9713	9717	9722	9727
9.4	9731	9736	9741	9745	9750	9754	9759	9763	9768	9773
9.5	9777	9782	9786	9791	9795	9800	9805	9809	9814	9818
9.6	9823	9827	9832	9836	9841	9845	9850	9854	9859	9863
9.7	9868	9872	9877	9881	9886	9890	9894	9899	9903	9908
9.8	9912	9917	9921	9926	9930	9934	9939	9943	9948	9952
9.9	9956	9961	9965	9969	9974	9978	9983	9987	9991	9996
N	0	1	2	3	4	5	6	7	8	9

ASSIGNMENTS

22–1   Basic Learning Curves. The Wilkes Company manufactures large grape presses. The firm generally experiences a learning effect on new models, at least through the first 75 or so units. Data on a new press appear below.

Labor time for first unit	800 hours
Labor rate	$10 per hour
Variable overhead	$8 per labor hour
Materials	$6,000 per press

The manager of the firm wants to know the expected total cost of making the first 32 units assuming a learning effect on labor of 80 percent, and of 85 percent.

Required:

1. Prepare schedules showing the cumulative average times for all doubling points up through 32 units for an 80 percent learning rate.
2. Repeat for an 85 percent rate.
3. Determine the total costs for the first 32 units estimated under each assumption.

22–2   Learning Curves and Volume. The managers of the MZT Computer Company expect that the new desk-top model they are about to introduce will sell 100,000 units in the next two years if it is priced at $800, and 75,000 units if it is priced at $1,000. The main reasons for the differences are that potential competitors will be more likely to bring out their own models if MZT's price is high.

Cost estimates for the first 10,000 units are, per unit:

Materials	$400
Direct labor and variable overhead	300

Direct labor and variable overhead are expected to drop, reflecting an 80 percent learning curve, which is what the firm has experienced on its new products.

Required: Determine which price you would charge, and justify your answer.

22–3   Bidding and Target Contribution Margin. The Icarus Aircraft Company is preparing to bid on sixteen amphibious airliners of a type that it has never made before. The potential buyer is West Pacific Airlines, which plans to use the airliners to service small islands that do not have landing fields. The managers of Icarus believe that their major competitor, Birch Airplane Company, will bid $6 million per plane.

The managers of Icarus want to earn an average contribution margin of $800,000 on the planes. They have developed the following estimates:

Materials and purchased parts, per plane	$2,800,000
Labor and variable overhead for first plane	3,800,000
Learning curve on labor and variable overhead	85%

Required:

1. Determine whether or not Icarus can meet the $6 million bid and still earn its target contribution margin.
2. Determine the learning curve that will make Icarus just meet the target contribution margin at a price of $6 million per plane.

22-4 Production Scheduling. The Rockland Manufacturing Company has received an order for 25 machines of a type that it has not previously made. The customer wants all 25 delivered by the end of 19X5, and the production manager of Rockland is not at all certain that he can make it. He has summarized information from several sources.

Total labor time available until year end	14,000 hr
Labor time committed on existing orders	8,800 hr
Estimated time for first machine	500 hr
Estimated learning rate	80%

The production manager does not want to disrupt any of the existing orders. He wants to know whether or not he can finish the new order in 5,200 labor hours.

Required: Determine whether or not the firm will be able to finish the order by year end.

22-5 Standard Costs and Learning Curves (CMA adapted). The Horace Company uses a standard cost system. In developing standard costs the firm builds in an 80 percent learning effect for direct labor based on its past experience.

The firm is planning for an automobile electrical timing device that requires assembling purchased components. Each production lot will have five units, and the firm expects the learning effect to disappear after the eighth lot. The first lot required 90 direct labor hours. The standard wage rate is $6 per hour.

Required:

1. Determine the standard amount that the firm should establish for total direct labor cost for the first eight lots.
2. Discuss the factors that the managers of the firm should consider in establishing the direct labor requirements for each unit produced beyond the eighth lot.

22-6   Learning Curve in a Service Function.   The manager of the claims department of the Midwest Insurance Company has studied the productivity of the workers who do some very basic operations in processing forms, such as making sure that all of the lines are filled out, that the policy number is correct, and so on before the claims forms go to adjusters who examine them more closely. The manager is especially interested in the apparent improvement in productivity because the turnover of these employees is very high. The findings appear below.

Total Claims Processed	Total Time to Process (in hours)
1,000	200
2,000	320
3,000	420
4,000	520

The data are all cumulative. Thus, a worker who has processed 2,000 claims forms usually requires about 120 hours to process the second 1,000 (320 − 200), and so on.

Required:

1. Estimate the learning curve.

2. Suppose that the learning curve will continue until the worker has processed 16,000 forms. How long will it take the worker to do all 16,000?

22-7   Learning Curves, Regression Analysis.   The general manager of the components department of the Chicago Machine Works has known for some time that workers become more efficient as they produce more of a particular component, but he is unsure just how much more efficient they become. He has collected the following data and wants you to analyze them and tell him how rapidly the workers improve so that he can use the information in planning.

Number of Batches	Total Time (in hours)
1	200
2	330
3	420
4	520
5	590

Required: Determine the learning rate using regression analysis.

22-8   Variance Analysis and Learning Effects.   The Jepson Company makes industrial products used by a wide variety of firms. Nearly all its business is done on contracts ranging from one to three years, over which Jepson delivers the products according to a schedule set by the contract. In determining a price per unit for each contract, Frances Miller, the controller, incorporates a 90 percent learning effect for labor and variable overhead.

The firm uses job order costing and Miller makes periodic comparisons of actual and budgeted costs. She has recently been working on a special project for the president and has asked you to analyze two jobs to see whether or not they are going smoothly. Data on the jobs appear below.

	Job	
	XZ-456	UH-040
Total number of units to be delivered	12,000	6,000
Number completed to date	7,000	2,000
Labor and variable overhead costs to date	$162,180	$ 78,300
Cost of first 100 units = budget	$ 3,800	
Total budgeted cost for entire order		$192,000

The cost of the first 100 units is not available for job UH-040 because of clerical oversight. Ms. Miller has mislaid the estimated cost to produce the entire order of job XZ-456.

Required: Determine the costs that should be accumulated for each job at its current state of completion.

22–9   Make-or-Buy Decision.   The Warner Company has been buying a number of components from the ICC Company for a number of years. One of them, called part #65-198, has cost the Warner Company $34.50 for the past several years. A representative of ICC has notified Warner that the price will rise to $39 for the coming year, with prices in future years likely to rise as well. However, ICC is willing to negotiate a five-year contract to supply the part at $42.

Upon learning of the price increase, managers of the Warner Company began to explore the possibility of making the part internally. The firm has sufficient capacity but lacks some sophisticated machinery of the type that ICC uses. There is a considerable lead time on acquiring this machinery, so that if Warner decided to make the part, it would have to use much more hand labor than ICC. The best estimates available appear on page 882.

The fixed costs included in the cost to make the part are all incremental. The production manager believes that the firm would experience a learning effect in making the part and that the effect would be confined to direct labor time. The best estimate of the learning effect is 85 percent, but that is a very rough estimate. Whatever the learning effect turns out to be, the best estimate is that the direct labor time on page 882 will be the average for the first 14,000 units. In other words, the first year's output is the first batch.

	Cost to Make Part #65-198
Direct labor hours	2.50
Direct labor and variable overhead per hour	$10.50
Direct labor and variable overhead per unit	$26.25
Materials cost per unit	8.65
Total variable cost per unit	$34.90
Annual requirements, in units	14,000
Total annual variable cost	$488,600
Additional fixed costs per year	175,000
Total annual cost	$663,600
Cost to buy, 14,000 × $42	588,000
Advantage to buying	$ 75,600

Required: Ignore the time value of money.

1. Determine the total cost of making part #65-198 over the next five years, with a learning effect of (a) 85 percent, (b) 80 percent.

2. Determine the learning effect that would make the total cost of making the part the same as the total cost of buying it under the five-year contract.

3. What advantages might there be to buying the part under a one-year arrangement at $39? What disadvantages?

4. What added information would you like before making a decision?

22–10 Make or Buy and Learning Curves. Philip Riccardi, the production manager of the Brison Company, has asked for your assistance. The firm has obtained a contract to supply radar systems to a major aircraft manufacturer over the next three years. The managers of Brison had expected to subcontract one assembly of the system to the Holt Electronic Company at a cost of $500 each. Riccardi has since learned that he can purchase machinery costing $180,000 that can be used to make the assembly internally. The machinery has an estimated useful life of six years but would probably not be suitable for use after the contract expired and would be sold for about $30,000.

Riccardi developed the following estimates related to internal production. His estimates were based on similar types of work that the firm had been doing for several years, so that he was reasonably confident of their validity.

Materials cost per unit	$100
Direct labor hours, per unit in first year	10 hours
Direct labor rate in first year	$ 12 per hour
Variable overhead rate in first year	$ 8 per labor hour
Total annual fixed overhead	$65,000

Riccardi believes that the only incremental fixed overhead would be $50,000 in depreciation expense, based on the cost less estimated salvage value of the machinery. He anticipates a 10 percent increase in the direct labor rate and a 5 percent increase in the variable overhead rate to take effect at the beginning of the second year. He believes that both rates will increase an additional 4 percent at the beginning of the third year.

The order will be filled in three batches; the firm will deliver 300 units at the ends of each of the first two years and 600 units at the end of the third year. Riccardi is confident that the firm will experience an 80 percent learning effect on the labor time. He states that the firm uses a 16 percent cutoff rate of return and is subject to a 40 tax rate.

Required: Determine what course of action Brison Company should follow. Be prepared to discuss the significance of the learning curve for the decision.

22–11 Scatter Diagram. The accompanying figure shows cumulative output and cumulative average time on a log-log plot.

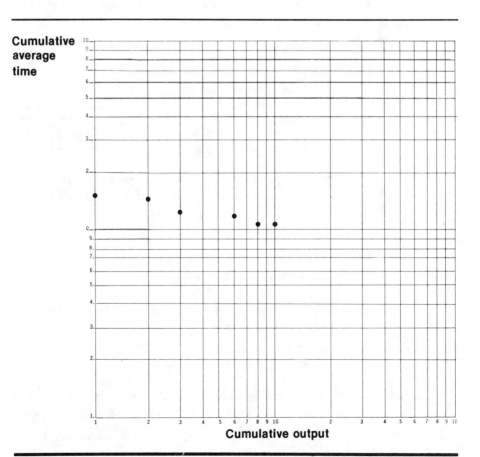

Required: Use the plot to determine the values that you would need for predicting times in the future.

22-12 Service Function, Employee Requirements. A large state operates a program that gives college students rebates on tuition at the state university. The department manager in charge of processing the applications hires workers for a six-week period, during which she must get all the work done. The applications must be in by the first of June, and the applicants must be notified of the amount of the rebate by July 15.

The manager expects about 20,000 applications in 19X6. From past experience, she is confident that the average worker will start out slowly and improve over the period. The pattern has been that the average worker takes 20 hours to do the first ten applications and improves at an 80 percent rate. The total working time for the six-week period is 240 hours per worker.

Required: Determine how many workers the manager should hire for the period.

22-13 Learning Effects and Income Statements. In August of 19X5 the Moore Company began work on a contract to make 30 printing presses for the Wynnant Newspaper chain. Results for 19X5 and 19X6 showed the following:

	19X5	19X6
Presses completed and shipped	12	18
Materials used	$120,000	$180,000
Direct labor cost	500,000	400,000
Variable overhead cost	250,000	200,000
Fixed overhead applied	60,000	90,000

The selling price was $70,000 per press. There were no inventories of in-process or finished goods at the end of 19X5. All costs were incurred as budgeted.

Required:

1. Prepare conventional income statements for each of the two years, down to gross margin.

2. Prepare income statements using the format on page 874, with cost of sales based on the expected cumulative average unit cost over the life of the contract.

3. Comment on the usefulness of the two sets of statements for internal reporting and for reporting to shareholders.

22-14 Job Orders, Learning Curves, and Cost Analysis. The Lahti Company produces high-quality gear assemblies used in several types of industrial machinery. Although each order is custom-built, it usually includes a good many standard parts that are combined with specially made components. Late in 19X8 the firm received an invitation to bid on 300 assemblies of a type it had not made before. The invitation was from the Brockton Tool and Die Company, which had never done business with Lahti.

Jon Miller, Lahti's sales manager, hoped that he could submit a good bid because he thought that there was considerable opportunity for future business from Brockton. He had learned that a competitor was prepared to bid about $61 per unit for the assemblies.

The estimating department developed the analysis of costs that appears below. Miller was unhappy with the $81.80 price, because he was sure that Brockton would not accept it. He then asked George DiLello, the production superintendent, whether the estimates looked reasonable.

	Analysis of Costs
Materials	$13.55
Purchased parts	17.80
Assembly labor	14.50
Overhead at 150% of labor	21.75
Total manufacturing costs	67.60
Allowance for selling and administrative expenses at 10%	6.76
Total cost	74.36
Allowance for profit at 10%	7.44
Price	$81.80

DiLello told Miller that the estimates had been based in part on observations of workers asked to perform a couple of the required operations. He said that the firm usually experienced a learning effect somewhere in the range of 85 to 90 percent on fairly large orders of new assemblies and that this effect should be taken into consideration when a final bid was determined.

Miller then went to Tod McMaster, the firm's controller, to ask about the incremental components of the cost estimate. McMaster said that materials, purchased parts, and labor were variable, along with 70 percent of overhead. Overhead generally varied closely with labor cost. The allowance for selling and administrative expenses was not itself variable: it was based on total expected expenses for the year. McMaster believed that selling and administrative expenses tended to vary with sales dollars, at a rate of about 2 percent.

Miller felt strongly that the firm should underbid the competition so long as it did not take an incremental loss. He knew that Brockton Tool and Die could be a source of a good deal of business. However, he did not want to bid so low that Brockton would expect unreasonably low prices on future business.

Required: Make a recommendation, supporting it with whatever analyses you believe relevant.

SELECTED REFERENCES

Andress, Frank J., "The Learning Curve as a Production Tool," *Harvard Business Review*, 32:1 (January–February 1954), 87–97.

Kollaritsch, Felix P., and Raymond B. Jordan, "The Learning Curve: Concepts and Application," chap. 35 in Homer A. Black and James Don Edwards, eds., *The Managerial and Cost Accountant's Handbook* (Homewood, Ill.: Dow Jones-Irwin, 1979), pp. 971–1017.

Morse, Wayne J., "Reporting Production Costs That Follow the Learning Curve Phenomenon," *The Accounting Review*, 47:4 (October 1972), 761–73.

Introduction to Simulation

Chapter 23

Simulation is a broad and diverse subject. It is a management tool used in many different types of situations, of which we consider only one major type in this chapter: the use of computer-based models to examine problems involving uncertainty.[1] We have dealt with uncertainty in two principal ways in this book: (1) by the use of expected values (means) and variances or standard deviations, and (2) by the use of sensitivity analysis. Simulation provides the means to analyze more complex, more realistic problems than do either of the techniques mentioned above.

In a broader sense, **simulation** is any process of modeling, of representing real activities in mathematical or other form. Thus, cost-volume-profit analysis simulates the behavior of profit under various conditions of costs and prices. Cash budgeting simulates the flow of cash through a firm under specified conditions relating to costs, prices, and patterns of collections of receivables and payments of obligations. Recall the discussion of budget simulators in Chapter 14. Additionally, sensitivity analysis simulates the behavior of an important variable (such as profit, cash flow, net present value) under changing conditions. Accordingly, we have been doing a form of simulation throughout this book. However, we have not yet dealt with simulation as a tool for dealing with uncertainty.

---

[1] Simulation does not necessarily deal with uncertainty. It is often used when either complexity or cost makes it difficult or impossible to obtain information in some other way. The use of scale models of aircraft wings in wind-tunnel tests is an example. Some people restrict the use of the term *simulation* to the modeling and analysis of dynamic systems, ones that operate over time. We consider such simulations later, as well as simpler ones that involve primarily cost-volume-profit relationships for a single period.

ANALYZING PROBLEMS OF UNCERTAINTY

When analyzing problems of uncertainty, we have usually assumed that only one variable (such as demand for a product or variable cost of production) was stochastic. Other variables were assumed to be known with certainty. We have usually assumed either that the stochastic variable was approximated by a normal distribution or that it could take on only a few values (such as four or five levels of demand). We noted that one of the major reasons for such assumptions is that computations become extremely burdensome without such restrictions.

The computational burdens of allowing many possible values of a stochastic, but not a normally distributed, variable are not the only problem.[2] Suppose that we allowed both contribution margin per unit and volume to be stochastic and normally distributed. The resulting probability distribution of total contribution margin might not be normal or even symmetrical. While the mean and variance of total contribution margin could be easily calculated from the means and variances of volume and contribution margin per unit, means and variances (or standard deviations) are summary statistics and, with the exception of the normal distribution, do not tell you all you would like to know about a probability distribution. We explore this important point in more detail shortly.

Sensitivity analysis is useful in dealing with uncertainty, but its limitations become apparent when more than one variable is stochastic. Consider one example. A manager preparing a cash budget may have reasonable ideas about the probabilities of several variables such as sales, average collection period, production costs, and so on. A decrease of 15 percent in sales might produce a cash shortage, as might an increase of 20 percent in the average collection period, or a 25 percent increase in production cost per unit. Thus, it might be that a 9 percent decrease in sales, coupled with a 15 percent increase in the average collection period and a 6 percent increase in production costs, could also create a cash shortage. In fact, the variety of combinations of changes that could create a cash bind is limitless. Attempting to list the most likely fifteen or twenty possible combinations might prove difficult, as well as fruitless. There would simply be so much information that a manager would have trouble assimilating it.

Simulation is a way to approach problems where many variables are stochastic, whether they are discretely or continuously distributed, so long as the form of the probability distribution of each variable is reasonably well defined. The next section illustrates the basics of a simple simulation.

Before we proceed, we should state that our objectives in this chapter are limited. We do not intend to make you competent in developing and

---

[2] A number of writers have dealt with the question of the distribution of profit when more than one variable is stochastic. Some of these writings are listed in the Selected References at the end of the chapter.

running simulations. Specialists will do most of that work. However, as an accountant or other type of manager you will probably work with such specialists in providing data for simulations and in reviewing results. You will also spot problem areas where simulation might be useful. Therefore, it is desirable that you have a basic understanding of the technique, its value, and its limitations.

Illustration: How Simulation Works

We begin with a simple illustration to show how simulation works. The problem is a cost-volume-profit analysis involving discrete probability distributions, rather than continuous ones. To reduce the number of variables, we assume that fixed costs are known with certainty and we work only with total contribution margin. The data for the problem appear in Exhibit 23–1.

EXHIBIT 23–1
Data for Illustration

Volume		Selling Price		Variable Cost	
Amount	Probability	Amount	Probability	Amount	Probability
8,000	.30	$20	.10	$ 8	.40
10,000	.40	25	.70	10	.30
12,000	.30	30	.20	12	.30

In this simple case we could determine the probability distribution of total contribution margin using a probability tree, as described in Chapter 4. Exhibit 23–2 presents the probability tree for this situation. The 27 possible values arise because there are three different values for the three different variables involved ($3 \times 3 \times 3 = 27$). Each value for total contribution margin has a probability equal to the joint probability of the occurrence of the required values. For example, the probability of total contribution of $64,000 is .009, the joint probability of volume of 8,000 units, selling price of $20, and variable cost of $12 (.30 × .10 × .30 = .009). The expected value of total contribution margin is $157,000 and the standard deviation is $40,207.[3]

---

[3] In a case like this we can determine the expected value of profit using the expected values of the variables. The expected value of volume is 10,000 units, of selling price is $25.50, and of variable cost is $9.80. These are calculated in the usual way; for example, variable cost is ($8 × .40 + $10 × .30 + $12 × .30 = $9.80). The standard deviation is given by,

$$\sigma = \sqrt{\sum_{i=1}^{n} (x_i - \bar{x})^2 p_i}$$

where x_i = each observed value
$\bar{x}$ = the mean of contribution margin
p_i = the probability of occurrence of the observed value

EXHIBIT 23–2
Probability Tree for CVP Problem

Volume	Selling Price	Variable Cost	Contribution Margin	Expected Value[a]
		$ 8 (.40)	$ 96,000	$ 1,152
	$20 (.10)	10 (.30)	80,000	720
		12 (.30)	64,000	576
		8 (.40)	136,000	11,424
8,000 (.30)	25 (.70)	10 (.30)	120,000	7,560
		12 (.30)	104,000	6,552
		8 (.40)	176,000	4,224
	30 (.20)	10 (.30)	160,000	2,880
		12 (.30)	144,000	2,592
		8 (.40)	120,000	1,920
	20 (.10)	10 (.30)	100,000	1,200
		12 (.30)	80,000	960
		8 (.40)	170,000	19,040
10,000 (.40)	25 (.70)	10 (.30)	150,000	12,600
		12 (.30)	130,000	10,920
		8 (.40)	220,000	7,040
	30 (.20)	10 (.30)	200,000	4,800
		12 (.30)	180,000	4,320
		8 (.40)	144,000	1,728
	20 (.10)	10 (.30)	120,000	1,080
		12 (.30)	96,000	864
		8 (.40)	204,000	17,136
12,000 (.30)	25 (.70)	10 (.30)	180,000	11,340
		12 (.30)	156,000	9,828
		8 (.40)	264,000	6,336
	30 (.20)	10 (.30)	240,000	4,320
		12 (.30)	216,000	3,888
			Total expected value	$157,000

[a] Example: the first contribution margin of $96,000 has a probability equal to .012, the product of the probabilities of each event. And $96,000 × .012 = $1,152.

It should be clear that if we had many, many values for each variable, it would be awfully burdensome to make the calculations of all possible values of total contribution margin. However, simulation will provide about the same information as an exhaustive enumeration of all possibilities. In using simulation we make a large number of iterations of possible values for each variable, calculating total contribution margin for each possibility. We can then find the expected value and standard deviation, using statistical packages designed for that purpose.

In this context a simulation may be regarded as a large number of tries, with each try using one value for each of the stochastic variables. Because the variables are subject to probability distributions, we must ensure that each value of each variable (for example, a $25 selling price in our illustration) occurs approximately in accordance with its probability. Thus, if we do 1,000 iterations of our illustrative problem, we should find volume of 8,000 units about 300 times (30 percent), of 10,000 units about 400 times (40 percent), and so on with the other values of each variable.

To ensure that we achieve the objective stated above, we assign random numbers to each possible value of each variable. On each iteration of the simulation we select a number at random and use that number to assign the value to each variable. Thus, on each iteration of our illustrative problem, we would assign a value to volume, selling price, and variable cost through the selection of a random number for each. In making the assignments of random numbers we must consider the probabilities of occurrence of each possible value of each variable. In this case we would need only ten random numbers, because all the probabilities are in even tenths.[4]

Suppose that we assign random numbers zero through 9 as shown below. Notice that a value with probability of .30 is assigned three numbers, one with a probability of .40 four numbers, and so on.

Sales Volume		Selling Price		Variable Cost	
Value	Random Numbers	Value	Random Numbers	Value	Random Numbers
8,000	0, 1, 2	$20	0	$ 8	0, 1, 2, 3
10,000	3, 4, 5, 6	$25	1, 2, 3, 4, 5, 6, 7	$10	4, 5, 6
12,000	7, 8, 9	$30	8, 9	$12	7, 8, 9

There is no special significance to the particular assignment of random numbers. We could have assigned any three digits to 8,000 units, say 6, 3, 2 or 5, 8, 9, just as well as 0, 1, and 2. All that matters is that the number of random numbers corresponds to the probability of occurrence of the value (in this case, 3 out of 10). We now draw one-digit numbers at random, in groups of three.[5] The first denotes the sales volume, the second selling price, and the third variable cost. We repeat the process a large number of times (1,000 is a commonly used number of iterations), until we are reasonably sure that the results correspond to the underlying pattern.

[4] If the probabilities of particular values were, say, .34 or .87, we would need 100 random numbers. We consider continuous distributions shortly.

[5] There are many ways to draw random numbers. Tables are available (see Table 23–1 at the end of the chapter), as are computer programs. The problem is to make sure that the numbers are random. Thus, you could not open a telephone book and pick the *first* digit in each telephone number because the digits 0 and 1 are never the first.

To illustrate this technique let us go through the process four times and obtain the following sets of three random numbers: 9, 9, 5; 8, 2, 7; 6, 3, 1; 0, 1, 8. The values selected and associated contribution margins are:[6]

| Iteration | Volume | | Selling Price | | Variable Cost | | Contribution Margin |
	Random Number	Value	Random Number	Value	Random Number	Value	
1	9	12,000	9	$30	5	$10	$240,000
2	8	12,000	2	25	7	12	156,000
3	6	10,000	3	25	1	8	170,000
4	0	8,000	1	25	8	12	104,000
			Total contribution margin				$670,000
			Average contribution margin ($670,000/4)				$167,500

Four iterations are obviously too few to use to draw any worthwhile conclusions. However, a computer program designed to simulate this problem operates in much the same way as our example, only much faster. Figure 23–1 presents a graphic picture of the results of 1,000 iterations that took less than a dollar's worth of computer time. The program essentially drew three random digits on each iteration, assigned the associated values for volume, selling price, and variable cost, calculated contribution margin, and stored the value for further use. The stored values of contribution margin were used to calculate the mean and develop the frequency distribution in Figure 23–1. They were also used as input to a statistical package that determined the standard deviation.

Figure 23–1 reveals that contribution margin tends to cluster in the range between $125,000 and $150,000. The expected value and standard deviation developed in the simulation are not significantly different from the results determined analytically. The figure also shows that the probability distribution of contribution margin is skewed to the right. The mean is to the right of the median because the very high possible values of contribution margin pull up the mean. The median is below $150,000, as evidenced by the .512 probability that contribution margin will be less than $150,000 (.008 + .062 + .145 + .297 = .512).

ANALYZING PROBABILITY DISTRIBUTIONS

One of the advantages of simulation is that its results may be presented in the form of probability distributions like that in Figure 23–1. Managers

---

[6] In this case we could have used two random numbers, one for volume and one for contribution margin per unit. There are nine possible values for contribution margin (three prices × three variable costs). We would then have had to use two-digit random numbers, because some of the joint probabilities for contribution margin have two digits. For example, an $8 contribution margin has a probability of .03, with price of $20 and variable cost of $12, so that .10 × .30 = .03. We would need 100 random numbers to model these probabilities.

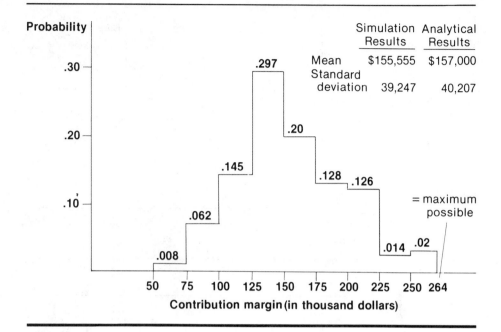

FIGURE 23–1
Simulation of CVP Problem

can frequently obtain more information from a visual inspection of a probability distribution than from simply knowing its mean and standard deviation. The mean and standard deviation are summary statistics. They do not tell us all that we want to know about a probability distribution, except in the case of the normal distribution and some other well-defined ones.

Skewness is an important aspect of probability distributions, as is kurtosis. We saw that the distribution in Figure 23–1 was skewed to the right: its right-hand tail was longer than its left-hand tail. Kurtosis refers to the *peakedness* of a distribution. A distribution with a high degree of kurtosis contains more observations near the mean and more observations far away from the mean than does the normal distribution. Thus, it has a tighter body, as well as fatter tails. A distribution with less than normal kurtosis is flat-topped, with short tails and a thicker body than the normal distribution.

The importance of examining probability distributions is illustrated by those in Figure 23–2 on page 894. The two distributions have the same mean and standard deviation but are obviously quite different. They are, in fact, mirror images of one another. The two distributions represent costs using two different production processes.

Both processes show the same average cost of $200,000. Process A shows a long right-hand tail, indicating the probability of very high costs, and this long tail pulls up the mean. The left-hand tail is truncated, so that the probabilities of relatively low costs are very small. The distribution is

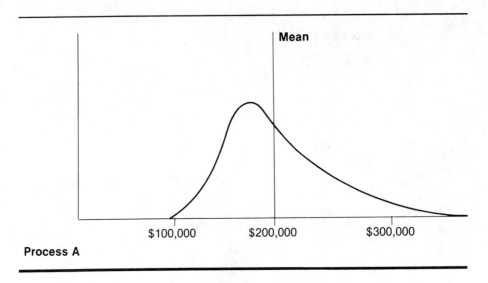

Process A

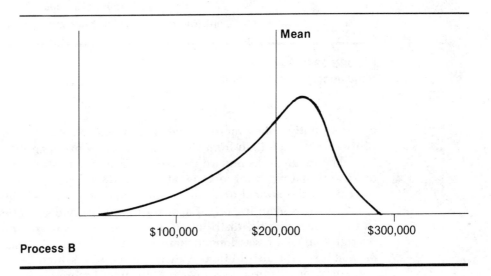

Process B

FIGURE 23–2
Probability Distributions of Cost

skewed to the right, in contrast to that of process B, which is skewed to the left.

Process B shows significant probabilities of relatively low costs. However, the bulk of the distribution lies to the right (higher cost) of the bulk of the distribution of process A costs. In other words, most of the time, process B will show higher costs than process A, but process B will not show the extremely high costs that process A could. Just knowing the mean and standard deviation of the distribution of costs for the two processes is not enough, because these statistics, being the same for both distributions, would indicate that the manager should be indifferent between them.

It should be clear that the two processes are not alike and that some thought must go into the decision to use one or the other. Which would you choose? If you wished to minimize risk, you would choose process B. You could be virtually assured that costs would never be higher than $300,000. Additionally, process B holds the possibility of very low levels of cost. However, you would find that process B would give higher costs than process A most of the time. The bulk of the distribution of costs of process A is lower than that of process B.

The question for the manager is whether he or she is willing to take the chance of showing some very high costs by selecting process A over process B. In return for accepting some dismal periods, he would expect to show lower costs in most periods. The answer depends on the manager's attitudes about risk and return. The two distributions are obviously contrived to show that even when the means and variances of two distributions are equal, the distributions are not necessarily the same. Thus, we need to look at the probability distribution of the variable of major interest, rather than relying on just the mean and standard deviation.

CONTINUOUS DISTRIBUTIONS

Discrete probability distributions with only three possible values are unlikely to be of interest in the real world. Most managerial problems will involve distributions with enough possible values that they may be treated as if they were continuous. It is helpful to understand the basics of generating random variables using computers, and so the next section describes some of the properties of computer codes that generate random numbers from continuous distributions. For simplicity, we limit the discussion to normal distributions, but most computers have packages that can be used to draw random numbers from almost any well-defined probability distribution. Operations research textbooks, as well as books on simulation, describe ways to generate random numbers using mathematical operations.

Generating Normally Distributed Random Numbers

Generating many random numbers is obviously best done by computer, not by hand.[7] Special simulation languages usually have subroutines for drawing random numbers from various types of probability distributions. Simulations written in general-purpose languages such as FORTRAN or BASIC

---

[7] Computers cannot do anything truly at random, so that we should call numbers that they generate pseudo-random numbers. For most practical purposes, pseudo-random numbers are usable as if they were truly random. We shall use the term random numbers to include pseudo-random numbers.

usually make use of system subroutines that generate random numbers. A subroutine usually requires a *seed*, a number provided by the user to get the generator working. The seed is usually a large number (six to ten digits) and is the basis for the mathematical calculations that result in the set of random numbers. An advantage gained when the user provides the seed is that he can run the same simulation with the same series of random numbers at some later time. That is, if you use the same seed twice, you get the same sequence of random numbers. This can be advantageous when you wish to run the simulation over again, but with different values for some of the variables (making a change in the mean or standard deviation of a variable).

Some subroutines generate random numbers from the **standardized normal distribution.** The standardized normal distribution has a mean of zero and a standard deviation of one. The user converts these values to the corresponding values from the desired distribution by using the following formula:

$$V = (R \times S) + M$$

where V = the value of the random variable
R = the value of the variable returned by the random number generator
S = the standard deviation of the random variable
M = the mean of the random variable

Some programs will do the conversion automatically when the user provides the mean and standard deviation as inputs. Suppose that you wish to draw random numbers from a normal distribution with a mean of 12,000 and standard deviation of 2,500. Suppose further that the subroutine generating the random numbers from the standardized normal distribution returns the value -1.25 (the value returned will usually be eight or ten digits, but we use a three-digit number here for simplicity). The random number that you want is 1.25 standard deviations *below* the mean. Your program will then perform the operation shown above and give the value 8,875 from $(-1.25 \times 2,500) + 12,000$. Likewise, if the random number returned were 0.75, your program would convert it to 13,875 from $(0.75 \times 2,500) + 12,000$.

Illustration: New Product, Bronson Company

Managers of the Bronson Company are considering a new product. They have analyzed historical data for similar products and have made some forecasts based on their expectations about future competition and other factors. They are reasonably sure about the values of the following variables:

Selling price	$30
Life of product	10 years
Annual fixed costs requiring cash	$200,000
Future tax rate	40%
Cost of capital	15%

While the managers are fairly confident about some variables, they are less so about others. Market research and engineering studies have revealed some parameters that they are willing to accept along with the assumption that the following variables will be normally distributed:

	Mean	Standard Deviation
Volume	50,000	7,000
Variable cost	$18	$2
Investment in plant and equipment	$1,100,000	$80,000

The firm uses straight-line depreciation for tax purposes and expects no salvage value from the fixed assets at the end of the expected ten-year life.

The first step is to evaluate the project, using the means of the stochastic variables. In essence, this is what we show in the discussion of discounted cash flow techniques in Chapter 15. The schedule below shows that the project seems desirable, with a net present value of over $325,000.

Operating Flows

Volume	50,000	
Contribution margin per unit ($30 − $18)	$12	
Total contribution margin	$600,000	
Fixed costs requiring cash payment	200,000	
Pretax operating flows	400,000	
One minus the tax rate	.60	
After-tax operating flows	$240,000	
Present-value factor, 10 years, 15%	5.019	
Present value of operating flows		$1,204,560

Tax Shield From Depreciation

Annual depreciation ($1,100,000/10)	$110,000	
Tax rate	.40	
Annual tax shield	$ 44,000	
Present-value factor	5.019	
Present value of tax shield		220,836
Total present value		$1,425,396
Investment		1,100,000
Net present value		$ 325,396

Let us now perform some sensitivity analysis to get some idea of the riskiness of the proposed investment. We shall ignore the investment in this analysis and concentrate on the volume and variable cost.[8] First, if the tax shield remains constant, the annual pretax flows from operations must be about $175,000 for the investment to return just 15 percent. The calculations appear below, using the technique described in Chapter 16.

Investment	$1,100,000
Present value of tax shield	220,836
Required present value of operating flows	879,164
Divided by:	
Present-value factor	5.019
Equals:	
Required annual operating net cash flows	$ 175,167
Divided by:	
One minus the tax rate	0.60
Equals:	
Required pretax operating flows	$ 291,945
Fixed costs requiring cash	200,000
Required total annual contribution margin	$ 491,945

Because the expected contribution margin is $600,000 (50,000 × $12), the firm can fall short by $108,055 ($600,000 − $491,945) before the net present value will go below zero. The critical changes in volume and variable cost are calculated below:

$$volume = 9,005 \text{ decrease } (\$108,055/\$12)$$
$$variable\ cost = \$2.16 \text{ increase } (\$108,055/50,000)$$

Each of these values assumes that the other will equal its mean. That is, if variable costs are $18 and, therefore, contribution margin per unit is $12, a drop in volume of 9,005 units (50,000 to 40,995) would bring the net present value to zero. The same reasoning applies to the critical change in variable cost.

Because we have the probability distributions of volume and variable cost, we can also calculate the probabilities that each will change unfavorably far enough to bring the net present value to zero. We simply divide the critical changes by the standard deviations and look up the associated probabilities in Table A–1 on page 926:

---

[8] The net present value is not very sensitive to investment in plant and equipment. You might wish to verify that the following calculation gives the amount of investment that would result in a zero net present value if operating flows materialized at the expected value: $I - (I/10 \times .40 \times 5.019) = \$1,204,560$. I is the investment, $1,204,560 is the present value of the operating flows, and the term in parentheses is the present value of the depreciation tax shield. The value of I is $1,507,132.

volume 9,005/7,000 = 1.29 standard deviations below the mean,
with probability of about 9.8%
variable cost $2.16/$2.00 = 1.08 standard deviations above the mean,
with probability of about 14%

We see that there is a 9.8 percent probability that the net present value will be less than zero if volume falls while variable cost is incurred as expected, at $18. Similarly, there is a 14 percent probability that variable cost will be higher than the $20.16 figure ($18 + $2.16) needed if volume is 50,000 units. For example, we have explored this type of sensitivity analysis and uncertainty in Chapters 4 and 16. The problem is that there are many combinations (an infinite number, actually) of volume, variable cost, and investment that would put net present value below zero. Moreover, there is no straightforward analytical technique for determining the total probability of a zero (or less) net present value involving all these variables.

What is the probability that some combinations of volume and variable cost (as well as investment) will produce a negative net present value? Sensitivity analysis works with one variable at a time. However, there are infinitely many possible combinations that would make the investment undesirable. In such cases, simulation provides a reasonable way to evaluate the risk of a proposal.

Figures 23–3 and 23–4 on pages 900–901 present the results of 1,000 iterations of the problem. The cost to do the simulation, including some statistical analysis and development of histograms, was about $1.40. Figure 23–3 shows the probability distribution of net present value, while Figure 23–4 shows the cumulative probability that net present value will fall below specified levels. The computer program used to develop the results appears in Appendix 23–A.

Figure 23–3 shows that the distribution is skewed to the right, with the very high values pulling up the mean. Put another way, the range above the mean is greater than below it because the right-hand tail is considerably longer than the left-hand tail. The mean obtained by simulation ($320,160) is a bit less than the mean that we determined earlier using the means of each variable. Small differences like this will usually exist even with a simulation of 1,000 iterations. One reason is that random number generators rarely generate a distribution of exactly what is specified by the user. Remember, too, that we cannot know that a particular variable will have a particular exact distribution in the future.

Figure 23–4 provides some useful information in a more direct way than does Figure 23–3. A manager is likely to be interested in such questions as the probability of net present value's being greater than or less than some specified level. Obviously, the breakeven point, where NPV = zero, is of considerable interest. The manager can read from Figure 23–4 the probability that NPV is less than any particular value. Of course, subtracting that probability from one gives the probability that NPV will be greater than the value.

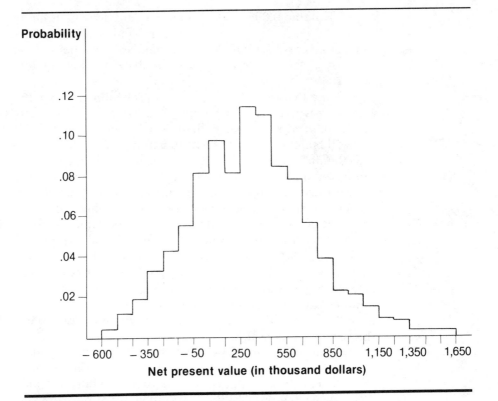

FIGURE 23–3
Probability Distribution of Net Present Value

Interval width = $100,000
Mean = $320,160
Standard deviation = $389,060

For example, Figure 23–4 shows that the probability of NPV's being less than zero is just about 20 percent. Similarly, the probability of its being less than $325,000 is about 52 percent. There is virtually zero probability of its being below about minus $625,000. Figures 23–3 and 23–4 provide information not readily obtainable by ordinary sensitivity analysis. Recall that the probabilities that volume and variable cost would be sufficiently unfavorable to bring the NPV to zero were 9.8 and 14 percent, respectively. Although these values are interesting in themselves, they are of less concern than the overall probability of the proposed investment's showing a negative NPV, because of the interaction of several variables.

Either Figure 23–3 or Figure 23–4 can be used to determine the probabilities of NPV's being within some range of interest, say from $200,000 to $300,000. Figure 23–4 affords more flexibility in making this kind of analysis because Figure 23–3 uses arbitrarily selected intervals. For example, the

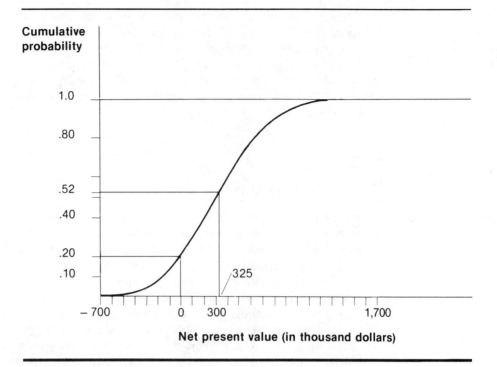

Net present value (in thousand dollars)

FIGURE 23–4
Cumulative Probability—Net Present Value Less Than Specified Levels

probability of NPV's being between zero and $325,000 is about 32 percent, which is the 52 percent probability of its being less than $325,000 minus the 20 percent probability of its being less than zero.

Refining the Simulation

This fairly simple simulation could be made much more sophisticated. We could incorporate investment in working capital based on the generated values of sales volume. We could also put limits on productive capacity and, therefore, put limits on sales volume. For example, if the capacity of the plant were 70,000 units, we would make that value the upper limit on unit sales. Other variables such as fixed costs requiring cash, useful life, and selling price could be made stochastic. Cash flows could be calculated year by year, rather than as an annuity. That is, the simulation could pick separate values for volume and variable cost for each year. The probability distributions of volume and variable cost could be widened in each successive year to reflect greater uncertainty of estimates that are further away in time.

Again, our purpose in this chapter is to introduce some of the basic ideas of simulation. In the future, you may be involved in evaluating the assumptions incorporated into a simulation, and you should have some idea of how various factors interact. In our illustration, one example is the implicit assumption that volume is not constrained by productive capacity. Another is the assumption that volume will be the same in each year of the life of the product.

PRACTICAL CONSIDERATIONS AND PROBABILITY DISTRIBUTIONS

So far we have made one of two assumptions about probability distributions of relevant variables. Either the variable can take on only one of a given number of values (usually three to five possible values), or the variable is assumed to be normally distributed. In real life, both of these assumptions are questionable. Although one or the other assumption may fit some circumstances, they cannot always give us reasonable results.

In many cases, about the best that managers can do is to make estimates of the probability that a variable will take on a value no greater than some specified level (or no less than that level). For example, a sales manager might be willing to state that volume for a particular product will almost certainly be at least 8,000 units, but less than 30,000 units. She might be willing to make other estimates, such as that the probability that volume will be at least 15,000 units is about 75 percent. This is equivalent to saying that the probability that volume will be less than 15,000 units is about 25 percent (100 percent − 75 percent). If the manager is willing to specify a few such levels of volume and associated probabilities, it is possible to construct a continuous cumulative probability distribution by assuming that each level of volume within a given range has an equal probability of occurrence.

The idea will become clearer as we proceed through an illustration. Suppose that the sales manager has made the following estimates of volume and associated probabilities that volume will be less than the specified level.

Level of Volume	Probability That Volume Will Be Less Than the Level
8,000	.00
15,000	.25
20,000	.70
25,000	.90
30,000	1.00

Notice that the probabilities given are not the probabilities that volume will be equal to the specified levels. They are cumulative probabilities that volume will be less than each specified level. This kind of probability statement is more realistic than ones where a variable is allowed to take on only four or five values. Here, we are saying that volume can take on any value from 8,000 to 30,000. It is reasonable to assume that within each of the ranges (for example, 8,000–15,000 or 20,000–25,000), each level of volume has an equal probability of occurrence (a uniform distribution). Thus, because there is a probability of 25 percent that volume will fall in the 8,000 to 15,000 range, each value within that range has a probability of .00003571 (.25/7,000). Similarly, each value from 25,000 to 30,000 has a probability of .00002 (.10/5,000), because there is a 10 percent probability of volume's being in that range (100 percent − 90 percent).

Now, how can we draw random numbers so that their corresponding values for volume will have the desired probability distribution? We could not draw random numbers from a uniform probability distribution ranging from 8,000 to 30,000 because of the different probabilities within each of the ranges. For example, volumes in the range from 8,000 to 15,000 units have higher probabilities of occurrence than those in the 25,000 to 30,000 unit range, as calculated above.

The technique to be used can best be explained graphically. Figure 23–5 on page 904 shows the plot of the cumulative probability distribution of volume. Volume is plotted on the vertical axis, with the cumulative probability that volume will be less than the specified amount plotted on the horizontal axis.[9] Plotting this way, rather than the other way around, as in Figure 23–4, makes it easier to visualize the technique. The graph shows straight-line segments connecting each point, consistent with our assumption that each value within a given range has an equal probability of occurrence. That is, we have used linear interpolation between the points specified by the sales manager. This assumption is also likely to be more realistic, in many situations, than assuming that volume (or any other variable) is normally distributed or distributed in conformance with some other well-defined and analytically tractable probability distribution.

Look carefully at Figure 23–5. Each point on the horizontal axis represents the cumulative probability that volume will be less than the corresponding level on the vertical axis. Given our assumption of equal probabilities within each range of volume, we can interpolate to find, say, the probability that volume will be less than 18,500 units, or any other level of interest. Now, look at the horizontal distances that each of the line segments covers. Notice, for example, that the segment from 15,000 to 20,000 units is longer than the one from 20,000 to 25,000 units. The two segments cover the same vertical distance, 5,000 units, but quite different horizontal distances. In fact, the horizontal distance that each line segment covers equals the probability that volume will fall within that range. The line segment from 15,000 to 20,000 units occupies 45 percent of the length of the horizontal

---

[9] Plotted this way, the function is usually called the inverse of the cumulative probability function.

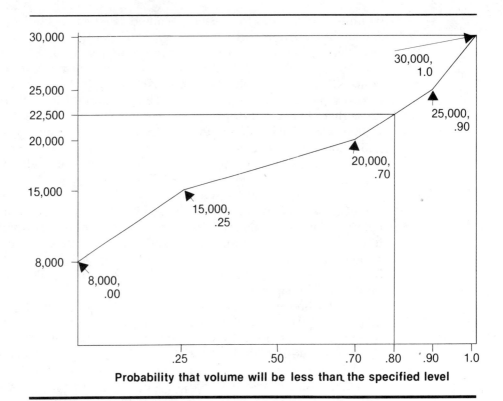

FIGURE 23–5
Cumulative Probability Distribution of Volume

axis. It runs from .25 to .70, which is .45, and the total length of the axis is 1.00. Similarly, the segment from 20,000 to 25,000 units occupies 20 percent of the horizontal axis, from .70 to .90, and so on. The sharper the slope of the line segment, the less horizontal distance it occupies and the lower the probability of each level of volume in the range.

Suppose that we selected numbers at random from a uniform distribution ranging from zero to one. That is, every number within that range has an equal probability of being selected. If we then drew a line up from the number on the horizontal axis to the line segment above it, the corresponding value on the vertical axis would be a randomly selected level of volume. For example, if we selected the number .80, we would find that the volume is 22,500 units.

Please verify for yourself that this method does not mean that every level of volume from 8,000 to 30,000 has an equal probability of being selected. The different horizontal lengths and the slopes of the line segments take care of that. About 45 percent of the time, the random number will be in the range from .25 to .70, about 10 percent of the time from .90 to

1.0, and so on. Notice also that each random number in a single range has an equal probability of being drawn. For example, each of the numbers from .25 to .70 is equally probable. This means that within the 15,000 to 20,000 unit range, each level of volume is equally probable. Accordingly, the weighting of the probabilities of each level of volume is taken care of by the widths of the line segments in each range.

Obviously, drawing random numbers and finding their corresponding volumes on a chart such as Figure 23–5 would be tedious and subject to error. We would want to use random numbers with several digits (perhaps five or six), and so the visual approach would lead to some errors. What we would do, then, would be to generate the random numbers by computer, determine the range in which each falls, then use linear interpolation to find the associated level of volume. The formula given below will do the job, once the range has been determined:

$$Q = Q_u - \frac{(P_u - R)(Q_u - Q_l)}{P_u - P_l}$$

where

Q = the selected volume
Q_u = the upper value for volume in the range
Q_l = the lower value for volume in the range
P_u = the cumulative probability at the upper
     level of volume in the range
P_l = the cumulative probability at the lower
     level of volume in the range
R = the random number drawn

For example, if the random number were .63592, the corresponding volume would fall within the range 15,000 to 20,000, since this range goes from .25 to .70. Inserting the appropriate values into the formula above gives:

$$Q = 20,000 - \frac{(.70 - .63592)(20,000 - 15,000)}{.70 - .25}$$
$$= 19,288$$

The method that has just been described gives us a great deal of flexibility. We are not forced to make possibly unrealistic assumptions about the probability distribution of a variable, nor are we limited to using only a few values for a variable. Managers are used to thinking in the terms suggested here—that it is possible to make reasonable statements about the probability of a value's being greater than (or less than) some specified level. To the extent that such statements are made based on judgment and intuition, the method succeeds in incorporating these factors into a fairly sophisticated model.

DYNAMIC SYSTEMS

The simulations that we have looked at so far have been static systems. A static system operates within a period of time, but not over time. For example, CVP analysis is single-period modeling. We can use CVP analysis for one month, then another month, and so on, but the results of one month do not affect those of the following month. Dynamic systems do operate over time, with the results of one period affecting those of the next. For example, cash budgeting by day or week over a three-month period is a dynamic process. The ending cash balance of one period becomes the beginning balance of the next period. The sales made in one week affect cash receipts in the following weeks, and so on with purchases, production, and other variables in cash budgeting.

Simulation is most widely used to model dynamic systems. Among the foremost types is the queuing, or waiting-line, model, where some type of station provides some type of service. Examples are supermarket checkout stands, bank teller windows, and gasoline pumps. A bank manager might request a simulation of the teller windows during the lunch period (say 11:30 A.M. to 1:30 P.M.). She would want to know the average length of the waiting line (queue) in number of persons, and the average waiting time per person if two windows were open, three windows open, and so on. She might set objectives of keeping the queue below six persons 95 percent of the time and the average waiting time below eight minutes. The cost accountant's role in this kind of situation would be to assess the potential benefits and costs of having different numbers of windows open. The potential benefits of having more windows open is increased business for the bank. Put another way, failing to have enough windows open to keep the queue and waiting time down to reasonable levels could lead to lost business.

Illustration: Cash Budgeting

Cash budgeting is the dynamic process that most directly involves the accountant. The treasurer of the firm is responsible for ensuring that the firm has sufficient cash available to meet its needs and that excess cash is invested in income-producing securities until it is needed. The treasurer and accountants working with him will want to know the probabilities of running out of cash, the probable balances at various points in the future, and the likely amounts of interest income and expense.[10]

For illustrative purposes, we shall show hypothetical results of a single

[10] It is possible to simulate a cash budget using a general-purpose computer language such as BASIC or FORTRAN, but there are more efficient simulation languages such as GPSS, SIMSCRIPT, and GASP. Special languages are easier to code than are general-purpose languages. Of course, to use one, you must learn it, so that for simpler simulations you are probably better off using a general-purpose language.

run of a simple cash flow simulation. Of course, we would want to have a great many more runs to see how the underlying patterns develop. The data below relate to the Northwood Department Store.

	Mean	Standard Deviation
Daily cash sales, normally distributed	$22,400	$4,200
Daily credit sales, normally distributed	$43,200	$7,560
Average days to collection of credit sale normally distributed (includes time from sale to next monthly billing and time from billing to receipt of payment)	47	8
Daily purchases, determined by inventory at the end of the previous day, which is kept current by point-of-sale recording system		
Time from purchase to payment of accounts payable normally distributed, in days	22	4
Other cash disbursements, normally distributed:		
Payroll, every 15th day	$11,000	$1,000
Miscellaneous cash disbursements	$12,000	$2,500

Suppose that we obtain the following selected results for one run of the simulation for a period of 360 days. Results are rounded to the nearest $100.

Day	Beginning Balance of Cash	Cash Sales	Collections of Credit Sales	Payments of Accounts Payable	Other Cash Disbursements
82	$14,100	$27,300	$48,500	$18,300	$ 7,600
83	64,000	18,400	38,400	27,300	19,500
84	74,000	22,600	31,200	24,200	27,900

How are these results derived? Cash sales and other cash disbursements are simply generated according to their respective distributions. The cash effects of these transactions are immediate. Collections of credit sales and payments for purchases of merchandise (accounts payable) lag the transactions that give rise to the cash flow effects (sales on credit and purchases of merchandise). The collections of credit sales on day 82 are determined by the credit sales made earlier, mostly from about days 28 to 42 or so (the average collection period is 47 days, so that $82 - 47 = 35$). The simulation generates credit sales by day, then makes the payments of receivables based on the distribution of the time to payment. Thus, after determining credit sales for, say, day 25 according to the distribution given, the simulation will assign randomly selected amounts of that day's sales to be collected on each subsequent day. The bulk of the collections will fall around 47 ± 8 days (one standard deviation) from the day of sale.

The payments of accounts payable do not require as much work as the collections of receivables. Purchases are uniquely determined by the inventory at the end of the previous day. The only stochastic process is the time to payment. Once purchases for a given day are determined, the payments by day are generated according to the distribution given. Notice why this simulation is dynamic.

Values generated for credit sales on any given day affect the inventory level at the end of the day (as do the cash sales for that day), which then determines the purchases for the following day. In turn, these purchases determine cash payments on later days. Credit sales for one day also determine cash receipts on later days.

After a number of runs of the simulation, the accountant would develop some ideas about the distribution of cash flows. The store might seek financing to meet possible cash shortages, or might alter some policy to speed up cash flows. Customer bills might be prepared more quickly than before in order to reduce the average time to payment. Of course, there would be additional costs to speed billing.

Most department stores and other firms that grant credit to large numbers of customers use cycle billing. Rather than bill everyone at the end of a month, the firm bills a portion of its customers virtually every day. Customers with names beginning with A and B might be billed on the first of each month, those from Sa to Sl on the 18th of each month, and so on. Assuming about 22 working days per month, about 1/22 of the customers would be sent bills each day.

You can see that a simulation could be extremely complex. For example, a department store's sales tend to be different on different days of the week, with Saturdays usually being heavy in some departments, Wednesdays heavy in others. The persons preparing the simulation might do each department separately, using different distributions for each of the days of the week, which would make the program a good deal more realistic, but more costly to develop and run.

The accuracy of a simulation depends on the accuracy of the expectations about the conditions that the firm faces. This includes the accuracy of the statements of probability distributions as well as unit variable costs, selling prices, and other variables. Of course, any managerial analysis that uses numbers (such as cost-volume-profit analysis or budgeting) depends on the accuracy of expectations. An advantage of simulation is that it is usually fairly easy to try different sets of values once the basic computer program is running. A manager working on a cash budget could go through the budget many times using different values (prices, costs, probability distributions of volume, cash collection period, and so on) to get an idea of how cash flows would behave under different conditions.

Stating the results of simulation in the form of probability distributions is likely to give results that are easier to interpret than the results of ordinary sensitivity analysis. In fact, simulation allows you to do extensive sensitivity analysis in a relatively short time.

LIMITATIONS OF SIMULATIONS

Simulation is not a cure-all, nor do its advocates claim that it is. Like any stochastic analysis, its results are accurate only to the extent that the actual probability distributions of relevant variables conform to the distributions used in the simulation and that all assumptions are reasonably accurate. Of course, any deterministic analysis suffers from the defect of failing to consider the variability of the relevant variables. Perfect predictions are a rarity in the business world, and simulation provides the advantage of showing how results are likely to be shaped by stochastic variables.

Theoretical Limitations

The major uses of simulation are in ongoing operations where the laws of probability have a chance to work. Simulation can be valuable in one-shot decisions such as large capital-budgeting situations, but generally less so than in day-to-day, dynamic processes. Over time, the arrivals and service times of a work station in a plant will be likely to come close to an assumed probability distribution. However, major plant expansions will not be repeated enough times for the manager to be able to take full advantage of the tendency of variables to conform to probability distributions. In other words, when a great deal of money is at risk in a one-shot decision, it is of little comfort to know that over the long run, given many opportunities, the decision is correct. This amounts to no more than saying that most people would not flip a coin with heads giving them $20,000, tails losing them $5,000, if they had only one chance to play the game, even though the expected value is $7,500.

Simulation involves repeated iterations with given probability distributions. It is a brute-force technique of running these iterations on a computer and getting an output to interpret. Many managers and academics feel this is a weakness of simulation, since it does not solve problems analytically. Thus, simulation is often used as a method of last resort when others fail.

It is sometimes possible to develop analytical solutions to problems involving stochastic variables. For example, if one normally distributed variable is subtracted from another, the mean of the resulting distribution is the difference between the two means and the variance is the sum of the variances of the two variables. The distribution is also normal. In a problem involving only such subtractions, simulation adds nothing because the analytical solution is known. Depending on the forms of the distributions of the relevant variables and the operations to be carried out (addition, subtraction, multiplication, division), the form of the resulting probability distribution may or may not be known. Therefore, although it is best to have analytical solutions, it is not always possible. Simulation may then be the only applicable technique.

Cost Limitations

Simulation can be a very expensive technique, as can any computer model of a complex process. A complicated simulation may require several person-years to develop and program. As a result, simulation may be undesirable in some situations. The cost to develop the simulation might outweigh the advantages of better decisions. Fortunately, several canned programs are available for solving some of the more common problems where simulation is useful. There are also some simulation languages that provide managers with the capability of simulating their particular processes at relatively low cost.

SUMMARY

Simulation provides techniques for analyzing complex problems in a systematic fashion. At times it may be the only feasible way to approach a problem, because the complexity may be so overwhelming that attempts to find analytical solutions are bound to fail.

Relatively simple simulations can be done quickly and easily using ordinary computer languages such as BASIC and FORTRAN, but more complicated problems require special simulation languages. A simulation, like any other approach to solving a problem, is only effective when the data used as inputs are reasonably good.

USING THE TABLE OF RANDOM DIGITS

Table 23–1 opposite contains 1,000 random digits, arranged in 20 rows and 50 columns. The five-digit groupings are for convenience in reading the table. Each digit is a separate number, and there is no special significance to the five-digit arrangement. Your objective is to select digits at random, in whatever quantity you need (one, two, four, or whatever) for the particular problem. To ensure a random selection, you need a randomly selected starting point. The following procedure will give reasonable results.

Stab at the table with a pencil and find the four digits to the right of (or left of, or above, or below) the point. Treat the first two digits as the column number and the second two as the row number where you will start. Thus, each set of two digits is a single number, ranging from 00 to 99. Treat 00 as 100. If the number is greater than 50 (for column number) or 20 (for the row number), just subtract 50 and use the result for the column number. For instance, 65 would give you 15. For the row number, subtract 20 until you get to 20 or below. Thus, 65 would be 05 (65 − 20 − 20 − 20).

Go to the starting point and select digits going to your right, or left, or up, or down. Take as many as you need to form the required random num-

TABLE 23-1
Random Digits

Row	01 05	06 10	11 15	16 20	21 25	26 30	31 35	36 40	41 45	46 50
01	84672	51485	43533	05350	74235	76889	09329	52788	80226	45472
02	79763	81275	44912	71365	67168	58062	83762	42098	09330	74430
03	99551	90450	23357	58449	34883	50294	85141	91792	38753	52326
04	89001	14074	20922	52804	32200	86563	73981	04581	56771	17056
05	59745	64968	84463	74856	03383	90892	71095	82448	07959	91822
06	11452	77755	53303	76131	73402	04712	79913	62285	40048	68919
07	74708	64717	59268	76757	29521	38194	12864	74353	83232	53653
08	54511	22553	56240	04654	90672	95552	79386	61851	79644	22467
09	20205	04398	28907	43338	49346	89203	54359	00654	33917	21038
10	70215	20219	16811	99855	98391	04175	51864	35208	08662	23147
11	88805	24729	94632	98871	32291	55727	13691	68933	02295	02875
12	75683	32757	88433	89968	08546	08197	36943	41603	53269	78825
13	48189	84550	12991	68777	78182	57932	02681	17036	77961	29385
14	72651	10047	32725	94693	50742	34889	87852	85786	78261	35700
15	11043	61106	68077	63682	95279	63360	10895	29025	79479	04050
16	50929	48837	73517	22111	94395	05880	78202	60443	48183	13327
17	36298	72775	01392	17467	50179	65405	78629	28664	16220	83208
18	06290	47502	78663	49556	52841	29791	03444	87922	25150	49579
19	63141	51482	82787	37012	55876	95633	52487	05780	09923	98758
20	02141	96104	40431	49062	66673	05742	54825	66394	48345	17718

Column

bers. When you come to the end of a row or column, go to the next one. If you finish row 20, go to row 01, if you finish column 50, go to column 01. This procedure is not strictly random but is close enough for our purposes.

In general, the random numbers that you will want are decimals, so simply place a decimal point to the left of the set of digits that forms each random number.

Illustration

Suppose that you need two-digit random numbers and that your stab at the page gave you 9503. You begin in column 45, row 03. If you are going to move to the right, your first four random numbers will be 35, 23, 26, and 89. The last, 89, is from row 04, columns 01 and 02.

APPENDIX 23–A: COMPUTER PROGRAM FOR CAPITAL-BUDGETING SIMULATION

The FORTRAN program listed below solves the simulation of a capital-budgeting problem involving a new product, or an increase in capacity to increase production of an existing product. The tax rate of 40 percent, cost of capital of 15 percent, useful life of ten years, and straight-line depreciation are built into it. Changing any of those values requires changing the program. It would be a simple matter to allow these values to be inputs, rather than embedded values. However, the more flexibility allowed in changing inputs, the more inputting that needs to be done and the longer it takes to solve a problem. As written, the program calculates the relevant values and writes the present value of future flows, amount of investment, and net present value to unit 7, which is a temporary or permanent file. The data are then read into a canned statistical package for calculation of means, standard deviations, measures of skewness and kurtosis, and other statistical tests. Most statistical packages provide frequency counts for use in developing graphs of the probability distributions of any of the variable of interest.

The program logic is fairly straightforward. However, a few items require some comment. The READ statements use FORMAT statements, but the data are input separated by commas. The FORTRAN used for the program allows commas to be used to designate the ends of fields, which makes it unnecessary to count columns as you input the data. Most installations allow this valuable leeway.

The calls to GGNMP draw the pseudo-random numbers from the standardized normal distribution. A total of 5,000 numbers are drawn, 1,000 for each of the variables. The arguments for the subroutine are the seed (the starting point for the drawing), the number of numbers to be drawn for each

EXHIBIT 23A–1

```
C          NOTATION IS STANDARD, Q=VOLUME,P=PRICE, ETC. INV=INVESTMENT,PV=PRESENT
C          VALUE, NPV=NET PRESENT VALUE, CF=CASH FLOW
C          'M' AT END OF VARIABLE =MEAN OF VARIABLE, 'S' AT END =STANDARD DEVIATION
           DIMENSION CF(10000),Q(10000),P(10000),V(10000),F(10000)
           DIMENSION PV(10000),INV(10000),NPV(10000)
           REAL INV,NPV,INVM,INVS
     1     FORMAT('ENTER MEAN,SIGMA OF VOLUME,PRICE,VARIABLE COST,FIXED COST')
     2     FORMAT('AND INVESTMENT. COMMAS AFTER EACH ENTRY, USE DECIMAL POINTS')
     3     FORMAT('FOR EXAMPLE, 90000.,9000.,. . .100000.,')
     4     FORMAT('ENTER SEED AND NUMBER OF ITERATIONS, UP TO 10000, ')
     5     FORMAT('DO NOT USE DECIMAL POINTS, DO USE COMMAS, E.G., 514133,1000,')
     6     FORMAT(10F12.4)
     7     FORMAT(2I10)
     8     FORMAT(3F12.0)
     9     FORMAT(7F12.3)
    10     FORMAT(I12)
           WRITE (6,1)
           WRITE (6,2)
           WRITE(6,3)
           READ (6,6)QM,QS,PM,PS,VM,VS,FM,FS,INVM,INVS
           WRITE (6,4)
           WRITE (6,5)
           READ (6,7) ISEED, ITIMES
           CALL GGNMP(ISEED,ITIMES,Q)
           CALL GGNMP(ISEED,ITIMES,P)
           CALL GGNMP(ISEED,ITIMES,V)
           CALL GGNMP(ISEED,ITIMES,F)
           CALL GGNMP(ISEED,ITIMES,INV)
           DO 600 I=1,ITIMES
           Q(I)=Q(I)*QS+QM
           P(I)=P(I)*PS+PM
           V(I)=V(I)*VS+VM
           F(I)=F(I)*FS+FM
           INV(I)=INV(I)*INVS +INVM
           CF(I)=((Q(I)*(P(I)-V(I))-F(I))*.6)+((INV(I)/10)*.4)
           PV(I)=CF(I)*5.019
           NPV(I)=PV(I)-INV(I)
           WRITE(7,9)Q(I),P(I),V(I),F(I),CF(I),INV(I),NPV(I)
   600     CONTINUE
           STOP
           END
```

variable (ITIMES), and the label for the result.[11] These random numbers are then converted into distributions with the desired mean and standard deviation by multiplying by the standard deviation and adding the mean.

The calculated values for the stochastic variables are then used to determine cash flows, present values, and net present values. Finally, the

[11] GGNMP calculates a new seed for each call, so you need only one seed—for the first call.

present values, investments, and net present values are written to a file for subsequent use. We used the Michigan Interactive Data Analysis System (MIDAS) to calculate means, standard deviations, and measures of skewness and kurtosis, as well as to generate histograms used to develop Figures 23–3 and 23–4.

ASSIGNMENTS

23–1 **Cost-Volume-Profit Simulation, Assigned RNs.**   The Targon Company makes a product that sells for $100 and has direct fixed costs of $800,000 per year. Volume is uniformly distributed between 20,000 and 30,000 units, and variable cost is also uniformly distributed from $60 to $70.

Required: Simulate the behavior of profit for five iterations. Draw random digits from Table 23–1 in the following manner. Begin with row 2, column 1, and select two-digit numbers going across row 2. The first set of two digits is for volume, the second for variable cost on each iteration. Thus, your first random number for volume is .79, your second for volume is .38. Your first and second numbers for variable cost are .76 and .12. Use linear interpolation to determine the volumes and variable costs.

23–2 **Simulation Results.**   The operations research group in your firm has developed a simulation of the firm's cash flow patterns using historical data and policies on inventory and payments to suppliers. The summarized results appear below. They represent 1,000 iterations of a simulation of cash balances at month end for the first six months of the year. Sales generally rise rapidly over the first four months of the year, then begin to decline.

Month	Average Ending Cash Balance	Standard Deviation	Percentage of Times Cash Negative
January	$134,287	$ 95,209	6.4%
February	118,432	103,190	11.0
March	86,120	82,087	14.8
April	51,407	67,420	22.9
May	78,912	56,097	8.5
June	116,078	67,942	3.9

Required: Comment on the results. What do they tell you, not tell you? What actions might you take as a result of your analysis?

23–3 **Product Demand.**   The sales manager of the Portsmouth Company has requested your assistance in analyzing a new product. Because the product is much like one that the firm has made for a number of years, he is confident of the following estimates of demand and probabilities:

Monthly Demand	Probability That Actual Demand Will Be Less Than Estimate
10,000	.00
12,000	.10
15,000	.40
18,000	.80
20,000	1.00

The product is expected to sell at $10 and have variable costs of $4. Monthly fixed costs associated with the product are expected to be $70,000. The sales manager believes that the probabilities of demand figures within ranges are equal. For example, each level of demand from 10,000 to 12,000 has probability of .00005 (.10/2,000).

Required: Simulate the demand and resulting profit for the product. Do ten iterations, using random digits drawn from Table 23–1. Use two-digit numbers and round to the nearest unit.

23–4 **Cumulative Probability Distributions.**   The production manager of your firm is considering acquiring some machinery he thinks could reduce costs notably. The industrial engineering staff have simulated the new process, based on data obtained from other firms that use it. Their results are in the form of a cumulative probability distribution, shown on page 916, for the firm's normal output of 40,000 units per month. The process now used averages $580,000 per month for 40,000 units, with a low of $560,000 and a high of $600,000. The distribution is fairly uniform within the range: any value of cost seems to have an equal probability of occurrence.

Required: On the graph on page 916, draw in a line representing the cumulative probability distribution under the existing process. Comment on the results in the graph and make a recommendation.

23–5 **Interpreting Simulation Results.**   The chief operations research analyst of your firm simulated the effects of using two alternative production methods for a new product. She used historical data, adjusted for changes in prices of materials, labor, and overhead elements, from the firm's experiences using the two methods for other products. She gave you the results in the form of probability distributions, shown at the foot of page 916.

Process B is one that has been used for some time. Process A is newer and requires much finer machine settings. The differences in costs under the two processes relate primarily to the quantity of scrap that each process generates. Process A might produce very low amounts, or very high amounts of scrap, while process B keeps scrap within a fairly narrow range.

Required: Which method would you select and why?

ASSIGNMENT 23-4—Cumulative Probability Distributions

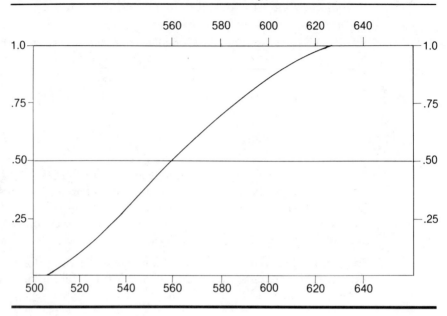

ASSIGNMENT 23-5—Probability Distributions

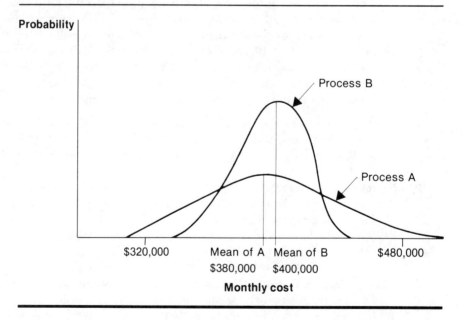

23-6 CVP Analysis, Two Random Variables. The Torgeson Company makes a single product. The sales manager has developed the following estimates of volume and selling price for the coming year, each with the associated cumulative probability that the actual value will actually be less than the one given. Because of conditions in the market for the product, the price and volume do not seem to be interdependent.

Volume	Cumulative Probability	Price	Cumulative Probability
10,000	.00	$10	.00
14,000	.40	12	.30
18,000	.80	14	.80
20,000	1.00	15	1.00

The sales manager believes that linear interpolation is appropriate because he considers it likely that the probabilities are uniform within each range. Variable costs are $8 per unit, and total fixed costs are $50,000.

Required: Simulate the behavior of profit for ten iterations. Use Table 23–1 to draw random numbers to two places (for example, .24, .78) for both volume and price. Thus, you will need twenty random numbers, ten for each variable.

23–7 A Concessionaire. Hart and Crane are partners in a food service business. They can sell hot dogs and soft drinks at 50 events to be held at the local civic center during the coming year and want to decide how much food and drink to buy for each event. Their experience indicates that each person attending an event buys $2 worth of food and drink. Contribution margin is 60 percent of sales, and the partners must throw out any unsold items.

Historical results and judgment about the likely effects of such changes as higher gasoline prices have led Hart and Crane to the following estimates of attendance and assigned cumulative probabilities:

Attendance	Cumulative Probability
7,000	.00
11,000	.40
15,000	.50
19,000	.90
23,000	1.00

Hart has suggested that they buy enough food and drink for 18,000 people, while Crane would prefer to buy enough for 15,000, believing it safer. The distributions within each range shown above seem to be relatively uniform, so that linear interpolation is reasonable.

Required: Using Table 23–1 to draw two-digit random numbers, simulate the behavior of profit under each suggested strategy for ten iterations. Be prepared to make a recommendation.

23-8 Inventory Policy. The Gregson Company is a wholesaler of a variety of consumer goods. It receives orders from retailers daily, and if it does not have sufficient stock to fill the order, provides what it does have. The retailer then goes to another wholesaler for the rest of its requirements. In the past, Gregson has maintained a large supply of all fast-selling items, but rising carrying costs have made this policy questionable.

Ben Gregson, the owner of the firm, has asked for your assistance in determining inventory policies. You decide to prepare a pilot study using a single item, for which the following data are available:

Price	$3.00
Cost (purchase)	2.50
Contribution margin	$0.50

Weekly Demand	Probability
10,000	.10
5,000	.10
3,000	.30
2,000	.30
0	.20
	1.00

Carrying costs for this item are $0.10 per week. For simplicity, assume that demand can take on only one of the five values given above. The item can be ordered from the manufacturer in any quantity. Delivery is made one week after the order is placed. Gregson orders, if necessary, at the end of each week. Sales are assumed to take place evenly over each week.

Required: Simulate the behavior of inventory and profit for a ten-week period, using the policy assigned by your instructor. The beginning inventory is 3,000 units. Carrying costs per week are given by the formula:

$$\text{carrying costs} = (\text{beginning inventory} \times \$0.10) - (\text{sales} \times \$0.05)$$

Assign the digits 0–9 to the various levels of demand, using Table 23–1 to draw the digits.

The following example may be helpful. Assume that you are to order 5,000 units if inventory is equal to or less than 3,000 units. Assume further that demand determined by the random number draws is 5,000 in week 1, 2,000 in week 2.

Week	Beginning Inventory	Order	Sales	Received at End of Week	Ending Inventory
1	3,000	5,000	3,000[a]	5,000	5,000
2	5,000	0	2,000	0	3,000

[a] Only 3,000 units on hand, so that sales are less than demand.

Profits—week 1: $(3,000 \times \$0.50) - [(3,000 \times \$0.10) - (3,000 \times \$0.05)]$
$= \$1,350$

week 2: $(2,000 \times \$0.50) - [(5,000 \times \$0.10) - (2,000 \times \$0.05)]$
$= \$600$

23–9 **Ordering Strategy.** *The Bugle* is a weekly newspaper published in a large city. The managers of the paper have analyzed the demand for it and have come up with the following cumulative probabilities associated with demand:

Demand	Cumulative Probability That Actual Demand Will Be Less
20,000	.00
25,000	.40
30,000	.70
35,000	1.00

The paper sells for $0.15 and has variable production costs of $0.04. Any unsold papers are sold to a dealer for $0.01 each.

Required: Simulate the behavior of profit for five iterations, using the strategy of printing 30,000 copies. Repeat using 35,000 copies. Use linear interpolation and two-digit random numbers from Table 23–1.

23–10 **New Product, Two Random Variables.** Working with people in market research, production, and engineering, Walter Burke developed the following data related to a digital watch that the PMP Company was going to introduce soon.

	Expected Value	Range
Monthly sales volume	100,000	80,000–120,000
Unit contribution margin	$14	$12–$16
Monthly fixed costs	$1,200,000	$1,200,000

"Monthly fixed costs are virtually certain, but the other key variables are not," said Burke's boss. "I know that both selling price and variable manufacturing cost are likely to vary, and of course so should volume, but I am not sure what to do with these numbers. For instance, if we sell 80,000 in a month, we need a contribution margin per unit of $15 to break even. How likely is it that we won't break even in any given month, or that we'll earn more than $500,000? These are the kinds of things that I'd like to have some idea about. I know that we are dealing with estimates and that we cannot pin things down much better than you already have, so far as the estimates are concerned. But can't you give me a better idea of what is likely to happen?"

Required: Simulate the behavior of monthly profit for ten iterations, using two-digit random numbers from Table 23-1 and assuming that the probability distributions are uniform within the ranges.

23-11 **Stockout Costs, Information.**   The Blake Company manufactures a number of products, using over 120 different raw materials and purchased components. The firm uses the economic-order-quantity model for planning its purchases but has no formal system for determining when to replenish the stock of a material or component. The production manager has complained that he often runs out of a critical item, necessitating costly shifts in the production schedule. Accordingly, he has been arguing that the firm carry higher stocks.

The treasurer has argued that the firm should keep its inventories as low as possible because of high holding costs. She has no objection to stocking a six- or eight-month supply of a small, cheap item, but she wants the stock of high-value items kept to a minimum.

The firm recently hired Jan Smith, a graduate of the state university with a degree in accounting and a minor in operations research. Smith has made the suggestion that simulating the behavior of inventory and associated costs would be a good initial step in getting a handle on the situation.

Required: Outline the steps that you would take in gathering information for the simulation. What kinds of information would you want to have and how would you expect to get each kind of information? How would you cope with the problem that some of the required information is likely to be very subjective and not very amenable to an accurate quantitative determination?

23-12 **Stockout Costs, Simulation.**   Jan Smith had collected a good deal of information about one important component (see the preceding assignment) and developed the following procedure for simulating the behavior of stockout costs.

1. Select a lead time at random.
2. Simulate the total use during the lead time by drawing, at random, values for daily use for the number of days during the lead time. For example, if the lead time were five days, Smith would draw five values for daily use and sum them to determine total use.
3. Calculate the number of units stocked out, if any.
4. Calculate the cost of stockouts.

Smith decided to start with replenishment points of 3,000 units and 4,000 units. Stockout costs are $100 per unit, and the following data describe, as well as Smith can estimate, the lead time and daily use.

Lead Time		Daily Use	
Number of Days	Probability	Number Used	Cumulative Probability
2	.60	500	.00
5	.40	800	.20
		1,200	.60
		1,500	1.00

Thus, lead time is discrete while use is continuous. Smith believes that linear interpolation to determine use each day is quite reasonable. The firm orders the component five times per year.

Required: Simulate the behavior of inventory under each replenishment policy for five iterations (one year). Determine the total stockout cost for the year under each policy.

23-13 Information (CMA). Shotz Company is a major producer and distributor of a regional brand of beer. The beer is marketed in thirteen states along the east coast of the United States. Recent decisions by some states to ban nonreturnable bottles and cans and the expectation that more states will do the same have led the Shotz management to reappraise its bottling function. Shotz has automatic bottling and canning facilities that can handle three sizes of nonreturnable bottles and two sizes of cans.

Demand for beer in cans and nonreturnable bottles will be reduced drastically in the next few years, owing to the ban of nonreturnables. However, demand for beer in returnable bottles is expected to increase sufficiently to offset the reduced sales of beer in nonreturnables. The present canning equipment cannot be adapted for use in the returnable-container environment. The bottling equipment can be adapted for use in bottling returnable bottles. Therefore, the company will have to acquire more automated bottling equipment to replace the capacity lost from the discarded canning equipment. The new equipment should enable the company to have adequate capacity for the next five years. Should returnable cans be developed, the company would be prepared to invest in the necessary equipment five years from now.

The company's largest bottling plant, which is located in New Jersey, produces approximately 75 percent of the firm's total output split evenly between bottles and cans. The present canning equipment will be replaced by new automated bottling equipment. The new equipment is technologically superior to the present automated bottling equipment. The major decision plant management must now make is how large the New Jersey plant's maintenance and repair staff should be to keep both the new and adapted automated equipment running efficiently.

The maintenance and repair staff is responsible for both the preventive maintenance conducted according to a planned schedule and the repairs arising from any breakdowns. Comprehensive accounting records regarding the maintenance and repair function exist for the past five years of operations. Records on the number of breakdowns for each three-month quarter during the past five years are classified by kind, length of time, and type of product being processed (bottle or can identified by size). Total costs of the maintenance and repair department consisting of labor, supplies, equipment, and an allocation of general factory overhead have averaged $500,000 a year for the past five years.

Two separate ten-person maintenance and repair staffs have been used to service the bottling and canning operations for each of the two eight-hour shifts. The total staff has averaged 40 persons for the past five years.

There no longer will be the need for two separate maintenance and repair staffs on each shift, because the canning equipment is to be replaced by new bottling equipment. Further, the management believes that it may be able to reduce the size of the maintenance and repair staff on each shift to less than twenty persons. However, the staff will not be reduced unless operations can be maintained as efficiently as in the past. The plant will not be able to hire temporary service persons because the servicing of the automatic bottling equipment requires a relatively high level of skill.

Because a great deal of uncertainty is associated with this decision, plant management has decided to use a simulation model in its analysis. Simulation models have been used by the company in the past to analyze other problems, and they have proved very useful.

Required:

1. The use of a simulation model to analyze the size of the maintenance and repair staff for the New Jersey plant requires the accumulation of certain costs.
   a. Identify the different types of costs that should be included in the simulation model and briefly justify their inclusion.
   b. Indicate the source for each of the cost inputs identified.

2. Assuming the decision problem can be adequately simulated, explain the typical types of information that will be generated from the simulation model that will assist the New Jersey plant management in its decision regarding the appropriate size for the maintenance and repair staff.

23–14 **Linear Programming and Simulation.** The Balmoral Company makes two types of basketball backboards, wood and glass. Each requires work in two production departments, fitting and assembly. The firm has limited capacity in both departments, so one of its managers formulated the following linear programming problem to determine the optimal mix, per week:

$$
\begin{aligned}
\text{Maximize:} \quad & \$30G + \$18W \\
\text{Subject to:} \quad & 3G + 2W \le 1{,}000 \text{ (fitting)} \\
& 8G + 2W \le 2{,}000 \text{ (assembly)} \\
& G, W \ge 0
\end{aligned}
$$

The optimal mix is 200 of each backboard at these values, yielding $9,600 contribution. However, the firm experiences a good deal of variation in the time required for wood backboards in the fitting department. The time can range from one hour to three hours per unit, and the distribution seems to be uniform. The hourly cost in the fitting department is $4, so that contribution margin on the wood backboards varies with the time required. Thus, at one hour per board, contribution margin will be $22 [$18 + $4(1)] and at 2½ hours would be $16 [$18 − $4(.50)].

In view of the uncertainty regarding the wood boards, one manager suggested that the firm make only glass boards, 250 per week with a near-certain contribution margin of $7,500. Another suggested that the firm make only wood boards, pointing out that uncertainty works both ways and that if it took only one hour of fitting time to make a wood board, the firm could make 1,000 with contribution margin of $22,000.

The setup of the fitting department is such that if the firm follows the strategy of making both types of backboards, it must make the glass ones first. Thus, following that strategy, the firm would make 200 glass boards per week and devote the remaining 400 hours to making wood boards, making as many as it can, up to 200, depending on the time per board. (It cannot make more than 200 wood boards because it cannot assemble more than 200 of each.)

Accordingly, production of wood boards under the strategy of making both is given by:

$$Q_w = 400/\text{time per board}$$

where Q_w = the number of wood boards, $Q_w \leq 200$

Required: Simulate contribution margin for ten iterations under each strategy: (a) make only wood backboards; (b) make 200 glass backboards and as many wood ones as possible, up to 200. Use two-digit random numbers (from Table 23–1) to determine the hours per wood board in the fitting department. Use the same random numbers for each strategy on each iteration: that is, determine the contribution margin that the firm would earn following both strategies based on the same event (hours per wood board). Thus, you need ten random numbers, not twenty. Be prepared to make a recommendation. (Remember that the firm can be virtually certain of $7,500 per week making only glass boards.)

23–15   **Cash Budget.**   The treasurer of the Chandler Company, a wholesaler of dry goods, is concerned about meeting $225,000 in bank loans that fall due in six months. She believes that the firm should have enough cash by that time, but she would like to be more certain. The firm's sales vary between $400,000 and $600,000 per month, and the distribution appears to be nearly uniform over the entire range. Cost of sales is 60 percent of sales and monthly purchases equal cost of sales. The firm pays for purchases immediately. Cash expenses other than merchandise are $140,000 per month.

The firm's collection experience is that between 60 and 80 percent of sales are collected in the month after sale, the remainder in the second month after sale. The distribution is uniform within that range. The firm has $100,000 in cash at the beginning of month 1. Existing receivables should bring in $500,000 cash in month 1, $150,000 in month 2. The firm will also collect some cash in month 2 from sales made in month 1.

Using the expected values of $500,000 for monthly sales and 70 percent collections in the month after sale, the treasurer has determined that the balance at the end of six months will be $460,000. The uncertainty about sales and collections bothers her, though, and she decides that a simulation would be appropriate.

Required: Simulate the firm's sales, cash receipts, cash disbursements, and cash balances for six months. Use two-digit random numbers from Table 23–1 for both sales and the percentage of sales collected in the month after sale. Make any recommendations that you think are appropriate.

23–16 Cash Budget, Three Random Variables.   After you performed the analysis for the Chandler Company (assignment 23–15), the treasurer told you that the firm was going to handle some different product lines from those that she had originally known about. The effect is that sales mix will make some difference in the percentage of cost of sales. Specifically, the ratio of cost of sales to sales should follow the probability distribution shown below.

Cost-of-Sales Percentage	Cumulative Probability
.50	.00
.60	.40
.70	1.00

All other data remain the same as they were in assignment 23–15.

Required: Redo your simulation from assignment 23–15. Use the same values for monthly sales and for the percentages collected in the month after sale. Thus, the only differences will be in cash disbursements and cash balances. Use two-digit numbers to determine monthly cost of sales.

SELECTED REFERENCES

Ferrara, William L., Jack C. Hayya, and David A. Nachman, "Normalcy of Profit in the Jaedicke-Robichek Model," *The Accounting Review*, 47:2 (April 1972), 299–307.

Hillier, Frederick S., and Gerald J. Lieberman, *Operations Research*, 2d ed. San Francisco: Holden-Day, Inc., 1974, chap. 15.

Jaedicke, R. K., and A. Robichek, "Cost-Volume-Profit Analysis under Conditions of Uncertainty," *The Accounting Review*, 39:4 (October 1964), 917–26.

Kottas, John F., Amy Hing-Ling Lau, and Hon-Shiang Lau, "A General Approach to Stochastic Management Planning Models: An Overview," *The Accounting Review*, 53:2 (April 1978), 389–401.

————, and Hon-Shiang Lau, "Direct Simulation in Stochastic CVP Analysis," *The Accounting Review*, 53:3 (July 1978), 698–707.

Wagner, Harvey M., *Principles of Operations Research*. Englewood Cliffs, N.J.: Prentice-Hall, Inc., 1969, chap. 21.

Appendix

TABLE A-1
Area Under the Standard Normal Curve Between the Mean and Successive Values of z

Example: If z = 1.87, the area between the mean and 1.87 standard deviations is .46926 and the area to the right of z is .03074 (.50000 − .46926).

z	.00	.01	.02	.03	.04	.05	.06	.07	.08	.09
.0	.00000	.00399	.00798	.01197	.01595	.01994	.02392	.02790	.03188	.03586
.1	.03983	.04380	.04776	.05172	.05567	.05962	.06356	.06749	.07142	.07535
.2	.07926	.08317	.08706	.09095	.09483	.09871	.10257	.10642	.11026	.11409
.3	.11791	.12172	.12552	.12930	.13307	.13683	.14058	.14431	.14803	.15173
.4	.15542	.15910	.16276	.16640	.17003	.17364	.17724	.18082	.18439	.18793
.5	.19146	.19497	.19847	.20194	.20540	.20884	.21226	.21566	.21904	.22240
.6	.22575	.22907	.23237	.23565	.23891	.24215	.24537	.24857	.25175	.25490
.7	.25804	.26115	.26424	.26730	.27035	.27337	.27637	.27935	.28230	.28524
.8	.28814	.29103	.29389	.29673	.29955	.30234	.30511	.30785	.31057	.31327
.9	.31594	.31859	.32121	.32381	.32639	.32894	.33147	.33398	.33646	.33891
1.0	.34134	.34375	.34614	.34849	.35083	.35314	.35543	.35769	.35993	.36214
1.1	.36433	.36650	.36864	.37076	.37286	.37493	.37698	.37900	.38100	.38298
1.2	.38493	.38686	.38877	.39065	.39251	.39435	.39617	.39796	.39973	.40147
1.3	.40320	.40490	.40658	.40824	.40988	.41149	.41309	.41466	.41621	.41774
1.4	.41924	.42073	.42220	.42364	.42507	.42647	.42785	.42922	.43056	.43189
1.5	.43319	.43448	.43574	.43699	.43822	.43943	.44062	.44179	.44295	.44408
1.6	.44520	.44630	.44738	.44845	.44950	.45053	.45154	.45254	.45352	.45449
1.7	.45543	.45637	.45728	.45818	.45907	.45994	.46080	.46164	.46246	.46327
1.8	.46407	.46485	.46562	.46638	.46712	.46784	.46856	.46926	.46995	.47062
1.9	.47128	.47193	.47257	.47320	.47381	.47441	.47500	.47558	.47615	.47670
2.0	.47725	.47778	.47831	.47882	.47932	.47982	.48030	.48077	.48124	.48169
2.1	.48214	.48257	.48300	.48341	.48382	.48422	.48461	.48500	.48537	.48574
2.2	.48610	.48645	.48679	.48713	.48745	.48778	.48809	.48840	.48870	.48899
2.3	.48928	.48956	.48983	.49010	.49036	.49061	.49086	.49111	.49134	.49158
2.4	.49180	.49202	.49224	.49245	.49266	.49286	.49305	.49324	.49343	.49361
2.5	.49379	.49396	.49413	.49430	.49446	.49461	.49477	.49492	.49506	.49520
2.6	.49534	.49547	.49560	.49573	.49585	.49598	.49609	.49621	.49632	.49643
2.7	.49653	.49664	.49674	.49683	.49693	.49702	.49711	.49720	.49728	.49736
2.8	.49744	.49752	.49760	.49767	.49774	.49781	.49788	.49795	.49801	.49807
2.9	.49813	.49819	.49825	.49831	.49836	.49841	.49846	.49851	.49856	.49861
3.0	.49865									
4.0	.49997									

Courtesy of Professor Lyn Pankoff, Washington University.

TABLE A–2
Critical Values of Student's *t* Statistic

Degrees of Freedom	Levels of Significance for One-Tailed Test				Degrees of Freedom	Levels of Significance for One-Tailed Test			
	.10	.05	.025	.005		.10	.05	.025	.005
1	3.078	6.314	12.706	63.657	16	1.337	1.746	2.120	2.921
2	1.886	2.920	4.303	9.925	17	1.333	1.740	2.110	2.898
3	1.638	2.353	3.182	5.841	18	1.330	1.734	2.101	2.878
4	1.533	2.132	2.776	4.604	19	1.328	1.729	2.093	2.861
5	1.476	2.015	2.571	4.032	20	1.325	1.725	2.086	2.845
6	1.440	1.943	2.447	3.707	21	1.323	1.721	2.080	2.831
7	1.415	1.895	2.365	4.499	22	1.321	1.717	2.074	2.819
8	1.397	1.860	2.306	3.355	23	1.319	1.714	2.069	2.807
9	1.383	1.833	2.262	3.250	24	1.318	1.711	2.064	2.797
10	1.372	1.812	2.228	3.169	25	1.316	1.708	2.060	2.787
11	1.363	1.796	2.201	3.106	26	1.315	1.706	2.056	2.779
12	1.356	1.782	2.179	3.055	27	1.314	1.703	2.052	2.771
13	1.350	1.771	2.160	3.012	28	1.313	1.701	2.048	2.763
14	1.345	1.761	2.145	2.977	29	1.311	1.699	2.045	2.756
15	1.341	1.753	2.131	2.947	30	1.310	1.697	2.042	2.750
					∞	1.282	1.645	1.960	2.576

To find the critical value for a two-tailed test, simply multiply the levels of significance by 2. That is, the values for the one-tailed test with significance of .10 are also those for a two-tailed test with .20 significance, and so on.

Table courtesy of Jeannine A. Myer, Southern Illinois University at Edwardsville.

TABLE A–1

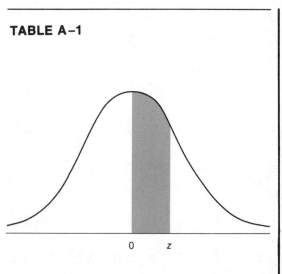

TABLE A–2

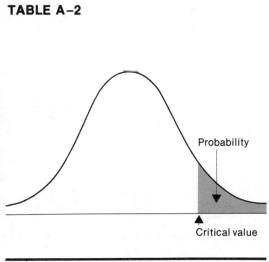

TABLE A-3
Present Value of $1

$$\frac{1}{(1+r)^t}$$

t/r	4%	5%	6%	7%	8%	9%	10%	11%	12%	13%	14%	15%	16%	17%	18%	19%
1	.9615	.9524	.9434	.9346	.9259	.9174	.9091	.9009	.8929	.8850	.8772	.8696	.8621	.8547	.8475	.8403
2	.9246	.9070	.8900	.8734	.8573	.8417	.8264	.8116	.7972	.7831	.7695	.7561	.7432	.7305	.7182	.7062
3	.8890	.8638	.8396	.8163	.7938	.7722	.7513	.7312	.7118	.6931	.6750	.6575	.6407	.6244	.6086	.5934
4	.8548	.8227	.7921	.7629	.7350	.7084	.6830	.6587	.6355	.6133	.5921	.5718	.5523	.5337	.5158	.4987
5	.8219	.7835	.7473	.7130	.6806	.6499	.6209	.5935	.5674	.5428	.5194	.4972	.4761	.4561	.4371	.4190
6	.7903	.7462	.7050	.6663	.6302	.5963	.5645	.5346	.5066	.4803	.4556	.4324	.4104	.3898	.3704	.3521
7	.7599	.7107	.6651	.6227	.5835	.5470	.5132	.4817	.4523	.4251	.3996	.3759	.3538	.3332	.3139	.2959
8	.7307	.6768	.6274	.5820	.5403	.5019	.4665	.4339	.4039	.3762	.3506	.3269	.3050	.2848	.2660	.2487
9	.7026	.6446	.5919	.5439	.5002	.4604	.4241	.3909	.3606	.3329	.3075	.2843	.2630	.2434	.2255	.2090
10	.6756	.6139	.5584	.5083	.4632	.4224	.3855	.3522	.3220	.2946	.2697	.2472	.2267	.2080	.1911	.1756
11	.6496	.5847	.5268	.4751	.4289	.3875	.3505	.3173	.2875	.2607	.2366	.2149	.1954	.1778	.1619	.1476
12	.6246	.5568	.4970	.4440	.3971	.3555	.3186	.2858	.2567	.2307	.2076	.1869	.1685	.1520	.1372	.1240
13	.6006	.5303	.4688	.4150	.3677	.3262	.2897	.2575	.2292	.2042	.1821	.1625	.1452	.1299	.1163	.1042
14	.5775	.5051	.4423	.3873	.3405	.2992	.2633	.2320	.2046	.1807	.1597	.1413	.1252	.1110	.0985	.0876
15	.5553	.4810	.4173	.3624	.3152	.2745	.2394	.2090	.1827	.1599	.1401	.1229	.1079	.0949	.0835	.0736
16	.5339	.4581	.3936	.3387	.2919	.2519	.2176	.1883	.1631	.1415	.1229	.1069	.0930	.0811	.0708	.0618
17	.5134	.4363	.3714	.3166	.2703	.2311	.1978	.1696	.1456	.1252	.1078	.0929	.0802	.0693	.0600	.0520
18	.4936	.4155	.3503	.2959	.2502	.2120	.1799	.1528	.1300	.1108	.0946	.0808	.0691	.0592	.0508	.0437
19	.4746	.3957	.3305	.2765	.2317	.1945	.1635	.1377	.1161	.0981	.0829	.0703	.0596	.0506	.0431	.0367
20	.4564	.3769	.3118	.2584	.2145	.1784	.1486	.1240	.1037	.0868	.0728	.0611	.0514	.0433	.0365	.0308
21	.4388	.3589	.2942	.2415	.1987	.1637	.1351	.1117	.0926	.0768	.0638	.0531	.0443	.0370	.0309	.0259
22	.4220	.3418	.2775	.2257	.1839	.1502	.1228	.1007	.0826	.0680	.0560	.0462	.0382	.0316	.0262	.0218
23	.4057	.3256	.2618	.2109	.1703	.1378	.1117	.0907	.0738	.0601	.0491	.0402	.0329	.0270	.0222	.0183
24	.3901	.3101	.2470	.1971	.1577	.1264	.1015	.0817	.0659	.0532	.0431	.0349	.0284	.0231	.0188	.0154
25	.3751	.2953	.2330	.1842	.1460	.1160	.0923	.0736	.0588	.0471	.0378	.0304	.0245	.0197	.0160	.0129
30	.3083	.2314	.1741	.1314	.0994	.0754	.0573	.0437	.0334	.0256	.0196	.0151	.0116	.0090	.0070	.0054
35	.2534	.1813	.1301	.0937	.0676	.0490	.0356	.0259	.0189	.0139	.0102	.0075	.0055	.0041	.0030	.0023
40	.2083	.1420	.0972	.0668	.0460	.0318	.0221	.0154	.0107	.0075	.0053	.0037	.0026	.0019	.0013	.0010
45	.1712	.1113	.0727	.0476	.0313	.0207	.0137	.0091	.0061	.0041	.0027	.0019	.0013	.0009	.0006	.0004
50	.1407	.0872	.0543	.0339	.0213	.0134	.0085	.0054	.0035	.0022	.0014	.0009	.0006	.0004	.0003	.0002

TABLE A–3 (Cont.)
Present Value of $1

$$\frac{1}{(1 + r)^t}$$

t/r	20%	21%	22%	23%	24%	25%	26%	28%	30%	32%	34%	36%	38%	40%	45%	50%
1	.8333	.8264	.8197	.8130	.8065	.8000	.7937	.7813	.7692	.7576	.7463	.7353	.7246	.7143	.6897	.6667
2	.6944	.6830	.6719	.6610	.6504	.6400	.6299	.6104	.5917	.5739	.5569	.5409	.5251	.5102	.4756	.4444
3	.5787	.5645	.5507	.5374	.5245	.5120	.4999	.4768	.4552	.4348	.4156	.3975	.3805	.3644	.3280	.2963
4	.4823	.4665	.4514	.4369	.4230	.4069	.3968	.3725	.3501	.3294	.3102	.2923	.2757	.2603	.2262	.1975
5	.4019	.3855	.3700	.3552	.3411	.3277	.3149	.2910	.2693	.2495	.2315	.2149	.1998	.1859	.1560	.1317
6	.3349	.3186	.3033	.2888	.2751	.2621	.2499	.2274	.2072	.1890	.1727	.1580	.1448	.1328	.1076	.0878
7	.2791	.2633	.2486	.2348	.2218	.2097	.1983	.1776	.1594	.1432	.1289	.1162	.1049	.0949	.0742	.0585
8	.2326	.2176	.2038	.1909	.1789	.1678	.1574	.1388	.1226	.1085	.0962	.0854	.0760	.0678	.0512	.0390
9	.1938	.1799	.1670	.1552	.1443	.1342	.1249	.1084	.0943	.0822	.0718	.0628	.0551	.0484	.0353	.0260
10	.1615	.1486	.1369	.1262	.1164	.1074	.0992	.0847	.0725	.0623	.0536	.0462	.0399	.0346	.0243	.0173
11	.1346	.1228	.1122	.1026	.0938	.0859	.0787	.0662	.0558	.0472	.0400	.0340	.0289	.0247	.0168	.0116
12	.1122	.1015	.0920	.0834	.0757	.0687	.0625	.0517	.0429	.0357	.0298	.0250	.0210	.0176	.0116	.0077
13	.0935	.0839	.0754	.0678	.0610	.0550	.0496	.0404	.0330	.0271	.0223	.0184	.0152	.0126	.0080	.0051
14	.0779	.0693	.0618	.0551	.0492	.0440	.0393	.0316	.0254	.0205	.0166	.0135	.0110	.0090	.0055	.0034
15	.0649	.0573	.0507	.0448	.0397	.0352	.0312	.0247	.0195	.0155	.0124	.0099	.0080	.0064	.0038	.0023
16	.0541	.0474	.0415	.0364	.0320	.0281	.0248	.0193	.0150	.0118	.0093	.0073	.0058	.0046	.0026	.0015
17	.0451	.0391	.0340	.0296	.0258	.0225	.0197	.0150	.0116	.0089	.0069	.0054	.0042	.0033	.0018	.0010
18	.0376	.0323	.0279	.0241	.0208	.0180	.0156	.0118	.0089	.0068	.0052	.0039	.0030	.0023	.0012	.0007
19	.0313	.0267	.0229	.0196	.0168	.0144	.0124	.0092	.0068	.0051	.0038	.0029	.0022	.0017	.0009	.0005
20	.0261	.0221	.0187	.0159	.0135	.0115	.0098	.0072	.0053	.0039	.0029	.0021	.0016	.0012	.0006	.0003
21	.0217	.0183	.0154	.0129	.0109	.0092	.0078	.0056	.0040	.0029	.0021	.0016	.0012	.0009	.0004	.0002
22	.0181	.0151	.0126	.0105	.0088	.0074	.0062	.0044	.0031	.0022	.0016	.0012	.0008	.0006	.0003	.0001
23	.0151	.0125	.0103	.0086	.0071	.0059	.0049	.0034	.0024	.0017	.0012	.0008	.0006	.0004	.0002	.0001
24	.0126	.0103	.0085	.0070	.0057	.0047	.0039	.0027	.0018	.0013	.0009	.0006	.0004	.0003	.0001	.0001
25	.0105	.0085	.0069	.0057	.0046	.0038	.0031	.0021	.0014	.0010	.0007	.0005	.0003	.0002	.0001	.0000
30	.0042	.0033	.0026	.0020	.0016	.0012	.0010	.0006	.0004	.0002	.0002	.0001	.0001	.0000	.0000	
35	.0017	.0013	.0009	.0007	.0005	.0004	.0003	.0002	.0001	.0001	.0000	.0000	.0000	.0000	.0000	
40	.0007	.0005	.0004	.0003	.0002	.0001	.0001	.0001	.0000	.0000			.0000	.0000		
45	.0003	.0002	.0001	.0001	.0001	.0000	.0000	.0000								
50	.0001	.0001	.0000	.0000	.0000			.0000								

TABLE A–4
Present Value of an Annuity of $1

$$\frac{1 - \dfrac{1}{(1 + r)^t}}{r}$$

t/r	4%	5%	6%	7%	8%	9%	10%	11%	12%	13%	14%	15%	16%	17%	18%	19%
1	.9615	.9524	.9434	.9346	.9259	.9174	.9091	.9009	.8929	.8850	.8772	.8696	.8621	.8547	.8475	.8403
2	1.8861	1.8594	1.8334	1.8080	1.7833	1.7591	1.7355	1.7125	1.6901	1.6681	1.6467	1.6257	1.6052	1.5852	1.5656	1.5465
3	2.7751	2.7232	2.6730	2.6243	2.5771	2.5313	2.4869	2.4437	2.4018	2.3612	2.3216	2.2832	2.2459	2.2096	2.1743	2.1399
4	3.6299	3.5460	3.4651	3.3872	3.3121	3.2397	3.1699	3.1024	3.0373	2.9745	2.9137	2.8550	2.7982	2.7432	2.6901	2.6386
5	4.4518	4.3295	4.2124	4.1002	3.9927	3.8897	3.7908	3.6959	3.6048	3.5172	3.4331	3.3522	3.2743	3.1993	3.1272	3.0576
6	5.2421	5.0757	4.9173	4.7665	4.6229	4.4859	4.3553	4.2305	4.1114	3.9975	3.8887	3.7845	3.6847	3.5892	3.4976	3.4098
7	6.0021	5.7864	5.5824	5.3893	5.2064	5.0330	4.8684	4.7122	4.5638	4.4226	4.2883	4.1604	4.0386	3.9224	3.8115	3.7057
8	6.7327	6.4632	6.2098	5.9713	5.7465	5.5348	5.3349	5.1461	4.9676	4.7988	4.6389	4.4873	4.3436	4.2072	4.0776	3.9544
9	7.4353	7.1078	6.8017	6.5152	6.2469	5.9952	5.7590	5.5370	5.3282	5.1317	4.9464	4.7716	4.6065	4.4506	4.3030	4.1633
10	8.1109	7.7217	7.3601	7.0236	6.7101	6.4177	6.1446	5.8892	5.6502	5.4262	5.2161	5.0188	4.8332	4.6586	4.4941	4.3389
11	8.7605	8.3064	7.8869	7.4987	7.1390	6.8052	6.4951	6.2065	5.9377	5.6869	5.4527	5.2337	5.0286	4.8364	4.6560	4.4865
12	9.3851	8.8633	8.3838	7.9427	7.5361	7.1607	6.8137	6.4924	6.1944	5.9176	5.6603	5.4206	5.1971	4.9884	4.7932	4.6105
13	9.9856	9.3936	8.8527	8.3577	7.9038	7.4869	7.1034	6.7499	6.4235	6.1218	5.8424	5.5831	5.3423	5.1183	4.9095	4.7147
14	10.5631	9.8986	9.2950	8.7455	8.2442	7.7862	7.3667	6.9819	6.6282	6.3025	6.0021	5.7245	5.4675	5.2293	5.0081	4.8023
15	11.1184	10.3797	9.7122	9.1079	8.5595	8.0607	7.6061	7.1909	6.8109	6.4624	6.1422	5.8474	5.5755	5.3242	5.0916	4.8759
16	11.6523	10.8378	10.1059	9.4466	8.8514	8.3126	7.8237	7.3792	6.9740	6.6039	6.2651	5.9542	5.6685	5.4053	5.1624	4.9377
17	12.1657	11.2741	10.4773	9.7632	9.1216	8.5436	8.0216	7.5488	7.1196	6.7291	6.3729	6.0472	5.7487	5.4746	5.2223	4.9897
18	12.6593	11.6896	10.8276	10.0591	9.3719	8.7556	8.2014	7.7016	7.2497	6.8399	6.4674	6.1280	5.8178	5.5339	5.2732	5.0333
19	13.1339	12.0853	11.1581	10.3356	9.6036	8.9501	8.3649	7.8393	7.3658	6.9380	6.5504	6.1982	5.8775	5.5845	5.3162	5.0700
20	13.5903	12.4622	11.4699	10.5940	9.8181	9.1285	8.5136	7.9633	7.4694	7.0248	6.6231	6.2593	5.9288	5.6278	5.3527	5.1009
21	14.0292	12.8212	11.7641	10.8355	10.0168	9.2922	8.6487	8.0751	7.5620	7.1016	6.6870	6.3125	5.9731	5.6648	5.3837	5.1268
22	14.4511	13.1630	12.0416	11.0612	10.2007	9.4424	8.7715	8.1757	7.6446	7.1695	6.7429	6.3587	6.0113	5.6964	5.4099	5.1486
23	14.8568	13.4886	12.3034	11.2722	10.3711	9.5802	8.8832	8.2664	7.7184	7.2297	6.7921	6.3988	6.0442	5.7234	5.4321	5.1668
24	15.2470	13.7986	12.5504	11.4693	10.5288	9.7066	8.9847	8.3481	7.7843	7.2829	6.8351	6.4338	6.0726	5.7465	5.4509	5.1822
25	15.6221	14.0939	12.7834	11.6536	10.6748	9.8226	9.0770	8.4217	7.8431	7.3300	6.8729	6.4641	6.0971	5.7662	5.4669	5.1951
30	17.2920	15.3725	13.7648	12.4090	11.2578	10.2737	9.4269	8.6938	8.0552	7.4957	7.0027	6.5660	6.1772	5.8294	5.5168	5.2347
35	18.6646	16.3742	14.4982	12.9477	11.6546	10.5668	9.6442	8.8552	8.1755	7.5856	7.0700	6.6166	6.2153	5.8582	5.5306	5.2512
40	19.7928	17.1591	15.0463	13.3317	11.9246	10.7574	9.7791	8.9511	8.2438	7.6344	7.1050	6.6418	6.2335	5.8713	5.5482	5.2582
45	20.7200	17.7741	15.4558	13.6055	12.1084	10.8812	9.8628	9.0079	8.2825	7.6609	7.1232	6.6543	6.2421	5.8773	5.5523	5.2611
50	21.4822	18.2559	15.7619	13.8007	12.2335	10.9617	9.9148	9.0417	8.3045	7.6752	7.1327	6.6605	6.2463	5.8801	5.5541	5.2623

TABLE A–4 (Cont.)
Present Value of an Annuity of $1

$$1 - \frac{1}{(1 + r)^t}$$
$$\frac{}{r}$$

t/r	20%	21%	22%	23%	24%	25%	26%	28%	30%	32%	34%	36%	38%	40%	45%	50%
1	.8333	.8264	.8197	.8130	.8065	.8000	.7937	.7812	.7692	.7576	.7463	.7353	.7246	.7143	.6897	.6667
2	1.5278	1.5095	1.4915	1.4740	1.4568	1.4400	1.4235	1.3916	1.3609	1.3315	1.3032	1.2760	1.2497	1.2245	1.1653	1.1111
3	2.1065	2.0739	2.0422	2.0114	1.9813	1.9520	1.9234	1.8684	1.8161	1.7663	1.7188	1.6735	1.6302	1.5889	1.4933	1.4074
4	2.5887	2.5404	2.4936	2.4483	2.4043	2.3616	2.3203	2.2410	2.1662	2.0957	2.0290	1.9658	1.9060	1.8492	1.7195	1.6049
5	2.9906	2.9260	2.8636	2.8035	2.7454	2.6893	2.6351	2.5320	2.4356	2.3452	2.2604	2.1807	2.1058	2.0352	1.8755	1.7366
6	3.3255	3.2446	3.1669	3.0923	3.0205	2.9514	2.8850	2.7594	2.6427	2.5342	2.4331	2.3388	2.2506	2.1680	1.9831	1.8244
7	3.6046	3.5079	3.4155	3.3270	3.2423	3.1611	3.0833	2.9370	2.8021	2.6775	2.5620	2.4550	2.3555	2.2628	2.0573	1.8829
8	3.8372	3.7256	3.6193	3.5179	3.4212	3.3289	3.2407	3.0758	2.9247	2.7860	2.6582	2.5404	2.4315	2.3306	2.1085	1.9220
9	4.0310	3.9054	3.7863	3.6731	3.5655	3.4631	3.3657	3.1842	3.0190	2.8681	2.7300	2.6033	2.4866	2.3790	2.1438	1.9480
10	4.1925	4.0541	3.9232	3.7993	3.6819	3.5705	3.4648	3.2689	3.0915	2.9304	2.7836	2.6495	2.5265	2.4136	2.1681	1.9653
11	4.3271	4.1769	4.0354	3.9018	3.7757	3.6564	3.5435	3.3351	3.1473	2.9776	2.8236	2.6834	2.5555	2.4383	2.1849	1.9769
12	4.4392	4.2784	4.1274	3.9852	3.8514	3.7251	3.6059	3.3868	3.1903	3.0133	2.8534	2.7084	2.5764	2.4559	2.1965	1.9846
13	4.5327	4.3624	4.2028	4.0530	3.9124	3.7801	3.6555	3.4272	3.2233	3.0404	2.8757	2.7268	2.5916	2.4685	2.2045	1.9897
14	4.6106	4.4317	4.2646	4.1082	3.9616	3.8241	3.6949	3.4587	3.2487	3.0609	2.8923	2.7403	2.6026	2.4775	2.2100	1.9931
15	4.6755	4.4890	4.3152	4.1530	4.0013	3.8593	3.7261	3.4834	3.2682	3.0764	2.9047	2.7502	2.6106	2.4839	2.2138	1.9954
16	4.7296	4.5364	4.3567	4.1894	4.0333	3.8874	3.7509	3.5026	3.2832	3.0882	2.9140	2.7575	2.6164	2.4885	2.2164	1.9970
17	4.7746	4.5755	4.3908	4.2190	4.0591	3.9099	3.7705	3.5177	3.2948	3.0971	2.9209	2.7629	2.6206	2.4918	2.2182	1.9980
18	4.8122	4.6079	4.4187	4.2431	4.0799	3.9279	3.7861	3.5294	3.3037	3.1039	2.9260	2.7668	2.6236	2.4941	2.2195	1.9986
19	4.8435	4.6346	4.4415	4.2627	4.0967	3.9424	3.7985	3.5386	3.3105	3.1090	2.9299	2.7697	2.6258	2.4958	2.2203	1.9991
20	4.8696	4.6567	4.4603	4.2786	4.1103	3.9539	3.8083	3.5458	3.3158	3.1129	2.9327	2.7718	2.6274	2.4970	2.2209	1.9994
21	4.8913	4.6750	4.4756	4.2916	4.1212	3.9631	3.8161	3.5514	3.3198	3.1158	2.9349	2.7734	2.6285	2.4979	2.2213	1.9996
22	4.9094	4.6900	4.4882	4.3021	4.1300	3.9705	3.8223	3.5558	3.3230	3.1180	2.9365	2.7746	2.6294	2.4985	2.2216	1.9997
23	4.9245	4.7025	4.4985	4.3106	4.1371	3.9764	3.8273	3.5592	3.3254	3.1197	2.9377	2.7754	2.6300	2.4989	2.2218	1.9998
24	4.9371	4.7128	4.5070	4.3176	4.1428	3.9811	3.8312	3.5619	3.3272	3.1210	2.9386	2.7760	2.6304	2.4992	2.2219	1.9999
25	4.9476	4.7213	4.5139	4.3232	4.1474	3.9849	3.8342	3.5640	3.3286	3.1220	2.9392	2.7765	2.6307	2.4994	2.2220	1.9999
30	4.9789	4.7463	4.5338	4.3391	4.1601	3.9950	3.8424	3.5693	3.3321	3.1242	2.9407	2.7775	2.6314	2.4999	2.2222	2.0000
35	4.9915	4.7559	4.5411	4.3447	4.1644	3.9984	3.8450	3.5708	3.3330	3.1248	2.9411	2.7777	2.6315	2.5000	2.2222	2.0000
40	4.9966	4.7596	4.5439	4.3467	4.1659	3.9995	3.8458	3.5712	3.3332	3.1250	2.9412	2.7778	2.6316	2.5000	2.2222	2.0000
45	4.9986	4.7610	4.5449	4.3474	4.1664	3.9998	3.8460	3.5714	3.3333	3.1250	2.9412	2.7778	2.6316	2.5000	2.2222	2.0000
50	4.9995	4.7616	4.5452	4.3477	4.1666	3.9999	3.8461	3.5714	3.3333	3.1250	2.9412	2.7778	2.6316	2.5000	2.2222	2.0000

TABLE A-5
Present Value of the Tax Savings From Sum-of-the-Years'-Digits Depreciation for an Asset Worth $1 Depreciated Over t Years With No Salvage Value

t/r	4%	5%	6%	7%	8%	9%	10%	11%	12%	13%	14%	15%	16%	17%	18%	19%	20%
3	.93712	.92251	.90830	.89449	.88105	.86797	.85525	.84286	.83079	.81904	.80758	.79642	.78553	.77492	.76456	.75446	.74460
4	.92526	.90810	.89149	.87541	.85984	.84476	.83013	.81596	.80221	.78887	.77592	.76335	.75114	.73927	.72774	.71653	.70563
5	.91363	.89403	.87515	.85695	.83941	.82248	.80614	.79037	.77512	.76039	.74615	.73238	.71904	.70614	.69364	.68153	.66980
6	.90222	.88029	.85927	.83909	.81971	.80110	.78321	.76600	.74944	.73350	.71814	.70334	.68907	.67530	.66201	.64918	.63678
7	.89102	.86688	.84382	.82179	.80073	.78057	.76128	.74279	.72507	.70807	.69176	.67609	.66103	.64656	.63263	.61923	.60632
8	.88004	.85377	.82880	.80504	.78242	.76086	.74030	.72068	.70194	.68402	.66689	.65050	.63479	.61974	.60531	.59147	.57817
9	.86926	.84097	.81419	.78882	.76475	.74191	.72022	.69959	.67995	.66126	.64343	.62643	.61020	.59470	.57987	.56569	.55211
10	.85868	.82846	.79997	.77310	.74771	.72371	.70099	.67947	.65906	.63969	.62128	.60379	.58713	.57127	.55615	.54173	.52796
11	.84830	.81624	.78614	.75786	.73126	.70620	.68257	.66026	.63918	.61924	.60035	.58245	.56547	.54934	.53401	.51942	.50553
12	.83812	.80429	.77268	.74310	.71537	.68936	.66491	.64192	.62026	.59984	.58056	.56234	.54510	.52878	.51330	.49862	.48467
13	.82812	.79262	.75958	.72878	.70003	.67315	.64798	.62439	.60224	.58142	.56182	.54336	.52594	.50948	.49392	.47920	.46524
14	.81830	.78121	.74683	.71490	.68521	.65755	.63174	.60763	.58507	.56392	.54408	.52543	.50789	.49136	.47576	.46104	.44712
15	.80867	.77006	.73441	.70144	.67089	.64253	.61616	.59160	.56869	.54728	.52725	.50848	.49086	.47430	.45872	.44404	.43019
16	.79921	.75915	.72232	.68838	.65704	.62806	.60120	.57626	.55306	.53146	.51129	.49244	.47479	.45825	.44271	.42811	.41435
17	.78992	.74849	.71054	.67570	.64366	.61412	.58683	.56157	.53815	.51639	.49613	.47725	.45961	.44311	.42766	.41315	.39952
18	.78080	.73806	.69906	.66340	.63071	.60067	.57302	.54750	.52390	.50203	.48173	.46285	.44525	.42883	.41348	.39910	.38561
19	.77185	.72786	.68788	.65146	.61818	.58771	.55974	.53401	.51027	.48834	.46803	.44918	.43166	.41534	.40011	.38587	.37254
20	.76306	.71788	.67699	.63986	.60606	.57521	.54697	.52107	.49724	.47528	.45500	.43621	.41878	.40258	.38749	.37341	.36025
21	.75442	.70813	.66637	.62860	.59433	.56314	.53469	.50866	.48478	.46282	.44258	.42388	.40657	.39051	.37557	.36166	.34867
22	.74594	.69858	.65602	.61766	.58297	.55150	.52286	.49674	.47284	.45091	.43075	.41216	.39498	.37907	.36430	.35056	.33776
23	.73760	.68923	.64593	.60703	.57196	.54025	.51148	.48530	.46140	.43953	.41946	.40099	.38396	.36821	.35362	.34007	.32745
24	.72942	.68009	.63609	.59670	.56130	.52938	.50051	.47430	.45044	.42864	.40869	.39036	.37349	.35791	.34350	.33014	.31771
25	.72138	.67114	.62649	.58666	.55097	.51889	.48994	.46373	.43992	.41823	.39840	.38022	.36352	.34812	.33390	.32073	.30850

TABLE A–5 (Cont.)

Present Value of the Tax Savings From Sum-of-the-Years'-Digits Depreciation for an Asset Worth $1 Depreciated Over t Years With No Salvage Value

t/r	4%	5%	6%	7%	8%	9%	10%	11%	12%	13%	14%	15%	16%	17%	18%	19%	20%
26	.71348	.66238	.61713	.57689	.54096	.50874	.47975	.45356	.42983	.40825	.38856	.37055	.35402	.33881	.32478	.31180	.29977
27	.70572	.65381	.60800	.56740	.53124	.49892	.46991	.44378	.42014	.39869	.37915	.36131	.34497	.32995	.31611	.30333	.29149
28	.69809	.64541	.59909	.55816	.52183	.48943	.46043	.43436	.41083	.38952	.37015	.35249	.33633	.32150	.30786	.29527	.28362
29	.69059	.63719	.59039	.54917	.51269	.48025	.45127	.42529	.40188	.38072	.36153	.34405	.32808	.31345	.30000	.28761	.27615
30	.68322	.62914	.58191	.54045	.50382	.47136	.44243	.41654	.39328	.37228	.35326	.33597	.32020	.30576	.29251	.28031	.26904
31	.67598	.62126	.57362	.53192	.49522	.46275	.43389	.40812	.38500	.36417	.34534	.32824	.31266	.29842	.28536	.27335	.26227
32	.66887	.61353	.56553	.52363	.48686	.45441	.42564	.39999	.37703	.35638	.33773	.32083	.30545	.29140	.27854	.26672	.25582
33	.66187	.60597	.55763	.51556	.47875	.44634	.41766	.39215	.36935	.34888	.33043	.31372	.29854	.28469	.27201	.26038	.24966
34	.65499	.59856	.54991	.50771	.47086	.43851	.40994	.38458	.36195	.34167	.32341	.30690	.29191	.27826	.26577	.25432	.24378
35	.64823	.59130	.54237	.50005	.46320	.43092	.40247	.37727	.35482	.33473	.31667	.30035	.28556	.27210	.25980	.24853	.23816
36	.64158	.58418	.53501	.49260	.45576	.42356	.39525	.37021	.34794	.32805	.31018	.29406	.27947	.26619	.25408	.24298	.23279
37	.63504	.57720	.52781	.48533	.44852	.41642	.38825	.36338	.34130	.32160	.30393	.28802	.27361	.26052	.24859	.23767	.22764
38	.62861	.57037	.52078	.47824	.44148	.40949	.38148	.35678	.33490	.31359	.29792	.28220	.26798	.25508	.24333	.23257	.22271
39	.62229	.56367	.51391	.47134	.43464	.40277	.37491	.35040	.32871	.30940	.29213	.27660	.26257	.24985	.23827	.22768	.21797
40	.61607	.55710	.50719	.46460	.42798	.39624	.36855	.34422	.32273	.30362	.28654	.27121	.25737	.24483	.23341	.22299	.21344
41	.60996	.55065	.50062	.45804	.42150	.38990	.36238	.33824	.31694	.29803	.28115	.26601	.25235	.23999	.22874	.21848	.20908
42	.60394	.54434	.49419	.45163	.41519	.38374	.35640	.33245	.31135	.29264	.27596	.26100	.24752	.23533	.22425	.21414	.20489
43	.59802	.53814	.48791	.44538	.40905	.37775	.35059	.32684	.30594	.28743	.27094	.25616	.24287	.23085	.21993	.20997	.20086
44	.59220	.53207	.48176	.43928	.40307	.37194	.34496	.32141	.30070	.28239	.26609	.25150	.23838	.22652	.21576	.20595	.19698
45	.58647	.52610	.47575	.43333	.39724	.36628	.33949	.31614	.29563	.27751	.26140	.24699	.23405	.22235	.21174	.20208	.19324
46	.58084	.52026	.46987	.42751	.39157	.36078	.33418	.31102	.29072	.27279	.25687	.24264	.22986	.21833	.20787	.19835	.18964
47	.57529	.51452	.46411	.42184	.38603	.35542	.32902	.30606	.28596	.26822	.25248	.23843	.22582	.21444	.20413	.19475	.18617
48	.56983	.50889	.45847	.41630	.38064	.35021	.32401	.30125	.28134	.26380	.24824	.23436	.22191	.21060	.20052	.19127	.18283
49	.56446	.50337	.45296	.41038	.37539	.34514	.31913	.29658	.27686	.25951	.24413	.23042	.21813	.20706	.19703	.18792	.17959
50	.55917	.49795	.44756	.40559	.37026	.34020	.31439	.29204	.27252	.25535	.24015	.22661	.21448	.20355	.19366	.18468	.17647

Index